THE
RECORD OF
MANKIND

FOURTH EDITION

THE

RECORD

OF MANKIND

A. Wesley Roehm / *Morris R. Buske* / *Hutton Webster* / *Edgar B. Wesley*

D. C. HEATH AND COMPANY
Lexington, Massachusetts

A. Wesley Roehm: Chairman of the Department of History
and Social Sciences, Oak Park and River Forest
High School, Oak Park, Illinois

Morris R. Buske: World Civilization Humanities Coordinator, Oak Park
and River Forest High School, Oak Park, Illinois

Hutton Webster: Formerly Professor Emeritus of Sociology,
Stanford University

Edgar B. Wesley: Formerly Professor of Education,
University of Minnesota

Library of Congress Number 70-106073

FOREWORD *to the fourth edition*

In his book *Human Destiny* Lecomte du Noüy says: "The only history which makes any sense is universal history. Outside of certain purely local facts, generally without great importance, nothing takes place in a country which is not linked to the events unfolding in bordering or distant countries. . . . This is truer in our day than a century ago, and will be still more marked in the future. An inextricable network of veins and arteries, invisible from the exterior, renders all nations solidary with the whole. To isolate arbitrarily the history of one country is equivalent to sectioning these veins which are thus transformed into unexplainable stumps." [1]

If the authors of *The Record of Mankind* have a thesis, the above quotation comes very close to expressing it. They have tried to present, within the limits of a one-year course, a world history that "makes sense" and that leaves no "unexplainable stumps." They have tried to weave the threads of man's past into a meaningful pattern (1) by using simple, direct language, comprehensible to the average high school student; (2) by employing a logical and coherent organization; (3) by incorporating usable teaching and learning aids, and illustrations and maps closely integrated with the text; and (4) by emphasizing the growing interdependence of peoples and nations in a world of vanishing distances.

In an age of ever-accelerating change, world history acquires a new significance in the 1970's. When the last edition of *The Record of Mankind* appeared, no man had landed on the moon, De Gaulle was secure in the French presidency, and peace talks over the Vietnam War seemed very remote. These examples are merely representative of the pace of change that requires man to have a greater adaptability to his environment than ever before. Indeed, the world must appear to high school students like a "perpetual seesaw." It is therefore the major purpose of this edition of *The Record of Mankind* to help young Americans adapt to a rapidly changing world and to develop the historical perspective needed for making the most of man's "usable past."

To that end, some extensive revisions of the text have been made. First, in order to bring it thoroughly up to date, nine chapters have been rewritten in whole or in part. Second, this edition embodies a new balance and a different emphasis. There is much more material on cultural history (literature, the arts, and science) and on the non-Western world. Third, an entirely new feature of the fourth edition is the inclusion of a number of boxed quotations. These excerpts from the "raw materials" of history are designed to stimulate the student to make his own discoveries and draw his own conclusions. Finally, *The Record of Mankind* has many new illustrations and maps, all of which should facilitate the learning process.

As in the past, we owe a debt of gratitude to a number of our colleagues on the staff of Oak Park and River Forest High School for their helpful suggestions. We also wish to thank Mrs. Peter Saecker for revising the study aids and bibliographies; Dr. Paul V. Lemkau of the Johns Hopkins University for advice on modern medical history; and the editor, Mrs. Joan E. Schuman, for her patience and wise counsel in the preparation of this edition. Finally, to our wives, Mildred C. Roehm and Dorothy Buske, we are grateful beyond measure for their understanding and moral support during the throes of producing a new edition.

THE AUTHORS

[1] Quoted with permission of Longmans, Green & Company, Inc., from *Human Destiny* by Lecomte du Noüy, 1940.

TABLE OF CONTENTS

MAPS AND CHARTS

SPECIAL TOPICS IN COLOR

THE
RECORD OF
MANKIND

THE OLDEST KNOWN RECORD OF MANKIND is this picture writing on a limestone tablet found at the ruined city of Kish, Iraq. Dated about 3500 B.C., the tablet contains the symbols for head, hands, and foot; for a threshing sledge; and for numerals. It was probably used to record an agricultural transaction.

PART ONE

THE DAWN OF CIVILIZATION

Your textbook is named *The Record of Mankind* because it tells man's story from his early beginnings up to the present time. The book is divided into nine parts, or units. You are about to begin the study of Part One, which deals with early man and the beginning of civilization.

Scientists tell us that man today differs but little in physical appearance from his ancestors living 100,000 years ago. Mankind has undergone no essential change during this time, but man's way of living has changed amazingly. In Part One we shall trace "the record of mankind" from the age of living in caves up to the point at which civilizations appeared and became well established. We shall visit some of the first civilizations: those which arose in Egypt, in Babylonia, and in other countries of the ancient Middle East; and those which developed in India and China.

On the next few pages you will find explanations of the meaning of some terms which will help you to understand history. Additional study aids appear at the close of each chapter and part. As your study proceeds, you will also find it helpful to use the Table of Significant Dates and other materials in the Reference Section, located at the back of the book.

Part One has no definite beginning in time, since we cannot be sure of the exact time of man's first appearance on earth. However, we shall bring man's record in the Middle East up to about 300 B.C., and in the Far East to A.D. 500.

1 What History Means to Us

GOING TO SCHOOL, then and now. The modern classroom presents a striking contrast to the school scene found carved in an ancient Roman tomb.

". . . The word history is used to denote not only the record of what has been learned by inquiry, but also the course of events themselves."
—Allen Johnson, *The Historian and Historical Evidence.*

"History is the witness of the times, the light of truth, the life of memory, the teacher of life, the messenger of antiquity."
—Marcus Tullius Cicero, 106–43 B.C.

"History is . . . the record of what one age finds worthy of note in another."
—Jakob Burckhardt, 1818–1897

". . . history . . . is indeed little more than the register of the crimes, follies, and misfortunes of mankind."
—Edward Gibbon, *Decline and Fall of the Roman Empire,* 1776–1788

"The history of all hitherto existing society is the history of class struggles."
—Karl Marx and Friedrich Engels, *The Communist Manifesto,* 1848

History and Civilization

What is history? As the quotations above show, history can mean many different things to many different people. In short, it is the record of what men have thought and said and done in building today's civilization. We should add, though, that history comes to us mostly secondhand, from the pens of historians rather than from original documents. And, while historians will generally agree on what the facts are, they will, being human, often differ on what the facts mean.

History deals with groups of people. Civilization comes only when men live in co-operating groups. Consequently, the story of civilization must deal with group life. When individual persons enter the story, it is only because they are important members of their groups. Just as biography describes the life of individuals, so history describes the life of social groups such as churches, armies, states or countries, trading companies, and villages. History, then, is the story of human beings living in groups, rather than the account of the lives of individuals.

Formerly, history was largely concerned with kings, monarchies, constitutions, laws, diplomacy, and wars. These were, and still are, important parts of life; but they are by no means the whole story. Today, history deals with the entire life of a people: their houses, furniture, clothing, and food; the occupations they followed; the schools they had; the beliefs and superstitions they held; the amusements and festivals they enjoyed; the inventions and discoveries they made. Whatever is interesting or important in the life of a people comes within the scope of history.

Steps toward civilization. Civilization has been a long time in the making. Man was first a savage, then a barbarian, and finally a civilized being. The *savage* depends almost entirely on nature. He secures food from wild plants and wild animals; he knows nothing of metals but makes his tools and weapons of stone, wood, and bone; he wears little or no clothing; and his home is merely a cave, a rock shelter, or a hut of bark. Such primitive folk still live in the interior of Africa and Australia. The *barbarian* has gained more control over nature than the savage. He plants seeds, has domesticated animals, and uses some metal implements. Most American Indians before the coming of Columbus and many natives of Africa may be classified as barbarians. In contrast to the savage and the barbarian, the *civilized man* is one who, to a large extent, can change his surroundings to fit his needs and wants.

What is civilization? It is hard to say at what point the barbarian becomes a civilized man. The change is very gradual. Civilized men know how to control many things in their environment. They have learned how to transport goods, build cities, and organize governments. They have developed languages which enable them to think better than the barbarian. More important still, civilized men have learned to write and to keep records. To have a civilization a social group must have developed many arts and crafts. The Egyptians and Babylonians reached this stage of development about six thousand years ago. They cultivated the soil, laid out roads and canals, worked mines, built cities, organized stable governments and religious ceremonies, and kept written records.

History and Culture

While the historian deals primarily with civilized peoples who kept written records, he must also give attention to primitive peoples who made progress toward civilization by acquiring culture. Culture consists: (1) of *material things,* such as tools, houses, roads, machines, and books; (2) of *institutions,* such as laws, governments, and churches; and (3) of *ideas,* such as democracy, truth, immortality. A people's culture arises and grows from three sources: inheritance, cultural interchange, and invention. *Cultural inheritance* —consisting of such things as language, writing, customs, institutions—is what our predecessors have accomplished and passed on to us. To this each generation adds its own contributions. But *cultural interchange* also takes place, since no social group is completely isolated from other groups. This is the process of receiving ideas and ways of doing things from people outside one's own group. Among civilized men cultural interchange is promoted by means of trade, travel, and communication. The third source of culture is *invention,* a term applied to all improvements in culture. The invention may be an improved method of performing any activity, whether it is work, play, war, government, the education of the young, or the care of the sick.

The spread of culture. The history of civilization is the story of the development of culture as it grew and spread from land to land. We can trace the origins of culture in America through the British Isles, western Europe, Rome, and Greece back to the ancient Middle East. Similarly, China and India in the Far East have been the cultural mothers of many Oriental peoples. Our study of history will teach us how true it is that the roots of the present lie deep in the past.

The Peoples of History

The world's races. The world's population of about three billion people is divided into more or less distinct groups called races. We are not yet sure how they originated. Racial differences are based on physical traits, of which the most prominent is skin color. There are three main races, generally called Negroid, Mongoloid, and Caucasoid. We also use color labels—black, yellow, and white as convenient, though less accurate terms.

Distribution of races. When history began, each race occupied a separate geographical area. Thus we have come to associate the beginnings of the Negroid group mainly with Africa, and the Mongoloid peoples with Asia and the New World. (The American Indians

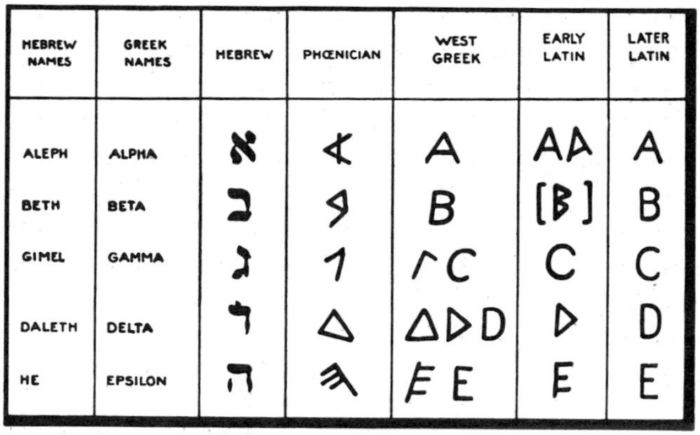

HEBREW NAMES	GREEK NAMES	HEBREW	PHŒNICIAN	WEST GREEK	EARLY LATIN	LATER LATIN
ALEPH	ALPHA	א	⟨	A	AΛ	A
BETH	BETA	ב	⌐	B	[β]	B
GIMEL	GAMMA	ג	1	⌐C	C	C
DALETH	DELTA	ד	△	△▷D	▷	D
HE	EPSILON	ה	�	ⱶE	ⱶ	E

SEVERAL FORMS OF THE ALPHABET. The Latin alphabet was derived from the Greek, and the Greek was derived from the Phoenician. Both the Hebrew and the Phoenician alphabets are thought to have had their beginnings in Egypt.

are Mongoloid.) The Caucasoid race was at first confined to Europe, northern Africa, and southwestern Asia. The Polynesians, a brown-skinned people who live in Oceania, seem to be a blend of Mongoloid and Caucasoid.

Besides the division of mankind into races, smaller groupings called nations, or nationalities, have developed. A nation consists of a group of people bound together by ties of common language, history, customs, and devotion to similar ideals. In modern times nations, or nationalities, are usually organized as separate political communities called states, occupying definite territories. For example, the French and the English are nations, or nation-states. It is inaccurate to speak of them as the French race or the English race. Both peoples belong to the Caucasoid race.

Man's migrations. Men have always been creatures who moved from place to place. From the cradleland, possibly central Asia, men roamed in all directions in quest of food, a pleasant climate, and plunder. Sometimes enemies pushed them onward. Extensive migrations began long before written records existed. Stone Age relics in Europe show this to be true. Furthermore, it is believed that the American Indians entered North America from Asia by way of the Bering Strait, spreading eastward and southward until they reached the tip of South America. Later, recorded history shows how Romans pushed

in upon Celts in Britain, only to give way in turn to Anglo-Saxons, to Danes, and to Normans. On the European continent, Germans and Slavs were hard pressed by Huns, Mongols, and Turks, who came from Asia during the Middle Ages. The Northmen, or Vikings, from Scandinavia furnish still another example of man's habit of wandering. Their settlements reached westward to Iceland, Greenland, and even to North America, and eastward through Russia and the borders of the Mediterranean. For us, the most significant migratory movement in history is the colonization of America by millions of Europeans.

Adaptability of man. Throughout all of these wanderings, man has shown a wonderful ability to adapt himself to changed surroundings. In order to gain a living, he has adjusted himself to extremes of heat and cold, to high altitude and to lowland.

Naturally, migrations have led to various degrees of intermixture, or fusion, of peoples. To indicate this mingling of peoples, we sometimes apply such terms as "crossroads of civilization" or "melting pot" to certain parts of the world. Indeed, it can hardly be said today that any pure races exist, if they ever did. To what race does the modern Egyptian or the modern Latin American belong? The question has no simple answer, for these peoples, like nearly every modern nation, are a fusion of many races.

AN EARLY WATER WHEEL. The water wheel above is an example of man's ability to adapt to his surroundings. Located near Alicante, Spain, it was used by early farmers to irrigate their dry fields. Below, "primitive" man is shown coping with the heat—a forerunner of our modern airconditioner.

Unity of Man. The tendency of modern science is to stress resemblances rather than differences among races and nations. All human beings have a common ancestry, even though it may be remote. The physical traits separating the races are numerous but do not seem to go deep. The same is true of mental traits. Besides, the languages, religions, superstitions, arts, and sciences of all mankind are similar. Nature has created no superior racial or national groups, although there are superior individuals. The peoples of the earth are by nature about equal in intelligence, in morality, and in capacity for social progress. Essentially mankind is one; and history, broadly speaking, is the story of all mankind.

REVIEWING THE CHAPTER

TERMS TO UNDERSTAND: *social group, savage, barbarian, invention, race, nation, fusion, cultural interchange, melting pot, cradleland.*

PLACES TO LOCATE: *Europe, Asia, Africa, Malaya, Bering Strait, Polynesia.*

QUESTIONS TO ANSWER

1. (a) Give a definition of history in your own words. (b) Distinguish between history and biography. (c) Do you think a history book should tell more than the political story? Why or why not?
2. (a) What are the outstanding characteristics of *civilized* peoples? (b) Distinguish between culture and civilization. (c) From what sources do people develop culture?
3. (a) What is the approximate population of the earth? (b) Into what main races are the world's people divided? (c) What characteristics distinguish one race from another? (d) Name a division, or group, of mankind which is smaller than a race. (e) Are the French people a race? Explain why they are or are not.
4. (a) Why have men constantly migrated? (b) What has been the effect of migrations on the races of mankind?
5. Why should we stress the resemblances of people more than their differences?

2 Prehistoric Man

THREE TYPES OF EARLY MAN. A study of the bones dug up by scientists has made it possible to reconstruct the features and appearance of primitive man. From left to right: Java man, Neanderthal man, and Cro-Magnon man.

CENTERS OF EARLY CIVILIZATION

This chapter is called "Prehistoric Man" because it deals with a stage of man's development before the time of written records. We must obtain our ideas of this long period (possibly two million years) from fossils, bones, tools, ashes of fires, fragments of pottery, and cave paintings. The account based on such remains is called prehistory. The historic age, on the other hand, begins in any region of the world when the inhabitants keep written records from which we can get some sort of picture of how they lived. Thus, in Egypt and Babylonia history began between 4000 B.C. and 3000 B.C. Written records in China and India go back beyond 1500 B.C., while those of Greece and Rome do not begin much before the seventh century B.C. In Central America writing dates from about 200 B.C. Most of Europe did not enter the historic age until after the opening of the Christian era. We need to remind ourselves, however, that the historic age, or the civilized portion of the human story, accounts for less than one four hundredth of man's total time on this earth.

Man Makes a Beginning

The expanding story of prehistory. Our knowledge of the prehistoric period is constantly growing and changing. This is so because trained scientists, using improved skills, have been roaming the world "digging" up new evidence of man's past. These are the archaeologists and the anthropologists, whose work is closely related. An *archaeologist* searches for the remains of centuries-old dwelling places, long since buried under windblown dust and sand. The relics he finds can often shed new light on the kind of life led by early humans and their ancestors. The *anthropologist* is interested in the same relics with a view to tracing the development of man and his culture from the earliest beginnings. But neither archaeologist nor anthropologist works as a "lone wolf." Today when an expedition goes on a "dig" at an ancient site, the team of experts frequently includes not only archaeologists and anthropologists, but geographers, geologists, surveyors, chemists, and possibly engineers. Even then, their findings must await careful examination by other specialists around the world.

Radioactive time clocks. To aid those who seek to unlock the remaining mysteries of man's remote past, new tools have become available. The most useful perhaps are two radioactive dating methods, by-products of atomic fission. (See pages 342–343.) One is the radiocarbon method, developed in 1946 by Willard F. Libby, an American chemist. It is based on the fact that all living (organic) materials such as bone, wood, and clothing contain the radioactive element carbon-14, which decays or breaks down at a known rate. For example, if the wood from an ancient cave fire gives off a radioactive count of 108 (measured by a Geiger counter), we know that the tree died 11,500 years ago. This method is fairly accurate in determining dates up to about 30,000 years ago. The other radioactive tool, the potassium-argon method, has been developed more recently. It can be used to measure into millions of years the age of volcanic rocks which encase the fossil remains of once-living creatures.

In search of man. Scientists have not yet determined with certainty when and where man first appeared on the earth. They are also uncertain as to which, if any, of the so-called man-apes, or primitive human types, are among our direct ancestors. They do agree that we descended, through a very long evolutionary process, from this kind of creature.

This idea follows the Darwinian theory, to be explained later.

The most productive trail in recent years has led to East Africa. At Olduvai Gorge in what is now Tanzania, the British anthropologist, Louis S. B. Leakey, over a period of many years uncovered a treasure of manlike fossil bones. One of the most significant of his finds came in 1964, when he unearthed the fossil parts of five individuals which he identified as hominids (the zoological family to which man belongs). He named the apparently new species *Homo habilis,* or skilled man, because of his tool-making ability. This newly found "man" evidently walked erect, had a fairly high forehead, a larger brain capacity than his predecessors, and presumably ate meat. Leakey claimed for him the distinction of being modern man's direct ancestor, with an age of roughly 1,750,000 years.

In 1967, Leakey added a new chapter to the story of man's evolution. At two sites in Kenya he found fossil fragments which showed that the family of man was distinct from the apes as long ago as 20,000,000 years. *Kenyapithecus africanus,* as he called the new pre-man, was different from his cousin the ape in the teeth and the jaw structure. Meanwhile, teams of anthropologists were exploring the sites of hominid remains in Ethiopia. Their discoveries all tend to push back the age of man's ancestry, but there is still much disagreement among anthropologists about when man first emerged. As Leakey himself has said, "We shall never be able to point to a specific time and a specific creature and say here man began." What is becoming more and more certain, perhaps, is that man's origins were in Africa, rather than in Asia.

The East African discoveries, plus the new radioactive dating methods, may change man's idea of his ancestral tree. Nevertheless, along man's evolutionary path earlier finds marked important stages of development.

The oldest known manlike remains before *Homo habilis* were those of the ape-man of Java, Pithecanthropus. Discovered in 1891 by Dr. M. Eugene Dubois, Java man's age is now estimated at over a half million years. Next in time, possibly 360,000 years ago, was Sinanthropus, or Peking man, unearthed in China in the late 1920's. Java and Peking men made skillfully shaped stone tools and used fire, although they had comparatively small brains. In Europe the first discovery of a manlike type was Neanderthal, named after the valley in Germany where his bones were first found in 1856. Since then, Neanderthal type remains have come to light in widely scattered places of the world—in Spain, North Africa, the Middle East, and Central Asia. If Neanderthal man were to be given an age, it might be roughly set at more than 100,000 years.

In appearance, Neanderthal man was still quite unlike "modern man," or unlike us in other words. His short, thickset body held up a long, flat-topped head, with retreating chin, sloping forehead, and pronounced eyebrow ridges. For reasons not clear, Neanderthal man disappeared in Europe and the Middle East about 35,000 years ago.

His place was taken by a hominid generally regarded by anthropologists as truly "modern man," or *Homo sapiens.* In Europe this type is broadly referred to as Cro-Magnon man, named after the French cave where five skeletons were uncovered in 1868. What distinguishes him from the earlier near-men are the refined head features—a taller skull with thinner walls, a finer and more prominent nose, slightly developed eyebrow ridges, a well-developed chin, and a larger brain case. The head is supported by a straight and slender neck, unlike the bullish neck of Cro-Magnon's predecessors. Where did he come from, or from whom was he descended? We can only say that perhaps he came into Europe about 35,000 B.C. and that the peoples of Europe, North Africa, and the Middle East may be his direct descendants.

Early man's environment. The story of man is closely bound up with the story of his home, the earth. Geography and climate have had a great influence on the development of human customs and habits.

Man first appeared during a geological period known as the Pleistocene or Ice Age. It began possibly more than 2,000,000 years ago. Although scientists still disagree over details about dates, divisions, and varying effects of the Ice Age in different parts of the world, we can outline its general characteristics. During this period an immense coating of ice, hundreds of feet thick, formed in the lands surrounding the North Pole and gradually moved southward. This icy mass covered North America as far south as the valleys of the Ohio and Missouri rivers, and much of northern Asia, Russia, and western Europe as far south as the valleys of the Thames and Rhine rivers. Glaciers (ice sheets) also arose in the Alps, the Pyrenees, and the Caucasus, and descended from these mountains into the plains. Moreover, the ice sheet made several major advances and retreats, beginning about 600,000 years ago and producing alternate cold and warm periods on the earth. In all, four such major cold, or glacial periods and three warm, or interglacial periods occurred during the Ice Age. We are now living in a fourth warm period called postglacial. The movements of the ice sheet also caused changes in land surfaces. For example, glacial action produced the Great Lakes in Mid-America.

Another effect of the Ice Age was to change the kind of animal and plant life in various areas of the earth. As the glaciers advanced and retreated, they moved climate zones with them. Changes in climate caused changes and variations in the kinds of animals and plants. Thus, the fossils of large mammals like the elephant and the lion have been found in England, far away from their present homes.

The changing phases of the Ice Age also affected man's living habits. He had to take refuge from the cold in caves or in crude brush shelters which he built above ground. He had to regulate his diet according to the kind and variety of available animals and plants in his region. His tools also had to be adapted to the particular needs of the hunt and the harvest wherever he lived. In short, to survive, man had to depend more and more on his inventiveness and ingenuity, characteristics which distinguish him from all other living creatures.

Early man's culture. The Neanderthalers and Cro-Magnons lived in a period of human development, or culture epoch, known as the Old Stone Age. Scientists often call it the Paleolithic Age, from paleolith, meaning "old stone." During the Old Stone Age, beginning possibly 1,000,000 years ago or more, this early dawn age man was still a savage. What he learned was the result of accidental discovery and his own resourcefulness. In fact, the only advantages he possessed over wild animals were his upright posture, which gave him the use of his hands, his flexible hand with its apposite thumb, and thinking ability.

Nature furnished man his first tools and weapons. These were branches, sticks, and rough stones, which he used as spears, clubs, missiles, and pounders. Man arrived at an important turning point when he developed from a tool-user into a toolmaker. Eventually he found that shaped implements were far more serviceable than those that nature provided; so he began chipping stones, especially flints, into crude hand-axes, knives, spearheads, borers, and the like. In addition to these crude stone tools, he gradually learned to make implements of bone, mammoth ivory, and reindeer horns. He also shaped tools for special uses, such as awls, wedges, saws, bone needles, drills, stone chisels, and barbed harpoons.

A still more important landmark in early man's progress was the discovery—perhaps 500,000 years ago—of how to make fire and how to keep it burning. We know that fire occurred by natural means, as the result of lightning or volcanic eruption. It was when man learned to create it artificially, perhaps by striking flints and producing sparks, that he turned a new corner. At any rate, the discovery of the uses of fire made it possible for men to protect themselves at night against wild beasts, to cook food instead of eating it raw, to preserve meats by smoking them, and to make their shelters more comfortable.

By exploring Paleolithic caves and rock shelters, we have been able to learn much about the home life of primitive men. In the many layers of ashes of successive generations, scientists have traced the slow steps by which man improved his living conditions. Some of the bone remains are those of animals like the woolly mammoth, the bison, the reindeer, and especially the steppe horse. As their weapons improved, men killed and ate these beasts, and thereafter their food was not confined to wild berries, roots, herbs, birds' eggs, shellfish, grubs, and small game. The presence of flint scrapers and bone needles tells us that men made clothing from the pelts of animals.

Cave life also brought out the artistic side of Paleolithic man. He spent time in decorating stone and bone implements with engravings, in making stone and ivory statuettes, and in covering the walls of his caves with drawings and paintings. The subjects are generally animals and the best are remarkably lifelike. (See pages xvi A and 15.) Furthermore the cave dwellers seem to have had a rude form of religion. Offerings of food, implements, and ornaments, found with buried bodies, indicate that men of the Old Stone Age believed in life after death. We can suppose, too, that family life had appeared and that people lived in small groups or communities under the leadership of a chief or a council of elders.

The Neolithic Revolution

Age of more rapid change. Man's accomplishments in the Old Stone Age had bettered his lot considerably. He had discovered fire, was adding handles to his weapons and implements, was making garments of skin, and perhaps was beginning to use the bow and arrow. These improvements marked the approach of a new culture period, the New Stone, or Neolithic, Age. It began about 10,000 years ago, probably somewhere in the Middle East (the region extending from the eastern shores of the Mediterranean to India). But it did not occur at the same time among peoples everywhere. There was much overlapping with older culture patterns. And although progress was much more rapid than before, it was uneven and no doubt was marked by a number of setbacks.

The implements used by Neolithic people were still of stone, bone, and wood, but they

THE STAGES OF MAN AND HIS CULTURE

PALEOLITHIC AGE	
1,750,000 (1.7 million) B. C.	Australopithecus, Homo habilis, Olduvai Gorge
1,000,000 (1 million) B.C.	Crude stone tools found in Africa and Europe
500,000 B.C.	Java Man, Peking Man
100,000 to 30,000 B.C.	Neanderthal Man, Hand axes
25,000 to 10,000 B.C.	Cro-Magnon Man
NEOLITHIC AGE	
8,000 B.C.	Invention of Agriculture (Jarmo)
4,000 B.C.	Beginning of Civilization (Sumerian cities)

were greatly improved. Man now polished his arrowheads and sharpened his stone axes by grinding. Neolithic people made pottery, chiefly for cooking and for storing food. They also plaited baskets, spun and wove textiles, prepared leather, built boats, and used wheeled carts. But most important of all, New Stone Age men cultivated some grains and raised food animals. As they changed from the hunting and gathering stage to the agricultural stage, they also began to settle in permanent villages.

From food gathering to food growing. When man began to grow the food he ate instead of gathering and hunting it, he made perhaps the most radical change in his whole history. All of his civilized achievements sprang from this transition, as we shall see.

We cannot be sure exactly how man became a farmer, except that it must have been by chance and by very slow steps. As a food gatherer he had harvested grass-like wild grains, such as wheat and barley, over a long span of time. He found that these could easily be stored for future use. No doubt he returned often to places where wild grains grew in abundance. By accident he might have strewn or spilled some of the ripe kernels on the ground while harvesting or storing them. Observing that they sprouted and grew, Neolithic man then took the crucial step—he deliberately sowed the seed to raise a crop.

It is more difficult to reconstruct the story of the domestication of animals. For some time after he raised crops of grain, the hunter-farmer depended on wild animals to fill out his diet. Some anthropologists believe that man first made pets of certain animals, es-

THE GREATEST SINGLE CHANGE

Then, about 8000 B.C., and somewhere in the Near East (as far as we know), the Neolithic way of life began ... It means a state of culture in which food is planted and bred, not hunted and gathered—in which food is domesticated, not wild. If we had to choose the greatest single change in human history right up to the present, this would be it. I mean, of course, a change by cultural evolution, as distinct from a biological change like standing erect, or gradually becoming able to use culture and language in the first place. And I do not mean that the change was sudden, or dramatic to those who were changing, as though a light were being switched on. It was dramatic, but long after, in its consequences, because everything else we have achieved flowed out of this as a beginning.

—William Howells, *Back of History— The Story of Our Own Origins.*

pecially the young, and that eventually these reproduced in captivity.

From cave and camp to village. Freed from the necessity of wandering about in search of food, Neolithic people began to settle in more or less permanent village-farming communities. Such settlements arose within perhaps a thousand years after the sowing of grains had begun. Digging into flat-topped mounds called tells, archaeologists have recently discovered the oldest known towns on earth. One is Jericho, north of the Dead Sea in present-day Jordan. Others equally old are Jarmo in northern Iraq and Tepe Sarab in Iran. All three, according to radiocarbon dating, go back to between 7000 and 6500 B.C.

At Jarmo, perhaps our best example, about twelve layers of habitation have been identified. The village at first consisted of something like two dozen mud-walled houses for 150 people. Here kernels of wheat and barley were found, as well as the bones of cattle, sheep, goats, pigs, and dogs. Moreover, the presence of stone mortars and pestles (for

grinding) indicates that the villagers made their grain into flour. Although the people of Jarmo still hunted and gathered some of their food, they now had time to develop other interests. Remains of pottery, woven baskets and rugs, and clay figures of animals and fertility goddesses tell us that they had religion and handicrafts. The beginnings of commerce are also evident.

By about 5000 B.C. farming villages such as Jarmo had spread into the lower Tigris-Euphrates valley, or Mesopotamia, "the land between the rivers." Eventually the new way of life reached eastward beyond the Caspian Sea and westward to the shores of the Mediterranean and into the great river valleys of Europe.

On the road to civilization. When man no longer had to worry about getting his next meal, his energy and thought could be directed into new channels. In order to eat, not everybody had to produce his own food any longer. Some people became skilled in certain crafts, making things that other people required and exchanging these things for food. In other words, specialization of task and division of labor began to develop. The result was larger communities in which handicraft industries and the exchange of goods could be carried on more easily. Contacts among people in such communities stimulated man's thinking and inventiveness as never before.

Neolithic man had now progressed from a wandering hunter and food gatherer to farmer and then to village and city dweller. In short, he had passed from savagery into barbarism. He needed only to acquire the use of metals and the art of writing to be called "civilized."

The Age of Metals

The use of stone for implements had its disadvantages. Stone is not pliable; it tends to split easily; and it is hard to grind and polish. In time men began to seek substitutes for stone in the softer metals—copper, gold, silver, and tin. When found in a pure state, these can be readily mined and worked cold. The widespread use of the softer metals marks the close of the Stone Age and the opening of the Age of Metals. This change first occurred at the eastern end of the Mediterranean basin, where Neolithic culture existed earlier than in Europe.

Copper. The Egyptians mined copper on the peninsula of Sinai at least as early as 4000 B.C. They seem to have been the first people to get metal from ore by means of heat, a process called smelting. The Babylonians were also skilled workers with copper at an early date.

Bronze. Implements made of copper were comparatively soft and would not keep an edge. Some ancient smith, doubtless through a lucky accident, discovered that the addition of a bit of tin to the copper produced a hard, tough alloy called bronze. Where this simple but most important discovery took place, we cannot say. Bronze made its appearance in Egypt by 3000 B.C., and somewhat later in Cyprus, Crete, Asia Minor, and on the coast of Greece.

Iron. At an early date metal workers must have noticed the great wearing qualities of iron. In contrast to copper and tin, however, iron is difficult to mine and smelt; therefore, its use came later than that of bronze. The Egyptians seem to have made little use of iron before 1500 B.C. They called it the "metal of heaven," a name which may indicate that

they obtained some of it from meteorites. Western and northern Europe became acquainted with iron only in the last thousand years before Christ.

Dawn of Civilization

Centers of early civilization. To develop the arts of civilized life, certain favorable circumstances are necessary. Among these we may mention especially a fertile soil, a moderate climate, and some natural barriers against invaders. Civilizations arose first in areas that had these advantages. In the Old World these regions were Egypt, Babylonia, northern India, and central China. Those in the New World—where civilization developed at a much later date—were Mexico, Central America, and Peru. From these original centers civilization has spread until it now covers most of the globe. (See map, page 10.)

Subdivisions of history. For the sake of convenience, historians divide the whole historic age into three periods—Ancient, Medieval, and Modern. Ancient history begins with the peoples of the Middle and Far East, where the arts of civilization first developed, about 3000 B.C. It deals next with the so-called golden age of the Greeks and ends with the decline of the Roman empire about 500 A.D. Medieval is a term that applies chiefly to the history of the peoples of eastern and western Europe. It covers about a thousand years, from the breakup of the Roman Empire to the discovery of America near the close of the fifteenth century, A.D. From about 1500 to the present we regard as Modern history. It is no longer the story of Asia or of Europe and the Americas, but of the whole world.

There is another division of time which historians commonly use. You have noticed that in the chapter the initials B.C. and A.D. have occasionally appeared. When following a number, B.C. indicates years before Christ, or before Christ's birth. Likewise, A.D., standing for *anno Domini* or the year of our Lord, refers to time since Christ was born. Thus, from 25 B.C. to A.D. 50 is 75 years. In this connection it is also well to understand the numbering of centuries, or hundred-year periods. When we speak of the nineteenth century we mean the span of time from 1801 to 1900. The first year of this century is 1901. A.D. is understood when no initials appear with the number. This dividing line of history arose as the result of the influence of Christianity.

REVIEWING THE CHAPTER

TERMS TO UNDERSTAND: *prehistory, history, archaeologist, anthropologist, carbon-14, hominid,* Homo sapiens, Homo habilis, *Pithecanthropus, Neanderthal, Cro-Magnon, Pleistocene, Paleolithic, Neolithic, tell, pestle, glacier.*

PLACES TO LOCATE: *Olduvai Gorge, Jarmo, Tepe Sarab, Jericho, Middle East, Mesopotamia, Caspian Sea, Egypt, India, China, Dead Sea, Caucasus Mountains, Asia Minor.*

QUESTIONS TO ANSWER

1. (a) How do we distinguish between prehistory and history? (b) Approximately where is the dividing line in time? (c) By what means have we been able to expand our knowledge of prehistory?
2. (a) Why is there so much uncertainty about the evolution of man? (b) What distinguishes "modern man" from his ape-like predecessors?
3. (a) Explain the change in man from tool-user to toolmaker. (b) Why was the discovery of fire such an important landmark in man's progress? (c) How do you account for early man's artistic and religious interests?
4. (a) What is meant by "the Neolithic revolution"? (b) How, perhaps, did man become a farmer? (c) What changes did living in village-farming communities bring about?

3 Civilization Arises in the Middle East

THE ROSETTA STONE. Found by Napoleon's soldiers near Rashid, Egypt, in 1799, it provided a vital clue to the translation of the hieroglyphics. It took the linguist Champollion fourteen years to decipher.

Bright is the earth when thou risest in the horizon.
When thou shinest as Aton by day
Thou drivest away the darkness.
When thou sendest forth thy rays,
The two Lands are in daily festivity,
Awake and standing upon their feet
When thou hast raised them up.
Their limbs bathed, they take their clothing,
Their arms uplifted in adoration to thy dawning.
Then in all the world they do their work.

—Ikhnaton

Geography of the Middle East

To understand how man's first civilizations began, we need to know something of the geography of the Middle East. Briefly, we may say that the Middle East includes southwest Asia and northeast Africa. Today the Middle East includes the countries of the Persian Gulf: Iraq, Iran, Saudi Arabia and its neighbors; and countries of the Red Sea and eastern Mediterranean: Egypt, Sudan, Israel, Jordan, Lebanon, and Syria, among others. As the map on this page shows, the three continents of Europe, Africa, and Asia come together in the Middle East. For this reason it has been called "the crossroads of the world." In the Middle East men of many nations have met since the beginning of history. (For a larger view of the region, turn to the map in color on pages xvi D and E.)

Little rainfall occurs in the Middle East; much of the region is desert or semidesert where people can raise food only with great difficulty. Two wonderfully fertile river valleys, however, provided favorable living conditions for early men. These valleys were formed by the Nile, which empties into the Mediterranean, and the Tigris and Euphrates,

emptying into the Persian Gulf. The valley dwellers needed little shelter and clothing in the hot, dry climate. They could raise three crops a year of grain and vegetables on the rich soil which the rivers brought down from the uplands. The streams also furnished water for irrigation. Moreover, the valleys yielded clay which, molded into brick and dried in the sun, became *adobe,* the cheapest building material imaginable. Stone and wood for building were found in the mountains. The rivers, and the seas into which they emptied, provided convenient means of transportation. All these advantages helped the valley dwellers to build the earliest civilizations.

The Rediscovery of Ancient History

We have long known something about the ancient civilizations of the Middle East. Much information has come from the Bible and from Greek and Latin writings. Within recent times, however, the extent and accuracy of our knowledge have been greatly increased. Archaeologists have uncovered the ruins of famous cities and interesting buildings. New finds of pottery, tools, and inscriptions are constantly being made. And, most important of all, we have learned how to read some of the most widely used kinds of ancient writing.

The Rosetta Stone. The rediscovery of ancient Egypt began when we learned to read the Egyptian hieroglyphs. These strange symbols, which covered the walls of tombs and temples, were long a puzzle to all inquirers. In 1799 one of Napoleon's soldiers found a stone slab (see page 18) having a face covered with inscriptions. Since it was found near the Rosetta mouth of the Nile it has become known as the Rosetta Stone. It bears inscriptions in three languages: at the top, hieroglyphs; in the middle, a later and simpler form of Egyptian writing; and at the bottom, Greek. Scholars assumed that the three inscriptions contained the same message. By comparing the known Greek letters with the unknown hieroglyphs they were finally able to read the other inscriptions on the stone. With this key, other Egyptian writing could be read. Thus, after centuries of silence, the records placed on pyramids, monuments, temples, and tombs have become known to us.

The Behistun Rock. A similar exploit resulted in the decipherment of Babylonian cuneiform writing used by the ancient inhabitants of the Tigris-Euphrates valley. The Behistun Rock, a limestone cliff, contained a long historical record carved by the order of Darius I of Persia. Three languages were used: Persian, Susian, and Babylonian. A series of pictures told the same story. One of the languages, Persian, was partly known. It furnished clues which led to the decipherment of the writing of the Babylonians.

Egyptian discoveries. The pyramids and other tombs of the Egyptians were furnished with objects for the use of the soul of the person buried there. Vessels for food and drink, furniture, jewelry, weapons, tools, toilet articles, playthings—these and other articles have been uncovered by modern investigators. One of their most famous discoveries was that of the tomb of Tutenkhamon, who ruled Egypt about 1360 b.c. Another sensational find, the Tell el-Amarna tablets, threw light on the international affairs of the Egyptian Empire at about the time of the reign of Ikhnaton. The tablets are clay bricks on which cuneiform writing appears. Most of the tablets are letters written over thirty-two hundred years ago and sent to Egyptian rulers by the kings of other countries.

The mounds of Babylonia and Assyria. The immense mounds lining the banks of the Tigris and Euphrates are the remains of extensive palaces, temples, and other public buildings. These structures, built of sun-dried brick and wood, decayed more quickly than the stonework of the Egyptians; they col-

DETAIL FROM THE BEHISTUN ROCK, showing Darius I facing nine rebel chiefs whose hands are bound behind them. An account of Darius's deeds was repeated in three kinds of cuneiform writing. The Persian portion, which was known, enabled scholars to read the Babylonian cuneiform symbols.

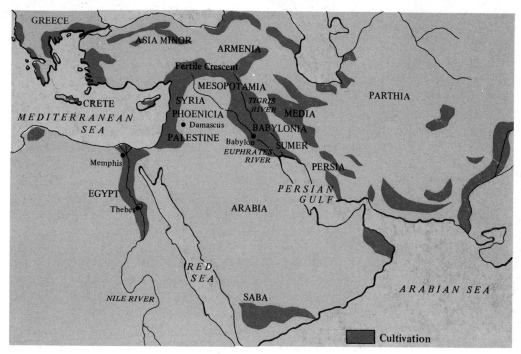

THE MIDDLE EAST IN ANCIENT TIMES

lapsed into shapeless mounds. Excavations within the mounds disclosed records, household articles, and works of art which tell the story of the past. Similar remarkable discoveries have also been made in Palestine, Syria, Asia Minor, and Persia. The knowledge thus gained throws light upon almost every aspect of life and thought in the ancient world of the Middle East.

Egyptian History in Ancient Times

The Nile. Egypt owes its existence to the Nile. This great river rises in the lakes of east central Africa and flows rapidly northward through Upper Egypt. The valley of Upper Egypt is five hundred miles long and thirty miles wide; a strip averaging only eight miles in width may be cultivated. Not far south of modern Cairo the hills inclosing the valley fall away, the Nile divides into numerous branches, and the delta of Lower Egypt begins.

The stream now becomes sluggish as it passes through a region of mingled swamp and plain. Lower Egypt has been created by the constant accumulation of silt at the mouth of the Nile. The river overflows its banks each summer and deposits a thin layer of rich sediment on the narrow plain through which it runs and over the delta, thus renewing annually the fertility of the soil. Rainfall in Egypt is so scanty that water has to be taken from the Nile to irrigate the farms after the annual flood is over.

Prehistoric Egypt. Stone Age men lived in the Nile valley thousands of years ago. They made beautiful implements of polished flint, fashioned pottery, built with brick and stone, sailed boats, raised domestic animals, and tilled the soil. In time the early Egyptians began to make tools from copper and to keep written records. The Egyptians probably lived at first in separate tribes, under the rule of chiefs. As civilization advanced, the tribal organization gave way to city-states. These were small, independent communities, each one centering about a town or city. The city-states by 3500 B.C. had combined into two kingdoms, one in the Delta, the other in Upper Egypt. The end of the prehistoric period is considered to be about 3000 B.C., when the Egyptians began to keep written records of yearly events.

At first the Egyptians wrote in pictures, such as the American Indians used. From these pictures were developed the hieroglyphs in which the later Egyptians wrote. The hieroglyphs were phonetic signs—that is, each stood for a sound, generally the sound of a syllable. By 3000 B.C. the Egyptians had arranged an alphabet of twenty-four letters, which is probably the source of our own al-

phabet. The Egyptians wrote with a small brush dipped in ink, drawing their hieroglyphs upon a material called *papyrus*. They made papyrus from a reed several inches thick which still grows along the Nile. They split the pith into thin strips, soaked them, and then pasted them together to form long sheets. The sheets were rolled up when not in use. Our word *paper* has come from Egyptian papyrus.

The Pyramid Age, c. 3000–c. 2100 B.C. The history of Egypt begins about 3000 B.C., when a ruler named Menes (mē′nēz) made himself king over both Upper Egypt and the Delta (Lower Egypt). Menes was the first of a long line of kings, or pharaohs as they are called in the Bible, who ruled in Egypt for over two thousand years. The union of Upper and Lower Egypt enabled the kings to suppress rebellions, extend the nation's boundaries, regulate irrigation, and promote prosperity. Proof of the power of the pharaohs can be seen in the great pyramids which they built during the first period of Egyptian history. We call this period the Pyramid Age or the Old Kingdom.

The Age of the Nobles, c. 2100–c. 1580 B.C. As time went on a class of landholding nobles grew strong enough to challenge the power of the kings. The period in which the nobles were strong is known as the Feudal Age or the Age of the Nobles. Civil wars broke out, bringing confusion and weakness to Egypt. About 1680 B.C. the fierce Hyksos (hĭk′sōs) from western Asia entered and conquered most of Egypt. These conquerors ruled for over one hundred years.

The Empire Age, 1580–1150 B.C. Upper Egypt never passed completely under the control of the Hyksos. The Egyptians learned to use the iron swords and horse-drawn chariots of their enemies and finally drove out the invaders. The pharaohs themselves then began a career of conquest. They raised great armies, invaded Palestine, Phoenicia, and Syria, and

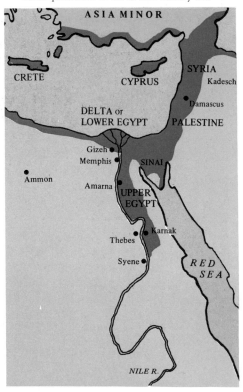

THE EGYPTIAN EMPIRE ABOUT 1450 B.C.
Weakened by civil war and invasion, Egypt lost its possessions in the twelfth century B.C.

ASIA MINOR

CRETE

CYPRUS

SYRIA
Kadesch

Damascus

DELTA or
LOWER EGYPT

PALESTINE

Gizeh
Memphis

SINAI

Ammon

Amarna

UPPER
EGYPT

Karnak

Thebes

Syene

RED
SEA

NILE R.

Man Emerges from Prehistoric Times

Old Stone Age cave painting, Lascaux, France

In prehistoric times men learned to use tools and weapons made of wood, bone, and stone. During the Old Stone Age man fashioned rough stone implements and drew pictures on cave walls. Almost always the artist pictured animals; almost never did he picture himself. At their best the drawings are remarkably lifelike and vigorous. It is even more remarkable that their colors have endured for as much as twenty thousand years. The scenes from Lascaux Cave, in France, date from the late Old Stone Age. Probably the pictures of animals were intended to give magical aid to the hunter when he went out in search of food, and they also may have played a part in religious ceremonies.

Lion of Ishtar, Babylon

The use of metals and the growth of systems of writing are among the marks of civilization. Iron, that most useful of metals, came into general use in the region which is now Turkey. Among the earliest masters of iron smelting were the Hittites. Remains of their cities still dot the Turkish plain, where modern excavation is bringing them to light. The picture at the top of page C shows that the Hittites, like the Egyptians, desired massive monuments.

Other civilizations appeared in the Tigris-Euphrates valley. Here stone was scarce, so builders turned to the use of brick. The use of glazed tiles set into a brick wall such as the lion from Babylon's Ishtar gate shows that man's desire and ability to express himself grew with each succeeding age. Later artists who made stained glass windows or mosaic pictures have developed and improved a Babylonian art.

Hittite sphinxes

Jaffa Gate, Jerusalem

Boreal forest
Midlatitude forest
Grassland
Mediterranean type
Savanna
Open forest

GREENLAND

ARCTIC

ATLANTIC OCEAN

Iceland

BRITISH ISLES

North Sea

SCANDINAVIAN PEN.

White Sea

Baltic Sea

GREAT EUROPEAN PLAINS

URAL MTS.

PYRENEES

ALPS

CARPATHIANS

Danube R.

Grassland

Dniepr

Don R.

Volga R.

Ural R.

G

MEDITERRANEAN SEA

BLACK SEA

CAUCASUS MTS.

Caspian Sea

Aral Sea

Amu R.

ATLAS MTS.

PLATEAU OF ANATOLIA

ELBURZ MTS.

PLATEAU OF IRAN

HINDU

S   A   H   A   R   A

FERTILE CRESCENT

Euphrates R.

Tigris R.

ZAGROS MTS.

SEISTAN DESERT

Niger R.

L. Chad

S   U   D   A   N

Nile R.

ARABIAN PEN.

RED SEA

Persian Gulf

Gulf of Oman

Equator

Congo R.

White Nile

Blue Nile

PLATEAU OF ETHIOPIA

Gulf of Aden

ARABIAN

Rainforest

L. Victoria

INDIA

22D

The Theater of the

Legend
- Ice pack
- Ice cap
- Tundra
- Desert
- Rain forest
- Cultivation
- Hills
- Mountains
- Salt pans

Early History of Mankind

In the Nile valley, the Egyptians built in stone on a scale so colossal that men still marvel. Much of the building was done for religious purposes. Thus we find immense temples, like the Temple of Luxor at Thebes, the pyramids, and the Sphinx. Many people besides the Hittites and Egyptians carved sphinxes, usually giving them a religious significance. Worship of the gods also played an important part in Egyptian writing. We give the name hieroglyph, *or sacred writing*, to the symbols used by the Egyptians, for writing was performed mostly by priests or scribes in the temples.

Sphinx and Pyramid of Cheops

Statues of Rameses II at Temple of Luxor

Various themes run through the works of ancient man. Religious feeling demanded expression growing nobler as man found his way from the cave to Jerusalem. Man's desire for artistic expression also made itself felt in the things he left behind. The paintings on walls of caves or tombs, the carving and rich decoration of statues, the erection of monuments, all show artistic feeling. Ways of living have changed, but the yearnings of man in the past are the yearnings we feel today. That is why to understand ourselves we need to understand the past.

Egyptian fishing and fowling skiff of painted wood

extended their rule beyond the Euphrates. Even the islands of Cyprus and Crete were under Egyptian influence. The Egyptian Empire lasted from 1580 to 1150 B.C., when its foreign possessions were lost. Egypt was conquered in turn by Ethiopia, Assyria, Persia (525 B.C.), and Rome (31 B.C.).

Egyptian Society and Culture

Ancient Egypt had no caste system, but there were, as in other countries, several more or less distinct classes. In Egypt the officials, priests, farmers, slaves, artisans, traders, and professional men, such as physicians and scribes, each formed a separate class. High officials, landholding nobles, and other wealthy persons formed an aristocratic group.

The king and his helpers. At the top of the social order stood the king, who was considered the earthly representative of the gods. Temples were erected to him and offerings were made to his sacred majesty. He had many duties. He was commander, judge, and high priest, all in one. In time of war he led his troops and faced the perils of the battlefield. In time of peace he held meetings with officials, hearing complaints, settling disputes, and issuing commands. The king was also occupied with a continuous round of sacrifices, prayers, and other religious ceremonies. Next to the king was the viceroy, who acted for the king during his absence; a host of other officials carried on the work of government. Faithful officials were rewarded by advancement, a practice which usually gave the kings efficient helpers.

Administration of law. Criminal law was crudely administered. Witnesses were tortured, and magic was employed in determining the guilt of the accused. The penalties for crime, however, were not extremely severe. Death was inflicted for only a few crimes, such as murder and stealing from temples. Laws relating to property and individual rights were much more highly developed than criminal law. Definite rules governed contracts, loans, leases, mortgages, partnership, marriage, and the family. The legal position of woman was high; she had full rights of ownership and inheritance and could engage in business on her own account.

Priests and religion. The priests formed an influential group. The people respected them, and in some periods they even performed political duties. Their principal concern, of course, was with religious matters. Egyptian religion was essentially nature worship. The sun became an object of particular adoration and was represented by several deities: Amon, Re, and Aton, and by Horus, god of the rising sun. Other popular divinities were Osiris, god of the dead, Isis, goddess of life, and Set, god of evil. Animals also played an important religious role. The jackal, bull, ram, hawk, crocodile, snake, and scarab (a beetle) received reverence because they were thought to be symbols of various gods. Thus Horus, son of Isis, was pictured as a hawk.

Toward monotheism in Egypt. A remarkable feature of Egyptian history was the movement toward a belief in one God (monotheism). The pharaoh Ikhnaton (ĭk·nä′t'n), who ruled about 1370 B.C., ordered the Egyptians to worship only the sun-god Aton as the creator and ruler of the world. Ikhnaton, who is pictured at worship on page 2, has been called the world's first monotheist. However, his reverence for the sun-god differed a good deal from monotheism as we know it today.

It is interesting to note that the Hebrews were then living in Egypt. Their beliefs also tended toward monotheism, although they were not as yet (according to one authority) "monotheistic in the usual sense of the word." Scholars have debated whether the Hebrews influenced or were influenced by the thinking of Ikhnaton. His "Hymn to the Sun," quoted at the beginning of this chapter, bears a striking resemblance to some parts of Psalm 104 of the Old Testament. (For more on Hebraic monotheism, see page 32.)

Naturally, some of his subjects resisted Ikhnaton's attempt to change their religion. Disturbances arose among the people and caused Ikhnaton to neglect the outlying parts of his empire. Appeals for help from his subjects along Egypt's frontiers are included in the clay tablets found at Tell el-Amarna, where he built a new capital city. Many of the appeals were ignored, and Egypt's empire shrank under attacks of invaders. After Ikhnaton's death his opponents brought back the old nature worship under his son-in-law, Tutenkhamon, and other rulers.

Belief in the future life. The Egyptians believed that man has a soul which survives the death of the body. They thought, however,

DISCOVERY OF TUTANKHAMEN'S TOMB. Opened in 1922, it was the first tomb of an Egyptian king to be discovered intact. The body was preserved in a solid gold casket.

that the soul would cease to exist if the body was not preserved. This explains the care with which the embalmed body (mummy) was prepared and protected; the pyramids were built to protect the bodies of kings. The Egyptians came to think of the hereafter as a place of rewards and punishments. They believed that a man's heart was weighed in the scales of judgment before the throne of Osiris, god of the dead. The righteous soul was admitted to the happy land, where it joined Osiris. If the scales turned against the soul it was cast to waiting monsters.

Economic life. The land in Egypt was owned largely by the king and other wealthy persons. It was divided into great estates rather than small farms. The work was done by peasants and slaves, who led a dreary, monotonous existence. Their labor is pictured in great variety and detail on Egyptian monuments. Most of the work was done by hand with crude tools, but work animals pulled the wooden plows. The farms, when properly irrigated, produced large crops in spite of the primitive methods of the workers. Wheat and barley were the principal grains; vegetables and fruit grew in great abundance. Cattle, sheep, goats, and pigs were raised. Oxen and asses were the usual work animals. The horse, introduced under the Hyksos, was used chiefly by the army.

Blacksmiths, carpenters, stonecutters, weavers, potters, glass blowers, and workers in ivory, silver, and gold lived in every city. The creations of these ancient craftsmen often exhibited remarkable skill. Egyptian linens were so wonderfully fine and transparent as to merit the name of "woven air." Egyptian glass, with its lines of different hues, was much prized. Fine vases, linen, jewelry, and papyrus were produced in great quantities for export to other lands.

The Egyptians carried goods up and down the Nile, the natural highway for trade among themselves. They also traded with

EGYPTIAN BOOK OF THE DEAD. The gods are passing judgment on a dead man, whose heart is being weighed on the scale of truth. If the gods decide against the dead man, his soul will be devoured by the monstrous animal seen in the center.

other countries both by overland routes and by sea. The Egyptians, pioneers in so many fields of human activity, probably built the first seagoing ships. As early as the thirtieth century B.C. they began to venture out into the eastern Mediterranean. Soon they had a thriving trade with both Cyprus and Crete, which lay not far from the mouths of the Nile. The ships of the pharaohs also sailed up and down the entire length of the Red Sea, bringing ebony and cinnamon from the east coast of Africa. Ivory, gold, and ostrich feathers were brought overland from the region south of Egypt, and from Syria came fish, wine, and incense. During early times goods were simply exchanged; eventually the Egyptians used small pieces of gold, each of which was equal to the value of a cow. They weighed the metal whenever a purchase was made. The weigher with his scales appears in many pictures on Egyptian monuments.

Egyptian literature. Next to historical inscriptions, the most interesting type of Egyptian literature is that which deals with religion. Hymns and magic sayings have been found in great numbers. The best-known work is the *Book of the Dead,* a collection of hymns, prayers, and magical phrases to be recited by the soul on its journey beyond the grave. A chapter from this work usually covered the inside of the mummy case. In addition to historical and religious writings, a number of poems, folk songs, and tales have been discovered.

Houses and architecture. Aristocratic families lived in large, well-built houses made of wooden frames covered over with brick. The latticed windows with their colored curtains gave the houses an air of charm. Well-planted gardens and orchards supplied abundant food, and numerous servants gave respectful attention to the wishes of their masters. The poor people lived in one-room houses made of mud bricks. In the cities the houses had only a single wall between them. Narrow alleys marked off blocks of such hovels. Although many Egyptian houses showed skill in building, Egyptian architecture appeared at its best in the tombs of the kings and the temples of the gods. These structures, even in their ruins, leave upon the observer an impression of peculiar massiveness, solidity, and grandeur. They seem to have been built for eternity.

Engineering. The art of stonemasonry arose in Egypt earlier than anywhere else in the world. It soon produced the Great Pyramid, the largest stone structure ever erected in ancient or (until recently) in modern

COLUMNS FROM THE TEMPLE OF KARNAK AT THEBES

times. This huge tomb originally towered almost 500 feet above a square base, which measured 756 feet on each side. One must walk over half a mile in circling the Great Pyramid. It was made of 2,300,000 limestone blocks, with an average weight of two and one-half tons. The largest and finest example of Egyptian temple building is the Karnak Temple, at Thebes. The Egyptians learned how to raise buildings with vast halls, the roofs of which were supported by rows of columns (colonnades). Windows at the sides of an upper story (clerestory) furnished light for the interior of these halls. The column, the colonnade, and the clerestory were adopted by Greek and Roman builders, from whom they have descended to us. Another example of Egyptian engineering genius was the canal built to connect the Nile with the Red Sea four thousand years ago.

Egyptian science. Conspicuous advance took place in the exact sciences. A very old Egyptian manuscript contains arithmetical problems with fractions as well as whole numbers, and geometrical formulas for computing the capacity of storehouses and the area of fields. The Egyptians also knew something of astronomy. By 2780 B.C. they had formed a solar calendar consisting of twelve thirty-day months, with five extra days at the end of the year. This calendar, improved by the insertion of leap years, is the one we use. In medicine the Egyptians made some progress. An old medical treatise which has been preserved distinguishes various diseases and notes their symptoms. The curious characters by which druggists indicate grains and drams are of Egyptian origin.

Schools. Such schools as existed in Egypt were attached to the temples and were conducted by priests or scribes. Reading and writing formed the chief subjects of study. A pupil who learned to read and write might become a scribe. When a man received a letter he usually employed a scribe to read it to him and to write the reply. The scribes also compiled and copied the papyrus rolls which were the Egyptian books. Only the well to do could afford these books or even learn to read them. The common people remained grossly ignorant.

Babylonia in Ancient Times

The Tigris and the Euphrates. Two famous rivers rise in the mountains of Armenia—the Tigris and the Euphrates. Flowing southeastward, they approach each other to form a single valley, proceed in parallel channels for the greater part of their course, and unite shortly before reaching the Persian Gulf. In antiquity each river had a separate mouth. The soil which the Tigris and Euphrates bring down every year fills up the Persian Gulf at the rate of about three miles a century. Their delta was therefore much less extensive five or six thousand years ago than it is today. In ancient times it was a plain about 170 miles long and 40 miles wide. It is best known to us as Babylonia, after Babylon, which became its leading city and capital, or as *Mesopotamia,* meaning "the land between the rivers."

Babylonian history. Babylonia, like Egypt, offered many advantages to early man. The fertile valley of the two rivers yielded abundant harvests, workable clay, and the nutritious fruit of the date palm. Since large stone deposits were lacking, the Babylonians used clay for building and even for writing material. For this reason their civilization is said to have been "built on mud."

Wars were frequent in ancient Babylonia. Tribes of hunters from the northern mountains and tribes of herdsmen from the southern grasslands often tried to conquer this rich land. The *Sumerians* were the earliest inhabitants from whom we have written records. They had entered Babylonia by 3700 B.C. and gradually settled down to a life of farming. A number of independent city-states grew up, each with its king and patron god. By

HAMMURABI RECEIVING HIS CODE OF LAWS FROM THE SUN–GOD. Hammurabi is at the left, standing before the god. The king had this sculpture carved at the top of a stone shaft on which was inscribed his body of laws, c. 1750 B.C.

about 1750 B.C. the Sumerian city-states were conquered and united by Semitic invaders from Arabia. Hammurabi (häm'ŏŏrä'bĕ), the Semitic king who completed the work of unification, made Babylon the capital city of what was henceforth called Babylonia. For about three hundred years Babylonian civilization was at a high level, but it declined under successive invasions from both north and south.

Babylonian culture. The upper class of Babylonia consisted of officials, priests, nobles, and wealthy merchants. A middle class in-

RUINS OF BABYLON. Babylon was the center of a flourishing civilization nearly four thousand years ago. Destroyed by the Assyrians, it was later rebuilt by the Chaldeans.

cluded small farmers, artisans, and shopkeepers. Slaves made up the lowest class. The distinction between classes was sharper and more rigid than in Egypt. Slaves and poor freemen who broke the laws were punished more severely than were members of the upper class.

The king governed all Babylonia after it was united by the Semitic conquest. A host of tax collectors and inspectors carried out the royal orders. Written laws placed some limits on the power of the king and protected the rights of his people.

The Babylonians were a very legal-minded people. When a man sold some wheat, married a wife, bought a slave, or made a will, the transaction was recorded on a contract tablet. The soft clay tablets were written upon with a wedge-shaped stylus. We call such writing *cuneiform* (from Latin *cuneus,* meaning "wedge"). Every property owner had a seal which he could stamp, as a signature,

upon his contract tablets. A completed tablet was dried or baked until hard, and was protected by a clay case or envelope. These tablets have given us a wealth of information.

Hammurabi is famous for his code of laws, as well as for his unification of Babylonia. We have discovered an almost complete text of these laws. Recent discoveries show that Hammurabi's code was based in part on a still earlier code. Hammurabi's code shows, in general, a keen sense of justice. A man who tried to bribe a witness or a judge was to be severely punished. A farmer who carelessly allowed his irrigation dikes to break and flood his neighbor's land was compelled to pay for the damage he caused. Other laws provided harsh punishment for personal injuries. For instance, a son who struck his father was to have his hands cut off. The nature of the punishment depended, moreover, on the rank of the injured party. A person who

NEW YORK CITY. The center of a great civilization today, will New York someday exist only in ruins like those of Babylon? Or will modern man learn to preserve and enrich his great urban centers?

caused the loss of a "gentleman's" eye was to have his own plucked out; but if the injury was done to a poor man, the culprit had only to pay a fine. These laws give us a vivid picture of Babylonian society twenty centuries before Christ.

Economic life. The earliest records of Babylonia contain references to canals and irrigation ditches. The cost of constructing and maintaining an irrigation system was considerable; consequently most of the land was owned by persons of wealth, such as nobles and merchants. Slaves and tenant farmers worked the estates. Wheat, barley, and dates were the principal crops. Great numbers of sheep were raised to supply wool, which was one of the principal exports.

As active businessmen, the Babylonians improved upon the commerce and industry which the Sumerians had developed. Skilled craftsmen made fine woolen and linen garments, tapestries, leather goods, and jewelry. Manufactured goods and farm produce were sent in ships to India; caravans followed overland roads as far east as China and as far west as Egypt and Asia Minor.

Architecture. The architecture of the Tigris-Euphrates peoples differed entirely from that of the Egyptians, because brick rather than stone formed the chief building material. In Babylonia the most typical structure was the temple. It was a solid square tower, rising in stories (usually seven) to the top, where the shrine of the deity stood. Each story was smaller than the one below, so that each side had the appearance of a flight of stairs. These temples were centers of business as well as of religion.

Religion. The Babylonians, like the Egyptians, practiced nature worship. Their chief gods were Marduk, god of the earth; Ea, god of the waters; and Anu, god of the heavens.

The Babylonians believed that they were constantly surrounded by a host of evil spirits who caused insanity, sickness, accidents, and death. To protect themselves against these spirits, the Babylonians wore charms and put the image of a god at their doors. Magicians recited incantations over sick people.

The Babylonians believed in *divination* (foretelling the future) by interpreting dreams, by casting lots, and by examining the entrails of animals slain in sacrifice. They commonly used a sheep's liver for this prac-

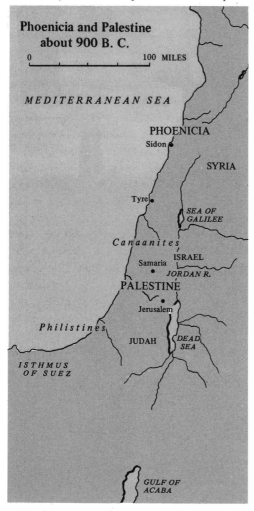

SYRIA, PHOENICIA, AND PALESTINE about the time of Solomon. Palestine was known in ancient times as Canaan. Since 1948 it has been called Israel.

tice. Divination by the liver was studied for centuries in the temple schools of Babylonia, and the practice afterward spread to the Romans. The Babylonians also tried to read their fate in the stars. The five planets then recognized, as well as comets and eclipses, were thought to exercise an influence for good and evil on the life of man. *Astrologers,* who seek to tell the future from the stars, still carry on a practice which the Babylonians began.

Education and libraries. Schools existed in Babylonia at an early date. The students learned to read, write, and work problems in arithmetic. They practiced writing with the stylus by copying moral sayings; some of the copybooks of children who went to school four thousand years ago have been preserved. We have also discovered parts of immense libraries which Babylonian kings collected long ago.

Literature. Parts of two famous Babylonian epics (long poems) have been preserved on clay tablets found in a royal library. The epic of the Creation tells how the god Marduk slew a terrible dragon; with half the body of the dragon he made a covering for the heavens, in which he placed the stars and moon. Last he created man, in order that the service and worship of the gods might be established forever. The second epic contains an account of a deluge, sent by the gods to punish sinful man. The rain fell for six days and nights and covered the entire earth. All people were drowned except the Babylonian Noah, his family, and his relatives, who safely rode the waters in a boat.

Mathematics and science. The Babylonians developed great skill in mathematics. They understood many of the principles of algebra and geometry, and knew how to solve complicated problems in arithmetic. Instead of counting by units of ten, as we do in the decimal system, they counted by units of sixty. We use the Babylonian system in our reckoning of time, for we divide the hour into sixty minutes and the minute into sixty seconds. We are also indebted to the Babylonians for founding the science of astronomy. They took interest in the movements of the planets and recorded unusual events such as eclipses of the sun and moon.

New Nations Arise

The western Fertile Crescent. The Egyptians and Babylonians speak in their records of smaller nations which arose in or near the western Fertile Crescent. You will find the Fertile Crescent marked on the map of the ancient Middle East, page 21. The Fertile Crescent is the name given to a strip of rich soil which curves like a half-moon from the Tigris-Euphrates valley to the shore of the Mediterranean Sea. Babylonia lay at the eastern end; at the western end there grew up a number of smaller nations which made important contributions to our civilization. As we shall see, the Hittites, Lydians, Phoenicians, and Hebrews each influenced history.

A civilization built on iron. The map on page 21 shows the Hittites' homeland in Asia Minor (now Turkey), just north of the Fertile Crescent. Here the Hittites built a number of cities whose sites are now being excavated. (Hittite sphinxes are shown on page xvi B.) Clay tablets found in the ruins of their cities make it clear that the Hittites had become civilized by 2000 B.C., and that in the following centuries they held a loosely organized empire including part of the Fertile Crescent.

Probably the most notable accomplishment of the Hittites was their mastery of ironworking. Although the Egyptians knew something of iron (see page 21), it was the Hittites who first learned to mine and smelt iron on a large scale. Armed with iron weapons, Hittite armies advanced along the Mediterranean coast toward Egypt. In 1285 the two empires met head-on at the Battle of Kadesch. Neither side won decisively, and both empires began

---

LANGUAGE GROUPS

Semitic languages were spoken, in general, by people living west and south of the Tigris-Euphrates valley. Among the Semitic languages were those used by the Assyrians, the Babylonians, the Phoenicians, and the Chaldeans. Modern Arabic and Hebrew are Semitic languages.

Indo-European languages include those spoken by both Persians and Hindus in Asia, as well as Greek, Latin, German, English, and others in Europe.

---

to decline soon afterward. Egypt's Empire Age ended by 1150 B.C. The Hittite Empire disappeared at about the same time.

The Lydians invent coinage. West of the Hittites, on the coast of the Aegean Sea, lived the people whom we know as Lydians. They are remembered for trade, not for conquest, and for the use not of iron but of gold. Mines in their country gave the Lydians a supply of gold and silver which they began to use as money. Some forms of money had been used previously in other lands: the Chinese, for instance, circulated bronze articles as money by the 13th century B.C. However, the Lydian government was the first to issue coins which had been stamped to indicate their value.

Phoenicians carry the alphabet. The Phoenicians lived in the western Fertile Crescent on a narrow strip of Mediterranean coast (see map at the left). Since their tiny land could not support a large population by farming, the Phoenicians became a nation of sailors, merchants, and artisans (skilled craftsmen). By the 14th century B.C. they were writing with an alphabet of twenty-nine characters. They produced fine carpets and glassware, artistic works in silver and bronze, and beautiful purple cloth. These goods were carried to the east by caravan and to the west by ships: east to Babylon and perhaps to India, west to seaports on the Mediterranean Sea. The map on page 61 shows numerous settlements which the Phoenicians established in Europe and North Africa. Of these, the most famous was Carthage. Wherever the Phoenicians came ashore, they influenced the culture of the natives with whom they traded. Thus we find that the Greeks and Romans based their alphabets on that of the Phoenicians. In fact, many ancient and modern alphabets have descended from the alphabet of the Phoenicians.

Origin of the Hebrews. The Hebrews lived in Palestine, south of Phoenicia (see map). The story of the Hebrews is one of almost constant struggle with poor soil, active enemies, and oppressive rulers. Famine in Palestine forced them to move to Egypt, where they dwelt peacefully in the Delta for many generations. But after the Egyptians enslaved them they fled into the desert of Sinai, and for forty years they wandered before settling once more in Palestine.

The Hebrew kingdom. After years of struggle the twelve Hebrew tribes conquered Palestine. The most glorious period in Hebrew history followed. In the eleventh century B.C. the tribes united under a ruler named Saul. David, Saul's successor, overthrew their enemies the Philistines and made Jerusalem the Hebrew capital. In the reign of David's son Solomon (c. 973–c. 933 B.C.), the Hebrew kingdom reached the height of its power. Shortly after Solomon's death the kingdom split into two parts, Israel and Judah. The Assyrians conquered Israel, and the Chaldeans annexed Judah. In 586 B.C. the Chaldeans destroyed Jerusalem and led most of the people to captivity in Babylonia. When the Persians captured Babylon (538 B.C.), they permitted the Hebrews to go home.

Importance of the Hebrews. Hebrew religion and literature have played an important part in shaping modern civilization. In their years of wandering, these people formed a religious conception—a belief in one God, Jehovah, ruler of all mankind. Moses brought the Ten Commandments down from Mt. Sinai as a guide to righteous conduct. The Hebrews also gave Christianity to the world through the life and teachings of Jesus.

The power of ideas. The record of the Hittites, Lydians, Phoenicians, and Hebrews should remind us that ideas can sometimes change history more effectively than conquering armies. Although these nations never dominated the ancient Middle East, they left an indelible mark on the record of mankind. It is difficult to imagine our world without iron (from the Hittites), coined money (from the Lydians), an alphabet for writing (developed by the Phoenicians), and the concepts of worshiping God and following an ethical or moral code (bequeathed by the Hebrews).

Assyrians, Chaldeans, and Persians

The empire builders. The early history of the Middle East records the growth of several more or less separate civilizations. After 800 B.C. these civilizations were conquered and organized into great empires by military powers. The conquering nations made few contributions of their own to civilization. They are important because their empires

NINEVEH, CAPITAL OF ASSYRIA. Located on the Tigris River, this walled city contained vast palaces and imposing temples. The palace buildings alone covered twenty-five acres.

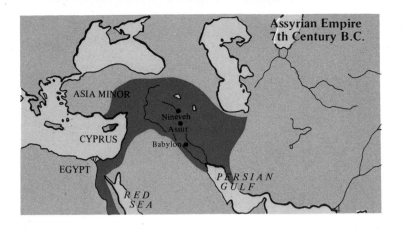

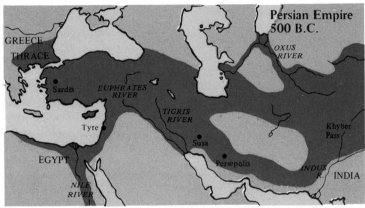

TWO ANCIENT EMPIRES. Conquerors of ancient times spread death and destruction as they struggled to dominate the Middle East. Of all the empire builders the Assyrians were the most cruel and destructive, while the Persians did most to spread civilization.

united the older civilizations and thus helped to speed the exchange of arts and ideas. The Assyrians, Chaldeans, and Persians built the greatest empires of the Middle East in ancient times.

The Assyrians. The Assyrians were the terror of the ancient world. They came from the region of the upper Tigris River, where their capital, Nineveh, was built. Assyrian armies, equipped with horses, chariots, and iron weapons, had conquered all the Fertile Crescent, part of Persia, and much of Egypt by about 750 B.C. (See the map above.) The Assyrians organized their empire into several

districts, each governed by an official responsible to the king. Many roads were constructed to promote trade, the movement of troops, and the carrying of messages. Great palaces—the characteristic structures of Assyrian architecture—give evidence of the power of the kings. They collected large libraries containing writings drawn from many parts of the Middle East. However, the harshness and cruelty of the Assyrians finally drove their subjects to revolt. At the same time the Assyrians had to meet attacks by Medes from the north and Chaldeans from the south. After a terrible siege the great capital of Nineveh was taken by storm (612 B.C.), and the Assyrian empire fell. It had dominated the Fertile Crescent for a century and a half.

The Chaldeans. The Chaldeans, whose empire has been called the Second Babylonian Empire, now became rulers of the Fertile Crescent. They made the ancient city of Babylon their capital. The best-known Chaldean king was Nebuchadnezzar (605–562 B.C.), who waged several successful wars of conquest. It was he who captured Jerusalem in 586 B.C., brought the kingdom of Judah to an end, and carried the Hebrews to Babylonia. Nebuchadnezzar also built the Hanging Gardens of Babylon, one of the Seven Wonders of the World. The Chaldean empire lasted less than one hundred years; a powerful alliance of Medes and Persians overthrew it in 538 B.C., when they captured Babylon. The Bible tells how the prophet Daniel foretold the fall of Babylon when he interpreted "the writing on the wall."

The Persians. The Persians and their kinsmen, the Medes, were an Indo-European group. By the time they entered Babylon, the Persians had already conquered a great belt of territory to the north, and had become united with the Medes under a king known as Cyrus the Great (550–529 B.C.). He and his successors led the Persian armies to a notable series of victories. They enlarged the empire until it included Egypt and part of Europe and extended east into northwestern India. (See the map on page 33.) The Persians were able to maintain their vast empire for over two hundred years, partly because of an efficient system of administration. The entire empire, excluding Persia proper, was divided into about twenty provinces ruled by governors (satraps). Special agents traveled about to investigate the conduct of the royal officials. The empire was further united by a system of military roads.

In religion the Persians approached monotheism. The great prophet Zoroaster taught that Ahura Mazda, the heaven deity, is the maker and upholder of the universe. As a god of light and order, of truth and purity, he opposed the forces of darkness and evil. Man, by doing good and avoiding wrong, can help Good to triumph over Evil. Zoroastrianism still survives in some parts of Persia and among the Parsees (Persians) of India. The Persians were the heirs of Babylonian and Assyrian culture. They used cuneiform writing and imitated Assyrian architecture, sculpture, and military tactics. In several fields the Persians advanced beyond anything that had been done before. Their art was developed to the highest degree of any ancient civilization and its influence is still noticeable today. Many fruits, vegetables, and flowers familiar to us were first grown by the Persians. Their experiments and progress in animal husbandry have also benefited both eastern and western civilizations.

The Persians spread civilization. As a result of uniting the ancient world the Persians aided the spread of civilization. They abolished many old frontiers when they brought different nations under one government, and thus broke down isolation. Persian kings developed their military roads into the finest system of highways which existed before the Romans. Along these highways moved the caravans of traders from many lands, carrying new customs and ideas throughout the Persian empire. Persia also dug a "Suez" canal between the Nile and the Red Sea, partly for use by the Persian fleet but also as an aid to seaborne commerce. Ease of transportation and travel, the protection given by Persia's army and navy, the profits to be gained from selling goods throughout the vast empire—all encouraged communication. The best work and thought of each nation passed to other peoples and became the property of all. Although the Greeks called the Persians "barbarians," the Persians in fact were the friends of civilization.

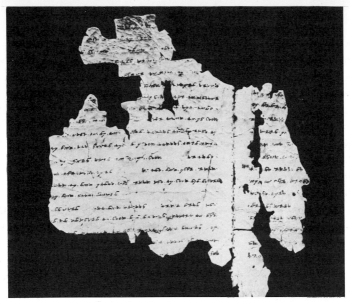

DEAD SEA SCROLL. The fragment above is from the historic Dead Sea Scrolls, found in 1947 near the Dead Sea. Made of parchment, they are more than two thousand years old.

REVIEWING THE CHAPTER

TERMS TO UNDERSTAND: *adobe, hieroglyph, cuneiform, delta, city-state, papyrus, pharaoh, pyramid, nature-worship, monotheism, viceroy, colonnades, clerestory, solar, scribe, divination, astrology, astronomy, satrap.*

PERSONS TO IDENTIFY: *Menes, Tutenkhamon, Ikhnaton, Hammurabi, Saul, David, Solomon, Moses, Zoroaster, Nebuchadnezzar, Cyrus the Great.*

PLACES TO LOCATE: *Middle East, Nile River, Tigris River, Euphrates River, Assyria, Lydia, Phoenicia, Palestine, Fertile Crescent, Thebes, Carthage, Nineveh, Babylon, Jerusalem, Kadesch, Mesopotamia.*

QUESTIONS TO ANSWER

1. (a) Where is the Middle East? (b) List five advantages which the river valleys offered to the men who built the earliest civilizations.
2. How have scholars learned about the first civilizations in the Middle East?
3. Describe the method of writing developed by the early Egyptians.

4. (a) Into what three periods is the ancient history of Egypt divided? (b) Give the approximate dates and the chief events of each. (c) What empire conquered Egypt?
5. (a) Describe the main features of Egyptian legal and religious practices. (b) What occupations of the Egyptians are still followed in our country? (c) What are some advantages a country gains from foreign trade?
6. Make a list of Egyptian achievements in engineering and the sciences.
7. (a) Why do we say that civilization in the Tigris-Euphrates valley was "built on mud"? (b) Name some of the chief occupations of the Babylonians. (c) How did they try to foretell the future? In so doing what science did they begin?
8. Name the four countries which arose at the western end of the Fertile Crescent. For what do we remember each?
9. (a) Name three countries which built great empires in the ancient Middle East. (b) Which one was most noted for its cruelty? (c) Which was largest? How did it contribute to the spread of civilization?

4 Early Civilizations Arise in India and China

"SCHOLARS COLLATING CHINESE CLASSIC TEXTS." Among the most important works of Chinese literature are the "Classics," which include the ancient works compiled by the great teacher Confucius and his disciples. The scholars in this painting lived around the tenth century A.D. during the Sung dynasty, under whose rule Chinese arts, literature, and science reached new heights.

The Middle East did not have the only civilizations which appeared in ancient times; others were developed by the peoples of India and of China. We know less about them than we do about ancient Egypt and Babylonia. The writing used in the first Indian civilizations has not been deciphered, and archaeological work in China has been limited by the Communists. Although our knowledge is still limited, it is becoming increasingly clear that civilizations were built more or less independently in many places by many peoples. The arts and skills of civilization belong to all races of mankind.

Lands and Peoples of Asia

The continent of Asia. In our discussion of the ancient Middle East we became acquainted with only a small part of Asia. The map in color on pages 22 D and E suggests Asia's enormous size. It is the largest of the continents, making up nearly one third of the earth's land surface. As the map shows, Europe and Asia are part of a single land mass. Asia is separated from Europe by the Mediterranean Sea, the Black and Caspian seas, and the Caucasus and Ural mountains.

The Asiatic continent is varied as well as vast. It extends from the equator (which passes through the East Indies) to a point north of the Arctic Circle. Asia therefore has some of the hottest regions of the world as well as some of the coldest. The climate of Asia is also affected by marked changes in altitude, which ranges from 1200 feet below sea level at the Dead Sea basin to nearly 30,000 feet (more than five miles) above sea level on lofty Mount Everest in the Himalayas. Much of central Asia is desert or semidesert; some lands nearer the coast, on the other hand, have rainfall ranging to more than four hundred inches per year.

Asia's coastline is rather uniform and unindented, so good harbors are rare. The mighty mountains, the deserts and barren plateaus, and the scarcity of navigable rivers also make travel difficult. Consequently, the early civilizations of Asia tended to remain more remote and isolated than did those in the Middle East.

Population of Asia. Asia contains over half of the world's population. Yet most of the continent is sparsely settled, for the mountain slopes, the steppes (plains) of central Asia, the deserts, the forests, and the tundras (treeless Arctic plains) support few inhabitants. The people who live in these regions support themselves chiefly by hunting and herding. The bulk of Asia's population is found in southern and southeastern Asia, where agriculture forms the principal means of livelihood.

Asiatic races. All the races of man are found in Asia. The Negroid race is represented by the dwarf blacks found in the Malay Peninsula. Some people in southern India also have Negroid characteristics. Members of the Caucasoid, or white, race have occupied India and the greater part of western Asia since historic times began. By far the greater number of the inhabitants of Asia, however, belong to the Mongoloid, or yellow, race, represented by the Mongols, Chinese, and Japanese.

History of Ancient India

Geography of India. South Asia includes the present-day countries of India, Pakistan, Nepal, and Ceylon, shown in the Reference Section map "Asia Today" on page 675. Compared with the rest of Asia, this region looks small, but South Asia is almost as large as Europe if Russia is excluded. In ancient times, Pakistan and India were not separated; there-

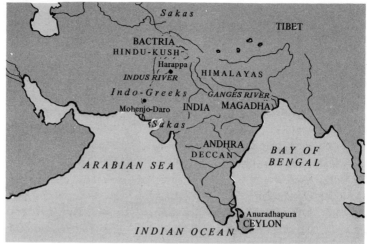

INDIA, about 3000 B.C.

fore in this chapter they will be considered together under the heading of "India."

India is a triangular-shaped peninsula projecting far south into the Indian Ocean. Its coastline is long but it is so regular that it contains few good harbors. To the north, India is bounded by the formidable range of the Himalayas. From the eastern and western ends of the Himalayas lower ranges extend to the sea. Passes and open stretches in the lower ranges permit entry into India on both her northwestern and northeastern frontiers. Northern India is a broad plain containing India's two great rivers, the Ganges and the Indus. The Deccan, a rough and rocky plateau, covers the southern half of India.

Harappa and Mohenjo-Daro. Since 1920 archaeologists have unearthed in the Indus valley the remains of a civilization long unknown. Like the civilizations of Egypt and the Tigris-Euphrates valley, the Indus civilization had reached a high level by about 3000 B.C. The Indus people used irrigation canals to grow grains and vegetables, and found the Indus River useful for communicating and trading between their cities and towns.

Early civilization in the Indus valley centered about two cities, Harappa and Mohenjo-Daro (see map at the top). Both cities were planned with care. Wide streets, with sewers beneath them, separated blocks of brick houses, many of which had wells and bathrooms. Huge bins for the storage of grain indicate that strong rulers controlled to a certain extent food production and distribution.

Excavations show that men of the Indus valley passed through several cultural stages. First were Stone Age men, who gradually learned the use of metals. Then came a period of about 1400 years (3000–1600 B.C.) in which Harappa and Mohenjo-Daro flourished. Civilization seems to have appeared suddenly, suggesting that it may have been transplanted from the Middle East. At any rate, articles made in ancient Sumeria have been uncovered in Harappa, indicating trade between the Indus and the Tigris-Euphrates valleys. Indus workers also developed skills of their own. They may have been first in the making of cotton cloth, and their achievements in pottery-making and work with gold and silver ornaments are admirable.

Until 1969 Indus valley writing remained undeciphered, hiding the record of a civilization which had disappeared 3,500 years ago. In that year scholars with the aid of a computer managed to "break the code" of Indus writing. As translation of ancient inscriptions progressed it was announced that the civilization had been built by Dravidians, and that they had developed a caste system long before the Aryans arrived in India.

The Aryan invasions. The early inhabitants of India seem to have been dark-skinned people, most of whom belonged to the group known as Dravidians. Light-skinned nomads known as Aryans began to enter India through the northwest mountain passes about 1500 B.C. (Some authorities think that the invasions may have begun as early as 2000 B.C.) The Aryans spoke Sanskrit, a language belonging to the Indo-European group, which includes English and most European languages. After occupying the valley of the Indus, the Aryans spread eastward into the plain of the Ganges, conquering and enslaving the dark-skinned people they encountered and seizing their lands. Partly in order to preserve the superior position of the Aryans, India's unique *caste system* was maintained.

Although the caste system attempted to keep Aryans and Dravidians separate, considerable intermixture took place. In time the religious beliefs of the Aryans became merged with those of the conquered peoples; from these two sources there developed the Hindu faith described later in this chapter. Descendants of the Aryans form the majority of the population of northern India today. They are lighter in color than the Dravidians, who make up the bulk of the population of southern India.

The invasions of Darius and Alexander. About the end of the sixth century B.C., Darius the Great, king of Persia, annexed the Indus region to his dominions. It remained a part of the Persian Empire for nearly two hundred years. After Alexander the Great conquered Persia, he went into India and conquered the Indus region. The year of Alexander's invasion, 326 B.C., is the first exact date in the history of India. Alexander's empire lasted only a short time, but it opened the way for closer contact between India and the West. Greek styles in sculpture came to exert a strong influence on artists in India, and commerce between India and the eastern Mediterranean began to grow.

Invasions by Aryans, Persians, and Greeks weakened and divided the people of India. Civilization in the Indus valley, as we have noted, disappeared by about 1600 B.C. During many centuries which followed, India consisted mostly of small and backward states, each with its own petty ruler and local speech. (India is still handicapped by lack of a real national language. Although Hindi, derived from Aryan Sanskrit, is the official language, as recently as 1960 the Indian government recognized over eight hundred languages and dialects spoken in India.) Some ancient conquerors sought to unite India. The two most notable were Chandragupta (c. 322–c. 298 B.C.) and his grandson Asoka (c. 273–c. 232 B.C.). They established the Maurya Empire in northern India, and are described in Indian legends as ruling wisely. However, by 184 B.C. the Maurya Empire had fallen apart. India remained disunited until A.D. 320, when a second Chandragupta began a dynasty (the Gupta) which conquered northern India.

PODIUM OF THE GREAT GRANARY in Mohenjo-Daro. This podium was originally 150 feet by 75 feet. On one side was a brick platform where huge bins of grain were stored.

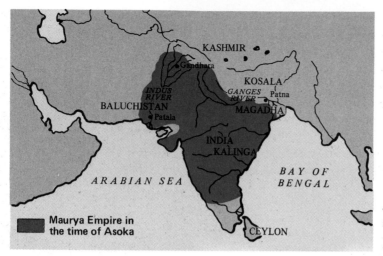

THE MAURYA EMPIRE
flourished during the reign of Asoka (c. 273–c. 232 B.C.) but declined soon after his death.

Indian Society and Culture

India today and yesterday. Most of the people of India today live much as their ancestors did centuries ago. They are bound to the ways of the past by the customs of the village community and the rules of the caste system, both of which may be traced back for several thousand years. It is therefore possible to learn much about the India of yesterday by studying the India of today.

The village community. Nine tenths of India's population are country folk. The village community, in which most of the people live, consists of peasant landowners and tenants, wage earners, and skilled workers such as blacksmiths, carpenters, and cobblers. The skilled workers receive for their labor a share of the harvest. There are also various public officials. Each village is economically independent, or self-sufficient. The organization of rural life in India closely resembles that which was found in medieval Europe a thousand years ago.

Caste. The caste system in India is unique, nothing quite like it being known in any other country. Under this system the people are divided into rigid social classes which are hereditary. No member of a caste may change to another caste. The people of any one caste are similar in color, occupation, religion, wealth, and social standing. The four original castes were: (1) the Brahmans, or priests and wise men; (2) rulers and warriors; (3) merchants and landowners; (4) humble workers, such as servants and peasants. These have divided and subdivided until today there are several thousand castes, including those which are purely local. The Brahmans are highest. Lowest are the outcastes, or "untouchables," who perform the most menial and odious tasks and are forced to live apart from other Hindus. They may not enter the temples, attend school, or use the wells and bathing places used by other Hindus. About fifty million people belong to this unfortunate group. The number of castes is constantly growing as old castes are divided and new ones arise. For instance, the caste of chauffeurs, which arose when automobiles came into use, has now been divided into subcastes; the members of each are restricted to driving cars of a particular make or value. Since all the castes are closely connected with the Hindu religion, no Moslem or Christian may belong to one of them. The caste system is gradually growing weaker, since modern industry draws its workers from all castes and forces them to mingle with one another. In 1949 the constitution of India officially abolished untouchability.

One who belongs to a caste must not marry outside it, must do no kind of work not approved by it, and must not eat or drink with a person of a lower caste. He must observe the ceremonies customary in his caste in connection with birth, marriage, and death; must eat no food regarded as impure; and must not render services to men of lower caste. When a member of an upper caste has touched one of a lower caste, he must purify himself by taking a bath. The person who breaks any of these rules loses caste and may become an outcaste.

Influence of caste. The caste system, by dividing the people of India into innumerable small groups, hampered the development of true national feeling. It also retarded economic development by restricting each individual's choice of occupation and activities. It was a powerful force in maintaining the traditional ways of living and thinking. The conservative Hindu defended the caste system on the grounds that it gave every man, no matter how humble, a recognized place in society.

Early Hinduism. The native religion of India is called "Hinduism." Our earliest knowledge of it comes from some sacred books, the Vedas, which were composed by the early Aryans and for centuries passed orally from generation to generation. The Vedas are written in poetic form and contain hymns, descriptions of forms of worship, charms and spells against evil, and the accumulated wisdom of the ancient Aryans. They worshiped many gods, including a god of the storm, a god of fire, and "Mother Earth." Contact with the people the Aryans found in India caused them to make changes in their early religious beliefs. Thus Hinduism developed out of a mixture of Aryan and other elements. Because the Brahmans, or priests, came to occupy an influential place in Hinduism, it is often called "Brahmanism."

Hindu beliefs. Hinduism teaches that there are three supreme gods: *Brahma,* the Creator, *Vishnu,* the Preserver, and *Siva,* the Destroy-

A GUPTA TEMPLE. Built during India's "Golden Age," it is an example of early Hindu architecture.

er. Hindus believe that mankind was from the first divided into castes, or social classes. Thus the Hindu religion upholds the caste system. Hindus also believe in the *transmigration of souls*—the doctrine that when a human being dies his soul enters into the body of a newborn infant or animal. Some Hindus will not kill any animal, even a poisonous snake or a mosquito, since it may contain a human soul. The progress of the soul is determined by *Karma,* the law of life, which says that good shall be rewarded by good and that evil shall be punished. Those who have led bad lives will be reborn as animals or as members of lower castes; those who have led good lives will rise to a higher caste. The upward process may continue until the soul is joined with Brahma in *Nirvana* (the ending of personal existence). The Hindus worship many gods who reside in trees, animals, persons, and idols. Some groups of Hindus pay reverence to various animals such as monkeys, serpents, and cattle. A strict Hindu would not dream of eating the flesh of cattle, which are held to be sacred.

Gautama Buddha, 563–483 B.C. During the fifth century B.C. a new religion, Buddhism, arose in India. Its founder, Gautama (gō'tȧmȧ), was the son of a noble who ruled a re-

The Buddhist concept of Nirvana is explained in a conversation between a king and a monk.

The King asked, "Is cessation Nirvana?"

"Yes, your highness."

"How is that?"

"All the foolish common people take delight in the senses, are impressed by them, are attached to them. Therefore they are not set free from birth, old age, and death, from grief, pain, and sadness. They are, I say, not set free from suffering. But the holy disciples do not take delight in the senses, are not attached to them, and in consequence their craving ceases; therefore they cease to know birth, old age, and death. It is thus that cessation is Nirvana."

The King asked, "Do all win Nirvana?"

"Only those win Nirvana who follow the correct rules."

The King asked, "Do those who have not won Nirvana know how happy a state it is?"

The monk answered, "Yes, they do."

"But how can one know this about Nirvana without having reached Nirvana?"

The monk answered, "How do we know how bad it is to have a hand or foot cut off?"

"From hearing the laments of those who have had a hand or foot cut off."

Then said the monk, "So it is by hearing the words of those who have reached Nirvana that one knows it to be a happy state."

—Adapted from *Buddhist Scriptures*.

gion at the base of the Himalaya Mountains. Life gave Gautama all he could ask for until he became aware of the suffering of others. Why, he thought, must there be poverty, suffering, and death? At the age of twenty-nine he left his wife, infant son, and all his possessions to go as a beggar in search of the truth. He learned everything that the Brahmans could teach, but their philosophy did not satisfy him. He then became a hermit and for six years led a life of severe penance, but this brought no answer to his questionings. Then one day, as he sat in meditation, illumination came and he found the truth which neither learning nor self-mortification had taught him. In that moment he became Buddha, the Enlightened.

Buddha's teachings. Buddha taught a modified form of Hinduism. He believed that the beginning of wisdom was Karma: "From Good must come Good, and from Evil must come Evil." From this he concluded that the Vedas and the Hindu gods were not sacred, for they could not change good to evil or evil to good. Although he did not attack the caste system openly, he taught that people should be divided only into those who are good and those who are bad. Since only good or bad deeds are important, men should not seek salvation through animal sacrifices and self-torture. Buddha taught four truths: (1) that human life is full of sorrow and suffering; (2) that sorrow and suffering come from cravings and desires; (3) that sorrow can be escaped by suppressing one's cravings and desires, and (4) that through the eightfold path of moderation in conduct (right views, right intention, right speech, right action, right livelihood, right effort, right mindfulness, right concentration) one can reach Nirvana. All true Buddhists strive to suppress desires and wants and to practice the most severe self-control, meditation, and holiness of thought in order to reach the final goal of Nirvana—a state of perfect peace, in which the individual is released from having to be born again.

Buddha's influence. Many people were attracted by Buddha's teachings, and the number of his followers grew. Buddhism in time became an organized religion with monasteries and temples, with saints and relics, and with sacred places thronged by pilgrims. The human personality of Buddha was lost in the mists of legend and his image became an object of worship, although he had denounced idol-worship. Buddhism flourished in India for more than a thousand years, but it gradually merged with Hinduism and by the thirteenth or fourteenth century it had almost ceased to exist as a separate religion in India proper.

Buddhism made its most lasting conquests outside of India. During the early centuries of the Christian era it entered Burma, Siam, China, Korea, and Japan. It also spread to Tibet, Turkestan, and Manchuria. Practically all the people of China and Japan have been influenced by Buddhist teachings, providing a primary cultural link between East Asia and India. About one fourth of the world's population today is Buddhist.

The Rise of Ancient China

An unbroken civilization. Although the civilization of China may not have begun as early as those in Egypt, Mesopotamia, and India, it has proved to be the most lasting. Invasion and conquest changed or destroyed each of the others, but China alone has kept its culture unbroken from generation to generation. China's stability rests in part on the size of its population and in part on its isolation today as Buddhist.

The land of China. China lies in East Asia and includes an area larger than that of the United States. Extensive though it is, China's territory consists mostly of deserts and mountains, unfit for farming. From earliest times, therefore, the population of China has centered in the more fertile eastern provinces near the Pacific coast.

Geography has given the Chinese people a number of advantages. Two great river valleys, those of the Yellow River (Hwang Ho) and the Yangtze, form the heartland of China. The rivers carry boats of the valley dwellers and bring down silt which enriches the valley farms. Chinese farmers irrigate some of their fields, but many parts of China enjoy a good rainfall. Nature also provided China generously with minerals—iron in the north, and copper, lead, and others in the south. Mention should also be made of the rich soil called *loess* in China's northwest provinces. This soil, extending over 100,000 square miles, is so fertile that the Chinese have farmed it for centuries without the need of fertilizer.

China's location cut her off from the rest of the ancient world. Travel by sea was difficult, for it required a long journey to the other early centers of civilization in India and the Middle East (see colored map, pages xvi D and E). Travelers by land faced a perilous

CHINA during the time of Confucius

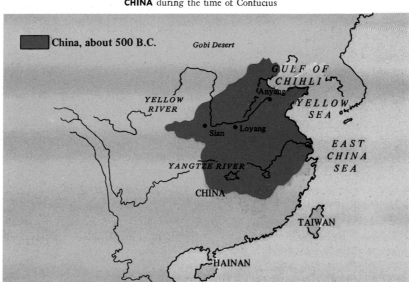

China, about 500 B.C.

Gobi Desert

GULF OF CHIHLI

Anyang

YELLOW RIVER

YELLOW SEA

Sian • Loyang

EAST CHINA SEA

YANGTZE RIVER

CHINA

TAIWAN

HAINAN

Hsia (shyä)—c.2205–c.1766 B.C.

This legendary dynasty, if it existed, probably ruled in the lower Yellow River valley. During this period civilization first appeared in China.

Shang—c.1766–c.1122 B.C.

The Shang rulers were not very strong. Mud walls were needed to protect farming villages, and human beings were sacrificed to appease the gods. Beautiful bronze vessels remain from the Shang period. Silk manufacture became widely practiced.

Chou (jō)—c.1122–256 B.C.

Chou rulers gradually lost authority, and by 800 B.C. were only figureheads. This period of weak government was of enormous importance in shaping Chinese civilization. Confucius and other scholars molded Chinese thought. Formal rules of conduct, laid down at this time, continued to be followed for centuries.

Ch'in—256–206 B.C.

Shih Huang Ti, who ruled during much of this half century, gave China its first strong government. China is named for this dynasty. Shih built most of the Great Wall, and burned all he could find of the books of ancient scholars.

Han—206 B.C.–A.D. 220

Ancient Chinese civilization reached its height under the Han dynasty. Literature, the arts, commerce, and good government were developed to a degree previously unknown in East Asia. China expanded into Manchuria, Mongolia, and Korea, and Chinese goods began to reach the Mediterranean area.

Feudal period

For four centuries after A.D. 220, invaders and petty warlords ruled China. To escape foreign rule, many Chinese fled to the south. During this time, Buddhism and Taoism made millions of converts. Among the invaders of China were the Huns, who also swept westward and helped to destroy the Roman Empire.

trip over mountains and barren plateaus. Mountain barriers were tallest toward the west and south. Consequently, invasions of China came most frequently from the north and northwest. Here the Chinese built their Great Wall for protection about two thousand years ago. The wall and natural barriers kept China in isolation.

China's people. Apparently China long has been the most populous nation on the earth, making up about a quarter of the total at any given time. Nearly all her people belong to the Mongoloid, or yellow, race. Characteristic features are prominent cheekbones, straight black hair, and a complexion varying from pale yellow to dark brown. Southern Chinese tend to be short, but those in the north often reach a height of six feet. Invasions have resulted in intermixture, with Tibetans, Manchus, and other peoples mingling with the original Chinese. However, invaders were never numerous enough to destroy the basic culture of the Chinese.

Civilization begins in the Yellow River valley. Man has long lived in China. One of the earliest known types, Peking man, dates from about 200,000 years ago (see chart, page 14). We know from the study of excavations that early man in China passed through both an Old and a New Stone Age thousands of years ago. The fertile plain of the lower Yellow River in northern China appears to have been the seat of the first Chinese civilization. By about 5000 B.C. men were living in villages, farming with stone tools, and making pottery. During the period from 2000 to 1500 B.C. many of the villages were united under a single ruler. Writing began (although historical records were not kept until much later), the manufacture of silk and the casting of bronze appeared, and China emerged as the fourth of the world's first civilizations. For the next two thousand years, a series of dynasties governed in China. The box on this page summarizes their periods of rule.

Chinese Society and Culture

The family. In China the family has traditionally been a peculiarly important institution. It included not only the father, mother, and children, but also grandparents, grandchildren, uncles, aunts, cousins, and even more distant blood relatives. Since every Chinese man wanted sons, young men married early, usually at about the age of twenty. If his father was prosperous, a young man brought his wife into the paternal home and stayed there even after he had children of his own. Thus the well-to-do family expanded, until sometimes an entire village was only an enlarged household. In every Chinese family both the father and the mother received great deference and respect from their children during life; after death parents were venerated.

The veneration of ancestors in China must have arisen in prehistoric times, judging from the references to it in the most ancient Chinese literature. According to Chinese tradition, ancestral souls resided in wooden tablets kept in the family dwelling. From time to time the members of the family burned incense and placed offerings of food before the tablets, and on important occasions performed acts of worship there or at the graves of the ancestors. Although the religious books declared that a good son ought to sacrifice to his ancestors without seeking anything from them in return, he made sacrifices to them partly because he hoped that by so doing he would win their aid.

Social classes. The traditional Chinese social system rested upon four classes—scholars, farmers, craftsmen, and traders. Practically, however, there were only two classes—officials and nonofficials. There was no hereditary nobility, except in the case of a few families whose ancestors had served the state, and even they had no special privileges.

Chinese government. The government of China from ancient times until 1912 was a monarchy, in which the emperor had almost unlimited power. He made laws merely by issuing decrees. Officials held their positions at his pleasure, and the people had no voice in the government. But the emperor was expected to govern justly. Should he prove to be a tyrant, the people might properly rebel

PORCELAIN VASE of the twenty-four filial pieties. An example of early Chinese brush-and-ink painting.

against him. Chinese history mentions several occasions when a bad emperor was compelled to resign. Government in China thus rested on a moral basis; there were social responsibilities which not even the emperor could evade.

The moral tone of China's government was strengthened by an unusual method of choosing and promoting officials. Appointment to office depended upon knowledge of ancient works (the "Classics") which included writings on philosophy, history, and especially the works of Confucius. Advancement in office depended on proving in examinations that the official knew these writings well. The higher the office, the greater was the knowledge that was expected. Since the "Classics" emphasized reverence for the past, they tended to turn the minds of officials against changes in Chinese government. Thus we may account for the changelessness of China by noting (1) her form of government, (2) her geographic isolation, (3) the sheer mass of her population, and (4) the influence of family life.

CHINESE SILK PAINTINGS made eleven hundred years apart. The painting below is of the Emperor Yang Ti. It dates from the T'ang dynasty (7th century). The painting above dates from the early 18th century.

Economic life. The great majority of the Chinese are peasants. From the days of the Ch'in dynasty until the Communists took control of the mainland in 1949, the peasants farmed their own land. (See page 612.) Their holdings were usually very small, partly because of inheritance customs. As a rule all sons inherited equal shares of the father's estate. Consequently, with the passage of time the farms became smaller and smaller. With three acres a family was thought to be well off; with ten acres it was thought to be wealthy. The Chinese have long been familiar with intensive cultivation, fertilization, and rotation of crops. For centuries they have added to the amount of cultivated land by irrigating dry land, building terraces on mountain slopes, and draining low-lying fields. All this work has gone on with incredible patience and an immense expenditure of human effort.

The principal manufactures of China have been porcelain, silk, and cotton goods. Chinese silk was popular in the Roman Empire many centuries ago. India ink, fans, furniture, lacquer ware, straw matting, dyes, and varnished tiles are other Chinese products. Until recently, China knew nothing of power-driven machinery for manufacturing. Goods were made by hand in households and small shops.

The Chinese gained early mastery over many principles of engineering. Their most notable engineering feat was construction of the Great Wall. Knowledge of mechanics is shown in Chinese waterwheels and other appliances for irrigation, such as windmills. Before A.D. 500 they also used waterwheels as a source of power to drive trip-hammers and to force air into furnaces. The Chinese also pioneered in the casting of iron in molds, in building suspension bridges, and in the digging of deep wells from which to obtain water and natural gas. They used coal and gas for heating hundreds of years before Europeans did. As early as the second century after Christ they had learned to make paper. Wallpaper, the folding umbrella, and playing cards are other Chinese inventions.

Contacts with the outside world. By A.D. 500 China had developed trade connections with India and the Middle East, and to some extent with the Roman Empire. Overland caravans carried silk to the west by 200 B.C. Records show that a Chinese diplomat who was sent out in 138 B.C. returned twelve years later with information about lands as far west as the Middle East. He also brought alfalfa and grapevines, which had been unknown to the Chinese. In return, China has given the world oranges, peaches, pears, cinnamon, rhubarb, tea, the soybean, and flowers such as the azalea, peony, camellia, tea rose, and chrysanthemum.

Cultural achievements. The practical character of the Chinese did not prevent their having a genuine appreciation of the beautiful. Chinese painting developed from the Chinese system of writing, itself a form of painting with use of a brush and ink. From the forming of graceful written characters with a brush to the painting of pictures was but a short step. Chinese painters usually represented landscapes and still life rather than human personality. Chinese painting was marked by great delicacy and serenity. Much early painting was done on silk, although paper became popular following its invention. (See Chinese painting, page 229.)

Chinese literature had an unbroken development from distant antiquity. All forms of literature—histories, biographies, geographies, philosophical writings, essays, dramas, novels, and poetry—were represented. Some of the earliest were written on bamboo strips, which

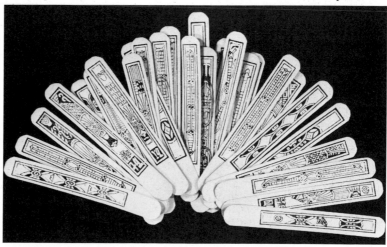

PLAYING CARDS. An early Chinese invention; these date from the 19th century.

proved to be durable. The most important literature in all Chinese history was contained in the so-called "Classics." Included in the "Classics" were writings ascribed to the great teacher Confucius and some of his followers. To more fully understand the Chinese people and their history we need to examine the religious and ethical beliefs taught by Confucius and others.

Religious beliefs. Some ancient Chinese seem to have believed in one god. They regarded him not as the creator of the universe or of man, but as a personal Supreme Ruler, who rewarded the good and punished the wicked. In time other gods, such as sun, moon, stars, and earth, were recognized, but they were thought of as ministers to the Supreme Ruler. The mass of the Chinese believed that spirits populated the country as densely as its human inhabitants and caused accidents, eclipses, earthquakes, disease, and insanity. Ancestor veneration and the teachings of Confucius, Lao-tzu (lou′dzŭ′), and Buddha have also held important places in Chinese religious life.

PORTRAIT OF CONFUCIUS based on ancient traditions. Confucius tried to give his people rules of good conduct under all circumstances.

SAYINGS OF CONFUCIUS

Confucius taught a system of morality, rather than a religion. Some of his sayings were put together by his pupils in the *Lun Yü,* from which the following have been taken.

The higher type of man is calm and serene; the inferior man is constantly agitated and worried. . . .

. . . A man of inward virtue will have virtuous words on his lips, but a man of virtuous words is not always a virtuous man. . . .

. . . Surely the maxim of charity is such: —Do not [do] unto others what you would not they should do unto you. . . .

. . . Alas! I have never met a man who could see his own faults. . . .

. . . Before we know what life is, how can we know what death is? . . . .

—Lionel Giles, *The Sayings of Confucius.*

Confucius, 551–479 B.C. The great Chinese sage K'ung-Fu-tzŭ, whom we call Confucius, was born in what is now the province of Shantung. His father came from an aristocratic family, but his death when Confucius was only three left the family in poverty. Confucius nevertheless managed to acquire a good education and at the age of twenty-two set up as a public teacher. Pupils came to him in increasing numbers, and his reputation grew rapidly. During this period in his life he is said to have spent much of his time collecting and editing materials in the Chinese "Classics," with which his name has ever since been associated. When Confucius was about fifty-two years of age he had a chance to apply his teachings to government, for he was made minister of justice in the duchy of Lu. After he took office crime almost disappeared and the duchy prospered. Neighboring rulers, jealous of the progress in Lu, succeeded in getting the duke to dismiss Confucius. For the remaining years of his life he traveled, taught, and wrote. After his death his disciples began to collect his writings and set down his words. Temples were erected to him and many Chinese came to regard him as a god.

The teachings of Confucius. Confucius was not a religious prophet or even an especially religious man, and he did not teach a new way of life. He lived during the turbulent period of the later Chou dynasty, and hoped to restore stability to China by inducing the people to return to the ways of the past. He emphasized particularly the virtues of devotion to ancestors, respect for parents, benevolence toward relatives, propriety of conduct, and reverence for learning. The noblest expression of Confucianism is the negative form of the Golden Rule: "What you do not want done to yourself do not do to others." The Chinese can quote many such sayings, for Confucius stated rules about almost all phases of human conduct. (See box on opposite page.) His teachings continue to influence all Chinese.

Lao-tzu and Taoism. Chinese traditions tell of a man about fifty years older than Confucius, the famous Lao-tzu. Unlike Confucius, who was concerned with practical matters, Lao-tzu was a highly speculative thinker who devoted his attention to spiritual matters. He believed that there was an indefinable Something, a way of the universe, which he called *Tao* (dou). Man should try to bring himself into harmony with Tao, said Lao-tzu, by practicing the three great virtues of humility, frugality, and contentment (ceasing to strive for wealth or fame). He declared: "To them that are good I am good, and to them that are not good I am also good; thus all get to be good." Most of Lao-tzu's teachings are not clear. Taoism degenerated as the masses took it up. Beginning as a system of philosophy which was opposed to all forms of worship, it became a religion with many gods, among whom Lao-tzu himself held a prominent place. It accumulated countless saints and protecting spirits, each with temples, monasteries, priests, and forms of worship.

Followers of three teachers. Many Chinese became followers of Buddha (see page 43) as early as the first century after Christ. For a long time the Buddhists and the Taoists were bitter opponents, but eventually these rival faiths came to exist peaceably together. Each borrowed a great deal from the other and from the teachings of Confucius. For centuries nearly every Chinese has been influenced by all three bodies of teaching: those springing from Confucius, Lao-tzu, and Buddha.

REVIEWING THE CHAPTER

TERMS TO UNDERSTAND: *steppe, tundra, Aryan, Dravidian, caste, Sanskrit, Hindi, Vedas, Hinduism, Karma, transmigration of souls, Buddhism, loess, Confucianism, Taoism.*

PERSONS TO IDENTIFY: *Gautama Buddha, Shih Huang Ti, Confucius, Lao-tzu.*

PLACES TO LOCATE: *Ural Mountains, Caucasus Mountains, Caspian Sea, India, Ceylon, Ganges River, Harappa, Indus River, Mohenjo-Daro, Nepal, Yellow River, Yangtze River, Mongolia, Manchuria.*

QUESTIONS TO ANSWER

1. (a) What geographical features helped to keep the early civilizations of Asia more remote and isolated? (b) What races are found in Asia? (c) Where is most of the population located?

2. (a) What are the main geographical divisions of India? (b) Where did the first civilization in India begin? (c) Briefly describe

what has been learned about this first civilization in India. (d) Name the various groups which invaded India before 300 B.C.

3. (a) Describe village life in India. (b) What rules are followed by caste members? (c) Explain the main beliefs of the Hindu faith. Of Buddhism. (d) To what Oriental countries has Buddhism spread?

4. (a) What advantage has geography given the Chinese people? (b) Name the geographic features which have tended to isolate China.

5. (a) Where did the first civilization in China begin? (b) Summarize some of the important things which happened during the Shang, Chou, Ch'in, and Han dynasties.

6. (a) Show the influence of religion upon family life in China. (b) What four factors may account for the changelessness of Chinese culture? (c) Describe Chinese methods of farming. Of manufacturing. (d) What are some of their engineering achievements and inventions? (e) Describe the characteristics of Chinese painting. (f) In Chinese literature what are the "Classics"?

7. State the teachings of Confucius and Lao-Tzu.

FURTHER ACTIVITIES FOR PART ONE

1. Find three examples to show that "the roots of the present lie deep in the past."

2. On an outline map of the world name the continents and locate the cradlelands of the world's races.

3. Read Thomas De Quincey's *The Flight of a Tartar Tribe* and prepare a class report on the migration described there.

4. Prepare a chart of the most important contributions made by prehistoric man to civilization. In parallel columns list inventions, discoveries, plants domesticated, animals domesticated, and progress in teamwork, or social co-operation. At the left of the chart place in order the names of the ages, or culture epochs, during which these developments took place.

5. Look up the word "archaeology" in the dictionary and be prepared to tell how the work of the archaeologist and that of the historian are related.

6. Select one of the men mentioned in Chapter 3 or 4 and prepare a report on his life from an encyclopedia or from the references listed below.

7. Draw an outline map of Asia, and on it show the countries studied in Part One. Locate on the map the places listed under *Places to Locate* at the end of Chapters 3 and 4.

8. Prepare one or both of the following time lines. (a) Draw a line beginning with the Ice Age, and continuing to the present. On it mark the four glacial periods, the chief types of early man, and the Old Stone Age, the New Stone Age, and the beginning of the Age of Metals. (b) Draw a line to show the chief events in the history of the ancient Middle East and Asia from 3000 B.C. to 300 B.C.

FURTHER READING FOR PART ONE

(Stars indicate easier books)

HISTORY

ANDREWS. *Meet Your Ancestors.* Viking.
*BOTHWELL. *The Story of India.* Harcourt.
BOUQUET. *Everyday Life in New Testament Times.* Scribner.
BRAIDWOOD. *Prehistoric Man.* Chicago Museum of Natural History. (paperback)
BULLOCK. *The Doubleday Pictorial Library of World History; Civilization from Its Beginnings.* Doubleday.
CASSON. *Ancient Egypt.* Time-Life.
CERAM. *Gods, Graves, and Scholars.* Knopf.
——. *Secret of the Hittites.* Knopf.
CHIERA. *They Wrote on Clay.* Chicago. (paperback)
CHUBB. *Nefertiti Lived Here.* Crowell.
COON. *The Story of Man.* Knopf.
COTTRELL. *Anvil of Civilization.* Mentor. (paperback)

——. *Land of the Two Rivers*. World.

——. *Life under the Pharaohs*. Holt.

——. *Lost Cities*. Grosset. (paperback)

*——. *Lost Pharaohs*. Grosset. (paperback)

——. *Secrets of Tutankhamen's Tomb*. Dell. (paperback)

DESROCHES–NOBLECOURT. *Tutankhamen*. New York Graphic Society.

FAIRSERVIS. *The Origins of Oriental Civilization*. Mentor. (paperback)

FITCH. *Their Search for God: Ways of Worship in the Orient*. Lothrop.

FITZGERALD. *History of China*. American Heritage.

GAER. *How the Great Religions Began*. Dodd.

GOLDMAN. *First Men: The Story of Human Beginnings*. Collier. (paperback)

HEATON. *Everyday Life in Old Testament Times*. Scribner.

HORIZON MAGAZINE. *The Horizon Book of the Arts of China*. American Heritage.

——. *The Horizon Book of Lost Worlds*. American Heritage. (also Dell, paperback)

HOWELLS. *Back of History*. Anchor. (paperback)

*LAMPREY. *All the Ways of Building*. Macmillan.

LI. *The Ageless Chinese*. Scribner. (paperback)

*LIFE (periodical). *The World's Great Religions* (Special edition for young readers). Golden Press. (paperback)

*LINTON. *Man's Way from Cave to Skyscraper*. Harper.

LLOYD. *The Art of the Ancient Near East*. Praeger. (paperback)

McNEILL, BUSKE, ROEHM. *The World . . . Its History in Maps*. Denoyer-Geppert.

*MEADOWCROFT. *Gift of the River*. Crowell.

*MILLS. *Book of the Ancient World*. Putnam.

——. *The People of Ancient Israel*. Scribner.

MONTET. *Everyday Life in Egypt in the Days of Rameses the Great*. St. Martin.

ORLINSKY. *Ancient Israel*. Cornell. (paperback)

PARRINDER. *The Faiths of Mankind*. Crowell.

POOLE. *Carbon–14, and Other Science Methods That Date the Past*. McGraw.

*QUENNELL and QUENNELL. *Everyday Life in Prehistoric Times*. Putnam.

*SAMACHSON and SAMACHSON. *Good Digging*. Rand McNally.

SCHAFER. *Ancient China*. Time-Life.

SCHULBERG. *Historic India*. Time-Life.

*SEEGER. *The Pageant of Chinese History*. McKay.

SHIPPEN. *Portals of the Past: The Story of Archaeology*. Viking.

*SPENCER. *The Land of the Chinese People*. Lippincott.

STEINDORFF and SEELE. *When Egypt Ruled the East*. Chicago. (paperback)

WHITE. *Everyday Life in Ancient Egypt*. Putnam. (paperback)

WINER. *Life in the Ancient World*. Random House.

BIOGRAPHY

NOBLE. *Egypt's Queen Cleopatra*. Messner.

FICTION

BARRINGER. *And the Waters Prevailed*. Dutton.

*BAUMANN. *The World of the Pharaohs*. Pantheon.

*BERRY. *Honey of the Nile*. Viking.

BUCK. *The Good Earth*. World.

*COTTRELL. *The Land of the Pharaohs*. World.

*GAER. *The Adventures of Rama*. Little, Brown.

——. *The Fables of India*. Little, Brown.

KJELGAARD. *Fire-Hunter*. Holiday.

*McGRAW. *The Golden Goblet*. Coward-McCann.

*——. *Mara, Daughter of the Nile*. Coward-McCann.

*MALVERN. *Behold Your Queen*. McKay.

*——. *The Foreigner: The Story of a Girl Named Ruth*. McKay.

MORRISON. *The Lost Queen of Egypt*. Lippincott.

WALTARI. *The Egyptian*. Putnam.

ATHENA, patron goddess of Athens.

PART TWO

THE GLORY OF GREECE AND THE GRANDEUR OF ROME

In Part One we watched the dawn of civilization in the Middle East and in India and China. Now we shall see how Europe in turn rose out of barbarism into the light of history.

The first civilization in Europe appeared in Greece and the nearby islands. There, amidst rugged natural surroundings, the Greeks built a culture rarely if ever equaled since their time. They displayed a wonderful feeling for balance and harmony in everything they made or did—in their buildings, sculpture, and literature, and especially in their daily lives, seeking to develop a sound mind in a sound body. They probed for the meaning of man's existence, and in doing so, contributed much to our knowledge of science, mathematics, literature, and philosophy.

The Romans, on the other hand, were largely a practical-minded people. More doers than philosophers, they distinguished themselves as engineers, conquerors, organizers, and empire-builders. Their influence has been as enduring as that of the Greeks. For example, our Senate is named for that of Rome; the dome of our national Capitol follows Roman design; our language is studded with words derived from Latin, spoken by the Romans; and Roman law has become the basis for most of the legal systems of the world. Our heritage owes much to the civilizing influence of both the Greeks and the Romans.

The span of history covered in Part Two extended for more than a thousand years, from about 776 B.C. to A.D. 500. The Table of Significant Dates in the Reference Section will highlight and summarize the leading events which you will study in Part Two.

5 The Greeks Assume Leadership

BATTLE SCENE from the *Iliad* shows Greeks fighting Trojans. This illustration, produced between the third and fifth centuries A.D., is the earliest existing example of a Greek illustrated book.

Although civilization first appeared in Egypt and Babylonia, for the last twenty-five centuries it has centered in the West. For the most part it was the Europeans who gave us modern industry and commerce, government, art, literature, and science. They carried their languages, laws, customs, and religions to the New World and to many parts of Asia and Africa. The first Europeans to distinguish themselves for their high culture were the Greeks. This chapter will tell the story of their origin and development, their wars with outsiders and among themselves, and the final loss of their political independence.

The European Setting

Geographical advantages of Europe. Considering its great influence, Europe is surprisingly small. It has less than half the area of North America, and a little more than one fifth that of Asia. Geographically it is *not* a continent but a peninsula of Asia. Despite its small size, Europe enjoys many favorable physical features and a varied climate. It has a long coast line, with numerous bays and harbors; there are many rivers, navigable for long distances; and the fertile lowlands are extensive. In addition, Europe's location in north temperate latitudes assures that neither extreme heat nor cold will hinder man's activities. A mountain barrier, formed by the Pyrenees, the Alps, and the Balkans, has been an historical dividing line between northern and southern Europe. Twenty-five centuries ago the Europeans dwelling north of these mountains were still barbarians.

The Mediterranean basin. The Mediterranean is the largest inland sea in the world. It is about 2500 miles long, from 400 to 600 miles wide, and washes the shores of three continents. The climate of this area is midway between tropical and temperate. The rainfall is, on the whole, scanty, with the result that the grape and the olive have long been important products. Here, too, men early took to the sea, for the surrounding lands were too unfruitful to support more than a few herdsmen and farmers. Moreover, good harbors were plentiful, islands numerous, and the sea was free from high tides. From the most ancient times the Mediterranean became an "avenue of commerce." In trade people exchange not only goods but ideas. Such communication between peoples spreads civilization. We shall observe many examples of this as we proceed with the story.

The Aegean Sea. Particularly at its eastern end, the Mediterranean was a "highway of nations." Here the Aegean Sea, between Greece and Asia Minor, forms a branch of the Mediterranean. Bounded by the long and narrow island of Crete on the south, it is dotted with hundreds of smaller islands. These served as a bridge over which the culture of the Orient passed to Europe.

The Aegean Age

Aegean civilization. Until late in the 1800's we knew nothing of a remarkable civilization which was old when the Greeks arrived. Modern excavations have shown that this civilization centered in the island of Crete and spread by commerce and colonization to the nearby islands, the coast of Asia Minor, and the shores of Greece.

Our knowledge of Aegean civilization comes largely from the work of two men, Heinrich Schliemann and Sir Arthur Evans. Schliemann believed the stories in Homer's *Iliad,* and in 1870 began digging in a hill called Hissarlik in northwestern Asia Minor. In time he uncovered there the remains of nine successive cities, each built on the ruins of its predecessor. The seventh of these from the bottom was probably the Troy (Ilium) of Homer. In its ashes were found powerful walls, well-fortified gates, and stone palaces. Schliemann made excavations of other Homeric sites at Mycenae and Tiryns on the plain of Argos in Greece. (See maps, pages 19, 50.) These places proved to be the northern extension of a mighty Cretan empire. Shortly after 1900 Sir Arthur Evans uncovered many relics of the art and culture of the Cretans. At Cnossus, the capital of Crete, he found the remains of an enormous palace with numerous rooms and passages. Wall paintings show scenes of many human figures, as well as the Cretan sport of bull-leaping. This dangerous pastime consisted of gripping a charging bull by the horns and somersaulting over its back.

Aegean culture. The discoveries of Schliemann and Evans indicate that Aegean civilization entered the Age of Metals as early as 3000 B.C., and that it reached its peak between 1600 and 1400 B.C. The peoples of this region lived in villages and cities. They had despotic rulers, who lived in huge stone palaces. Some of these buildings had conveniences such as bathrooms with pipes and drains. They were beautifully decorated with paintings and sculpture. Aegean artists decorated walls, made plaster reliefs, carved ivory, engraved gems, and inlaid metals. Rock-hewn graves, containing many objects of everyday use, show that the Aegeans believed in life after death.

Downfall of Aegean civilization. For many years the so-called "sea kings" of Crete controlled the commerce of the Mediterranean. Products of Cretan art have been found in Egypt, Babylonia, and as far west as Spain. The Cretans built a prosperous civilization through the peaceful methods of trade. However, they failed to fortify Cnossus and depended solely on their navy for defense of the

island. About 1400 B.C. barbarous tribes from the Greek mainland overran Crete. The great palace at Cnossus went up in flames, and the invaders brought an end to Aegean civilization.

The Early Greeks

Rise of the Greek people. Long before the downfall of Aegean civilization, tribes of wandering Indo-European barbarians had moved southward into the Greek peninsula. The principal tribes were the Achaeans, the Dorians, and the Ionians. They differed from the short and dark-skinned Aegean peoples in that they were tall and light in complexion. Armed with iron weapons, the invaders overcame the inhabitants of Crete and western Asia Minor, who still used bronze implements. Frequently the conquerors settled among their victims and intermarried with them. The result of this mixture was the Greek people. However, many tribal differences interfered with the development of unity among the Greeks. Even without tribal differences unity is hard to achieve in a land divided by numerous mountain ranges.

The Homeric Age. Historic times did not begin in the Greek world until about 750 B.C. Information on the period before that date comes chiefly from the *Iliad* and the *Odyssey*. According to the Greeks, a blind poet named Homer wrote these two epics; therefore we call that period the Homeric Age. The *Iliad*

A GREEK WARSHIP, about 500 B.C.

tells the story of a Greek expedition against Troy led by Agamemnon (ăg'à-mĕm'nŏn), king of Mycenae. The *Odyssey* relates the wanderings of the Greek hero, Odysseus, on his way home from Troy.

Homeric culture was rude compared with Aegean civilization. Many Greeks still lived the life of shepherds. They knew of iron but more often used bronze for weapons and tools. They had no coined money and therefore traded little. Their only contact with the outside world came through the Phoenicians, whose merchants stopped at Greek ports. Few Greeks of this period were skilled workmen, so that luxuries were scarce. The people carried on warfare almost constantly, and they considered piracy an honorable occupation. Murders were frequent. They did not bring the murderer to trial, but permitted the victim's family to punish him.

Early Greek religion. The Greeks worshiped many gods and goddesses. Twelve of the most important deities formed a council, which was supposed to meet on snowcapped Mount Olympus in northern Thessaly. At its head was Zeus, "father of gods and men," as Homer calls him. He made storms and hurled the thunderbolt. His brother, Poseidon, ruled the sea. His wife, Hera, presided over the life of women and had charge of marriage ceremonies. Apollo, his son, was the god of light, who became the ideal of manly beauty and the patron of music, poetry, and the art of healing. Athena, his daughter, stood for wisdom and womanly virtues. The Greek deities possessed the weaknesses of human beings, but possessed superhuman power and the gift of immortality. The Greeks had very dismal ideas of the future life. The abode of the dead was a dark and gloomy place in the underworld called Hades; the souls of all men went to Hades after death and there passed an eternally joyless existence.

Oracles. Prophecy played an important part in Greek religious and political life. The

ZEUS, chief of the Olympian gods

Greeks believed that messages from the gods were received at certain places called oracles. The oracle of Apollo at Delphi became the most famous. Many inquirers, including some from foreign lands, came to seek advice from the prophetess through whom Apollo spoke. The oracle was honored until the fourth century after Christ, when a Roman emperor banned it.

The Olympian games. The Greeks admired physical strength, and therefore held many athletic festivals. The most popular were the Olympian games in honor of Zeus, presented every fourth year at Olympia in the city-state of Elis. The first recorded celebration of the games occurred in 776 B.C., and from this year the Greeks reckoned all dates. The festival

THE PANKRATION. This was one of the chief contests of the Olympian games. It was a violent combination of wrestling and boxing, in which the contestants generally followed the rule that almost "anything goes." They did, however, have a referee, pictured at the left. The scene is taken from a painted vase, the only kind of Greek painting that has survived.

lasted for five days in midsummer. Thousands of spectators from every part of the Greek world gathered to watch contests in running, the broad jump, discus and javelin throwing, and other sports. The winning athlete was crowned with a wreath of wild olive, while at home his fellow citizens showered him with gifts and adoration. These games were religious celebrations, for it was thought that the gods were pleased with the display of manly strength. The Olympian games were also like great fairs, where merchants set up their shops and sold their goods. On these occasions, too, the crowds enjoyed art exhibits, poetry reading, and oratory. During the games all peoples of Greek blood gave up their petty quarrels and a sense of brotherhood prevailed among them.

The Greek City-States

The city-state. The Greeks were noted for a type of community called the city-state. It included not only the area within the walls of a city but also the surrounding countryside. The city-state was independent and self-governing; it could declare war, make treaties, and form alliances. It had a very small population. Athens, at her greatest, had perhaps a quarter of a million inhabitants. Thebes, Argos, and Corinth, the next in size, probably had between fifty thousand and one hundred thousand each; and Sparta, probably less than fifty thousand. These numbers included citizens, and also slaves and resident foreigners.

The citizens. Citizenship in a city-state was considered a great privilege. The citizens believed that they had descended from a common ancestor and they looked to a common god, or hero, for protection. These ties of religion and blood relationship gave the group a feeling of unity and patriotism. A person could acquire citizenship only by birth, and if he moved to another city-state, he lost his citizenship.

Government of the city-state. In Homeric times the government consisted of the king, the council, and the assembly. The king was commander in chief, judge, and priest; but he did not have absolute power, as in Egypt or Persia. A council of nobles advised him. In matters of great importance, such as making war, he had to consult an assembly of the common people. As time went on the nobles in some city-states abolished kingship. Monarchy, the rule of one, thus gave way to aristocracy, the rule of the nobles. In other city-states one man seized control of the government by force or guile. A ruler of this kind was called a "tyrant." Athens went through all these changes in government, from kingship to aristocracy, to tyranny, and finally, to democracy.

Sparta and Athens

Rise of Sparta. The two most prominent city-states were Sparta and Athens, whose ways of life were in sharp contrast. Sparta was located in the southern peninsula of Greece, called the Peloponnesus, which had been settled by Dorian invaders. The Spartans lived largely by agriculture. As their numbers grew, they needed more land for farming. Consequently, Sparta began to expand through conquest. By 500 B.C., she had brought most of the Peloponnesus under her rule. Sparta neglected industry and commerce, as well as art, literature, and philosophy.

Sparta had an unusual arrangement of two kings who reigned at the same time. But the real management of affairs was in the hands of five overseers, called *ephors,* who were elected every year by the citizens. The ephors advised the kings, guided the activities of the council of nobles and the assembly, and in general supervised all life in the city-state.

Life in Sparta. Spartan education had a single purpose—to produce good fighting men. At birth the unsound of body were left to die. The state took charge of a boy at the age of seven. He was trained in marching, fighting, and gymnastics at a military school. He learned to be brief in speech, or *laconic* (from Laconia, the district in which Sparta is located). Above all, the Spartan youth had to endure hardship without complaint. Summer and winter he wore a single garment and went barefoot. Public flogging was a regular part of his training. At twenty the youth became a warrior and lived in barracks. He became a full citizen at thirty and a member of the popular assembly. Compelled to marry, he still had to continue military training. The state did not release him from the strict discipline of a soldier's career until he was sixty years old. As an Athenian sarcastically remarked, "A Spartan's life is so unpleasant that it is no wonder he throws it away lightly in battle."

Athens as a city-state. The Athenian city-state included all the inhabitants of the towns and villages of Attica, a district in east central Greece. A man was an Athenian no matter in what part of Attica he lived. The soil of this part of Greece was rocky and unproductive. It was best suited for raising grapes and olives, or sheep and goats. From an early period, therefore, the Athenians looked to the sea for a livelihood.

THUCYDIDES ON THE SPARTANS

. . . you have never considered what manner of men are these Athenians with whom you will have to fight, and how utterly unlike yourselves. They are revolutionary, equally quick in the conception and in the execution of every new plan; while you are conservative—careful only to keep what you have, originating nothing, and not acting even when action is most necessary. They are bold beyond their strength; they run risks which prudence would condemn; and in the midst of misfortune they are full of hope. Whereas it is your nature, though strong, to act feebly; when your plans are most prudent, to distrust them; and when calamities come upon you, to think that you will never be delivered from them. They are impetuous, and you are dilatory; they are always abroad, and you are always at home.

—Thucydides.

A WEDDING PROCESSION as it appeared on a black-figured Greek vase of about 560 B.C.

While Sparta was building a military state, Athens was laying the foundations of a democratic state. Instead of fighting for territorial conquest, early Athens fought her battles within—political battles which developed freedom-loving citizens.

Draco's code, 621 B.C. By the eighth century B.C., the kings of Athens had lost their power to the nobles. This change, however, did not bring better government, for the rule of the nobles was harsh and unjust. Their mistreatment of the poor aroused much discontent, which sometimes threatened to break out in open revolution. Fortunately, in these troubled years three great lawgivers rose to power. Each in his turn made reforms which helped to establish democracy in Athens. The first lawmaker, Draco, gave the Athenians a written code of laws. Before his day the judges, who were all nobles, applied the unwritten laws in such a way as to favor their own class. Draco's code abolished the feud as a means of punishing a murderer. The fate of a killer was now left to the courts. Most

provisions of the new laws, however, were very severe. The penalty for most offenses, even the smallest theft, was death. We still use the word *draconic* to mean harsh, or cruel.

Reforms of Solon, 594–593 B.C. Solon's name has come down to us as a synonym for a wise lawmaker. He improved the condition of the Attic peasants by canceling the debts which they owed to their landlords, by freeing all those who had been enslaved for debt, and by limiting the amount of land a noble might own. He also encouraged industry and commerce by offering citizenship to foreigners who were skilled craftsmen. Finally, he admitted even the poorest citizens to the popular assembly and to membership in the courts. Thus Solon gave the people a greater share in the government and promoted democracy in Athens. When invited to make himself a permanent dictator, he declined, saying that dictatorship was "a very fair spot, but there was no way down from it."

Clisthenes. After Solon's time tyrants controlled Athens for more than half a century. They were not all bad rulers. Pisistratus (pĭ-sĭs′trȧ-tŭs), who ruled from 554–527 B.C., was outstanding. He made little change in Solon's laws and Athens prospered under his rule. After Pisistratus, however, a period of revolution and turmoil followed. Then a third great lawgiver, Clisthenes (klĭs′thḗ-nēz), appeared (508 B.C.). He furthered the democratic movement begun by Draco and Solon by enlarging the Assembly and increasing its powers. Clisthenes also established the practice called *ostracism*. According to this custom, the Assembly, by a majority vote, might send into exile (ostracize) any prominent man for ten years. Despite the opposition of powerful families, Clisthenes built a democratic government that stood, with little change, for nearly two centuries. Later we shall describe the Athenian democracy at its height and some of its contributions to mankind. (See page 64.)

COLONIAL EXPANSION OF THE GREEKS AND PHOENICIANS, 750–500 B.C. The Greeks and Phoenicians founded many colonies bordering the Mediterranean. The ancient Greek city of Massilia was the ancestor of present-day Marseilles. Gades, an old Phoenician colony on the Spanish coast, was the forerunner of Cádiz.

Expansion of the Greeks

Age of colonization. Following the Homeric Age the Greeks began to plant colonies throughout the Mediterranean and Black Sea regions. The great age of colonization covered the period from about 750 B.C. to 500 B.C.

Trade was one motive for colonization. The Greeks found it very profitable to exchange their manufactured goods for the food and raw materials of the outside world. Land hunger furnished another incentive. The poor soil of Greece could not support the increasing number of inhabitants. For many the only solution was emigration. A third motive was the desire for greater freedom. During the rule of nobles and tyrants, many poor and dissatisfied men hoped to find freedom from oppression in new lands.

The Greeks tried to pattern the life of their colonies after that of the mother cities. The colonists called themselves "men away from home." Mother city and daughter colony traded with each other and in time of danger helped each other. The sacred fire, carried from the public hearth of the old community to the new settlement, was a sign of the close ties between them.

Nature of the colonies. Beginning nearest home the Greeks moved into the islands of the Aegean Sea and on both sides of the passages leading into the Black Sea. Among the colonies was Byzantium, on the site of Constantinople (now Istanbul). The Black Sea itself was fringed with colonies, which furnished fish, wood, grain, meats, wool, and slaves. Southern Italy, because of its pleasant climate, was even more attractive to the Greeks. So many settlements were made there that it came to be known as Great Greece (*Magna Graecia*). Among the important cities established by the Greeks in southern Italy were Cumae, Tarentum, Rhegium, and Crotona. In Sicily the outstanding colony was Syracuse, founded by the city-state of Corinth. In western Sicily, Corsica, Sardinia, and the coast of Spain, the Carthaginians prevented the Greeks from getting much of a foothold. At the mouth of the Rhône, however, the Greeks settled Massilia (Marseilles). They founded other colonies on the southern coast of Asia Minor, in northern Africa, and on the Nile Delta.

Greek colonial expansion is important in history because it spread Greek culture over many lands. The Greeks everywhere identified themselves as Hellenes, to distinguish them from the foreigners, or "barbarians." Hellas, their country, came to include all the territory possessed by Hellenic peoples. Thus the "glory that was Greece" was not held within the narrow limits of the Aegean Sea.

PLAIN OF MARATHON. Located twenty-six miles from Athens, the plain is seen here from the top of a burial mound. In 490 B.C. it was the site of the Battle of Marathon between Persia and Athens. Led by the able general Miltiades, an Athenian force of barely 10,000 defeated a force twice that size of Persians under Darius. More than 6000 Persians died in the battle, which left only 192 Greeks dead.

The Greeks Clash with the Persians

We have already related how the Persians, under Cyrus the Great and his successors, expanded to the Aegean Sea and into Egypt. In the course of these conquests many Greeks came under Persian rule. When Darius I came to the throne of Persia, he determined to extend his control still farther. He therefore sent an expedition to the lower Danube region, Macedonia, and Thrace. As a result he extended his sway over the Greek settlements at the western end of the Black Sea. Gradually the Persians were encircling the Greek homeland.

The Ionian revolt, 499–493 B.C. The clash of the Greeks with the Persians started when the Ionian cities of Asia Minor revolted against Persian rule. The Spartans refused to take part, but the Athenians sent aid to their Ionian kinsmen. After temporary success the revolting cities again fell under Persian control.

Battle of Marathon, 490 B.C. Darius now decided to punish Athens for helping the Ionian cities in their revolt. The first attempt failed when the Persian fleet, supporting land forces, was wrecked off Mount Athos. Two years later another large Persian fleet sailed straight across the Aegean and landed at Marathon, twenty-six miles from Athens. The Athenians were in a state of great excitement. They had scarcely ten thousand soldiers, about half the number in the Persian force. The Spartans had promised support but delayed sending any troops. Despite these handicaps, the able Greek general, Miltiades (mĭl-tī′à-dēz), ordered his men to attack. The outcome was a complete rout of the Persians. The invaders lost more than 6000 men and the Greeks only 192. Today the burial mound of the Athenian dead may still be seen.

Thermopylae and Salamis, 480 B.C. Ten years later Xerxes, son of Darius, sent a third expedition against Greece. Coming by way of the Dardanelles Strait, the Persians advanced to the Pass of Thermopylae, which guarded the entrance to central Greece. Here a brave band of a few thousand Greeks, led by the Spartan king, Leonidas, stood off the Persians for two days. Then the enemy found a way around the pass, and all of its remaining defenders died at their posts.

Meanwhile, the Athenians had withdrawn from their city, and all fighting men took to the ships. The Greek fleet, under Themistocles (thē-mĭs'tō-klēz), awaited the Persian navy between the island of Salamis and Attica. In these narrow waters the Persians gave battle. Their large navy was so handicapped in these close quarters that they suffered heavy damage at the hands of the Greeks. The Persian fleet withdrew to Asia Minor, while the land forces of Xerxes retreated into Thessaly.

Plataea and Mycale, 479 B.C. After a winter's preparation in Thessaly, the Persian general, Mardonius, ventured forth to meet the Greeks near Plataea, in Boeotia. He now faced a combined force of Spartans, Athenians, and their allies. In a final great effort the Greek forces turned back the enemy. At about the same time the remainder of the Persian fleet suffered a crushing defeat at Mycale on the Ionian coast. These Greek victories practically ended the Persian effort to conquer Greece.

The Persian wars were more than a clash of arms. They represented a struggle of East and West, between the despotism of the Orient and the newly developing ideas of freedom in the Occident. The defeat of Persia left Greece free to develop a rich culture, which has benefited all mankind.

The Rise of Athens

Greatness of Athens. The leadership of Greece passed to Athens after the Persian wars. From 479 B.C. to 404 B.C. was the great period of Athenian glory. During this period Athens built an empire, established democracy, and became the intellectual and artistic center of the world. Even when wars ended its political and economic greatness, Athens remained a leader in culture.

Athenian leaders. Following the Persian wars, Themistocles remained the outstanding figure in Athens. He rebuilt the city's walls, which protected the people in case of attack. He also repaired and enlarged the port of Piraeus to handle the growing commerce of Athens. Aristides, who next assumed the leadership, formed the Delian League to safeguard Athens against further attacks by the Persians. His successor, Cimon, extended the power and influence of the League. The greatest Athenian leader, however, was Pericles. He was not only a military genius but also an orator, a builder, and a promoter of art, poetry, and learning. The Age of Pericles is the name often given to his period of leadership. Let us see how Athens developed under these men.

The Athenian Empire. The Delian League, formed by Athens for protection against Persia, soon developed into an Athenian empire. This came about because Athens commanded the League's navy and frequently used it to make the members obey Athenian commands. In this way Athens forced the more than two hundred city-states of the League to accept governments like her own. She also sent garrisons of Athenian soldiers to these city-states, compelled them to furnish recruits for her armies, and exacted an annual tribute. The treasury of the League was transferred from Delos to Athens. What had started out as a voluntary association of free and independent city-states thus ended by becoming an Athenian empire. (See map, page 66.)

Athenian democracy. Among the gifts Athens left to the world, none is so important as the ideal of democracy. Under the Athenian system of government every male citizen had a part in public affairs. He might hold office, serve in the courts, and help make the laws. These privileges were open to rich and poor alike. The offices, moreover, were numerous (fourteen hundred in all), and most of them were for a term of one year. Election to office was usually by lot. This did away with favoritism and allowed the poor man a chance in politics equal to that of the man of wealth or of noble birth. It should be remembered, however, that slaves and foreigners were not citizens and therefore had no voice in the government. Furthermore, the women of Athens exercised no political rights. The proportion of the population who could take part in the government was therefore small. This fact does not make the contribution of Athens less important. Never before had the world seen a government in which the people had so large a part.

The Assembly. The center of Athenian democracy was the Assembly, which consisted of all male citizens who had reached twenty years of age. It met on the slopes of a hill called the Pnyx. The meetings were frequently disorderly and very trying to the speakers. Voting was by show of hands, except in cases concerning individuals, when the ballot was used. Whatever the decision of the Assembly, it was final.

The Ten Generals. Many officers and magistrates assisted the Assembly. Among these, the Ten Generals held the leading place. They guided the discussions of the Assembly and carried out the orders of that body. Since the office of general was elective, it was open to men of ability and influence. Pericles served sixteen years in succession as one of the Ten Generals.

Popular courts. The courts were composed of citizens selected by lot. Any citizen might present himself as a candidate. A court was both judge and jury. It decided by majority vote, and from its decision there was no appeal. Trials of public officers and disputes between cities of the empire, besides all ordinary legal business, came before these bodies.

Democracy, then, developed to a high degree in ancient Athens. The citizens ruled and they ruled directly. This system worked well in a small city-state like Athens, but it did not benefit the empire. The subject communities of the Delian League were not represented at Athens. They were ruled in a dictatorial fashion by the Athenians.

Athenian economic life. Athens had many skilled workmen—mostly foreigners—who produced fine pottery, metal wares, and objects of art. In the country districts of Attica people raised olives, grapes, and figs on small farms and large estates. These articles and products formed the bulk of the exports of the city-state. Athens imported salt, fish, hides, timber, wool, and wheat. These products came mostly from the Black Sea region and the Aegean. To make sure that in time of war there should be no interruption of food supplies, the Athenians built the so-called Long Walls between the city and its port of Piraeus. Henceforth they felt safe from attack as long as their navy ruled the Aegean.

Artistic Athens. As the chief commercial city of the Greek world, Athens became wealthy. The Athenians spent much of their wealth in adorning their city with beautiful buildings, sculptures, and other works of art. The finest buildings arose on the Acropolis, the hill overlooking Athens. This steep rock was reached through a superb entrance gate, or Propylaea. It looked like the front of a temple, with columns and pediment (gable). A huge bronze statue of the goddess Athena, by the sculptor Phidias, stood just beyond the Propylaea. On the crest of the Acropolis were two temples. The smaller one was named Erechtheum (ĕr′ĕk-thē′ŭm), for a legendary king. The larger one, called the Parthenon, was dedicated to Athena. Because of its

THE PARTHENON AND A MODERN BANK BUILDING in Philadelphia. The building on the right is living proof that Greek architecture is still admired. Compare it with the ruins of the Parthenon, dedicated to Athena in 438 B.C.

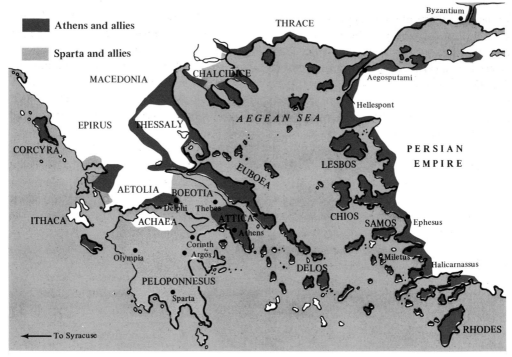

Athens and allies

Sparta and allies

THRACE

Byzantium

MACEDONIA

CHALCIDICE

Aegosputami

Hellespont

EPIRUS

THESSALY

AEGEAN SEA

CORCYRA

PERSIAN
EMPIRE

LESBOS

AETOLIA

BOEOTIA

EUBOEA

Delphi Thebes

CHIOS

ITHACA

ACHAEA

ATTICA

SAMOS

Ephesus

Athens

Corinth

Olympia

Argos

Miletus

DELOS

Halicarnassus

PELOPONNESUS

Sparta

To Syracuse

RHODES

THE ATHENIAN EMPIRE AND THE GREEK STATES, 431 B.C. The second Peloponnesian War, beginning in 431 B.C., was one of three wars fought between Athens and Sparta. The third war left Sparta in control.

perfect construction and fine proportions, it is regarded as a masterpiece of architecture.

Athens, the "School of Hellas." At this time Athens was the heart of Greek intellectual life. The greatest poets, historians, philosophers, and orators of Greece were Athenians, either by birth or by residence. Pericles rightly remarked of his native city, "Athens is the school of Hellas."

Class rule. There were, however, some weaknesses in the life of this noble city. In the first place, slaves, who were mostly war prisoners, did the work on the large estates, in mines and quarries, and on ships. Slavery enabled many Athenians to live in leisure, but it made manual labor dishonorable and tended to prevent the rise of the poorer citizens to important positions. In the second place, not all the freemen of Athens were citizens. As mentioned before, citizenship was inherited. Foreigners living in Athens could

not vote, could not buy land in Attica, and could not legally marry Athenian women.

The Greeks Fight among Themselves

After the Persian wars the Greek city-states renewed their quarrels. Common blood, language, and religion were not enough to unite them. The larger and stronger city-states would not allow the smaller ones to remain independent. That led to the destruction of small, self-governing city-states.

The Peloponnesian Wars, 459–404 B.C. Athens, supreme upon the sea, and Sparta, the chief military power, were rivals for the leadership of Greece. When Athens tried also to become a military power, Sparta declared war.

This conflict lasted, with brief intervals of peace, for more than fifty years. Each side had its allies, who sometimes renewed the fight after peace terms had been arranged.

In the early stages of the struggle a disastrous plague broke out among the Athenians. They had gathered between the Long Walls for protection against the invading Spartans. Among the victims was the great Pericles. His death removed the only leader who might have brought success to the Athenians. The last stage of the war was marked by an Athenian naval attack upon Syracuse, an ally of Corinth and Sparta in Sicily. The outcome was a disaster for Athens. Only a handful of the force ever reached home again. The Spartans quickly renewed the contest, occupied most of Attica, and finally destroyed the Athenian fleet near Aegospotami on the Hellespont (Dardanelles). Athens now had to accept the harsh terms which Sparta offered. The Long Walls were destroyed, the remainder of the fleet surrendered, and the empire was broken up. Worst of all, Athens was forced to recognize the supremacy of Sparta (404 B.C.).

Further struggles. Spartan rule of Greece proved cruel and despotic. Dissatisfaction with such leadership soon led Thebes, a city-state in central Greece, to revolt. In 371 B.C. her great general, Epaminondas, defeated the Spartans at Leuctra. For a brief time thereafter Thebes became the supreme state among the Greeks. But unity brought about by force could not last. At the battle of Mantinea (362 B.C.), Thebes, in turn, suffered defeat at the hands of Sparta and Athens. Exhausted by these long wars, the Greek states could not beat off invaders from the north.

The Rise of Macedonia

North of Thessaly was a rough region inhabited by the Macedonians, distant cousins of the Greeks. They had learned something of Greek civilization through commerce and war. Unlike the Greeks, however, the Macedonians lived under a single ruler. When Philip II became their king in 359 B.C., he determined to conquer and unite the Greeks.

Philip II, 359–336 B.C. Philip II had spent a part of his youth as a hostage at Thebes, where he had learned the art of war and something of Greek politics. Profiting by these lessons, he first formed a standing army of professional soldiers. He improved the Greek phalanx, composed of soldiers massed in rows, and added strong forces of cavalry to attack the enemy's flanks. Moreover, Philip used the catapult, a machine which could throw darts and huge stones into the ranks of the opposing side. Thus Philip made his army stronger than any fighting force that ever existed until the days of the Roman legion.

Demosthenes. Philip's conquests in northern Greece found favor with some people in Athens, Thebes, and Sparta. They saw in his advance the only means of uniting Greece. One leader strongly opposed Philip's invasion. He was Demosthenes (dĕ-mŏs′thĕ-nēz). In stirring speeches this Athenian urged his fellow citizens to lead Greece against Philip. These orations have given us the word "philippic," meaning a spirited speech against some person.

Battle of Chaeronea, 338 B.C. The appeals of Demosthenes had little effect until Philip entered central Greece. Then a hastily formed alliance made a stand against the invader, but it was too late. At Chaeronea, in Boeotia, the well-drilled and disciplined Macedonians overcame the citizen-soldiers of Greece. Philip now became the master of all the Greek states except Sparta, which managed to preserve its liberty. The city-states never again became first-rate powers.

The next step in Philip's ambitious program was the conquest of Asia Minor and perhaps even of Persia. At a meeting in Corinth the Greek states promised to help in this large plan. However, Philip never led his armies into Asia. He was struck down by an assassin less than two years after the Battle of Chaeronea. The task now fell to his young son, Alexander.

ALEXANDER THE GREAT

Alexander the Great Builds an Empire

Alexander became king of Macedonia when only twenty years old. He had his father's vigorous body, keen mind, and iron will. He developed into a splendid athlete and had the advantage of an excellent education. His tutor, Aristotle, was the most learned man in Greece, and made Alexander a lifelong admirer of Greek civilization.

Alexander and the Persians. The Persian Empire was a collection of many peoples, loosely held together by a common loyalty to the Great King. Despite its enormous resources, this empire could not stop the attack of the youthful Alexander. His small but well-drilled army crossed into Asia Minor near Troy, driving the enemy from the western and southern parts of the peninsula. Meanwhile, Darius III, king of Persia, assembled a large force on the narrow plain of Issus, between the Syrian Mountains and the Mediterranean Sea. Here, after a stubborn fight, the Persians fled before the forces of Alexander (333 B.C.). Proceeding southward, the Macedonians laid siege to and destroyed the great seaport of Tyre, ancient Phoenician stronghold. Alexander then entered Egypt, where he was welcomed as a deliverer. At the western mouth of the Nile he founded Alexandria, which replaced Tyre as an important commercial center. Turning eastward, the young conquerer crossed the Tigris and the Euphrates, and again defeated the forces of Darius at Arbela (331 B.C.). This victory decided the fate of the Persian Empire. Babylon surrendered without a struggle, and Susa, the Persian capital, fell to Alexander.

Alexander in Iran and India. Alexander might well have returned at this point, but he could not rest while there still were lands to conquer. He continued to march eastward into the valley of the Indus and added northwestern India to his possessions. Alexander would have pressed forward to the Ganges River, but his troops refused to go farther. They had had their fill of war.

Death of Alexander, 323 B.C. Alexander then returned to Babylon, a city which became the capital of his empire. While planning expeditions against the Arabs, Carthage, and the Italian states, he suddenly became ill and died. He was not quite thirty-three years of age. The empire he had built in such haste soon fell apart.

Results of Alexander's conquests. The *immediate result* of Alexander's conquests was the removal of the barriers which had so long shut in the Oriental world. Greek colonists of many different professions and occupations followed the Macedonian armies. They brought their arts and culture and became the teachers of those whom they called "barbarians." The *final result* of Alexander's conquests was the joining of East and West. He gave Persians positions of trust; he organized the government of his provinces on a system similar to that of Darius I (see page 32); and he admitted Persian soldiers to his armies. He also encouraged marriages with Orientals, and himself married Roxana, the daughter of the last Persian king. Moreover, Alexander

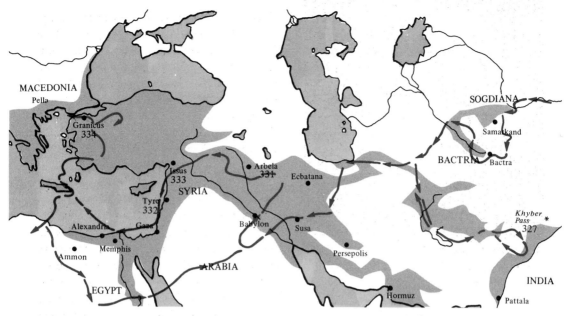

MACEDONIA
Pella
Granicus 334
Issus 333
Tyre 332
SYRIA
Alexandria
Gaza
Memphis
Ammon
EGYPT
ARABIA
Arbela 331
Ecbatana
Babylon
Susa
Persepolis
Hormuz
SOGDIANA
Samarkand
BACTRIA
Bactra
Khyber Pass 327 *
INDIA
Pattala

ALEXANDER'S ROUTE OF CONQUEST AND HIS EMPIRE AT THE TIME OF HIS DEATH, 323 B.C.

founded no less than seventy cities, which helped to hold his dominions together and provided centers of communication. This joining of Greek ideas and customs with those of the Middle East produced a new kind of culture, known as Hellenistic.

The Hellenistic Age

Nature of the Hellenistic Age. The Hellenistic Age was the third stage of Greek development. The first stage had been the development of a civilization in the Greek peninsula by the Achaean, Dorian, and Ionian barbarians. The second consisted of the spreading of Greek culture through colonization. When the Greeks themselves were conquered and joined their civilization to that of their conquerors, the Hellenistic Age began. It lasted from 338 B.C., until Rome conquered the Hellenistic kingdom.

With Alexander's death, his empire broke up into a number of kingdoms, including Macedonia, Syria, and Egypt. They were ruled by despotic descendants of Alexander's generals until the Romans conquered them.

Alexander's successors continued to build cities. Unlike the Greek city-states, they were not independent but formed parts of kingdoms. For the most part, these cities enjoyed self-government, but the old Athenian spirit of democratic liberty had disappeared. In appearance, too, Hellenistic cities differed from those of Greece. They had broad, well-paved streets, a water supply, baths, theaters, gymnasiums, and parks. In these population centers Greek became a language understood by all.

Communication between East and West. Many Hellenistic cities became thriving business centers through which Asiatic products reached Greece. This trade raised the standard of living because it introduced luxuries which the earlier Greeks did not know. Still more important was the exchange of ideas. What the Greeks had accomplished in art, literature, philosophy, and science became familiar to the Egyptians, Babylonians, and others. These peoples, in turn, passed on to the Greeks their own cultural achievements.

RAMLEH STATION, ALEXANDRIA, EGYPT. In this view of the modern city there is little to suggest Hellenistic culture.

Alexandria. Alexandria in Egypt was a crossroads for commerce and peoples. On that account it came to be the foremost Hellenistic city. By the time of Christ its population ranked next to that of Rome. Its public buildings were magnificent and its learning great. The royal museum became a genuine university. The library of this school contained over five hundred thousand papyrus and parchment (sheepskin) rolls. Learned men translated Oriental literature into Greek, including the Hebrew Old Testament. They also made progress in mathematics, astronomy, geography, medicine, and other branches of knowledge.

The Aetolian and Achaean Leagues. The Greek city-states had learned through bitter experience that close union could be an advantage to them. Consequently, after Alexander's death they formed the Aetolian League in central Greece and the Achaean League in the Peloponnesus. The latter was the more important. An assembly, or congress, handled for all its members such matters as taxation, war and peace, and foreign affairs. This league was the first genuine federation that the world had ever known. American statesmen looked to it as an example when they were drafting our constitution. Athens and Sparta remained outside these leagues. Without them, neither association could achieve lasting success.

Cosmopolitanism. The Greeks who left their homeland for Egypt or western Asia became "cosmopolitans," or citizens of the world. Henceforth, the difference between Greek and barbarian gradually faded away, and the eastern Graeco-Oriental world grew into one unit. The *eastern* Mediterranean civilization was now to come in contact with a growing power in the *western* Mediterranean—Rome.

REVIEWING THE CHAPTER

TERMS TO UNDERSTAND: *oracle, city-state, monarchy, aristocracy, tyrant, ephor, laconic, draconic, ostracism,* Magna Graecia, *Hellas, Occident, Acropolis, Parthenon, phalanx, philippic, federation, cosmopolitanism.*

PERSONS TO IDENTIFY: *Schliemann, Evans, Homer, Agamemnon, Odysseus, Zeus, Xerxes, Leonidas, Themistocles, Aristides, Pericles, Epaminondas, Demosthenes, Roxana.*

PLACES TO LOCATE: *Aegean Sea, Hissarlik, Mycenae, Tiryns, Cnossus, Mt. Olympus, Athens, Sparta, Peloponnesus, Constantinople, Marathon, Dardanelles (Hellespont), Thermopylae, Salamis, Attica, Plataea, Mycale, Macedonia, Chaeronea, Tyre, Alexandria, Arbela.*

QUESTIONS TO ANSWER

1. (a) What geographic features helped give Europe so important a place in history? (b) Why did the Mediterranean Sea become an "avenue of commerce"? (c) What is meant by the "Aegean bridge"?

2. (a) Name the centers of Aegean civilization. (b) Who uncovered them? (c) When did Aegean civilization reach its peak? (d) Compare it with the earlier civilizations in the Middle East. (e) What brought about its downfall?

3. (a) From what tribes did the Greek people develop? (b) When did historic times begin among the Greeks? (c) Of what value are the *Iliad* and the *Odyssey* to the historian? (d) Describe the culture of the Homeric Age. Compare it with Aegean civilization. (e) Name five Greek deities and tell what each represented. (f) What part did oracles play in Greek religious life? The Olympian games?

4. (a) Define "city-state." (b) Who were citizens in a Greek city-state? (c) Through what stages did the government of the city-state pass?

5. (a) Compare Spartan and Athenian life and government. (b) How did Draco, Solon, and Clisthenes change the government of Athens?

6. (a) For what reasons did the Greeks establish colonies? (b) Locate seven areas colonized by the Greeks. (c) Why have Greek colonies been called "patches of Hellas"?

7. (a) What caused the clash between the Persians and the Greeks? (b) Give the chief events of each of the three Persian invasions. (c) What was the importance of Greek victory?

8. (a) In what century did Athenian culture reach its height? (b) How did Athens make the Delian League into an Athenian empire? (c) In what respects did Athenian democracy differ from our ideas of democracy? (d) What did Pericles mean when he said, "Athens is the school of Hellas"? (e) What is meant by the Age of Pericles?

9. (a) Why did the Greek city-states fight among themselves? (b) Explain the statement: "The road from Aegospotami, Leuctra, and Mantinea led directly to Chaeronea." (c) Describe Philip's new war methods.

10. (a) Trace Alexander's campaigns in the east, giving battles, events, and results. (b) How did Alexander's conquests lead to the Hellenistic Age? (c) Describe Hellenistic culture as represented by life in Alexandria.

6 Our Debt to the Greeks

ARISTOTLE. Pupil of the great philosopher Plato and tutor of Alexander the Great, Aristotle was known in his day as the "wisest man in Greece." He was a physical scientist as well as a philosopher, and his findings in physics and biology went unchallenged for a thousand years. He is credited with having written between 400 and 1000 books.

In the previous chapter we learned about the geographic setting of Greece and traced the story of its military and political life. Now we turn to another side of Greek life—the great activity in art, literature, science, and philosophy. This intellectual activity did not stop when the Greeks lost their independence, but continued for several centuries, far into the Roman period. In Chapter 6 we shall find out how the Greeks lived and what ideas they contributed to civilization. We shall discover that the ancient Greeks were in some ways strikingly modern.

Greek Home and Social Life

Clothing and housing. Because of the mild Mediterranean climate of Greece the Greeks wore a simple and scanty costume. It did not change with the whims of fashion but remained the same for centuries. Men's dress consisted of tunic and mantle. The tunic was an undergarment of wool or linen without sleeves. Over this was thrown a large woolen mantle, so wrapped about the body as to leave free only the right shoulder and the head. The mantle was usually worn only out of doors. In rainy weather the mantle could be pulled up to cover both head and face; hats were seldom worn. Women's garments were much the same as those of men, but with greater variety in shape, draping, color, and ornamentation. For both men and women, footwear consisted of sandals indoors and leather shoes outdoors. To go barefoot in public, however, was not considered out of place. The Greeks liked simplicity and usefulness in dress.

The same sort of simplicity appeared in the Greek house. Built of sun-dried brick, it stood close to the street in the city. The outside was extremely plain. In a two-story house a narrow, paneless window or two and a clay tile roof relieved the blank appearance. Inside was an open court, from which doors led to a living room, dining room, sleeping quarters, storerooms, and a small kitchen. The floors were of earth, with a hard-beaten surface of pebbles. The house contained no plumbing or piping of any kind. Springs or wells furnished the water supply, which was carried into the house in jars by slaves. The only means of heating was by pans of charcoal, or braziers. Moreover, very little furniture adorned the Greek home, although it was often elaborately carved. One could also find in the Greek house such objects as metal utensils, bronze mirrors, and lovely painted jars, vases, and dishes.

The position of women. Greek society was largely a man's world. The only schooling the young girl received was in the duties of housekeeping. On the rare occasions when she went outside, she was closely chaperoned by her parents. Neither she nor her future husband had a voice in their marriage plans. The parents on both sides arranged the match and agreed on how large a dowry the bride's father was to give his daughter.

Marriage did not bring the young woman freedom. In Homeric times women seem to have occupied a position more nearly equal with that of men. In Sparta women were highly respected, and the girls received gymnastic training. But in many of the city-states, and particularly in Athens, the wife lived largely within the four walls of her home. She did not appear in public except at festivals, and then only by permission of her husband and under escort. She took no part in the feasts and entertainments which her husband gave. In fact, on such occasions women were confined to their own quarters of the house. An Athenian wife also had no legal rights. If her husband mistreated her, she found it difficult to secure a separation. In case of divorce, the children remained with the father. The inferior position of Athenian women did not necessarily mean that they were unhappy with their lot. Greek literature is full of examples of affectionate and contented family life.

The class system. There were other divisions in Greek society. As mentioned before, only male citizens had a voice in the conduct of public affairs, and they were outnumbered in Athens by the resident foreigners (*metics*) and slaves. The citizen population itself represented a wide range of economic well-being, from the very wealthy to the very poor. Many wealthy Athenians lived on the income from their lands and could afford to devote much of their time to political and social matters. Prosperous businessmen frequently bought land in order to gain the social standing and influence associated with landholding. These Athenian aristocrats considered themselves superior men and ran the city-state until the fifth century B.C., when they lost most of their power to the popular Assembly.

The greater part of the citizen class, however, consisted of the small farmers who lived

STATUETTE OF A GIRL RUNNING

in Attica, outside the city of Athens proper. They formed a fairly prosperous middle class before the Peloponnesian wars, but most of them did not participate regularly in the political affairs of the city-state. The small size of their farms and frequent warfare made conditions increasingly hard for this class; as a result, many lost their land and became tenants on the estates of aristocrats. Another large group of citizens were the poor people of the city—small shopkeepers, skilled workers, manual laborers, sailors, peddlers, and the unemployed. Many of these were no better off than slaves, although under Pericles thousands were given employment in the navy, on public works, and in the government; others were sent abroad as colonists. A considerable number, it is thought, took part in the Assembly.

Unlike most of the other Greek city-states, Athens opened its gates rather freely to foreigners. The *metics*, as they were called, were welcomed to satisfy the growing need for manpower in industry and in the navy. They paid a special poll tax and a higher income tax than citizens during wartime, ordinarily could own no land, and had no political rights. On the other hand, the metics served in the army in time of war, and could achieve wealth and social standing on a basis of equality with citizens.

The lowest class in Greek society was the slaves. Their number in Periclean Athens has been estimated at about one third of the total population. The rapid increase in slavery after the Persian wars resulted from the need for labor both in industry and in domestic service, and from the large number of available war prisoners. They were largely non-Greeks, some of whom served in responsible positions as personal attendants, skilled artisans, overseers, and children's nurses. The state also owned a number of slaves, using them on public works and sometimes as secretaries and accountants. For the most part, slaves were treated with kindness, the big exception

GREEK GAME. This relief from the base of an Athenian statue shows boys using a ball and sticks in a game similar to modern hockey.

being those who worked in the mines, where conditions were extremely wretched. In small shops and on farms, slaves often worked side by side with their masters, sometimes receiving pay in addition to their keep. Freeing slaves became fairly common in Athens, and the freedmen assumed the status of metics. Slavery was generally accepted by the Greeks, as by all other ancient peoples, as part of the natural order of things. A few Athenians, however, considered it degrading to the natural dignity of man. The dramatist Euripides spoke for these when he said:

> Slavery,
> That thing of evil, by its nature evil,
> Forcing submission from man to what
> No man should yield to.

An Athenian's day. It has been said that the Greeks prized leisure above everything else except glory. Even the average freeborn Athenian enjoyed an abundance of leisure. In the middle of the morning he usually made his way to the Agora, the great marketplace. Here he not only did his shopping (with the help of a slave, if he owned one), but also met friends to discuss public affairs. In the late afternoon the Athenian would visit one of the gymnasiums, such as the Lyceum or the Academy, in the city's suburbs. He might

take part in vigorous exercises but, if an older man, he would probably be content with talking to his friends. In the evening a citizen sometimes attended a banquet instead of eating with his family. The host and his guests reclined on couches arranged about one or more tables. The meal consisted of several courses, served in a leisurely fashion. Afterward, the tables were cleared and the *symposium* (drinking together) began. This was more than a mere drinking bout. It was entertainment, to which each guest contributed with poetry, songs, wit, riddles, or serious discussion of a suggested subject. Thus we get the present meaning of the word "symposium"—a series of viewpoints on some topic, presented by several persons.

Greek education. From what we have learned about the position of women in Greece it should not surprise us that education was for boys and not for girls. In early childhood, Greek boys, as well as girls, remained under the care of their mothers. A slave woman usually helped to watch over the children. In most parts of Greece, when a boy reached seven his formal education began and continued until he was fourteen. During this period a slave called a *pedagogue* was his constant companion, teaching him good manners, helping him select his friends, and accompanying him everywhere—to and from school, to the athletic field, and about the house.

Although Athens and other Greek cities had no public schools, the Greeks took it for granted that all male citizens would be educated. They were thus the first people to realize the importance of widespread schooling. The many private schools were open to boys of all classes at moderate fees. No matter how poor his parents, a Greek boy could get at least what we would regard as an elementary education.

The curriculum. The training of the Greek schoolboy consisted of grammar, music, a little arithmetic, and gymnastics. Grammar included instruction in writing and the reading of literature, especially poetry. The boy began by tracing his letters with a stylus on wax-coated wooden tablets. When he had learned to read and write, he studied the works of the great poet Homer, the *Fables* of Aesop, and other literary compositions. He memorized much of the poetry. Some boys could recite the whole of Homer's *Iliad* and *Odyssey*. These studies taught the Greek youth to admire the heroic deeds of his ancestors and to use his own language well. The study of foreign languages never became a part of Greek education.

Young men did not study music to become fine musicians but to fit themselves for pleasant social fellowship. They learned to play the seven-stringed lyre and to sing to their own accompaniment. This was enough to enable a man to take part in the entertainment on social occasions. The Greeks also thought that music, through its beauty and rhythm, purified the emotions and strengthened the moral side of man's nature.

Boys took their gymnastic exercises in the *palestra,* an open stretch of ground on the outskirts of the city. They received instruction in running, boxing, jumping, wrestling, discus hurling, and javelin throwing. Before the contests the participants usually rubbed their bodies with olive oil and afterward cleaned themselves with a scraper. Often the youth also swam in a nearby stream. The daily physical training in the open air served to produce healthy bodies.

The formal education of a boy ended at the age of fourteen, but his daily exercises on the athletic field or in the gymnasium continued so long as he was able. He also continued to learn by attending dramatic festivals and by discussing public affairs with his elders in the Agora. Perhaps he was fortunate enough to enroll in an advanced school such as Plato's Academy, or in one conducted by a sophist. At eighteen an Athenian youth took an oath of loyalty and was accepted as a full-fledged citizen.

The Greek educational system aimed at producing a sound mind in a sound body. It prepared the citizen not only to perform his duties to the state but also to develop the complete man by encouraging him to pursue excellence in all things. Strictly vocational training—that is, training for money-making occupations—was therefore not a part of Greek education. That could be gained through apprenticeship. The typical Greek valued knowledge for what it could do in making him a well-balanced individual and an honored member of his city-state. The reward of high achievement or excellence was the praise of his fellowmen and of succeeding generations. As Plato remarked, the Greeks had a "passionate thirst for fame, 'to leave behind them,' as the poet says, 'a name for all succeeding ages.' " The type of education that would lead to this goal was the Greek ideal—the ideal of a truly "liberal" education rather than a "practical" one.

Religion in Greek Life

Humanlike gods and godlike men. As we have already learned, the Greeks of the Homeric Age had developed a flourishing polytheism (worship of many gods). The number of gods increased as time passed. Every object in nature, every human quality and vice, every vocation, art, and profession, and every city had its own particular god. Indeed, "All things are full of gods," as the astronomer Thales said. Moreover, the Greek gods usually took human form, with all the virtues and weaknesses of human beings. This gave the Greeks a sense of companionship with their deities.

Connected with each god was a myth or story, telling of the god's origin and explaining the special ceremony or ritual that honored him. These myths, like the gods themselves, were not created by priests or prophets, who remained outside the routine of ordinary living. They were rather an attempt by poets, philosophers, and artists to explain things around them—things that they saw in nature which could not be accounted for otherwise. From the stories of the gods came the inspiration and the themes for most of the literature of the Greeks, and the subjects that artists used for their numerous paintings and sculptures.

Changes in religious thought. As time passed, Greek religion changed. Homer's gods no longer met the needs of men who were al-

ways trying to find life's purpose and to solve its mysteries. The Greeks became more and more aware of what life required of them and therefore demanded higher standards of their gods. Zeus, for example, became a god of justice, who cared for the poor as well as for the powerful. In other words, the Greek religion was increasingly concerned with morality, that is, with questions of right and wrong. By the sixth and fifth centuries B.C. the poets and dramatists were using the stories of the gods to teach lessons in human conduct. Their religion was that of Apollo, the god of purity and light, with the watchwords "know thyself" and "nothing in excess." The dominating ideal, which every Greek wished to strive for, was excellence, or virtue. A man must exert his utmost efforts to achieve the best, and the driving energy to do this came, he believed, from the gods.

At the same time that fifth-century poets and dramatists were calling for a nobler standard of conduct, Greek religion entered a new phase. It was marked by quarrels between the philosophers and the poets. The philosophers, such as Socrates and the sophists (see page 79), appealed to scientific reason to teach the truth. Hence they promoted the growth of doubt and of a critical attitude toward the old religious ideas. Protagoras, for example, said, "With regard to the gods I know not whether they exist or not, or what they are like." And he added, "Man is the measure of all things." He was banished from Athens, for the fifth-century Athenian still showed a deep loyalty to traditional forms of worship. Plato, on the other hand, tried to reconcile the mysteries of religion with the "new learning," that is, with scientific reasoning. His thinking represented the Greek genius for recognizing the place in life of both the ideal and the actual.

Religion and the state. Greek religious life cannot be understood apart from loyalty and devotion to the city-state. The city-state was a religious as well as a political unit. The government officials of each city took charge of and protected the official religion and the places of worship. They regarded religion as vital to maintaining law and order. Whereas in Egypt and Mesopotamia the priests controlled the state, in Greece the state exercised religious leadership. The priests were merely minor officials in the temples. They received no special training, had no organized profession, and sometimes could buy their positions. A citizen did not voluntarily "join a church," but was automatically a member of a religious as well as a political community. He practiced his religion by taking part in the official ritual in honor of the city's gods. This was his patriotic duty. There was thus no separation of church and state in ancient Greece.

Religious festivals. Among the Greek religious celebrations several were outstanding. The Olympian festivals, with their games and throngs of people, have already been described (see page 57). Almost as important was the Great Panathenaea, held at Athens every fourth year. On this occasion masters gave their slaves many privileges and women came out of their seclusion. The celebration was in honor of Athena, patron goddess of Athens. To mark this holiday, Athenians held sacrifices, feasts, and processions, as well as athletic and poetry contests. Another festival, open to all Greeks, was the annual celebration of the Eleusinian Mysteries in the little town of Eleusis. These "mysteries" were secret ceremonies connected with the worship of Demeter, goddess of vegetation and of nature. Those to be initiated into the mysteries, or secret rites, witnessed a play which gave them a kind of living picture of life after death. Of a less religious nature were the festivals in honor of Dionysus, god of wine. These took place in midwinter and spring in various cities, especially in Athens. For three days people gathered in the local theater to watch the performance of tragedies and comedies, both old and new. The citizens voted a prize each day to the poet whose play had pleased

them most. Some of these dramas have survived to this day as excellent examples of Greek literature.

The Greeks as Philosophers

The first philosophers. In the sixth century B.C., long before the Persian wars, a few thinkers in Greece began to inquire into the mysteries of nature. They were not satisfied with the explanation that the gods caused thunderstorms, eclipses, changes in seasons, and other such occurrences. On the contrary, said these bold thinkers, such happenings must have natural causes; there must be some *reason why* they happen. These men with inquiring minds may be called the first *philosophers,* or "lovers of wisdom." By trying to understand why things happened, they became pioneers in both philosophy and science.

The sophists. Shortly after the Persian wars another class of thinkers arose in Greece. They declared that instead of studying what happens in nature people should study man and his activities. The knowledge thus gained would be true wisdom. In time these thinkers became known as *sophists,* or "wise men." Many of them were brilliant men who helped to spread more reasonable ideas about politics,

---

PERICLES PRAISES ATHENIANS

. . . An Athenian citizen does not neglect the state because he takes care of his own household; and even those of us who are engaged in business have a very fair idea of politics. We alone regard a man who takes no interest in public affairs, not as a harmless, but as a useless character; and if few of us are originators, we are all sound judges of a policy. The great impediment to action is, in our opinion, not discussion, but the want of that knowledge which is gained by discussion preparatory to action. For we have a peculiar power of thinking before we act and of acting too . . .

—*Thucydides.*

morals, and religion. They traveled throughout Greece, teaching for pay any young men who wished to learn the art of debate. They questioned whether justice was possible, whether the gods really lived and had power over the lives of men. Older citizens became alarmed and looked upon the sophists as dangerous. True, many sophists were not real lovers of wisdom, but merely talkers who used tricky and deceitful reasoning in order to win an argument. The name sophist thus came to be used with disrespect. We still use the word in that sense. When anybody's reasoning is only a clever attempt to deceive, we call it *sophistry*.

Socrates, lover of wisdom. About the time of the Peloponnesian wars (459–404 B.C.), one of the most interesting characters in all history appeared in Athens. This was Socrates (sŏk′rȧ-tēz), who had given up sculpture to become a teacher and philosopher. He had a homely and bulky appearance, but also a kindliness and simplicity that won the love of his followers. In time his name spread throughout Greece, and in Athens he became a unique public figure.

Such a person was bound to make enemies as well as friends. Among those who had reason to dislike Socrates were the sophists. He did not believe in accepting pay for teaching, as they did. It is not surprising, therefore, to learn that Socrates and his family lived in poverty. He also thought that many of the sophists boasted too much about their wisdom, thus causing their pupils to become conceited. To think one's self wise was wrong, according to Socrates. Hence he would not allow anyone to call him a sophist, or wise man; instead, he was content to be known as a lover of wisdom, or philosopher. To him the philosopher was a humble seeker after knowledge, or truth. Wisdom would lead to right conduct and happiness, while ignorance accounted for all evil. To become truly wise, Socrates thought that a man should examine carefully what such ideas as justice, honor, virtue, duty, and patriotism meant to him. "Know thyself" was the motto of Socrates.

The Socratic method. Socrates' method of getting men to discover the meaning of ideas has become famous. Unlike the sophists, he did not deliver ranting lectures to his pupils.

MEN OF WISDOM in the academy of Plato. This mosaic pictures dates from the Graeco-Roman period. Its exact subject is no longer known. Some authorities believe that it is intended to show Plato teaching in the Academy. Others believe that the artist represented famous Greek philosophers and poets from different ages, as they would appear if brought together.

Instead, he tried to point the way to truth by give-and-take discussion. Barefoot and clad in an old rumpled tunic, Socrates fell into conversation with men in the streets and market place of Athens. By asking searching questions he tried to get them to think more carefully about the meaning of the words and terms they used. He wanted them to take nothing for granted. The use of questions to make people think and arrive at conclusions is known as the *Socratic method*.

Death of Socrates. The Socratic method not only stirred up thought; it also stirred up many enemies for Socrates. Then, as now, men did not like to be made uncomfortable by having their long established beliefs questioned. So at the age of seventy Socrates was publicly accused of denying the existence of the gods (impiety) and misleading the city's youth. When brought to trial he said that his conscience, which he considered the voice of God, moved him to teach. He declared that if allowed to live he would still follow the same course. Consequently, he was condemned to death. He refused to plead for a pardon or to attempt escape. He drained the hemlock cup that brought him death—and also fame as one of the earliest martyrs to freedom of thought.

Plato, the idealist. Socrates left no writings. For information about his ideas we must go to the writings of his pupils. The greatest of these was Plato, a wealthy aristocrat. Plato often taught his pupils as he strolled with them in the Academy, which was a public park and athletic field. Upon his death (347 B.C.) at the age of eighty-one, he left his fortune to maintain a school in the Academy. It continued for over eight hundred years. We still apply the name "academy" to certain kinds of schools.

Plato left a number of writings in which he explained his ideas on government, education, religion, virtue, and justice. Each of these writings is in the form of an imaginary discussion, or dialogue, among several persons. Together these works are therefore known as the *Dialogues*. In most of them Plato makes his old teacher, Socrates, the chief speaker. The most important dialogue is the *Republic*, in which an answer is sought to the question "What is justice?" To define justice properly, Plato imagines an ideal state, where only the wisest men (philosopher-kings) are rulers, and everyone is doing the work for which he is best fitted. Plato did not believe that a society so perfect would ever exist on this earth. He did believe that good men should always keep in mind such a model and try to make their country as much like the ideal as possible. Throughout his writings Plato emphasized the importance and power of ideas, rather than wealth and material things. He also urged men to strive for perfection in thought and deed.

Aristotle, the all-knowing. Among Plato's pupils in the Academy was one so able and eager that Plato called him "the mind of the school." This pupil was Aristotle (384–322 B.C.), a Macedonian who had come to Athens to study under Plato. He returned to his native state at one time to become the tutor of Alexander. (See page 68.) Later, back in Athens, in the garden and gymnasium of the Lyceum, he founded a school which was called the Lyceum. He continued as head of it until Alexander died (323 B.C.); then an uprising of the Athenians against the Macedonians caused Aristotle to flee for his life. He died the following year, an old man in exile.

Aristotle probed into every field of knowledge. He studied the constitutions of over 150 Greek city-states as the basis for his *Politics*, a book on the principles of government. He examined the acts and beliefs of men, tried to find those which brought virtue and happiness, and then wrote a treatise called the *Ethics*. A study of Greek dramas led to the writing of the *Poetics*, which pointed out the difference between a good play and a poor play. Aristotle also did important work in botany and zoology by collecting and describ-

. . . Hence it is evident that the state is a creation of nature, and that man is by nature a political animal. And he who by nature and not by mere accident is without a state is either a bad man or above humanity; he is like the "Tribeless, Lawless, heartless one," whom Homer denounces—the natural outcast is forthwith a lover of war. . . .

Now, that man is more of a political animal than bees or any other gregarious animals is evident. Nature, as we often say, makes nothing in vain, and man is the only animal whom she has endowed with the gift of speech. And whereas mere voice is but an indication of pleasure or pain, and is therefore found in other animals, . . . the power of speech is intended to set forth . . . the just and the unjust. And it is characteristic of man that he alone has any sense of good and evil, of just and unjust, and the like, and the association of living beings who have this sense makes a family and a state. . . .

— Aristotle

ARISTOTLE

ing specimen plants and animals. He created the science of *logic,* or the principles of correct reasoning. These are but a few examples of his accomplishments. Apparently Aristotle's two great aims were to collect as many facts as possible and then to organize them for the purpose of finding out what they meant. He was thus not only a philosopher but also a scientist. Aristotle lacked Plato's creative imagination and striving for perfection. However, as a master of definitions, the scientific method, and the orderly classification of information, he has rarely, if ever, been equaled.

Epicureanism. In the early Hellenistic period another school near Athens was "the garden of Epicurus." Here Epicurus taught that pleasure is the sole good in life and pain the only evil. Today an Epicurean means a person who follows the motto "Eat, drink, and be merry, for tomorrow we die." But Epicurus himself taught no such belief. By "pleasure" he meant not so much the passing enjoyments of the hour as the permanent happiness of a lifetime. Indeed, he believed that to be happy, men must lead a simple life. He also thought that happiness came to virtuous men, because virtue brings less pain than does vice.

Stoicism. At the same time that Epicurus was teaching in his garden, Zeno was conducting a school in the Painted Porch, or Stoa. The ideas of Zeno and his followers have since become known as Stoicism. The Stoics said that the good life comes as the result of accepting whatever the laws of nature dictate. Thus, if a man's friend dies, no undue grief should be shown. A man's reason ought to teach him that such things must be. The Stoics stressed the importance of reason as a guide to conduct. They did not trust the emotions, and tried to be indifferent to grief, fear, pain, and pleasure. They believed that virtue is the highest good, and that it consists in co-operating with nature, or God. There is only one evil—moral wrong. Bad conduct is conduct not in harmony with nature, or God. Many Romans accepted the doctrines of Stoicism. It also had a marked influence on Christianity.

Science among the Greeks

Greek philosophy and science. The Greeks did not recognize the distinction we now make between philosophy and science. At that time they had not yet divided knowledge into many separate departments. We might call the early Greek philosophers scientists, since they tried to explain the wonders of nature. Some of the later philosophers also contributed to scientific knowledge. Democritus, a contemporary of Socrates, thought that all material things were made of moving atoms —particles so small that they could not be divided. (See page 341.) Plato and his followers did useful work in mathematics and astronomy. Aristotle and his students laid the foundations of the sciences of zoology, anatomy, and botany. His pupil Theophrastus (thē´ō-frăs´tŭs) classified the known plants, and thus ranks high as a botanist.

Mathematics. The Greeks' method of writing numbers was so clumsy that they never accomplished much in arithmetic. With geometry, however, they did a great deal. Euclid, who lived at Alexandria about 300 B.C., wrote a geometry textbook known as the *Elements.* We still use his theorems in modern books on the subject. Hipparchus, a second-century astronomer, developed trigonometry. Archimedes (är´kĭ-mē´dēz) of Syracuse (287–212 B.C.), who had studied at Alexandria, was the foremost mathematician of ancient times. He worked out theorems in regard to the sphere, cone, and cylinder. One of his achievements was the calculation of the value of π (pi) in figuring the area of a circle.

Physics. Archimedes also made physics a separate science. He discovered the principle of specific gravity and the law of floating bodies. He invented the compound pulley and cogged wheels and developed the theory of the lever. "Give me a place to stand, and I will move the world," he said. From Archimedes the Romans learned much about engineering.

Astronomy. In astronomy the Greeks went beyond the Babylonians. Aristarchus of Samos (310–230 B.C.) determined that the earth and all the planets revolve around the sun. Hipparchus was perhaps the greatest student of the stars in ancient times. He measured almost exactly the solar year and the lunar month, charted many stars, and devised the method of measuring distances by latitude and longitude. Unfortunately, he did not accept the idea of Aristarchus that the sun was the center of the universe. Instead, he made the earth the center of his system. Ptolemy of Alexandria copied this mistaken theory and developed it in the second century after Christ. It remained the accepted idea until Copernicus (kō-pûr´nĭ-kŭs) rediscovered the central position of the sun in the sixteenth century.

Medicine and anatomy. In the fifth century B.C. Hippocrates gained fame as the "father of medicine." He thought that all disease resulted from natural causes. He did much to free the art of healing from superstition. His high ideals of medical practice were embodied in the *Hippocratic Oath,* still recited by graduates of our medical schools. Alexandria became an important center for the study of medicine and anatomy. There doctors studied anatomy by performing human dissections, and also performed surgical operations. Greek scientists believed correctly that the brain is the center of the nervous system, and that the arteries carry blood to every part of the body. The supreme authority on medicine for more than a thousand years was Galen of Pergamum (A.D. 131–210). His extensive summaries were not revised until the Renaissance.

Geography. For early geographical information we owe much to Eratosthenes (ĕr´ȧ-tŏs´thĕ-nēz), who lived in Alexandria in the third century B.C. His greatest achievement was his calculation that the earth's diameter was 7850 miles, which is only 76 miles from the true figure. He did this by observing the shadows cast by the sun at two different places in Egypt, approximately 500 miles apart. Eratosthenes described the geography of the known world and even suggested that men might reach India by sailing westward. The

PORCH OF THE MAIDENS ON THE ERECHTHEUM. Six female figures support the porch roof of the Erechtheum, a temple honoring Athena. Located on the Acropolis, the building was erected during the Peloponnesian Wars, 425–405 B.C. The figure-columns shown here are variations of the orders of Greek architecture.

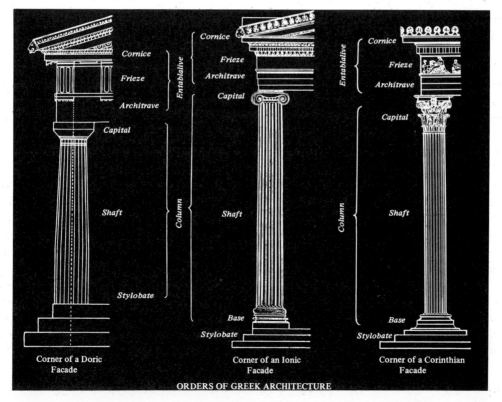

Cornice
Frieze
Architrave
Entablative
Capital

Shaft
Column

Stylobate

Corner of a Doric Facade

Cornice
Frieze
Architrave
Capital

Shaft

Base
Stylobate

Corner of an Ionic Facade

Cornice
Frieze
Architrave
Entablative

Capital

Shaft
Column

Base
Stylobate

Corner of a Corinthian Facade

ORDERS OF GREEK ARCHITECTURE

astronomer Ptolemy was also an eminent geographer. His famous map of the world was still in use at the time of Columbus. Further progress in geography did not come until late in the Middle Ages.

Lack of instruments. The scientific progress of the Greeks is all the more remarkable because they lacked elaborate instruments. They had no real telescopes or microscopes, no mariner's compass or chronometer, no delicate balances, and nothing like our modern laboratories. Modern scientists are perhaps no better thinkers than were the ancients, but they have far better equipment to carry on experiments. We should note also that, except perhaps in medicine, the Greeks did not use their science to solve everyday problems.

Greek Art

Architecture. Ruins of ancient Greek buildings still give the traveler some idea of the outstanding features of Greek architecture. The building materials were limestone and white marble. The Greeks did not use cement. Instead, they put metal clamps between the blocks of stone to hold them in place. They usually colored the ornamental parts of a temple and the open spaces that served as background for sculpture. The Greeks did not make use of the arch in order to support large ceilings. The flat ceilings of their temples rested on long rows of columns.

The Greek temple. The temple was the chief building in a Greek city. It was rectangular in shape, with doors but no windows, and was surrounded by a single or double row of columns. The *architrave,* a plain band of massive stones, connected the tops of the columns. Above this came the *frieze,* adorned with sculptured reliefs, and then the horizontal *cornice.* At each end of the building rose the *pediments,* or gables. Sometimes the Greeks decorated these pediments with statues. The temple did not serve as a meeting place for worshipers but only as a shrine for the deity. For that reason its interior usually had little ornamentation. Greek temples were seldom large and were not extravagantly decorated. Their beauty lies, most of all, in harmonious proportions. We still imitate their style in many of our public buildings.

SEMICIRCULAR THEATER AT EPIDAURUS, built c. 325 B.C. The seats were on a hillside and accommodated 15,000 spectators. The actors could be heard easily from any seat. The orchestra circle is set off by white limestone.

Sculpture. Few pieces of Greek sculpture remain. Most of the original statues have disappeared. Those we still have are mainly copies made in Roman times. The most famous fifth-century sculptor was Phidias, who became the artistic adviser of Pericles on matters relating to the beautification of Athens. All his statues have vanished, but some of the Parthenon bas-reliefs are probably his work, or were carved under his direction. Praxiteles (prăks-ĭt″l-ēz) was the leading sculptor of the fourth century B.C. His statue of the god Hermes holding the boy Dionysus (dī′ō-nī′-sŭs) has survived in the original. It was found at Olympia in the late nineteenth century.

Painting and handicrafts. Greek painters enjoyed a fine reputation in their own day. Unfortunately, they did their major work in water color and it has not survived. We possess some remarkable miniatures, produced by grinding colors in heated wax and applying them to wooden or ivory objects. We also have many of their painted vases, usually made by ordinary craftsmen but excellent in artistic quality. The same is true of their metal work, gems, and coins. Everything that a Greek workman made showed that he had a feeling for beauty.

Greek Literature

A present-day visitor to Greece would find it difficult to get an idea of ancient Greek life merely from the ruins that remain. To understand the life and thought of ancient Greece we would need to look into the many books which the Greeks have left. Thousands of people still read these books, which cover an enormous range of knowledge. They include songs and poems, plays, histories and biographies, treatises on animals, plants, politics, and logic.

Poetry. The earliest poetry of the Greeks was in the songs of wandering minstrels, who entertained in the palaces of kings. The minstrels sang to the accompaniment of the clear-toned lyre. In time, the singer gave up the lyre and relied only on the power of the story for effect. The Greeks finally combined minstrel songs into long poems called *epics*, which told the stories of famous events. The best epics are the *Iliad* and the *Odyssey*, works which the Greeks attributed to Homer. (See pages 56–57.) The Greeks also composed many short poems to express feelings. These poems were called *lyrics*. The love lyrics of the poetess Sappho, who lived on the island of Lesbos, were well known in her day. Unfortunately, only fragments of her writings have survived. The greatest Greek lyric poet was Pindar, who lived in Thebes. He wrote odes in honor of victorious athletes. It is said that when Alexander was punishing Thebes for rebellion, he ordered that Pindar's house be spared.

A MARBLE HEAD OF HOMER

Drama and theater. Greek plays were actually another form of poetry and in content were either tragedies or comedies. The three great masters of the tragic drama were Aeschylus, Sophocles, and Euripides. All three lived and wrote in Athens during the splendid half century between the Persian and the

GREEK POET WITH THEATRICAL MASKS. In portraying characters, the Greek actor made use of masks that had exaggerated features, especially a wide mouth. The Greek play had only three or four actors, so that each one had to change his mask to impersonate different characters.

Peloponnesian wars. The greatest Athenian writer of comedies was Aristophanes (ăr′ĭs-tŏf′a-nēz). He made many prominent citizens of his day appear ridiculous, to the great delight of the fun-loving audiences.

The Greeks performed their plays out of doors in an amphitheater built on a hillside. At the bottom of the outdoor auditorium was a circle called the orchestra, or the dancing ring. The stage was a long, high platform, which closed in one end of the amphitheater. The Greeks used comparatively little scenery in their theaters; the spectator had to imagine for himself the setting of the play. The actors were men, and usually numbered not more than three; each one, therefore, had to play several different parts in the same play. The costumes were elaborate; actors wore masks, padding, and thick-soled boots to make themselves appear larger than human. In the orchestra circle small choruses chanted hymns or danced between scenes. Dramatists frequently presented gods in their plays to teach lessons in patriotism, morality, and religion. The plays also helped to form political opinion by ridiculing or praising ideas.

History. Herodotus (hē-rŏd′ŏ-tŭs), who lived during the fifth century B.C., is often called the "father of history." He traveled widely in the Greek world and in the Middle East before he wrote an account of the rise of the Oriental nations and the struggle between Greece and Persia. Herodotus was a great storyteller and wrote with charm, but often accepted gossip and hearsay for truth. Thucydides (thū-sĭd′ĭ-dēz), on the other hand, tried to sift the truth from legend and fable. Thus he became the first scientific historian. His great work was the *History of the Peloponnesian War.*

The greatest Greek biographies appeared after Greece had become a province of the

Roman Empire. In the first century after Christ, Plutarch, a Greek who spent some time in Rome, produced his famous *Parallel Lives*. In this book he first relates the life of an eminent Greek, then of a distinguished Roman, followed by a comparison of the two men. Like Herodotus, Plutarch did not let accuracy interfere with the telling of a good story. Nevertheless, these biographies give us much information and have been popular reading for centuries.

Our debt to the Greeks. Our debt to the Greeks is above all an intellectual one. Greek civilization lives on in the fields of literature, philosophy, science, and art. It was the Greeks who first learned to be truly *human*—to balance their lives by training body, mind, and spirit. They had a wonderful feeling for the beautiful and an eager curiosity which led them to look for the causes of events and things. In these respects no other people has surpassed or even equaled them.

REVIEWING THE CHAPTER

TERMS TO UNDERSTAND: *metic, Agora, symposium,* palestra, *polytheism, myth, philosopher, sophists, logic, Epicureanism, Stoicism, Hippocratic Oath, architrave, frieze, cornice, pediments, epic, lyric, academy, lyceum, ethics.*

PERSONS TO IDENTIFY: *Aesop, Socrates, Plato, Aristotle, Zeno, Democritus, Euclid, Hipparchus, Archimedes, Aristarchus, Ptolemy, Hippocrates, Galen, Eratosthenes, Phidias, Praxiteles, Aeschylus, Sophocles, Euripides, Herodotus, Plutarch, Thucydides.*

QUESTIONS TO ANSWER

1. (a) Describe the clothing of the ancient Greeks. (b) Describe a Greek house and its furnishings.

2. (a) Name five social classes of Athenian society and describe how each class made its living. What part did each class play in political affairs? (b) Describe a typical day in the life of a well-to-do Greek. (c) Tell what he did at the Agora, the Lyceum, a symposium.

3. (a) Compare the upbringing of the Greek boy with that of the Greek girl. (b) Compare the duties of a modern pedagogue with those of a pedagogue in ancient Greece. (c) What was included in a boy's schooling? (d) What is meant by a "liberal" education?

4. (a) Explain the origin of the Greek myths. (b) What changes occurred in Greek religious thought from the Homeric Age to Plato? (c) Describe the relationship between the city-state and religion. (d) Describe three Greek religious festivals. (e) What part did drama play in these celebrations?

5. (a) What distinguished the first philosophers from other men? (b) Who were the sophists? (c) Why did Socrates refuse to call himself a sophist? (d) What is meant by sophistry? (e) What is the Socratic method? Could it be used in teaching history? (f) What did Plato try to do in his *Republic?* (g) Describe Aristotle's many-sidedness. (h) How did Stoicism influence Christianity?

6. (a) What did the Greeks contribute to mathematics? To physics? To astronomy? To medicine? (b) How did Erastosthenes calculate the earth's circumference?

7. (a) What are the main characteristics of a Greek temple? (b) Name three examples of classical Greek architecture in the United States. (c) Why have not Greek paintings survived?

8. (a) Of what did the earliest Greek poetry consist? (b) What are the best Greek epics? (c) Name the foremost Greek dramatists and the types of plays they wrote. (d) Compare the Greek theater with that of today. (e) What distinguishes the history writing of Thucydides from that of Herodotus? (f) What subject did each write about?

9. Summarize our debt to the Greeks.

7 The Romans Rise to Power

STATUE OF AUGUSTUS Adopted son and successor to Julius Caesar, Augustus became the first Roman Emperor in 27 B.C. During his reign he erected magnificent public buildings, repaired public highways, and revised the tax system. Although shown here in military dress, Augustus gave Rome over two hundred years of peace and prosperity—the Pax Romana, or Roman Peace.

In our study of Greek history we followed the path of civilization from the Middle East over to the nearby coast of Europe. Now we turn to the history of Rome, the carrier of civilization farther westward. Rome absorbed much of the civilization of the Middle East, added to it, and gave this higher culture to many barbarian peoples throughout Europe. The Roman story is a stirring one. Hampered by few seaports, the early people of Italy turned to farming rather than seafaring. From a village of poor farmer-soldiers Rome grew into the wealthy ruler of much of the known world. In Chapter 7 we shall see how the Romans lived through a thousand years of history—from about 500 B.C. to about A.D. 500.

As you read the chapter you may ask yourself why Roman history differed so markedly from that of the Greeks. Why were the Romans able to unite Italy under one government, whereas the Greeks could not unite their homeland? Why were the Romans, unlike the Greeks, able to conquer and rule an overseas empire? How did these conquests affect the lives of the Romans?

The Italian peninsula has a typical Mediterranean climate. The winters are mild, with little snow except in the mountains. Summers are warm and dry and the nights are cool. Italy and Sicily were once parts of a land bridge connecting Europe with Africa. Today, Sicily is about eighty miles from Africa and two miles from Italy at the closest point. Italy's position brought it within reach of the barbarians of the West and the civilized peoples of the East.

The Apennine Mountains divide Italy into three main regions. A northern plain extends two hundred miles along the Po River. It has a colder climate than the rest of Italy, but its soil is very rich. A large central plain, through which the Tiber flows, is also fertile. Southern Italy, although by no means level, has much land suitable for farming. There are few good seaports in Italy. The early peoples of Italy turned to farming rather than seafaring. Since Italy was less mountainous than Greece, it was more easily united under one central government.

Early Peoples in Italy

Italians. The Italians were an Indo-European people who spoke a language related to that of the Greeks. It is thought that shortly after the Greeks invaded the Aegean area the Italian tribes moved southward through passes in the Alps and settled in Italy. Wave after wave of these northerners arrived, until they had occupied most of the country. One group of tribes, called the Latins, settled in Latium on the central Italian plain. Latium lay south of the Tiber River between the mountains and the sea. The Latins, as they increased in number, gave up tribal life and established small city-states. To protect themselves better against common enemies, the Latin city-states united in the Latin League. The chief city in this league was Rome.

Etruscans. The earliest civilization in Italy was brought by the Etruscans. They came by sea, perhaps from Asia Minor. As early as 900 B.C., they founded a strong state on the west coast of Italy, just north of the Tiber. Modern Tuscany is named after the Etruscans. We have not yet been able to read their writing, but we do know that they were highly skilled workers in bronze, iron, and gold. They seem to have been good sailors and to have carried on an active trade with lands bordering the Mediterranean. They built up cities with massive walls, arched gates, paved streets, and underground sewers. The Romans adopted many features of Etruscan civilization.

Greek influence. After 750 B.C. the Greeks planted colonies in southern Italy and in Sicily. Trade brought the Greeks and Latins into frequent contact. The Romans probably acquired the Phoenician alphabet from the Greeks. Greek influence may also be observed in Roman standards of weights and measures and in Roman coins. The Greek colonies never extended deeply into Italy. Room was therefore left for the Italians, under the leadership of Rome, to build up their own civilization on the peninsula.

Gauls. The Gauls were also an Indo-European group. Like the Italians, they invaded Italy by way of the Alpine passes. They entered about 400 B.C. and settled in northern Italy, where they came into conflict with the Etruscans. The Etruscans were seriously weakened by the attacks of these fierce barbarians.

The Rise of Rome

Founding of Rome. The rise of Rome from an obscure Latin village to its place as the dominating city of a world empire is one of the great stories of history. Rome began as a little settlement on the Palatine Mount, a hill just south of the Tiber and fourteen miles

from its mouth. According to legend the city was founded by Romulus in the year 753 B.C. Whoever picked the site chose wisely. Rome was a natural trading center, for shallow water and an island made it easy for Latins and Etruscans to cross the Tiber there, and seagoing ships could come up the Tiber to Rome. The trading took place in a valley called the Forum. Latin tribes also founded villages on six other hills near by. When all these villages united with Rome, it became the "City of the Seven Hills."

For a time the Etruscans held control of Rome and even furnished its kings. The tyranny of the Etruscan rulers inspired the Romans with a bitter hatred of kings. In 509 B.C. they expelled the Etruscans and set up a republic.

Invasion by the Gauls, c. 400 B.C. The newly freed Romans faced danger from all sides. The Etruscans to the north were still powerful, and other Italian tribes envied Rome. However, her allies in the Latin League helped to protect Rome from her enemies. Rome at one time captured a city north of the Tiber while the Etruscans were busy

GROWTH OF ROMAN POWER IN ITALY. After driving out their Etruscan rulers (c. 509 B.C.), the Romans gradually conquered the neighboring tribes. By 264 B.C. they had won control of central and southern Italy and were ready to expand outside the Italian peninsula.

fighting the Gauls. Rome had little time to enjoy this triumph. About 400 B.C. the Gauls defeated the Etruscans and proceeded to burn and plunder Rome. Finally, we are told, the Romans induced them to leave by the payment of a large sum of gold. The Gauls then returned to the north and settled in the Po valley.

Rome supreme in central Italy, 290 B.C. After the Gallic tide had gone, Rome rose from her ashes mightier than before. About a half century later she was able to subdue her former allies, the Latins. Another fifty years of hard fighting brought victory over the remaining Italian tribes in central Italy. The strongest of these Italian tribes were the Samnites, who proved to be well matched with the Romans in numbers, courage, and military skill. Eventually, however, the Samnites were forced to recognize Rome's authority. The Etruscan territory also fell to Rome in the course of this struggle, for the Etruscans had joined with the losing side.

Rome supreme in southern Italy, 264 B.C. The wealthy Greek cities in southern Italy, as disunited as those in Greece, now fell to Rome one by one. Many of them received Roman governors and accepted the rule of the Roman Republic. But some cities continued the struggle for their independence. They were aided by Pyrrhus, a Greek king and the finest soldier of his day. Pyrrhus led twenty-five thousand troops into Italy—an army almost as large as Alexander's. The Romans could not break the bristling Greek phalanx, nor could they advance against the huge war elephants which Pyrrhus had brought with him. The invader won the first battle, but lost many of his best troops. The Romans also lost a second battle, but fought so bitterly that Pyrrhus declared, "Another such victory and I am lost." When further fighting proved indecisive, Pyrrhus returned in disgust to Greece. By 264 B.C. the remaining Greeks had been conquered, and Rome ruled all Italy south of the Po valley.

Early Roman Life

Roman traits. The early Romans were famous for their patriotism, their simplicity of life, their iron will, vigor, and strength. In times of peace they worked hard on their farms; in war they fought with bravery and skill. They regarded Cincinnatus as an ideal citizen. When Rome was in grave danger he left his farm to accept the dictatorship. As soon as the danger was past he gave up his power and went back to his plow.

The Roman family. The most notable feature of family life in early Rome was the unlimited authority of the husband and father. He could divorce his wife at will or sell her into slavery. Nevertheless, no ancient people honored women more highly than the Romans. A Roman wife was the mistress of the home, as her husband was its master. Though her education was limited, she frequently took part in public affairs and aided her husband in both politics and business. Husband and wife trained their children to be sober, silent, modest in their bearing and, above all, obedient. An early Roman father might even put his children to death for misdeeds. In time a more liberal attitude developed and the authority of the husband and father was restricted by law.

Economic conditions. Agriculture was the chief occupation of the early Romans. They raised cattle, sheep, and large crops of grain. Few citizens were very rich; few were very poor. The members of each household prepared their clothing from flax or wool, and made from wood or clay the simple utensils they needed. Their hardy life helped to make the Romans strong and independent.

Religion and Government

Religion in the family. The Romans regarded their dead ancestors as members of the living family. Ancestor worship greatly strengthened the father's authority, for it

NOBLE LADY HAVING HER HAIR DRESSED.
This scene from a tombstone exhibits the photographic realism which was typical of Roman sculpture. Details which remain recognizable after two thousand years include the wicker chair, the metal mirror, and the footstool. Corinthian capitals at both sides of the picture frame have been poorly executed.

made him the chief priest of the household. It also made marriage a sacred duty, so that a man might have children to continue the family. The Romans worshiped household deities who were thought to guard the home. One of these was Vesta, the spirit of the fire on the hearth.

State religion. Just as the household was bound together by the ties of common worship, so all the citizens were united in a common reverence for the deities that guarded the state. Some of these were taken directly from family worship. The temple of Vesta, in the Forum, guarded the sacred hearth of Rome. Six vestal virgins watched to see that the fire was always kept burning. The Romans also worshiped Jupiter, who sent rain and sunshine for the crops, and Mars, the god of war. Juno protected women, Ceres (sē′rēz) watched over the harvest, and Mercury carried messages for them all.

Divination. The Romans learned from their Etruscan neighbors how to predict the future by examining the entrails of animals. They also borrowed from the Etruscans the practice of looking for signs of the future in the number, flight, and actions of birds. Divination of this sort was called "taking the auspices." No public act, such as an election or a battle, could be begun unless the signs were "auspicious."

Heads of the Roman Republic. After they expelled the Etruscan kings, the Romans set up a republican government. Each year they elected two *consuls* to be heads of the government. The consuls had equal power and authority; each could veto a proposal of the other. This arrangement had the advantage of protection against one-man rule, but it did not give unity in time of danger. In emergencies the Romans sometimes appointed a dictator, for a term of not more than six months. The people put their property and lives entirely at his disposal during his period in office.

The Senate. The most important branch of the Roman government was the Senate. It contained about three hundred members, who held office for life. All weighty matters came before it for decision. The Senate well deserved its great power, for it conducted public affairs with foresight, energy, and success. An admiring foreigner once called it "an assembly of kings."

Growth of democracy. All high offices in the early republic were held by the nobles, or *patricians*. This caused dissatisfaction among the *plebeians* (common people). They demanded more voice in the government and more protection against unfair laws. These demands led to several reforms. The plebeians won the right to elect officers of their own, called *tribunes*. A tribune could veto any act of an official if that act seemed to be unfair to a citizen.

The plebeians also insisted on having written laws, so that everyone might know his rights and secure justice in the courts. This demand resulted in the writing of the Twelve Tables, the beginning of Rome's famed legal system. Later, the plebeians won the right to make new laws by voting in assemblies. The assemblies passed laws which gave more rights to the plebeians. Eventually, the plebeians were able to hold any office in Rome, even that of consul or senator.

Government of Italy. Rome ruled Italy wisely. She granted citizenship to many of the conquered peoples and gave the protection of Roman law to all. Italy was further united by the establishment of Latin colonies throughout the peninsula and by the building of roads. But the Romans never remedied the worst defect in their government—the lack of a representative system. Citizens could do their voting only in Rome. This meant in practice that the Romans alone controlled the government. Other people had no voice in public affairs.

Rome and Carthage

Carthage. The Phoenicians established Carthage in North Africa long before Rome conquered Italy. By 264 B.C. the Carthaginians ruled an imposing commercial empire. This empire included most of the coast of North Africa and settlements on the shores of Sicily, Sardinia, Corsica, and southern Spain. Trade made Carthage rich. She was thus able to support large armies and to maintain the strongest navy in the Mediterranean. Mistress of a wide realm, strong both on land and sea, Carthage proved to be Rome's most dangerous foe. The three wars between Rome and Carthage are known as the three Punic (that is, Phoenician) Wars; they are the most famous contests in ancient history.

First Punic War, 264–241 B.C. Rome and Carthage had little cause for conflict before 264 B.C. Both had opposed Pyrrhus—Carthage doing so in Sicily, and Rome in Italy. But when Pyrrhus went back to Greece the Carthaginians attacked the Greek cities in Sicily. The Romans feared that Carthage might next invade southern Italy, so they went to war to gain Sicily for themselves. At first the Carthaginians had the advantage, for the Romans had no strength at sea. With characteristic energy, however, the Romans built large fleets of warships and mastered the art of naval warfare. Finally, they won a complete victory over the enemy (241 B.C.), and forced Carthage to give up all claim to Sicily.

A period of preparation. During the next thirteen years Rome strengthened her position. She seized Sardinia and Corsica and conquered the Gauls in the Po valley. She also kept her navy stronger than that of Carthage. Carthage, meanwhile, expanded north into Spain. The Spanish silver mines filled the treasury at Carthage, and Spain's hardy tribes furnished soldiers for the Carthaginian army. The leader of this army was Hannibal, one of the great military figures of history. According to legend he went to Spain when only nine years old, after vowing always to be an enemy of Rome. When he grew older, he fought in his father's campaigns in Spain. Hannibal became a brilliant leader, the idol of his men. At the time of the second war with Rome he was twenty-six years of age.

The Second Punic War, 218–201 B.C. Bad faith on both sides brought on the Second Punic War. The Romans planned to fight in Spain and Africa, but Hannibal determined to attack Italy. He assembled his armies in Spain and in a famous march of five months he crossed the Alps and faced the astonished Romans in the valley of the Po.

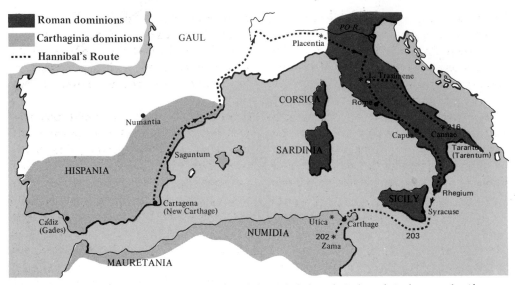

THE SECOND PUNIC WAR, 218–201 B.C. Hannibal marched through Spain and Gaul, across the Alps, and into Italy in 218 B.C. He returned to Carthage in 203 B.C. to defend it against a Roman army. A year later the Carthaginians were disastrously defeated at Zama.

Aided by the Gauls and other Roman subjects, he won brilliant victories against one Roman army after another. In 216 B.C. Hannibal reached the peak of his career when he won the Battle of Cannae against the largest army the Romans had ever sent out. After Cannae the Romans withdrew behind the walls of their cities. Hannibal could not take the fortified towns, but for thirteen years he moved through Italy almost at will. Meanwhile, the great Roman commander, Publius Scipio, drove the Carthaginians from Spain and invaded Africa. Hannibal returned to Carthage, and at Zama (202 B.C.) met his first and only defeat. In 201 B.C. the exhausted Carthaginians surrendered. They gave up Spain and destroyed all their warships. They also promised to pay a huge indemnity to Rome.

Third Punic War, 149–146 B.C. During the next fifty years Carthage recovered a part of her former prosperity. Rome watched this revival anxiously and at length determined to destroy the city. The Carthaginians were ordered to move ten miles from the sea. This was a sentence of death to a people who lived almost entirely by sea-borne trade. In desperation they took up arms again and for three years resisted the Romans. The city was finally captured and destroyed. The Romans plowed Carthage under, sowed salt in the furrows, and pronounced a curse over the spot.

The Beginnings of Empire

The Empire in the West. The Roman Empire began in the western Mediterranean. Rome gained Sicily in the First Punic War; she next took Sardinia and Corsica; in the Second Punic War she won a part of Spain; after the Third Punic War she annexed the lands of Carthage in North Africa. By 146 B.C. Rome had acquired an empire in the West.

The Empire in the East. Rome gained an empire in the East almost without trying. The process was quite simple. Even before the First Punic War, Alexander's empire had broken up into quarreling fragments. The divided East could not threaten Rome, nor did Rome take much interest in it. Her sole concern was to keep any single power from becoming strong enough to threaten her. When an eastern ruler showed signs of aggressiveness, Rome sent forces to defeat him, but as soon as the fighting ended the army and navy returned to the West. This left the people of the East weak and disunited, with little protection against pirates or invaders. Discontent grew when Rome began to send haughty orders, as if to subject peoples. Roman interference finally brought revolt throughout Greece and Macedonia. This time Roman armies stayed in the East. Macedonia became a Roman province, and Greece practically so (146 B.C.). The king who ruled Asia Minor died in 133 B.C., after having made a will leaving his kingdom to Rome. His lands became another Roman province—the province of Asia. To Rome had fallen the heritage of Carthage in the West and the heritage of Alexander in the East.

Effects of Foreign Conquests

The provincial system. Rome's rule of her new subjects overseas did not follow the methods that had proved so successful in Italy. The people outside Italy were not treated as allies, nor were they made citizens until much later. Rome adopted, instead, a system of *imperial* rule. She disarmed the inhabitants of the provinces, collected taxes from them, and forced them to obey officials sent out from Rome.

The Romans showed little desire to rule for the good of the subject peoples. A Roman governor exercised almost absolute sway over his province during his one-year term of office. He usually looked upon it as a source of personal gain and did everything possible to enrich himself at the expense of the inhabitants. They could complain to the Senate, but they rarely obtained justice. The senatorial courts were ignorant of conditions in the provinces and were often bribed by the governors. The people in the provinces also suffered terribly from the extortions of the tax collectors (publicans). These officials wrung all they could from the people, paid the correct tax to the Roman government, and kept the remainder for themselves—a system known as "tax farming."

Growth of luxury. The wealth that now poured into Rome from every province promoted the growth of luxurious living. Newly rich Romans spent money recklessly. They built fine houses adorned with statues, costly furnishings, and expensive paintings. They surrounded themselves with slaves, who were either war captives or the victims of slave raiders. Instead of plain linen clothes, the well-to-do Romans wore garments of silk ornamented with gold. At their banquets they spread embroidered carpets, purple coverings, and dishes of gilt plate. Pomp and splendor replaced the rude simplicity of earlier times.

Greek influence in Rome. The conquests brought Rome in closer touch with Greek culture. Roman soldiers and traders became acquainted with new customs and ideas in Greece. Thousands of educated Greeks, most of them slaves, also settled in Rome as actors, physicians, artists, writers, and teachers. As a result of their influence many Roman nobles began to take an interest in things other than farming, business, or war. They imitated Greek fashions in dress and manners, collected Greek books, and displayed Greek artistic works in their homes. Every aspect of Roman society felt the influence of the older, richer culture of Greece.

Disappearance of the small farms. The rich were becoming richer, but at the same time the poor were becoming poorer. Free farmers and artisans could not compete with slave labor. Furthermore, after Rome became mistress of the Mediterranean, her markets were flooded with cheap wheat raised in Sicily, North Africa, and Egypt. The price of wheat fell so low that Roman farmers could not raise enough to support their families and pay their taxes. They were forced to sell their farms, often for very little, to wealthy men, who built up great estates worked by gangs of slaves.

The city mob. The free farmers, who had once been the main strength of the Roman state, now thronged to the cities. There, if they could find any work, they labored for small wages. They lived mainly on bread, and dwelt in huge lodginghouses, three or four stories high. Many were unemployed and depended on the government for food. Since they voted in assemblies and thus controlled elections, they were courted by candidates for office, who gave them food and amusements. This large class of poor and unemployed people played an increasingly important part in Roman history.

The Decline of the Republic

Weakness of the Senate. The Senate had the power to remedy some of the evils which were undermining Roman society. But the Senate too had begun to show signs of weakness. The senators were no longer such able and patriotic men as those who led Rome while she was struggling for existence. They now thought less of the republic than of their own interests. Instead of helping, they used their power to block efforts at reform and to oppose reformers such as Tiberius and Gaius Gracchus (tī-bẹr'ĭ-ŭs and gā'yŭs grăk'ŭs).

Tiberius Gracchus. Tiberius Gracchus and his brother, Gaius, belonged to the highest nobility in Rome. Their mother brought them up to love their country more than their own lives. Tiberius was only thirty years old in 133 B.C. when he was chosen to be a tribune. He proposed at once a program to strengthen the small farmer class. Public lands which had been rented to the rich were to be taken back by the government and divided into small plots for landless citizens. The masses of poor city men favored this proposal, but it was vetoed by another tribune who was devoted to the wealthy class. The Senate also opposed the land reform. Tiberius then persuaded the popular assembly to remove the tribune who had cast the veto, and to put the reform law into effect without the Senate's consent. Both of these measures were unconstitutional. Soon afterward, a crowd of senators burst into the Forum and killed Tiberius. A century of violence had begun.

Gaius Gracchus. Nine years later Gaius Gracchus also became a tribune. He proposed that the government of the provinces be reformed; that landless men be allotted public lands in the provinces as well as in Italy; that grain should be sold at a low price to the poor; and that citizenship be given to men in the Latin colonies on the Italian peninsula. Part of his program became law. But rioting developed on an election day, the Senate called in troops, and the followers of Gaius were defeated. To escape assassination, he committed suicide. Nearly three thousand of his followers were executed without a trial.

The Senate loses control, 122–49 B.C. The Romans, weakened by discontent, their problems still unsolved, soon faced new dangers. German tribes appeared in the north, defeated five Roman armies, and demanded permission to settle inside the empire. A rebellion broke out in Africa, another in Spain, a third in Sicily, and slaves revolted in Italy. A social war occurred when Rome failed to grant citizenship to inhabitants of the Latin colonies on the peninsula. Pirates boldly preyed on shipping in the Mediterranean Sea, and a Roman senator formed a series of conspiracies to overthrow the government. The Senate proved incapable of real leadership in this time of trouble. Power slipped away from it and into the hands of able military leaders. These men built up large armies with which they defeated the rebels, the pirates, and the Germans. When the generals returned to Rome they usually acquired great influence over the government. Some were dictators, who cruelly stamped out all opposition. They brought a degree of peace—when they were not fighting each other—and added some territory to the empire. But they left Rome as weakened and divided as ever. This opened the door for one of history's greatest figures.

The Rule of Julius Caesar

Early life. Gaius Julius Caesar was born into a proud patrician family. As a young man he threw himself into the exciting game of Roman politics. He won a large following among the people by fiery speeches, bribes of money, and gifts of food and public shows. As his popularity grew, he won political office and in 59 B.C. became a consul. He and two other Romans, Pompey and Crassus, both former consuls, organized a political ring which controlled the government.

Caesar conquers Gaul, 58–50 B.C. Caesar had learned that a man could gain greater power by becoming a military leader. Accordingly, while still a consul he had the Senate appoint him governor of Gaul on both sides of the Alps. He raised an army and led it for nine years in a series of remarkable campaigns. The story is told in his *Commentaries,* which are still used as a text for studying Latin. He conquered most of what is now France and Belgium and made the Rhine a Roman frontier. Twice he bridged the Rhine and invaded Germany, and twice he crossed the Channel to invade Britain. Gaul adopted the Latin language, Roman law, and the customs and religion of Rome.

Caesar and Pompey. Pompey had won fame by conquering Syria and Palestine and by helping to crush rebellions and piracies. During the year that Caesar was consul, Pompey and Caesar worked together but the two did not always agree. Pompey favored the wealthy class, whereas Caesar appealed to the plebeians. While Caesar was in Gaul, the Senate voted to give Pompey the powers of a dictator. The wealthy senators and Pompey feared the return of Caesar from Gaul. His victories had made him very popular in Rome. If he

returned with his army, he would probably be able to replace Pompey as head of the government. In 49 B.C. the Senate ordered Caesar to give up the command of his legions. Caesar refused to obey the order and led his army across the Rubicon River into Italy. During the next four years Caesar waged war against the armies of Pompey and the senators. The struggle continued until Caesar had won supremacy. He had the power of a king, although he refused to accept a royal crown.

The rule of Caesar, 46–44 B.C. Caesar used his power wisely and well. With restless energy he entered on a series of far-reaching reforms. Free food was limited to those actually in need. The government of the cities was improved and order established. He founded overseas colonies for landless citizens and took steps to revive agriculture in Italy. He drew up plans for rebuilding Rome, for taking a census of the population, for improving the coinage, and for enlarging the empire. Caesar improved the calendar and gave his name to

---

CAESAR IN BATTLE

When his army gave way, he often rallied it single-handed, planting himself in the way of the fleeing men, laying hold of them one by one, and even catching them by the throat and forcing them to face the enemy; that, too, when they were in such a panic that an eagle bearer made a pass at him with the point as he tried to stop him, while another left the standard in Caesar's hand when he would hold him back.

His presence of mind was no less renowned, and the instances of it will appear even more striking. After the battle of Pharsalus, when he had sent on his troops and was crossing the strait of Hellespont in a small passenger boat, being met by Lucius Cassius, of the hostile party, with ten armoured ships, he made no attempt to escape, but went to meet Cassius and actually urged him to surrender; and Cassius sued for mercy and was taken on board. . . .

—Suetonius, *Lives of the Twelve Caesars.*

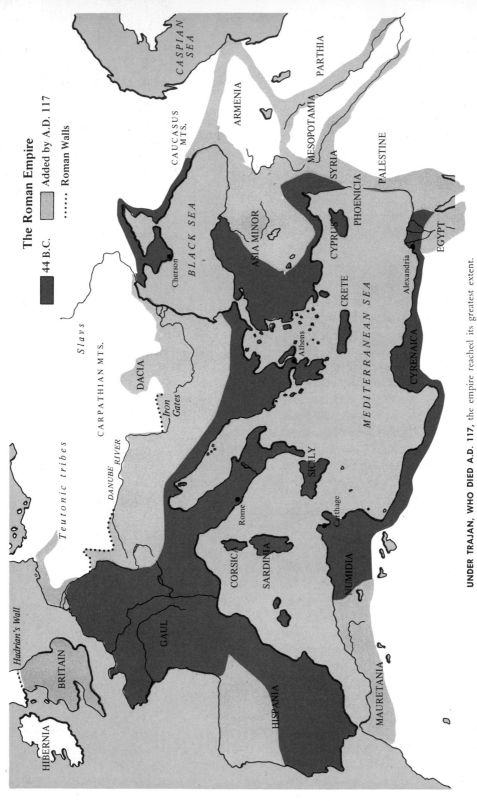

The Roman Empire

■	44 B.C.
▨	Added by A.D. 117
⋯⋯	Roman Walls

CASPIAN SEA

ARMENIA

PARTHIA

CAUCASUS MTS.

MESOPOTAMIA

SYRIA

PALESTINE

PHOENICIA

EGYPT

BLACK SEA

ASIA MINOR

CYPRUS

Cherson

CRETE

Alexandria

Slavs

CARPATHIAN MTS.

MEDITERRANEAN SEA

CYRENAICA

DACIA

Athens

Iron Gates

Teutonic tribes

DANUBE RIVER

SICILY

Rome

Carthage

CORSICA

SARDINIA

NUMIDIA

Hadrian's Wall

GAUL

HISPANIA

MAURETANIA

BRITAIN

HIBERNIA

UNDER TRAJAN, WHO DIED A.D. 117, the empire reached its greatest extent.

the month of July. He also reformed government in the provinces by providing for an honest collection of taxes and for the appointment of better officials. By giving citizenship and offices to conquered peoples outside Italy he sought to unite the empire. Few men have accomplished so much in so short a time. After little more than a year of undisputed power, "the greatest of the Romans" was treacherously stabbed to death by his political foes. His death plunged Italy and the empire into civil war.

PORTRAIT STATUE OF JULIUS CAESAR

Rome under the Emperors

Octavian becomes emperor, 27 B.C. The murderers of Caesar thought that all Rome would applaud them as saviors of the republic. But they were forced to flee to the East to escape the wrath of the people. Mark Antony, Caesar's friend, became the new ruler of Rome. Just as he seemed to be in full control, a new figure appeared on the scene. This was Octavian, Caesar's adopted son and heir. He was only nineteen, a student in Greece, when he heard of Caesar's death. He went to Rome at once and soon demonstrated great political skill. So popular did he become that Antony was forced to accept him as an equal in the government. Together they destroyed the armies of those who had killed Caesar. They then divided the Roman world between themselves, Antony taking the East and Octavian taking the West. Octavian ruled with moderation and success, but Antony showed less ability. He fell under the spell of Cleopatra, queen of Egypt, and gave her some Roman territory. The Senate then declared war on Cleopatra. Octavian, leading the Roman forces, crushed the navy of Antony and Cleopatra in a battle off the coast of Greece (Battle of Actium, 31 B.C.). Octavian pursued Antony and Cleopatra to Egypt. When their army deserted they killed themselves. Octavian annexed Egypt and then returned to

Rome to receive the title *Augustus,* meaning "His Sacred Majesty." The Roman Empire now had an emperor.

The Augustan Age, 27 B.C.–A.D. 14. Augustus (to use Octavian's new title) carried out many of Caesar's policies. He insisted on a just government in the provinces, and restored order everywhere. The system of "farming" taxes was abandoned. In Italy Augustus repaired the public highways and planted colonies in uninhabited districts. In Rome he erected magnificent public buildings. It is said that he "found Rome of brick and left it of marble." Impressive though his splendid roads and public buildings were, the greatest gift Augustus brought was peace. A century of conflict, which had begun in the days of Tiberius Gracchus, had ended.

The *Pax Romana,* 27 B.C.–A.D. 180. The *Pax Romana* (Roman Peace) lasted for more than two hundred years. For the Roman Empire this long period was a time of settled government and prosperity. With one exception, following the death of the cruel Nero, there was an orderly succession to the throne. Some fighting took place along the borders of the empire, but the clash of arms on the distant frontiers scarcely disturbed the serenity of the Roman world. Even when the city of Rome was disturbed by conspiracies, Italy and the provinces kept their prosperity. Commerce and industry thrived throughout the empire. Roads and cities were built on a vast scale. Education became more general, and the arts flourished. The narrow city law of

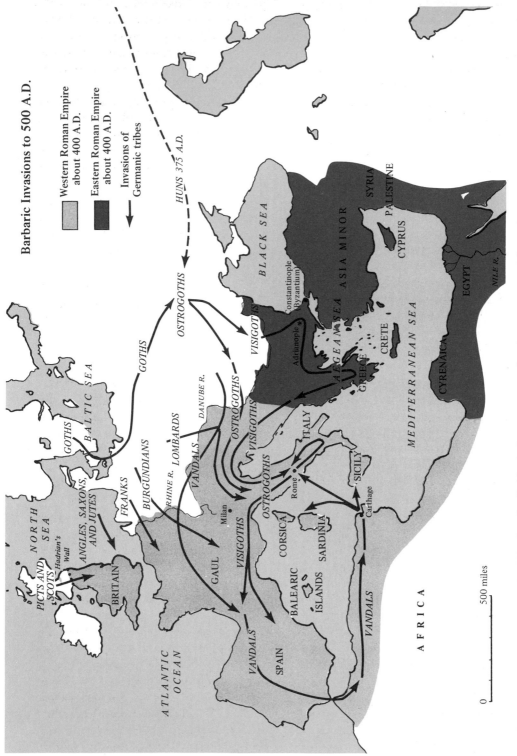

Barbaric Invasions to 500 A.D.

Western Roman Empire about 400 A.D.

Eastern Roman Empire about 400 A.D.

Invasions of Germanic tribes

BARBARIANS, as described by the Romans, were peoples who were not part of the Empire. In the fourth century these peoples began to invade the Empire.

Rome was altered and put into effect throughout the empire. The people everywhere in the empire were now regarded as belonging to the same state and equally entitled to justice and protection. The empire was enlarged by the conquest of Britain and the region north of the Danube (modern Rumania). (See map, page 98.) The time of the *Pax Romana* has become famous in history as the longest period of peace the Western world has ever known.

A century of violence, A.D. 180–284. Unfortunately for the Romans, one hundred years of violence and declining prosperity followed the *Pax Romana*. After A.D. 180 the death of an emperor often marked the beginning of a civil war to decide who should rule next. If an emperor proved to be weak or unpopular, he was likely to be overthrown by the Roman soldiers. Within a single year (237–238) six rulers were chosen and then murdered by their troops. This unsettled state of affairs threatened to wreck the empire. While rivals for the throne were fighting among themselves, ambitious governors of the provinces sometimes tried to establish independent kingdoms. To make matters worse, the Germans made constant raids along the northern frontier, while Persians (Parthians) invaded the empire in the East.

Diocletian and Constantine. Two famous emperors, Diocletian (284–305) and Constantine (324–337), made some progress in strengthening the empire. Diocletian restored order and reorganized the government to give himself absolute power. He wore a diadem of pearls and gorgeous robes of silk and gold like those of Asiatic monarchs, and revived the practice of emperor worship. He was regarded as a god, and everything that touched his person was sacred. Diocletian's abdication set off a civil war, which ended when Constantine became sole master of the Roman world. Constantine's reign is remembered for two events of lasting importance: (1) He recognized Christianity as one of the

legal religions of the empire and thus made possible the triumph of that faith over Roman paganism. (See pages 102–103.) (2) He changed his capital from Rome to the city of Byzantium, which soon came to be called Constantinople in his honor.

Two Roman empires. After the death of Constantine the eastern and western halves of the empire tended more and more to grow apart. After 395 there were usually two emperors, one ruling the western portion from his capital at Rome and the other ruling the eastern portion from his capital at Constantinople. From this time on, the history of the Eastern Empire is quite different from that of the Western Empire. The Eastern Empire lasted until 1453—a thousand years after Rome fell victim to invading German tribes.

Three groups of barbarians. German tribes lived along the northern frontier of the Roman Empire. Some had been allowed to enter the empire as soldiers or settlers. The Germans were tall, with fierce blue eyes and blond or ruddy hair. They were hospitable and prized liberty. They invaded the empire because they wanted land and plunder and because they were being pushed southward by the Slavs. The Slavic tribes lived in eastern Europe, in what is now Russia. Crowding upon the Slavs were the Huns, fierce warriors from Asia. Roman writers describe their olive skins, small turned-up noses, black beady eyes, and generally ferocious appearance. The Huns spent most of their time on horseback, sweeping over the country and leaving destruction and death behind them.

The Germans invade the empire in the West. So frightful were the attacks of the Huns that one German tribe, the Visigoths, begged permission to enter the empire. Their request was granted. But the Roman officials robbed them, withheld promised supplies of food, and even tried to murder their leaders. At length the Visigoths revolted. In the Battle of Adrianople in 378 they defeated the Roman legions and slew the Roman emperor.

The defeat at Adrianople was one of the decisive battles of the world. It meant that the Visigoths had come into the empire to stay, and that other tribes could follow. The Visigoths overran Greece, went on to conquer the city of Rome itself, and finally settled in Spain. The Franks, another German tribe, settled in Gaul and gave their name to modern France. Angles, Saxons, and Jutes overran Britain. The Vandals, coming from what is now Austria and Hungary, marched through Spain and crossed over to the coast of North Africa. There they turned to the sea and became pirates. In 455 their ships appeared at the mouth of the Tiber River. The Romans offered no resistance. For fourteen days the Vandals stripped Rome of her wealth. They took shiploads of plunder and thousands of Romans as slaves, including the widow and two daughters of an emperor.

A German emperor, 476. In 451 the Romans and Germans united to repel an invasion of

FOUR ROMAN EMPERORS: Constantine, Galerius, Diocletian, and Maximian. This sculpture from the Basilica of St. Mark dates from the twelfth century. The awkward figures contrast with the fine artistry of the Greeks and the Romans.

the Huns, but Roman prestige and authority had ended forever. The Germans set up barbarian kingdoms in Africa, Spain, Gaul, and Britain. Italy also fell into the hands of the Germans. In 476 they deposed the boy emperor, Romulus Augustulus, and put Odoacer, a German general, on the imperial throne.

The fall of Rome. Historians often use 476 as the date which marks the "fall" of the Western Roman Empire. By this they do not mean that the Western Empire ended within a single year. Just as Rome was not built in a day, so it did not fall in a year. As we have seen, the Western Empire declined gradually over a long·period of time. The dramatic events of 476 are merely a symbol of the end of Roman power.

Causes of the fall of Rome. Why did the Western Roman Empire fall? It is not enough to say that the Germans overthrew it, for they could not have succeeded if Rome had remained strong as in the days of the Roman Republic or of the *Pax Romana*. We can understand why Rome fell only if we look for weaknesses within the empire itself—weaknesses which made German conquest possible. They may be summarized as follows: (1) *Economic weaknesses.* When the independent farmers could no longer make a living on their land, many of them joined the idle city mob and were fed at public expense. Thus they became a drain on the state rather than a source of strength. By the end of the *Pax Romana* businessmen also had begun to suffer from declining prosperity, since the country people had less money to spend for goods. Businessmen found it hard to make ends meet when civil wars interfered with trade, and under the later emperors heavy taxes forced many of them into bankruptcy. Since many people could not afford to marry, the population decreased. (2) *Political weaknesses.* The people lost interest in political affairs as control passed from their hands into those of the emperors. Accustomed to direction from above, the people were helpless when anything happened to weaken the central government. A further political weakness was the size of the empire. It was so big as to be unwieldy. Even the best emperors found it hard to rule efficiently, and eventually, as we have seen, the empire split into two parts. Serious difficulties also arose from the failure to provide for regular succession to the throne. Good government was impossible while rivals were fighting for power. (3) *Religious weaknesses.* The Romans adopted several religions from the East. Formerly the family and state had been united by religion; the new religions, on the other hand, tended to divide the empire. (4) *Social weaknesses.* The idle city mobs were amused by degrading public shows in which men killed other men or were destroyed by animals. The amusements of the rich were equally vicious. Morality declined. (5) *Military weaknesses.* Fewer Romans were available for military duty, and not many of them were willing to serve. The government therefore brought in many barbarians to fill the ranks. The barbarians could not always be trusted to fight against their fellow tribesmen on the other side of the frontier.

REVIEWING THE CHAPTER

TERMS TO UNDERSTAND: *Forum, auspices, consul, dictator, patrician, plebeian, tribune, imperial, publican,* Pax Romana.

PERSONS TO IDENTIFY: *Romulus, Pyrrhus, Hannibal, Scipio, the Gracchi, Julius Caesar, Pompey, Octavian, Mark Antony, Cleopatra, Diocletian, Constantine, Romulus Augustulus, Odoacer.*

PLACES TO LOCATE: *Sicily, Apennine Mountains, Po River, Tiber River, Latium, Rome, Carthage, Cannae, Actium, Adrianople, Constantinople.*

QUESTIONS TO ANSWER

1. (a) Name and describe the three main geographical divisions of Italy. (b) How did geography influence the lives of the early people in Italy?
2. (a) Name four groups of people who were early settlers in Italy. (b) In what part of Italy did each settle?
3. (a) Describe Rome's early experience with rule by kings. (b) Describe the steps by which Rome conquered central and southern Italy.
4. (a) For what characteristics were the early Romans famous? (b) What was the position of the father in the Roman family?

5. (a) How did religion influence the early Roman family? (b) List five Roman deities and their supposed functions.
6. What steps marked the growth of democracy in Rome?
7. (a) Give the chief events of each of the three Punic wars. (b) How did Rome acquire an empire in the East?
8. (a) Describe Rome's government of her provinces. (b) How did foreign conquests affect the Romans? (c) Why did the Roman Republic decline?
9. (a) Trace Caesar's early life and conquests. (b) Why did Caesar wage war against Pompey? (c) What reforms did Caesar accomplish?
10. (a) How did Octavian become emperor? (b) List his achievements as emperor. (c) Do you think that the Romans were wise in allowing an emperor to be head of their government? (d) Why did the empire decline after the *Pax Romana?*
11. (a) Name and locate the three main groups of barbarians which pressed on the Roman Empire from the north. (b) Why did the German tribes enter the empire? (c) Tell where six of the tribes settled. (d) What date is used to mark the "fall" of Rome? (e) Why did the Roman Empire fall?

8 Our Debt to the Romans

RVINIS · SERVATAM · IVL · GAR · SIX · TI · IIII · PONT · NEPOS · HIC · STA

BAS-RELIEF FROM THE PORCH OF THE CHURCH OF SS. APOSTOLI in Rome.
The sculptural relief above represents an eagle with an oak leaf around it,
symbol of the second-century art work "The Apotheosis of Rome."

The history of the Romans is more than a record of what they did as warriors, rulers, and builders of states and empires. It includes a description of their private and community life and an account of their accomplishments in literature, philosophy, religion, and the arts. In this chapter we shall study the civilization of Rome and see how many of its features have been handed down to us.

Among the questions to be answered are these: How has the modern world been influenced by Roman law? Which branch of our legislature takes its name from the government at Rome? You may also wonder why the Romans, in contrast to the Greeks, erected huge public buildings rather than small and graceful ones, and dealt better with practical matters than with theories.

Roman Home and Social Life

Social classes in the Roman Empire. At the top of the Roman social order in imperial days were the aristocratic families (patricians) and the rich. As with the Greeks, wealthy Romans often sought to gain social standing by buying large estates in the country. The estates were rarely very profitable; wealth usually came from business, shipping, and holdings in mines or city real estate. Wealthy families often died out, a curious fact which has only recently been explained. Lead was used freely for tableware and water pipes in homes of the well-to-do. The resulting lead poisoning reduced the number of births and often caused early death.

A large middle class managed the business, professional, and political affairs of the empire. Those who made fortunes rose to the upper class. In the empire's later years government workers were especially numerous, and their salaries helped cause burdensome taxes. In the lower class were the free workers who performed the day-to-day labor needed in a complex social order. Roman society, like that of Greece, rested upon a base of slave labor. Some slaves earned enough money with which to buy their freedom, but most of them led bare, hard, hopeless lives.

What the Romans wore. The mild Mediterranean climate permitted the Romans, like the Greeks, to wear a simple, scanty costume. The *toga,* corresponding to the Greek mantle, formed the public dress of the citizens. It was a heavy woolen robe, white in color, covering the entire figure and reaching to the feet. Roman boys wore a toga with a crimson border. Patricians proclaimed their rank by wearing a broad purple stripe on their togas, and the togas of the rich bore a narrow stripe of purple.

Women's clothing was very similar to that of the men, but often of finer texture and more varied in color. They sometimes used elaborate hair styles or wore wigs, and on occasion bleached their hair. The Romans usually left their heads uncovered, except in rainy or stormy weather. Footgear consisted of sandals and shoes. Soldiers wore short tunics, leather armor, and boots on their feet.

The construction of Roman houses. A great misfortune that overtook two Roman cities has enabled us to learn many things about Roman houses. The two cities, Pompeii and Herculaneum, lay at the foot of Mount Vesuvius, near Naples. Mount Vesuvius was a volcano that had been inactive for centuries. In A.D. 79 it broke forth in a mighty eruption. Cinders, stones, and ashes buried both cities, and in time their very location was forgotten. The site of Pompeii was accidentally discovered in 1748. Since that date numerous excavations have laid bare a large part of that ancient city, with its streets, shops, baths, temples, and theaters. Some excavation work has also been done at Herculaneum. We thus have an invaluable source of information about Roman life in the days of the early emperors.

A visitor to the house of a well-to-do family at Pompeii stepped from the street into a small hallway. The passage was closed at the farther end by a heavy oaken door. Having announced his presence by using the knocker, the guest was ushered into the reception room, or *atrium*. This was a large room covered with a roof, except for an opening in the center admitting light and air. A marble basin or pool caught the rainwater which came through the opening. There were no windows in the atrium. It corresponded to the single room of the early Roman house, which had no windows or chimney. The Romans received formal visitors and business callers in the atrium.

A corridor from the atrium led into the *peristyle,* which was more of an enclosed garden spot than a room. Like the modern Spanish patio, it was open to the sky. Tall pillars formed a colonnade around the peristyle. This delightful spot, rather than the formal atrium, was the center of family life. The main part of the dwelling was built around the peristyle. Usually the house had two stories; from the peristyle one could enter the rooms on the ground floor—the bedchambers, bathrooms, dining room, kitchen, and other apartments of a comfortable mansion.

The Romans, like the Greeks, had few articles of furniture in their houses, but what they had was often beautifully made. They seem to have cared more for artistic forms than for comfort. Paintings and statues adorned the atrium, and statues might be found in the peristyle. What we think of as "modern" conveniences also appeared in the houses of the well-to-do; running water was piped to the bathrooms, and some houses had rooms heated by hot air piped from a central heating plant.

Daily life in Rome. For ordinary Roman families the day might begin in a crowded tenement building. Many of these "apart-ment houses" were poorly constructed. So many of them collapsed that the Emperor Augustus finally ordered that those facing busy streets could not be built more than seventy feet high. Poor sanitation and ventilation made life uncomfortable in even the better apartments.

Romans rose early so as to make full use of daylight. After a light breakfast the boys would leave for school and the father, or *pater familias,* would begin his day's activities. Women and girls busied themselves with the tasks of running a household. Shopping for food was a daily necessity, since meat and vegetables spoiled quickly without refrigeration. At eleven o'clock the Roman family ate lunch and then took the midday rest, or siesta. This practice became so common that at noon the streets of a Roman city were practically deserted.

In the afternoon Roman men not at work often took exercise out of doors or indoors at one of the city baths. Then came one of the chief pleasures of a Roman's existence—the daily bath. Rome's public bathing establishments were luxurious affairs, with fees so low that almost all could afford them. After undressing, the bathers entered a warm room and sat for a time on benches, in order to perspire freely. They then entered the hot bath, followed by an exhilarating cold plunge and anointment with perfumed oil. The poet Seneca, in describing the sounds of the bath, told of the grunts of a man exercising with leaden weights: "the racket of the man who always likes to hear his own voice in the bathroom, or the enthusiast who plunges into the swimming tank with [much] noise and splashing." After his bath a Roman might rest on a couch and pass the time in reading or conversation until the dinner hour.

The evening meal with the Romans, as with the Greeks, was the principal one of the day. Usually the meal consisted of three courses, varying from simple fare to great luxury. Wealthy men often vied with each other to see who could furnish the most exotic and expensive dishes, such as peacock tongues. Excessive eating and drinking were common, and accounts tell of noises made by drunken revelers returning home after a banquet.

However, a luxurious banquet was beyond the means of the poor. Their staple fare consisted of bread, olives, and grapes, with wine for drinking. These articles cost little during most of the empire's history. The working-men were able to enjoy the excitement of life in a great city. Numerous holidays, celebrated with games and shows, brightened their existence.

Roman Amusements

Dramatic shows. Unlike a Greek, the average Roman citizen did not enjoy sitting on the hard stone benches of an outdoor theater watching tragic dramas. Only the lighter comedies, adapted from Greek originals, were really popular at Rome. Pantomimes formed the staple amusement of the Roman theater. In these performances a single dancer, by movement and gestures, acted out mythological scenes and love stories; a chorus accompanied him with songs. There were also vaudeville entertainments by jugglers, rope-dancers, acrobats, and clowns, to amuse a people whose tastes were much less refined than those of the Greeks.

Chariot races. Chariot races drew great crowds to the Circus Maximus. Four horses were usually harnessed to a chariot, though sometimes the drivers showed their skill by handling as many as six or seven horses. The contestants raced seven times around the course. What we would call "fouling" was permitted and even encouraged. The driver might turn his team against another or might try to upset a rival's car. Spectators at the races were treated to the sight of broken chariots, fallen horses, and killed or injured drivers. Only the approach of darkness halted the exciting entertainment.

Animal shows. The Colosseum, a gigantic amphitheater, was often used for a variety of animal shows. Fierce wild beasts, brought from every quarter of the empire, were turned

CIRCUS PROCESSION IN ANCIENT ROME. The drawing is from a book published in 1600.

upon each other. There were also contests between savage animals and men. Sometimes the spectators watched animals tear condemned criminals to pieces.

Gladiatorial shows. Even more exciting were the contests between gladiators (Latin *gladius,* "sword"). Trained slaves were kept as gladiators, but sometimes free men and even women entered the arena. Some combats were between single opponents; others were arranged between groups of gladiators. The audience indicated, by turning thumbs up or down, whether the life of a fallen gladiator should be spared. Sometimes the Romans turned the arena into a lake and presented naval battles. Politicians who wished to become popular with the masses paid for many of the gladiatorial shows. The number of such exhibitions increased greatly during the im-

perial age. One emperor, in celebrating a victory, held gladiatorial combats in which ten thousand ill-fated war captives took part within the space of four months.

"Bread and the games of the circus." Gladiatorial combats, chariot races, and dramatic shows became the chief pleasures of life for the masses of people. There was no admission charge, and many people spent nearly half their time as idle spectators at the circus and the amphitheater. By the fourth century A.D. the Romans celebrated at least 175 holidays a year with public shows and games. The once sovereign people of Rome became a lazy, worthless rabble, fed by the state and amused with scenes of death and bloody combat. As an ancient author said, the Romans wanted only two things to make them happy —"bread and the games of the circus."

INTERIOR OF A ROMAN SHOP selling belts and pillows

The Cities

Growth of cities. As we have seen, the peace and prosperity which the Roman world enjoyed during the first two centuries after Christ fostered the growth of cities. Rome was the largest of these, her population being estimated at over a million. Numerous other cities rose to magnificence. Every city was a miniature Rome, with its forum and senate house, its temples, theaters, and baths, its circus for racing, and its amphitheater for gladiatorial combats. Most of the cities enjoyed an abundant supply of water, and some had good sewer systems and well-paved, though narrow, streets. Hundreds of such cities, like the one at Pompeii, could be found from the Danube to the Nile, and from Britain to Arabia.

City politics. The cities of Roman origin, especially those in the West, copied the local government of Rome. Each had a council, or senate, and a popular assembly which chose some of the officials. Many of the inscriptions found on the walls of Pompeii show how candidates appealed for votes. One inscription reads, "Vote for Gaius Julius Polybius, he provides fine bread"; another reads, "Vote for Bruttius Balbus, he will manage the city treasury well." Public officials provided banquets, festivals, wild beast hunts, and bloody contests of gladiators like those of Rome.

Support of the cities. The cities were not supported by direct taxes levied on the citizens. Some income came from mines, quarries, and other public property. Wealthy individuals also gave money for pavements, buildings, education, feasts, and games. Heavy contributions for such purposes were expected from all who held high city offices. Wealthy men were glad to win the applause of their fellows by splendid donations. During the later years of the empire, however, fewer people were able or willing to make gifts to the cities, and contributions had to be forced. The imperial government took more part in city management, and interest in local politics decreased. Since their citizens had lost the habit of independent action, the cities made little resistance when German tribes attacked.

Commerce and Industry

Promotion of commerce. The golden age of Roman commerce came during the first two centuries of the empire. Augustus and his successors kept the seas free from pirates, built lighthouses and improved harbors, policed the highways, and made travel by land both speedy and safe. Trade was promoted by having low tariff duties and a standard money system throughout the empire. Merchants traveled to distant countries and even imported goods from China.

The importation and sale of foreign goods at Rome furnished employment for many thousands of traders. There were great wholesale merchants and many retail shopkeepers. The shopkeepers might be either free men or slaves belonging to a wealthy noble.

Since the Tiber was too shallow to permit the passage of seagoing ships, the Romans built a harbor called Ostia at the river's mouth. Most of Rome's food came to Ostia, especially after the decline of farming in Italy. Thousands of workers were employed in unloading the ships and transporting their cargoes to Rome, either by road or by riverboat. Many government officials supervised the empire's trade, and soldiers guarded key ports.

Landholding. The class of small farmers almost disappeared from Italy during the later days of the republic. During the imperial age most of the land continued to be owned by a few wealthy men, who worked it with slave labor or else rented it out to the former peasant owners. The latter became tenants, dependent on the landlords and not much better off than slaves. The law often compelled them to work for their masters for a certain number of days each year without pay and forbade them to leave their farms in search of employment elsewhere. Such compulsory tenants are called "serfs." The Romans extended serfdom to Spain, Gaul, Britain, and other provinces, and it later became general throughout western Europe during the Middle Ages.

Roads. An effective system of communication and transportation was necessary to keep the commerce and government of the Roman Empire functioning. The first great road, known as the Appian Way, and other trunk highways were built in Italy. From the trunk roads a network of smaller highways penetrated every part of the peninsula. Under the emperors splendid paved roads were extended from the gates of Rome to every quarter of the empire. Along these highways sped the couriers of the Caesars. By using relays of horses, a courier could travel as much as 150 miles a day. The roads resounded to the tramp of Roman legions passing to their stations on the distant frontiers. Travelers by foot, horseback, or litter journeyed on them from one land to another, using the maps which described routes and distances. Traders used the roads for the transport of merchandise. The roads were so well built that some of them are in use today.

Education

Home training. In the early days of Rome the boy received only home training, which aimed to fix good habits rather than to impart knowledge. The father took his son into the fields to learn the work of the farmer and into the Forum to learn the duties of a citizen. The boy was also taught such manly exercises as riding, swimming, and the use of arms, so that he would be prepared for duty as a soldier. His father gave him some instruction in reading, writing, and arithmetic.

Elementary schools. Elementary schoolteachers gradually took over the task of instructing Roman boys. A boy began his school days at about the age of seven. He learned to read, to write with a stylus on wax tablets, and to cipher by means of the reckoning board, or abacus. He received a little instruction in singing and he memorized proverbs and maxims, besides the laws of the Twelve Tables. He studied under the watchful eyes of a harsh schoolmaster, who did not hesitate to use the rod on a pupil who made mistakes. A Roman poet tells us that if a boy missed a single syllable in his reading he was soon black and blue all over.

Grammar schools. By the second century B.C. educated Greeks had opened grammar schools in Rome. They gave instruction in the language and literature of Greece and, later, of Rome. The Latin works most frequently studied were Cicero's orations and the poems of Virgil and Horace. Roman boys were ready to assume the duties of citizenship by the time they had completed their studies in the grammar school. Very few schools were open to girls, though some taught them to sing, to dance, and to play a musical instrument.

Higher education. Young men who wished to do further study might attend rhetoric schools; here they learned the art of prose composition and practiced public speaking. Persons of wealth or noble birth might continue the training of the rhetoric schools by a university course. The most famous universities were located in Greek cities, such as Athens, Alexandria, or Rhodes. During the imperial age universities also arose in the West, particularly in Gaul and Spain. Rome had a university, the Athenaeum, teaching philosophy, law, medicine, architecture, mathematics, and mechanics. The universities attracted students from all parts of the empire.

Latin Literature and Science

The record of Roman thought. We have gained much of our knowledge of Roman civilization from the remains of Roman statues and buildings, especially in such cities as Rome and Pompeii. Latin literature has also given us a record of Roman life and thought. During the Middle Ages, when most Greek writers were either neglected or forgotten in western Europe, educated people read and enjoyed Latin literature. Indeed, we may still enjoy it today.

Cicero and Caesar. Cicero was an eminent author as well as a famous statesman. He created a style for Latin prose which has been admired and imitated by literary men even to our own day. Cicero's qualities as an author are shown in his *Orations,* a collection of his speeches to the Senate, and in the *Epistles,* a collection of letters which he wrote to friends and correspondents in all parts of the Roman world. They are models of what good letters should be—informal and delightful, yet beautifully written. As an orator, Cicero ranks with the leading Greek orator, Demosthenes. The writings of another statesman, Julius Caesar, are still counted among the literary masterpieces of all time. His *Commentaries* on the Gallic and Civil wars, though in parts rather dull, deserve praise for their simple, concise style.

Virgil and Horace. Latin literature reached its golden age in the reign of Augustus. The most famous poet of this period was Virgil, one of the world's greatest poets. The *Aeneid,* which he undertook at the suggestion of Augustus, is his best-known work. The *Aeneid* describes the adventures of the Trojan hero Aeneas, but its real theme is the growth of Rome under the fostering care of the gods. This work is probably the greatest single piece of writing in Latin literature. Another poet of the Augustan age was Virgil's friend, Horace. He is most famous for his *Odes,* which are considered flawless. Horace borrowed much from Greek poets, but added a charm of his own and a Roman point of view.

Livy and Tacitus. The most famous prose writer of the Augustan period was Livy. His *History of Rome,* beginning with Romulus and extending to Augustus, traced the triumphal rise and growth of the Roman state during eight centuries. It did in prose what Virgil's *Aeneid* had done in poetry. The other great Roman historian is Tacitus, who wrote about the events of Roman history which occurred from about A.D. 14 to A.D. 96. In his *Germania,* Tacitus has also given us information about the northern barbarians.

Roman science. The Romans did little to enlarge the boundaries of knowledge. They were interested in the applications of science, especially engineering, rather than in scientific research. Almost all they knew about nature came to them from the Greeks. It was summed up during the first century by Pliny the Elder. Using some two thousand books written by Greek and Latin writers, he compiled his *Natural History* which dealt with geography, botany, zoology, mineralogy, anthropology, and medicine. Pliny was not very critical, for side by side with sound science he describes imaginary beings such as winged horses and men with umbrella feet. Pliny preserved a great mass of knowledge and superstition, and his writings influenced men's thinking for centuries to come.

The Romans contributed to our knowledge of engineering, architecture, and city planning. Vitruvius, an engineer and architect, wrote a book on architecture that is still used today. Frontinus wrote about the water supply of Rome and the engineering problems to be considered in planning a water system. The Romans surveyed and mapped the principal roads of the empire, thus adding to geographic knowledge. They made little contribution to the science of medicine, but they did pay much attention to public health and sanitation. They were also interested in scientific agriculture and livestock breeding.

Roman Art and Architecture

The arch and dome. The temples and other public works of Greece seem almost insig-

PLAN OF A BASILICA, OR HALL. Roman judges held court in the semicircular apse (left). Early Christian churches copied the plan of the basilica, especially the apse, center aisle, and rows of columns.

nificant in size beside the stupendous buildings raised by Roman architects in every province of the empire. The use of the arch and dome enabled the Romans to build on a large scale. At first the arch was employed mainly for city gates, sewers, aqueducts, and bridges, but later it was used in the construction of vast buildings with enormous domes. The Roman arch and dome were round, rather than pointed. Some of the domes, as well as walls of buildings, were made of solid concrete. The triumphal arch is another characteristic example of Roman building.

Roman buildings. The Romans were a practical people. They built solidly and the remains of some of their work still stand. Roman theaters and temples were patterned after those of the Greeks, but the amphitheaters, where animal shows and gladiatorial combats took place, were a Roman invention. The gigantic Colosseum, which still stands in Rome, is an example of an amphitheater.

The basilica was another characteristically Roman structure. (The early Christians built their churches on the plan of the basilica. See illustration above.) Many of the Roman baths were constructed on a magnificent scale. In addition to the rooms for bathing, a typical bath included lounging and reading rooms, library, gymnasium, and perhaps a museum and an art gallery.

Roman art. The Romans showed more originality in architecture than in art. Roman sculpture owed much to Greek models; it also illustrates the tendency of the Romans toward realism in art. The sculptor tried to represent a historic person as he really looked, or an event as it actually happened. The portrait statues of Roman statesmen and emperors impress us with a sense of almost photographic reality.

Our knowledge of Roman painting is almost wholly confined to the wall paintings

ARCH OF CONSTANTINE, NEAR THE COLOSSEUM. The arch was erected at Rome in A.D. 315 to mark the victories over Licinius which made Constantine sole ruler of the Roman Empire in the West. After a second war with Licinius, Constantine ruled the entire Empire from 324 to 337.

found at Rome, Herculaneum, and Pompeii. They indicate that painters put less emphasis on realism than sculptors. What has survived consists mostly of scenes from classical mythology. The coloring is very rich, and the peculiar shade of red used is known today by the name of "Pompeian red." The ancient practice of wall, or mural, painting was passed on by the Romans to later European artists, and so to us.

Roman Law

Growth of Roman law. Rome made one of her most important contributions to civilization in her splendid system of law. The first written laws were the Twelve Tables. (See page 92.) The Romans enlarged and improved their legal system when they began to rule over conquered territories and became familiar with the customs of other peoples. Roman law took on an exact, impartial, liberal, and humane character. When properly enforced, it protected the weak and provided justice for all. It defined justice as "the steady and abiding purpose to give to every man that which is his own." After the fall of Rome her legal traditions lived on in the Eastern Empire. During the reign of Justinian (A.D. 527–565), legal experts collected and organized the principles of Roman law. The result was the famous code called the *Corpus Juris Civilis,* the "Body of Civil Law," also known as the Code of Justinian.

Influence of Roman law. The Justinian Code became the foundation of the medieval and modern legal systems of Italy, Spain, France, Germany, and other countries. The common law of England, which is followed in the United States and wherever English is spoken, owes many of its principles to this code. Both the canon law of the Christian Church and modern international law are based on Roman legal principles. The law of Rome is justly regarded as one of her greatest gifts to the world.

THE GOOD SHEPHERD. This early Christian statue, dating from the third century A.D., was found in the catacombs of Calixtus.

Rise and Spread of Christianity

Jesus. While Augustus was reigning over his mighty empire, there was born, in a faraway province on the fringe of the Roman world, a child who was destined to build an empire of another kind—and more lasting. The child Jesus, as is told in the *New Testament,* was born of humble Jewish parents in the little town of Bethlehem in Judea. He spent most of his short life in the village of Nazareth in Galilee; he is therefore called Jesus of Nazareth, the Nazarene, and the Galilean. When about thirty years of age, Jesus began to teach and preach throughout

Galilee and Judea. He soon attracted many followers, chiefly from among the common people. Twelve of these he chose as his disciples, to keep him company and go about with him from place to place. Jesus invited men to become members of a new kingdom. He warned them that this kingdom was not of this world, but that it existed in the hearts of men who repented of their sins and wished to do the will of God. After three years of teaching and preaching, Jesus died on the cross on a hill near Jerusalem about the year A.D. 29. (Owing to ancient errors in the calendar, we now reckon the date of Jesus's birth at between 8 B.C. and 4 B.C.)

Christianity among the Jews. Jesus had lived to preach his gospel for only three years. At first his disciples were stricken with sorrow and fear by his crucifixion. After becoming convinced of the resurrection of their master, they were fired with a new devotion and enthusiasm. They now said that Jesus was not only a great prophet whose coming had been foretold in the Jewish scriptures, but that he was a divine being, the Son of God, who had been raised from the dead and taken up into heaven. Some of them remained in Jerusalem, preaching and making converts, despite the opposition of Jewish leaders there. To escape persecution, many of the Christians withdrew to Samaria, Damascus, and Antioch, where there were large Jewish communities among whom they continued to teach and preach.

The Apostle Paul. Among those who were reached by this preaching was Saul of Tarsus, later known as the Apostle Paul. Though born a Jew, he received Greek training in the schools of Tarsus, a city in Asia Minor. He was then sent to Jerusalem to receive careful instruction in the Jewish scriptures. He became a zealous defender of the Jewish faith and helped to persecute the Christians. In fact, he was on his way to Damascus to help in the work of exterminating Christians, when he had a vision which he describes as

follows in the *Book of Acts:*

. . . as I made my journey, and was come nigh unto Damascus about noon, suddenly there shone from heaven a great light round about me.

And I fell unto the ground, and heard a voice saying unto me, Saul, Saul, why persecutest thou me?

And I answered, who art thou, Lord? And he said unto me, I am Jesus of Nazareth, whom thou persecutest.

After this vision, Paul showed as much zeal in promoting Christianity as he had formerly shown in opposing it. He turned his attention to extending Christianity among the Gentiles (non-Jews), and is hence known as the Apostle to the Gentiles. For over twenty years, sometimes alone and sometimes with companions, he traveled throughout Asia Minor, Macedonia, Greece, and the islands of the eastern Mediterranean, preaching and establishing churches. He encouraged these struggling young churches by writing them a series of letters, some of which have been preserved as the *Epistles of Paul* in the New Testament.

Conditions favoring the spread of Christianity. Christianity spread steadily among the Gentiles throughout the Roman world. At the close of the first century there were Christian churches throughout Asia Minor and even a few in Italy. The second century saw the establishment of churches in almost every province of the Roman Empire. "We are but of yesterday," says a Christian writer of those days, "yet we have filled all your places of resort—cities, islands, fortresses, towns, markets, the camp itself, the tribes, town councils, the palace, the Senate, and the forum. We have left to you only the temples of your gods." Two hundred years later there were missionaries along the Rhine, on the Danube frontier, and in distant Britain. It is important to notice these missionary activities among the Germans for, as a consequence, many of these people were already

Christians before they entered the Roman Empire.

Several factors contributed to the success of this gigantic missionary enterprise. (1) Credit must be given to the early Christian missionaries for the courage and fervor with which they preached the new gospel. (2) The growth of the Roman Empire had made it easier than in earlier times for people to travel and to exchange ideas. (3) Many of the early missionaries, including Paul, were Roman citizens. They enjoyed the protection of Roman law and profited by the ease of travel and communication which the imperial rule had made possible. (4) Since Greek and Latin were widely used throughout the empire, Christian writers and speakers could reach most of the people through one or the other of these languages. (5) Christianity had a special appeal to those who enjoyed few of the benefits of classical civilization—the poor, the sick, and the oppressed.

Appeal of Christianity. The new religion had many appealing aspects. In the first place, to the oppressed and unfortunate of this world it held out the hope of a blessed state in a life after death. Second, it stressed the great principle of love, which could make a better world here and now. In the words of Jesus (based in part on Deuteronomy),

Thou shalt love the Lord thy God with all thy heart, and with all thy soul, and with all thy mind.
This is the first and great commandment.
And the second is like unto it, Thou shalt love thy neighbor as thyself.

This teaching meant that all men were equal in the sight of God, that slave and master were brothers, and that it is a duty to show benevolence to the needy and the suffering. In the third place, Christianity, like Judaism, emphasized direct communion with God through prayer. By means of sincere prayer the humblest believer could obtain peace and comfort. In the fourth place, the writing of the Christian scriptures furnished a new guide to thinking and action. Believers found in them the assurance that they could learn the will of God.

Persecution and Triumph of Christianity

Popular hostility to Christians. Though the new religion had a great appeal for many, especially among the lowly, it aroused disapproval and even fear among many people in the middle and upper classes. They regarded the Christians as extremely unsociable. The Christians never appeared at public feasts and entertainments where they might be obliged to worship pagan gods. They would not join in the amusements of the circus or the amphitheater, for they held human life sacred and considered the gladiatorial combats to be thoroughly evil. Such people puzzled the ordinary citizen. It is not surprising, therefore, that the Christians were called "haters of mankind." Furthermore, the Christians aroused fear among the superstitious. Christians were accused of feasting on children and of being magicians who caused all sorts of disasters. It was not difficult, therefore, to excite crowds in the large cities to attack the Christians. Many followers of the new religion suffered wounds and death in street riots. Many more were executed. As a Christian writer said, "If the Tiber rises, if the Nile does not rise, if the heavens give no rain, if there is an earthquake, famine, or pestilence, straightway the cry is, 'The Christians to the lions.' "

Governmental hostility to Christians. The hostility of the public does not account for all the opposition which the early Christians had to endure. The government, too, long regarded them as a menace. The Christians denounced the pagan religion as sinful and idolatrous; they refused to worship the emperor by burning incense before his statue, which stood in every town; and they refused to serve in the army or to swear by the pagan gods in the law courts. It is therefore not surprising that the Roman government regarded them as disloyal and at various times ordered that Christians who refused to give up their religion should be put to death.

Persecution of the Christians. Various emperors ordered persecutions of the Christians. Nero did so in order to escape the charge that he himself had set fire to Rome. Another did so because the Christians had failed to pay certain taxes. Even some of the better emperors like Marcus Aurelius felt that it was necessary for the public good to persecute the Christians. The persecution beginning under Diocletian in 303 was the last and most severe. It continued, with some interruptions, for eight years. Only Gaul and Britain seem to have escaped its ravages. The government began by burning the holy books of the Christians, by destroying their churches, and by taking away their property. Members of the hated faith lost their privileges as full Roman citizens. Then sterner measures followed. The prisons were crowded with Christians. Some were thrown to wild animals in the arena, stretched on the rack, or burned over a slow fire. Many Christians welcomed torture and death, believing

it would gain them a heavenly crown. The word *martyr* is applied to those who paid the extreme penalty, death, for their faith.

Official toleration of Christians. Even while the Christians were being persecuted, they were in fact on the verge of triumph. When it became clear that persecution had failed to stamp out Christianity, the government gave up the struggle. In 311 the ruler of the Eastern Empire, Galerius, published an edict permitting the Christians to rebuild their churches and worship undisturbed. Two years later Constantine and his colleague, Licinius, issued the so-called "Edict of Milan," which proclaimed freedom to everyone to worship God according to the religion of his own choice. Constantine himself accepted Christianity and favored its followers throughout his reign. He surrounded himself with Christian bishops, freed the clergy from taxation, and spent large sums in building churches.

Triumph of Christianity. By the end of the fourth century Christianity had advanced from the position of the favored religion to that of the official state religion. In the year 392 the emperor Theodosius made Christianity the only legal religion of the empire.

THE CATACOMBS OF PALERMO. The catacombs were meeting-places and cemeteries for the persecuted Christians.

Sacrifices to the pagan gods were forbidden and their temples closed. Those strongholds of the old paganism, the Delphic oracle, the Olympian games, and the Eleusinian mysteries, were abolished. The worship of ancestors was prohibited. The early Roman household beliefs and ceremonies survived for a long time afterward, especially in country districts, but paganism as a religious force disappeared. Henceforth, Christians who taught doctrines condemned by the Church as false were guilty not only of a sin against the Church but also of *a crime against the state*. Such persons were called *heretics;* the state punished them after the Church had found them guilty. The use of political power to enforce religious conformity continued into modern times.

Development of the Christian Church

Christian communities. While Christianity was spreading throughout the Roman world, its followers were forming themselves into groups. These groups met, not in synagogues, as did the Jews, but in private houses. To escape persecution in the cities they sometimes went down into the catacombs (underground tunnels for the burial of the dead). Wherever they met, they sang hymns, listened to readings from the Holy Scriptures, and partook of a sacrificial meal in memory of the last supper of Jesus with the Twelve Apostles. This sacrificial meal was known as the Lord's Supper, or the Eucharist. Certain officers, called presbyters or priests (from a Greek word meaning "elders"), were chosen to conduct the services and instruct new converts. The chief priest received the name of bishop, which comes from a Greek word meaning "overseer," or "guardian." There were also deacons, who visited the sick and aided the poor. Every Christian community thus formed a little brotherhood of earnest men and women, united by common beliefs and common hopes.

EDICT OF MILAN, 313 A.D.

When I, Constantine Augustus, as well as I, Licinius Augustus, had fortunately met near Mediolanum and were considering everything that pertained to the public welfare and security, we thought that, among other things which we saw would be for the good of many, those regulations pertaining to the reverence of the Divinity ought certainly to be made first, so that we might grant to the Christians and to all others full authority to observe that religion which each preferred . . . We thought it fit to commend these things most fully to your care that you may know that we have given to those Christians free and unrestricted opportunity of religious worship. When you see that this has been granted to them by us, your Worship will know that we have also conceded to other religions the right of open and free observance of their worship for the sake of the peace of our times, that each one may have the free opportunity to worship as he pleases; this regulation is made that we may not seem to detract aught from any dignity or any religion.

The bishops. The increase in the number of converts and the growing number of churches led in time to a more elaborate organization, headed by the bishops of the chief cities. The bishops kept in touch with one another by visits and letters, and together formed a governing board for all the churches in a given district or province. In each district one of the bishops was made an archbishop and had the duty of presiding over the other bishops. The bishops of the five great cities of Jerusalem, Antioch, Alexandria, Constantinople, and Rome were given the title of patriarch (from a Greek word meaning the "chief," or "father of a family"); the patriarchs had authority over the archbishops. By the third century, the Christian Church was episcopal in form—that is, was ruled by bishops.

The Bible. Christian worship, as we have noted, consisted partly of reading from a collection of sacred writings called the Scriptures or, later, the Bible. These writings have been grouped into two large divisions, one of which is called the *New Testament*. It contains four accounts of the life of Jesus. These are called the Gospels, and are ascribed to Matthew, Mark, Luke, and John, who were apostles, or early followers, of Jesus. The New Testament also contains an account of the work and struggles of the early apostles. This is appropriately known as the *Acts of the Apostles*. Still another part of the New Testament is made up of epistles (letters) to the various churches, written by Paul and other apostles. The New Testament came to be the accepted statement of Christian doctrines.

The other large division of the Bible is called the *Old Testament*. Many parts of it were ancient even in the time of Jesus. It contains the old Jewish Scriptures, with which Jesus and his disciples were familiar and which they often quoted. These old writings were collected and accepted by Christians as part of their sacred literature. In its completed form the Old Testament consists of thirty-nine parts, or "books," which may be classified as historical, poetical, and prophetic.

The first great church council. As Christianity expanded and enrolled many followers from various parts of the known world, uncertainties and differences as to beliefs naturally appeared. The principal dispute was over the nature of Christ. A priest named Arius maintained that Christ the Son, having been created by God the Father, was necessarily inferior to Him. This doctrine was called *Arianism*. A priest named Athanasius opposed this view. He maintained that Christ was not a created being, but was in all respects equal to God.

In order to secure uniformity of belief on this and other disputed points, so that the Church would be strengthened, Constantine

called an assembly, or council, of bishops. The council met in 325 at the town of Nicaea in Asia Minor, not far from Constantinople. More than three hundred bishops or their representatives attended this meeting, the first general council of the Church. The principal work of the council was the settling of the dispute between Arius and Athanasius. The council accepted the arguments of Athanasius and condemned Arius as a heretic. The council then formulated a statement of fundamental beliefs, which is known as the Nicene Creed.

The Church. The different local churches had maintained close relations in order to strengthen one another in resisting the forces of paganism. Thus they came to regard themselves as members of a larger whole, which included all Christian believers throughout

Palace at Cnossus

The Glory That Was Greece and the Grandeur That Was Rome

On Crete, a beautiful island in the Mediterranean, Europe's first civilization appeared, then disappeared and was forgotten for thirty-two centuries. Excavation on Crete has proved to be wonderfully rewarding. Here had once been a civilization tied to the ancient Middle East. Ships came to Crete regularly and kept the island in touch with the older civilizations on the mainland. Egyptian influence was especially strong; for a time Crete was under Egyptian rule. Eventually Crete became independent, the center of a sea empire in the eastern Mediterranean. The sea kings of Crete built a capital of Cnossus, a portion of which still stands. On the fragment of plaster wall shown above we can see the portraits of cupbearers who served at royal banquets about 1500 B.C.

The marks of Cretan power also may be seen on the mainland of Europe. Just as eastern influence had come by sea to Crete, so Crete transmitted her culture to the shores of Europe. Outposts of Crete's empire have been discovered in Greece at Mycenae, Tiryns, and numerous other places.

When invaders put the torch to Crete, the Greeks continued independently. In time they developed a civilization towering far above anything known to that time. Their resources were few, and mountainous country kept them divided. In spite of difficulties, or because of them, the Greek genius flowered in a culture centered at Athens. We may still marvel that so few people in so poor a country should ever since have influenced men's thinking.

Modern Athens and view of Acropolis

The spirit of Greece still remains visible in many things: the Acropolis looking down on Athens; the ruins of temples reminding us of gods whom men no longer worship; or works of art of exceptional beauty. Much that the Greeks did was stamped with the seal of their special genius, which one can still sense in the silent sunlit ruins of their buildings.

Ruins of temple at Delphi

Just as Alexander had led the Greeks to conquest of the Middle East, so Greece in turn was conquered by Rome. At the time, Greek civilization far surpassed that of the Romans. A wave of admiration for all things Greek swept over Rome, and Greek ways became the fashion. It has been aptly said that "conquered Greece conquered her conqueror rude." The Romans copied Greek art forms, mosaics, statues, and wall paintings. Many of the columns shown on pages E, F, and G and Greek, of the Corinthian order. Frescoed wall paintings found among the ruins of homes in Pompeii are the product of a technique used fifteen hundred years earlier by the people of Crete. Running through these civilizations of Crete, Greece, and Rome is an unmistakable thread of continuity. Each one aided the progress of the next as civilization spread westward into Europe.

Alexander at the Battle of Issus from mosaic found at Pompeii

View from House of the Faun, Pompeii, looking toward Mt. Vesuvius

Roman Forum, looking toward the Colosseum

118F

That is not to say that the Romans were mere imitators. They changed the course of history by their conquests. Under Roman rule the ancient world knew peace and barbarian lands learned the arts of civilization. Roman rule was no passing thing, for what the Romans acquired they consolidated into a lasting empire. Roman ruins still convey a sense of stability and strength, and it is fitting that their capital should be known as the "Eternal City."

The Roman poet Virgil caught the essence of Roman character with these words: "Others, I doubt not, shall beat out the breathing bronze with softer lines; shall from marble draw forth the features of life; shall plead their causes better; with the rod shall trace the paths of heaven and tell the rising of the stars: remember thou, O Roman, to rule the nations with thy sway—these shall be thine arts—to crown Peace with Law, to spare the humbled, and to tame in war the proud."

We are debtors to Greece and Rome in many ways, especially in the arts and the field of thought. For a long time to come, it would seem, when men speak of "classical civilization" they will mean the civilizations of ancient Greece and Rome.

Roman architects borrowed ideas from many other civilizations. They copied Doric, Ionic, and Corinthian columns of Greece and the arch of the Etruscans. But the Romans were not attempting to match the perfection of Greek architecture. Instead, they were outdoing all people with great feats of engineering, many of which still stand.

Hadrian's tomb is an excellent example of the skill of the Roman builders. Hadrian was so greatly influenced by Greek ways that his palatial villa outside the city of Rome contained copies of Greek statues and a long pavilion supported by rows of Greek columns.

Castel Sant' Angelo in Rome, originally the tomb of the Emperor Hadrian

the world. This all-embracing Church became a great and powerful organization, with laws for the guidance of its members, with a graded series of officers (known as the *hierarchy*), and with councils or gatherings to decide important questions.

The Catholic Church. A Greek word, *catholic,* meaning "universal" or "general," was applied to the Church. The Church was catholic in two senses. In the first place, it included all local Christian churches in one organization. In the second place, it represented a religion that was intended, in contrast to the pagan and Jewish faiths, for all peoples and nations.

Christianity transmits classical civilization. As we have seen, Christianity often came into conflict with classical civilization. But when the story is carefully read, it shows the Christian Church depending upon classical civilization and utilizing many of its ideas. Men trained in Greek philosophy brought their skill in reasoning to the service of the Church and thus Christian doctrine came to include some of the classical heritage in philosophy. From the Roman government the Church borrowed many features of its organization. Church architects used many forms of classical architecture, and religious scholars copied and preserved much classical literature. In these various ways the Church helped to pass classical civilization on to the "barbarians" who, by the end of the fourth century, were already overrunning the Western Roman Empire and leading Europe into a "Dark Age."

REVIEWING THE CHAPTER

TERMS TO UNDERSTAND: *toga, atrium, peristyle, siesta, Circus Maximus, Colosseum, gladiator, serf, classical, edict, episcopal, catholic, martyr, heresy, hierarchy.*

PERSONS TO IDENTIFY: *Cicero, Virgil, Horace, Livy, Tacitus, Pliny the Elder, Justinian, Paul, Nero, Licinius, Theodosius, Arius, Athanasius.*

PLACES TO LOCATE: *Mt. Vesuvius, Pompeii, Rhodes, Galilee, Judea, Nicaea, Ostia.*

QUESTIONS TO ANSWER

1. Compare the Roman citizen with the Greek citizen in respect to dress, home, daily life, and amusements.
2. (a) Describe a typical Roman city in the age of Augustus. (b) How were public expenses met in most Roman cities?
3. (a) Why was the period of the *Pax Romana* favorable to the growth of Roman commerce? (b) During the imperial age, what was the condition of the working classes in the city? In the country?
4. (a) Describe the Roman school system. (b) Where were most universities located?
5. (a) Name six outstanding Roman writers and a literary work of each. (b) Name two characteristics of Roman architecture.
6. (a) State the basic principles of Roman law. (b) What was the *Corpus Juris Civilis*? (c) To what fields has its influence extended?
7. (a) Trace the life of Jesus. (b) How did Paul strengthen Christianity? (c) Account for the rapid spread of Christianity.
8. (a) Why did many people show hostility toward Christians? (b) Why was the Roman government hostile to Christians? (c) What was the significance of the Edict of Milan?
9. (a) Name the members of the clergy in the order of their rank. (b) What are the three main parts of the New Testament? (c) What is the source of the Old Testament?
10. (a) When and where did the first great church council meet? (b) What were its two most important acts? (c) How, other than in a religious sense, did the Church serve mankind during the Dark Ages?

FURTHER ACTIVITIES FOR PART TWO

1. Prepare a report on the Trojan War. Identify ten persons connected with it and tell the meaning of "Trojan horse tactics."
2. Name and locate the seven wonders of the ancient world and prepare a report on two of them.
3. Prepare a report comparing the ancient and the modern Olympic games.
4. Hold a debate on the question: *Resolved,* that Athens, though a democracy, was justified in turning the Delian League into an empire.
5. (a) Make a map to show the expansion of the Romans before, during, and after the Punic Wars through 133 B.C. (b) On another map trace the campaigns of Caesar or of Alexander.
6. Hold a debate on the subject *Resolved,* that I would rather have been a Roman citizen than an Athenian citizen.
7. Read parts of E. G. Bulwer-Lytton's *Last Days of Pompeii* and report to the class his description of the gladiatorial games and his vivid account of the eruption of Vesuvius which buried Pompeii and Herculaneum.
8. Prepare a report on the life of one of the leading Greeks or Romans.

FURTHER READING FOR PART TWO

(Stars indicate easier books)

HISTORY

ASIMOV. *The Greeks: A Great Adventure.* Houghton.

——. *The Roman Empire.* Houghton.

——. *The Roman Republic.* Houghton.

AUDEN, ed. *The Portable Greek Reader.* Viking. (paperback)

BOARDMAN. *Greek Art.* Praeger. (paperback)

BOWRA. *Classical Greece.* Time-Life.

BRUMBAUGH. *The Philosophers of Greece.* Crowell.

CHAMOUX. *Greek Art.* New York Graphic Society.

CHRISTENSEN. *A Pictorial History of Western Art.* Mentor. (paperback)

CLENDENIN. *Music History and Theory.* Doubleday. (paperback)

*COOLIDGE. *Caesar's Gallic War.* Houghton.

*——. *Greek Myths.* Houghton.

*——. *The Trojan War.* Houghton.

COTTRELL. *The Bull of Minos.* Grosset. (paperback)

COWELL. *Everyday Life in Ancient Rome.* Putnam.

*DAVIS. *A Day in Old Athens.* Allyn and Bacon.

*——. *A Day in Old Rome.* Allyn and Bacon.

DUGGAN. *The Romans.* World.

*FOSTER. *Augustus Caesar's World.* Scribner.

GARDNER. *Art Through the Ages.* Harcourt.

GLUBOK. *The Art of Ancient Greece.* Atheneum.

*GUERBER. *Myths of Greece and Rome.* London House.

HADAS. *Imperial Rome.* Time-Life.

*HALL. *Buried Cities.* Macmillan.

HAMILTON. *Echo of Greece.* Norton.

——. *Greek Way.* Modern Library.

——. *Roman Way.* Norton.

HERODOTUS. *Persian Wars.* Modern Library.

HORIZON MAGAZINE. *The Horizon Book of Ancient Greece.* Doubleday.

——. *The Horizon Book of Ancient Rome.* Doubleday.

*JOHNSTON. *Roman Life.* Scott, Foresman.

KIERAN and DALEY. *The Story of the Olympic Games.* Lippincott.

LIVY. *A History of Rome: Selections.* Modern Library.

McNEILL, BUSKE, ROEHM. *The World . . . Its History in Maps.* Denoyer-Geppert.

*MILLS. *Book of the Ancient Greeks.* Putnam.

*——. *Book of the Ancient Romans.* Putnam.

MIREAUX. *Daily Life in the Time of Homer*. Macmillan.

PAYNE. *Ancient Greece*. Norton.

*QUENNELL and QUENNELL. *Everyday Life in Roman and Anglo-Saxon Times*. Putnam.

*——. *Everyday Things in Ancient Greece*. Putnam.

RENAULT. *The Lion in the Gateway*. Harper.

*ROBINSON. *Everyday Life in Ancient Greece*. Oxford.

TACITUS. *On Britain and Germany*. Penguin. (paperback)

THUCYDIDES. *The History of the Peloponnesian War*. Dutton.

*TREBLE and KING. *Everyday Life in Rome in the Time of Caesar and Cicero*. Oxford.

VAUGHAN. *Those Mysterious Etruscans*. Doubleday.

VON HAGEN. *Roman Roads*. World.

WEBER. *The Western Tradition*. Heath.

BIOGRAPHY

BURN. *Alexander the Great and the Hellenistic Empire*. Verry.

——. *Pericles and Athens*. Verry.

COOLIDGE. *Lives of Famous Romans*. Houghton.

——. *Men of Athens*. Houghton.

COTTRELL. *Hannibal: Enemy of Rome*. Holt.

DUGGAN. *Julius Caesar*. Knopf.

*GOLDBERG. *Hippocrates: Father of Medicine*. Watts.

HARVEY. *The Quest of Archimedes*. Doubleday.

HORNBLOW. *Cleopatra of Egypt*. Random House.

*KOMROFF. *Julius Caesar*. Messner.

*LAMB. *Alexander of Macedon*. Doubleday.

*——. *Hannibal*. Doubleday.

MASON. *Socrates, the Man Who Dared to Ask*. Beacon Press.

MERCER. *Alexander the Great*. Harper.

ROBINSON. *Alexander the Great*. Watts.

*SILVERBURG. *Socrates*. Putnam.

WEBB. *Attila: King of the Huns*. Watts.

WHITE. *Plutarch's "Lives."* Putnam.

FICTION

ANDERSON. *For Freedom and for Gaul*. Biblo and Tannen.

——. *Slave of Catiline*. Biblo and Tannen.

——. *Swords in the North*. Biblo and Tannen.

——. *With the Eagles*. Biblo and Tannen.

*BAUMANN. *I Marched with Hannibal*. Walck.

BULWER–LYTTON. *Last Days of Pompeii*. Dodd.

COLUM. *The Adventures of Odysseus and the Tale of Troy*. Macmillan.

COOLIDGE. *Roman People*. Houghton.

*DARINGER. *Yesterday's Daughter*. Harcourt.

*DAVIS. *A Friend of Caesar*. Macmillan.

DONAUER. *Swords against Carthage*. Biblo and Tannen.

DOUGLAS. *The Robe*. Houghton.

*KENT. *He Went with Hannibal*. Houghton.

LAWRENCE. *Gift of the Golden Cup*. Bobbs.

*MALVERN. *The Secret Sign*. Abelard-Schuman.

*——. *Tamar*. McKay.

MAYER. *Olympiad*. Biblo and Tannen.

MITCHISON. *The Conquered*. Dufour.

PALMER. *At the Lion Gate*. Houghton.

*POWERS. *Hannibal's Elephants*. McKay.

RENAULT. *Bull from the Sea*. Pantheon.

——. *The King Must Die*. Pantheon.

SHORE. *Captive Princess: The Story of the First Christian Princess of Britain*. McKay.

SIENKIEWICZ. *Quo Vadis?* Little, Brown.

*SNEDEKER. *The Forgotten Daughter*. Doubleday.

*——. *White Isle*. Doubleday.

SON. *Eagles Have Flown*. Knopf.

SUTCLIFF. *Eagle of the Ninth*. Walck.

*——. *Silver Branch*. Walck.

*TREASE. *Message to Hadrian*. Vanguard.

WALLACE. *Ben-Hur*. Harper.

WALTARI. *The Roman*. Putnam.

WARNER. *The Young Caesar*. Little, Brown.

WHITE. *Unwilling Vestal*. Dutton.

"THE LORD OF THE MANOR," an early sixteenth-century frontispiece.

PART THREE

THE DECLINE AND REVIVAL OF CIVILIZATION IN WESTERN EUROPE

In the thousand years after the fall of Rome, new centers of power and civilization appeared in Asia. The Arabs and the Mongols proved to be the most successful of the new conquerors, while India and China reached high levels of civilization.

The story of Europe during this time is quite different. Collapse of Roman authority brought a decline of Europe's culture. Except in the Greek remnant of the old Roman Empire and a few scattered spots, Europe sank back into barbarism. The Christian Church alone remained as a unifying, civilizing influence in western Europe.

We speak of this period as the *Middle Ages,* because it came between ancient and modern times. The Middle Ages are also called "the medieval period." The Middle Ages in western Europe lasted for about a thousand years—from the fall of Rome to the discovery of America.

Part Three begins with a description of life in the Byzantine, or Eastern Roman, Empire. As you will see, this eastern empire not only kept civilization alive, it also protected western Europe against invasion by the Arabs. After their conversion to the faith of Mohammed, the Arabs conquered much of the old Roman Empire.

The remainder of Part Three shows how people in western Europe lived after A.D. 500. You will discover that most people huddled together in small farming villages, living close to the edge of starvation. The crusades, beginning about 1100, marked a turning point in medieval life. During the later Middle Ages times became better and people once more were interested in trade and travel.

9 Europe in the Early Middle Ages

MEDIEVAL CHURCHES required many workers in wood and stone for their construction. This illustration shows building in progress.

The Middle Ages begin. During the early Middle Ages much of Europe passed through a time of turmoil and confusion, of ignorance and lawlessness. Throughout the lands that had belonged to the Western Roman Empire, the invasions of the barbarians set civilization so far back that the early Middle Ages may justly be called the Dark Age.

Southeastern Europe, fortunately, had a different history. The Roman Empire in the East managed to survive for another thousand years and continued to uphold a number of Roman traditions. Its culture was a blend of Roman, Greek, Christian, and Oriental influences.

The Byzantine Empire

The capital of the Eastern Roman Empire was Constantinople, which had once been named Byzantium. The Eastern Roman Empire is usually called the Byzantine Empire. Beginning in the eleventh century the Turks gradually seized the Byzantine lands until the empire included only Constantinople and the territory close by.

Byzantine commerce and industry. While western Europe was in the Dark Age and commerce and industry there were at a standstill, the Byzantine Empire was prosperous. The products of Constantinople, especially silk and cotton cloth, tapestry, jewelry, and articles made of silver, found a ready market and were carried by Byzantine merchant ships to ports on the Mediterranean and the Black Sea. Byzantine wares were carried north by way of the Russian rivers and exchanged for slaves and furs. They were also carried east and exchanged for spices, drugs, and precious stones. Constantinople was indeed a center of world trade.

Byzantine art. The wealth brought to Constantinople by trade enabled many of the emperors to build lavishly. Byzantine architecture became a leading form of art. Its most striking feature is the dome. The exterior of a Byzantine church is usually without very much decoration, but the interior is adorned on a magnificent scale. The eyes of the worshipers are dazzled by walls faced with marble slabs of various colors, by tall columns of polished marble, jasper, and porphyry, and by brilliant mosaic pictures of colored glass. The impression is one of richness and splendor. Byzantine artists, though not very good painters and sculptors, excelled in decorative art. Their carvings in wood and ivory and their work in metal, together with their embroideries, enamels, miniatures, and mosaics, enjoyed a high reputation in medieval Europe.

Byzantine scholarship. One of Constantinople's great services to humanity was the preservation of the learning of Greece and Rome. The wisest men of the day resided in Constantinople, where they taught philosophy, law, medicine, and science to thousands of students. They made few new discoveries but they compiled huge encyclopedias, which preserved classical learning for future generations. Their best-known work was in the field of law. During the reign of the emperor Justinian (527–565), the laws then in effect were collected and organized into the Code of Justinian. (See page 99.)

The Greek Church. The breakup of the Roman Empire led to differences between the Latin Church and the Greek Church. They drifted apart because of disputes on points of doctrine and in 1054 formally separated. They have never reunited. Missionaries from the Greek Church succeeded in converting the barbarians who entered southeastern Europe during the early Middle Ages. Today

THE CITY OF CONSTANTINOPLE IN 1635. The old city walls, studded with towers, appear in the foreground. In the background, Moslem minarets have replaced the spires of Christian churches. Today Constantinople is known as Istanbul.

most of the inhabitants of the Balkan peninsula, including Greeks, Yugoslavs, Bulgarians, and Rumanians, belong to the Greek Orthodox Church. Its greatest victory was the conversion of the Russians, toward the close of the tenth century. The Russian ruler, having made up his mind to embrace Christianity, sent commissioners to visit both Rome and Constantinople. The commissioners reported in favor of the Greek Church. Their barbaric imagination had been so impressed by the majesty of the ceremonies performed in the great cathedral of Saint Sophia in Constantinople that "they did not know whether they were on earth or in Heaven." The numerous peoples whom the Greek Church converted to Christianity were influenced by other aspects of Greek civilization also. Thus the Greek as well as the Roman Church helped to bring a higher culture to the barbarians.

Constantinople. The heart of Byzantine civilization was Constantinople. It was the largest, most populous, and most wealthy city in medieval Europe. When London, Paris, and Venice were small towns, visitors to Constantinople found paved and lighted streets, parks, public baths, hospitals, theaters, schools, libraries, museums, beautiful churches, and magnificent palaces. The Northmen called it the "Great City"; the Russians knew it as the "City of the Caesars." Both names were fitting, but its own people described it as the "City guarded by God."

Importance of the Byzantine Empire. For over eleven hundred years—from the time that Constantine made Constantinople his capital in 330 until the Turks captured the city in 1453—the Byzantine Empire preserved the learning of classical civilization, formed a missionary center for Christianity, and stood as a bulwark which helped to protect Europe from eastern invaders, especially the Arabs and Turks.

The Arabs and Islam

A new religion. The Arabs, like the German tribes, took possession of parts of the Roman Empire. But unlike the Germans, the Arabs desired to spread their own religion. The religion of the Arabs was known as Islam. It began in the seventh century and grew with marvelous rapidity. For a time it promised to become the prevailing faith of Europe as well as of the Middle East and Northern Africa.

The Arabs. The Arabian peninsula is nearly four times the size of Texas. Except for occasional oases, the interior of the peninsula is a desert inhabited only by nomads, who are continually on the move with their sheep, cattle, horses, and camels from one pasturage to another. Some rain falls along the southern and western coasts of the peninsula, where the climate is very hot and the soil generally fertile. The Arabs who inhabited this favored region had reached a considerable degree of civilization by the sixth century—by the time the European Middle Ages began. They practiced agriculture, built cities and towns, and carried on a flourishing trade that reached even to India. There was much petty warfare between these settled Arabs and their nomad kinsmen of the interior.

Ancient Arabian religion. Every year for four months the Arabian tribes ceased fighting with one another and went on a pilgrimage to the city of Mecca, which is on the western coast near the Red Sea. Here stood the Kaaba, a famous building containing idols and a small black stone (probably a meteorite) which was regarded with religious awe. Although most Arabs worshiped idols, some Arabs believed that there was only one God—an understanding which was spread by the many Jews and Christians in Arabia. Thus the way was prepared for Mohammed, who preached a religion based on monotheism—the doctrine that there is but one God.

Mohammed's early life. The prophet Mohammed was born at Mecca about 570. Although he came from a prominent family, he received no regular education, since he was left an orphan at an early age. For some time he earned his living as a shepherd and camel driver. Then his marriage to a wealthy widow enabled him to settle down in Mecca as a prosperous, though still undistinguished, merchant.

As he grew older, Mohammed centered his thoughts more and more on religion. He could not reconcile the idolatry of the Arabs with that belief in one God which he himself had reached. His distress of mind led him often to withdraw into the wilderness, where he fasted and kept solitary vigils. During these lonely hours in the desert, strange scenes passed before his eyes and strange voices sounded in his ears. Mohammed at first thought that evil spirits possessed him, but his wife encouraged him to believe that his visions were a revelation from another world. One day, so he declared, the archangel Gabriel appeared to him and bade him preach a new religion to the Arabs. It was very simple, but in its simplicity lay its strength: "There is no god but God (Allah), and Mohammed is the prophet of God."

Mohammed preaches a new religion. Mohammed made his first converts in his wife, children, and friends. A few slaves and poor freemen became his followers, but most people regarded him as a madman. Mohammed's followers called themselves *Moslems*. They were persecuted by the citizens of Mecca, who resented the prophet's attacks on the worship of idols. Finally, in 622, Mohammed and his followers took refuge in the city of Medina, where some of the inhabitants had already accepted his teachings. The flight to Medina from Mecca is called the *Hegira*. The Moslems use this as the beginning date for their calendar, just as the Christians reckon time from the birth of Christ.

AN ARAB CAMP ON MOUNT CARMEL. Soon after Mohammed's death his followers conquered most of the Middle East.

Mohammed's religion is established. The people of Medina welcomed Mohammed and made him their chief magistrate. As his followers increased in numbers, he launched military attacks on nonbelievers. Many of the tribes which he conquered enlisted under his banner and at length captured Mecca for the prophet. He treated its inhabitants leniently but destroyed their idols. After the submission of Mecca most of the Arab tribes accepted the new religion. By the time Mohammed died, in 632, he had firmly established a new religion and had started his people on a career of conquest.

The Moslems write a sacred book. The religion which Mohammed taught is called "Islam," an Arabic word meaning "resignation" (to God's will). The sacred book of the Moslems is called the *Koran*. It contains speeches, prayers, and other utterances of Mohammed, which were collected in this one book soon after the prophet's death. Some parts of the Koran were dictated by the prophet to his disciples; other parts they wrote down from memory. The Koran has come down unchanged to the present day.

The Koran was influenced by Jewish and Christian teachings. It emphasizes the immortality of the soul and the idea that there is only one God. The Koran recognizes the existence of prophets, including Abraham, Moses, and others. It teaches that Jesus was a prophet but declares that Mohammed was a greater one. The Koran also contains descriptions of the resurrection of the dead, the last judgment, and the division of the after world into Paradise and Hell. One of Islam's important beliefs is that war against unbelievers is holy. "Whosoever falls in battle," the Koran says, "his sins are forgiven, and at the day of judgment his limbs shall be supplied by the wings of angels and cherubim." Moslems are told "Begin not hostilities."

Moral teachings of the Koran. The Koran furnishes a very strict moral code for the followers of Islam. It teaches many active virtues, including reverence toward parents, protection of widows and orphans, charity toward the poor, kindness to slaves, and gentle treatment of animals. It also prohibits certain acts; Moslems must not make images, engage in gambling, eat pork, or drink wine.

Duties required by the Koran. The faithful Moslem must accept five great obligations. (1) He must recite at least once in his life, aloud, correctly, and with full understanding, the short creed: "There is no god but God, and Mohammed is the prophet of God." (2) He must pray five times a day. The hour of prayer is announced from the tall minaret of the mosque by a crier. Before prayer the worshiper washes face, hands, and feet; during the prayer he turns toward the city of Mecca and bows his head to the ground. (3) During the ninth month of the Mohammedan year he must observe a strict fast from sunrise to sunset of each day. (4) He must give alms to the poor. (5) He must, "if he is able," undertake at least one pilgrimage to Mecca. Pilgrims also visit holy places near Mecca and Mohammed's tomb at Medina.

Arab conquests in the East, 632–651. The teaching of Mohammed that his religion might be spread by force, and the desire for richer lands outside Arabia, gave the Arabs two great motives for conquest. A few years after Mohammed's death Moslem warriors attacked with success the two strongest military powers then in the world—the Byzantine Empire and the Persian Empire. From the Byzantines they took the provinces of Syria and Egypt, and even laid unsuccessful siege to Constantinople itself. From the Persians they first took the Tigris-Euphrates district, and then went on to overthrow the Persian Empire, acquiring most of it by 651. Many Christians in Syria and Egypt and most of the Zoroastrians (see page 34) in Persia adopted Islam to avoid paying tribute and to acquire the privileges of Moslem citizens.

The Arabs advance westward until 732. After their remarkable conquests in the East, accomplished in less than twenty years, the Arabs turned westward. They established a capital at Cairo in Egypt and swept clear across North Africa to the Atlantic. In North Africa, Islam made one of its most perma-nent conquests. The Arabs and the natives of North Africa crossed the Strait of Gibraltar and for the first time confronted the Germans. The Visigoth kingdom in Spain fell before them. (See page 102.) They pressed northward through Spain, crossed the Pyrenees Mountains into Gaul, and there were finally stopped. The great Battle of Tours (732) decided that Europe would be Christian, not Moslem. Charles Martel, the grandfather of Charlemagne, led the forces which defeated the Moslem invaders. The Moslems held most of Spain for several centuries and held part of it until 1492.

The Arabs absorb and spread civilization. The conquests of the Arabs brought them into contact with the highly civilized peoples who lived in the Middle East and along the shores of the Mediterranean. What they

---

AN ESTIMATE OF MOHAMMED

. . . Mohammed was a great man, superior to his time and place. He not only preached but practiced a morality that was lofty for his society. If he could be ruthless, he was more often gentle, kind, generous, magnanimous. He could be Christlike in his sympathy for the weak and poor. Through the pious fog of tradition one catches many glimpses of an attractive humanity, as in his unfailing courtesy touched by shyness, his fondness for jokes and fun, his humble sharing of the household chores, his wry indulgence of the frailties of his womenfolk, his tolerance of the foibles of the companions. One can understand why he was so deeply loved by those around him. As one reads of his death and of the quiet, unaffected way in which he met it, one may almost share the grief of the companions, if not their bewilderment. Say the worst about his human limitations, and there remain a heroic and inspired life, a complete dedication to the service of his God, and a power of personality that made as deep an impression on his followers as Jesus made on his, in some ways a more lasting impression. . . .

—Herbert J. Muller, *The Loom of History*.

---

learned from Greeks, Syrians, Persians, Jews, and Hindus they absorbed, often improved upon, and carried to other lands. The Arabs built up a culture which for several centuries surpassed that of western Europe. They rivaled the Romans as absorbers and carriers of civilization, partly because their language was widely used. Moslems of many nationalities learned Arabic in order to read the Koran, which appeared only in Arabic.

The Arabs achieved a high civilization in many fields. In agriculture they practiced rotation of crops, employed fertilizer, and understood how to graft and how to produce new varieties of plants. They excelled in making brocades, tapestries, blades of tempered steel, armor, leather, rich silks, crystal and plate glass, and pottery. In commerce the Arabs were also outstanding. They traded with India, China, the East Indies, the interior of Africa, Russia, and even the Baltic lands. During the early Middle Ages, Europeans received the greater part of their fine manufactured articles through the Arabs.

Arabic scholarship and art. Their trade, their wide conquests, and their religious pilgrimages to Mecca vastly increased their knowledge of the world. Arab scholars compiled encyclopedias describing foreign countries and peoples, and calculated the size of the earth. They had a strong aptitude for mathematics and contributed to the development of both algebra and geometry. The so-called Arabic numbers, which they borrowed from India, were introduced by them into the Christian world, and it is probable that they were first to introduce the mariner's compass into Europe. They developed skill in chemistry, discovering a number of new chemical compounds, and made progress in the field of medicine, performing difficult surgical operations and using anesthetics. The Arabs also excelled in architecture. In many of their buildings swelling domes, vaulted roofs, arched porches, tall and graceful minarets,

and the exquisite decorative patterns known as "arabesques" are combined to make miracles of beauty. The walls of public buildings were richly decorated with mosaics made of colored glass or tile and with pierced stone filigreework. Paintings were little used except in private houses. The Arab architectural style was carried by the Spaniards to the New World.

Arabic universities. Moslem universities were one of the chief agencies in developing and spreading Arabic civilization. The largest university was at Cairo, where the lectures of the professors were attended by thousands of students. Famous universities also existed in Baghdad and at Cordova, Granada, and Toledo in Spain. Moslem scholars especially delighted in the study of philosophy and helped to revive the study of Aristotle's writings in western Europe. The Arabs also formed extensive libraries with thousands of manuscripts. The libraries, like the universities, were visited by many Christian students. Arab centers of learning in Spain exerted great influence on European thought.

Moslem caliphs. The Arab rulers who came after Mohammed were called *caliphs*. In time, disputes arose over the succession to the office of caliph, and there came to be three caliphs—one at Baghdad in Mesopotamia, one at Cordova in Spain, and one at Cairo in Egypt. The caliph at Baghdad was the most important of the three. The most famous of the caliphs at Baghdad was Harun al-Rashid (hä-roon' är-rå-shēd'), who lived at the same time as Charlemagne. Under him Baghdad became the largest and richest city in the Moslem world. Its splendor is reflected in the stories of the *Thousand and One Nights* (popularly called the *Arabian Nights*), a part of the world's great literature.

The Seljuk Turks invade the Middle East. The rich Arabian civilization, like that of Rome, fell under the onslaught of invading barbarians. In the eleventh century the Arab

PATIO DE LOS ARRAYANES of the Alhambra in Granada, Spain. The Alhambra is one of the finest examples of Moorish architecture in Spain.

dominions in the Middle East were overrun by the Seljuk (sĕl-jōōk´) Turks, fierce nomads from central Asia. The coming of the Seljuk Turks was a great misfortune, for these barbarians did nothing to preserve Arabic culture. They were converted to Islam, however, and began another era of Moslem conquest. Their conquests led the nobles and knights of western Europe to set out on the crusades.

German Tribes in the Early Middle Ages

Disorder in Europe after 476. The collapse of Roman government in western Europe marks the beginning of the Middle Ages. During the early Middle Ages, from 476 to about 1100, European civilization slipped back into semibarbarism. The chief cause of this decline was lack of a government which could keep order. The Germanic kingdoms which had been set up by 476 were unable to suppress violence. There were so many highway robbers that travel became dangerous. Europe suffered a decline in commerce and manufacturing, in education, in literature and the arts, and in almost all that makes possible a high civilization. Cities grew smaller and in some cases practically disappeared, and western Europe became a region of poverty-stricken farming communities, each virtually isolated from the rest of the world.

The Franks established in Gaul the strongest of the Germanic kingdoms. The early Frankish kings followed a policy of expansion until they ruled nearly all of what is now France, Belgium, and Holland, as well as a considerable part of western Germany. One of the ablest leaders was Charles Martel, who beat back the Moors in 732.

PORTRAIT OF CHARLEMAGNE in royal robes. He is shown holding the symbols of authority. Charlemagne disliked formality, and usually wore much simpler clothing.

Charlemagne. Charles Martel's grandson, called Charles the Great, or Charlemagne, was the greatest of the Frankish kings. He reigned over all the Franks from 771 to 814. His secretary describes Charlemagne as a tall, square-shouldered, strongly built man, with bright, keen eyes. Riding, hunting, and swimming were his favorite sports. He was simple in his tastes and temperate in food and drink. Charlemagne could use Latin as well as his native tongue and understood Greek when it was spoken. Although he never learned to write more than his own name, the "hero of the Middle Ages" was a well-educated man for his times and by no means a barbarian.

Charlemagne's conquests. Charlemagne's reign was filled with warfare. He practically doubled the territory which he inherited. Charlmagne conquered the Lombards,

who had taken northern Italy and threatened the possessions of the pope. From the Moslems he wrested a district called the Spanish March, which lay south of the Pyrenees Mountains. In east central Europe he conquered various of the Slavic peoples. Charlemagne's hardest task was subduing the Saxons, who lived in northern Germany. After almost thirty years of fighting they were forced to accept Christianity and Frankish rule. At the height of his power Charlemagne ruled over what is now France, Belgium, Holland, Switzerland, Austria, western Germany, northern Italy and northern Spain, besides a part of Czechoslovakia and Yugoslavia. This was truly a gigantic realm for one man to hold.

It seemed fitting that such a ruler should become the successor of the Roman emperors, especially since Rome itself lay within his empire. Charlemagne wanted the title of emperor, and the pope wanted him to have it as a reward for protecting the Church and converting heathen tribes. In old St. Peter's Church at Rome on Christmas Day, 800, the pope placed a golden crown on Charlemagne's head. This ceremony seemed to bring to life again the empire which had ceased when Romulus Augustulus was deposed by the Germans in 476. Actually, Charlemagne's empire was a new political creation resulting from the alliance of the Frankish king and the Roman Catholic Church.

Civilizing work of Charlemagne. Charlemagne did his best to bring orderly government to his dominions. He divided them into districts, over each of which he appointed a special officer. Other officials traveled from district to district, carrying orders and making sure that these orders were promptly obeyed. There is evidence that trade and city life revived in this period of better government. Charlemagne also encouraged education, which had almost disappeared except in the Church. He issued a number of orders to the clergy, requiring them to establish schools in the monasteries and cathedrals where the common people as well as the clergy might receive some education. He also formed his whole court into a palace school, in which learned men gave instruction to his own children and those of his nobles. He had the manuscripts of Latin authors collected and copied, so that the knowledge preserved in books should not be forgotten. All this civilizing work made his reign the brightest period of the early Middle Ages.

A setback for civilization. After Charlemagne died in 814, his empire began to fall apart. It had depended on his genius, and no successor of equal ability appeared. His son was a weak ruler, and Charlemagne's three grandsons quarreled among themselves. By the Treaty of Verdun (843) they divided the empire into three parts. One grandson took the west; his kingdom later became France. Another took the east, which later became Germany. The third grandson took northern Italy and a strip lying between the kingdoms of his two brothers. This strip of land, extending from the Alps to the North Sea, has since been a bone of contention between France and Germany. The division of Charlemagne's empire left western Europe without the unifying influence of a strong central government. There was an increase in petty warfare and in disorder; trade and education declined once again, and the number of city dwellers decreased. But conditions did not become so bad as they had been before Charlemagne. Indeed, civilization might have soon revived in western Europe had there not been a new series of barbarian invasions.

EUROPE IN THE TIME OF CHARLEMAGNE. His great Empire began to fall apart soon after his death in 814.

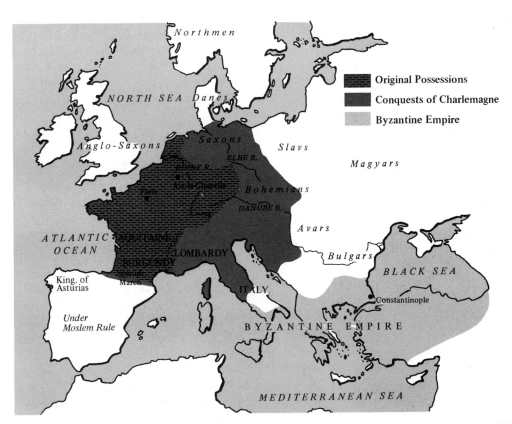

The Northmen. About the time of Charlemagne there began another—and the last—wave of Germanic invasions. The new barbarian invaders were the *Northmen,* most of whom lived in Norway, Sweden, and Denmark. According to their own writings, they were a restless, warlike people, cruel to their foes. They were excellent sailors. The Northmen fell first upon the coasts of western Europe, where they plundered and burned almost at will. They probably harmed civilization most by their attacks on churches and monasteries, for these were centers of learning as well as religion. A special prayer was inserted in the church services: "From the fury of the Northmen, good Lord, deliver us." But the attacks on religious institutions continued, for the Northmen had learned that there they would find the richest booty. Their fleets became larger year by year. They began to ascend the rivers, and their raids changed from mere summer forays of pirates to well-organized expeditions which stayed all winter. Eventually, many of the Northmen settled in the lands they visited, conquered the natives, and there set up their own governments.

One of the places which the Northmen visited was the faraway island of Iceland. It was settled by Norwegians, who brought to Iceland the language, customs, and literature of Norway. Eric the Red, one of the Icelanders, led an expedition still farther west to Greenland. Leif Ericsson, his son, voyaged even farther westward and visited the coast of North America about the year 1000. However, no lasting settlements were made in North America.

King Alfred and the Danes. Another group of Northmen, the Danes, made expeditions to England. They came in large numbers, made permanent settlements, and soon controlled all England north of the Thames. The Danes also ruled Ireland and part of Scotland for a time. Their advance in England was opposed by Alfred the Great, king of the Anglo-Saxon tribes which had previously settled in England. (See map on the next page.) Alfred, who reigned from 871 to 901, ranks with Charlemagne as a leading figure of the Middle Ages. He had the laws of the Anglo-Saxons collected and written down, tried to rebuild the ruined churches and monasteries, and labored to revive education. His court at Winchester became a literary center, where learned men wrote and taught. Alfred organized forces on land and sea to repel invaders, drove the Danes northward, and forced them to remain in northeastern England. This territory was later conquered by Alfred's descendants, and the Danes there, as well as those who came afterward, became a part of the English people.

Northmen settle in France. About the time the Danes began their invasions of England, another group of Northmen descended on northern France. The disunity of Europe after the death of Charlemagne left the empire nearly defenseless, and the Northmen came in ever greater numbers. They won the right to settle in a region around the lower Seine River, across the Channel from England. The Northmen quickly adopted the French culture, and came to be known as "Normans" (a softened form of "Northman"). The region they acquired is called Normandy.

Normans conquer England. The ruler of Normandy in 1066 was Duke William, later known as *William the Conqueror.* The duke claimed a right to the throne of England, and to gain it he crossed the Channel with an army of several thousand men. This proved to be the last successful invasion of England. Harold, the English king, met the Norman forces near Hastings. At the end of a day-long battle, Harold was killed by an arrow, and the surviving English soldiers fled. The Battle of Hastings settled the fate of England. Duke William marched on London and was crowned king of England on Christmas Day, 1066. William divided England among Nor-

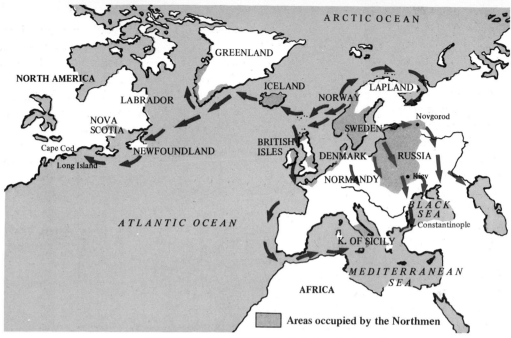

Areas occupied by the Northmen

DISCOVERIES AND SETTLEMENTS OF THE NORTHMEN

man nobles who promised to obey him. Norman merchants and workmen, as well as soldiers and nobles, came to England. The Normans became an important part of the English population, and left an enduring imprint upon the English language, customs, and government. This imprint consisted largely of French words and ideas.

Normans conquer Sicily and southern Italy. The Northmen had carried out raids in the Mediterranean as early as the time of Charlemagne. In the eleventh century the Normans followed with permanent conquests They created in Sicily and southern Italy a state known as the Kingdom of the Two Sicilies, which lasted until Italy was united under a single government in the middle of the nineteenth century.

The Swedes begin a Russian government. Another group of Northmen, the Swedes, crossed Russia by traveling along rivers from the Baltic to the Black Sea. They established a busy trade with the Byzantine Empire, and made Kiev and other Russian towns into important commercial centers. During the early

Middle Ages the Swedes became the chief carriers of Eastern goods to northeastern Europe. Rurik, one of the Swedish leaders, established a kingdom in the area around Novgorod about 862. He is regarded by the Russians as the founder of their country. The very name of Russia is derived from *Ros* or *Rous,* the Slavic name for these invaders. In time the Swedes in Russia were absorbed into the Slavic peoples by intermarriage, just as other Northmen intermarried with the natives of England, Ireland, Scotland, France, and Italy.

Non-Germanic invaders of Europe. The Moors who invaded Spain were only one of the non-Germanic tribes which overran Europe in the early Middle Ages. The Magyars, or Hungarians, were somewhat like the Huns, and like them came from Asia. At the time of the invasions of the Northmen the Hungarians were also raiding most of Europe. They looted and burned in the Byzantine Empire, Italy, France, and Poland but were finally defeated. They settled in Hungary, which is named for them.

CARCASSONNE, IN SOUTHERN FRANCE. One of the most spectacular of the walled medieval castles, Carcassonne was restored in the 1800's and is still inhabited. Most of the walls were erected during the 11th or 12th century, but some of the foundations date back to Roman times.

Feudalism in the Early Middle Ages

During most of the early Middle Ages the kings failed to protect the lives and property of their subjects. Nobles who held large tracts of land often became almost independent of the kings. In fact, attempts to seize the throne were frequent. Powerful nobles carried on private wars with each other and seized the property of their weaker neighbors. These conditions led to the growth of *feudalism*.

Nature of feudalism. Feudalism was a system of agreements, or ties, which linked lords and vassals together. A nobleman or other large landholder would promise to protect the family and property of a weaker neighbor. The person thus protected was called the *vassal* of the landholder. The vassal was a person of some importance and must not be confused with an ordinary worker. The vassal held a *fief,* which was land or an office with income enough to support at least one knight. The vassal and his protector, or lord, each accepted certain obligations.

Obligations of lord and vassal. The lord agreed to protect the life and property of his vassal and to see that in all matters he received just treatment. A vassal who felt he had been wronged by another lord could appeal to his own lord for help. This often led to fighting between lords.

The vassal promised loyalty to his lord, military service in time of war, and money payments on certain occasions. Three of these payments were called "aids"; they were paid when the lord's eldest son was knighted, when his eldest daughter was married, and when he was taken prisoner and had to pay a ransom in order to be set free. Women did not hold fiefs as a rule, since they could not fight for the lord. Usually fiefs passed from the vassal to his eldest son. The son assumed his father's obligations to the lord, and received a promise of the lord's protection.

Homage and investiture. The agreement between a lord and his vassal was made in formal ceremonies. One who wanted to become "a lord's man" (that is, to become a vassal and hold a fief) went through the ceremony of *homage* (from Latin *homo*, meaning "man"). He came bareheaded and unarmed into the lord's presence, knelt down, placed his hands between those of the lord, and promised to be his man. The lord then kissed him and raised him to his feet, whereupon the vassal swore a solemn oath to remain faithful to his lord.

The ceremony of *investiture* then followed, in which the vassal was given formal possession of his fief. The lord gave the vassal some object—a clod of earth, a lance, or a glove—in token of the vassal's possession of the fief. Henceforth, lord and vassal were bound to each other by mutual obligations and responsibilities.

The feudal pyramid. The fief which the vassal held was usually a grant of land. The supreme landlord was the king, who was supposed to hold his land from God. The vassals of the king were the great lords of the realm—dukes, marquises, counts, or barons. Their lands were divided and subdivided among other vassals, down to the smallest fief, which could support only one knight. The landholders might be thought of as forming a pyramid, from the humblest knight up to the king, with each person in the pyramid being the vassal of the person above him. In actual practice, feudal landholding was too complicated to be shown on a simple pyramid. Person *A* might be the lord of person *B* on one fief, yet on a different fief *A* might be the vassal of *B*. We must remember also that the feudal lords were often practically independent of the king and subject to him only in theory.

Military organization under feudalism. Feudalism provided a military organization, since the vassal promised to aid his lord in war. A feudal king might raise an army by calling for aid from the great nobles, who would in turn call on their vassals, and these vassals on their knights. The force thus raised was quite unlike a modern army, for it was composed of individuals who were fighting for their immediate overlords and felt no loyalty to the central command. A feudal army was unwieldy and hard to control.

Social classes under feudalism. In feudal society people were grouped according to station and rank in an arrangement that might also be compared to a pyramid. At the top was the king, below him the great nobles, and below them the lesser lords and knights, whose social position depended on their power and the size of their landholdings. At the bottom of the social scale were the great mass of serfs who worked on the estates of the lords and led a life of toil and poverty.

Local government under feudalism. Feudalism also provided for a system of government. The feudal lord lived on a landed estate, or *manor*. There was usually a village on the manor. All the people living on a manor were dependents and subjects of the lord of the manor. He could tax them; he could require them to give him military assistance; he could try them in his courts. The lord also enjoyed the privilege of declaring war, making treaties, and coining money. Most of the towns of feudal Europe were under the rule of a neighboring lord. This system of government prevailed wherever central authority had broken down—that is to say, throughout most of western Europe.

Economic activities under feudalism. Feudalism also provided an economic organization. In the early Middle Ages there was so little trade that each community had to produce almost everything that it used. Each manor therefore was a self-sufficient economic unit, in which farming was the main activity. Nearly all the goods used on the manor were homemade. The pastures, fields, and woods supplied raw materials; these were made into usable goods in the mill, blacksmith shop, bake ovens, and in the homes. This pattern was repeated on countless manors throughout feudal Europe. People learned to make things for themselves, or went without.

THIRTEENTH-CENTURY ARMOR   FOURTEENTH-CENTURY ARMOR

Activities of the nobles. The nobles spent their time mainly in hunting and fighting. Fighting enriched the victors since they plundered castles and villages, seized land, and held captives for ransom. The constant private warfare, though rarely very bloody, spread havoc through the country and was a major cause of the lack of progress in the early Middle Ages. In times of peace the nobles held mock fights called *jousts* and *tournaments*. The joust was a contest between two knights; the tournament, between two bands of knights. The contests took place in a railed-off space, called the "lists," about which the spectators gathered. Each knight wore upon his helmet the scarf or color of his lady. Victory went to the man who unhorsed his opponent or broke the greatest number of lances. The beaten knight forfeited horse and armor and had to pay a ransom to the victor. Sometimes when real rather than blunted weapons were used the defeated men were killed. The Church tried to stop these performances, but they remained universally popular until the close of the Middle Ages. When not engaged in real or sham fighting, the nobles spent much time in hunting.

Knighthood. The constant private warfare brought into existence a special class of warriors known as knights, whose chief duty was military service on horseback. Knights were drawn from the upper classes. A young man spent several years in apprenticeship before he could become a knight. During this period he was called a *squire;* he served his lord in the castle and fought beside him on the battlefield. When he reached the age of twenty-one and had become skilled in the use of arms, or when he performed a deed of bravery in battle, he might be made a *knight*. The customary ceremony for conferring knighthood was very elaborate. The young man kept a vigil in the church all night, heard Mass in the morning, and then knelt to receive a blow on the shoulder—the *accolade* —which made him a knight.

The medieval knight might almost be described as a living fortress. The early knights wore a cloth or leather tunic, covered with iron rings or scales, and an iron cap with a nose guard. Later the knights adopted chain mail. Still later they began to wear heavy plate armor, weighing fifty pounds or more, and helmets with visors which could be raised or lowered. Thus completely encased in metal, provided with shield, lance, straight sword, or battle-ax, and mounted on a powerful horse which was also armored, the knight could ride down almost any number of poorly armed peasants. It was not until the development of the long bow and gunpowder, which sent armor-piercing missiles, that the foot soldier again became important.

Chivalry. As manners softened and Christian teachings began to affect feudal society, the knight was expected to follow a code of conduct called *chivalry*. The chivalrous knight kept his promises; never took unfair advantage of another; defended women, children, and orphans against their oppressors; and sought to make justice and right prevail in the world. Needless to say, knights were more true to this code in ballads and in romance than in real life. Chivalry produced some improvement in manners, but it did nothing to lighten the burdens of the toiling peasants. The knight despised them and did his best to keep them in subjection.

The castle. We still may see in Europe the remains of many castles, built for defense in the days of feudal warfare. Often the castle was built on a high cliff or hill, or on an island, or in the center of a swamp. A castle without such natural defenses would be surrounded by a deep ditch, called a "moat," which was usually filled with water. A visitor to a castle crossed the drawbridge over the moat and approached the narrow doorway, which was protected by a tower on each side. If he was admitted, the iron grating (portcullis) rose slowly on its creaking pulleys, the heavy wooden doors swung open, and he found himself in the courtyard. Here stood the great central tower, or *keep,* the residence of the lord and his family in time of war. The keep was the final refuge in case enemies broke through the outer defenses of the castle. At the top of the keep was a platform where a sentinel watched the countryside for signs of danger; below the keep was the damp, dark dungeon where prisoners were kept. The castle walls also enclosed a hall for the lord's residence in time of peace, an armory, a chapel, storehouses, kitchens, and stables, as well as accommodations for the lord's servants and soldiers. Life in the castle could not have been very comfortable, for the rooms were dark, poorly heated and ventilated, and crudely furnished.

The manor. The typical rural community of the Middle Ages was the *manor,* a large tract of land occupied by the lord and his dependents. The manor naturally varied in size according to the wealth of its lord. In England, perhaps six hundred acres formed an average estate. Every noble had at least one manor; great nobles might have several scattered over the country. The manor contained some forest, some land used for pasture and haying, and some cultivated land. Part of the cultivated land was reserved for the use of the lord, and the rest of it was divided among the peasants.

Farming methods. The cultivated land of the manor was divided into hundreds of small strips, usually an acre or half an acre in size. Each peasant was assigned a number of small strips scattered over the manor. This method of dividing the land gave each peasant a portion both of the good land and the poor, but it cost him much time in going from one bit of land to another. Other farming practices were equally inefficient. The use of fertilizer and crop rotation was not understood. Each season all the cultivated land on the manor was divided into three fields, one being sown to winter crops such as wheat or rye, one to spring crops such as oats or barley, and the

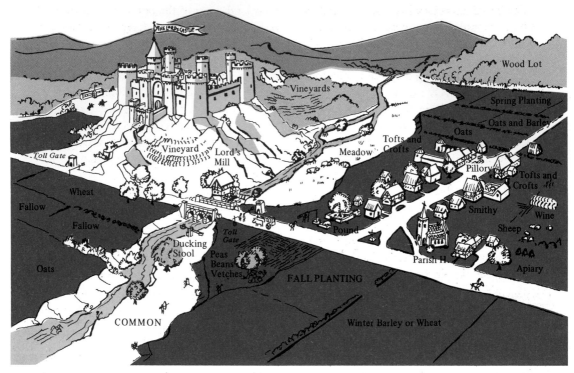

Fallow · Fallow · Wheat · Oats · COMMON · Ducking Stool · Toll Gate · Peas Beans Vetches · FALL PLANTING · Winter Barley or Wheat · Toll Gate · Vineyard · Lord's Mill · Pound · Meadow · Tofts and Crofts · Vineyards · Wood Lot · Spring Planting · Oats and Barley · Oats · Pillory · Tofts and Crofts · Smithy · Wine · Sheep · Parish H · Apiary · THE LORD'S CASTLE

PLAN OF A TYPICAL MANOR

third being left idle that year so that it might recover its fertility. The crops yielded little even in good years. Farm animals were small and unproductive because of poor care and poor breeding. Farm implements were few and clumsy, probably little better than those of the ancient Egyptians. It took five men a day to reap and bind the harvest of two acres. (Today, if each uses a modern "combine," five men can harvest 75 to 100 acres of grain in a day.)

Uncultivated land of the manor. Each peasant also had certain rights over the uncultivated land of the manor. He could cut a limited amount of hay from the meadow, and could turn some farm animals into the common pasture. He could cut some wood from the forest for fuel and building purposes but could not hunt there.

The medieval village. Medieval peasants lived in villages, which were built near the castle if the manor had one. The small, thatch-roofed, one-roomed houses were grouped about an open space (the "green"), or on both sides of a single, narrow street. The important buildings were the parish church, the parsonage, a mill, and possibly a blacksmith's shop. A village might contain from about one hundred to several hundred persons.

Village officials. A village had a regular staff of officials. First in a typical English village came the headman, or reeve, who governed the village and represented the peasants in their dealings with the lord of the manor. The constable, or beadle, carried messages around the village, summoned the inhabitants to meetings, and enforced the orders of the reeve. Then there were the poundkeeper, who seized straying animals; the watchman, who guarded the flocks at night; and the village carpenter, blacksmith, and miller. In return for their services the officials received an allowance of land which the other serfs cultivated for them.

The inhabitants of a village tried to produce at home everything they needed. They raised their own food, made their own clothes, tools, and furniture, and built their own houses. The chief articles which they had to buy were salt, iron, and millstones. Even these simple things were not easily obtained, for money was scarce and traders were few.

Condition of the peasants. The peasants labored from sunrise to sunset, ate coarse food, lived in huts, and if they were sick had only homemade remedies. They had no education and lived little better than their farm animals. They rarely or never left the manor where they were born. Unpleasant though it was, the peasant's life was better than that of the slaves in the days of the Roman Empire. The feudal system guaranteed the peasant certain rights as well as duties, and he shared with his fellows in the work, the sports, and the church services of the village. Festivities at Christmas, Easter, and other holy days, May Day, the end of plowing, and the harvest, also relieved the monotony of the peasant's life.

Serfdom. Slavery in western Europe died out during the early Middle Ages. This did not mean, however, that all classes had complete freedom. Although the manors had some freemen, who paid rent for the use of their land, most of the peasants were serts. A serf ranked lower than a freeman, because the serf had fewer rights. He was a part of the equipment of the manor, and could not leave it, marry, or bequeath his goods, without the lord's permission. He was "bound to the soil," which means that if the manor was transferred, the serfs as well as the land went to the new owner. The serf's land could not be taken from him so long as he performed his obligations.

Obligations of the serf. For the use of his land the serf owed certain obligations, including payments "in kind" and personal services. He had to work about half the time on the fields reserved for the lord, and had to perform other tasks such as cutting fuel for the lord and carting the lord's goods to distant places. The serf's payments in kind consisted of a substantial share of grain, honey, eggs, or other produce. When he ground the grain or pressed the grapes which grew on his land, he must use the lord's mill or the lord's wine press, and pay the customary charge. He must bake his bread in the lord's oven and give a share of the loaves as payment. Because of these obligations and the inefficient farming methods of the period, the serf usually had little left for himself. At best, he led a fairly drab life.

SERFS PUSHING A CART UPHILL during harvest time, as shown in a medieval manuscript

The Roman Catholic Church in the Early Middle Ages

Importance of the medieval Church. The most important unifying and civilizing agency in western Europe during the early Middle Ages was the Catholic Church. Several reasons may be given for its rise to leadership. (1) Active missionary work brought practically all people in western Europe under its influence. (2) People were probably more concerned with religious matters than they are today. They looked to religion to lead them to a happier life after death, when they would be released from the toil and suffering of this world. (3) The fall of the Roman Empire left western Europe without a central government; the Roman Catholic Church was the only unifying structure. (4) While Chris-

tendom in the Byzantine Empire was torn by theological disputes, the Roman Catholic Church stood by the Nicene Creed (see page 104) and preserved unity in western Europe on matters of doctrine. (5) In western Europe the Church, almost alone, carried on education and preserved the learning of the past. (6) Some leaders of the Church were unusually able men who greatly expanded its power and influence.

The popes as leaders. The Roman Catholic Church is headed by the pope. (Pope is a Latin word for "father.") The prestige of the papacy was raised by such men as Pope Leo I, who is said to have diverted Attila and his Huns from an attack on Rome in 452. Gregory the Great, pope from 590 to 604, was a man of uncommon ability and energy. He helped to keep the Lombards from overrunning central Italy, insisted that church officials recognize the authority of the pope, and sent out the mission which began the conversion of the English people. When his remarkable career came to a close, the papacy had reached a commanding place in western Christendom. The papacy attained the height of its power under Innocent III (1198–1216). He worked unceasingly to get the rulers of Europe to recognize the supremacy of the popes in temporal (worldly) as well as spiritual matters. Succeeding popes continued to press this claim. Throughout the Middle Ages the popes exerted great influence over both spiritual and temporal affairs.

Power of the papacy. The pope was the supreme lawgiver of the Church. His decrees might not be set aside by any other person. He made new laws, and by his "dispensations" he could in particular cases set aside old laws of the Church, such as the one forbidding cousins to marry. The pope was also the supreme judge of the Church, since all appeals from its lower courts came before him for decision. Finally, the pope was the supreme administrator of the Church. He confirmed the election of bishops and archbishops, deposed them when necessary, or transferred them from one post to another. He also exercised control over the monastic orders and called general councils of the Church.

Income of the papacy. To support the business of the papacy and to maintain the splendor of the papal court required a large annual income. This came partly from the gifts of the faithful, partly from payments by high church officials when the pope confirmed their election to office, and partly from "Peter's Pence," a tax of a penny on each hearth. It was collected every year in England and some continental countries until the time of the Reformation. Today "Peter's Pence" is a voluntary contribution made by Roman Catholics in all countries. The States of the Church were another source of papal income.

States of the Church. Shortly before the year 800 the pope acquired possession of the states of central Italy and ruled over them as a temporal sovereign. He did not lose them until Italy was united under one central government in the second half of the nineteenth century. He was again recognized as a temporal sovereign in 1929, but his state now includes an area of only about a hundred acres, called the Vatican City.

ST. PETER'S BASILICA in Vatican City

The clergy. As his assistants in administering the Church, the pope appointed a board, or college, of cardinals. In the eleventh century the cardinals received the right to elect the new pope. The number of cardinals may vary but usually there are seventy or more. Today there are several cardinals from the United States.

Below the cardinals were the archbishops. In England, for example, there were two archbishops, one residing at York and the other at Canterbury. Bishops ranked below archbishops and supervised the work of the parish priests. A church which contained the official throne of a bishop or archbishop was called a *cathedral*. It was ordinarily the largest and most magnificant church in the area.

Parish priests. In the Middle Ages, just as is the case today, the parish priest had charge of a parish, the smallest division of Christendom. He was the only church officer who came continually in touch with the common people. He watched over their deeds on earth and prepared them for the life to come. He was responsible to the bishop, who determined in what parish, if any; he should work.

The seven sacraments. Through the seven sacraments, the Church entered into all important events in a person's life from his birth to his death. Peter Lombard (1100–1160) defined the seven sacraments to be: baptism, confirmation, penance, eucharist, holy orders, matrimony, and extreme unction. The parish priests could administer all the sacraments except confirmation and holy orders, which were performed only by the bishops.

Church practices. The Catholic Church was distinguished for charitable work. It distributed large sums of money to the needy and built hospitals, orphanages, and asylums. Very little thought was given to the causes of poverty and the possibility that poverty could be prevented. The indiscriminate giving may have increased the number of beggars.

Religious leaders believed that men should deal fairly with one another in the prices they charged, the wages they paid, and the work they did. The taking of interest, called "usury," was forbidden to Christians. This naturally kept Christians from becoming moneylenders. As a result, the business of moneylending was left to non-Christians.

Disobedience to the regulations of the Church might be followed by *excommunication*. The excommunicated person could not attend religious services. By the law of the state he lost all civil rights and forfeited all his property. No one might speak to him, feed him, or shelter him. Such a terrible punishment was usually imposed only after the sinner had been brought to trial and had refused to repent.

Church institutions. Almost the only schools in western Europe during the early Middle Ages were those conducted by the clergy. The main purpose of these schools was to train young men for religious work, but some schools gave an elementary education to boys who were not entering the priesthood. This was especially true after the time of Charlemagne.

In the Middle Ages many cases came before the ecclesiastical (church) courts. Since marriage was a religious rite, the Church decided which marriages were lawful. It refused to sanction the divorce of two persons if both had been baptized Christians at the time of marriage. The Church dealt with inheritance under wills, for a man could not make a will until he had confessed, and confession was a religious rite. All contracts made binding by oaths came under church jurisdiction, since an oath is an appeal to God. The Church tried those who were charged with any sin against religion, including heresy, blasphemy, the taking of interest (usury), and the practice of witchcraft.

The Church and warfare. In general the Church used its influence for peace. It forbade attacks on all defenseless people, including priests, monks, pilgrims, merchants, peasants, and women. It also proclaimed a "Truce of God," which required all men to cease fighting from Wednesday evening to Monday morning of each week, also during Lent, and on various holy days. The truce would have given western Europe peace during about two thirds of the year, but it was never widely observed. The Church did not condemn warfare against heretics and infidels.

The Church and feudalism. The Catholic Church acquired much property through gifts and bequests. In many countries it became the greatest single landholder, with estates attached to church offices. Thus many church officials became feudal vassals holding lands as fiefs from feudal lords, who expected them to give homage before they were invested with their fiefs. (See pages 136–137.) In the ceremony of investiture the lord or the king gave the official not only land but also the symbols of his *religious* office. This situation led to disputes between the papacy and temporal rulers. The popes held that the investiture of religious officials should be conducted by the Church, since a religious official should not be under the control of a temporal lord. On the other hand, the lords believed that so long as churchmen held feudal lands they should be acceptable to and should do homage

to their feudal lords. The investiture question was really one of who would control the selection of church officials.

The investiture struggle. The pope came into conflict with the rulers of several countries over the investiture issue. The most notable conflict was with the Holy Roman emperors. Otto the Great, crowned at Rome in 962, attempted to revive the empire of Charlemagne. Otto's empire was mainly German, but also included northern Italy and several other areas. In theory Otto and his successors were the heirs of Charlemagne, but in practice they had much less power. This did not prevent them from interfering in church affairs, and even at times dictating the selection of popes. Gregory VII, who became pope in 1073, determined to end outside interference in the choice of church officials. He issued an order forbidding the investiture of a churchman by a lay ruler. This began a long conflict between popes and emperors. Henry IV, who was then emperor, had a council of German bishops declare that Gregory was no longer pope; Gregory replied by excommunicating Henry and deposing him. When most of the German nobles rallied to the side of the pope, Henry crossed the Alps in the win-

THE SACRAMENT OF BAPTISM, shown in a fifteenth-century Flemish tapestry. Sacraments marked the high points in the life of almost every person during the Middle Ages.

145

ter of early 1077 to reach the castle at Canossa, where Gregory was staying. One source says Henry stood, barefoot and penitent, for three days in the courtyard of the castle before the pope decided to forgive him. No incident in the Middle Ages gives a more dramatic illustration of the power of the papacy. Actually, nothing was settled at Canossa. Henry did not keep his promises of better behavior. The struggle was renewed, and Gregory was driven from Rome.

Concordat of Worms, 1122. The years of conflict over the investiture question were finally ended in 1122, at a conference in the old German city of Worms. It was agreed that bishops and abbots should be elected by the clergy and confirmed in office by the pope and should receive their symbols of office *only* from church officials. However, they were not to be installed in church positions until the emperor had invested them with

their feudal landholdings. This meant in practice that the emperors would continue to have some voice in the selection of bishops and abbots. Similar agreements were reached in other countries. (See pages 171–172.)

Regular and secular clergy. The church officials whose work has been described thus far were members of the *secular* clergy, so called because they dealt with worldly affairs in their churches. (Secular comes from the Latin *saecula*, "world.") There also arose a second religious group who withdrew from the world to monasteries, where they lived according to fixed rules. They were therefore called the *regular* clergy (from the Latin, *regula*, meaning "rule").

Monks and monasteries. Some early Christians in Egypt became monks, or hermits, and devoted their lives to solitary meditation and prayer. An able monk named Pachomius organized some of these scattered monks into

THE CHRISTIAN AND MOSLEM WORLDS AT THE TIME OF THE CRUSADES

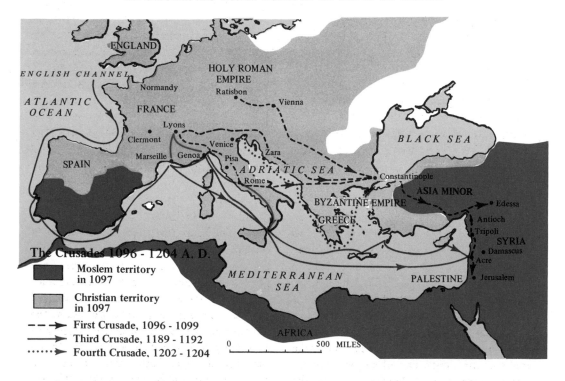

The Crusades 1096 - 1204 A. D.

Moslem territory in 1097
Christian territory in 1097
– – → First Crusade, 1096 - 1099
——→ Third Crusade, 1189 - 1192
······→ Fourth Crusade, 1202 - 1204

0   500 MILES

monasteries. The monks in a monastery spent much of their time in solitude, but co-operated in work and worship. Plans for Christian monasteries were carried from the Eastern Roman Empire to Italy and other parts of the Western Roman Empire at the beginning of the fifth century. In the West the aim of the monks came to be not merely to lead a life of seclusion and prayer, but actively to promote Christianity and spread civilization. St. Benedict became the outstanding figure among the monks of western Europe. He fled from the corrupting pleasures of Roman society and founded several monasteries. The most important one was at Monte Cassino, midway between Rome and Naples; it became the model of monastic life in the West.

Rule of St. Benedict, 529. To control the monks at Monte Cassino, St. Benedict framed a rule, or constitution. An abbot who held office for life presided over the monks. Every candidate for admission took a vow of obedience to the abbot. Any man, rich or poor, noble or peasant, might enter the monastery after a year's probation; having once been admitted to the order, he must remain a monk for the rest of his days. The monks lived under strict discipline. They could not own any personal property, nor leave the monastery without the abbot's consent; they accepted the abbot's allotment of work, food, and clothing. Nuns living in convents followed similar rules.

The monks and medieval civilization. By the careful cultivation of their lands, the monks set an example of good farming wherever they settled. They entertained pilgrims and travelers at a time when western Europe was almost without inns. They performed many works of charity—feeding the hungry, healing the sick who were brought to their doors, and distributing medicines freely to those who needed them. In their schools the monks trained boys who intended to enter the ranks of the clergy, and often gave instruction to others as well. Monks, too, were the

A BENEDICTINE ABBOT

most noted scholars of the age. By copying the manuscripts of classical authors, they preserved valuable books that would otherwise have been lost. The records they kept of the events of their time are the best source we have for medieval history.

The friars. The monks lived somewhat apart from their fellowmen. In order to reach laymen, two new religious orders were formed early in the thirteenth century; their members, called friars ("brothers"), devoted themselves to the salvation of others. One of these orders was founded in Italy by St. Francis of Assisi (1182–1226); the other was founded in Spain by St. Dominic (1170–1221). The Franciscans and Dominicans went on foot from place to place, wearing coarse robes tied around the waist with a rope. They possessed no property and lived on the alms of the charitable. The Franciscans worked especially among the poor in the cities; the Dominicans addressed themselves mainly to educated people and the upper classes. In the later Middle Ages both orders relaxed the rule of poverty and became wealthy. The individual members, however, did not own property. The Franciscan and Dominican orders still survive and carry on teaching and missionary activities.

Organization of the Church. The organization of the secular clergy may be compared to a pyramid, with the pope at the top. Below him were the cardinals, archbishops, bishops, and parish priests. The regular clergy had a similar organization. Below the pope were the heads of the orders of monks, friars, and nuns; next were the abbots and abbesses; and last were the monks and nuns themselves. The officials of the Church, arranged according to their rank, are known as the *hierarchy*.

The Crusades Mark the End of the Early Middle Ages

How the crusades began. By the end of the eleventh century the Seljuk Turks had conquered the Arab holdings in the Middle East. (See pages 116–117.) The fighting spirit of the Turks was heightened by their conversion to Islam, and they pressed into the Byzantine Empire until they threatened Constantinople. The emperor at Constantinople appealed to the pope for help—an indication of the high place the papacy then held in the affairs of Europe. Pope Urban II lent a willing ear and summoned a council of clergy and nobles, which met at Clermont in southern France in 1095. The council enthusiastically declared a holy war against the infidel Moslems and called upon Christian warriors to join in a crusade—a military expedition to recover the Holy Land. Thus began the crusading movement, which lasted for nearly two hundred years and produced seven major crusades.

Why the crusades began. The crusades were begun for a variety of motives. The main reason for the crusading enthusiasm was religion, and the main object of the crusades was the recovery of the Holy Land. Christians had long been accustomed to make journeys, called pilgrimages, to the scenes of Christ's life on earth. Men considered it a wonderful privilege to visit the spot where He was born, to kiss the spot where He died,

DEPARTURE OF KNIGHTS FOR THE CRUSADES. Knights led by nobles made up the most effective fighting forces in the crusades. Here they are gathering outside a castle to begin their long march to the Holy Land.

A CRUSADER ASSAULT on Jerusalem in 1099. This illustration is taken from a history of French crusades written in 1337.

ſ ſ r̄ei poͤint nͤre ſ̄emt. Se ne fuſt la delou

and to kneel in prayer at His tomb. The Arabs had not interfered with the stream of pilgrims from Europe, but after the Turks took Jerusalem (1071) reports came back of outrages committed by the Turks against the pilgrims and against Christian shrines. The crusaders, therefore, undertook to free the Holy Land from Moslem control. The Church promised to remove the penances it had imposed upon sinners if they went on a crusade. But religion was not the only force behind the crusades. The warlike nobles recognized an unequaled opportunity for acquiring fame, riches, lands, and power. The hope of reward in this world and the next caused thousands of men to start out on the greatest military enterprise of the Middle Ages.

Course of the crusades, 1096–1291. The first crusade got under way in 1096, the year after the Council of Clermont. In spite of great difficulties, the crusaders succeeded in capturing Jerusalem and setting up several small states in Syria known as the Crusaders' States. These possessions were defended by two orders of fighting monks, the Hospitalers and the Templars. The Christians managed to keep Jerusalem for nearly ninety years. An able leader named Saladin united the Moslem forces and recaptured the city in 1187. Of the later crusades which set out to free the Holy Land, none was successful. Perhaps the most famous crusader was Richard the Lion-Hearted, king of England, who became known for his valor in battles against Saladin. Unable to take Jerusalem, Richard reached an agreement with Saladin which permitted Christians to visit the city. During the next hundred years the Christians continued to lose ground. Acre, the last Christian post in Syria, fell to the Moslems in 1291. This event is commonly regarded as the end of the crusades.

Effects of crusades—on feudalism. The crusades, judged by what they set out to accomplish, must be accounted a failure. After two

A RICH VENETIAN MERCHANT awaits the arrival of a convoy of ships. As late as the eighteenth century Venice still carried on an active trade with the Orient. The engraving shown here was published in 1685.

centuries of conflict, and after a great expenditure of lives and wealth, the Holy Land remained in Moslem hands. The indirect results of the crusades were, nevertheless, important. First of all, they helped to undermine feudalism. Thousands of nobles mortgaged or sold their lands in order to raise money for crusading expeditions. Thousands more perished in Syria. If they died without heirs, their estates went back to the Crown. Thus the kings grew stronger, while the noble class became weaker. Moreover, private warfare, that curse of the Middle Ages, also tended to diminish with the departure for the Holy Land of so many unruly lords.

Effects of crusades—on commerce. The crusades also stimulated commerce. Shipowners profited by carrying crusaders and their supplies. When the crusaders arrived in eastern lands they longed to possess the silks, tapestries, precious stones, perfumes, spices, pearls, and ivory that they saw there. One enthusiastic crusader found the Orient so enchanting that he called it "the vestibule of Paradise."

EFFECTS of the CRUSADES {

Weakening of the nobles
which led to { Decline of feudalism
and
Rise of national states

Increase of trade
which led to { Growth of cities
and
Search for new
trade routes
which led to { Discovery of America

Greater knowledge
and
Spread of new ideas
which led to { Growth of universities
The Renaissance
The Reformation

When the crusaders returned home they brought with them eastern luxuries. Soon a lively trade grew up between Europe and the East. The products of Damascus, Alexandria, Cairo, and other cities were shipped across the Mediterranean to the Italian seaports, from which merchants carried them into all European lands.

Effects of crusades—on culture. The crusades also contributed to intellectual and social progress. They brought the inhabitants of western Europe into closer touch with one another, with their fellow Christians of the Byzantine Empire, and with other peoples of the Middle East. The meeting of Christians and Moslems gave most benefit to the Chris-

tians, because the Middle East at this time surpassed western Europe in civilization. The crusaders went out to see great cities, marble palaces, superb costumes, and people of elegant tastes and manners. They returned with many new ideas.

Beginning of a new era. As the preceding paragraphs indicate, the crusades helped bring great changes to western Europe— changes which eventually revolutionized the civilization there. Not all of these changes can be directly traced to the crusades, but the crusades were probably the most important immediate cause. The crusades may, therefore, be considered as marking the start of a new era, that of the later Middle Ages.

REVIEWING THE CHAPTER

TERMS TO UNDERSTAND: *Middle Ages, Dark Age, Kaaba, Moslem, Islam, Hegira, Koran, caliph, Northmen, Magyars, vassal, fief, homage, investiture, manor, joust, tournament, chivalry, serf, sacrament, Truce of God, usury, excommunication, friar, Seljuk Turks.*

PERSONS TO IDENTIFY: *Mohammed, Charles Martel, Harun al-Rashid, Charlemagne, Alfred the Great, Eric the Red, Leif Ericsson, William the Conqueror, Rurik, Gregory the Great, Henry IV, St. Benedict, Saladin, Richard the Lion-Hearted.*

PLACES TO LOCATE: *Arabia, Mecca, Medina, Tours, Baghdad, the Spanish March, Iceland, Greenland, Normandy, Novgorod, Worms, Acre.*

QUESTIONS TO ANSWER

1. (a) Why was the Byzantine Empire so called? How long did it continue? (b) What features of civilization were preserved by the Byzantine Empire?
2. Trace the beginnings of the Mohammedan faith. What are its main teachings?
3. (a) What regions were conquered by the Moslem Arabs? (b) Of what significance is

the Battle of Tours? (c) Describe Arabic culture. List several Arabic contributions to civilization.
4. (a) Why has Charlemagne been called the "hero of the Middle Ages"? (b) Indicate the extent of his empire. (c) Why did it fall apart?
5. Compare the work of Alfred the Great with that of Charlemagne.
6. "The Northmen laid the foundations of at least four modern European countries." Show specifically what this statement means.
7. (a) Why did the system of feudalism arise? (b) Describe the military, social, political, and economic organization of feudal society. What were the mutual obligations of lord and vassal?
8. (a) Compare the life of the feudal noble with that of the serf. (b) How did serfdom differ from slavery?
9. (a) Give reasons for the importance of the Roman Catholic Church during the Middle Ages. (b) Explain the organization of the secular clergy and the regular clergy. Describe the activities of each group.
10. (a) Why were the crusades begun? (b) Show their influence upon feudalism, commerce, and culture in western Europe.

10 Europe in the Later Middle Ages

As we have seen, the early Middle Ages was a period in which civilization declined in most parts of Europe. However, civilization continued to flourish in Spain and in the Eastern Roman Empire. During the later Middle Ages, about 1100 to 1500, civilization gradually reawakened in western Europe. More than any other single factor, the crusades, from 1096 to 1291, helped to shake western Europe out of its stagnation and to begin the transition to modern times. In the later Middle Ages changes appeared in many fields. Trade was increasing, cities were growing, serfdom was declining, kings were building national states, national languages were emerging, learning was increasing, and progress was being made in science, invention, and architecture. These changes, although slow and gradual, were significant. They brought new ways of thinking and acting which mingled with ancient traditions to produce modern civilization.

The Revival of Trade

The Italian cities. In the early Middle Ages, Moslem merchants controlled most of the trade in the Mediterranean. The Egyptian city of Alexandria was the chief trading center; it thrived at the time when trade had nearly disappeared in western and central Europe. In the same period the raids of the Northmen were interfering seriously with commerce in northern Europe. The first signs of a revival of European trade appeared in Italy. Some Italian city-states had enjoyed an increase of trade by the year 1000, and this trend was speeded up by the crusades. Ships were built to carry the crusaders and their equipment to and from the Middle East. Returning crusaders came back with a desire to own the silks, jewels, spices, fine weapons, and other luxuries they had seen. In meeting this demand Italian cities such as Venice, Genoa, and Pisa built up a thriving trade with both the Eastern Roman Empire and the Islamic lands. Italian merchants brought the luxuries of the Middle East back to Italy. From there traders carried them north. By the year 1200, goods from the Middle East had found their way into most European communities. This trade, and the development of other industries in Italy, brought great prosperity to the Italian cities.

A VIEW OF VENICE IN 1338. This city of many canals was built on islands and wooden piles driven into mud. By the thirteenth century Venetian merchants had made their city prosperous.

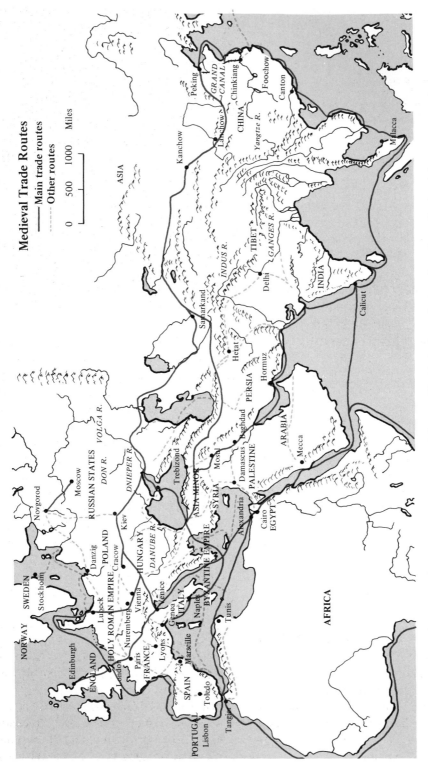

Medieval Trade Routes

—— Main trade routes
----- Other routes

0   500   1000   Miles

ASIA

Peking
Kanchow
Lanchow
Chinkiang
Foochow
CHINA
Canton
Yangtze R.
GRAND CANAL
Malacca
Samarkand
TIBET
INDUS R.
GANGES R.
Delhi
INDIA
Calicut
Herat
Hormuz
PERSIA
Baghdad
Mosul
ARABIA
Damascus
SYRIA
PALESTINE
Mecca
Trebizond
ASIA MINOR
Alexandria
Cairo
EGYPT
VOLGA R.
DON R.
Moscow
RUSSIAN STATES
DNIEPER R.
Novgorod
Kiev
DANUBE R.
Cracow
Danzig
POLAND
HUNGARY
Vienna
Venice
Genoa
ITALY
Naples
BYZANTINE EMPIRE
Tunis
Stockholm
SWEDEN
NORWAY
Lubeck
Nuremberg
HOLY ROMAN EMPIRE
Paris
FRANCE
Lyons
Marseille
London
ENGLAND
Edinburgh
SPAIN
Toledo
PORTUGAL
Lisbon
Tangier
AFRICA

BOTH EUROPEANS AND ASIATICS carried on considerable foreign trade throughout the medieval period.

PEASANTS PAYING TOLL FOR PASSING OVER A BRIDGE.
The practice of feudal lords in charging for the use of
bridges, roads, and fords on their estates greatly
hampered medieval trade and commerce.

The Hanseatic League. The Northmen returned home from their raids with many articles they had captured. Some of these goods they sold. From this beginning many of the Northmen became merchants, and they began to revive the trade they had helped destroy in the earlier raids. They developed a network of water routes that brought Middle Eastern goods across Russia to northern Europe. The expansion of trade encouraged the growth of cities as commercial and manufacturing centers. Many cities joined the Hanseatic League for mutual trade and protection. They kept their independence but co-operated in business and diplomatic affairs. The Hanseatic League was largely a German organization, but it also came to include cities in Russia, Scandinavia, Poland, Belgium, the Netherlands, France, and England. Trade between the member cities became very active and began to move over land as well as sea. Goods were brought by boat and by pack horse from Italy. Every year the Venetians sent a fleet loaded with Eastern products to be sold in the north. Manufacture, especially of cloth, began to flourish in many northern cities, especially those of Flanders. The Hanseatic League was at the height of its power in the fourteenth century.

Difficulties of commerce. A merchant who went by land from country to country found bad roads, few bridges, and poor inns. He transported his goods on pack horses instead of in wagons. Highway robbery was so common that travelers always carried arms and usually united in bands for better protection. The feudal lords, many of whom were not much better than highwaymen, demanded tolls at every bridge and ford and on every road. If the merchant proceeded by water, he had to face the danger of attacks by pirates, in addition to the hazards of storm and shipwreck.

Markets. Nearly every town of any size held a market, usually once a week, in the market place or in the churchyard. Market day was usually Sunday. Outsiders who brought cattle or produce for sale had to pay tolls to the nobleman who ruled the town, or to the town officers if it had bought its freedom from the overlord.

Medieval fairs. Many towns held fairs once or twice a year; they often lasted for a month or more. Merchants from distant places came to the fairs, bringing both goods and news from the outside world. A fair at an English town might attract Venetians with silk, pepper, and other spices from the East, Flemings with fine cloth, Spaniards with ironware and wine, Norwegians with tar and pitch from their forests, and Baltic merchants with furs, amber, and salted fish. Fairs had become common by 1200, and for a long time thereafter they were an important means of bringing buyers and sellers together. Their importance declined toward the end of the Middle Ages, especially in the cities, for city merchants began to have stocks of goods for sale the year around.

Revival of Cities

Origin of medieval cities. The cities which grew up in the later Middle Ages owed their prosperity to a favorable location for trade. They began as villages located at a road intersection, on a good harbor, or at a place where a river could be forded. In such a place merchants and craftsmen might settle permanently. Because there were jobs to be had, the population would grow. Some cities grew up on the sites of old Roman cities; some developed around cathedrals; some started as feudal fortresses.

A serf who ran away to a city and lived there for a year and a day became a freeman and could no longer be claimed by his lord. The chance to win freedom naturally attracted many runaway serfs. Freemen also came to the cities. The life of city workers was a hard one by modern standards, but it was easier than that of workers in the country and offered more variety and excitement. We do not have accurate figures to show the growth of cities in the later Middle Ages. However, we know that many cities outgrew their old bounds, for suburbs began to spring up outside the protection of the city walls. The growth of medieval cities came mainly after 1200.

A city from without. The visitor approaching a medieval city saw it clear in the sunlight, unobscured by coal smoke. It looked like a fortress from without, with walls, towers, gateways, drawbridges, and perhaps a moat. Beyond the walls he would see the spires of the churches and the roofs of public buildings and the larger houses. The general impression was of wealth, strength, and beauty.

A city from within. The visitor would not find things so attractive within the walls. The streets were narrow, crooked, and ill paved, dark during the day because of the overhanging houses, and unlighted at night. There were no open spaces or parks except a small

NUREMBERG IN THE LATE MIDDLE AGES. Note the strong wall with its close-spaced towers and the surrounding moat. This picture appeared in a book published in 1493.

market place. However, there were green fields and farmlands just outside the city walls. People hesitated to live in suburbs because they needed the protection of the city walls. Medieval London, for instance, covered an area of less than one square mile. The only water supply in a medieval city came from polluted streams and wells. Sewers and sidewalks were unknown. People threw refuse in the back yard or flung it into the street, where it was devoured by dogs and pigs. The living were crowded into houses several stories high, in which there was little air or light. The dead were buried close at hand in churchyards and in vaults under churches. Disease spread rapidly because of the unsanitary conditions, and the death rate always exceeded the birth rate. City populations would have declined quickly if people had stopped moving in from the country.

Buildings in the city. The inhabitants of the city took a just pride in the public buildings. The market place often contained a beautiful cross or shrine protected from the weather, and sometimes a market hall to shelter goods. Not far away stood the city hall, used for the transaction of public business and the holding of civic feasts. The hall might be crowned by a high belfry with an alarm bell. There were also handsome churches and abbeys and, if the city were the residence of a bishop, there would be an imposing cathedral. The cathedrals of the later Middle Ages were strikingly beautiful. All the people of the city contributed labor and money to build a cathedral. Sometimes the building and decoration of a cathedral extended over several centuries.

Merchant guilds. Men in medieval cities frequently joined together in guilds. A guild was an association of persons engaged in the same kind of work. The two most important kinds were the *merchant guild* and the *craft guild*.

The chief aim of a merchant guild was to keep for its own members a monopoly of trade within the town. The guild taxed all merchants who came there from outside the town and made rules for them to follow. Other rules were established for the guidance of guild members. It was required that goods meet certain standards of quality and sell for a certain price. The idea prevailed that goods

MEDIEVAL GUILDHALLS IN GHENT. The guilds in the leading cities of Europe during the Middle Ages became wealthy and powerful. Each guild had its own hall where it held its meetings.

should be sold at their "just price," which was not determined by supply and demand but by the cost of making the item. The "just price" was fixed by town laws as well as guild rulings, but it was not always observed.

Craft guilds. Skilled workmen (artisans) also joined together to form craft guilds. There were guilds of weavers, shoemakers, brewers, bakers, tailors, carpenters, blacksmiths, and other artisans. The members of a particular craft guild usually lived in the same street or quarter of a city. They marched together in parades, attended the same church, and contributed money for the aid of fellow members who were in distress. Like the merchants, they set up rules for the conduct of their affairs, so that products and prices would be uniform. Nearly everything made by a guild member was carefully inspected to see if it contained cheap materials or showed poor workmanship. If the products of a guild member failed to pass inspection, he was fined or perhaps expelled from the guild, in which case he could no longer stay in business. The monopoly possessed by the craft guild thus gave some protection to both producer and consumer.

Three levels of membership. Full membership in a guild was reached only by degrees. A boy started as an *apprentice,* or learner. He paid a sum of money to his master and agreed to work for him for a fixed period, usually seven years. The master in turn promised to provide the apprentice with food, lodging, and clothing, and to teach him all the secrets of the craft. The apprentice had to pass an examination by the guild at the end of his term of service. He would show his skill by submitting an article he had made. If he were found fit, he then became a *journeyman* and worked for daily wages. A journeyman who saved enough money could set up as a *master* in his own shop, where he would work with his own apprentices and journeymen. A master was at once workman and employer, laborer and businessman.

Rise of the middle class. In the later Middle Ages there was an increase in the number of people who belonged to the middle class. Persons such as merchants, skilled workers, and professional people, whose income is obtained from their own efforts plus investments in property or in training, are members of the middle class. Their numbers had declined during the early Middle Ages, but the revival of trade and manufacturing stimulated the growth of the middle class. The merchants were the most influential members of this group. Some of them accumulated fortunes and became the advisers of kings. A few kings permitted members of the middle class to enjoy a privilege formerly reserved for representatives of the clergy and nobles: they could sit in assemblies (parliaments) and help make the laws.

The city and feudalism. The city was at first a part of the feudal system. It grew up on the territory of a lord and its people owed obedience to him. The citizens enjoyed no political rights, for the lord collected the taxes, appointed officials, made laws, and punished offenders. As the city grew more populous and wealthy, many inhabitants began to demand the right to govern themselves in local matters. Sometimes they won their freedom by hard fighting; sometimes a king rewarded them with freedom for helping him subdue a noble; often they purchased their self-government, perhaps from some noble who needed money to go on a crusade. By the end of the Middle Ages the larger cities in western Europe had been freed of feudal restrictions.

Rise of National States

During the early Middle Ages most of the kings in western Europe had little power. After the time of Charlemagne the principal feudal lords had as much power as the king. Each lord was absolute in his own territory. He made laws and treaties, coined money, regulated trade, and often acted as though the king did not exist. A king became little more than a feudal lord. A king had no income and no soldiers except those he obtained from his own fiefs.

Why national states began. In the later Middle Ages the kings gained more power. Some of the reasons for an increase in royal power were: (1) The aid given by the cities to the king in his struggles with the feudal lords. The merchants preferred the rule of the king because he could help them in many ways. He could give them a single coinage system, protection against robbers and pirates, a single system of laws and courts, improved roads and bridges, and relief from the constant wars and taxes of the feudal nobles. (2) The new interest in Roman law, which emphasized the supremacy of the central government. (3) The growth of national languages in place of local dialects. People who spoke the same language had a feeling of belonging together and were more willing to be united under a single ruler. (4) The influence of the crusades in weakening the nobility. As a rule the nobles who went on the crusades were the more warlike and aggressive ones. Many a noble granted freedom to the towns on his fief in order to raise money for his journey to the Holy Land; thereby his power and future revenues were decreased. A large number of nobles did not return from the crusades; those who returned were weaker and more easily overcome by the kings. (5) The use of gunpowder, which came into common use in the 1400's. A king could arm peasants with guns whose bullets would penetrate a knight's armor and could thus form an army capable of defeating feudal forces. Royal armies also used cannon, with which they could batter down the castle walls of rebellious nobles. (6) The growing use of money. When taxes could be paid in money rather than in goods, central government became practicable. For these reasons, among others, the later Middle Ages was a period in which kings became rulers of national states. This was particularly true in western Europe.

Strong kings develop in England. England was the first country to emerge as a united nation. After William the Conqueror's victory in 1066 (see page 134), he gave English lands to his followers on the condition that they accept him as their ruler. He and his successors were able men, who laid the foundations of a strong central government in England. They also succeeded in enlarging their dominions. They annexed Wales in 1284, and conquered an area around Dublin in eastern Ireland. Their attempts to conquer Scotland and the rest of Ireland failed. The English kings made their greatest gains in France, through marriage and inheritance. Henry II (1154–1189), William the Conqueror's great-grandson, ruled all of western France from Flanders to Spain. His possessions in France were actually larger than those of the king of France. During the reign of King John, Henry's son, some of this territory was lost to the French king. All the rest, with the exception of Calais, was lost to the French in the Hundred Years' War (1337–1453). After this the English kings could concentrate on governing England. The central government thereupon strengthened its control over the nobles.

Beginning England's legal system. Henry II reorganized the court system of England. He issued orders which mark the origin of the system of trial by jury. He also sent judges on regular trips, or circuits, through England. The judges were expected to judge cases according to local custom, but they often ignored the variations of custom which had grown up in different localities. They developed a body of legal principles which applied throughout England. Thus England gradually acquired a national legal system. The decisions of the royal judges became the basis of the English *common law,* which is used today in the United States (except Louisiana) and in all other English-speaking countries. We have also inherited the use of circuit courts and jury trials.

Magna Carta. Some of the English kings made public promises to respect certain rights of the people. The most famous of these promises was signed by King John. His actions as king had made him feared and hated by many Englishmen. Nobles and church leaders opposed him, and for once the cities sided with the nobles; at one time John had only seven knights to support him and oppose his aroused subjects. The leading nobles met with King John at Runnymede in 1215 and

ENGLAND AT TIME OF ALFRED THE GREAT (871–901)

DOMINIONS OF WILLIAM THE CONQUEROR IN 1087

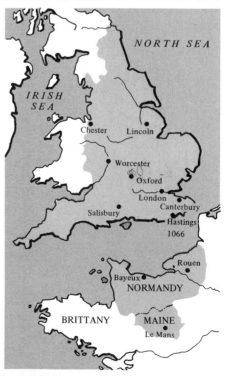

ENGLAND AND FRANCE IN THE REIGN
OF HENRY II (1154–1189)

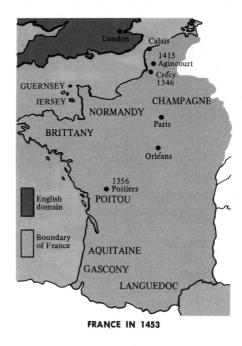

FRANCE IN 1453

forced him to sign the Great Charter (Magna Carta)—a series of written promises. He promised, among other things, that henceforth no one might be arrested, imprisoned, or punished in any way except after a trial by his equals (peers) and in accordance with the law of the land. Furthermore, the king could levy new taxes only with the consent of the Great Council, a group of nobles and church officials. Magna Carta contained legal principles upon which Englishmen ever afterward relied for protection against their rulers. It is one of the most famous documents in history.

Beginning of Parliament. The Great Council mentioned in Magna Carta was made up of nobles and church officials who met to advise the king. We would not call this system democratic, since the common people were not represented in the council. But in the reign of King John's son, Henry III, the practice began of having in the council men from the middle, or business, class. Later,

these men met separately in the House of Commons, while the nobles and church officials met in the House of Lords. The two houses together became known as *Parliament*. One of its most important powers, the control of taxes, was based on Magna Carta.

Beginning the unification of France. In the tenth century the old line of French kings who had descended from Charlemagne died out. In 987 a nobleman named Hugh Capet (kā′pĕt) founded a new dynasty. The Capetian line extended unbroken for more than three centuries and produced a remarkably able series of kings. They worked steadily to unite France into a real nation under a central government. This policy brought them into conflict with England, since much of France was ruled by the English king. The long struggle between France and England is known as the Hundred Years' War.

The Hundred Years' War, 1337–1453. An immediate cause of the Hundred Years' War was French aid to Scotland during her strug-

COLUMBUS BIDS FAREWELL TO FERDINAND AND ISABELLA. The place was Palos, a seaport on the southwest coast of Spain. The date was August 3, 1492.

gles with England. By weakening England in this and other ways, the French king hoped to be able to drive the English out of France. In 1337, Philip VI declared war on England and sent a fleet to attack the English coast. Edward III of England then put forth a claim to the French throne and led an army to France. The long contest that followed was not one of constant fighting; rather, it was marked by several battles with long periods of quiet between them. At first the English won, partly because of the English archers' skill with the longbow, and partly because the French knights refused to cooperate with their own common soldiers. At Crécy in 1346, Poitiers in 1356, and Agincourt in 1415, the English won decisive victories over large French armies. In 1429, just as the English were on the verge of seizing all of France, Joan of Arc appeared on the scene and was made leader of a French army. Clad in armor and wearing an ancient sword said to have been wielded by Charles Martel at the Battle of Tours, the young "Maid of Orleans" brought new spirit to the French. After

winning a series of victories, Joan was captured by the English and in 1431 was burned as a witch. Her patriotism and selflessness encouraged the French to greater effort. Their superior numbers and resources enabled them to advance steadily. By 1453 they had regained all the English holdings except Calais (a city just across the Channel from England).

Power of the French kings. After the Hundred Years' War the French king had great power, and he and his successors worked to increase the royal power. In the last half of the fifteenth century, the nobles who still dared to oppose the king were defeated. The king of France made laws, collected taxes, and acted as the sole ruler of the country. Kings who rule in this way are called *autocrats*. For the next three hundred years most of the French kings were autocrats—their powers were not limited until the French Revolution in 1789.

The unification of Spain. The Visigoths founded a Germanic kingdom in Spain after Roman rule collapsed. (See page 101.) Ger-

162   DECLINE AND REVIVAL

man rule lasted until Spain was invaded by the Moors. The Moors, who were Mohammedans, crossed over from North Africa in 711. They conquered most of Spain and established a civilization higher than any existing in western Europe at that time. The Moors revived commerce and manufacturing, erected beautiful buildings, and established universities which became famous. The Moors never wholly conquered a fringe of mountain territory in the extreme north of Spain. Here arose several Christian states, including Castile, Navarre, and Aragon. These states, beginning about the eleventh century, carried on a long series of wars which pushed the Moors back toward the Mediterranean. By the end of the thirteenth century the Moors held only Granada, a small kingdom along the southern coast of Spain. Meanwhile, the separate states were merging. They were virtually united in 1469 by the marriage of Ferdinand of Aragon and Isabella of Castile. In 1492 Ferdinand and Isabella captured Granada, thus ending Moorish rule in Spain. They could now afford to develop and support trade and exploration.

Autocracy in Spain. Ferdinand and Isabella established autocratic government in Spain. They and their successors ruled without any help from a parliament. They even gained the power to nominate the higher church officials in Spain. When gold from America began to pour into Spain in the early 1500's, the Spanish kings became the most powerful and wealthy rulers in Europe.

Other national states arise. Portugal first became a separate state in 1095, when the king of Castile gave some of his western territory to a nobleman who had helped him against the Moors. During the next century and a half Portugal was enlarged with territory taken from the Moors; by 1250 Portugal had reached its present boundaries. The kings of Portugal were strong and independent in the later Middle Ages, but afterward (1580–1640) Portugal was joined for a time to Spain.

During the later Middle Ages other autocratic kings rose to power in Austria and Scandinavia. In Poland and Scotland the power of the kings was more limited, though national states were formed. Thus in countries throughout western Europe national governments overcame the power of feudal lords. All classes—nobles, clergy, city folk, and peasants—began to think of themselves as belonging to one people and to develop a sense of loyalty to the entire nation. Germany and Italy were the most notable exceptions to this trend toward unity, for they did not become united until 1871.

Decline of Serfdom

Effects of the growth of trade. By helping the growth of cities, the revival of trade and commerce helped to bring about the decline of serfdom. The growth of the cities created a market where the serfs could sell their surplus farm produce for cash. This enabled many of them to pay a cash rent for their land and thus secure freedom from the old personal services to the lord. Both parties gained by the arrangement. The lord could hire labor which was more efficient than forced labor, and the serf could devote himself to the cultivation of his own holding instead of spending part of each week working on his lord's land. Some of the serfs added to their income by spinning, weaving, and other crafts.

The Black Death and serfdom. About the middle of the fourteenth century the decline of serfdom was hastened by the coming of the Black Death—an epidemic of bubonic plague which spread from Asia into Europe. The Black Death moved through the unsanitary towns and villages of Greece, Sicily, Italy, Spain, France, and Germany. It entered England in 1349. Within two years almost half the population of England was swept away. Crops rotted in the fields for want of hands to bring in the harvest; sheep and cattle, with no one to care for them, wandered through the countryside. The free peasants who survived demanded and received higher wages. The serfs were also helped by the shortage of labor, for they were able to demand better treatment by the landowners. Some of the serfs left their homes to seek work as hired laborers; many of those who remained were allowed to substitute money payments for personal services.

The decline of serfdom continues. The decline of serfdom continued throughout the 1300's and 1400's. By the end of the Middle Ages it had virtually disappeared in England and Italy and from many communities in France and western Germany. Serfdom lasted longest in eastern Europe. Prussian, Austrian, and Russian serfs did not secure freedom until the nineteenth century.

National Languages and Literatures

Latin as an international language. Latin was the international language of Europe throughout the Middle Ages. The Roman Catholic Church used it for papal bulls and other documents, and for church services. It was also the language of men of culture outside the Church. University professors lectured in Latin, students spoke Latin, and merchants used Latin in letters sent abroad. All learned books were composed in Latin until the close of the 1500's.

Two groups of national languages. During the Middle Ages the common people of Europe spoke a great variety of local dialects. The growth of trade and the rise of national states tended to develop in each country a national language. There are two main groups of these languages. The *Romance* languages (French, Italian, Spanish, Portuguese, and Rumanian) were derived from the Latin speech of the Roman Empire. In northern Europe the common people continued to use *Germanic* (*Teutonic*) tongues during the Middle Ages. Thus arose modern German,

Dutch, Flemish, Danish, Norwegian, Swedish, and Icelandic.

The English language. The English language occupies a position midway between the Romance and Germanic languages. Although Anglo-Saxon, or Old English, was originally a Germanic tongue, it was altered greatly after the Anglo-Saxons settled in England. They borrowed Latin words from British town-dwellers who had been Romanized, and Scandinavian words from the Danish invaders. Christian missionaries introduced Latin religious terms. Norman-French influence after 1066 resulted in the addition of a large number of French words, which of course were derived from Latin. By this time English grammar had been considerably simplified. About 1550 our language had reached the stage of development known as "Modern English

Songs of the troubadours. As the new national languages developed, new national literatures also arose. A pleasant glimpse of gay society in the twelfth to the fourteenth centuries is given in the songs of the troubadours. The troubadours were poets who journeyed from castle to castle in the south of France and in northern Spain and Italy. Many of them belonged to the nobility. They sang the verses they composed to the accompaniment of a musical instrument, usually the lute. The two themes most often used by the troubadours were love and brave deeds of chivalry. The songs of the troubadours influenced poets in other countries. In Germany the minnesingers used the same themes and, like the troubadours, traveled through the country.

National epics. Many long narrative poems (epics) appeared during the Middle Ages. Recited or sung from memory, they told of the exploits of mythical heroes or historic kings. *Beowulf* was written in Old English about the year 1000. Many French epics dealt with Charlemagne and his reign. The oldest and finest is the *Song of Roland,* written before the first crusade. It tells how Roland, one of Charlemagne's mighty warriors, fought against the Moors in Spain and died defending a pass in the Pyrenees so that Charlemagne might get through safely. The greatest epic composed in Germany during the Middle Ages was the *Nibelungenlied* ("Song of the Nibelungs"). It centers about the hero Siegfried, a legendary figure who is also mentioned in early Anglo-Saxon and Icelandic poems. It was written down about the year 1200.

King Arthur and his Knights of the Round Table were also important figures in medieval legend. Using the *romance,* a form of epic, medieval poets portrayed Arthur as the model knight, the ideal of noble chivalry. Sir Thomas Malory's *Morte d'Arthur,* one of the first books to be printed in England, contains many stories about Arthur. French versions of the Arthurian romances spread to Germany, where they inspired the epics *Tristan* and *Parsifal.* It is doubtful that Arthur ever lived; but if he did, he was probably a chieftain, not a king, who fought the Saxon invaders in southern Britain during the sixth century.

Ballads and fables. Ballads are narrative songs. They were especially popular among the country people. Some of the best-known old English ballads tell of Robin Hood, who led an adventurous life with his merry men in Sherwood Forest. He helped the weak

against the strong and robbed the rich to give to the poor. Fables, usually in verse, were much enjoyed by city folk. Often humorous, the fables tell how some important person was tricked, or relate an incident from everyday life to point up a moral. The characters in fables are often animals which speak and conduct themselves like human beings.

Chaucer and Dante. Two great writers in the later Middle Ages helped to establish their national languages. One of these was the English poet, Geoffrey Chaucer (1340–1400). His best-known work is the *Canterbury Tales,* a collection of stories told by a group of pilgrims as they traveled from London to the town of Canterbury. Chaucer wrote in the dialect used by Londoners, from which Modern English has developed. The other writer was

CHAUCER

DANTE

the Italian poet Dante (1265-1321). Dante's *Divine Comedy* describes an imaginary visit to Hell, Purgatory, and Paradise, and tells of his conversations with famous people of the past. The *Divine Comedy* is one of the finest literary works of all time. Dante wrote in the dialect used by the people of Florence. Largely through his influence Florentine became the national Italian language.

Customs and Manners

Popular beliefs. People in the Middle Ages had many superstitions. Various plants and minerals were credited with marvelous powers; for example, the sapphire, when powdered and mixed with milk, was supposed to heal ulcers and cure headaches. Magicians made charms, or lucky objects, and mixed powders which were supposed to inspire hatred or affection in the person taking them. Many days were regarded as unlucky, and various happenings were thought to foretell good luck or bad. Of all the superstitions of the time, the belief in witches was perhaps the most harmful. Witches were thought to have sold themselves to the Devil, receiving in return the power to work magic. At night they rode on broomsticks through the air and assembled in some lonely place for feasts, dances, and wild revels. There were various tests for the discovery of witches, the most usual being the ordeal by cold water. Thousands of innocent persons were put to death on the charge of being witches.

Games. It is pleasant to turn from the superstitions of the Middle Ages to the games, sports, and festivals which helped to brighten life for rich and poor. Some indoor games were of Eastern origin. Chess, for instance, arose in India as a war game. It was changed somewhat in Europe, and became one of the chief pastimes within the castles of the lords. Playing cards are another Oriental invention. They were probably introduced into Europe by Arabs or returning crusaders.

Many of our outdoor sports are derived from those played in medieval times. Modern football evolved from a sport in which each side tried to secure the ball and throw it over the goal line of the opposing side. The Persian game of polo, in which a man on horseback struck at a ball with a long mallet, spread to Europe and gave rise to the various games in which balls are hit with bats, including tennis, hockey, golf, baseball, and croquet. A common outdoor sport of the nobles was hunting. Deer, bears, and wild boars were hunted with spears and hounds; trained hawks, called falcons, were used for hunting smaller animals. Bearbaiting and cockfighting were popular.

Festivals. Many festivals of medieval times began as pagan celebrations. April Fool's Day was a relic of the festivities which celebrated the approach of spring. May Day was another ancient spring festival. The persons who acted as May kings and May queens represented the spirits of trees and of the budding vegetation. The lively Morris dance was especially associated with May Day and was often danced around a Maypole. On June 23, which marked the beginning of summer,

ORDEAL BY COLD WATER. This form of ordeal rested on the old belief that pure water would reject an impure person. Anyone accused of witchcraft might therefore be thrown bound into a stream. If he floated he was guilty; if he sank he was innocent and had to be rescued.

MEDIEVAL MUMMERS OF NUREMBERG. Farmers and villagers, wearing masks and outlandish costumes, produced crude plays and serenaded on holidays. Often they made fun of serious or even sacred subjects.

came the fire festival. People gathered in the evening to build fires and leap over them, to walk in procession with torches around the fields, and to roll burning wheels down the hillsides. Some of these ceremonies had begun with the sun worshipers of New Stone Age times.

Hallow Eve, so called from being the eve of All Saints' Day (November 1), is also a survival of a heathen celebration. Witches, fairies, and ghosts were supposed to assemble on this night. The festival of Christmas had some heathen features, such as the use of mistletoe, with which the Celtic priests once decked the altars of their gods. It is believed that the Christmas tree dates from the eighth century, when Boniface, an English missionary in Germany, adorned a fir tree in honor of the Christ child. Mumming had a particular association with Christmas. Mummers were bands of men and women who disguised themselves in masks and skins of animals and then serenaded the people outside their houses. The mummers often performed

little plays about Father Christmas, Old King Cole, and St. George.

The drama. Plays of a religious character were popular in the twelfth and thirteenth centuries. In England, France, and Germany the earliest were the *mystery* and *miracle plays*. These were dramatized scenes from the Bible and stories of the saints or martyrs, and were spoken in the language of the common people. At first the actors were priests, and the stage was the church itself or the churchyard. The religious setting did not prevent the introduction of clowns and buffoons. After a time the performance of mystery and miracle plays was taken over by the guilds. Singly or together the guilds of a town presented an annual exhibition. The exhibition might last for several days and have as many as fifty scenes, beginning with Creation and ending with Doomsday. *Morality plays* likewise began in the churches. The morality plays dealt with the struggle between good and evil, rather than with religious history. Characters such as Charity,

Faith, Prudence, Riches, Confession, and Death appeared and enacted a story intended to teach a moral lesson. The mystery, miracle, and morality plays helped prepare the way for the development of the modern drama.

Houses. As feudalism declined in the later Middle Ages, many huge and uncomfortable castles were either torn down or made over into country houses. Though less bare and inconvenient than castles, they were still poorly lighted, ill ventilated, and in winter scarcely warmed by the open wood fires. They became more comfortable when glass windows were substituted for wooden shutters or oiled paper, and when chimneys were introduced. In the cities wealthy people began to build large and often beautiful residences. The workers continued to dwell in dark, unsanitary houses. Country workers lived in cottages, usually with but one room, one small window, and no chimney.

Furniture. People in the Middle Ages, even the well to do, got along with little furniture. The great hall of a manor house contained a long dining table, with benches used at meals, and a few stools. The family beds were often placed in curtained recesses in the walls. Guests might have to sleep on the floor of the hall. Servants often slept in stables. The floors were strewn with rushes, for only the wealthy could afford rugs. Chests were used for storing clothes and household fabrics. Utensils were few, and articles of glass and silver practically unknown except in the houses of the very rich.

Costume. The pictures in old manuscripts give us a good idea of medieval dress. It varied according to time, place, and the social position of the wearer. Men did not begin to wear trousers until after the Middle Ages. The usual dress of the peasant was a single woolen garment, reaching to the knees and gathered at the waist with a belt or rope. The peasant seldom had shoes or underclothing. The upper classes wore clothing of a more expensive kind, and enjoyed the luxury of undergarments, stockings, and shoes. The headdresses of fashionable women were often of extraordinary size and shape. The moralists of the age were shocked, then as now, when tightly fitting garments which showed the outlines of the body became fashionable. The inconvenience of putting on tight garments led to the use of buttons and buttonholes. Men wore shoes with pointed toes. At one period these were so long that they hindered walking unless tied by a ribbon to the knees.

Food and drink. When they could afford something besides water, the common people drank ale and beer. Their food consisted mainly of porridge; heavy, dark bread; and dried peas and beans; supplemented occasionally by meat or fish and by home-grown vegetables and fruit. Famines were a frequent occurrence in the Middle Ages, for the peasants rarely had enough surplus food saved against a time of crop failure to last them through a poor season.

Medieval cookbooks show that people of means had a variety of elaborate and costly foods. Dinner at a nobleman's house might include ten or twelve courses, mostly meat and game, accompanied by several kinds of wine. The lord and his retainers sat down to a sumptuous feast and, as they ate and drank, watched the antics of a professional jester or "fool," listened to the songs and music of minstrels, and, perhaps, heard with wonder the tales of far-off countries brought by some traveler. Knives, forks, and napkins were conveniences unknown in medieval times. Food was conveyed to the mouth with the fingers and sometimes with hunting knives or daggers.

Education in the Later Middle Ages

Elementary schools. In the early Middle Ages learning in western Europe was kept alive by the Church. Monastic and cathedral schools trained boys who intended to be monks or priests. Charlemagne ordered that schools of this type be established or enlarged so as to teach reading to other boys in the neighborhood. (See page 133.) Pupils learned enough Latin grammar to read religious books, and enough music to follow the services of the Church. They also studied arithmetic by means of the awkward Roman numbering system, and sometimes gained a little knowledge of other subjects. Even this limited education was not available to the vast majority of boys in the early Middle Ages. The number of elementary schools increased considerably in the later Middle Ages. Guilds and private benefactors set up schools in addition to those maintained by churches and monasteries.

Medieval revival of learning. In the eleventh and twelfth centuries western Europe felt the beginning of a great intellectual revival. This came about largely as the result of increasing contacts with the culture of the Moslems and the Byzantines. Some Europeans went to Moslem and Byzantine universities to study. The returning crusaders also helped make Europeans aware of the knowledge of the cultivated people of the Middle East. A demand arose for schools of higher learning in western Europe. Some of the cathedral and monastic schools gradually developed into professional schools and universities. Many were modeled to a considerable extent on the Moslem colleges in Spain and Egypt. (See page 125.) By the end of the Middle Ages the universities numbered about eighty.

University of Paris. One of the first universities was established at Paris. Peter Abélard (1079–1142) went to Paris to attend the lectures given by a master of the cathedral school of Notre Dame. Abélard soon set himself up as a lecturer. Few teachers have ever attracted so large and so devoted a following. The fame of Abélard led to an increase of masters and students at Paris. By the end of the twelfth century the teachers organized themselves into a guild, or corporation,

UNIVERSITY OF PARIS in the late Middle Ages. These students appear to study in luxury while in most universities of this period students had neither benches nor texts.

known as a *universitas*. The University of Paris stressed the study of theology and philosophy. It furnished the model for Oxford University in England, and for universities in Scotland, Denmark, Sweden, and Germany.

University of Bologna. The revival of trade in the later Middle Ages resulted in a need for men who could draw up business contracts; consequently, there was a demand for legal training. In response to this demand the University of Bologna, in Italy, emphasized the study of law. This school arose at about the same time as the University of Paris. It made the Code of Justinian (see page 113) the chief subject of study, and thus spread the influence of the Roman legal system. Later universities in southern Europe were partly modeled on the University of Bologna.

The liberal arts. Beginning students at the universities studied the "seven liberal arts"— grammar, rhetoric, logic, arithmetic, music,

CONTRAST IN PRINTING METHODS. Above we see a sixteenth-century shop in France, equipped with a small hand printing press. Pictured on the right above is a modern color press. This machine prints four colors simultaneously on each side of the paper. It can print up to 300 books (like the one you are reading) in one hour.

geometry, and astronomy. The length of time spent at these studies depended upon the previous training of the individual student, and the speed with which he learned. If he passed certain examinations he was awarded a "bachelor's" degree.

To those who had completed the course in liberal arts, medieval universities offered three fields of advanced study. These were theology, law, and medicine. Each institution tended to specialize in one or more fields of learning. Thus, Paris was noted for theology, Bologna for law, and Salerno for medicine.

Materials and methods. A university did not have an extensive collection of libraries, laboratories, and museums. The only equipment consisted of lecture rooms. Not even benches or chairs were required, for students often sat on the straw-strewn floors. The high price of manuscripts compelled professors to give all instruction by means of lectures. The lectures were in Latin; students kept a notebook record of what was said.

Most medieval universities did nothing to encourage original research. Law students memorized the Code of Justinian. Medical students usually learned anatomy and physiology from old Greek books, rather than in the dissecting room. Theologians went to the Bible, the Church Fathers, or Aristotle for answers to the questions that perplexed them. Most scholars were satisfied to appeal to authority, rather than take the trouble of finding out things for themselves. This is not to say that there were no attempts to gain further knowledge, for some original work was done, especially in theology. Among the most famous medieval thinkers was St. Thomas Aquinas (1225?–1274?), an Italian monk who taught at Paris, Rome, Cologne, and Bologna. He helped make known Aristotle's writings and also wrote a large work entitled *Summa Theologica* (*Compendium of Theology*). In this great work Aquinas brought together harmoniously the philosophy of Aristotle and the beliefs of Christianity. His ideas were long opposed but eventually accepted by the Catholic Church.

Science and Invention

Progress in science. Many scholars in western Europe during the Middle Ages looked back to classical writings, particularly those of Aristotle, as the source of all information about nature. Breaking this habit was difficult, for those who wished to experiment for themselves had little apparatus and no accurate instruments. Yet in spite of this handicap considerable scientific progress was made in the later Middle Ages. Alchemists, who tried to turn other metals into gold, helped to lay the foundations of modern chemistry and physics. Peter of Albano, who lived about

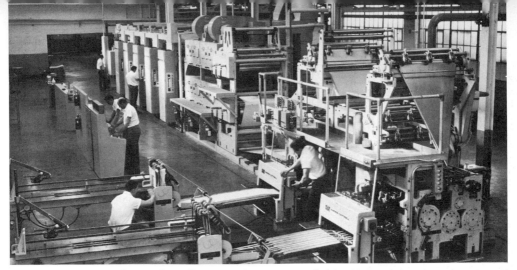

1300, knew of the theory that all matter is made up of atoms (see page 82), but doubted that it would ever be possible to find atomic weights. The study of astronomy made conspicuous progress. Medicine and geography began to advance. Valuable work was also done in arithmetic and algebra, mainly through Arab influence. It was in the later Middle Ages that Europeans adopted Arabic numerals, with their symbol for zero, in place of the clumsy Roman figures. Long encyclopedias were written in Latin. They contained the scientific information gathered by the ancients and by medieval observers. They included much misinformation but showed a healthy interest in scientific matters.

Important inventions. A number of important inventions were produced in the later Middle Ages. Lenses for spectacles were made by the end of the thirteenth century. Glass came to be used for windows and mirrors; and lead plumbing, mechanical clocks, and pipe organs were invented. An important invention in boat making was the keel, which extended into the water below the bottom of the boat and enabled it to sail against the wind. The rudder was invented when the last part of the keel was made movable. Roger Bacon (1214-1294) foresaw the time when ships would move swiftly without oars and men would make machines for flying.

The mariner's compass. The compass, a magnetized needle which points to the north, was probably invented by the Chinese and introduced to Europeans by the Arabs. The instrument, improved by being balanced on a pivot so that it would not be affected by choppy seas, was first used by Europeans in the thirteenth century. It enabled sailors to find their bearings even in murky weather and on starless nights. The compass and improvements in shipbuilding helped to make possible the long voyages of discovery which were undertaken in early modern times.

Gunpowder. Gunpowder seems to have been first used by the Chinese and later by the Arabs, but Europeans may have discovered it independently as early as the thirteenth century. At first it was used for fireworks, but at length it came to be used in small brass cannon for propelling stone or iron balls. Still later, muskets took the place of the bow, the crossbow, and the pike. The use of gunpowder caused a revolution in the art of warfare and helped to bring an end to feudalism. (See page 159.)

Printing. The Chinese were the first to print books by using movable type; that is, a type in which the letters are separate so that they can be arranged in any desired way for printing. The origin of printing in Europe is debatable, but it is known that a German printer, John Gutenberg of Mainz, was one of the first to print on a large scale. He, or someone else living at the same time, invented a method of casting metal type from a mold. In previous printing each letter had to be carved out by hand. The first large printed book which issued from Gutenberg's press was a Latin Bible, probably printed in 1454.

Printing brings a revolution. Movable cast type, plus the earlier development of a method of making cheap paper, brought a revolution in human affairs. The copying of books no longer needed to be done by hand on expensive parchment. Books could now be more accurate. They were so reduced in price that they became the possession of many, not the luxury of a few. Anyone who knew how to read could now enter the gateway to knowledge. The publication of newspapers, magazines, and pamphlets was made possible. Printing opened the way for public libraries and universal education and thus made possible a better life for all men.

Architecture in the Later Middle Ages

Architecture and the Church. The importance of the Church in the Middle Ages is shown in the great amount of building for religious purposes. The bishop wanted a great cathedral; the monks, a large monastery; and the parish priest, as fine a church as his people could erect. The people seem to have been as enthusiastic as the church officials. Consequently, church architecture was the most important kind of architecture in the Middle Ages. The two prominent styles were the Romanesque and the Gothic.

The Romanesque style. The Romanesque style was used in almost all religious buildings in the early Middle Ages. It was based on the design of the Roman basilica (hence the name "Romanesque"). The Roman basilica had a spacious central hall with one or two rows of columns on each side forming aisles. At one end of the hall was a semicircular space called the "apse." The outer wall at that end of the basilica was curved to conform to the apse. These features were reproduced in the Romanesque style, with some

new features added. One change was made by laying out the building in the form of a Latin cross. The short arm of the cross formed two wings called "transepts," which projected from each side. At the point where the transepts joined the central aisle (nave), a dome was often built. A third change was the enlargement of the apse to form the choir—a place reserved for the clergy—and a fourth change was the use of vaulted (arched) ceilings made of stone rather than concrete. The walls which carried the weight of the ceiling had to be thick and heavy, with few windows. Another Romanesque feature was the use of round, or semicircular, arches.

The Gothic style. Builders sought for a way to construct a wall which would admit sufficient light and yet support a high, vaulted ceiling. The Gothic style developed as the answer to the builders' problem. In a Gothic church a great number of stone ribs serve as rafters to support the ceiling. Each rib rests on a pillar. The pillars are braced by "flying buttresses," which rest on other pillars outside the walls of the church. (See diagram.) The walls, relieved from the pressure of the ceiling, now could be higher and could be opened up with high, wide windows. The roofs too could be higher.

The pointed arch. Gothic builders also made use of the pointed arch, which had long been known to the Arabs. The semicircular, or round, arch used in Romanesque churches can be only half as high as it is wide, but the pointed arch can rise much higher. It is lighter, more graceful, and offers more variety than the round arch.

Gothic ornament. The labors of the Gothic architect were admirably seconded by those of other artists. To adorn both the interior and exterior of the church, the sculptor carved many figures in stone—mostly religious figures, such as portrayals of saints, but sometimes expressions of fancy or humor, such as the figures of gargoyles perched atop the walls. The painter covered vacant wall spaces

GOTHIC VAULTING, *right,* **FLYING BUTTRESSES,** *left.* In the first diagram, the outer wall of the church appears at right. The left and center uprights are buttresses, which support the wall by means of the curved, connecting "flying" buttresses.

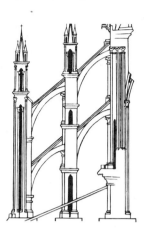
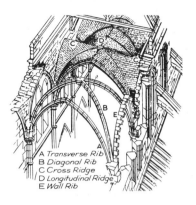

A Transverse Rib
B Diagonal Rib
C Cross Ridge
D Longitudinal Ridge
E Wall Rib

THE SAINTE CHAPELLE, PARIS. This beautiful church is often pointed out as a typical example of Gothic design. It was built by St. Louis (Louis IX, 1214–1270). Stained-glass windows fill the spaces between the tall stone columns and reach upward to the stone-vaulted roof. Statues, carvings, and pointed arches are also features of Gothic architecture.

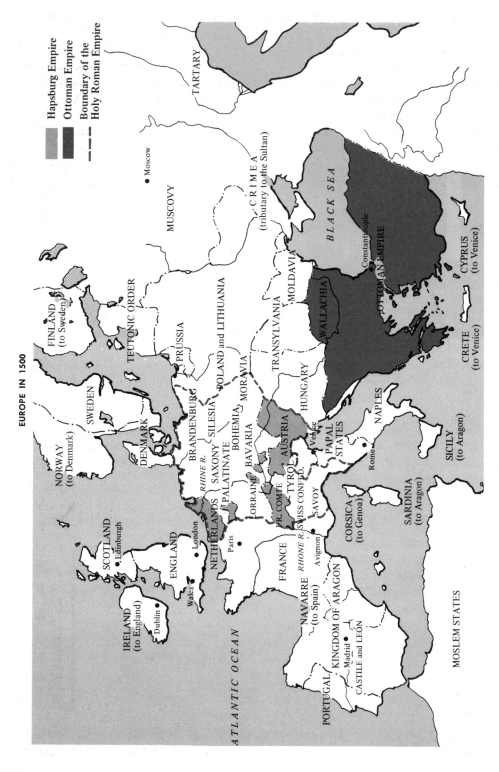

EUROPE IN 1500

Hapsburg Empire
Ottoman Empire
Boundary of the
Holy Roman Empire

TARTARY

MUSCOVY

• Moscow

CRIMEA
(tributary to the Sultan)

BLACK SEA

FINLAND
(to Sweden)

TEUTONIC ORDER

PRUSSIA

POLAND and LITHUANIA

MOLDAVIA

TRANSYLVANIA

WALLACHIA

OTTOMAN EMPIRE

Constantinople

CYPRUS
(to Venice)

NORWAY
(to Denmark)

SWEDEN

DENMARK

BRANDENBURG

RHINE R.

SAXONY
SILESIA

PALATINATE

BOHEMIA
MORAVIA

BAVARIA

HUNGARY

AUSTRIA

TYROL

Venice

PAPAL
STATES

NAPLES

CRETE
(to Venice)

SCOTLAND

Edinburgh

ENGLAND

London

NETHERLANDS

Paris

LORRAINE

FR. COMTE

SWISS CONFED.

SAVOY

Rome

SICILY
(to Aragon)

Wales

IRELAND
(to England)

Dublin

FRANCE

RHONE R.

Avignon

CORSICA
(to Genoa)

SARDINIA
(to Aragon)

ATLANTIC OCEAN

NAVARRE
(to Spain)

KINGDOM OF ARAGON

Madrid

CASTILE and LEÓN

PORTUGAL

MOSLEM STATES

174   DECLINE AND REVIVAL

with brilliantly colored pictures. The wood carver made exquisite choir stalls, pulpits, altars, and screens. Master workmen filled the windows with stained glass superior in coloring to the finest modern work. The rose windows were especially notable.

Other uses of Gothic. Gothic architecture, though at first confined to churches, came to be used for other buildings. Beautiful town halls, guildhalls, markets, and charming private houses are monuments of secular Gothic construction. But the cathedral remained the best expression of the Gothic style. In many ways it was the finest work of the later Middle Ages.

The End of the Middle Ages

Ottoman Turks threaten Christendom. The Ottoman Turks, kinsmen of the Seljuks, were driven from central Asia by the advance of the Mongols. (See page 226.) The Ottoman Turks settled in Asia Minor, where they enjoyed the protection of the Seljuks and from them accepted Mohammedanism. A chieftain named Othman (whence the name Ottoman) finally declared his independence of the Seljuks and founded another Turkish empire. By 1400 the Ottoman Turks were in Europe, wresting province after province from the feeble hands of the Byzantine emperors. Before long all that remained of the Eastern Roman Empire was Constantinople and a small district near the city.

Fall of Constantinople, 1453. In 1453 the army of the Ottoman Turks appeared before the walls of Constantinople. Only a crusade could have saved it but, despite frantic appeals for help, no crusaders arrived. The defenders of the city were a mere handful compared to the Ottoman hordes, yet they held out for nearly two months against the assault. At length the enemy scaled the walls and entered the city. They stripped the great cathedral of Saint Sophia of its crosses, images, and other Christian emblems, and proclaimed the faith of Mohammed. And so the "Turkish night" descended on this ancient home of civilization.

The end of the Middle Ages. Historians sometimes refer to 1500 as the approximate end of the Middle Ages. Fifteen hundred is chosen as an approximate date, because several important events at about that time signalize the change to modern times. These events include the fall of Constantinople and the end of the Hundred Years' War in 1453, the invention of movable cast type for printing, and the discovery of America. Although traces of feudalism have survived in Europe until the present, it is clear that by 1500 the medieval period was drawing to a close.

REVIEWING THE CHAPTER

TERMS TO UNDERSTAND: *guild, national state, common law, Magna Carta, autocracy, Black Death, troubadour, miracle play, morality play, alchemist.*

PERSONS TO IDENTIFY: *Henry II, King John, Hugh Capet, Joan of Arc, Ferdinand, Isabella, Roland, King Arthur, Robin Hood, Chaucer, Dante, Peter Abélard, Thomas Aquinas, Gutenberg, Othman.*

PLACES TO LOCATE: *Venice, Genoa, Pisa, Agincourt, Calais, Granada.*

QUESTIONS TO ANSWER

1. (a) Give the location and purpose of the Hanseatic League. (b) What handicaps to trade existed in western Europe in the Middle Ages? (c) Why did fairs decline in importance at the end of the Middle Ages?

2. (a) What locations favored the growth of

cities? (b) Describe the appearance of the medieval city as seen from without; from within. (c) Give reasons for the high death rate in medieval cities.

3. (a) Describe the organization and activities of the medieval guilds. (b) Do you think the idea of a "just price" should be adopted today? Why or why not? (c) Who are members of the middle class? (d) How did the cities free themselves from feudal restrictions?

4. (a) Account for the rise of national states in western Europe during the later Middle Ages. (b) What features of the English legal system have been transmitted to us? (c) Trace the development of the English Parliament.

5. (a) How did Joan of Arc change the course of the Hundred Years' War? (b) Compare the government of France after the Hundred Years' War with that of England. (c) In what other countries was autocratic government established?

6. (a) Give the two main reasons for the decline of serfdom. (b) Which of the two was the main cause of the decline?

7. (a) List the principal languages belonging to the Romance and the Germanic groups. (b) What are the chief sources of the English language? (c) Name the forms of popular medieval literature. Give an example of each.

8. (a) Mention five superstitions common in western Europe during the Middle Ages. (b) What modern games, sports, and festivals had their origin in medieval times?

9. How did the poor and well to do differ in regard to their houses? Clothing? Food?

10. (a) What caused the rise of medieval universities? (b) Describe the subjects they offered and the methods of instruction.

11. (a) Name two handicaps to the search for scientific knowledge in the Middle Ages. (b) In what fields of knowledge was progress made?

12. How did Romanesque and Gothic architecture differ?

13. What events marked the end of the Middle Ages in western Europe?

FURTHER ACTIVITIES FOR PART THREE

1. Draw a diagram showing the system of landholding in the feudal pyramid. The social classes may be shown in the same way.

2. From Haaren and Poland's *Famous Men of the Middle Ages* prepare a class report on Richard the Lion-Hearted's adventures in the crusades.

3. You will find in Boardman's *Castles* descriptions of the building and the defending of castles in the Middle Ages. Prepare a written summary of the information.

4. Imagine that you were an Italian merchant traveling by land from Genoa to Paris at the time of the crusades. Describe the events of your journey in a series of letters to your son or daughter in Genoa.

5. Prepare a list of superstitions in which people believe today. Ask your classmates for help in making the list as complete as possible. Mark with a star each superstition which came from medieval times.

6. Latin was an international language in the Middle Ages. Find out about "Basic English" and present arguments for its use as an international language today.

7. Make a time line of the history of Europe during the Middle Ages, beginning with 476 and ending with 1492. At appropriate intervals on the line write the names and dates of important events in the Middle Ages.

8. Arrange for the class to see the film *The Crusades,* available from Teaching Film Custodians, Inc., 25 West 43rd Street, New York, N.Y. This Paramount feature has been edited for classroom use with emphasis on the persons and events of the Third Crusade. The properties, costumes, and settings are accurate. Running time twenty-nine minutes.

FURTHER READING FOR PART THREE

(Stars indicate easier books)

HISTORY

ADAMS, GEORGE. *Civilization During the Middle Ages.* Barnes and Noble.

ADAMS, HENRY. *Mont-Saint-Michel and Chartres.* Houghton.

BAGLEY. *Life in Medieval England.* Putnam.

BOARDMAN. *Castles.* Walck.

*CHUBB. *The Byzantines.* World.

*DAUGHERTY. *The Magna Carta.* Random House.

*DAVIS. *Life on a Medieval Barony.* Harper.

*DONOVAN and KENDRICK. *The Vikings.* Harper.

DUGGAN. *Story of the Crusades, 1097–1291.* Doubleday. (paperback)

DURANT. *Age of Faith.* Simon and Schuster.

ELLIS. *The Arabs.* World.

FITCH. *Allah, the God of Islam.* Lothrop.

FREMANTLE. *Age of Faith.* Time-Life.

*HARTMAN. *Medieval Days and Ways.* Macmillan.

HITTI. *The Arabs: A Short History.* Regnery. (paperback)

HUYGHE. *Larousse Encyclopedia of Byzantine and Medieval Art.* Putnam.

KIELTY. *Fall of Constantinople.* Random House.

*LAMB. *Constantinople: Birth of an Empire.* Knopf.

*——. *The Crusades.* Doubleday.

*MILLS. *The Middle Ages.* Putnam.

MORRISON. *Armor.* Crowell.

PRICE. *Made in the Middle Ages.* Dutton.

*QUENNELL and QUENNELL. *A History of Everyday Things in England.* Putnam.

*SELLMAN. *The Crusades.* Roy. (paperback)

SHERRARD. *Byzantium.* Time-Life.

SIMONS. *Barbarian Europe.* Time-Life.

STEWART. *Early Islam.* Time-Life.

*TAPPAN. *When Knights Were Bold.* Houghton.

TREECE. *The Crusades.* Random House.

*WEST. *The Crusades.* Random House.

WILLIAMS. *Knights of the Crusades.* Harper.

*——. *Life in the Middle Ages.* Random House.

BIOGRAPHY

CHUTE. *Geoffrey Chaucer of England.* Dutton.

*DUGGAN. *The Falcon and the Dove: a Life of Thomas Becket of Canterbury.* Pantheon.

JEWETT. *God's Troubadour: The Story of St. Francis of Assisi.* Crowell.

KOMROFF. *Charlemagne.* Messner.

LAMB. *Charlemagne.* Doubleday.

MITCHISON. *The Young Alfred the Great.* Roy.

*REYNOLDS. *The Life of St. Patrick.* Random House.

WALSH. *Adventures and Discoveries of Marco Polo.* Random House.

WILLIAMS and LIGHTBODY. *Joan of Arc.* Harper.

FICTION

*BOWERS. *The Lost Dragon 'of Wessex.* Walck.

*BULLA. *Sword in the Tree.* Crowell.

CHUTE. *Innocent Wayfaring.* Dutton.

CLEMENS. *A Connecticut Yankee in King Arthur's Court.* Modern Library.

DOYLE. *The White Company.* Dodd.

*FAULKNER. *The Yellow Hat.* Doubleday.

*GRAY. *Adam of the Road.* Viking.

HUGO. *Hunchback of Notre Dame.* Dodd.

LEIGHTON. *Judith of France.* Houghton.

LEWIS. *Gentle Falcon.* Phillips.

MALCOMSON. *Son of Robin Hood.* Houghton.

PYLE. *Men of Iron.* Harper.

——. *Otto of the Silver Hand.* Scribner.

READE. *Cloister and the Hearth.* Modern Library.

SCOTT. *Quentin Durward.* Scribner.

——. *The Talisman.* Collins.

STEVENSON. *The Black Arrow.* Dell. (paperback)

SUTCLIFF. *The Shield Ring.* Walck.

ANTWERP was not only a thriving market, as the Latin legend in this 1515 woodcut boasts, but the site of an academy of painting and an influential center of humanistic studies.

PART FOUR

THE DAWN OF MODERN TIMES

In Part Four we shall study a period of transition, in which European civilization emerged from the isolation and backwardness of the Middle Ages and slowly developed modern ways of life and thought. The period of transition from medieval to modern times in the western world was notable for three important movements: the Renaissance, the Reformation, and geographical exploration.

The Renaissance was an intellectual rebirth, or awakening, noted for enormous creativity in literature, art and science. Partly as a result of the Renaissance, the Protestant Reformation began. It was marked by revolts against the authority of the Church and by the rise of new religious movements. The Catholic Reformation led to reforms within the Church and the establishment of new religious societies, or orders.

Meanwhile, geographical discoveries and explorations served to bring the various parts of the world closer together. European nations developed a worldwide trade on a scale never known before. They grew rich from this trade, and from the colonial empires they founded. All around the globe the Europeans' colonies flourished, and became the cause of global wars.

In the final chapter of Part Four we return to the story of mankind in Asia and then move to Africa. We shall see how civilizations in India and China from A.D. 500 to 1800 were at times far superior to those in Europe, and how civilization spread to Japan and Southeast Asia. In Africa, we shall trace the rise of early civilizations and wealthy empires only recently beginning to be known and appreciated.

11 Renaissance and Reformation

ERASMUS of Rotterdam, an engraving by Albrecht Dürer. A philosopher and reformer, Erasmus took issue with many of the Church practices prevailing at the time. However, Erasmus, unlike Luther, counseled reform rather than revolution.

The French word renaissance *means rebirth, or revival. The word is usually applied to the rebirth, or revival, in western Europe of the literature and art of ancient Greece and Rome. Classical masterpieces were brought to light and enthusiastically admired, then used as models by Renaissance writers and artists. They broke away from many medieval customs, thus beginning a new age in the culture of western Europe.*

Man's view of himself and of the world changed fundamentally during the Renaissance. As a result, his views of man's relationship to God and to the Christian Church changed also. During the Renaissance many teachings of the Church were brought into question. Questioning led to a re-forming of some Christian teachings in the movements known as the Protestant Reformation and the Catholic Reformation.

The Renaissance of Classical Literature and Art

Italy and the Renaissance. Italy was the original home of the Renaissance, and the scene of its highest development. Here, even during the Dark Age, admiration for Roman civilization never died out. During the later Middle Ages many Italians gained wealth as a result of the revival of trade. They had the means to reward richly the artists who could produce beautiful pictures, statues, and buildings, and the writers whose work found favor.

Petrarch and the Renaissance. If the beginning of the Renaissance may be traced back to any individual, that person is Petrarch (1304–1374). He has been called the first modern scholar and man of letters. A native of Florence, Petrarch devoted himself to the study of Latin classics. He traveled widely in Italy and other countries in search of ancient manuscripts. Sometimes he kept as many as four copyists in his house, busily copying the manuscripts that he had discovered or borrowed. "My tireless spirit pores over the pages," he wrote, "until it has exhausted both fingers and eyes, and yet I feel neither hunger nor cold." Other scholars copied and translated Greek writings. Ancient manuscripts black with dust were brought out of monasteries and cathedrals, where they had lain neglected for centuries. They were read with delight by men who seemed to see a new world opening before their eyes. After the fall of Constantinople in 1453, many learned Greeks went to Italy, where they further stimulated the study of Greek. "Greece had not perished, but had emigrated to Italy."

Growth in study of the classics. In Italy it became the fashion to study the ancient Greek and Latin languages and literatures. These studies were known as humanities (from Latin *humanitas,* meaning "culture"). In the universities the humanities replaced philosophy as the chief subject of instruction. From the universities the study of the humanities spread to the lower schools, and then throughout the Italian peninsula. Wealthy men gave money to build libraries for the safekeeping of classical manuscripts, to establish professorships of the ancient languages, and to support scholars engaged in research. The popes shared in the zeal for the humanities. One of them founded the Vatican Library at Rome, which has the most valuable collection of ancient manuscripts in the world. From Italy interest in the study of the classics spread in all directions. Until a hundred years ago most students who progressed beyond the elementary grades in the United States were required to devote much time to classical studies.

. . . Thus it is well to seem merciful, faithful, humane, sincere, religious, and also to be so; but you must have the mind so disposed that when it is needful to be otherwise you may be able to change to the opposite qualities. And it must be understood that a prince, and especially a new prince, cannot observe all those things which are considered good in men, being often obliged, in order to maintain the state, to act against faith, against religion. And, therefore, he must have a mind disposed to adapt itself according to the wind, and as the variations of fortune dictate, and, as I said before, not deviate from what is good, if possible, but be able to do evil if constrained.

A prince must take great care that nothing goes out of his mouth which is not full of the above-named five qualities, and, to see and hear him, he should seem to be all mercy, faith, integrity, humanity, and religion. And nothing is more necessary than to seem to have this last quality . . .

—Machiavelli, *The Prince*.

Renaissance architecture. While scholars were reviving classical literature, Renaissance architects drew inspiration from studying the old Greek and Roman designs. They turned away from the Byzantine, Romanesque, and Gothic styles to develop new styles, partly based on Greek and Roman ideas. The dome, placed on a drum, was often the central feature of a Renaissance building. Round arches and long rows of Greek columns were much used. Vertical spires and bell towers ending in columned belfries are among the inventions of the period. The new architecture appeared not only in churches but also in public buildings, palaces, and villas.

Sculpture. Changes in architecture naturally stimulated changes in the related arts such as sculpture and painting. The Italian sculptors began to copy the ancient bas-reliefs and statues preserved in Rome. The greatest of Italian sculptors was Michelangelo (1475–1564), who was a native of Florence. He won fame in architecture and painting as well as in sculpture. The dome of St. Peter's was finished according to his designs, while the paintings (frescoes) on the ceiling of the Sistine Chapel in the Vatican display his genius as a painter.

Painting. During the Renaissance, Italian artists, as well as scholars and sculptors, began to turn away from medieval styles. The painters endeavored to make lifelike pictures. They had superlative skill in the art of painting portraits of people. They were less successful with landscapes. Often the artists were commissioned to decorate churches and monasteries with paintings based on themes taken from the Bible or the lives of the saints. Much of their work was done in colors mixed with egg white and applied directly to the plaster walls of churches and palaces. Such paintings are called frescoes. Many frescoes painted during the Renaissance have suffered severely from injuries to the walls and from the effects of moisture, dust, and light. After discovery of the process of mixing the colors with oils instead of water, pictures on wood or canvas became common. Michelangelo, Leonardo da Vinci, Raphael, Titian, and Correggio—all of whom lived between 1450 and 1600—are called "Old Masters" of Italian painting.

The Renaissance elsewhere. The intellectual, literary, and artistic movement that had begun in Italy was carried on by scholars and artists in Germany, France, England, and other countries. Outstanding was Erasmus (1466–1536), a Hollander. His travels and extensive correspondence brought him in touch with many learned men of the day. The most important achievement of Erasmus was an edition of the New Testament in the original Greek. It was the source from which the Scriptures were translated into the modern European languages.

Italian architects found a cordial reception in France, Spain, the Netherlands, and other countries, where they introduced classical styles of building and ornamentation. The

Old Roman walls at Ávila, Spain

From Classical Times to the Renaissance

On the surface the Middle Ages may appear as a time of stagnation and sleep. It is true that the early Middle Ages witnessed few changes in European life. Yet in fact the Middle Ages as a whole made a deep and varied contribution to Europe's culture. Many different elements, including traditions from classical Greece and Rome, united to produce a new civilization.

After Roman government passed from the scene, feudal lords carried on many of the functions of government. They lived in castles whose fortifications were probably designed after heavy stone walls built by the Romans. The castles stood as stern reminders of the nobles' political, economic, and military power.

182A

Even in times of peace the nobles played at war in jousts and tournaments. These gay affairs are typified by a tournament held near Calais about 1385, where three French knights challenged all comers for thirty days. Many knights from England, France and elsewhere went to accept the challenge, even though France and England were supposedly at war. Colored tents, coats of arms, the sound of bugles, and the rich trapping of feudal lords all contributed to the excitement of the tournament.

The picture on the right shows the peaceful day-to-day life within the castle walls. This illustration by a medieval French artist seems to stress the easy life of the noble in sharp contrast to the life of back-breaking, manual labor of the serf.

Tournament held near Calais about 1385

Manuscript illumination of a French castle garden

182C

A deep interest in man characterized the Renaissance. It is no wonder that the art of this age expresses man's deep interest in man. No other age has brought together so many great painters, sculptors, and architects, all of whom seemed to have a "reborn" interest in man.

One of the first of these Renaissance painters was Giotto. From the moment when this 14th century painter broke with medieval tradition, art was never the same again. Although the painting by Giotto on page E emphasizes a religious subject, notice the great interest of the painter in the natural environment and, especially in the humans found in the landscape.

"Battle of San Romano" (1432), by Uccello

"St. Francis Preaching to the Birds," by Giotto

"The Queen of Sheba," by Piero della Francesca

Desire for beauty and variety in expression, a reaction against medieval monotony, underlies all Renaissance art. Although religious themes appear frequently, they are treated in glowing color and rich detail. The Renaissance was indeed a "rebirth" of classical humanism, but modified by feudal and religious influences. On pages F and G, ancient ideas were interwoven with religion to produce Renaissance masterpieces. The Queen of Sheba is depicted kneeling in prayer as she recognizes the Holy Tree which had been revealed to her in a dream. Michelangelo's Moses portrays a Biblical figure with power and realism typical of Renaissance artists.

"Moses," by Michelangelo

"Erasmus," by Hans Holbein

Italy, as the home of the Renaissance, became for a time "the schoolmistress of Europe." New ideas radiated out from Italy and found a special welcome in northern Europe, where the revival of trade produced a wealthy group of patrons of the arts. Northern Europeans admired the products of Italian artistic and intellectual genius and the spirit of Italian "humanism." We can see Italian influence, but typically Northern style and subject matter, in such famous works as Vermeer's "Woman Weighing Gold" and Holbein's portrait of the scholar Erasmus.

So fresh and alive was the Renaissance spirit that it outgrew even the continent of Europe. In the Age of Discovery, even then beginning, Europeans carried their new outlook to our own land and many others.

"Woman Weighing Gold," by Vermeer

classical style in sculpture also spread throughout Europe. Painters in northern countries at first followed Italian models but afterward developed a style of their own. The German artists, Albrecht Dürer (1471–1528) and Hans Holbein (1497–1543), were two of the greatest northern painters.

The New Literature and Science

The growth of secularism. By the end of the Middle Ages a growing *secularism,* or concern with the affairs of this world, began to displace the other-worldliness of medieval thought. The popularity of classical writings encouraged the growth of secularism, for the classical authors wrote mostly about worldly subjects. The revival of trade, by bringing more opportunities for making money and for enjoying life, also encouraged the growth of worldliness. The secular spirit combined with the classical tradition of good writing to produce a new trend in literature.

Growth of the new literature. We have seen that late in the Middle Ages there began in western Europe the development of native, or *vernacular,* literatures. (See pages 164–165.) The growth of venacular literature was held back somewhat by the revived interest in the classics. Many scholars preferred to show off their learning by writing in Latin or Greek. However, some authors began to write in their native languages because in this way they could reach a greater number of people. These authors developed a new kind of literature. We may note three important features of their work: (1) They tried to maintain the high standards of classical writing. (2) They wrote for the most part about nonreligious subjects. (3) By writing in the vernacular, they helped develop *national* literatures throughout western Europe. The invention of movable cast type for printing (see page 171) made possible a wide reading of the new literature.

A remarkable array of gifted writers contributed to the growth of the new literature. They contributed in different ways to a concept of man as the center of the universe—a concept which went back to the classical thought of ancient Greece and Rome. Only a few of the more outstanding authors can be mentioned here.

(1) Niccolò Machiavelli (mä′kyä-věl′lĕ, 1469–1527) was a statesman and philosopher of Florence who wrote *The Prince,* a guide for rulers. Machiavelli wished fervently for the unification of Italy. He believed that this noble aim would make it permissible for a prince to use any tactic, no matter how unprincipled or ruthless. Machiavelli said that it is unnecessary for a ruler to be good; he need only *appear* to be virtuous, since success was the important thing. Machiavelli thus reflected the new age, which seemed to have

LORENZO DE MEDICI (1449–1492), was known as "Lorenzo the Magnificent." He supported artists and scholars of the Renaissance and in a sense represented the peak of the Renaissance movement begun by Petrarch. As a leader of Florence he brought prosperity to the city and helped make its speech the national language of Italy.

rejected the restraints of religion and morality. Many dictators have since followed his doctrine that "the end justifies the means."

(2) Michel de Montaigne (1533–1592) was a French nobleman whose wealth gave him leisure in which to master the classics and to reflect upon man and his place in the universe. Whereas Machiavelli had looked outward to the world of affairs, Montaigne looked inward to the human heart. He wrote what he called essays, or attempts to express his thoughts. In his *Essays* he gave the world not only a new literary form but also a self-portrait in which all men could recognize themselves. His views reflected at once the philosophy of Greece and Rome, Christian teachings, and the skeptical spirit of the Renaissance. Montaigne believed in the unity of mankind and in a concept of man as a unit, with both body and soul worth acceptance as part of the human condition. Be glad you live, he said, but try to make your life a good one.

(3) Miguel de Cervantes (sĕr-văn′tēz, 1547–1616), a Spanish writer, looked not to the new age but backward to the old. He made fun of the romantic tales of medieval chivalry in his most famous book, *Don Quixote*. Clad in rusty armor and mounted upon an ancient nag, accompanied by one faithful servant, the hero set out from La Mancha to do knightly deeds. Don Quixote's adventures, such as an attack upon windmills which he mistook for a group of giants, made amusing reading, but the book was more than a satire or an adventure novel. Its sympathetic description of people in all walks of life has given it a permanent place in the world's great literature.

(4) William Shakespeare (1564–1616), English poet and dramatist, produced plays whose timelessness and insight into human character rivaled the best works of the ancient Greek playwrights. Characters in Shakespeare's plays—such as Romeo and Juliet, Hamlet, and Falstaff—are known around the globe. Like Cervantes, Shakespeare had a keen sense of humanity's problems at every social level. Although he has rightly been called a man for all time, he was also a product of his age. Shakespeare's plays speak of the zest for life and the exciting times when England began its rise to world power under the first Elizabeth.

(5) Sir Francis Bacon (1561–1626) was a gifted leader in the fields of English law and politics, but his most striking achievements came in the field of science. As he put it, he was "fitted for nothing so well as for the study of truth." Bacon's search for truth took him far from medieval reliance on statements by authorities. He urged instead that men collect complete scientific data and then draw conclusions from them. He called this procedure *inductive* reasoning and expected it to replace the deductive reasoning advocated by Aristotle. The plan Bacon proposed has turned out to be impractical because it is rarely possible to gather *all* the facts bearing upon any research. Consequently, scientists have also had to rely upon their imagination in forming hypotheses.

The new science. Science, like literature, reflected the trend away from medieval ways of thinking. Students in western Europe during the Middle Ages had mostly been satisfied to accept without questioning the teachings of Aristotle and other ancient philosophers. (See page 80.) The new science rested on the method of *observation* and *experiment*. Scientists learned to take nothing for granted, even the statements of wise men of the past; they went straight to nature for their facts. Sir Francis Bacon gave a clear statement of the modern scientific method when he said: "All depends on keeping the eye steadily fixed upon the facts of nature, and so receiving their images as they are, for God forbid that we should give out a dream of our own imagination for a pattern of the world."

The earth and the universe. Throughout the Middle Ages most people had believed that the earth was the center of the universe. Beginning with the sixteenth century, a succession of astronomers and mathematicians demonstrated that the earth is only a minor member of the solar system.

First place among these men must be given to Copernicus (1473-1543), the founder of modern astronomy. Patient study and calculation led him to the conclusion that the earth turns upon its own axis and, together with the other planets, revolves around the sun. The Copernician theory met much opposition, not only in the universities, which clung to the time-honored Ptolemaic system (see page 82), but also among theologians, who thought that it contradicted statements in the Bible. Moreover, many people could not easily accept the idea that the earth is only one member of the solar system—that it is only one of many worlds.

An Italian scientist, Galileo (1564-1642), made one of the first telescopes. It was only thirty-two times as powerful as an opera glass, yet he turned it on the heavenly bodies with wonderful results. He found the sun moving unmistakably on its axis, and he noted the movements of the planets. Galileo rightly believed that his discoveries confirmed the theory of Copernicus.

Another man of genius, the German Kepler (1571-1630), worked out the mathematical laws which govern the movements of the planets. He made it clear that the planets revolve around the sun in elliptical instead of circular paths, or orbits.

Sir Isaac Newton (1642-1727), continuing Kepler's work, showed by mathematical calculation that the motion of the planets about the sun, and of the moon about the earth, can be explained as due to the same force of gravity which makes an apple fall to the ground. The discovery that the heavenly bodies move in accordance with a single physical law is a landmark in the history of science.

Anatomy and physiology. Two other scientists gained fame in a field far removed from astronomy. Vesalius (1514-1564), a Fleming who studied in Italian medical schools, published a careful description of the human body based on actual dissection. His findings contradicted many ancient errors and established the modern study of anatomy. Harvey (1578-1657), an Englishman, after careful observation of living animals, described the movements of the heart and the circulation of the blood. This was a great forward step in the study of human physiology.

The Church Drifts toward Disunity

Religious upheavals. The new movements in literature, art, and science were accompanied by sweeping changes in the field of religion. The Reformation, as it is called, affected deeply the lives and beliefs of all those persons who brought European civilization to the New World. The story of the Reformation is thus part of the story of America today. In tracing this story we shall notice: (1) the development of disagreements among the Christians of western Europe; (2) the formation of the Protestant churches; and (3) the Catholic Reformation.

Church versus state. In the thirteenth century the popes were the greatest sovereigns in Europe. They ruled a considerable part of Italy and had much influence in the political affairs of other countries. From their capital at Rome they sent forth ambassadors called "legates" to every European court and issued laws binding on western Christendom. In feudal times, when kings were weak and nobles were strong, the activity of the Church in political affairs proved useful and even necessary. But when the kings began to subdue the feudal lords and establish their own authority, they sometimes came into conflict with the popes. The kings tried to weaken the political power of the Church and even interfered in religious matters. This policy naturally led to friction between popes and kings, between church and state.

THE PEASANTS' REVOLT, 1381. John Ball, the English priest who helped stir up the revolt, is shown addressing armed peasants. He urged the abolition of class distinctions, asking, "When Adam delved and Eve span, who was then the gentleman?" The king, Richard II, received representatives of the rebels and promised to abolish serfdom. As soon as he could collect an army, however, he put down the revolt. John Ball and about one hundred others were hanged.

The "Babylonian Captivity." One of the most violent of the disputes between church and state resulted in a victory for Philip IV, the king of France. In 1296 he objected when the pope denied that the king had a right to tax the French clergy. The quarrel finally ended when the pope gave way and permitted the taxation. Soon after this, in 1305, Philip secured the election of a French clergyman as pope and thereby gained control of the papacy. This French pope moved the papal court away from Rome, to Avignon (àv′ē′nyôn′) on the French frontier. The popes lived in Avignon from 1309 to 1377. This period of nearly seventy years is usually called the "Babylonian Captivity of the Church." (This phrase originally referred to the time Nebuchadnezzar took the people of Judah as captives to Babylon.) The prestige of the popes declined during the time the papal court was in Avignon. Many people objected to the pope's absence from Rome, to the requests for large sums of money needed for the new papal court, and to French influence in papal affairs. The pope who was in office in 1377 moved the papal court back to Rome, but this action alone could not restore papal prestige.

Conflict within the Church: the Great Schism. The Babylonian Captivity resulted from a quarrel between the pope and a king; it was soon followed by a quarrel within the Church. In 1378 an Italian was elected pope by the college of cardinals. Some of the French cardinals objected to him and elected another pope to live at Avignon. Thus there came to be two popes, each with a large number of followers and each with a college of cardinals which could elect a successor and continue the rivalry. Finally, there were three popes. The third one was chosen at a joint meeting of the two groups of cardinals in 1409. Western Christendom could not decide which one to obey. This division, or schism, within the Church is known as the "Great Schism." It continued for nearly forty years (1378–1417). The Great Schism injured the papacy more than anything else that had happened to it. A church council at Constance ended the schism in 1417 by obtaining the resignation of one pope, deposing the other two, and electing a new one who was recognized by all. But it was not easy to revive the former undivided loyalty to the papacy.

Abuses within the Church. A number of the popes took much interest in the Renaissance movement. They kept up splendid courts, collected manuscripts, paintings, and statues, and erected magnificent palaces and churches in Rome. To meet the expenses involved, the popes needed additional income. They levied an income tax called the tithe, or "tenth," although it was usually less than a tenth of a person's income. In early Christian practice the tithe had been voluntary, but now it came to be required of almost everyone. Occasionally, papal revenue was increased by the sale of high church offices (a practice called "simony"). At times large fees were asked for the performance of religious services. Church income was also enlarged by the practice of accepting alms money in exchange for indulgences. An indulgence was a letter of pardon relieving the sinner from some or all of the penances (punishments) which the Church would otherwise impose upon him. The sinner, of course, had to be truly sorry (penitent) for his sin, and he had to do some pious act like going on a pilgrimage, joining a crusade, or contributing money for the erection of a church or convent. Thus the sinner who was penitent and had done one of these "good works" as a penance might receive a letter of pardon—that is, an indulgence. Catholics did not deny the right of the pope to grant indulgences, but many did object to the increase of church revenue through the granting of indulgences. People complained not only about financial abuses but also about the worldly living of some of the clergy. It must be remembered, however, that most of the clergy led entirely proper lives. The Catholics who criticized abuses wished to strengthen and reform the Church from within.

Growth of heretical movements. The Church was also weakened by a number of people who demanded fundamental changes in Catholic belief and worship. Such people were called *heretics,* and their teachings were denounced as heresies. Some heretical movements during the later Middle Ages spread over wide areas and attracted great numbers of followers. Four important heretical groups were the Albigenses, the Waldensians, the Lollards, and the Hussites.

The Albigenses were named after the town of Albi in southern France, where many of them lived. In the thirteenth century the pope preached a crusade against them, and the movement was stamped out by wholesale massacres. The Waldensians were followers of Peter Waldo; most of them lived in France. They regarded the Bible as a sufficient guide to religious life, and condemned the luxurious living of some of the clergy. The Waldensian sect survived severe persecution and now forms a branch of the Protestant church in Italy.

The Lollards, as the followers of John Wycliffe were called, held beliefs similar to those of the Waldensians. Wycliffe was the master, or head, of an Oxford college and a popular preacher. He and two friends translated the Bible into English. He organized bands of "poor priests" sworn to poverty, who went about preaching in English to the common people; in their sermons they attacked many beliefs and practices of the Church and also demanded social reforms. The Lollards were severely persecuted. John Huss, a priest and professor in the University of Prague, was influenced by the doctrines of Wycliffe. Huss attacked the actions of some of the clergy in sermons and pamphlets and urged that the powers of the pope be limited. In 1415 he was excommunicated from the Church and burned as a heretic. His followers, known as *Hussites,* survived years of religious war. They kept alive his teachings, which influenced Martin Luther.

The Protestant Reformation

Martin Luther, 1483–1546. The founder of the Protestant Reformation was Martin Luther. Luther was the son of a German miner. Although he was brought up in poverty, his father managed to give him a good education. Luther took the degrees of Bachelor and Master of Arts and then began to study law. Soon,

SELLING OF INDULGENCES. A woodcut depicting the selling of indulgences by religious leaders. It was this practice that Luther criticized.

however, his interest in religion caused him to enter a monastery. A few years later he visited Rome and was disturbed by the city's worldliness. He returned to Germany in 1511, was granted the degree of Doctor of Divinity, and became a professor of theology in the University of Wittenberg. This school had been founded a short time before by the elector (ruler) of Saxony. Luther's sermons and lectures attracted large audiences. Students began to flock to Wittenberg, and the elector took pride in the rising young teacher who was making his university famous.

Tetzel and indulgences. Before long there came into the neighborhood of Wittenberg a Dominican friar named Tetzel, who granted indulgences in return for money to be used for the completion of St. Peter's Church in Rome. Luther attacked the indulgences because they were likely to be misunderstood and misused. He pointed out that most people could not understand the Latin in which the letters of pardon were written, and that ignorant persons often thought that these indulgences wiped away the penalties of sin, even without true repentance.

Luther posts his theses, 1517. Luther set forth these and other criticisms in ninety-five theses (short statements he was willing to defend in debate). He posted his theses, written in Latin, on the door of the church at Wittenberg, where other scholars might see them.

Such an action was not unusual for a medieval scholar. At the time Luther had no thought of attacking the Church; he opposed the use being made of indulgences and wished to reform the abuse.

Salvation through faith. It is unlikely that Luther expected his theses to stir up any trouble. They were translated into German, printed, and spread broadcast over Germany. Their effect was so great that before long the granting of indulgences in that country almost ceased. For the next three years Luther studied, wrote, debated, and finally came to attack some of the basic precepts, or doctrines, of the Church. His teaching centered around the view that the road to salvation is through *faith*—faith in Christian teachings which each person can find for himself in the Bible. (The Church taught that salvation is through faith *and* good works.) Luther, the scholarly critic of indulgences, found himself in the position of publicly arguing for beliefs very much like those of Wycliffe and Huss. Luther's views were expressed in books and pamphlets which found a wide audience.

Luther burns a papal bull. The pope had at first paid little attention to the controversy about indulgences, declaring it "a mere squabble of monks," but by 1520 the situation was more serious. Luther was now preaching not merely reform but heresy. In 1520, therefore, the pope issued a decree, or bull, ordering

Luther to repent or be excommunicated. Luther's answer was dramatic and stirred all Germany. In the presence of a throng of students and townsfolk, in the square of Wittenberg, he burned the papal bull.

Luther is tried as a heretic. In January, 1521, the pope declared Luther to be excommunicated, and urged the Holy Roman emperor, Charles V, to deny Luther the protection of the laws of the empire. The emperor was willing to comply, but agreed to the demand of the German princes that Luther should be given a trial. Accordingly, Luther was summoned before a great assembly, or diet, of princes and religious leaders at Worms. Here he refused to retract anything he had written, unless his statements could be shown to contradict the Bible. "It is neither right nor safe to act against conscience," said Luther. Since he would not recant, the Diet at Worms proclaimed Luther a heretic and an outlaw. Luther escaped death because the elector of Saxony protected him.

Why Lutheranism became popular. In Germany the Reformation made a wide appeal. To patriotic Germans it seemed a revolt against a foreign power—the Italian papacy. To the pious it offered the attractions of a simple faith based directly on the Bible. Worldly minded princes welcomed an opportunity to seize church lands and revenues for themselves. Lutheranism became the dominant religion in most parts of northern and central Germany. South Germany, however, has remained Roman Catholic to the present time.

The followers of Luther, known as Lutherans, organized local congregations. Often they met in the same church buildings where they had worshiped previously as Catholics. Luther made a German translation of the Bible, which the printing press soon multiplied into thousands of copies. He composed many hymns and a catechism. He also introduced changes in the religious services. The support of powerful friends enabled Luther to

defy both pope and emperor and to continue as leader of the Reformation in Germany as long as he lived.

Peace of Augsburg, 1555. If he had acted quickly after the Diet at Worms, the emperor might have stamped out Lutheranism. However, he spent the next ten years in Spain, from which he directed a war against France. He did not return to Germany until 1530. Although he then defeated and captured some of the Lutheran princes, he was finally forced to accept a compromise on the religious question. This compromise, known as the Peace of Augsburg (1555), provided that the ruler of each German state might decide whether the religion of his subjects should be Catholicism or Lutheranism. Germany then contained over three hundred states. The Peace of Augsburg failed to establish religious toleration, since all Germans had to believe as their prince believed. However, it recognized Lutheranism as a legal religion and ended the attempts to crush the Reformation in Germany.

Lutheranism in Scandinavia. Luther's doctrines also spread into Scandinavian lands. The rulers of Denmark, Norway, and Sweden closed the monasteries and compelled the Roman Catholic bishops to surrender church property to the Crown. Lutheranism was established as the official religion of these three countries.

The Reformation in Switzerland. Huldreich Zwingli, who lived at the same time as Luther, was the leader of the Reformation in Switzerland. From his pulpit in the cathedral of Zurich, Zwingli began to question the teachings of the Church. He soon broke with it completely and set up a new faith. Unlike Luther, Zwingli rejected most of the Catholic forms of worship. Some of the Swiss cantons (districts) accepted his teaching. Others have remained Catholic.

John Calvin, 1509–1564. A Frenchman, John Calvin, ranks with Luther as a leader of the Protestant movement. In his youth Calvin planned to enter the priesthood, but later changed to the study of law. He became a Protestant and fled from persecution to Switzerland. After nearly two years of travel and writing in Switzerland Calvin was appointed preacher at the cathedral in Geneva. He gradually became leader of the city in political as well as religious matters. The government, he believed, should look to the Church for guidance. He used his power to prohibit festivals, playing cards, dancing, and masquerades. Stage plays were permitted only if they were based on the Scriptures. All the citizens had to attend two sermons on Sunday and to agree, outwardly at least, to the reformer's doctrines.

Calvin's *Institutes of the Christian Religion*. Calvin gained fame as a religious reformer through the publication of *The Institutes of the Christian Religion*. This work presented in an orderly, logical manner the main principles of Protestant religious beliefs. He provided for a very simple form of worship, consisting of Bible reading, a sermon, extemporaneous prayers, and hymns sung by the congregation. These same features of Calvinism are found today in the Presbyterian,

JOHN CALVIN. His *Institutes* presented Protestant beliefs in logical form.

Congregational, and many other Protestant churches. Calvin also believed in "predestination." According to Calvinist doctrine this means that a child at birth is already destined to reach either Heaven or Hell. Human will could not alter this "predestination."

Spread of Calvinism. The French Protestants, called "Huguenots," accepted the doctrines of Calvin. Conflict between the Catholics and the Huguenots led to a long period of civil war in France. These struggles ended in 1598, when King Henry IV issued the celebrated Edict of Nantes. The edict permitted the Huguenots to hold private worship everywhere in France and allowed them to worship publicly in a large number of villages and towns. A great European state thus took an important step toward religious liberty. Calvinism became firmly established in Holland and Scotland, and it won many followers in England. In the 1600's the Puritans carried Calvinism across the sea to New England, where it was the dominant faith in colonial times.

The Reformation in the Netherlands. Both Lutheranism and Calvinism appeared in the Netherlands. In the 1500's the Netherlands belonged to Catholic Spain. The Spanish ruler was a despot; his rule was so harsh as to rouse both Catholics and Protestants to revolt. The ten southern provinces of the Netherlands, from which modern Belgium grew, soon made peace with Spain. Belgium has remained mainly Catholic. The seven northern provinces, after a long and hard contest for independence, won their freedom from Spain. In these provinces, which we now know either as Holland or the Netherlands, Calvinism is the dominant religion.

The Reformation in England. Well before Luther had posted his theses on the Wittenberg church door, English scholars and politicians, as well as the Lollards, had been dissatisfied with the activities of the prelates of the Church. As early as 1515 the relations of church and state had been bitterly criticized

HENRY VIII AND ANNE BOLEYN. Central figures in the English Reformation. Their daughter, Elizabeth I, restored Protestantism to England after Henry's first daughter, Mary Tudor, had for a short time re-established Catholicism.

in the House of Commons. Many Englishmen preferred that their church be English and not Roman in her allegiance. It fell to Henry VIII (1509–1547), king of England, to play the leading role in England's break with the papacy.

Henry was an able though despotic ruler, who was accustomed to having his own way. He had married Catherine of Aragon, the widow of his brother. Such a marriage was contrary to church law and was made possible only by special dispensation (permission) from the pope. Later, Henry wished to divorce Catherine so he could marry Anne Boleyn, a lady-in-waiting at the royal court. Henry appealed to the pope for a divorce on the grounds that the marriage to Catherine never had been lawful. For moral reasons the pope hesitated to permit the divorce. Besides, he did not want to offend the powerful king of Spain and Holy Roman emperor, Charles V, who was Catherine's nephew. While the pope hesitated, King Henry acted. He induced an English court to grant him the divorce and influenced Parliament to pass, in 1534, the

Act of Supremacy. This law declared the king, not the pope, to be head of the church in England.

The break with the papacy was accepted by those Englishmen who had been influenced by the teachings of Wycliffe and the reformers on the Continent and by those who desired that no foreign power exist in England. Henry gained other supporters by distributing church lands and offices among the English nobility. He took firm measures to suppress those who opposed his religious policies. The church in England became known as the *Church of England,* with an unbroken tradition dating back to the coming of St. Augustine from Rome to Kent in 597. Many features peculiar to Roman Catholicism were dropped, the service was translated into English, and the king became the political head of the church. Henry's followers considered that they thereby united the virtues of the Reformation with those of the ancient Catholic tradition. The Episcopal Church in America follows most of the beliefs and practices of the Church of England.

Let every member recognize that not only when he makes his [vows], but throughout his life, he is subject to the present Pope and to his successors. We are bound beyond the ordinary by a particular vow in this regard. If . . . the . . . Pope . . . should send us for . . . propagation of the faith to the Turks . . . or to heretics . . . , we are to obey without evasion or excuse. Wherefore, those who would join us should consider long before taking this load upon their shoulders . . . In everything touching the rule, let obedience be given to the general. He in turn is always to be mindful of the goodness, gentleness, and love of Christ. All should be concerned for the instruction of youth in Christion doctrine and the Ten Commandments.

—B. J. Kidd, *Documents Illustrative of the Continental Reformation.*

The Catholic Counter Reformation

The reforming popes. The rapid spread of Protestantism soon led to a new movement, the Catholic Reformation. The popes now turned from the cultivation of Renaissance art and literature to the defense of the Church. They made needed changes in the papal court and appointed to church offices men distinguished for virtue and learning. This reform of the papacy dates from the time of Paul III, who became pope in 1534.

The Society of Jesus. The most important agency of the Catholic Reformation was the Society of Jesus, founded by a Spanish soldier and nobleman, Ignatius Loyola (loi-ō′là, 1491–1556). The Jesuits, as members of the society came to be called, formed an army of

THE RELIGIONS OF EUROPE, 1648

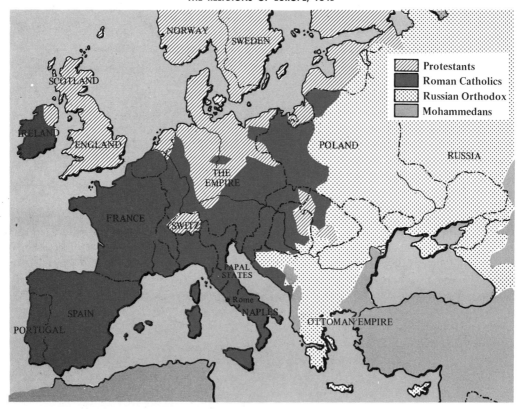

Protestants
Roman Catholics
Russian Orthodox
Mohammedans

spiritual soldiers, living under the strictest obedience to their head, and fighting for the Church against heretical beliefs. They served as preachers, confessors, teachers, and missionaries. Their activities in Poland, Hungary, Bohemia, and other countries did much to roll back the rising tide of Protestantism in Europe. The Jesuits also entered lands outside Europe. In India, China, the East Indies, the Philippines, Africa, and the two Americas their converts were numbered by hundreds of thousands.

Council of Trent, 1545–1563. Another agency in the Catholic Reformation was the great church council summoned by Pope Paul III. The council met at Trent, on the borders of Germany and Italy. It continued, with intermissions, for nearly twenty years. The Council of Trent made no essential changes in Roman Catholic doctrines, which remained as theologians had set them forth in the Middle Ages. It declared that the pope was supreme over spiritual matters throughout Christendom. It authorized the continued use of the Vulgate, or Latin Bible, as the correct version of the Scriptures and reserved to the Church the right of interpreting the Scriptures. The council also forbade the sale of ecclesiastical offices and issued decrees requiring bishops and other prelates to attend strictly to their duties.

The Index. The council authorized the pope to draw up a list, or index, of works which Roman Catholics might not read. This action was not an innovation or novelty. The Church from an early day had condemned and destroyed heretical writings. The invention of printing, by making it easier to spread new ideas which might endanger the existing order, led to stricter regulation of thought. Today, both Protestants and Catholics have relaxed their censorships. The Church ended the "Index of Prohibited Books" in 1966, and left choice of reading to "the mature conscience."

The Inquisition. The Catholic Reformation gained further strength from the Inquisition. This was a system of ecclesiastical courts for the discovery and punishment of heretics. Such courts had been set up in the Middle Ages to suppress heresies such as the Albigensian movement. (See page 187.) After the Council of Trent the courts of the Inquisition redoubled their activity, especially in Italy, the Netherlands, Spain, and the Spanish colonies. The Inquisition probably did much to prevent the spread of Protestantism in Italy and Spain. In the Netherlands, on the other hand, the Inquisition only aroused hatred, and helped to provoke the successful revolt of the northern provinces (Holland) from Spain. To this day most of the Dutch people are members of Protestant churches.

Results of the Reformation

Extent of Protestantism. In 1500 the Roman Catholic Church embraced all Europe west of Russia and the Balkans. By 1600 nearly half of its former members had renounced their allegiance. The greater part of Germany

---

PROFESSION OF FAITH

I hold unswervingly that there is a purgatory and that the souls there detained are helped by the intercessions of the faithful; likewise also that the Saints who reign with Christ are to be venerated and invoked; that they offer prayers to God for us and that their relics are to be venerated. I firmly assert that the images of Christ and of the ever-Virgin Mother of God, as also those of other Saints, are to be kept and retained, and that due honour and veneration is to be accorded them; and I affirm that the power of indulgences has been left by Christ in the Church, and that their use is very salutary for Christian people.

I recognize the Holy Catholic and Apostolic Roman Church as the mother and mistress of all churches; and I vow and swear true obedience to the Roman Pontiff, the successor of blessed Peter, the chief of Apostles and the representative of Jesus Christ.

—Henry Bettenson, ed., *Documents of the Christian Church.*

---

and Switzerland and all of Denmark, Norway, Sweden, Holland, England, Wales, and Scotland became independent of the papacy. The religious unity of western Christendom, which had been preserved throughout the Middle Ages, thus disappeared. It has not since been restored, although its absence has caused concern to many churchmen.

Divisions among Protestants. The Protestants denied the authority of popes and church councils. Instead, they turned to the Bible for religious guidance. But there were various ways of interpreting the Bible. Consequently, Protestantism split up into many sects, or denominations, and the number of these is still growing. Nearly all, however, are offshoots from the two main varieties of Protestantism—Lutheranism and Calvinism—

which appeared in the sixteenth century.

Religious wars. Religious disagreements sometimes played a part in military conflicts. Of the four most important wars of religion, we have already mentioned three: the conflict between Huguenots and Catholics in France, the struggle of the Netherlands for independence from Spain, and the fighting in Germany which was ended by the Peace of Augsburg in 1555. The last and most terrible of the religious wars was the Thirty Years' War in Germany, which continued from 1618 to 1648. Denmark, Sweden, France, the Holy Roman Empire, and various German states took part in the struggle. Beginning as a religious civil war within Germany, it quickly became an international war for political power. Germany lost over half its

EUROPE IN 1648, AFTER THE THIRTY YEARS' WAR

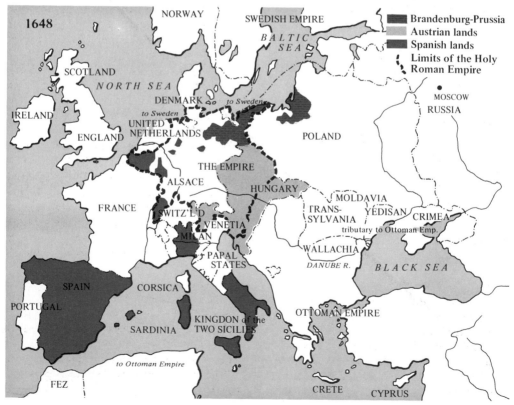

population, whole cities and towns were wiped out, and the people who remained alive led a miserable existence. Gustavus Adolphus, who led the Swedish forces, was one of the few noble leaders produced by this horrible war. Peace was finally restored by the Treaty of Westphalia in 1648. According to the peace terms, Switzerland and Holland were recognized as independent countries. France obtained Alsace, the power of the Holy Roman emperor in Germany was reduced, and the German princes were permitted to choose Calvinism as well as Lutheranism and Catholicism for themselves and their subjects.

The Reformation and freedom of thought. Religious liberty as we understand it today was not introduced by the Reformation or by the religious wars. Nothing was further from the minds of Luther, Calvin, and other Protestant reformers than the toleration of beliefs unlike their own. The early Protestant sects punished dissenters as zealously as the Roman Church punished heretics. Complete freedom of conscience and the right of private judgment in religion have been attained only within the last hundred years.

International law. The religious wars led, indirectly, to the founding of international law. Among those shocked by savage atrocities in the Thirty Years' War was Hugo Grotius. In 1625 this Dutch lawyer and statesman published his famous work: *On the Laws of War and Peace*. His attempt to replace international lawlessness with reason has given him the title "father of international law."

REVIEWING THE CHAPTER

TERMS TO UNDERSTAND: *Renaissance, classics, humanities, fresco, secularism, vernacular, Babylonian Captivity, Great Schism, tithe, indulgence, papal bull, diet, Peace of Augsburg, Huguenots, dispensation, Society of Jesus, Index, Inquisition.*

PERSONS TO IDENTIFY: *Petrarch, Erasmus, Hans Holbein, Sir Francis Bacon, Copernicus, Galileo, Kepler, Sir Isaac Newton, Vesalius, Harvey, John Wycliffe, John Huss, Luther, Tetzel, Zwingli, Calvin, Henry VIII, Ignatius Loyola, Grotius.*

PLACES TO LOCATE: *Avignon, Wittenberg, Netherlands, Belgium, Trent, Westphalia.*

QUESTIONS TO ANSWER

1. (a) Why did the Renaissance begin in Italy? (b) Explain the interest of Renaissance scholars in the classics.
2. Describe the styles which mark the work of Renaissance (a) architects, (b) sculptors, (c) painters. (d) Name the leading figures in each field.

3. (a) What were the two main influences which helped to produce the new literature? (b) Who were the leading writers of the new literature?
4. (a) Explain what is meant by the scientific method. (b) What findings resulted from the application of the scientific method in the Renaissance period to astronomy? Anatomy? Physiology?
5. Why did the influence of the Church in western Europe decline during the Renaissance?
6. (a) What was the basic difference between Catholic beliefs and those of Luther? (b) Explain the popularity of Lutheranism. (c) In what countries did Lutheranism become the official religion? (d) Did Calvin's beliefs most closely resemble those of Zwingli or Luther? Explain your answer.
7. (a) What areas were influenced by the teaching of Calvin? (b) Describe the religious settlement in Belgium, Holland, and England.
8. Explain three steps taken in the Catholic Reformation to meet the Protestant revolt.
9. (a) List the four main wars of religion. (b) Give the terms of the Treaty of Westphalia.

12 Europeans Build Colonial Empires

MARCO POLO on his travels through Asia, as shown in a detail of a fourteenth-century map. After he returned to Italy, Marco was captured in a battle between Genoa and Venice. While he was imprisoned, Marco dictated the story of his travels to a fellow prisoner. His book gave Europeans their first reasonably accurate picture of the Far East.

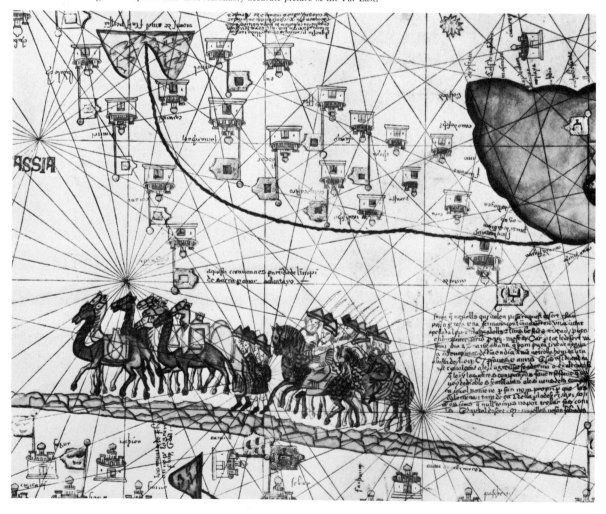

While the Renaissance and Reformation movements were developing, a third movement was also bringing changes in the lives of Europeans. Geographical discovery, exploration, and colonization led to a vast increase of commerce and to the opening of the New World to European civilization. Thus new knowledge of geography, together with the new attitudes developed during the Renaissance and Reformation, played an important part in bringing about the transition in Europe from medieval to modern times.

Geographical Discovery

Knowledge of geography in the Middle Ages. The Greeks and Romans had become familiar with a large part of Europe, Asia, and North Africa, but much of their learning was forgotten during the early Middle Ages. The Arabs, whose conquests and commerce extended from the Atlantic to the Pacific, far surpassed the Christian peoples in knowledge of the world. In the late Middle Ages, however, western Europeans began to learn more about geography. The crusades excited interest in foreign lands, and encouraged religious pilgrimages and missions in both the Middle and Far East. Merchants who visited the Orient also helped to awaken interest.

The Polos in the Far East, 1271–1295. Among these merchants were the Venetians, Nicolo and Maffeo Polo, and Nicolo's son, Marco. The Polos made an adventurous journey through the heart of Asia to the court of Kublai Khan, at what is now Peiping in China. The Mongol ruler received them in a friendly manner. They gained much wealth by trade. Marco entered the Khan's service and went on several expeditions to distant parts of the Mongol realm. When the Polos finally returned to Venice, after an absence of twenty-four years, their relatives did not recognize them.

Marco Polo's book. The story of the Polos, as written down at Marco's dictation, became one of the most popular works of the Middle Ages. In this book people read of far Cathay (China), with its wealth, huge cities, and swarming population; mysterious and secluded Tibet; Burma, Siam, and Cochin-China, with their palaces and pagodas; the East Indies, famed for spices; Ceylon, abounding in pearls; India, little known in Europe since the days of Alexander the Great, and Cipango (Japan), which Marco described from hearsay as an island whose inhabitants were civilized and so rich that the royal palace was roofed and paved with gold. These accounts made Europeans more eager than ever to go to the Far East.

Trade with the Far East. Europeans wanted to reach the Far East chiefly for purposes of trade. Among the eastern goods they most desired were spices—cinnamon, pepper, cloves, nutmeg, and ginger. In those days spices were used freely to preserve food and to disguise the unpleasant flavor that developed in meat kept without refrigeration. Precious stones, drugs, perfumes, gums, dyes, and fragrant woods from the Far East also found a ready market in Europe. Goods from the East were enormously expensive by the time they reached the European markets. Of the three routes over which Oriental products were carried to the eastern Mediterranean, every one involved some costly overland transportation. (See map, page 154, for the three routes traders used.) During the journey, the goods passed through the hands of various merchants, each of whom marked up the price so as to make a profit for himself. Finally, tolls charged by the Ottoman Turks (see page 174) added to the cost of trade between Europe and the Far East.

Rivalry for the eastern trade. Italian merchants monopolized most of the carrying trade from the eastern Mediterranean to Europe. Portuguese and Spanish merchants noted their high profits with envious eyes. About 1450 the Portuguese and Spanish entered the eastern trade in competition with the Italians. They hoped to find an *all-water* route to the Indies, thus avoiding Turkish tolls in the Middle East, reducing transportation costs, and concentrating in their own hands the profits other middlemen had been making. In this way trade rivalry led to exploration; the wonderful geographical discoveries which soon followed were at first merely a by-product of the search for a new and less expensive route to the fabled Far East.

Prince Henry of Portugal. The Portuguese succeeded in finding a new route to the Far East partly because of the able work of Prince Henry the Navigator. The son of the king of Portugal, he gave up a military career and for more than forty years devoted his wealth, learning, and enthusiasm to geographical discovery. He believed that the Indies could be reached by sailing south around Africa. Under his direction better maps were

made, Portuguese ships were equipped with compasses, and learned men were brought to Portugal to instruct seamen in all the nautical knowledge of the time. Prince Henry dispatched expedition after expedition southward to explore the African coast. By the time of his death (1460), Portuguese seamen had reached about a third of the distance to

THE POLOS begin their journey to Cathay.

the southern tip of Africa. More expeditions followed, and finally Bartholomew Diaz rounded the southernmost point of Africa (1486). The king of Portugal, recognizing its importance as a stage on the route to the Indies, named it the Cape of Good Hope.

Da Gama reaches India, 1498. The great problem of finding an all-water route to the Far East was solved by the Portuguese mariner, Vasco da Gama. He went past the Cape of Good Hope with four tiny ships, and in 1498 arrived at Calicut, a seaport on the southwest coast of India. When Da Gama returned to Portugal, he brought back a cargo of spices which repaid sixty times the cost of the expedition. The Portuguese king received him with high honor and named him Admiral of the Indies.

Spain enters the competition. In 1492 King Ferdinand and Queen Isabella of Spain conquered Granada, the last Moorish stronghold in Spain. (See page 163.) With their country united at last, the Spanish rulers could take part in the rivalry for the rich eastern trade. Six years before Vasco da Gama cast anchor in the harbor of Calicut, the Spaniards dispatched a mariner to find new trade routes.

Christopher Columbus. The mariner sent out by Spain was Christopher Columbus, a native of Genoa, Italy. He had devoted most of his life to the sea and had become convinced that the world was round and therefore one could reach the Far East by sailing west. The idea was not new. Ptolemy and other ancient geographers had known that the world was round, and their teachings had been familiar to the Greeks and Romans and to educated men throughout the Middle Ages.

Behaim's globe, shown on this page was made in 1492. It shows that geographers believed the world was round, although they did not have an accurate knowledge of the distance from Europe to Asia. Columbus is justly famed, not because his ideas were original but because he dared to act upon them.

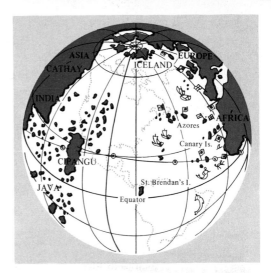

BEHAIM'S GLOBE. Made in 1492, it proves some geographers believed the world was round.

Columbus discovers America, 1492. Queen Isabella aided Columbus in outfitting a fleet of three small ships. When he started out, he firmly believed that a journey of only four thousand miles would bring him to the Far East. After a voyage of several weeks, he reached a group of islands off the southeastern coast of North America. The first land sighted was the island of San Salvador, on October 12, 1492. Columbus, thinking the world was smaller than it actually is, believed he had reached the Indies. He therefore called the natives "Indians." The islands he discovered are still known as the West Indies. Years passed before the Spaniards realized that they had found the New World.

Significance of the discovery. When Columbus returned to Spain in 1493, he carried no valuable cargoes of gold or spices—just a few naked savages and some worthless beads. His three later voyages to the Western Hemisphere were no more profitable, and Columbus died a disappointed man. Da Gama's voyage in 1498 won greater praise at the time than did the work of Columbus. Today, however, we realize that the discovery of America by Columbus was one of the most significant events in world history. It shifted the main

Prima ego velivolis ambivi Cursibus Orbem
Magellane novo te duce ducta freto.
Ambivi, meritoq pocor VICTORIA sunt mi
Vela, alæ, preciu gloria pugna mare.

VICTORIA.

Conveniunt rebus nomina sepe suis. G.

MAGELLAN'S SHIP, THE *VICTORIA*. This was the only one of the original five ships to complete the voyage around the world, and only eighteen men survived. Magellan died in the Philippine Islands, which were named for Philip II, son of the Emperor Charles V.

stream of European commerce from the Mediterranean to the Atlantic, opened the way for a great expansion of European civilization, and marked the beginning of modern times.

Magellan's fleet sails around the world, 1519–1522. Ferdinand Magellan, a Portuguese navigator in the service of Spain, believed that a route to the Indies could be found by sailing around the barrier of land which had stopped Columbus. The Spanish ruler, Charles I, grandson of the Isabella who had supported Columbus, looked with favor upon Magellan's ideas, and provided a fleet of five vessels for the undertaking. Magellan crossed the Atlantic and sailed southward along the eastern coast of South America. At last he rounded the tip of the continent by sailing through the passage which is called, in his honor, the Strait of Magellan. The ocean which he now entered was so much more quiet and peaceful than the Atlantic that he named it the Pacific Ocean. Magellan continued sailing across the Pacific for more than a hundred days, and finally reached the Philippine Islands, where he was killed in a fight with the natives. A single ship carried back to Spain the few sailors who survived the hardships of the voyage. They returned nearly three years after the start of the journey.

Significance of Magellan's voyage. In the history of geographical discovery, three events stand out as supremely important. The first of these was Da Gama's discovery of the water route to India; the second was Columbus's discovery of the New World; the third was the voyage of Magellan's men around the world—the first circumnavigation of the globe. (The map facing this page shows the routes they followed.) Magellan's voyage proved that America, at least on the south, had no connection with Asia, and that the western sea route to the Indies really existed. Furthermore, it revealed the enormous extent of the Pacific Ocean and led to the discovery of many large islands in the East Indies. Men now were sure that the earth is round. In the distance covered by Magellan they had a rough approximation as to its size. Magellan stands beside Da Gama and Columbus in the company of great explorers.

Beginning of the Portuguese and Spanish Empires

Establishing a Portuguese empire. After Da Gama's voyage, the Portuguese made haste to secure the wealth of the Indies. By the middle of the sixteenth century they had won trading rights in a large area, including the western coast of India, Ceylon, and key trading stations in the Indies. Portugal established almost a complete monopoly of the spice trade, and her cities displaced the Italian

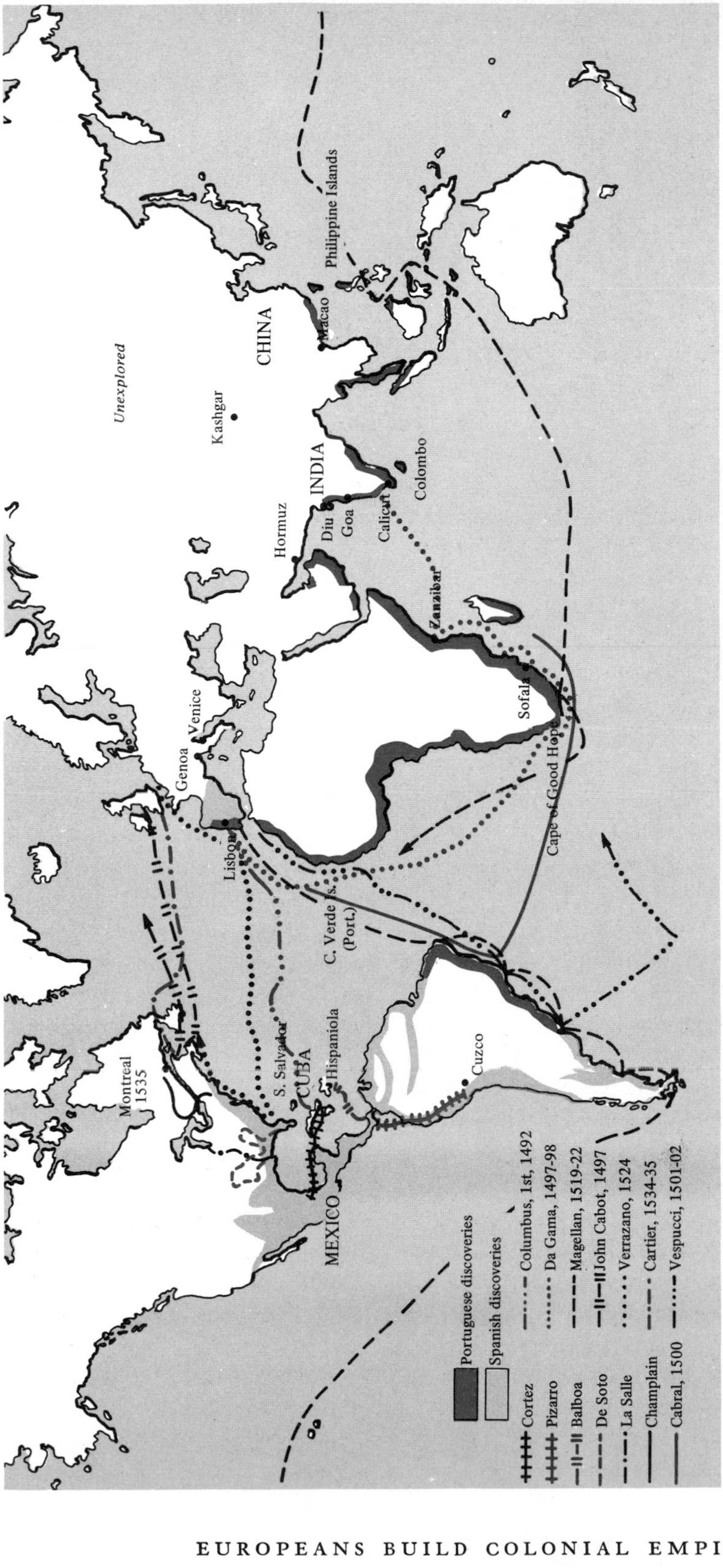

VOYAGES OF DISCOVERY

Portuguese discoveries
Spanish discoveries

++++ Cortez	—·—· Columbus, 1st, 1492	
++++ Pizarro	········ Da Gama, 1497-98	
—||—|| Balboa	—|| —|| Magellan, 1519-22	
—— De Soto	—||—|| John Cabot, 1497	
—··— La Salle	········ Verrazano, 1524	
—·—· Champlain	—·—· Cartier, 1534-35	
—— Cabral, 1500	—— Vespucci, 1501-02	

Unexplored

CHINA
Kashgar
Philippine Islands
Macao
INDIA
Hormuz
Diu
Goa
Calicut
Colombo
Zanzibar
Genoa
Venice
Sofala
Cape of Good Hope
Lisbon
C. Verde Is. (Port.)
Montreal 1535
S. Salvador
CUBA
Hispaniola
Cuzco
MEXICO

cities as distribution centers for spices in Europe. Venturing further in the Far East, the Portuguese opened up commerce with China and with Japan. In Africa they built numerous posts along the coast, which served as centers for trade with the natives. In South America Portugal conquered the area we know as Brazil and held it as a colony until 1822. The language, literature, and customs of Brazil are still in large part those of Portugal.

Establishing a Spanish empire. Spain led the way in the exploration of the New World that Columbus had discovered. Ponce de León discovered Florida in 1513; Balboa sighted the Pacific in the same year after crossing the Isthmus of Panama. Cortés overthrew the Aztec power in Mexico; Pizarro conquered the Incas of Peru; De Soto discovered the Mississippi; and Coronado explored in what is now the southwestern part of the United States. These men laid the foundations of the Spanish colonial empire. It included the southern part of the United States as well as Mexico, Central America, the West Indies, and all South America except Brazil. Outside of the New World, Spain also held the Philippine Islands in the Pacific.

The Spaniards meet the Indians. When the Spaniards first arrived in the New World they met a people previously unknown to them. The natives of America, whom Columbus called Indians, resemble Mongoloid peoples in some physical features, such as the reddish brown complexion, the uniformly coarse and black hair, and the high cheekbones. On the other hand the large aquiline nose, the straight eyes, never oblique, and the

LIMA, PERU. Founded in 1535 by the conqueror Pizarro, the "City of the Kings" shows careful planning. The streets fan out from a number of *plazas*, or squares, the first of which was the Plaza de Armas.

tall stature of some tribes are not typical of Mongoloids. It seems safe to conclude that the Indians came from Asia originally but developed racial characteristics of their own during long centuries of isolation from the rest of mankind.

Indian culture. The Indians, because of their isolation, had to work out by themselves many arts, inventions, and discoveries. The various groups spoke over a thousand languages and dialects, and not one has yet been traced outside of America. Anthropologists have identified fourteen culture groups, each differing in major ways from the others, and ranging all the way from savagery to civilization. Although most of the Indians used implements of polished stone, some groups also had tools made of unsmelted copper, while a few advanced groups in Mexico and Peru learned to make tools of bronze. The Indians did not know the use of iron. There was no one system of government or religion practiced by all Indians. For the most part, Indian religion consisted of nature worship. All nature was recognized as the abode of spiritual powers, whom men ought to conciliate by prayers and sacrifices. Three crops now grown throughout the world—corn (maize), tobacco, and the potato—were first cultivated by the Indians. They had domesticated the dog, and some groups in Latin America had domesticated the llama, vicuña, and the alpaca. Most of the American Indians were not savages but barbarians fairly well advanced in culture.

The Mayas. Indian culture reached its highest development in Mexico, Central America, and Peru. The earliest great civilization was that of the Mayas, who settled in Yucatán, Guatemala, and Honduras about 1000 B.C. The remains of their cities—the Ninevehs and Babylons of the New World—lie buried in tropical jungles. The temples, shrines, altars, and statues in these ancient cities show that the Mayas had made much progress in the fine arts. They knew enough about astronomy to devise a solar calendar of three

MAYAN STATUE OF ASTRONOMER, made to commemorate a Mayan astronomical congress held in A.D. 503

hundred and sixty-five days, and enough mathematics to use a symbol for zero and to employ numbers exceeding a million. In writing, the Mayas had advanced beyond the use of pictures and were beginning to make use of symbols for the sounds of words and syllables. When, if ever, their hieroglyphs have been completely deciphered, we shall learn much more about this gifted people. The Mayas were conquered by the Toltecs about A.D. 1200.

The Aztecs. The Aztecs were an Indian people who came down from the north early in the 1200's and established themselves on the plateau of central Mexico. They conquered neighboring tribes and formed an empire. When the Spanish came, the ruler was Montezuma. The capital was on the site of the present Mexico City. The Aztecs borrowed much of their art, science, and knowledge of writing from their Maya and Toltec neighbors. They built houses and temples of stone or sun-dried brick; constructed aqueducts, roads, and bridges; and excelled in the dyeing, weaving, and spinning of cotton. Advanced in some fields of art, they made beautiful ornaments of silver, gold, and gems. They worshiped many gods and sacrificed war captives to them.

The Incas. The lofty tablelands of the Andes in South America were also the seat of an advanced Indian culture. The greater part of the territory now included in Ecuador, Peru, Bolivia, and northern Chile came under the sway of the Incas, the "Children of the Sun," as they called themselves. The Inca power centered in the Peruvian city of Cuzco and on the shores of Lake Titicaca, which lies twelve thousand feet above sea level. In this region of magnificent scenery the traveler views with astonishment the ruins of deserted cities, which were built either by the Incas or by the Indians whom they conquered or displaced. The Incas displayed great skill in the manual arts; they were expert goldsmiths, silversmiths, and potters; as cultivators and engineers they surpassed their European conquerors.

Intermarriage of Spaniards and Indians. The Spaniards brought few women with them and hence had to find their wives among the Indians. Intermarriage between the two peoples became common at an early date. The result was the mixed race of *mestizos* found today throughout most of Spanish America. The Indian strain predominates, because almost everywhere the natives were far more numerous than the white settlers.

Conversion of the Indians. Many of the Indians were converted to Christianity. Devoted monks penetrated deep into the American continents, bringing with them not only the Christian religion but also European civilization. The natives were usually gathered into permanent villages, or "missions," each one with its church and school. Converts who learned to read and write sometimes became priests or entered the monastic orders. The monks also took much interest in the material welfare of the Indians and taught them European methods of farming, building, spinning, weaving, and cooking.

Spanish-American culture. When we recall the often brutal treatment of the Incas and Aztecs by the Spaniards, the civilizing work done by the Spaniards in the New World should not be forgotten. Here were the earliest American hospitals and asylums; they were for the use of Indians and Negroes as well as Spaniards. Here were the first American schools and colleges. Twelve institutions of higher learning arose in Spanish America during the colonial period. The fine arts also flourished in the Spanish colonies. Architects of the United States have copied the beautiful churches and public buildings of Mexico and Peru. Spain gave her language, religion, law, political institutions, and economic system to half the New World.

Mercantilism Stimulates Further Colonial Expansion

Decline of Spain and Portugal. By the beginning of the 1600's both Portugal and Spain had begun to decline as colonizing and commercial nations. Portugal lost ground after

AZTEC CALENDAR STONE. Aztec knowledge of astronomy on which this calendar was based probably came in part from the Mayas.

INCA RUINS. Machu Picchu, the lost city of the Incas, was found by archeologists lying in a saddle between two peaks. A complex of terraces, temples, sacred plazas, and residences were discovered during its excavation.

she was united with Spain in 1580. Spain proved unable to prevent the advance of three new rivals for commerce and colonies. The new rivals who came forward in the 1600's and 1700's were the Dutch, French, and English.

Motives for colonization. Various motives inspired colonial expansion. National rivalry had considerable weight. Holland, France, and England wanted possessions overseas to balance those obtained by Portugal and Spain. Religion also played a part, as when Jesuit missionaries braved the American wilderness to convert the Indians to Christianity, and when the Pilgrim fathers sought in the New World a refuge from persecution. However, the main motive for colonization was economic. Colonies were set up as a means of increasing the wealth of the mother country, especially its supply of gold and silver.

Mercantilism. By the seventeenth century most of the leaders in European politics and commerce believed in an economic doctrine called "mercantilism." The mercantilists held that a country should so regulate its foreign trade as to attract to itself the largest possible amount of money. One of the chief aims of the mercantilists was to have gold and silver coming into the country. The mercantilists desired a large supply of money for two reasons. It would provide capital for investment in business pursuits, and it would provide funds for the army and navy in time of war. The mercantilists believed that a country prospered by *encouraging the export of manufactured goods* and by *discouraging their importation*. By selling more than it bought, a country would have money coming in; it would enjoy a "favorable balance of trade." Although economists tell us that a country cannot prosper unless it imports as much as it exports, the doctrine of mercantilism still influences many governments, including our own. Countries use tariffs, for instance, to

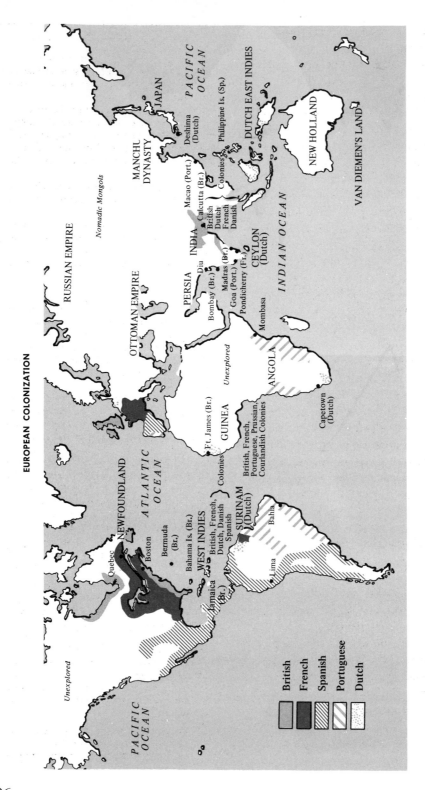

EUROPEAN COLONIZATION

British
French
Spanish
Portuguese
Dutch

PACIFIC OCEAN

Unexplored

NEWFOUNDLAND

ATLANTIC OCEAN

Quebec

Boston

Bermuda (Br.)

Bahama Is. (Br.)

WEST INDIES

Jamaica (Br.)

British, French, Dutch, Danish Spanish

Colonies

SURINAM (Dutch)

British, French, Portuguese, Prussian, Courlandish Colonies

Lima

Bahia

Ft. James (Br.)

GUINEA

Unexplored

ANGOLA

Capetown (Dutch)

RUSSIAN EMPIRE

Nomadic Mongols

OTTOMAN EMPIRE

PERSIA

INDIA

Diu

Bombay (Br.)

Madras (Br.)

Goa (Port.)

Pondicherry (Fr.)

Calcutta (Br.)

British
Dutch
French
Danish

CEYLON (Dutch)

Mombasa

INDIAN OCEAN

MANCHU DYNASTY

JAPAN

Deshima (Dutch)

Macao (Port.)

Philippine Is. (Sp.)

Colonies

DUTCH EAST INDIES

PACIFIC OCEAN

NEW HOLLAND

VAN DIEMEN'S LAND

discourage imports, and bounties to encourage "home" industries.

Mercantilism and colonial policy. The doctrine of mercantilism led naturally to a desire for colonies. Colonies could produce raw materials needed by the mother country, and the money paid for these raw materials went to citizens of the mother country, not to citizens of a foreign country. Moreover, the colony could furnish a market for the manufactured goods of the mother country. This thinking prompted the colonial ventures of Holland, France, and England. Each country passed laws regulating the economic activities of its colonies. They were given bounties for producing articles needed by the homeland, and were discouraged from manufactures which would compete with those at home. The colonies were permitted little or no trade with foreign countries, since it was thought that such trade would benefit foreign countries rather than the mother country. Colonies were viewed simply as estates to be worked for the advantage of the country fortunate enough to possess them. Portugal and Spain first adopted this colonial policy. Holland, France, England, and other European countries later followed their example.

Trading companies. The home government did not itself engage in colonial commerce, nor did it leave this privilege open to all citizens. Instead, it granted the privilege of trading with a given colony or trading area to a single private company. In return for the monopoly of trade with the inhabitants of a colony, the trading company was expected to govern and protect them. Trading companies were very numerous. For instance, Holland, France, England, Sweden, Denmark, Scotland, and Prussia each chartered its own "East India Company." The state of New York was originally founded by the Dutch West India Company. English companies established the colonies of Virginia and Massachusetts.

REASONS FOR ENGLISH COLONIZATION

A brefe collection of certaine reasons to induce her Majestie and the state to take in hande the westerne voyadge and the plantinge there.—

The soyle yeldeth, and may be made to yelde, all the severall comodities of Europe, and of all kingdomes, domynions, and territories that England tradeth withe, that by trade of merchandize cometh into this realme.

The passage thither and home is neither to longe nor to shorte, but easie, and to be made twise in the yere.

The passage cutteth not nere the trade of any prince, nor nere any of their contries or territories, and is a safe passage, and not easie to be annoyed by prince or potentate whatsoever.

. . . . .

At the firste traficque with the people of those partes, the subjects of this realme for many yeres shall chaunge many cheape comodities of these partes for thinges of highe valor there not estemed; and this to the greate inrichinge of the realme, if common use faile not.

By makinge of shippes and by preparinge of thinges for the same, by makinge of cables and cordage, by plantinge of vines and olive trees, and by makinge of wyne and oyle, by husbandrie, and by thousandes of thinges there to be done, infinite nombers of the Englishe nation may be set on worke, to the unburdenynge of the realme with many that nowe lyve chardgeable to the state at home.

Wee shall by plantinge there inlarge the glory of the gospell, and from England plante sincere relligion, and provide a safe and a sure place to receave people from all partes of the worlde that are forced to flee for the truthe of Gods worde.

. . . . .

Many men of excellent wittes and of divers singular giftes, overthrowen by . . . some folly of youthe, that are not able to live in England, may there be raised againe, and doe their contrie goodd service; and many nedefull uses there may (to greate purpose) require the savinge of greate nombers, that for trifles may otherwise be devoured by the gallowes. . . .

—Richard Hakluyt, "Discourse Concerning Westerne Planting," *Old South Leaflets*.

The Dutch Establish a Colonial Empire

How the Dutch became traders. The Dutch, living in a small territory which was never capable of supporting more than a fraction of the inhabitants by farming, naturally became seamen. After the discovery of the Cape of Good Hope route to the East Indies (see page 199). Dutch traders met Portuguese merchants at Lisbon and there obtained spices and other eastern commodities for distribution throughout Europe. When the Dutch won their independence from Spain (see page 190), they were in a position to enter the competition for overseas trade. They sent their first trading expedition to India in 1595, and by 1601 had sent fourteen more to the Far East. Well constructed and skillfully manned, their merchant fleet ranked far ahead of French and English shipping on the high seas.

The Dutch in the Far East. In 1652 the Dutch government chartered an East India Company and gave it a monopoly of Dutch trade and rule throughout the East from the Cape of Good Hope to the Strait of Magellan. Competition in trade with Spain and Portugal quickly developed into open fighting. The Dutch captured many Portuguese and Spanish ships and seized trading posts in the Far East. The Portuguese lost nearly all their Asiatic possessions. Ceylon, Malacca, Sumatra, Java, Celebes, and the Moluccas, or Spice Islands, fell into the hands of the Dutch. The Dutch also began to trade with China and Japan; by the middle of the 1600's they had won control over commerce with the Far East.

The Dutch in South Africa. In 1652 the Dutch East India Company began a settlement called Cape Town at the Cape of Good Hope. The company officials intended to make Cape Town merely a supply station, where ships could pick up fresh food and water for the long voyage to the Indies. Before long, however, numbers of Dutch emigrants began to arrive, together with French Protestants who had left their native land to escape persecution. The Dutch farmer-settlers, called Boers, gradually moved into the interior and laid there the foundation of Dutch sway in South Africa. The Cape of Good Hope became a British possession at the opening of the nineteenth century, but the Boer republics retained their independence for another hundred years.

The Dutch in America. Fired by their success and enriched by their gains in the East, the Dutch laid plans for founding another colonial empire in the New World. In 1609 they sent out Henry Hudson (an Englishman) to search for a northern passage to the Indies. He failed to find a passage, but he did discover the Hudson River and Hudson Bay. The Dutch at once opened up a fur trade with the Indians along the Hudson River and built a fort on Manhattan Island, at the river's mouth. The little station on Manhattan Island grew into a flourishing port, which the Dutch named New Amsterdam, and Dutch settlers moved inland to settle along the banks of the Hudson. In 1655 the Dutch seized the Swedish settlements on the Delaware River. The Dutch also secured part of Guiana, on the northeast coast of South America, as well as some of the West Indies.

Dutch colonial policy. The Dutch established colonies mainly for the purpose of promoting trade. They gave trading companies almost unlimited control over the colonies. The Dutch West India Company held a monopoly on all trade with people living along the Atlantic coasts of Africa and the Americas. This company also governed all Dutch colonies in the Atlantic basin. In the Far East, Dutch colonies and trade were controlled by the Dutch East India Company. The companies ruled in an autocratic way, but for a time they were highly successful. By the middle of the 1600's the Dutch were the commercial leaders of Europe.

The French Enter the Colonial Field

The French in America. France sent two early explorers to North America: Verrazano (1524) and Cartier (1534–1540). Although the voyages of these men gave France a claim to North America, a series of wars in Europe prevented her from entering at once into the race for colonies. In 1608 the French established their first successful colony at Quebec on the lower St. Lawrence River. From Quebec they moved into the heart of North America, making new settlements, opening up the fur trade, and converting many of the Indians to Christianity. In 1718 they founded New Orleans at the mouth of the Mississippi. It became a trading center and a base of supplies for other French settlements, which were extended farther north until France held a chain of posts from New Orleans to the mouth of the St. Lawrence. By 1750 about 80,000 Frenchmen occupied the vast St. Lawrence–Mississippi area. They prospered through control of the fur trade. Many French traders and trappers lived among the Indians and, like the Spanish, chose Indian wives. The French also settled several islands in the West Indies, where they built up thriving sugar plantations.

The French in India. In 1664 the French chartered their own East India Company, giving it a monopoly on French trade with India. Agents of the company made their headquarters at Pondicherry, on the southeastern coast of India, and established trading stations on both the east and west coasts. The natives of India offered little opposition to the French. Mogul (i.e., Mongol) emperors had ruled India since early in the 1500's (see page 222), but their power was declining by the time the French arrived. During the 1700's India consisted of separate and virtually independent provinces, each ruled by a native prince.

Dupleix leads French expansion. For over seventy years the French East India Company

QUEBEC, the only walled city in America. This view is from the ramparts of the old Citadel. The modern city appears below, and in the distance, the spires of the famous hotel, Château Frontenac.

TWO SPANISH TREASURE GALLEONS being captured by English ships off the coast of Peru. Attacks such as these led to war between Spain and England in the late 1500's.

concerned itself only with trade and did not attempt to annex territory in India. This policy was changed by Dupleix (dü-plĕks′), an able soldier who became governor general of Pondicherry in 1741. Dupleix saw clearly that the breakup of the Mogul empire and the defenseless condition of the native states opened the way to European conquest. An empire for France and glory for himself seemed to lie within his grasp. He entered into alliances with some of the native princes, fortified Pondicherry, and managed to form an army by enlisting native soldiers (sepoys), who were drilled by French officers. Skillful in both diplomacy and war, Dupleix by 1751 brought southern India under French control.

French colonial policy. The French East India Company enjoyed almost complete freedom to govern French possessions in India. For a time the French colonies in America were also directed by various companies, but after 1731 the king took charge of Canada (most of which lay north of the Great Lakes) and Louisiana (in the Mississippi valley). The king's policy toward his colonies was one of paternalism (rigid control from above, as by a stern father over his family). He appointed colonial officials and made all the laws. The colonists were allowed to trade only with other Frenchmen and with the Indians. None but Roman Catholics were permitted to settle in the colonies.

Founding the British Empire

Cabot discovers North America. The English, like the Dutch, turned naturally to seafaring. During the later Middle Ages they built up a thriving trade with other European countries, exporting wool, sheepskins, copper, and tin, and importing cloth, metalware, glass, and other manufactured goods. They also began to look for new commercial opportunities. In 1497 King Henry VII sent John Cabot on an expedition to find a northwest passage to the Indies. Cabot failed to find the passage, but as the effective discoverer of North America he gave England a claim to that continent.

English conflict with Spain. Conflict between England and Spain during the 1500's grew out of a variety of causes. The Spaniards disliked the Reformation in England, denounced English claims to North America, and resented the activities of English merchants who carried on an illegal trade with the Spanish colonies in America. Still worse were English raids on Spanish treasure fleets coming from the New World.

Defeat of the Spanish Armada, 1588. The Spanish king laid plans to end both English attacks and English Protestantism. He gathered together a great fleet, called the Invincible Armada, from the united navies of Spain and Portugal. The Armada was to carry an invading army to England. Before it was ready to sail, Sir Francis Drake carried the fight to Spain. He sailed into Cádiz, the chief Spanish port, and destroyed a vast amount of stores and shipping. This exploit, which Drake called "singeing the King of Spain's beard," delayed the expedition for a year. The Armada at last set out in 1588. It suffered severely in a nine days' fight in the English Channel, and a storm wrecked many of the remaining ships off the Scottish and Irish coasts. Spain and Portugal never recovered their naval and colonial supremacy. During the 1600's the Dutch took the place of Portugal as the dominant commercial power in the East, and the English succeeded in planting colonies in the New World in defiance of Spanish claims there.

Early English colonies in America. The British Empire began in 1607, when the London Company started the settlement of Jamestown in Virginia. In 1620 the Pilgrims founded Plymouth in New England, as a place where they might find religious freedom. Other groups of Englishmen came later to find havens of their own along the eastern coast of North America. In 1664 the English captured the Dutch colony of New Netherland, and by the middle of the 1700's English colonies stretched along the whole seaboard from New England to Georgia. At that time they contained about two million people. Most of the colonists were English, but there were many Irish, Scottish, and Germans, and some Dutch, Swedes, and French Huguenots. In addition to the mainland colonies, England also settled some of the West Indies.

English and French rivalry with the Dutch. The expanding colonial and commercial activities of the English and French brought them into conflict with the Dutch. Both countries passed laws designed to help their own merchants and shippers at the expense of the Dutch. The rivalry broke out into open warfare during the latter half of the 1600's. It was during one of their wars with the Dutch that the English captured New Netherland. By 1700 the Dutch had been driven from India and North America and had lost their supremacy in European commerce. They continued, however, to rule the East Indies.

FORT NEW AMSTERDAM on Manhattan Island, 1626–1628. Though somewhat inaccurate, this picture is important as the earliest known view of New York.

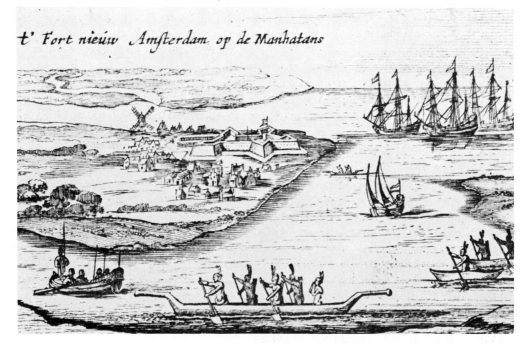

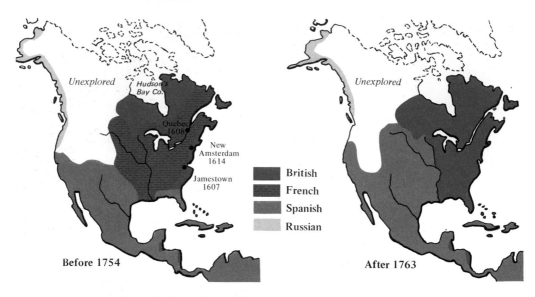

EUROPEAN CLAIMS IN NORTH AMERICA before and after the French and Indian War

Before 1754

Unexplored

Hudson's Bay Co.

Quebec 1608

New Amsterdam 1614

Jamestown 1607

British
French
Spanish
Russian

After 1763

Unexplored

England and France struggle for North America. With the power of the Dutch reduced, England and France entered upon a long and costly struggle for colonies, for commercial domination, and for leadership in Europe. The wars in which the two engaged, sometimes collectively called the "Second Hundred Years' War," are listed in the chart on page 200. England enjoyed several advantages in the contest for control of North America. The English navy was almost always superior to that of France; English colonists greatly outnumbered the French in America; and the English colonies, concentrated along the coast, were better situated both for attack and for defense than were the scattered French outposts. Only the aid of their numerous Indian allies enabled the French to keep the struggle on nearly equal terms. The final contest, known as the French and Indian War, began in 1754 as a struggle for control of the Ohio valley. In 1756 it merged with the Seven Years' War in Europe. At first the war went against the English. When William Pitt became Prime Minister, he strengthened the English efforts by

sending additional troops and supplies and abler commanders to America. In co-operation with the colonists, the English attacked and captured one French stronghold after another. In 1759 Wolfe defeated the gallant Montcalm under the walls of Quebec, and the city surrendered soon afterward. Montreal was taken in the following year. The British flag was then raised over Canada.

Peace of Paris, 1763. The Peace of Paris in 1763 marked the end of the war. France ceded Canada to England, as well as all her North American possessions east of the Mississippi, except for two small islands off the coast of Newfoundland, which were kept for fishing purposes. Spain, which had entered the war on the side of France, gave up Florida and received all the French territories west of the Mississippi. The city of New Orleans, although it lay east of the Mississippi, was also ceded to Spain. (The maps on this page show the changes made by the Peace of Paris.)

Anglo-French rivalry in India. Rivalry between England and France also brought the two countries to blows in India. The English organized an East India Company in 1600, and established agencies at Bombay, Madras, and Calcutta. Both the English and French companies were interested primarily in profits and long remained at peace even when their countries were at war. By the middle of the 1700's, however, the English had become alarmed by the aggressive policies of Dupleix. (See pages 209–210.) Fortunately for the British East India Company, a leader appeared in India who showed a genius even greater than that of Dupleix. Robert Clive began his career in India as a clerk in the company's office at Madras. He volunteered his service in the company's armed forces when fighting with the French began. After training a force of native soldiers (sepoys), he led his men to victories against an army of French and natives in southeastern India. The British East India Company thus became master of that region. Because his policies were not fully understood at home Dupleix was recalled in disgrace to France, where he died a disillusioned and unhappy man.

Battle of Plassey, 1757. Clive found an opportunity for even greater service in the northeast. The native ruler of Bengal suddenly attacked and captured Calcutta. He allowed one hundred and forty-six British prisoners to be confined in a tiny room, where they passed a sultry night without water. Next morning only twenty-three emerged alive from the "Black Hole." This atrocity was avenged by the victory of Plassey, in which Clive, with about thirty-two hundred soldiers, defeated an Indian army of fifty thousand men. The British East India Company then put on the throne of Bengal a ruler whom it could control. The Battle of Plassey marked the beginning of British rule in India, a rule maintained for nearly two hundred years—until 1947.

The Seven Years' War in India. When the Seven Years' War broke out in Europe, the French and English renewed their contest in India. The English were completely successful, for their control of the sea enabled them

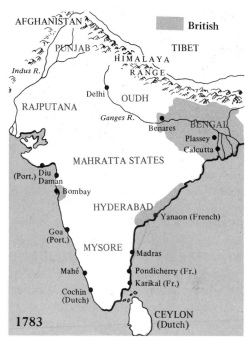

INDIA IN 1783. The English controlled the important province of Bengal and much of the eastern coast. The French, Portuguese, and Dutch controlled a number of scattered ports.

to prevent the French from sending reinforcements to India. The Peace of Paris in 1763 provided that France would recover her Indian possessions but should not fortify them. This meant that she gave up her dream of an empire in India and that England would have a free hand in extending her own control. After 1763 the English continued their expansion in India, partly through military action and partly through alliances with native princes. (The map on this page shows possessions of the European powers in India in 1783.)

How England governed her colonies. The East India Company governed British India until the middle of the nineteenth century. The directors of the company in London decided on the policies to be carried out by company officials in India. In America, on the other hand, colonial affairs were supervised more closely by the English government. The king appointed governors in most of the colonies, and Parliament passed laws regulating colonial trade and manufacturing. In general, the colonists governed themselves in local matters. The voters in each of the thirteen mainland colonies elected local officials and chose an assembly to make laws for the colony. The thirteen colonies prospered under this arrangement and by 1776 had reached a population of about two and one-half millions. Colonists enjoyed practically the same freedom and privileges as did citizens in England; in this respect English colonial policy was superior to that of any other European power. The colonists did not begin to ask for independence until fear of the French was removed in 1763 and English taxes and controls were increased. In Canada, England also pursued an enlightened policy. She allowed the French residents to observe their own religious and legal traditions, thus keeping their loyalty during the American Revolution. (See page 264.)

EUROPEAN AND COLONIAL WARS   1689–1783

In Europe	Dates	In America	Contestants	Treaty
War of the League of Augsburg	1689–1697	King William's War	France *vs.* Great Britain, Holland, Spain, Austria, Sweden, etc.	Ryswick
War of the Spanish Succession	1701–1713	Queen Anne's War	France, Spain, Bavaria *vs.* Great Britain, Holland, Austria, Portugal, Savoy, Prussia, etc.	Utrecht and Rastadt
War of the Austrian Succession	1740–1748	King George's War (1744–1748)	Prussia, France, Spain, Bavaria *vs.* Austria, Great Britain, Holland	Aix-la-Chapelle
Seven Years' War	1756–1763	French and Indian War (1754–1763)	Prussia, Great Britain *vs.* Austria, France, Russia, Sweden, Saxony	Paris and Hubertusburg
War of the American Revolution	1776–1783	Revolutionary War	Great Britain *vs.* United States, France, Spain, Holland	Paris and Versailles

Hanseatic merchants with their Hansekoggen (merchant ships) shown in the background

Europeans Venture Forth

214A

Taj Mahal at Agra, India

Medieval life in Europe, narrowly shut in, opened up to embrace the whole world at the close of the Middle Ages. By the year 1500, trade and exploration had begun to lure Europeans into the far corners of the earth.

At first, medieval trade had expanded into the waters near Europe. Trade in northern Europe during the later Middle Ages centered in the North Sea and the Baltic. To the south, the Crusades had stimulated Italian trade in the Mediterranean. Italian cities grew extremely wealthy, enabling them to finance the art and scholarship of the Italian Renaissance.

It was a wonderful new world which appeared before European eyes as modern times began. The pictures in these pages suggest scenes from lands which Europeans were just beginning to visit five hundred years ago.

214B

Assault by Tamerlane on the fortress of the
Knights of St. John at Smyrna, 1402

214C

A Dutch trader in the Indies points to his ships in the Dutch-built port of Batavia, painted by Albert Cuyp.

Many Europeans eventually settled in Asia,
as is the case with the Dutch trader who points with
pride to his ships in the East Indies harbor of Batavia.
Some other lands had been previously unknown.
Africa's interior held new scenes, such as the tremendous Victoria Falls.

214E

Of all the regions to be found, America proved to be the one most important for its impact on world events. At first the American land mass seemed to be an unfortunate mistake of nature, blocking passage from Europe to Asia. A French map of 1547 shows with amazing accuracy the Caribbean area, where men long hoped to find a passage to the Pacific. Explorers also probed deep into North America in search of a Northwest Passage to Asia. Actually the passage does exist, at least under today's climatic conditions. Bellot Strait, recently discovered, permits a ship to travel from the Atlantic to the Bering Sea through waters which are not ice-bound the year around.

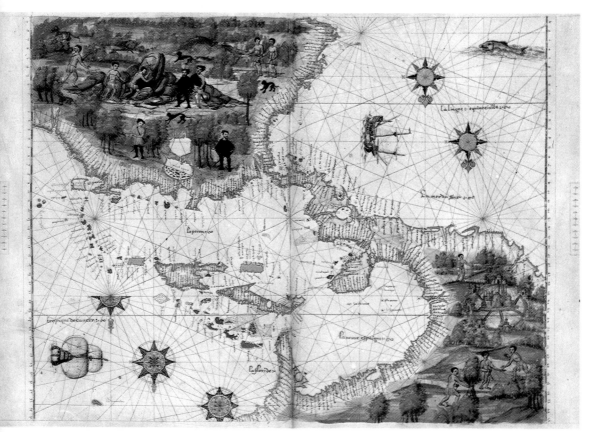

Map of the Caribbean, 1547

Bellot Strait

Victoria Falls, Southern Rhodesia

214G

Man-made wonders also awaited European explorers of the Americas. The ruins of the once great Inca city of Macchu Pichu in Peru stand as testimony to the magnificence of the Inca civilization. This civilization was far ahead of their European conquerors in many fields, especially government and civil service. It seems strange to think of its crumbling before the sword of the conquistador. But the day of the Inca has passed. Instead, European culture took root in the Americas. The vital New World grew to a strength rivaling that of the Old.

Macchu Pichu, Inca ruins in Peru

How Discovery and Colonization Brought Change to Europe

Increased supply of gold and silver. The Age of Discovery brought an age of change to Europe. Whether he knew it or not, each adventurer who helped to explore an unknown land or to conquer an overseas empire for his king was also helping to transform life in Europe. One result of the discoveries was an increased supply of gold and silver in Europe. During the Middle Ages businessmen had suffered from a shortage of money, but more money became available when large amounts of the precious metals began to pour into Europe from America. The Spaniards plundered the Indians of Mexico and Peru of their stored-up gold. Even larger supplies of silver were obtained by the Spaniards as soon as they put their Indian subjects to work in the wonderfully rich silver mines of Potosí in Bolivia. It has been estimated that by the end of the 1500's the supply of gold in Europe had doubled and the amount of silver had multiplied ten times.

Consequences of increased money supply. The Spaniards used most of their newfound wealth to pay for goods they bought from other European countries. A greater amount of money thus came into circulation throughout Europe. As a result the prices of manufactured goods shot upward, and businessmen made high profits which they could use to expand their enterprises. Wages also rose and attracted more workers to the cities. Serfs found it easier to obtain money with which to buy their freedom. European monarchs grew stronger because they could collect more money through taxes.

Rise in the standard of living. The European standard of living rose as more goods became available. From America came many commodities unknown before. Among these were the potato (which soon became "the bread of the poor" in Europe), chocolate and cocoa made from cacao seeds, quinine, to-

THE BANKER AND HIS WIFE. Weighing gold was an important part of business. This couple are displaying their possessions—furs, fine garments, a rare book—in the portrait they commissioned.

bacco, dyewoods, and mahogany. America also sent to Europe large supplies of cane sugar, molasses, fish, whale oil, and furs. The highly prized spices and other products of the Far East became more plentiful and cheaper as ocean commerce replaced the old caravan traffic. People in every class could now obtain more goods and lead more comfortable lives.

Social effects of the discoveries. The discoveries changed the social standing of many Europeans. The increased money supply led to higher pay for wage earners and freedom for many serfs. People in the lower classes also benefited from the new opportunities offered in America. Hundreds of thousands emigrated, especially to the English colonies, where many gained farms of their own and rose to the middle class. Others remained in Europe after securing promises of better treatment. Even more notable was the rise of the middle class. Its numbers and wealth grew as trade and manufacturing expanded. At the same time, the landowning aristocrats tended to lose power, though they remained at the top of the social scale. The nobles moved from their feudal castles to more pleasant country homes or to the gayer social life of the royal courts.

Shifting of trade routes. In the Middle Ages the Mediterranean and Baltic seas had been the principal highways of commerce. Columbus's discovery of America, however, followed immediately by Da Gama's voyage to India, shifted European trade routes to the Atlantic Ocean. Venice, Genoa, Hamburg, Lübeck, and Bruges gradually lost ground as trading centers, while Lisbon and Cádiz, Bordeaux and Cherbourg, Antwerp and Amsterdam, London and Liverpool gained. One may say, therefore, that the year 1492 opened the Atlantic period of European history.

Political effects of the discoveries. The Atlantic-facing countries, first Portugal and Spain, then Holland, France, and England, became the great powers of Europe. For centuries their trade rivalries and contests for colonial possessions brought repeated wars to Europe. Inside these countries, too, political changes appeared, the most notable being the growing influence of the middle class. Merchants and bankers made loans to the kings; the kings, in turn, gave trading privileges and high government positions to the businessmen. Later, during the Age of Revolution, the middle class helped to reshape governments so that they were less autocratic.

The discoveries and religion. The New World offered ample room for those who wished to escape religious persecution. Puritans came to New England, Roman Catholics to Maryland, and Quakers to Pennsylvania. French Huguenots and other persecuted groups scattered throughout the English colonies. At the same time, the discoveries tended to reduce the violence of religious disputes, for men began to give more thought to making money and enjoying life than to quarreling over religious differences.

THE BANKER FUGGER AND CHARLES V. Fugger grew rich from mining and the spice trade. He served as papal banker, and in 1519 financed the election of Charles V as Holy Roman Emperor.

REVIEWING THE CHAPTER

QUESTIONS TO ANSWER

1. (a) What was the goal of the early explorers? (b) List ten articles which were brought to Europe from the East. (c) Why were they so expensive?

2. (a) Tell the story of the Portuguese search for an all-water route to the East. (b) What areas were acquired by the Portuguese?

(c) Why were the voyages of Columbus and Magellan important?

3. (a) Name the explorers who laid the foundation of the Spanish empire in America. (b) Describe the culture of the most advanced groups of Indians before the Spanish came. (c) How did the Spanish change the Indian way of life?

4. (a) Explain why European nations desired colonies. (b) Trace the growth of the Dutch and French colonial empires.

5. (a) Describe the conflict between the English and French in North America; in India. (b) How did England govern her colonies in India? In America? (c) In what respects was English colonial policy superior to that of other countries?

6. (a) Explain how the opening of the New World led to higher prices in Europe. (b) What groups in Europe were affected by the higher prices? (c) Why did Mediterranean cities lose ground as trading centers? (d) Indicate the political and religious effects of the discoveries.

13 Civilization Expands in Asia and Africa

A WESTERN MERCHANT SHIP IN JAPAN. This scene was painted in the early seventeenth
century, just before most European traders were expelled from Japan and the Japanese
were forbidden to travel abroad. Japan was virtually isolated from Western influences until
the mid-nineteenth century, when Commodore Perry forced the Japanese to open some
of their harbors to American ships.

In recent chapters we have traced the story of civilization in the western world. We have seen how, after the fall of Rome, the Eastern Roman Empire kept civilization alive while western Europe suffered a return to barbarism in the early Middle Ages. The Middle East experienced a burst of activity with the rise of Islam. Then, at the time of the Renaissance, western Europe awakened from the Middle Ages. There was a quickening of activity in the arts, religion, politics, and business. Exploration and colonization were also intensified as merchants, missionaries, and empire-builders traveled around the globe and brought East and West together as never before.

In this chapter we shall go back to ancient times in Asia and Africa. We shall trace developments in India and China and the Middle East, and also note developments in regions where newer civilizations arose—in Japan, Southeast Asia, and Africa. Thus it will be possible to understand how the people of these areas lived, and how their lives were affected when they had contact with the West.

The Middle East to A.D. 1800

Establishing a Moslem empire. As we noted in Chapters 9 and 10, Islam inspired the Arabs to conquer a huge empire. By A.D. 750 this empire included lands stretching from the Atlantic Ocean on the west to the borders of India in the east. Seven centuries later the Moslem world had reached its greatest extent. Included within it were Spain and North Africa, Asia Minor and the Fertile Crescent, Persia, northern India, and parts of Southeast Asia. Within this vast area a remarkable civilization arose and contributed greatly to the rest of the world in many ways (see pages 127–131).

Disunity in the Moslem world. Religious and political quarrels among the Arabs led to a breakup of their empire, with each part being governed by a different caliph, or ruler. Invasions also weakened Moslem unity, as did the continual struggles between the nomadic tribes and the sedentary civilization. Seljuk Turks in the eleventh century, Mongols in the thirteenth century, and Ottoman Turks in the fourteenth century invaded the Middle East, weakening the previously established communities. Although the invaders generally adopted the Islamic faith, they never succeeded in conquering all the Islamic world. As a result, several separate states arose: the Mogul (Mongol) Empire in India, the kingdom of Iran (Persia), and the Ottoman Empire, which centered in what is now Turkey. As we shall see, these states from about 1100 on entered upon a gradual decline in prosperity and culture.

Shifting frontiers of the Moslem world. For a time this economic and cultural decline was hidden by military victories. The Christian crusaders, at first successful, were driven from the Holy Land by the Seljuk Turks. In 1453 the Ottoman Turks besieged and scaled the walls of Constantinople. The fall of this ancient fortress opened the way to Ottoman invasion of eastern Europe. Turkish armies advanced through the Balkans until they reached the gates of Vienna. The battle for Vienna, like that at Tours in 732, had decisive effects for the future of Europe. The final Turkish effort to take Vienna in 1683 failed, thus marking the high-water point of Turkish expansion in Europe. From then on the Turkish tide receded slowly. The sultan at Constantinople (now renamed Istanbul) continued to hold most of the Balkans for nearly two hundred years, but lands north of the Black Sea gradually passed into the hands of Catherine the Great and her successors (see page 253).

Elsewhere the Turks were also in retreat. The rulers of Spain drove out the last of the Moslems by 1492 and then carried the war to North Africa. By 1800 only Libya and Egypt remained in the Ottoman Empire, and even here the sultan had no real authority. As the map on page 409 shows, by 1800 the Ottoman Empire had shrunk to three areas: the Balkans, present-day Turkey, and the "Fertile Crescent" lands extending from Palestine to Mesopotamia.

Meanwhile, the Mogul Empire in northern India had become so weak by the 1700's that the way was opened for a European take-over (see pages 195–196 and 198–199). Persia, or Iran, had experienced a series of invasions by Turks and Mongols. By 1300 the Mongol khan (ruler) of Persia had adopted Islam as his faith, further increasing the influence of that religion. Persia now expanded and became one of the great powers of Asia. It remained a truly great empire, continually expanding until by 1800 it too had become unprogressive and stagnant. Gone were the days when Moslems carried nearly all long-distance trade between the leading civilizations of the world. No longer were the Moslems in the center of world affairs. After 1700 their role as leaders of civilization and holders of world power had passed into the hands of the Europeans.

Life in the Moslem world. By 1800 conditions were such that the average person in the whole region from North Africa to northern India lived in grinding poverty as a peasant or herdsman. In Mesopotamia numbers of the ancient canals fell into neglect. Lacking drainage during floods and without a source of water in dry periods, the land which had been fertile since the days of the Sumerians began to return to swamp or desert. Moslem trade with other nations also dwindled, bringing increasing poverty to even the largest cities from the eleventh century onward. The universities, once the centers of Moslem intellectual leadership, now substituted mere memorization of facts for creative thought. Gone were the days when thousands of Christian students sat at the feet of Moslem professors, and when Moslem geographers and astronomers mapped the world and charted the stars. Moslem thought seemed to have drawn in upon itself and to have become frozen in a pattern of the past.

Islamic literature also suffered, with the exception of Persian poetry. The verses known as the "Rubáiyát of Omar Khayyám" are examples of poetry which for several centuries set a high standard of excellence. Artistic work declined in quality, with the exception of architecture. Moslem rulers, whether Turkish, Persian, or Indian, put up splendid buildings when they could afford the cost. During the sixteenth and seventeenth centuries especially, beautiful mosques and palaces arose throughout the Moslem world. The Taj Mahal, shown on page 214 B, is the best known of these structures.

Why did the Islamic world lose world leadership? Several reasons may help explain the stagnation which had fallen upon the Moslem world by 1800. One cause is to be found in the military tradition of the Turks and Mongols. Accustomed to war, they were successful in overcoming the Arabs and other peoples they conquered in the Middle East. However, they did little to carry on the intellectual activities which had marked the Arabs. Eventually, even the military prowess of the conquerors was softened by luxury. The Turks, for example, began to conscript Christian boys as a way of filling out their army ranks. These boys, brought up as Moslems and trained as fierce warriors, became the famed "Janizaries," the elite troops of the Turkish army. But the Janizaries became corrupt and more of a threat than a support to the sultan. Their influence was especially bad by the mid-1600's. A sultan finally had them massacred in 1826.

A second cause of stagnation in the Islamic states grew out of religious controversies. Violent quarrels over interpretation of the Koran and other questions divided Moslems during the sixteenth and seventeenth centuries. The winning side was the one which taught rigid adherence to the past. Consequently, young people were taught to avoid new ideas.

European expansion also helped to shut in and weaken the Moslem world. Not only was territory lost as a result of European attacks in North Africa and near the Black Sea, but Spain and Portugal also struck at Moslem trade routes and ports in Asia. Later the Dutch, French, and English joined in the contest for trade routes and ports. Thus by 1800 the immense profits of trade in Asia and in the Mediterranean had been torn from Moslem hands.

This situation was the reverse of conditions a thousand years earlier. During the early Middle Ages it was the Moslems who attacked Europe, preventing western Europeans from trading on the Mediterranean. At that time Europeans borrowed extensively from Moslem thought, language, learning, and technology. Now the Moslems would have to rely upon European advancements in all spheres of life. The greatest centuries of Arabic culture corresponded to some of the darkest times in Europe. By 1800, however, the tables had been turned; European expansion and superior economic competition had helped to bring about a Dark Age in the Middle East.

India to the Nineteenth Century

Indian history, A.D. 500–1800. By A.D. 500, as we noted in Chapter 4, many basic patterns of Indian life had become established. Nearly

ORNAMENTED PAGE OF A KORAN dating from the fourteenth century.

all the people lived in farming villages. Like western Europeans during the Middle Ages, they worked in the fields by day and returned to their villages at nightfall. Similarly, the people of India never came under the rule of a single government. Instead, many states flourished in disunited India.

Some rulers managed to form empires which endured for a time. The Maurya Empire united the Ganges and Indus valleys and most of central India into a single state (see map, page 222). After the Maurya Empire broke up, a new dynasty, the Gupta, arose. By A.D. 300 the Gupta kings ruled in northern India; their empire lasted for two and a half centuries. During this time much of India enjoyed peace and prosperity. The Gupta rulers promoted the Hindu religion, although they were tolerant of Buddhism as well. Their government—a strong absolute monarchy—provided services for its people ranging from distribution of food to the poor in times of famine to the building of roads and canals to providing jobs for the unem-

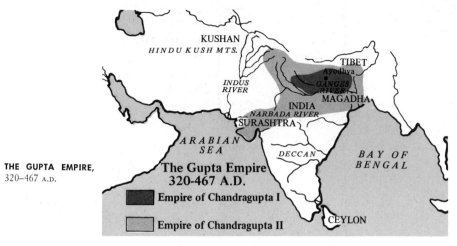

THE GUPTA EMPIRE,
320–467 A.D.

The Gupta Empire
320-467 A.D.

Empire of Chandragupta I

Empire of Chandragupta II

ployed and inspecting food, markets, and shops. Hindus, during the Gupta period, also made far-ranging advances in astronomy, mathematics, and chemistry. Most Gupta rulers encouraged and sponsored art and learning. As a result, art, architecture, sculpture, and literature flourished as never before, causing the period to be considered the "Golden Age" of India.

Soon after A.D. 1000 a new element in Indian life was introduced through invasions by Moslem Turks. For the next two hundred years waves of invaders entered through passes in the Himalayas. The Turks seized the north and then moved into the central highlands and finally the south. By 1313, Turkish-Moslem states governed most of India. The Turks thought the Indians were infidels and were shocked by Hindu and Buddhist use of idols; they slaughtered many followers of these faiths.

From time to time Mongols also invaded India. They made no lasting conquests, however, until the appearance of a chieftain named Baber. He marched into India in 1525 and in two great battles won the north. Baber and his successors ruled over what came to be known as the empire of the Moguls (a corruption of the word *Mongols*). Baber set up his capital at Agra; others were established later at Delhi and Lahore. The Moguls were Moslem, having been converted to Islam before

entering India. Akbar, Baber's grandson, united many Moslem states, and created the largest Indian empire prior to British rule. Both Akbar and Baber were tolerant of the Hindus and other religious groups. They were also interested in arts and literature and in bringing peace to their large domain.

Soon after 1700 the Mogul Empire began to break up. Division and weakness played into the hands of Europeans, particularly the English and French, who became the chief rivals for mastery of India. By 1800 the English were well on the way to control of the great subcontinent.

Indian culture during the Gupta Age. As we have mentioned, Indian culture entered a golden age during the prosperous Gupta period (c. 320–480). At this time two Indian epics, the great *Mahabharata* and the *Ramayana,* took final form. The first somewhat resembles Homer's *Iliad* and *Odyssey* in that lives of gods and men were interwoven in the story of an ancient war. The shorter *Ramayana* recounts the exciting adventures of Rama, a heroic and adventurous figure. Both these epics are still studied, and continue to influence Indian thought today. Indian writers also produced numbers of animal fables. Some were told only for amusement; others pointed a moral. This was also a time of rich production of plays and historical poetry.

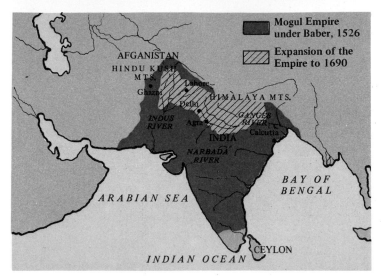

Mogul Empire
under Baber, 1526

Expansion of the
Empire to 1690

THE MOGUL EMPIRE,
1526–1690

Religious life in the Gupta Age was marked by the retreat of Buddhism in the face of a Hindu revival. Buddhist monks withdrew from the world instead of preaching to the masses as Buddha had done. Sanskrit, the sacred language of Hinduism, came to be used by the Gupta kings for their laws, and even the Buddhists adopted Sanskrit for many of their own writings. The decline of Buddhism in India is all the more remarkable when we remember that at the same time it was winning millions of converts elsewhere in Asia (see page 43).

Surprisingly enough, Indian religious art during the Gupta Age dealt more with Buddhist than with Hindu themes. As with Christian churches during the Renaissance, wealthy Buddhist monasteries employed numerous painters and sculptors. They have left us with many figures of Buddha, usually carved but also shown in fine fresco paintings such as those in the Ajanta caves. In style the paintings somewhat resemble the work of early Italian Renaissance artists.

In science, Indian culture advanced far. Study of medicine came to center about observation rather than superstition. Indian doctors were accomplished in bone setting and plastic surgery of the eyes, nose, and lips. For years they had used inoculation and sterilization of operating instruments. In chemistry the Hindus became world leaders in the chemical arts of dyeing, tanning, soapmaking, glassmaking, and cementmaking. Knowledge of Greek mathematics had reached India by this time and was taught in the schools and universities. India also made an original and highly important contribution of its own in mathematics—the invention of "Arabic" numerals. These numbers, with their symbol for zero, may have been invented earlier, but it is known that during the Gupta period they came into wide use. Hindu mathematicians are also given credit for inventing many algebraic symbols, especially the idea and use of the negative sign which is so important to algebraic equations. These developments rank with the alphabet (also a gift of Asia to the world) as invaluable tools for thought and communication.

Although the Gupta period brought a flowering of Indian culture in literature, science, and art, these achievements were largely unknown to the mass of Indians. Indian thought continued to be "otherworldly" and to ignore the problems of daily living. Little was done to make practical inventions which might have lightened toil, or to educate a large number of students. Even the keeping of historical records was largely ignored. Our best information about events in India comes from the accounts of foreigners who visited there.

BODHISATTVA. A tempura wall painting found in a cave-temple at Ajantá, India, dated between 600–700 A.D. The Bodhisattva was a merciful intermediary between Buddha and man.

Effects of the Moslem invasions. Indian culture was deeply affected by the Moslem invasions. Since the invaders came by land from the north, their blows fell first upon the main centers of Indian civilization—those in the Ganges and Indus valleys. The Moslems sacked impartially both Hindu and Buddhist temples, partly for their wealth and partly in order to destroy the idols which to Moslems were an abomination. Buddhism in India, already weak by the year 1000, never recovered from the Islamic attacks. Thus it was that Islam rose to take a place beside Hinduism as one of the two leading religions in India. Attempts to make lasting peace between Moslems and Hindus failed and eventually resulted in the division of India into two parts after World War II (see page 622).

The Moslems naturally influenced the arts, especially in northern India. Here the Moslem taste for graceful minarets, pointed arches, and rounded domes was expressed in their buildings. Examples are the Taj Mahal, completed about 1648 as the symbol of an emperor's love for his wife, and magnificent palaces rivaling those of European kings. (See picture, page 214 B.) The Moslems also brought India out of its isolation. Through their extensive trade and contacts with the West, they brought back not only western goods but ideas as well. By these same routes they spread the literature and scientific advancement of India to the western world.

Chinese History to the Nineteenth Century

Cycles in China's history. The history of China in the period A.D. 500 to 1800 continued to record the rise and fall of ruling dynasties. As we saw in Chapter 4, China was united by the first emperor, Shih Huang Ti. His family ruled briefly and was followed by that of the Han (206 B.C.–A.D. 220), under whom ancient Chinese civilization reached its highest point.

For nearly four centuries after the overthrow of the Han (from A.D. 220 to 618) China endured invasion and disorder. Several times in Chinese history we find this pattern repeating itself: a strong dynasty seized power, ruled well at first but then grew weaker, and was followed by a time of disorder until a new dynasty came to the throne. Often the time of disorder was made worse by foreign invasion. This cycle has not been limited to the experience of China. As we noted in ancient Egypt, the Age of the Nobles, or feudal period, interrupted rule by the pharaohs. Later, in western Europe, invaders helped cause the fall of the Roman Empire and the rise of feudalism. While feudalism was developing in western Europe, feudalism in China was ended by a new dynasty known as the T'ang.

China under the T'ang dynasty, 618–907. During the three centuries of T'ang rule China was the most civilized country on earth. Fine arts, such as painting, reached a high degree of perfection. Printing of books had begun by the year 868; the books that have survived show a fine craftsmanship. Printing stimulated both literature and learning, since authors could be widely read and books became more easily available to students. During the T'ang period the government began the practice, continued for a thousand years, of promoting officials who showed in examinations that they had mastered the "Classics" and the teachings of Confucius. The box on page 226 describes examination conditions at this time. China's prosperity was fostered by trade with much of the known world, and by the extension of China's frontiers (see map). As we shall note later, China's trade and conquests helped spread Chinese culture to many parts of Asia.

The Sung dynasty, 960–1280. The T'ang emperors gradually lost power and China once more suffered from a long series of civil wars. A new dynasty, the Sung (sŏong), restored order and prosperity during its reign. It failed, however, to repel invasions by the Mongols.

There were, however, brilliant achievements in the arts and in economics under the Sung dynasty. Among these were a series of economic reforms devised by a government official named Wang An-shih. His program had four main provisions which he hoped would bring about a better way of living for the poor of China while also making the country's economy sound. The first provision was that the government would agree to make loans to farmers at a very low interest rate for that time. The loans would be used for seed and equipment needed to grow crops. The second provision set up a market exchange system in which prices could be controlled through government buying and selling. The third provision abolished forced labor by taxing all men in proportion to their ability to pay. Public works programs were then to be established with these taxes to provide jobs for the unemployed. The fourth provision reduced the size of the standard army, thereby cutting down on military expenses.

Chinese culture also continued to expand under the Sungs. Poetry and art flourished and education became more important and more highly cherished than ever before. Education was further enhanced by the inven-

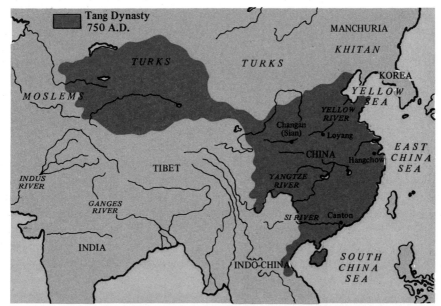

CHINA UNDER THE TANG DYNASTY, 750 A.D.

Tang Dynasty
750 A.D.

MANCHURIA

KHITAN

TURKS

TURKS

KOREA

MOSLEMS

YELLOW SEA

YELLOW RIVER

Changan (Sian)

Loyang

EAST CHINA SEA

CHINA

Hangchow

TIBET

INDUS RIVER

GANGES RIVER

YANGTZE RIVER

SI RIVER

Canton

INDIA

INDO-CHINA

SOUTH CHINA SEA

... The approach to this most critical moment of a scholar's life was always filled with keen excitement, tense hope, and a nervous fear of failure. It was the moment to which all his years of grinding labor and hours of burning the midnight oil were supposed to lead. The candidates had to get up in the middle of the night and come to the palace at dawn, bringing their cold meals with them, for they would not be able to leave until the examinations were over. During the examinations they were shut up in cubicles under the supervision of palace guards. There was a rigorous system to prevent bribery or favoritism. The candidates' papers were recopied by official clerks before they were submitted to the examiners, to avoid recognition of their identity by their handwriting. In the recopied papers the writers' names were taken out and kept on file. While the candidates were let out after the examinations, the judges themselves were shut up within the palace and forbidden to have any contact with the people outside, usually from late January till early March, until the papers were properly graded and submitted to the Emperor ...

—Lin Yutang, *The Gay Genius:*
The Biography of Su Tungpo.

tion of printing. So highly developed was this process that by 1000 it was widely used by the Chinese.

Mongol rule of China, 1279–1368. The Mongols who entered China were fierce nomads who swept down from what is now northern Mongolia. They lived in tribes which had fought one another constantly for cattle and pasture lands until they were united by the famous Genghis Khan (1162?–1227). They then set out to attack neighboring peoples and succeeded in building up one of the largest empires in history. As we have seen, Mongol rule was established in Russia, Persia, and many other lands. In 1279 Genghis Khan's grandson, Kublai (kū'blī), put an end to the Sung dynasty and made himself emperor of all China. Kublai, however, interfered little with Chinese laws and customs.

His splendid court at Peking, his great public works, and his patronage of art and scholarship made his reign notable in Chinese history. It was at this time that the Venetian traveler Marco Polo visited and described the "Celestial Empire." Since the Mongols never completely trusted the Chinese and often appointed foreigners to high positions, he was given posts of importance.

The Ming dynasty, 1368–1644. The Chinese could never forget that the Mongols were aliens. After a number of revolts they drove out the Mongols in 1368. A native dynasty which took the name Ming ("Brilliant"), mounted the imperial throne, and held it until 1644. A notable event at this time was the coming of European traders and missionaries.

Manchu rule, 1644–1912. The last of China's imperial dynasties was that of the Manchus. They were foreigners, like the Mongols, and entered China from Manchuria during a revolt in which the last Ming emperor was dethroned. The Manchus, also like the Mongols, made few changes in Chinese society and government. Confucius continued to be highly honored, and both Taoism and Buddhism remained as the national religions. However, the Manchus never allowed the Chinese to forget who was master. They kept Manchu troops throughout the country to hold the people in subjection, and required the Chinese to follow the Manchu custom of shaving the front of the head and braiding the back hair in a queue. Thus the queue, for over two hundred years one of the distinguishing marks of a Chinese, began as a sign of his rule by a foreign overlord.

Under the Manchus, commerce between China and the West grew rapidly. Some traffic overland between Russia and China existed by the end of the eighteenth century. Most trade was seaborne, however, and was confined to two ports: Macao, dominated by the Portuguese, and Canton, which far outranked Macao in volume of commerce. The

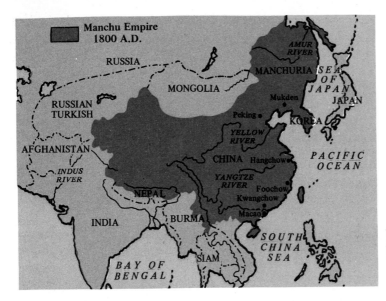

THE MANCHU EMPIRE
AT ITS GREATEST EXTENT,
1800

Canton trade was mainly in the hands of the British and the Dutch. American merchants entered the "China trade" in 1784, when their first ship arrived in Canton.

The two greatest Manchu emperors were K'ang-hsi (käng'shē', 1662–1722) and Ch'ien Lung (chĕ-ĕn' lŏong', 1736–1796). Their conquests (see map, at the top) made China larger than ever before. Success on the battlefield convinced them of the superiority of Chinese ways over those of all foreign "barbarians." Since China was the wealthiest and most populous country in the world, they saw no need for any diplomatic or cultural ties with the West. In 1793, when King George III of England suggested an exchange of ambassadors, Ch'ien Lung scornfully replied that "this request is contrary to all usage of my dynasty and cannot possibly be entertained." In the next century the Chinese paid dearly for this attitude. They remained bound to traditional ways while the West surged ahead in a revolution of science and technology. Only after the overthrow of the Manchus in the twentieth century did China attempt to catch up in those fields.

Growth of foreign influence. Chinese life in the centuries from 500 to 1800 continued to rest on an economic base of village agriculture. As in the past (see Chapter 4), most of the Chinese people lived by tilling with tireless care and effort the fields outside their villages. Village social life centered in the family, with its deeply rooted customs of reverence for ancestors both living and dead. Regard for the teachings of Buddha, Lao-tzu, and Confucius also strengthened the hold of the past upon Chinese thought and action.

Although life went on much as before during these centuries, foreign influences brought some change to "unchanging China." Invasions by tribes who crossed the Great Wall from the north forced many Chinese to move southward. Consequently, the northern part of China, where civilization had first appeared, lost its place as the only center of Chinese life. From southern China, especially the Yangtze valley, Chinese merchants made increasing contacts with other countries. Trade brought new goods to China, including tea, which is mentioned in records of the south before A.D. 900. Similarly, conquerors in the north introduced new customs, such as the use of coal.

Chinese art and thought were also affected by contact with other lands. Art in China about A.D. 500 felt the influence of India, as shown in statues of Buddha, page 224. Similarly, the influence of Arabs and Greeks may be traced in art works of the T'ang dynasty. Chinese religious life also absorbed ideas from Islam and Christianity. Probably the most lasting of all foreign influences, however, was that of Buddhism.

Buddhism in China. Buddhist missionaries had carried their faith to China at least as early as A.D. 65, but their religion took hold slowly. The problem of translating Buddhist writings into Chinese was extremely difficult and occupied several centuries. More important in delaying the adoption of Buddhism was the fundamental conflict between Confucian and Buddhist doctrines. Buddhism taught a belief in reincarnation, in which a man is reborn to a higher or lower state according to the life he has led. Followers of Confucius, on the other hand, believed in reverence for ancestors, whose spirits presumably remained unchanged after death. The two doctrines were opposed; logically, one could not accept both beliefs at the same time. Since the Chinese were firmly committed to Confucius, they at first persecuted the Buddhists.

Eventually, however, the Chinese decided to overlook the contradictions between Buddhism and Confucianism. By about A.D. 500 Buddhism had become widely popular in China, and indeed was spreading rapidly elsewhere. Zen, one of the branches of Buddhism, entered China from India soon after A.D. 500, and was later carried to Japan.

Changes in Chinese culture. As noted earlier, Chinese artists wrought beautiful work in the T'ang period. Excavations have revealed fine carvings (usually of animal figures), lacquer ware, and porcelain made at

GANDHARAN AND CHINESE SCULPTURAL STYLES. The head of Buddha at left illustrates Gandharan sculpture, a blend of Hellenistic and Indian styles. The standing statue of Buddha at right (477 A.D.) is one of the earliest surviving examples of Buddhist sculpture from China.

SUNG VASE. This water bottle, dating from the Sung era, is an example of the exquisite porcelain work done at that time.

this time. In the late T'ang era, Buddhist influence appeared in sculpture, for the human form was more often shown, in keeping with Buddhist art. The T'ang era has also been called "the greatest age of Chinese poetry," as well as a time when drama and novels first appeared.

The Sung era saw the perfection of porcelain work; Sung vases are much admired today. This was also an age which produced fine painters. In the field of invention, the first use of gunpowder in war is recorded in 1126, when the Chinese besieged a city. By this time the Chinese were using printing quite widely. Works of all sorts were produced in quantity and are still preserved in the vast storehouse of Chinese literature. Poetry continued to be popular. The greatest scholar-philosopher of the era was Chu Hsi (1130–1200). He brought the philosophy of Confucius up to date in his commentaries on the "Classics," thus helping Confucianism keep its hold on Chinese thought. The drama (sung, somewhat like our opera) was greatly

improved in the Sung and Mongol periods, as was the novel.

Under the Ming dynasty the Chinese once again ruled themselves. Hatred of the Mongols caused them to emphasize those things which were distinctively Chinese. As a result we have many surviving paintings and other works of art, buildings, and literary productions. They show that Chinese culture revived and flourished after Mongol neglect. Selection of officials according to their knowledge of the "Classics," halted by the Mongols, was restored by the Mings.

Unlike the Mongols, the Manchus acted as patrons of Chinese culture. They encouraged the gathering of knowledge and the editing and publishing of ancient texts. Original writing, as in novels and poetry, also was favored. Chinese painters did some experimenting but generally remained faithful to traditional styles.

Expansion of China's influence. Despite the Chinese yearning for isolation, contacts with the outside world resulted from conquests, trade, and religious missions. Under the Han and T'ang rulers, traders carried Chinese customs into central Asia with some regularity, and one trading mission is said to have reached the Roman Empire. Ming China, as we have seen, made a special effort to shut the door against the outside world. However, one of the Ming emperors took the quite unprecedented step of building a fleet of huge ships. These were sent out in several voyages southward around Malaysia to Burma, India, and Africa. The voyages, lasting from 1405 to

MUSICIANS FROM THE T'ANG ERA. These figures show a definite Buddhist influence.

1433, established Chinese domination over Southeast Asia and the Indian Ocean. Rulers of islands in the East Indies sent tribute to the emperor in recognition of his authority. Many Chinese settlers migrated to the Philippine Islands and to other parts of Southeast Asia, where their descendants continue to live today. China might have maintained a huge sea empire, but later Ming emperors allowed the fleet to decay. As we have seen, Arab sea power had also declined by 1500. Europeans, therefore, met little opposition when they began to trade and colonize in the East.

Chinese expansion reached its peak under the Manchus. They ruled, either directly or through vassal kings, not only China proper but also Mongolia, Sinkiang, Tibet, eastern Siberia, Korea, Burma, and Siam. Taiwan (Formosa) was also made a part of the Manchu Empire (see map, page 227). To the Manchus, their conquests were another proof of China's superior culture. Consequently, they felt content with their ancient ways at the very time when they needed most to keep up with a rapidly changing world—at the beginning of the nineteenth century. Yet to the neighbors of the Manchus and to those they had conquered, Chinese influence was strong. This is illustrated in the case of the Japanese.

AINU COUPLE living on the northern island of Hokkaido.

Japan to the Nineteenth Century

Geographic features. The islands which make up Japan stretch in the shape of a crescent off the coast of eastern Asia. Most of the islands are very small, and many are uninhabited. Four large islands are the real homeland of the Japanese. They are Honshu, the main island, and Shikoku, Kyushu, and Hokkaido. The Japanese call their country Nippon ("Land of the Rising Sun"). Because of its generally mountainous character, little more than one sixth of the area of Japan can be cultivated. Japan has an enormous extent of coast, with many harbors.

The Japanese people. The Japanese probably descended, in part, from Malay people and, in part, from Koreans and North Chinese who reached the islands several hundred years before the birth of Christ. When the ancestors of the modern Japanese arrived in Japan, they found much of the land occupied by the Ainus. It required many centuries for the Asiatic invaders to subdue the Ainus and drive them into the northern islands where their descendants now live. The Japanese today are shorter than most Chinese, but in other respects they closely resemble their Chinese neighbors.

According to Japanese legend, their emperors are direct descendants of the Sun Goddess. Jimmu Tenno, the first emperor, is said to have ascended the throne in 660 B.C. Archaeologists have found evidence that men lived in Japan hundreds of years before 660 B.C., and that they passed through a period of New Stone Age culture. A Chinese writer of the first century after Christ describes the Japanese of that time as being in what we would call the stage of barbarism.

Introduction of Chinese culture. The Japanese became civilized after contact with the Chinese. During the fourth and fifth centuries after Christ numbers of Chinese and Koreans emigrated to Japan, bringing with them their arts and crafts. The Japanese also sent representatives to China to learn at first hand its language, customs, and religions. The Japanese borrowed a great deal from China. They adopted the moral system of Confucius. They formed a system of writing based on Chinese characters. Japanese literature, philosophy, art, medicine, law, and education all reflect Chinese influence. The Japanese did not accept many of the internal forms of Chinese life, however. The strong family unit and anti-militaristic beliefs were replaced in Japan with a culture based on the tribal, militaristic clan.

The Shogunate. The Japanese emperor, or mikado, held little power in the early period of Japanese history. During the seventh century after Christ the emperor began to exercise real authority, but control of the government gradually passed into the hands of leading families. Later, in 1192, one of the military leaders, Yoritomo, made himself master of the empire. His title of "shogun" (shō'-goŏn') was used by his successors, who made the emperor a mere figurehead. The shogunate lasted until 1867—a period of 675 years. The period of the shogunate was also a period of feudalism in Japan. As recently as a century ago fewer than three hundred great nobles, or daimios (dī'myōz), held two thirds of the farming land. They lived in fortified castles on their great estates and enjoyed much the same powers as those held by feudal lords in medieval Europe. A large number of fighting men called "samurai" formed a warrior class somewhat like that of the medieval knights. The masses of people labored to support the samurai and daimios.

Bushido. The code, or customs, of *bushido* (the way of the warrior) guided the conduct of the knightly samurai. He was ready to give up wife, family, and life for the sake of his lord. The code demanded that he revenge the smallest insult or injustice to himself or his lord. The *bushido* code did not disappear with the passing of Japanese feudalism, but loyalty to one's lord was transformed into loyalty to the nation and to the mikado.

Religion in Japan. The ancient national faith of Japan is Shinto, meaning the "Way of the Gods." Shinto may be described as a mixture of nature worship and ancestor worship. To the Japanese the dead are as real as the living. Departed ancestors are supposed to watch over their descendants, rejoice in their prosperity, and find satisfaction in their prayers and offerings. Shintoism recognizes countless spirits, or *Kami,* including those of ancestors, ancient heroes, and nature gods. The chief Shinto deity is the Sun Goddess, from whom the emperors are supposed to be descended.

Buddhism was also adopted throughout Japan after it was introduced from Korea. For many centuries most Japanese have worshiped at both Shinto and Buddhist shrines. Zen, a branch of Buddhism, won many followers. Zen combined Taoist with Buddhist beliefs, and taught that one should seek to understand both life and one's own self through study and meditation. Shin, the most popular Buddhist sect, was formed during the twelfth century. It preached the idea of salvation by simple faith.

Japan closes her doors to the world. During the 1500's it seemed that Japan might adopt many features of European civilization. The Japanese welcomed Portuguese, Spanish, English, and Dutch traders to Japan and sent Japanese envoys to Lisbon, Madrid, and Rome to learn about the West just as earlier missions had learned about China. In 1549 an eminent Roman Catholic missionary, St. Francis Xavier (zāv'ĭ-ēr), carried Christianity to Japan. Within a few years so many thousands had been baptized that authorities became alarmed. At first missionaries were banned; later, Japanese Christians were persecuted relentlessly. By 1638 Christianity had been stamped out in Japan.

Spanish and Portuguese traders were also expelled during the first half of the seventeenth century. Only the Dutch were allowed to remain. They operated a single trading station on a small island in the harbor of Nagasaki. All other Europeans faced the death penalty if they entered Japan, and the same fate awaited any Japanese who went abroad. Even the building of ocean-going ships was prohibited. For over two centuries the Japanese kept their doors closed to the outside world. As a result, Japan remained untouched by the Industrial Revolution and knew little of the West's scientific and industrial achievements.

Southeast Asia

The land and people of Southeast Asia. As we have noted, numbers of Chinese migrated to Southeast Asia after the Ming emperor sent naval expeditions there. The term *Southeast Asia* refers to the "corner" of Asia between India and China. It includes Indo-China (Laos, Cambodia, and Vietnam), Thailand, Burma, Malaya, the Philippine Islands, and Indonesia (formerly called the East Indies). The map on page 619 shows that Southeast Asia is a vast region, larger than the United States if one counts water acreage. The equator passes through Southeast Asia, and the climate is tropical. Rainfall is generally very heavy. On the mainland the land rises to mountain chains which branch from the Himalayas. Dense forests cover much of the high country in Southeast Asia, and many of the lowlands, to be farmed, must be retrieved from swamp or jungle.

Islands form a notable feature of Southeast Asia's geography. They include Indonesia, the largest group of islands in the world, as well as the Philippines. Among the natural resources are oil, tin, gold, and other minerals. Spices and precious stones also have attracted merchants from many lands.

The people of Southeast Asia are typically brown-skinned, slender and rather short, and black-haired. Anthropologists call them Malay or Indonesian peoples, or Malayo-Polynesian. (The word *Polynesian,* meaning "many islands," refers to the fact that the inhabitants of thousands of islands extending all the way from Madagascar to the mid-Pacific are of the same racial stock.) The original Malayan people in Southeast Asia seem to have come from central Asia thousands of years before Christ. After reaching the coast they scattered—some to Japan, as we have seen, and others to even more distant islands. Since then the movements of other peoples (Indians, Europeans, and especially Chinese and other Mongoloids) have led to much intermixture.

History and culture of Southeast Asia. Through the centuries four major religions have been brought to Southeast Asia and have had a marked influence upon its culture. By A.D. 200, Hindu priests and Indian traders were coming to both the mainland and islands, and in both seem to have established numerous Indian-Hindu kingdoms. Later, Buddhist monks appeared. As a result of the Hindu and Buddhist influences, civilization in most of Southeast Asia arose on a base of Indian writing, religion, and government. The major exception was the northern section of Indo-China, where Chinese culture was dominant.

In 111 B.C. soldiers of the Han dynasty entered Vietnam. They established Chinese rule, which was enforced by garrisons stationed throughout the country. Many other Chinese followed as opportunities opened for officials and merchants. Although Vietnam's culture became Chinese in many respects, most of the people never ceased to hope for independence. Many revolts broke out. None had more than temporary success during the next thousand years. Then in A.D. 959 a native Vietnamese finally freed his country from Chinese rule and began a period of independence which lasted

TEMPLES AT ANKHAR CAVES IN CAMBODIA. While Europeans were building cathedrals such as Chartres, a Cambodian people known as the Khmers built this temple city of Anghor Thom.

until the 1800's. (For the beginnings of French rule in Vietnam, see page 620.)

Chinese contacts with other parts of Southeast Asia came later and were related to Buddhism. Buddhist monks often traveled by water from China to India, an easier route than that across the Himalayas. Accounts of journeys during the T'ang period refer to Cambodia as ruling much of the mainland in Southeast Asia. Cambodian culture and political influence were at their peak from about A.D. 600 to 1300. Today the immense ruins of their temples serve as reminders of Cambodia's ancient power. Chinese pilgrims also reported kingdoms in Siam, Sumatra, and Java as being Buddhist. (To locate these places, see the map on page 227.)

When Marco Polo returned to Europe by water through Southeast Asia, he found that a new religious influence was at work—that of Islam. Arab merchants carried the faith of the Prophet to both the islands and the mainland in the 1200's. By the early 1500's, Islam had become the dominant religion in the central part of Southeast Asia. It had reached the Philippines, where many natives in the south remain Moslem today. The conversion of all the Philippines was prevented, however, by the introduction of Christianity. Within a few years after Magellan's landing in 1521 the Spanish had mastered the islands. Thus the Philippines came to be civilized for the first time. The civilization was European and Catholic, making Philippine culture quite different from that of the other parts of Southeast Asia.

Portuguese mariners were the first Christians to reach the East Indies, arriving soon after Da Gama's voyage in 1498. Their superior sea power enabled them to drive out the Arabs and to establish bases. The Portuguese dealt harshly with the Moslem natives and as a result of their intolerance won few converts to Christianity. Without native support the Portuguese lost their bases and trade monopoly to the Dutch in the 1600's. Until World War II the Dutch claimed most of Indonesia. At first the Dutch East India Company governed the islands, giving more thought to profit than to the welfare of the natives. In 1798 the Dutch government took over the governing of the islands.

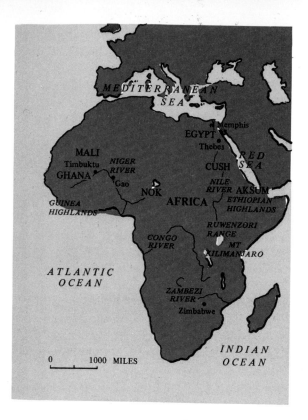

Sahara), the longest river (the Nile), some of the mightiest waterfalls (such as Victoria Falls, shown in color on page 214 G), the fourth-largest island (Madagascar), and the second-largest fresh-water lake (Lake Victoria). In resources it is one of the richest of continents: from it are taken over 90 per cent of the world's diamonds and about half the gold. It contains vast reserves of oil and other minerals as well. Great herds of wild animals have also been a feature of the African scene, although slaughter by hunters has now much reduced their size.

The equator cuts across central Africa in the region of the Congo River (see physical map of Africa, page xvi D). Accounts of the dense foliage and hot, humid climate there have given the impression that all Africa is covered by tropical jungle. The facts are quite different. Both to the north and the south of the Congo Basin lie broad stretches of grassland, somewhat similar to the plains of western North America. The grasslands could produce immense supplies of food if it were not for the tse-tse (tsĕt-sĕ) fly, which carries sleeping sickness. Beyond both grassland belts are deserts—the vast waste of the Sahara in northern Africa and the Kalahari Desert in the south. Beyond these, the northern and southern edges of Africa contain rich food-producing regions with a pleasant climate.

Far from being low or flat, much of Africa consists of high plateau or mountain country. In northwestern Africa, facing Spain, are the Atlas Mountains; south of them, just under the bend of West Africa, are the Guinea Highlands. The southern tip of Africa rises sharply to the Drakensberg Mountains, and east central Africa is marked by the Ethiopian Highlands and the Ruwenzori Range, or Mountains of the Moon, the latter capped by perpetual snow. Africa's chief rivers are the Niger, which rises in the Guinea Highlands; the Zambezi, in southern Africa; and the Congo and the Nile, both of which begin

African Civilizations to 1800

The unknown continent. Today African studies arouse particular interest. Because Africa south of the Sahara was never one of the centers of world civilization, she was rarely studied in as great detail as Europe or Asia. Now that African states have gained their independence and have a greater voice in world affairs, their importance has increased. As a result, historians are now taking more interest in the history of the many societies that make up the African continent.

Africa is remarkably vast and varied. It outranks all other continents except Asia in size. It also contains the world's largest desert (the

in the region of the Ruwenzori Range (see map, page xvi D).

African conditions long served to discourage explorers. Many of Africa's rivers, coming from high country inland, fell to sea level at the coast in rapids and waterfalls, making water travel dangerous. Jungles and deserts turned back travelers on land, and diseases threatened all who came to Africa for the first time.

The peoples of Africa. As we noted in Chapter 2, the discoveries of Dr. Leakey suggest that man first appeared in East Africa. Other evidence of human life has recently been found in the Sahara Desert. Rock-shelter paintings, the largest collection of prehistoric paintings yet known, tell much about life before the Sahara became a desert. Up to about 2500 B.C. the Sahara was fertile, and the people who left the paintings lived as hunters, herdsmen, and farmers. Their culture reached its peak from about 5500 B.C. to 2500 B.C. After the rains ceased, some of the people moved with their flocks and herds to live along the Mediterranean coast. Others settled in the Nile valley. Still others migrated southward, following the retreating pasturelands. Thenceforth the Sahara Desert separated the peoples of northern and southern Africa.

In previous sections of this book we have traced the history of northern Africa. We have seen how the Egyptians developed one of the world's first civilizations, and how Greek and Phoenician colonies were planted along the Mediterranean coast. Eventually, Rome dominated all North Africa. Later, as Rome's power declined, her place was taken first by German tribes, then by the Arabs, and (to 1800) by the Turks.

Less well known is the record of the people living south of the Sahara. This part of the continent is largely occupied by four broad racial groups—Negro, Pygmy-Bushman, Ethiopoid, and Caucasian. Studies indicate that Negroes originally lived in west central Africa north of the forest belt, and that groups migrated toward the east and south. In East Africa they came into contact with dwellers in the Nile valley, known as "Ethiopoids"—an ancient racial mixture of Negroes and white people, and eventually were affected by this civilization. The Negroes who migrated south united with others to form the large culture group known as Bantu. In Southwest Africa they found people related to the present day Bushmen, and in the Congo forests they found the Pygmies. Madagascar, now called the Malagasy Republic, was settled by Malaysians, and some tribes in eastern Africa may be descended from Chinese who came during the Ming dynasty voyages. In modern times other settlers have come to central and southern Africa. Arabs and Europeans represent the Caucasian race. There are also many (now perhaps a million) who are descended from recent Asiatic immigrants—Malaysians, Chinese, and Indians. The Negro peoples now occupy most of the continent, although at one time they inhabited only the north.

Since Africans have never united under a single government, no common language has developed. Instead, several hundred dialects or languages are spoken. Many reflect the influence of traders and colonizers. The language of Madagascar is Malaysian, and that of Ethiopia is Semitic, related to Arabic. Swahili, a combination of Arabic and Bantu, is widely used in east central Africa for business and government.

Hunters, herdsmen, and farmers. Physical conditions in Africa vary so greatly that Africans have had to make many adaptations in their lives. Although they have developed a great variety of life patterns, the basic ones are those of the hunters and food-gatherers, the herdsmen, and the farmers.

From the time of the Sahara dwellers, many Africans have lived by hunting. One type of hunter-gatherers still remaining are

AFRICAN PLAIN AND MT. KILIMANJARO

the Bushmen of the Kalahari Desert, in southern Africa. They have learned to find food and water where neither seems to exist. The Pygmies of the Congo basin live under quite different conditions, being overwhelmed by moisture and vegetation. Yet both groups have survived by hunting in groups and by willingly sharing with each other. Although they live at the level of bare subsistence, they take pride in maintaining their customs and freedom of movement.

For centuries a much larger number of Africans have lived as herdsmen, as did the Sahara people of 6000 years ago. Like the hunters, they have prized their independence. Among the herdsmen in Africa today are the Watusi, the world's tallest people. (Their average height of seven feet contrasts with that of the Pygmies, who at four to four and a half feet are the world's smallest people.)

By 1800 most Africans south of the Sahara were living as farmers. Their crops included rice, corn, and potatoes, raised by hoe agriculture rather than the use of plows. Land was regarded as belonging to the village group, not to individuals.

Traders and empire-builders. Until recently, Africans were thought of only as hunters, herdsmen, and farmers. Discoveries since World War II have revealed another side of Africa's past. Explorers have found the remains of African cities, temples, and tombs, some built on a massive scale. Although study of these remains is far from complete, it is now clear that for a thousand years and more in the past Africans also excelled as miners and metal-workers, traders and seafarers, and builders of cities and empires. Perplexing is the fact that Africa missed out on the Bronze Age and remained technologically backward from 2500 B.C. to 500 B.C. Then, suddenly, she went directly from the New Stone Age to the Iron Age.

East Africa entered the Iron Age before the time of Christ. Meroë, which became the capital city of the Kush Empire, was by 200 B.C. a busy center of iron mining and smelting. In West Africa, gold mining was likewise carried on from an early date. Accumulation of metals and other products, such as ivory, salt, and grain, led naturally to the development of commerce. Most trading was carried on within Africa, but African goods also reached Europe and Asia. Wealth from trade led to the growth of several empires in Africa.

The Kushite Empire. Kush, a territory south of Egypt and once ruled by it, became independent in 750 B.C. The Kushite kings then invaded Egypt and conquered it, only to be driven out by the Assyrians about 650 B.C. Although Kush thereafter remained separate from Egypt, its culture remained Egyptian in many ways. Meroë as capital and iron-working center is the best known of several Kushite cities. From them trade was carried on with India and Arabia, and for a time ambassadors were sent to Rome. By A.D. 320 Meroë had been captured by invaders, and her empire was dissolved. Inscriptions on Kushite pyramids and temples cannot as yet be read, but if they are deciphered they doubtless will explain much about the beginnings of civilization in east central Africa.

The rise of Ethiopia. While Kush was declining, a new state was rising in eastern Africa. This was Ethiopia, after which the eastern highlands are named (see map, page 234). Ethiopian traders steered their ships to India, Ceylon, and Mediterranean lands. In this process they came into contact with Christianity. In 333 Ethiopia was converted to Coptic Christianity, which it has followed to the present. For a long time Ethiopia was cut off from the rest of the world. Beginning about A.D. 800, Arab merchants entered Africa's east-coast trade, and soon controlled it. Although Arabs nearly surrounded Ethiopia, they could not conquer her. Ethiopia maintained her independence except for a brief period just before and during World War II, and claims to be the world's oldest country.

West African empires. Meanwhile, other empires were formed in west central Africa, in the region of the Niger River. Three of the largest were those known as Ghana (700–1200), Mali (1200–1500), and Songhai (1350–1600). The empire of Mali extended from the Atlantic coast far into Africa, and included the fabled city of Timbuktu (see 1830 map, page 420). The city at that time was one of the largest in the world, famous for its library and university. Although Mali was politically independent, it adopted the religion of Mo-

hammed. In the 1300's, when an emperor of Mali made a pilgrimage to Mecca, he left a lasting impression wherever he went. Records of the time say that he took with him thousands of servants and over $12,000,000 for expenses.

Songhai was the largest, richest, and last of the West African empires. It absorbed nearly all of Mali and other territory as well, so that at its peak Songhai ruled territory as large as all of Europe. Desire for Songhai's wealth led to a successful invasion by Moslems in 1591.

The prosperity of West Africa's empires was based on trade. Their merchants served as middlemen, trading salt mined in the Sahara for gold along the western "Gold Coast." The gold was taken by caravans to Arab markets on the Mediterranean Sea and Indian Ocean. Since the Arabs were eager for the gold, and since the people of central and western Africa needed salt, the West African merchants made enormous profits. Their skill in trade was widely respected. However, their favorable position was weakened when Arab armies conquered Songhai at about the same time Europeans entered the gold trade of the west coast.

AFRICAN RELIGIOUS FAITH

. . . It fills the fisherman's net; it ripens the husbandman's corn; it gives success to the trader's adventure; it protects the traveller by sea and land; it accompanies the warrior, and shields him in battle; it stays the raging pestilence; it bends heaven to its will, and refreshes the earth with rain; it enters the heart of the liar, the thief, and the murderer, and makes the lying tongue to falter, quenches the eye of passion, withholds the covetous hand, and stays the uplifted knife, or it convicts them of their crimes, and reveals them to the world; it even casts its spells over malignant demons, and turns them for good or ill according to its pleasure.

—K. A. Busia, *Africa in Search of Democracy.*

The coming of the Europeans. As the Arabs had taken over trade on the east coast, so Europeans eventually dominated the west. First to come were the Portuguese, inspired by Prince Henry. Their profits in ivory, gold, and slaves led them to set up trading posts on the west coast and (later) the east. Dutch and English slave traders next ventured to the African coast in hope of financial gains. The slavers purchased their human cargoes from coastal tribes who obtained the slaves from the interior through war or barter. The slave-hunters often traded their captives for guns, enabling them to capture more slaves. Exact figures are unavailable, but it is clear that millions of people were victimized in this grim and horrid traffic. Perhaps half of them died aboard ship on their voyage to the Americas.

With the coming of the Europeans, African life was permanently changed. Giving guns to the coastal tribes made them stronger than those in the interior, where empires had been centered. Secondly, the slave trade destroyed many villages and upset the cultural life and economy of large parts of Africa. It is unfair to blame the Europeans alone for the slave trade. Slavery had existed in Africa from the days of ancient Egypt, before the Europeans came. Furthermore, most of the slaves were captured and sold by their fellow Africans. However, settlement of America after 1500 opened a new market for slaves, and the ravages of the trade were much greater than ever before. It now appears that, left to herself, Africa by 1800 would have led a reasonably stable and peaceful existence. The farming villages and tribes of herdsmen had learned to produce food enough for their own needs. There was no land shortage, and merchants were conducting profitable businesses.

African culture. The variety of cultures in Africa was so great that generalizations are dangerous in the extreme. Perhaps it is safe to say, however, that the strongest feature of African culture was religion. Religious faith touched upon all aspects of life on the Gold Coast in the early 1800's. Other evidence indicates that the lives of most Africans had long been similarly influenced. In addition to native beliefs which may be classed as nature worship, both Islam and Christianity had footholds in Africa by 1800.

The dance also occupied a central position in African culture from early times. The Stone Age paintings in the Sahara Desert show dances of prehistoric groups. Through the centuries, Africans developed complicated and sophisticated rhythms in their dances and accompanying music. Dances might be religious or social, formal or informal, narrative or emotional.

African art, once considered "primitive," is now highly regarded. It appears in stone and wood sculpture and in castings of bronze and other metals. These works of art often showed great strength and versatility in design, and were characterized by religious feeling. Some experimentation was done in abstract designs. Modern sculptors and painters have been affected in considerable degree by African art (see page 360).

Summarizing the chapter. During the period A.D. 500–1800 large empires were established in the nonwestern world—in the Middle East, India, China, Southeast Asia, and Africa. Each empire made progress both in gaining material wealth and in developing its own art, architecture, and literature. Religious movements also stimulated each. However, by 1800 these cultures had generally ceased to be active and the empires had ceased to grow. China and Japan made special efforts to shut out new ideas. The more aggressive Europeans found it relatively easy to establish trading posts and then expand them into colonies. By 1800 this movement was beginning to have profound effects on the peoples of the nonwestern world.

REVIEWING THE CHAPTER

TERMS TO UNDERSTAND: *khan, Janizaries, Shintoism, Zen Buddhism, Shin Buddhism, mikado, shogun, daimio, samurai, bushido, Polynesian, Swahili, Coptic Christianity.*

PERSONS TO IDENTIFY: *Baber, Genghis Khan, Kublai Khan, Marco Polo, Chu Hsi, Jimmu Tenno, Yoritomo, St. Francis Xavier.*

PLACES TO LOCATE: *Istanbul, Peking, Macao, Canton, East Indies (Indonesia), Siberia, Korea, Taiwan (Formosa), Japan, Indo-China, Malaya, Philippine Islands, Madagascar, Kalahari Desert, Niger River, Ethiopia, Timbuktu, Zambezi River.*

QUESTIONS TO ANSWER

1. (a) What was included in the Moslem world at its greatest extent? (b) Explain why several separate states arose in the Moslem world. (c) Describe the culture of the Moslem world by 1800.

2. (a) Describe Indian culture during the Gupta Age in the fields of literature, religion, science, mathematics, and art. (b) Why were achievements of the Gupta Age largely unknown to the mass of Indians? (c) Discuss some of the effects of the Moslem invasions in India.

3. (a) What pattern repeats itself in Chinese history? (b) Describe Chinese culture under the T'ang dynasty and under the Sung dynasty. (c) What were the roots of Chinese life from 500 to 1800? Describe some of the changes brought by foreign influences in this period.

4. (a) Name the four main islands of Japan. (b) How has Japanese civilization been influenced by that of China? (c) Describe the Japanese government and social system during the feudal period. (d) Briefly describe the beliefs of Shintoism, Zen Buddhism, and Shin Buddhism. (e) How did Japan close her doors to the world in the 1600's?

5. (a) What geographical areas are included in the term *Southeast Asia?* (b) Name the groups of people who have intermixed in Southeast Asia. (c) Name the four major religions brought to Southeast Asia and tell what specific areas were affected by each.

6. (a) Give eight examples of ways in which Africa is vast and varied. (b) Name some of the civilizations which flourished in North Africa and some of the groups who settled south of the Sahara Desert. (c) What have discoveries since World War II revealed about Africa's past? (d) Explain how the Europeans changed African life. (e) Briefly describe African culture in the fields of religion, dance, and art.

FURTHER ACTIVITIES FOR PART FOUR

1. Read in Dorothy Mills's *Renaissance and Reformation Times* the account of the wonderful age of the Renaissance. Prepare a written report on your reading.

2. Give a class report on the start of one of the world's great religions. Clear and interesting explanations are given in Joseph Gaer's *How the Great Religions Began.*

3. Write an imaginary diary telling the adventures of one of the great explorers. Leonard Outhwaite's *Unrolling the Map* is one of the best references you can use.

4. A committee may prepare maps showing colonization by the European powers. One map should show the Spanish Empire at its peak; others should do the same for Portugal, Holland, France, and England.

5. Prepare a list of products and inventions we have received from the peoples of Asia. Cornelia Spencer's *Made in China* will be especially helpful.

6. Prepare a report on the building of the Great Wall of China.

7. Find out more about one of the African kingdoms and report your findings to the class. Basil Davidson's *African Kingdoms* and

Henri Labouret's *Africa Before the White Man* will be helpful.

8. Construct a time line to show the events in Europe which were discussed in Part Four. On a separate line show the events which occurred in Asia and the Americas.

FURTHER READING FOR PART FOUR

(Stars indicate easier books)

HISTORY

*BERGER and WROTH. *Discoverers of the New World.* Harper.

*BIXBY and SANTILLANA. *The Universe of Galileo and Newton.* Harper.

BURTON. *The Pageant of Elizabethan England.* Scribner.

CHAMBERLAIN. *Everyday Life in Renaissance Times.* Putnam.

CHRISTENSEN. *The Pictorial History of Western Art.* Mentor. (paperback)

CLENDENIN. *Music History and Theory.* Doubleday. (paperback)

DAVIDSON. *African Kingdoms.* Time-Life.

——. *The Lost Cities of Africa.* Little, Brown. (paperback)

*DAVIS. *Life in Elizabethan Days.* Harper.

*DILTS. *Pageant of Japanese History.* McKay.

DURANT. *The Story of Civilization.* Simon and Schuster.

*DUVOISIN. *They Put Out to Sea: The Story of the Map.* Knopf.

EMBREE. *Indians of the Americas.* Houghton.

FAGG and PLASS. *African Sculpture.* Dutton. (paperback)

GAER. *How the Great Religions Began.* Dodd.

HALE. *Renaissance.* Time-Life.

——. *Age of Exploration.* Time-Life.

*HEWES. *Spice Ho!* Knopf.

HITTI. *The Arabs: A Short History.* Regnery. (paperback)

HORIZON MAGAZINE. *The Horizon Book of Christianity.* American Heritage.

——. *The Horizon Book of the Renaissance.* American Heritage.

JENYNS. *A Background to Chinese Painting.* Schocken. (paperback)

KENTON. *With Hearts Courageous.* Liveright.

KOMROFF, ed. *The Travels of Marco Polo.* Liveright.

LABOURET. *Africa Before the White Man.* Walker. (paperback)

LATOURETTE. *The History of Japan.* Macmillan.

——. *Short History of the Far East.* Macmillan.

LEWIS. *Istanbul and the Civilization of the Ottoman Empire.* University of Oklahoma.

MACHIAVELLI. *The Prince.* Mentor. (paperback)

McKINNEY. *Music in History, the Evolution of an Art.* American Book.

McNEILL, BUSKE, ROEHM. *The World . . . Its History in Maps.* Denoyer-Geppert.

*MILLS. *Renaissance and Reformation Times.* Putnam.

*MODAK. *The Land and the People of India.* Lippincott.

MOOREHEAD. *The White Nile.* Dell. (paperback)

PRICE. *Made in the Renaissance.* Dutton.

REISCHAUER. *Japan Past and Present.* Knopf.

SAVAGE. *The Story of Africa South of the Sahara.* Walck.

SHOR. *After You, Marco Polo.* McGraw.

SIMON. *The Reformation.* Time-Life.

SPENCER. *Made in India.* Knopf.

*VAUGHAN. *The Land and People of Japan.* Lippincott.

BIOGRAPHY

ALLEN. *The Story of Michelangelo.* Roy.

BAINTON. *Here I Stand: A Life of Martin Luther.* Abingdon.

*BAKER. *Amerigo Vespucci.* Knopf.

*——. *Sir Walter Raleigh*. Harcourt.

BRODRICK. *Galileo*. Harper.

COUGHLAN. *The World of Michelangelo, 1475–1564*. Time-Life.

CRISS. *Isabella, Young Queen of Spain*. Dodd.

*FERMI and BERNARDINI. *Galileo and the Scientific Revolution*. Basic Books.

*FOSDICK. *Martin Luther*. Random House.

*GARST. *Three Conquistadors*. Messner.

HAHN. *Mary, Queen of Scots*. Random House.

*HODGES. *Columbus Sails*. Coward-McCann. (paperback)

HORIZON MAGAZINE. *Leonardo da Vinci*. American Heritage.

——. *Marco Polo's Adventures in China*. American Heritage.

JENKINS. *Elizabeth the Great*. Coward-McCann.

*KOMROFF. *Marco Polo*. Messner.

LAMB. *Genghis Khan*. Doubleday.

MORISON. *Christopher Columbus, Mariner*. New American Library. (paperback)

RIESENBERG. *Balboa: Swordsman and Conquistador*. Random House.

RIPLEY. *Michelangelo, a Biography*. Walck.

——. *Raphael*. Lippincott.

——. *Rembrandt*. Walck.

ROSEN. *Galileo and the Magic Numbers*. Little, Brown.

SANCEAU. *Henry the Navigator*. Shoe String.

SOOTIN. *Isaac Newton*. Messner.

SPERRY. *The Voyages of Christopher Columbus*. Random House.

SUGIMOTO. *A Daughter of the Samurai*. Tuttle.

*VANCE. *Elizabeth Tudor*. Dutton.

WALLACE. *The World of Leonardo, 1452–1519*. Time-Life.

WEDGWOOD. *The World of Rubens, 1577–1640*. Time-Life.

WELCH. *Ferdinand Magellan*. Phillips.

FICTION

BAUMANN. *Sons of the Steppe: The Story of How the Conqueror Genghis Khan Was Overcome*. Walck.

BENNETT. *Master Skylark*. Grosset.

CHUTE. *Wonderful Winter*. Dutton.

*CLEMENS. *The Prince and the Pauper*. Scott, Foresman.

*FINGER. *Courageous Companions*. McKay.

HAYCRAFT. *The Reluctant Queen*. Lippincott.

——. *Too Near the Throne*. Lippincott.

*HEWES. *Spice and the Devil's Cave*. Knopf.

IRWIN. *Elizabeth, Captive Princess*. Harcourt.

KELLY. *Trumpeter of Krakow*. Macmillan.

*KENT. *He Went with Marco Polo*. Houghton.

*——. *He Went with Vasco da Gama*. Houghton.

KINGSLEY. *Westward Ho!* Scribner.

*LOWNSBERY. *The Boy Knight of Reims*. Houghton.

MARKANDAYA. *Nectar in a Sieve*. Day,

*RITCHIE. *The Golden Hawks of Genghis Khan*. Dutton.

SCOTT. *Kenilworth*. Macmillan.

SETH–SMITH. *The Black Tower*. Vanguard.

STONE. *Michelangelo: Sculptor*. Doubleday.

WIBBERLEY. *The King's Beard*. Hale.

VOLTAIRE, ROUSSEAU, AND FRANKLIN, pictured on the cover of a snuff box.
These men were leading figures in the eighteenth-century revolt against authority.
European scientists and philosophers treated Franklin as an equal. He was very popular
as America's minister to France during the Revolutionary War.

PART FIVE

AN ERA OF POLITICAL REVOLUTIONS

In Part Four we traced the story of the widening horizons of European peoples. They revived ancient learning and challenged the ideas and customs of the Middle Ages. They also ventured forth boldly into the far corners of the world in search of trade and wealth.

Part Five will give an account of the far-reaching effects of Europe's new awakening. First we shall see how the power to rule was concentrated in the hands of strong kings and dynasties (families of hereditary rulers). They wielded absolute authority over their peoples and realms, although some, called "enlightened despots," tried to promote the welfare of their subjects. The so-called Age of Autocracy reached its peak during the reign of Louis XIV of France, whose lavish court life was widely imitated. Most of the autocrats, however, made only halfhearted efforts to wipe out the class injustices and inequalities left over from feudal times. As a result, the whole system of autocratic rule came under attack by seventeenth- and eighteenth-century thinkers, especially by the "philosophers" of the Enlightenment. Their ideas helped to bring on a revolutionary era that sowed the seeds of democracy and nationalism, two of the important continuing forces or themes in modern times.

It may be well to make clear at this point what we mean by revolution. In a general sense revolution may be defined as any far-reaching change in ways of living and thinking. It may take place in a number of fields of human activity—in government, in science and invention, in manners and customs, in religion, or in art and literature. Usually, revolutionary change affects all these areas of human endeavor at about the same time, for life is not a series of separate compartments. Revolutions may also take place gradually or suddenly. They may be accompanied by violence or be peaceful. In Part Five we shall study revolutions which brought about new political and social conditions in most of the western world.

14 The Age of Autocracy

PALACE AT VERSAILLES. Louis XIV ordered its construction, as a symbol of his greatness, on a barren marshland twelve miles from Paris. French nobility spent most of their time at this splendid court, seeking the king's favor. With them were the country's foremost artists and scholars, along with visiting counterparts from throughout Europe.

As the Middle Ages drew to a close, the kings had gained greater power than the nobles in many European countries. Wherever they could, the kings then made themselves autocrats, or absolute masters of their domains. In this chapter we shall follow the colorful careers of the autocrats in Spain, France, Russia, and Austria during the seventeenth and eighteenth centuries—a period known as the Age of Autocracy.

The Rise of Spain to Leadership in Europe

Why Spain became powerful. In 1492 Ferdinand and Isabella finally succeeded in bringing all Spain under their control. (See page 163.) Spain was then neither wealthy nor powerful, yet during the next century it became the leading nation of Europe. Three reasons may be given for the remarkable growth of Spanish power and influence: (1) Ferdinand and Isabella established a strong central government in Spain. They ended the private warfare of the nobles, reorganized the army, and encouraged industry and agriculture. (2) Discoveries and explorations helped to strengthen Spain. She acquired a vast empire and used a part of the gold and silver brought from America to build the mightiest fleet and army in the world. (3) Spanish influence was extended through "political" marriages arranged for the descendants of Ferdinand and Isabella. Following the custom of the times, they were wed to the sons and daughters of other royal families so as to give Spain allies throughout most of Europe.

Spain rises to leadership under Charles V. Under Charles V, who was born in 1500, Spain became the dominant power in Europe. His mother was Joanna, the daughter of Ferdinand and Isabella. Charles inherited the Spanish throne and all the Spanish colonial possessions, as well as Sicily and parts of southern Italy. His father was Philip of Hapsburg, son of the Holy Roman emperor.[1] Charles inherited the Netherlands, a Hapsburg possession, and after his grandfather's death he was chosen Holy Roman emperor. Some called Charles the "Lord of the World." Certainly his possessions were extensive (see map on this page), and he had the difficult task of governing many different and scattered peoples. His reign (1519–1556) was filled with wars, some growing out of the Reformation in Germany and some out of rivalry with other rulers. The French, who were practically encircled by his possessions, looked upon Charles as their most dangerous foe and tried in every way to weaken him. He was at war with France during most of his reign. In Spain, Charles continued Ferdinand and Isabella's policy of strengthening the central government. He alone ruled Spain; in short, he was an autocrat. Charles had considerable ability and a desire to rule well, but at last he tired of war and responsibility. In 1556 he gave up all his titles and possessions and retired to a Spanish monastery. His son Philip received Spain, the Netherlands, and Spain's colonial and Italian possessions. Ferdinand, the younger brother of Charles, had previously inherited Austria and come into possession of Hungary and Bohemia. He became Holy Roman emperor after Charles abdicated. Thus there arose two

[1] The Holy Roman Empire included several hundred small states, most of which were German. The heads of seven of the states elected the Holy Roman emperor. In 1438 Albert of Austria, a Hapsburg, was chosen Holy Roman emperor. After him the imperial title became practically hereditary, since all but one of the succeeding emperors were Hapsburgs. The Hapsburgs held the title of emperor until 1806, when the empire was dissolved after Napoleon's victory over Austria. The Hapsburg ruler then took the new title of Emperor of Austria.

245

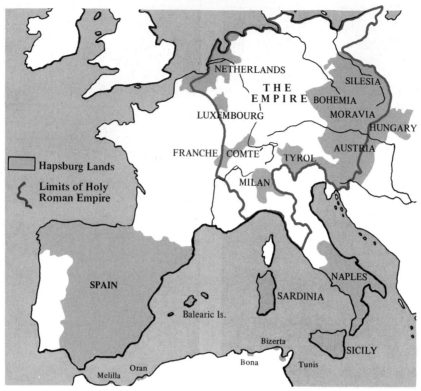

HAPSBURG LANDS DURING THE REIGN OF CHARLES V, 1516–1556

Map legend:
Hapsburg Lands
Limits of Holy Roman Empire

Map labels: NETHERLANDS, THE EMPIRE, SILESIA, LUXEMBOURG, BOHEMIA, MORAVIA, HUNGARY, AUSTRIA, FRANCHE COMTE, TYROL, MILAN, SPAIN, SARDINIA, NAPLES, Balearic Is., Bizerta, SICILY, Bona, Tunis, Oran, Melilla

powerful branches of the Hapsburg family: one in Austria, and one in Spain.

Spain under Philip II. Philip II, who succeeded Charles, was a cold and haughty man. During his reign (1556–1598) Spanish influence reached around the globe. His wife, Mary, was queen of England from 1553 until her death in 1558. Philip's mother was a Portuguese princess. Because of this connection he acquired Portugal in 1580, together with the Portuguese colonies and the monopoly on Oriental trade. Although Spain reached the peak of its power under Philip, his policies eventually led to its decline. He drove the Netherlands to revolt by his harshness. (See page 190.) In 1588 his attempted invasion of England ended with the defeat of the Spanish Armada and the weakening of Spanish and Portuguese sea power. The defeat of the Armada was a blow from which Spain never fully recovered. During the following century Portugal regained its independence, and Spain had to recognize the independence of the United Netherlands. Although Spain held its colonies until the 1800's, after the days of Philip II it no longer dominated European politics.

Autocracy Flowers in France

The Bourbons. The Bourbons established in France an autocracy similar to that of the Hapsburgs in Spain. Henry of Navarre, the first member of the Bourbon family to reign in France, came to the throne in 1589. He inherited, together with the throne, a bitter struggle between Catholics and Huguenots. Although he was a Protestant, Henry sought to please the Catholic majority in France by accepting their faith, remarking cynically,

"Paris is worth a Mass." To the Huguenots he granted the right to hold public office, and a limited religious freedom. (See page 190.) In the reign of his son, Louis XIII (1610–1643), the power of the French monarchy increased enormously. This growth was due chiefly to the political genius of Cardinal Richelieu (rēsh′ ē lōō), the king's leading minister.

Louis XIV. The third Bourbon, Louis XIV, whose reign (1643–1715) is the longest in European history, ranks among the most able of French monarchs. He was a man of handsome appearance, slightly below the average in height, with a prominent nose and abundant hair, which he allowed to fall over his shoulders. In manner he was dignified, reserved, and courteous. He was as majestic in his dressing gown as in his official robes. Louis possessed much natural intelligence, an extremely good memory, and great capacity for work. It must be added, however, that his general education had been neglected, and that throughout his life he remained ignorant and superstitious. Vanity formed a striking trait in his character. He accepted the most extravagant compliments and delighted in being known as the "Grand Monarch" and the "Sun King."

The French court. Louis gathered around him a magnificent court at Versailles, near Paris. Here a whole royal city, with palaces, parks, groves, terraces, and fountains, sprang into being at his order. The gilded salons and mirrored halls of Versailles were soon crowded with members of the nobility. They now spent little time on their estates, preferring to remain at Versailles near the king, who gave them offices, pensions, and honors. The splendor of the French court cast its spell upon Europe. Every king and prince looked to Louis as the model of what a ruler should be and tried to imitate him. French language, manners, dress, art, and literature became the accepted standards of polite society throughout Europe.

United Provinces
Spanish Provinces

THE NETHERLANDS IN 1581. In that year the seven northern provinces (known as the United Provinces) split off from the remainder of the Spanish Netherlands and declared their independence from Spain. In an attempt to conquer the United Provinces Spain fought until 1609.

Autocracy in France. The famous saying "I am the State," though not uttered by Louis, did express his conviction that in him were embodied the power and greatness of France. Conditions in that country made possible his autocratic government. Previous rulers had been successful in strengthening their royal authority. There was no parliament to give the people a voice in the government, nor was there a Magna Carta, as in England, to limit the powers of the king. The French, furthermore, did not have independent courts of law which could interfere with the king's actions. The king was indeed the state.

The work of Colbert. Louis of course kept all authority in his own hands, but he could not attend to all the details of governing. He had to rely upon advisers, or ministers, to bring him information and to carry out his

Never did man give with better grace than Louis XIV, or augmented so much in this way, the price of his benefits. Never did man sell to better profit his words, even his smiles,—nay, his looks. Never did disobliging words escape him, and if he had to blame, to reprimand, or correct, which was very rare, it was nearly always with goodness, never, except on one occasion . . . , with anger or severity. Never was man so naturally polite, or of a politeness so measured, so graduated, so adapted to person, time, and place. Towards women his politeness was without parallel.

As for the King himself, nobody ever approached his magnificence. His buildings, who could number them? At the same time, who was there who did not deplore the pride, the caprice, the bad taste seen in them? He built nothing useful or ornamental in Paris, except the Pont Royal, and that simply by necessity; so that despite its incomparable extent, Paris is inferior to many cities of Europe. . . . He built at Versailles, on, on, without any general design, the beautiful and the ugly, the vast and the mean, all jumbled together . . .

—Leon Bernard and Theodore B. Hodges, eds., *Readings in Modern World Civilization.*

orders. Colbert was the most notable of Louis's ministers.

Colbert believed thoroughly in the principles of mercantilism. (See page 205.) He tried to foster manufactures by placing heavy duties on all goods imported from abroad and by giving financial assistance to new industries. He helped to establish trading companies, and he encouraged colonial activities that would yield raw materials for French factories. Under his direction many islands in the West Indies were acquired, Canada was developed, and Louisiana was opened up to settlement. Colbert also built roads and canals in France and so improved the methods of tax collection that he was able to turn the government's annual deficit into a surplus.

The wars of Louis XIV. Four great wars occupied a large part of Louis's reign. The first three were undertaken to extend the dominions of France as far as the Rhine, which Louis regarded as the natural boundary between France and Germany. He did secure several strips of territory to the east and northeast of France, particularly Alsace. (The map on page 194 shows the extent of France early in his rule.) The Alsatians, though of Germanic extraction, in time came to think of themselves as French. The wealthy duchy of Lorraine was added to France during the reign of Louis's successor, and the Lorrainers, like the Alsatians, became thoroughly French in feeling. Germans long maintained, however, that France should give up both Alsace and Lorraine, and eventually Germany seized these provinces.

The War of the Spanish Succession, 1701–1713. The fourth great war arose over the question of succession to the Spanish throne. The king of Spain, who lacked children or brothers to succeed him, left a will naming one of Louis's grandsons as his heir. He hoped that the French might be strong enough to keep the Spanish dominions from being divided. Louis was pleased at the prospect of a vast expansion of French influence, but other European rulers looked on with dismay. England, Austria, Holland, Portugal, and several of the German states formed a Grand Alliance against France and Spain in the War of the Spanish Succession. The war continued for more than a decade in all parts of the world until both sides were exhausted. In 1713 the belligerents signed the compromise Peace of Utrecht. The Allies agreed to recognize Louis's grandson as king of Spain and her colonies, but only on condition that the French and Spanish crowns should never be united. Louis was allowed to keep the territories acquired in Europe during his reign, but he had to surrender to England part of his possessions in North America, including Acadia (now Nova Scotia), Newfoundland, and the Hudson Bay region. (See map, page 212.) The war and the peace that

LOUIS XIV, THE SUN KING. During his long reign, he brought to its peak the concept of absolutism. As the most important ruler of his age, he constantly strove to fulfill his enormous obligation and drive France to its greatest heights. As a benefactor of culture he was widely imitated. However, his constant wars left France bankrupt.

followed it thwarted his ambitious plans for gaining the mastery of western Europe.

Effect of the wars on France. All the gains produced by Colbert's economic reforms were swallowed up by the costs of the king's warlike policy. France suffered famine and pestilence. Excessive taxes and huge war debts impoverished her people. Louis, now a very old man, survived the Peace of Utrecht only two years. As he lay dying he turned to his little heir and said: "Try to keep peace with your neighbors. I have been too fond of war; do not imitate me in that, or in my too great expenditure."

Russia Becomes a Nation

Geography of European Russia. European Russia lies on the borderland between Asia and Europe, and has therefore been influenced by both the East and the West. The land of Russia is a part of the great plain which stretches across northern Europe and Asia. Rising above the plain, the Ural Mountains form a natural boundary separating Russia from Asia. Generally level though it is, the land of Russia shows some variations in altitude. The highest part of the Russian plain is the region around Moscow; here begin all of the main Russian rivers. They flow slowly toward the White and Baltic seas on the north or toward the Black and Caspian seas on the south. Northern Russia is a land of lake and swamp and forest, with bitterly cold winters. Central Russia also has extensive marshes, but most of the land is suitable for farming when cleared of trees. In southern Russia, especially in the Ukraine, farming conditions are almost ideal. A belt of rich black soil yields abundant crops of wheat and rye, causing the region to be called the "breadbasket" of Russia. Russia is rich in timber, coal, iron, oil, manganese, and other resources.

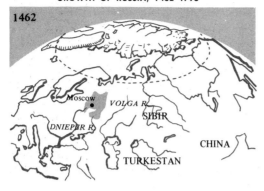

GROWTH OF RUSSIA, 1462–1796

1462

Moscow
VOLGA R.
SIBIR
DNIEPER R.
CHINA
TURKESTAN

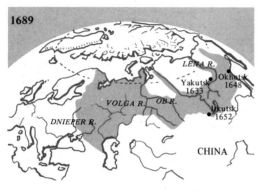

1689

LENA R.
Yakutsk
1633
Okhotsk
1648
VOLGA R. OB R.
DNIEPER R.
Irkutsk
1652
CHINA

1725

1697
KAMCHATKA
St. Petersburg
1703
CHINA

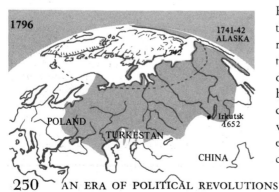

1796

1741-42
ALASKA
1742
POLAND
Irkutsk
1652
TURKESTAN
CHINA

The Slavs. As we have seen, Slavic tribes had settled in eastern Europe by the time the Roman Empire fell. (See page 102.) Most of the Slavs found homes in what is now Russia, but others pushed farther west into Poland or turned south into the Balkans. During the Middle Ages the Slavs began to come under the influence of other European peoples. They traded with the Eastern Roman Empire and in the tenth century adopted from it the Greek Orthodox faith. The Slavs were still more influenced by Northmen from Sweden, who opened trade routes from the Baltic to the Black Sea, following the natural highways formed by the Russian rivers. The Northmen established cities and trading posts and built up the first great Russian state, which for a short time claimed to rule all the Slavs. (See page 135). This state soon broke up into a large number of quarreling principalities.

The Mongols. Through the activities of traders, diplomats, and religious leaders, the people of Russia kept in touch with the Eastern Roman Empire and western Europe. A new influence came in during the thirteenth century when the Mongols under Genghis Khan conquered Russia. These nomad horsemen held the Russians in subjection for more than three hundred years, forcing the Russian princes to pay tribute to the khan, three thousand miles away. While the Mongols did not interfere with the laws, customs, religion, or language of their subject peoples, the Mongol occupation left an indelible imprint on Russian society and government. As a result, Russia came to be more nearly a part of Asia than of Europe. Gradually the Mongol hold relaxed, however, and in the fifteenth century the various Russian states asserted their independence. The strongest state was that headed by the prince of Moscow. By conquest, purchase, or diplomacy each Muscovite prince who came to the throne tried to enlarge his dominions. (See maps in the left column.) In 1547 the prince of Moscow took upon himself the title of czar, or "Caesar." He and his successors claimed the title "ruler of all Russia," but until the rise of the Romanov dynasty the nobles were often as powerful as the czars.

The Romanovs. Michael, the first of the Romanovs, came to the throne in 1613. His descendants were to rule for three hundred years—until the Russian Revolution in 1917. When Michael became czar, Russia was isolated from the rest of the world. It extended to neither the Black Sea nor the Baltic, and had not yet revived its earlier contacts with Europe. Most of the Russians were ignorant, superstitious peasants, who lived secluded lives in small farming villages scattered over the plains and through the forests. The Romanovs began the twofold task of acquiring seaports through which to trade with the outside world, and of bringing European civilization to Russia.

Russia advances into Siberia. The czars' easiest expansion was eastward into Siberia, which was thinly settled. Northern Siberia is largely wasteland, but below it lies a vast and valuable belt of forest with treeless steppes still farther south. Although the Russians did not know it, Siberia also contained a wealth of minerals. In 1581 a small band of Cossack cavalrymen crossed the Ural Mountains and defeated the Khan of Sibir (Siberia). Peasants then began an eastward migration to settle on the newly opened lands.

Meanwhile, Cossack forces pushed ahead until in the 1640's they reached the Pacific. Defeated by China in an effort to move south, the Russians sent Captain Vitus Bering on two Pacific voyages. His visit to Alaska in 1741 led to a few settlements in America and to Russia's claim to Alaska.

Peter the Great. The greatest of the Romanovs was Peter the Great, who reigned from 1689 to 1725. Peter became czar when only seventeen years of age. An Englishman who knew him well described him as "a man of very hot temper, soon inflamed, and very

brutal in his passion." After a mutiny of his bodyguard he personally sliced off the heads of the culprits. In order to quell opposition in his family, he had his wife whipped and his son tortured and executed. Yet Peter could often be good-humored and frank, and he was as loyal to his friends as he was treacherous to his foes. He possessed a quick mind and a powerful body, and used both unsparingly in what he thought to be the best interests of Russia. Whatever his weaknesses, few men have done more than Peter to change the course of history.

Europeanization of Russia. Peter decided that Russia should take Europe, not Asia, as its model. He sent fifty young Russians of the best families to Venice, Holland, and England, instructing them to absorb European ideas. He himself spent two years in Germany, Holland, and England, traveling un-

---

RECOLLECTIONS OF PETER THE GREAT

. . . The Czar came this winter over to England, and stayed some Months among us; I waited often on him, and was ordered, both by the King and the Archbishop and Bishops, to attend upon him, and to offer him such Informations of our Religion and Constitution, as he was willing to receive: I had good Interpreters, so I had much free discourse with him. He is a man of a very hot temper, soon inflamed, and very brutal in his Passion; he raises his natural heat by drinking much Brandy, which he rectifies himself with great application: He is subject to convulsive Motions all over his Body, and his Head seems to be affected with these; he wants not Capacity, and has a larger measure of Knowledge than might be expected from his Education, which was very indifferent: A want of Judgment, with an instability of Temper, appear in him too often and too evidently . . . After I had seen him often, and had conversed much with him, I could not but adore the depth of the Providence of God, that had raised up such a furious man, to so absolute an Authority over so great a part of the World . . .

—Leon Bernard and Theodore B. Hodges, eds.,
Readings in Modern World Civilization.

der an assumed name. He even worked for a week as a laborer in a Dutch shipyard. Upon his return to Russia he proceeded to introduce to his people the arts and customs of western Europe. He ordered the Russian nobles to take off their long Asiatic robes and replace them with short German jackets. Long beards, which the people considered sacred, had to be shaved, or else the wearer must pay a tax for the privilege of wearing one. Women of the richer classes, who had previously been kept in seclusion, were permitted to appear in public without veils and to mingle with men at social gatherings and entertainments. The Bible was translated into the language of the people and sold at popular prices. Peter adopted the Julian calendar in place of the old Russian calendar which began the year on the first of September. He

organized the Russian army after the German fashion and built a fleet modeled upon that of Holland. He opened mines, dug canals, laid out roads, introduced sheep breeding, promoted silk culture, and aided woolen manufactures. He established a police system, a postal service, and schools of medicine, engineering, and navigation, and framed a code of laws based upon those of western Europe.

"Windows to the West." The Europeanization of Russia formed only half of Peter's work. His foreign policy was equally ambitious. By the time he came to the throne, Russian forces had advanced eastward across Siberia to the Pacific. However, Peter took less interest in developing that vast region than in opening a "window to the West." He wanted a seaport, on either the Black Sea or the Baltic, through which Russia could trade with Europe. Peter made little headway against the Turks, who controlled the Black Sea, but after twenty years of intermittent warfare with the Swedes he won most of the eastern shore of the Baltic. Here in the swamps along the shore Peter built a new and splendid capital, giving it the name St. Petersburg (now Leningrad). Peter had at last realized his long-cherished dream of opening a "window" into Europe.

CATHERINE THE GREAT, Empress of Russia from 1762 to 1796.

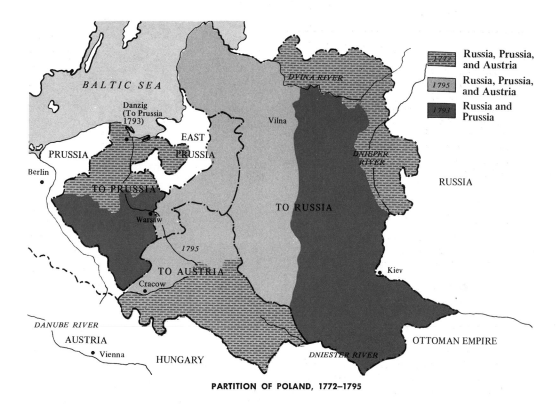

BALTIC SEA

Danzig (To Prussia 1793)

Vilna

DVINA RIVER

EAST PRUSSIA

PRUSSIA

Berlin

TO PRUSSIA

Warsaw

DNIEPER RIVER

TO RUSSIA

RUSSIA

1795

TO AUSTRIA

Kiev

Cracow

DANUBE RIVER

AUSTRIA

Vienna

HUNGARY

DNIESTER RIVER

OTTOMAN EMPIRE

PARTITION OF POLAND, 1772–1795

Catherine the Great. Catherine the Great, who ruled from 1762 to 1796, was another notable Russian ruler. She moved Russia's frontier toward the west by annexing large sections of Poland—territory she acquired by diplomacy rather than by war. In 1772, at the suggestion of the rulers of Austria and Prussia, she agreed to a "partition" of Poland in which the three great powers each took a piece of that helpless country. Russia and Prussia seized additional Polish land in 1793. Two years later they joined with Austria in a third partition which wiped Poland off the map. (See map above.) In the south Catherine conducted two successful wars against the Turks and won territory on the coast of the Black Sea. Thus a second "window" was opened into Europe. (For Russian acquisitions under Peter and Catherine, see the maps on page 250.) Catherine's government was thoroughly despotic, but she used her power to introduce further European reforms. She allowed a limited degree of religious toleration, began a few schools and hospitals, abolished torture of criminals, and substituted exile to Siberia for capital punishment. Catherine did nothing for the lower classes and left the serfs worse off than before.

The Rise of Prussia

The Holy Roman Empire. As we have already noticed (see page 245), Germany contained several hundred states at the close of the Middle Ages. These, together with other states in central Europe, were united into what was called the Holy Roman Empire. The emperor, elected by the heads of the member states, had very little power. Each state went its own way, waging wars, making alliances, and acting for the most part as though it were an independent country. Historians have generally agreed with Voltaire's remark that the empire was neither holy, nor

Roman, nor an empire. Actually, most of its people were German. The Hapsburgs of Austria held the office of emperor after 1438. (See note, page 245.) As the map on page 246 reveals, their possessions were widely scattered throughout Europe, a fact which kept the Hapsburgs from giving their attention entirely to German affairs. In time another German state, Brandenburg, arose to challenge the leadership of Austria and eventually to unite Germany. Brandenburg, later known as Brandenburg-Prussia and finally as Prussia, was on the northeast border of the Holy Roman Empire. (See map, page 255.)

The Hohenzollerns. The Hohenzollern family began ruling in Brandenburg in 1415. It would be hard to name another European dynasty with so many able and ambitious rulers. The Hohenzollerns prided themselves on the fact that almost every reigning member of the family enlarged the possessions received from his ancestors. They did this by purchase, by inheritance, by shrewd diplomacy, and by hard fighting. (The maps on the opposite page show how well they succeeded.) They believed in absolute government, with the ruler working as hard as any of his subjects to promote the welfare of the state. Efficiency became a Hohenzollern watchword. These active rulers fostered agriculture, industry, and commerce, promoted education, and made the best use of the limited resources in their possessions. By 1740 these possessions included East Prussia, Brandenburg, and smaller territories in central and western Germany; together they formed the kingdom of Prussia.

The Hohenzollerns wanted an army strong enough to defend a kingdom made up of scattered provinces without natural defenses. They used conscription (forced enrollment) to bring peasants into the ranks. They provided the army with the most up-to-date equipment. Carefully trained officers, appointed from the nobility and advanced only on merit, enforced an iron discipline. The sol-

FREDERICK THE GREAT, King of Prussia from 1740 to 1786 and foremost among the "enlightened despots"

diers, it was said, feared their commanders more than they did the enemy.

Frederick the Great. Frederick the Great became king of Prussia in 1740 at the age of twenty-eight. He was rather below the average height, with fair hair and blue-gray eyes of extraordinary brilliancy. During his youth Frederick disliked military life and showed a deep interest in books and music. After he became king, however, he proved to be energetic, ambitious, cynical, and extremely capable as a military leader. He was not a man to inspire affection, yet he was popular with the mass of his subjects.

War of the Austrian Succession, 1740–1748. In 1740, the year Frederick began his reign in Prussia, Maria Theresa became queen of Austria and the many Hapsburg possessions. Her father, realizing that after his death neighboring rulers might try to seize her realm, had made treaties in which every important European power promised to respect her right to the throne. The ruler of Bavaria had not agreed to this arrangement, and as soon as the young queen came to the throne he claimed that he was the rightful heir. Frederick saw his chance to seize some of Maria Theresa's territory and determined to act while others were disputing. He marched his army into the Hapsburg province of Silesia, which lay next to Brandenburg, and overran the country without much difficulty. Frederick's action led to a general European conflict—the War of the Austrian Succession. France, Spain, and Bavaria, hoping for a share of the Hapsburg lands, allied themselves with Prussia. Great Britain and Holland took the side of Austria. Things might have gone hard with Maria Theresa but for her courageous and energetic leadership and the loyal support of her subjects. Neither side was able to strike a decisive blow and at last, in 1748, the warring powers signed the Peace of Aix-la-Chapelle. It recognized Maria Theresa as the rightful Hapsburg heir, but required that she give up Silesia to Frederick.

The Seven Years' War, 1756–1763. Maria Theresa still hoped to recover her lost province. Within a few years she succeeded in forming a coalition of Russia, France, Sweden, Saxony, and Austria against Frederick. Great Britain, long opposed to France, became

Prussia's only ally. The British sent gold and troops to aid Frederick and fought the French in India, America, and on the sea. Frederick conducted a purely defensive warfare, thrusting against one attack and then turning swiftly to meet another. Fortunately for him, his slower-moving adversaries never learned to act together and exert their full force all at once. Even so, the struggle was desperately unequal. The Russians occupied East Prussia, penetrated Brandenburg, and even occupied Berlin. Faced by the gradual wearing down of his armies, an empty treasury, and an impoverished country, Frederick more than once thought of committing suicide. His cause was saved by the death of his enemy, the czarina (empress) of Russia. The czar who then came to the throne happened to be a warm admirer of the Prussian king and at once made peace with Frederick. Maria Theresa, deprived of her eastern ally, now had to come to terms and agree once more that Frederick might keep Silesia. Soon after-

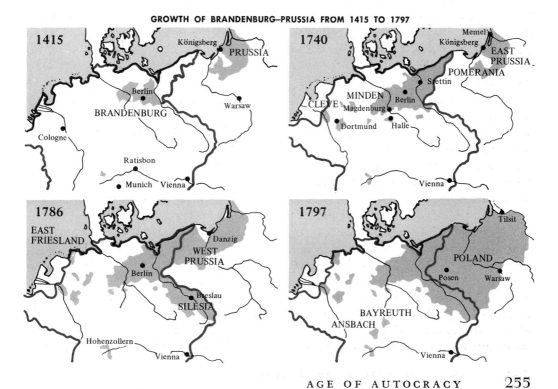

GROWTH OF BRANDENBURG–PRUSSIA FROM 1415 TO 1797

ward the Peace of Paris between France and
Great Britain brought the Seven Years' War
to an end.

Frederick rebuilds Prussia. Until his death
in 1786 Frederick labored unceasingly in the
interests of his people. He worked harder and
had fewer pleasures than any other ruler of
his day. His vigorous measures soon restored
the prosperity Prussia had lost during the
war. Under him Prussia became the best-gov-
erned state in Europe. He founded elementary schools so that his subjects could at least
learn to read and write, and reformed the
courts so that everyone from high to low

might hope for impartial justice. A liberal in
religion, Frederick declared that everybody
should be allowed to get to Heaven in his own
way. He backed up his declaration by putting
Roman Catholics on an equal basis with
Protestants. In 1772 he joined with Maria
Theresa of Austria and Catherine the Great
of Russia in the first partition of Poland.
Frederick secured the territory lying between
Brandenburg and East Prussia, thus uniting
the two most important parts of his kingdom.
He left to his successors a strong and progressive state, around which the German Empire
was formed in 1871.

GROWTH OF THE AUSTRIAN EMPIRE FROM 1500 TO 1789

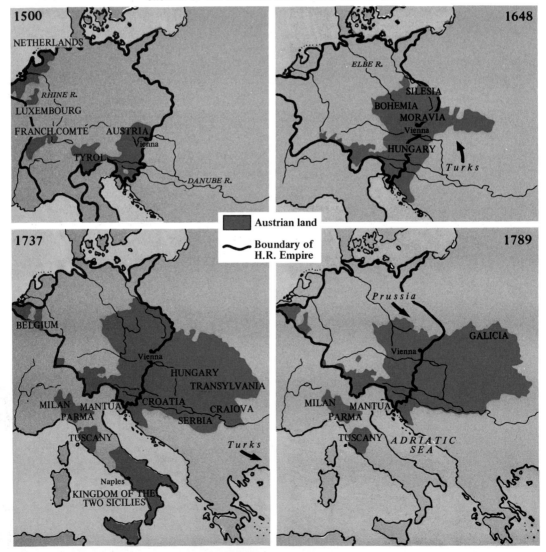

The **"enlightened despots."** Frederick was the foremost of a group of eighteenth-century rulers who have been called "enlightened despots." They practiced absolute government but tried to rule in the interests of their people. The "enlightened despots" borrowed many of their ideas on government from the French philosophers Montesquieu, Voltaire, and Rousseau. (See pages 269–270.) Urging reform of the social system, these radical French thinkers attacked abuses such as religious intolerance, the slave trade, cruel criminal laws, and unjust methods of taxation. Frederick especially came under French influence, as is shown by his reforms in Prussia. Despite his many duties he wrote no less than thirty volumes in French, and for a time played host to Voltaire in Berlin. Catherine the Great, although less sincere than Frederick, at least paid lip service to the ideas of the noted French thinkers. In Austria, Maria Theresa and her son Joseph II also introduced reforms in government. Most of the autocrats of western Europe followed the fashion, and adopted more or less enlightened policies.

Why despotism failed. Despotic government had two serious weaknesses: (1) Despotism failed to provide *continuous good government*. A country might prosper under an able and liberal-minded ruler, only to be plunged into misery through the incompetence of the next king. In Prussia, for instance, much of Frederick's work was undone by his weak and indolent successor. Other countries had similar experiences.

(2) Despotism failed to give the people a voice in the government. If the ruler was cruel or oppressive, his subjects must either submit or risk their lives and property in a revolt against him. Gradually there arose a demand for a more democratic system, in which the people could make *peaceful* changes in government policies. The clash between ideas of autocracy and democracy led to the Age of Revolution, which is described in the next chapter.

REVIEWING THE CHAPTER

TERMS TO UNDERSTAND: *Peace of Utrecht, autocracy, czar, Peace of Aix-la-Chapelle, coalition, Peace of Paris, enlightened despot.*

PERSONS TO IDENTIFY: *Charles V, Philip II, Henry of Navarre, Louis XIV, Colbert, Michael Romanov, Peter the Great, Catherine the Great, Frederick the Great, Maria Theresa.*

PLACES TO LOCATE: *Austria, Hungary, Bohemia, Versailles, Alsace, Lorraine, Ural Mountains, Ukraine, Moscow, St. Petersburg, Holy Roman Empire, Prussia.*

QUESTIONS TO ANSWER

1. (a) Give three reasons for Spain's rise to leadership in Europe. (b) List the territorial possessions of Charles V. (c) What policies of Philip II led to Spain's decline?
2. (a) Describe the French court under Louis XIV. (b) Explain three measures which Colbert took to strengthen the economic system of France. (c) Give the causes and results of the wars of Louis XIV.
3. (a) Describe the geography of Russia. (b) How did Mongol rule influence the Russians? (c) What were the two main aims of the Romanovs? (d) To what extent were these aims realized by Peter the Great? By Catherine the Great?
4. (a) What territory was included in the Holy Roman Empire? (b) Describe the policies of the Hohenzollern rulers. (c) What was Frederick's purpose in starting the War of the Austrian Succession? (d) Give the dates, causes, and results of the Seven Years' War in Europe. (e) What territory did Frederick later add to Prussia?
5. (a) Describe the policies of the "enlightened despots." (b) Give the two main reasons for the failure of despotism.

15 The Revolt against Autocracy

JOHN LOCKE

THOMAS JEFFERSON

JEAN JACQUES ROUSSEAU

THE DEMOCRATIC THEORIES AND PRACTICES which formed the basis for many of the
societies and nations which were to come later were, in large part, found in the writings
of Rousseau and Locke. Jefferson built upon these ideas and created the
foundations of the American democracy.

Americans have always been especially interested in the two English revolutions of the seventeenth century—the Puritan Revolution and the Glorious Revolution. In these revolutions the English people checked the growing power of their kings, expressed a hatred of tyranny, and established the principle that rulers are responsible to their subjects. In the eighteenth century these ideas helped to stir up the American Revolution and the French Revolution. As a result, a long struggle to establish and maintain democratic governments began. The contest between the forces of democracy and autocracy dominated the history of the western world until the middle of the nineteenth century. In this chapter we shall examine the causes and effects of this revolutionary movement.

The English People Check Autocracy

Parliament checks the growth of the king's power. In the late Middle Ages England had developed a national lawmaking body known as Parliament. Although it was supposed to represent the different classes of people (see pages 160–161), it was not a democratic body chosen by popular vote. Nevertheless, it did prevent the king from becoming an autocratic ruler—that is, a ruler who governs without respect for the wishes of the people or their representatives. In England, Parliament controlled the expenditure of the government's money. The kings often called meetings of Parliament to ask for more money. On these occasions Parliament could demand certain reforms in exchange for grants of money for carrying on the government. Thus, in the late Middle Ages England was already on the road to representative government.

Tudor kings check the power of Parliament. At the end of the Wars of the Roses in 1485, Henry VII, the first of the Tudor kings, came to the throne. The war had resulted from a fierce struggle among the English nobles for the crown. It had created a demand for a strong monarchy which could keep order and prevent strife among the nobles. Henry VII and his successors in the Tudor line met that demand. It has already been pointed out that one of them, Henry VIII,

made the Church dependent upon the king and that another Tudor, Elizabeth, humbled the great king of Spain. (See pages 210, 246–247.) Members of the Tudor family sat on the English throne for over a hundred years (1485–1603). During that period they helped to give England order, prosperity, and prestige; and they were popular with the influential middle class in town and country. The Tudors kept Parliament under their thumbs. Henry VII called Parliament together only five times during his reign. His son, Henry VIII, seems to have persuaded or frightened it into doing anything he wished, while Elizabeth consulted it as little as possible. Under the Tudors, Parliament did not give up its claims to a share in the government, but it had little chance to do anything.

James I and Parliament. The death of Elizabeth in 1603 ended the Tudor dynasty and brought James I, the first of the Stuarts, to the English throne. Unlike the Tudors, who did not boast of their power, James openly proclaimed his absolute right to make laws without the advice of Parliament. He was a most outspoken supporter of the theory of *divine right*. According to this theory, the king did not receive his power from the people but from God. Consequently, the king was responsible to God alone for his acts and not to the people or their representatives. But when James needed money, Parliament refused to grant him any unless certain complaints were satisfied. The king would not give in. He got along as best he could by levying tariff duties, selling titles of nobility, and imposing large fines. Parliament protested, but to no avail.

Puritanism. A religious dispute helped to embitter the quarrel between James and Parliament. The king, who was a devout Anglican, made himself very unpopular with the Puritans. This group wished to "purify" the Church of England of certain customs which they described as "Romish." Among these were the use of the surplice (an outer garment of white linen worn by Anglican clergymen), the ring in the marriage service, and the sign of the cross in baptism. The Puritans had a large majority in the House of Commons. For that reason the struggle against Stuart absolutism became also a religious contest.

Charles I and Parliament. The political and religious difficulties of the reign of James I did not end with his death. His son, Charles I, who came to the throne in 1625, almost immediately began to quarrel with

Parliament. When that body refused to vote money, Charles forced wealthy people to make "loans" to him and even imprisoned a number of persons who refused to contribute. Such acts of tyranny led Parliament to assert its authority. In 1628 it presented to Charles the famous Petition of Right. One of the important provisions said that loans and taxes without parliamentary approval were illegal. Another clause declared that no one should be arrested or imprisoned except according to the law of the land. The Petition of Right thus reaffirmed some of the leading principles of Magna Carta. (See page 160.) The people of England, speaking this time through their elected representatives, asserted once more their right to limit the power of kings.

Outbreak of the Puritan Revolution. Charles signed the Petition of Right but failed to observe it. He dismissed Parliament in 1629 and resumed his autocratic ways. His attempt to rule without Parliament, together with his harsh treatment of the Puritans, finally led in 1642 to revolution and civil war. Those who supported the king were called *Cavaliers*. They included the upper classes, the Anglican clergy, and the Roman Catholics. The parliamentary party, which opposed Charles, was referred to as the *Roundheads;* its members cropped their hair close because they disliked the long locks of the aristocrats. The Roundheads were largely from the trading classes in the towns or from the class of small landholders in the country. Most of the working people remained indifferent and took little part in the struggle.

Cromwell. Fortune favored the Cavaliers until Oliver Cromwell took command of the parliamentary forces. A country gentleman, Cromwell had represented the University of Cambridge in Parliament, where he had boldly opposed the royal government. An unfriendly critic at this time described "his countenance swollen and reddish, his voice sharp and untuneable, and his eloquence full of fervor." He was a zealous Puritan, who believed himself to be the chosen agent of the Lord. At the same time Cromwell was fond of "honest sport," of art and music. In public life he was an able administrator and a military genius. His victories over the king's armies resulted in the final collapse of the royalist cause and the triumph of the Roundheads (1646).

Execution of Charles I, 1649. The victors now tried Charles I before a high court of justice composed of his bitterest enemies. He refused to recognize the right of the court to try him and made no defense whatever. Charles was speedily convicted and sentenced to be beheaded "as a tyrant, traitor, murderer, and public enemy to the good of the people." He met death with quiet dignity on a scaffold in London. The king's execution again reminded the English that rulers are responsible to their subjects.

The Commonwealth and the Protectorate. Soon after the execution of Charles I, Cromwell's party made sweeping changes in the government, and proclaimed England to be a free Commonwealth, or republic. The kingship and the House of Lords were abolished,

leaving the House of Commons in complete control of lawmaking. The executive functions of the government were carried on by a council of forty-one members. But the real power was in the army, of which Cromwell was the head. The Commonwealth gave way to the Protectorate when Cromwell made himself a military dictator with the title of "Lord Protector." His power was as great as that of any previous English king, although he refused to accept the royal title. His authority came from the Instrument of Government, the only written constitution England has ever had. As lord protector, Cromwell ruled efficiently, if not always wisely, until 1658, when his death left the nation without a strong leader. Confusion began to spread throughout the land as political and religious factions renewed their old quarrels. In these circumstances Parliament called from exile the eldest son of the executed Charles I. Amid great rejoicing this son was crowned Charles II in 1660. This event, by which the Stuart line was restored to the throne, is known as the *Restoration*.

Importance of the Puritan Revolution. It seemed, indeed, as if the Puritan Revolution

CROMWELL DISSOLVING PARLIAMENT. In 1653, when Cromwell returned from quelling insurrections in Scotland and Ireland, he found Parliament quarreling and sent its members home. Although the English people had disliked the Stuart absolutism, they also objected to Cromwell's dictatorship. After Cromwell's death the Stuarts were restored to the throne.

KING JAMES II fleeing after the Battle of the Boyne, 1690. Many Irish, loyal to James, revolted against the rule of William and Mary. The revolt was put down, and the English then enacted severe laws to repress the Irish.

had been a complete failure. But this was hardly true. The revolution stopped the growth of autocracy and divine right in England. The events preceding and following the revolution created among Englishmen a lasting hatred of despotic rule, whether exercised by king, parliament, protector, or army. Furthermore, these events strengthened the belief in *popular sovereignty,* that is, the belief that the people, or their representatives, should have supreme authority. This belief helped to bring about revolutions in America and France in the eighteenth century.

Reign of Charles II. The Restoration showed that the English people wished to have a king, but not a king of unlimited power. Charles II, less stubborn and more clever than his father, recognized that he must tread warily. He swore to observe Magna Carta, the Petition of Right, and Parliament's religious policy. He always avoided serious trouble with Parliament by yielding to its wishes at the right time. Whatever happened, he used to say, he was resolved never to set out on his travels again. In spite of his grave faults of character, Charles's charm of manner and genial humor made him popular. He was described as a king who "never said a foolish thing nor ever did a wise one."

Habeas Corpus Act, 1679. One of the most important events of the reign of Charles II was the passage by Parliament of the Habeas Corpus Act. *Habeas corpus* is a Latin phrase, meaning "You may have the body." A writ of *habeas corpus* is an order, issued by a judge, requiring that a person held in prison be brought before the court. If there is evidence that the prisoner has committed a crime, he is to be given a trial; otherwise, he must be released. English courts had used this writ for a long time, but kings had frequently defeated its purpose by maintaining that the command of the king was sufficient answer to the writ. The Habeas Corpus Act established the principle that every man not charged with, nor convicted of, a known crime is entitled to his liberty. Most of the English-speaking world has accepted this basic principle of personal freedom.

Whigs and Tories. The reign of Charles II also marked the beginning of the modern party system of Parliament. Two opposing parties took form as the result of a religious controversy. The king's long exile in France made him sympathetic to Roman Catholicism. His brother, James, the heir to the throne, was converted to the Roman Catholic faith in 1672. This aroused the fears of many members of Parliament, who introduced a bill to keep James from becoming king. The supporters of the bill were called Whigs; they wanted a strong Parliament.

Those who opposed the bill were nicknamed Tories; they were mostly Anglicans who were willing to have a Roman Catholic king in order to avoid civil war. The bill did not pass the House of Lords. The two parties continued to divide on other questions. They survive today as the Liberals and the Conservatives.

Reign of James II. In his brief rule of three years (1685–1688), James II stirred up opposition throughout his kingdom. He lacked the attractive personality of his brother Charles and was a staunch believer in the divine right of kings. He shocked the Tories by creating a standing army, which was regarded as a threat to the people's liberties. He made enemies of most of the Whigs. They disliked him because he "suspended" the laws discriminating against Roman Catholics and appointed them to important positions. For a time the people tolerated these acts. They hoped that James's Protestant daughter, Mary, would soon succeed him. But in 1688 his Roman Catholic wife gave birth to a son. The prospect of a Catholic successor to the throne was the last straw. A number of influential Whigs and Tories now invited Mary's husband to come and rule in England. He was William of Orange, the governor general of Holland. His coming was the first step in the so-called "Glorious Revolution."

Arrival of William and Mary. William landed in England with a small army and marched unopposed to London. James II, soon deserted by his supporters, fled to France. There he lived out his days at the French court. Parliament granted the throne to William and Mary jointly, and provided that in case they had no direct heirs, the succession was to go to Mary's sister, Anne.

The Bill of Rights, 1689. In giving the crown to William and Mary, Parliament took care to preserve its own authority. It enacted a Bill of Rights, which ranks with Magna Carta and the Petition of Right among the great landmarks of English history. The Bill of Rights provided that the king must henceforth be a member of the Anglican Church. It prohibited his "suspending" the laws, or levying taxes, or maintaining a standing army without the consent of Parliament. It also declared that there should be no interference with the free election of members of Parliament or with freedom of speech and action within the two houses of Parliament. No excessive bail was to be required, nor excessive fines imposed, nor cruel and unusual punishments inflicted by command of the king. Finally, it affirmed the right of subjects to petition the sovereign and ordered that Parliament hold frequent meetings. These ideas were not new, but now the English people were strong enough to make them into binding laws. The same principles are contained in the first ten amendments to the Constitution of the United States.

The Glorious Revolution. The English through a bloodless revolution had thus struck a final blow at absolutism and the belief in the divine right of kings. Henceforth, an English king was the servant of Parliament and might be deposed if Parliament wished. It is well to remember, however, that the Revolution was not a popular uprising and that it brought few advantages to the common people. It was a successful struggle of the upper classes to make Parliament supreme. The English government was still far from being a democracy.

John Locke's new theory of government. The Glorious Revolution produced a book of lasting influence. It was written in 1689 by an eminent English philosopher, John Locke. He wished to show that the revolution was reasonable and just because the people consented to it. According to his *Two Treatises of Government,* all men have natural rights to life, liberty, and property. To preserve these rights, people create governments by entering into a contract with one another. They agree that the majority shall have power to make and enforce laws. If a government

GEORGE III tried to restore the waning power of the English monarchy. His colonial policy helped start the American Revolution.

ceases to protect man's natural rights, then the people may overthrow it and establish a new one. In other words, the basis of government is the consent of the people, and political power exists and must be used for the public good. The American Declaration of Independence and the French Declaration of the Rights of Man (1791) contain these same basic ideas.

Act of Settlement, 1701. Another outcome of the Glorious Revolution was the passage of the Act of Settlement. It provided that in case William III or his sister-in-law Anne died without heirs, the crown should pass to a German princess, Sophia of Hanover. She was the granddaughter of James I and a Protestant. This arrangement deliberately overlooked a number of nearer representatives of the Stuart family because they were Catholics. Parliament thus asserted in the strongest way the right of the English people to choose their own rulers.

Queen Anne died in 1714, and in accordance with the Act of Settlement, the son of Sophia of Hanover came to the throne as George I. He was the first member of the Hanoverian dynasty, which has continued to reign in Great Britain ever since. In 1917 popular dislike for things that were German led the English ruling family to change its name to "House of Windsor."

The American Revolution

The American colonies drift away from England. English colonists in the New World had long been cutting their ties with Englishmen in the Old World. Pioneer conditions developed the colonists' energy, self-reliance, and love of freedom. In their local assemblies they received valuable training in self-government. Furthermore, the part they played in the French and Indian War gave them confidence in their ability to take care of themselves; indeed, the Peace of Paris (see page 212) marked a turning point in the history of the English colonies. Freed now from the French danger on the frontiers, the colonies had less need of the mother country.

Mercantilism and the English colonies. Most European statesmen of the time believed in mercantilism. (See page 191.) According to this theory, colonies existed for the benefit of the mother country. They were to furnish her with raw materials and to buy manufactured goods from her in return. Therefore, the British government passed laws which discouraged the manufacture in the colonies of goods that could be made in England. It also passed navigation laws intended to prevent the colonies from carrying on trade with any country except England. These laws did little harm for several reasons. (1) They were not well enforced and the colonists easily evaded them. (2) Great Britain was a good market for most colonial products. (3) The mother country granted bounties for the production of certain raw materials. (4) Colonial shipping flourished because ships built in the colonies enjoyed the same privileges in the carrying trade as British-built ships. In considering the treatment that the colonies received from England, it must also be remembered that England spent large sums in defending the colonies.

England's new policy. After the close of the French and Indian War (1763), England was deep in debt. She thought it only reasonable that the colonies should share the expense of keeping troops on the newly won frontiers in the Mississippi and St. Lawrence valleys. To carry out this policy, Parliament took steps to enforce the old trade regulations and passed several new laws to raise revenue. Among these were the Stamp Act (1765) and the Townshend Acts (1767).

English and colonial views of the new policy. Many colonists feared that the British troops were being sent to suppress them rather than to protect them. As to the revenue laws, they argued that taxes could be rightfully voted only by their own representative assemblies. To be taxed by Parliament was to be taxed without their consent, and was against the traditional "rights of Englishmen," they said. Some British statesmen, such as Edmund Burke and William Pitt, sided with the colonists. But the general British view was that Parliament represented all Englishmen and hence might tax them wherever they lived.

At first the colonists had no thought of separation from England; they merely resisted the policy of parliamentary taxation. A series of events after 1770, however, aroused sentiment for independence. The hated tax on tea led a number of Boston citizens to board tea ships and dump the cargo into the harbor. In 1774 Parliament replied to the "Boston Tea Party" by closing the port and by depriving Massachusetts of self-government. These

THE BOSTON TEA PARTY. A group of Boston patriots made a spectacular protest against the English tax on tea. When East India Company tea was sent over, Americans refused to buy it. They disguised themselves as Indians, boarded three tea ships, and dumped the cargoes into Boston harbor.

stern measures only stirred up more opposition and led all the colonies, except Georgia, to send delegates to the First Continental Congress. The congress recommended a policy of no further trading with Great Britain until the colonists had recovered their "just rights and liberties."

Declaration of Independence. The Second Continental Congress, which met after the battles of Lexington and Concord in 1775, feared that war would come and appointed George Washington to command the colonial forces. However, it sent a respectful petition to the king, seeking a peaceful solution, and waited several months for a reply. Hope of peace faded when the king proclaimed the colonists to be rebels and took steps to force them to submit. Desire for independence grew with the appearance of a stirring pamphlet entitled *Common Sense*. Its author, Thomas Paine, an immigrant from England, declared the time had come for complete separation from England. On July 4, 1776, the Continental Congress declared that "these united colonies are, and of right ought to be, free and independent states." The author of the Declaration of Independence was Thomas

Jefferson, an ardent champion of liberty who had read the writings of Locke and the eighteenth-century French philosophers. At the beginning of the Declaration, Jefferson restated the natural rights doctrine.

The "Tories." Even after the Declaration of Independence many "Loyalists," or "Tories," continued to favor the British cause. At the end of the war many of them went to Canada, where they were the first English settlers. They prospered in their new home, and their descendants form a considerable part of the Canadian population. Today they are among the most devoted members of the British Empire.

The French alliance, 1778. The lack of unity in resisting Great Britain was not the only handicap of the Americans. They could not match the population, the wealth, the trained armies, and the powerful navy of the British. However, when France came to the aid of the revolutionists, the advantage was no longer with Great Britain. France, still smarting from the losses suffered in the Seven Years' War (known in America as the French and Indian War), wished to regain some of her colonial possessions and her prestige. After

DRAFTING THE DECLARATION OF INDEPENDENCE. The Declaration was drawn up by Jefferson with the help of Adams and Franklin. Then it was submitted to a special committee appointed by the Continental Congress. The members of the committee were (left to right) Robert Livingston, Roger Sherman, John Adams, Thomas Jefferson, and Benjamin Franklin.

the American victory at Saratoga, France therefore entered into an open alliance with the rebellious colonies.

Close of the Revolutionary War. The war now became also a world-wide struggle, in which Spain and Holland joined France to fight Great Britain. Great Britain needed all her energies to prevent rebellion in Ireland, defend Gibraltar, and keep her possessions in the West Indies and India. She could not prosecute the war in America with much vigor. The struggle in America practically ended in 1781, when Cornwallis surrendered at Yorktown. The French fleet had prevented his escape by water, while the combined French and American armies closed in on him by land. Nearly two more years passed before the peace treaty was signed.

Treaties of Paris and Versailles, 1783. The Treaty of Paris between Great Britain and the United States recognized the independence of the former thirteen colonies. Their territory was now bounded by Canada and the Great Lakes, the Atlantic Ocean, Florida, and the Mississippi River. The Treaty of Versailles between Great Britain, France, and Spain restored to France some minor possessions and gave Florida back to Spain. (Florida had been taken by the English during the French and Indian War.) By a separate peace with Great Britain, Holland gave up some trading posts in India and allowed British merchants to trade in the East Indies.

Articles of Confederation. In 1781 the thirteen states adopted the Articles of Confederation, which set up a very weak central government to succeed the Continental Congress. The new government could not levy taxes, could not regulate interstate commerce, and had no power to enforce obedience on either a state or an individual. Economic depression added to the difficulties, and the young republic was threatened with collapse. The period from 1781 to 1789, when the Constitution went into effect, is therefore known as the Critical Period.

Formation of the Constitution. To save the newborn nation, a number of leaders urged a revision of the Articles of Confederation. For this purpose the Constitutional Convention met in Philadelphia in 1787. Among the fifty-five delegates present were Washington, who presided, Benjamin Franklin, James Madison, and Alexander Hamilton. Instead of merely amending the Articles, the convention prepared an entirely new plan of government, or constitution. It established a federal system, under which powers are divided between the national government and the states, but with the national authority supreme.

The founding of the new government brought into the limelight one of history's great men—George Washington. His military ability, practical wisdom, and courage contributed greatly to the winning of independence. After the revolution he was largely responsible for setting the new ship of state on a steady course. He presided at the Constitutional Convention and was President of the United States during the first eight critical years. To Washington we rightfully apply the proud words—"Father of His Country."

America teaches by example. The American War of Independence had an immediate effect upon Europe. Popular leaders in France now rallied the people in a struggle for "liberty, equality, and fraternity." The French Revolution of 1789 was the child of the American Revolution. Early in the nineteenth century still another revolutionary movement stripped Spain and Portugal of their colonies in the New World. America was, indeed, teaching by example.

The French Revolution

The Old Regime. The English revolutions of the seventeenth century and the American Revolution had dealt heavy blows to absolutism and the doctrine of the divine right of kings. Still more effective in destroying autocracy was the French Revolution. It con-

THE THIRD ESTATE triumphs over the first and second estates. This painting shows the National Assembly celebrating their ascendency over the higher clergy and nobility.

The clergy. Kings and lords revered the Church and therefore gave it rich and broad lands. Not only in France but also in Spain, Italy, and southern Germany, the higher clergy ruled as princes and paid few or no taxes to the government. They came mainly from the noble families and naturally took the side of the absolute monarchs. The lower clergy—the thousands of parish priests who came from the common people—just as naturally favored the popular cause.

The nobility. Some of the nobles were descendants of the feudal lords of the Middle Ages; others had been granted titles of nobility by the king for various services and favors. The nobles were usually great landholders. They did not have the military obligations of feudal days. They held most of the important offices in the government, the army, and the Church, and were largely exempt from taxation. Many of the nobles lived in idle luxury at the court of the king.

Beneath these two privileged orders, or estates, came the unprivileged class, known as

sisted of a tremendous struggle against a system of society known as the Old Regime (râ-zhēm′). The two outstanding features of the Old Regime were (1) autocracy in government and (2) inequalities in social, political, and economic life. Some parts of this system carried over from feudal times; others developed in the late Middle Ages and early modern times. Eighteenth-century France presented a typical example of the Old Regime.

The three estates. The Old Regime maintained the class distinctions of feudal times. There were three classes or, as they were called, *estates*. The first estate was composed of the clergy, the second estate of the nobles, and the third estate of everyone else (the "commons"). The first two, the privileged classes, were a very small minority of the population in any European country, but they possessed great influence.

THE RIGHTS OF MAN

1. Men are born and remain free and equal in rights. Social distinctions can be based only upon public utility.

2. The aim of every political association is the preservation of the natural and imprescriptible rights of man. These rights are liberty, property, security and resistance to oppression.

3. The source of all sovereignty is essentially in the nation; no body, no individual can exercise authority that does not proceed from it in plain terms.

4. Liberty consists in the power to do anything that does not injure others; accordingly, the exercise of the natural rights of each man has no limits except those that secure to the other members of society the enjoyment of these same rights. These limits can be determined only by law.

—*French Declaration of the Rights of Man,* 1791.

---

the third estate. It included the great majority of the people and consisted of three main divisions—the middle class, the artisans, and the peasants.

The third estate. (1) The *middle class,* or *bourgeoisie* (from French *bourg,* meaning "town"), included all those who were not manual laborers. It was made up of professional men such as magistrates, lawyers, physicians, and teachers, together with bankers, manufacturers, merchants, and shopkeepers. The British middle class enjoyed representation in Parliament and frequently entered the nobility. The French bourgeoisie, on the contrary, could not hold positions of great honor in the government. Though well educated and often wealthy, they were considered to be inferior to the nobles. They therefore supported the cause of political liberty and social equality.

(2) The *artisans,* or craftsmen, also lived mainly in towns and cities. The craft guilds of the Middle Ages had begun to disappear in Great Britain but still maintained their importance on the European continent. The guilds tended to become more and more exclusive. Membership fees were so high that few could afford to pay them. Journeymen found it difficult to rise to the position of masters; they often remained wage earners for life. Moreover, the number of apprentices that a master could take was strictly limited. The result was that most artisans no longer benefited from the guild system. It interfered with making a living and they wanted it abolished.

(3) The *peasants* were by far the largest division of the third estate. In eastern Europe and in Spain they were still serfs and owed various obligations to their lords. (See page 127.) In France the great majority of peasants were not serfs; they were legally free and many of them owned their own farms. But even the free peasants of France carried a heavy burden. The king imposed the hated land tax (*taille*), assessing a certain amount

on each village. Still worse was the *corvée,* or forced labor on roads and public works, which the government required from time to time. In addition, the clergy demanded tithes (page 187), and the nobles levied various feudal dues for the use of oven, mill, and wine press, and collected tolls for the use of roads and bridges. The farmers were also obliged to allow the game of their own and neighboring lords to invade their fields and damage their crops. It is not hard to understand why the peasants were discontented and anxious for any change which would better their hard lot.

The reform movement. On the whole, the abuses of the Old Regime were not much greater in the seventeenth and eighteenth centuries than they had been for hundreds of years before. Now, however, the Old Regime was seriously attacked by thinkers—the so-called "philosophers." They believed that the human race could achieve perfection if men used reason in solving their problems. In the eighteenth century their ideas formed the basis of the so-called Age of Enlightenment, or Age of Reason. John Locke (see page 264) was a forerunner of the Age of Enlightenment, and his ideas had great influence upon the French thinkers of the eighteenth century. By 1750 the people were better prepared than in Locke's lifetime to receive and to act upon the new ideas.

Montesquieu, 1689–1755. One of the French thinkers of the Enlightenment was Montesquieu, a nobleman, lawyer, and judge. His *Spirit of Laws,* which he spent twenty years in writing, is a classic in political science. There was nothing revolutionary in Montesquieu's conclusions. He examined each form of government in order to determine its merits and defects. The British constitution seemed to him the best. He thought that it combined the virtues of monarchy, aristocracy, and democracy. To avoid the possibility of tyranny, Montesquieu recommended separating the executive, legislative, and judicial

... tolerance has never brought civil war; intolerance has covered the earth with carnage ...

What! Is each citizen to be permitted to believe and to think that which his reason rightly or wrongly dictates? He should indeed, provided that he does not disturb the public order; for it is not contingent on man to believe or not to believe; but it is contingent on him to respect the usages of his country; and if you say that it is a crime not to believe in the dominant religion, you yourself then accuse the first Christians, your ancestors, and you justify those whom you accuse of having martyred them ...

I shall not cease, my dear sir, in spite of the complaints of your priests and the [outcries] of ours, to preach tolerance from the roof-tops as long as persecution does not cease. The advances of reason are slow; the roots of prejudices are deep. Doubtless I shall not see the fruits of my efforts, but they will be seeds that perhaps will sprout some day.

—Voltaire.

branches of government instead of combining them in a single ruler. This idea impressed the French revolutionists and also the framers of the Constitution of the United States.

Voltaire, 1694–1778. The foremost figure among the philosophers was Voltaire, who belonged to the bourgeoisie. For more than half a century he poured forth a succession of poems, dramas, essays, biographies, histories, and other works. He wrote so clearly, so wittily, and so sensibly that he won a large following of devoted readers. Voltaire did not confine his criticisms of the Old Regime to politics; he also condemned the religious intolerance of the age and the restrictions on free speech.

Rousseau, 1712–1778. If Voltaire was the destroyer of the old, Rousseau was the prophet of the new. He was a man of weak moral character, of excitable temperament, and of a fine but unsteady intellect; in fact, there is little doubt that in his later years he was not wholly sane. Nevertheless, Rousseau did more than any other author to inspire the French Revolution. For the boasted civilization of the age he felt only contempt. He loved to picture what he supposed was once the "state of nature," before governments had arisen, before the strong had begun to oppress the weak, when nobody owned the land, and when there were no taxes and no wars. "Back to nature" was Rousseau's cry. In his most important book, the *Social Contract* (1762), he laid down the essential principles which he thought must form the basis of every rightful society. These may be summed up in the phrases "Liberty, Equality, Fraternity," and "government by consent of the governed." The idea that governments and laws arise by voluntary agreements among men, who may overthrow them when necessary, was not new. Locke had stated it (see page 264), but Rousseau first made it widely popular. His countrymen read the *Social Contract* with intense interest and during the French Revolution tried to put its democratic teachings into effect.

The Encyclopedists. Rousseau, Voltaire, and Montesquieu were among the contributors to the famous *Encyclopedia*, edited chiefly by Diderot (dēd'rō'). The work ran to seventeen volumes, the first of which appeared in 1751. It formed a storehouse of all the scientific and historical knowledge of the age. The Encyclopedists, as its editors are known, were radical thinkers who attacked religious intolerance, the slave trade, the cruel criminal law, and the unjust system of taxation. They even dared to criticize absolutism in government. Their writings set in motion a current of revolt that did much to weaken the Old Regime.

Why the revolution started in France. The attack upon the Old Regime began in France. The misery of the people was not worse in France than in other parts of the Continent, but France was then the most advanced of the continental countries. Next to Great Britain, France contained the most numerous, prosperous, and influential bourgeoisie, or middle class. Members of this class furnished the revolution with its principal leaders. Even the nobility and clergy included many men, notably the Marquis de Lafayette, who condemned the abuses of the Old Regime. Another reason why France led the revolutionary movement on the continent of Europe was that the French philosophers had more influence upon their countrymen than the thinkers of other countries had upon theirs. Then too, the examples of the English and American revolutions affected French opinion. Finally, nowhere in Europe was the ruling class so extravagant, inefficient, and corrupt as in France. This fact brought the French monarchy face to face with financial ruin.

Reign of Louis XV, 1715-1774. The financial difficulties which furnished the immediate cause of the French Revolution had been developing for a long time. Under Louis XIV, four wars in rapid succession had wasted the wealth which had been built up by Colbert. (See page 249.) Louis XV allowed the government to fall more and more into the hands of courtiers and adventurers. Their main interest was to enrich themselves at public expense. Consequently, the treasury every year faced a deficit. To meet this condition more money was borrowed, while the clergy and nobility continued to be exempt from taxation. Thus the government brought France to virtual bankruptcy.

Instead of remedying the causes of dissatisfaction, Louis XV did his best to stifle complaints. His government rigidly censored the press; opened letters and revealed their contents to the king; burned books and pamphlets critical of the government; and imprisoned those who wanted reforms. No man's personal liberty was safe. If provided with a sealed letter (*lettre de cachet*) signed by the king, the police could send anyone to jail. Persons arbitrarily imprisoned sometimes waited for years without trial. Such measures of oppression only increased the opposition to the monarchy. Yet Louis XV asserted just before he died that he "owed an account of his conduct to God alone."

Reign of Louis XVI, 1774-1792. Louis was succeeded by his grandson, who became Louis XVI. Only twenty years old when he came to the throne, the new king was honest and well-meaning but slow of thought. He would much rather have spent his time hunting and tinkering with machinery than running the affairs of government. His queen, Marie Antoinette, presided over the gay court of Versailles. She was the daughter of Maria Theresa of Austria and had many enemies in France because of her foreign birth. Marie Antoinette was also disliked because the king sometimes followed her whims in public affairs and because she spent money lavishly on herself and on her favorites. Her enemies called her "Madame Deficit."

Turgot's plans for reform. The young king began his reign well by appointing Turgot (tür'gō') to the position of minister of finance. Turgot was a friend of Voltaire and a writer for the *Encyclopedia*. He drew up a program of reforms to correct the chief economic wrongs of the time. The changes he recommended included the following: (1) Pensions to useless courtiers were to be cut off. (2) The taxes bearing most heavily on the third estate were to be replaced by a general tax on all landowners. (3) Work without pay on public highways and bridges was to be discontinued. (4) The old guilds which hampered industry, were to be abolished. (5) The annoying tolls and duties on the passage of grain from one province to another were to be swept away. Turgot also recommended freedom of the press, a national system of education, and more political power for the bourgeoisie. If these reforms had been carried out, they might have given France a bloodless and orderly revolution. But Turgot's policies aroused strong opposition. The privileged classes would not give up their privileges without a struggle. Turgot was dismissed in 1776.

Financial chaos. The government's finances went from bad to worse. Turgot's successors relied mainly on fresh loans to cover the deficits. From the viewpoint of French interest, Louis XVI made a serious mistake in helping the Americans in their Revolutionary War. America was freed and Great Britain humbled, but the war raised the public debt of France by leaps and bounds. When at last it became impossible to borrow more money, the king consented reluctantly to call a meeting of the Estates-General. Absolutism had failed.

The Estates-General. The Estates-General was the old feudal assembly of France. It consisted of representatives of the three classes or estates—the clergy, the nobles, and the unprivileged group of peasants, artisans, and bourgeoisie. On the eve of the French Revolution the Estates-General had not met for 175 years. Now, in 1789, the representatives of the three estates appeared at Versailles to advise the king on his financial problems. In all, there were over twelve hundred members. A little less than half of these belonged to the two privileged orders—the first and second estates. It is important to note that of the delegates representing the third estate a few were liberal nobles, about two thirds were lawyers, and less than a dozen were from the lower classes. Indeed, the two leaders of the third estate were Count Mirabeau and the Abbé Sieyès (à′bā′ syā′yĕs′), both members of the privileged classes. As a whole, therefore, the Estates-General represented the most prosperous and best-educated classes of people in France.

The Estates-General had been called to save France from bankruptcy. Many of the members, however, were determined to make thoroughgoing reforms in French government and society. They had the help and support of numerous other Frenchmen, who had written letters (*cahiers*, kä′yä′) of complaint and suggestion. While these *cahiers* did not recommend overthrow of the monarchy, they did breathe the spirit of reform which had been made popular by the philosophers. The problem before the Estates-General was to do away with political, social, and economic abuses. The immediate question was how to organize the assembly in order to attack this problem.

Reorganizing the Estates-General. Formerly the three estates had sat separately and voted "by orders"; that is, each estate had one vote. Thus the nobles and clergy, with their two votes, could easily outvote the third estate with its one vote. In 1789, however, the third estate insisted that the Estates-General represented not feudal France or particular social groups, but a new united nation. Its members demanded, therefore, that every delegate be allowed to vote as an individual. Representatives of the third estate could then outvote the representatives of the other two estates.

Establishment of the National Assembly. For several weeks the Estates-General debated the question of whether to organize itself into a single body representing the people of France or to meet separately in the three feudal orders. The debate reached a deadlock. Then, on the motion of the Abbé Sieyès, the third estate boldly declared itself to be the National Assembly, with the right to act for the nation as a whole. The king opposed this move and placed troops before the entrance of the hall that had been set apart for the third estate. When the representatives found that they could not enter their meeting place, they assembled in a nearby building which had been used as a tennis court. Here they took a solemn oath, called the "Tennis Court Oath," never to separate and to continue to meet until they had drawn up a constitution for France. This action brought to their side the lower clergy (*curés*), who favored reform. The king then summoned the three estates

THE STORMING OF THE BASTILLE. Built as a city fortress in 1370, the Bastille was later used as a prison for people who offended the king. The revolutionists attacked and destroyed it on July 14, 1789. Ever since then the French have celebrated that date as a national holiday, comparable to our July 4.

and told them that they should meet separately. The higher clergy and nobility at once withdrew to their own quarters, but the third estate did not stir. "We are here by the will of the people," declared Count Mirabeau. "Bayonets alone shall drive us away." The king dared not use force; he therefore reversed himself and ordered the rest of the clergy and nobles to join with the third estate in the National Assembly. The common people had won an important victory.

Fall of the Bastille, July 14, 1789. The National Assembly was about to begin its work when news spread that Louis XVI had changed his mind and was determined to dismiss it. A large number of troops gathered near Paris. It looked as if the king were going to use force against the assembly. This aroused the people of Paris to action. Mobs of the poor and unemployed armed themselves and began to riot. They looted shops, attacked officers of the king, and for several days created wild disorder. In their search for more arms the angry masses stormed and captured the Bastille, a fortress where political prisoners had often been kept. At this time, however, it held only seven offenders, all there for good reason. However, the Bastille stood for the tyranny of the Old Regime, and its fall created a tremendous sensation throughout France and even abroad. When Louis XVI heard the news, he is said to have exclaimed, "Why, this is a revolt!" "No, Sire," replied a courtier, "this is a revolution."

The revolution spreads. The country provinces quickly copied the example set by Paris.

The peasants plundered and burned many castles. They took particular pains to destroy the legal documents by which the nobles bound the people to feudal service. Royal officials left their posts, courts of justice ceased to act, and people stopped paying their taxes. From end to end of France the Old Regime broke down in the midst of widespread disorder and violence.

The end of feudalism. The revolution in the provinces led directly to one of the most striking scenes of French history. On the night of August 4-5, 1789, the National Assembly was considering what might be done about the uprisings. Suddenly one of the nobles urged that all the remaining feudal rights of the lords be abolished. Then, amid hysterical enthusiasm, noble after noble and cleric after cleric arose to propose sweeping reforms. Equality of taxation, the surrender of hunting rights, the abolition of tithes, tolls, and pensions, were among the measures voted by the assembly on that eventful night. In their final form the decrees contained the bold declaration that the National Assembly "hereby completely abolishes the feudal system." Within a few days the king gave his approval to these revolutionary changes. The reforms which Turgot labored in vain to secure thus became accomplished facts. The Old Regime was finished.

The revolution reaches the king's palace. The king had not learned the lesson of July 14. Reports of new plots to overthrow the revolution circulated in Paris. To make matters worse, hunger and hard times added to the discontent of the people. They were quite willing to believe rumors that the court and the aristocrats were deliberately causing a famine. It was also reported that during an army officers' banquet on October 1 those present expressed their loyalty to the king and queen and trampled under foot the new national flag, the tricolor. This was the spark which lit another explosion. On October 5 a hungry mob, composed mostly of women

and armed with every sort of weapon, including scythes and pitchforks, set out for Versailles to demand bread of the king. Early the following morning some of the mob broke into the palace, killed the sentinels, and entered the rooms of Marie Antoinette. The queen escaped with difficulty. Only the arrival of Lafayette at the head of the National Guard prevented further rioting and bloodshed. The rioters finally quieted down when the king promised to remove to Paris. That afternoon the royal family made its way to the capital, accompanied by a crowd which yelled, "We have the baker, the baker's wife, and the baker's little boy—now we shall have bread." The National Assembly also established its headquarters in Paris. Both the king and the assembly were now under the watchful eye of the citizens of Paris.

The National Assembly governs France. For the next two years the National Assem-

THE TRIUMPH OF MARAT, 1793. This shows the leader of the extreme revolutionists as the idol of the sans-culottes, or ragamuffin mobs of Paris.

bly continued in session. Its purpose was to write a constitution, but in the meantime it had to govern France. In doing so a number of changes were made. First, the Assembly changed the system of local government. The old provinces had varied greatly in size, each with its own privileges, customs, and laws. They were now replaced by eighty-three departments, approximately equal in size and population. Second, the Assembly reorganized the Church in France. It took over church lands and sold them to the peasants, abolished monasteries, fixed the salaries of the clergy, and took their appointment out of the hands of the king and the pope. Third, the Assembly assumed control of national finances. It passed a decree providing for the issue of paper money to the value of four million francs, with the former church lands as security. These notes were called *assignats*. If the printing of assignats could have been limited, as Mirabeau desired, they might have been a safe means of raising revenue. However, the government continued to add to the flood of assignats. The result was that they steadily declined in value. Gold and silver, now the only money of real value, disappeared from ordinary use. Prices rose so high that the time came when a basket of assignats was needed to buy a pair of boots. Inflation had got out of hand. In the end the assignats became practically worthless.

The National Assembly writes a constitution. In 1791 the National Assembly completed the writing of a new constitution. It provided for a Legislative Assembly of a single chamber with wide authority over every branch of the government, severely limited the powers of the king, and gave the privilege of voting only to citizens who paid substantial taxes—a provision which kept political control in the hands of the propertied classes. An important step had been taken, however, in transforming the government from an absolute monarchy into a limited monarchy. The constitution of 1791 was in effect only a short time. Of far greater influence was the Declaration of the Rights of Man, which formed an introduction to the constitution.

Declaration of the Rights of Man. This memorable document stands alongside the English Bill of Rights (1689) and the American Declaration of Independence (1776) as a great charter of human liberty. Revealing Rousseau's influence in nearly every line, it consists of a statement of the principles underlying the French Revolution. All persons, said the declaration, shall be equally eligible to all public offices according to their abilities. No person shall be arrested or imprisoned except according to law. Anyone accused of crime shall be presumed innocent until found guilty. Every citizen may freely speak, write, and print his opinions, including his religious views, but he may be held responsible for abuse of this freedom. Law is the expression of the general will, and every citizen has a right to participate in its formation, either personally or through his representative. No one shall be deprived of his property, except for public purposes, and then only after due compensation. These clauses of the declaration reappeared in the later constitutions of France and other countries.

Why the new constitution failed. The first phase of the revolution had ended. The work of the National Assembly had brought sweeping political, economic, and social changes. Many believed that France would now settle down to the enjoyment of peace and prosperity. But the revolution was not over. It soon entered a second phase, because many people opposed the new government. Among these were the king and queen, most of the nobles, most of the clergy, and the radicals. Each of these groups helped to bring the revolution into a second and more violent phase.

Flight of the king and queen. Louis XVI and Marie Antoinette naturally disliked the constitution, which took away so much royal power. They therefore decided to flee from Paris and join the royal troops near the northeastern frontier of France. The king might then return at the head of an army and suppress the revolution. Disguising themselves, Marie Antoinette as a Russian lady and Louis as her valet, they escaped from the palace of the Tuileries during the night of June 20, 1791. The adventure was doomed to failure. The king and queen were recognized at the little village of Varennes, near the northeastern border of the country. They were arrested and soon brought back to the capital. The attempted flight caused the French people to lose confidence in their king and made them despise even more the "Austrian woman," their queen.

Emigrant nobles. Many of the nobles also sought to undermine the new government. This was especially true of those who emigrated during the revolution (*émigrés*). These emigrant nobles gathered in small armies on the northeastern boundary of France and plotted with the rulers of Austria and Prussia for the overthrow of the revolutionary government.

Nonjuring clergy. The new government also made an enemy of the Church. The National Assembly confiscated church property and took control of the French Church away from the pope. The pope therefore refused to allow the clergy to take the oath of loyalty to the new constitution. Until this time the parish priests had generally supported the revolutionary cause. They now turned against it, carrying with them their peasant followers. The clergy who refused to swear loyalty to the constitution were called the *nonjuring* clergy.

Radicals. Some people opposed the new constitution because it was not radical enough; that is, they thought its reforms did not remedy the real troubles of France. They were against the monarchy, the property qualifications for voting, and the control of the government by the bourgeoisie. The radicals formed clubs to promote their views, and established newspapers to attack government

by the well-to-do middle class. The most famous of their organizations was the Jacobin Club, and the most able of their leaders were Marat (mà′rä′), Danton, and Robespierre. The radical movement naturally centered in Paris, where there were large numbers of poverty-stricken, discontented workingmen; yet Jacobin clubs were formed throughout France. The course of events was soon to give the radicals their opportunity.

The monarchs of Europe interfere. With the overthrow of absolutism in France, the monarchs of Austria and Prussia began to fear for their thrones. Urged on by the *émigrés,* they now announced their intention of suppressing the revolution by force. This threat was answered by the Legislative Assembly with a declaration of war against Austria (April 20, 1792). Prussia immediately joined her ally against France. Thus began a conflict which was to last for almost twenty-three years and was to sweep over all Europe. The French troops, poorly organized and disciplined, met severe reverses. The French masses turned more and more against the monarchy because they suspected Louis and Marie Antoinette of secretly revealing the French plans to the enemies. This suspicion turned into hatred when the commander of the invading army, the Duke of Brunswick, issued a provoking manifesto. It declared that the allies were going to restore Louis to his rightful powers, and threatened Paris with destruction if any harm came to the royal family. The proclamation served to anger the French radicals and to seal the fate of Louis XVI.

The radicals take charge of the government. The Jacobins under Danton replied to the Brunswick Manifesto by organizing a popular uprising. On August 10, 1792, a mob stormed the Tuileries, massacred the Swiss Guard, and forced the Legislative Assembly to suspend the king from his duties until his fate could be decided. A new assembly, known as the National Convention, was sum-

THE EXECUTION OF LOUIS XVI. Although a weak ruler who never liked to face responsibilities, Louis met death with dignity and courage. His executioner, Sanson, reported the king's last words: "Sirs, I am innocent of that of which I am accused! I hope my blood will consolidate the happiness of all Frenchmen."

moned to prepare another constitution for France. Meanwhile, the Parisian mobs, stirred up by Jacobin leaders, caused more bloodshed. Suspected opponents of the revolution, including priests, were arbitrarily executed. More than one thousand persons met death in the "September massacres." Shortly afterward the National Convention by a unanimous vote decreed the monarchy at an end and established the First French Republic. In 1793 a constitution was drafted but never put into effect.

Dealing with the enemies of the republic. The tremendous problems facing the Convention were not solved merely by setting up a republic. Two urgent questions had to be decided: (1) what to do with the king, and (2) how to defend the country against the foreign invaders and the enemies at home. Those of extreme views, who now controlled the Convention, wanted to try Louis for treason. "Louis must die, that the country may live," said Robespierre. So the National Convention, by a small majority vote, sent the king to the guillotine. Danton, railing against the enemies of France, could now declare, "We have thrown them as gage of battle the head of a king." One of the enemies of the republic was gone. Meanwhile, the French

forces not only hurled back the foreign armies but took the offensive and overran the Austrian Netherlands.

After the execution of Louis XVI, Austria, Prussia, Great Britain, Holland, Spain, Portugal, Sweden, Naples, and Sardinia formed a coalition to overthrow republican France. At the same time revolts broke out in the cities of Lyon, Marseilles, and Bordeaux, where the bourgeoisie resented the radicalism of the Parisian Jacobins. A new agency, the Committee of Public Safety, put down these insurrections with great cruelty.

Committee of Public Safety. The National Convention had created the Committee of Public Safety as an executive body which could deal effectively with the enemies of the republic. It consisted of twelve members. At first Danton, and later Robespierre, was the leading figure. The Committee exercised almost unlimited authority over the life and property of everyone in France. It proceeded to put into effect a general levy, or conscription, which placed all males of military age at the service of the armies. This earliest of draft laws also imposed duties on women, old men, and even on children. The new national army, drilled and disciplined, went forth to battle singing a new patriotic song, the *Marseillaise*. The coalition of the European powers broke down under their attack, and France enlarged her territory by annexing parts of the Netherlands and part of Germany lying west of the Rhine.

The Reign of Terror. To deal with the increasing resistance at home, the Committee of Public Safety started a program of terrorism. A law was passed declaring suspect every noble, everyone who had held office before the revolution, every person who had had any dealings with an emigrant noble, and every person who could not show a certificate of citizenship. Adoption of this law started the so-called Reign of Terror, which lasted for about ten months, from September, 1793, to July, 1794. People from all classes of society were arrested and tried. About 3 or 4 per cent of those arrested were sentenced to death. Among the victims of the terror were Marie Antoinette and, ironically, both Danton and Robespierre. The execution of Robespierre, who had been the pitiless leader in this policy, ended the Reign of Terror. It has been estimated that seventeen thousand persons were put to death under form of law, while many more were killed without the pretense of a trial. No wonder, then, that Madame Roland, an early supporter of the republic, should utter before her execution, "O Liberty! what crimes are committed in thy name!"

Constitution of 1795. It must not be forgotten that the National Convention had been summoned in 1792 to write a new constitution for the republic. After the end of the Reign of Terror the Convention again took up its task and produced the constitution of 1795. The new constitution provided for a legislature of two houses, and placed the executive power in the hands of a committee of five members known as the Directory. While the Convention was still writing the constitution, a mob attacked the Tuileries, where the Convention was in session. A young artillery officer now stepped into the limelight. He scattered the rioters by a cannonade of grapeshot, leaving many of their number dead in the streets. The officer was Napoleon Bonaparte. His activities were to shake Europe to its foundations. Before turning to his career, let us summarize some of the principles of revolutionary France.

Revolutionary principles. The French Revolution differed sharply from previous revolutionary movements. The Puritan Revolution and the Glorious Revolution in England were carried out by men of the upper and middle classes who wished to limit the king's power and establish the supremacy of Parliament. The American Revolution was led by conservative statesmen who were concerned for the rights of property as much as for the rights of man. The French Revolution also began as a middle class movement. However, it soon reached the poorer classes and thus went deeper into the roots of society. The new spirit given to the French Revolution by the common people was expressed in the famous motto, "Liberty, Equality, Fraternity."

MARIE ANTOINETTE on her way to the guillotine. The artist David made this rough sketch of the queen as the death cart passed along the street. Her hair had been cut and her hands tied behind her.

The Age of Kings Leads to the Age of Revolt

"Armada Portrait" of Elizabeth I, by Marc Gerarts. "Good Queen Bess" reigned in England from 1558 to her death in 1603.

"These unfortunate kings, of whom so much evil is spoken, have their good points now and then." So said a Frenchman in the eighteenth century. Perhaps the faint praise for royalty contained in these words was a sign of the changing times. Certainly, by this time the job of being a king was becoming less and less secure, despite the efforts of some "enlightened" kings to take more interest in the welfare of their subjects.

The Peterhof Palace, Leningrad, restored after World War II. The grounds are now a park, visited by thousands of Soviet citizens on Summer weekends.

An old tapestry showing the abdication of the Hapsburg emperor Charles V, who had grown weary of his burdensome responsibilities

The monarchs of the Age of Autocracy believed that they received their authority from heaven and that therefore it was wrong to oppose a king. This so-called theory of divine right justified rulers in exercising absolute control over their subjects. Its meaning was well expressed in the remark attributed to Louis XIV, "L'état, c'est moi" (I am the state); or again in the statement of Frederick William I of Prussia, "Salvation belongs to the Lord; everything else is my affair."

Sometimes royal projects were merely for "show"—monuments to the vanity of the ruler. Peter the Great built as a summer residence a lavish palace surrounded by the lovely Peterhof gardens. The Palace of Versailles was planned on a most grandiose scale and the interior ornately decorated with the richest of furnishings. It remains today as a monument to a lavish monarchy.

The ornate Queen's Chamber, Palace of Versailles

278D

Divine-right monarchy as a system of government had serious weaknesses. Few kings had the ability to handle alone the mass of details connected with ruling. Yet they tried. Saint-Simon, one of the courtiers at Versailles, in his *Memoirs* has left us the following picture of Louis XIV: "Naturally fond of trifles, he ceaselessly concerned himself with the most petty details of his troops, his household, his mansions: would even instruct his cooks, who received, like novices, lessons they had known by heart for years." Likewise, the historian Motley says of Peter the Great, "He felt that he must do everything himself, and he did everything." Naturally, much inefficiency, waste, and many errors of judgment occurred. In other words, autocrats were not miracle men. Even if they had been, there was no assurance that their successors would not be knaves or fools.

The magnificent Palace of Versailles, built by Louis XIV at an estimated cost of more than $100,000,000

Long before divine-right monarchy was threatened by internal defects, another theory had arisen to challenge it. It was the idea that government is man-made, based on the consent of the governed. Thus, if the ruler violated certain "natural rights" of the people, they had the right to revolt.

The conflict of these two theories laid the foundation for an era of revolution. Beginning in England in the seventeenth century, revolutionary movements for self-government spread throughout the western world—in the American colonies of Great Britain and Spain, in France, and in various countries of Europe up to the middle of the nineteenth century. The results were far-reaching as nation after nation turned away from a monarchy to some form of elective government.

Robespierre, leader of the French Revolution
during the Reign of Terror

"The Battle at Bunker Hill" by the American painter John Trumbull. General Joseph Warren, (center) was killed when the British attacked the American forces in one of the early battles of the American Revolution.

When the revolutionary ideas of liberty, equality, and fraternity spread from the French mainland to the colonies in Latin America, the slaves in the French colony of Saint-Dominique in Hispaniola found a great leader, Toussaint L'Ouverture. Under his leadership, on January 1, 1804, the blacks proclaimed complete independence from France. For the first time a Latin American land had broken away from a European country.

The fortress in the picture was built by Henri Christophe, a leader who followed L'Ouverture during the revolution from France; and who later ruled Haiti from 1811 to 1820.

The Citadel, Haiti, a fortress built on a precipice
by Henri Christophe, revolutionary leader against the French

Liberty, Equality, Fraternity. "Liberty" meant that the government was to be carried on according to the will of the people, and that they had certain "natural rights"— life, liberty (freedom of thought, speech, worship), and ownership of property. "Equality" meant the abolition of class privileges. All citizens were to be equal in the eyes of the law. "Fraternity" meant that all individuals belong to a human brotherhood.

France teaches by example. The principles of 1789 were not confined to France. In fighting their outside enemies, the revolutionary armies of France went beyond the borders of the homeland. They overturned the Old Regime in the Netherlands, in western Germany, and in northern Italy. In these countries the masses of the people had grievances and ambitions like those of the French. During the nineteenth century the revolutionary spirit spread to other European countries and to Latin America. It resulted everywhere in a demand for the removal of the special privileges of wealth, birth, and social position.

The Era of Napoleon

Every now and then in history some person of genius comes forward to dominate men and events. Such a man was Napoleon. The course of human affairs would undoubtedly have been different without him. For fifteen years Napoleon's life was so much a part of the history of France and of western Europe that it seems fitting to speak of that period as the Era of Napoleon.

Early life of Napoleon. Napoleon Bonaparte was born at Ajaccio, Corsica, in 1769, only a year after that island became a French possession. He was the second son of an Italian lawyer of noble birth but poor means. At the age of nine Napoleon was sent to a military school in France, where he finished the course of study with credit at fifteen. Mathematics and history seem to have been his favorite subjects. After a brief period of mili-

NAPOLEON as a student at the military school in Brienne. He admitted that he was not very popular in school.

tary training in Paris, he was commissioned a sublieutenant in an artillery regiment. Thus he realized his boyhood desire to be a soldier. He was not happy, however, for he was poor, friendless, and without family influence. His aristocratic schoolmates laughed at him because of his poverty and short stature.

Rise of Napoleon. Napoleon took a keen interest in the reform movement then stirring France. He was a devoted admirer of Rousseau's ideas and hated class privileges and aristocracy. For a time, at least, he became a Jacobin. The revolution gave him his first opportunities. He was an artillery officer under the First French Republic and helped suppress an insurrection in southern France; two years later he defended the National Convention against the Parisian mob. Shortly afterward the Directory gave him command of the French army in Italy.

Napoleon in Italy. France was still at war with Austria. Therefore, the Directory decided to attack the Austrian possessions in Italy. Napoleon's army, small and poorly equipped, seemed a weak force for such an attack. But to the "Little Corporal," as his men nicknamed him, nothing was impossible. "Soldiers," he cried, "I desire to lead you into the most fertile plains in the world. Rich provinces and great cities will be in your power; you will find there honor, glory, and wealth. Soldiers of France, will you be wanting in courage and constancy?" Napoleon did not find them wanting in anything. Within less than two years Napoleon and his army had overcome the Sardinians and the Austrians. By the Treaty of Campo Formio, 1797, he forced them to give control of northern Italy to France.

Napoleon in Egypt. England was the most persistent enemy of France. Napoleon convinced the Directory that England could be weakened by interfering with her trade in the eastern Mediterranean Sea. He also foresaw that victories in the east might make him the "man of the hour" if a new coalition should be formed against France. In May, 1798, he therefore set sail with a large expedition for Egypt. There he defeated the Turks, but in Syria he met reverses. Furthermore, the English Admiral Nelson had completely destroyed Bonaparte's ships at Alexandria. This action cut off the French troops from going home. Meanwhile, news of trouble at home made Napoleon decide to return to France. Leaving his army to its fate, he escaped from Egypt and was hailed as a savior when he reached the shores of France in October, 1799. His claims of victory in the Middle East were greatly exaggerated. The only important results of the Egyptian campaign were the added fame it gave Napoleon and the discovery of the Rosetta Stone, by means of which Egyptian hieroglyphic writing was deciphered.

Napoleon's *coup d'état*. As Napoleon had expected, affairs went badly for France during his absence. Great Britain, Austria, and Russia formed a second coalition against the republic, put large armies in the field, and drove the French from Italy. Most Frenchmen now looked to Napoleon as the one man

who could bring victory abroad and order at home. His first step was to enter a conspiracy with the Abbé Sieyès and others to overthrow the government of the Directory. The conspirators persuaded three of the directors to resign, placed the other two under military guard, and at bayonet-point forced the two legislative houses to dissolve. Such a seizure of the government is called a *coup d'état*—literally, a "stroke of state." Napoleon was now master of France. "I found the crown of France lying on the ground," he once remarked, "and I picked it up with a sword."

Constitution of 1799. After the *coup d'état* Napoleon proceeded to give France its fourth constitution since the beginning of the revolution. The new document provided for a government known as the Consulate. It placed the executive power in the hands of three consuls, appointed for ten years. The first consul was supreme, and Napoleon himself took this office. To him belonged the command of the army and navy, the right of naming and dismissing all the chief officials, and the right to propose all new laws. The legislative power was exercised by no less than four assemblies, with none having any real authority. Napoleon submitted the constitution to the people for approval. A "yes" or "no" vote, known as a *plebiscite*, showed an overwhelming majority in favor of the new government. "What is there in the constitution?" someone asked. "There is Bonaparte!" came the reply.

Napoleon soon showed himself to be as able an administrator as he was a general. He put the local governments of all France directly under his control by placing a prefect over every department and naming the mayors of the towns and cities. This centralizing of authority enabled Napoleon to make his will felt promptly throughout France.

Napoleon's reforms. The same desire for unity and order led him to complete the codification of French law. Before the revolution nearly three hundred different local codes had existed in France. The National Convention had begun the work of replacing these various systems of law—Frankish, Roman, feudal, royal, and revolutionary—by a single uniform code. Napoleon and a committee of legal experts finished the task after some four years' labor. The *Code Napoléon* expressed many democratic principles, such as social equality, religious toleration, and jury trial. These principles were carried into the foreign lands conquered by the French. It is still used in France, and has greatly influenced the legal systems of Belgium, Holland, Italy, Louisiana, Spain, and Spanish America.

Napoleon felt it necessary to please the Catholics, who formed so large a part of the population of France. He therefore made an agreement, or *Concordat,* with the pope, providing for the restoration of Catholicism as the official religion. Napoleon retained the right of nominating bishops and archbishops, and the pope gave up all claims to the church property taken by the state.

Return of the *émigrés*. Nor did Napoleon forget the emigrant nobles, or *émigrés*. He soon granted amnesty, or pardon, to those members of the aristocracy who had fled from France to escape the revolutionists. More than forty thousand families now returned to their native land.

Other peaceful activities of Napoleon. Napoleon showed his statesmanship in a number of other ways. He founded the Bank of France, which helped to restore financial order. He established the first public school system of Europe, although he used it for propaganda purposes. He also began the construction of a vast system of canals and military highways. The taste for building led Napoleon to erect many of the monuments which today decorate Paris. Even more appreciated by the war-weary French was the temporary peace that Napoleon brought about. In 1800 he defeated the Austrians at Marengo in Italy and the next year agreed to the Treaty of Lunéville. Two years later he signed the Peace of Amiens with England. For the first time since 1793 France was at peace.

NAPOLEON visiting a cotton factory at Rouen. The emperor was eager to have the French textile industry compete successfully with that of the British. Prizes were offered to French inventors who would build improved textile-making machines. One prize was offered specifically for the "machine which would do most injury to British commerce."

NAPOLEON'S PLAN FOR INVADING ENGLAND. After the renewal of war in 1803, Napoleon built a fleet of boats and barges on the channel coast, planning to launch an attack on England. But when the Russian and Austrian armies began to move, and when Nelson won at Trafalgar, Napoleon gave up his invasion plan.

Napoleon becomes emperor, 1804. Napoleon enjoyed the support of all Frenchmen except the radicals and the royalists. The radicals would not admit that the revolution had ended, and the royalists wished to restore the Bourbon monarchy. His widespread popularity moved Napoleon to take two more steps in satisfying his ambition for absolute power. In 1802 he asked the people to vote on the question, "Shall Napoleon Bonaparte be consul for life?" The answering "ayes" numbered over three and a half millions, the "noes" only a few thousand. Two years later another plebiscite decided by an equally large majority that the first consul should become emperor. Before the high altar of Notre Dame Cathedral at Paris and in the presence of the pope, the modern Charlemagne placed a golden laurel wreath upon his own head. Thus he became Napoleon I, Emperor of the French.

Imperial glory and despotism. The new emperor restored the etiquette and ceremony of the Old Regime. Already he had estab-

lished the Legion of Honor to reward those who most faithfully served him. Now he created a nobility. His relatives and ministers became kings, princes, dukes, and counts; his ablest generals became marshals of France. "My titles," Napoleon declared, "are a sort of civic crown; one can win them through one's own efforts." Under the spell of so much glory, France forgot that she had yielded to the rule of one man. The secret police smothered what opposition might have arisen against Napoleon. They arrested and imprisoned hundreds of persons. Napoleon demanded that even the schools and the churches should be tools of the new government.

The Peace of Amiens did not last long. To keep the affections of his people, Napoleon needed military glory. "My power proceeds from my reputation," he said, "and my reputation from the victories I have won. My power would fall if I were not to support it with more glory and more victories. Conquest has made me what I am; only conquest can maintain me."

Napoleon at war with Europe. The immediate cause of the renewal of war was a dispute over the evacuation of English troops from the island of Malta. A deeper reason lay in Napoleon's attempt to exclude British goods from the countries which he controlled. The war that followed involved most of Europe. On the sea England was victorious. Off Cape Trafalgar, Lord Nelson won a great triumph over the French fleet in 1805, and put an end to any plan which Napoleon might have had for invading England. On the other hand, in 1805 Napoleon marched swiftly into Germany (then part of the Holy Roman Empire) and defeated the Austrians at Ulm. At Austerlitz in Moravia he won a victory over the combined forces of Russia and Austria. At Jena (1806) he shattered the Prussian army and entered Berlin in triumph. Then he met and defeated the Russians at Friedland in East Prussia (1807). Thus Napoleon had again proved his ability as a conqueror. His enemies, except England, now sued for peace.

Napoleon remakes the map of Europe. When told the news of Napoleon's victory at Austerlitz, the English prime minister, William Pitt, exclaimed, "Roll up the map of Europe; it will not be wanted these ten years." By his new conquests Napoleon did, in fact, make a map of Europe out of date. (See map, page 284.) In the first place, he enlarged France by the annexation of neighboring areas, including Holland, parts of Germany, the States of the Church (including Rome), and northwestern Italy. Thus France proper now extended from the Baltic on the north to the Adriatic on the south. In the second place, he created a belt of dependent states, governed by himself or his appointees. These dependencies included northern Italy, the kingdom of Naples, Switzerland, and the grand duchy of Warsaw, formerly part of Poland. Finally, Napoleon compelled other states to become his allies, including Spain, Denmark, Norway, Prussia, and Austria.

Confederation of the Rhine, 1806. Napoleon exercised control over the central European dependencies through the Confederation of the Rhine. In its final form this organization included all the German states except Austria and Prussia. As "Protector" of the Confederation, Napoleon could use its military forces and had charge of its foreign relations. The formation of the Confederation of the Rhine gave the death blow to the Holy Roman Empire. When Napoleon declared that he would recognize it no longer, the Hapsburg ruler laid down his ancient crown and contented himself with the title of Austrian emperor.

Napoleon versus England. Napoleon had conquered the European continent. Its countries were under his control. But across the English Channel was a relentless foe whom Napoleon could not defeat—England, mistress of the seas. She had defeated his navy at Trafalgar and he could not reach her with his army. Napoleon therefore resorted to a commercial war. At Berlin and Milan (1806–1807) he issued decrees barring English goods from continental markets. He also ordered French ships to seize neutral vessels which traded with England. This policy was intended to destroy the trade between the Continent and England. It is called the "Continental System." It was not effective for two reasons. In the first place, England controlled the seas. Napoleon could not blockade her ports nor prevent her ships from carrying on trade. In the second place, the continental countries, including France, suffered as much as England, because they needed England's manufactured goods. Napoleon's own soldiers wore British cloth and shoes. The continental allies and dependencies of France complained against the Continental System, and England was not brought to her knees.

Growing resentment against Napoleon. Until this time Napoleon had been fighting kings, not nations; and he had been altogether successful. His fortunes were about to

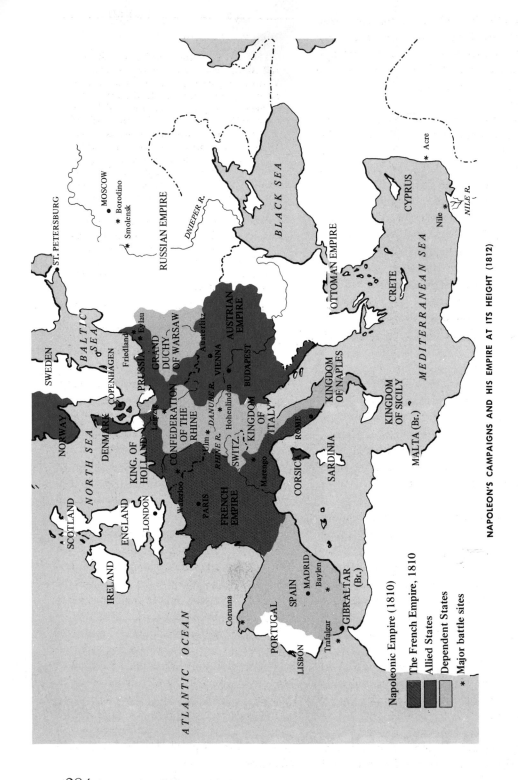

NAPOLEON'S CAMPAIGNS AND HIS EMPIRE AT ITS HEIGHT (1812)

Napoleonic Empire (1810)

The French Empire, 1810

Allied States

Dependent States

* Major battle sites

change. His demands upon the conquered countries, his despotic government, and the hardships imposed by the Continental System produced hatred. One after another the nations of Europe rose against their common oppressor.

Napoleon at war again. From 1808 to 1814 Napoleon was almost continually at war. He invaded Spain and Portugal to stop some leaks in the Continental System, but the people rose in revolt and called in the English. Under the future Duke of Wellington, the English drove the French from Portugal and forced Napoleon to keep a large army in Spain. Encouraged by the resistance shown in Spain and Portugal, Austria again declared war but was defeated at Wagram (1809). In 1812 Russia abandoned the Continental System and Napoleon declared war. With an army of 400,000 men, he invaded Russia. He reached Moscow, only to find the city in flames. Napoleon was without supplies, and the czar showed no signs of offering peace. The only course left was retreat. The Russian winter took a terrible toll of lives as the French armies made their way back to western Europe. Only about 20,000 soldiers escaped from Russia. Napoleon tried to make a comeback. He gathered fresh forces and at Leipzig faced the greatest allied army ever to oppose him. The "Battle of the Nations" followed; it involved every European people except the Turks. Napoleon was defeated and withdrew into France, but the allies pressed their advantage and in 1814 captured Paris. Napoleon was banished to the little island of Elba in the Mediterranean. Meanwhile, the allied diplomats gathered at Vienna to try to undo his work.

Waterloo. While the diplomats were busy at Vienna, they were startled to hear that Napoleon had escaped to France. They refused to allow the French to restore him to the throne and declared him an international outlaw. Napoleon quickly gathered another army and hurried to meet the allied forces, which

Was Napoleon a Great Man?

The opinion of the world is still divided, and perhaps will always be, on the question, Whether Napoleon did in fact deserve to be called a great man? . . . If the era of the Revolution was, as its admirers think, the most brilliant, the most glorious epoch of modern history, Napoleon, who has been able to take the first place in it, and to keep it for fifteen years, was, certainly, one of the greatest men who have ever appeared. If, on the contrary, he . . . found nothing around him but the *débris* of a social condition ruined by the excess of false civilisation; if he has only had to combat a resistance weakened by universal lassitude, feeble rivalries, ignoble passions, in fact, adversaries everywhere disunited and paralysed by their disagreements, the splendour of his success diminishes with the facility with which he obtained it . . .

—*Memoirs of Prince Metternich.*

were assembling in Belgium. At Waterloo, near Brussels, the opposing forces met on Sunday, June 18, 1815. Caught between the English under Wellington and the Germans under Blücher, Napoleon's army was crushed. It became a disorganized mob. Napoleon himself escaped with difficulty to Paris, where he again gave up his claims to the throne of France. The Prussians had orders to take Napoleon dead or alive. Therefore he hastened to surrender himself to the English because, as he said, they were "the most generous" of his enemies. The English exiled the fallen emperor to the lonely little island of St. Helena in the South Atlantic. There he lived the remaining six years of his life, surrounded only by a few intimate friends.

The Napoleonic legend. After Napoleon's death, France forgot the sufferings he had caused her and remembered only his glorious deeds. Poets, painters, and singers created a legendary figure of the "Little Corporal." They made the world despot appear as a fighter for liberty and a foe of tyrants. In this guise the French people fondly remembered Napoleon.

Napoleon's achievements. The Napoleonic legend was not without some foundation. Despot though he was, Napoleon certainly enjoyed the support of the great majority of Frenchmen. Through his plebiscites he at least paid lip service to the idea of popular sovereignty. Under him citizens of all ranks might compete freely and equally for offices, honors, wealth, and other distinctions. Furthermore, the tremendous campaigns of his armies through Europe united the French by a common bond of national feeling. Thus Napoleon to some extent promoted the revolutionary principles of liberty, equality, and fraternity.

Napoleon was an agent of the revolution in still other ways, not only in France but elsewhere. Wherever the Code Napoléon went, feudal customs, class privileges, and social inequalities tended to disappear. The trained officials sent out by the emperor reformed finances, built roads and bridges, improved harbors, encouraged trade, and advanced education. The inhabitants of many states of western Europe learned for the first time what it meant to have an efficient government. Could Napoleon's activity have ended with these achievements, he would have earned the thanks of mankind.

The Diplomats Try to Undo the Revolution

Congress of Vienna, 1814–1815. At a great international congress at Vienna, the diplomats now took up the task of rebuilding the states of Europe and rearranging the European map. The powers represented were Great Britain, Austria, Prussia, Russia, Sweden, Portugal, Spain, and France. The Congress of Vienna formed a brilliant assemblage of emperors, kings, princes of every rank, and titled diplomats. Amidst a bewildering round of banquets, balls, and other festivities, the monarchs and their advisers undertook the reconstruction of Europe. But,

as one observer remarked, "the real purpose of the congress was to divide among the conquerors the spoils taken from the vanquished." This meant satisfying the selfish claims of rulers rather than the wishes of the people.

The allied powers were opposed to all the democratic and liberal tendencies which had been awakened in Europe since 1789. The French Revolution appeared to them merely as an enemy of the social order and a destroyer of property and of countless lives. Those who had fought against the French revolutionists and then against Napoleon did not understand the strength of the demand for liberty and equality. They sought only to bring back the Old Regime of absolutism, privilege, and divine right. Their ideal was Europe as it was before 1789. They may be described therefore as *reactionary,* that is, in favor of a return to "the good old days."

The demand for self-determination. The French Revolution and Napoleon's conquering armies aroused the patriotic feelings of European peoples. The result was a growing demand by the people of each nationality for the recognition of their national existence and national rights. Patriots in one country after another boldly declared that no nation, however small or weak, should be governed by foreigners. Every nation, on the contrary, ought to be free to choose its own form of government and manage its own affairs. This principle is called the "self-determination of nations." Many peoples, known as *submerged nationalities,* did not enjoy this right. Such were the Belgians, Bohemians, Poles, and Magyars. To them the principle of self-determination held out the hope of independence. Such also were the Italians and the Germans, who cherished the hope of being united under governments of their own. But the rulers and diplomats at Vienna disregarded national ambitions. For example, they joined Belgium to Holland and granted Norway to Sweden, while they left the German, Italian, and

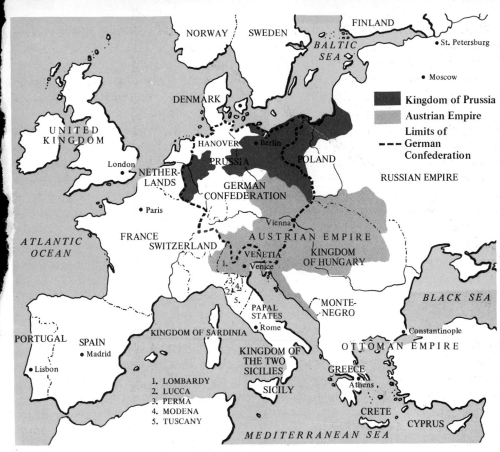

EUROPE IN 1815, AFTER THE CONGRESS OF VIENNA

Polish peoples divided into many political units. In general, the Vienna peacemakers treated the European peoples as pawns in the game of diplomacy. As a result, the peace settlement led to revolutions and wars.

Restoration of the dynasties. The Congress of Vienna thought its first business was to restore the former or "legitimate" rulers to their thrones and positions of authority. Spokesmen for the allied powers asserted the right of European monarchs to govern their former subjects regardless of the people's wishes or the claims of the rulers whom Napoleon had set up. Accordingly, a brother of Louis XVI became king of France as Louis XVIII. (The young son of Louis XVI, "Louis XVII," is supposed to have died in a revolutionary prison in 1795.) Another Bourbon king, Ferdinand VII, went back to Spain. Still other

legitimate princes recovered their thrones in Italy. Some of them governed without constitutions or parliaments, using their absolute power to get rid of every trace of the revolutionary period. The restoration of the dynasties spelled reaction.

Territorial readjustments. The leaders at Vienna tried to give territorial compensation to the great powers for losses suffered in the Napoleonic wars or as a result of restoring former rulers. Austria obtained a piece of northern Italy, while Prussia received some large slices of land belonging to other German states. Russia widened her boundaries by annexing Finland and a former portion of Poland. Great Britain, who did not desire continental territories, received additional colonies. These included the islands of Malta and Ceylon, and Cape Colony in southern

PRINCE METTERNICH. Between 1815 and 1848, this Austrian statesman and diplomat tried to keep autocracy alive in Europe.

Africa. One unit which Napoleon had destroyed was not restored, namely, the Holy Roman Empire. In its place the Congress of Vienna created the German Confederation, consisting of thirty-eight small states, under the domination of Austria. None of these settlements satisfied either the democratic or the national aspirations of European peoples. They served only to establish a "balance of power" among the chief states.

Reactionary Austria. After the Congress of Vienna, Austria consisted of more than a score of territories inhabited by Germans, Magyars, Slavs, Rumanians, and Italians. To keep them united under a single authority, the Hapsburgs put down all agitation for independence or self-government. The Hapsburgs also felt it necessary to discourage every popular movement in the countries bordering their dominions for fear it might spread to their own peoples. "My realm," confessed an Austrian emperor, "is like a worm-eaten house; if a part of it is removed, one cannot tell how much will fall." These circumstances placed Austria at the head of the reaction against democracy and nationalism.

The Metternich system. Prince Metternich of Austria seemed to embody the spirit of re-action. An aristocrat to his fingertips—polished, tactful, clever—this man became the real head of the Austrian government and the most influential diplomat in Europe. He regarded absolutism and divine right as the foundations of good government. Consequently, he believed that all demands for constitutions, parliaments, and the basic liberties must be opposed; spies and secret police must be multiplied; press and pulpit must be gagged; and all agitators must be exiled, imprisoned, or executed. Such despotic measures seemed quite workable at a time when the majority of European people were ignorant peasants, far removed from public life. Democratic ideas could only find followers among the workingmen of the cities and the bourgeoisie. Both, however, were very weak against governments based on class privilege and military force. Metternich found little difficulty in maintaining absolutism in Austria. He also extended his reactionary system to many states of Germany.

Trying to prevent change. In 1815 the allies who overthrew Napoleon became the masters of Europe. Great Britain, Austria, Prussia, and Russia renewed their alliance in order to preserve peace and the *status quo.* Their partnership was called the Quadruple Alliance. France under Louis XVIII was soon admitted into this circle of allied powers. One clause of the treaty between the powers provided that they should hold congresses from time to time to consider measures to maintain peace in Europe. Metternich summoned four such congresses. He also persuaded the sovereigns of Austria, Prussia, and Russia to sign an agreement to use their combined forces for the suppression of any popular uprisings. Metternich's coalition became a sort of international police force to keep order in Europe. Sometimes the Quadruple Alliance is called the Holy Alliance. However, the Holy Alliance, proposed by Czar Alexander, was a separate organization which nearly all of Europe's divine-right rulers joined.

More Revolutions in Europe

Revolutions of 1820–1823. The rulers of Austria, Prussia, and Russia soon had an opportunity to carry out their reactionary policy. In 1820–1823 revolutions occurred in Naples, Sardinia, Spain, Portugal, and Greece. An Austrian army quickly occupied Naples and Piedmont (part of the Sardinian kingdom) and restored an absolute government there. Liberal leaders were hurried to the dungeon and the scaffold. French troops, acting for Metternich's coalition, invaded Spain and put the cruel and stupid Ferdinand VII back on his throne. Ferdinand then carried on a reign of terror—exiling, imprisoning, and executing liberals by the thousands. However, the revolution of the Greeks against their Turkish overlords presented a different problem. The Turks were non-Christian and the traditional enemies of Russia. Russia, therefore, would not agree to intervention against the Greeks, and in the end she even joined the fight on the side of the rebels. Greece became independent of Turkey in 1829.

Britain leaves the alliance. Great Britain also refused to aid in suppressing the revolution in Greece; in fact, she gave her patronage and, eventually, her armed support to the cause of the Greeks. The foreign policy of the British government under the leadership of George Canning opposed intervention in countries where the liberals were trying to overthrow despotism. The reasons for this attitude were: (1) Britain herself had a representative government and her people were naturally sympathetic to the struggle for representative government in other countries; and (2) intervention was not healthy for British commercial interests. Thus, by 1820 Britain had dropped out of the Quadruple Alliance.

Revolution in France, July, 1830. The first revolutionary movements in Italy and Spain did not succeed. In France, on the other hand, another revolution soon won a victory for freedom. It came as the result of the reactionary rule of Charles X, who succeeded his brother, Louis XVIII, as king of France. The revolution broke out at Paris in July, 1830, when Charles issued the so-called "July Ordinances." These took away some of the liberties granted by Louis XVIII in 1814 when he began his reign. In protest, workingmen and students raised barricades in the narrow streets and defied the government. After several days of fighting, the revolutionists gained control of the capital. Thereupon Charles X fled to England, and the old republican tricolor was once more raised in France. The workingmen wanted a republic, but they found little support among the liberal bourgeoisie, who feared that a republican France would soon be at war with the monarchies of Europe. The aged Lafayette persuaded the Republicans to accept another king in the person of Louis Philippe, a member of the younger branch of the Bourbon family. He took the crown and promised to respect the constitution and the liberties of Frenchmen.

Effect of the July Revolution. The events in France created a sensation throughout Europe. Reactionaries were alarmed at the sudden outburst of a revolutionary spirit which they had been trying to keep down; liberals were encouraged to renew their struggle for self-government and national rights. Widespread disturbances in the Netherlands, Poland, Italy, and Germany discouraged Metternich from trying to restore Charles X in France.

Revolution in Belgium. Without regard for national feeling, the Congress of Vienna had united the Belgians and Dutch in one state under a Dutch king. Differences in language, religion, and occupations soon led to trouble between the two peoples. The success of the July Revolution in France encouraged the Belgians to start a revolt. It quickly spread from Brussels to the provinces and brought about a demand for complete separation from Holland. Louis Philippe of France, eager to

A CARICATURE OF LOUIS PHILIPPE, who tried to appear as a "man of the people"

make himself popular, favored Belgian independence. As a supporter of small nationalities, Great Britain also gave her approval. The three eastern European powers would gladly have stepped in to prevent such a violation of the Vienna settlements; but Austria and Russia had disorders of their own to quell, while Prussia did not want to risk, single-handed, a clash with France. Consequently, the revolution succeeded and Belgium became a constitutional monarchy, with Leopold of Saxe-Coburg as king (1831). The king of Holland did not recognize Belgian independence until 1839, when all the great powers signed a treaty declaring that Belgium was to be a "perpetually neutral state." This meant that Belgium would not make any alliances, and that the other signers would defend her against attack. It proved an important agreement in the light of future events. (See page 450.)

Failure of other revolutionary movements. The attempts of other submerged nationalities to secure freedom at this time were not successful. The Poles, whose territory had been partitioned in the late 1700's among Austria, Russia, and Prussia, started a revolt, but Russian troops quickly crushed it. Metternich's Austrian soldiers again put down an insurrection in Italy. Autocracy thus remained supreme in most of Europe, in spite of setbacks in France and Belgium.

Preparation for further revolution. No real victories for democracy or nationalism were produced in Europe from 1830 to 1848. Italy and Germany were still disunited, Bohemia and Hungary were subject to the Hapsburgs, and Poland was subject to the Hapsburgs, Romanovs, and Hohenzollerns. Metternich, though growing old and weary, still kept his

power at Vienna. The new rulers who came to the throne in this period were no less autocratic than their predecessors. Beneath the surface, discontent and unrest grew. Dissatisfaction became all the stronger as governments placed checks on the people's liberties. Journalists, lawyers, professors, and other liberal-minded men adopted radical views and sought to teach them to the working classes of the cities—the hungry proletariat. Murmurs of another storm were heard; soon it burst in France.

The February Revolution in France, 1848. Louis Philippe posed as a thoroughgoing liberal and liked to be called the "citizen king." He walked the streets unattended, dressed in frock coat and top hat and carrying an umbrella. He also gave an appearance of being democratic by sending his sons to public schools and by opening the royal palace to visitors, who might even shake hands with the head of the state. But Louis's republican simplicity was only skin deep. The "citizen king" had all the Bourbon itching for personal power. He did everything he could to gain the favor of the new capitalist class, or bourgeoisie—a group which was becoming powerful as a result of the Industrial Revolution. (See Chapter 16.) Nevertheless, he had many enemies. Both the Legitimists, as the supporters of Charles X were called, and the Bonapartists, who wished to restore the Napoleonic dynasty, heartily disliked him. The Republicans, mostly workingmen, felt themselves cheated by the outcome of the Revolution of July, 1830. Many of them had accepted the new doctrines of socialism (see page 298), and detested Louis Philippe for catering to the capitalist class. The growing discontent with the monarchy produced a number of plots, strikes, and riots, which were cruelly suppressed. The government required that all societies submit a record of their activities to it for approval. Editors of outspoken newspapers were jailed, fined, or banished. The authorities prohibited all criticism or cartooning of the king. Finally, on February 22, 1848, riots broke out in Paris. Workingmen armed themselves, erected barricades, and raised the cry, "Long live the Republic!" Louis Philippe, losing heart and fearing to lose his head as well, gave up the throne and sought refuge in England as plain "Mr. Smith."

Second French Republic. The revolutionists in Paris now proclaimed a republic, and the people outside the capital supported this move. The constitution of the Second French Republic was a thoroughly liberal document. It guaranteed freedom of speech and of assembly, prohibited capital punishment for political crimes, and abolished all titles of nobility. There was to be a parliament of one house and a president, both chosen by universal manhood suffrage. The extension of the vote to the masses is a landmark in the history of French democracy. The Revolutions of 1789 and 1830 destroyed absolute monarchy and privileged aristocracy in France; the Revolution of 1848 overthrew the rule of the middle class and established political equality.

Louis Napoleon, president of France. In the bitter "June days" of 1848 a socialist uprising was put down at the cost of the lives of fifteen hundred soldiers and ten thousand workingmen. The voters then elected Louis Napoleon to the presidency. Louis, a nephew of the more famous Bonaparte, had taken full advantage of the Napoleonic legend. (See page 288.) During the reactionary rule of the Bourbons and the dull, bourgeois monarchy of Louis Philippe, the tradition had grown that Napoleon was noble and heroic. The stories told at every peasant's fireside, the pictures on every cottage wall, kept his mem-

ory fresh. To the mass of the French people the name of Napoleon stood for prosperity at home and glory abroad. Their votes now swept his nephew into office. "Why should I not vote for him," remarked a Napoleonic veteran, "I, whose nose was frozen at Moscow?"

Effect of the February Revolution. France had once more lighted the revolutionary torch. This time eager hands took it up and carried it throughout the Continent. Within a few months half the monarchs of Europe were either deposed or forced to grant liberal reforms. No less than fifteen separate revolts marked the year 1848. Those in the Austrian Empire, Italy, and the German states had most importance.

Fall of Metternich. Vienna, the center of reaction, was one of the first scenes of a popular uprising. Mobs, which the guards refused to drive away, set fire to Metternich's palace and forced the old, white-haired minister to resign. His name had become a synonym for illiberal and oppressive government. For a time after Metternich's downfall, a revolutionary committee of students and citizens ruled Vienna. The Hapsburg emperor had to grant a constitution; he also promised many other reforms which, however, he soon forgot.

Revolts in Bohemia and Hungary. Other peoples of the Hapsburg realm soon caught the spirit of revolt and began movements for national liberation. The Czechs, as the Slavic inhabitants of Bohemia are called, believed that the hour had struck to regain their liberties. The Magyars also revolted and established an independent Hungarian republic. Its first and only president was the patriot Louis Kossuth. He made himself the Hungarian national hero by attacking the tyranny of the Hapsburgs. The revolts in Bohemia and Hungary were crushed by the armies of the Austrian monarch and his ally, the Russian czar. Kossuth escaped to Turkey and later went to America. Many liberal leaders who remained were executed.

Revolts in Italy. The revolutionary flood of 1848 also spread over the Italian peninsula. Charles Albert, king of Sardinia, assumed the leadership of the revolution and declared war on Austria. But the dream of a free united Italy faded when Charles Albert lost the Battle of Novara (1849) and went into exile. His son and successor, Victor Emmanuel II, then made peace with Austria. The day of Victor Emmanuel was yet to come. (See page 394.) Meanwhile, French troops occupied Rome and destroyed the republic which the revolutionist Mazzini had set up. Mazzini's day was also yet to come.

Revolution in Germany. Almost all the German states had revolutionary disturbances in 1848. The demand arose everywhere for constitutions, parliaments, and civil liberties. A national assembly chosen by popular vote met at Frankfort-on-Main to frame a constitution for a united Germany. The majority of the assembly favored a federal empire with a hereditary sovereign. The emperorship was offered to Frederick William IV, king of Prussia, but he refused it. He showed his contempt for the people by saying that he did not wish to "pick up a crown from the gutter." Moreover, he knew that the Hapsburgs would not consent to a Hohenzollern as emperor. The efforts of the assembly to unite the Germans therefore failed. Some of the more radical leaders then tried to set up republics in the individual German states by force of arms. In this desperate venture for freedom, some of the noblest men in Germany took part. Among them were Carl Schurz and Franz Sigel, who afterward emigrated to America and fought in the War between the States. Their efforts in Germany were in vain. Prussian troops suppressed the uprisings and defeated the attempt to establish German republics. Germany was doomed to continue for more than twenty years as a collection of disunited states.

Results of the revolutions of 1848. Almost everywhere in Europe the revolutions had failed. Yet some gains in the direction of democracy and nationalism had been made. Feudalism was abolished in the Hapsburg Empire. Nearly every state in Germany now had a parliament. The Frankfort assembly, although a failure, marked the first effort to unite Germany—an effort which the people did not easily forget. The masses of Frenchmen gained the vote and thereby set an important example for other countries. All in all, the Metternich system suffered a severe check in 1848.

The Independence of Latin America

The burden of Spanish rule. It has already been shown that Spain, like other colonial powers, governed her colonies for her own benefit. In following the mercantile system (see page 205), the mother country required that the colonists buy only Spanish goods and sell only to Spain. She prohibited the manufacture of any articles that might compete with those produced at home. As the demand for revenue increased, taxes in the colonies grew larger and multiplied in number until there were more than forty different kinds. Tax collectors were often dishonest and their methods of collection vicious and cruel. Moreover, the authorities kept the Indians, mestizos, and mulattoes in poverty and ignorance, and frequently mistreated them. It was the *Creoles,* or American-born Spaniards, who were the most dissatisfied. Although often wealthy and well educated, they could hold none of the important offices in church or government. These positions went to the *Peninsulars,* or Spaniards born in Spain, who formed a privileged caste in the colonies. The Creoles' distaste for Spanish rule was further increased by censorship of books and the press. The Creoles became the leaders in the revolutionary movement. By the end of the eighteenth century their discontent became still greater because of certain influences from outside Latin America.

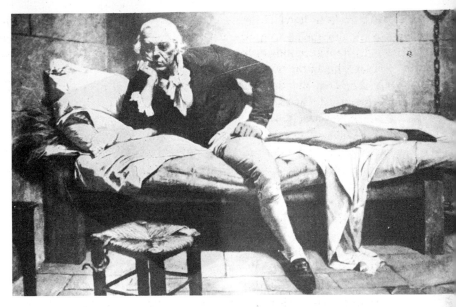

FRANCISCO MIRANDA in prison. Inspired by the French Revolution, Miranda attempted to liberate Venezuela from Spanish control. His success was short-lived. Less than a year after independence, Venezuela was returned to the Royalists. Miranda was arrested and imprisoned in Spain, where he died in 1816.

Example of the United States. One of these influences was the stirring story of the American Revolution and the formation of a great republic based on principles of liberty. French translations of the Declaration of Independence and Spanish translations of the Constitution of the United States soon found their way southward. Washington was regarded as a hero by Creole leaders. The example of the United States led many of the southern republics to adopt the federal system of government after winning independence.

Influence of France. Even before 1789, some educated Spanish Americans had become acquainted with the writings of Montesquieu, Voltaire, Rousseau, and the Encyclopedists. (See pages 269–270.) A Spanish edition of Rousseau's *Social Contract* spread the doctrines of popular sovereignty and natural rights. The colonial leaders not only read French books but watched with interest the revolution in France. After their own struggle for independence began, they made "Liberty, Equality, Fraternity" their watchword, took the liberty cap for their emblem, and formed secret revolutionary societies upon French models. France, too, gave the Latin Americans lessons in liberty.

The long hand of Napoleon. The struggle for Latin American independence was closely connected with events in Europe. In 1808 the power-hungry Napoleon Bonaparte overthrew the Bourbon monarchy in Spain and placed his own brother, Joseph, on the Spanish throne. The Spanish Americans refused to recognize this "intruder king." Instead, they set up *juntas*, or councils, in a number of cities. These bodies proceeded to take charge of local affairs, while declaring their loyalty to Ferdinand VII, the rightful Spanish king. The taste of self-government was enough to convince many colonial leaders that complete separation from the mother country was desirable. Others had already determined to seek independence even before Napoleon invaded Spain.

Miranda (1750?–1816), "Forerunner of Independence." Foremost among the early agitators for independence was Francisco de Miranda, a Venezuelan Creole. Napoleon once said of him, "The man has sacred fire in his soul!" The remark seemed fitting in view of the fact that Miranda devoted thirty years of his life to freeing his countrymen from the yoke of Spain. He began his career as an officer in the Spanish army, fought

SIMON BOLIVAR. Called "the Liberator," he freed northern South America from Spain.

against the British in Florida and the West Indies during the American Revolution, and later served as a general in the French revolutionary armies. As a military man, however, he never succeeded.

After 1790 Miranda spent most of his time in England, where he plotted the liberation of Spanish America. He hoped to get British help for his plan, but the British found it necessary to ally themselves with the Spaniards against Napoleon. Finally, Miranda returned to his native land and persuaded the revolutionary congress to declare Venezuela independent (July 5, 1811). Misfortune, however, dogged his footsteps. A disastrous earthquake occurred on March 26, 1812. The priests, most of whom were royalists, told the people that the earthquake was a sign that God disapproved of the revolt. Consequently, many deserted the patriot cause, and Miranda was forced to sign an armistice with the Spanish commander, Monteverde. Some of Miranda's subordinates thought he had deserted them. They therefore betrayed him into the hands of the Spaniards. The old warrior, his work a seeming failure, died in a dungeon in Spain (1816).

Bolívar (1783–1830), the "Liberator." Among the young officers who thought Miranda was a traitor to the patriot cause was

Simon Bolívar, later known as "the George Washington of South America." Like Miranda, Bolívar was a native of Caracas and a well-to-do Creole. He had been educated by private tutors and had traveled widely in the United States and Europe, where he had absorbed the liberal doctrines of the eighteenth-century philosophers. After Miranda's defeat, Bolívar fled from Venezuela. In 1813 he returned and for a time held Caracas. However, Ferdinand VII, who regained his throne after Napoleon's downfall, sent ten thousand fresh troops to put down the revolution in South America. Once more Bolívar fled, this time to Jamaica. But in 1816 he came back. In the following six years he proved himself a brilliant military commander. The forces he commanded liberated, in turn, Colombia, Venezuela, and Ecuador. Out of these three countries he created a new state, called El Gran Colombia or Great Colombia, and became president for life. After an unsuccessful conference with San Martín (see below), the Liberator moved southward into Peru. There, in 1824, his army won the decisive battle of the war at Ayacucho. But the people were not ready for self-government, and Bolívar was faced with jealousies and bickering on every hand. El Gran Colombia fell apart when Venezuela and Ecuador seceded. Then Bolívar, broken in health, resigned as president. His discouragement was expressed in the despairing words, "Those who have served in the revolution have plowed the sea." He died soon after at Santa Marta, Colombia (1830).

San Martín, 1778–1850. While Bolívar was freeing northern South America from Spain, José de San Martín was winning freedom for the southern part of the continent. Born in the mission district of northeastern Argentina, he was the son of an army officer. As a youth San Martín went to Spain, where he served for twenty-two years in the army. In 1812 he resigned his commission and offered his services to the revolutionists at Buenos

UNITED STATES

NEW SPAIN

FLORIDA

CUBA

HAITI
(independent)
1804

SANTO DOMINGO

PUERTO RICO

Mexico City

Caracas

Barcelona

British

Bogota

Dutch

GUIANAS

French

Quito

NEW GRANADA

AMAZON R.

Guayaquil

BRAZIL

Lima

Callao

Pisco

PERU

PARAGUAY R.

RIO DE
LA PLATA

Rio de Janeiro

Valparaiso

Santiago

Buenos Aires

Spanish possessions

Bolívar's route

San Martín's route

* Battles

THE CAMPAIGNS OF
BOLÍVAR AND SAN MARTÍN
1813–1824

Aires. A junta had made the region self-governing in 1810, although independence was not declared until 1816.

Meanwhile, San Martín saw that independence must be won by attacking the Spaniards at their strongest point—Peru. With the aid of the Chilean, Bernardo O'Higgins, he spent nearly three years training an army at Mendoza in western Argentina. Early in 1817 San Martín made his famous march across the Andes into Chile. Only the marches of Hannibal and of Napoleon over the Alps rank with San Martín's feat. In two decisive battles San Martín freed Chile (1818) and moved northward by sea to Peru. San Martín occupied Lima, while the Spanish troops fled into the mountains. The revolutionary army could not pursue them without rein-

forcements. San Martín therefore sought the help of Bolívar at a famous conference in Guayaquil, Ecuador. The leaders failed to agree on the command of the armies and the type of government for the liberated colonies. San Martín thereupon gave up his command and left to Bolívar the task of winning Peru from the Spaniards. "There is not room in Peru for both Bolívar and myself," wrote San Martín to a friend. "Let him enter, that America may triumph." With this act of self-sacrifice San Martín retired to France—a hero who was to remain unsung until after death.

The independence of Mexico. The struggle for independence in Mexico began in 1810, when the mestizos and Indians revolted against their white landlords. They were led by a liberal priest, Miguel Hidalgo. His followers got out of his control and spread terror through the central provinces. They shouted their famous battle-cry, "Death to the Spaniards! Down with bad government!" The trained forces of the Spanish, however, soon defeated the revolutionists. Hidalgo was captured and shot. His successor, José María Morelos, likewise a priest, was an able military leader. Morelos gained many a victory over the royalists and in 1813 declared Mexico independent. Like Hidalgo, Morelos fell into the hands of the enemy, was condemned by the Inquisition, and executed (1815).

For a time the revolutionary movement died down. Then, in 1821, Agustín de Iturbide, former Creole officer on the royalist side, deserted to the patriots. Under his leadership, Mexico completed the struggle for independence. Iturbide was a self-seeker and soon set himself up as emperor of Mexico. His arbitrary rule was short-lived. Revolt broke out against him and he was forced to abdicate. In 1824 Mexico became a republic, although its future did not look promising.

Central America. The Central American part of the Spanish Empire, known as the Captaincy-General of Guatemala, followed the lead of Mexico and in 1821 proclaimed its independence. The unprincipled Iturbide, however, forced the new state into the Mexican Empire. After the downfall of Iturbide

LATIN AMERICA IN 1828. The map shows the date when each country gained its independence.

in 1823, a confederation called the United Provinces of Central America was established. This state lasted until 1838, when it split into five republics.

The West Indies. In 1697 Spain was forced to cede the western part of the island of Santo Domingo, or Hispaniola, to France. This French possession came to be known by its Indian name, Haiti, meaning "land of mountains." The independence movement in Haiti began in 1791 with the outbreak of a slave insurrection. The slave leader, Toussaint L'Ouverture, soon gained control of the whole island and wished to set up a self-governing colony under French rule. Napoleon would not tolerate such an arrangement and sent an army of twenty thousand men to suppress the movement. The Negro leader was captured and died in France. His followers, aided by yellow fever, defeated the French forces and in 1804 declared Haiti to be an independent republic—the first free nation in Latin America.

The French loss of Haiti affected the history of the United States. It was an important reason for Napoleon's sudden decision to sell Louisiana to the United States in 1803, for no longer could Haiti be used as a steppingstone to a great French empire in America. The eastern end, or Spanish part, of Santo Domingo separated from Haiti in 1844. Cuba, the so-called "Ever-Faithful Isle," did not break away from the mother country until 1898, as a result of the Spanish-American War.

The independence of Brazil. Brazil won her independence from Portugal without bloodshed. When Napoleon invaded the Iberian Peninsula in 1807, the royal family of Portugal fled to Brazil. In 1815 King John VI made the colony a part of his kingdom and removed most of the colonial restrictions. But on the demand of a new Cortes (parliament) in 1821, the king reluctantly returned to Portugal, leaving his son, Dom Pedro, as regent in Brazil. The Cortes next ordered Dom Pedro to return to Europe. Backed by strong

TOUSSAINT L'OUVERTURE led the slave rebellion and ruled Haiti until captured by the French in 1802.

sentiment for independence among the people, Dom Pedro defied the home government and uttered the famous Cry of Ypiranga: "The time has arrived. Independence or Death! We are separated from Portugal!" (September 7, 1822.) The constitution, which was drafted two years later, established a limited monarchy. Dom Pedro became the first emperor of Brazil. His illiberal rule turned the people against him, and in 1831 he abdicated in favor of his infant son. Brazil prospered under the kindly rule of the second Pedro, who was the last monarch to occupy an American throne (1831–1889).

The Monroe Doctrine. The wars for independence on the mainland of Latin America lasted for nearly fifteen years (1810–1825). The United States followed the struggle with sympathetic eyes and sent commissioners to establish commercial relations with the revolting colonies. Great Britain also encouraged them with money, ships, and war materials. When it appeared that Metternich's Quadruple Alliance might help Spain to win back her colonies, both Great Britain and the United States were alarmed. George Canning, the British foreign minister, made it clear to the governments of France, Austria, Prussia, and Russia that Great Britain would oppose any foreign interference in Latin

PRESIDENT MONROE discussing his famous doctrine. Under this doctrine the United States at first assumed the role of protector of its weaker neighbors. Today the nations of the Americas co-operate as partners in defense against foreign aggression. During World War II they worked together with notable effectiveness.

America. In an exchange of notes with Russia over the boundaries of Alaska, the United States had already warned the world that the American continents were "henceforth not to be considered as subjects for future colonization by any European powers." Canning suggested that the two governments proclaim these principles in a joint statement. But President Monroe and Secretary of State John Quincy Adams thought it best for the United States to make its own statement of policy. This the President did in a notable message to Congress in December, 1823. The political system of the European powers, he said, was fundamentally different from that of America. Therefore, the United States would "consider any attempt on their part to extend their system to any portion of this hemisphere as dangerous to our peace and safety." In other words, the Monroe Doctrine said to Europe, "Hands off!" By 1824 both the United States and Great Britain had recognized the independence of the Latin American republics.

Many years passed before the Spanish government did the same.

Latin America after the wars for independence. Independence did not bring order to the Latin American countries. All of the freed states except Brazil and Haiti promptly became republics, with constitutions modeled upon that of the United States. From the beginning, however, these new governments proved unstable. The chief reasons were: (1) the great social inequalities between the Creole aristocrats and the masses of the people, most of whom were mestizos, Indians, and Negroes; (2) widespread illiteracy; (3) lack of experience in self-government; and (4) disunity created by natural barriers of mountains and jungles. Under these circumstances, military chieftains called *caudillos* easily imposed their will upon the people of Latin America. The growth of democracy has been very slow, but in some countries *caudillismo,* or dictatorship, is now a thing of the past.

REVIEWING THE CHAPTER

TERMS TO UNDERSTAND: *revolution, divine right, Puritan, Cavaliers, Roundheads, Restoration, Wars of the Roses, Bill of Rights,* habeas corpus, *Whig, Tory, Old Regime, absolutism, bourgeoisie,* taille, lettre de cachet, *Estates-General, assignats, nonjuring, Jacobin,* coup d'état, *Reign of Terror, émigrés, Directory, Peace of Amiens, Code Napoléon, plebiscite, Concordat, amnesty, Continental System, Napoleonic legend, reactionary, submerged nationality, proletariat, Creole, junta,* caudillo, *Cry of Ypiranga, Monroe Doctrine.*

PERSONS TO IDENTIFY: *Cromwell, William and Mary, Locke, Burke, Paine, Jefferson, Montesquieu, Voltaire, Rousseau, Marie Antoinette, Turgot, Diderot, Abbé Sieyès, Mirabeau, Danton, Robespierre, Metternich, Wellington, Louis Philippe, Louis Napoleon, Kossuth, Mazzini, Miranda, Bolívar, San Martín, Hidalgo, L'Ouverture, Dom Pedro I, Canning, Lafayette.*

PLACES TO LOCATE: *Yorktown, Hanover, Marseilles, Versailles, Trafalgar, Ulm, Jena, Austerlitz, Moscow, Friedland, Leipzig, Waterloo, Elba, St. Helena, Vienna, Bohemia, Malta, Cape Colony, German Confederation, Ayacucho, Mendoza, Guayaquil, Caracas.*

QUESTIONS TO ANSWER

1. Why should Americans be especially interested in the English revolutions of the seventeenth century?

2. (a) Contrast the position of Parliament under Tudor and under Stuart kings. (b) What were the issues in the quarrels between Parliament and the Stuarts? (c) Did Cromwell get along with Parliament? (d) What was the Instrument of Government? (e) Why do you agree or disagree with the statement: "The execution of Charles I was a great injustice"? (f) Did the Restoration of the Stuarts indicate that the Puritan Revolution was a failure?

3. (a) What party was opposed to permitting James, the brother of Charles II, to become king? Why? (b) What party was willing that James become king? Why? (c) What was accomplished by the Glorious Revolution? (d) How did John Locke justify it? (e) In what respects are Magna Carta, the Petition of Right, and the Bill of Rights alike?

4. (a) How and why did England change her treatment of her American colonies after 1763? (b) What led the colonists to desire independence? (c) Where did the ideas in the Declaration of Independence come from? (d) Describe the Critical Period. What brought it to a close?

5. (a) What is meant by the Old Regime? (b) What groups belonged to each of the three estates? (c) How did the teachings of the "philosophers" help to break down the Old Regime? (d) Why did the revolution begin in France?

6. (a) How was the rule of Louis XV tyrannical? (b) What reforms did Turgot propose? Why was he dismissed? (c) Why did Louis XVI call the Estates-General? (d) How did the Estates-General transform itself into the National Assembly? (e) What was the "Tennis Court Oath"? (f) What was the importance of the fall of the Bastille?

7. (a) What reforms did the National Assembly put through? (b) Summarize the principal clauses of the Declaration of the Rights of Man. (c) What groups opposed the Constitution of 1791? Why?

8. (a) How did the revolutionary government get into war with foreign powers? (b) What was the effect of the Brunswick Manifesto? (c) How did the Committee of Public Safety deal with its enemies outside and inside France? (d) What marked the end of the Reign of Terror?

9. (a) How did the French Revolution differ from previous revolutionary movements? (b) Explain the meaning of "Liberty, Equality, Fraternity."

10. (a) What first brought Napoleon into the limelight? (b) By what steps did he make himself emperor? (c) What reforms did he

carry out in France? (d) Describe how he remade the map of Europe. (e) What were the causes of Napoleon's downfall?

11. (a) To what extent did Napoleon preserve and spread the principles of the French Revolution? (b) Summarize the work of the Congress of Vienna. (c) What principles did the peacemakers at Vienna disregard? (d) Why did Britain leave the Quadruple Alliance?

12. (a) What changes were made in France by the revolutions of 1830 and 1848? (b) What were the results of the revolutions of 1848 in Europe?

13. (a) What caused the Spanish colonies in America to revolt? (b) Describe the careers of Miranda, Bolívar, and San Martín. (c) How did the independence movement in Brazil differ from that in the Spanish colonies? (d) Why were the new Latin American governments unstable? (e) State the principle of the Monroe Doctrine.

FURTHER ACTIVITIES FOR PART FIVE

1. Prepare a chart of the Tudor and Stuart periods, giving dates, names of rulers, and chief events during the rule of each.

2. Prepare a report on the fall of the Bastille, based on the account in Thomas Carlyle's *The French Revolution.*

3. Prepare a table of Napoleon's battles, giving names, locations, dates, and results of each.

4. Write a report on the similarities and differences between the American Revolution and the Latin American independence movement.

5. (a) On an outline map of Europe indicate the changes made by Napoleon. (b) On another outline map indicate the settlements decided upon by the Congress of Vienna.

6. Prepare an oral report on the styles and costumes of the eighteenth century. You will find excellent pictures and explanations of various costumes in Hansen's *Costumes and Styles,* Dutton.

7. Prepare a chronological chart of the rulers of each great European country during the seventeenth and eighteenth centuries.

8. Debate: *Resolved,* that the able rule of one man is preferable to democratic government.

FURTHER READING FOR PART FIVE

(Stars indicate easier books)

HISTORY

BLITZER. *Age of Kings.* Time-Life.

CARLYLE. *The French Revolution.* Dutton.

CHRISTENSEN. *The Pictorial History of Western Art.* Mentor. (paperback)

CHURCHILL. *The Age of Revolution.* Bantam. (paperback)

CLENDENIN. *Music: History and Theory.* Doubleday. (paperback)

DEFOE. *Journal of the Plague Year.* Penguin. (paperback)

DURANT. *The Story of Civilization.* Simon and Schuster.

GAY. *Age of Enlightenment.* Time-Life.

GERSHOY. *The Era of the French Revolution, 1789–1799.* Van Nostrand. (paperback)

GOTTSCHALK. *Era of the French Revolution.* Houghton.

HOBSBAWN. *The Age of Revolution, 1789–1848.* New American Library. (paperback)

HORIZON MAGAZINE. *The French Revolution*. American Heritage.

——. *Horizon Book of the Age of Napoleon*. American Heritage.

*KOMROFF. *The Battle of Waterloo*. Macmillan.

LEVEY. *From Rococo to Revolution: Major Trends in 18th Century Painting*. Praeger. (paperback)

*LINDQUIST. *The Age of Revolution*. Golden Press.

LOOMIS. *Paris in the Terror, June 1793–July 1794*. Lippincott.

McKINNEY. *Music in History, the Evolution of an Art*. American Book.

McNEILL, BUSKE, ROEHM. *The World . . . Its History in Maps*. Denoyer-Geppert.

MATTINGLY. *The Armada*. Houghton. (paperback)

——. *Catherine of Aragon*. Houghton. (paperback)

*MOSCOW. *Russia under the Czars*. American Heritage.

SPENCER. *Song in the Streets*. Day.

STEARNS. *Pageant of Europe: Sources and Selections from the Renaissance to the Present Day*. Harcourt.

TAPIE. *The Age of Grandeur: Baroque Art and Architecture*. Praeger. (paperback)

*VILLIERS. *The Battle of Trafalgar*. Macmillan.

WALLACE. *The Rise of Russia*. Time-Life.

*WILLIAMS and SMITH. *The Spanish Armada*. American Heritage.

BIOGRAPHY

*BAKER. *Peter the Great*. Vanguard.

*CARR. *Men of Power*. Viking.

CARUSO. *Liberators of Mexico*. Peter Smith.

*CASTELOT. *Queen of France*. Harper.

CRONIN. *Louis XIV*. Houghton.

*GUÉRARD. *Napoleon I: A Great Life in Brief*. Knopf.

*GURKO. *Tom Paine: Freedom's Apostle*. Crowell.

KIELTY. *Marie Antoinette*. Random House.

KNAPTON. *Empress Josephine*. Harvard.

KOMROFF. *Napoleon*. Messner.

*NOBLE. *Empress of All Russia: Catherine the Great*. Messner.

OLDENBOURG. *Catherine the Great*. Pantheon.

SAINT–SIMON. *The Age of Magnificence: The Memoirs of the Duc de Saint-Simon*. Putnam. (paperback)

THOMSON. *Catherine the Great and the Expansion of Russia*. Macmillan. (paperback)

*VANCE. *The Empress Josephine*. Dutton.

*——. *Marie Antoinette, Daughter of an Empress*. Dutton.

WHITRIDGE. *Simón Bolívar, the Great Liberator*. Random House.

FICTION

*BEATTY and BEATTY. *At the Seven Stars*. Macmillan.

BEYER. *The Sapphire Pendant*. Knopf.

BOYD. *Drums*. Scribner.

*DICKENS. *A Tale of Two Cities*. Dutton.

DU MAURIER. *The Glass-Blowers*. Doubleday.

HARDY. *Trumpet Major and Robert His Brother*. St. Martin. (paperback)

*ORCZY. *Scarlet Pimpernel*. Grosset.

*SABATINI. *Scaramouche*. Houghton.

SELINKO. *Désirée*. Morrow.

STENDHAL. *The Red and the Black*. Modern Library.

TOLSTOY. *War and Peace*. Modern Library.

WATSON. *Lark*. Holt.

WILLIAMSON. *Jacobin's Daughter*. Knopf.

THE NEW YORK CRYSTAL PALACE EXHIBITION of 1853–1854 showed the industrial progress of nations around the world. It featured demonstrations of the first passenger elevator and the sewing machine.

PART SIX

INDUSTRIALISM TRANSFORMS WESTERN CULTURE

In Part Five we observed the emergence of two of the most powerful forces in modern times, namely, democracy and nationalism. Both of these upset the older patterns of political organization and customs, creating new struggles and new problems. At the same time another major force in modern history was silently and gradually changing man's ways of living. It was industrialism—the economic organization of society based on the factory system and machine-made goods. Beginning with some key inventions in eighteenth-century England, it spread to most of the nations of the western world during the next century. The pace of its advance was uneven, as we can easily see from the fact that the economic life of some peoples today remains largely agricultural.

The Industrial Revolution (as we call the series of changes which produced industrialism) passed through several stages. As time passed, it gained momentum, until by the late nineteenth century It gave rise to a new era, the machine age, or the Second Industrial Revolution. The scientist and the inventor-engineer now combined their talents to tap new sources of power, produce new labor-saving devices, and make available myriads of new products for man's pleasure and convenience. The machine age has also brought new problems, many of which man is still struggling to overcome.

As a mirror of life, the literature and arts of the machine age expressed how man thought and felt about the new environment he had created. They revealed widely differing moods and reactions to the industrial and scientific world of modern times. Part Six will bring the story of the machine age into the twentieth century. The story will be brought down to the present in the final chapter of the book.

16 The Industrial Revolution

MACHINES. Stephenson's *Rocket* (left) was one of the earliest successful locomotives, built by the "founder of railways." Elias Howe's sewing machine (bottom left), patented in the United States in 1846, did not interest people at first. Later, Howe made a large fortune from his invention. The *Savannah* (below) was the first vessel using steam power to cross the Atlantic. However, the engine was operating only about one fifth of the time.

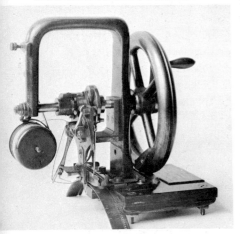

For the sake of convenience, the hundred years from about 1770 to 1870 may be described as the period of the First Industrial Revolution. It was marked by the following developments: (1) the introduction of machines which reduced the need for hand labor in making goods; (2) the substitution of steam power for water, wind, and animal power; (3) the change from manufacturing in the home to the factory system; (4) new and faster methods of transportation on land and on water; and (5) the growth of modern capitalism, with greatly increased conflicts between employer and employee. After about 1870 the Industrial Revolution entered a period of more rapid change. This stage, called the Second Industrial Revolution, is marked by the use of new sources of power to drive machinery, by the creation of new products through scientific research, and by the rapid growth of cities.

The Coming of the Industrial Revolution

Why the Industrial Revolution began in England. In the late eighteenth century England had all the things necessary for the growth of industry. She possessed money to invest, or capital, an ample labor supply, and the essential natural resources. Since the sixteenth century wealth had been pouring into England from colonies in America and trading posts in Asia. Substantial sums were thus available for investment in new manufacturing enterprises. Her large merchant fleet brought her an abundance of raw materials— more than could be used under the old system of manufacture. This surplus and the growing demand for goods encouraged the development of new and faster methods of manufacture. Another favorable factor in England was the supply of cheap labor. The "enclosure acts" (see page 314), which increased the size of the large estates at the expense of the small farmer, sent many people to the city. The comparatively early breakdown of feudalism and the guild system also promoted migration from farm to factory. These changes meant that workers could move about freely and employers had greater liberty in deciding what to make and how to make it. Finally, the presence of large

amounts of coal made possible the extensive use of steam power, while the plentiful supply of iron encouraged the manufacture of tools and machinery. No other country in Europe had such favorable conditions for a vast increase in production.

Inventions before the Industrial Revolution. The process of invention is always gradual. Every invention is based on some previously known principle, idea, or model, and one invention frequently produces another. This is shown by our Patent Office records. In prehistoric times men had already developed an impressive list of inventions including levers, rollers, and wedges; bows and arrows, slings, and lassos; oars, sails, and rudders; fishing nets, lines, and hooks; the plow and the wheeled cart; the needle, bellows, and potter's wheel; the distaff and spindle for spinning; and the hand loom for weaving. Not many inventions of basic importance were added to this list in ancient times, even by highly civilized peoples such as the Egyptians, Babylonians, Greeks, Romans, and Chinese. The Middle Ages in Europe were also strikingly lacking in inventions. It was only toward the close of the medieval period that gunpowder, the mariner's compass, paper, and movable type reached Europe from Asia. (See page 171.) The sixteenth and seventeenth centuries produced the telescope, microscope, thermom-

Too true too true

eter, barometer, clocks and watches run by weights, sawmills driven by wind or water, an improved form of the windmill, and many minor inventions such as the wheelbarrow. Manufacturing and transportation, however, continued to be carried on in much the same crude way as before the dawn of history.

Improvements in Manufacturing

The cotton industry. The revolution in manufacturing began with the cotton textile industry. Although cotton has been used for cloth since ancient times, it was not known in England until the seventeenth century, when the East India Company brought "calico" (named for Calicut) from India. The new fabric quickly became the fashion, in spite of the bitter opposition of the makers of woolen goods. Shrewd businessmen with capital were soon importing raw cotton and making it into cloth. The guild regulations which restricted the older industries did not apply to cotton manufacturing. Hence the new industry grew rapidly. Workers using the old spinning wheel and hand loom, however, could not keep up with the increasing demand for cotton clothes. Faster ways of spinning and weaving were greatly needed.

The flying shuttle. In the eighteenth cen-tury weaving was still done on the hand loom. To operate this simple machine, a man had to push the shuttle containing the warp, or crosswise, thread all the way across the loom and then pull it back. In 1733 an Englishman, John Kay, invented the flying shuttle. By this device the operator could send the shuttle back and forth by pulling a cord.

Three revolutionary inventions. One invention soon led to another. Since Kay's shuttle doubled the speed of weaving, the spinners, who still used the spinning wheel, could not keep up with the weavers. Prizes were offered for a better spinning machine. In 1764 James Hargreaves, a poor workman of Lancashire, invented the spinning jenny—named after his industrious wife. The machine carried eight spindles turned by cords or belts from the same wheel. Though hand-operated, it spun eight threads at one time and thus greatly speeded up the process of spinning. Another improvement in spinning occurred in 1769, when Richard Arkwright patented the famous water frame. Arkwright's machine, run by water power, drew out the cotton fibers between two sets of rollers and twisted them into thread on revolving spindles. In 1779 Samuel Crompton combined the chief features of the spinning jenny and the water frame into what became known as the "mule," because of its hybrid origin. This mechanism produced a finer thread than that made in India and at a lower price. Consequently, more people could wear cotton clothes.

Cartwright's power loom. The three inventions just mentioned again upset the balance in the textile industry. Now the spinners could produce more thread and yarn than the weavers could make into cloth. To fill the need for a better weaving machine, Edmund Cartwright invented the power loom in 1785. He was a clergyman, and although he had never seen a weaver at work, he constructed a loom with an automatic shuttle operated by water power. When this machine had been improved, a single operator could produce more cloth than two hundred men could weave on the old-fashioned hand loom. One of the immediate results was a drop in the price of cloth and hence a much larger demand for cloth.

Whitney's cotton gin, 1793. The growing demand for cloth called for an increasing supply of raw cotton. The need was met as a result of the invention of the cotton gin in 1793 by an American, Eli Whitney. The new device made it possible to separate the seeds from the cotton about three hundred times as rapidly as it could be done by hand. It encouraged the production of cotton to such an extent that between 1791 and 1800 the export of raw cotton from the United States increased tenfold. Whitney is also remembered for having worked out and applied the principle of standardization of parts. He did this in his gun factory in Connecticut. Today this principle is used in all mass production industries.

The steam engine. In ancient times men knew that water when heated expands in the form of steam. They did not put this knowledge to practical use, however, until late in the 1600's, when Savery invented a steam pump to get rid of water in mines. This, the first practicable steam engine, was soon displaced by Newcomen's engine, patented in 1705. It was a crude affair. After the steam entered the cylinder and pushed the piston upward, cold water had to be sprayed into the cylinder in order to condense the steam.

SPINNING SILK in France in the 1700's. The spinning wheels used by these boys were turned by means of a crank held in the right hand. Simple as it was, the spinning wheel represented an important advance over the distaff, with which thread had been spun since the New Stone Age. The picture is from a book published in 1773.

A COTTON GIN. This machine, a much later model than Whitney's original gin, separates the cotton seeds from the fibers. The name *gin* is a short form of *engine*.

Such alternate heating and cooling used too much coal and took too much time.

In 1769 James Watt, an instrument maker at the University of Glasgow, patented an improved steam engine. He appropriately named it "Beelzebub." Watt had overcome the two greatest defects of the old steam pump by providing a separate condenser to cool the steam and by enclosing the cylinder in an airtight jacket to maintain its heat. He continued to improve his engine and finally found a way to make it drive machinery. The inventor himself was a poor man, but he entered into a partnership with a wealthy manufacturer of Birmingham, Matthew Boulton, who financed the new machine.

With Watt's engine, the Industrial Revolution quickened its pace. In 1785, the year of Cartwright's invention of the power loom, the Watt engine was introduced in factories to turn spinning and weaving machines. However, steam power did not soon displace water power, for manufacturers had already invested much money in water-driven cotton mills. Nevertheless, a great victory over nature's forces was at hand. Factories with steam power could be located almost anywhere without regard to the presence of a stream or a waterfall. The "age of steam" had dawned. (See page 311 for discussion of the steamboat and locomotive.)

The age of coal and iron. The growing demand for machinery called for an increased production of iron. The smelting of iron, in turn, required an abundant supply of coal. Thus iron and coal became the twin necessities of modern industry. Abundant deposits of both of these materials were present in England, and various improvements in mining cheapened their production. One of the most notable improvements was Sir Humphry Davy's safety lamp, in which the flame was enclosed in wire gauze to prevent the flame from exploding the gas called firedamp, should it be present. This simple device, invented in 1816, made it possible to work the most dangerous mines in comparative safety.

Blast furnaces. Coke (made by heating coal in an oven to remove the volatile gases) was first used for the smelting of iron early in the 1700's. To make a coke fire produce sufficient heat for smelting, a strong blast of air is necessary. From this we get the name "blast furnaces." In 1760 a steam blower was invented to take the place of the leather bellows which had formerly been used to keep a coke fire burning constantly.

The Bessemer process. Steel is a harder form of iron, made by removing most of the impurities. It was not produced on a large scale until after 1850. An early method of making steel was the "puddling" process, discovered by Henry Cort in 1783. Of far greater importance was the invention of the Bessemer process by an Englishman, Henry Bessemer, in 1856. An American, William Kelly, invented the same process earlier, but his method was not widely known or adopted. This method of removing the carbon from iron consists of forcing a blast of cold air through the molten metal. The Bessemer process reduced the cost of a ton of steel to less than one seventh of what it had been before. It introduced the "age of steel." Other improvements in steelmaking soon brought into use extensive fields of low-grade iron ore in France, Germany, and other countries. Steel became the mainstay of industry.

The beginnings of electric power. In ancient times men were acquainted with certain properties of amber and lodestone. When rubbed with wool, amber accumulates a charge of static electricity and will then attract small pieces of pith or paper. Lodestone is a natural magnet and attracts bits of iron and nickel. In 1600 William Gilbert, physician at the court of Queen Elizabeth, pointed out the difference between magnetic and electrical activity. A century and a half went by before anyone again gave serious attention to the study of electrical energy. Then in 1752 Benjamin Franklin identified lightning as an electric discharge. He probably made the first practical application of the mysterious force by inventing the lightning rod. In 1800 an Italian, Volta, found that he could produce an electric current by immersing a strip of copper and one of zinc in an acid. The device was known as a voltaic cell and led in time to the invention of the storage battery. Soon after, the work of the French physicist, Ampère, laid the foundation of the science of electromagnetism. No one did more to harness electricity for use than the English scientist, Michael Faraday (1791–1867). In a well-planned experiment in 1831, he produced an electric current by rotating a copper disc between the poles of a magnet. This led to the invention of the electric dynamo, or generator. A practical dynamo was not exhibited until 1877. It produced electricity so cheaply that the current could be used for commercial lighting and for turning machinery. Electricity was first used for operating streetcars about 1882, and soon after began to turn the wheels of factories in Europe and America. The "age of electricity" had begun.

The vulcanization of rubber. Columbus observed natives in the West Indies playing with balls made of the gum of a certain tree. Europeans seem to have found no use for this sticky substance until the late 1700's. Then someone discovered that it would erase pencil marks. This quality, plus the fact that it came from the Indies, gave the gum the name "India rubber." In 1820 an American shipmaster brought a pair of rubber shoes from Brazil to Boston, and soon New Englanders were making shoes, coats, and other articles of rubber. Goods made of this material, however, proved impractical because heat and warm weather made them sticky. It remained for an American, Charles Goodyear (1800–1860), to discover how to "cure," or "vulcanize," rubber so that it would resist both heat and cold. After many years of experiment during which he was hampered by poverty, he succeeded in producing a durable rubber. This he accomplished in 1839 by mixing the gum with sulphur and heating it. By the time Goodyear died he had taken out sixty patents on rubber articles, and the rubber industry was giving employment to sixty thousand persons. But the great era of rubber production awaited the coming of the automobile.

Improvements in Transportation and Communication

Roads. At the opening of the Industrial Revolution the roads in western Europe and America scarcely deserved the name; they were little more than beaten tracks, either deep with mud or dusty and full of ruts. Passengers in stagecoaches seldom made more than fifty miles a day, while heavy goods had to be moved on pack horses. Late in the 1700's, roads in Great Britain were improved, for cheap and rapid transportation was needed to distribute the large quantity of goods produced by the new machinery. To help meet the need, private companies built turnpikes —roads on which tolls were charged. These proved very profitable, and soon a network of highways spread over England. They were now made of layers of broken stone, well drained and smooth surfaced. John McAdam devised the new method of construction and

GOODYEAR'S VULCANITE COURT at the Crystal Palace Exhibition of London, 1851. Goodyear spent about $30,000, a very large sum at the time, on this beautiful exhibit. In it he displayed products made of vulcanite, a hard rubber which could be readily cut and polished. In the same year, Goodyear set up a rubber-manufacturing company in Europe.

such roads were called "macadamized." Turnpike tolls, however, were high and the turnpikes therefore did not fully satisfy the demand for cheaper and faster means of transportation.

Canals. The expense of sending goods by road led people to make use of rivers wherever possible. Where rivers were lacking, canals were sometimes built. Canal building in Europe began near the close of the medieval period, especially after the invention of locks for the control of the flow and level of the water. The great era in the use of canals was between 1775 and 1850, not only in Great Britain and on the European continent, but also in the United States. Canals relieved the highways of a large part of the growing traffic, but both suffered through the growing competition from railroads. Some ship canals between oceans, seas, and lakes have retained their importance.

The steamboat. Frequently an invention is the result of the work of a number of men

experimenting independently on the same problem. So it was with the steamboat. Near the close of the eighteenth century several inventors applied steam power to navigation. No successful steamboat service was established, however, until Robert Fulton launched the *Clermont* on the Hudson River in 1807. His boat, a side-wheeler equipped with a Watt engine, immediately began to make regular trips between New York and Albany. Twelve years after the *Clermont's* first voyage, an American vessel, the *Savannah,* crossed the Atlantic in twenty-nine days. It had both sails and a steam engine. The first ship to cross without using sails or recoaling on the way was the *Great Western*. The voyage, made in 1838, took her fifteen days. Various improvements soon added greatly to the efficiency of ocean steamers. Iron, and later steel, replaced wood in their construction, giving the vessels added strength and buoyancy. By the 1850's the clumsy paddle wheels had given way to screw propellers.

The steam locomotive. Wooden or iron rails had long been used in mines and quarries to enable horses and human beings to draw heavier loads. As early as 1803 a horse-car line was opened in the suburbs of London. Among the first to experiment with steam locomotion on land was an Englishman, Richard Trevithick, who built a locomotive to travel on the highways. However, it could not pull a heavy load.

The invention of the "iron horse" is associated mainly with the name of an English engineer, George Stephenson. In 1814 he constructed a successful locomotive for hauling coal from mine to port. He improved his model, and in 1825 operated it on the Stockton and Darlington Railway, the first line to carry passengers and freight by steam power. Stephenson also built the Liverpool and Manchester Railway, which was opened in 1830. His famous engine, the *Rocket,* pulled a train of cars over this line at the then astonishing rate of twenty-nine miles an hour.

Growth of railways. After 1830 the building of railways went forward rapidly, not only in England but also in America and on the continent of Europe. The steam railways in Britain alone increased from 49 miles in 1830 to 15,300 miles in 1870. Many technical improvements accompanied this growth, such as T-shaped steel rails (1857), the Pullman sleeping car (1859), the Welch block-signal system (1863), and the Westinghouse air brake (1869). Short lines were gradually combined into great "trunk" systems, with branches, or "feeders," reaching into the remotest districts. The year 1854 marked the construction of the first line across the Alps, and in 1869 the first transcontinental line was completed in the United States. By 1870 the usefulness of the railroad far surpassed the dreams of its early promoters.

The telegraph. Scientists of the eighteenth century often discussed the idea of using electricity to send messages. However, no such apparatus appeared until the nineteenth century, when the telegraph was invented. As in the case of the steamboat, a number of men contributed to the invention of a workable telegraph instrument. An American, Joseph Henry, and an Englishman, Charles Wheatstone, helped prepare the way. Samuel F. B.

SOLID RUBBER TIRES FIRST USED ON STEAM TRUCKS, 1867. This omnibus pulled by a steam truck was operated in India by Thomson and Burrell about 1871. Four years earlier Thomson had constructed a rubber layer for steam truck wheels which was used successfully on Burrell's machine. The trucks weighed eight and a half tons.

Morse, an artist by profession, deserves perhaps the greatest credit. By 1844 his telegraph was a success. It found an immediate use on railroads and in sending government messages. Soon it became an invaluable aid to journalism and business.

Submarine cables. At first, few believed that a telegraph message could be carried across the sea. Experiments soon showed that wire cords, protected by wrappers of gutta-percha, a rubberlike substance, would conduct electric current under water. In 1851 a cable was laid under the English Channel from Dover to Calais. A group of American promoters, including Cyrus W. Field, then took up the project of an Atlantic cable, which should "moor the New World alongside the Old." Discouraging and costly failures marked the enterprise. The first cables broke; when finally laid, the insulation on the wires proved defective. Not until 1866 did Field's efforts result in successful contact between the New World and the Old by undersea telegraph cable. Before long, cables connected all the continents.

The postal service. A regular postal service under government management existed in Europe as early as the seventeenth century, but it was slow, expensive, and little used. Postage stamps were unknown, prepayment of postage was considered an insult to the recipient of the letter, and the rates increased according to distance. Modern postal service began in Great Britain in 1840. It was marked by prepayment of postage, the adoption of a uniform charge regardless of distance, and the use of gummed stamps. These reforms soon spread to other countries and everywhere resulted in a great increase in the use of the mails. The International Postal Union, established in 1879 at Berne, Switzerland, sets the rates to be charged for foreign postage and promotes co-operation in handling mail sent from one country to another.

Newspapers. Weekly and daily newspapers began to appear in the 1600's, but only the middle and upper classes could read and afford them. Cheap newspapers for the masses developed much later, and only after there was widespread public education. In 1814 the *London Times* installed the first steam printing press. A paper-making machine, which produced wide sheets of unlimited length, came into use shortly thereafter. These inventions lowered the cost of printing and brought newspapers within reach of an ever growing number of readers. European governments, however, for a long time tried to keep newspapers from getting into the hands of the common people. First, they imposed stamp taxes; then they taxed paper and advertisements. The upper classes feared that a cheap press would spread democratic ideas and hence would undermine their position of privilege and authority. Restrictions on the circulation of newspapers have disappeared in most countries, although even today in many countries there is a censorship of what is printed. (See page 505.) Low postal rates

SAMUEL F. B. MORSE. Famous as an artist as well as an inventor, Morse first built a successful telegraph in 1835. After years of discouragement, he was granted $30,000 by the United States Congress to put up a line between Washington and Baltimore. In 1844 Morse sent over this wire the memorable words "What hath God wrought?"

have also helped to increase the circulation of newspapers.

The Revolution in Agriculture

During the century from 1770 to 1870 changes in agriculture and industry went hand in hand. As a result of the Industrial Revolution, cities grew very rapidly and the demand for food and raw materials increased. To meet this demand, farmers produced larger quantities of farm products. The Industrial Revolution helped farmers to step up production by providing them with better agricultural implements and faster means of transporting goods. Thus farm and factory were linked together in a series of changes which have made modern civilization what it is today.

Agriculture in the seventeenth and eighteenth centuries. The agricultural system of the Middle Ages (see pages 139–140), with its "open fields" and fallow land, its backward methods and poor crops, was disappearing in the seventeenth and eighteenth centuries. The Dutch were among the first to develop better farming methods, and from them the English learned many improved ways of tilling the soil. The pioneer of scientific agriculture in England was Jethro Tull. In order to do away with the wasteful method of sowing seeds broadcast, he invented a drill which sowed the seeds in rows (1701). He also advocated the practice of pulverizing the soil between the rows with a horse-drawn cultivator. Another revolutionary development was crop rotation—a system by which a field is planted to a different crop each year for several years, after which the series is repeated, rather than growing the same crop on the same land, year after year. Viscount Townshend introduced this improvement in the middle of the eighteenth century. Rotation helped conserve the mineral contents of the soil and made it unnecessary to have the land lie fallow every

third year. The introduction of new crops, such as turnips, clover, and cabbage, helped to increase food production. The experiments of another Englishman, Robert Bakewell, in the eighteenth century did much to put animal husbandry on a scientific basis. The new methods in farming became better known through the writings of Arthur Young, who traveled widely and was a keen student of farm problems. His influence led the English government in 1793 to establish a Board of Agriculture to encourage farmers to adopt the new methods.

Machinery on the farm. The farmers of the 1700's had no better tools than the Roman farmers had in Caesar's day. Crude wooden plows, sometimes tipped with iron, did little more than scratch the soil. The ancient scythe, sickle, and flail were still in general use. At the end of the eighteenth century cast-iron plows began to take the place of wooden ones, although at first many farmers refused to use them, believing that they poisoned the soil. A great improvement came when Jethro Wood, an American blacksmith, invented a cast-iron plow in three parts (1814); a broken part could be replaced without buying an entire new plow.

The reaper. Machines to cut grain first appeared in England and Scotland, but the greatest laborsaving machine for the farm was an American invention. It was the reaper, patented in 1833 by Cyrus Hall McCormick, who was a man of vision as well as a skillful mechanic. In 1847 he set up a factory in Chicago, for he believed that it would become the center of a new grain-growing region. Here he manufactured many kinds of farm implements and laid the foundations of a large industry.

The thresher. Another invention which made large-scale farming possible was the thresher, which separates grain from the straw and the chaff. Threshing machines were built in England as early as 1732, and in the first quarter of the nineteenth century

HARVESTING GRAIN. This primitive cradle consisted of a scythe with a row of curved teeth above the blade to lay the cut grain aside in bunches. The modern combine (*above*) is a power-driven machine that cuts and threshes the grain in one operation. It did not come into general use until after World War I.

Americans imported and copied them. Small farmers, of course, could not afford such expensive machinery. The thresher could be used profitably only on large farms.

The beginning of chemical agriculture. Farmers had known for a long time that soil loses its fertility when planted with the same crops year after year. To remedy this condition, tillers of the soil first tried fallowing, then rotation, and after that used manure as a fertilizer. In the 1840's chemistry came to the aid of the farmers when a German professor, Justus von Liebig, showed that artificial fertilizers could restore the necessary minerals to the soil. As a result of his teachings, the English soon afterward began to manufacture and sell superphosphate of lime for use as a fertilizer. Another way had been found to increase the production of food without increasing the number of farm workers.

Enclosures. The revolution in farming methods was bound to change the system of landholding. The medieval "open-field" method of cultivation (see page 139), by which a farmer tilled many small strips in different parts of the manor, was wasteful of time and labor. Moreover, under this system all who held strips in one field had to plant the same crop. Farmers therefore began to exchange their scattered strips for larger pieces of land which could be enclosed with hedges or fences and cultivated independently. The enclosure movement began in England in the 1500's. It continued in western Europe until about 1840, when nearly all the open fields had given way to separate farms.

British landlordism. Enclosures meant better farming, but in Great Britain they also helped to create the large estates which have been so common there. The lord of the manor, not satisfied with enclosing his own lands, often managed by unfair means to enclose those of the peasants as well—even the meadows and forests, which the villagers had formerly used in common. There was, of course, a greater efficiency in farming large estates. More food could be produced with less labor. But as a result of the enclosures many farmers lost their small holdings and were forced to leave the farms. In his narrative poem, *The Deserted Village,* Oliver Goldsmith gives a vivid picture of the sad lot of those driven off the land by enclosure.

Landholding on the Continent. In France much of the farm land belonged to the peasants even before the French Revolution. Their holdings increased in the revolutionary period as the result of laws which took away the estates of the king, the Church, and the nobles. France is still a country of small farmers. The land reforms of the French Revolution spread to Belgium, Switzerland, western Germany, and northern Italy, where the ownership of small farms by the peasants had long been common. In other parts of Europe, however, the medieval manorial system remained throughout the nineteenth and well into the twentieth century. There a few noble families owned the land, which was worked by peasants, either as tenants or as day laborers.

Landholding in Russia. After the abolition of serfdom in Russia (1861), the nobles were required to sell a portion of their estates to the peasants. About half of the agricultural area of Russia thus changed hands. The farming land was now entrusted to the entire village, or *mir.* It was divided into small strips, which were redistributed among the inhabitants every few years. All that the peasant possessed in his own right was a house and a garden plot. The peasants were not satisfied with this arrangement, for they wished to become owners of individual farms. As we shall see (page 497), one of the first acts of the revolutionists of 1917 was to take over and distribute the huge holdings of the czar and many of the estates belonging to the nobility.

Development of Modern Capitalism

The domestic system. Toward the close of the medieval period the craft guilds grew more and more exclusive, so that most journeymen were never able to become masters. (See page 158.) Consequently, workers often left the cities and settled in villages that had no guild restrictions, where they could set up shops of their own. The movement gave rise to the domestic, or "putting out," system. For example, in the British cotton industry, a middleman with some ready money would purchase a supply of raw cotton and distribute it ("put it out") to the spinners and weavers in their homes. They, in turn, made the raw cotton into thread or cloth on their own spinning wheels or hand looms. The middleman then collected the finished materials, paid the workers an agreed price, and marketed the goods at a profit. The workmen usually eked out their small earnings by cultivating a garden plot. The domestic system was formerly common in rural New England. Something like it has survived in the system of industrial home work found in modern cities, where clothing and novelties are made in the workers' homes at so much a piece.

The factory system. Clearly, under the domestic system the middleman provided the raw materials, took most of the risks, and received most of the profits. He was a merchant capitalist. The workers, on the other hand, had to accept such pay and conditions as he was willing to offer. The sharp division between laborers and employers, which was marked under the domestic system, became complete under the factory system. One of Arkwright's, Crompton's, or Cartwright's machines was too expensive for a single family to own, too large and heavy for use in a private house, and besides, could be operated only by water or steam power. The result was that the worker left his household shop and went with hundreds of others to work in a mill or factory. The employer now provided not only the raw materials and sold the finished product but also owned the machinery and the workshop. The word "manufacturer" (Latin *manu + facere,* to make by hand) no longer applied to the handworker, but to the person who employed others to work for him.

Division of labor. Under the factory system, workers perform many separate and specialized tasks. There are about forty operations in the manufacture of ready-made clothing, nearly one hundred in the manufacture of shoes, and over a thousand in the construction of a fine watch. In each case an individual worker performs a single operation, and many workers contribute to the finished product. A worker, for example, may drill holes in metal or turn bolts on a piece of machinery all day long. Such a minute division of labor tends to make jobs in modern industry very monotonous. The employee does not take the pride in the completed article which he might take if he had produced it entirely

by himself. On the other hand, through an efficient system for dividing labor, many men working together can turn out in a few minutes an article which would otherwise require weeks or months to produce. The greater efficiency may also result in lower prices and wider markets for factory-made goods.

Large-scale production. The use of machinery, the factory system, and the division of labor made it possible to manufacture goods in enormous quantities for world-wide markets. A great expansion in trade naturally followed on the heels of the Industrial Revolution. The value of cotton exports in Great Britain increased nearly threefold in the years from 1830 to 1870. Similar increases occurred in other textile manufactures. So-called mass production in the heavy industries, such as steel and machinery, came a little later.

Capitalism. Machinery, the factory system, and large-scale production account, finally, for modern capitalism. The word "capitalism" may be briefly defined as the private ownership and control of the means of production. *Capital* is wealth used in producing more wealth. The *capitalist* is the man who invests money in an enterprise from which he expects to make a profit. If his expectations are realized, he may become wealthy, as did Arkwright, the "father of the factory system." At the start he runs the business alone or in partnership with others; in either case he gives it his personal attention. Should the business continue to expand and require more capital for buildings, machinery, and raw materials, he may organize a *corporation.* A corporation sells shares of stock to people who wish to invest their money. The management of the enterprise is entrusted to a board of directors. The profits are divided among the stockholders in the form of dividends. The corporate form of business has become more and more common. Practically all businesses of medium size or larger are incorporated. Until about 1870 most corporations were small. The "age of big business,"

Conditions in Factories and Mines

. . . At what age did you first go to work in [a factory]?—Eight.

How long did you continue in that occupation?—Four years.

Will you state the hours of labor at the period when you first went to the factory, in ordinary times?—From 6 in the morning to 8 at night.

Fourteen hours?—Yes.

With what intervals for refreshment and rest?—An hour at noon.

When trade was brisk what were your hours?—From 5 in the morning to 9 in the evening.

Sixteen hours?—Yes.

With what intervals at dinner?—An hour. . . .

Sadler Committee, 1832.

---

marked by gigantic corporations, began about 1870 and is spoken of as the Second Industrial Revolution. (See Chapter 17.)

Capital and labor. Capitalism is not new. Since the beginning of civilization there have been rich men who can hire others to work for them and poor men who have only their labor to sell. There has always been private ownership of some kinds of capital. Modern capitalism, however, has developed a distinct, well-marked "working class," consisting of skilled and unskilled workers in commerce and industry. Between the wage earner and his employer there is seldom any close personal relationship; indeed, the employer is often a corporation. Though free *politically*, as slaves and serfs in former days were not, wage earners are *economically* dependent. When depressions come, many lose their jobs and join the unhappy ranks of the unemployed. Even when employment is steady, in many instances wage earners have been overworked and underpaid. This was especially true in the years before the twentieth century. Since then, society has become increasingly concerned with the protection of the welfare of industrial workers. We shall now see what steps were taken to control the capitalistic system so that workers and employers could live in greater harmony.

Controlling an Industrialized Society

New conditions bring new ideas. With the changes produced by the Industrial Revolution came new problems. One of the most important of these concerned the relationship between industrial workers and their employers. Efforts were made to improve the workingman's lot by: (1) the formation of trade unions, (2) obtaining the passage of labor laws, and (3) obtaining public ownership of some industries.

Rise of trade, or labor, unions. Trade unions are organizations of wage earners for the purpose of improving the conditions under

... I never went to day-school; I go to Sunday-school, but I cannot read or write; I go to pit at five o'clock in the morning and come out at five in the evening; I get my breakfast of porridge and milk first; I take my dinner with me, a cake, and eat it as I go; I do not stop or rest any time for the purpose; I get nothing else until I get home, and then have potatoes and meat, not every day meat. I hurry in the clothes I have now got on, trousers and ragged jacket; the bald place upon my head is made by thrusting the corves, ... I hurry the corves a mile and more under ground and back; they weigh 300 cwt. ..

—Lord Ashley's Mines Commission, 1842.

which they work. Such associations began to appear in Great Britain during the eighteenth century as the domestic system gave way to the factory system. Under the changes which the factory system brought with it, the employer lost personal touch with his employees. At the same time, the workers in any one trade were thrown more closely together than they had been under the domestic system. They came to realize their common interests and the need for organization.

Trade unions prohibited. The trade unions immediately met opposition. Under the common law they were treated as illegal conspiracies "in restraint of trade." Moreover, the employers used their influence in Parliament to have laws passed against what were called "unlawful combinations of workers." The last of these measures, passed in 1800, provided harsh prison terms for persons who combined with others to demand higher wages, shorter hours, or better working conditions.

Trade unions gradually made legal. Agitation by trade union leaders forced Parliament in 1824 to repeal all laws against combinations of wage earners. A year later Parliament enacted a new measure permitting laborers to meet for the purpose of agreeing on the wages they would accept and the hours they would work. However, such agreements could apply only to those present at the meeting. In

Lewis Hine

CHILD LABOR in a southern United States cotton mill. During the late nineteenth and early twentieth centuries twenty per cent of all boys and ten per cent of girls between the ages of ten and fifteen were employed. Working conditions were often unsanitary and dangerous.

France, workingmen did not win the right to form unions until 1884, although agreements to stop work were legal after 1824. Finally, laws passed in England between 1871 and 1876 declared that nothing done by a group of laborers should be considered illegal unless it was also illegal when done by a single person. As a result, workingmen achieved the full right to organize and to strike—rights which they had long sought.

Trade unionism in the United States. Early in the nineteenth century American courts followed English courts in passing stern sentences on workers who tried to organize. Not until the 1840's did courts decide that workers had the right to join unions. After the War between the States labor unions grew rapidly. Working conditions in the United States were better than those in Europe because it was possible for workers to obtain cheap land and become farmers. Consequently, effective labor organizations developed more slowly. Most of the trade unions, which were composed of skilled workers, eventually banded together in the American Federation of Labor, founded in 1886.

Evils of the factory system. Improvement in the lot of wage earners has come not only through the activity of trade unions but also through government regulation of industry. As the Industrial Revolution spread, the need for such regulation increased. The factories were crowded and unsanitary. Hours of work were from sunrise to sunset. Wages were on the starvation level. Furthermore, the use of machinery permitted the employment of women and children, who would work for lower wages than men. Their hard toil amid unhealthful surroundings and their meager diet caused a high rate of sickness and death among the workers. There was some truth in the passionate words of one reformer who said that the slave trade was "mercy compared to the factory system."

The "laissez-faire" policy. The poor conditions in factories and other places of employment were naturally most prominent in Great Britain, where the Industrial Revolution was farthest advanced. At first, little effort was made to remedy these evils. Wage earners exercised no political influence; indeed, the laws against combinations had prevented them from forming unions for self-protection. However, statesmen felt improvement could result by practicing the *laissez-faire,* or "let-alone," policy. This idea originated with the eighteenth-century French economists who called themselves "physiocrats" (from physiocracy, "the rule of nature"). The government, they declared, should not regulate trade and industry, for such interference would be against the "natural laws" of supply and demand, which alone should determine wages and prices. A hands-off policy on the part of the government would secure the greatest good to the greatest number of people. This doctrine was put forward to oppose the accepted doctrine of mercantilism. (See page 205.) Adam Smith, a Scottish professor, carried the ideas of the physiocrats to England, and expanded and changed them somewhat in a famous book, *Wealth of Nations,* published in 1776.

Appearing in the year of American independence, Smith's work was a declaration of independence for industry and commerce at a time when the state exerted a rigid control over economic activity. According to Smith, the state should limit itself to three duties: "First, the duty of protecting the society from the violence and invasion of other independent societies; secondly, the duty of protecting, as far as possible, every member of the society from the injustice or oppression of every other member of it, or the duty of establishing an exact administration of justice; and thirdly, the duty of erecting and maintaining certain public works and certain public institutions, which it can never be for the advantage of any individual or small number of individuals to erect and maintain." After these three duties have been carried out, every man should be left "perfectly free to pursue his own interest in his own way, and to bring both his industry and capital into competition with those of any other man or order of men." This doctrine of laissez-faire, or let alone, made a deep impression on businessmen and statesmen. As a result the doctrine of mercantilism lost most of its supporters. Recently the doctrine of laissez-faire has been modified to meet changing economic conditions, and governments now do a great deal to encourage business and also to regulate it.

Early labor legislation. While the doctrine of laissez-faire led to an attack on the harmful practices of mercantilism, it also gave comfort to selfish employers. Many of them sought to keep the wages of the workingmen at the lowest possible levels. Fortunately, some humane employers felt that the state ought to protect those who could not protect themselves. After some agitation, especially by country gentlemen who opposed the growth of industry, and by clergymen and labor leaders, Parliament in 1802 passed the First Factory Act. It limited the working hours of pauper children bound out as apprentices in cotton mills to twelve hours a day. The law was poorly enforced. The Second Factory Act (1819) forbade the employment of children under nine years of age in the cotton industry. It also prescribed the twelve-hour day for children who were not pauper apprentices. In 1833 a third act was passed, applying to all textile factories, not merely to cotton mills. It prohibited the employment of children under nine years of age; limited the number of working hours for those between the ages of nine and thirteen to nine hours a day, and for persons under eighteen to twelve hours a day; and forbade night work. Skilled inspectors saw that the law was enforced. Another humane measure was a statute of 1842, which outlawed the employment in mines of women and girls, and of boys under ten. Five years later Parliament took the still more radical step of passing the Ten-Hour Act, which limited the labor of women and children in textile factories to ten hours a day. This measure became a law in spite of fierce opposition on the part of manufacturers. It proved so beneficial, however, that henceforth the public showed a more favorable attitude toward the idea of labor legislation. Soon the laissez-faire policy was seriously challenged.

Socialism

What is socialism? As the Industrial Revolution advanced, some reformers became convinced that laws to protect wage earners were not enough. They were disturbed by the fact that while vastly more wealth was now produced, it was very unequally distributed. The few seemed to have too much; the many had too little. The reformers therefore proposed to set up a new economic order called *socialism*, to take the place of the capitalistic system. It is important to note that in the course of its history socialism has had many prophets, who have not always agreed upon its meaning. Essentially, however, socialism may be defined as the idea that the community as a whole, or the government, should own and control the *means of production* (or at least, the principal means of production). Means of production include land, capital, mines, railroads, machines, tools, trucks, and other things used in producing goods. Socialists disagree as to how much the state should own. Some say only basic industries like steel, coal, and railroads; others want government ownership of all means of production. Socialists claim that their proposals would result in a fairer distribution of the wealth produced by industry and commerce.

The Utopian Socialists. Early in the nineteenth century there appeared a group of pioneer Socialists called "Utopians." They were named for Sir Thomas More's book,

Utopia (1516), which pictures an ideal society. They believed that by improving man's environment he would be both good and happy.

The first reformer of this group was a French aristocrat, Saint-Simon (săn′ sē′môn′, 1760–1825). He proposed a new society in which men would not exploit men, but would co-operate with others to exploit nature. The leading French Utopian was Fourier (foo′ryā′, 1772–1837). He presented a detailed scheme of social reform, centered in a small co-operative community which he called a *phalange*. The people in each phalange would own local enterprises in common and share the profits. While Fourier's ideas had little effect in France, they were influential in America. Many Fourier groups were formed here, the most famous of which was Brook Farm in Massachusetts.

Another of the early Socialists was Robert Owen (1771–1858), a wealthy Scottish manufacturer. In his cotton mills at New Lanark he established excellent working conditions; he was also a strong supporter of labor legislation and of trade unions. Among the things he introduced were co-operative stores, owned by their customers, who divided the profits among themselves. The principle of co-operative *distribution*, or consumer co-operation, was very successful in England and Owen deserves credit as its originator. He also advocated co-operation in *production*. His remedy for the ills of society was the formation of small co-operative communities similar to those advocated by Fourier. Such a community would support itself on a tract of land and its members would produce in common everything needed for their existence. Owen's experiments in co-operative production all failed, including the one at New Harmony, Indiana, which he established in 1825. But his ideas led in 1844 to the formation in England of the Rochdale Equitable Pioneers' Society, a consumers' co-operative for workers that achieved notable success. Co-operatives on

NEW HARMONY, INDIANA. Founded by the Utopian socialist Robert Owen in 1825, this experiment in co-operative living failed two years later. Every inhabitant received an equal share of life's goods and was supposed to contribute an equal amount of work. But too many of the people turned out to be shirkers and not workers.

this pattern sprang up throughout Britain and spread to the continental countries and to America.

Louis Blanc and "social workshops." Between the socialism of the Utopians and that of the Marxians (see page 322) was the socialism advocated by Louis Blanc (1813–1882), a French journalist and author. Somewhat more practical than his predecessors, he was one of the earliest of the Socialists to assert that workers could improve their condition only through their own efforts. Blanc believed that every man has a right to a job. To provide work for the unemployed, he proposed that the state should furnish the funds to set up "social workshops." The laborers themselves were to manage these factories and divide the profits, getting rid of the capitalists altogether. The revolutionary government of 1848 set up a system of national workshops. However, the men in charge of the workshops were not in sympathy with Blanc's plan. They therefore did not follow it, with the result that "battalions of paid idlers" ate up the public funds. The experiment was a miserable failure. For a time after 1848 socialism almost died out in France.

Karl Marx, 1818–1883. Before Marx, socialism was largely a dream or ideal which made little appeal to wage earners. Marx gave socialism a set of principles and a program of action to achieve its goals. He is therefore known as the "father of modern socialism," and his system is known as "scientific socialism," to distinguish it from Utopian socialism.

Born of a well-to-do German family, Karl Marx as a young man studied philosophy and history in several universities. He soon became interested in economics and started a Socialist newspaper to help the cause of the workers. He supported the revolutionary movement of 1848–1849, but when it failed the government exiled him from Germany. Eventually he went to London, where he spent the rest of his days in study and writing. He carried on his work despite the grinding poverty resulting from his lack of gainful employment. The result of his efforts was an epoch-making book, *Das Kapital* (*Capital*). The first volume appeared in 1867. It is a tremendous work, covering the whole field of economics, and has been translated into many languages. It has had a wide influence upon human thought and action.

KARL MARX

Marxism. Marx's ideas are set forth briefly and strikingly in the *Communist Manifesto,* which he and his friend, Friedrich Engels, wrote in the revolutionary year of 1848. This document showed Marx's impatience with the idealistic schemes of the Utopian socialists. He described these schemes sarcastically as "pocket editions of the New Jerusalem." To distinguish his program from that of the earlier Socialists, he gave it the name *communism*. Put in its simplest form, Marxian socialism, or communism, asserts that in every historical period economic conditions alone determine the kind of society which develops. Thus a capitalist society is the inevitable result of the Industrial Revolution. It forms a necessary stage, like feudalism, in the development of mankind. But, said Marx, all stages of history have been marked by struggles between classes. Under capitalism, the struggle is between the *bourgeoisie,* or middle class, who own the means of production and control the government, and the *proletariat,* or wage-earning class, whose labor is exploited for profit. While labor, Marx asserted, is the source of all value, laborers in fact receive only a fraction of what they produce. All the rest goes to the capitalistic bourgeoisie. Marx believed that the ruling class would become richer and the workers poorer, and that the class struggle would end with the overthrow of the capitalists by the wage earners. The proletariat would then be the ruling class and would put all means of producing wealth in the hands of the state. In its first stages the political system would be a "dictatorship of the proletariat." Later, as the socialist commonwealth gained experience in practicing co-operation, there would follow a "withering away of the state." The *Communist Manifesto* concludes with the appeal: "The proletarians have nothing to lose but their chains. They have a world to win. Workers of the world, unite!"

Revisionism. The Marxian doctrines raised a great deal of debate, even within the ranks of Socialists. One point of argument was whether the working class state was to come as the result of violent revolution or by democratic, legal means. Late in the 1800's a number of Socialists in England and Germany claimed that Marx favored constitutional and peaceful methods to achieve his goal of a proletarian state. They also believed that Socialists ought to co-operate with existing governments in approaching the goal gradually through labor legislation. In other words, they wished to make socialism *evolutionary* instead of *revolutionary*. The followers of Marx who wished to revise his ideas in this way are called "revisionists," "Social Democrats," or simply "Socialists."

Socialism and politics. During the 1870's the followers of Marx in Germany founded the Social Democratic Party. It became a model for similar organizations of Marxian Socialists in Great Britain, France, Italy, Austria, Russia, Australia, Japan, and the United States. At the outbreak of World War I (1914), the Socialists throughout the world polled about eleven million votes and elected over seven hundred representatives to the various parliaments. The revisionists dominated the Socialist parties. Only in Russia did the opponents of revisionism gain control. There they clung to the belief in the violent overthrow of capitalism, and in 1917 they succeeded by revolution in setting up a proletarian state. The Russian Socialists regard themselves as the true Marxians. They are referred to as *Communists* to distinguish them from the revisionists, or Socialists.

International socialism. To have his program succeed, Marx realized he would need the united support of workingmen all over the world. In 1864 an assembly of workers from many countries met in London and formed an organization which became known as the First International. Marx drew up a Socialist constitution for the group. In doing this he started so many quarrels that the as-sociation came to an end in 1873. A Second International took shape in 1889 at a meeting in Paris. Unlike the delegates at the London conference, the representatives to the Second International were all members of Socialist parties who believed in the revisionist ideas. By 1914 it included twelve million members from twenty-seven countries. It broke up during World War I, when Socialists generally supported their own nation rather than the cause of international socialism. A Third International was established in Moscow in 1919. From the start it was dominated by the Russian Communists.

REVIEWING THE CHAPTER

TERMS TO UNDERSTAND: *calico, "Beelzebub," standardized parts, crop rotation, enclosure, vulcanize,* Clermont, Great Western, Rocket, *domestic system, factory system, capitalism, corporation, trade union, laissez faire, Factory Acts, phalange, consumer co-operation,* Das Kapital, *socialism, revisionism.*

PERSONS TO IDENTIFY: *Kay, Hargreaves, Arkwright, Cartwright, Whitney, Watt, Davy, Bessemer, Franklin, Volta, Ampère, Faraday, Goodyear, Fulton, Stephenson, Henry, Morse, Field, McCormick, Townshend, Adam Smith, Fourier, Owen, Blanc, Engels, Marx.*

QUESTIONS TO ANSWER

1. (a) Distinguish between the First and Second Industrial Revolutions. (b) Why did the Industrial Revolution begin in England?

2. (a) Name the basic inventions in the textile industry and their inventors. (b) Explain how one invention led to another in this industry.

3. (a) Of what special advantage was the use of steam power in factories? (b) Explain the connection between Watt's improved steam engine and the coming of the "age of steel." (c) What are the twin necessities of modern industry? Why?

4. (a) Describe the condition of transportation in Europe and America on the eve of the Industrial Revolution. (b) Show how inventions slowly changed this condition. (c) What improvements in transportation and communication between continents had been made by 1870?

5. (a) What improvement in farm machinery and farm methods came in this period? (b) What were the contributions of Robert Bakewell and Arthur Young? (c) Describe the systems of landholding in England and on the Continent.

6. (a) Distinguish between the domestic system and the factory system. (b) Point out advantages and disadvantages of the division of labor. (c) Explain: "Wage earners are *politically* free but *economically* dependent."

7. (a) By what three means did workingmen try to improve their condition? (b) Give examples of each means. (c) Explain the theory of laissez faire. (d) What gains had labor made by 1870?

8. (a) Distinguish between Utopian and scientific, or Marxian, socialism. (b) What fallacies can you point out in the latter? (c) Distinguish between Communists and Socialists. (d) Who dominated the Third International?

17 Technology and Science in the Machine Age

THE AUTOMOBILE INDUSTRY revolutionized American business and society. It pioneered new methods of production, finance, marketing, management, and labor relations. A new life style emerged in response to the new means of rapid mobility.

The Industrial Revolution moved from one stage to another with ever-increasing speed. This chapter will tell how a new industrial age brought about many changes in man's living conditions during the period from about 1870 to 1914. In some instances the story will be carried down to the present day. We shall see how the invention of a new labor-saving device, the discovery of a new chemical process, or the ups and downs of the business cycle may influence the daily life of people as much as a new constitution or the overthrow of a dictator.

The Second Industrial Revolution

A new industrial age. It has already been pointed out that about 1870 the Industrial Revolution entered a period of more rapid change. (See page 305.) The discovery of new sources of power, the application of science to industry, and the increase in the size of business enterprises created a new industrial age. This may be called the Second Industrial Revolution.

Science, the handmaiden of industry. Science has made possible the amazing progress of industry. Science may be defined as an organized body of knowledge gained by exact observation and experiment. Until the nineteenth century men did not make extensive use of scientific knowledge to improve living conditions. For the most part, science was not yet advanced enough to be of great practical use. During the Second Industrial Revolution, however, science and industry became inseparable partners. Industry employed increasing numbers of scientists to help solve business and manufacturing problems. Research laboratories, first established by German chemical and electrical companies, grew to be a normal part of the factory system. Out of these poured hundreds of new inventions and processes to improve both the quality and the quantity of industrial products. Applied science, or technology, is largely responsible for the machine age.

An age of electricity. During the past century the science of physics has made possible the "age of electricity." The pioneer work of the English scientist Michael Faraday (see page 309) has already been mentioned. In the basis of Faraday's discoveries, a Belgian engineer named Gramme produced the first generator that was a commercial success (1872). Then followed the wonderful developments which made it possible to carry electric power for many miles to light cities, draw trains, and run factories. In making electric power serve mankind, Americans led the way. Foremost was Thomas Alva Edison (1847–1931), who in 1879 invented the incandescent lamp, the first practical electric light for indoor use. Between 1868 and 1900 alone, he patented nearly eight hundred devices, mostly electrical.

Electricity did not do away with coal as a source of power. In fact, coal is still used to produce a large portion of electrical energy. It provides the heat which makes the steam used to spin the generators, or dynamos. Much electricity, however, is produced by hydroelectric plants at natural waterfalls, such as the falls at Niagara. Huge dams have also been constructed. Outstanding are the Wilson and Norris dams in the Tennessee valley of the United States, and the Dnieper dam in Russia. More recently, atomic power plants have become an important source of electricity.

An age of oil. Petroleum has sometimes been called "liquid gold." Certainly the machine age owes as much to this substance as it does to any other. For some time after the first oil well was sunk in Pennsylvania in 1859, the chief use of oil was for lighting. It was refined into kerosene and burned instead of whale oil in lamps. The invention of the internal-combustion engine (see page 329) rapidly increased the demand for gasoline, which is one product in the refining of petroleum. Petroleum also became important as a lubricant. Mechanical devices cannot operate without lubrication. The invention in 1879 of the Diesel engine created still another use for oil. Today many Diesel-powered ships and locomotives operate efficiently on a cheap product of petroleum. More recently oil has proved important in making explosives and synthetic rubber. (See page 328.) In wartime oil can be vital to a nation's security. Modern industrial states, particularly those which are oil-poor, compete for its control in underdeveloped countries. Thus, in the Middle East, where at least two-thirds of the world's oil reserves are located, "oil politics" has frequently made for trouble.

The oil industry furnishes one of the best examples of the uses of technology. The increasing demand for oil products and the threat of shortages have led geologists (scientists who study the earth's composition) to search for new reserves under the seas and in the shale of mountains. Meanwhile, with new processes, chemists have been producing substantial amounts of oil from coal.

An age of steel and light metals. Perhaps no term describes modern industrial progress so well as the "age of steel." Despite the amazing growth in the use of plastics and light metals, steel continues to be the basic material on which all industry depends. The automobile, building, and railroad industries are the largest users of steel. It plays an essential part in the manufacture of thousands of other products. The average household in the United States is said to contain about 660 pounds of steel in various articles ranging from a refrigerator to tin cans and knives.

The steel age dawned in 1856 with the invention of the cheap Bessemer process for making steel. (See page 308.) Further improvements in steel manufacture came in the next two decades. The Siemens-Martin, or open-hearth, method was one; another was the Thomas-Gilchrist process, by which low-grade iron ore can be turned into good-grade steel. In the present century the science of metallurgy has contributed to the development of the steel industry. Metallurgists have discovered how to remove more impurities from the iron ore and how to make different kinds of steel alloys by adding other minerals. For these purposes they have used electric furnaces. The principal minerals added to steel in making alloys are carbon, manganese, nickel, chromium, vanadium, and tungsten. They add hardness and strength to the steel and therefore increase its usefulness.

Developments in metallurgy have also led to a rapid increase in the use of metals lighter than steel. The most important of these is aluminum. For a long time scientists had known that it existed, but not until 1886 did anyone discover how to separate it easily from its principal ore, bauxite. This discovery was the work of an American, Charles Martin Hall, and a Frenchman, Paul Louis Héroult. The Hall-Héroult process has given the world hundreds of aluminum products. A number of qualities account for the popularity of this metal. It is light in weight, spreads heat quickly and evenly, conducts electricity, corrodes less than other metals, and is non-poisonous. At first aluminum was used mostly to make cooking utensils. After World War I it became a very important material in the building of ships, trains, automobiles, and especially airplanes.

The Miracles of Applied Chemistry

Chemistry and everyday living. Chemistry is constantly at work in the daily lives of the people of modern countries. Their clothes, their food, their houses, and many articles of everyday convenience are in some degree the products of chemistry. Out of the chemical laboratory have come illuminating gas, friction matches, powerful explosives such as dynamite and nitroglycerine, Portland cement for concrete roads and buildings, artificial fertilizers, aluminum, stainless steel, woodpulp paper, and beet sugar. Among the most remarkable products of applied chemistry are the articles derived from coal tar, a by-product of coal after the gas is removed from it. When touched by the chemist's fairy wand, this black, sticky substance becomes the source of many useful things, including aniline dyes, perfumes, flavoring extracts, healing medicines, carbolic acid, naphtha, and saccharine. The chemist now creates innumerable other substances, most of them in the research laboratories of industrial firms. Some of these materials had never existed before or else had been produced only by plants or in the bodies of animals. Artificial substances of this kind are called *synthetics*. One branch of the synthetics industry deserves special mention, namely, plastics.

Plastics. The first commercially successful plastic came into being in 1869, when John Wesley Hyatt of Albany, New York, tried to invent a substitute for the ivory in billiard balls. The result was celluloid. It was made from cellulose, nitric acid, and camphor. By 1890 the Celluloid Corporation had found 25,000 different uses for the new substance, including the making of men's collars and cuffs. The chief defect of celluloid was its inflammability. In 1907 Dr. Leo H. Baekeland, a Belgian chemist who had come to the United States, developed a noninflammable plastic material called "Bakelite." The basic ingredients of this compound come from coal tar and wood alcohol. Bakelite weighs less than metal or stone, yet is very strong and will not rust or corrode. Soon after its invention it was used in manufacturing telephones and electrical insulating equipment. It won for Dr. Baekeland the reputation of "father of the plastics industry."

During both World Wars I and II, the search for wood and metal substitutes speeded up the development of the plastics indus-

PLASTIC HOUSE. The Monsanto Home of the Future was designed to show how plastics could be used structurally.

try. By 1945 the United States alone was producing more than twenty different kinds of plastic materials. Among the most useful are the cellulose plastics for making synthetic textiles (rayon, nylon), and the phenolic or coal tar plastics, for the manufacture of solid articles, such as football helmets. In recent years, polyethylene plastics, derived from natural gas and from petroleum, have taken the lead. These are formed into containers of various sorts, packaging materials, and even underground pipes. Polyethylene plastics make up a large portion of the so-called petrochemical industry. Another important plastic is synthetic rubber, which World War II brought into the limelight. To trace its story we must go back to the earlier history of rubber.

The story of rubber. The modern rubber industry is also an offspring of chemistry. The story of the discovery of vulcanization by Charles Goodyear has already been told. (See pages 309-310.) In 1890, nearly fifty years later, the rubber industry was still small. It was then producing rubber boots, shoes, raincoats, belting and hose for machinery, and a variety of smaller articles. The industry really began to boom in the early 1900's, when the automobile came into use. (See page 329.) By 1910 the world's output of crude rubber was 75,000 tons, as against 10,000 in 1870. The year 1910 marked another milestone in rubber production. In that year America received its first cultivated, or "plantation," rubber from the Far East. Before that time most of the world's rubber came from the wild trees of Brazil. In 1876 Sir Henry Wickham took some of the seeds of the Brazilian wild rubber tree to England. There he raised seedlings and shipped them to Ceylon, Malaya, and the Netherlands Indies. Gradually the cultivated rubber trees of this area outstripped the wild rubber trees of Brazil in high yield and low cost. By 1940 only 3 per cent of the world's rubber came from its original home.

Getting a steady and inexpensive supply of natural rubber from distant sources proved difficult. Therefore, chemists in the industrialized nations tried to find ways of making artificial rubber. Led by the Germans, by the 1930's rubber research had made progress in a number of countries. Under the pressure of war demands, the United States turned out large quantities of synthetic rubber during World War II. Most of it went into tires for motor vehicles. By 1968, synthetic rubber production in the United States accounted for more than three-fourths of the total output.

Chemistry and the farmer. Chemistry has also come to the aid of agriculture. It provides artificial fertilizers, spraying compounds for the control of insect pests and weeds, and methods to test soil fertility. Moreover, chemistry has given us many new uses for farm plants. For example, Dr. George Washington Carver (1864?-1943), humble American ex-slave, performed wonders with the peanut and the sweet potato. Through "chemical gymnastics," as he said, he transformed the peanut into such different products as face powder, shampoo, butter, creosote, dandruff cure, soaps, and wood stains.

Thus chemistry added another dimension to the efficiency and productivity of the farm. Already the farmer's job had been lightened and made more profitable by the use of new machinery, by the tractor and motor truck, by electricity, and by the scientific selection and breeding of plants and animals—a contribution of applied biology. The net result was an immense increase in the output of food and a decrease in the labor needed to produce it. The Second Industrial Revolution made agriculture a mass-production industry.

The Transportation Revolution

The technology of the Second Industrial Revolution also brought about remarkable changes in transportation. It led to vast improvements in many of the old ways of conquering distance and to the development of a number of new means of travel.

Railroads. Railroad transportation since the 1870's has been marked by greater speed, safety, and comfort. Steel has taken the place of wood in the building of cars; the refrigerator car has made it possible to ship food safely for long distances; and electric signaling and switching devices have added to the safety of railway travel. Increased speed has become a yardstick of railroad development. In 1904 an English train on a special run attained an average speed of 84.6 miles per hour—a record that was to stand for thirty years. Today a streamlined, Diesel-driven train can travel over one hundred miles an hour, and on long, regular runs can average well over seventy miles an hour. Railroads are making ever-increasing use of Diesel locomotives and electric locomotives. These operate more efficiently than steam locomotives. Electric traction on street railways had already become common during the 1880's, when the faster trolley car began to take the place of the horsecar in cities. Motor vehicles and airplanes have taken a larger and larger share of passenger business away from the railways. As freight carriers, however, the railroads are still the most important agency.

The automobile. No creation of man's inventive mind has changed his way of living more than has the automobile. With it have come countless new jobs, many new industries, and a new style of home and community life.

The pioneer self-propelled vehicle was a steam-powered "road engine." A French inventor built a crude, three-wheeled road engine in 1770. An American built a steam carriage in 1787. In 1801 an English inventor built a steam carriage for passengers. (See page 311.) Repeated efforts to popularize the new vehicle failed because the roads were bad and people looked upon it as a nuisance. A successful automobile had to wait for the in-

vention of a practicable, high-speed internal-combustion engine. Throughout the nineteenth century inventors in several countries worked on this problem. In the 1880's a German, Gottlieb Daimler (dīm'lĕr), invented a gasoline motor, which was soon used to propel a "horseless carriage." By the early 1900's Americans had taken the lead in the improvement of the new means of transportation. The name of Henry Ford stands out among the pioneers in automobile manufacture. His great contribution was assembly-line production. This means that parts are assembled on a moving platform, or conveyor; every workman does one operation only; and corresponding parts are exactly alike and interchangeable. Motorcars displaced horse-drawn vehicles almost entirely and brought about a decline in the use of trolley cars. Today they compete with the railroads for both passengers and freight.

Aviation. From earliest times man had envied flying birds. Ancient legends and fables told of gods and mythical heroes with wings.

HENRY FORD and his Quadricycle, his first car, built in 1896. Ford produced inexpensive cars by using mass production. By 1923, he had sold over a million and a half automobiles.

A DIRIGIBLE prepares to land. This type of lighter-than-air craft was first designed by Count Zeppelin in 1900. By the time noncombustible gases were developed to keep the airships aloft safely, the airplane had taken over.

Leonardo da Vinci, Renaissance genius (see page 182), studied the flight of birds and built a model flying machine. But man did not actually get off the ground until 1783, when the Montgolfier brothers of France launched a hot-air balloon. Experiments with lighter-than-air craft continued throughout the nineteenth century. In 1900 Count Zeppelin, a German army officer, built a rigid, cigar-shaped airship powered by gasoline motors. This type, the dirigible, was further improved so that by 1932 the Germans had established regular transatlantic airship service. Unfortunately, the giant gas bags ran into a series of fatal mishaps. The worst was the explosion of the *Hindenburg* as it was landing at Lakehurst, New Jersey, in 1937. Thereafter commercial travel by dirigible ended. A small, nonrigid airship, the blimp, is still used.

Meanwhile, heavier-than-air flying machines were proving safer and faster than the lighter-than-air type. Among the early pioneers of the airplane was S. P. Langley, an American scientist. In 1903 he built a heavier-than-air craft with a gasoline engine. It was abandoned during its first trials because of accidents. Where Langley had led the way and failed, the Wright brothers of Dayton, Ohio, succeeded. On December 17, 1903, at Kitty Hawk, North Carolina, Orville Wright made the first successful flight in a heavier-than-air machine. It lasted only twelve seconds, but it

ushered in a new era in transportation. "They done it!" cried a fisherman who looked on. "They done it. Danged if they ain't flew!"

The air age was not long in coming. The Wrights rapidly improved their airplane and in 1906 made a flight of over forty miles. In 1909 a Frenchman, Louis Blériot, flew across the English Channel. Five years later, in World War I, aviators were assisting in military operations in France and Germany. In 1919 Captain John Alcock and Lieutenant A. W. Brown of England made the first nonstop flight across the Atlantic. More spectacular was the achievement of Charles A. Lindbergh in flying alone from New York to Paris (3160 miles) in 1927. This event helped make the public aware of the immense possibilities of aviation. During the 1920's regular airlines for carrying mail and passengers were established in both Europe and America. Still further revolutionary advances in air transportation came as a result of World War II.

Passenger air travel increased by leaps and bounds. Transoceanic scheduled flights became common. World War II also gave rise to jet and rocket planes, some of them capable of exceeding the speed of sound (about 760 miles per hour). In 1958 the British began jet passenger flights between Europe and the United States. Ten years later, the world's first supersonic passenger transport (SST), the British-French *Concorde,* made its appearance. Similar American planes were to be in production by 1971. It was anticipated that speeds up to 1800 miles per hour would be attained by such airliners, cutting transatlantic flying time to less than two hours.

The submarine. Unlike other kinds of modern transportation the submarine has been designed almost exclusively for wartime use. As far back as the Revolutionary War an American inventor built a tiny submarine which tried unsuccessfully to sink a British warship. Robert Fulton was encouraged by Napoleon to make several submarines. One of them remained underwater for four hours and blew up a small vessel with a torpedo. During the American War between the States the Confederates used underwater boats propelled by steam power. Thereafter in several countries inventors made improvements on the submarine. One of the most successful inventors was an Irish-American, J. P. Holland, who in 1900 sold a boat named after himself to the United States. During World War I the Germans used the submarine extensively and with deadly effect. (See page 456.) World War II also saw a great deal of activity by undersea boats.

Modern Communication

Modern means of transportation have not been the only conquerors of distance. Man has achieved even more rapid communication by sending signals and the human voice over electrified wires and air waves.

The telephone. The word *telephone* comes from the Greek words meaning "at a distance" and "voice." Experimentation with crude forms of the telephone began in the same decade which produced the telegraph. (See page 310.) Little progress took place until 1876, when Alexander Graham Bell, a native of Edinburgh residing in Boston, first sent the human voice over wires. Since that time, Bell, Thomas A. Edison, and others have made many improvements in the telephone. Long-distance messages are transmitted overland by wire and across the seas by means of submarine cables or by radio.

Wireless telegraphy. The invention of wireless telegraphy and the radio grew out of a basic discovery made by a German, Heinrich Hertz. In 1886 he demonstrated the existence of electromagnetic waves, or vibrations, known after him as "Hertzian waves." It remained for an Italian, Guglielmo Marconi, to turn this discovery into a great world force. In 1896 Marconi took out his first patent on the wireless. Three years later wireless messages were sent between France and England across the Channel, and in 1901 Marconi sent the first wireless signals across the Atlantic. The first transatlantic radiogram appeared in a London newspaper on March 30, 1903. Marconi's invention set the stage for the development of both radio and television, which we shall describe later.

Motion pictures. Today the "movies" are among the leading communications industries. They furnish the world's peoples with a large share of their entertainment.

The development of motion pictures began in the 1860's, but little progress was possible until after the invention of celluloid film and the projector. In 1887 an American named Goodwin invented the transparent, flexible celluloid film. Edison made use of it in his kinetoscope, a kind of "peepshow" motion picture machine (1889). The showing of life-size pictures to groups of people was not possible until 1895, when Jenkins in America and the Lumière brothers in France invented the projector. At first, motion pictures were shown in connection with stage programs. Not until 1905 did a theater offer films exclusively. Attempts soon followed to have a musical or spoken accompaniment for the pictures. Edison, among others, constructed a device for this purpose, but it was not a success. In 1926 Warner Brothers introduced the vitaphone, the first successful machine for projecting sound pictures. Thereafter, "talkies" rapidly took the place of silent films. Today, color movies and wide-screen projection have added to the viewer's pleasure.

The Industrial Revolution and Population

One of the most important features of the machine age has been the enormous growth of the world's population. In 1650, not long after the Thirty Years' War, the total number of the earth's people was about half a billion. Another two hundred years passed before it doubled. But in the next eighty years, between 1850 and 1930, it doubled again.

IMMIGRATION to the United States from European countries during the nineteenth century was often caused by increased population growth. Here German emigrants for New York embark on a Hamburg steamer.

Although population growth began to show a distinct upward trend by about 1650, it was the Industrial Revolution that brought the sharpest climb in numbers of people. Population experts (called *demographers*) do not all agree on what the most important reasons are. Nevertheless, with improved farming methods and better health and sanitation standards, we know that food output increased and people lived longer. Despite this seemingly bright prospect, Thomas Malthus, an English clergyman, took a gloomy view of the future. In 1798 he published *An Essay on the Principle of Population*. He concluded that even though famine, pestilence, and war at times would act to check population growth, the increase in the number of people would outstrip the food supply. Therefore, he thought, many human beings were doomed to a miserable existence.

What Malthus did not foresee was that the continuing progress of science and technology could enable man to produce ample food for a constantly growing population. This does not mean that undernourishment and actual starvation have reached the vanishing point throughout the world. It means that wherever man's scientific knowledge has been applied and shared, people need not go hungry. The world can produce enough food for far more people than now exist. The number of people who can be supported in a given region does not depend primarily on the amount of food that they raise. It depends more on their production of raw materials and manufactured goods which they can exchange for food.

Effects of the Machine Age on Population

Migrations. Another characteristic of the machine age is the migration of people from one country to another. During the past century there has been an extraordinarily large emigration of Europeans to lands beyond the seas. The United States received about 38.5 million immigrants between 1820 and 1945. Nearly all of them came from Europe. Millions more went to the British colonies and South America. Emigration from Europe increased rapidly after the middle of the nineteenth century. The many improvements in steam navigation at that time lowered the cost of ocean travel and thus encouraged people to emigrate. More important as causes for leaving Europe were the unsettled political and economic conditions and the better opportunities for making a living in the newer areas of the world.

In the twentieth century some governments have limited the number of immigrants by applying various tests. In this way they have tried to select those they considered the most desirable. After World War I, the United States, long a haven for the world's poor and oppressed, adopted a strict new policy. It set up a quota for each nationality (excepting the Americas), a system which favored western and northern Europeans. Asiatics were excluded until 1945. In 1965 Congress abolished the national origins quota system. Immigrants are now "admitted on the basis of their skills and their close relationship to those already here."

Growth of cities. The population of the leading industrial countries is mostly concentrated in cities. The rapid growth of the cities came largely as the result of the rise of the factory system, the mechanization of farming, and the improvement in the means of travel and transportation. Moreover, immigrants, especially in the United States, tended to crowd into the cities because they lacked money to buy farmland and jobs were more available in the industrial centers. At the opening of the nineteenth century western Europe was still mainly rural, as southeastern Europe is today. In 1800 Europe had only fourteen cities of more than one hundred thousand inhabitants; in 1900 it had one hundred and forty. Now there are many more. London in 1800 contained under a million inhabitants; today Greater London has about 8,500,000 within its borders. Paris contains more than five times as many people as it had shortly before the French Revolution. Before World War II Berlin had over twenty times as many people as it had during the reign of Frederick the Great. Tokyo, Japan, in a nation late to become industrialized, leaped from a population of two million in 1900 to four million in 1923. Today its people number about nine million. In 1800 the United States had only six cities of over eight thousand inhabitants. By 1960 it had nearly three hundred cities with a population of over fifty thousand each.

Distribution of wealth. Science and invention have made it possible for the civilized world to satisfy the material needs of a large and expanding population. Life, therefore, should be healthier and happier for everyone. Yet there is poverty in the midst of plenty. We have invented the machinery for mass production and have solved the problems of making vast quantities of goods at low cost. Yet the markets are sometimes filled with goods that cannot be sold because the power to purchase them is lacking. Peoples living in modern industrial nations have not yet got to the point of distributing properly year in and year out the vast quantities of goods they are able to produce. Thus the comforts and luxuries of modern industrial society are not within the reach of all.

Effects of the Machine Age on Commerce

Expansion of commerce. A tremendous expansion of commerce came on the heels of the Industrial Revolution. It is estimated that the commerce of the world increased over

1200 per cent in the nineteenth century. The expansion continued until 1929, when a world-wide depression began.

Many hindrances to trade which existed in the Middle Ages have disappeared in modern times. As national governments grew strong, they suppressed robbery on their highways and piracy in their territorial waters. Moreover, with the death of feudalism feudal lords no longer imposed burdensome tolls on transportation and travel. In the late 1700's a movement began to reduce the high duties levied by European states on imports and exports.

Free trade in Great Britain. Great Britain went still further in the 1800's and adopted free trade; that is, she abolished tariffs. Great Britain enjoyed almost a monopoly in most lines of industry. She had no reason to fear the competition of foreign manufacturers.

CORN LAWS REPEALED. This 1846 cartoon from *Punch* applauded the repeal of the tariff on wheat and other grains.

PEEL'S CHEAP BREAD SHOP,
OPENED JANUARY 22, 1846.

Therefore it was to her advantage to lower or do away with the duties on imports, especially those raw materials. William Pitt the Younger began the work of tariff reform; Sir Robert Peel continued it in the 1840's; and Gladstone completed it.

For many years the corn laws restricted or prohibited the importation of wheat and other grains into Great Britain. The corn laws were intended to encourage grain production by British farmers. Manufacturers and factory workers objected to the high prices that resulted. In 1846, after much agitation, the hated corn laws were repealed. Since then Great Britain has secured the bulk of her food abroad. She has paid for imports of food with the products of her mines and factories.

The major trading nations. Until World War I Great Britain led the world in trade. There are several reasons for this. The Industrial Revolution began in Great Britain, and for many years she alone had large quantities of manufactured goods for export. Furthermore, Great Britain's success in acquiring colonies promoted her commerce. The bulk of the trade of British dependencies was with the mother country. Finally, Britain was mistress of the seas. This position protected her trade in time of war; besides, it gave her ample numbers of ships, docks, and sailors for carrying on trade. Although Great Britain is no longer the commercial leader of the world (see page 527), she still relies largely on foreign trade for a living. She imports most of her foodstuffs and raw materials, and exports chiefly manufactured goods, as well as machinery, chemicals, textiles, iron and steel.

Germany's foreign trade increased threefold between 1871 and 1914. This was a part of the remarkable industrial development which followed her unification. (See page 398.) On the eve of World War I, Germany ranked next to Great Britain among commercial nations. Her imports were mostly foodstuffs to supply the rapidly growing population, and raw materials for her expanding factories. Exports consisted mainly of manufactures (chemicals, dyestuffs, optical goods, machinery), coal, and beet sugar.

In 1914 France stood third among European countries in volume of foreign trade. The French people are skilled in the creation of such artistic luxuries as millinery, laces, gloves, perfumes, and fine chinaware. These, together with silks and wines, make up the bulk of their exports.

The resources of the United States are so great and so varied that internal trade furnishes a large part of her needs. This country is more nearly self-sufficient than any other leading country. Nevertheless, in the twentieth century many American industries produced more goods than they could sell profitably at home. Hence the export of manufactured articles grew steadily until the world depression of 1929.

The return to protective tariffs. In the second half of the nineteenth century the United States, Germany, and France broke away from the liberal policy of free trade and returned to a policy of protective tariffs. Other national states soon followed their example. They sought in this way to protect their "infant industries" against competition from foreign goods. They hoped that their own factories then would be able to supply the home market and even to compete with Great Britain in the markets of the world. Protectionism formed a part of the nationalistic movement which swept through Europe in the nineteenth century.

After World War I the United States led the way in boosting tariffs to new high levels. American duties reached their peak in the Hawley-Smoot Act of 1930, which raised rates 20 per cent above previous levels. Other governments were quick to follow our example. By early 1932 more than twenty of them had increased their tariffs. Some did so as a reprisal against the United States. Even Great Britain, long a free-trade stronghold, turned to protectionism. In 1931 Parliament imposed comparatively high duties on a long list of imported manufactures. However, the products of British colonies and dominions were given more favorable rates than foreign goods.

Tariff barriers stifle international trade. Nations found it difficult to sell their surpluses and buy what they needed. In 1934 the United States began an effort to revive trade by passing the Reciprocal Tariff Act. It gave the President power to raise or lower duties by as much as 50 per cent in bargaining with other countries for reduced tariffs on American goods. Before World War II over twenty governments had signed agreements with the United States for mutual tariff reductions. The result was a marked increase in trade.

The Effects of the Machine Age on the Economic System

The age of big business. The Second Industrial Revolution brought a marked change in the size of business concerns. Machine methods and improved transportation led to a concentration of manufacturing in the hands of a comparatively small number of large corporations. In mass-production industries big units have certain advantages over small ones. They can make maximum use of expensive machinery, employ skilled managers and research experts, carry the division of labor to the point of greatest efficiency, and make savings through large-scale purchases of raw materials. Large companies found that it paid to operate at full capacity. In an effort to sell an increasing amount of goods they tried to capture the markets of rival firms by carrying on costly price-cutting battles. Such cutthroat competition generally led to the combination of the competing companies and often to the establishment of a monopoly. Either one company would defeat and absorb its competitors, or the rivals would join forces to avoid collapse. The resulting combination might then become a monopoly. That means it would control the production or sale of a commodity to the extent that it could fix prices above a reasonable profit level.

In Europe monopolistic combinations are known as cartels; in the United States they are often referred to as trusts. Large business combinations that are international in scope are also called cartels. In these, agreements are made among like corporations in two or more countries to fix prices, limit production, and divide raw materials and sales territory. International combinations of this sort have been formed in the steel, oil, aluminum, electrical, chemical, and other industries. Many people believe that, by maintaining artificially high prices, trusts and cartels interfere with full production and full employment. In some countries, particularly the United States, laws have been passed to curb monopolistic practices. However, such efforts to restrict big business have met with little success.

In Europe the trend toward consolidation was especially marked in Germany and England. However, combinations there did not, by and large, reach the gigantic size of those in the United States, as, for example, the United States Steel Corporation or the Standard Oil Company. The very large corporations in America comprise only about 5 per cent of the total number of industrial companies, but they employ about 70 per cent of all the workers employed by industrial companies and produce 90 per cent of the manufactured goods.

The marketing system. Improvements in transportation have brought remarkable changes in the selling of goods and services. Today the producer seldom disposes of his goods directly to the consumer. In place of the old system of weekly markets and annual fairs, a complicated marketing system has developed that maintains a steady flow of goods from producers through wholesalers and retailers to consumers. As business expands, the number and variety of middlemen increase. Among them are commission merchants, jobbers, managers of produce and stock exchanges, and brokers. Some of these middlemen perform valuable services in making commodities available to large numbers of customers. For example, co-operatives aid farmers in selling their products.

To aid in the buying and selling of goods, banking has played an increasingly important part. Although banking is an ancient business, its operations expanded greatly after the Industrial Revolution, which multiplied the wealth of the western world. Many owners of capital (savings or profits) entrusted it to bankers for safekeeping or investment and received interest for its use. Bankers also made (and still make) loans to businessmen and other individuals who needed cash to buy goods or to tide them over bad times. The borrower, of course, paid interest on such loans.

Every aspect of business enterprise involves risk of loss. It is now possible to get insurance against almost every kind of misfortune. The farmer insures his crops against hail or windstorm; the merchant insures his goods against theft or fire; and the shipowner insures his vessel against loss at sea. Marine insurance arose in medieval Italy, but for centuries it has centered in London in the great firm of Lloyd's. The first fire insurance policies were written after the great fire in London during the reign of Charles II (1666). Other forms of business insurance (theft, liability, workmen's compensation, and so on) originated much later. In recent decades life insurance companies have experienced an extraordinary growth.

To encourage the purchase of their products, business firms besiege the public with every imaginable appeal in newspapers, mag-

DEPRESSION, 1930

azines, billboards, electric signs, and over the radio and television. They believe that "it pays to advertise."

Technological unemployment. The machine age has also brought with it what is known as "technological unemployment." Each time a labor-saving machine or process is introduced, some workers are displaced. They may or may not be able to find jobs in the same or other industries. At best they will be unemployed for a time. This means loss of purchasing power, suffering, and discontent. Over a long period of time, however, machines may tend to increase the number of jobs. They lower the costs of production and thus bring lower prices, increased sales, and a demand for additional workers. Machines do not necessarily have this effect in monopolistic industries, where prices may be kept high despite lower production costs.

The business cycle. The capitalistic, or free-enterprise, system has run a somewhat unsteady course between good times and bad. The change from prosperity to depression and back again is known as the "business cycle." During the past century depressions have grown more and more severe. At least

they have brought suffering to a larger number of people. Moreover, a depression arising in a major industrial country, particularly in the United States, nowadays spreads like a contagion to all other countries for which it is a market.

Economists have offered various explanations of the causes of the business cycle. No explanation has proved thoroughly satisfactory. One widely accepted theory says that depressions are due to overproduction and underconsumption. According to this explanation, during boom phases of the cycle, corporations and individuals save too large a portion of their incomes and spend too little for consumers' goods and for wages. The result is that industry produces more goods than can be sold. Investment in new or expanding industries falls off, and idle savings accumulate in banks and other savings institutions. Surplus goods pile up, prices and profits fall, and merchants with large stocks on hand go into bankruptcy. Manufacturers, receiving fewer orders, reduce their outputs or shut down their plants entirely. Investment to establish new enterprises or expand old ones comes to a stop. Widespread unemployment and suffering follow. Before good times return, millions of people may be forced to accept public relief. As discontent grows, governments are sometimes endangered. Throughout much of the world this sequence of events marked the great depression of the early 1930's.

Attempts to remedy our economic ills. Our economic difficulties are man-made; the solution of them must also be man-made. The machine age is a mighty achievement of modern civilization. Few would wish to retrace their steps to an age when there were no labor-saving machines, no rapid transportation, and no mass-production industries. Machinery now does much of the roughest and hardest work, saves human labor, and makes possible an enormous production of goods. But it should also be possible to distribute purchasing power widely enough so that people can buy all the goods and services they need for a decent standard of living. Uninterrupted mass consumption is just as essential as mass production. In recent times efforts have been made to maintain the purchasing power of low-income groups and to provide them with greater security. Governments have enacted social legislation, such as laws which reduce the hours of labor and provide insurance benefits for unemployment, sickness, accidents, and old age. Other efforts have aimed at a greater control, and sometimes outright ownership, of business enterprise by the state.

Government regulation and ownership. Government regulation of industry began in the nineteenth century. (See page 319.) As time went on, these restrictions increased in number. Nowadays most governments limit the employment of children so that they need not be absent from school. Governments also limit the hours of work, not only of women and children in most industries, but frequently also of men in mines and factories. They require employers to install safety appliances in their plants. In general, govern-

ments have made employers responsible for the lives, limbs, and health of their employees while at work. Government control of the conditions of labor was carried furthest in the countries which after World War I set up dictatorships—Italy, Germany, and Russia. There people gave up their liberty in the hope of having greater economic security. But even democratic governments have found it necessary to pass more laws for the regulation of industry and for the protection of people with small incomes. Besides the Factory Acts (see page 319) of the last century, Great Britain has had social insurance in some form since 1897, Germany since 1883, and France since 1898. Today Britain has "cradle to grave" protection against unemployment and sickness; and the government provides pensions for widows, orphan children, and the aged. Canada has a system of family allowances to aid parents of small and average income to support their children. France in 1930 and Germany in the 1920's (see page 530) enlarged their programs of social insurance. In the United States the Social Security Act of 1935 set up a national plan of insurance for the jobless, the aged, dependent children, and the blind. Some Latin American countries have developed social insurance systems. Among the most advanced in this respect are Mexico, Brazil, Chile, and Uruguay.

It is clear that the modern state is no longer merely an agency to keep law and order. To a greater or lesser extent, in all countries it has also become a social welfare agency. This means that the state takes action to protect the less fortunate members of society. Thus, as already noted, the state regulates private enterprise to an ever-increasing degree. But it does not stop there. The state itself operates some business enterprises. Indeed, in Communist countries the state has abolished practically all private enterprise.

In modern times, postal service and coinage have always been in government hands.

Likewise, railways, telegraph and telephone service, and public utilities have for years been state enterprises in Great Britain, most other European countries, and Japan. Even the United States, where public ownership of business has been unpopular, made a new departure in 1933. In that year the government established the Tennessee Valley Authority. It built dams which, among other things, were used to produce electricity. "Democratic socialism," as some call it, perhaps reached a peak in 1945, when the Labor party came into power in Great Britain. It proceeded to nationalize, or place under government ownership, the coal mines, the Bank of England, major transportation facilities, and the steel mills. Subsequently, in 1953, the Conservative party returned the steel industry to private ownership. Sweden, too, furnishes a notable example of government control of the economy. The Swedish state operates one third of the mines of the country, owns railroads which compete with private lines, and controls more than a third of the electric power industry. Besides, the government encourages and aids both producers' and consumers' co-operatives.

Thus, in economic matters there has been a tendency to abandon the policy of laissez faire, or "let alone." Like it or not, the machine age has led governments more and more to direct the economic life of their citizens. Nevertheless, countries with the highest standard of living have not gone to extremes. They have what economists call "mixed economies," that is, systems in which there is considerable government regulation and yet a wide area of freedom for private business.

Physical Sciences in the Machine Age

The nature of modern science. As we have seen, the marvels of the new industrial age owed much to the use of applied science. It was the combined efforts of the thinker and

the craftsman, of the pure scientist and the engineer or inventor, that resulted in changing almost every aspect of life in the western world.

A few bold and original thinkers of the seventeenth century had laid the intellectual foundations of modern science and technology. They provided both a spirit of inquiry and a method of approach for unraveling the mysteries of the world of nature. One of these pioneers, Sir Francis Bacon, though not a researcher himself, gave us the essentials of the scientific method, namely, observation and experiment. (See page 184.) He recognized that the causes of things in the physical world may lie deeply hidden in nature, but that man through his power of reason could discover these causes and also determine their effects. Another pioneer of scientific thought, Sir Isaac Newton (see page 185), went a step further. With Galileo's work as a starting point, he discovered that the whole universe is regulated by the same natural laws and that these laws can be expressed in mathematical terms. Newton thus applied with epoch-making results the scientific method which Bacon had urged men to use. This way of thinking about man's natural surroundings, based on collecting facts and testing them, furnished the foundation for all later scientific progress.

The effects of the so-called Newtonian revolution went far beyond the realm of science. The eighteenth-century "philosophers" of the Enlightenment (see page 269) used the scientific method to test the soundness of all human ideas and institutions. Through it they justified the overthrow of traditional ideas about government, religion, and the class structure of society. Freedom of thought became their watchword. "We think," said Diderot, "that the greatest service to be done to men is to teach them to use their reason, only to hold for truth what they have verified and proved." Man could, indeed, fashion his world as he saw fit and become master of his destiny.

We shall now turn to some of the major accomplishments of theoretical (pure) science, although it becomes more and more difficult to draw the line between applied and pure science.

Astronomy. Oldest of the sciences, astronomy did not in any sense become "scientific" before Galileo, Kepler, and Newton had made their special contributions. (See page 185.) In modern times it has become closely linked with the other physical sciences—chemistry, physics, and geology. All are concerned with matter and energy. It is the special task of astronomy to study the size, movements, distances, and composition of bodies beyond the earth. It has furnished the basis for keeping correct time, for guiding navigators over sea and land and through the air, and for making accurate maps. Moreover, by studying the pressure and heat of the stars, astronomers have added to man's knowledge of the nature of matter.

For since the qualities of bodies are only known to us by experiments, we are to hold for universal all such as universally agree with experiments. . . . We are certainly not to relinquish [give up] the evidence of experiments for the sake of dreams and vain fictions of our own devising.

—Sir Isaac Newton, *Principia*.

With improved telescopes, eighteenth-century astronomers brought within eye range additional stars and planets. The greatest stargazer of this period was Sir William Herschel (1738–1822), a musician-turned-astronomer. Besides discovering the planet Uranus, he built the best telescope of his time and mapped the stars of the Milky Way. In doing so, he added further proof of Newton's law of universal gravitation. In the nineteenth century, astronomers located another planet, Neptune, and began the immense task of photographing the heavens. But the most important breakthrough came with the development of the spectroscope by two German scientists, Gustav Kirchhoff and Robert Bunsen, one a physicist and the other a chemist (a significant example of the interrelationship of the sciences). In 1859, using their new instrument to study the sun's rays, they found spectra (bands of different colors as through a prism) that were identical with those produced by earthly substances. The result was that they could determine what chemical elements existed on the sun. Kirchhoff and Bunsen thus founded a new branch of astronomy called astrophysics. Other scientists have since developed spectrum analysis to the point where they can tell the temperature of a star by analyzing its light.

Twentieth-century astronomers have had the advantage of vastly improved telescopes, such as the two-hundred-inch reflector type on Mt. Palomar, California. They have, however, used the telescope increasingly to make photographs rather than to gaze directly at the heavens. In our own day the radio telescope, used for locating stars not visible through an ordinary one, has become an important tool of the astronomer.

The beginning of modern chemistry and physics. The chemist tells us primarily what solids, liquids, and gases are composed of and how they may be broken down and put together again into new combinations, as in synthetic products. The physicist is interested primarily in explaining the energy in matter, aside from its chemical changes. But the interactions of matter and energy are continuous. Therefore, no exact distinction between the two sciences can be made. In fact, all modern sciences overlap; we shall become more aware of this as we study their history.

In the eighteenth century, attempts to discover the real nature of heat furnished a bridge between physics and chemistry. In 1774, Joseph Priestley, an Englishman, discovered the gas that is necessary to the burning process, namely, oxygen. Another Englishman, Henry Cavendish (1731–1810), found a new gas which he named "inflammable air," later to be called hydrogen. It remained for a Frenchman, Antoine Lavoisier (1743-1794), to use the discoveries of Priestley and Cavendish to create a revolution in chemistry, just as Newton had done in physics. Lavoisier solved the problem of combustion by showing that fire is the result of the rapid combination of other chemical elements with oxygen. He also proved that water is a compound of hydrogen and oxygen. Moreover, his careful experiments led him to conclude that although matter may be altered in form, it does not change in amount. This is called the law of conservation of matter. It was accepted as true until the work of Einstein.

Lavoisier's accomplishment earned for him the title "father of modern chemistry." Unfortunately, his life was cut short when he fell victim to the guillotine during the Reign of Terror. "It required but a moment to cut off his head; it will take a century to produce another like it," sadly remarked a scientist friend.

The world of the atom. The discoveries of Priestley, Cavendish, and Lavoisier disproved the old Greek idea that earth, air, fire, and water compose the original "elements" out of which everything else is made. Democritus, a Greek who lived in the fifth century B.C., pro-

ANTOINE LAVOISIER

posed a theory which modern physicists have recently used to revolutionize their science. Democritus thought that all material things were made of atoms—particles so small that they could not be divided. (See page 82.) It was not until the nineteenth century that this theory was really tested.

In 1803 John Dalton, an English Quaker schoolmaster, advanced the theory that all forms of matter are composed of atoms—indivisible and unchangeable particles. He believed that atoms are of different kinds, that each kind represents a chemical element, and that one chemical element can be distinguished from another by the relative weight of its atoms. Thus, hydrogen atoms weigh less than those which form oxygen. Dalton also thought that atoms of different elements unite, forming what we now call "molecules," the smallest particles in chemical compounds. For example, the union of two atoms of hydrogen with one atom of oxygen always produces a molecule of water (H_2O). Dalton believed that atoms unite in fixed proportions which can be measured. The main aspects of Dalton's atomic theory have been proved; yet Dalton had never seen an atom. Not until 1957 was the human eye able to view an atom. Even then, it was not a direct view, but a photograph taken through a microscope.

After Dalton's time chemists demonstrated that all matter exists in a solid, liquid, or gaseous form, and that matter can be changed from one of these forms to another by adding or removing heat. In 1869 a Russian chemist, Mendeléef (měn′dĕ-lā′yĕf), worked out the so-called Periodic Table, in which he classified all the known elements according to their atomic weights. He predicted that additional elements would fit into certain gaps in his list. These elements have since been discovered. Moreover, during and since World War II, research in connection with nuclear energy has led to the production of a number of new elements. Over one hundred are now known.

Electricity and the atom. The common ground shared by physicists and chemists becomes especially clear with regard to the atom. Physicists for many years tried to find answers to the questions "What is electricity?" and "Where does it come from?" Men such as Franklin, Volta, Faraday, and Hertz explored the nature of electrical activity without fully answering these questions. (See pages 287, 330.) In 1895 a German, Roentgen (rûnt′gĕn), opened a new door of science. He discovered that an electric current sent through gases produces radiations which can penetrate solid substances. Not knowing what these radiations were, he called them X rays. Three years later a Frenchman, Pierre Curie, assisted by his Polish wife, obtained from the mineral pitchblende the marvelous element radium. It proved to be a better source of gamma rays—exactly like X rays in character—than any other element then known. Madame Curie and her husband, along with Henri Becquerel (bĕk′rĕl′), shared the Nobel prize for their outstanding discovery in science. After her husband's death Madame Curie herself received the prize in 1911 for her distinguished service to science. She died in 1934, perhaps the greatest woman scientist in history.

The discovery of X rays and the rays emitted by radium opened a new world to physicists. They soon found many other radioactive substances and proved that the rays emitted by them are composed of particles of electricity. In 1897 an English physicist, J. J. Thomson, discovered the particles of one of these rays and called them *electrons*. He showed that electrons form a part of every atom. Thus he upset Dalton's idea that the atom is the smallest unit of matter and cannot be divided. Further research by a number of scientists has given us a better picture of the atom's makeup. We know that atoms are composed of a great many infinitesimal electrified particles. The principal ones are protons, electrons, and neutrons. We have also learned that most elements consist of two or more sorts of atoms, each having a slightly different weight but all behaving chemically alike. Atoms having different weights but the same properties are called *isotopes*. The form of matter depends on how the particles are arranged within the atom. Thus the principal isotope of hydrogen has but one electron, which revolves around one proton as a nucleus. The uranium atom is the heaviest atom found in nature. When scientists learned how to split the uranium atom by artificial means, a new age was born.

Conversion of mass into energy. Some atoms, notably those of radium, are in a constant process of breaking up. This means that

IGY expedition to Antarctica in 1957 58

Electronic memory tape
used by telephone companies

Machine-Age Living Takes Over

Over two thousand years ago Archimedes boasted, "Give me a place to stand, and I will move the earth." Ever since then man has increasingly put his scientific knowledge to work. In the twentieth century, science has become more "practical" than ever before. That is to say, it has been used to solve problems in industry, in agriculture, and in medicine. More and more the scientist and the inventor-engineer have combined their efforts to save man time, labor, and inconvenience.

342A

A revolutionary result of their teamwork has been the use of new sources of power. When man harnessed the energy of the atom and the thrust of rocket fuels, he opened the door to a different world. Although frightful in their destructive possibilities, the atomic reactor and the rocket promise great benefits to mankind. The rocket, for example, has become the means for probing the mysteries of outer space. The launching of numerous space vehicles since the first in 1957 foreshadowed the day when man himself would be able to travel beyond the earth's atmosphere. Such initial space pioneers as Yuri Gagarin and John Glenn were followed by a host of intrepid space travellers. For instance, in the summer of 1969, the United States through its Apollo moon project successfully explored the moon.

Launching a rocket at Cape Kennedy, Florida

To pave the way for such daring ventures, much scientific experimentation has taken place. In medicine, for instance, researchers have made studies of the motion of the human body under the strains and stresses of space travel, and of the problems of humans during periods of weightlessness.

Space scientists have also been interested in the causes of the "common cold," for the astronauts have suffered from ordinary earth-bound colds and flu during space travel. Finally, this age of space exploration has added to the development of many new technological breakthroughs, especially those associated with automation.

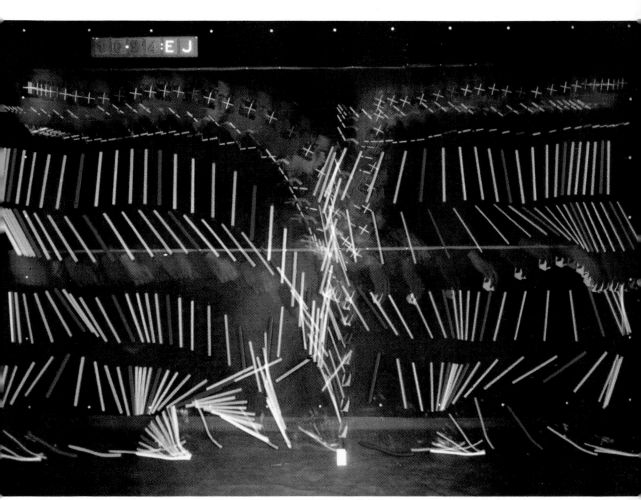

Study of the body movement of a man as he picks up an object, recorded by a camera with changing filters

Less spectacular have been the scientific probings of "inner space." The world around us has become the object of intensive study. During the International Geophysical Year scientists uncovered a vast store of information in Antarctica. At the same time, in industry and in agriculture, technology has scored additional victories for "inner space" man. The new science of electronics has passed beyond the stage of the radio and television to the wonders of automation and the mechanical brain. Likewise, chemical technology has furnished the basis of new industries, such as plastics and synthetic fertilizers, and has become the indispensable partner of many others. Meanwhile, great steel mills have continued to form the sinews of industrial might, while the energy from hydroelectric plants and oil produced in refineries across the world has shown no signs of diminishing usefulness.

Modern steel mill at night

Some of the most astonishing technological developments have been those associated with agriculture. Giant combines, machines that now can do the work of a hundred men, planters, balers, tractors, and all types of mechanical harvesters have made farming an almost automated enterprise. Coupled with these developments are the great strides taken toward the development of better seeds, hybrid plants, chemical fertilizers, and insecticides and pesticides to kill harmful animal pests and weeds. It is no wonder that agricultural production has increased in the last decade faster than at any other time in man's history. However, the consistent increase in the world population still finds hunger and famine a continuing threat in many parts of the world.

Harvesting with modern machines
on a collective farm in Russia

Oil refinery in Venezuela

Modern Painting and sculpture by artists from many countries on display at Carnegie Institute in Pittsburgh

Machine-age technology has also had a striking influence on art and architecture. Painters and sculptors have shown a trend toward new line and form, frequently geometrical and severe in appearance. Their works are abstract, not resembling anything that can be easily recognized. Modern artists have been willing to experiment as a scientist or inventor does in his laboratory. Often the results seem weird and meaningless to viewers because the artist has tried to express ideas and emotions he himself might not have fully understood.

In architecture, the expression "form follows function" has become a leading principle. The aim of the architect has been to design something that will most efficiently serve the needs of the user. Whether the buildings be schools, churches, apartment houses, skyscrapers, or small suburban homes, they must now be practical and convenient. To help make them so, architects have made greater use of the newer materials of concrete, metal, and glass. Incorporating the mechanization of the machine age, modern architecture has proportion, harmony, and beauty of its own.

Church of the Holy Cross in Oak Creek Canyon, Arizona

Despite all of the comforts and conveniences that technology has given to man, a basic question still remains: How can these wonderful devices of the machine age be best used to bring happiness as well as material comfort to modern man? Advanced agricultural methods do not mean that all people eat well. Nor do beautiful buildings necessarily indicate good schools. Better means of communication and transportation mean little unless they are available for use everywhere. Man must learn to make the machines work for him, not to grow more automatic, more mechanical, more of a machine himself.

Workers on First National City Bank building crouch above Park Avenue, New York.

342H

some of their electrical particles are thrown off—that is, their mass is converted into energy. The idea that mass can be changed into energy and energy into mass was proposed in 1905 by a German physicist, Albert Einstein, who became a citizen of the United States. He regarded the matter in the nucleus of the atom as a highly concentrated packet of energy. Einstein worked out what has been called "probably the most important equation ever devised by man," namely, $E = mc^2$. This means that energy (E) is equal to mass (m) multiplied by the square of the speed of light (c^2). This amount of energy seems fantastic. For example, if we could convert one entire pound of matter, the resulting energy would be the same as that produced by burning one and a half million tons of coal. Einstein's equation was one of the results of his famous theory of relativity. This is the idea that space, time, and matter have no absolute meaning. They can only be measured in relation to an observer.

The earth sciences: geology and geography. The study of the structure of the earth furnishes another example of the close interrelationship of the sciences. The fundamental materials of geology are rocks and fossils. Physicists and chemists help identify and test rock formations. Astronomers and physicists furnish knowledge to explain how the earth originated. Geologists have furnished biologists clues to the theory of evolution.

The Newtonian revolution and the eighteenth-century Enlightenment had cast doubt on the older explanations of the earth's formation. No longer were the ideas of divine creation or cataclysms (sudden violent movements) acceptable. Men now looked for the *natural* causes that would account for mountains, valleys, plains, lakes, seacoasts, and layers of the earth. Two men led the way in creating geology as a science. A Scotsman, James Hutton (1726-1797), set forth the idea that natural forces (wind, rain, frost, ocean waves,

etc.) which men can observe made the earth what it is. Moreover, these forces were continuing to change the earth's contours. In the next century an Englishman, Sir Charles Lyell (1797-1875), refined Hutton's work. He said that the changes brought about in the earth's structure and surface were the result of (1) the contraction of the globe, (2) erosion by water, glaciers, frost, and wind, and (3) earthquakes and volcanoes. It took immense periods of time (now called geologic ages), measured in billions of years, to produce the effects we now see. The presence of fossils in the earth's layers of rock supported Lyell's theories.

The practical value of geology today can be appreciated when we ponder the benefits to man of petroleum and the many minerals which the earth yields.

A close scientific partner of geology is geography. It deals not with structure, but mainly with the earth's terrain, bodies of water, resources, and variations in climate. Geography also involves man to a very large extent, studying the relationships between human beings and the conditions of their natural surroundings. Thus, for example, geographers have a keen interest in the conservation of water, soil, and mineral resources in order that man may not plunder these gifts of nature and suffer as a consequence.

From the beginning, maps have been the language of the geographer. As soon as civilized man began to travel any distance, he mapped the new places he explored. As we have seen, the Greeks were perhaps the first systematic students of geography. The Age of Exploration (see page 197) did much to enlarge man's geographical knowledge. Behaim and Mercator were the leading cartographers (map makers) of that day. But by 1800 half the globe was still unmapped. Most of the Americas and Africa, and much of Asia, were still a closed book. Within little more than a century later, however, man's adventurous spirit had carried him to the limits of his planet. Not only had virtually every corner of the habitable earth been mapped, but both North and South poles had been reached. The time had come for earthlings to look for new worlds to conquer.

The Life Sciences

Biology and the cell theory. Whereas physicists and chemists investigate the nature and meaning of nonliving things (matter and energy), biologists study the world of plants and animals. They (and their allies—botanists, medical scientists, physiologists) try to find laws and principles that explain all life processes. Once again, however, it is important to emphasize the interdependence of all the sciences. Biologists and physicians owe much to both physics and chemistry in analyzing living tissues and in developing drugs to treat diseases. In addition, their microscopes, X rays, and electrical equipment and their use of radioactivity are products of the science of physics. And in biochemistry we have a good example of the merger of two branches of science to study living matter.

Eighteenth-century explorers brought back to Europe from America and the Pacific many new kinds of plants and animals. With the aid of this new material scientists made great strides in the study of living things. A Swede, Linnaeus (lĭ-nē′ŭs), helped to make botany an orderly body of knowledge by carefully classifying plants. His French contemporary, Buffon, performed much the same service for zoology, the study of the structure of animals.

What the atom is to physics and chemistry, the cell is to biology. In 1838–1839 two German naturalists, Schleiden and Schwann, set forth the cell theory. According to their conclusions, all living things, both plants and animals, are composed of tiny units, or cells. Further studies proved the cell theory correct.

CHARLES DARWIN

Biologists also found that cells contain a transparent jelly, protoplasm, which is the basis of life. The study of cells was possible because physicists had made remarkable improvements in the microscope.

Darwin and evolution. Of even greater importance than the cell theory was the theory of evolution. Its influence was to extend far beyond the field of biology. The man chiefly remembered for this idea was an Englishman, Charles Darwin, who in 1859 published *The Origin of Species*. Even before the appearance of this book, some scientists believed that existing species of plants and animals, as well as the earth itself, were not created in their present form. They thought that living things had developed, or evolved, from simpler, or at least different, cell structures. Darwin was the first to suggest that natural selection was an important factor in the changes in living things through the ages. He pointed out that many more individuals of each species are born than can possibly live and have offspring; consequently, there is a constant struggle for existence. Darwin believed that in this struggle only the fittest survive. They are the strongest, the swiftest, the most cunning, or otherwise the most adaptable. According to Darwin, the characteristics that make for survival are inherited and tend to become more and more prominent in following generations, since individuals lacking these characteristics are likely to perish without leaving offspring. Finally, Darwin thought that by the slow accumulation of slight changes entirely new species arise, more complicated in form than their ancestors.

What Darwin had done was to extend the idea of endless change from the plant, animal, and physical worlds to the realm of man himself. Some refer to this as the Darwinian revolution. As with all important revolutionary ideas, it raised a storm of protest. It was charged that Darwin made man the descendant of the apes, that evolution contradicted the story of creation in the Bible, that war and disease might be justified as eliminators of the weak in the "struggle for existence," and that if only the "fit" survive, success alone is what counts. By World War I the angry argument had largely subsided. Most people came to recognize that Darwinism is, as its author intended, a biological and not a religious or social theory.

Investigators since Darwin have made important contributions to the theory of evolution. An Austrian monk, Mendel, was able in 1860 to formulate certain laws of inheritance by experimenting with the breeding of plants. His conclusions led biologists to give more attention to genetics, the study of heredity. They have found that mutations—sudden variations from normal—occur frequently in nature and that new types of plants and animals often arise as a result of mutation. The plant and animal breeder searches for mutations in order to produce improved types more useful to mankind. Mutations can be brought about artificially in

---

DARWIN ON THE DESCENT OF MAN

The main conclusion of the whole work is simply that man is descended body and mind from the lower animals. I regret to think that this conclusion will be highly distasteful to many people, who will regard it as inimical to both morality and religion. But we scientists are not concerned with hopes or fears—only with the truth as far as we are able to discover it. Having considered the evidence, it seems to me that we must acknowledge that man still bears indelible and unmistakable traces of his lowly origin. His body is still the body of an animal, and the mark of the beast is still clearly discernible in all his mental and moral faculties.

—Charles Darwin, *The Descent of Man.*

---

plants and animals. Social customs have prevented genetic experiments with human beings. However, scientists have learned much about human heredity by studies of families and population figures and by comparisons with the genetics of animals.

Modern medicine and the germ theory. Medicine furnishes perhaps the best example of the practical application of science to human needs. The big strides in its development date from the late 1600's when a Dutchman, Leeuwenhoek (lā'věn-hōōk), made an amazing discovery. While gazing through his microscope at a drop of water, he saw many kinds of creatures with one or a few cells, which wriggled about and devoured food. He called these creatures animalcules (little animals) because they moved. We know from his descriptions that Leeuwenhoek saw both plant and animal microorganisms and that among them may have been some bacteria.

Late in the next century Dr. Edward Jenner (1749-1823), an Englishman, made one of the most important contributions in fighting harmful bacteria. He began the practice of vaccination to prevent the dread disease smallpox. The method consists of injecting into the body a substance containing some of the bacteria (in weakened form) which cause the disease. A mild form of the disease results and makes the individual immune from later attacks of the germ.

During the nineteenth century a French chemist, Louis Pasteur (1822–1895), went a step further. His microscopic research revealed that bacteria (germs) multiply like all other living things. Thus he destroyed the old theory of "spontaneous generation," that is, that germs simply appeared in matter without cause. He proved that harmful germs cause many diseases and applied Jenner's technique of immunization. But unlike Jenner, who did not know why vaccination worked, Pasteur based his cures on scientific knowledge of causes. He found that germs, or microbes, are responsible not only for animal and human diseases, but also for putrefaction (decay), fermentation, and souring. These findings were invaluable to industry and agriculture (wine- and silk-making, for example), as well as to medicine. A process called "pasteurization," developed by Pasteur, has saved multitudes of lives. It consists of heating a liquid, such as milk, until the harmful germs it contains are destroyed, without changing the chemical makeup of the liquid.

A Prussian named Koch continued Pasteur's beneficial work in developing methods of immunization. In 1882 he identified the germs which cause tuberculosis and cholera. More recently, scientists have isolated the bacteria which cause such scourges as diphtheria, typhoid fever, pneumonia, lockjaw, bubonic plague, polio, and measles. In many cases it is possible to inject an antitoxin to fight the toxin, or poison, produced by a particular kind of bacteria. However, certain diseases do not respond to treatment with antitoxin. Some of these diseases may be combated by using chemicals that kill or prevent the growth of harmful bacteria while leaving the body cells undamaged. Among the most effective drugs of this kind have been sulfa medicines and the antibiotics, such as penicillin and streptomycin. A continuing problem, however, with the use of antibiotics is that bacteria can build a resistance to them. In some cases this makes them less effective. It also emphasizes what Darwin made clear —that all living organisms can adapt to their environment and make changes in order to survive.

Further medical victories. Early in the present century experimenters discovered that animals do not thrive on a diet consisting of pure proteins, carbohydrates, and fats. This discovery led to the finding of certain substances known as *vitamins*. These substances occur in minute amounts in many natural foodstuffs and are necessary for health and for growth. A dozen or more vitamins are now known. Most of these can be produced artificially. When the diet is deficient in one or more vitamins, a vitamin-deficiency disease may result. Such a disease is treated by supplying the needed vitamin.

Medical researchers continue to win victories against some of mankind's most deadly diseases. Thanks to the electron microscope, they can now study viruses—disease-producing parasites that are smaller than bacteria. Many of them look and act like living things. Viruses cause a number of sicknesses, including influenza and infantile paralysis. The use of radioactive isotopes, particularly in cancer research, marks another great advance (see page 342). The remarkable progress of medical science is indicated by the increase in the average life span. In the days of Queen Elizabeth I the average expected lifetime of a male at birth was only about twenty years. By 1850 it had increased in western countries to about thirty-five years. Today in the United States a male has a life expectancy of sixty-eight and a female has one of seventy-five. Europeans enjoy a comparable long-life expectancy, but in most countries of Africa, Asia, and Latin America it is much lower. Where public health laws and regulations have been enforced, the life span has lengthened.

Psychiatry. An increasingly important branch of modern medicine is psychiatry— the study and treatment of mental illnesses or behavior disorders. As early as the fifth century B.C. Hippocrates (see page 82) recognized such ailments and argued that they resulted from natural causes. Nevertheless, until the nineteenth century many people still thought the mentally sick were possessed of demons or witches. Consequently, such people were often feared or shunned, and sometimes chained and imprisoned. Then a number of doctors began to study mental patients more carefully, tracing their experiences (histories), listening to them talk, and classifying their disorders. The greatest pathfinder in this effort was an Austrian, Sigmund Freud (1856–1939). He developed many theories of the causes of mental illnesses. He came to believe that many of them originated in the unpleasant relationships between children and their parents. Such experiences may be repressed (forgotten), only to appear later in distorted ways as anxiety, dreams, or physical symptoms. In other words, Freud stressed the influence of the subconscious mind on conduct. He treated patients by encouraging them to talk freely in order to unburden themselves of their pent-up emotions.

Modern American psychiatry and medical education owe much to the Swiss-born Adolf Meyer (1866–1950), who worked for many years at the Johns Hopkins University. Meyer called the science of man's behavior psychobiology. It regards the individual as a single unit, with thinking and feeling as important as other body functions. Meyer was especially concerned with the prevention of diseases of the mind through mental hygiene.

In recent years two methods of treatment of psychiatric patients have produced signifi-

SIGMUND FREUD

cant results. One is electroshock, used to relieve mental ailments marked chiefly by depressed moods. More important, however, is the use of an increasing number of tranquilizing drugs. These methods, along with community mental health programs, have caused a steep drop in the number of psychiatric patients requiring hospital care.

Advances in surgery. Meanwhile, the use of anesthetics has made possible marvelous advances in surgery. Before 1840 few patients were able to survive the shock caused by a serious operation. In the 1840's two Americans, Crawford Long and W. T. G. Morton, independently discovered that ether is an effective anesthetic. At about the same time other doctors here and abroad began to use nitrous oxide ("laughing gas") and chloroform to produce anesthesia. Anesthetics saved the patient from pain and enabled surgeons to perform long and difficult operations. However, a large proportion of surgical patients died as a result of infection. An English surgeon, Joseph Lister, following the discoveries of Pasteur, showed how to reduce the danger of infection when he began the practice of antiseptic surgery in 1865. He carefully cleaned his instruments and the wounds of his patients with a solution of carbolic acid to prevent infection. Surgeons gave increasing attention to this practice, called *asepsis*—that is, freeing their instruments and dressings from germs by sterilizing them. Other advances in surgery have resulted from the use of electronic devices. Foremost among these is the X-ray machine. It reveals the presence of foreign substances in the body and the condition of the bones and internal organs. It is used also in the treatment of cancer. Surgeons now perform many kinds of operations by electrosurgery. This means that they use an electric knife, which closes the smaller blood vessels immediately and makes the operation practically bloodless. This has become especially important in the delicate operation of organ transplants. (See page 66.) Another indispensable aid to successful surgery is the blood transfusion. Not until 1900 was it discovered that there are four basic blood types. During World War I large-scale blood transfusion became common. Nowadays blood and its plasma may be stored for future use.

Anthropology and psychology. The late nineteenth century saw the rapid development of the newer life sciences, anthropology and psychology. As we have already seen (see page 11), the anthropologist, as a partner of the archaeologist, plays an important role in "digging up" new evidence of man's prehistoric past. But he is also interested in man's historic experience. He tries to explain human behavior in terms of man's different cultural patterns. For example, he sees the differences in behavior between the Chinese, the Navajo Indian, the Eskimo, the African Watusi, and ourselves as differences in cultural development. And to the anthropologist culture is the sum total of what man has learned in response to various surroundings—in oth-

er words, his customs. (See page 13.) Thus anthropology overlaps a number of fields of knowledge, for example, history (in tracing all human activity), biology (in studying different physical and racial traits), sociology (in accounting for the origin of languages, laws, moral codes, etc.), and even art and literature (as a means of expressing imaginatively people's reactions to their particular environments).

The father of anthropology, Edward Burnett Tylor (1832–1917), organized the School of Anthropology at Oxford University. In his book *Primitive Culture* (1871) he defined the word *culture* and called for the use of scientific methods in studying it. Since then, the effect of anthropologists' research has been to explode the myth of racial and natural superiority. No race, nation, or culture, they indicate, is "better" than any other in a scientific sense. Hence they emphasize the essential unity of mankind.

Psychology, too, pointed in new directions. As a science of human behavior, only a fine line separates it from psychiatry. The latter is a medical science, seeking the causes and cures of mental illnesses. Psychologists focus their attention on such problems as the development of intelligence and personality, the learning process, and group as well as individual behavior. Wilhelm Wundt (1832–1920), a German physiologist, first tried to make psychology a science. He opened the first psychological laboratory, experimenting with the behavior of animals. A Russian, Ivan Pavlov (1849–1936), also a physiologist, found that in dogs, and presumably in human beings, conditioned reflexes (automatic responses) control much of their behavior. In other words, many activities are performed without conscious effort or reasoning. Freud, as we have seen, likewise stressed the subconscious drives of human beings. They all seemed to raise the important question: "Is man primarily a thinking creature after all?"

REVIEWING THE CHAPTER

TERMS TO UNDERSTAND: *Second Industrial Revolution, "oil politics," synthetics, plastics, dirigible, supersonic, Hertzian waves, demography, free trade, corn laws, protectionism, reciprocal tariff, monopoly, cartel, technological unemployment, business cycle, nationalized industries, laissez faire, scientific method, spectroscope, atom, molecule, x-rays, electron, isotope,* $E = mc^2$, *cell theory, natural selection, genetics, mutation, vaccination, germ theory, pasteurization, antibiotics, psychiatry, anthropology, psychology.*

PERSONS TO IDENTIFY: *Gramme, Edison, Bessemer, Baekeland, Carver, Daimler, Ford, Zeppelin, Wright brothers, Lindbergh, Holland, Marconi, Malthus, Herschel, Priestley, Lavoisier, Dalton, Thomson, Einstein, Lyell, Darwin, Mendel, Leeuwenhoek, Jenner, Pasteur, Freud, Lister, Pavlov.*

QUESTIONS TO ANSWER

1. (a) What is science? Technology? (b) What advances in technology brought about the wide use of electricity? Oil? Steel? Aluminum? (c) Make a list of synthetics. Discuss their importance. (d) Explain how the Second Industrial Revolution made agriculture a mass-production industry.

2. Explain three key developments in each of the following fields: (a) railroads, (b) automobiles, (c) aviation, (d) motion pictures.

3. (a) Give figures to show the increase in modern times of population, of migration, and of cities. (b) How are these changes related to the Industrial Revolution? (c) Why is there often "poverty in the midst of plenty"?

4. (a) Give three reasons for Great Britain's commercial supremacy following the Industrial Revolution. (b) Trace the tariff policies of the major countries since the Industrial Revolution.

5. (a) What led to the development of large-scale business units? (b) Explain the functions of the following in modern commerce: middlemen, banking, insurance, advertising. (c) How may the business cycle be explained? (d) Give examples to show that the policy of laissez faire is being abandoned.

6. (a) Discuss some of the effects of the Newtonian revolution. (b) What are some of the achievements of modern astronomers? (c) Why is Lavoisier called the "father of modern chemistry"? (d) What did each of the following contribute to modern chemistry or physics: Dalton, Mendeléef, Roentgen, Madame Curie, Thomson, Einstein. (e) Explain how the study of the structure of the earth furnishes an example of the close interrelationship of the sciences.

7. (a) Show how biology, physics, and chemistry are interdependent. (b) What is the importance of the cell theory? The germ theory? The theory of evolution? (c) Who was responsible for the development of each of these theories? (d) What does the increase in the life span of human beings indicate?

8. (a) What was Freud's contribution to the development of psychiatry? (b) What did Meyer contribute to this field? (c) Describe the advances made in surgery over the past hundred years. (d) What myths has anthropological research exploded? (e) Distinguish between psychology and psychiatry.

18 Literature and the Arts in the Machine Age

A REFLECTION OF THE TIMES. Twentieth century art turned more and more away from realism and toward abstractionism. Charles Sheeler came close to abstraction in his paintings (*above*) and photographs of barns and later of grain elevators and factories.

In every age, man has expressed in various ways his thoughts and feelings about "the human condition." His writings, his art, his music, his philosophy, his religious and social customs—all have served to mirror his hopes and fears, his achievements and failures, as he tried to derive some meaning and satisfaction from life. In this chapter we shall see how these activities and interests of man revealed the temper of the times, mostly in the period since the First Industrial Revolution.

Philosophy in Modern Times

What is philosophy? The word *philosophy* means literally a love of wisdom. Thousands of years before the development of modern science, men pondered such questions as why people behave as they do and what man's place in the universe is. This thinking was based on rather vague and often mistaken ideas of the nature of things. Consequently, the philosophers differed widely in their answers to these questions. Today the study of philosophy has split into two camps—the natural philosophers, or scientists, and the speculative and religious philosophers (whom we call respectively "philosophers" and "theologians"). The scientists deal with things they can measure (like electricity), and are pretty much agreed on what they believe at any one time. The philosophers and theologians deal with such questions as good and evil, order and freedom, life and death—answers to which we must take on faith. There is no agreement in this field except in a very general way. For example, most philosophers would subscribe to the maxim "Love thy neighbor." The practical applications of such beliefs are difficult to determine.

Foundations of modern philosophy. A Frenchman, René Descartes (dā-kärt'), has been called the "father of modern philosophy." A scientist and mathematician, as well as a philosopher, he stands alongside Newton and Bacon as a great pioneer in promoting the scientific method. In his book *Discourse on Method* (1637) he made doubt the key to his thinking on every problem. The only thing he could not question was his own existence. "I think, therefore I am," he said. This frame of mind (see box) set the stage for the eighteenth-century Enlightenment, or age of reason, as we have seen. It was a period when reason was enshrined as a deity, almost replacing religion as a guide to art, thought, and government. Nothing was to be respected simply because it was old, nor accepted because someone in authority had said it was true. Reason, it was confidently believed, could bring about a new society of justice and order, in perfect harmony with the physical universe.

The spirit of the Enlightenment penetrated every aspect of human activity. In philosophy it was the starting point for the thinking of a German, Immanuel Kant (1724–1804). Kant, however, concluded that pure reason was limited in what it could accomplish for man. It might conceivably lead him into error if he did not heed his inborn sense of "good will." This sense, said Kant, would be man's chief guide to conduct and would impel him to help his fellow man. Reason would tell him when to exercise his good will. Such faith in man's progress, which philosophers call idealism, was in keeping with the Enlightenment. It also led Kant to draw up a grand plan for a league of nations to assure lasting peace.

As the Industrial and Scientific revolutions went forward, the idealism of Kant gave way to more practical thinking about what makes man "tick." Such English philosophers as Jeremy Bentham (1748–1832) and John Stuart Mill (1806–1873) supported the idea of material well-being as the basic motive, or guide, for conduct. They believed that society should aim to create the greatest good for the greatest number of people. Another English philosopher with a materialistic point of view was Herbert Spencer (1820–1903). He built up a system of thought based on Darwin's theory of evolution. (See page 344.) Thus he formed a link between the older philosophers and the modern scientists.

Two leading American philosophers, William James (1842–1910) and John Dewey (1859–1952), also took a practical view of things. Their philosophy is called "pragmatism"—that is, the belief that the truth of an idea can be tested by its consequences. An idea is good if actual experience proves it so. Dewey is best known for applying his philosophy to education. He believed that the school should teach people how to live in the machine age. It should teach through practice, using the experimental methods of science. In other words, we should learn to do by doing. Dewey's influence has reached into almost every schoolroom in America, as well as to many in other countries.

Philosophy's offspring. The search of the philosophers for some controlling principle in human society gave rise to a new and related field of learning—the social sciences. As students of man and society, social scientists applied the scientific method to the study of human behavior. A French philosopher, Auguste Comte (1798–1857), was a leader in this effort. He believed that man could rely only on science for absolute knowledge and that its highest form was the science of society. This he called *sociology,* the study of how languages, laws, moral codes, religions, and customs arise and develop. By 1900 it was accepted as a separate subject.

Literature Mirrors the Moods of the Age

Literature and life. Ever since man has become civilized, he has reflected the predominant moods of his times in what he has written, as well as in other artistic ways. Literature has played an especially important role in his experience. It has not only been shaped by events, but it has also helped to shape them. For example, the writings of the thinkers of the Enlightenment did much to produce the French and American revolutions. Thus the interaction between what man thinks and feels, and what he does, has always influenced the course of human history.

The romantic revolt. In the half century after 1775 a new mood took possession of all fields of literature and the arts in the western world. It was foreshadowed in the idealism of Rousseau and Kant. Known as *romanticism,* it marked a sharp turnabout from the *rationalism* (emphasis on reason as a guide to truth) of the Enlightenment. The romanticists held that man's feelings, emotions, and natural instincts, rather than reason, opened a sure path to wise conduct. For, they might have asked, where had faith in reason gotten them? Politically, it had produced the Reign of Terror and the Napoleonic Wars. The dream of "liberty, equality, and fraternity" had not been fulfilled. The Congress of Vienna, too, had seemed to turn back the clock. (See pages 287–288.) Moreover, the expanding Industrial Revolution brought with it, especially in England, some miserable living conditions which did not spell progress.

The disillusionment of the romanticists expressed itself in all the arts and in a number of different ways. It was in literature, however, that it became most evident. Here the romantic protest gave free play to sentiment and imagination, as it sought escape from the harsh realities of everyday life. Poets glorified nature (see box), not only for its beauty, but as the embodiment of the divine spirit of the universe. The simple, unspoiled rural life was to be preferred by far to the artificial existence of the city-dweller. The romanticists also glorified the past. They revived an interest in Greek and Roman classics, and especially in the literature and art of the Middle Ages. This was another form of escape from everyday reality. Escape was also sought in the supernatural world of magic and miracles. Fairies, ghosts, demons, and witches appeared in poetry, drama, and fiction to excite the imagination of readers who were miserable or bored. Finally, romantic writers displayed a stubborn confidence in their ability to remold society according to their own individual desires. They lacked definite plans and programs, they dreamed impossible dreams, and they were full of contradictions. Yet they expressed a side of the human spirit, its idealism, that continued to spur man toward a better life. Several examples will suffice to show how the romantic spirit dominated literature.

Some romantic "greats." German and British writers led the way in the movement. The many-sided Johann Wolfgang von Goethe (1749–1832) was Germany's greatest literary genius. His masterpiece, the poetic drama *Faust,* ranks among the world's best literary works. Based on an old European legend, it tells the story of a man who sells his soul to the devil in order to enjoy the pleasures of eternal youth. In the end he redeems his soul after realizing that it is more worthwhile to work for human welfare. The return to medieval folklore portrayed here was characteristic of the romantic writers. But more striking in *Faust* is the idealism expressed in man's struggle to overcome his weaknesses. "Man still must err, while he doth strive," said Faust. Goethe also excelled as a lyric poet, a favorite form of romantic expression. Many of his poems were based on themes of love, as were the ballads of his good friend Friedrich von Schiller (1759–1805). But Schiller's reputation rests mainly on his historical dramas. The most famous one, *William Tell,* idealized the resistance of the Swiss people to the oppression of an Austrian ruler. Here we have reverence for the past coupled with a rising sense of nationalism, or feeling of devotion to one's own national culture. This force was to play an increasingly important part in nineteenth-century Europe, especially in Germany and Italy. (See pages 376–415.) Thus romanticism and nationalism were closely linked in this period.

In England the romantic revolt was perhaps best expressed in the *Lyrical Ballads* of William Wordsworth (1770–1850) and Samuel Taylor Coleridge (1772–1834). Their reaction against classicism (cold, formal style) and the Enlightenment was emphatic. Wordsworth sought to make poetry appeal to the common man by simplifying its language and speaking of commonplace things. Both were inspired by the beauty and simplicity of nature. Not reason but nature could develop man's "immortal spirit," or soul. Coleridge made use of the supernatural element in his *Rime of the Ancient Mariner,* which told of a curse that overtook a seaman who killed an albatross. England produced other great romantic poets in Shelley, Keats, and Byron. Of these, Shelley was the most rebellious, turning against everything that interfered with individual liberty. Byron, in his own career and in his poetry (*Don Juan,* for example), portrayed the restless adventurer and hero. Ironically, he died while fighting in the Greek revolution (1824). Keats achieved fame for his immortal odes, written in elegant style. *Ode on a Grecian Urn* expressed his faith in the ultimate value of the beautiful: "Beauty is truth, truth beauty,—that is all/Ye know on earth, and all ye need to know." English romanticism had its prose writers, too. Sir Walter Scott (1771–1832) collected medieval folk ballads and wrote more than thirty popular historical novels. *Ivanhoe,* one of his best, extols the age of chivalry.

In France, Victor Hugo (1802–1885) became the recognized leader of the romantic movement. When his play *Hernani* was staged in 1830, it created a sensation by discarding all the traditional rules of dramawriting. It also set an example for a revolution in the other arts. Hugo's *Notre Dame*

GREECE expiring . . . by Delacroix in 1827

de Paris was in many ways the typical romantic novel—sentimental, picturesque, and harking back to the past. In his most widely read book, *Les Misérables,* he turned from the past to the romance of life in his own time. But his lyric poetry has perhaps been the most enduring of his works. It embodies the romantic ideals of optimistic faith in man's goodness, a sympathy for the poor and helpless, and a hatred of injustice. His contemporary, Alexandre Dumas, specialized in writing fascinating adventure stories, such as *The Count of Monte Cristo* and *The Three Musketeers.* Again, they represented a flight from the present into the past.

Russia's greatest poet, Alexander Pushkin (1799–1837), was in many ways a romanticist. He scorned the patterns of the French classic school which had prevailed in Russia and turned to native themes, much to the delight of his countrymen. In *Eugene Onegin,* a novel in verse, he celebrated much in the life and traditions of his own land. It furnished the story for one of Tchaikovsky's operas. It can be said that Pushkin founded Russian national literature.

Influenced by Europe, America, too, experienced a romantic mood. In the early 1800's Washington Irving (1783–1859) and James Fenimore Cooper (1789–1851) worshiped nature and called forth the past, whereas Edgar Allan Poe (1809–1849) wrote eerie stories of murders and tormented people. Irving expressed the mood aptly when he said, "I longed . . . to escape from the commonplace realities of the present, and lose myself among the shadowy grandeurs of the past."

From romanticism to realism and naturalism. Romantic writers had overpraised the beauty and goodness of human life. They had dwelt on the world as it should be instead of on the world as it is. Some romantics, such as Hugo, had become increasingly aware that they were losing themselves in a dream world that did not come to grips with society's needs. New scientific discoveries and the acceleration of the Industrial Revolution helped to produce a new mood in literature and the arts. It was called *realism*, the attempt to reflect the actual world of man reliably and accurately, without exaggeration and flights of fancy.

By the middle of the nineteenth century this realistic approach to life had largely captured literature. But the break with romanticism was not sharp or sudden. Some writers, like Hugo, who began their careers as romanticists, ended by picturing society as it really was. It is also difficult to fit the realists into a neat classification. One can say, however, that they reflected a great variety of actual experience, and that they generally found fault with the business culture of the dominant class of their age, the bourgeoisie. Furthermore, the preeminent form of literary expression of the realists was the novel, just as poetry had been the chief medium of the romanticists.

Germany produced no realistic novelists of first rank. The poet Heinrich Heine (1797–1856) represented best the changeover from romanticism to realism. His superb lyric poems, many of which have been set to music, display a great variety of romantic moods. The well-known *Lorelei* and *You Are Like a Flower* are examples. But Heine also expressed a realistic awareness of the trends of the times. In his poem *The Weavers* he sympathized with the Silesian weavers whose strike had been cruelly suppressed: "A curse to the king, and a curse to his coffin,/The rich man's king whom our plight could not soften. . . ."

In France, Honoré Balzac (1799–1850) pointed the way to realism in fiction. His *Human Comedy,* a whole collection of novels, showed up the shabbiness of man's grasping for money and power to the neglect of basic human values. Gustave Flaubert (1821–1880) carried the realistic mood further in his masterpiece, *Madame Bovary,* which exposed the shallowness of middle-class morals and ambitions. Toward the end of the century an even more extreme school of realists appeared, led by Émile Zola (1840–1902). They called themselves naturalists, dealing with man as if he were a specimen in a science laboratory. The result was generally to concentrate on the seamy and ugly aspects of life. Zola shocked prudish people who thought he was capitalizing on the exposure of vulgarity. His long series of novels, called *Les Rougon-Macquart,* set the stage for the twentieth-century literature of discontent and protest that portrayed middle-class society in a state of decay. This pessimistic note marked much of the literature that followed. It was encouraged, perhaps, by the increasing influence of socialistic and communistic doctrines.

English fiction of the so-called Victorian Age (the reign of Queen Victoria) also came to grips with the facts of an industrial society. Charles Dickens (1812–1870) was the most popular novelist of the period. In such stories as *Oliver Twist* he gave his readers a sympathetic picture of the paupers, delinquents, and criminals of the London slums. His contemporary, William Thackeray (1811–1863), on the other hand, poked fun at the pretensions and snobbery of middle- and upper-class people in his popular novel, *Vanity Fair.* In the later Victorian era, Thomas Hardy (1840–1928) followed the naturalistic trend in uncovering without feeling the ugly side of life in rural England (*The Return of the Native,* for example). Victorian poetry, however, departed less from the traditions of romanticism. Such poets as Alfred Tennyson (1809–1892) and Robert Browning (1812–1889) tended to accept the values of middle-class Englishmen.

Some of the greatest realistic literature of the nineteenth century came out of Russia. Nikolai Gogol (1809–1852) is said to be the "father of modern Russian realism." Both in his popular comedy *The Inspector General* and in his outstanding novel, *Dead Souls,* he ridiculed the inefficiency and corruption of the government of his day. His work revealed an underlying note of sadness, which can be found in all Russian literature. Gogol set the pace for the great trio of Russian novelists who followed. Ivan Turgenev (1818–1883) depicted in *Fathers and Sons* the thoughts of the educated Russians who opened the way to reform. He contributed the word *nihilist* to our vocabulary.

Fëdor Dostoevski (1821–1881) portrayed in *Crime and Punishment* the conflicts in the minds of abnormal individuals. Count Leo Tolstoi (1828–1910) produced one of the world's masterpieces in his historical novel of the Napoleonic period, *War and Peace.* The brutality of war and the questioning of its meaning brought out the realistic qualities of the long and involved story. In his psychological novel *Anna Karenina,* Tolstoi revealed his own emotional conflicts and inner contradictions. During his life he questioned every traditional institution: church, state, family, marriage, and education.

Elsewhere the realistic mood also prevailed. In *The Doll's House* the Norwegian dramatist Henrik Ibsen (1828–1906) raised the question of woman's role in the home and in society. With painful frankness he aired a problem that aroused a heated argument in Europe and America. In the United States, too, literature reflected the changes brought by the Scientific and Industrial revolutions. William Dean Howells (1837–1920), leader of the realists, said that fiction should ". . . cease to lie about life; let it portray men and women as they are. . . ." He did that in writing about a self-made businessman in *The Rise of Silas Lapham.* American naturalists, like Stephen Crane (1871–1900) and Frank Norris (1870–1902), laid bare some of the seamier sides of life which Howells had shied away from.

Literature of discontent and protest. The early 1900's continued the trend toward an extreme realism. The problem novel, the problem play, and the problem short story became the common forms of the literature of the western world. Writers generally took a dim view of the materialistic culture created by the Industrial Revolution. They subjected man and society to a microscopic examination, exposing especially their shortcomings. They also cast aside older styles and experimented with new ones. The continuing influence of Freud led some writers to produce psychological studies of human personality. Others turned to a form called symbolism, hiding their real thoughts behind make-believe characters or events.

Representative of twentieth-century realism in the theater were the problem plays of George Bernard Shaw (1856–1950), a native of Ireland. A disciple of Ibsen, Shaw used his keen wit and satire to deflate the ego and conceit of smug middle- and upper-class minds. He supported new and unpopular ideas and causes, for example, socialism. In *Pygmalion* he ridiculed the false standards of the upper classes by transforming an illiterate flower girl of the London streets into a society belle. Later this became the basis of the popular musical *My Fair Lady.*

A new kind of novel appeared in the works of another Irishman, James Joyce (1882–1941). In *Ulysses* he used the myth of the ancient Greek adventurer to portray the search of a twentieth-century wanderer for his lost self. This kind of symbolism was a way of pointing up the disorder and futility of present-day existence. Likewise, a French novelist, Marcel Proust (1871–1922), used symbolism in his *Remembrance of Things Past,* a long, semiautobiographical work. He tried to find the basic mystery and anguish of life in unconscious memories. In the United States, William Faulkner (1897–1962) wrote in symbolic form a series of novels revealing the mind and spirit of the South through the complicated stories of various families in an imaginary county.

In poetry, T. S. Eliot (1888–1965), an American-born British writer, also turned to a symbolic technique. *The Wasteland* criticized the dreariness of a society of false gods and empty diversions. The abrupt contrasts, "difficult" words, and veiled references to obscure things gave Eliot's poetry a rather narrow appeal. Many twentieth-century poets have experimented with new forms, discarding to a large extent the older styles of rhyme and meter.

Symbolism was only one aspect of literature in this century. American writers such as Theodore Dreiser (1871–1945), Sinclair Lewis (1885–1951), and Ernest Hemingway (1899–1961) expressed in more direct and blunt language the disillusionment and disgust of man with his environment. But despite their realistic and naturalistic exposure of their world, they were not all pessimistic. Lewis, for example, held out hope for the middle class which he mercilessly lampooned, and Hemingway showed a real concern for man's conduct and honor. Furthermore, one should not get the impression that the literature of scorn and protest attracted the only readers. Writers on sentimental and traditional themes—love, cloak-and-dagger romances, faraway places—still had a large following. They gave their middle-class audiences a chance to escape from the humdrum of everyday life.

Art and Architecture in the Machine Age

As in literature, modern painting, sculpture, and architecture generally reflected the moods and social conditions of the times. There were, however, greater exceptions to the prevailing patterns and more experimentation with individual styles.

From classicism to romanticism. In the half century following the French Revolution, classic and romantic trends in painting were in keen competition. Neoclassicism (new classicism) still held its own, due largely to the influence of a Frenchman, Jacques David (1748–1825), official painter of the revolutionary party. Reacting against the ornate baroque style of the preceding period, with its flattering portraits of royalty and aristocracy, David revived the cold and sharp lines of classical art. He painted scenes from Roman literature ("Oath of the Horatii"), revolu-

OATH OF THE HORATII
by Jacques David

CONSTABLE responded lyrically to nature in this English country scene, *Dedham Lock and Mill.*

tionary events ("Tennis Court Oath"), and the triumph of empire ("Napoleon's Coronation"). The use of traditional techniques to depict contemporary events indicated that classicism and romanticism were not in absolute contradiction.

Another artist who stood outside the main trend of romanticism was a great Spanish painter, Francisco de Goya (1746–1828). His portraits of Spanish royalty and his "Disasters of War" (the atrocities of Napoleon's troops in Spain) showed a stark realism. On the other hand, his passionate patriotism brought him close to the romantic temper.

Romanticism in painting came into its own with the works of John Constable (1776–1837) and Joseph M. W. Turner (1775–1851) in England, and of Eugène Delacroix (1798–1863) in France. Constable and Turner, like Wordsworth in poetry, turned to nature for inspiration. Their striking landscapes, marked by the free use of color and the brilliance of lighting effects, typified the romantic mood. Delacroix emphasized still more the importance of color and light. He had learned much from the flamboyant colors used by a seventeenth-century Flemish painter, Rubens. Delacroix's "Massacre of Scio," a bloody scene

from the Greek War of Independence, stirred the emotions of its viewers.

Sculpture was slower in freeing itself from the rigid lines and forms of classicism. The neoclassical works of an Italian, Antonio Canova (1757–1822), and of a Dane, Bertel Thorvaldsen (1768–1844), dominated the art until the mid-1800's. They displayed an obvious enthusiasm for the ancient Greek and Roman masterpieces. It was a Frenchman, Jean Carpeaux (1827–1875), who broke away from the stern classical pattern. Instead of goddesslike Greek figures, he shaped warm human beings.

Realism and impressionism in art. After 1850, as western society became more industrialized and democratic, painting took a realistic turn. Here again the French led the way. Jean François Millet's paintings reflected his peasant upbringing. Without sentimentality or false idealism he portrayed the simple worker with dignity and sincerity. "The Angelus" was perhaps his masterpiece. What Millet did for the peasant, Honoré Daumier (1808–1879) did for the underprivileged workers of Paris. Daumier's caricatures of middle-class failings were especially amusing. Gustave Courbet (1819–1877) continued

CEZANNE reduced natural forms to geometrical planes. In *Mill at Pontoise* Cezanne abandoned literal appearance in order to express structural simplicity.

the interest in common people and commonplace things. He mocked his critics with the comment "Show me an angel and I will paint one." Nineteenth-century American painters, such as Winslow Homer (1836–1910), generally followed the European patterns. Homer's great sea paintings of the Maine coast revealed his knack for reporting on canvas the objects as the eye saw them.

After 1870, realism gave rise to an even more experimental and innovative school of art known as *impressionism.* The impressionists attempted to record in painting a single fleeting impression of a scene. Taking a cue from the physicists, they tried to break down light as through a prism and put it together again on their canvases. This "divided-color" technique gave their works a shimmering brilliance. It also made them outcasts from the conservative academies of art. They were considered too *avant garde,* that is, ahead of their times. The leading impressionist was a Frenchman, Claude Monet (1840–1926), whose paintings, landscapes mostly, gave one the feel of the open air. His contemporaries, Édouard Manet (1832–1883) and Pierre Auguste Renoir (1841–1919), although less bold in their experimentation with technique, distinguished themselves by painting ordinary people in luminous settings.

Toward the end of the century still another school of painters, known as postimpressionists, came to the fore. The greatest of these was Paul Cézanne (1839–1906), a Frenchman who is often called the "father of modern painting." He emphasized color, design, and surface over subject matter and produced striking scenes by what has been termed the "architectural use of color." By breaking up his canvases into separate areas and blending blocks of color into the whole, he achieved a three-dimensional effect. His objects took on the basic shapes of either a cone, a cylinder, or a sphere. Other postimpressionists, such as a Dutchman, Van Gogh (1853–1890), who was influenced by Japanese painting, and a Frenchman, Gauguin (1848–1903), developed their own individual styles. Both, however, shared with Cézanne the belief that a painter need not represent objects as they really appear.

Meanwhile, in sculpture, new and experimental styles also appeared. The leading sculptor of the late nineteenth century was a Frenchman, Auguste Rodin (1840–1917). His realistic and impressionistic figures were characterized by simplified contours and irregular lines, often blending into rough stone areas. But they also gave a feeling of life and motion. "Man with a Broken Nose" suggests one kind of subject matter he worked into stone and bronze. Rodin's American contemporary, Augustus Saint-Gaudens (1848–1907), brilliantly caught human expressions in marble, such as his figure of Abraham Lincoln in Washington, D.C.

Modern abstract art. Twentieth-century art turned more and more away from realism and toward *abstractionism;* that is to say, it portrayed objects and figures that bore little resemblance to their actual appearance in real life. Paintings (and sculptures, too) of this style have no photolike quality. Distorted figures, tangled lines, topsy-turvy landscapes, clashing colors, and often unidentifiable objects reflect the artist's feelings about the world around him.

One school of abstract painting was cubism. Led by a Spaniard, Pablo Picasso (1881–), the cubists owed much to the geometrical patterns of Cézanne. To the cone, sphere, and cylinder of his works they added flat planes and cubes. There is an oversimplification and distortion of bodies and forms, and these are frequently interchanged, making recognition difficult. Extremely inventive and original, Picasso's art passed through various stages of development. For example, at one point he adapted for his own purposes the faces on African Negro masks. A Frenchman, George Bracques, and a Russian, Marc Chagall, were among Picasso's foremost followers.

Another school of abstract painting was known as *surrealism*. The outstanding painter of this school was also a Spaniard, Salvador Dali (1904–). His work reveals the world of dreams and the subconscious, suggesting the influence of Freud. At first glance, a painting such as "The Persistence of Memory," with its bent-time watches, appears nightmarish and absurd. But surrealism, like most modern abstract art, is strongly personal and individualistic, and has a special meaning for the artist unrelated to the viewer's tastes.

Architecture in the industrial age. The same romantic spirit which expressed itself in the literature and art of the early nineteenth century affected architecture as well. The flights of poetic and artistic imagination that glorified the past brought a revival of classical and Gothic styles in the buildings of the western world. The French Revolution introduced a Roman fashion, reaching a peak in Napoleon's Triumphal Arch and the Church of the Madeleine. In America, Thomas Jefferson was an ardent supporter of neoclassical styles. They were embodied in his home and in the buildings of the University of Virginia, which he designed. The most famous example of neoclassical architecture in the United States is the federal capitol, with its Renaissance dome and Corinthian colonnades. In England neoclassical styles, strongly influenced by the work of Sir Christopher Wren in the seventeenth century, continued in vogue. By 1825, however, the medieval Gothic style had taken over. Stimulated by the romantic longing in such books as Scott's novels, Gothic became the fashion not only for churches, banks, and public buildings, but also for fancy villas and smaller dwellings. The British Houses of Parliament, rebuilt by Sir Charles Barry between 1840 and 1860, furnish a good example of the Gothic revival.

In the late nineteenth century entirely new architectural styles developed. They came in response to the Second Industrial Revolution. Classical and Gothic buildings, despite their eye appeal, were not well suited to the practical needs of an age that placed high value on the efficient use of space and lighting. The possibilities of the new building materials, concrete and steel, also helped to create a new kind of architecture.

The pioneer in revolutionary building methods was an American, Louis Henri Sullivan (1856–1924). His guiding principle was "form follows function," meaning that the structure of a building should fit its purpose. The steel-skeleton framework, the simple and unadorned lines, and the large window openings of his office buildings carried out this idea. He started the era of the modern skyscraper, which has become a symbol of American business activity. Sullivan's functionalism, as it is called, influenced almost all subsequent architectural styles. His pupil, Frank Lloyd Wright (1869–1959), applied it not only to business buildings but to dwellings as well. The modern house should meet modern living needs, Wright held. "Organic architecture," as he called this idea, "is honest because it is true to the place, the time, and the man for whom it is built." Wright's Midwest prairie houses—with their flat, low lines, wide overhanging eaves, and interiors of open space—are typical of his modern living concept.

In Europe, although the skyscraper became much less common, functional architecture also took a firm hold in the twentieth century. A French-Swiss architect, Le Corbusier (1887–1965), and a German, Walter Gropius (1883–1969), developed what came to be called the international style. Their buildings used glass, concrete, and metal in new arrangements and combinations, including ramps and the "split-level" principle.

In architecture, as in all the other arts, there remained followers of more conservative trends. But these did not represent the defiant mood of the industrial age, which broke with tradition and experimented with new forms and styles.

Music Follows Changing Moods

Music, the listener's art. Like literature and painting, music in modern times has followed rather closely the changing moods of the times. But more than any of the other forms of art, music has had an international appeal. No matter in what age or in what style it is composed, it involves the emotions of the listener to a high degree. This gives music a universal quality not found as often in the other arts. It also makes music more difficult to identify as classical, romantic, or impressionistic. Changes from one style to another were not as complete or as abrupt as

FAGUS FACTORY, the first industrial building designed by Walter Gropius in 1911.

in the visual arts. Each period built solidly on the preceding one, and there has been much mixing and overlapping of styles.

Moreover, the shift in styles was directly connected with the kind of audience for whom the music was composed. Until about 1600 music was written chiefly for religious use, reflecting the predominant influence of the church in life. Composers wrote for singers, keeping the instruments in the background or omitting them entirely. From 1600 on, secular music grew in importance. Composers wrote more and more to satisfy the tastes of the drawing-room audiences of nobility and royalty. Court composers were commonly employed. Instruments now came into greater prominence, freeing them from mere dependence on vocal parts. New dramatic forms of musical expression, the opera and oratorio, became popular. (The oratorio is a drama, usually on a Biblical theme, set to music. It differs from the opera in that it has no action, scenery, or costumes.) Then, as the Industrial Revolution spread in the eighteenth century, composers responded with works designed for public concert-hall audiences, and suited to the tastes of middle-class listeners.

From classical to romantic music. The eighteenth century, particularly from 1750 to 1800, marked the heyday of what is termed "classical" music. It corresponded to the age of reason. (See pages 269, 270.) Man was in a questioning mood as he turned from faith to reason as his guide. He sought orderliness and regularity, balance and restraint, which he thought were always present in the natural world. His outlook on life, therefore, was supposedly cool and impartial (objective) instead of personal and emotional (subjective).

In the early eighteenth century, classical music was dominated by the towering figures of Johann Sebastian Bach (1685–1750) and George Frederick Handel (1685–1759). Bach excelled in organ and voice compositions with sacred themes, which tied him to the older tradition of religious music. A master of the art of harmony, he is considered by many the greatest composer in the history of music. Handel distinguished himself by writing oratorios and operas, producing more than forty of the latter. In the second half of the century, classical music reached its height in the works of Joseph Haydn (1732–1809) and Wolfgang Mozart (1756–1791) and in the earlier compositions of Ludwig van Beethoven (1770–1827). Instrumental music came into its own in this period, the string quartet and the symphony orchestra became standard, and the piano replaced the older harpsichord. The short-lived Mozart exemplified the genius of the classical school. Within the accepted forms of rhythm and harmony he experimented with all sorts of combinations of instruments and voice arrangements, and in his light operas, *The Marriage of Figaro* and *Don Giovanni,* satirized the aristocracy of the day in a manner reminiscent of Voltaire.

It was the German composer Beethoven who began the transition to romantic music. During his early career he maintained close ties with classicism, which he had learned from his teacher, Haydn. But the French Revolution and the Napoleonic era, in which he lived, left its marks. As faith in reason declined, old restraints broke down and feelings and emotions were given full expression. Music, always having a basic emotional appeal, now achieved a new freedom. Beethoven's works echoed this change. Whereas Haydn seemed to be untouched by the French Revolution and the changes it wrought, Beethoven was tremendously influenced by his times and surroundings. This influence comes through in the outpouring of feeling and of personality—of Beethoven the man—in his music. He also used nature themes, as in the *Pastoral Symphony,* which bore the notation "Cheerful feelings upon arrival in the country." Here the musical sounds imitate flowing water, storms, and birdcalls. Beethoven's famous piano sonatas—such as *The Moonlight Sonata,* and his nine symphonies, of which the *Ninth* is the most elaborate—marked him as one of the world's greatest composers.

The changes in style, such as the less classical forms and more daring harmonies and rhythms, introduced by Beethoven influenced a whole generation of his followers. These composers began to write for larger orchestras. Emphasis was placed on the use of new and better developed instruments—such as wind, brass, and percussion instruments. Dramatic use of tone color through new instrumental techniques could now be employed. There was constant innovation in form, style, and harmony which culminated, as we shall see, in Wagner's use of excessive tonal colors and massive instrumentation in the orchestrations of his operas.

Many of the leaders of the romantic movement in music were Germans and Austrians. Franz Schubert (1797–1828), although he composed in many forms, was the master of the German *lied* (song), in which he especially captured the romantic mood by a blending of voice and piano parts. His more than six hundred songs were natural and personal outpourings of the soul. Many of them were based on the poems of Goethe and Schiller. The romantic impulse came to full flower in the songs of Robert Schumann (1810–1856). His solo piano works and symphonies, as well as his poetic songs, used novel rhythmic arrangements and showed quickly changing moods. Similarly, lyrical pieces for piano were among the outstanding compositions of Felix Mendelssohn (1809–1847). His *Songs Without Words* achieved wide popularity, although he, too, composed in all forms.

With Johannes Brahms (1833–1897) began a heightened interest in symphonic music. His four great symphonies combined classi-

LUDWIG VAN BEETHOVEN

cal forms with the beauty and sentiment of romantic expression. He was also a master of vocal music, some of which is based on Goethe's poems. Together with Bach and Beethoven, he has been referred to as one of the "three B's" in the great music of the world.

Romantic music thrived not only in Germany and Austria. Frédéric Chopin (1810–1849), of Polish-French parentage, found new possibilities in making the piano "sing like an orchestra." His mazurkas, polonaises, and waltzes, although dance rhythms, were in a new concert style. Meanwhile, Gioacchino Rossini (1792–1868) and Giuseppe Verdi (1813–1901) gave Italian opera a new life. Verdi produced such masterpieces as *Aïda,* written to celebrate the opening of the Suez Canal, *Rigoletto,* and *Il Trovatore,* remembered for its "Anvil Chorus." He combined admirably the vocal parts with the rich effects of choruses and orchestra. The older Italian operas emphasized solo performances.

But the greatest departure in romantic opera came with the compositions of a German, Richard Wagner (1813–1883). His superb contribution was the overpowering musical drama, in which he wove together voices, instruments, and action in an "endless melody." The themes of such masterpieces as *Tann-*

häuser, Tristan and Isolde, and the *Ring of the Nibelung* were based on old, heroic Teutonic legends. They gave Wagner's work a strong nationalistic flavor, which was to become a dominant trend in music after 1850. Wagner's spectacular operas aroused heated controversy. Some regarded them as too noisy, heavy, and showy. Today, however, they are generally recognized as among the greatest of all time.

From postromanticism to impressionism. Wagner's works marked a new turning point in music. They inspired composers in other countries to write operas and symphonic pieces based on their own folk songs, national history, and customs. This spirit of nationalism in late nineteenth-century music marked the so-called postromantic or post-Wagnerian period. It reflected the political and diplomatic developments that were to reach a climax in World War I. (See Chapter 21.)

The movement arose first in Russia, where Modest Moussorgsky (1835–1881) and Peter Ilyich Tchaikovsky (1840–1893) were perhaps its best representatives. Moussorgsky's *Boris Godunov* is considered by some critics Russia's greatest opera. Based on Pushkin's play, it pays little attention to formal rules but concentrates on expressing in sounds and tones the deep feelings of the murderer-hero, Boris. Tchaikovsky, too, wrote music that came from the heart, with a strong element of pessimism and melancholy. His best works were probably the symphonic poems based on stories, such as *Romeo and Juliet;* the popular ballet music *Swan Lake* and *Nutcracker Suite,* making use of folk tunes and fairy tales; and the *1812 Overture,* celebrating the defeat of Napoleon in Russia. He also wrote symphonies, concertos, and operas.

National music spread widely to other parts of Europe. Edvard Grieg (1843–1907), Norway's leading composer, put in his music the special qualities of his homeland—its fjords, forests, folk songs, and dances. A Finnish composer, Jean Sibelius (1865–1957), similarly reflected the character of Finland in his symphonic poems, based on the national epic and folk-song themes. His best-known *Finlandia* reveals the ruggedness of his native land. Less nationalistic but more romantic were the works of a Hungarian, Franz Liszt (1811–1886). Considered the greatest concert pianist of all time, as a composer his fame rests solidly on his symphonic poems, a term that he originated. It describes the short, single-movement composition based on a painting, a drama, a story, or a poem. Schiller, Hugo, Byron, and others furnished Liszt his literary material. His nationalism showed through especially in his Hungarian rhapsodies, which included Magyar melodies with gypsy elements. Finally, among the postromantics who upheld the German reputation for music, was Richard Strauss (1864–1949). A worthy successor to Wagner, he was master of both the symphonic poem and the opera. Of the former, *Till Eulenspiegel's Merry Pranks* is outstanding. Based on old German legend, it realistically imitates the sounds of hoofbeat, honking geese, and the falling trapdoor at a hanging. *Der Rosenkavalier (Cavalier of the Rose)* brought light opera to a new peak, with charming waltzes and rollicking melodies. He defied old forms and rules and gave his music a strong individuality.

Meanwhile, toward the end of the century in France, music headed in still another direction. With Claude Debussy (1862–1918) impressionism as a musical style was born. Like other impressionistic art, its aim was to record the artist's fleeting impression of an event or a scene. There is, therefore, a blurring and haziness of themes, with many dissonances (mixing of chords in different keys). In *Pelléas et Mélisande* he fused drama and music almost to perfection in the only great impressionistic opera. But impressionism was short-lived. Debussy's countryman, Maurice Ravel (1875–1937), for a time used its techniques, especially in his piano works. Like Cézanne in painting, however, Ravel tried to add something solid and less vague. By World War I a new revolutionary trend had set in.

Twentieth-century expressionism. The new trend reflected the frustration and disillusionment of an industrial society that was to see its hopes blasted in a worldwide conflict. In music the pioneer in the ultramodern style, as it is sometimes called, was an Austrian, Arnold Schönberg (1874–1951). His complete break with the past came in 1909 with the appearance of his *Three Piano Pieces*. A radical *atonal* approach in which the composition has no single fixed key, together with the use of a twelve-tone scale instead of the customary eight-tone, marks his compositions.

The works of the Russian-born Igor Stravinsky (1882–   ) were equally innovative and extreme. When in 1913 his ballet *Rite of Spring* was first presented in Paris, it caused a riot. Based upon the religious ceremonies of Russian pagan tribes, it was full of wild rhythms, dissonant and harsh sounds, and offbeat chords. Unlike Schönberg, however, Stravinsky turned to the old classical forms but at the same time used radical harmonic structures. These early works of Stravinsky were known as his neoclassical period. Before long, the use of atonality in compositions by contemporary composers would be quite common. Throughout the twentieth century composers and musicians would be experimenting with this concept of replacing instruments with electronic devices.

At the same time, the United States was making its unique contribution to music— jazz. Although its origins are obscure, the American Negro played a key part in its development. It was firmly based on Afro-American blues, folk songs, and spirituals. With its syncopated rhythms (unusually accented or offbeat), jazz left room for a large variety of styles, from the "hot" to the "sweet." Individual brass bands originated their own special techniques. Jazz harmonies and rhythms also found their way into the serious music of many composers. Foremost among these perhaps was George Gershwin (1898–1937), whose *Rhapsody in Blue* for orchestra and folk opera, *Porgy and Bess,* captured the particular spirit and atmosphere of America.

Social Reform in the Industrial Age

The humanitarian impulse. The idea that man should be concerned with the welfare of his fellow man is as old as history. Ancient prophets and philosophers (both Oriental and Occidental), medieval monks, and modern religious leaders have all preached the brotherhood of man and condemned injustice and cruelty. But the impulse to care for society's poor and oppressed grew with the advance of the Industrial Revolution and the spread of the democratic doctrines of equality and fraternity. "Man's inhumanity to man" came under strong attack from the thinkers of the Enlightenment. They believed society should permit each individual to enjoy "life, liberty, and the pursuit of happiness." This idea underlay much of the reform effort that followed.

Abolition of slavery. Slavery had all but died out in Christian lands by the close of the Middle Ages. It was revived on a much larger scale after the era of geographical discovery. At that time Africa became a source of slaves and America a field for their profitable use. (See page 238.) Antislavery agitation began in the 1600's with the Quakers, who excluded slaveowners from their religious society. Denmark was the first country to declare the trade in African slaves unlawful. In 1807 Great Britain forbade her citizens to engage in the slave trade. In 1808 the United States prohibited the importation of slaves. The

French revolutionists abolished slavery in the colonies of France, but Napoleon restored it. In 1833 the British Parliament freed the slaves throughout the Empire and voted to pay one hundred million dollars to their former masters as compensation. This measure is a monument to the labors of a great humanitarian, William Wilberforce, who devoted his wealth, his energies, and his powerful oratory to the cause of the oppressed Negroes. Slavery afterward disappeared peacefully in the colonial possessions of France, Portugal, and Holland. In the United States it took a costly civil war (1861–1865) to bring an end to this evil. Brazil abolished slavery in 1888. After World War I the League of Nations undertook to bring about the final abolition of slavery. It has not yet entirely disappeared in isolated parts of Africa and Asia.

Crime and punishment. In Europe, up through the eighteenth century, the treatment of criminals and those suspected of crime was barbarous. To torture an accused person to obtain a confession was common. Prisons were usually places of horror. Men, women, and children were herded together, the sick with the well, the hardened criminals with the first offenders. For small crimes the com-

mon punishments were branding, flogging, and exposure in the pillory. Death was imposed for murder, arson, burglary, forgery, counterfeiting, and many other crimes down to the stealing of a small amount of money. In Great Britain death was the punishment for as many as 160 offenses. The authorities often substituted exile in America or Australia for the death penalty. Executions took place in public, in the belief that the spectators would be deterred from committing crimes by the memory of the punishment.

Late in the 1700's reformers attacked these appalling conditions. An Italian nobleman, Beccaria (bāk′kä-rē′ä), ranks as the founder of modern criminology (the study of the prevention and punishment of crime). His work *On Crimes and Punishments,* which appeared in 1764, was translated into twenty-two European languages. It condemned both torture and the death penalty. In France the Revolution hastened penal reform. Great Britain began in the early nineteenth century to reduce the number of capital offenses—that is, crimes for which the death penalty was inflicted. By 1861 high treason, piracy, and murder were the only capital offenses that remained. A number of European and Latin-American countries have now abolished capital punishment, and many states in the United States do not inflict the death penalty.

Reform of prisons went along with reform of the penal code. Mrs. Elizabeth Fry (1780–1845) in England and Dorothea Dix (1802–1887) in America were pioneers in calling attention to the wretched conditions of jails and the miserable treatment of prisoners.

Within the past century much has been done to improve sanitary conditions in prisons and to do away with striped clothing, the lock step, and other practices which humiliate prisoners. The idea behind many of the prison reforms is to change the inmates so that they may become useful members of society.

Control of intoxicating liquor. The fight against alcoholism is another phase of the social reform movement. With the growing urbanization and mechanization of modern life has come increasing recognition of the evils of drunkenness. In the nineteenth century many countries began to experiment with laws to regulate the liquor traffic. Places where alcoholic liquors were sold were required to obtain a license. During World War I most of the belligerents restricted or prohibited the manufacture and consumption of alcoholic liquors, and afterward many of these nations continued public regulation in some form. Sweden and Norway placed the liquor business under government-controlled corporations; others made it a state monopoly.

In the United States agitation for total prohibition of the manufacture and sale of liquor began in the 1830's. Prohibition sentiment at length led to the adoption, in 1919, of the Eighteenth Amendment to the Constitution. It forbade the manufacture, sale, transportation, or importation of intoxicating liquors anywhere in the United States. The hopes of the reformers were not realized; prohibition proved impossible to enforce. Besides, in the hard years of 1930 to 1933 the government desired additional revenue from the taxation of liquor. In 1933 the Eighteenth Amendment was repealed. The sale of alcoholic beverages is now regulated by state and local governments.

Woman's rights. A century ago woman's position in Europe was what it had been in the Middle Ages—a position of dependence on her husband or male relatives. She received little or no education, seldom had any paid employment, and for support relied on husband, father, or brother. After marriage she became subject to her husband. In Great Britain she could neither make a will nor enter into a contract without his consent. All her possessions belonged to him. Any money she earned or inherited was her husband's and might be taken to pay his debts. The law gave the husband control over his children, and if he chose he could take them away from their mother. Similar restrictions existed on the continent of Europe and in America.

The humanitarian sentiment expressed in the French Revolution freed both slave and serf; soon it was to demand the emancipation of women as well. The improvement of woman's position was made possible as a result of new opportunities for women to support themselves. With the development of factories and modern commerce, women could find paid work, and their economic dependence on men was lessened. The agitation for woman's rights steadily increased. Today most civilized countries permit women to own property, engage in business on their own account, and enter the professions. Educational opportunities have also widened.

National woman suffrage scored its first victories in Finland and Scandinavia. Finland granted suffrage to women in 1906, Norway in 1913, and Denmark in 1915. In Great Britain the Equal Franchise Act of 1918 gave women over thirty the right to vote. In 1928 the age limit was lowered to twenty-one years, the same as that for men. (See page 384.) Most European countries and all the British commonwealths now have woman suffrage. Almost all Latin American countries, China, and Japan have also given women the right to vote. In the United States the constitutional amendment for woman suffrage, which had been constantly before Congress for forty years, was approved in 1920.

Socal welfare agencies. In modern times many organizations have been formed to help people who are in need and to provide social services of various kinds. Among other things, these organizations conduct clinics, hospitals, settlement houses, workshops for the blind, and fresh-air camps for underprivileged children, and provide family counseling, visiting housekeepers, and visiting nurses.

The so-called social settlement furnished a good example of such agencies. Founded by private individuals or groups, it arose in the crowded slum areas of industrial cities in the late nineteenth century. Social settlements carried on various activities designed to help improve the lot of the underprivileged. They conducted citizenship courses, vocational training programs, clubs for recreational purposes, nurseries, and employment bureaus. Settlement workers led in sponsoring labor laws and slum-clearance projects. The first such settlement was founded in London by Oxford University men in 1884. It was called Toynbee Hall after its founder, Arnold Toynbee, who had lived and worked among London's slum-dwellers. In the United States the best-known social settlement was Hull-House in Chicago, founded by Jane Addams in 1889. Today public welfare agencies do much of the social-settlement work in the cities.

A different kind of social welfare agency is the International Red Cross. It owed its beginning to a young Swiss, Henri Dunant, who had witnessed one of the bloody battles of the Austro-Sardinian War. (See page 392.) This experience led him to urge the formation of relief societies for the care of sick and wounded soldiers. The result was an international gathering at Geneva in 1864 and the framing of an agreement, or convention, by the representatives of sixteen nations. The agreement provided that every country signing it should set up a wartime civilian agency to help the army medical corps care for the sick and wounded. The "American Amendment" to the Geneva Convention, adopted in 1884, extended the humanitarian work of the Red Cross to peacetime relief during floods, earthquakes, and other disasters. Over sixty nations belong to the International Red Cross.

Education and Religion in Modern Life

Education expands and becomes secular. About the time of the Reformation the demand for education grew stronger. Several factors account for this: (1) the invention of printing, which made more and more books available; (2) the growth of commerce and industry; and (3) the Protestant belief that an individual's religious life should be guided by his own private reading of the Bible.

The task of educating the young, however, remained largely in the hands of the clergy. Not until the Enlightenment and the revolutionary period of the late eighteenth century did a demand arise for secular education, that is, education controlled by laymen. It was part of the overall attack on the old regime, of which the church was a despised symbol. Reason, not ancient tradition, was now to be the guide for conducting schools. The most drastic reforms of the time were suggested by Rousseau (see box) in his book *Émile*. He had his pupil, Émile, abandon books for the most part and learn by observing nature and the operation of nature's laws. Moreover, discipline was not to be imposed. These ideas may have seemed impractical, but they strongly influenced a Swiss educator, Johann Pestalozzi (1746–1827), who applied them to his own classroom. His experiments had much in common with the "learning by doing" method of twentieth-century educators such as John Dewey (see page 352), whose ideas gave rise to the progressive education movement.

The fight for free public schools. The battle for the secularization of education continued through most of the nineteenth century. At the same time, the movement for free public

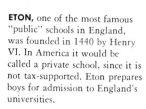

ETON, one of the most famous "public" schools in England, was founded in 1440 by Henry VI. In America it would be called a private school, since it is not tax-supported. Eton prepares boys for admission to England's universities.

schools gained strength as democratic doctrines spread in the western world. In most countries, however, the upper classes looked with disfavor upon the idea of broadening educational opportunity. Universal education, they thought, would make the people unfit for manual labor, add to the burden of taxation, and encourage the masses to upset the *status quo.* "If a horse knew as much as a man, I should not like to be its rider," declared a lord in the British Parliament as he voted against a measure for extending public education. After the workingmen won the vote in Britain (1867), the government set up for the first time a national system of schools (1870). Some private schools (called "public" in England), such as Eton and Harrow, remained as prestige institutions for the wealthy. Until recently, they furnished virtually the only avenue into the major universities. Britain now requires school attendance until age fifteen.

In France the revolutionists of the 1790's prepared an elaborate scheme for public schools but never put it into effect. Napoleon also aimed to set up a public education system from primary grades through the *lycées,*

or high schools. But the close of the Napoleonic era still found a majority of French children attending church schools. Not until the 1880's did France secure a truly national system of education.

Elsewhere in Europe, Germany became a leader in public education. Frederick the Great had made elementary school education compulsory in 1763. In the next century Bismarck made Germany's educational system a model for the world. Schooling became free and compulsory for all between the ages of six and fourteen. In most other European countries public schools developed more slowly.

In the United States the real battle for public education came between 1825 and 1850. No one did more for the advancement of education than Horace Mann, who in 1837 became

---

ROUSSEAU ON EDUCATION

Life is the trade I would teach him. When he leaves me, I grant you, he will be neither a magistrate, a soldier, nor a priest; he will be a man.

—Jean Jacques Rousseau, *Émile.*

---

secretary of the Massachusetts State Board of Education. He founded the first normal schools for the training of teachers, and worked for the better support and equipment of schools. In the United States, state and local governments regulate the public schools and supply them with funds. In most other countries the national government controls public education.

Wherever free public education has become the rule, the percentage of illiteracy has declined markedly. It is still relatively high in Italy, Spain, Portugal, and the Balkan nations of Europe, and in the underdeveloped countries of Africa, Asia, and Latin America. Unfortunately, poverty and ignorance inevitably go together.

Colleges and universities. With the democratic movement and industrialization came a demand for greater opportunities for higher education. In the first place, the spread of free public schools brought a need for more and better-trained teachers. After 1850 the normal school (a two-year teachers' college) was introduced in all advanced countries. As the standards for entering the professions and the business world were raised, most of these schools eventually became four-year liberal arts colleges. Moreover, the Second Industrial Revolution created a need for new knowledge and special skills, particularly in science, engineering, and business management. New universities were founded, many at government expense, and graduate schools were added to the older ones. The curriculum was changed to meet the demands of an industrialized society. Medicine and law, already well established in the curricula of universities, became more specialized. Medical schools reflected the scientific spirit of the age, whereas law schools responded to the enormous increase in legal work required by the growth of big business. Government employment (the civil service) also called for an increasing number of legally trained persons as well

as many others with college degrees. Many educators and business executives, however, still believed that the best-prepared minds were the products of a general or liberal arts education, and that on-the-job training should take care of whatever specialized knowledge was required.

The growth of religious toleration. The secular movement in education was only one sign of the changing attitudes toward religion in modern times. Ever since the Reformation the unity of western Christendom had been crumbling. The Newtonian revolution of the seventeenth century and the Enlightenment of the eighteenth cast further doubt on the authority of organized religion, especially as exercised by established churches (those officially supported by governments). The free thinking stimulated by these movements led in the first place to the multiplication of Protestant sects, for Protestant leaders did not always agree on the meaning of the Bible. It also led to a demand for religious toleration—respect for each individual's right to worship as he pleased. A third and related effect was the demand for complete separation of church and state—the idea that government should not support an official religion nor interfere in religious matters.

Limited freedom of worship had begun in modern times with the publication in France of the Edict of Nantes in 1598, although it was revoked by Louis XIV. (See pages 190–191.) The British Toleration Act of 1689 marked another step forward, but it excluded Catholics and Unitarians from its protection. In the eighteenth century the movement gained strength owing largely to the influence of the philosophers of the Enlightenment. Of these, none was more influential than Voltaire, who carried on a lifelong battle for tolerance. A victim of intolerance himself, he was imprisoned for a year in the Bastille and spent three years in exile in England. While in England he noted that because of the competition of thirty religious groups the people enjoyed religious toleration. Voltaire's friend, the enlightened despot Frederick the Great of Prussia, established religious toleration in the late 1700's. The French revolutionists in the Declaration of the Rights of Man (1791) announced that no one should be disturbed on account of his religious opinions. In the United States freedom of worship was guaranteed by the First Amendment to the Constitution. Freedom of worship was secured in many parts of Germany, in Austria-Hungary, and in Italy only during the nineteenth century.

Separation of church and state. As religious toleration increased, many people opposed the use of tax money to support an official religion. More and more they wanted the church completely separated from the state. America had the first communities that took religious matters entirely out of the hands of the government. In the 1600's Roger Williams separated church and state in Rhode Island, and William Penn did the same in Pennsylvania. The First Amendment to the Constitution of the United States provides that Congress may not make any law "respecting an establishment of religion." No state in the United States has had an established church since the early 1800's.

Few countries today support an official church. Where they do, religious toleration is granted to other sects. In England the Anglican Church is still the state church. Italy and Spain continue to recognize Roman Catholicism as the established religion, whereas in Denmark, Norway, and Sweden the Lutheran Church is supported by the state. Except in Turkey, church and state are virtually one in Moslem countries.

REVIEWING THE CHAPTER

TERMS TO UNDERSTAND: *Enlightenment, pragmatism, idealism, sociology, rationalism, romanticism, nationalism, realism, naturalism, symbolism, neo-classicism, impressionism, avant garde, abstractionism, cubism, surrealism, Gothic revival, functionalism, "International Style," oratorio, symphonic poem, expressionism, jazz, established church.*

PERSONS TO IDENTIFY: *Descartes, Dewey, Comte, Goethe, Wordsworth, Scott, Hugo, Dumas, Pushkin, Dickens, Tolstoy, Shaw, Hemingway, David, Monet, Cézanne, Rodin, Picasso, Dali, Wren, Sullivan, Wright, Bach, Beethoven, Brahms, Wagner, Tchaikovsky, Debussy, Gershwin, Wilberforce, Beccaria, Susan B. Anthony, Jane Addams, Dunant, Rousseau, H. Mann.*

QUESTIONS TO ANSWER

1. (a) What is philosophy? Into what two camps has it split? (b) Describe briefly the main emphasis in the ideas of Descartes and Kant. (c) Name some leading English and American philosophers. What is their common characteristic? (d) What is John Dewey's philosophy of education? His influence? (e) Briefly explain how the social sciences came into being.

2. (a) Explain some of the reasons for the romantic revolt in the half century after 1775. (b) Distinguish between romanticism and realism in literature. What did each attempt to do? What was the chief medium of each? (c) Give three examples of romanticism and three examples of realism, and briefly explain how each example typifies either romanticism or realism. (d) What were some of the trends in literature in the early 1900's? Name six authors who reflected these trends.

3. (a) Give brief definitions for the following schools of art: neo-classicism, romanticism, realism, impressionism, cubism, surrealism. (b) Name artists who typify each school. (c) What factors helped create a new kind of architecture in the second half of the nine-

teenth century? (d) Name four architects of the new architecture and tell the contributions of each.

4. (a) Why does music have a universal quality not found as often in the other arts? (b) Show how shifts in musical styles have been directly connected with the kind of audience for whom the music was composed. (c) Define each of the following musical styles: classical, romantic, post-romantic, impressionist, expressionist. (d) Name composers of each style.

5. (a) What belief underlay much of the reform effort after the Enlightenment? (b) Tell the story of reform in the treatment of criminals. The insane. (c) Tell about the improvement in the position of women. The fight against alcoholism. (d) What did each of the following contribute to social betterment: Wilberforce, Beccaria, Elizabeth Fry, Dorothea Dix, Susan B. Anthony, Henri Dunant?

6. (a) Explain why there has been an increased demand for education in modern times. Include the demand for higher education. (b) Why is *Émile* important in the history of education? (c) When did England and France first have a national system of education? (d) What have been some of the effects on religion of the free thinking stimulated by the Newtonian revolution and the Enlightenment? (e) Give some notable steps in the growth of religious toleration.

FURTHER ACTIVITIES FOR PART SIX

1. Debate the question: *Resolved,* that labor is the source of all value.
2. Read Mrs. Browning's poem "The Cry of the Children" and Thomas Hood's "Song of the Shirt." Explain the social conditions which led to the writing of these poems.
3. Prepare a chart entitled "Modern Science and Invention." In a column at the left list between twenty and fifty leading modern scientists and inventors. In successive parallel columns give the nationality, the dates of birth and death, and the principal inventions or contributions of each.
4. (a) On a time line indicate the chief landmarks of modern science. (b) On another time line show the chief steps in modern social and cultural progress. Place the names of persons beside their achievements.
5. Prepare an oral report on one of the persons discussed in Part Six.
6. Prepare a musical program for the class. Use records to illustrate the different kinds of music discussed in Chapter 18.
7. Prepare a visual program for the class. Use pictures or slides to illustrate various schools of art or architecture discussed in Chapter 18.

FURTHER READING FOR PART SIX

(*Stars indicate easier books*)

HISTORY
ASHTON. *The Industrial Revolution, 1760–1830.* Oxford.
*ASIMOV. *Inside the Atom.* Abelard-Schuman.
BAUER and PEYSER. *How Music Grew.* Putnam.
BERGERE and BERGERE. *From Stones to Skyscrapers.* Dodd.
BLAKE. *The Master Builders.* Knopf.

*BLOW and MULTHAUP. *Men of Science and Invention.* Harper.
BRION. *Art of the Romantic Era.* Praeger. (paperback)
BRITTEN and HOLST. *The Wonderful World of Music.* Doubleday.
BUTTERFIELD. *Short History of Science.* Anchor. (paperback)
CHENEY. *Story of Modern Art.* Viking.
CHRISTENSEN. *Pictorial History of Western Art.* Mentor. (paperback)

CLENDENIN. *Music: History and Theory.* Doubleday. (paperback)

CRAVEN. *The Rainbow Book of Art.* World.

DUKE and LANCHBERY. *Saga of Flight.* Avon. (paperback)

EBERLE. *Modern Medical Discoveries.* Crowell.

FOX. *Milestones of Medicine.* Random House.

FROST. *Basic Teachings of the Great Philosophers.* Doubleday. (paperback)

GEORGE. *England in Transition.* Penguin. (paperback)

GOMBRICH. *The Story of Art.* Oxford. (paperback)

*HARTMAN. *The World We Live In and How It Came to Be.* Macmillan.

KAINZ and RILEY. *Understanding Art: People, Things and Ideas.* Abrams.

*LAMPREY. *All the Ways of Building.* Macmillan.

McKINNEY. *Music in History, the Evolution of an Art.* American Book.

MACY. *The Story of the World's Literature.* Liveright.

*MEYER. *World Book of Great Inventions.* World.

*MONTGOMERY. *Story Behind Great Inventions.* Dodd.

NEAL. *From Spinning Wheel to Spacecraft.* Messner.

*SHIPPEN and SEIDLOVA. *The Heritage of Music.* Viking.

TAYLOR. *An Illustrated History of Science.* Praeger.

THOMAS. *Understanding the Great Philosophers.* Doubleday.

WRIGHT and RAPPORT. *Great Adventures in Science.* Harper.

BIOGRAPHY

*BAKELESS. *Story-Lives of Great Composers.* Lippincott.

*BOLTON. *Famous American Authors.* Crowell.

*——. *Famous Men of Science.* Crowell.

BRYAN. *Susan B. Anthony, Champion of Women's Rights.* Messner.

*BURLINGAME. *Inventors Behind the Inventor.* Harcourt.

——. *Machines That Built America.* Harcourt.

——. *Scientists Behind the Inventors.* Harcourt.

CURIE. *Madame Curie.* Garden City.

*DE KRUIF. *Men Against Death.* Harcourt.

*——. *Microbe Hunters.* Harcourt.

EBERLE. *Edward Jenner and Smallpox Vaccination.* Watts.

FANNING. *Fathers of Industries.* Lippincott.

FORSEE. *Frank Lloyd Wright: Rebel in Concrete.* Macrae Smith.

GOSS. *Beethoven, Master Musician.* Holt.

——. *Deep Flowing Brook.* Holt.

GRAHAM. *The Story of Charles Dickens.* Abelard-Schuman.

*HARTMAN. *Machines and the Men Who Made the World of Industry.* Macmillan.

*HILL. *Robert Fulton and the Steamboat.* Random House.

*JUDSON. *City Neighbor: The Story of Jane Addams.* Scribner.

KNIGHT. *Robert Koch: Father of Bacteriology.* Watts.

KOMROFF. *Mozart.* Knopf.

LARSEN. *Men Who Changed the World: Stories of Invention and Discovery.* Roy.

MANTON. *A Portrait of Bach.* Abelard-Schuman.

MEYER. *Dynamite and Peace.* Little, Brown.

SEROFF. *Frédéric Chopin.* Viking.

*SHIPPEN. *Men of Medicine.* Viking.

*SOOTIN. *Michael Faraday: From Errand Boy to Master Physicist.* Messner.

SUMMERSON. *Sir Christopher Wren.* Shoe String.

VALLERY–RADOT. *Louis Pasteur.* Knopf.

FICTION

BECKER. *Introducing Charles Dickens.* Dodd.

*DICKENS. *Hard Times.* Dutton.

*——. *Oliver Twist.* Dutton.

HUGO. *Les Misérables.* Washington Square. (paperback)

*LOBDELL. *Thread of Victory.* McKay.

QUEEN VICTORIA (1837–1901). Her long reign coincided with a new era in England. During this period (a historian has stated) the ethics of the prosperous industrialists and businessmen dominated English manners as they dominated English economic life. The race for colonies was an important aspect of England's economy.

PART SEVEN

RIVALRY AMONG THE GREAT POWERS LEADS TO WAR

In Part Five we saw how in some countries autocratic governments replaced feudal anarchy, and how autocracy led men to revolt. Meanwhile another revolution, the Industrial Revolution, was quietly gathering force.

In Part Seven we shall see how democracy and nationalism moved forward in several countries of Europe and the Americas. At the same time, forces unleashed by the Industrial Revolution began to shape international events. The new industries increased a demand for markets, cheap raw materials, and investment opportunities; the industries also turned out powerful new weapons. Consequently, rather abruptly after 1870, a new colonial rivalry sprang up. Within a quarter century or so the industrial nations had seized large parts of Asia, nearly all of Africa, and most of the islands of the seas.

The race for colonies helped to produce bitter feelings among nations. To add to the unfriendliness, newly unified Germany was challenging the dominant position of Great Britain, France, and Russia in European and world affairs. Still another source of trouble was the increasing discontent of Europe's "submerged" nationalities.

By 1914 the great powers, armed to the teeth, had formed two opposing alliances. Suspicious of each other, rivals for colonial empires, quick to resent any slur on national honor, they needed only an excuse for war. The excuse came with the assassination of Austria's Archduke Francis Ferdinand. Eventually these powers were drawn into what became known as World War I.

Toward the close of the war, many men hoped that there might be established a world organization which would represent all nations and would put an end to war. However, their hopes were disappointed in the "lost peace."

19 The Growth of Democracy and Nationalism

GLADSTONE addressing the House of Commons in 1882. As prime minister
four times, he helped democratize British institutions, both political and
social. His reforms ranged from achievement of universal manhood suffrage
to an employers liability act. In an era of rising nationalism, England,
with its industrial might and stable government, played a unique role in
world affairs.

The revolutionary era from about 1775–1848, which we examined in Chapter 15, resulted in substantial gains for democratic institutions. But democracy is a developing or evolutionary process and is therefore never quite complete. We shall undertake in this chapter to show how democracy, and the spirit of nationalism that accompanied it, grew and spread in the Western world to about the end of the nineteenth century. As we shall see, these forces still have a powerful impact on the life of peoples and nations today.

Modern Democracy

What is democracy? The word "democracy" comes from the Greek and means government by the people. It is thus distinguished from autocracy, the rule of one, and from both aristocracy and oligarchy, the rule of a few. Since the late eighteenth century, when the American and French revolutions took place, democracy has had a slow but persistent growth, and has been a powerful influence in shaping modern history.

In ancient Greece "government by the people" was limited. All the people did not have a vote, even in those Greek cities considered most democratic. (See page 64.) The numerous slaves had no political rights, while freedmen and foreigners were seldom allowed to take part in public affairs. A democratic state today does not recognize any slave class, admits foreigners to citizenship, and gives the vote to all native-born and naturalized citizens, regardless of birth, property, or social condition. Within recent years many countries have extended the suffrage to women. This step broadens the idea of "the people" to include practically all adult citizens.

Majorities and minorities. As a working system of government, democracy means majority rule. People are seldom of one mind regarding proposed measures or policies. Of course, a unanimous or nearly unanimous decision is best; failing that, it is necessary to "count heads" and see which side has the more supporters. A government which did not carry out the will of the majority would not be democratic. How far should the rule of a majority go? If it goes so far as to suppress the civil liberties of individuals, then there is little to choose between the absolutism of a democracy and the absolutism of an autocrat. A majority can be as tyrannical as any divine-right king. In a true democracy, therefore, the rights of all minorities must be safeguarded, lest the majority abuse its power. After a decision has been reached on a question, the minority should still have the opportunity to try to change the view of the majority by free and open argument. Democratic constitutions assure that minorities shall have this right by providing for freedom of speech, press, and assembly.

Direct and representative democracy. Ancient democracy was direct, while that of today is representative. Every citizen of Athens had a right to appear in person and vote in the popular assembly. This was direct democracy and was suited to the needs of a small city-state. In a modern state the population is too large and the distances are too great for all the citizens to meet in one public gathering. The voters therefore choose someone to represent them in a parliament or congress.

The Greeks and Romans were acquainted with the representative system but made little use of it. Representation in government developed during the Middle Ages, when such countries as Denmark, Sweden, the Netherlands, France, and England established advisory bodies representing the three estates of clergy, nobles and commoners. (See page 272.) Most of these medieval councils afterward disappeared or became unimportant, but the English Parliament continued to hold a strong place in the government. It furnished a model for the American colonies and later for revolutionary France. During the past hundred and fifty years its influence has spread to nearly all European countries and to many other parts of the world.

Republics and democratic monarchies. In the United States and France democracy has long been associated with a republican form of government. A republic is a government in which the supreme power rests in the elected representatives of the people, instead of in a king. But democracy does not require a republican form of government. Great Britain and certain European states developed governments which, though monarchies in form, are democratic in operation. The king still reigns by hereditary right but he does not rule. The prime minister, leader of the majority party in the legislature, has far more power.

Constitutions. Every democracy has a constitution. It consists of the accepted ideas, or principles, regarding how the government shall be organized, what powers its officers are to exercise, and what rights shall be guaranteed to the people. A democratic nation usually has some one document, or charter, containing its basic ideas of government. Great Britain has no one document of this nature; its constitution is set forth in a series of charters and laws dating back to the Magna Carta. Some of the basic ideas of government may not be written; instead they may be found in customs that have long been accepted. For example, the method actually followed in choosing a President in the United States depends on custom, not upon our Constitution. It is considered part of our "unwritten constitution." The government of Great Britain rests so much upon custom that some people say it has no written constitution.

Early written constitutions. Among the earliest written constitutions for an entire country was the Union of Utrecht (1579), by which the Dutch provinces of the Netherlands bound themselves together "as if they were one province" to maintain their liberties "with lifeblood and goods" against Spain. Another was the Cromwellian Instrument of Government (1653), which was in force for several years. The Constitution of the United States, which went into effect in 1789, was more nearly complete than any of its forerunners. It influenced the first French constitution, adopted in 1791. All these documents, it should be noted, were of *revolutionary* origin. The people won them by successful rebellions. During the nineteenth century other European and American nations gained constitutions through revolution.

An important feature of a democratic constitution is its provision for making changes in the government by peaceful and orderly means. Unless a government adjusts itself to new conditions and new needs, it runs the risk of being overthrown. A truly democratic government is flexible, not rigid.

Modern Nationalism

What is a nation? In molding modern history the idea of nationalism has been at least as powerful as that of democracy. The word "nation" should not be confused with "state," which means the entire political community, nor with "government," which refers to the legislative, executive, and judicial agencies of the state. A "nation" may be defined as a group of people bound together by a common history, and by common customs and ideals, whether or not they have a government of their own.

What makes a nation? The development of national feeling, or consciousness, in a group of people does not depend on their belonging to the same race. Indeed, pure races can be found nowhere. In most parts of the world the inhabitants are of greatly mixed blood. National feeling does depend, in part, on common language. People with different languages do not easily unite. The examples of bilingual Belgium and trilingual Switzerland show, however, that nations may exist without a common language. A common religion also tends to bring people together; nevertheless, most modern nations include groups having different faiths. National feeling is essentially a historic product—the result of sharing experiences as a national group. Because of these shared experiences a nation has a common heritage of memories of the past and hopes for the future. Ireland was long joined to England, but Irish nationality did not disappear. Bohemia, long subject to the Hapsburgs, never lost her national spirit. The Polish nation still lived, even after Poland vanished from the map of Europe. (See page 253.) While national feeling remains, a nation cannot perish. Devotion to one's nation, and a desire that it be independent, is known as nationalism.

Localism. So long as travel and communication were difficult and the average individual spent his entire lifetime in the community where he was born, national feeling was not strong. When the nation was attacked, the soldiers fought under the leadership of a local chief or nobleman and gave him, rather than some distant king, their loyalty. Their patriotism took the form of *localism* rather than nationalism. Members of the upper, or ruling, class had more opportunity to develop a sense of nationality because they had wider contacts and traveled more than the masses of people. Yet in feudal times each petty lord fought with the neighboring lords and resisted the efforts of the king to rule the entire nation.

The rise of nationalism. Toward the close of the Middle Ages, however, the spirit of nationalism blossomed in most parts of Europe. A number of reasons account for the

A STOPPAGE to a STRIDE over the GLOBE

rise of nationalism: (1) the development of the king's power at the expense of the feudal nobles; (2) the growth of the middle class, or bourgeoisie, which is far more national in its attitude than the clergy and the nobles; (3) the rise of national languages and literatures, replacing Latin among the educated and local dialects among the uneducated; (4) the danger of conquest by foreigners, which greatly promoted patriotic feeling and a sense of unity among those threatened with attack; (5) finally, the spread of education and of better means of trade and communication. The masses of people in each land began to feel themselves bound together by a common government and common interests and to call themselves a nation.

Nationalism and the French Revolution. The French Revolution did much to develop national sentiment in France. The revolutionists substituted the French nation for the French kingdom; for loyalty to a monarch they substituted love of country. When a coalition of European powers attempted to crush the revolution, the revolutionists rose as one

man in a citizen army, and to the inspiring
strains of the *Marseillaise,* drove the invaders
from the "sacred soil" of France. The common struggle against outside enemies gave
the French people a greater sense of national
unity than they had ever felt before.

Not satisfied with defending the revolution at home, the French started to spread it
abroad by force of arms. They posed as liberators; very quickly they proved to be conquerors. A republican general, Napoleon
Bonaparte, made the members of the citizen
army into professional soldiers devoted to his
personal fortunes. He led these soldiers to victory on a score of battlefields. Napoleon himself was a man without a country and felt
little sympathy for nationalism. Out of a Europe composed of many independent states,
he wished to create a unified Europe upon the
model of Charlemagne's empire. "I wanted,"
he said at St. Helena, "to found a European
system, a European code of laws, a European
court of appeal; there would have been but

one people throughout Europe." He even intended, had he been successful in the Russian
campaigns, to move the capital of his dominions to the banks of the Tiber. There he
would have revived the glories of imperial
Rome. The European peoples refused to submit to the Napoleonic yoke. Throughout the
Continent, Napoleon aroused a nationalistic
resistance which finally destroyed his empire.

**The Congress of Vienna fails to check na-
tionalism.** After the Congress of Vienna the
rulers of Europe tried to turn the clock back.
(See page 268.) They blocked, but could not
destroy, the national hopes of European peoples. Nationalism, combined with all the liberal and democratic sentiments aroused by
the French Revolution, provoked a series of
revolutions between 1815 and 1848. (See
pages 289–291.) These upheavals were only
partly successful. In the following years, however, nationalism won notable victories in the
unification of Italy (substantially completed
by 1866) and of Germany (achieved in 1871).

How Great Britain Achieved Political Democracy

What is included in Great Britain. Great
Britain is an island consisting of England,
Scotland, and Wales. England is the largest,
most populous, and wealthiest of these divisions. Wales, to the west of England, was
conquered in the thirteenth century, and in
the sixteenth century became a part of the
English parliamentary system. Scotland and
England were combined under one ruler in
1603, when the Scottish king inherited the
throne of England and became king of both
countries. This ruler was James I, the first of
the Stuarts. By the Act of Union in 1707,
Scotland and England came under a common
parliament. In 1800 Ireland was united with
Great Britain. Together they formed the
United Kingdom. Since 1922 a large part of
Ireland has been a self-governing country.

Thus, from 1800 to 1922 the term English, or British, government meant the government which controlled England, Scotland, Wales, Ireland, and certain near-by islands.

Great Britain was undemocratic. In the early 1700's Great Britain was still an undemocratic country. The Glorious Revolution (page 263) had preserved the liberty of the upper classes, but had not given most Englishmen any share in electing the members of Parliament. The legislative body was by no means democratic. The members of the House of Lords, composed of nobles and bishops, inherited their seats or were appointed by the king. The members of the House of Commons were indeed elected, but by only a fraction of the British people.

In the counties, or shires, only certain landowners could vote; in the towns, or boroughs, only a handful of well-to-do people could vote. There were even some boroughs where a rich man, generally a nobleman, had the privilege of appointing a representative. For that reason he was said to carry the borough in his pocket, and his district was called a "pocket borough." At that time in the British Isles as a whole only one person in a hundred had the privilege of voting for members of the House of Commons.

Representation was not based on population. Elections to the House of Commons were also undemocratic because of the unequal population of the election districts. These districts had been set up in the late Middle Ages. Each shire and each borough, regardless of its population, sent two representatives. Since the Middle Ages, however, many of the medieval towns had disappeared, and nothing remained of them but a house or two, a green mound, a park, or a ruined wall. Yet such a town still had representatives in Parliament who were appointed by the man owning the site. Such places were called "rotten boroughs." On the other hand, the towns that had grown up since the Middle

Ages had no representation. Outstanding examples were towns that had become busy manufacturing centers because of the Industrial Revolution. Among them were the flourishing cities of Manchester, Leeds, Birmingham, and Sheffield.

The need for reform. Restrictions on the right to vote and inequalities in representation would have been sufficient reasons for a reform movement. In addition, however, the elections were accompanied by dishonest practices. Because voting was not secret but public, individual voters were frequently bribed or intimidated. Rotten boroughs and pocket boroughs were often sold outright to the highest bidder.

Agitation for parliamentary reform. Efforts to improve these conditions began in the eighteenth century, but for a long time they accomplished nothing. Sober people, alarmed by the revolution in France, saw in the demands for parliamentary reform only radical plots against the government. After 1815, however, the Reign of Terror and Napoleon Bonaparte were no longer bugbears. Public opinion steadily became more hostile to a system of representation which denied political power to so many educated, prosperous members of the middle class. The Whig nobles also took up the liberal cause and made it a party question. The Tories, on their side, stood firm against anything which looked like democracy. The Duke of Wellington, who had become prime minister, even declared that nothing better than the existing system could be devised "by the wit of man." This stubborn refusal to make the slightest reform caused the downfall of the duke's ministry. In 1830, the year of the July Revolution in France (see page 289), the Whigs, under Earl Grey, returned to office. They promised to introduce a bill for parliamentary reform.

Passage of the First Reform Act, 1832. The events which followed show how the parliamentary system works in England. The reform bill introduced by Earl Grey, the Whig prime minister, failed to pass the House of Commons. Parliament was then dissolved and a general election called to test the opinion of the country. The Whigs won, and the Whig ministry, or cabinet, twice more tried to put through a reform bill. Each time the House of Lords turned it down. Popular excitement rose to fever pitch. England seemed on the verge of revolution. In one mass meeting after another the lords were denounced as corrupt and selfish. The prime minister, Earl Grey, advised the king to create a number of new peers, or lords, who would favor reform. The new peers would, of course, be members of the House of Lords and would vote for the reform bill. The king refused to comply with this request, and the prime minister and his cabinet resigned from office. The Duke of Wellington tried to form a Tory ministry but did not succeed. The king then promised to create the necessary peers, and Earl Grey came back as prime minister. The king did not have to create new lords. The mere threat of doing so brought the House of Lords to terms, and in 1832 the long-debated bill quietly became law.

Provisions of the Act. The Reform Act corrected some of the worst evils in the system of electing representatives to the House of Commons. In the first place, the act did away with most of the rotten and pocket boroughs. This left a large number of seats for towns and counties which had too few representatives or none at all. In the second place, the act gave the franchise, or right to vote, to all men in the towns who owned or rented houses worth fifty dollars a year and to those who rented land of a certain value in the country. These two provisions of the act were important steps in bringing political democracy to Great Britain. Nevertheless, the majority of the population, consisting of workingmen, farm laborers, and women, still remained without a vote.

Significance of the Act. The Reform Act brought about a great change in British politics. The revolution of 1688–1689 had transferred the chief power from the king to the upper class, or landed aristocracy. (See pages 263–264.) The parliamentary revolution of 1832 shifted the power to the middle class of merchants, manufacturers, and professional men—the class corresponding to the French bourgeoisie. Henceforth for many years the middle class ruled Great Britain. Furthermore, the events of 1832 proved that the Tory aristocracy, entrenched in the House of Lords, could not permanently go against the popular will. The lords had yielded, however reluctantly, to popular opinion. Their action meant that for the future Great Britain would possess in her parliamentary system a means for orderly reform.

The Chartist movement. Even after the passage of the Reform Act of 1832, only about one ninth of the grown men in Great Britain could vote. Farm laborers, day laborers in the cities, and many of the middle class were left without the franchise because they could not meet the requirements laid down by the First Reform Act. The desire for further parliamentary reform grew, particularly among the laborers. A depression in 1837 which threw many of them out of work deepened their dissatisfaction. In 1838 a group of workers issued a document known as the "People's Charter." It demanded annual meetings of Parliament, universal manhood suffrage, equal electoral districts, the secret ballot, and other reforms considered radical at the time. The workingmen also made their wants known through mass meetings and petitions to Parliament. Chartism, as the movement was called, lost ground during the 1840's because some Chartists staged violent uprisings. It made a temporary comeback in the revolutionary year of 1848, when a huge procession was planned to deliver a monster petition to Parliament. The government prohibited the

WILLIAM EWART GLADSTONE

of Scottish birth, had been educated at aristocratic Eton and Oxford. When only twenty-four years old he entered Parliament from a pocket borough. To many he seemed the "rising hope of the stern, unbending Tories." His advancement was rapid, for he had wealth, family influence, an attractive personality, wide knowledge of both books and men, enormous energy, and great oratorical ability. All things considered, no Englishman of Gladstone's generation equaled him as a public speaker. He was an impressive figure, whether in the House of Commons or on the platform. In time he disappointed his political backers by joining the Liberal party. It was as a Liberal that Gladstone four times became prime minister of Great Britain.

Disraeli, 1804–1881. Benjamin Disraeli belonged to a converted Jewish family of London. His father, a well-known author, had him educated privately. The public first knew him as a novelist. In book after book he heaped ridicule upon the upper classes and called attention to the sufferings of the common people. He entered Parliament as an independent radical. At first, his flowery language and dashing clothes—as a young man

parade, and it was found that the petition contained many forged signatures. The resulting ridicule put an end to Chartism, but almost all the Chartist demands have since become a part of English law.

The promise of further reform. The death of the Chartist movement did not end political unrest. The outcome of the American War between the States was regarded by many Englishmen as a triumph for democracy. It encouraged their demands for popular sovereignty. It seemed absurd that British workingmen should be denied the vote when it was about to be granted to former slaves in the United States. Moreover, two of the leading statesmen of Great Britain became supporters of further parliamentary reform. One of these was Gladstone, a leader of the Liberal party (formerly the Whig party). The other was Disraeli, a leader in the Conservative party (formerly the Tory party).

Gladstone, 1809–1898. William Ewart Gladstone, the son of a rich Liverpool merchant

BENJAMIN DISRAELI, Lord Beaconsfield

he wore bright-colored waistcoats and decked himself with rings—provoked only amusement. Gradually, however, his intelligence, courage, and intense patriotism overcame the prejudice against him. As he gained experience, he toned down his radical viewpoint and before long became a Conservative. Thereafter, he was a staunch defender of the Crown, the established church, and the aristocracy. However, he insisted that they serve the welfare of the people. His program came to be known as "Tory democracy." Disraeli was an expert in parliamentary rules of procedure and was always feared in debate. For thirty years he dominated the Conservative party and twice became prime minister.

The Second Reform Act, 1867. In 1866 Gladstone, then Liberal leader of the House of Commons and the prime minister, introduced a bill providing for further extension of the right to vote. Gladstone's bill was defeated and his ministry overthrown. The Conservatives now returned to power with Disraeli as their real leader, though he was not prime minister. Popular demonstrations throughout the country convinced Disraeli that an extension of the right to vote could no longer be delayed. With Gladstone's aid, he secured the passage of the Second Reform Act in 1867. Under this act the voting population was more than doubled, and most of the factory workmen were enfranchised. The agricultural laborers remained as the only considerable class of men without the vote.

The Third Reform Act, 1884. In the next election after the Reform Act of 1867, the Liberal party returned to power with Gladstone as its leader. In 1872 he secured the passage of a bill providing for the secret, or Australian, ballot. The Ballot Act did away with the old opportunity to buy votes and to threaten voters. Under Gladstone's leadership democratic reform was carried still further in 1884 by passage of the Third Reform Act, which gave the vote to farm laborers. After

its passage the United Kingdom enjoyed practically universal manhood suffrage, such as had already been established in France, Germany, and the United States. The following year another democratic step was taken when Gladstone's government made the election districts of the country practically equal in population.

Parliament Act, 1911. The drive for political democracy in Great Britain carried over into the present century. It now took the form of an attack upon the House of Lords. That body did not represent the people, and yet it frequently blocked legislation which public opinion favored. In 1911 another Liberal, David Lloyd George, led both the Liberal and the Labor parties in securing passage of the famous Parliament Act. The lords agreed to it only when threatened, as in 1832, with being "swamped" by a large number of newly created Liberal peers. The Parliament Act deprived the upper chamber of all control of money bills—that is, bills levying taxes or making appropriations. The act further provided that any bill passed by the Commons in three successive sessions should become law after two years, even though not approved by the House of Lords. Thus by 1911 the real authority in British government was in the hands of the people's representatives— the House of Commons.

Woman Suffrage. About the time of the passage of the Third Reform Act (1884) a campaign began for "votes for women." This demand aroused the anger and ridicule of Liberals and Conservatives alike. Nevertheless, the supporters of woman suffrage were persistent. They formed organizations to promote their cause, debated on the platform and in the newspapers, and introduced bills into Parliament proposing equal political rights for women. The movement made slow progress. A few women, impatient with peaceful methods, became "militant suffragettes." They broke up public meetings, smashed shop windows, slashed paintings in art galleries, and committed other outrages to bring their cause prominently before the people.

Then came World War I. The patriotic service of British women in the hospitals, in munitions factories, and on the farms strengthened the cause of woman suffrage. In 1918 Parliament passed the Equal Franchise Act, granting the right to vote to women who were thirty years of age or older. Ten years later (1928) the government made the qualifications for voting the same for both sexes.

Democratic Great Britain. Great Britain thus abandoned the old feudal idea that voting is a *privilege* attached to the ownership of property, especially land. Voting is now a *right* to be enjoyed by every citizen. The will of the majority of the people guides the actions of Parliament. Politically, Great Britain ranks among the most democratic of modern countries. She has set an example which has been widely followed.

Government of the United Kingdom

The written constitution. The British constitution is partly written and partly unwritten. The written part consists of: (1) such documents as Magna Carta and the Bill of Rights, which represent agreements between king and people; (2) parliamentary statutes, such as the Habeas Corpus Act, the Act of Settlement, and the various reform acts; (3) international treaties, including the Union with Scotland and the Union with Ireland; and (4) the common law as expressed in court decisions. These various documents have never been brought together in one complete statement as in the constitutions of the United States, France, and other modern countries.

The unwritten constitution. The unwritten part of the British constitution includes a mass of customs followed by both Crown and Parliament. Some of them reach back to medieval times, but others are more recent,

SUFFRAGETTES parading with sandwich boards in London in 1902.

such as those relating to the cabinet. Traditional usages of this sort grow up in every government. In the United States custom gives the two major political parties an important part in carrying on the government, although the Constitution does not provide for political parties. The party system has become part of our unwritten constitution.

The Crown. So far as appearances go, the sovereign of Great Britain is a monarch who rules by divine right. Whatever the government does, from the arrest of a criminal to the declaration of a war, is done in his (or her) name. Coins and proclamations still say that he rules "by the grace of God" (*Dei gratia*). But everyone knows that the British sovereign now acts only by and with the advice of his responsible ministers (that is, ministers responsible to the people). He reigns but does not rule. The figurehead king (or queen) occupies, nevertheless, a useful place in the British system of government. As the representative of the entire nation, he often exercises a restraining or moderating influence upon public affairs, especially through his conferences with politicians of both parties. He himself stands above party. A common loyalty to the Crown, as an ancient, dignified, and permanent institution, also helps to bind together Canada, Australia, and the other self-governing dominions of the British Commonwealth.

Parliament. British legal theory makes Parliament consist of the Crown, the House of Lords, and the House of Commons. However, the word "Parliament" is often used to refer to the House of Commons alone. The part played by the Crown is now limited to giving approval to a bill after its passage by the Commons and the Lords. The monarch is expected to give assent to every bill passed. The royal veto has not been expressly taken away, but this privilege was last exercised by Queen Anne in 1707. Nor may the courts set aside an act of Parliament as unconstitutional, for every statute is a part of the constitution. An American student, accustomed to the division of powers between President, Congress, and the federal courts, finds it hard to realize that supreme authority resides in the British Parliament. The only check upon it is the good sense of the British people.

The British cabinet. Parliament works through a committee known as the cabinet. This body developed during the eighteenth century and exists purely by custom. It has no place whatever in the written constitution of Great Britain. The cabinet includes about twenty members of Parliament, all of whom usually belong to the party in power. During both world wars and also in 1931, there was a "coalition" cabinet, representing all parties. Except when there is a coalition government, a caucus of the majority party in Parliament selects members of the cabinet. The prime minister, who is the recognized leader of the party and a member of Parliament, must approve the selection of cabinet members. The cabinet acts together in all matters, thus presenting a united front to Parliament and the country. If the people do not like what the administration does, it is easy to fix the blame.

Cabinet government in the United Kingdom. The cabinet exercises both executive and legislative powers. It appoints officials and is responsible for carrying laws into effect. At the same time the cabinet introduces all important bills into the House of Commons. The Commons may amend the measures, though amendments are usually few and unimportant. If the Commons votes against a major cabinet bill or passes a resolution of "no confidence," one of two things follows. Either the cabinet resigns, or it asks the king to dissolve Parliament and order a general election. In case the cabinet resigns, the king invites the leader of the opposition party to form a cabinet. If an election is called and the voters choose a majority favorable to the cabinet, it may remain in office; otherwise the prime minister and his colleagues give way to a cabinet formed by the opposition. Unless the king dissolves Parliament under the circumstances just described, elections for members of the House of Commons take place at least once every five years.

The French Achieve a Stable Republic

Louis Napoleon. Much of European history from 1848 to 1871 centers about the personality of the second French emperor, Louis Napoleon. He influenced the fortunes of France, Italy, Germany, Austria, and Russia almost as much as had his uncle, Napoleon Bonaparte, a half century earlier. Louis Napoleon's early life was a succession of adventures. When Louis XVIII came to the throne, Louis Napoleon was exiled from France. He found his way to many lands, and in Italy even became a member of a revolutionary secret society. Twice he tried to provoke an uprising in France. The first time he was captured and deported to the United States. The second time the authorities sentenced him to life imprisonment, but after six years he escaped to England. There he waited, confident in his destiny as a Bonaparte, until the events of 1848 called him home. His election to the presidency of the Second French Republic followed. (See page 291.)

President Napoleon becomes emperor. According to the republican constitution of 1848, the president was limited to one term of four years. But Louis Napoleon did not intend to retire to private life. As the fourth and last year of his presidency approached, he put through a *coup d'état.* On December 2, 1851, he dissolved the legislature, arrested his chief opponents, and stationed loyal troops throughout Paris. He then drafted a new constitution, which made him president for another term of ten years with almost absolute authority. In a carefully controlled *plebiscite,* or popular vote in which the voter was limited to saying "yes" or "no," the people approved these changes overwhelmingly. There remained only one more step to complete Louis Napoleon's ambition. In 1852, with almost no opposition, another plebiscite authorized him to accept the title of Napoleon III, hereditary emperor of the French. Thus began the Second French Empire.

Government under Napoleon III. The French people had welcomed Napoleon III for several reasons. The Napoleonic legend made a powerful appeal to a people who longed to see France restored to first rank among European nations. Moreover, the bourgeoisie feared the growth of socialism among the workingmen, who had fought against the republican government during the terrible "June days" of 1848. Under Napoleon III, France had all the machinery of popular rule—a constitution, universal manhood suffrage, and a legislature. Nevertheless, it soon became clear that real democracy did not exist. Candidates for office were nominated and elected under the direct supervision of the government. The legislature could consider only the measures presented to it by the

EMPEROR NAPOLEON III

emperor, could not question the government's ministers, could not regulate the expenditure of money, and could not publish its own discussions. A General Security Act permitted the government to imprison or exile political suspects without trial. Newspapers which criticized the emperor were, after two warnings, suppressed. In the universities, liberal-minded professors lost their positions.

Prosperity under Napoleon III. The people of France were more willing to accept the loss of freedom because under the Second Empire they enjoyed material prosperity. Napoleon III's government provided vast public works and many holidays. Unemployment was overcome. Paris was rebuilt into the most beautiful and modern city in the world. Napoleon's admirers called him "emperor of the workmen." During this period businessmen profited by the remarkable development of banks, factories, railways, canals, and steamship lines. The progress made was strikingly displayed at the first Paris Exposition in 1855, to which foreign visitors flocked to see the products of French industry and art.

The imperial court under Napoleon III. Napoleon III failed to marry into any royal family of Europe because he was regarded as an adventurer.. He therefore married a Spanish lady, Eugénie de Montijo. Her beauty and elegance helped to make the court at the

Tuileries a center of European fashion such as it had been under the Old Regime. From Eugénie's day until World War II, Paris continued to be the social capital of the world.

Napoleon III's foreign policy. At first, success seemed to follow Napoleon in his dealings abroad. In 1854 he joined England in the Crimean War against Russia. (See page 407.) By his alliance he established cordial relations with England and won honor for France. Furthermore, at the close of the war in 1856 Napoleon III presided at the peace conference in Paris. This gave him added prestige and influence. In 1859 he was able to annex Savoy and Nice as a result of having aided Sardinia in its war against Austria. (See page 393.) He completed the conquest of Algeria in North Africa, acquired some islands in the Pacific, secured valuable trading privileges in China, and laid the foundations for French Indo-China. Fortune smiled upon Napoleon III, but only temporarily.

Napoleon III meets reverses. One check to Napoleon's ambitions came in connection with the Seven Weeks' War in 1866 between Prussia and Austria. (See page 397.) The war was part of a carefully laid plan of Bismarck, the Prussian chancellor, to unite Germany under Hohenzollern rule. Napoleon III wanted a disunited and weak Germany and believed that the conflict between Prussia and Austria would keep it so. He therefore remained neutral in exchange for Bismarck's vague promise that France might secure compensation in territory along the Rhine. Prussia's quick and unexpected victory alarmed Napoleon. He tried in vain to get compensations (Belgium, the Rhenish Palatinate, Luxembourg) to balance Prussia's new power. Bismarck blocked his efforts.

In 1867 Napoleon's foreign schemes suffered another setback. During the American War between the States, his troops had overrun much of Mexico on the pretext of collecting debts owed to French citizens. His real motive became evident when he overthrew the liberal republic under Juárez and established the Austrian Archduke Maximilian as emperor of Mexico. The United States protested against this violation of the Monroe Doctrine, and the French troops were withdrawn. The Mexicans then executed the ruler who had been forced upon them, and Napoleon's dream of an empire in America came to an end.

By 1867 Napoleon had few friends among the nations. Russia, Prussia, Austria, Sardinia, the United States, and even England distrusted and disliked him. His failures abroad and his despotism at home had lost him many supporters. Napoleon saw the rising tide of opposition and tried to meet it by liberal reforms, including a new constitution. They came too late. Events were shortly to bring about his overthrow.

Franco-Prussian War, 1870–1871. A revolution had broken out in Spain, and the liberals there had offered the throne to a cousin of William I, the Hohenzollern monarch of Prussia. Napoleon III at once informed the Prussian monarch that he would regard the acceptance of the Spanish crown by a Hohenzollern as a sufficient reason for war. William then gave way and persuaded his cousin to refuse the throne. Napoleon was not satisfied. He further demanded that William promise never to allow a Hohenzollern to become a candidate for the Spanish throne. William declined to make his pledge, and from the town of Ems, a vacation place where he was staying, he telegraphed his decision to Bismarck at Berlin. Bismarck seized the opportunity to provoke France into war, which he regarded as a sure method to complete the unification of Germany. Making certain that the Prussian forces were ready for war, he gave the king's statement to the newspapers, not in its original form but in an edited version. The abbreviated telegram had two results: (1) It caused the Prussians to feel that the French ambassador had insulted their king. (2) It caused the French to feel that the Prussian king had insulted their ambassador. Bismarck himself said later that the Ems dispatch was intended to have the effect "of a red flag on the Gallic bull." Soon after receiving it, France declared war. What followed left Europe breathless. Fighting began in mid-July. On September 2, 1870, the main army of the French, under Napoleon III and Marshal MacMahon, was defeated and captured at Sedan, less than eighty miles from Paris. Napoleon himself became a prisoner, and the Germans besieged Paris.

GAMBETTA proclaims the Third French Republic.

The French proclaim the Third Republic, 1870. Two days after news of the disaster at Sedan reached Paris, revolt broke out in the capital. Empress Eugénie fled with her son to England, and the absent emperor was deposed as being responsible for the "ruin, invasion, and dismemberment of the country." The revolutionists then set up a provisional republican government. Lyons, Marseilles, Bordeaux, and other provincial cities took similar action. This time Paris did not impose a republic upon the rest of the country; the cities in the provinces declared for it of their own accord. The fact is important in helping to explain why the Third Republic lasted so much longer than its predecessors.

France makes peace with Germany, 1871. The provisional government undertook the task of driving the Germans from French soil. Gambetta, the most prominent republican leader, escaped from Paris in a balloon, roused the fighting spirit of the French people, and for several months carried on a brave but hopeless struggle against the Germans. The diplomatic efforts of Adolphe Thiers to enlist foreign aid for France were equally useless. Paris could not be saved. After the fall of the capital an armistice was arranged, and the French people elected a National Assembly. The assembly promptly ratified the humiliating Treaty of Frankfort, by which

France agreed: (1) to pay an indemnity of one billion dollars within three years, (2) to support a German army of occupation until this sum was paid, and (3) to cede to Germany the province of Alsace and most of the province of Lorraine. France never accepted the loss of these two provinces. Her anger over their loss helped to bring on World War I, which broke out in 1914.

Adolphe Thiers sustains France. Fortunately for France, during these troubled times she had an able statesman at the head of affairs. Adolphe Thiers (tyâr) was seventy-three years old when the Franco-Prussian War broke out. He had long been famous as a historian of the revolutionary and Napoleonic era, as a journalist whose vigorous pen helped to overthrow the reactionary Charles X (see page 289), as the prime minister of Louis Philippe, and as the most effective critic in parliament of the short-sighted policies of Napoleon III. The downfall of the Second Empire gave Thiers a great opportunity and he took advantage of it. The National Assembly promptly appointed him head of the government and soon afterward made him president of the republic. He negotiated the peace treaty with Germany and quickly raised the billion dollars to pay the indemnity. By 1873 the German armies of occupation were out of France. More difficult was the problem of the Parisian revolutionists, who were called "Communards." They were Socialists and radical republicans who violently opposed the National Assembly, which was full of monarchists. The Communards believed in decentralizing the government. They wished to establish local self-governing units, or *communes*, run by workingmen. The Paris Commune engaged the troops of Thiers's government in a bloody street fight that lasted two months (April–May, 1871). Both sides resorted to the use of cruel methods. In the end, the Commune was suppressed, with a greater loss of life and more destruction to property than marked the Reign of Terror.

Gambetta sustains the Third Republic. A long time passed before France became republican in much more than name. The provisional republican government was left in control because the quarreling factions who opposed a republic could not agree upon a monarch. Their quarrels played into the hands of the republicans under the leadership of Léon Gambetta. To him the salvation of France lay in having a republic. He made it his mission to spread republican ideas among conservative Frenchmen. No one was better fitted for the work. Gambetta's services during the Franco-Prussian War endeared him to the masses, while his oratory and lively personality fascinated even his political opponents. More and more of the people who had formerly been monarchists now accepted the republic as permanent. The result was that in 1875 the National Assembly passed a series of basic laws which became the constitution of the Third Republic.

Stability of the Third Republic. For seventy years the Third Republic weathered all the storms which threatened its existence. The monarchists faded into political unimportance; the army ceased to be a hotbed of antirepublican agitation; the clergy gradually accepted the loss of the privileged position which they enjoyed before 1905, when the Third Republic completely separated church and state. By the time of World War I, the republic had the support of nearly every Frenchman.

The French government. The form of government provided by the constitution of 1875 was a parliamentary republic. The legislature, or National Assembly, consisted of the Chamber of Deputies and the Senate. The deputies were elected for a term of four years by universal manhood suffrage, and the senators were chosen indirectly for a term of nine years by electoral colleges in the departments. The premier, or prime minister, and his cabinet were responsible to the Chamber of Deputies. The cabinet, or ministry, had to resign if a majority in the Chamber of Deputies did not support its measures. The ministry was the real head of the government rather than the president, who was largely a figurehead.

Under the Third Republic, France had no real parties but only political groups. For lack of a better name, these groups are usually spoken of as "parties." Most members of the Chamber of Deputies were republicans of various shades of opinion. There were several groups, or parties, of Socialists, as well as a few monarchists who wanted to restore either the Bourbons or the Bonapartes. The monarchists sat at the extreme right of the presiding officer and the Socialists at the extreme left. The other groups were in the center of the chamber. This arrangement gave rise to the terms "Right," "Left," and "Center" to indicate shades of political opinion.

Ministerial changes. The existence of many political groups explains why changes of ministry occurred so frequently in France. No ministry could be formed except one which represented a coalition, or bloc, of several groups; no ministry could live long unless it kept the support of several groups. In fact, all ministries under the Third Republic were short-lived. From 1875–1940 France averaged more than one ministry a year, usually re-appointed to different positions. This made for continuity of government policy. Another stabilizing influence was the large body of permanent officials (the bureaucracy) who continued in office when a ministry fell.

The Third Republic survives crises. For seventy years the Third Republic weathered many storms. Perhaps the most serious crisis occurred over the famous Dreyfus case. In 1894 Alfred Dreyfus, a Jewish army officer, was sentenced by a military court to life imprisonment. The charge was that he gave military secrets to a foreign power. Convinced of his innocence, a number of supporters of the republican government demanded that the case be reopened. Among them was the novelist Émile Zola, who accused the army of shielding the real traitor. Dreyfus was finally exonerated in 1906 by the highest French court. The outcome discredited the military men, monarchists, and clergy who had been against Dreyfus and were enemies of the Republic. The Third Republic now got its second wind.

The Italians Achieve National Unity

Italy before the French Revolution. From about 1550 to the outbreak of the French Revolution Italy had been in a state of decline. The glories of Renaissance art, literature, and scholarship had become but a memory. The Italians were still divided into many petty states, just as they had been since the late Middle Ages. (See map, page 392.) For the most part they were ruled by despots, whose bitter quarrels and rivalries made Italy an easy prey for foreign aggressors. Centuries of misrule, civil strife, and foreign interference had stifled the energies of the nation. Moreover, prosperity had steadily declined as a result of the shifting of trade centers from the Mediterranean to the Atlantic. This shift was brought about by the discovery of the New World and of a new route to India around the southern tip of Africa. Divided, dependent, and poor, Italy had fallen on evil days.

Italy during the revolutionary and Napoleonic era. The French Revolution came as a shock to the Italian people. It stirred a new spirit in them. The armies of revolutionary France drove the Austrians out of Italy, set up republics in the northern part of the peninsula, and swept away the abuses of the Old Regime. (See page 268.) The Italians began to think that they too needed to make over their country. Napoleon Bonaparte, himself an Italian by birth, continued the unifying work of the French revolutionary army. Except for the islands of Sardinia and Sicily, he made all Italy either a part of France or dependent on France. Throughout Italy he introduced personal freedom, religious toleration, equality before the law, and the justice of the Code Napoléon. (See pages 280–281.) Most Italians welcomed these reforms and were determined to keep them.

Italy between 1815 and 1848. The decisions of the Congress of Vienna in 1815 (page 286) were a cruel disappointment to patriotic Italians. Again they saw their country dismembered, made subject to Austria, and placed under reactionary princes. People who had once experienced more enlightened rule would not stand for this restoration of the Old Regime. The bourgeoisie, many of the nobles, and some of the better educated artisans now began to work for the overthrow of Austrian power in the peninsula. They also wanted to form constitutional governments in the various states. Unable to agitate in public, the Italians had to resort to underground methods. A number of secret societies sprang up. Foremost among these was the *Carbonari,* or charcoal burners, which started the first unsuccessful uprisings against Austria in 1820.

In the 1830's a new movement for national unity sprang up in Italy. It is known as the *Risorgimento,* or "resurrection." Its leaders

COUNT CAMILLO CAVOUR

1815

1861

were well educated, spirited young men. The most outstanding of these was Mazzini, who in 1831 organized Young Italy, another revolutionary society. Its motto was "God and the people"; its purpose, the creation of a republic. Many patriotic men who did not favor republican principles hoped to form a federation of the Italian states under the pope. Many more put their faith in a constitutional monarchy under the Sardinian king.

Sardinia and Italian unity. The kingdom of Sardinia included not only the island of that name but also Savoy and Piedmont on the mainland. (See map above.) In 1850 Sardinia ranked as the leading state in Italy. It was, moreover, almost the only Italian state not controlled by Austria. In the revolutionary year of 1848 Sardinia had led a valiant but unsuccessful effort to drive the Austrians from Italian soil. (See page 292.) The pope had shown himself unwilling to head the national movement, and Mazzini had failed in an attempt to set up a Roman republic. (See page 292.) Hence the eyes of Italian patriots turned more and more for leadership to the king of Sardinia, Victor Emmanuel II.

Cavour. Fortunately, Victor Emmanuel II had a great minister in Count Cavour. His plain, square face, fringed with a ragged beard, his half-closed eyes that blinked through steel-bowed spectacles, and his short, burly figure did not suggest the statesman. Cavour, however, was finely educated and widely traveled. He knew England well, admired the English system of parliamentary government, and felt a deep hatred of absolutist principles. Unlike the poetical and rash Mazzini, Cavour had all the patience, caution, and mastery of details essential for successful leadership.

Sardinia under Cavour. In 1852 Cavour became the Sardinian premier, a position which he continued to fill, with but one brief interruption, until his death nine years later. Faithfully supported by Victor Emmanuel II, Cavour bent every effort to develop the economic resources of the kingdom, promote education, and reorganize the army. He made Sardinia a strong and liberal state—strong enough to cope with Austria and liberal enough to attract to herself all the other states of Italy. At the same time he managed foreign affairs most skillfully. He joined England and France against Russia in the Crimean War. This gave him the opportunity at the peace conference to call the attention of Europe to

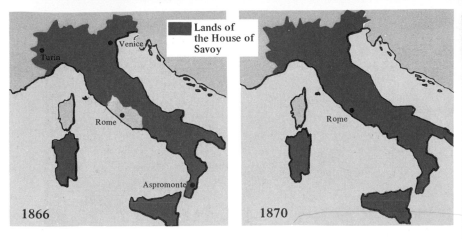

GIUSEPPE GARIBALDI

THE UNIFICATION OF ITALY. Out of a collection of petty states, Victor Emmanuel II, his shrewd premier, Cavour, and Garibaldi welded a united Italy around the kingdom of Sardinia. In doing so they extended the rule of the house of Savoy over the entire peninsula.

the sad condition of Italy. Then he made an alliance with Napoleon III, who promised to send an army to help Sardinia drive the Austrians from Italy. In return for his aid, Sardinia was to give France the duchy of Savoy and the port of Nice. (See map above.)

Quarrel between Austria and Sardinia. Once he had struck the bargain with Napoleon, Cavour had to provoke the Austrian government into a declaration of war. He wanted Austria to appear the aggressor. Cavour's agents secretly stirred up disturbances in Lombardy and Venetia. In an outburst of reckless fury Francis Joseph I, the Hapsburg emperor, finally sent an ultimatum to Sardinia. It offered the choice between disarming in three days or war. Cavour joyfully chose war. "The die is cast," he exclaimed, "and we have made history."

Austro-Sardinian War, 1859. The fighting which followed lasted only a few months. Sardinia and France carried everything before them. They won the important battles of Magenta and Solferino. They drove the Austrians out of Lombardy and might have driven them out of Venetia as well, but Napoleon III suddenly decided to withdraw from the war. He had not counted on the unifica-

tion of all Italy, and the outburst of national feeling that accompanied the conflict promised to bring that result. Napoleon did not welcome the prospect of a strong national state as a neighbor of France and therefore he ceased to help Italy. Victor Emmanuel II and Cavour, left in the lurch by their ally, were obliged to make peace with the Hapsburg ruler. Lombardy was ceded to Sardinia, but Venetia remained in Austrian hands. However, the first step in Italian unification had been taken.

Central Italy annexed, 1860. The people of central Italy voluntarily took the second step in unification. Tuscany, Parma, Modena, and Romagna expelled their rulers and declared for annexation to Sardinia. Napoleon III accepted this action after Cavour handed over to him both Savoy and Nice. Cavour did so despite the fact that the French ruler had not carried out his part of the agreement to free Italy "from the Alps to the Adriatic."

Garibaldi. The third step in unification was taken by Giuseppe Garibaldi, a sailor from Nice. He was a picturesque, heroic figure. At the age of twenty-four Garibaldi joined Young Italy, took part in an insurrection, and was condemned to death. Escaping to South

America, he fought many years in the revolutionary struggles there. He returned to Italy during the uprising of 1848 and won renown in the defense of Mazzini's Roman Republic. The collapse of the revolutionary movement made him once more a fugitive. He lived for some time in New York, later became the skipper of a Peruvian ship, and finally settled down as a farmer on a little Italian island. In 1859 he left his farm to take part in the Sardinian war against Austria.

Garibaldi and the Kingdom of the Two Sicilies. In the following year, 1860, Garibaldi with one thousand red-shirted volunteers went to the aid of the Sicilians, who were revolting against their Bourbon king. It seemed a foolhardy expedition—one thousand against the Bourbon king's hundred thousand. Within a month, however, Garibaldi and his "Red Shirts" had conquered the entire island of Sicily. From there they crossed to the mainland and soon entered Naples in triumph. The Kingdom of the Two Sicilies, as the union of Sicily and southern Italy was called, voted for annexation to Sardinia. Garibaldi then handed over his conquests to Victor Emmanuel II. The two liberators rode through the streets of Naples side by side, amid the enthusiastic applause of the people.

Kingdom of Italy. Thus within two years the diplomacy of Cavour, the aid of Napoleon III, Garibaldi's sword, and the will of the people united the larger part of Italy. In 1860 a national parliament met and conferred the crown upon Victor Emmanuel II. The new kingdom added Venetia in 1866, when Italy joined forces with Prussia against Austria in the Seven Weeks' War. (See page 397.) Rome remained as the chief hindrance to the completion of Italian unification. The pope refused to recognize the kingdom of Italy, and Rome was defended by a French army, sent in 1849 by Napoleon III. (See page 292.) Upon the outbreak of the Franco-Prussian War, however, Napoleon withdrew his troops. The Italians took quick advantage of the opportunity to seize Rome. The temporal power of the papacy (its rule over an earthly state), dating back to the Middle Ages, thus came to an end. The States of the Church disappeared, and the territory ruled by the pope was limited to the land occupied by the Vatican and Lateran palaces in Rome. In 1871, the "city of the Seven Hills," once the capital of the Roman Empire, became the capital of the unified, modern kingdom of Italy.

Italy after unification, 1871–1914. "We have united Italy. It remains for us to unite the Italians," remarked an Italian statesman in 1870. For thirty years thereafter the new kingdom struggled with little success against a number of handicaps. The government of Italy was based on the Sardinian constitution of 1848, which had been patterned after Great Britain's. But Italians were not used to a parliamentary system nor a centralized government. Moreover, only about 30 per cent of them could read or write and those who could not do so were not permitted to vote. Consequently, the middle and upper classes ran the government. The Roman question also divided the Italians. The pope called upon Catholics not to co-operate with the new regime because it had taken away most of his temporal power. Finally, Italy was a poor land. Her soil could not support her growing population, and her industries suffered for lack of iron and coal.

By 1900, however, the tide had turned; Italy began to overcome her handicaps. Under Giovanni Giolitti, prime minister during most of the period from 1900–1915, the government helped to develop hydroelectric power to turn the wheels of industry, spent considerable sums on education, nationalized the railroads and insurance companies, established a system of old age pensions, and in 1912 granted universal manhood suffrage. Meanwhile, Italy's trade more than doubled. The net result was a revival of national spirit among the people. It found expression in a drive for more territory.

Unredeemed Italy. After 1871 there was still some Italian territory under Austrian rule. The district around Trent in the Alps, or the Trentino, and the district around Trieste at the head of the Adriatic remained parts of the Hapsburg empire. These areas were called *Italia Irredenta* or "Unredeemed Italy." The desire to round out the Italian kingdom by adding to it *Italia Irredenta* was one of the reasons which led Italy to take the side of the Allies in World War I.

The German States Achieve Unity

The German states. The political unification of Germany was another striking victory for nationalism. The German movement did not involve the removal of a foreign power, as was the case in Italy. At the opening of the French Revolution, the map of Germany was a crazy quilt of independent kingdoms, duchies, principalities, and free cities. These independent states had grown out of the feudal system. Each made its own laws, held its own courts, conducted its own foreign affairs, and had its own army, tariff, and coinage. Here then, in central Europe, was a large, populous, and wealthy area which lacked a national government such as had existed for centuries in England, France, Spain, and Russia.

Napoleon promotes unification in Germany. It is a peculiar fact that Napoleon Bonaparte was responsible for the first steps toward German unification. He secured for France the German lands west of the Rhine and thus took away the territories of nearly a hundred princes. He afterward reorganized much of Germany east of the Rhine, with the idea of setting up a few large states as a barrier between France on the one side and Austria and Prussia on the other. This work survived the emperor's downfall. The German Confederation in 1815 included only thirty-eight independent states, as compared with more than three hundred that existed in 1789.

The way was now open for a closer union of the "Germanies."

German nationalism also owed much to Napoleon Bonaparte. The struggle of the states against him drew them together, at least for the moment, in support of a common patriotic cause. Prussians, Saxons, and Bavarians rose in arms, not to seek conquests but to protect a common fatherland. "I have only one fatherland," wrote the Prussian minister of state, Baron vom Stein. "That is called Germany."

The German Confederation hinders national unity. In 1815 the hopes of German nationalists were dashed by the Congress of Vienna. It had no sympathy with the popular agitation for a national state. Instead, the congress provided for a German Confederation, which was a union of rulers rather than of states. Each member of the confederation continued to be independent except for foreign affairs, which were controlled by a diet, or parliament, under the leadership of Austria. The diet was composed of delegates sent by the reigning princes of each of the thirty-eight states in the confederation.

The *Zollverein* promotes national unity. Meanwhile the German states were becoming economically unified. The tariff duties levied by each member of the confederation against the goods of every other member greatly hampered commerce and industry. To meet this difficulty, Prussia led the way in 1834 by forming a tariff union, or *Zollverein* (tsŏl'fĕr-īn'). By 1842 it included nearly all the German states except Austria. Free trade prevailed among the members of the *Zollverein*, while high protective duties shut out imports from abroad. The *Zollverein* showed the German people some of the advantages of union and encouraged them to look to Prussia as the leader in further steps toward unity.

Why Prussia was the leader in German unification. The Prussian kingdom seemed to be the natural core of a unified Germany. Her population, except for the Poles, was en-

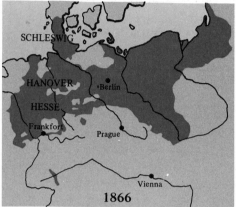

tirely German; she had led Germany in the heroic struggle against Napoleon; and since 1850 she had possessed a constitution which, while not democratic, at least established some measure of representative government. The interests of Austria, on the contrary, were divided between her German and numerous non-German peoples, and the Austrian government was thoroughly autocratic. Neither nationalists nor democrats could expect help from the Hapsburgs. As for the central and southern states—Saxony, Bavaria, Württemberg, Baden, Hanover, and the rest—none was large enough or strong enough to attempt the task of unification. But if the Hohenzollerns undertook it, how would they carry it through? Would they merge Prussia in a German nation, as Sardinia had been merged in Italy, or would they dominate Germany?

Bismarck, 1815–1898. The guiding star of German unification was the famous statesman Otto von Bismarck. He was a member of an aristocratic landowning family, well educated, and conscious of the superior position of his class. During the revolutionary period of 1848, he strongly denounced parliamentary government. Throughout his career he remained antidemocratic in his sentiments. The most valuable training for his task of unifying Germany was service as a delegate to the diet of the German Confederation and as ambassador to Russia and France. In 1862 he became chief minister of William I, king of Prussia. Bismarck was now convinced that Germany could be unified only by force, or by a policy of "blood and iron." This meant the building up in Prussia of a great war machine. Accordingly, Bismarck and the able general Von Moltke bent every effort to make the Prussian army the best in Europe, as it had been in the days of Frederick the Great. (See page 254.) In accomplishing this purpose, Bismarck defied the parliament by levying taxes without its consent. Nothing was to stand in the way of his goal—the unification of Germany under Prussian leadership. How well he succeeded events soon showed.

Prussia goes to war with Austria, 1866. To place Prussia at the head of Germany meant a conflict with Austria, for that power would never willingly surrender her leadership in the German Confederation. Bismarck deliberately set about to stir up trouble with Austria. To do this, he first made Austria his ally in the so-called Schleswig-Holstein dispute. In 1863 Denmark had annexed these two duchies, largely German in population, contrary to an agreement among the great powers made in 1852. A short war followed between Denmark on the one side and Austria and Prussia on the other (1864). As a result the king of Denmark gave up all claims to Schleswig-Holstein. Bismarck had foreseen that it would be easy to start a quarrel with Austria over what should be done with the two duchies. He first made certain that France would not interfere in a conflict between Prussia and Austria and that Italy would be his ally. (See pages 318, 324.) Then he goaded the Austrians into declaring war. Thanks to the careful preparation of the Prussian army, to the use of a new rifle called a "needle gun," and to Von Moltke's brilliant strategy, it turned out to be a Seven Weeks' War (1866). The Austrians suffered a crushing defeat at Sadowa, and Francis Joseph I, the Austrian emperor, had to sue for peace. Bismarck did not humble Austria by making the peace terms too harsh. He required simply that the German Confederation should be broken up, that Austria should not be a member of any new confederation, that the Schleswig-Holstein duchies should become a part of Prussia, and that Venetia should be given to Italy.

Prussia forms a new confederation. Bismarck now had a free hand in Germany. He began by annexing several small German states to bring together the scattered Prussian lands. He then required all the remaining German states north of the river Main to enter a North German Confederation controlled by Prussia. The four states south of the Main, which had fought on the side of Austria, did not enter the new confederation. They agreed, however, to place their armies at the disposal of Prussia in case of a conflict with France.

Prussia goes to war with France, 1870–1871. Bismarck believed that combined action by the North German and South German states against a common foe would arouse national feeling and complete the work of unification under Prussia. He also believed that war between the Germans and the French was inevitable. The French emperor was ready to risk a struggle with the Germans. He thought that a victory over Prussia would appeal to the French people and strengthen his waning prestige. The conflict came in 1870, and ended in a victory for the Germans. (See pages 388–389.)

Formation of the German Empire, 1871. The time had now come to organize a German national state under the leadership of Prussia. Bismarck did not miss the opportunity. While the conquering German armies were still besieging Paris, and before the Treaty of Frankfort (see page 319) had been signed, a united Germany came into existence. The four South German states—Bavaria, Württemberg, Baden, and Hesse-Darmstadt—now agreed to enter the North German Confederation, which was renamed the German Empire. On January 18, 1871, in the Hall of Mirrors in the French city of Versailles, the Hohenzollern ruler, William I, took the title of German emperor.

Government of the German Empire. The federal empire set up in 1871 became one of the powerful countries of the world. Its constitution remained practically unchanged until World War I; consequently, its main outlines are of interest to us. The chief executive power was in the hands of the kaiser, or emperor, who commanded the army and navy, carried on foreign affairs, and exerted a dominating influence in domestic matters. The legislative power was vested in the *Bundesrat* and the *Reichstag*. The *Bundesrat,* or federal council, consisted of delegates appointed by the hereditary rulers of the various states making up the empire. Prussia's delegates numbered seventeen out of a total of twenty-five; hence she controlled the activities of this body. The *Bundesrat* drew up the bills to be considered by the *Reichstag* and had a veto power over acts passed by the *Reichstag*. The *Reichstag,* or imperial parliament, contained nearly four hundred members elected by manhood suffrage. It could debate and postpone, but eventually it had to accept the will of the kaiser and the *Bundesrat*. The kaiser exercised much of his power through a chancellor, or chief minister, who was appointed by and solely responsible to the kaiser. Thus the federal empire was unlike the governments of Great Britain, France, or the United States. Its government was constitutional but autocratic.

Achievements of the new national government. For almost twenty years after 1871, William I and his chancellor, Bismarck, shaped the policies of the new German Empire. They provided the empire with a uniform code of criminal and civil law, a supreme court, an imperial bank (the *Reichsbank*), an imperial coinage with the mark as its basis, and an imperial bureau to control the railroads. Germany became a pioneer in social legislation. Bismarck feared the growth of socialism. He believed that by granting reforms and thus stealing the thunder of the Socialists he would prevent the workingmen from joining revolutionary parties. Accordingly, in the 1880's laws were passed regulating hours of labor and providing workers' insurance benefits in case of sickness, accident, and old age. "In Prussia," Bismarck once remarked, "it is the kings, not the people, who make revolutions." The activities of the empire in colonial affairs will be treated later. (See page 420.)

Germany becomes an industrial power. Germany's industrial progress matched her sensational advance as a political power. The Industrial Revolution came late in Germany, but the unification of the country speeded its pace remarkably. Large deposits of coal and iron, an excellent railway system, fine technical training for workmen, and the use of the most modern methods and machinery all helped in bringing about a rapid increase in factory production. By 1912 Germany had surpassed England in the production of steel and in the export of machinery. The government took steps intended to promote industrial prosperity. Bismarck put through a high tariff in 1879 to protect the "infant industries" of Germany against foreign competition. Similar protection was soon extended to agricultural products. The government also helped create prosperity by its wise management of the state-owned railways and by its construction of a system of canals throughout Germany. As a result, transportation became cheaper and more convenient. At the beginning of the twentieth century the young industrial giant, Germany, had become a strong rival of Great Britain and the United States for leadership in world trade.

Bismarck's struggle with the Catholics and the Socialists. Bismarck achieved unusual success as the pilot of the new German ship of state. Nevertheless, two of his policies met with complete failure. One was his attempt to weaken the influence of the Catholic Church in German politics; the other was his effort to suppress the Socialists. Bismarck and many Germans looked upon Catholicism and socialism as dangers to the independence and unity of Germany. The Catholics expressed loyalty to an authority outside the empire, namely, the pope at Rome. The Socialists were part of an international movement that

EMPEROR WILLIAM I during the Franco-Prussian War. The emperor is in the center with the crown prince at the left. On the right of the emperor is Von Moltke, while in the rear of the crown prince is Bismarck.

aimed to overthrow existing governments or to introduce radical changes in them. (See page 301.) Both the Catholics and the Socialists in the *Reichstag* nettled Bismarck by opposing many of his plans. Moreover, many patriotic Germans developed a dislike for groups with foreign connections. In 1872 Bismarck opened his anti-Catholic campaign by expelling the Jesuit order from Germany. The "May laws" that followed provided for government control of the education and selection of Catholic clergymen. The laws also made civil marriage compulsory. That is, persons married by a clergyman must also go through a civil marriage ceremony. When the pope declared these provisions null and void, German Catholics stiffened their opposition to Bismarck's policies. Meanwhile, the Catholic Center party in the *Reichstag* gained new supporters. Bismarck now realized he had stirred a hornet's nest. He decided to give up the *Kulturkampf,* or "battle for civilization," as his anti-Catholic policy was called. In 1886 most of the measures objectionable to the Catholics were repealed.

Bismarck regarded socialism as an even greater menace to German unity than Catholicism. The Socialists had organized the Social Democratic party in 1875 and were gaining

steadily in strength. Bismarck soon found an excuse to launch an attack upon them. In 1878 two attempts were made to assassinate the Emperor William I. Bismarck blamed the Socialists and had the *Reichstag* pass a series of anti-Socialist laws. These forbade the circulation of socialist writings and gave the police special power to break up socialist meetings and to punish violators of the laws. The result was merely to drive the movement underground. Meanwhile, the Social Democrats increased their membership in the *Reichstag* from twelve in 1877 to thirty-five in 1890. In the latter year the laws against the Socialists were not renewed.

Germany under William II. William I died in 1888 and was succeeded by his son, who died within a few months. Then William's grandson, a young man of twenty-nine, came to the throne as William II. The youthful ruler could not work well with the old chancellor, who for so many years had been the real ruler of Germany. William II was conceited and domineering. He held to the old belief in divine-right monarchy, claiming that authority to rule was given him "by the grace of God alone, and not by parliaments or the will of the people." There was not room in the government for two such headstrong personalities as the emperor and Bismarck. They disagreed on an alliance with Russia and on the renewal of the laws against the Socialists. Finally, in 1890 William II "dropped the pilot" who almost single-handed had molded modern Germany. The young monarch then set forth upon a reign marked by energy and ambition. He strove to gain for Germany "a place in the sun," that is, a colonial empire, and he created a large navy to protect this empire and Germany's growing foreign trade. These policies helped to bring about World War I. Defeat in that conflict led to the fall of the Hohenzollern family and the overthrow of the imperial government. As we shall see, World War I also sealed the fate of other dynasties in Europe.

The Problem of Nationalism in Austria-Hungary

The creation of Austria-Hungary. After the defeat by Prussia in 1866, Austria faced the necessity of changing her government. The old Holy Roman Empire was gone; the German Confederation was no more; and

EMPEROR FRANCIS JOSEPH I OF AUSTRIA–HUNGARY

Austria was excluded from acting as leader of the German states. The growing restlessness of her submerged nationalities forced her to rearrange her internal affairs. On the suggestion of the Hungarian leader, Deák (dā′äk), a new constitution was drawn up. This was the *Ausgleich* (ous′glīk), or Compromise of 1867. It provided for the Dual Monarchy, which consisted of the empire of Austria and the kingdom of Hungary. Each had its own parliament, ministry, courts, officials, language, and capital (Vienna and Budapest). Both had one flag, one army and navy, and one sovereign, who reigned as emperor of Austria and king of Hungary. There was also a common tariff, a common coinage, and a common administration of foreign affairs. This political arrangement survived until the revolutionary year of 1918.

Francis Joseph I and the Dual Monarchy. The relations between Austria and Hungary under the Dual Monarchy were not always friendly. Perhaps the strongest tie holding the two countries together was a deep-seated loyalty to Francis Joseph I. He ruled for sixty-eight years (1848–1916), almost as long as Louis XIV ruled France. The emperor's reign bridged the wide gap between the era of Metternich and World War I. A succession of personal tragedies filled his life—the execution of his brother Maximilian, whom Napoleon III had set on the throne of Mexico and then deserted; the suicide of his only son; the murder of his wife by an anarchist; and the assassination of his nephew and heir in 1914. Despite these tragedies, Francis Joseph never forgot the duties of a monarch. He mixed freely among the people and received them in public audience, speaking now one, now another, of the many languages used in his dominions. All in all, he worked harder at the business of governing than any of his ministers. In 1916 the emperor-king died. The crowns of Austria and Hungary then passed to his grandnephew, Charles I, who reigned less than two years.

Nationalities in Austria-Hungary. The principle of nationality, so effective for union in Italy and Germany, made for disunion in Austria-Hungary. The ruling family was German, and the German language was favored over all the others. But out of a total population of about 50,000,000 in 1914, there were only 12,000,000 Germans. The other nationalities included Hungarians, or Magyars (10,000,000), Slavs (24,000,000), and Rumanians and Italians (4,000,000). Thus the Dual Monarchy was really only a league between the Germans and the Hungarians, or Magyars, both of whom forced their languages and customs upon the Slav, Rumanian, and Italian subjects. The attitude of the ruling groups toward the subject nationalities was expressed by the Austrian Count von Beust, who is reported to have told the Hungarians, "You take care of your barbarians and we will take care of ours." The result was increasing bitterness between dominant and subject peoples. The discord between the nationalities helped to bring on World War I and to destroy the Dual Monarchy.

Russia Struggles for Popular Government

Importance of modern Russia. Russian history during the hundred years preceding World War I has special significance. This period produced the conditions which led to the overthrow of the Romanov dynasty and the establishment of the Soviet Union. By 1914 Russia controlled an immense and continuous territory, nearly equal in size to the scattered areas of the British Empire. In this extensive region, much of it in Asia, lived about 175,000,000 people under one central government. The majority of them were Slavs; but some were of other nationalities, for in the nineteenth century Russia acquired Finland, Bessarabia, most of Poland, and the Caucasus. Non-Russians, including Jews, Finns, Lithuanians, Poles, and others, were often harshly treated. An autocratic czar ruled over this conglomeration of peoples long after western Europe had turned toward democratic government. By the late 1800's, however, a growing number of democrats, Socialists, and anarchists had begun to assail the despotic rule of the czars. (The anarchists believed that all forms of government are oppressive and should be abolished.) Let us see what produced this revolutionary spirit.

Russia in the early nineteenth century. In 1801 Alexander I became "Czar of all the Russias." He surrounded himself with a number of liberal young nobles who had caught the spirit of the French Revolution. He toyed with the idea of emancipating the serfs, granted Poland a constitution (1815), and considered plans for a constitutional government for Russia. For a few years a new era of freedom seemed at hand. However, secret societies began to agitate for more thoroughgoing reforms, and the Poles showed a desire for complete independence. Consequently, Alexander turned away from reform at home and began to follow the advice of the reactionary Metternich in foreign affairs. As Metternich remarked, Alexander "stirred everything up but built nothing." His successor, Nicholas I (1825–1855), was a complete despot and permitted not even a pretense of liberty. Like other czars, his motto was "submit and obey." A strict censorship of the press was enforced; universities were closely supervised; and arrest, exile, or death threatened anyone who expressed opinions unfavorable to the government. Nicholas died during the Crimean War. (See page 407.) His reign was remembered by one exile as a "plague zone which extended from 1825 to 1855."

Reform and reaction under Alexander II. Alexander II came to the throne in 1855. It seemed that he might prove to be a more enlightened ruler than his immediate predecessors had been. He pardoned political offenders, eased the censorship of the press, and issued a new code of laws based on those of western Europe. He also improved the courts of justice, long noted for their dishonesty and inefficiency. More important still, he set up district assemblies, or county councils, called *zemstvos,* which had charge of roads, poor relief, schools, churches, and other local concerns. The zemstvos were elected by all classes of the people. Alexander's most memorable achievement came in 1861 when he abolished serfdom, which had lasted longer in Russia than in any other European country. The emancipation decree, however, did not make the peasant an individual property owner, nor did it give him full civil rights. It allotted the land to the village, or *mir,* which assigned it to families and was responsible for making payments to the government for its use. Such halfway measures did not satisfy everyone. The cry arose for more self-government, including a constitution and a national parliament. In 1863 the Poles staged another revolution for independence, but it was crushed by military force. Radical organizations increased their anti-government activity. Alexander II now turned reactionary, for he believed that his liberal efforts had merely

encouraged disloyalty. He fell back upon the oppressive methods used by Nicholas I.

Nihilism. The intense disappointment of the educated classes, or the *intelligentsia,* at Alexander's return to autocratic ways gave rise to *nihilism.* The young people who accepted this doctrine had lost all faith in the existing order of things; they declared that they believed in nothing (Latin *nihil*). Russia, they urged, must make a clean sweep of autocracy, of the Orthodox Church, and of every other institution that had come down from an unreasoning, unscientific past. When the ground had been thus cleared, it would be possible to build a new and better society. Before long the nihilists began to seek followers among the masses, most of whom were peasants. The government got wind of the movement and imprisoned or exiled those who took part in it.

Political terrorism. Some nihilists decided that since the government ruled by terror, it should be fought with terror. A secret committee of nihilists at St. Petersburg marked for death a number of prominent officials, spies, and members of the hated secret police. In some cases the terrorists succeeded in assassinating those they had condemned. In 1881, on the day that Czar Alexander II had agreed on some sort of constitution for Russia, he was killed by a bomb. His son, Alexander III, succeeded him. The revolutionists offered to abandon their campaign of violence if a representative assembly elected by manhood suffrage was summoned, and if freedom of speech, press, and assembly was granted. Alexander III, embittered by the murder of his father, determined to crush the revolutionists. His director of police sought out and punished the leading terrorists with such cruelty that revolutionary nihilism, or terrorism, almost disappeared. Autocracy was too strongly entrenched to be overthrown by a handful of terrorists. It commanded the support of the official classes, of the Orthodox Church with its numerous priests, and of the

---

A FRENCHMAN VIEWS CZARIST RUSSIA

"The Russian government is the discipline of the camp substituted for the civic order— it is a state of siege become the normal state of society . . .

"The more I see of Russia, the more I agree with the Emperor when he forbids Russians to travel and makes access to his own country difficult to foreigners. The political system of Russia could not withstand twenty years of free communication with Western Europe . . .

"The diplomatic corps and Westerners in general have always been considered by this government, with its Byzantine spirit, and by Russia as a whole, as malevolent and jealous spies . . .

". . . In Russia, fear replaces, that is to say paralyzes, thought . . ."

—Marquis de Custine, *Journey for Our Time* (1846).

RUSSIA IN EUROPE, 1796–1881. In the period from 1796 to 1881, Russia gradually expanded its boundaries in the west and the south. It did not succeed, however, in obtaining control of the Black Sea. In consequence, it feared that other powers might deny it access to the Mediterranean.

ignorant, conservative peasants, who formed the bulk of Russia's millions.

Beginning of industrialism in Russia. It was at this time that the Industrial Revolution began to reach Russia. The emancipation of the serfs allowed many of them to flock to the cities, where they furnished an abundant supply of cheap labor. The government also started railroad building on an extensive scale and persuaded foreign capitalists to invest in Russian coal mines, iron mines, oil fields, and other natural resources. Factories sprang up like mushrooms, and millions of Russians, especially in the western part of the empire, became factory workers. These economic changes could not fail to affect the life of the people in many ways. Old cities grew rapidly

and new ones developed. A middle class appeared, together with an industrial proletariat more intelligent and far less conservative than the peasantry. The workingmen organized trade unions, conducted strikes and, as in Germany, lent a willing ear to socialist agitators. The middle and lower classes proved fertile soil for the seeds of revolution.

The Revolution of 1905. Alexander III had apparently suppressed all opposition to autocracy. Nevertheless, during the reign of his successor, Nicholas II (1894–1917), a new wave of anger against the government broke out. Not only the intelligentsia, but also many other Russians, now took up the liberal cause. Enlightened members of the nobility, as in France before the revolution, added their voices to the rising volume of criticism. Then came defeat in the Russo-Japanese War of 1904–1905 (see page 433), which revealed the shameful inefficiency and corruption of the government. On Sunday, January 22, 1905, an event occurred which stirred public feeling to its depths. A radical priest organized a procession of working people, men and women, to march through the streets of the capital and lay their grievances before the "Little Father" in person. When they reached the royal palace, they were received, not by the czar but by Cossack soldiers, who greeted the defenseless crowd with gunfire. This was the massacre of "Red Sunday," in which over a thousand unarmed people were killed.

The months which followed witnessed an epidemic of strikes throughout Russia. Every strike had a twofold purpose—the improvement of economic conditions and the securing of a constitution. In October, 1905, workers in St. Petersburg and other large cities left their jobs. Railway transportation all over the empire came to a halt. The strike fever extended to the middle class. Teachers dismissed their classes and judges left their courts; merchants closed their stores and doctors their offices; ballet dancers would not dance. With life in the cities virtually at a standstill, nothing remained for the government but to give in. The czar then promised the people freedom of conscience, speech, meeting, and association. He further promised that a representative assembly, or *Duma,* should be elected on the basis of a broad suffrage. Henceforth, every law must have the Duma's consent.

The czar and the Duma. The first Russian parliament, or Duma, met the following year, 1906. It spent most of its time struggling with the czar, who finally dissolved it. Three other Dumas met between 1907 and 1914. The czar so changed the requirements for voting that the membership of the Duma was confined mainly to large landowners, wealthy manufacturers, and other representatives of the conservative classes. Even these he distrusted. Meanwhile, Nicholas II relied more and more upon the advice of the Empress Alexandra, who reminded him constantly of his coronation oath to uphold autocracy. The empress, in turn, was under the evil influence of the mystical peasant monk, Rasputin. She regarded him as a saint because of his seeming power to heal her sickly son, who was heir to the throne. Rasputin used his favor at court to support reactionary policies. Under these circumstances the Duma was blocked

RED SUNDAY. On January 9, 1905, a procession led by the priest Georgi Gapon was met by the Czar's soldiers at the Winter Palace. Over a thousand people were killed.

in its efforts to win liberty for the people and to reform the methods of government. Consequently, when Russia was drawn into the whirlpool of World War I, its political and economic structure could not meet the strains put upon it. Before the war was over, the czar had been driven from the throne and the country was in chaos. The Russian people then entered on a series of radical experiments —social, economic, and political. (See pages 481–490.)

The Rise of Nationalism in the Balkans

The Balkans under Turkish rule. In 1453 the Turks had established a foothold in Europe by the capture of Constantinople. (See page 175.) They gradually extended their control over the whole Balkan peninsula—the peninsula lying between the Black and Adriatic seas. (See map, page 409.) The Turkish advance into Europe reached high tide in 1683 at the gates of Vienna. Thereafter it began to recede. Most of the European subjects of the Turkish sultan were Christian in religion and Slavic in language and culture. This fact, however, did not unite them. Jealousies and quarrels constantly arose among the different nationalities—Serbs, Bulgarians, Albanians, Rumanians, and Greeks. Sometimes their disputes and wars were caused by the fact that small national groups were separated from their homelands. Thus, there were Greeks in Serbia, Rumanians in Bulgaria, and Albanians in Greece. Sometimes the Balkan peoples clashed bitterly over religious matters. The patriarch, or head, of the Greek Orthodox Church, to which most of the people belonged, was always a Greek. He was appointed by the sultan, who was at the same time leader of the Mohammedan faith. Christians outside Greece regarded the patriarch as a tool of the Turkish ruler. The Turks made the most of the discord among their European subjects, whom they called *rayahs*, or "cattle." The sultan encouraged the ill feeling of one

NICHOLAS II, Alexandra and their daughters

subject nationality for another and crushed uprisings with the harshest cruelty. Moreover, he oppressed the non-Moslems by forbidding them to possess arms, by taxing them heavily, and by taking promising Christian boys from their families to be brought up in the Mohammedan faith. These boys were trained to serve in the armies and public offices of the Turkish government. The Balkan peoples naturally awaited a chance to throw off the despotic yoke of the Ottoman Empire.

The decay of the Ottoman Empire. The sultan had the powers of an absolute monarch, had he chosen to use them. As a rule the sultan was a luxury-loving recluse who spent his days idly in his imperial palace at Constantinople. The management of affairs was left to the grand vizier, or chief official, and a host of councilors. Bribery was the usual means of gaining office. Once in power the officials put pressure on their subordinates to raise more money. Private individuals collected the taxes and in so doing tried to get rich as quickly as possible. The heaviest sufferers under this vicious system of tax farming were the Christian subjects in Europe, who had never enjoyed equality of treatment with the Moslems. Corruption was not confined to government officials; it extended also to the professional army, or *Janissaries*. By the end of the eighteenth century they had degenerated into a disorderly band of plunderers. When at last two exceptional sultans, Selim III (1789–1807) and Mahmud II (1808–1839), tried to introduce honesty and efficiency into the governing system, their efforts were blocked by the Janissaries. Turkey, as Czar Nicholas I expressed it, was indeed the "sick man of Europe."

The great powers watch the "sick man." The subject Balkan peoples were not the only ones interested in expelling the Turks from Europe. Some of the great powers wanted to gain control of the lands which they hoped the "sick man" would leave behind when he died. Ever since the time of Peter the Great, Russia had hoped to win command over Constantinople and the straits of the Bosporus and Dardanelles. Control of these places would insure that Russia would have free access to the Mediterranean. This was important for her commerce and also to lessen the danger of blockade in time of war. The czars had another reason for wanting to dismember the Ottoman Empire in Europe. The Russians were Slavic people and followers of the Greek Orthodox faith. They felt sympathy with the Slavic Christians who were oppressed by the sultan, and were only too glad to act as the "big brother" of the Balkans. Austria-Hungary too was anxious to see Turkey fall apart, so that she might annex some of the Balkan regions near her southern border. England, later aided by France, favored keeping Turkey alive. England did not want to see Russia or any other strong power acquire the port of Constantinople. Possession of that vital base by a strong state could mean control of the eastern Mediterranean sea lanes and would thus endanger the British approaches to India. Hence, England intervened several times in the nineteenth century to keep Russia from dealing a death blow to the "sick man." The problem of what to do with the "sick man's" European lands was called the "Near Eastern question." This question had two sides: (1) the struggle of subject nationalities to win their freedom from Turkey, and (2) the interference of the great powers in Balkan affairs to win some advantages for themselves.

Emerging nationalities in the Balkans. In the nineteenth century the peoples of the Balkans were stirred by the same enthusiasm for unity and freedom that inspired the Italians and Germans. In 1799 the sultan was forced to recognize the independence of the tiny mountain state of Montenegro on the Adriatic. Five years later the Serbs began the first large-scale revolt against the authority of the Porte, or Turkish government. Under the leadership of Karageorge, who was a sort of Serbian Robin Hood, and then of Obrenovich, the Serbs compelled the sultan to grant them self-rule within the Ottoman Empire (1829). Their liberation was bound up with that of the Greeks, who in 1821 started an insurrection in Morea (the Peloponnesus). The fires of revolution soon spread to northern Greece and the Aegean islands. Both Greeks and Turks committed shocking massacres. At first the European governments held aloof from the struggle. Popular sympathy, however, was on the side of the Greeks, and scores of volunteers went to help in the struggle for Greek independence. Among them was the romantic English poet Lord Byron, who in 1824 died of a fever in the service of the rebels. Despite such help to the Greeks, it appeared that the sultan would succeed in suppressing the uprising, for he had won the assistance of Mehemet Ali, head of the self-governing Turkish province of Egypt. In 1827 Athens fell to the Moslems. The European powers now changed their earlier attitude and decided to intervene. England, Russia, and France demanded that hostilities cease and that Greece be granted self-government within the Ottoman Empire.

When a combined fleet of the three allies sailed into the Bay of Navarino to enforce their demands, a major naval battle took place (1827). The result was the destruction of the Turkish squadron.

Greeks gain independence. Czar Nicholas I soon took advantage of the "sick man's" plight by declaring war on the sultan. According to the Treaty of Adrianople which ended the war in 1829, Turkey was obliged to leave the fate of Greece to the three allied powers. Consequently, Greece became completely independent. In addition, the sultan granted autonomy to Serbia and to the Danubian provinces of Moldavia and Wallachia. Russia had come nearer to her goal of easing the "sick man" into his grave.

The Crimean War, 1854–1856. The gains made against Turkey in the Treaty of Adrianople merely whetted the appetite of Czar Nicholas I. Impatient because the "sick man" was so slow in dying, the czar sought an excuse for another attack upon the sultan. The opportunity came in 1853, when the Roman and Orthodox Catholics in Palestine quarreled over the protection of the holy places there. Nicholas demanded of Turkey a treaty upholding the rights of the Greek Church and making him the protector of all the Orthodox Christians in Turkey. When the sultan turned down these demands, the Crimean War followed. England, alarmed lest Russia become too powerful in the eastern Mediterranean, sided with Turkey. France and Sardinia joined England. (See page 388.) After enduring a long siege at Sevastopol, Russia suffered defeat, and thus Turkey in Europe secured a new lease on life. The peace conference assembled at Paris in 1856. By the terms of the treaty Russia gave up her claim to act as protector of the Greek Christians in Turkey and of the principalities of Serbia, Moldavia, and Wallachia. Furthermore, the Black Sea was neutralized—that is, all warships and fortifications were forbidden within its boundaries—and the lower Danube was

declared free to the commerce of all nations. Finally, in their anxiety to keep Russia out of Constantinople, England and France abandoned their traditional claim that the Turks were a barbarous people. Henceforth, Turkey was to be treated as a recognized member of the European family of nations.

The Russo-Turkish War, 1877–1878. The main provisions of the Peace of Paris were scrapped within fifteen years. In 1875 the Turkish provinces of Bosnia and Herzegovina revolted. The revolt spread in the following year to the Bulgarians, upon whom the sultan took a terrible revenge. He loosed on a number of Christian villages some barbarous Turkish militiamen, who put to the sword no less than ten thousand men, women, and children. The Bulgarian massacre aroused all Europe. Gladstone called for punishment of the "unspeakable Turk" in bitter terms. Czar Alexander II threatened to act alone if the European powers did not take united action. An international conference at Constantinople demanded that the sultan make reforms, but England would not join the other countries in enforcing the demands. As a result, Russia declared war on Turkey (1877) and won a decisive victory. The Treaty of San Stefano (1878) forced Turkey to recognize the independence of Serbia, Montenegro, and Rumania. (Rumania was created out of the former principalities of Moldavia and Wallachia.) Of more importance was the establishment of a "Greater Bulgaria," combining Bulgaria, Macedonia, and Rumelia into a self-governing state under the nominal rule of Turkey. (See map, page 409.) To England and Austria this arrangement looked like a scheme to insure Russian control of the whole peninsula. They demanded that the treaty be submitted to a conference of the powers for revision. When the other governments agreed, Russia reluctantly consented.

The Congress of Berlin, 1878. The conference met at Berlin under the chairmanship of Bismarck. Within a month the delegates had drafted a new settlement. It recognized the independence of Serbia, Montenegro, and Rumania, but broke up Greater Bulgaria. The powers gave Austria the right to occupy and administer the Serb provinces of Bosnia and Herzegovina on her border. Great Britain received the island of Cyprus. The congress tried to soothe Russia by giving her southern Bessarabia and the cities of Kars and Batum in Asia Minor. The Italian delegate, whose country received nothing, summed up the work of the congress thus: "Everybody was telling everybody else to take something which belonged to somebody else."

The Turkish Revolution of 1908. In 1908 the Near Eastern question took a new turn. A revolution broke out in Turkey itself. This was the work of the Young Turks, a group of patriotic reformers who aimed to revive and westernize the Ottoman Empire. They won the support of the army and carried through a sudden, almost bloodless, *coup d'état*. They forced the terrified sultan, Abdul Hamid II, to restore the constitution granted in 1876 but long since abandoned. His despotism now seemed at an end, and the Ottoman Empire, with an elective parliament, a responsible ministry, and a free press, took on the appearance of a democratic state. Everyone rejoiced, including the Christian dependencies of the sultan in Europe. It soon became evident, however, that the Young Turks were more nationalistic than liberal. They intended to weld together all the peoples of the Ottoman Empire into a single nation, with Turkish as the favored language and Islam the only privileged faith. Hence, the program of the Young Turks filled the Balkan Christians with fear and alarm.

The Balkan Wars, 1912–1913. The Turkish Revolution weakened rather than strengthened the Ottoman Empire. In 1908 Bulgaria took advantage of the situation to proclaim herself an independent kingdom. Austria saw an opportunity to expand her dominions and in the same year seized Bosnia and Herzego-

vina, which she had administered since 1878. In 1912 Albania likewise made the most of the Turkish Revolution by forcing the Turks to grant her self-rule. In the same year Italy took from Turkey the African possession of Tripoli (Libya). (See page 421.) These attacks upon the Ottoman Empire showed the weakness of the Young Turk government.

The Balkan Christians believed that the time was ripe for pushing Turkey completely out of Europe. Greece, Bulgaria, Serbia, and Montenegro forgot their mutual hatreds for a moment, formed an alliance, and declared war on their ancient enemy. The result was an overwhelming defeat for Turkey. The peace treaty, signed at London, left to the Ottoman Empire in Europe only Constantinople and the nearby area.

The Balkan allies began to quarrel over the Turkish spoils. Serbia, who had been deprived of her Albanian conquests by the treaty made at London, wanted Macedonia. But Bulgaria refused to give up her claim to Macedonia. Consequently, a second Balkan war broke out, with Bulgaria on one side, and Serbia, Montenegro, Greece, Rumania, and Turkey on the other. Bulgaria stood no chance and speedily lost the war. The Treaty of Bucharest (1913) stripped Bulgaria of most of her former conquests. Macedonia was divided between Serbia and Greece, while Rumania acquired an additional strip on the Black Sea. Greece received the island of Crete. In a separate treaty Turkey regained Adrianople and a small part of Thrace.

The Balkan volcano. Thus nationalism had led the Balkan peoples to rise up against the "sick man" and all but thrust him from Europe. But the intense nationalism of the new states, plus the meddling of the great powers, prevented the peaceable division of what had been won from Turkey. The Balkan region was indeed a volcano, whose periodic eruptions continued to disturb the peace of Europe. It was another Balkan eruption which started World War I. (See page 448.)

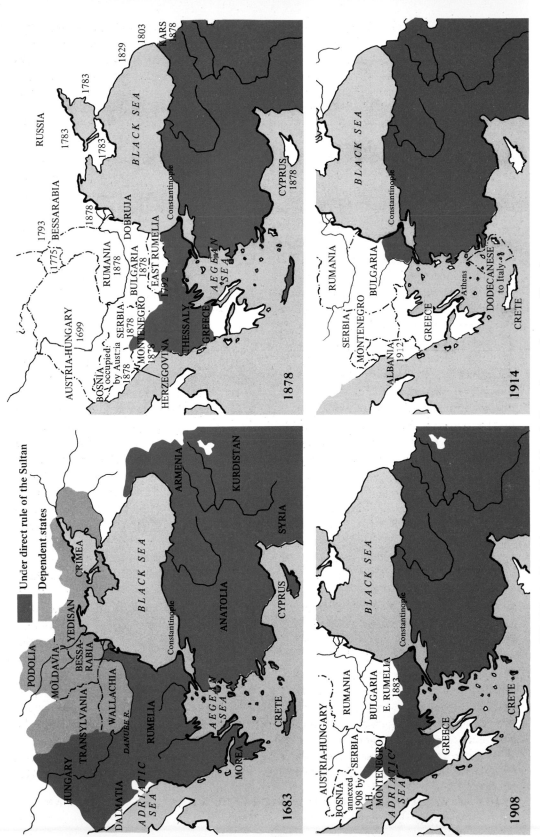

THE OTTOMAN EMPIRE lost most of its holdings in Europe between the years 1683 and 1914.

1683

Under direct rule of the Sultan

Dependent states

HUNGARY
TRANSYLVANIA
PODOLIA
MOLDAVIA
YEDISAN
BESSA-RABIA
CRIMEA
WALLACHIA
DANUBE R.
DALMATIA
RUMELIA
MOREA
ADRIATIC SEA
AEGEAN SEA
CRETE
BLACK SEA
Constantinople
ARMENIA
KURDISTAN
ANATOLIA
SYRIA
CYPRUS

1878

RUSSIA
AUSTRIA-HUNGARY 1699
1775
1793
BESSARABIA 1783
1783
1783
1783
1803
KARS 1878
BLACK SEA
RUMANIA 1878
DOBRUJA 1878
1829
BULGARIA 1878
EAST RUMELIA 1878
BOSNIA occupied by Austria 1878
SERBIA 1878
MONTENEGRO 1878
HERZEGOVINA 1878
1792
THESSALY
GREECE
AEGEAN SEA
Constantinople
CYPRUS 1878

1908

AUSTRIA-HUNGARY
BOSNIA annexed 1908 by A.H.
SERBIA
MONTENEGRO 1883
RUMANIA
BULGARIA
E. RUMELIA
GREECE
ADRIATIC SEA
BLACK SEA
Constantinople
CRETE

1914

RUMANIA
SERBIA
MONTENEGRO
ALBANIA 1912
BULGARIA
BLACK SEA
Constantinople
GREECE
Athens
DODECANESE to Italy
CRETE
CYPRUS 1878

Nationalism and Democracy in the Americas

Nationalism in the United States. The movements toward greater democracy and nationalism also appeared in the Americas. In the United States the spirit of nationalism expressed itself in a rapid expansion westward. This expansion began in 1803 with the purchase of the Louisiana territory from France. (See page 297.) Thus in one step the borders of the United States were pushed more than halfway across the continent. The southeastern area was rounded out by the acquisition of Florida from Spain (1819). The young republic extended its boundaries still farther west and south by the annexation of Texas in 1845. This step led directly to the Mexican War, out of which the United States gained New Mexico, Upper California, and an undisputed claim to Texas (1848). The addition of the Oregon country by agreement with Great Britain in 1846 completed the northwestern borders of the United States. In 1853 the Gadsden Purchase from Mexico rounded out the southwestern boundaries. These territorial gains were accompanied by a growing faith of the people in the greatness and "manifest destiny" of their nation. The test of whether it was to remain one nation came in the War between the States. Under President Lincoln's leadership, the war determined that the nation would remain united.

Democracy in the United States. Meanwhile, democracy as well as nationalism was growing in the United States. As early as 1791 the new state of Vermont provided for manhood suffrage. By 1850 most of the states had removed property and religious restrictions on voting. The frontier states took the lead in extending the vote to all male citizens; then the older states followed. After the War between the States the vote was given to Negroes. In 1920, following World War I, women won the right to vote. The United States now has nearly universal suffrage. Each state determines for itself most educational, residence, and other qualifications for voting.

Disunited Canada. The population of Canada in 1763 was almost entirely French. During the American Revolution Canada received a large number of "Tories" from the Thirteen Colonies, and later received many immigrants from Great Britain. The new settlers had so many quarrels with the French Canadians that the British Parliament divided the country into Upper Canada for the British and Lower Canada for the French. Nova Scotia, New Brunswick, and Newfoundland continued to be separate provinces.

The United States and Canada. The War of 1812 between Great Britain and the United States came as the result of a dispute over freedom of the seas—that is, over the right of a neutral country to use the seas without interference by warring countries. It will be remembered that Europe at that time was in the midst of the fight against Napoleon. To many people in the United States the War of 1812 seemed to furnish a good opportunity for the conquest of Canada. British and French Canadians, however, united in defense of their country and drove out the American armies. The treaty of peace left matters as they were before the war. In 1818 the United States and Great Britain agreed to do away with fortifications and warships along the boundaries between the United States and Canada. Both sides have observed this agreement faithfully ever since. The unfortified boundary from the Atlantic to the Pacific is eloquent proof of the good relations between Canada and the United States.

Lord Durham's report, 1839. Canada had done her duty to the British Empire during the War of 1812, but she waited more than thirty years for her reward in the form of self-government. The British government, after losing the Thirteen Colonies, did not favor any measures which might lead to Canadian independence. Consequently, political discontent increased, until Parliament sent

CANADIAN PARLIAMENT BUILDINGS in Ottawa, Ontario. The original buildings were built in 1860. In 1916 a fire demolished everything but the library. The present buildings were completed in 1920.

over a wise statesman, Lord Durham, to investigate the causes. In his report in 1839, Lord Durham declared that the only method of keeping distant colonies is to allow them to rule themselves. If the Canadians received freedom to manage their own affairs they would be more, and not less, loyal, for they would have fewer causes of complaint against the mother country. The Durham report produced a lasting effect on British colonial policy. By 1849 Great Britain had granted self-government to the Canadian provinces. Later she gave the same privileges to Australia, New Zealand, and South Africa.

Unification of Canada 1867. In 1867 Ontario or Upper Canada, and Quebec or Lower Canada, joined with Nova Scotia and New Brunswick to form a federal union known as the Dominion of Canada. It has a governor general, representing the British king; a Senate, whose members hold office for life; and an elective House of Commons, to which the cabinet of ministers is responsible. Each Canadian province also maintains a parliament for local legislation. The distinguishing feature of the Canadian constitution is that all powers not definitely assigned by it to the provinces belong to the dominion. In that respect it is unlike the basic law of the United States, which gives definite, "enumerated"

powers to the federal government and leaves the remainder to the states.

The new dominion expanded rapidly. It purchased from Hudson's Bay Company the extensive territories out of which the provinces of Manitoba, Saskatchewan, and Alberta have been created. British Columbia and Prince Edward Island soon came into the federation. All the remainder of British North America, except Newfoundland, was annexed in 1878 to the Dominion of Canada. Newfoundland enjoyed dominion status after World War I but returned in 1933 to the status of a colony because of financial difficulties. In 1948 the Newfoundlanders voted to join Canada. One government now holds sway over the whole region from the Great Lakes to the Arctic Circle.

Latin America before World War I. It has already been noted that the Latin American republics began their independent existence under many handicaps. (See page 298.) The result was a long period of revolution, civil war, and dictatorship. These conditions lasted in some countries for fifty years after independence had been won, in others for a century or more. Despite the turmoil that characterized Latin American political life, some states made encouraging progress toward democracy and stable government.

Those which made the greatest advance before World War I had a large proportion of Europeans in their population, and were developing their industries so as to attain a larger measure of self-sufficiency in their economic life.

The Central American republics. The vast majority of the inhabitants of Central America are *mestizos,* or persons of mixed white and Indian blood. After the breakup of the United Provinces of Central America in 1838, the people of this region separated into five small republics. The secession of Panama from Colombia in 1903 added a sixth republic to this number. Factional strife and a succession of military dictators plagued the Central American republics throughout the nineteenth century and beyond. One of them, Costa Rica, began to achieve political order in the late 1800's. There the population is largely white, the farms are mostly small, and foreign interference has been infrequent. By 1914 orderly elections, a free press, free compulsory education, and generally sound finances had become the rule in this small country.

The early Mexican Republic. From the winning of independence to World War I the history of Mexico may be summarized in the careers of three men. The first was Santa Anna, who dominated Mexican politics from 1830 to 1855. He had no fixed principles; indeed, he was as changeable as a chameleon. During his regime Mexico was continually in a topsy-turvy condition and suffered the loss of more than half her territory in the war with the United States. (See page 410.)

President Juarez, 1861–1872. With the overthrow of Santa Anna in 1855, a period of liberal reform began under the leadership of Benito Juárez (hwä′rās). Juárez, a full-blooded Indian, is sometimes referred to as "the Abraham Lincoln of his country." In 1857 Juárez and his fellow liberals drafted a new constitution. Together with the reform laws of 1859, it deprived the Church of its lands, proclaimed religious liberty, approved civil marriages, and abolished special church and military courts. The constitution also provided a federal form of government, manhood suffrage, freedom of speech, of the press, and of teaching. This program led to the War of Reform (1858–1860), in which Juárez and his liberal followers defeated the armies of the conservatives. In 1861 Juárez was elected president. Soon he had to flee before the invading troops of Napoleon III, who set up Maximilian of Austria as emperor of Mexico. (See page 388.) When the French troops were finally withdrawn in 1867, Juárez resumed office. He became president a fourth time in 1871 and died the following year. Juárez had given the masses of the people, especially the Indians, new hope that their rights would be recognized.

Mexico under Díaz, 1877–1911. The third dominant personality of Mexican politics was Porfirio Díaz (dē′äs), who had been an able lieutenant of Juárez and a valiant fighter for the liberal cause. In 1867 he broke with Juárez and opposed his re-election as president. In a comparatively short time Díaz changed from patriot to power-hungry *caudillo*—the name which Spanish Americans used for a military chieftain. He gained the presidency in 1876 and began the longest period of personal rule in Latin American history. Díaz brought Mexico peace and order, new industries, railroads, public works, and schools. On the surface his record was impressive. Foreign governments favored Díaz's rule, because he paid off Mexico's debts and invited foreign capitalists to exploit Mexico's resources. But the profits of the thriving industries went into the pockets of the upper classes and foreigners. The laborers in the towns and the peons, or farm workers, in the country received little or no benefit from the amazing industrial development. Three fourths of the people remained poverty-stricken. Díaz would not tolerate trade unions. He permitted big landowners to enlarge their holdings at the expense of Indian tribes and poor peasants. At the same time the Church regained a great deal of its economic and political power. Thus the work of Juárez was largely undone by Díaz. A seething discontent developed. It did not break forth until 1911, when Díaz was re-elected for his seventh consecutive term as president. Then a successful revolution, led by Francisco Madero, overthrew him and he retired to Europe.

The Mexican Revolution. The expulsion of Díaz was only the beginning of a long struggle by the common people of Mexico to free themselves from oppression by the privileged classes. To the Mexicans, that struggle, rather than the one for independence, is known as "the Revolution." Its principles are summed up in the popular cry, *tierra y libertad,* or "land and liberty." Nearly thirty years were needed to carry out its main purposes. Like the French Revolution, it reached to the roots of the social and economic evils of Mexican society. The first decade of the revolution was violent. The most notable accomplishment during this period was the drafting of the constitution of 1917. It was a revolutionary document and embodied the ideals of the reformers from Juárez's time onward. The new constitution provided for the division of the large estates among the peons and Indian villages; for the ownership by the state of all minerals beneath the surface of the earth; and for the protection of the laborer through the eight-hour day, minimum wages, and guarantee of the right to strike. The constitution also set up new restrictions against the Church. Religious organizations were forbidden to own property or to conduct primary schools. The large landowners, foreign capitalists, and the Church thus became the chief losers by the constitution of 1917. No serious effort was made to enforce the provisions until 1920, when President Obregón came into office.

Argentina. Except for Brazil, Argentina is the largest republic of South America in size, population, and wealth. Until 1853 Argentina was a victim of armed struggles and dictatorship. The most remarkable dictator was Juan Manuel de Rosas (1829–1852), who tried "to make of terror a system of government." He has been called the "Robespierre of South America." After his overthrow the Argentines adopted a federal constitution modeled upon that of the United States. A period of increasing political order and material prosperity followed. Grain and cattle growing became the chief enterprises. Two presidents in particular promoted the rapid progress of Argentina: Bartolomé Mitre (1862–1868) and Domingo Faustino Sarmiento (1868–1874). They made the central government powerful and respected. In addition, Sarmiento, the "schoolmaster president," was the outstanding pioneer of free public education in Latin America. Argentina became the most literate of the Latin American countries. The successors of Mitre and Sarmiento, though less distinguished, were mostly able and public-spirited men. Armed revolts against the government practically ceased. An important democratic reform came in 1912 with the passage of a law providing for compulsory secret voting.

Brazil. Portuguese-speaking Brazil is nearly as large as the United States and richer in natural resources. By 1910 she was producing almost three fourths of the world's coffee and nine tenths of the natural rubber. A decade later she had lost most of her rubber trade to the East Indies. In recent years Brazil has made a rapid industrial advance; at present she is ahead of all Latin American nations so far as industrialization is concerned.

Unlike her Spanish American neighbors, Brazil lived under a constitutional monarchy until 1889. During the long reign of Dom Pedro II (1840–1889), the country enjoyed liberal, tolerant, and enlightened leadership. The emperor built railroads, welcomed immigrants, organized schools, and maintained orderly government. In 1887 slavery was completely abolished. This angered the great land-holders, who with other dissatisfied groups forced Dom Pedro to resign. The last monarch in America retired to Europe, and Brazil became a republic. The new constitution of 1891 was closely modeled after that of the United States. Pedro's example in promoting order and progress was not lost. For nearly forty years the republic of Brazil, ruled by an intelligent minority, was faithful to constitutional methods. In 1930 it passed into the control of a military dictatorship which lasted twenty-five years. (See page 537.)

Chile. Chile, the "shoestring republic," has enjoyed domestic peace almost from the beginning. After 1833, when the conservatives drafted a new constitution, the government was mostly in the hands of the feudal landowners of the Central Valley. Nevertheless, the nation moved forward. Some of its leaders distinguished themselves by their progressive spirit. They established schools, libraries, and other agencies of public education; built railways and telegraph lines; and encouraged industry. By the War of the Pacific (1879–1883) Chile gained the rich nitrate fields of the Atacama Desert and deprived Bolivia of a coastline. The export of nitrates filled the Chilean treasury with money. General prosperity followed, especially during the presidency of Balmaceda (1886–1891), who spent large sums on public works. With his overthrow in 1891, the period of the autocratic presidents came to an end. Thereafter the executive was subject to the will of the majority in congress. In the twentieth century the middle and lower classes have had an increasing influence in politics. As a result, Chile has developed one of the most advanced social security systems in the New World. It includes retirement pensions, medical care, and low-cost housing for wage earners. Chile faced very serious economic problems after World War I, when the production of artificial nitrates abroad reduced the value of her natural nitrates.

Colombia. The republic of Colombia lives under geographical handicaps. The country is pierced by three fingers of the Andes. Most of her people live in the mountain valleys and on the plateaus, for the coasts are hot and humid. Until recent years these conditions have made it hard for Colombians to communicate with one another and with the outside world.

During most of the nineteenth century there was much strife between the conservative and the liberal factions. But unlike her neighbors, Colombia fought over ideas rather than personalities. Dictators of the usual Latin-American type have been rare. Colombia suffered two severe shocks near the beginning of the twentieth century: a costly civil war (1899–1902), and the secession of Panama. (See page 437.) These events seem to have had a sobering influence. From that time until 1948 a respect for freedom of speech and press became the rule. Then another civil war broke out, ending ten years later with a truce between the rival parties. (See page 597.)

Other states of South America. With one exception, the other South American republics—Venezuela, Ecuador, Bolivia, Peru, Uruguay, and Paraguay—made much slower progress toward stable and democratic government. The exception is Uruguay. After seventy-five years of almost constant turmoil, this tiny state entered the twentieth century with a lively interest in good government. Under President José Batlle (bät′yä, 1903–1907, 1911–1915), the beginnings of really democratic rule appeared. Batlle introduced a number of social and economic reforms to better the lot of the workers. He established the eight-hour day, government banks to help small farmers and laborers, and a state monopoly of the production of electric light and power. In more recent years Uruguay has passed laws which provide retirement pensions, unemployment and sickness insurance, and minimum wages for rural laborers.

REVIEWING THE CHAPTER

TERMS TO UNDERSTAND: *democracy, republic, constitution, nationalism, franchise, liberal, conservative, pocket borough, rotten borough, Chartists, Communards, ministry, Right, Left, bureaucracy,* Risorgimento, Carbonari, *Seven Weeks' War, kaiser,* Bundesrat, Reichstag, Kulturkampf, *zemstvo, nihilism, Duma, autonomy, Janissaries, "sick man of Europe," Young Turks, War of the Pacific,* caudillo.

PERSONS TO IDENTIFY: *Earl Grey, Gladstone, Disraeli, Thiers, Gambetta, Mazzini, Cavour, Victor Emmanuel II, Francis Joseph I, Garibaldi, Bismarck, Rasputin, Giolitti, Karageorge, Abdul Hamid II, Lord Durham, Santa Anna, Juárez, Díaz, Rosas, Sarmiento, Batlle.*

PLACES TO LOCATE: *Indo-China, Ems, Sedan, Sardinia, Savoy, Piedmont, Lombardy,* Italia Irredenta, *Venetia, Schleswig-Holstein, Budapest, Finland, Bessarabia, Balkan Peninsula, Morea, Serbia, Moldavia, Wallachia, Sevastopol, Bosnia, Rumania, Macedonia, Tripoli, Nova Scotia, New Brunswick, Newfoundland, Costa Rica, Ecuador, Uruguay.*

QUESTIONS TO ANSWER

1. (a) Distinguish between direct democracy and representative democracy. Between a democracy and a republic. (b) What are the safeguards against the tyranny of majority rule? (c) How does the British constitution differ from that of the United States?

2. (a) How does the term "nation" differ in meaning from "state" and "government"? (b) What conditions led to the rise of nationalism at the end of the Middle Ages? (c) How did nationalism help bring about Napoleon I's overthrow?

3. (a) Name and identify the divisions of the British Isles. (b) Why did the British parliamentary system need reform? (c) Name and explain five great reform acts. (d) Distinguish between a right and a privilege. (e) Explain the part played by each of the following in the British government: king, Lords, Commons, cabinet.

4. (a) Trace the steps by which Louis Napoleon (Napoleon III) made himself emperor. (b) In what ways did Napoleon try to please different groups of Frenchmen? (c) What were the aims of his foreign policy? (d) State the causes and results of the Franco-Prussian War. (e) List, with dates, the five French republics. (f) Describe the government of the Third French Republic.

5. (a) What did Mazzini, Cavour, and Garibaldi each do for Italian unification? (b) How did Napoleon III help? (c) What problems did Italy face after unification?

6. (a) Who was responsible for the first steps toward German unification? (b) How did the *Zollverein* promote German unity? (c) By what methods did Bismarck seek to unify Germany? (d) Trace the steps by which he did so. (e) Why did Bismarck put through a program of social legislation in Germany? (f) Which two of Bismarck's policies failed? (g) Why did Kaiser William II "drop the pilot"?

7. (a) Explain the origin of the Dual Monarchy. (b) How did the principle of nationality make for disunion in Austria-Hungary?

8. (a) What was the greatest reform accomplished in Russia during the nineteenth century? (b) In the early 1900's how did Russia lag behind western Europe? (c) How successful was the Revolution of 1905?

9. (a) What were the two sides of the Near Eastern question? (b) What were Russia's aims in the Balkans? Britain's? (c) What were the results of the Crimean War? The Congress of Berlin? The two Balkan wars?

10. (a) How did nationalism express itself in the United States? (b) In Canada? (c) In Latin America?, (d) Compare the policies of Juárez and Díaz in Mexico. (e) To the Mexicans, what is "the Revolution"? (f) Name four of the most progressive of the South American republics and tell what steps they had taken toward democracy by World War I.

20 A New Race for Colonies

TWO BRITISH COLONIES in the 1890's. By 1914, some 200 million Europeans controlled over 900 million non-Europeans, mostly in Africa and Asia. Above is the harbor of Zanzibar, a tiny island off the east African coast that was rich in spices. On the left is the Bultfontein diamond mine, South Africa.

As we have seen, a remarkable expansion of Europe began at the close of the Middle Ages. At first Spain and Portugal led in the race for colonies; later Holland, France, and England made aggressive bids for leadership. The struggle for colonies helped to cause frequent wars among the European powers during the sixteenth, seventeenth, and eighteenth centuries. By about 1825, however, rivalry for colonies had slackened. The Napoleonic wars, the struggle for political liberty, and the beginning of the Industrial Revolution all tended to center the attention of Europeans on affairs at home. Furthermore, a growing number of people began to feel that colonies did not pay. They pointed to the high cost of maintaining armies of occupation and colonial officials and to the huge expense of wars fought to obtain or to hold distant possessions. During the middle of the nineteenth century, therefore, there appeared to be a decline in the rate of European expansion.

Revival of the colonizing movement. Imperialism came back with a rush during the last quarter of the nineteenth century, as the great powers began another race to secure dependencies. Why did this new burst of imperialism take place? One reason may be found in national pride. Italy and Germany were each newly united, and the United States and Japan were just emerging as strong nations. Leaders in each of these countries felt that colonial possessions gave prestige to a nation. Thus the old urge for "keeping up with the Joneses" helped to bring the younger countries into the colonial field.

As the Industrial Revolution progressed, it provided a second and even more important cause for a revival of imperialism. The greater the output of manufactured goods, the greater was the demand for markets and raw materials. Colonies could furnish industrial nations with markets, raw materials, and opportunities for the investment of surplus capital. Moreover, improvements in means of transportation (railroads, steamships, and canals) permitted easy travel to distant places. Improved communication (the telegraph, telephone, and submarine cable) made easier the occupation and government of remote dependencies. Better firearms and stronger naval vessels also provided more effective means

for the conquest and continued rule of "backward" peoples.

Imperialism. The word "imperialism" conveniently describes all this activity of the different nations in reaching out for colonial dependencies. Imperialism took several forms. Sometimes it resulted in the outright annexation of a territory, with or without the consent of the inhabitants. In other cases the colony, although keeping its own government and the appearance of independence, would really be dominated by another power and become a *protectorate* or a *sphere of influence*. Sometimes imperialism was mainly economic, as when special trading or investment privileges (*concessions*) were secured in underdeveloped countries. Economic imperialism often led to the establishment of a protectorate or even to outright annexation.

Regardless of the form in which it appeared, the "new imperialism" proved to be unprofitable. Arguments used against imperialism in the 1700's turned out to be equally valid in the 1800's and 1900's: it was expensive to administer colonies, to put down revolts, and to fight off rivals. As it turned out, the imperialistic nations paid dearly for their attacks on weaker peoples.

On the other hand, we must remember that many people went out to the colonial areas not for profit but for service. Missionaries braved hardships and devoted their lives in efforts to bring what they thought were better beliefs, medicines, and education to "backward" peoples. Some colonial administrators sought to govern well, although their attitude was generally as condescending as that shown in Kipling's "The White Man's Burden." (See the boxed quotation on this page.)

The New Imperialism in Africa to 1914

"The Dark Continent." In ancient times, little more than the Mediterranean shore of Africa was known to Europeans. Even as late a period as the Middle Ages found the Arabs almost alone among white men who had much knowledge of Africa. Not until they had mastered ocean navigation in the time of Diaz and Columbus were the shores of Africa within reach of Europeans. As we have seen in Chapter 13, the Portuguese set up trading posts on the east and west coasts, and the Dutch planted a colony at the southern cape. Little effort was made to reach the interior of the Dark Continent for various reasons.

Opening up the Dark Continent. The penetration of Africa was mainly accomplished by following the course of its four great rivers—the Niger, the Nile, the Zambezi, and the Congo. In the last decade of the eighteenth century the British African Association sent Mungo Park to explore the Niger River. He and his successors charted the course of the upper Niger and confirmed the existence of the mysterious city of Timbuktu, which had never previously been visited by Europeans. Shortly after the middle of the nineteenth century, the sources of the Nile River were found. About the same time, an intrepid Scottish missionary and explorer named David Livingstone traced the course of the Zambezi. Starting from the Cape of Good Hope, he worked his way northward to the Zambezi. While following the river toward the coast he discovered the wonderful Victoria Falls. On

DAVID LIVINGSTONE, who explored the Zambezi River and discovered Victoria Falls

his third (and final) journey, Livingstone disappeared for years; the *New York Herald* sent an explorer-reporter, Henry M. Stanley, to look for him. In 1871 Stanley found Livingstone in the heart of Africa, greeting him with the now famous words, "Dr. Livingstone, I presume?" After his Livingstone expedition, Stanley carried out many explorations in Africa, following the mighty Congo all the way to its mouth and making many important geographical discoveries.

The European nations, just entering upon a new period of imperialism, took a great interest in the findings of explorers in Africa. The second largest continent in the world lay open to any who wished to stake out claims there, and there was no lack of claimants. Spain, Portugal, Belgium, Italy, France, Germany, and Great Britain each took part in the scramble for territory, particularly during the 1880's and 1890's. With astonishing ease they won control over nearly all of Africa. The white men often made themselves master of a region by striking a bargain with the local chieftain. They gave him a few presents— some trinkets, a little money, perhaps a flashy uniform—and promised to keep him in office if he would accept European rule. Frequently a force of native soldiers was organized under white officers to keep the rest of the inhabitants subdued. By these means Europeans dominated the continent, although they were a mere handful in comparison with the native population.

The Spanish and Portuguese in Africa. Once ruler of an immense empire, Spain today holds only a few colonies. All of them lie along the coast of Africa. Spain owns the Canary Islands and Spanish Sahara (formerly Rio de Oro) on the northwest coast of Africa; along the Gulf of Guinea coast she also holds some islands and Rio Muni. The Spanish colonies are small and poorly developed. Portugal, more fortunate than Spain, controls the two valuable regions of Angola (Portuguese West Africa) and Mozambique (Portuguese East Africa), as well as a number of islands, and Portuguese Guinea on the westernmost edge of Africa.

The Belgians in Africa. Stanley's exploration of the Congo basin attracted the attention of Leopold II, king of the Belgians. Stanley had recognized the wealth of rubber, ivory, and palm oil available in the Congo basin. Leopold employed him to return there and establish trading stations and claim territory. In 1885 the European nations agreed to recognize Leopold's possession of a vast area. He ruled this territory as his private property. Leopold grew rich from the sale of Congo products, which were collected through the forced labor of the natives. Cruel punishments such as mutilation were inflicted upon those who did not produce their required quotas of rubber and ivory. Because

---

CONDITIONS IN THE BELGIAN CONGO
ABOUT 1906

Senator Picard . . . traveled in the Congo Free State, in the 'cultivated' district . . . Here are his impressions: 'The inhabitants have disappeared. Their homes have been burned; huge heaps of ashes amid neglected palm hedges and devastated, abandoned fields. Inhuman floggings, murders, plunderings, and carryings-off . . .' Near Stanley Pool, on the caravan road, he notices 'a continual succession of Negroes carrying loads upon their heads; worn-out beasts of burden with projecting joints, wasted features, and staring eyes, perpetually trying to keep afoot despite their exhaustion. By thousands they pass, in the service of the State, handed over by the chiefs whose slaves they are and who rob them of their wages. They totter along the road with bent knees and protruding bellies, crawling with vermin, a dreadful procession across hill and dale, dying from exhaustion by the wayside, or often succumbing even should they reach home after their wanderings . . .

—Ludwig Bauer, *Leopold the Unloved.*

these methods were severely criticized, Le-opold finally let the Belgian government take over his holdings in Africa (1908). They became a colony known as the Belgian Congo. Its area was increased by the addition of former German territories after World War I.

The Germans in Africa. Soon after Germany became united, she made her appearance among the colonial powers. Through treaties with the native chiefs and through annexations she acquired extensive regions: Southwest Africa, East Africa, the Camer-

oons and Togo. These were all taken from her by the Allies at the end of World War I.

The Italians in Africa. Italy also found that Africa provided her best opportunity for gaining territory. In the 1890's Italy secured Eritrea on the Red Sea and Italian Somaliland. In 1912, after a short war with Turkey, she obtained Libya. The Italians also hoped to conquer Ethiopia, or Abyssinia, a large country located in eastern Africa. In 1896, at the Battle of Adowa the Ethiopians inflicted a humiliating defeat upon an invading Italian

THE EXPLORATION AND PARTITION OF AFRICA BY EUROPEANS

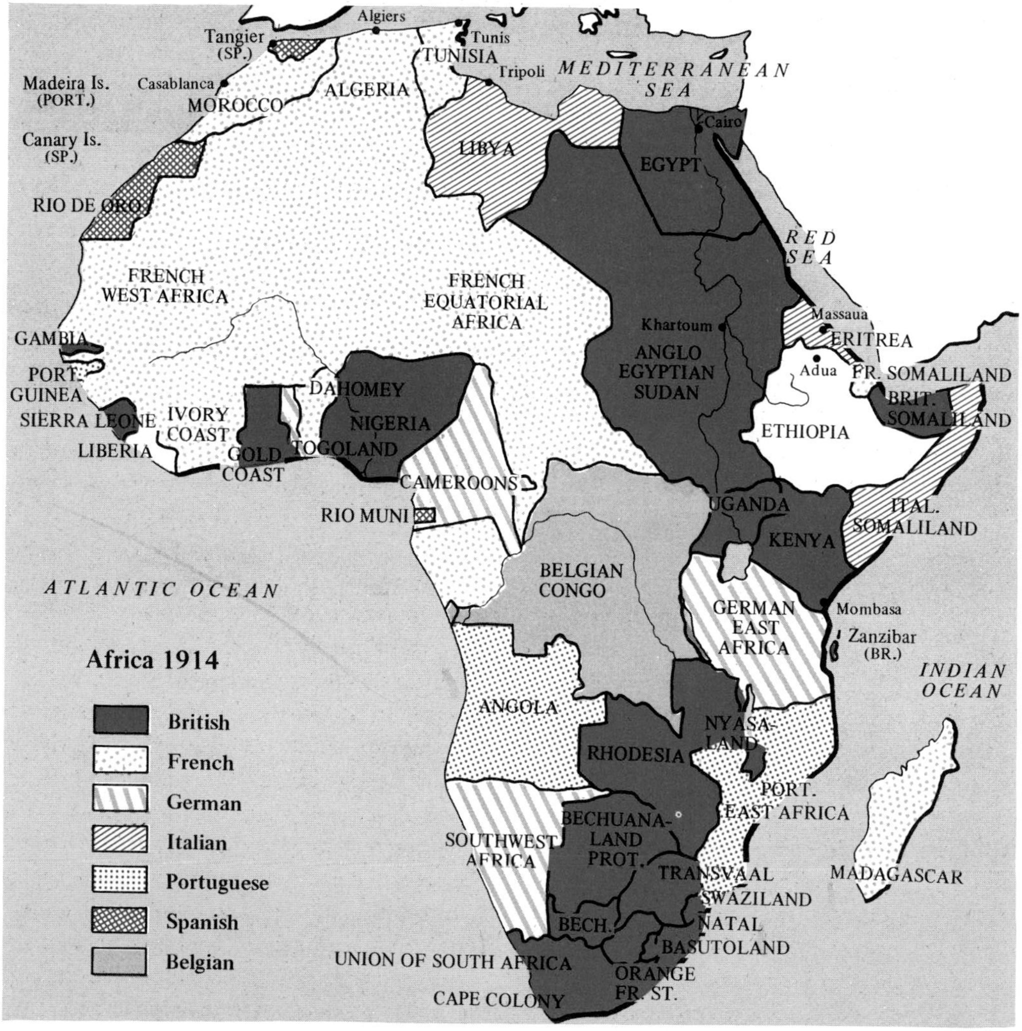

Africa 1914

- British
- French
- German
- Italian
- Portuguese
- Spanish
- Belgian

army. Italian forces succeeded in conquering Ethiopia in 1935–1936, but a British army forced them to surrender it during World War II. Ethiopia then became once more an independent state. (See pages 544, 633.)

The French in Africa. The beginnings of French dominion in Africa reach back to the seventeenth century, when Louis XIV began to acquire trading posts along the western coast and on the island of Madagascar. It was not until the nineteenth century, however, that the French entered seriously upon the work of colonization in Africa. France eventually possessed immense areas in north and west Africa, several thousand square miles in central Africa, and the island of Madagascar. The French holdings in Africa were larger than those of any other power, but much of the area had little value, since it lay in the Sahara Desert.

Cape Colony. Great Britain secured, if not the lion's share, at any rate the most valuable share of Africa. Besides extensive possessions on the Guinea coast, she held a solid block of territory all the way from the Cape of Good Hope to the borders of Egypt. Cape Colony, at the tip of the continent, was captured from the Dutch during the Napoleonic wars. Though small in extent, it had great importance as a halfway station on the route to India and to Australia. It also provided a base for expansion northward into Africa.

Natal, Orange Free State, and the Transvaal. The Dutch farmers, or Boers, in the Cape Colony did not take readily to British rule. Many of them, with their families and flocks, moved inland toward the north and east. This wholesale emigration—the "Great Trek"—resulted in the formation of the Boer republics of Natal, Orange Free State, and the Transvaal. Natal was soon annexed by Great Britain, but the two other republics remained independent. Then in 1885 the world's richest gold mines were discovered in the Transvaal. Many adventurers flocked

A GOLD MINE in South Africa in 1888. Today the South Africans mine nearly half of the world's annual gold production, and own some of the world's richest diamond and uranium resources.

in. Most of them were Englishmen who, since they settled down and became taxpayers, soon demanded a share in the government. The champion of British interests was Cecil Rhodes, who had found wealth in the Kimberley diamond fields of South Africa. The Dutch settlers, headed by President Paul Kruger of the Transvaal, were determined to keep the government in their own hands. Disputes between the two peoples resulted in the Boer War (1899–1902). The Boers put up a brave struggle for independence, but they were overcome by sheer weight of numbers.

Union of South Africa. Great Britain showed a wise liberality toward her former foes and granted them self-government. In 1908 representatives of the Transvaal, Orange Free State, Natal, and the Cape Colony met to work out plans for a union of the four colonies. Both British and Boers met in a spirit of compromise. They succeeded in forming the Union of South Africa, which came into being in 1910. The Union was a self-governing dominion, with a parliament for making its own laws.

Recently, agitation toward a larger share of self-government or complete independence has appeared throughout British holdings in Africa. In some cases independence has been granted and in others new status in the Commonwealth of Nations has been offered a restless colony. (See pages 631–632.)

The Suez Canal. The Suez Canal may be considered a monument to the genius of the great French engineer, Ferdinand de Lesseps. He dreamed of cutting a channel through the Isthmus of Suez, so that ships would no longer have to go around Africa on voyages between Europe and the East. In 1854 De Lesseps secured from the ruler, or *khedive* (kĕ-dēv′), of Egypt a concession permitting the building of a canal. He then organized a company to construct and operate it. The company raised funds by selling 400,000 shares

of stock. Despite numerous difficulties De Lesseps finally succeeded in completing the canal. It has no locks but lies at sea level throughout its length of about one hundred miles. The first ships passed through the canal in 1869, and within a few years so many were paying tolls that the company prospered. British vessels made up the largest number of ships passing through the canal. People began to speak of the Mediterranean-Suez route to India as the "life line of the British Empire." The British government, although at first opposed to the building of the canal, came to realize that the canal was important to the security of the empire.

Because of the attitude of their government, no British investors had bought stock in the Suez Canal Company, and therefore the British had no part in managing the canal. Within a short time, however, they found an opportunity to remedy this situation. The opportunity came about as a result

THE SUEZ CANAL IN 1880. Only after the canal was opened by the French did the British realize its importance as a "lifeline" connecting the mother country with India and other possessions in the East. Although the French continued to manage the canal, the British took over its defense after 1875.

of the financial policies of the khedive of Egypt. He had spent money recklessly for projects to modernize his country and for personal indulgence. He also invested heavily in stock of the Suez Canal Company, and came to own over 176,000 shares. Six years after the canal was opened the bankrupt khedive offered his shares for sale. Disraeli, who was then prime minister of Great Britain, arranged to have his government buy the stock. From this time on the British played an important part in the management and defense of the canal. The administration of the canal remained mostly in French hands. Under the terms of the khedive's concession to De Lesseps, the canal was to become Egyptian property in 1968. (See page 629.)

Growth of British interest in the Suez Canal. The khedive's financial policies also made possible the growth of British influence in Egypt. He had raised money by obtaining loans at high interest rates, and he met the interest payments by obtaining more loans. Eventually, of course, the khedive's credit was exhausted. To protect those who had lent money to the khedive, the French and British governments set up a dual control over Egyptian finances. The arrangement was not popular in Egypt, and a native revolt began. It was suppressed by Great Britain alone in 1882, France having refused her cooperation. The British now had a free hand in Egypt. They built roads and schools, extended the irrigation system, and reformed the administration and financial practices of the government. In 1898 the Egyptians and British together recovered the Sudan, a region directly south of Egypt, after a revolt had occurred there. The two countries then agreed on a plan for joint control of what was henceforth called the Anglo-Egyptian Sudan. Throughout the period of British domination, the Egyptians carried on a campaign for independence. Not until 1922, following World War I, were most of their demands granted. Egypt then became an independent kingdom.

European control of Africa. The revival of imperialism which began in the 1870's resulted in European control over nearly all of Africa. By 1914 only two independent states remained on the continent. Ethiopia (Abyssinia) has already been mentioned. The second was Liberia, a tiny Negro republic on the west coast of Africa. (See map, page 420.) An American society founded Liberia as a place where American Negroes might settle. The first permanent settlement was begun in 1822. Liberia has since been under the informal protection of the United States.

Up to 1914 the colonial powers governed in Africa much as they pleased. Some colonies suffered under cruel officials. Reforms came only when news of bad conditions stirred home governments to action. Thus Belgium in 1908 (see page 420) and Germany in 1907 made much-needed reforms in colonial administration. For the most part, the natives remained helpless under European control.

European Imperialism in Asia and the Pacific, 1800–1914

The European advance in Asia. Asia, where half the people on earth live, offered alluring prospects to nineteenth-century imperialists. By 1800 Europeans had gained control of only part of Asia. Russia ruled the vast stretches of Siberia; Britain had begun to penetrate India in the south; and Spain and Holland held islands off the Asiatic coast. Further expansion into Asia would give access to raw materials for European factories, would provide opportunities for profitable investment of capital, and would open up new markets for European products.

True, there were obstacles in the way of an imperialist advance in Asia. The obstacle of distance was partly overcome by the invention of the steamship and the building of the Suez Canal. A greater obstacle was the opposition of Asiatic peoples to European imperialism. In western Asia the empire of the

Ottoman Turks stood ready to oppose aggression. The Ottoman Empire extended over Mesopotamia, Asia Minor, and the Balkans in Europe. Oddly enough, the French and British, whose imperialism threatened the Turks in Asia, helped to protect Turkey in Europe against imperialism. They wished to keep Turkey strong in Europe—so strong that it could prevent Russia from taking over the Balkans. (See page 406.) In eastern Asia the Chinese and Japanese kept their backs turned upon the rest of the world. Like the Turks, they opposed change, but they lacked the foreign protection that the Turks possessed. Events proved that the Chinese, Japanese, and others could not keep out the soldiers, traders, and missionaries who came to Asia during the nineteenth century.

British conquest of India. We have already seen how the British East India Company gained a foothold in India during the seventeenth century. (See pages 212–213.) After the close of the Seven Years' War in 1763 the British continued their advance into India. Sometimes the British made alliances with native princes, to whom protection was given in return for a promise to support British rule. When a prince refused to co-operate he was ousted, and his land was taken over as a British province. By about 1850 these methods had given the East India Company control of practically all of India. It ruled directly over about two thirds of the country, and indirectly, through allied princes, over the remaining third.

The Sepoy Mutiny, 1857. Officials of the East India Company governed India until 1858. Many of the natives wished to drive out the company officials, partly because they were foreign and partly because they had caused taxes to be increased. Native unrest led to a revolt against the British in 1857—a revolt touched off the mutiny of sepoys (sē′pois), the native soldiers in the British army of northern India. The sepoys had been given a new type of cartridge for use in their army rifles. Before they could fire the cartridges, they had to bite off the paper tips which covered the greased bullets. The Mohammedan soldiers, who regarded pork as unclean, heard rumors that the bullets they put in their mouths were greased with pig fat. The Hindu soldiers, who regarded cows as sacred, heard that the bullets were greased with fat from cows. Many of the sepoys rose in revolt. They killed all the British they could lay hands on and besieged the forts where the rest took shelter. For a time it seemed that all northern India would be lost, but the British rushed troops from the south and finally put down the revolt. They punished the mutineers with acts as cruel as those of the mutineers themselves: some of the rebels were tied to the mouths of cannon and blown to pieces. The Sepoy Mutiny cost the lives of over a hundred thousand people, most of whom were natives.

British government of India. The British people at home were shocked when they heard the story of the Sepoy Mutiny. In 1858 popular feeling led Parliament to pass an "Act for the Better Government of India," which transferred the task of ruling India to the British government. The new officials built schools for the natives and made progress in reducing the death rate from famines and plagues. Partly as a result of British public health work the population of India has increased rapidly. Today the population of India and Pakistan stands at about 600,000,000, about one sixth of the world's population.

British investors used part of their profits from India to build railroads, factories, and canals in India. Although India probably enjoyed greater prosperity and well-being than before, many of the people continued to ask for self-government. The British replied by throwing native leaders into prison. Not until World War I did the British give serious attention to Indian demands for home

QUEEN VICTORIA and her Indian assistant. The queen took great pride in her title of "Empress of India," which Disraeli secured for her from Parliament. In her reign, the longest in British history, Britain reached the peak of prosperity and world power. Victoria embodied the feeling that British ways were superior and that Britain would always win. Told that things were going badly at the start of the Boer War, she said, "We are not interested in the possibilities of defeat."

rule, and not until after World War II was India granted independence.

The British settle Australia. Captain Cook had raised the British flag over Australia in 1770 on his first voyage of discovery in the Pacific. Australia, an island continent, contained only a few savages, who were among the most primitive on earth. They had Australia all to themselves until 1788, when the British began to ship convicts to Botany Bay on the east coast. A few settlers began to come voluntarily when they learned that sheep raising was profitable on the southern plains of Australia. After gold was discovered in 1851 more people came in search of fortunes. Today there are eleven million people in Australia. Most of them live near the eastern and southern coasts, where there is ample rainfall and the climate is cool. In recent years manufacturing and commerce have developed, but agriculture remains the most im-

portant activity of the country. Australia is the world's largest exporter of wool and one of the chief producers of wheat and beef. In 1901 the five states of Australia, together with the neighboring island of Tasmania, united to form the Australian Commonwealth. The Australians set up a federal government like that of the United States, with a written constitution, a senate, and a house of representatives. Australia is a self-governing dominion in the British Commonwealth of Nations. It governs several nearby islands and has claimed authority over much of the Antarctic continent.

The Dominion of New Zealand. Twelve hundred miles east of southern Australia are the two islands which form New Zealand. Their temperate climate, abundant rainfall, and luxuriant vegetation attracted British settlers, who now number more than two and a third million. Most of the people earn their

THE TRANS-SIBERIAN RAILWAY in 1911. Built to link European Russia with the Pacific coast, the Railway opened up the vast area of Siberia to colonization.

living by farming. The New Zealanders are perhaps best known for their social legislation, which includes sickness and old age insurance and a plan for free medical care. New Zealand, like Australia, is a self-governing British dominion. It controls a number of small nearby islands.

The British and French in Indo-China. The peninsula of Indo-China, bordering on India and China, caught the eye of imperialists. In 1800 Indo-China included Burma, Thailand, Cambodia, Laos, Vietnam, and several states in the long Malay Peninsula. By 1914 the British and French had taken over most of Indo-China. The British added Burma to their empire in 1886, and ruled it as part of India. They also set up a protectorate over the states at the tip of the Malay Peninsula. Here, after World War I, they built a great naval base at Singapore—the so-called "Gibraltar of the Far East." (See map, page 427.)

The French began to enter Indo-China dur-

ing the middle of the nineteenth century. Like the British in India, the French made alliances with native princes and enlisted native troops under white officers. Through force and diplomacy they made Laos, Cambodia, and Vietnam into "French Indo-China," a colony larger than France itself. Thus by 1914 the kingdom of Siam was the only independent state in Indo-China.

The Russians in eastern Asia. The Russians also joined the imperialist parade in Asia. As we have seen, they already held Siberia. (See page 251.) They had made little use of eastern Siberia, partly because transportation difficulties kept it isolated from the rest of the world. During the latter half of the nineteenth century the Russians attacked the problem of transportation in two ways: (1) They opened traffic by sea. As a preliminary step they persuaded the Chinese to give up a long strip of coast near Japan (1860). Here the Russians promptly built the port of Vladivostok to serve as an outlet for Siberian products. (2) To improve land transportation, the Russians connected Vladivostok with Moscow by constructing the Trans-Siberian Railway. This single-track line, 5500 miles in length, was completed in 1905. In 1896 the Chinese gave the Russians permission to build a short-cut line across northern Manchuria to Vladivostok. (This short cut was called the Chinese Eastern Railway.) Unfortunately, the Vladivostok port was choked with ice during the winter. The Russians wanted a warm-water port which could be open to shipping the year around. They got it in 1898, when the Chinese granted them a twenty-five-year lease on Port Arthur, at the southern tip of Manchuria. The Chinese also gave them the right to build a railway connecting Port Arthur with the Chinese Eastern Railway. The two rail lines and the Port Arthur lease gave the Russians an opportunity to dominate Manchuria. Meanwhile, in 1861 the czar abolished serfdom in Russia.

Imperialism in the Far East to 1914

| British | Dutch |
| French | Russian |

IMPERIALISM IN THE FAR EAST, 1914

This meant that the peasants could leave their villages to look for better opportunities. Many of them moved into Siberia. Perhaps two and one-half million did so between 1861 and 1871. Naturally this speeded up the development of Siberia. Some of the peasants even went beyond Siberia and settled on the island of Sakhalin off the east coast. In 1875 the Japanese gave up their claims to Sakhalin in return for Russia's recognition of Japanese claims to the Kuril Islands. (See map, 427.)

The Russians in central Asia. The Russians also expanded southward into central Asia. Much of the region was dry and thinly populated. After the Russian serfs were freed, large numbers of them moved to central Asia to cultivate the land wherever there was sufficient rainfall.

The Russians continued southward until they reached the northern boundaries of India, Afghanistan, and Persia. The Russian advance alarmed the British, who regarded both Afghanistan and Persia as within their "sphere of influence." For a time it seemed that the two powers might go to war. A mutual fear of Germany helped to draw them together, however, and in 1907 they signed a treaty which settled most of their difficulties. (See page 442.) They agreed that Persia should be divided into three zones. Britain took south Persia as a sphere of influence, Russia took north Persia as its sphere, and central Persia was left open to investments by both British and Russians. Both countries recognized the independence of Persia and Afghanistan.

The Opium War breaks down Chinese isolation. All the imperialist powers wanted to have China opened to foreign trade. Before the nineteenth century the Chinese did their best to remain isolated. They regarded foreigners as barbarians and called them "foreign devils." Only a few missionaries and traders were allowed to enter China. Practically all foreign trade was restricted to the port of Canton. (See page 230.) Foreign merchants at Canton had frequent disagreements with Chinese officials. The merchants did not wish to obey Chinese laws, some of which they thought unjust. They objected especially to the practice of punishing a whole colony of merchants for a crime committed by one of them. The Chinese officials, on the other hand, objected to the smuggling of opium into China. Merchants from several countries took part in the illegal drug traffic. In 1839 the Chinese determined to stamp out the opium smuggling and took measures against the foreign merchants. As a result the First Opium War (1839–1842) broke out between Great Britain and China. The British, with their modern fleet and army, had an easy victory. In 1842 they compelled the Chinese government to give them the island of Hong Kong, near Canton, and to open four additional ports to British traders.

Foreign powers push into China. After the First Opium War the Chinese began to grant to other merchants the same trading privileges they had given the British. They also gave foreigners the privilege of "extraterritoriality." Extraterritoriality meant that foreigners in China, when accused of crime, would be judged according to the laws of their own country rather than the laws of China. The Second Opium War (1856–1860) resulted in new concessions to foreigners. Five more ports were opened to foreign merchants; Europeans were permitted to travel in China; and protection was promised for Christian missionaries and converts.

Foreign powers annex Chinese territory. By 1860 the imperialist powers had begun to annex parts of China. As we have seen, the French entered Indo-China in the south, and in the north the Russians obtained the region north of Vladivostok. Toward the end of the century the Japanese, just beginning their national expansion, fought a short war with China over Korea (Sino-Japanese War, 1894–

HONG KONG, an island city of contrasts. Perched high on a hill, a shiny new apartment house looks down upon a settlement of squatters' huts. A British Crown Colony for over one hundred years, Hong Kong is one of the great ports of the Far East. Many refugees have settled here since the Communists seized mainland China.

1895). The Japanese won an unbroken series of victories. In 1895 they compelled the Chinese to recognize the independence of Korea and to give the island of Formosa to Japan. Only the combined protests of Russia, Germany, and France prevented Japan from annexing part of southern Manchuria as well. The three powers soon asked China to pay heavily for their help. France added some more Chinese territory to French Indo-China; Germany received the port of Kiaochow (jyou'jō'); and Russia obtained Port Arthur and railway rights in Manchuria. The British enlarged Burma at China's expense and leased the port of Weihaiwei (wā'hī'wā') for as long as the Russians should remain at Port Arthur. France, Russia, Germany, Great Britain, and Japan then proceeded to map out spheres of influence for themselves in China. Some observers predicted that the spheres of influence would soon be transformed into colonies, and that China would cease to exist as an independent nation.

The "Open Door" in China. At this point the United States took steps to protect China's independence. The American people had been busy at home during the latter part of the nineteenth century and had taken little interest in Chinese affairs except to support missionary activities there. The Americans had made their country a powerful industrial nation with goods to sell and capital to invest abroad. American leaders wanted the Chinese market kept open for American goods. Therefore, in 1899 John Hay, then Secretary of State, wrote notes to the great powers, urging them to agree that merchants of all nations should be treated equally everywhere in China— even in leased territories and spheres of influence. Hay's suggestion was called the "Open Door" policy. Great Britain approved of the Open Door policy, and the other powers rather reluctantly followed her example. For some years they gave at least lip service to the principle that no foreign country should enjoy special commercial privileges in any part of China. Hay's diplomatic action helped to keep China independent, because under the Open Door policy there was nothing to gain by carving up China.

The Boxer uprising, 1900. The Chinese also took steps to protect their independence. A Chinese organization, popularly called the "Boxers," began an antiforeign movement. It spread like wildfire throughout North China. In an outburst of violence in 1900 the Boxers destroyed churches, business houses, and residences belonging to Europeans, and murdered missionaries and native Christians. The foreigners in Peking took refuge in the legation quarter (the part of the city where the diplomats lived) and fought desperately against Chinese attacks. Their situation may well be compared to that of the British in India during the Sepoy Mutiny. In August, 1900, the foreigners were rescued by an international army composed of European, Japanese, and American troops. The powers then forced China to accept a humiliating settlement. They insisted that China destroy some of her forts, permit foreign troops to be stationed in Peking for protection of the diplomats, and pay about $330,000,000 for damage done during the Boxer uprising. Later, the United States gave nearly three fourths of its share of the Boxer indemnity back to the Chinese. China used most of the money to send Chinese students to American colleges.

The Chinese Revolution, 1911–1912. The Boxer uprising revealed fully the weakness of China. Men in all parts of the "Celestial Empire" began to demand changes for the purpose of strengthening their country. Some felt that the best way to get reform would be to overthrow the unprogressive Manchu dynasty, which had ruled China for nearly three hundred years. The leader of the reformers was Dr. Sun Yat-sen (soon'yät'sĕn'), the "George Washington of China." He and other educated Chinese saw clearly that China must abandon the ways of the past and adopt

SUN YAT–SEN

western ideas and methods. In 1911 a mutiny of part of the army touched off the Chinese Revolution. Everywhere people rose against the government, and early in 1912 the child emperor was compelled to abdicate. China then became a republic.

The Chinese become divided. After the Manchus were overthrown, two opposing groups struggled for control of the government. Yuan Shih-kai (yoo-än'shē'kī') led one group, which may best be described as the conservative faction. He had the support of the army and of the men who had held offices under the Manchus. Yuan was elected president of the republic. Opposed to Yuan was Dr. Sun Yat-sen. He led the National People's Party, or Kuomintang (gwō'mĭn-täng'), which wished to establish a democratic government in China. Soon after becoming president, Yuan made himself dictator. He dismissed the national legislature and forced Sun Yat-sen and other Kuomintang leaders to flee from China. Yuan died in 1916. The following year the Kuomintang set up a government at Canton in opposition to the government at Peking. The weak and divided Chinese entered upon a long period of almost continual civil war.

Japan Becomes a World Power

Opening the door to Japan. Japan remained in the grip of feudalism until the middle of the nineteenth century. The emperor, or mikado, was a mere figurehead during the feudal period. The real ruler of Japan was the *shogun* (shō'gōōn'), a military leader who held office for life. By 1639 the shoguns had adopted a "closed door" policy for Japan, shutting out all foreigners except a few Dutch traders. (See page 231.) During the first half of the nineteenth century the Russians, English, French, Dutch, and Americans made unsuccessful attempts to open the door to Japan. The man who finally succeeded in opening Japan to foreign trade was Commodore Matthew Perry of the United States Navy. In 1853 he sailed into Yedo Bay with four warships and a request from the American government for the right of shelter for our fishing craft and the privilege of trade for our merchants. In the following year the shogun signed an agreement permitting Americans to trade at two Japanese ports. The diplomatic ice having thus been broken, various European nations soon made similar treaties with Japan and won the right to trade at several other ports.

The Japanese Revolution. After Perry's visit thoughtful Japanese realized that their country was weaker than the western nations. A group of barons therefore set to work to strengthen Japan. Their first step was an attack on the feudal system. In 1867 they persuaded the shogun to resign and made the emperor once more the head of the government. The emperor left his isolated inland capital and moved to the shogun's capital on the coast—the city of Yedo, renamed Tokyo. (Yedo Bay, which Perry had entered, was renamed Tokyo Bay.) Japan then entered the *Meiji* (mā'jĭ) *Era*, or "Era of Enlightened Government." By 1871 most of the feudal system was swept away; the nobles gave up many of their feudal privileges, and serfdom

PERRY'S EXPEDITION TO JAPAN, shown in an illustration from the report of his 1853 visit. The Japanese were much impressed by the miniature railroad, telegraph, and other mechanical marvels brought to them by Commodore Matthew Perry and his men. Later the Japanese sent a delegation to tour the United States.

was abolished. The emperor later granted his people a written constitution providing for a legislature of two houses and a cabinet. This does not mean that Japan became a democracy. The authority of the emperor was supreme and was even increased through the revival of the ancient Shinto (shǐn′tō′) religion, which taught that the emperor was descended from the gods.

Japan adopts western ideas. The Japanese revolution was more than a change in government; it revolutionized Japanese life as well. Few countries have altered so greatly in so short a time. The Japanese set out to borrow the best ideas that the West could offer. They brought in British experts to establish a strong navy, German officers to train a modern army, and American educators to plan a national school system. The Japanese also copied western building styles, railroads, steamships, and industrial methods. By 1900 the Japanese had built about seven thousand factories and were turning out low-priced goods through the use of abundant water power and cheap labor.

Effects of change on Japanese life. The changes brought by the Meiji Era had a profound effect on the Japanese. City populations grew as factories provided employment opportunities and as scientific and medical knowledge lowered the death rate. On the average, Japan's population grew at the rate of a million persons per year; Tokyo became one of the largest cities in the world.

For Japanese farmers the Meiji Era brought freedom from feudal restrictions. Since they were no longer bound to the soil, farmers could move to the city or to better farming areas. They could keep more of their produce for themselves, and could hope that their children, through education, might rise in society.

Chief beneficiaries of Japan's new policies, however, were the businessmen. Previously they had been scorned by the nobles; now they acquired wealth and power. The government often developed model industries and then sold them cheaply to business firms. Other firms received government assistance in the fields of banking, shipbuilding, mining, and utilities, and were encouraged to manufacture weapons for Japan's armed forces. Profits tended to center in the hands of a few wealthy families called the *Zaibatsu*. The *Zaibatsu* worked in partnership with the Imperial government and often influenced its decisions.

The old feudal nobility, on the other hand, suffered a loss of power, prestige, and wealth. The nobles had their incomes reduced by about nine tenths overall, and the class of *samurai* (feudal knights) was abolished. The only nobles remaining in power were those who served the government. They included men with hereditary seats in the upper house of the parliament, as well as many of the emperor's ministers. Influential families controlled the army and navy, for example, and held almost hereditary posts in the cabinet. A group of nobles called the "Elder Statesmen" also had great influence on the emperor. They had helped to shape the policies of the Meiji emperor, and had advised him regularly until his death in 1912. The nobles worked to limit the influence of Japan's parliament and to enhance the emperor's prestige. They encouraged Shintoism, which by glorifying the emperor and Japan's heroes helped prepare the Japanese people for war.

Japan begins to expand. The Japanese observed with great interest the methods used by the western powers in acquiring colonies. Before long the Japanese determined that they too would enlarge their possessions. Conquest appealed to the nobles and military leaders as a way of gaining prestige for Japan. Japanese merchants and manufacturers wanted opportunities for money-making abroad, and Japanese leaders wanted lands for settlement by the growing population. As we have noted (see pages 428–429), Japan went to war with China in 1894–1895, winning Formosa and bringing Korea under Japanese influence. During the next few years Russian and Japanese interests clashed head on. Japan wished to expand in Russian-held Manchuria, while Russia sought greater influence in Korea. Each country was able to check the other by diplomatic maneuvers, and therefore neither could advance as it wanted.

The Russo-Japanese War, 1904–1905. In order to end the stalemate the Japanese took two steps which had world-wide repercussions: (1) They made a treaty of alliance with Great Britain in 1902. Each country promised to remain neutral if the other went to war in defense of its own interests, and each promised to enter the war if the other had to fight more than one power. (2) The Japanese then made a surprise attack on Russia in February, 1904. To the amazement of the world, the Japanese proceeded to win victory after victory. The inferiority of the Japanese in numbers and resources was more than made up by their bravery, the ability of their leaders,

and the thoroughness of their war preparations. The Russians were handicapped by having part of their fleet icebound at Vladivostok and by not yet having completed the Trans-Siberian Railway. The Japanese quickly overcame the Russian fleet and then landed troops on the mainland of Asia. The army advanced across Korea into Manchuria, captured Port Arthur, and pushed the Russians northward. The Russians sent their European fleet halfway around the world to join in the fighting, only to have almost all their ships destroyed in a single battle with the Japanese navy (Battle of Tsushima, May 27-28, 1905). The Japanese had won brilliant victories, but they were almost at the end of their resources by the spring of 1905. The Russians were also in bad condition. They had suffered heavy losses, and revolutionary groups were urging the people to revolt. Both governments therefore accepted the suggestion of President Theodore Roosevelt that they meet and write a peace treaty.

SHIPYARD AT KOBE, twenty miles west of Osaka. Kobe ranks second to Yokohama as a major port in Japan. Today, Japan is the world's foremost shipbuilding nation.

The Treaty of Portsmouth, 1905. Representatives of Russia and Japan met at Portsmouth, New Hampshire, where they drew up and signed the Treaty of Portsmouth. Russia agreed to give Japan the southern half of .the island of Sakhalin, as well as Port Arthur and part of the railway running north from it. The Russians also recognized Japanese interests in Korea, and both Russia and Japan promised to withdraw their armies from Manchuria.

Japan becomes a world power. The Russo-Japanese War had at least two important results: (1) It gave the Japanese a chance to expand. They made a series of agreements with Russia by which the two countries divided Manchuria into spheres of influence. In 1910 the Japanese took control of Korea in name as well as fact by annexing it to their empire. (2) A second result of the war was the recognition of Japan as a world power. People throughout the Far East hailed Japan as a champion of Asiatic rights. She had reversed the trend of centuries of European imperialism, had defeated an imperialist power singlehanded, and had destroyed the myth that a western power could not be defeated.

The great powers also recognized Japan's new place in world affairs. In 1905 Great Britain signed a second treaty of alliance with Japan. The alliance was renewed in 1911. Meanwhile both France and Russia reached a friendly understanding with Japan in regard to Far Eastern questions. Because of her treaty obligations Japan entered World War I on the side of the Allies.

Japan in 1914 was a far different nation from the one Commodore Perry had entered in 1853. Instead of a hermit country, Japan had become a great power. Business and military leaders, rather than feudal lords, were now the most powerful men in Japan. The Japanese took pride in their busy factories, their increasing trade, their expanding railroad and steamship lines, and their growing empire. Japan's future looked promising indeed.

The United States Becomes a World Power

Agricultural development of the United States. We have already seen how the United States expanded across the continent to the Pacific. (See pages 410–411.) The American people thus came to possess a vast area, part of which was ideally suited for farming. During the nineteenth century American farmers began to cultivate the new lands in the West, and food production increased by leaps and bounds. In 1862 Congress encouraged the settlement of new land by passing a Homestead Act, which gave a farmer 160 acres of government land free after he had lived on it for five years. Millions of immigrants came from Europe to obtain land for farming. Food production was also increased by the use of new types of farm machinery which did work formerly done by hand. By using machinery each farmer could cultivate more land and raise more food. A vast network of railroads was built across the continent, enabling the farmers to send their produce to city markets or to seaports for shipment to other countries. As a result of all these developments the United States became the world's largest producer and exporter of farm products.

Industrial development of the United States. After the middle of the nineteenth century manufacturing increased enormously in the United States. Immigration helped to provide the labor needed in factories; abundant natural resources, such as iron, copper, coal, and oil, furnished raw materials for manufacturing; and railroads provided efficient transportation. In manufacturing, as in agriculture, new inventions and new processes speeded up production. By 1894 the United States was turning out more manufactured goods than any other country in the world, and its foreign trade was expanding rapidly.

The United States enters world politics. During most of the nineteenth century the American people took little interest in for-

WRECK OF THE *U.S.S. MAINE*. For thirteen years the ship lay on the bottom of
Havana harbor, partly exposed and creating a menace to navigation. Finally
the ship was raised, examined, and sunk in deeper water. The examination failed
to reveal the cause of the explosion, which is still a mystery.

eign affairs. They did not worry about being attacked, because they had peaceful neighbors on the north and south and broad oceans on the east and west. Neither did they plan to attack other countries, for they were busy enough with the development of their own land. At the end of the nineteenth century most Americans probably wished to continue the traditional American policy of isolation. With every year that passed, however, they found it harder to remain aloof from the rest of the world. Modern means of transportation and communication in effect brought other countries closer to the United States. At the same time the growth of the United States made it necessary for the government to become more active in foreign affairs. Producers expected government help in finding foreign markets for the flood of goods pouring from American farms and factories. The government also sought to aid American shipping by obtaining coaling stations on Pacific islands for American ships and by building a canal across Central America. Furthermore, the government took steps to protect the

United States by enforcing the Monroe Doctrine (see page 298) and by acquiring outlying naval bases.

The United States in Samoa. During the early part of the nineteenth century American merchant and whaling ships frequently stopped at the Samoan Islands for fresh supplies. In 1872 the United States acquired the harbor of Pago Pago—one of the best harbors in the Pacific. A little later both Germany and Great Britain secured from the natives the right to trade in the Samoas. A number of Americans, Germans, and Englishmen came to the islands and began a brisk competition for control of the native trade. In 1888 the natives killed some German citizens. When Germany sent warships to avenge the deaths, both Britain and the United States feared that Germany might end by seizing the islands. They therefore sent naval vessels also. Fighting might easily have broken out between the squadrons, but a hurricane destroyed or put out of action all but one of the warships. The three countries then organized a commission, composed of representatives of all three, to "protect" the Samoans. Great Britain withdrew from the commission in 1899, and the Germans and Americans then divided the islands. The United States got Tutuila, on which Pago Pago is located, and five other islands, while Germany kept four inhabited islands until World War I.

The United States annexes Hawaii. American ships usually put in at the Hawaiian Islands on voyages to China. During the nineteenth century Americans became owners of most of the Hawaiian sugar plantations, and in 1887 the United States leased Pearl Harbor as a naval base. A few years later the native queen took away some of the rights which she had granted to foreigners. Americans in Hawaii joined with natives in a revolt against her. The new government promptly asked the United States to annex the islands. Five years later, in 1898, the United States accepted the offer.

The Spanish-American War. In 1898 the United States became involved in a war with Spain. Spain had lost nearly all her American colonies early in the nineteenth century. (See pages 292–297.) She retained only the islands of Cuba and Puerto Rico in the Caribbean Sea. By the end of the nineteenth century the Cubans were making a strong bid for independence. They rose in revolt in 1895, beginning a bitter struggle that dragged on for several years and was marked by cruelties on both sides. Lives were lost, property destroyed, and trade disrupted. People in the United States watched the contest with great interest, most of them because they sympathized with the rebels, and some of them because of the large American investments in Cuba. American feeling against Spain grew stronger after the battleship *Maine* blew up in Havana harbor. The cause of the disaster is still in doubt, but at the time most people in the United States thought that Spain was responsible. In April, 1898, largely because of popular demand stirred up by the newspapers, the government of the United States declared war on Spain.

The fighting lasted less than four months. On May 1, Admiral Dewey destroyed Spain's Pacific fleet at Manila Bay in the Philippines and on July 2, Spain's Atlantic fleet was sunk outside the harbor of Santiago in Cuba. American troops landed on Cuba, Puerto Rico, and the Philippines, and defeated the Spanish without much difficulty.

The United States annexes Puerto Rico, Guam, and the Philippines. Spain and the United States made peace in December, 1898. They agreed to give Cuba her independence, but the United States kept Puerto Rico, Guam, and the Philippines. The Filipinos had hoped that an American victory would bring them independence. When they learned that they had merely changed masters, they rose in rebellion. The revolt was put down only after three years of bitter jungle warfare.

The United States as a Pacific power. By the end of the nineteenth century the United States had become one of the strongest powers in the Pacific. Her purchase of Alaska from Russia in 1867 had given her a dominating position in the North Pacific. She had also obtained strategic posts in the South and Central Pacific: the Midway Islands in 1867; Guam, the Philippines, and the Hawaiian Islands in 1898; part of the Samoan Islands in 1899; and the island of Wake, which she occupied in 1900. The United States was also beginning to take an active part in Chinese affairs. We have already noted how she obtained agreement on the Open Door policy in 1899 so as to keep China's markets open, and how in 1900 the United States helped put down the Boxer Uprising. Many Americans regretted our growing activity in world affairs; others welcomed our emergence as a world power. Some isolationists as well as expansionists approved of the Panama Canal and supported the Monroe Doctrine.

Building the Panama Canal. Ferdinand de Lesseps tried to build a canal across the Isthmus of Panama during the 1880's, but tropical diseases and financial troubles caused his attempt to fail. After the Spanish-American War many Americans urged that the United States should build a canal. They argued that the canal would (1) bring a reduction in freight rates, and (2) make it easier for the Navy to defend both coasts and the new island empire of the United States. President Theodore Roosevelt gave enthusiastic backing to the canal project. Shortly after he became President (in 1901), the British agreed that the United States alone might build the canal, provided it was kept open to ships of all nations. (In 1850 the United States and Britain had agreed to be partners if either began work on a canal.) Roosevelt then opened negotiations with Colombia, which owned the Isthmus of Panama. Colombia wanted a higher price for the right to build a canal than the United States offered her. The people of Panama broke the deadlock by revolting against Colombia and granting the United States the right to build a canal and to control a strip of land ten miles wide stretching across the isthmus. Excavation began in 1906. The first ship passed through in 1914.

Enforcement of the Monroe Doctrine. The Monroe Doctrine is the most famous single statement of American foreign policy. On several occasions the government of the United States has taken vigorous action to enforce the doctrine. We have noted (see page 388) how Napoleon III tried to make Mexico a colony of France at the time of the American War between the States. After the war ended the United States sent an army to the Mexican border, and French troops left Mexico. President Cleveland also invoked the Monroe Doctrine in 1895, when Great Britain and Venezuela were in dispute over the boundary of British Guiana. Cleveland practically threatened war unless the British agreed to let a board of judges arbitrate the dispute. The British agreed. In 1904 Theodore Roosevelt gave a new interpretation to the doctrine when he entered a dispute involving the Dominican Republic. The little republic had fallen deeply in debt to several European countries, who were threatening to collect their money by force. Roosevelt asserted that the Monroe Doctrine gave the United States the right to exercise "an inter-

BUILDING THE PANAMA CANAL. Ferdinand de Lesseps, successful with the Suez Canal, failed in Panama. The United States then completed what has been described as "the greatest liberty man has ever taken with nature."

PRESIDENT GABRIEL TERRA OF URUGUAY inaugurates the Seventh Pan American Conference in Montevideo, December 3, 1933. Today, the Organization of American States seeks to improve relations among American nations.

national police power"—namely, to intervene in the affairs of its neighbor republics in case of long-continued wrongdoing or mismanagement. Accordingly, he arranged with the Dominican president to have the United States take charge of Dominican finances for some years. Under this agreement American officials collected tariffs in the Dominican Republic and used part of the money to pay the Dominican debts.

The United States dominates the Caribbean. By 1916 the Caribbean had become "an American lake." Panama had leased the Canal Zone to the United States and had even agreed to let American troops enter Panama if necessary to keep order. By a treaty ratified in 1916 the United States also received the right to build and fortify a canal through Nicaragua. Cuba gave the United States a naval base. The United States owned Puerto Rico, and in 1916 purchased the Virgin Islands from Denmark to strengthen the Pan-

ama Canal defenses. Between 1906 and 1916 American troops had entered Cuba, Nicaragua, the Dominican Republic, and the republic of Haiti at various times to preserve order. These four countries, as well as Panama, had become protectorates of the United States. Latin Americans were beginning to complain of "Yankee imperialism," and to express fear that the United States would continue to expand southward.

Inter-American co-operation. Pan Americanism, or the "inter-American co-operation" movement, has encouraged more cordial relations between the United States and Latin America. Those who believe in inter-American co-operation point out that the countries in the Western Hemisphere form a distinct geographic family of nations, with common interests. The inter-American movement aims to strengthen commercial and cultural ties between the American nations, and promote peaceful settlement of disputes.

Inter-American conferences. The ideal of Pan Americanism, or inter-American co-operation, may be said to date back to 1826, when Bolívar invited all the countries of the Western Hemisphere to send delegates to a conference at Panama. Only four nations were represented at the conference. It met without the delegates from the United States, for one of them died on the way and the other turned back when he found he could not reach Panama in time. The first successful conference of the American republics met at Washington in 1889. Secretary of State James G. Blaine, who presided, had long been a leader in the Pan American movement. During the conference he worked unceasingly for the adoption of two programs: (1) tariff reduction and (2) arrangements for the peaceful settlement of disputes. Although the conference did not adopt his suggestions, Blaine started the American nations on the path of closer co-operation.

One result of the First International Conference of American States (1889) was the establishment of the Pan American Union. It was an organization maintained in Washington by the twenty-one American republics to promote friendly relations among them. It acted as a clearing house of information on the American nations and arranged for conferences at fairly regular intervals. In 1948, at the Ninth International Conference of American States, meeting at Bogotá, Colombia, a further step was taken. Under a charter of its own, the Pan American Union was transformed into the Organization of American States (OAS) as a regional organization of the United Nations.

REVIEWING THE CHAPTER

TERMS TO UNDERSTAND: *Boers, khedive, Sepoy Mutiny, extraterritoriality, Open Door policy, Boxer Indemnity, Pan Americanism.*

PERSONS TO IDENTIFY: *David Livingstone, Henry M. Stanley, Leopold II, Cecil Rhodes, Ferdinand de Lesseps, John Hay, Sun Yat-sen, Matthew Perry, Admiral Dewey, Theodore Roosevelt, James G. Blaine.*

PLACES TO LOCATE: *Morocco, Belgian Congo, Madagascar, Cape Colony, Isthmus of Suez, Liberia, Indo-China, Port Arthur, Sakhalin Island, Afghanistan, Peking, Isthmus of Panama.*

QUESTIONS TO ANSWER

1. Give three reasons for the revival of the colonizing movement.
2. Describe the various forms of imperialism.
3. (a) What men led the way in exploring Africa? (b) What countries took part in the race for African possessions? List the posses-

sions each acquired. (c) Tell the story of the building of the Suez Canal.
4. (a) By what methods did Britain gain control of India? (b) How was the government of India changed in 1858? Why?
5. (a) Describe the settlement of Australia and New Zealand. (b) What areas did Britain and France acquire in Indo-China? (c) Trace the expansion of Russia in Asia to 1914.
6. (a) How did the Opium Wars serve to break down Chinese isolation? (b) Why did the United States favor the Open Door policy in China? (c) Explain the effects on China of the revolution of 1911–1912.
7. (a) How was Japanese isolation ended? (b) Describe the ways in which Japan copied the West. (c) What possessions did Japan acquire before World War I?
8. (a) Why did the United States abandon its policy of isolation? (b) Locate territories which the United States came to control in the Pacific and the Caribbean. (c) Trace briefly the development of the Pan American movement.

21 World War I

WAR AND PEACE. Tanks were a British development, first tried in combat in 1916. At first they caught the Germans by surprise, but they were too few and too slow to win the war. Only after attacks by massed men and the slaughter of millions was victory won. Signing of the armistice brought deep rejoicing in Britain, for it was believed that the war would end all war forever. But peace brought new problems: during the 1920's the empire began to fall apart, and unemployment brought widespread suffering.

Man's progress is never complete, nor unmarred by setbacks. The advances of democracy, nationalism, and industrialism in the Western world during the nineteenth century produced an atmosphere of optimism and hope. But these forces also gave rise to new rivalries and frictions among nations. Almost unconsciously Europe drifted into a war that nobody wanted or expected. The United States, abandoning a long tradition of aloofness from European entanglements, was inevitably drawn into the conflict. The "war to end war" was the most extensive and the most costly up to that time, and it raised more problems than it solved. How it came about and how it was won by the Allied powers will be the subject matter of this chapter.

The Trend toward War

Germany's position among the nations. From the hour of its birth the German Empire took first place among the nations on the European continent. The other countries regarded the newcomer with distrust, for Germany's rise upset the balance of power. For a long time after the French Revolution the diplomats of Europe had watched France as a possible troublemaker. After 1870 they looked upon Germany as a threat to European peace. The bold strokes with which Bismarck had built the German Empire were bound to arouse suspicion and fear. (See pages 397–398.) Bismarck was fully aware of this. His aim therefore was to win friends and allies for Germany and at the same time to keep France from finding allies. This required some skillful diplomacy.

Germany wins an ally. The "Iron Chancellor" turned first to Austria-Hungary. He had prepared the way for good relations with that empire by granting moderate peace terms at the close of the Austro-Prussian War in 1866. (See page 397.) After the war, Austria had begun to seek compensation in the Balkans for the territory which she had lost to Germany and Italy. Shortly after establishing the German Empire, Bismarck had the opportunity to win the good will of Austria by supporting her Balkan policy against Russian ambitions. At the Congress of Berlin in 1878

(see page 407), Bismarck approved the Austrian occupation of the Balkan provinces of Bosnia and Herzegovina, formerly owned by Turkey. He also successfully opposed the extension of Russian influence in the Balkans. In 1879 Germany and Austria-Hungary made a secret treaty known as the Dual Alliance. It provided that each member would come to the aid of the other if either should be attacked by Russia or by another power which had the help of Russia.

The Triple Alliance. Bismarck scored a further triumph in 1882 by persuading Italy to throw in her lot with Germany and Austria-Hungary. This group became known as the *Triple Alliance*. Italy, like Germany, was a newly unified country in need of friends and allies. Moreover, Italy was angry because France had just established a protectorate over Tunis. This Turkish province, the region of ancient Carthage, contained a large Italian population, and Italy herself had hoped to snatch it from the sultan's feeble hands. In 1883 the new Balkan country of Rumania secretly joined the group. Henceforth the Triple Alliance was really, though not in name, a quadruple alliance. The alliance continued unbroken until after the opening of World War I.

The beginning of another alliance. The creation of the Triple Alliance was a challenge to France and Russia. Russia, the "big brother" of the Slavs in the Balkans, resented

Austria-Hungary's attempt to keep the southern Slavs under its thumb. France was smarting from its defeat by Germany in 1870–1871 and was alarmed by Germany's growing power in European affairs. Thus the time was clearly ripe for a Franco-Russian understanding. The two countries had already shown a tendency to co-operate. To build the Trans-Siberian Railroad and develop Russian industries, the czar's government had sold large amounts of stock to French investors. In 1892 France and Russia signed a secret military agreement, which was ratified two years later. They agreed that if either country was attacked by its neighbor the other would come to its assistance. France no longer stood alone, and Germany now had a possible enemy on its eastern flank. It was the "nightmare coalition" so feared by Bismarck.

The diplomatic position of Great Britain. Great Britain was not yet entangled in any alliances. Britain was not friendly toward either France or Russia, for the colonial aims of France in Africa and of Russia in Asia clashed with Britain's own. On the other hand, while Bismarck was chancellor the British looked with favor on Germany and the other members of the Triple Alliance. To avoid offending Great Britain, Bismarck carefully refrained from violating Belgian neutrality during the Franco-Prussian War. For the same reason he long opposed the acquisition of colonies by Germany. Toward the end of the century, however, Great Britain and Germany began to draw apart. One reason for the change was the amazing industrial development of Germany, which made it a serious competitor of Great Britain in foreign markets. Another reason was Germany's aggressive colonial policy, begun in 1888 under Kaiser William II. The most important reason was Germany's declared purpose to build up a great navy as well as a great army. To the average Britisher the new German navy seemed a dagger pointed at his country's heart. Furthermore, before and during the Boer War (see page 421), the kaiser's sympathetic attitude toward the Boers had placed an added strain on Anglo-German relations.

Great Britain reaches an understanding with France. In the early years of the twentieth century, therefore, Great Britain was seeking new friendships on the Continent. The first step was an understanding with France. In 1904, after an exchange of visits by King Edward to Paris and by President Loubet to London, the two countries signed a treaty, providing for the adjustment of their colonial claims. France recognized the superior rights of Great Britain in Egypt; Great Britain gave France a free hand in Morocco. The nations also made agreements relating to other regions. These agreements did not set up a formal alliance. They did not provide for military measures, either for offense or defense. Nor did they have special reference to Germany or any other power. They merely established an *Entente Cordiale* (än'tänt' kôr'dyàl'), or "cordial understanding." The importance of the agreements lay in the fact that they ended the ancient quarrels of the two nations and paved the way for closer co-operation between them.

The Triple Entente, 1907. Three years later Great Britain and Russia overcame their differences. For half a century they had been jealously watching each other's expansion in Asia. The Anglo-Russian agreement in 1907 settled the troublesome questions relating to Persia, Afghanistan, and Tibet. Persia was divided into Russian and British spheres of influence with a neutral zone between. Britain disclaimed any intention of altering the political status of Afghanistan, and Russia recognized the country as outside the Russian sphere of influence. Both powers promised not to interfere in Tibet. Thus in 1907 Russia and Great Britain had an agreement; France and Great Britain had an agreement; and France and Russia had an alliance. This triangular relationship became known as the *Triple Entente,* or "triple understanding."

It was still in operation at the outbreak of World War I, when the three countries became allies.

The new balance of power. The year 1907, then, found the chief European powers lined up in two diplomatic camps. On the one hand was the Triple Alliance, composed of Germany, Austria-Hungary, and Italy, with Rumania as a secret ally. On the other hand was the Triple Entente, composed of France, Russia, and Great Britain, with Japan as an ally of Great Britain. As time went on the interests of the two groups clashed frequently in many parts of the world. Let us see how this came about.

Diplomatic Clashes and Crises

Germany's "place in the sun." As a latecomer in the family of nations, Germany found that the best regions for colonization had already been taken by other powers. The colonies which she acquired in Africa and the Pacific were of little value. They did not attract settlers, provided no important markets, and were costly to maintain. It began to seem that if Germany were to secure a "place in the sun," it could only be at the expense of other countries. Germany's ambitions soon clashed with those of France in North Africa and of Great Britain and Russia in the Middle East.

Disputes over Morocco, 1905–1911. France lost no time in taking advantage of the *Entente Cordiale* as it applied to Morocco. While the Moroccans were staging frequent revolts against their sultan, France and Spain negotiated a treaty recognizing each other's special rights in the disturbed country. Then in 1905, hoping to increase French control over Morocco, France made demands upon its ruler. The Germans were aroused because they felt they should have been consulted. Besides, Germany was trying to weaken the Anglo-French entente. Kaiser William II therefore, in a speech at Tangier, asserted the

THE MOROCCAN CRISIS. An English cartoonist pokes fun at the kaiser's visit to Tangier in 1905. The kaiser alarmed several countries by his words and actions in North Africa.

independence of Morocco and the equal rights in that country of all foreign powers.

Talk of war was heard on every hand. The German chancellor, Bülow, demanded an international conference to settle the matter. France was reluctant to join a conference, but the American president, Theodore Roosevelt, persuaded France to meet the other nations. The conference met in 1906 at Algeciras, Spain. By its decision France and Spain were to train a police force and take charge of reforms in Morocco. While the decision was a victory for France, it only led to another and more serious crisis. After repeated disorders, in 1911 France sent an army to Fez, the Moroccan capital, to restore order. In protest Germany sent a warship to the port of Agadir.

Again the diplomatic atmosphere was tense with anxiety. Britain declared that France had complete British support. France and Germany entered into negotiations. Germany agreed to recognize that France had a right to establish a protectorate over Morocco. In return France promised to give Germany a part of the French Congo region. The two Moroccan crises were damaging to German prestige. Further, they indicated that the entente between France and Great Britain had taken on the character of an alliance.

The Berlin to Baghdad railroad. A glance at the map on page 472 shows that Germany and her ally, Austria-Hungary, together formed a solid block of territory which stretched southeastward toward the Balkans. Extending into Asia was the Ottoman, or Turkish, Empire. In his ambition to find Germany a "place in the sun," the kaiser early in his reign turned his attention toward Asiatic Turkey. He saw in the fertile regions of Asia Minor and Mesopotamia (then part of Turkey) many opportunities for German investors, merchants, and colonists. The Germans could not take advantage of these opportunities, however, without easy and quick communication.

In 1903 German investors launched a project to build a railroad through Asiatic Turkey from Constantinople to Baghdad. Since there was already a railroad from Berlin to Constantinople, the new line would establish a direct connection between Berlin and Baghdad. Much of the main railroad had been completed and a number of branch lines had been started by the beginning of World War I. This ambitious undertaking naturally aroused the suspicion and jealousy of Britishers. They felt that the German activities in this region would endanger British control of the Suez Canal and the route to India. Besides, the kaiser had announced himself as the protector of all Mohammedans. Since many of them lived in colonies or protectorates of England, France, and Russia, these three nations regarded the kaiser's announcement as a serious threat.

Austria-Hungary creates a Balkan crisis, 1908. Germany's peaceful penetration of Asiatic Turkey formed only a part of the kaiser's policy. With the co-operation of Austria-Hungary, he planned also to "Germanize" the Balkan countries, thus making them part of a "Middle Europe" controlled by Germany and Austria. His scheme gained ground in 1908 when Austria-Hungary suddenly annexed Bosnia and Herzegovina. The Congress of Berlin (1878) had given Austria-Hungary the right to occupy and administer these Balkan provinces, which had formerly belonged to Turkey. (See page 407.) Their annexation raised a storm of protest in Serbia. The inhabitants of Bosnia and Herzegovina are Slavs. Serbia expected some day to unite them and the Montenegrins into a Greater Serbia which would stretch from the Danube to the Adriatic. The Russians also were angry, for they considered the annexation an insult to Slavic peoples by a Germanic power.

Russian troops began to move toward the Austrian border (1908). Germany took the side of Austria-Hungary. A general European war would have resulted had France and Great Britain not refused to aid Russia. Thereupon Russia, not yet recovered from the recent struggle with Japan (see page 433), gave way and withdrew support from Serbia. The Slavic peoples felt humiliated by the action of the Central Powers (Germany and Austria-Hungary). Their hatred smoldered as all Europe became increasingly nervous over the rivalries in the Balkans.

The second Balkan crisis, 1912–1913. In 1912–1913 the Balkan cauldron boiled over again. We have already noted that two Balkan wars resulted. (See page 408.) In the first war, Greece, Bulgaria, Serbia, and Montenegro quickly defeated their old enemy, Turkey, but quarreled over the division of the spoils. Consequently, there was a second war, in which Serbia, Greece, and Rumania turned on Bulgaria and defeated it. Early in the conflict the Serbs and Montenegrins pushed to the Albanian coast on the Adriatic Sea. Austria-Hungary and Italy had no intention of allowing Serbia to become an Adriatic state. With Germany's backing, they demand-

THE BALKAN POT threatens to boil over, while European powers try to hold down the lid. A cartoonist's view of the continuing Balkan crisis in the years before World War I.

ed that the Serbs and Montenegrins leave the coastal towns which they had captured. At first, Serbia and Montenegro, supported by Russia, refused. A general war loomed near. The crisis was overcome when the Slav states agreed to the creation of an independent Albania ruled by a German prince.

The two Balkan wars had far-reaching effects: (1) Turkey was practically ousted from Europe. (2) Bulgaria was eager for revenge against its neighbors, who had snatched from it the fruits of victory. (3) Serbia, though denied an outlet on the Adriatic, nearly doubled its area by expanding southward. The result was that the Serbs revived their dream of a Greater Serbia, and Austria felt menaced by Serb expansion. In fact, Austria was so alarmed that it made ready to attack Serbia in 1913. However, Austria's allies, Germany and Italy, refused to co-operate. One thing was certain—storms lay ahead.

The Race for Armaments

Between 1871 and 1914 there were wars in the Balkans, in Asia, and in Africa. The nations of western Europe did not come into armed conflict. Yet at no other period had

they maintained such large standing armies and big navies. Western Europe had peace, but it was an "armed peace" based upon fear.

New means of destruction. New applications of science to warfare produced weapons more deadly than ever. War now required expert technical knowledge both on the battlefield and in the munitions factory. Among the new or improved means of destruction were the breech-loading and repeating rifles, the machine gun, smokeless powder, and cannon which fired projectiles of much longer range and higher explosive force. In death-dealing efficiency the new weapons made the earlier tools of war seem like toys. Having done so much to create modern civilization, science appeared ready to destroy it.

Europe becomes an armed camp. In early modern times the comparatively small army of a European ruler was made up of volunteers and of soldiers hired from some other ruler. The French revolutionists introduced a general levy, or conscription (see page 277), and Napoleon continued this method of keeping his military ranks filled. After being defeated by Napoleon, Prussia adopted universal military service in peacetime as well as wartime. All able-bodied men were to receive several years' training in the army and were then to pass into the reserve. If war broke out, the government could call them to active duty. During the nineteenth century all the European countries except Great Britain adopted this system. It was a sign of the growing distrust among the nations which accompanied the rise of nationalism and imperialism. Europe thus became an "armed camp," with five million men constantly under arms and with more millions immediately ready for the call to arms.

THE HAGUE PEACE CONFERENCE IN 1899

Rivalry on the sea. Great Britain found sufficient protection in her fleet. The British had long followed a policy of keeping their navy as strong as the combined navies of any two other powers. Germany, however, would not be content as long as the British were supreme on the sea. The ambitious kaiser wanted a navy second to none. Germany therefore started to build a mighty fleet. Helgoland, off the mouth of the Elbe, was converted into a naval base. It became a second Gibraltar. In 1914 Germany enlarged the Kiel Canal so that it could accommodate the largest warships passing between the Baltic and the North Sea. Great Britain watched these preparations with growing dismay. The answer was the complete reorganization of the British fleet, the scrapping of nearly two hundred old vessels, and the construction of dreadnoughts and superdreadnoughts. The naval rivalry became so expensive that British statesmen twice proposed a "naval holiday," that is, an agreement to slow down the building of ships. Germany refused to enter into an arrangement which would leave Great Britain the mistress of the seas.

The crushing burden of standing armies and navies led to a popular demand in many countries for the abolition of war. To promote this movement, Czar Nicholas II in 1898 proposed an international conference to arrange a general disarmament. The czar pointed out with remarkable clearness the direction in which Europe was heading. He said: "The preservation of peace has been put forward as the object of international policy. In its name the great states have concluded between themselves powerful alliances; the better to guarantee peace, they have developed their military forces in proportions hitherto unprecedented, and still continue to increase them without shrinking from any sacrifice. . . . It appears evident, then, that if this state of things continues, it will inevitably lead to the very cataclysm which it is desired to avert, and the horrors of which make every thinking being shudder in anticipation."

The Hague peace conferences, 1899 and 1907. Delegates from twenty-six states met in 1899 at The Hague, Holland, in the first International Peace Conference. In 1907 a second International Peace Conference of forty-four states assembled at the same place. The representatives at these meetings adopted rules to lessen the horrors of war. For instance, they agreed to prohibit the use of poison gases and the bombardment of cities from the air. They also set up a Permanent Court of Arbitration (Hague Tribunal) to settle international disputes. The court consisted of a panel of judges, four from each national state. Nations wishing to submit a dispute to arbitration could choose an arbitration board from the panel. The court had no power to make governments submit their disputes to it or to enforce its decisions. The conferences failed to agree on the most important topic before them, namely, the limitation of armaments. It was clear that many statesmen were not seriously interested in ridding the world of war.

Summary of the Basic Causes of World War I

Nationalism. We have noted that long before 1914 mighty forces were working toward war in Europe. One of the most powerful was nationalism, which had gained ground steadily all through the nineteenth century. Nationalism had helped unify Italy and Germany. These nations rapidly became aware of their newly won strength and lost no time in letting the world know that they wished to be ranked among the first-rate powers. On the other hand, in Austria-Hungary and the Balkans nationalistic feelings had been suppressed. The submerged nationalities seethed with resentment against their overlords and awaited the day of liberation from foreign rule. (See page 401.) Elsewhere nationalistic ambitions took still other forms. In France the people hoped to regain the "lost provinces" of Alsace and Lorraine, which they had given up after the Franco-Prussian War. (See page 388.) Bitter memories of that conflict strained the relations between France and Germany and helped to promote the armament race. A similar sore spot was *Italia Irredenta,* which the Italians longed to annex to the fatherland. This area consisted of the Italian regions of Trentino and Trieste that were still in the hands of Austria-Hungary. (See page 395.) Thus the spirit of nationalism bred ill will among European peoples. It made difficult any real sympathy or understanding among them. Each nation developed an exaggerated sense of "national honor" and stood ready to fight over any insult to its government or even to a single citizen. This "chip-on-the-shoulder" attitude led the English historian Froude to remark, "Nations are but enlarged schoolboys."

Economic imperialism. The story of the nineteenth-century drive for colonies has been told in Chapter 20. The Industrial Revolution was largely responsible for the new imperialism. The production of increasing quantities of manufactured goods brought a struggle for new markets, sources of raw materials, and places to invest surplus capital. The competition became keener in the late 1800's and early 1900's. At that time Germany and Italy, recently unified, entered the race for colonial possessions. Imperialism was also shown in the establishment of high protective tariffs (see page 417), which added to the irritation caused by colonial rivalries. The result was a clash of ambitions and the growth of ill feeling among the leading industrial countries.

Secret diplomacy and alliances. The cause of peace suffered further because the European powers aligned themselves into two opposing groups. Nations that fear and suspect one another feel more secure against attack if they have partners. Thus the nations of Europe formed partnerships, or alliances, in secret, and hid their real strength from their enemies. Under the system of secret diplomacy the ambassadors and ministers of foreign affairs wielded enormous power. They often made binding agreements without disclosing them to the people or even to their own parliaments. The alliances made governments bolder and more reckless in their diplomatic relations. They sometimes cast caution to the winds, knowing their allies would back them up rather than risk finding themselves alone among hostile neighbors. Fear of attack was all the greater because there was no international organization designed to stop an aggressor nation. A nation's only hope of security seemed to be in an alliance with a powerful neighbor.

Militarism. Militarism was another force bringing Europe nearer to war. "If you wish for peace, prepare for war" was an idea generally held by European statesmen. They felt that a country with huge armaments was secure against attack and could more easily have its way in disputes with its neighbors. *Power politics* (diplomacy backed up by a display of might) became the fashion among the great powers. This was especially true after 1870, when German military might seemed to challenge the rest of Europe. But where would an armaments race lead? If one power enlarged its army or built more battleships, its neighbors felt obliged to do the same thing. The result was a mad scramble that could only produce fear, suspicion, and hatred among nations. Many professional military men encouraged the armament competition, for it gave them added prestige and importance. The manufacturers of firearms and war supplies also used pressure to promote large armament programs. In an age of extreme nationalism it was not difficult to persuade the people to accept any measures intended for national defense. Newspapers often helped to inflame nationalistic hatreds by beating the war drums. As 1914 approached, therefore, Europe was a powder keg. It took only a spark to make it explode.

How World War I Began

The Sarajevo assassination. The spark which touched off the explosion was the assassination of the Archduke Francis Ferdi-

nand and his wife. The crime took place at Sarajevo (sä′rȧ-yĕ-vô), the capital of Bosnia, on June 28, 1914. Ferdinand was the nephew of Francis Joseph I, the Hapsburg emperor of Austria-Hungary, and heir to the Austrian throne. The murderers were Bosnians and therefore Austrian subjects. A Serbian officer, who belonged to a secret society called the Black Hand, supplied weapons. It is now known (but was not at the time) that some members of the government of Serbia were aware of the plot but took no steps to prevent the tragedy. The Sarajevo assassination was a political crime. It was the natural outcome of the bitter feelings of the Yugoslavs, or southern Slavs, against Austria-Hungary, which had prevented the Yugoslavs from gaining national unity. (See page 444.)

Austria's ultimatum to Serbia. Nearly a month passed before Austria-Hungary acted. Then, on July 23, she sent Serbia a harsh ultimatum (a note laying down final conditions or terms). The ultimatum demanded that Serbia suppress anti-Austrian publications and societies; dismiss from the army and the government all those having anything to do with the anti-Austrian propaganda; get rid of anti-Austrian teachers and textbooks in the public schools; and allow agents of the Austro-Hungarian government to take part in the investigation on Serbian soil of the Sarajevo crime. The Serbian government was given only forty-eight hours to accept or reject the Austrian terms. In making these demands, the Austrian foreign minister, Count von Berchtold, saw a chance to squelch once and for all the Greater Serbia movement that threatened to dismember the Dual Monarchy. If Austria failed to act against Serbia now, Berchtold and his advisers feared that the enemies of their country would gain strength. In that case the submerged nationalities of the Austrian Empire might succeed in breaking the empire into fragments.

Serbia's reply. Serbia replied to the ultimatum within the given forty-eight hours.

The reply agreed to all the Austrian demands except those requiring that Austrian officials enter Serbia to help investigate the Sarajevo crime. Serbia pointed out that such an arrangement would violate its rights as a sovereign state—would make it, in fact, an Austrian vassal. Serbia also expressed willingness to submit the entire dispute to arbitration by the Hague Tribunal or to the mediation of the great powers. Austria-Hungary rejected the Serbian reply as unsatisfactory and on July 28 declared war upon its neighbor. The next day the Austrians bombarded Belgrade, the Serbian capital, firing the first shots of what was to become World War I.

The quarrel threatens to spread. So far the conflict was between Austria-Hungary and the small Slav state of Serbia. But Russia, the "big brother" of the Balkan Slavs, could not allow the conquest of Serbia. If Russia attacked Austria-Hungary, Germany must come to the aid of Austria-Hungary, its ally. Furthermore, France, which was bound to Russia in firm alliance, would be obliged to attack Germany. Thus instead of preserving peace, the alliances of the great powers threatened to produce a general European war. Efforts to prevent such a catastrophe began at once. Europe could remain at peace only if Austria-Hungary and Russia did not clash in battle.

Attitude of Austria-Hungary and Germany. The Triple Entente first asked Austria-Hungary to extend the time limit for the answer from Serbia. Austria-Hungary refused. Great Britain and France then urged Serbia to make its reply to the ultimatum as acceptable as possible. After Serbia had sent its reply, Sir Edward Grey, British minister for foreign affairs, invited Germany, Italy, and France to confer with his government in London in a last-minute effort to settle the dispute. France and Italy accepted the proposal. Germany would not accept on the ground that the whole quarrel concerned only Austria-Hungary and Serbia.

WAR'S MISCALCULATIONS

. . . No one in 1914 took the dangers of war seriously except on a purely military plane. Though all, except a few fighting men, abhorred its bloodshed, none expected a social catastrophe. In the days of Metternich, and even afterwards, statesmen had feared that war would produce "revolution"—and revolutionaries had sometimes advocated it for that very reason. Now they were inclined to think that war would stave off their social and political problems. . . .

The Balkan wars had taught a deceptive lesson. Everyone supposed that decisive battles would be fought at once, and a dictated peace would follow. The Germans expected to take Paris, the French expected to break through in Lorraine. The Russian "steamroller" would reach Berlin; more important, from the Russian point of view, their armies would cross the Carpathians and take Budapest. Even the Austrians expected to "crush" Serbia. The British expected to destroy the German fleet in an immediate naval engagement and then to establish a close blockade of the German coast; apart from that, they had no military plans, except to applaud the victories of their allies and perhaps to profit from them.

None of these things happened.

—A. J. P. Taylor, *The Struggle for Mastery in Europe, 1848–1918.*

Attitude of Russia and France. Russia had given in to the Central Powers in the Balkan crises of 1908 and 1913. (See pages 444–445.) This time, however, Russia's foreign minister, Sazonov, could count without fail upon French support, which had been lacking previously. The president of France, Raymond Poincaré, and his advisers had made it perfectly clear that France would fulfill its obligations under the alliance. Therefore, when news came of the bombardment of Belgrade, Russia started a partial mobilization of its armies along the Austrian frontier. Soon a general mobilization along the entire western border of Russia was ordered. Russia thus served notice to the Central Powers that it would fight rather than let them take away

GERMAN TROOPS INVADE BELGIUM

Serbia's independence and destroy Russian influence in the Balkans.

Germany declares war on Russia and France. The general mobilization of Russian troops forced Germany to mobilize its armies at once. The Germans could not afford to wait until their slower-moving opponent had brought large forces into position for attack. The kaiser's government, therefore, sent an ultimatum to Russia ordering that country to begin demobilization within twelve hours or accept the consequences (July 31). Russia did not reply. Germany then declared war on Russia (August 1). War with Russia meant war with its ally, France, as well. France had already begun to mobilize. When Germany asked what France would do in a Russian-German conflict, France replied that it would be guided by its own interests. Germany therefore declared war on France (August 3).

Great Britain declares war on Germany. The German plan of campaign called for a swift, crushing blow at the French before the Russians could complete their mobilization. Such an attack could best be made through the small, neutral state of Belgium. A comparatively level plain stretches across Belgium into France, reaching almost to Paris. Furthermore, the fortifications on France's Belgian border were not so strong as those on the German border. The European powers, however, including France and Prussia, had guaranteed the neutrality of Belgium in 1831 and 1839. In addition, Great Britain had for centuries believed that its security depended on having no strong military power occupy the Belgian coast and thus threaten British control of the Channel. Since the success of the German plan depended upon speed and timing, the Germans decided to disregard

Belgian neutrality and risk the chance of provoking a British declaration of war. The German government addressed a note to Belgium demanding permission to move troops across the country into France. When Belgium refused, the German army fought its way into that small country against brave resistance (August 4). Thereupon the British government sent an ultimatum to Germany, demanding assurances by midnight that Belgian neutrality would be respected. Germany would not give such assurances. About midnight, August 4, Great Britain declared war on Germany.

The line-up of forces at the outbreak of the war. The opposing forces were now lined up for combat. At the outbreak of hostilities the members of the Triple Entente, Great Britain, France, and Russia, quickly transformed their understanding into a firm alliance. They became known as the *Allies*. They promised not to make peace separately and to accept a general peace only on terms agreeable to all of them. From the beginning of the war Belgium, Serbia, and Montenegro fought on the side of the Allies. As the ally of Great Britain, Japan joined this group on August 23 by declaring war on Germany. Great Britain, with its fleet, its money, and eventually its army, formed the keystone of the coalition.

The Central Powers were less populous and wealthy than their opponents, but in the German army they possessed the finest war machine in the world. They also had unity of command, for the German general staff took almost complete charge of military operations. Above all, they were prepared. Austria-Hungary had already massed part of its army against Serbia. Germany, by means of its strategic railroads, could move and concentrate troops on its eastern and western frontiers with greater speed than either Russia or France. In a short war the Central Powers seemed likely to win, despite the fact that Italy refused to join its Triple Alliance partners. (See page 454.)

The Allies Win the War

Our interest in the war. Military engineers and students of military history delight in examining small details of the campaigns and strategy of wars. Even the average citizen in 1914–1918 followed eagerly the newspaper stories of a half-mile advance or retreat in a remote part of the battle front. Today we are interested less in the details of the war than in the overall picture. It is sufficient if we can grasp the general course of the war and can appreciate the vast numbers who took part, the enormous cost, and the reasons for the victory of the Allies. Let us then try to get a bird's-eye view of World War I.

The Allies save Paris. Fighting between the two opposing sides began in the west. The German army poured across the frontiers of Belgium and smashed the heavy fortifications of Liége and Namur with the new sixteen-inch siege guns. The unexpectedly stubborn resistance of the Belgians delayed by at least twelve days the arrival of the Germans on the borders of France. This delay gave the French time to complete their mobilization. Meanwhile, the British were able to send an expeditionary force of one hundred thousand men. The Anglo-French army could not hold back the German invaders, who crossed the Marne River and came within fifteen miles of Paris. The French government fled to Bordeaux. Then followed the Battle of the Marne, which lasted an entire week (September 6–12, 1914). In this engagement alone, 2,500,000 men took part along a front of more than one hundred miles. The French generals, Joffre (zhôf'r') and Foch (fôsh), launched attacks against the right flank and the center of the Germany army. They forced the Germans to retreat with heavy losses of men and materials on both sides. German plans for a speedy victory were upset and Paris was saved.

Deadlock on the western front. Both sides now made a dash northward to the sea. If

0 — 100 miles

NETHERLANDS
The Hague

ENGLAND
London

NORTH
SEA

BELGIUM
Ypres
Brussels
Meuse R.

GERMANY

ENGLISH
CHANNEL

Rhine R.

LUXEM-
BURG

Seine R.
Argonne
Forest
Saar R.

Paris
Château-
Thierry
Versailles
Marne R.
Verdun
Lorraine
St. Mihiel

Alsace

SWITZERLAND

Central powers
Allied powers
Farthest German advance, Sept. 1914
Armistice Line, Nov. 11, 1918
Major battle sites

THE WESTERN FRONT. The German armies came within fifteen miles of Paris in 1914. When the war ended they still had a foothold on French soil and occupied most of Belgium.

the Germans gained control of the coast, they would keep England from sending help to France by the most direct route. The British and French forces reached the sea first and in the first Battle of Ypres (ē'pr'), late in 1914, maintained their lines against the hammer blows of the Germans. Fighting now became general along a six-hundred mile front extending from the Vosges Mountains on the Swiss border to the North Sea. Along this crooked line the opposing armies dug deep trenches. From time to time small groups went over the top, crossed the deadly "no man's land," and hurled grenades into the enemy's trenches. During 1915 both sides tried to break the deadlock on the western front. The outstanding engagement that year was the second Battle of Ypres, in which the Germans made the first extensive use of poison gas. This terrible weapon wrought havoc, but the Germans were unable to follow up their advantage. In 1916 each side made a tremendous effort to smash through its opponent's

lines. The Germans launched a long siege against the key fortress of Verdun (February–September, 1916). In this battle, one of the fiercest of the war, the French held fast, inspired by the cry, "They shall not pass!"

Meanwhile, to ease the pressure on Verdun, the Allies made a counterattack along the Somme River (July–November, 1916). The Battle of the Somme marked the introduction of another new weapon, the tank. Invented by the British, this armored car with caterpillar treads could pass over trenches and through barbed wire with ease. The desperate fighting along the Somme cost each side well over half a million men and forced the Germans to give up their attack on Verdun. Under Field Marshal Hindenburg the Germans prepared a new defense position near Cambrai and Saint-Quentin. From April to December, 1917, the Allies steadily pounded the Hindenburg line. The approach of winter put an end to active operations, and the deadlock on the western front continued into another year.

THE EASTERN FRONT. The poorly equipped Russian armies were no match for the well trained and efficient Germans. When Russia quit the war she had to give up one fourth of her population.

Russia's part in the war, 1914–1917. There was no similar deadlock on the eastern front. As soon as the war started the Russians began to put large forces in the field. They planned to advance at the same time against the Germans in East Prussia and the Austrians in Galicia, a province in eastern Austria-Hungary. In East Prussia the Russians promptly met reverses. There in August, 1914, Hindenburg surprised the Russian armies and almost wiped them out at the Battle of Tannenberg. The following January the Russians again entered East Prussia and again met with overwhelming defeat. In Galicia the Russians had better luck. They overran all of this Austrian province and by the spring of 1915 began to filter through the Carpathian passes into Hungary. The Germans then sent troops from the western front. Under the command of Hindenburg the armies of the Central Powers started a terrific drive in Poland and Galicia. The Russians were pitifully lacking in arms and ammuni-

tion. The Germans, on the other hand, made full use of poison gas and a smothering fire of high-explosive shells.

By the end of 1915 the Central Powers had extended their conquests in the east until that front stretched from the Gulf of Riga to the borders of Rumania. (See map above.) In 1916 the Russians made a counterattack which was temporarily successful. By the opening of 1917 Russia's power was spent. The inefficient government of the czar was collapsing and in March, 1917, the Russian Revolution began. The party which finally gained control in Russia quit the war and made peace with the Central Powers. The story of this revolution and its results will be told in Chapter 22.

Turkey in the war. Soon after the outbreak of hostilities Turkey entered the war on the side of the Central Powers. This action was not surprising, for Turkey had long feared Russia's schemes to take Constantinople. (See page 406.) Moreover, Germany had won the friendship of Turkey by investing money in such projects as the Berlin to Baghdad railroad. With Turkey in possession of the Dardanelles, the Central Powers would be able to bottle up Russia in the Black Sea. Therefore, the Allies tried to strike a blow against Turkey by capturing Constantinople. An Anglo-French fleet in 1915 tried to force its way to that city through the Dardanelles Straits, heavily defended by the Turks. The effort did not succeed. Then the Anzacs (Australian and New Zealand troops), aided by Anglo-French forces, made heroic efforts to get a foothold on the Gallipoli Peninsula. Again the Turkish defenses proved too strong, and the Allies withdrew after suffering heavy losses. Plans for a renewed effort were abandoned because of the threatening Balkan situation.

The war in the Balkans. Stretching across southeastern Europe, a belt of Balkan states cut off Turkey from her allies. As soon as the war broke out, one of the Balkan states, Montenegro, joined Serbia against the Central Powers. Three others—Bulgaria, Rumania, and Greece—at first remained neutral. After long hesitation Bulgaria threw in her lot with the Central Powers (October, 1915), because she bitterly remembered that Serbia had been her most successful foe in the Second Balkan War only two years before.

The war in the Balkans now took a different turn. Little Serbia, which earlier in the war had twice pushed back the Austrians, quickly collapsed under the double attack of the Austro-German armies from the north and the Bulgarians from the east. The Central Powers also overran Serbia's ally, Montenegro, together with northern Albania. These moves opened railroad communication from Berlin to Constantinople. Rumania, however, decided to join the Allies (August, 1916). Its armies promptly invaded Austria-Hungary. A counterstroke by Germans, Austrians, and Bulgarians drove the Rumanians out and led to the conquest of two thirds of

their country. The Rumanian collapse brought great advantages to the Central Powers. It gave them the grain fields and oil wells of Rumania; it shortened their battle front by five hundred miles; and it allowed easier communication with Bulgaria and Turkey.

Allies gain control of Greece. King Constantine of Greece managed to keep his country neutral until the middle of 1917. Then the Allies entered Greece and deposed him, for they had feared that he would lead his country into the war on the side of the Central Powers. At the same time Venizelos (vĕn´ē-zā´lŏs), a vigorous champion of the Allies, became prime minister. Thus, in 1917 the Allies had control of only one country in southeastern Europe, Greece.

Italy in the war. Before 1914 Italy had been a member of the Triple Alliance. (See page 427.) But at the outbreak of World War I it remained neutral. The treaty of alliance, Italy declared, did not bind it to assist the Central Powers in an aggressive war, and Italy regarded them as the aggressors. The Allies therefore made a strong bid for Italy's help. They offered it a chance to win back *Italia Irredenta*. They also promised Italy a large share of Dalmatia and a part of Albania. These territories would give Italy control of the Adriatic Sea. Lured by these offers, Italy entered the war in May, 1915, on the side of the Allies. Italy's entrance created another front and almost completed the encirclement of the Central Powers. During 1915 and 1916 the poorly equipped Italians succeeded in holding their own against the Austrians in the Isonzo Valley. But when Russia quit the war after its revolution (see page 453), the Central Powers were able to mass large forces against Italy. Late in 1917 at Caporetto, an Austro-German attack threw the Italians back as far as the Piave River. When French and British reinforcements arrived there, the disastrous Italian retreat ended.

The outlook at the end of 1917. The military situation in Europe at the end of 1917 clearly favored the Central Powers. (United States troops did not play an active part in the war until 1918.) On the western front the Central Powers held Luxembourg, nearly all of Belgium, and a broad strip of northern France containing valuable coal and iron mines. On the eastern front they held the richest industrial districts of the Russian Empire. They had overrun Serbia, Montenegro, northern Albania, and a large part of Rumania. They had taken most of Venetia from the Italians. Their own territorial losses to the Allies were not important in area and population. Moreover, in 1917 German submarines had seriously crippled Allied shipping. Outside of Europe, however, the picture was not favorable for the Central powers.

The Allies capture the German colonies. Except for the submarine, the sea power of the Allies was far stronger than that of the Central Powers. For this reason Germany could not protect her colonial possessions. The British and French, aided by the South Africans and Belgians, seized the German colonies in Africa. In the Pacific the Australians and New Zealanders took over the German possessions south of the equator, while those north of the equator (including Kiaochow in China) fell to the Japanese.

The Allies free some Turkish lands. Turkey also lost parts of her scattered empire. At the beginning of the war Great Britain proclaimed a protectorate over Egypt and set up a new ruler who was to be independent of the sultan at Constantinople. In 1916 Colonel T. E. Lawrence, a young British archaeologist who knew the Arabic language, organized a revolt of the Arabs against the Turks. Arab troops soon occupied Mecca and Medina, the sacred cities of Arabia. They also set up the kingdom of Hejaz, which extended along the eastern coast of the Red Sea. In the same year a British force invaded Mesopotamia by way of the Tigris River and entered Baghdad in triumph. Another British army, led by General Allenby, invaded Palestine from Egypt and took possession of Jerusalem (October, 1917). Thus that holy city, after nearly thirteen centuries under the Moslems, was again under Christian control. By these victories the British had saved the Suez Canal and preserved their life line to India and the Pacific.

Allied control of the sea. The fleets of the Allies quickly swept the merchant ships of the Central Powers from the ocean and forced German warships to seek the shelter of their home ports. Only once did the German fleet slip out of Kiel Harbor. That time it was met by British battle cruisers off the coast of Jutland (May 31, 1916). Both sides suffered heavy losses in the battle which followed. With the approach of nightfall the German ships stole away to the safety of their anchorage. During the remainder of the war the regular warships of Germany did not venture forth again; the submarine was Germany's only threat to Allied control of the sea. Throughout the war the Allies maintained a blockade of Germany and Austria-Hungary. Three results followed: (1) the Allies were able to import food and raw materials freely from their colonies and from neutral states; (2) they kept the ocean lanes safe for the transportation of troops from Africa, Australia, India, and Canada; (3) they destroyed the commerce of their enemies. Because of the Allied blockade the Central Powers were hard pressed to find the necessary materials of war for their armies and food for their people.

Allied blockade grows tighter. The Allied blockade of the Central Powers grew tighter and tighter. At first it affected only German importation of military supplies. But in 1915 Great Britain declared foodstuffs contraband. (Contraband consists of goods which neutral powers are forbidden to ship to warring countries. A belligerent may seize contraband materials which are on the way to an enemy port in neutral ships.) Eventually Great Britain was seizing as contraband almost everything sent to Germany and to the neutral states on Germany's borders.

The submarine menace. Determined to break the British blockade, Germany struck back with the submarine, or U-boat. During the first months of the war the submarines attacked only enemy warships; but before long they began to destroy enemy merchantmen as well. According to international law, a merchant ship must be warned before being sunk, and the attacking vessel must provide for the safety of the merchant ship's passengers and crew. A submarine could not do these things without danger to itself. It was a new weapon, not covered by the existing rules of international law. The Germans would not accept any regulations which limited the usefulness of the submarine. In 1915, after the British made food contraband, Germany declared the waters around the British Isles to be a war zone. Within this area Germany promised to sink on sight all enemy merchant vessels and refused to be responsible for the safety of their passengers and crews. Neutral ships were warned to keep out of the zone lest they be mistaken for enemy ships.

The German submarine campaign reached its peak in the early months of 1917. For a while the U-boats sank Allied ships two or three times faster than new ones could be built. In April one out of every four vessels that left Great Britain was torpedoed. Had the sinkings continued at this rate, the Allies would have lost the war. Fortunately, they learned how to strike back at the submarine. They developed an instrument to detect it when under water and depth bombs to destroy it. They organized powerful convoys to escort merchant vessels. Finally, the building of new ships to replace those sunk by submarines was enormously increased, especially in the United States. Germany's desperate submarine campaign eventually failed, but not before it had brought the United States into the war.

American neutrality. When the war broke out, President Wilson declared that the United States would be neutral. But neutrality proved impossible. In the first place, many Americans were foreign born or the children

THE SINKING OF THE *LUSITANIA*. In 1915 a German submarine torpedoed the British liner with the loss of 128 American lives. American protests caused Germany to limit her submarine attacks. However, in 1917 several American ships were sunk, and the United States then declared war on Germany.

of immigrants. They naturally took sides in the conflict. In the second place, the United States was a rich source of war materials, which each side tried to keep the other from getting. Our country was caught between two fires.

Our rights as a neutral were freely violated by both sides. More than once President Wilson sent strong protests to Great Britain for interfering with our rights at sea. The British irritated our government by taking American merchant ships bound for Europe into British ports to determine whether or not the vessels carried contraband goods. Contraband goods were seized, but the shippers were paid their full value. German violation of our neutrality was more serious in nature. The proclamation of a war zone endangered not only American property but American lives. President Wilson protested at once. He declared that the United States would hold the German government to a "strict accountability" for American ships destroyed or American citizens killed. Germany said that American ships entering the war zone might be sunk by accident and Germany would not be responsible for such accidents.

The United States enters the conflict. Then came a test of our toughness. On May 7, 1915, a German U-boat torpedoed the great British liner *Lusitania,* with the loss of 1198 persons, including 128 American men, women, and children. Submarines had also sunk American ships and those of other neutral nations. Wilson sent several sharp notes of protest to the German government. Finally, Germany promised not to sink passenger ships at all and not to sink merchant vessels without warning unless they tried to escape or offered resistance. A few months later, in January, 1917, Germany withdrew its promise. The American government was notified that Germany would sink on sight all ships, both enemy and neutral, found within a new war zone. This zone included a broad area near the British Isles and France and the greater

part of the Mediterranean. Inside the barred zone the Germans would permit a small number of neutral ships to pass through narrow "safety lanes" to one British port and to Greek waters. The United States was authorized to send only one ship a week to Europe. President Wilson refused to accept these restrictions on our commerce and early in 1917 broke off diplomatic relations with the German government. Within a few weeks eight American ships were sunk. Finally, on April 6, 1917, the President asked Congress to declare war on Germany and Congress did so. In December we declared war against Austria-Hungary. Our government broke off diplomatic relations with Turkey and Bulgaria but did not declare war on them. The United States did not make a military alliance with the Allies but acted as their associate in the war.

A world "safe for democracy." In his war message to Congress President Wilson said that the people of the United States had no quarrel with the people of Germany; our quarrel was with their autocratic government which had led them blindly into war. We would fight, declared the President, "for the ultimate peace of the world and for the liberation of its peoples, the German peoples included: for the rights of nations great and small and the privilege of men everywhere to choose their way of life and of obedience. The world must be made safe for democracy. Its peace must be planted upon the tested foundations of political liberty. We have no selfish ends to serve. We desire no conquest, no dominion. We seek no indemnities for ourselves, no material compensation for the sacrifices we shall freely make. We are but one of the champions of the rights of mankind."

The United States gets ready. America had to prepare with all possible speed. The Germans believed that we could not send a fighting force to Europe in time to save the Allies. The speed of our operations amazed both the Allies and the Germans. We immediately

HERBERT HOOVER (center) was United States food administrator during World War I. He is shown with American sugar producers who met with him in Washington to discuss the nation's food problem. His introduction of food rationing during the war gave rise to the word "Hooverize," meaning to ration.

sent part of our Navy to Europe. Among the warships were torpedo boats and destroyers to fight the German submarines. With assistance from the British fleet, our naval forces planted more than seventy thousand mines in the North Sea between the Orkney Islands and Norway. This deadly string of explosives shut out German submarines from the Atlantic, for the Allies had already sown mines and stretched nets across the narrow Dover Strait. Congress passed a draft law, believing the draft to be the most rapid and democratic method of raising an army. Within two months after the declaration of war, over ten million young men registered for service under the draft. To train a vast citizen army, the War Department set up thirty-two cantonments, or camps, each housing forty to fifty thousand men. In France the War Department had to build docks, storage depots, barracks, and even entire railroads to accommodate our troops and supply their needs. By the end of 1917 America had about two hundred thousand men in France. At the close of

the war two million American soldiers were in Europe. The American Expeditionary Force (AEF) was under the command of General John J. Pershing.

Congress appropriated huge sums of money to carry on the war. It was spent for training and supplying the armed forces, for munitions, for building cargo ships and airplanes, and for loans to the Allies. The money came partly from increased taxation and partly from the sale of "liberty bonds." To mobilize the entire nation behind the war effort, the government had to exercise emergency powers. Congress provided for a fuel administration to control the production and distribution of fuel and set up a food administration, which was directed by Herbert Hoover. Spurred by the slogan "Food will win the war!" the American people voluntarily produced and saved enough food to supply our own needs and those of the Allies as well. During the war the government also took charge of the railroads, express companies, and telegraph and telephone lines.

Allied and German war plans, 1918. We have noted that at the end of 1917 the Central Powers held the advantage on the continent of Europe. The Powers had finally forced the Russians out of the war; they had overrun most of the Balkans; and they had taken a large slice of northern Italy. The Central Powers were now free to turn their attention to the western front. Great Britain, France, and Italy knew this and prepared to stay on the defensive until the United States could throw its full might into the struggle.

The Allies were under the vigorous leadership of Lloyd George in Great Britain, Clemenceau (klā-män′sō′) in France, and Orlando in Italy. These leaders felt that their side could afford to wait. The Central Powers, on the other hand, could not afford to wait. They were choking from the blockade. Meanwhile, the Allies were receiving large loans from the United States and vast quantities of supplies. Streams of transport ships were bringing fresh American troops in ever larger numbers to France. Germany realized that it must make a supreme effort for victory in 1918 or it would be too late.

Germany's last drives. Field Marshal Hindenburg and General Ludendorff gathered every available German soldier and gun and in March, 1918, started a drive against the Allies on the western front from Arras to La Fère. The battle which followed dwarfed all previous clashes on this front. By terrific massed attacks the Germans took back in a few days all the ground won by the Allies in the offensives of 1916 and 1917. In April the Germans launched another drive to the north between Arras and Ypres. The British, who were guarding the Channel ports, bore the full brunt of this attack. The enemy drove a deep wedge into the British line. French reinforcements arrived in time to check the German advance. At the end of May the Germans made a third drive between Soissons and Reims. On this push they once more reached the Marne. French and American troops halted the German advance at Château-Thierry, only forty-three miles from Paris. In two drives in June and July, the Germans again tried to pierce the Allied line and reach Paris. Again they failed. The tide of battle was about to turn.

ALLIED MILITARY LEADERS, WORLD WAR I. From left to right: Marshal Joseph Joffre, Marshal Ferdinand Foch (supreme commander of Allied armies), General Maxime Weygand, Field Marshal Douglas Haig, General John J. Pershing, and Marshal Henri Pétain.

ANTIAIRCRAFT FIRE IN WORLD WAR I. These French marines are firing at German planes. During the war airplanes began to carry guns and bombs.

The beginnings of aerial warfare. Meanwhile, the fighting forces were experimenting with a new weapon—the airplane. In the first year of the war (1914) airplanes flew over enemy lines on scouting, or reconnaissance, flights. They observed enemy positions and strength and took photographs. Soon airmen were directing gunfire by wireless. They became the eyes of the artillery. Fliers also carried on small-scale bombing and strafing expeditions. As each side tried to force its enemies from the skies, aerial "dogfights" between individual airmen and later between whole squadrons became common. "Aces" like Fonck of France, Von Richthofen of Germany, and Rickenbacker of the United States were looked upon as national heroes. For a time the Germans held the upper hand in aerial combat, but by 1917 the Allies had gained superiority. While air fighting created much excitement, it was not important in determining the outcome of the war.

The turn of the tide. The crisis which the Allies faced in 1918 led them to set up a united military command under the French general, Ferdinand Foch. His fighting forces now included reinforcements sent by Great Britain and Italy and more than a million American soldiers under General Pershing. Some of the Americans had already seen action at Cantigny, Belleau Wood, and Château-Thierry. On July 18, 1918, the Allies launched a series of rapid counterstrokes all along the line from Switzerland to the sea. It was the beginning of the end for the Central Powers. In quick succession the French and Americans pushed the Germans out of the Marne salient (a position jutting out from the main line); the Americans, in their first independent operation, swept the enemy from the Saint-Mihiel salient south of Verdun and then drove east of the Argonne Forest to Sedan; the British, with French and American help, broke the Hindenburg line; and the Belgians, British, and French liberated Flanders. (See map, page 452.) At the end of September General Ludendorff told the German kaiser that the war was lost.

Collapse of Germany's allies. Facing disaster in the west, Germany no longer could support its allies in the other theaters of the war. In the Balkans a strong offensive by British, Greek, Serbian, French, and Italian troops brought Bulgaria's unconditional surrender (September 29, 1918). This victory cut off Turkey from Germany and Austria-Hungary. On October 30 she signed an armistice that took her out of the war. The collapse of Austria-Hungary was not far off. General Diaz and his Italian troops pushed the Austrians out of northern Italy, occupied Trentino and Trieste, and captured six hundred thousand prisoners and seven thousand guns. On November 3, Austria-Hungary signed an armistice which amounted to an unconditional surrender. The Austrian emperor abdicated, and the Dual Monarchy began to break up.

The end of the war. During the summer and autumn of 1918 the unhappy German people began to taste the bitterness of defeat. They now demanded peace and a democratic government. The kaiser feared for his throne and appointed a liberal chancellor, Prince Maximilian of Baden. But it was too late to save the monarchy. Revolutionists hoisted their flag over the German fleet at Kiel, and soon Berlin and other cities fell into their hands. William II abdicated and fled to Holland. A group of socialists led by Friedrich Ebert turned Germany into a socialist republic. On November 11, 1918—a memorable day in the history of the world—the new German government signed an armistice with the Allies and the United States. Millions of people throughout the world rejoiced that the "war to end war" was over.

Terms of the armistice. The terms of the armistice left Germany at the mercy of the Allies. The defeated nation agreed to return all prisoners of war and to surrender its submarines, the best part of its fleet, and huge quantities of guns and other war materials. In addition, Germany promised to take its troops out of Belgium, Luxembourg, France, and Alsace-Lorraine. Allied and American troops were to occupy all the territory west of the Rhine, together with the main bridgeheads, or crossings, of the Rhine at Mainz, Coblenz, and Cologne. The Germans signed the armistice with the understanding that the peace settlement would follow President Wilson's "Fourteen Points." The Allies had already accepted these, with certain reservations, as a statement of their peace plans.

The Fourteen Points. President Wilson announced his famous peace program in an address to Congress on January 8, 1918. What were the "Fourteen Points"? Here is a brief summary of the principal ones: to put an end to secret diplomacy; to keep the seas free and open to the navigation of all countries; to remove the economic barriers between nations; to reduce national armaments; in adjusting colonial claims, to consider the interests of colonial peoples; to give back Belgium to the Belgians and Alsace-Lorraine to France; to restore all Russian territory taken by Germany and give Russia a chance to develop "under institutions of her own choosing"; to readjust Italy's boundaries on the basis of the nationality of the people living in disputed areas; to create an independent Poland; to let the different peoples of Austria-Hungary and Turkey decide for themselves under what government they wished to live (the principle of self-determination of nations); and finally, to form an association, or league, of nations to guarantee political independence "to great and small states alike."

The Costs of World War I

A world-wide conflict. World War I cast a dark shadow over almost the entire globe. No conflict so widespread or so costly had ever happened before. Twenty-eight countries and their colonial dependencies took up arms. Five more in Latin America broke off diplomatic relations with Germany. Only sixteen countries, with less than one sixteenth of the world's population, remained neutral. These were Spain, Switzerland, Holland, Denmark, Norway, Sweden, Abyssinia, Persia, Afghanistan, Mexico, El Salvador, Colombia, Venezuela, Chile, Paraguay, and Argentina. Involved were Europe, most of the Americas, much of Africa, and two thirds of Asia.

The cost in human lives. A total of about 65,000,000 men fought in World War I. Of these about 42,000,000 were on the Allied side and 23,000,000 on the side of the Central Powers. It is estimated that about 8,500,000 died in battle or of wounds. (In all the wars from the French Revolution to 1914 not more than 5,000,000 men died in battle.) In addition 7,000,000 men were listed as prisoners or missing; many of these never returned. Probably 22,000,000 men were wounded and about a third of these were permanently disabled. To these casualties we must add an estimated 13,000,000 civilians who lost their lives as the result of famine, disease, and massacres. The total of deaths due to World War I has been placed at 26,000,000.

WOUNDED AMERICAN SOLDIERS in a Red Cross hospital at Paignton, England, 1918. Besides providing hospital care, the International Red Cross sent medicines, food supplies, and clothing to many war-torn lands.

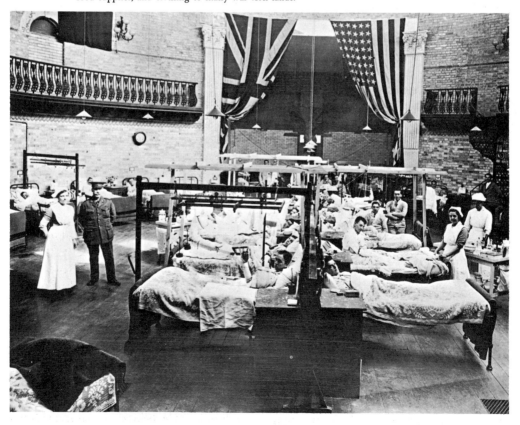

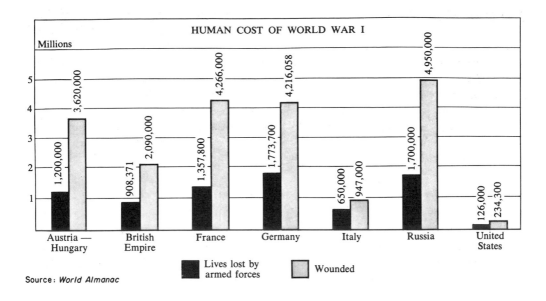

HUMAN COST OF WORLD WAR I

Millions

	Lives lost by armed forces	Wounded
Austria — Hungary	1,200,000	3,620,000
British Empire	908,371	2,090,000
France	1,357,800	4,266,000
Germany	1,773,700	4,216,058
Italy	650,000	947,000
Russia	1,700,000	4,950,000
United States	126,000	234,300

■ Lives lost by armed forces   ▢ Wounded

Source: *World Almanac*

The men who fell in the war were mostly picked men. They had passed tests for physical and mental fitness; they were in the prime of life and health and strength. Had they lived they would have been the fathers of the next generation. Moreover, they would have contributed heavily to the productivity of their nations. Their loss greatly weakened their countries and in some it was doubtful if the loss could ever be made up. France, for instance, lost 60 per cent of its young men in the war.

The cost in money. The direct cost of World War I to the fighting powers has been estimated at 186 billion dollars for military operations alone. This tremendous sum does not include any indirect costs, such as the destruction of property, the loss of trade and of factory production, the payments for war relief and soldiers' pensions. The total direct cost was equal to the value of all buildings, land, and other property in the United States in 1912. The indirect costs were even larger than the direct costs, which at the peak in 1918 amounted to 10 million dollars per hour.

Financing the war. The war powers raised part of the money necessary to carry on the war by increasing taxes, but chiefly by issuing

inflation currency and bonds. Most European governments issued vast quantities of inflation currency—paper money which could not be exchanged for gold or silver. The more of this money there was in circulation, the less people could buy with it. Since the governments controlled the banks, however, they could easily force their creditors to accept inflation money in payment of debts. The amount of money raised by bond issues in each country, including the United States, was far greater than expected. The governments sold their bonds, or promises to pay, to all who would buy them. Citizens considered it their patriotic duty to buy bonds to give their governments money to spend.

The governments of Europe had borrowed mostly from their own people, but during and soon after the war the Allies had also borrowed heavily from the United States. The principal owed the United States was more than ten billion dollars. Accumulated interest added much more. (The problem of paying the war debts to the United States is discussed in Chapter 21.)

National finances after the war. At the end of the war the world's financial affairs were in disorder. The belligerents faced the future under the burden of gigantic national debts. For example, in 1919 the debt of the United States was about 26 billions, more than twenty times our debt in 1916. Great Britain's debt in 1920 was 40 billions. The other countries owed even larger sums of money, many of them being close to bankruptcy. Great Britain and the United States were the only major powers whose finances were sound.

All the belligerents in Europe had to collect heavy taxes to pay the interest on their huge debts and to repair the damage caused by the struggle. Most countries continued to issue inflation currency. Some of them—notably Germany and Russia—issued so much paper money that it became practically worthless. The French franc and the Italian lira declined to a fraction of their prewar value. A number of European nations simply repudiated, or refused to pay, their national debts. After the 1917 revolution, the new Russian government would pay neither the internal nor the external debt of the czar's government. The new Turkish government repudiated the foreign debts of the old Ottoman Empire.

The end of an era. Most students of history consider that the close of World War I marked the end of an era in the history of civilization. After a struggle so wide in scope and so costly, a different world was bound to emerge. It was a world that faced trying times. The problems of making the peace were harder to solve than those of winning the war. The global nature of the war had shown the closeness of the relationship among the countries of the world. In the twentieth century nations may still have political independence, but economically and socially they are interdependent. How statesmen grappled with the world's postwar problems is the topic of the following chapter.

REVIEWING THE CHAPTER

TERMS TO UNDERSTAND: *balance of power, "Iron Chancellor," "nightmare coalition," militarism, secret diplomacy, power politics, Middle Europe, submerged nationality, conscription, Hague Tribunal, mobilization, aggressor nation, ultimatum, contraband,* Lusitania, *Anzacs, Italia Irredenta.*

PERSONS TO IDENTIFY: *Bülow, Nicholas II, Francis Ferdinand, Berchtold, Grey, Sazonov, Poincaré, Joffre, Foch, Hindenburg, Ludendorff, Venizelos, Lawrence, Wilson, Pershing, Allenby, Hoover, Lloyd George, Clemenceau. Orlando, Ebert.*

PLACES TO LOCATE: *Tunis, Afghanistan, Tibet, Agadir, Mesopotamia, Hejaz, Baghdad, Montenegro, Albania, The Hague, Sarajevo, Belgrade, Ypres, Marne River, Helgoland, Liége, Verdun, Somme River, Gallipoli, Arras, Galicia, Tannenberg, Flanders, Dalmatia.*

QUESTIONS TO ANSWER

1. (a) Explain Germany's desire to make allies after 1870. (b) Trace the steps, from 1873 to 1882, by which the Triple Alliance was formed.
2. (a) How and why did British and German interests clash after 1890? (b) Trace the steps by which the Triple Entente was formed. (c) Distinguish between an *entente cordiale* and an *alliance.*
3. (a) What situation led to the calling of a conference at Algeciras? What was decided there? (b) What was the result of the two Moroccan crises? (c) How did the Berlin to Baghdad railroad enter into international politics? (d) What far-reaching effects were produced by the Balkan wars?
4. (a) After the French Revolution by what system did the European countries maintain their armies? (b) What was the mainstay of British defense? How did Germany chal-

lenge it? (c) Discuss the purposes and results of the peace conferences at The Hague. (d) Explain the four basic causes of World War I.

5. (a) What terms did Austria-Hungary demand of Serbia following the crime at Sarajevo? (b) What did Serbia reply? What did Austria-Hungary do then? (c) Tell how and when each of the following countries was brought into World War I: Russia, Germany, France, Great Britain. (d) What was the line-up of opposing forces at the beginning of the war?

6. (a) Summarize the events of the war during the first three years: (1) on the western front, (2) on the eastern front, (3) in southeastern Europe, and (4) in the Middle East. (b) Why did Turkey enter the war on the side of the Central Powers? (c) Why did not Italy enter the war until 1915? (d) What was the military situation in Europe at the end of 1917?

7. (a) What results did the Allied blockade bring about? (b) How serious did the German submarine campaign become? (c) How were American neutral rights violated?

8. (a) Why did the United States enter the war? When did we declare war? (b) What did the United States contribute to victory? (c) What were the principal military events of 1918? (d) What part did the airplane play in World War I?

9. (a) What were the terms of the armistice? (b) Summarize Wilson's "Fourteen Points."

10. (a) What was the cost of the war in human lives? (b) What was the cost of the war in money? (c) Describe the effects of the war on national finances.

22 The Peace that Failed

PARIS PEACE CONFERENCE, 1919. Diplomats of twenty-seven nations, excluding the defeated Central Powers, gathered to "make the world safe for all the peoples who live upon it . . ." These were the aims embodied in Woodrow Wilson's Fourteen Points.

World War I, like all wars in history, left in its wake a number of grave problems. Not since the Congress of Vienna (see page 286) at the end of the Napoleonic wars in 1814–1815 had Europe been in such disorder. Widespread hunger, disease, and destruction were not likely to create an atmosphere favorable to reason and calm deliberation. On the contrary, these conditions made it very hard for the nations to even consider, much less work out, a "just and durable peace." This chapter will show how the Paris Peace Conference dealt with the problems left by the war. It will also point out the successes and failures of the peace-keeping efforts in the decade or so afterward. As we shall see, the part played by the new League of Nations in these efforts proved disappointing. Why this was so we shall also try to determine.

Making the Peace of Paris, 1919–1920

The Peace Conference. On January 18, 1919, the Peace Conference met at Paris to deal with the knotty problems left by the war. Seventy official delegates attended the meeting. They represented most of the countries which had fought against the Central Powers. In addition the conference admitted representatives from neutral states when questions affecting their countries came up for discussion. No one was present to speak for the Central Powers and their allies. The victors did not allow the defeated countries a voice in the conference. Nor was the new Russian government invited to participate.

The peacemakers. Over a thousand experts came with the official delegates to the conference. They advised the peacemakers on such matters as boundaries, the nationality of people living near disputed borders, international law, and commerce. A host of secretaries and clerks helped to keep records of the deliberations. By unanimous vote the delegates elected Premier Clemenceau of France as chairman of the conference. The two chief delegates of each of the five great powers—the United States, Great Britain, France, Italy, and Japan—formed a Supreme Council to direct the business of the conference. This council of ten

was soon reduced to five members. Then both Italy and Japan dropped from the inner circle, leaving only the "Big Three"—Clemenceau of France, Lloyd George of Great Britain, and President Wilson of the United States. The Big Three decided many of the most important questions in secret session, then referred their decisions to the whole conference for its formal approval. Many people criticized this seeming return to the ways of the old and discredited diplomacy. Yet any other procedure would have greatly delayed the writing of the peace treaties. The need for speed was urgent. Already much of Europe was in the grip of revolution, and wartime hatreds appeared to increase while the Peace Conference deliberated. In these circumstances the peacemakers faced a thankless task.

The terms of peace. In addressing the Peace Conference, the president of France reminded the delegates of their solemn duty in these words: "Gentlemen, you hold in your hands the future of the world." If true, the gentlemen decided the world's future in a comparatively short time. Within six months the conference completed the most important treaty, that with Germany. Representatives of the German government were summoned to Paris to sign the treaty. They protested that its harsh terms did not carry out Wilson's

Fourteen Points. They objected especially to the "war guilt" clause, which held Germany alone responsible for the war. Nevertheless, they secured only slight changes and were forced to sign the hated document. The ceremony of signing took place in the Hall of Mirrors at Versailles on June 28, 1919—five years to the day after the crime of Sarajevo. The treaty is called the Treaty of Versailles.

In the same year Austria and Bulgaria signed treaties (Treaties of Saint Germain and Neuilly), and in 1920 Hungary and Turkey settled with the victorious powers (Treaties of Trianon and Sèvres). The Turkish government, however, never ratified the signature of its delegates. The five treaties, together with other agreements among the Allies themselves are known as the Peace of Paris (1919–1920).

The peace treaties written at Paris were lengthy documents. That with Germany alone covered 230 large pages of print. We cannot consider them in detail, but we can get a general idea of their contents. (1) The Treaty of Versailles changed many boundaries and created some new states. (See pages 469–473.) (2) The victorious powers forced Germany to make good in money, materials,

or labor some of the damage which her armed forces had caused. The damage payments were called *reparations*. (See pages 473–475.) Germany also had to pay the cost of Allied occupation of a part of her territory. (3) The Peace Conference drew up a plan for the League of Nations and made it a part of the different treaties. This plan was dear to the heart of President Wilson. He had recommended "a general association of nations" in the fourteenth of his famous Points, and insisted that it should be included in the peace treaties. We shall consider the League later in this chapter. (See pages 478–473.) (4) The victors took away all of Germany's colonies. Most of them were given as mandates to one or the other of the Allies. (See page 465.) (5) Germany had to disarm. She was to reduce her army to 100,000, give up compulsory military training, destroy her fortifications on the Rhine and the Baltic, stop making munitions, and surrender most of her navy and most of her merchant ships. (6) The other treaties broke up the Austro-Hungarian and Turkish empires.

The United States and the Peace of Paris. The United States did not ratify the treaties made at Paris. Her delegates signed them, but

THE BIG FOUR AT PARIS.
From the beginning of the Peace Conference in 1919 these men dominated the discussions. They were, from left to right, Lloyd George, Orlando (who later dropped out), Clemenceau, and Wilson.

the Senate refused to approve them by the necessary two-thirds vote. The chief stumbling block to Senate approval was the Covenant (constitution) of the League of Nations, which formed a part of the four major treaties. Article 10 of the Covenant stated that the League would protect the territory and political independence of all its members against aggression. Some senators feared that this provision would give the League the power to summon our military and naval forces, along with those of other League members, to restrain an aggressor. They said that it might drag us into war against our will and that it would take away from Congress its constitutional power to declare war. On a speaking tour of the country, President Wilson tried to clear up the misunderstanding about Article 10 and the League. His efforts were in vain. A number of senators wanted to amend the Treaty of Versailles by writing into it reservations, that is, conditions on which the United States would accept it. Twice the amended form failed to pass by the necessary two-thirds vote. The treaties were not yet ratified by the time of the presidential campaign of 1920. Consequently, the League of Nations became an issue in that campaign. In general, the Republicans opposed our joining the League and the Democrats favored it. The victory of the Republican candidate, Warren G. Harding, doomed American acceptance of the League. In the summer of 1921 Congress passed a resolution which declared the war between the United States and Germany at an end. The President promptly signed this resolution. The Senate later ratified separate treaties with Germany, Austria, and Hungary.

Remaking the Map of Europe

Why the map of Europe was remade. We have already learned that before World War I, Germany, Austria-Hungary, and Russia contained a number of submerged nationalities, or minorities. These minorities were groups of people bound together by ties of common ancestry, language, traditions, and aspirations. Yet they did not rule themselves; they were governed by other nationalities. In other words, they did not enjoy the right of national self-determination, a principle which President Wilson included in his Fourteen Points. When the Central Powers lost the war, revolutions broke out in Germany, Austria-Hungary, and Russia. The time was ripe for the submerged nationalities to win their political independence or to unite with related people across the border. The Peace Conference recognized this fact and tried to win self-determination for the minorities.

The peacemakers also remade the European map to satisfy the national ambitions of some of the victorious powers. Italy wanted to complete her national unification by gaining from Austria *Italia Irredenta,* or "unredeemed provinces" of Trentino and Trieste. Likewise, France wanted back the lost provinces of Alsace and Lorraine. Because they were on the winning side, Italy and France had no trouble in getting the desired boundary changes. In short, the defeat of the Central Powers, the revolutions following the war, and the victors' wishes at the Peace Conference each had something to do with remaking the map of Europe. Let us take a journey through Europe and see how and why the peacemakers redrew boundaries and set up new states. (See map, page 472.) We shall begin in western Europe on the Franco-German frontier.

The new map of western and northern Europe. The Treaty of Versailles compelled Germany to give back Alsace and Lorraine to France. Germany also had to turn over to France the coal mines in the Saar basin just north of Lorraine. The treaty placed the government of this area under a commission of the League of Nations. At the end of fifteen years, the people there were to vote whether they wished to remain under the control of

PRAGUE, the capital of Czechoslovakia. Located on both banks of the Vltava River, this charming old city dates back to the eighth century. It became the capital of an independent republic after World War I, but in 1948 was seized by the Communists, and in 1968 occupied by the Russians.

the League, return to German rule, or live under French rule. (See page 586.) These provisions of the treaty were intended to repay France for the destruction of her property.

Moving northward, we arrive at the border between Germany and Belgium. On this frontier Belgium received the small areas of Eupen, Malmédy, and Moresnet as the result of a plebiscite, or popular vote, of the inhabitants of each area.

Continuing northward and eastward, we come to the border between Denmark and Germany. Here a narrow strip of land separates the North and Baltic seas. It also is the connecting link between Germany and Denmark. On this strip are the provinces of Schleswig and Holstein, which Germany annexed in 1864. (See page 397.) The Versailles Treaty said that the boundary between Germany and Denmark would be fixed accord-

ing to the wishes of the people. After two plebiscites in 1920, northern Schleswig became a part of Denmark, while southern Schleswig remained with Germany.

Moving eastward across the Baltic, we come to a tier of new states that had been a part of Russia before World War I. Out of the territory Russia had once governed were created the four small republics of Finland, Estonia, Latvia, and Lithuania.

On the south shore of the Baltic, at the mouth of the Vistula River, stands the old and commercially important city of Danzig. Before the war Danzig and the surrounding area belonged to Germany. We cannot understand what happened to Danzig until we have seen how the Poles brought their state back to life. Let us turn now to Poland.

How the Polish question arose. When World War I broke out, the so-called "Polish question" had been troubling Europe for over a hundred years. Late in the eighteenth century Poland's three neighbors, Austria, Russia, and Prussia, divided Poland among themselves. (See page 253.) As a result, the Poles were scattered under the rule of three different governments. Polish patriots resented foreign control and longed to re-establish their own state. Several times during the nineteenth century they tried to regain their independence but without success. During World War I their lot was hard indeed. Russian Poles often had to fight against German and Austrian Poles. When revolution swept over eastern Europe at the close of the war, the Poles combined and set up an independent republic. The Peace Conference gave its blessing to the new state and helped to define its boundaries.

The Polish Republic. The new Poland was about the size of our state of Montana. In Europe that is a comparatively large country. It was carved out of Austria, Russia, and Germany—the countries which had partitioned Poland in the eighteenth century. The new republic had but one possible outlet to the sea. That was by way of the Vistula River, which flowed northward through German territory to the city of Danzig on the Baltic coast. If this city and the surrounding area were to remain in German hands, Poland would be cut off from the sea. The Peace Conference therefore made Danzig a *free city* under the protection of the League of Nations. Poland also received a narrow strip of territory connecting Danzig and Poland proper. This neck of land was known as the *Polish Corridor*. It cut off East Prussia from the rest of Germany. The Corridor gave Poland control of an avenue to the sea.

Remaking the map of central Europe. Southwest of Poland in central Europe we find another war-born republic. During the conflict the Czechs and the Slovaks, like the Poles, had to fight for a country that they did not regard as their own, namely, Austria-Hungary. When the Dual Monarchy fell to pieces after the war, the Czechs and Slovaks organized their own state. It included the former districts of Bohemia, Moravia, Austrian Silesia, Slovakia, and Ruthenia. The old Bohemian city of Prague became the capital. The young republic of Czechoslovakia was fortunate to have Thomas G. Masaryk (1850–1937) as its first president. He had been a liberal professor of philosophy at Prague, was married to an American, and had many friends in the United States. He skillfully guided Czechoslovakia through its early years as an independent state.

The old Dual Monarchy of Austria-Hungary vanished when its subject nationalities broke away. Only the parent states of Austria and Hungary remained. Almost immediately after the downfall of the Hapsburg monarchy, Austria became a republic. It was now a small, landlocked state, German in culture and mainly German in population. The Versailles Treaty forbade its union (*Anschluss*) with Germany except with the consent of the League. Hungary, which borders Austria on

THOMAS G. MASARYK

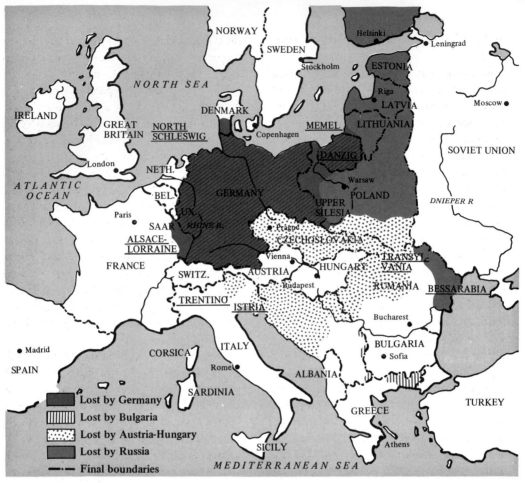

EUROPE AFTER THE PEACE SETTLEMENT, 1923

the east, was reduced to one fourth of its former size. The Treaty of Trianon gave slices of the old Hungary to its neighbors, Czechoslovakia, Rumania, and Yugoslavia.

East of Hungary lies Rumania. By the peace settlement Rumania nearly doubled its area. She received the large Russian province of Bessarabia, which she had lost in 1878 by the Treaty of Berlin. (See page 407.) In addition, Rumania acquired Bukovina, the Hungarian province of Transylvania, and reacquired the province of Dobruja.

Remaking the map of southeastern Europe. South of Hungary, along the eastern coast of the Adriatic Sea, live the Serbs, Croats, and Slovenes, together known as the Yugoslavs, or South Slavs. Before the war they were scat-

tered among the independent states of Serbia and Montenegro and in several provinces of Austria-Hungary. By the Peace of Paris both Serbia and Montenegro gave up their separate governments. They now joined with their brother Slavs in the provinces of Austria-Hungary to form the "kingdom of Serbs, Croats, and Slovenes," commonly called Yugoslavia.

South of Yugoslavia the little principality of Albania came out of the war with a shaky government. In 1925 it became a republic, but its boundaries were not fixed until the following year. Albania's president, Ahmed Zogu, soon made himself a dictator and in 1928 was proclaimed King Zog I. Meanwhile, he had signed a defensive alliance with Italy which made Albania practically an Italian protectorate.

Italy came out of the war with substantial gains in territory. To the northeast she annexed the Austrian Tyrol and Trentino. She also obtained the Adriatic coastal region that includes Trieste and Fiume.

In the far southeast of Europe, Bulgaria had to give up part of Thrace to Greece and thus lost its outlet on the Aegean Sea.

The remade map of Europe. We have now surveyed the principal boundary changes brought about by the war, revolutions, and the Peace of Paris. The outcome made Germany essentially a national state, for she had lost most of her alien nationalities. Likewise, Austria and Hungary, shorn of their subject peoples, became national states. The new map showed Yugoslavia, Czechoslovakia, Poland, Lithuania, Latvia, Estonia, and Finland as independent countries. Each of these now had a population composed mostly of one nationality. Other countries completed their national unification: France by regaining Alsace-Lorraine; Italy by securing *Italia Irredenta;* and Rumania by adding adjoining territory. The peace settlements recognized more than ever before the principle of national self-determination. The number of subject peoples in Europe was reduced from 54,000,000 to 17,000,000. Most of the 17,000,000 lived in border regions where the nationalities were mixed or where the need for a defendable frontier overrode the home rule ideal. As we shall see, they became the source of future trouble.

The Problem of Reparations and War Debts

Germany's "war guilt" obligations. The Treaty of Versailles placed the entire blame for World War I on Germany and her allies. It therefore required that Germany pay "for all damage done to the civilian population of the Allied and Associated Powers and to their property." Military pensions were included as a part of the damage. At first the Allies did not fix the amount of reparations, or damage payments. They set up a Reparations Commission to find out how much Germany could pay and to make out a schedule of payments. After much wrangling the commission arrived at a total sum of about thirty-three billion dollars. Germany was to pay this amount over a period of years by issuing bonds, that is, by borrowing. France was to receive 52 per cent of the reparations, Great Britain 22 per cent, Italy 10 per cent, and Belgium 8 per cent. All other victor powers were to share the remaining 8 per cent. The German government accepted these terms only after the Allies threatened to occupy additional German territory.

The riddle of reparations. Merely to tell Germany what she had to pay did not end the reparations problem. Germany could not get the gold to meet her reparations payments unless she could sell large quantities of goods abroad. That would mean the building up of German industry and trade. But Germany's creditors did not want German goods to compete with their own, either at home or in foreign markets. They erected high tariff walls to keep out German goods. It seemed that the creditor nations wanted to eat their cake and have it too.

A number of economists foresaw Germany's predicament, but many statesmen did not. By 1922 heavy borrowing and the issuance of worthless paper money had brought Germany to the brink of financial ruin. She claimed that she could no longer keep up her reparations payments. Therefore she asked for a postponement (moratorium) of her obligations until the end of 1924. Great Britain favored the request, for she now realized that a prosperous Germany would be a good customer for British goods. France, however, refused to listen, for she feared that if Germany grew strong there would be another war.

The Dawes and Young plans. In January, 1923, French and Belgian troops seized the rich industrial region of Germany called the Ruhr. They took possession of coal and iron mines and steel plants. Although the Germans declared themselves practically bankrupt, the French and Belgians said they would stay in the Ruhr until Germany made further payments. Meanwhile, the embittered Germans waged a campaign of "passive resistance" against the invaders; that is, they refused to obey orders. Industry and transportation came to a standstill. The deadlock was broken in 1924 when the Reparations Commission approved the proposals of a committee headed by an American banker, Charles G. Dawes. The Dawes Plan called for removal of French and Belgian troops from the Ruhr, foreign control of German finances, and a reduction in the yearly reparations payment. Germany made payments under this plan until 1929. But it was merely a stopgap arrangement. It did not reduce the total sum of reparations, and Germany insisted that she could not continue to pay, even with the aid of American loans.

In 1929 the Young Plan was adopted. It took its name from an American, Owen D. Young, who served as chairman of a new committee. The Young Plan scaled down Germany's total reparation debt to approximately $9,000,000,000, plus interest. It was to be paid over a period of fifty-nine years. In addition, Allied troops were to leave the Rhineland. No sooner had the Young Plan gone into effect than the world depression began. It became impossible for Germany to make payments. Therefore, in 1931 President Hoover proposed a moratorium of one year on all reparations and debt payments between nations. The proposal met with general approval.

The Lausanne agreement. When the moratorium ended, Germany was less able to pay her debts than before. In 1932 debtors and creditors met in a conference at Lausanne, Switzerland. There they reached an agreement to wipe out German reparations once and for all. Germany was to pay a lump sum of about 750 million dollars. She was to deposit bonds to this amount with the Bank of International Settlements, or World Bank. The Young Committee had established this bank at Basle, Switzerland, to handle reparations payments.

Germany's creditors, however, decided they could not ratify the Lausanne agreement until the United States had given them better terms on the debts they owed to her. The United States refused to do this. Our government would not admit that reparations and war debts were linked together, so the Lausanne agreement fell through. Agreement or no agreement, Germany had stopped paying and never started again.

The inter-Allied debts. During and immediately after World War I the Allies borrowed heavily from the United States. Great Britain and France received 80 per cent of the loans made by the United States. The principal that the Allies owed the United States was more than ten billion dollars. The borrowers agreed to pay this amount, plus interest, over a period of sixty-two years.

At the Peace Conference of 1919 the British said they would cancel the war debts owed to them if the United States would do the same. (Great Britain had lent eight billion dollars to her war partners.) The United States turned a deaf ear to this suggestion. Our government likewise refused to heed all later pleas and arguments for cancellation of the debts, although it did reduce the interest rate. Europeans resented the stand taken by the United States. They gave a new meaning to the initials U.S.—"Uncle Shylock." They argued that since they could not collect reparations from Germany, they should not have to pay their debts to the United States. Besides, the only way they could pay their debt to the United States was with goods, and the high American tariffs shut out their goods. The

American government would not accept this reasoning. The people in the Allied countries also thought that the United States should cancel the debts on the ground that they represented supplies used in fighting the common enemy. The Allies had expended a far larger number of men than we had; should we not be willing to contribute the munitions and foodstuffs that enabled the Allies to keep on fighting?

After the Hoover moratorium most of the governments stopped paying on their war debts to the United States. Only Finland continued to pay until World War II.

The Peace Movement

The abolition of war. The disastrous struggle of 1914–1918 gave new strength to the movement to abolish war. The horrors of armed conflict made a deep impression on thoughtful people everywhere. They knew that another war would be global in scope and many times more destructive than the last. They realized, furthermore, that the roots of war lie deep in the past, and that all civilized nations must share in some degree the blame for wars. Was it not time, they asked, to take steps to end forever this scourge of mankind? The world had been largely rid of cannibalism, human sacrifice, witchcraft persecution, slavery, and other savage practices. Why then not abolish war? This would require the united efforts of all peoples. They must work through international organizations which seek to remove the causes of war. Attempts to build such organizations and to arouse sentiment against war constitute the peace movement. Let us trace its development.

GERMAN MARKS being baled as waste paper in a German junk shop. This inflationary paper money was issued in such large amounts after World War I that it became almost worthless. By 1923 it took nearly 15½ billion paper marks to equal one gold mark. Workers hurried to spend their wages before the purchasing power declined further.

Early Christianity and warfare. The Christian Church formed the first peace society and launched the first peace movement. The Christians introduced into Europe the idea that human life is sacred. The Church condemned homicide of any kind and therefore looked upon war as sinful. However, after Christianity became the official religion of the Roman Empire, the pacifist attitude of the Church began to disappear. The Romans had built their empire by successful warfare, and only by warfare could they defend it against barbarian foes. The use of the cross on the standards of the imperial army showed that Christianity was no longer thought to condemn war.

The medieval Church and warfare. The Church in the Middle Ages was by no means a pacifist organization, but it generally attempted to use its influence to preserve peace. It deserves credit for trying to stamp out private warfare among feudal nobles. (See page 138.) On the other hand, the Church encouraged warfare against heretics and infidels. For example, it declared a holy war against the Moslems—a fierce struggle which we call the crusades. (See page 148.) The Church also showed its warlike side by supporting the military orders of monks, such as the Templars and Hospitalers. (See page 149.)

Protestantism and warfare. The rise of Protestantism did not change the attitude of official Christianity toward war. Most of the Protestant churches were state churches. Their ministers therefore considered themselves to be in the public service and supported any war their government carried on. Nevertheless, some Christian sects opposed *all* war. The English Lollards in the fourteenth century taught that the New Testament forbids killing in war. The sixteenth century Anabaptists in Germany believed that Christians should not bear arms or offer forcible resistance to wrongdoers. The Society of Friends (Quakers), founded in 1648, likewise has staunchly supported pacifism.

Promoting sentiment for peace. Through the centuries isolated reformers have voiced strong protests against war. Among these were Erasmus (1466–1536) and Voltaire (1694–1778). In the nineteenth century numerous peace societies arose in many countries. In 1843 they held their first international congress in London. Thereafter these societies met regularly and maintained a permanent office at Bern, Switzerland. They helped to arouse public opinion in favor of arbitration of disputes between nations, reduction of armaments, and the gradual removal of the causes of war. As the peace movement gained in strength, it began to influence governments. In 1890 the twenty-one American republics organized the Pan American Union (see page 438) to promote friendly relations in the Western Hemisphere. Wealthy individuals also contributed to the cause of peace. In 1897 Alfred Nobel, the Swedish inventor of dynamite, established the now well-known Nobel Peace Prize. This is awarded annually to the person or society that renders the greatest service for the cause of human brotherhood. Another promoter of the peace movement was the capitalist Andrew Carnegie. In 1910 Carnegie gave ten million dollars to establish the Carnegie Endowment for International Peace. Its purpose is to hasten the abolition of war, "the foulest blot on our civilization," by promoting good will and understanding among nations. The fund was particularly intended to encourage studies in economics, history, and international law. In this way Carnegie hoped that the world's peoples might learn more about each other and so avoid quarrels.

International arbitration. Another step toward peace was the growing custom of settling disputes by arbitration. This means that quarreling states voluntarily agree to submit their differences to a board of judges, or arbitrators chosen by themselves. The disputing parties agree in advance to accept the award, or decision, of the judges. During the nineteenth century, arbitration courts made over two hundred awards, and every one was carried out. After 1900 many countries signed arbitration treaties with one another. By these treaties they promised to submit to arbitration all quarrels except those involving national honor or vital interests, such as independence. In 1902 Argentina and Chile went still further. They bound themselves to arbitrate *every* dispute which might arise between them. The United States has also been a staunch supporter of the method of arbitration. While William J. Bryan was secretary of state (1913–1915) under President Wilson, we made no less than thirty conciliation treaties. The parties to each treaty agreed to refer their disputes to an international body for investigation and to delay a full year before going to war to settle any dispute. The nations known as the Central Powers declined our invitation to enter into arbitration treaties with us.

The Permanent Court of Arbitration. The two Hague Conferences of 1899 and 1907 (see page 446) gave further encouragement to the use of arbitration in settling international disputes. Although the delegates failed to agree on the limitation of armaments, they revised the laws of war and they set up a Permanent Court of Arbitration, sometimes called the Hague Tribunal. The "Court" was really not a court at all. It consisted of a list, or panel, of judges, from which disputing states might choose arbitrators to settle their difficulties. A new tribunal (board of arbitration) was picked for every dispute. No state was bound to submit its quarrel to a tribunal. By the beginning of World War I the Permanent Court of Arbitration had settled fifteen cases. The success of this court led to a demand for a court that would meet continuously and that would base its decisions on international law, rather than merely trying to settle disputes by compromise.

The idea of an international league. The idea of a league of nations to keep the peace

ALFRED NOBEL, the Swedish chemist, established the Nobel Peace Prize for the greatest contribution to brotherhood.

goes far back into the past. The confederations of the Greek city-states suggest a kind of international organization. During the period when Rome ruled the Western world, no general association of states was possible. Likewise, in medieval times feudal disorder and the lack of strong central governments prevented the development of any international league. But as national states emerged out of feudal confusion, some men began to dream of joining the states of the world into a union. Every major war gave birth to such schemes. None of these was put into effect until the twentieth century, for statesmen rarely took them seriously, but some of them are interesting as forerunners of the League of Nations and the United Nations.

Plans for an international league. Two noteworthy blueprints for an international organization of states appeared in the seventeenth century. One was the "Grand Design" of Henry IV, king of France (1589–1610). It provided for a general council of fifteen European powers. Each of the great powers was to have four representatives on the council and each of the smaller ones, three. The council members would consider and settle all disputes among the nations. To enforce its decisions and to keep peace, the council would have at its command an international army and navy. The other scheme was the brain child of a French monk, Eméric Crucé. In 1623 he wrote *Le Nouveau Cynée,* in which he proposed a world union of states, including the European nations, Persia, China, and the Indies. The peace machinery of Crucé's plan consisted of a world assembly and a world court. In later years other reformers urged similar plans to organize the world for peace. Worth mentioning are those of William Penn, the founder of Pennsylvania (1693), Abbé Saint-Pierre (1713), Jean Jacques Rousseau (1761), and Immanuel Kant (1795). The schemes of these men had a common purpose—the prevention of war. Each called for an international organization, league, or confederation, with a representative assembly to settle disputes among nations. Nearly all the plans provided for the

---

PENN'S PEACE PLAN

. . . Now if the sovereign princes of Europe . . . would . . . agree to meet by their stated deputies in a general diet, estates, or parliament, and there establish rules of justice for sovereign princes to observe one to another; and thus to meet yearly, or once in two or three years at farthest, or as they shall see cause, and to be styled, the Sovereign or Imperial Diet, Parliament, or State of Europe; before which sovereign assembly should be brought all differences depending between one sovereign and another that cannot be made up by private embassies before the sessions begin, Europe would quietly obtain the so much desired and needed peace . . .

—William Penn, *The Peace of Europe; the Fruits of Solitude; and Other Writings* (1693).

---

use of force against states that broke the peace. This last provision is important in the light of later peace plans.

A lesson of World War I. After World War I, statesmen were ready to take seriously the so-called "vision of dreamers." The enormous sacrifices of the struggle would have been in vain unless some way could be found to prevent future wars. Obviously, the world would have to *organize for peace.* An international league began to seem not a utopian idea but a practical necessity. President Wilson, David Lloyd George, William Howard Taft, and other American and Allied statesmen repeatedly said that a "world league for peace" must follow the war. "Every lover of mankind, every sane and thoughtful man, must take that for granted," declared the American president.

The League of Nations and the World Court

As soon as the Peace Conference opened at Paris, a committee of the victorious powers set to work on a plan for an international organization. This committee drafted a constitution for the League of Nations and presented it to the conference. On April 28, 1919, the peace delegates accepted it unanimously. The constitution, called the *Covenant,* was a short, simple, and dignified document. Its chief author was President Wilson. The Covenant was inserted in the various peace treaties. When the Versailles Treaty went into effect on January 10, 1920, the League of Nations officially was born.

Membership in the League. At one time or another, more than sixty sovereign states belonged to the League. The list of members included every important country except the United States. The victorious powers that signed the treaty automatically became full members. Any self-governing state, dominion, or colony might be admitted by a two-thirds vote of the Assembly. After two years' notice, any member could withdraw from the League. At first Russia and the defeated powers were not allowed to join, but eventually each of them was admitted.

Organization of the League. The League had three main parts—the Assembly, the Council, and the Secretariat. The Assembly was composed of not more than three delegates from each member state. The voting, however, was not by individuals but by states, with each state having one vote. The Assembly met once a year in Geneva, Switzerland, to deal with "any matter within the sphere of action of the League or affecting the peace of the world." It elected new members to the League and chose three of the nonpermanent members of the Council. It also approved or rejected the Council's nomination for the position of secretary general, and jointly with the Council chose the judges of the World Court. In addition, the Assembly could propose amendments to the Covenant, supervise the work of the special agencies, and prepare the annual budget of the League.

The Council was a smaller body than the Assembly. It was made up of five permanent members, who represented the leading states, and from four to ten nonpermanent, or rotating, members, who represented the lesser powers. It met about four times a year. The activities of the Council were as numerous as those of the Assembly. Its most important function was the settlement of international disputes. The Council also supervised mandates (see below) and internationalized areas (Danzig, Saar basin), carried out recommendations of the Assembly, and prepared plans for disarmament. All important decisions of the Council required a unanimous vote.

The Secretariat consisted of a secretary-general and a staff of assistants, with headquarters at Geneva, Switzerland. It handled the research and clerical work, the preparation of programs for meetings, the translation of speeches, and the publication of a multitude of reports on all phases of international affairs. The Secretariat employed some five hundred persons.

Purpose and duties of the League. The preamble of the Covenant stated that the purpose of the League was "to promote international co-operation, and to achieve international peace and security." To carry out this purpose the Covenant gave the League four principal tasks: (1) to take charge of internationalized areas, such as the Saar basin and Danzig; (2) to supervise mandates and protect minorities; (3) to promote the improvement of social and economic conditions in the world; and (4) to prevent war. Let us examine some of these duties more closely.

The League and mandates. A mandate was an order given by the League of Nations to an "advanced" nation to assume control over some "backward" area or country. The word *mandate* was also used to refer to an area so controlled. The League set up as mandates the former colonies of Germany and the countries liberated from Turkey. The mandate system was a welcome change from the usual way of parceling out conquered territories among the victors. The conquerors were not to annex the former enemy territories but were to govern them under the supervision of the League. The nations in charge of mandates were known as *mandatories*. They were required to submit annual reports to the Permanent Mandates Commission of the League, which had the power to decide whether the mandatories had carried out their duties properly. The mandate system rested on the idea that backward, or undeveloped, countries are not yet able to achieve or preserve independence. Therefore, an international organization ought to act as their guardian and protect them from the greed of imperialistic powers. If these good intentions could be realized, the mandates would be spared the evils of imperialistic control.

The League and minorities. The peace settlement went a long way toward putting into practice the principle of national self-determination. (See page 473.) The breakup of Austria-Hungary and the redrawing of boundaries brought unity and independence to a number of nationalities. But one object of the peacemakers in designing the new map was to strengthen the victor powers. At the same time they wanted to cripple the defeated states as much as possible. Besides, it was impossible to draw boundaries in a way that would include all people of one nationality under the same government. As a result, the peace treaties still left about 17,000,000 Europeans under alien rule. For example, over 3,000,000 Germans found themselves in Czechoslovakia, nearly 1,500,000 Magyars were in Rumania, and almost 4,000,000 Ukrainians were in Poland. Such groups are called "national minorities" or "submerged nationalities." Before World War I governments often tried to force minorities to adopt the language and culture of the majority group. This led to resistance, disorder, and sometimes war. To avoid such troubles, the

Peace Conference made the League of Nations the protector of the rights of minorities. The rights were defined in treaties signed by the new states with the Allied powers. The treaties guaranteed the minority groups equality of civil and political rights, freedom to use their own language and religion, and the right to have schools. The Council of the League was to receive complaints and recommend remedies if any government violated the treaty guarantees. Unfortunately, this arrangement did not solve the minorities problem in Europe. As we shall see, the problem raised its head dangerously in the 1930's.

The League's social and economic activities. It is in the field of social and economic cooperation that the League made its greatest contribution. It set up the International Health Organization to prevent and control epidemics, and the Advisory Commission on the Traffic in Opium and Other Dangerous Drugs. It created special agencies to deal with the problems of slavery and the slave trade, the return of war prisoners and refugees, and

THE PALACE OF NATIONS in Ariana Park, Geneva, Switzerland. This building, completed in 1937, was the home of the League of Nations. The vast structure, overlooking beautiful Lake Leman, was the gift of John D. Rockefeller, Jr.

the protection and welfare of children. These agencies, or committees, often co-ordinated the work of national organizations dealing with the same subject. Through them the League was able to accomplish much good. For example, in eastern Europe it checked epidemics of typhus and bubonic plague that might easily have spread over an entire continent or possibly over the world. It also returned to their homes about 300,000 prisoners of war.

The League promoted co-operation in economic matters. It established the Communications and Transit Organization to deal with problems of international waterways, railroads, ports, and electric power lines. It created the Economic and Financal Organization, which prepared reports on special problems at the request of the League Council. Another agency connected with the League, although it had its own charter, was the International Labor Organization (ILO). The Covenant of the League had promised "to secure and maintain fair and humane conditions of labor for men, women, and children" everywhere. The ILO has tried to achieve this goal by promoting the adoption of uniform labor laws throughout the world. It draws up proposed treaties, or conventions, designed to improve labor conditions and submits them to member states for approval. If a national legislature approves a convention, it is expected to take steps to enforce it and to report these steps to the ILO. By 1947 member nations had ratified individual conventions in 946 cases. Though never a member of the League, in 1934 the United States joined the ILO. At the beginning of World War II the ILO moved its headquarters from Geneva to Montreal. In December, 1946, the ILO became one of the specialized agencies of the United Nations Economic and Social Council. (See page 568.)

The League and the prevention of war. By far the most important task of the League was the prevention of war. On its success in that effort the League was to stand or fall. In the Covenant the League members promised to do certain things to preserve peace. They pledged themselves "to respect and preserve as against external aggression" the boundaries and independence of every other member (Article 10). If an aggressor attacked a member, the Council was to decide what action should be taken. Such a decision had to receive unanimous approval. Furthermore, the Covenant declared that any war or threat of war was a matter of concern to the whole League (Article 11). All signers of the Covenant agreed to settle disputes among them by arbitration or judicial decision, or else let the Council adjust their differences. If the Council failed to arrive at a unanimous decision, then the members would be free to act as they pleased. In no case, however, were they to go to war until three months after the Council, or other arbitrators, had issued a report (Article 12).

What if a country broke its promises and went to war? In that case the Covenant said the wrongdoer would have "committed an act of war against" the entire League. Then the Council might ask the members to cut off all trade and financial relations with the aggressor nation. Penalties of this kind are called "economic sanctions." If these did not bring the peace-breaking country to terms, the Council as a last resort might recommend that the League members use force against the offender. Beyond that the League could not go. It had no army or navy of its own. If members refused to lend their armed might to back the League, the whole peace machinery would break down. We know that the peace machinery did break down and that the League failed in its biggest undertaking—the prevention of war.

As a part of its peace program, the League also had the task of drawing up plans for the reduction of armaments. Another provision of the Covenant required that any treaty between League members be registered with the Secretariat and published. Unless so registered, it would not be binding. This rule was designed to abolish the evils of the old secret diplomacy.

The League deals with political disputes. In the twenty years before World War II, about forty political disputes came before the League of Nations. The Council took care of most of these cases, while the Assembly and World Court each handled a few. In general, the League was more successful in settling the differences between small nations than it was in settling those between major powers. The large states were quick to claim that a League investigation was an interference with their sovereign rights. Besides, they sometimes used undue pressure to gain a favorable decision.

The League's successes. Nevertheless, the League headed off a number of serious clashes between European countries. In 1920–1921 it settled an argument between Finland and Sweden over the Åland (ō'land) Islands in the Baltic. The Council gave the island to Finland, but ordered that they were to be self-governing and neutral. In the same year the very troublesome question of the Polish-German boundary in Upper Silesia came before the League Council. The award called for a new frontier line and both countries accepted it. In 1925 the League settled the boundary dispute between Turkey and Iraq.

The League's failures. On the other hand, the League's efforts in a number of cases came to nothing. In 1920 the Poles seized the border town of Vilna after a League commission had given it to Lithuania. France stood behind Poland, and the League did nothing. In 1923 the newborn Fascist government in Italy denied that the League had authority to settle its dispute with Greece over the island of Corfu. Italy finally accepted the recommendations of the Conference of Ambassadors, who decided the matter largely in her favor. Small states began to doubt that the League could protect their rights. The League also failed

to stop the Gran Chaco War between Bolivia and Paraguay (1932–1935); and its efforts to prevent aggression broke down completely in 1931 when Japan invaded Manchuria. When the League held Japan to be in the wrong, Japan resigned. (See page 542.) Although the League failed to prevent Japan's conquest of Manchuria, the League's action marked the first time that an international body had condemned the conduct of a major power. Likewise, when Italy attacked Ethiopia in 1935 (see page 544), the League decided that the Italian government was the aggressor. It recommended that economic sanctions be applied against Italy—that is, that member states refuse to supply Italy with war materials. The sanctions had two weak spots: (1) Germany and the United States did not participate, and (2) the list of banned goods did not include gasoline or oil. The League wished to add gasoline and oil to the list, but Italy threatened to attack anyone who tried to enforce the sanctions. Consequently, Italy continued to get war supplies. Thereafter the great powers did little to support the League when the Covenant was violated. Instead, they fell back upon the old balance-of-power politics. In 1933 Germany also withdrew from the League, followed in 1937 by Italy. After that the chances of keeping the peace were poor indeed.

The World Court. Closely linked with the League, and provided for in the Covenant, was the Permanent Court of International Justice, or World Court. All the major countries except Russia and the United States, and most of the minor countries, signed the statute, or constitution, of this court. The Court began its sessions at The Hague in 1922. It consisted of fifteen judges, chosen by the Council and Assembly of the League for a term of nine years. At all times the members represented a number of different nationalities and systems of law. Unlike the Permanent Court of Arbitration (see page 567), the World Court was more than a body of arbi-

HAILE SELASSIE, Emperor of Ethiopia, appearing before the League of Nations in 1935. He appealed to the League to take action against Italy for attacking his country. The League was unable to stop Italian aggression.

trators. It settled disputes according to the principles of justice, whereas the Permanent Court of Arbitration settled them by compromise. It could hear and decide any legal question—that is, one relating to the meaning of a treaty or to a matter of international law. Its jurisdiction, however, was voluntary. That means it could decide only such cases as the states concerned were willing to bring to it. At the request of the Council or Assembly of the League, the Court also gave advisory opinions on legal points connected with the League's work. The Court's record of impartial judgment gave it a place of great importance in the League system. Although the Court had no power to enforce its decisions and opinions, in practice these were always accepted.

Other Roads in Search of Security

Buttressing the League system. The League of Nations and the World Court were the foundation stones of the peace structure. Their efforts alone, however, were not enough to ensure peace and security. In the first place, not all the major powers belonged to the League. The United States never joined and Russia remained outside until 1934. Their absence greatly handicapped the League. Second, as we have already noted, many small states felt that the League was run by the big powers to further their own interests. Little states, therefore, did not depend on the League alone for their safety; they formed defensive alliances with other states. The great powers too failed to rely entirely on the League machinery to maintain peace. Some feared that it would be used to change the *status quo* (the existing state of affairs), and others, that it would be used to maintain the *status quo.* For these reasons the nations took various steps to ensure their own safety, regardless of the work of the League. In the years from 1920 to 1935 they tried unsuccessfully to agree on disarmament; they signed many nonaggression, mutual aid, and arbitration treaties; and they even resorted to the old-style system of alliances.

Progress toward disarmament. After World War I, statesmen realized that huge armaments had been a cause of the conflict. They also knew that disarmament can come only by international action. One nation cannot safely disarm while its rivals remain armed. Before 1914 international agreements to reduce or limit armaments were few in number and rarely effective. A noteworthy exception was that between the United States and Great Britain. In the Rush-Bagot agreement, ratified in 1818, the two governments agreed to eliminate forts and armed vessels along the American-Canadian boundary. This pact is still in force. On the other hand, the Hague Conferences of 1899 and 1907 (see page 446) failed to accomplish anything on the question of limiting armaments. Following World War I the peace treaties forced Germany to reduce her standing army to 100,000 and to give up her navy. The other defeated powers likewise had to accept substantial disarmament. This was a one-sided arrangement, but the Treaty of Versailles held out the promise that all the nations would agree to limit their forces. To that end the League of Nations was to draw up plans for the reduction of armaments.

All nations were ready to admit that armaments ought to be reduced "to the lowest point consistent with domestic safety." Yet by 1920 a new armament race was already in the making, especially among the naval powers. The United States and Japan had prepared plans to build up their navies to a strength approaching or surpassing that of Great Britain. France and her satellites in Europe still sought security by building up huge standing armies. The crushing financial burden of this armed rivalry seemed unbearable, particularly among the poverty-stricken and war-torn states of Europe. The great powers were already spending the larger part of their income in paying for past wars and preparing for future wars. Common sense dictated that the nations should get together to halt the armaments race. But who was to take the first step?

The Washington Conference, 1921–1922. Although the United States kept aloof from

the League of Nations and World Court, she started a movement in the direction of disarmament. In 1921 President Harding called a Conference on the Limitation of Armaments at Washington. Nine nations took part in it —the United States, Great Britain, France, Italy, Japan, Belgium, Holland, Portugal, and China. The first five were to discuss the question of limiting navies. The others were invited to join in considering Pacific and Far Eastern problems in which they had a direct interest. Three principal treaties came out of the conference. By the Treaty Limiting Naval

"MORE UP TO DATE. THE FOUR-POWER TREATY REPLACES THE CLOAK OF ISOLATION."

Armament, or Five-Power Treaty, the five great powers agreed to scrap sixty-eight capital ships (battleships and heavy cruisers), which were already built or planned. They also promised to observe a ten-year building "holiday," during which they would not construct any new capital ships. After that the United States and Great Britain were each to have a tonnage of 525,000, Japan 60 per cent of that amount, and France and Italy smaller tonnages. The ratio for the five powers was set at 5 : 5 : 3 : 1.67 : 1:67. Japan consented to the treaty only when the United States promised not to strengthen its fortifications and naval bases in the Aleutians, the Philippines, and on Samoa and Guam. This meant that the Japanese navy would be supreme in the Far Pacific, for the United States lacked adequate bases there.

Two other treaties were signed in Washington. The Four-Power Treaty pledged the United States, Great Britain, Japan, and France to respect each other's rights in their island possessions in the Pacific Ocean. This treaty replaced the Anglo-Japanese Alliance. (See page 432.) More important was the Nine-Power Treaty, in which Belgium, Holland, Portugal, Italy, and China joined the four great powers in a promise to respect the independence of China and to maintain the Open Door policy. (See page 429.)

The return to alliances in the 1920's. Some European states tried to find safety outside the League system by making alliances. France was the leader in this effort to find security. Hardly had World War I ended when France began to look for protection against another German attack. Even after the League took form, French statesmen did not place full confidence in it. They trusted more in the old diplomacy than in the new and untried League machinery. The old diplomacy called for military alliances. France wanted her recent allies to promise to defend her if Germany tried to upset the Versailles Treaty. Fear of Germany, who had attacked her twice since 1870 and whose population was half again as large as that of France, explains the constant French demand for guarantees against attack.

France and her satellites. In 1919 France thought that she had achieved security against future German aggression. At that time she drew up the so-called Guarantee Treaties with Great Britain and the United States, by which these two governments promised to come to the aid of France if Germany made an unprovoked attack upon her. The agreements never were ratified. The United States Senate turned down the American treaty.

That action killed the British treaty, which was to go into effect only if the United States entered the agreement. France then turned to the "succession states" to build her defenses. These were the states that the Peace of Paris had created or enlarged. They too wanted to maintain the *status quo*. France therefore made alliances with Poland (1921), Czechoslovakia (1924), Rumania (1926), and Yugoslavia (1927). All the treaties provided for mutual aid in case of attack. Czechoslovakia, Rumania, and Yugoslavia had already joined in the Little Entente to protect themselves against Hungary and Bulgaria. Likewise, Poland and Rumania had signed an alliance to help one another in case of attack by Russia (1921). To cement the friendship of her satellites, France lent them money for munitions and improvements.

Other alliances. Meanwhile, Germany and Russia did not like being outcasts. They feared that the French bloc was hostile to them. Consequently, they drew close together in the Treaty of Rapallo (1922), which reestablished trade relations between them. In 1926 they signed a treaty of friendship and neutrality. Italy too protected herself by alliances with Yugoslavia (1924), Albania (1926), and Spain (1926). She did this to counterbalance French control of the western Mediterranean.

By the end of the 1920's Europe again showed signs of splitting into armed camps. Conditions grew worse during the 1930's as the League system of collective security weakened and finally broke down.

The Locarno Pacts, 1925. Nations also sought to organize peace through special and regional agreements. One of the most notable of these was made in 1925 at the Swiss town of Locarno, where representatives of Great Britain, France, Germany, Italy, Belgium, Poland, and Czechoslovakia signed a series of seven treaties, or pacts. The heart of the pacts drawn up at Locarno was the one known as the Security Pact, which guar-

---

---

anteed the boundaries between Germany, France, and Belgium as fixed by the Treaty of Versailles. If any of the three countries attacked one of the others, all the parties to the treaty, including Great Britain and Italy, promised to take up arms against the aggressor. They also promised to settle all disputes between them by peaceful means. Locarno thus raised the hopes of all lovers of peace. Germany had now accepted of her own accord the western borders "dictated" at Versailles. She and her former foes had at last agreed to shake hands. Soon after, in 1926, the powers welcomed Germany into the League of Nations.

Further attempts at naval disarmament. Although no conference was so successful as that at Washington, there were other conferences on naval disarmament. In 1927 President Coolidge invited Great Britain, Japan, France, and Italy to join us in a conference at Geneva to discuss naval disarmament. The purpose was to limit the construction of types of naval vessels not covered in the Washington Treaty. France and Italy refused to attend, and the conference broke up without results. Again in 1930, at London, the five great powers tried to reach an agreement to limit navies. All five consented to continue until 1936 the building holiday in capital ships. But France refused to give in to the Italian demand for parity (equality) with her in cruisers, destroyers, and submarines. Britain, the United States, and Japan did agree to limit such vessels. They established a ratio of 10 : 10 : 7 for cruisers and destroyers, and equality in submarine tonnage. An "escape" clause, however, provided that any one of the three chief powers might build beyond the agreed limits if its "national security" required. This provision made the treaty almost meaningless. Finally, in 1934 the last hope for naval disarmament vanished. Japan demanded equality of tonnage in capital ships with the United States and Great Britain. When this was refused, she announced that she would not renew the naval treaties at the end of 1936. Once more the naval race was on.

The Geneva Disarmament Conference, 1932–1934. Since 1925 a special commission of the League of Nations had been at work on plans for general disarmament—land, sea, and air. It had struggled with some very thorny questions. For example, how was the military strength of a nation to be measured? Merely by size of armies or amount of equipment? Or was quality of armaments as well as quantity to be considered? Should governments agree to limit each kind of weapon, or should they place restrictions on the money spent for all armaments? What about a nation's resources and manpower? Ought they to take these into account? By 1930 the commission submitted a "draft treaty" full of high-sounding but indefinite proposals. It was a "skeleton lacking flesh and blood." Nevertheless, the General Disarmament Conference met in February, 1932, at Geneva to discuss this plan. Representatives of all League members were present, as well as delegates from the United States and Soviet Russia.

An immediate conflict flared up between Germany and France. Germany, disarmed by the Versailles Treaty, wanted the other powers to reduce their armaments to a level with hers, or else permit her to rearm. France refused to consider a reduction in her armaments unless the other great powers guaranteed to help her if attacked. In short, German demands for equality clashed with French demands for security. The United States and Great Britain were unwilling to promise that they would go to war to defend France or the *status quo* in Europe. When Hitler came to power in Germany (see page 497), the chances of success at Geneva faded. Germany failed to get the equality she demanded. She therefore quit the conference and announced that she would also leave the League. That meant the conference was as good as dead.

The Pact of Paris, 1928. Still another attempt to buttress the League's peace machinery was the Kellogg-Briand Pact, or Pact of Paris. In 1927 Aristide Briand, the French Minister of Foreign Affairs, suggested to the American Secretary of State, Frank B. Kellogg, that their two nations enter an agreement to outlaw war. Secretary Kellogg welcomed the idea, but replied that such an agreement should be *multilateral*—that is, open to all countries. The outcome of the discussions was a General Treaty for the Renunciation of War (1928). By 1930 almost every nation on earth had signed it. The pact was a declaration of noble intentions. The parties solemnly stated that they would not use war "as an instrument of national policy" (Article I). They also agreed to settle all disputes "by pacific means" (Article II). The pact contained no sanctions or guarantees such as the agreements made at Locarno provided. In other words, there was no force behind it except moral force. Furthermore, it did not ban wars undertaken in self-defense. That left a serious loophole. A government that wishes to fight can always say that it is acting in self-defense. Hence the Pact of Paris proved ineffective. It expressed the desire of the world for peace, but it failed to provide the means to achieve it. Within three years (1931) Japan openly flouted the pact by invading Manchuria. (See page 542.)

REVIEWING THE CHAPTER

TERMS TO UNDERSTAND: *Versailles Treaty, reparations, covenant, free city, war guilt clause, self-determination, moratorium, passive resistance, Lausanne agreement, pacifism, arbitration tribunal, mandate, mandatory, national minority, ILO, economic sanctions,* status quo, *collective security, 5 : 5 : 3, Little Entente, French bloc, multilateral, succession states.*

PERSONS TO IDENTIFY: *Harding, Masaryk, King Zog I, Dawes, Young, Erasmus, Voltaire, Nobel, Bryan, Crucé, Penn, Rousseau, Kant, Kellogg, Briand.*

PLACES TO LOCATE: *Saar basin, Finland, Estonia, Latvia, Lithuania, Danzig, Czechoslovakia, Bukovina, Transylvania, Bessarabia, Dobruja, Yugoslavia, Tyrol, Trentino, Trieste, Fiume, Ruhr.*

QUESTIONS TO ANSWER

1. (a) Describe the organization of the Peace Conference. Where did it meet? (b) What countries were not invited to participate? (c) Name the "Big Three" at the Peace Conference. (d) Name five principal provisions of the Peace of Paris.

2. (a) Why did the United States Senate refuse to ratify the treaties made at the Peace Conference? (b) How did the United States make peace with Germany, Austria, and Hungary?

3. (a) What were two main motives in remaking the map of Europe at the Peace Conference? (b) What boundary changes were made in western and northern Europe? (c) Explain the origin of the Polish question. (d) Why was Danzig made into a free city? Why was the Polish Corridor established?

4. (a) What areas and peoples were included in Czechoslovakia? Austria? Hungary? (b) Was the creation of Yugoslavia based upon the principle of national self-determination? (c) What other boundary changes were made in southeastern Europe? (d) To what extent did the Peace of Paris give independence to submerged nationalities?

5. (a) What were Germany's "war guilt" obligations? (b) Give the date and provisions of the Dawes Plan. The Young Plan. (c) What was the "riddle of reparations"? (d) Why did not Germany continue to pay her war debts? (e) What reasons did the Allies give for cancellation of their debts to the United States?

6. (a) What is meant by the "peace movement"? (b) Trace the attitude of the Christian Church toward war. (c) Give examples of the successful arbitration of international disputes. (d) Describe two seventeenth-century blueprints for a league of nations. (e) Describe the Permanent Court of Arbitration.

7. (a) Name the three principal parts of the League of Nations organization. (b) What were the functions of each? When and where did each meet? (c) List the purposes and duties of the League.

8. (a) Describe the mandate system. On what idea did it rest? (b) What is the minorities problem? Do you believe this problem will ever be solved? (c) In what field was the League most successful? Describe its activities in this field. (d) What was the League's most important task? Did it accomplish anything here? (e) What action could the League take against an aggressor? (f) What did the League do in the Italian-Ethiopian conflict? What was the result? (g) How did the World Court differ from the Hague Tribunal?

9. (a) What was provided by the principal treaties made at the Washington Conference in 1921? (b) Account for the return to the old system of alliances in the 1920's. (c) By what pacts did Germany agree to accept the western borders "dictated" at Versailles? (d) Why did the General Disarmament Conference of 1932 fail? (e) What were the provisions of the Pact of Paris? Did it have any loopholes?

FURTHER ACTIVITIES FOR PART SEVEN

1. After reading brief accounts of the lives of Cavour and Bismarck, prepare a report which points out the differences and similarities in their family background and training, their political views, their ability to get along with people, and the methods they used in achieving their ambitions.

2. Write an essay on the Dreyfus case. Show how it influenced French politics and how its final outcome was a victory for democracy. (If available, Schechter's *The Dreyfus Affair* would be a good source of information.)

3. (a) On a time line indicate the chief events in the imperialistic expansion of the western countries from about 1850 to 1914. (b) On another time line trace the events of WWI.

4. Prepare a class report telling how Commodore Perry opened the door to Japan.

5. Read Rudyard Kipling's poem "The White Man's Burden." Mention some historical events which furnished the background for the poem. Does Kipling show a definite point of view?

6. In two parallel columns list the places where the principle of self-determination was carried out by the Peace of Paris and the places where it was violated. Locate these areas on a blank map, using different colors to indicate the places listed in columns one and two.

7. Write a comparison of the mandate system and the imperialistic system for dealing with dependent areas. Point out the advantages and disadvantages of each system.

8. Compare the personalities of Wilson, Lloyd George, and Clemenceau. A good reference is Parkman, *Fighters for Peace*.

FURTHER READING FOR PART SEVEN

(Stars indicate easier books)

HISTORY

AMERICAN HERITAGE. *American Heritage History of World War I*. Dell. (paperback)

ARON. *Century of Total War*. Beacon. (paperback)

*BALDWIN. *World War I: An Outline History*. Grove. (paperback)

BROGAN. *French Nation: From Napoleon to Pétain, 1814–1940*. Harper Colophon. (paperback)

BURCHELL. *Age of Progress*. Time-Life.

*—— and ISSAWI. *Building the Suez Canal*. Harper.

CHRISTENSEN. *The Pictorial History of Western Art*. Mentor. (paperback)

*COWLEY. *1918: Gamble for Victory*. Macmillan.

CZERNIN. *Versailles—1919*. Capricorn. (paperback)

DERRY. *Short History of 19th Century England*. Mentor. (paperback)

DOS PASSOS. *Mr. Wilson's War*. Doubleday.

FALLS. *The Great War, 1914–1918*. Capricorn. (paperback)

FAY. *The Origins of the World War*. Free Press.

*FOOTMAN. *The Russian Revolutions*. Putnam.

HART, *Real War, 1914–1918*. Atlantic–Little, Brown. (paperback)

HERRING. *A History of Latin America*. Knopf.

HORNE. *The Price of Glory: Verdun, 1916*. St. Martin.

KENNEDY. *Short History of Japan*. Mentor. (paperback)

KIRK. *Short History of the Middle East: From the Rise of Islam to Modern Times*. Praeger. (paperback)

MACK SMITH. *Italy*. University of Michigan.

McNEILL, BUSKE, ROEHM. *The World . . . Its History in Maps*. Denoyer-Geppert.

*MARTIN. *A Picture History of Russia*. Crown.

MAUROIS. *History of France*. Funk and Wagnalls.

MOOREHEAD. *The Blue Nile*. Dell. (paperback)

——. *Cooper's Creek*. Dell. (paperback)

——. *The Fatal Impact*. Dell. (paperback)

——. *Gallipoli*. Harper. (paperback)

——. *The Russian Revolution*. Bantam. (paperback)

——. *The White Nile*. Dell. (paperback)

*NAZAROFF. *Land and People of Russia*. Lippincott.

OLIVER and FAGE. *Short History of Africa*. Penguin. (paperback)

*PECK. *Pageant of South American History*. McKay.

PRATT. *Battles That Changed History*. Doubleday.

*QUENNELL and QUENNELL. *A History of Everyday Things in England, 1733–1851*. Putnam.

*QUINN. *Picture Map Geography of Asia*. Lippincott.

READER. *Life in Victorian England*. Putnam.

REEDER. *The Story of the First World War*. Duell.

*REYNOLDS. *They Fought in the Sky*. Rinehart.

SCHECHTER. *The Dreyfus Affair*. Houghton.

SEAMAN. *From Vienna to Versailles*. Harper Colophon. (paperback)

SELLMAN. *The First World War*. Criterion.

*SNYDER. *First Book of World War I*. Watts.

STEARNS. *Pageant of Europe*. Harcourt.

STERLING and KIMBLE. *Exploration of Africa*. Harper.

STEVENS. *Egypt, Yesterday and Today*. Holt. (paperback)

STORRY. *History of Modern Japan*. Penguin. (paperback)

TAYLOR. *The Fall of the Dynasties*. Doubleday.

TUCHMAN. *Guns of August*. Macmillan.

——. *The Proud Tower*. Macmillan.

——. *The Zimmermann Telegram*. Dell. (paperback)

*WALN. *House of Exile*. Little, Brown.

WALSH. *Russia and the Soviet Union*. University of Michigan.

*WERSTEIN. *The Franco-Prussian War*. Messner.

*——. *The Many Faces of World War I*. Messner.

*——. *Ten Days in November: The Russian Revolution*. Macrae Smith.

WHITAKER. *Nationalism and International Progress*. Chandler. (paperback)

*WILLIAMS. *Africa: Her History, Lands, and People, Told with Pictures*. Cooper Square. (paperback)

YOUNG. *Victorian England: Portrait of an Age*. Oxford. (paperback)

BIOGRAPHY

*BAKER. *Garibaldi*. Vanguard.

*——. *Juarez, Hero of Mexico*. Vanguard.

*——. *Sun Yat-sen*. Vanguard.

BENÉT. *Stanley, Invincible Explorer*. Dodd.

BUCK. *Man Who Changed China: The Story of Sun Yat-sen*. Random House.

*CARR. *Men of Power*. Viking.

CASTOR. *America's First World War: General Pershing and the Yanks*. Random House.

COWELES. *The Kaiser*. Harper.

*DAVENPORT. *Garibaldi, Father of Modern Italy*. Random House.

*EATON. *David Livingstone, Foe of Darkness*. Morrow.

GUÉRARD. *Napoleon III*. Knopf.

HALL–QUEST. *With Stanley in Africa*. Dutton.

*HATCH. *Woodrow Wilson*. Holt.

*KOMROFF. *Disraeli*. Messner.

*LOCKHART and WOODHOUSE. *Cecil Rhodes: The Colossus of Southern Africa*. Macmillan.

LONG. *DeLesseps, Builder of Suez*. McKay.

MASSIE. *Nicholas and Alexandra*. Dell. (paperback)

MAUROIS. *Cecil Rhodes*. Shoe String.

——. *Disraeli*. Modern Library.

MEYER. *Champions of Peace*. Little, Brown.

NOLAN. *Florence Nightingale*. Messner.

PAYNE. *The Life and Death of Lenin*. Simon and Schuster.

PEARE. *The Woodrow Wilson Story*. Crowell.

STRACHEY. *Eminent Victorians*. Capricorn. (paperback)

——. *Queen Victoria*. Harcourt.

*STREATFIELD. *Queen Victoria*. Random House.

TAYLOR. *Bismarck, the Man and the Statesman*. Random House.

*WOODHAM–SMITH. *Lonely Crusader: The Life of Florence Nightingale, 1820–1910*. McGraw.

FICTION

BUCHAN. *Greenmantle*. Nelson.

*COLES. *Drink to Yesterday*. Norton.

FENNER. *Over There! Stories of World War I*. Morrow.

FORESTER. *The African Queen*. Modern Library.

HILTON. *Random Harvest*. Little, Brown.

LAMPEDUSA. *The Leopard*. New American Library. (paperback)

*MUKERJI. *Gay Neck, the Story of a Pigeon*. Dutton.

*NORDHOFF and HALL. *Falcons of France*. Little, Brown.

PASTERNAK. *Doctor Zhivago*. Modern Library.

REMARQUE. *All Quiet on the Western Front*. Little, Brown.

WERFEL. *Forty Days of Musa Dagh*. Viking.

WIBBERLEY. *Kevin O'Connor and the Light Brigade*. Farrar, Straus.

GUERNICA, by Pablo Picasso, is an intense expression of man's pledge to life.
Profoundly shocked by the Spanish Civil War, Picasso presented the horrors of war
in stark, haunting images. The painting has a terrible timeliness in an era
dominated by war.

PART EIGHT

CIVILIZATION AT THE CROSSROADS

The Great War, as World War I was called, brought an end to the economic, social, and political stability which had prevailed generally in the western world since 1815. In a sense, the war marked the end of the nineteenth century and the beginning of the twentieth. The new era turned out to be markedly different from the old. The war had destroyed many monarchies and empires and had weakened other governments, it shook the social order in numerous parts of the world, and it wrecked or damaged the economies of many nations. Perhaps the most terrible effect of the war, however, came from the exposure of millions of men to the sight of human slaughter. Veterans, accustomed to killing and to the loss of human dignity during the war, returned home and often supported or at least accepted brutal dictatorships in the 1920's and 1930's.

After the war most European countries adopted democratic forms of government, and during the prosperous years of the early 1920's it seemed that they might thrive. The Great Depression which began in 1929 shattered this hope, for the depression brought economic problems which were more than the democracies could handle. Consequently, fascist dictatorships sprang up in a number of countries, notably in Italy, Germany, and Japan. Russia had already turned to a different kind of undemocratic rule in 1917.

During the depression years the democracies tended to withdraw from world affairs, and to concentrate instead on their problems of business failures and unemployment. The dictatorships, on the other hand, looked to foreign adventures as a way to regain prosperity. Beginning with Japan's attack on Manchuria in 1931, they began a series of attacks which led to World War II. Although the democracies were disunited and ill prepared, as were their allies the Russians, they proved that free peoples can stand together in a common cause. In the end the Axis lost.

23 The World between Two Wars

PRIME MINISTER CHAMBERLAIN, with his famous umbrella, returning from a conference with Hitler. All Europe became an armed camp during the crisis over Czechoslovakia. Chamberlain tried to appease Hitler so as to avoid another war, whose tragic results are symbolized by the scene of old women rummaging for food in Berlin garbage dumps in 1918.

World War I destroyed much of the social, economic, and political stability which we associate with the reign of Queen Victoria in the late 1800's. The period of the 1920's and 1930's, therefore, was one in which men sought for new social, economic, and political systems to replace those the war had overturned.

In politics, men turned first to democracy but then to dictatorship, especially after the Great Depression began in 1929. In economics, "free enterprise" was replaced by government management in the dictatorships, and even in democratic countries the governments took greater part in regulating the production and distribution of goods. As for new social systems, activities ranged all the way from forming the "classless society" of communism to attempts in the democracies to bring a better life to the underprivileged. This chapter, then, deals with the world at a time of profound change.

Europe after World War I

Creating new states out of old. At the close of World War I a wave of revolutions in Europe swept away the autocratic governments of Russia, Germany, and Austria-Hungary. As the old regimes fell in these countries, the "submerged nationalities" set up independent governments of their own. Out of former Russian territory emerged the four new states of Finland, Estonia, Latvia, and Lithuania. Austria, Hungary, and Czechoslovakia were created from the empire of Austria-Hungary. A new Slav state, Yugoslavia, united Serbia and Montenegro with part of the former Austro-Hungarian Empire. Poland, the largest of the new nations, was made up of territory that had been held by Germany, Russia, and Austria-Hungary. (See map, page 472.)

The triumph of democracy. The war "to make the world safe for democracy" at least made Europe unsafe for monarchy. Revolutions overthrew the Russian czar, the German kaiser, the Austro-Hungarian emperor, and other sovereigns. A crowd of princes, dukes, and grand dukes also lost their special privileges. The most violent revolution occurred in Russia. Practically all the Russian nobles who survived the revolution fled to other countries with only the possessions they could carry.

In most countries where monarchy was overthrown, the people set up republics with constitutions based on democratic principles. Before the war there were only four republics in Europe; after the war there were sixteen. France, Switzerland, Portugal, and tiny San Marino had adopted republican governments before the war; the republics established after the war were Germany, Austria, Czechoslovakia, Poland, Lithuania, Latvia, Estonia, Finland, Greece, the Irish Free State, Soviet Russia, and Turkey (which may be included since it still holds a small piece of territory in Europe).

The constitutions of the new republics gave the vote to all men and usually women as well. They provided for separation of church and state and for religious freedom. They also established systems of common schools, so that the people might be educated for good citizenship. In the monarchies which survived in Europe (and in the four new ones established in Hungary, Yugoslavia, Albania, and Iceland) constitutions limited the powers of the kings. In Britain and the Scandinavian countries, for example, the kings ruled in name only, for law and custom had long guaranteed democratic government to the people. In practice Spain was probably the least democratic of the monarchies, although the Spanish constitution gave political rights to the people. In short, nearly all the countries of Europe west of Russia seemed to be started on the road to political democracy.

Economic problems of Europe. With the end of the war, the people of Europe turned to the task of repairing the damage caused by the fighting. In some ways reconstruction was more difficult than the war itself. The work of rebuilding Europe had to be done without the help of the millions of young men killed or disabled in battle. Many people suffered from shortages of food and clothing and other necessaries, and could work for only a few hours at a time. In their weakened condition they succumbed quickly to disease, especially influenza, which took a toll of millions of lives in a worldwide epidemic near the close of the war.

The governments of Europe could do little to relieve suffering and speed reconstruction, for the war had left most of them in grave financial difficulties. The creation of several new states also hindered economic recovery in Europe, since each of them placed tariffs on goods that crossed their borders and thus interfered with the flow of trade. The United States and other countries gave aid in the form of gifts of food and clothing and cash loans. Conditions gradually improved, but for years Europeans continued to suffer from the economic effects of the war. For a short time, during the late 1920's, prosperity seemed to be returning. Then in 1929 a worldwide depression began, bringing economic collapse and severe unemployment in most countries in Europe.

Why democracy lost followers. Because of the unsatisfactory economic conditions in Europe, political unrest continued. Many people, impatient for a return of prosperity, began to have doubts about the effectiveness of democratic government. They wanted freedom indeed, but they also wanted bread. Some people, especially those who were unemployed, were willing to exchange their freedom for better living conditions. Democ-

racy was challenged by leaders who promised to restore prosperity if they were given sweeping powers. They organized their followers into active political groups which used force to frighten their opponents. If possible these men made themselves dictators. Democracy held its ground in countries like England and France where the people had long-standing traditions of self-government. Of the twelve new republics, however, only three managed to avoid dictatorship. They were Finland, Czechoslovakia, and the Irish Free State. In many other countries the people fell into step behind a "strong man" who promised to bring better times. In effect these nations entered a new Age of Autocracy.

Meaning of dictatorship. A dictator disregards the constitution of his country and violates the civil rights of individuals as he chooses. He cannot be removed from office by popular vote—only a revolution can overthrow him. The dictator makes the laws, although he may permit a legislature filled with his followers to go through the motions of passing the laws he wants. He does not permit criticism; he demands unquestioning obedience. In modern times dictators have usually risen to power in countries where a democratic government has failed to solve national problems, and where the people have had little experience with democracy. The dictator may gain office through popular election, but once in power he keeps a large army on hand to support him. The idea of dictatorship is not new. Julius Caesar and Augustus in ancient times, and Napoleon I and Napoleon III in modern times are familiar examples of strong men who pushed their way to supreme power.

Soviet Russia

The downfall of the Romanovs. As we have already pointed out (see page 453), the inefficient and corrupt government of the czar could not stand the strain of World War I. Hundreds of thousands of Russian soldiers had died for lack of ammunition and supplies, and as a result of military blunders by their generals. Many people believed that the czarina and other persons in high places were pro-German and guilty of treasonable activities. Unrest mounted and disorders spread over the country. In March, 1917, a severe food shortage in the capital city of Petrograd (St. Petersburg) brought matters to a crisis. Hungry mobs paraded through the streets shouting "Bread!" Thousands of striking workers joined the unruly throngs and ignored the czar's order to return to their jobs. The government called out troops to put down the rioting. Instead of firing on the crowds, the soldiers joined the demonstrators. The czar's authority broke down completely. The Duma, or national assembly, disobeyed an order to adjourn and persuaded the czar to abdicate. Thus, after three hundred years of absolute rule, the Romanov dynasty ended.

The provisional government fails. Czardom had collapsed of its own weight. What was to take its place? The leaders of the Duma who now came into power belonged to the moderate parties. They represented the middle class, and did not hold radical views. They set up a provisional, or temporary, government and proclaimed many liberal reforms. Among these were liberty of speech and press, a general amnesty (pardon) for all political prisoners and Siberian exiles, and a popular assembly to draw up a constitution for Russia. It seemed to the outside world that Russia was on the road to liberal democracy. The Allied powers promptly recognized the provisional government. They were especially pleased because the new Russian leaders promised to continue the war.

The provisional government was not equal to its task. The people were thoroughly sick of the war and in no mood for halfway measures. After centuries of repression, they now resorted to direct action. In the country many

peasants, unwilling to wait for government reforms, seized and divided their landlords' estates. On the war front, soldiers befriended their German foes and sometimes shot their officers. Thousands of deserters trudged home. Factory workers added to the confusion by striking or slowing down work and by insisting on electing their own factory managers. Chaos reigned everywhere.

The socialists took advantage of the disorder to undermine what they called the "bourgeois" government and to press for more sweeping reforms. They strengthened the revolutionary councils, or *soviets,* which had been set up in cities by representatives of the workers and soldiers after the 1905 revolution. Others now sprang up in the army and among the people in rural villages. Soon they began to challenge the authority of the provisional government. At first the soviets were led by the moderate socialists—Mensheviks and Social Revolutionaries. As time passed, the radical socialists, or Bolsheviks, gained control of the soviets. They promised to give the people what they wanted: "Peace, bread, and land!"

The Bolshevik program. The word "Bolshevik" means "member of the majority." Actually, in the beginning the Bolsheviks were not in the majority. By trickery they forced their views on a meeting of exiled Russian socialists held at Brussels in 1903. In 1918 they changed their official name to the Russian Communist party. The Bolsheviks were ardent followers of Karl Marx. (See page 322.) They believed in the complete overthrow of the capitalistic system— by persuasion if possible, by violence, if necessary. In its place they wanted to establish a dictatorship of the proletariat, or workingmen.

Under the leadership of Lenin and Trotsky, the Bolsheviks called for: (1) immediate peace, based on "no annexations and no indemnities"; (2) division of the big estates among the peasants, with no compensation to the former owners; (3) operation of the fac-

NICOLAI LENIN

LEON TROTSKY

tories by the workers; (4) government control of production and distribution of goods; (5) "all power to the soviets!" in place of the provisional government; and (6) the denial of political rights to propertied people.

The Bolsheviks take over, November, 1917. This program appealed to many people. By the fall of 1917 the Bolsheviks had charge of the most important soviets, including the Petrograd Soviet of Workers' and Soldiers' Deputies. Meanwhile, the provisional government had changed hands. Kerensky, a moderate Socialist, took the helm and tried to rally the Russians to continue the war against Germany. His efforts ended in failure. In November, 1917, the Petrograd Soviet led a second revolution which easily overthrew the Kerensky government. The Bolsheviks were now in the saddle. Let us take a brief look at their leaders.

Lenin and Trotsky. Nicolai Lenin (1870–1924), a "plump little man, with a high bulbous forehead, a snub nose, and bald head," was the son of a Russian teacher and school inspector. As a youth he was embittered by the execution of his brother, who had plotted against the life of Czar Alexander III. Lenin began the study of law at the University of Kazan but was soon expelled for carrying on revolutionary agitation. That was only the beginning of his trouble with the czar's gov-

ernment. In 1895 he was exiled to Siberia for five years. Upon his release he spent much time in England, France, and Switzerland, where he engaged in underground activities against the czarist regime.

Leon Trotsky (1877–1940) did not throw in his lot with the Bolsheviks until after the March Revolution. Nevertheless, he soon ranked next to Lenin as a party leader. He came of a middle class family and early in his career became a professional revolutionist. Twice the czarist authorities exiled him to Siberia and twice he escaped. Trotsky then went to western Europe and later to the United States.

After the Revolution of March, 1917, both Lenin and Trotsky hurried back to Russia. They led the assault on the Kerensky government which brought the Bolsheviks into power in November, 1917 (the so-called "October Revolution"). Lenin became premier and Trotsky foreign minister (later war minister) in the new government.

The Treaty of Brest-Litovsk, March 3, 1918. The Bolshevik leaders faced the immediate problem of taking Russia out of the war. The Russian army had broken down completely, leaving the country at the mercy of the Germans. The Germans were eager to eliminate the eastern front in order to bolster their armies in the west. In the end Russia had to accept extremely harsh terms. By the Treaty of Brest-Litovsk in 1918, she agreed to give up eastern Poland, the Ukraine, Lithuania, Estonia, and Latvia. These areas fell under German control. Russia also recognized the independence of Finland. The treaty thus took away about one fourth of Russia's population and a fourth of her tillable land. She lost the richest agricultural regions, the chief industrial districts, most of the iron and coal mines, and a large proportion of her railways. Besides all this, she had to pay a huge war indemnity. Lenin had a hard time persuading his party to accept this humiliating peace. He thought the peace terms would be changed later, for he expected Germany to lose the war. Meanwhile, peace would furnish the breathing spell necessary to set up the "dictatorship of the proletariat."

Civil war and Allied invasion. The Treaty of Brest-Litovsk did not bring peace to Russia. For about three years, 1917–1920, the new government had to fight for its life against enemies within and without. From the very outset the bourgeois classes resisted the Bolshevik government and tried to bring about its downfall. Former czarist officers organized an army in southern Russia to fight the Bolsheviks. Anti-Bolshevik forces, known as "Whites," also sprang up in other parts of the country. They fought many battles against the Bolsheviks, or "Reds." The White armies were backed by the Allied nations. England, France, the United States, and eleven other countries sent men, money, and supplies to fight the Reds. The Allies worked for the overthrow of the Soviet regime because it was a threat to their economic system. They were also angry because the Bolsheviks refused to pay the czarist government's debts and had quit the war against Germany. For a time it looked as though the Reds would be overwhelmed by their foes. Two things, however, gained them popular support. (1) Patriotic Russians resented the presence of foreign soldiers on Russian soil; and (2) the peasants feared that a White victory would bring the return of landlordism. As a result, the volunteer Red army organized by Trotsky stopped the advances of the anti-Bolshevik forces. By 1919 the Allies except Japan had withdrawn and by 1920 the Reds were in power. Allied intervention helped to create a lasting distrust of the western powers by the Soviets.

The Red Terror. The Bolsheviks had to fight not only the White armies and foreign troops. They had to deal with individual counterrevolutionists, as the enemies of the regime were called. Against these the Soviet government used the same methods that the czarist government had employed—arbitrary arrest, exile, or execution. Lenin said, "No dictatorship of the proletariat is to be thought of without terror and violence." Acting upon this idea, the Communists crushed all opposition to their program. They organized the Cheka, or secret police, which launched the "Red Terror" against enemies of the Soviet government. Among the victims of the Red Terror were the former czar and his whole family. The local soviet murdered them in a cellar at Ekaterinburg (now Sverdlov) near the Ural Mountains. The Cheka arrested and executed thousands of counterrevolutionists. Later the secret police went by other names and initials, most recently, KGB.

The First Communist constitution. While Lenin's government was fighting for its life, it proclaimed the first constitution of the Russian Socialist Federated Soviet Republic. The constitution of July, 1918 declared that all land, factories, mineral wealth, banks, railroads, and others means of production belonged to the workers' and peasants' state. Only "productive" workers over eighteen might vote. This left most of the middle class, the former noblemen, and the clergy without political rights. Oppression of national minorities was forbidden.

Communists set up the USSR. At first the Soviet Republic consisted of only a fraction of the old Russia. The Treaty of Brest-Litovsk had stripped away a broad belt of territory along the western border of Russia. After the Allied victory, Germany had to give up control of this area, but the Communists did not recover it. It was divided into the new republics of Finland, Estonia, Latvia, Lithuania, and Poland. During the civil war extensive areas were occupied by foreign nations, but by 1922 all of these areas except Bessarabia had been regained by the Communists. By a treaty of union in 1923 a new and larger federation came into being—the Union of Soviet Socialist Republics (USSR). The federal constitution and that of each of the member republics followed closely the constitution of the RSFSR. By 1929 the number of republics in the Soviet Union had risen to eleven. There are now fifteen. Each republic is self-governing in a limited number of matters, but in most affairs is controlled from Moscow, the capital of the Union government since 1918. We shall discuss the organization of the government in a later paragraph. (See page 505.)

Early Communist setbacks. The three years of civil war had seriously interfered with Lenin's plans to establish a Communist state. There had been widespread destruction of crops and property. Food and consumers' goods were extremely scarce. Factory workers grew lax because of hunger and because pay was according to need and not according to work done. The inexperienced workers' councils knew little about managing industry. As a result, factory output fell 80 per cent below the 1913 level. Moreover, the decrepit railway system broke down, and extreme inflation drove people to use barter. To prevent starvation in the cities and to obtain food for the army, the government seized the peasants' crops, leaving them only enough for their own use. The government also took what manufactured goods it could lay hands on and distributed them to those most in need. This policy of "war communism" drew little opposition while the fighting was still going on. But when peace returned, the long-suffering Russians looked for the good times they had been promised. The peasants were especially disappointed to find that they were not to be their own bosses. They had not counted on giving to the state all food beyond a certain amount allowed as wages. When the government began to seize grain by force, many peasants raised only enough for their own needs. To make matters worse, in 1921 a bad crop failure threatened millions with starvation. Discontent grew and cries of "Down with the Soviet government!" were heard at meetings of peasants and workers.

The New Economic Policy, 1921. Lenin now called a halt to the rapid communization of Russia. "We must retreat two steps to go forward one," he said. He therefore ordered a modified program called the New Economic Policy, or NEP. Under it the peasants got back the right to sell all their crops which remained after paying a large tax in produce. Some of the more able or energetic peasants profited by this arrangement. They were able to lease land and hire laborers. These comparatively well-to-do peasants were called "kulaks." The government still owned the land and large-scale industries. Factories employing less than twenty workers might be privately owned and operated. Workers were paid according to output, not need. The NEP was clearly a breathing spell. Lenin wanted to restore production before resuming the march toward the Communist state. Under the NEP, Russia recovered rapidly, although Lenin admitted that it meant "the restoration of capitalism in no small degree."

In 1924 Lenin, the father of Soviet communism, died. His enormous tomb in Moscow's Red Square became a Russian Mecca. In his honor Petrograd was renamed Leningrad, and his speeches and writings became the Bible of communism.

Stalin takes the helm. After Lenin's death two of his dedicated followers struggled for leadership of the Communist party and the

Soviet government. They were Leon Trotsky and Joseph Stalin. Their views clashed sharply. Trotsky was for speeding up the long-awaited world revolution, in which, according to Marx, workingmen everywhere would unite to overthrow capitalism. Stalin wanted to soft-pedal the world revolution and concentrate on establishing communism in one country. Stalin was a master of political maneuver. As secretary-general of the Communist party, he had the backing of a powerful political machine. Consequently, he gained the upper hand. In 1929 Trotsky had to leave the country. In 1940 he was assassinated in Mexico by a man believed to be a Soviet agent.

Stalin was born in 1879 in the Caucasus. He was the son of a shoemaker and his real name was Joseph Dzhugashvili (jōō′gȧ-shvē′lē). Lenin called him Stalin, or "man of steel." While still in his teens he joined the revolutionary movement against the czar's government. He suffered long periods of exile and several times made daring escapes. The Revolution of March, 1917, gave him a chance to show his great organizing ability. Stalin built the Communist party into an effective organization. Through it he became practically dictator of the Soviet Union.

The Five-Year Plans. The NEP had put Russian industry and agriculture back on their feet, but Russia remained a very poor and backward country. Convinced that world revolution would have to wait, Stalin asked the nation to begin an all-out effort to raise Russia's standard of living. For that purpose the Soviet government launched a Five-Year Plan to make Russia self-supporting. It was prepared by the State Planning Commission, or Gosplan, and was to cover the years 1928–1933. The goals of the first Five-Year Plan were: (1) to turn the Soviet Union into a powerful industrial nation, which need not fear "capitalist encirclement"; (2) to force the peasants to give up farming individual plots of land and to join big collective farms, on which the village would work together,

THE SOVIET CONSTITUTION

Article 123.—Equality of rights of citizens of the U.S.S.R., irrespective of their nationality or race, in all spheres of economic, government, cultural, political and other public activity, is an indefeasible law.

Article 124.—In order to ensure to citizens freedom of conscience, the church in the U.S.S.R. is separated from the state, and the school from the church. Freedom of religious worship and freedom of anti-religious propaganda is recognized for all citizens.

Article 125.—In conformity with the interests of the working people, and in order to strengthen the socialist system, the citizens of the U.S.S.R. are guaranteed by law:

a) freedom of speech;
b) freedom of the press;
c) freedom of assembly, including the holding of mass meetings;
d) freedom of street processions and demonstrations.

using machinery; (3) to do away completely with private business; and (4) to wipe out illiteracy. A second Five-Year Plan, with higher production goals, was completed in 1937. The third Five-Year Plan, begun in 1938, was interrupted by World War II. After the war, large-scale planning was resumed.

Under each Five-Year Plan the national planning agency fixed goals of production for each industry and then for each mine and factory. It determined the kind and amount of goods to be produced and wage and price levels. It based its estimates upon the advice given by government leaders, economic experts, factory managers, and the workers in each individual plant. By means of propaganda and by offering prizes, the government spurred the workers to go beyond the quotas assigned to them. "Overtake and pass America" became a slogan of the day.

Russia's industrial revolution. The first Five-Year Plan pushed the construction of heavy industries such as steel plants, tractor factories, hydroelectric plants, and new railroads. Later plans called for an increase in consumers' goods. The program of industrialization ran into many snags. There were few experienced managers, technicians, and skilled workers. Shortages of all kinds slowed up progress. As a result, production was very uneven and bottlenecks developed. Consumers' goods remained scarce and poor in quality because the planning agency was interested first of all in building heavy industry. If a quota was not met, the government tried and punished someone as a "wrecker." Some industries reached their goals ahead of time; others failed by a wide margin. By 1930 the 1100-mile Turkestan–Siberian Railroad was completed more than a year ahead of schedule. In 1932 the huge Dnieper River dam at Dnepropetrovsk was finished under the direction of American engineers. In the same year, at Magnitogorsk in the Urals, one of the largest steel works in the world began operations. All in all, by 1932 industrial output had increased 119 per cent under the plan.

The agricultural revolution. The agricultural plan called for the wholesale consolidation of small farms into large state and collective farms. The state farms are run with hired workers by government-appointed managers. A collective farm is operated by a co-operative association of peasants. The members of a collective own the machinery and most of the livestock in common. They divide the farm income which remains after

BARLEY HARVEST on a collective farm in the Uzbek Republic in 1947. During this period, the Soviet government mounted a new offensive to turn farm workers into Soviet Socialists.

paying the government a fixed quota of produce as a tax, and after setting aside other amounts for tractor service, seed, and improvements. Under this system, each collective elects its own manager, who is almost always a Communist party member. Each family owns its own house and an acre or so of land, besides pigs, fowl, and perhaps a cow.

The Communists met greater obstacles in agriculture than in industry. Eighty per cent of the Russian people were peasants. Their farming methods were out of date and their ways hard to change. Many of them did not understand what the government was trying to do. The kulaks, or prosperous peasants, particularly resisted the government's program for collectivizing the farms. Some killed their cattle rather than turn them over to the collective. The government treated the kulaks harshly, taking their belongings and sending them as slave laborers to concentration camps. The plan for agriculture also suffered from crop failures in 1931 and 1932. Starvation for many was the result. The food shortage meant also that Russia could not export enough grain to buy all the machinery needed for carrying out the industrial part of the plan.

Nevertheless, by 1933 the Communists had won the battle of collectivization. The peasants gave in and accepted the new order in agriculture. They had learned through bitter experience that resistance did not pay. In 1938, 242,400 collective farms and 3961 state farms accounted for more than 99 per cent of all land tilled.

The constitution of 1936. In 1936 Stalin said that the first phase of communism had been largely achieved. The "exploiting" classes had been eliminated; only workers and peasants remained. Furthermore, the country had passed from a predominantly agricultural state to an important industrial nation. It now seemed safe to make political changes. Therefore a new constitution was adopted.

The framework of Soviet government. Article I of the 1936 constitution calls the Union of Soviet Socialist Republics "a Socialist state of workers and peasants." But alongside the social, or government, ownership of the means of production, the constitution permits the existence of small private businesses based on the personal labor of their owners. An individual may also own his own home, furnishings, and personal belongings. Work is a duty, and the reward, or pay, is according to the amount and kind of work done. This marks a departure from the Marxist ideal of taking from each according to his ability and distributing to each according to his needs.

The constitution imitates those of the western democracies in many respects. It provides for the direct election of the people's representatives from geographical districts. It gives all citizens over eighteen the right to vote by secret ballot. On paper at least it guarantees the citizen freedom of speech, press, assembly, and worship. The constitution also recognizes rights that Communists claim are ignored in "bourgeois" democracies. These are the right to work, the right to rest and leisure (including an annual vacation with pay), the right to medical care, the right to security in old age, the right to education, and equality of rights regardless of nationality, sex, or race. The Russians hailed the new constitution as the most democratic in the world. Outside critics thought that some of its features, such as the guarantee of civil rights, would not be put into effect. The critics have proved to be right.

A pyramid of councils. The government of the USSR is carried on through a pyramid of soviets, or councils—in village, city, district, region, province, and member republic. The highest authority in the all-union, or central, government is the Supreme Council, or Soviet. It corresponds to a national parliament and consists of two houses, the Council of the Union and the Council of Nationalities. Through the latter each national minority is assured of a voice in the government. The Su-

V. I. LENIN PROCLAIMS SOVIET POWER. This painting by V. Serov is an example of "socialist realism" in the arts. This concept refers to a realistic depiction of life in a revolutionary social context. As the Communist party had its own view of life, socialist realism often turned into a crude propaganda.

preme Soviet meets twice a year. Between sessions the Presidium, or executive committee of the Supreme Soviet, exercises many of the legislative duties of the larger body. The day-to-day activities of the central government are carried on by the Council of People's Ministers, or Commissars. It is chosen by the Supreme Soviet and may be compared to a cabinet. Each minister heads a department, of which there are many, since the government directs every phase of the economic life of the country. The Supreme Soviet also elects the supreme court and special courts.

The same pattern of government exists in the fifteen federated republics. In practice their activities must harmonize with the policies of the Union government and the Communist party. The constitution gives the Union republics the right to secede, but a demand for separation would doubtless be regarded as counterrevolutionary. The fif-

teen members of the federation vary greatly in size and in population. Together they occupy one sixth of the earth's surface, or an area as large as the United States, Canada, and Central America combined.

Communist dictatorship. On paper the Soviet system of government appears little different from that of the western democracies. Actually, a wide gap separates them. The difference lies in the part played by the Communist party, which controls Russian political and economic life from top to bottom. No other political party may exist. The people may vote, but only for the candidates put forward by the Communist party or by Communist-dominated organizations. The Communists defend one-party rule by saying that since there is only one class, there need be only one party, composed of the leaders of that class. Their duty is to direct and train the masses. In doing so the party claims it has to guard against the influence of class enemies by a strict censorship of speech and press. The government also finds it necessary to maintain a secret police and "corrective labor camps" to deal with those who refuse to follow the "party line." The party line is the policy which the party leaders consider best at any one time. A citizen may criticize and make suggestions about the running of factories, farms, or mines; but he dare not question the Communist form of society or the basic policies of the party. It is assumed that no others are worth while. Thus the Soviet idea of democracy is radically different from ours.

Party organization and membership. The Communist party operates through units, or cells, in every factory, office, or local soviet. Its organization parallels that of the government. At the top of the pyramid is the All-Union Party Congress, which meets ordinarily every two years. It chooses a Central Committee of less than a hundred to direct affairs between sessions of the Congress. Still more important is the Presidium, formerly the Politburo, an inner circle of fifteen full members and eleven alternates elected by the Central Committee. Here is the real seat of authority. The Presidium makes party policy and really runs the USSR, for all leading government officials are party members. The most influential member of the Presidium is the secretary-general of the Communist party. This key post was first held by Lenin, followed by Stalin and later by Khrushchev. Their power over Russia has been as absolute as that of the czars. The dictatorship of the proletariat seems to have boiled down to the dictatorship of one man and his associates in the Presidium.

The number of members in the Communist party has always been small. In 1921 it was 650,000; today it is estimated at about 3 per cent of the population. Strict discipline has made it possible for this minority to rule Russia. Applicants for membership are carefully trained and their loyalty severely tested. Successful party members receive special privileges. Those who fail in their tasks are quickly dropped from the party. Disloyal members risk harsh punishment. Periodic "purges," or house cleanings, have swept thousands from the party ranks, some to exile, prison camps, or death. Especially sweeping were the purges of 1937 and 1938, which took the lives of leading generals and officials, and also thousands of humbler persons.

Education in Soviet Russia. "Citizens of the USSR have the right to education," says the Soviet constitution. The Communist leaders had a two-fold purpose in promoting education. Schools would prepare managers, technicians, and skilled workers to run the factories and farms; and schools would help in developing loyalty to the Communist way of life. The government therefore launched an ambitious program of education from the kindergarten to the university. The program includes many vocational and technical schools and workers' study groups. The Soviet goal of "a school for every person and every person in school" has not been reached, but educational progress has been noteworthy. By 1932 three times as many pupils were enrolled in the elementary schools as during the czarist regime. Under the czars about 75 per cent of the people could not read or write. Today, according to Soviet authorities, illiteracy has been "almost completely wiped out in the Soviet Union."

The Soviet attitude toward religion. Before the revolution the Orthodox Church was the state church and the staunch supporter of czarism and aristocracy. The Communists regarded it as their enemy. Furthermore, they believed with Marx that "religion is the opiate of the people"—something that makes them satisfied to accept their earthly miseries. The government, therefore, attacked the church at every turn, although it did not forbid religious worship. Most of the churches had to close. The authorities turned many of them into schools, clubrooms, museums, or industrial plants. They circulated anti-religious literature, and jailed or executed members of the clergy who resisted the attack on the church. Nevertheless, the Communist efforts to destroy organized religion failed. As the commissar of education admitted, "Religion is like a nail; the harder you hit it the deeper it goes into the wood." After 1938 the Soviet government toned down its anti-religious propaganda. Training schools for priests, closed for many years, were permitted to re-open. In 1943, in the midst of the war against the Nazis, the government approved the election of a new patriarch, or head, of the Russian Church.

Communist foreign policy. Marx and Lenin regarded communism as a revolutionary movement that would overthrow capitalism everywhere. To help spread revolutionary propaganda abroad, the Soviet leaders set up the Third International, or Comintern, in 1919. It replaced the Second International which had been controlled by moderate socialists. (See page 323.) The Comintern, however, failed to undermine capitalism. Meanwhile, Lenin had to modify communism at home to save it from collapse. (See page 500.) Russia needed foreign money, machinery, and engineers. To obtain them she had to get along with the capitalist world. The Soviet government therefore sought to re-establish trade and diplomatic relations with other countries. By the end of 1924 every major power in Europe had recognized the Soviet regime. The United States did not do so until 1933.

Under Stalin the country needed peace to insure the success of the Five-Year Plans. Talk of world revolution was replaced by talk of co-operation. Russia now sent representatives to peace conferences, signed nonaggression pacts with each of her near neighbors, and in 1934 joined the League of Nations. Her able foreign minister, Litvinov (lĭt-vē´-nôf), boldly called for general disarmament, but his proposals proved impracticable. Meanwhile, the anti-Communist policies of Hitler Germany alarmed the Soviet government. But in the midst of negotiations with Great Britain and France to form an anti-Nazi pact, Russia reversed her policy sharply. As we shall see in the next chapter, the Soviet government suddenly signed a nonaggression treaty with Germany in 1939.

Fascist Italy

Italy after World War I. The Italians entered a period of confusion after World War I. Their government carried a heavy burden of debt which grew greater every year. Over 600,000 of the Italian youth lost their lives in the war, and those who returned home found prices rising, factories closing, and unemployment increasing. Since the government failed to improve conditions, the workers and the unemployed began to look for ways to help themselves. Many of them joined revolutionary groups and sought to set up a government like that of Russia. Workers began a wave of strikes for higher wages; street fighting broke out in the cities; and peasants, refusing to pay rent, began to riot against the owners of large estates. The Italian government failed completely to preserve law and order. Then Mussolini and his Fascists appeared on the scene.

Mussolini and the rise of Fascism. Benito Mussolini was born in 1883, the son of a blacksmith who was active in the Socialist movement. To escape service in the army young Mussolini went to live in Switzerland. After returning to Italy he taught school for a time, then turned to journalism, and showed such ability that he became editor of the Socialist party newspaper. Shortly after World War I broke out he switched from his former pacifism and began to urge Italian entry into the war. Suspected of having accepted a French bribe for changing his views, he was expelled from the Socialist party. He edited a newspaper of his own in Milan until he was called

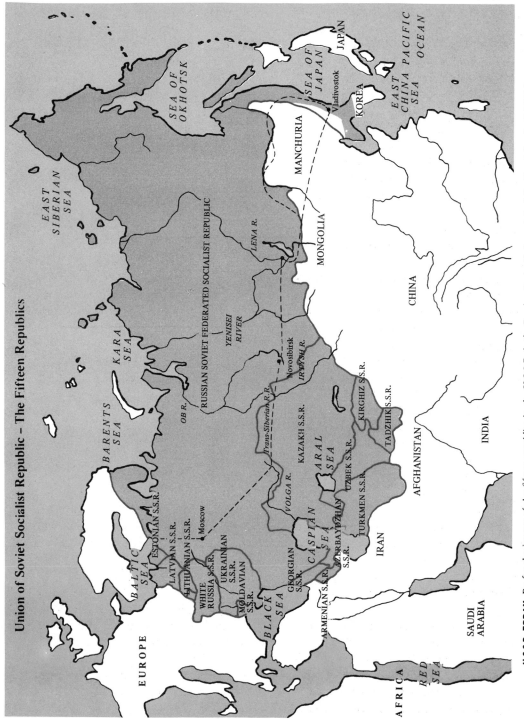

Union of Soviet Socialist Republic – The Fifteen Republics

EUROPE

AFRICA

BALTIC SEA

ESTONIAN S.S.R.

LATVIAN S.S.R.

LITHUANIAN S.S.R.

WHITE RUSSIA S.S.R.

UKRAINIAN S.S.R.

MOLDAVIAN S.S.R.

Moscow

BLACK SEA

GEORGIAN S.S.R.

ARMENIAN S.S.R.

AZERBAYDZHAN S.S.R.

CASPIAN SEA

RED SEA

SAUDI ARABIA

IRAN

TURKMEN S.S.R.

UZBEK S.S.R.

ARAL SEA

KAZAKH S.S.R.

VOLGA R.

AFGHANISTAN

INDIA

TADZHIK S.S.R.

KIRGHIZ S.S.R.

CHINA

OB R.

Trans-Siberian R.R.

IRTYSH R.

Novosibirsk

YENISEI RIVER

RUSSIAN SOVIET FEDERATED SOCIALIST REPUBLIC

LENA R.

MONGOLIA

MANCHURIA

KOREA

Vladivostok

JAPAN

SEA OF JAPAN

EAST CHINA SEA

PACIFIC OCEAN

SEA OF OKHOTSK

EAST SIBERIAN SEA

KARA SEA

BARENTS SEA

U.S.S.R. TODAY. By far the largest of the fifteen republics in the U.S.S.R. is the Russian Soviet Federated Socialist Republic, the R.S.F.S.R.

up as a private in the army when Italy declared war on the Central Powers. Mussolini
served with bravery for nearly two years until, having been wounded, he was sent home.
He resumed his newspaper work and organized a new party—the Fascist (*Fascisti*). The
party took as its emblem the old Roman
axe in a bundle of sticks called a *fasces,* a symbol of authority. Party members wore black
shirts. The first Fascists were mostly young
war veterans. Mussolini organized them,
trained them as a military force, and filled
them with enthusiasm for reviving the ancient greatness of Italy. The Black Shirts used
violence and threats of violence to intimidate
Communists and other opponents. During
1920 and 1921 Fascist bands fought nearly a
hundred skirmishes against groups of Communists and Socialists.

The march on Rome. The Fascist movement grew steadily. Mussolini drew to his
party increasing numbers of veterans who
wanted work, businessmen who feared communism, and patriots who wanted to end the
nation's weakness and confusion. The party
also contained gangsters and other undesir-

able persons who became Fascists as a cloak
for criminal activities. By October, 1922, the
Fascists controlled much of Italy. Mussolini
now believed that his party should take over
the government. "Either the Government will
be given to us," he proclaimed, "or we will
seize it by marching on Rome." He was not
speaking idly. When the cabinet ministers refused to give him full power, about fifty
thousand armed Fascists marched to the capital and occupied it without any real opposition. The cabinet resigned, and on October
29 King Victor Emmanuel III appointed
Mussolini as prime minister. The weak-kneed
parliament voted him dictatorial powers to
last until the end of 1923. He remained dictator for nearly twenty-two years.

The Fascist dictatorship. At first Mussolini
made few changes in the outward appearance
of the government. Victor Emmanuel III remained on his throne, and the Italian parliament continued to pass laws. Actually, Mussolini soon controlled every action of the government. He issued regulations having the
force of laws. He decided which topics parliament might debate. He appointed and dis-
charged government employees and commanded the armed forces. He even began to
appoint the officials of the towns and cities,
who had formerly been elected by the people.
Mussolini tried to suppress all criticism of his
regime. His opponents were beaten, imprisoned, or murdered. In 1926 he abolished all
political parties except his own. Newspapers
could print nothing that had not been approved by his officials. Teachers were dis-
charged and textbooks banned if they taught
anything contrary to "the healthful spirit of
Fascism." A force of secret police arrested
anti-Fascists and brought them to trial by
special military courts which meted out
speedy and drastic punishment. Mussolini
worked systematically to wipe out every trace
of democracy and liberalism in Italy.

Material progress under Fascism. Mussolini
devoted his great energy and organizing abil-

ity to the task of making Italy a strong, prosperous nation. To a certain extent he succeeded. He restored order by suppressing liberty. He borrowed money abroad for industrial and hydroelectric enterprises. His admirers boasted that he "made the trains run on time." The government provided work for the unemployed by increasing armament production and also by carrying on a program of public works, such as the construction of roads, power plants, and public buildings. The old trade unions were abolished. Laborers lost the right to strike, but they received small payments when unemployed, disabled, or on annual vacations. Workers who had been employed before Mussolini came to power worked longer hours and had a lower standard of living as a result of his policies;

workers who had been unemployed usually had work and therefore enjoyed a greater income under Mussolini. Farmers received some help also. Thousands of acres of swampland were drained and divided among landless peasants. Agricultural experts taught the farmers how to improve their crops and awarded prizes to the best farmers. In an effort to make Italy less dependent on imported food, Mussolini urged that more land be devoted to the growing of wheat. As a result, imports of grain were reduced 80 per cent. However, so much land and labor were devoted to "the battle of wheat" that olive and fruit production declined sharply. Businessmen probably profited most under Mussolini. He gave them loans for beginning new industries, and placed high tariffs on imports

MUSSOLINI, at the head of a military parade, goes to meet Hitler. At first the two men were rivals, especially since each sought to control Austria. Later they joined forces in the so-called Rome-Berlin Axis. For a time it appeared that they could not be stopped in their attempted conquest of Europe.

which would compete with Italian products. Industrial production rose. Mussolini also balanced the government budget, mainly by increasing taxes.

The Corporate State. Arguing that democracy, socialism, and capitalism had all failed, Mussolini constructed a new type of government—the Corporate State. In the Corporate State the Fascist party planned and controlled the life of the nation. Mussolini, of course, guided the planning. He decided, for instance, which industries should be expanded and which crops should be encouraged. Representatives of employers, of laborers, and of the government met together to make plans for reaching the goals Mussolini had set. In order to carry out the plans efficiently the producers of the country were organized into twenty-two "corporations." The laborers in each "corporation" banded together, and the employers formed a separate organization. Each group was led by Fascists or those acceptable to the Fascist party. Representatives of the employers met with representatives of the laborers to settle wage disputes and other problems, but there was nothing like genuine collective bargaining. If the two groups could not agree the dispute went before a court whose decision was final.

Mussolini's Corporate State combined features borrowed from capitalism, socialism, and the medieval guild system. In 1939 Mussolini wiped out the last trace of democracy in Italy by replacing the elected Chamber of Deputies with an appointed Chamber of Fasces and Corporations. The new chamber was made up of representatives of the Fascist party and the corporations. Mussolini presided at meetings of the chamber.

The Lateran Accord. One of Mussolini's achievements was the settlement of a long-standing dispute between the papacy and the Italian government. Government troops had seized Rome in 1870, and the city had then become the capital of Italy. The popes maintained that they were the rightful rulers of Rome and refused to recognize the government's action. Ever since 1870 each pope had remained within the Vatican as a "voluntary prisoner." In 1929 the pope and the Italian government signed three agreements known together as the "Lateran Accord." The Italian government agreed that the pope should rule the Vatican City (a new and entirely independent state of a little more than one hundred acres in Rome), and the pope recognized the right of the government to rule the rest of Rome. The Lateran Accord provided for compulsory religious training in Italian schools and settled many other questions.

Fascist militarism. Mussolini emphasized militarism as part of his program for making Italy the strongest state in the Mediterranean. Boys began their training at the age of six, when they entered semi-military organizations. As they grew older their military training received increasing emphasis. They wore uniforms, practiced marching and the use of weapons, and learned the principles of Fascism. Boys who made good records in the youth organizations could enter the Fascist party at the age of twenty-one. During their twenty-first year all young men began a period of compulsory military training in the armed forces. Once their training was completed, many joined the Fascist militia, a force of about 300,000 armed men maintained by the Fascist party. Others joined the regular army, navy, or air force. Mussolini did everything possible to transform the Italians into a warlike nation. In a characteristic statement he said: "War alone brings all human energies to their highest tension, and imprints a seal of nobility on the peoples who have the virtue to face it."

The Rise of Nazism in Germany

The German Revolution. In the years before World War I many German workingmen came to believe in the principles of socialism as taught by Karl Marx. They wished to abolish capitalism and set up a state in which the government owned the factories and other means of production. The socialists could not agree, however, on the *method* to be used in setting up a Socialist state. The radical socialists (Communists) favored the method of revolution. They would seize the property of the capitalists and set up a dictatorship controlled by the workers. The moderate socialists, on the other hand, wished to introduce socialism peacefully and above all, to preserve and strengthen democracy. They believed in majority rule, and therefore wanted socialism to begin only when the people had voted for it. Most of the German socialists were moderates, united in a political party called the Social Democrats. Before the war the Social Democrats provided the chief opposition in the *Reichstag* to militarism and autocracy in Germany, and in 1914 a bold minority of them opposed entry into the war. Germany's defeat in 1918 strengthened the hands of the Social Democrats. Many workers had suffered from the severe shortage of food and clothing during the war, while the well to do continued to live in comfort. The Germans who suffered remembered that the socialists had held the ruling classes responsible for war. As defeat loomed nearer in the closing months of the war, and it became clear that all the sacrifices had been in vain, great numbers of Germans grew dissatisfied. Even the famous discipline of the armed forces began to crack. In October, 1918, the sailors in the German fleet at Kiel refused to go to sea for a last desperate battle with the British navy. The mutiny at Kiel spread swiftly to other ports and touched off a revolutionary movement. Social Democratic leaders throughout Germany demanded that the kaiser abdicate. On the morning of November 9, large crowds of unarmed workers marched to the center of Berlin to ask that a republic be set up. The soldiers in the capital refused to fire on the workers; in fact, some of them joined the revolutionists. The kaiser then fled to Holland, where he remained for the rest of his life.

Creation of the German Republic. The kaiser's chancellor (prime minister) handed control of the government over to Friedrich Ebert, a leader of the Social Democrats. Ebert set up a temporary government composed of Socialists, which at once took steps to end the war. An armistice was signed on November 11. (See page 461.) Ebert and his associates then turned to the task of giving Germany a democratic, constitutional government. In January, 1919, they held elections in which the German people chose delegates to a national assembly. The assembly met at Weimar (the German Republic is therefore sometimes called the Weimar Republic) and began the task of writing a constitution. Before the constitution was finished the assembly received the Treaty of Versailles from the Allies. A large majority of the assembly delegates thought the treaty was too harsh. They protested especially against the "war guilt" clause. But when the Allies threatened to renew the war unless Germany signed the treaty, the assembly voted to sign. Thus those responsible for establishing the German Republic were made responsible for the acceptance of a harsh peace—a fact which later helped those who wished to abolish the republic.

In August, 1919, the new constitution went into effect. It provided for a genuinely democratic government, with universal suffrage and freedom of press and assembly. The president of the republic was elected by the people for a term of seven years. He appointed a cabinet which stayed in office as long as it was supported by a majority in the *Reichstag,* or lower house of the legislature. The people elected the *Reichstag* members. Members of the *Reichsrat,* or upper house, were appointed by the governments of the German states. The *Reichsrat,* however, had little power. A chancellor presided at cabinet meetings and held powers similar to those of the prime minister in England.

President von Hindenburg. Friedrich Ebert, the first president of the German Republic, died in 1925. He was succeeded by the national hero, Field Marshal Paul von Hindenburg. When World War I broke out Hindenburg was a retired army officer living on his estate in East Prussia. He returned to active service at the beginning of the war and rose to supreme command of the German armies. After the war he once more retired, only to be summoned back to public life by popular demand. The affection of the people for him was shown by his re-election in 1932, although he was then eighty-five years old. He died two years later.

Economic problems of postwar Germany. Germany faced staggering economic problems during the early days of the republic. Her foreign trade had practically disappeared, and many of her factories had closed down after the armistice. The German government spent a great deal of money to aid the suffering and unemployed. Reparations payments to the Allies put a further strain on the German treasury. Instead of trying to balance the budget by putting higher taxes on those who could pay, the government followed the easier practice of printing paper money. Each issue of new money drove the value of the mark downward, and caused prices of goods to rocket upward. In late 1923, at the height of the inflation, over four trillions of paper marks were needed to buy goods worth one dollar. As a result of the inflation the people of the middle class lost practically all their savings.

The republic nearly fails. In 1923 the German Republic came close to disaster. The government had asked the Allies for permission to halt reparations payments for three years, so that there would be time to settle the financial crisis at home. The French refused to agree and in January, 1923, French and Belgian troops entered the rich industrial district in the Ruhr Valley. The French announced that they would keep control of the Ruhr Valley until Germany began to make full reparations payments. Ruhr workmen refused to produce coal or iron for the French and lived on grants from the German government. The decline of production in the Ruhr crippled German industry, increased unemployment, and led to still more inflation. The crisis strengthened the hands of those who wished to overthrow the republic. The Communists grew in numbers, and so did nationalist parties who demanded a dictatorship or a return to monarchy. The government succeeded in putting down several revolts, the most famous being a *putsch* in Bavaria led by Adolf Hitler and other nationalists. Unless conditions improved, however, other revolts were sure to follow. By the fall of 1923 German leaders realized that they could save the republic only by putting an end to inflation and by co-operating with the Allies.

German recovery, 1924-1928. In November, 1923, the government finally checked inflation. It issued a new mark of the prewar value (4.2 to the dollar) and began to take the old marks out of circulation. At the same time the government balanced the budget. Under the new policy of reconciliation with the Allies, the German government ordered the Ruhr workers back to their jobs and indicated that it would try to pay reparations. Germany soon benefited from these actions. By the Dawes Plan of 1924 (see page 460) the Allies reduced Germany's reparations payments and provided loans. Aided by a sound currency, by the resumption of iron and coal production in the Ruhr, and by foreign loans, German industry prospered from 1924 to 1928. During these years Germany remained on friendly terms with her former foes. She joined the League of Nations and the World Court, and signed the Locarno pacts and the Kellogg-Briand Pact of Paris. (See pages 486 and 487.) By 1929 Germany had become a respected and prosperous member of the family of nations.

Effects of the depression on Germany, 1929-1933. The economic depression which began in the United States in 1929 and soon swept over the world brought severe hardships to the German people. Foreign trade declined, factories closed, and upwards of six million workers lost their jobs. Loans from abroad practically ceased, making it impossible for Germany to continue reparations payments. The government budget went out of balance once more as a growing number of unemployed people applied for aid. Millions of Germans reached the point where they would accept any program or leader offering hope of better times. Their despair made possible the dictatorship of Adolf Hitler.

Early life of Hitler. Adolf Hitler was born in Austria in 1889, the son of a customs inspector. Hitler's early years contained many failures and disappointments. His home life was unhappy, and at school he did good work only in drawing. When he applied for a scholarship to study art in Vienna, his application was rejected. His parents died while he was still in his teens, and he moved to Vienna, where he earned a bare living by doing odd jobs. In 1912 he went to Munich, Germany, and became a house painter. At the outbreak of World War I he volunteered for service in the German army; although he served for four years, he never rose above the rank of corporal. After the war Hitler returned to Munich. There he helped organize the National Socialist German Workers party (usually called the "Nazi" party). His ability as an organizer and his fiery speeches soon made Hitler the recognized leader of the new party.

The Nazi party. Like Mussolini's Fascists, Hitler's Nazis had a party uniform—brown shirts; an emblem—the swastika; and a salute (the Nazis used the Fascist salute of extended arm with palm out). Similarly, the Nazis copied the Fascist method of organizing a private party army which could attack or frighten opponents. The two parties stood for similar principles. Both glorified war, lauded dictatorship, stressed patriotism, denounced communism, scorned democracy, and held that the state should be supreme in all human affairs. In addition, Hitler made promises which would have particular appeal to Germans. He shouted that he would tear up the Treaty of Versailles, by which he meant that he would restore Germany's lost colonies and European territories and put an end to the hated "war guilt" clause. He would rearm Germany and restore her to the ranks of the great powers.

All Germans would prosper, he said, if they made him dictator. He told the Germans that they were a superior "race" whose defeat in the war and whose postwar troubles came from Jewish plotting—"the true creator of all suffering."

Hitler's words made a deep impression upon Germans who did little thinking. He attracted others who hoped to profit under a Nazi regime—for instance, a number of army men who expected him to revive militarism in Germany, and some industrialists who saw in him a bulwark against communism. In 1923 Hitler felt strong enough to attempt a revolt at Munich. The *putsch* failed, and Hitler served eight months of a five-year sentence. He spent his imprisonment in writing *Mein Kampf* (*My Battle*). This rambling account of his life and aims became the Bible of the Nazi movement. After leaving prison Hitler continued the work of building up his party. He united his followers on the basis of their hatreds—hatred of foreign countries; hatred of Communists, pacifists, and those who were held responsible for signing the peace treaties; above all, hatred of the Jews. As long as good times lasted Hitler made little progress.

The growth of Nazi power. After the depression set in at the end of 1929, millions of Germans became disgusted with the government for its failure to bring back prosperity. Some of them became Communists; many more joined the Nazis. By 1932 Hitler's followers formed the largest single party in Germany. Hitler then demanded that President Hindenburg make him chancellor. Hindenburg refused. Three chancellors held office in 1932, but each failed to muster a majority of votes in the *Reichstag*. The German government seemed close to collapse, and as a last resort the president decided to give Hitler the chancellorship.

In January, 1933, when Hitler became chancellor, he headed the largest party but not the majority party in the *Reichstag*. Since his position would be stronger if he could win a vote of confidence from the German people, he insisted upon holding new elections promptly. The Nazis threw all their energies into the pre-election campaign. Besides repeating their previous promises as an appeal to the voters, they used strong-arm methods to silence opposition speakers and newspapers. In Prussia, for instance, the police were ordered to "shoot first and inquire afterward." One night shortly before the election the *Reichstag* building caught fire. Although it is almost certain that they had set the blaze themselves, the Nazis promptly blamed the fire on the Communists.

Hitler becomes dictator. In the election the Nazis won 288 seats out of a total of 648 in the *Reichstag*. Hitler made sure of having a Nazi majority by refusing to allow the 81 Communist deputies to take their seats. The remaining deputies voted to give Hitler almost unlimited power for four years. The *Reichstag* then adjourned. Thus the dictatorship of Adolf Hitler replaced the government of the German Republic.

Hitler wipes out opposition. By swift and ruthless action Hitler paralyzed opposition to his policies. The Nazis outlawed all political parties except their own, abolished labor unions, and arrested, shot, or administered beatings to every person they suspected of working against Nazi rule. Even among Hitler's closest associates, the price of disloyalty to him was death. During the "Blood Purge" of June, 1934, a number of leading Nazis were shot by Hitler's command because they had disagreed with him. After the "Blood Purge" few Germans dared speak out against Hitler. Most Germans seem to have accepted his rule willingly; practically all the rest remained silent through dread of the secret police and the concentration camps. On the death of Hindenburg in 1934 Hitler at once assumed the powers of the president. He might have taken the title as well but he had no need of it, for he was the undisputed master of Germany. In a plebiscite held shortly after Hindenburg's death about 88 per cent of the voters indicated their support of Hitler's leadership.

Hitler's economic policies. Hitler aimed to make Germany self-sufficient. His government set production goals for both agriculture and industry. Imports into Germany were held to the barest minimum. Synthetic rubber and oil and other substitute raw materials and fuels were developed. To make control of business easier, the government dissolved many small corporations and reduced the power of stockholders in the remaining firms. Large corporations grew larger under the Nazis. For all practical purposes German banks became agencies of the government.

Hitler solved the unemployment problem in Germany by building public works and by rearmament. The construction of public buildings, dwellings for workers in slum areas, and a network of splendid highways put men to work. In 1935 Hitler began openly to make Germany an armed camp. Military conscription took millions out of the labor market. Other millions were needed to produce goods for the armed forces. It has been estimated that the rearmament program directly affected 60 per cent of Germany's industries. By 1938 unemployment had practically disappeared in Germany. Yet the workers of Germany, like those of Italy, had gained little if anything under dictatorship. Under the drive for rearmament the work week had been lengthened, wages had been held down despite the rising cost of living, and strikes had been forbidden. Grievances of the workers were laid before "labor trustees"—officials with judicial powers in the settlement of labor disputes. In exchange for their freedom the workers were given a voice in minor matters of plant management and cheap tickets for vacation travel. They were told that as Germans they belonged to a superior "race" and that their sacrifices would enable Germany to take her rightful place in world affairs.

Regimenting German youth. Hitler made every effort to attract German youth to his banner. The schools became centers of Nazi propaganda. At the age of ten boys and girls were enrolled in the organization known as "Hitler Youth." Their activities, songs, and slogans were designed to instill a fanatical patriotism. Boys were taught the duties of the soldier; girls were prepared for lives as wives and mothers in the new Germany. All learned to recite: "We believe on this earth solely in Adolf Hitler. . . . We believe that God has sent Adolf Hitler so that Germany may receive a foundation for its existence through all eternity. Adolf Hitler! Hail Victory!"

Persecution of the Jews. In their persecution of the Jews the Nazis reached the depths of inhumanity. Laws deprived the Jews of their rights as citizens, barred them from practically all business, professional, and political occupations, and forced them to pay special taxes. The hatreds which Hitler had so long been fanning burst into flame in the spring of 1933. While the police stood by, anti-Jewish mobs roamed the streets, committing deeds of violence which horrified people throughout the world. During the next five years upwards of half the Jews fled the country; among them were many of the leading scholars and scientists of Germany. In 1938 those who had been unable or unwilling to leave suffered from a new, carefully organized campaign of terror. The excuse was the murder of a minor German official by a young Jew. Hundreds of Jews were killed by mobs and thousands, less fortunate, were herded by police into concentration camps. The policy of Jewish persecution now changed to a policy of extermination. The Gestapo, or secret police, decided who should be put into the concentration camps. It held the power of life and death over those imprisoned. During World War II the prisoners included Jews from Germany and the conquered countries and many non-Jewish opponents of the Nazis. They were without sufficient food and had practically no medical care. When this treatment failed to produce death quickly enough, the prisoners were sent to special extermination camps, which operated during the years 1942–1944. Usually the Gestapo used gas to kill its victims in the murder factories. It is estimated that six million Jews were slaughtered by the Nazis in concentration camps and elsewhere.

Rearming Germany. Hitler never ceased to denounce the Treaty of Versailles for limiting Germany's military power. Soon after he became chancellor he began to arm Germany secretly. In 1935 he thrust pretense aside and armed in open violation of the treaty. In an amazingly short time "the little man with the funny mustache" became the head of an enormous military machine. Conscription provided millions of soldiers, German factories produced excellent arms, and the small

---

DUTIES OF NAZIS

The National Socialist commandments:
   The Führer is always right!
   Never go against discipline!
   Don't waste your time in idle chatter or in self-satisfying criticism, but take hold and do your work!
   Be proud but not arrogant!
   Let the program be your dogma. It demands of you the greatest devotion to the movement.
   You are a representative of the party; control your bearing and your manner accordingly! . . .
   Practice true comradeship and you will be a true socialist!
   Treat your racial comrades as you wish to be treated by them!
   In battle be hard and silent!
   Spirit is not unruliness!
   That which promotes the movement, Germany, and your people, is right!
   If you act according to these commandments, you are a true soldier of your Führer.

—Mosse, Cameron, Hill, and Petrovich, eds.,
Europe in Review.

---

army which had been permitted by the treaty had been used as a training school for a large number of officers. "Guns instead of butter" became the Nazi slogan. Herman Goering (gû'rĭng), one of Hitler's most able lieutenants, assumed the task of building up an air force with terrific striking power. In 1936 German troops occupied the demilitarized zone in the Rhineland, on the French frontier. When Hitler thus tore another clause from the Treaty of Versailles the democracies took no action against him.

Other Dictatorships in Europe

The spread of dictatorship. The dictators discussed above are the most famous, but by no means the only ones to appear in Europe after World War I. In country after country, by one method or another, new dictators rose to power. Together they represented a definite movement away from democracy. No two dictators had identical careers; to be understood they must be examined separately.

Political changes in Spain. Spain has never developed a large middle class. The mass of the people are very poor. Radical ideas attracted many workers during and after World War I, leading to demands for economic reforms and for a more democratic government. The prestige of King Alfonso XIII declined, especially after his army suffered a bad defeat by native tribes in Spanish Morocco in 1921. To save his throne the king gave dictatorial powers to General Primo de Rivera. De Rivera's regime (1923–1930) was efficient but unpopular. Finally he resigned and left Spain. King Alfonso restored the constitution in 1931 and permitted an election to fill local offices. Reformers won a sweeping victory and proclaimed a republic. King Alfonso then followed De Rivera into exile.

Under the new republic Spain experienced a number of changes. Church and state were separated, schools were secularized, and some

FRANCO AND HITLER meet at the Spanish-French frontier. German planes and Italian soldiers and supplies enabled Franco to overthrow the Spanish republic.

large estates were divided up among peasants. The government suppressed revolts by conservatives, who felt that reform had gone too far, and by radicals, who felt that reform had not gone far enough.

At an election in 1933 the Republicans were defeated and conservatives came into power. Church subsidies were in part restored. A repressive labor policy was adopted. To combat conservatives, the Republicans joined with the radicals in a so-called Popular Front. At an election in 1936 the Popular Front was victorious. This was the signal for civil war.

The Spanish civil war. General Francisco Franco led the Nationalists, as opponents of the republic were called. He was backed by much of the army, by monarchists and members of the aristocracy, and by many supporters of the Church. The Republicans, or Loyalists, drew their strength from the working class. Both sides received foreign aid, with Russian support for the Loyalist cause.

(See page 529.) Throughout the conflict Mussolini and Hitler aided Franco on a large scale. When Franco finally announced his victory, the war had lasted three years, taken a million lives, and devastated much of Spain. Franco set up a fascist-type dictatorship patterned after that of Mussolini. He restored to power the groups which had dominated Spain under the monarchy.

Fascism in Portugal. A republican government replaced the Portuguese monarchy in 1910. During the next sixteen years no less than eighteen revolts occurred, and forty ministries held power for varying lengths of time. A revolt in 1926 brought about the dictatorship of General Carmona. Although General Carmona continued to hold office as president, his powers gradually passed into the hands of Premier Salazar. In 1933 the voters adopted a constitution creating a Corporate State.

Austria, pawn of the powers. The republican government set up in Austria after World

War I had to deal with distress even greater than in Germany. Stripped of the lands formerly belonging to the Austro-Hungarian Empire, the new Austria was far too small to achieve prosperity. One third of its people lived in Vienna. The surrounding territory was not large enough to supply the wants of a great city or to furnish a market for its manufactures. Many Austrians believed that a union with Germany (*Anschluss*) was an economic necessity. The peace treaties forbade *Anschluss*. Economic conditions grew worse and by 1931 Austria was on the verge of collapse. When Austria asked the League of Nations to permit a customs union with Germany, the request was turned down.

After Hitler came to power in Germany, a strong Nazi movement rose in Austria. To maintain Austrian independence, Premier Dollfuss (dôl'foos) decided to rule by decree. He accepted Mussolini's support, which was given on condition that Austria become a Fascist state, that the Socialists be destroyed, and that Austria break with the League of Nations. Dollfuss launched a bloody attack on the Social Democrats and outlawed all political parties. He was murdered by a band of Austrian Nazis. Their bid for power had

been made too soon; Hitler was not yet ready to support them openly. Schuschnigg (shoōsh'nĭk), one of Dollfuss's associates, continued the dictatorship. After Hitler and Mussolini formed the Rome-Berlin Axis, Mussolini withdrew his support from Austria. Early in 1938 Hitler forced Schuschnigg to appoint a number of Nazis to the Austrian cabinet. A month later Schuschnigg was forced from office and Hitler's troops marched into Austria. The country then became a part of the new Germany.

Hungary. Like Austria, Hungary became an independent republic after the breakup of the Austro-Hungarian Empire. Communists ruled Hungary for a few months in 1919, but were forced to flee when a Rumanian army occupied most of the country. After the Rumanians withdrew, Admiral Horthy became head of an anti-Communist government (1920). A national assembly, elected the following year, voted to make Hungary a monarchy, with Horthy acting as regent until the Hapsburg king returned. The king returned twice in 1921; twice he was forced out by foreign pressure. Hungary thus remained a monarchy without a monarch, and Horthy continued to rule with dictatorial powers. During the 1930's he followed a policy of friendship with Germany and Italy, and as a result Hungary was rewarded with a good

VIENNA in the days of the Anschluss. Austrians decorated their shops with symbols and slogans welcoming Hitler. The poster reads, "The auto plants greet the Fuehrer."

deal of territory while the Axis dominated Europe.

Poland. Perhaps no country suffered more devastation than Poland from 1914 to 1918. In 1919 the impoverished country became an independent nation. A republican constitution went into effect in 1922, but so many parties arose that the government was unstable. A severe inflation led to economic chaos. The very existence of the nation was in doubt. At this juncture Marshal Pilsudski led a march on Warsaw and made himself dictator (1926). Pilsudski showed sympathy with Hitler and Mussolini. After Pilsudski's death in 1935, a constitution with Fascist features was adopted. The president was all-powerful and could even designate his successor.

Finland, Estonia, Latvia, and Lithuania. The independence of Finland, Lithuania, Latvia, and Estonia, which formerly belonged to Russia, was recognized by Russia in 1920. Situated between Germany and Russia, all four faced a difficult task in maintaining friendly relations with both countries. Finland led an attempt soon after World War I to establish a defensive bloc of the four Baltic states, but the effort came to nothing. All four established democratic governments and carried out the division of large estates. An enlightened dictatorship was established in Lithuania in 1926 and in Estonia and Latvia in 1934. The dictators claimed that they seized unconstitutional powers in order to prevent fighting between rival political groups. A pro-German government was set up in Finland in 1933. The dictator in Latvia was also pro-German. Estonia adopted a new constitution in 1937 and returned to democratic government.

Dictatorships in the Balkans. World War I left five states in the Balkans: Albania, Yugoslavia, Rumania, Bulgaria, and Greece. (Turkey also held some Balkan territory.) By the time World War II began all five of the nations were ruled by dictators. Because politics in the Balkans are traditionally complicated and turbulent we will take time to review only main events in the rise of Balkan strong men.

Albania. Little *Albania* became a republic in 1925. Zog, the first president, made himself king (1928) and ruled autocratically. Italian troops drove him out in 1939 and added Albania to the Italian Empire.

Yugoslavia. *Yugoslavia* was created in 1918 by bringing the Serbs, Croats, and Slovenes together under a limited monarchy. Parliamentary government worked badly because the various groups rarely agreed. In 1929 King Alexander proclaimed a dictatorship. After he was assassinated four years later, his powers passed to his brother, Prince Paul.

Rumania. During the 1920's *Rumania*, like Yugoslavia, was a parliamentary monarchy. By 1933 King Carol II had made himself dictator. He later abolished the constitution and set up a Corporate State.

Bulgaria. In *Bulgaria* soon after King Boris III came to the throne in 1918, a peasant party obtained control of the parliament. The peasant leaders used high-handed methods in suppressing opposition. In 1923 a middle-class revolt overthrew the peasant government and put a number of its members to death. Mid-dle-class rule fell before a conservative and Fascist *coup d'état* in 1934. Boris gradually took the reins of government into his own hands and steered his country away from the more extreme Fascist policies.

Greece. At the end of World War I *Greece*, with Allied approval and some Allied aid, sent troops to win Turkish territory inhabited by Greeks in Asia Minor. The fighting lasted for over two years and ended in disaster for the Greeks. King George II, never very popular with his subjects, received part of the blame for the defeat. He was deposed (1924) and Greece became a republic. The royalist party remained strong, however. In 1935 it executed a military *coup* and secured the return of George II. The next year he appointed General Metaxas as premier. Claiming that there was danger of a Communist uprising, Metaxas made himself dictator. He was friendly with the Axis powers until Italy invaded Albania.

BUDVA, YUGOSLAVIA, a picturesque old town on the Adriatic. After World War I Yugoslavia gained territory, but political unrest led to dictatorship.

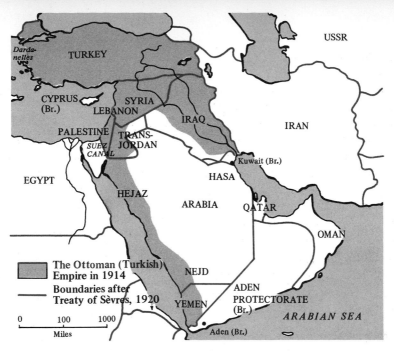

TERRITORIES LOST BY TURKEY AS A RESULT OF WORLD WAR I

Problems of the Middle East

Allied plans for Turkey. During World War I the Entente Powers made plans to dismember the Ottoman, or Turkish, Empire. Russia was to receive Constantinople and part of European Turkey; Great Britain, France, and Italy were each to receive part of Turkey in Asia. After the Russian Revolution the Allies had to revise their plans, for they did not want to see a Communist regime in control of the Straits (the waterway into the Black Sea). In 1920 the Allies finally agreed to the Treaty of Sèvres, by which Turkey was to lose nearly all her non-Turkish population. The Straits were to be controlled by an international commission.

The Turkish nationalists take charge. The sultan indicated his willingness to accept Allied terms. Angered by his attitude, Mustafa Kemal (mŏŏs′tä-fä kĕ-mäl′) and the Turkish nationalists organized a new government at Ankara. (Constantinople, the sultan's capital, was controlled by the Allies.) The nationalists succeeded in dividing the Allies by promising to give France and Italy investment privileges in Turkey. These two countries remained aloof when Mustafa Kemal struck back at the Greek army in Asia Minor and, as we have noted, drove it out of Turkey. The nationalists then deposed the sultan and declared Turkey a republic.

Treaty of Lausanne, 1923. Confronted by Turkish victories which their jealousies had made possible, the Allies consented to a new treaty. It was signed at Lausanne in 1923. The treaty and a number of separate agreements provided that no limit would be placed on the size of Turkey's armed forces. Unlike the other Central Powers, Turkey need not pay reparations to the Allies. Greeks living in Asia Minor were to be exchanged for Turks living in Greece, thus removing a possible cause of dispute in the future. A large transfer of population was subsequently carried out.

End of Turkish claims in Africa. The Turks renounced all claims to Egypt and the Sudan, which had been nominally a part of the Ottoman Empire although actually controlled by the British. Italy and France were also confirmed in their possession of former Turkish territory in North Africa.

Turkey under Mustafa Kemal. After World War I Mustafa Kemal was the national hero of Turkey. He had helped greatly to win the victory over the Allies at Gallipoli, had turned back the Greek invasion, and had secured favorable terms from the Allies at Lausanne. By a unanimous vote the national assembly elected him the first president of the Turkish Republic. Mustafa Kemal's policies were comparable to those of Peter the Great in Russia, for both set out to westernize their countries. Turkish women were freed from the harem, polygamy was abolished, church and state were separated, the solar calendar replaced the lunar calendar followed in Moslem lands, and the Latin alphabet replaced the cumbrous Arabic characters previously used. Education was encouraged, with the result that in ten years illiteracy was reduced by half.

MUSTAFA KEMAL

MUSTAFA KEMAL CHANGES TURKEY

. . . Then a law was passed forbidding the wearing of the fez. Here and there the law met silent resistance, but there was no open manifestation of it. A reform thought impossible had taken place simply and smoothly.

"Now we need a new law to do the same thing with the veils of women," Atatürk was told by his political friends.

"Oh no," he said. "You can't catch me doing that. When religious prejudice and men's jealousy over their women's faces being seen in public are coupled in this problem, it becomes most difficult to cope with. No legislation about veils! There is a natural law which will take care of it more easily than any written law. It is called 'fashion.'"

—Ahmed Emin Yalman, *Turkey in My Time.*

Mustafa Kemal sought to increase the wealth of Turkey. He rewarded farmers who made good use of their soil, and himself maintained a model farm. The government furnished most of the capital for building factories, railroads, and hydroelectric plants, and exercised general control over the nation's industries. Naturally Mustafa Kemal could not transform Turkey overnight, but he did succeed in giving better health to the "Sick Man," as his country had formerly been called. When he died in 1938 Ismet Inonu (ĭ-nû-nü′) was elected in his place. In general he followed the course Mustafa Kemal had set.

New Arab states. A number of new states, mostly Arab in population, arose out of the ruins of the Ottoman Empire. (The map on page 521 shows the new boundaries in the Middle East.) *Iraq,* at first a British mandate, received independence in 1932. The kingdom of *Saudi Arabia* includes most of the Arabian peninsula. Since it contains the Moslem holy cities of Mecca and Medina, the kingdom has an important place in the Arab world. *Syria* and *Lebanon,* on the Mediterranean coast, were held as mandates by the French until

World War II. *Palestine* and *Transjordan* also became new, predominantly Arab states.

Palestine. Palestine, just south of Syria, became a British mandate. By the Balfour Declaration of 1917 Great Britain expressed approval of "the establishment in Palestine of a national home for the Jewish people." Under this policy the British opened Palestine to Jewish immigrants, at the same time promising to protect the rights of the Arabs in Palestine. (Transjordan, included in the mandate for Palestine, was not opened to Jewish immigration.) When Jewish immigrants arrived in the "much promised" land, they applied modern methods to agriculture and industry, achieving remarkable results. The Arabs were at first not alarmed by Jewish immigration, since they outnumbered the Jews by eight to one and expected to remain in the majority. After 1933 Hitler's persecution of the Jews drove increasing numbers of them to seek refuge in Palestine. Immigration into Palestine jumped from five thousand a year to sixty thousand—a rate which, if continued for ten years, would make the Jewish population in Palestine equal to that of the Arabs. Arab guerrilla bands had made attacks on the Jews during the 1920's. After 1933 they stepped up their activities. Since the British were responsible for keeping the peace, they had to increase their garrisons. The British fought numerous skirmishes with the Arabs. No agreement could be reached on British proposals to divide the country between Jews and Arabs. Armed clashes of the two groups with each other and with the British became more frequent. The British found a temporary solution to the puzzle in Palestine by getting nearly all the Jews and Arabs to agree to cease fighting each other during World War II. (For postwar developments see page 625.)

Nationalism in Iran and Afghanistan. Persia, on the eastern border of Turkey, experienced a nationalist revival somewhat similar to Turkey's. Although Persia was theoretically an independent kingdom it had been divided into spheres of influence by Russia and Great Britain. (See page 428.) After the Russian Revolution the British took over Russian interests in Persia and exercised a general supervision over the country. In 1925 Riza Khan (rĭ-zä′ kän), leader of a patriot party, ousted the shah, or king, and took the title himself. He changed his name to Riza Shah Pahlevi (pă′lá-vē) and the name of his country to Iran. Under the new government Iran successfully asserted her independence. She won a much larger share of the profits made by British companies from the development of Iran's rich oil fields. While the Iranians were securing freedom from foreign control they went ahead with a program of modernization like that in Turkey.

Afghanistan, which lies between Iran and India, also put an end to British control (1922). The amir failed, however, to enlist the support of his Moslem subjects for his plan to westernize Afghanistan.

The Far East in Ferment

How India was governed to 1919. Throughout the early twentieth century the British Parliament continued to be the supreme authority over India. Policies decided upon in England were carried out by a viceroy who resided in India. Officials under his direction had charge of the various provinces which made up British India. These provinces included about two thirds of the country. The remaining third of India consisted of states ruled by native princes. The British rarely interfered in the government of the princely states. Two councils—the Executive Council and the Legislative Council—advised the viceroy. In some of the provinces there were councils to assist the British provincial officials. By the time World War I began the British were permitting Indians to hold some of the seats on the various councils.

MAHATMA GANDHI, who used passive resistance in winning India's freedom

Provision for partial self-government. World War I helped to bring partial self government to India. The people as a whole loyally supported Britain in the war, although many of them disliked British rule. About 1,300,000 men served overseas as soldiers or laborers, and nearly three quarters of a billion dollars was loaned for the war effort. In 1919, partly as a reward for aid during the war and partly as a means of quieting unrest, the British gave the people of India a greater share in their government. A legislature of two houses was created, and voters in British India were allowed to elect a majority of the members in each house. Since very few people were eligible to vote, and since the legislature could do little more than debate, India was still a long way from democracy in its central government. In the provincial governments greater changes appeared. The voters in each province elected at least 70 per cent of the members of a provincial legislative council, which had control of such matters as education and public health. British officials remained in charge of the provincial police, tax collection, and the courts, and thus had great influence.

Mahatma Gandhi. The new political arrangement was attacked from all sides. Government in the provinces was complicated by the division of authority between British and native officials, as the British admitted. The loudest complaints were made by the Indian nationalists, who wanted complete independence and found themselves little nearer to it. The movement for Indian independence crystallized around the personality of Mohandas K. Gandhi. A Hindu of good family, he studied law in London and for several years thereafter practiced his profession in South Africa. There he became prominent as a champion of the downtrodden Indians and other Asiatics who had settled in Cape Colony. Returning to India, Gandhi threw himself wholeheartedly into the movement for Indian home rule. His earnestness and sincerity, his ascetic life of prayer and fasting, and his eloquence soon made a deep impression on the unlettered people who listened to him. They thought of him as a saint and gave him the title of Mahatma, or Great Soul. Gandhi opposed the use of violence. He hoped to end British rule by a campaign of civil disobedience, or "nonviolent non-co-operation." His followers tried to avoid army service, shunned public offices, refused to pay taxes, and boycotted British goods. The ordinary methods of repression failed to stamp out this passive resistance. Whenever Gandhi was arrested he usually went on a hunger strike, forcing the British to free him for fear that his death would set all India aflame.

The constitution of 1935. After a number of conferences with Gandhi and other Indian leaders, the British announced a new constitution for India in 1935. The powers of the viceroy were reduced, those of the central legislature were increased, and government in the provinces was practically transferred to the Indians. These changes, substantial though they were, failed to satisfy the nationalists. They continued to agitate for "a united, free, democratic country."

It is a superstition and ungodly thing to believe that an act of a majority binds a minority. Many examples can be given in which acts of majorities will be found to have been wrong and those of minorities to have been right. All reforms owe their origin to the initiation of minorities in opposition to majorities. If among a band of robbers a knowledge of robbing is obligatory, is a pious man to accept the obligation? So long as the superstition that men should obey unjust laws exists, so long will their slavery exist. And a passive resister alone can remove such a superstition.

To use brute-force, to use gunpowder, is contrary to passive resistance, for it means that we want our opponent to do by force that which we desire but he does not. And if such a use of force is justifiable, surely he is entitled to do likewise by us. And so we should never come to an agreement. We may simply fancy, like the blind horse moving in a circle round a mill that we are making progress. Those who believe that they are not bound to obey laws which are repugnant to their conscience have only the remedy of passive resistance open to them. . . .

Passive resistance, that is, soul-force, is matchless. It is superior to the force of arms. How, then, can it be considered only a weapon of the weak? Physical-force men are strangers to the courage that is requisite in a passive resister. Do you believe that a coward can ever disobey a law that he dislikes? . . . But a passive resister will say he will not obey a law that is against his conscience, even though he may be blown to piece at the mouth of a cannon.

—William Theodore de Bary, ed.,
Sources of Indian Tradition.

The Dutch East Indies. A nationalist movement also threatened Dutch control of their highly valuable empire in the East Indies. In 1918 a Dutch East Indies parliament was created, with natives holding half the seats. Although the parliament could do little more than give advice to the Dutch governor general, he followed its wishes in most matters. Before World War II very few of the nationalists sought to win independence by revolt.

Independence for the Philippines. As they came to appreciate the benefits of rule by the United States, the Filipinos gradually forgot their bitterness at American conquest. Some actually came to favor a permanent American administration of the islands. Most Filipinos, however, never ceased to hope for the day when they would be set free. In 1934 the Congress of the United States promised the Philippines independence after a trial period —a pledge that was carried out on July 4, 1946. Some military bases in the islands have been retained by the United States.

Civil war in China. The Revolution of 1911–1912 freed China from rule by the Manchus, but not from the curse of civil strife. Ever since the imperial government fell, China has been kept in turmoil, because of the greed for power and plunder on the part of military leaders and governors, the activities of the Communists, and the raids of bandits. Dr. Sun Yat-sen, the revered leader of the revolution, governed only the south of China. When he died in 1925 his party (the Kuomintang, gwō'mĭn-täng') contained two factions. One group wished to improve the condition of the masses; it contained a number of Communists. The other group believed that the first need of China was a strong central government which could unite the country. Chiang Kai-shek led the second group. He won control of southern China, then conquered most of the north, and made himself virtual dictator. By the end of 1928 he appeared to be at the head of a united nation. Yet in reality China was as divided as ever. Under Chiang the common people were if anything worse off than before, and great numbers of them were easily converted to communism. The Communists beat off several military expeditions Chiang sent against them. In their search for a place of greater safety several hundred thousand made a remarkable march to northwest China in 1934. By that time the Japanese had conquered Manchuria in an undeclared war with China. Three years later

Chiang and the Communists agreed to cease fighting each other so as to present a united front against Japan. The wisdom of this decision soon became apparent, for in July, 1937, the Japanese began a campaign to conquer China.

Japan's urge to expand. Modern Japan has shown a decided tendency to expand her empire. The desire for more territory arose, in part, from the belief that the emperor was descended from the gods and had a "divine mission" to rule over all the East. A second cause for conquest was the pressure of economic conditions. As a secluded feudal nation Japan had been self-supporting; as a rising industrial nation she needed to import food and raw materials. Her population increased at the rate of nearly a million a year after World War I. Even with their best efforts the Japanese farmers and fishermen could scarcely

CHIANG KAI–SHEK REVIEWING TROOPS. Much of Chiang's early life was devoted to military affairs. After graduation from a Japanese military school he taught at a Chinese military academy. During the early 1920's he developed the army of the Kuomintang government.

supply the additional needs. Meanwhile new factories were increasing the need for more raw materials and markets. Military and business leaders of Japan found in these economic conditions good reasons for territorial expansion.

The Twenty-one Demands. Across the narrow Sea of Japan the coast of Asia seemed to beckon to Japan's expansionists. Before World War I they gained mastery of Korea and a sphere of influence in Manchuria. (See pages 432–433.) In 1915, while the western powers were occupied with World War I, the Japanese presented to China a list of Twenty-one Demands. Among other things the Chinese were asked to give the Japanese special economic privileges in Manchuria and China, and posts as advisers to the Chinese government. Refusal would have meant war. The Chinese government at Peking agreed to most of the demands.

A halt in Japanese expansion. Events combined to protect the Chinese from further demands during the 1920's. The Nine-Power Treaty signed at the Washington Arms Conference pledged the Pacific powers to respect China's independence. (See page 484.) By strengthening the Chinese government Chiang Kai-shek imposed a further barrier to Japanese aggression. Meanwhile, the Japanese were becoming less warlike. During the 1920's politicians representing the business interests controlled the government. Much to the disgust of the military leaders the government held fast to a peaceful foreign policy as the best means of promoting trade with other countries. Japan's prosperity during the 1920's showed that this policy was succeeding.

The depression hits Japan. To the Japanese, dependent as they were on foreign trade, the economic depression of the 1930's was a major catastrophe. All over the world people lost purchasing power. In an attempt to keep the domestic market entirely for domestic producers, nations raised tariff walls, thus reducing the market for Japanese goods. The Japa-

ENGLISH WORKERS COLLECTING DOLE. The dole gives unemployed people enough to keep alive, but results in loss of skills and self-respect. The dole is much less costly than government work projects, however.

nese closed many factories for lack of orders and laid up ships for lack of cargoes. As the expansionists saw it, there was only one solution to the economic crisis—military conquest. A group of hot-headed young patriots, mostly army officers, spread terror and death among officials who favored peace. Gradually the military leaders took over the government. During the 1930's they transformed Japan into a dictatorship, not unlike Nazi Germany and Fascist Italy. They suppressed all opposition, abolished political parties, preached a fanatical patriotism, and built a strong military machine. Aiming at the creation of a "New Order" in Asia, they launched Japan on a search for new conquests.

The British Empire in Transition

The world's largest empire. World War I, resulting in the capture or destruction of most of the German fleet, confirmed Great Britain's position as mistress of the seas. Her fleet was the largest in the world, and her naval bases dominated nearly all the great trade routes. The United Kingdom (England, Scotland, Wales, and Ireland) was the center of an empire which included approximately one fourth of the habitable area of the globe and

one fourth of the world's population. No such wide dominion had ever been built up before, either in ancient or in medieval times. All the races of man, all stages of culture from savagery to civilization, all the principal religions, and nearly all the principal languages of mankind were represented within the British Empire.

England after World War I. Shortly after the close of World War I an economic decline began in England. Her prosperity, like that of Japan, depended chiefly upon foreign trade. But England, having been the first nation to become industrialized, used many machines and methods which were now out of date. Countries with more efficient production methods, such as Japan and the United States, sold goods for a lower price and took markets away from England. Furthermore, many of England's customers in Europe were impoverished by World War I. The loss of foreign trade was reflected in England's unemployment figures, which rose to one million in 1920 and to more than three million in 1932. The government gave the unemployed a "dole," or small payment which would enable them to keep alive. Because of the extra burden on the treasury, taxes, especially those on incomes, were raised to a high level. In an effort to increase employment England

IRELAND SINCE 1922. The Republic of Ireland was originally called Eire. Northern Ireland continues to be part of the United Kingdom, which also includes England, Wales, and Scotland.

Divisions of the British Empire. The British Empire emerged from World War I as a complex organization of many types of government. It consisted of (1) the United Kingdom, (2) India, (3) protectorates and spheres of influence, (4) the Crown colonies, and (5) the dominions. Each part of the empire was controlled to some extent by the British Parliament. As we shall see, Parliament's authority over the empire tended to decline after the war.

Ireland becomes Eire. For centuries the Irish were unhappy under British rule. In 1801 the separate Irish parliament was abolished and Ireland now sent representatives to the British Parliament. This change brought no lessening of Irish agitation against the Anglican Church, British landlords, and the union of Ireland with England. During World War I members of the Sinn Fein (shĭn′ fān) party occupied some public buildings in Dublin and proclaimed a republic. (The words "Sinn Fein" are Irish for "we ourselves.") The revolt in Dublin was soon suppressed by British troops, but for several years fighting persisted in other parts of Ireland.

In 1921 the British agreed to the creation of the Irish Free State. The Free State was given dominion status, like that of Canada. Ulster, the northern and Protestant part of Ireland, refused to join the Free State and continued to send representatives to the British Parliament. Nationalists in the Free State, demanding complete separation from England, carried on a bitter struggle against the settlement of 1922. They won most of their demands in 1937 when a new constitution was adopted. The constitution was a virtual declaration of Irish independence. Under it the Irish Free State became a republic with the name of "Eire" (â′rĕ), the Gaelic word for Ireland. In 1949 an act of the British Parliament separated Eire from the Commonwealth of Nations and proclaimed it the Republic of Ireland.

abandoned its traditional policy of free trade and put a tariff on imports which competed with English products. In 1932, at the Imperial Economic Conference in Ottawa, a tariff wall was erected around the whole British Empire.

One of the most significant political changes in England was the growth of the Labor, or Socialist, party. It urged that the coal mines, the transportation system, and some industries be taken over by the government. Leaders of the Labor party emphasized their belief in democracy and said that their aim was a peaceful change to a partly socialized economy. Although it had been organized only a few years before the war, the Labor party grew rapidly until by 1922 it had become the second largest party in England. The Conservative party held its own, controlling the government during most of the 1920's and 1930's, while many Liberals swung over to the Labor party. Another significant shift in politics came when women received the right to vote. So many men had been lost in the war that women voters outnumbered the men by nearly a million and a half.

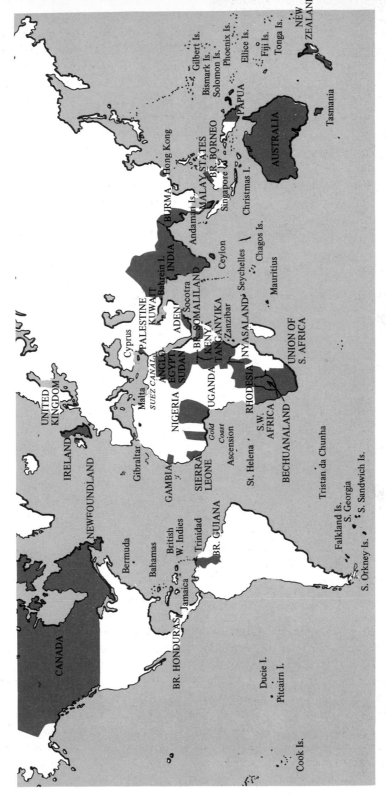

THE BRITISH EMPIRE AND COMMONWEALTH IN 1939

Protectorates, spheres of influence, and mandates. Great Britain's hold over her protectorates also tended to relax. As we have seen, Egypt was allowed almost complete freedom in 1922 (see page 423), although the British stayed in the Anglo-Egyptian Sudan. Meanwhile, Iran and Afghanistan asserted their independence and thus ceased to be British spheres of influence. (See page 523.) A nationalist movement in India also reduced British authority there. With the exception of Iraq, which became independent in 1932, Great Britain retained the mandates granted to her by the Allied powers until World War II began. In the South Pacific, New Zealand and Australia governed former German possessions.

The Crown colonies were the most numerous of the British possessions, for example, Gibraltar, the Bahama Islands, and British Guiana. Each had a governor appointed by the British government. In some of the Crown colonies the colonists elected a council to assist the governor, as was the practice in some American colonies before the Revolution.

The Statute of Westminster, 1931. Because of her contribution to victory, Canada demanded that her representatives be granted seats at the Paris Peace Conference in 1919. The British agreed, and gave the same right to the other dominions. Thus the dominions, already self-governing in domestic matters, became equal partners with Great Britain in foreign affairs. In 1931 the Statute of Westminster set forth definitely the position of the dominions. They were described as self-governing communities, "united by a common allegiance to the Crown, and freely associated as members of the British Commonwealth of Nations. Every self-governing member of the Empire is master of its destiny. In fact, if not always in form, it is subject to no compulsion whatever." Each of the dominions is bound to the British Commonwealth of Nations by no more than allegiance to the British sovereign.

France after World War I

The problem of reconstruction. The French people paid dearly for their victory in World War I. They suffered 5,300,000 casualties in battle, and the destruction of one quarter of their productive property, such as factories, mines, and livestock. The government promised to restore the property losses of its citizens, and expected Germany to foot the bill through reparations payments. Although the payments Germany actually made amounted to no more than a quarter of the expense involved, the French government managed to rebuild most of the devastated area within a few years.

Economic problems. The French government borrowed a great deal of money for use in the war and in reconstruction. On paper the French foreign debts were nearly balanced by the loans France made to her allies, especially to Russia and Belgium. After the war the Soviets repudiated the czarist debts. Belgium was unable to pay her debt to France because of the devastation she had suffered.

The French were therefore caught between the demands of their creditors and the default of their debtors. For a time it appeared that the French franc would suffer the fate of the German mark and lose all its value. By heroic efforts, however, the government managed to stabilize the franc in 1926 at about 20 per cent of its prewar value. This meant that Frenchmen who held government bonds lost about 80 per cent of their investment. During the financial storms of the 1930's the franc was further devaluated. Unemployment did not become as serious a problem in France as in a number of other countries, partly because cheapening the franc made it easier for foreign consumers to buy French goods. During the depression the French adopted for workers a comprehensive system of social insurance which provided benefits for sickness, injury, retirement, and other needs.

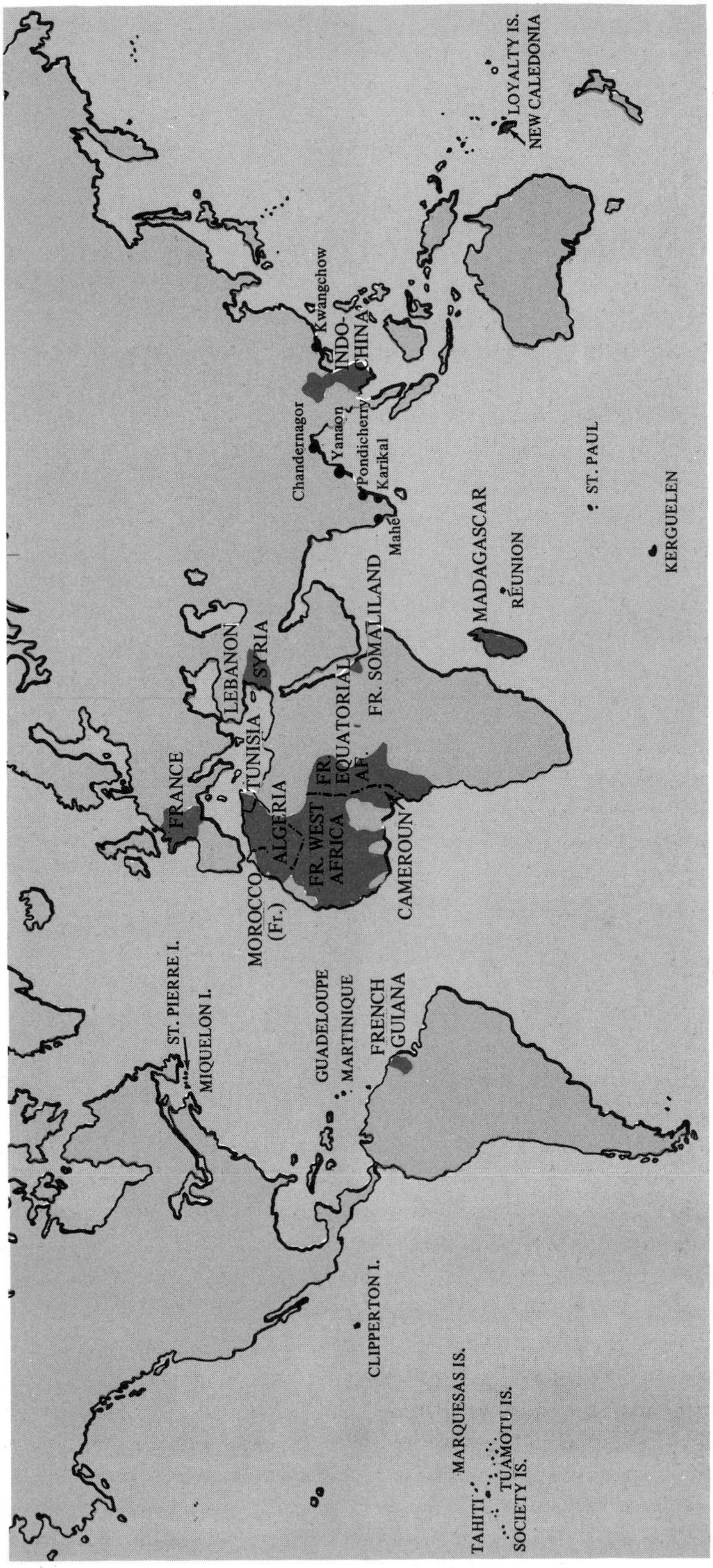

THE FRENCH EMPIRE IN 1939

LOYALTY IS.
NEW CALEDONIA

Kwangchow
INDO-
CHINA

Chandernagor
Yanaon
Pondicherry
Karikal
Mahé

ST. PAUL

KERGUELEN

MADAGASCAR
RÉUNION

FRANCE
LEBANON
SYRIA
TUNISIA
ALGERIA
MOROCCO
(Fr.)
FR. WEST
AFRICA
FR.
EQUATORIAL
AF.
FR. SOMALILAND
CAMEROUN

ST. PIERRE I.
MIQUELON I.

GUADELOUPE
MARTINIQUE
FRENCH
GUIANA

CLIPPERTON I.

MARQUESAS IS.
TUAMOTU IS.
TAHITI
SOCIETY IS.

THE WORLD BETWEEN TWO WARS

... that General Gamelin had settled down into the certainties of what may be called the *Credo* of the Maginot Line. Here are the central articles of this faith:

... Men defending fieldworks can hold out against an offensive, even if they are outnumbered three to one, or if the attack is carried out with bombers and tanks in massive quantities. This is even more true of the defense of concrete and steel fortifications. ...

The French Command was well aware that tanks would be launched against our lines in a density of one hundred units to the kilometer . . . But this avalanche of steel did not worry the High Command. Besides, they ignored that there was such a thing as air artillery which was to work in conjunction with fortresses on wheels. . . .

. . . Besides, the Maginot Line has replaced the fieldworks of twenty-five years ago. These works were continuous; the Maginot Line is not only continuous, it has a strength far above anything we have ever seen. . . .

—Pertinax, *The Gravediggers of France.*

The search for security. With memories of two wars with Germany fought on their soil in one generation, the French sought anxiously for security against another invasion. For more than a decade after World War I they maintained the largest standing army in Europe. Their statesmen signed treaties of alliance with a number of other countries (Poland, Czechoslovakia, Rumania, Yugoslavia) and helped draw up the pacts outlawing war. (See page 487.) For additional protection the French built the Maginot Line, a costly and complicated defense system stretching along the Franco-German frontier. The French overestimated the value of the Maginot Line and therefore failed to keep their army and military equipment up to date.

The French Empire. The French, with an empire second in size only to that of the British (see map, page 515), sought to preserve and to strengthen the ties which bound the colonies to France. French colonial officials in Africa were encouraged to treat the natives as equals and to give them administrative

A MAGINOT LINE installation. It was never used.

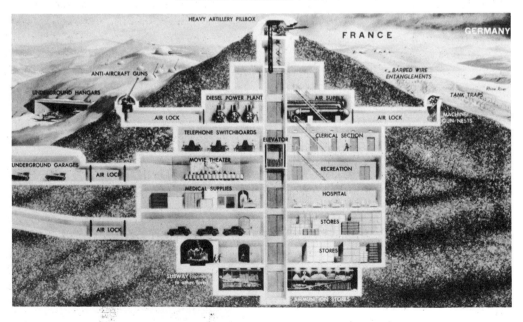

posts whenever possible. Algeria was made a part of France and its representatives were given seats in the parliament at Paris. By their generally fair treatment the French won the friendship of most of their colonial subjects in Africa, the chief exception occurring in French Morocco. Here the Riff tribes set up an independent state, and a costly war (1925–1926) was necessary to subdue them. The French also had difficulty in keeping the upper hand in Syria. In putting down Arab revolts they used strong measures, including two bombings of Damascus. French policy in Syria was criticized by the Mandates Commission of the League of Nations. French Indo-China in the Far East ranked first in population and second in size of all the French colonies. Here too there were demands for self-government, at least in local matters. The French made only a few concessions to the native people and put down uprisings by force.

The American Republics between Wars

The "dizzy twenties" in the United States. After World War I the United States tried to turn its back on the world. Most Americans were tired of the anxieties and sacrifices of wartime and showed little interest in President Wilson's program for peace abroad or reform at home. They desired to return to what President Harding called "normalcy." Many bent their efforts as never before to the making and spending of money. A period of reckless speculation set in. The hope of getting something for little or nothing became a craze. People risked their money to gamble in real estate and industrial stocks, which boomed to unheard-of price levels. Spurred by high-pressure advertising and installment buying, many families bought comforts and luxuries beyond their means. Business prospered and grew bigger. The government gave it every encouragement. Presidents Harding,

Coolidge, and Hoover believed that the government should not interfere with business but should give it friendly help. Hence the antitrust laws were not enforced; industry was protected against foreign competition by higher and higher tariffs (see page 335); a greater share of the tax burden was shifted from the shoulders of the rich to those of the middle and low income groups; and Congress voted generous subsidies to aviation companies and shipowners.

Depression hits the United States. Events soon showed that the prosperity of the twenties was built on sand. The optimistic talk about "a chicken in every pot and two cars in every garage" was misleading. The general business prosperity did not reach to the farmers or to all groups of workingmen. From the mid-twenties onward farm income dropped steadily. Europe no longer needed so much of our food, and our export market fell off. High tariffs also damaged our foreign trade. Moreover, the earnings of many wage earners lagged behind the rising prices. Most people disregarded these danger signals. Then, with a rude suddenness, the bubble burst in October, 1929. Stock prices tumbled until by the end of the year stockholders had lost forty billion dollars. The stock market crash was the beginning of the worst and longest business depression in history. It soon spread to the whole world. Banks collapsed, business houses and factories closed, millions were thrown out of work, and foreign trade came almost to a standstill. Once more the business cycle had reached its low point. (See page 337.)

The New Deal. Under Herbert Hoover the government for the first time in American history took steps to stem the tide of depression. In 1933, when Franklin D. Roosevelt was inaugurated president, the attack on the depression became much broader. By that time the economy of the United States seemed to be on the brink of ruin. President Roosevelt proposed to give the country a "New

Deal," consisting of bold measures designed both for recovery and for long-range reform. To revive business and furnish employment, the New Deal embarked upon a vast program of government lending and spending. This was called "priming the pump." Besides pump priming, the government increased its control over business and enacted much social legislation. (See page 338.)

The New Deal marked a break with the past in the United States. It cast aside some ideas of laissez faire and introduced ideas of social welfare, wherein the state tries to regulate economic affairs in order to bring security to the whole population. The voters continued to approve the New Deal. President Roosevelt was re-elected in 1936, and in 1940 he shattered the two-term tradition by being elected a third time. In 1944 during World War II, President Roosevelt won an unprecedented fourth term in office.

Between isolation and international co-operation. Between 1918 and 1940 the foreign policy of the United States followed a wavy path. It moved unsteadily between isolation from the rest of the world and co-operation with it. On the one hand, we refused to join the League of Nations and the World Court; we erected high tariff walls; we nearly cut off immigration; and we insisted that the hard-pressed Europeans pay us their war debts. (See pages 335, 469, 474.) President Roosevelt killed the London Economic Conference of 1933, which had met to deal with world money problems. Moreover, as war clouds gathered in Europe during the 1930's, Congress tried to keep trouble at arm's length by passing the Neutrality Acts of 1935 and 1937. These prohibited the sale of munitions and the lending of money to any nation at war. The President could also forbid the sale of important raw materials to warring countries unless they paid cash and carried the goods away in non-American ships. The neutrality legislation was based on the popular belief that our entry into World War I had

been a blunder. It was thought that we might avoid repeating such a mistake by giving up our neutral rights in wartime.

On the other hand, the United States took some steps in the direction of co-operation with other nations. We have already noted the part played by our government in the Washington and London Naval Conferences (1921, 1930), the Pact of Paris to outlaw war (1928), the General Disarmament Conference of the League of Nations (1932–1934), and in the reduction of tariffs through the Reciprocal Trade Agreements Act (1934). (See pages 335, 484, 486.) The United States also joined with the League of Nations in condemning Japan's invasion of Manchuria in 1931. (See page 542.) In the late 1930's the aggressive actions of the Axis powers in Europe and in Asia alarmed some Americans. They began to feel unsafe behind the isolationist wall. In October, 1937, at Chicago, President Roosevelt denounced aggressors and proposed to "quarantine" them. He named no names, but obviously he referred to Japan, Germany, and Italy. When Hitler's mechanized divisions swept into Poland on September 1, 1930, it became clear that isolation and neutrality could no longer safeguard the United States. In November, 1939, Congress repealed the arms embargo and permitted trade with warring powers on a cash-and-carry basis. This favored the countries with whom we sympathized—France and Great Britain. The policy of isolationism had proved unworkable.

The policy of the "Good Neighbor." The greatest contribution of the United States to international co-operation was the Good Neighbor policy, which flowered under President Franklin D. Roosevelt. It marked a complete turnabout in our relations with Latin America. From about the beginning of the twentieth century until the Good Neighbor policy was adopted, the United States had assumed a "big brother" attitude toward its southern neighbors. In the name of the Mon-

THE QUINTET, by Emilio Pettoruti of Argentina.

roe Doctrine and in order to protect American investments, we had intervened time and again in the countries around the Caribbean. (See page 437.) We had tried to keep order and to make weak governments pay their debts. This policy increased Latin American distrust and fear of the "Colossus of the North."

In the late 1920's we began to change our policy. Our relations with Mexico improved under the sympathetic guidance of Ambassador Dwight Morrow. We withdrew our marines from the Dominican Republic (1924) and Nicaragua (1933). In 1930 our State Department announced that the Monroe Doctrine did not justify armed intervention in the internal affairs of Latin American republics.

The most important changes, however, came after Franklin D. Roosevelt became president. In his first inaugural address (1933) he said: "I would dedicate this nation to the policy of the good neighbor." Soon after, at the Seventh Inter-American Conference in Montevideo, Uruguay, Secretary of State Hull signed an agreement for the United States declaring: "No state has the right to intervene in the internal or external affairs

of another." The Latin Americans were pleased, but wondered if we meant what we said. They soon found that we did. In 1934 we gave up our protectorate over Cuba and took our occupation force out of Haiti. In 1936 we signed a treaty that gave Panama its way on most matters relating to the Canal Zone. Meanwhile, Secretary Hull negotiated a number of trade agreements which improved our commercial relations with Latin American countries. The United States also took steps to promote a better knowledge and understanding among the American republics. In 1938 the Department of State set up a Division of Cultural Relations, and in 1940 an independent government agency, the Office of Inter-American Affairs, was established.

We share the Monroe Doctrine. The Good Neighbor policy helped bring the American republics into a close partnership to deal with the menacing signs of approaching war. In 1936 President Roosevelt called a special Inter-American Conference for the Maintenance of Peace. It met at Buenos Aires. There the delegates agreed that a threat to the peace and safety of any one of the American republics was the concern of all. They pledged themselves to consult one another on measures for dealing with such a threat. This agreement was a milestone in inter-American relations. It is said to have "continentalized" the Monroe Doctrine. In other words, the United States would henceforth share the responsibility for defending the hemisphere with the other American states. Thus the Monroe Doctrine was changed from a purely United States policy into an inter-American policy.

Hemisphere solidarity. The need for a solid front against threats to American security became increasingly clear. After 1933 Nazi Germany was a serious menace to the Americas. Her secret agents tried to stir up fear and distrust of the United States and to destroy faith in democracy. They also took steps to gain economic and eventually military control of the Latin American countries. In the face of this danger, the Eighth International Conference of American States, meeting at Lima in 1938, reaffirmed the "continental solidarity" of the American nations. It also provided for emergency meetings of the foreign ministers.

When World War II broke out in Europe in 1939, inter-American co-operation stood the test. Special meetings of the foreign ministers at Panama (1939) and at Havana (1940) speedily reached agreement on establishing an inter-American neutrality zone and on measures to forestall Nazi seizure of French and Dutch colonies in America. The Panama conference also set up the Inter-American Financial and Economic Advisory Committee. This committee made plans to help the Latin American countries out of the distress that resulted from their wartime loss of European markets. The United States government aided its neighbors to the south by lending them money for industrial development and by sending them defense materials under the Lend-Lease Act. (See page 553.)

The Rio Conference of 1942. The severest test of inter-American co-operation came in December, 1941, when the Japanese launched their surprise attack against the United States at Pearl Harbor. Would the American republics demonstrate their solidarity by taking common action against the aggressors? In

SOUTH AMERICAN INDUSTRY. Crude copper is being molded into "pigs" at a Chilean smelter. Chile is the second largest producer of copper, the United States ranking first.

January, 1942, the special conference of foreign ministers at Rio de Janeiro gave the answer. It recommended that all the American states should break off diplomatic relations with the Axis powers. Ezéquiel Padilla (pä-dē'yä), Mexican foreign minister, made a stirring appeal for support of the United States. He said: "Let us stand together as one solid block against those who would divide and conquer us." Within a short time all the republics except Argentina and Chile had cut off relations with the Axis. Before the end of World War II all twenty Latin American states had declared war. (In contrast, only eight entered World War I.) The Rio conference also organized committees to decide on measures for common defense. Soon the United States was given the right to use strategic bases in most countries of Latin America. The Good Neighbor policy had paid off handsomely.

Latin American progress between wars. In domestic as well as in foreign affairs Latin America moved in new directions. In the years between the two world wars two developments stand out: (1) the beginnings of industrialization, and (2) the struggle of the submerged masses (mostly Indians and mestizos) for political and economic democracy.

Industrial advance. The establishment of industries was an uphill fight. Latin America had always been shackled to a "colonial economy," that is, an economic system based on the production of raw materials and the purchase of finished goods from abroad. Sparse population, a lack of capital, and a lack of skilled workers hindered industrial growth. World War I led to the first big step forward. With much of their European trade cut off by the war, our southern neighbors could no longer get the manufactured goods they needed. They began to make many articles themselves—chiefly textiles, leather products, processed foods, and other light consumers' goods. Argentina, Brazil, Chile, and Mexico experienced the greatest industrial development. However, only in Brazil and Argentina did the value of industrial products equal or surpass the value of agricultural products.

Growth of democracy in the 1920's. Until the depression of the 1930's, the trend toward democracy went hand in hand with the trend toward industrialization. Liberal governments sprang up in a number of republics. They tried to introduce some far-reaching economic reforms, for the people wanted bread as much as liberty. The depression upset the political applecart. People chafed under hard times and blamed those in power. Thirteen governments were overthrown. They were replaced by new ones of various complexions.

Dictatorships in Brazil and Argentina. In 1930 Getulio Vargas became Brazil's first long-term dictator, although a benevolent one. He was ousted in 1945, but was returned to office in a free election in 1951. He took his own life without completing his term. In Argentina, the "radical" government of Irigoyen was turned out in 1930. The large landholders then installed a conservative regime. It continued in power until 1943 when a military *coup d'état* brought a new kind of dictatorship to Latin America. The new regime gradually took on the earmarks of European fascism. After a series of behind-the-scenes struggles for power among the leaders, Juan Perón, an army colonel, established himself firmly as dictator. In 1946 he was legally elected to the presidency, with the support of large numbers of workingmen. In 1955, a group of army officers forced Perón out of office. He was compelled to leave the country.

Social reform in Mexico and other countries. On the other hand, Mexico, Chile, Colombia, Cuba, Peru, and Venezuela moved in the direction of more democracy and social reform. Mexico's revolution, which started in 1910, reached its peak during the term of President Cárdenas (1934–1940).

IRRIGATION FARMING IN MEXICO. Some farmers prefer to use mules for cotton cultivation because they believe that tractors pack down the earth, resulting in a poorer crop.

THE TWO LATIN AMERICAS

There are two Americas: the visible and the invisible. The visible America, the America of presidents and embassies, expresses itself through official organs, through a controlled press. This America takes its seat at the conference table of the Pan American Union and has many votes in the United Nations. And there is the mute, repressed America, which is a vast reservoir of revolution. Both Americas are misleading in appearance.

Under its dictatorial regimes, visible America makes fervent protestations of its democratic faith, signs charters of liberties, manufacturing one line of goods for foreign and another for domestic consumption. This double personality has achieved a dexterity that is almost unbelievable. Even though everywhere and in all periods of history there has been something of this same split between what is said and what is done, the contrast has rarely been so brutal as that afforded by the Latin American dictatorships. . . .

Like visible America, invisible America lives. The humble folk know that they cannot say what they think, and the upper classes have learned this too . . . In invisible America, where a vast mass of the population lives with the cold breath of terror on its neck, the least word may bring reprisals. The part of prudence is to keep quiet, to wear a mask. Where machine guns have the floor a deep silence reigns. Life goes on under the cover of conventional phrases, lip-service, extorted votes . . . Nobody knows exactly what these 150,000,000 [now] silent men and women think, feel, dream, or await in the depths of their being . . .

—Germain Arciniegas, *The State of Latin America.*

The government continued its distribution of land to the peasant farmers, took over the foreign oil properties, passed laws to protect the laborer, established many new schools in a vigorous campaign against illiteracy, and encouraged industrialization. Cárdenas's successors, Camacho and Alemán, were less ardent reformers. They followed a middle-of-the-road policy. Mexico stands out as one of the most progressive of the Latin American republics.

Looking back on the chapter. As we look back at the events discussed in this chapter, we can see at least three important trends in world affairs during the 1920's and 1930's. First was the widespread demand for freedom by people who wanted a government of their own choosing. This demand led (1) to the setting up of republics in most of Europe and (2) to colonial independence movements. A second trend was toward more regulation by governments of the economic activities of their citizens. In the democracies as well as in the dictatorships the state increased its supervision over agriculture, industry, and labor, especially during the depression years. A third trend was the growing reliance on force as a means of solving problems. Dictators, who substituted decrees for debate, arose in countries which had little democratic experience. Having used force successfully against their opponents at home, some dictators were encouraged to try the same approach to international relations. We shall see the results of their actions in the next chapter.

REVIEWING THE CHAPTER

TERMS TO UNDERSTAND: *soviet, Bolshevik, Treaty of Brest-Litovsk, kulak, collectivism, party line, fascism, Corporate State, Lateran Accord, Weimar Republic*, Mein Kampf, *Nazi*, Anschluss, *Twenty-one Demands, dole, Sinn Fein, Maginot Line, Good Neighbor policy.*

PERSONS TO IDENTIFY: *Kerensky, Lenin, Trotsky, Stalin, Litvinov, Mussolini, Victor Emmanuel III, Ebert, Hitler, Goering, De Rivera, Franco, Salazar, Dollfuss, Schuschnigg, Horthy, Pilsudski, Carol II, Boris III, Metaxas, Mustafa Kemal, Mahatma Gandhi, Chiang Kai-shek, Franklin D. Roosevelt, Vargas, Perón, Cárdenas.*

QUESTIONS TO ANSWER

1. (a) Name and locate the new states which arose in Europe after World War I. (b) Why were many Europeans willing to exchange democratic government for dictatorship?

2. (a) Why was the rule of the czar overthrown in Russia? (b) Why did the Kerensky government fall? (c) Describe the policies of Lenin. (d) What changes were made by the Five-Year Plans in Russian industry? In agriculture? (e) Contrast the Soviet and American ideas of democracy. (f) What have been the policies of the Soviet Union in regard to education? Religion? Foreign relations (to 1939)?

3. (a) Trace the rise of Mussolini to power in Italy. (b) By what methods did he govern? (c) Describe the Fascist Corporate State.

4. (a) Describe the founding of the German Republic. (b) What problems confronted the German Republic in its early years?

(c) Why did Germany first recover and then lose its prosperity? (d) In what ways was Hitler's program similar to that of Mussolini? (e) Tell how Hitler carried out his policies of economic control. Of persecution of the Jews. Of rearming.

5. (a) What changes were made when Spain became a republic? (b) How was the Spanish Republic overthrown? (c) Describe the movement toward dictatorship in Austria. Poland. Yugoslavia. Bulgaria. Greece.

6. (a) In what ways did Mustafa Kemal seek to modernize Turkey? (b) What states arose from former Turkish territory?

7. (a) Describe progress toward self-government after World War I in India. In the Dutch East Indies. In the Philippines. (b) Why did civil strife continue in China? (c) How did the Japanese justify their conquest of more territory?

8. (a) What economic and political changes occurred in England after World War I? (b) Give examples of the weakening of England's hold over her empire during this period.

9. (a) Describe the postwar economic problems of France. (b) By what means did France seek security against invasion? (c) What policies did the French adopt in dealing with their colonies?

10. (a) Trace postwar changes in the United States concerning domestic policies. Concerning foreign policies. (b) What were the two main developments in Latin America between World Wars I and II?

11. Summarize three important trends in world affairs in the period between World Wars I and II.

24 World War II

D-DAY, June 6, 1944

After World War I people everywhere felt strongly that war does not pay and that peace must be made permanent. To enforce peace the statesmen at the Versailles Peace Conference established the League of Nations. The League was based on the idea that all nations should co-operate in settling disputes that might cause war, and that if any nation should resort to war in defiance of the League, the members would combine to resist its aggressions. Within a few years the League system of collective security broke down and the world was on the brink of a still more terrible conflict. The period from 1919 to 1939 had proved to be only a twenty-years' truce in preparation for another war. How was the peace lost?

The Road to War

The lost peace. After World War I people everywhere felt strongly that war does not pay and that peace must be made permanent. To enforce peace the statesmen at the Versailles Peace Conference established the League of Nations. The League was based on the idea that all nations should co-operate in settling disputes that might cause war, and that if any nation should resort to war in defiance of the League, the members would combine to resist its aggressions. Within a few years the League system of collective security broke down and the world was on the brink of a still more terrible conflict. The period from 1919 to 1939 had proved to be only a twenty-years' truce in preparation for another war. How was the peace lost?

Weakness of the League. We have already considered the failures of the League. (See page 482.) It was greatly handicapped from the start because the United States was not a member. It had no authority to enforce its decisions, since it was not a world government but only a loose confederation of sovereign states similar to that of the United States under the Articles of Confederation. Under the most favorable conditions its task would have been extremely difficult.

World conditions unfavorable for peace. World conditions were far from favorable.

The war had left fierce hatreds in its wake. The peace settlement, made up of compromises, was fully satisfactory to no one. It had not been possible to apply the principle of self-determination to all the nations of Europe, and a number of national minorities had been left under foreign rule. (See page 480.) Sometimes their hardships were real, sometimes imaginary. German minorities were among the loudest complainers. Moreover, the German people chafed under the "dictate" of Versailles. The treaty had imposed heavy reparations upon them, and in the "war guilt clause" had charged that Germany and her allies were solely responsible for causing the war. Questions connected with reparations caused disagreements among Great Britain, France, and the United States. Great Britain did not agree with France's desire to keep Germany a weak nation. In spite of these various disagreements and frictions, the League might still have managed to succeed had it not been for the world economic collapse that began in 1929.

The great depression undermined the foundations of the peace machinery set up after World War I. Unemployment and unrest strengthened the grip of the dictators in Germany, Italy, and Japan. Each dictator claimed that prosperity would be restored if his nation could expand its territory, that is, gain *Lebensraum* (living space). The depression caused each of the industrial nations to try to advance its own economic interests regardless of what happened to other nations. This policy of economic nationalism made the depression worse.

Failure of "appeasement." Divided and weakened, the democratic powers did not take steps to check the aggressive moves of the dictators until it was too late. Instead, Britain and France adopted a policy of "appeasement," believing that the dictators' appetites could be satisfied. Appeasement only encouraged the dictators in their contempt for peace treaties and international law. Step by step during the 1930's they advanced along the road to World War II.

JAPAN ATTACKS MANCHURIA

. . . The Commission has come to the following conclusions:

Tense feeling undoubtedly existed between the Japanese and Chinese military forces. The Japanese, as was explained to the Commission in evidence, had a carefully prepared plan to meet the case of possible hostilities between themselves and the Chinese. On the night of September 18th–19th, this plan was put into operation with swiftness and precision. The Chinese . . . had no plan of attacking the Japanese troops, or of endangering the lives or property of Japanese nationals at this particular time or place. They made no concerted or authorised attack on the Japanese forces and were surprised by the Japanese attack and subsequent operations. An explosion undoubtedly occurred on or near the railroad between 10 and 10:30 P.M. on September 18th, but the damage, if any, to the railroad did not in fact prevent the punctual arrival of the southbound train from Changchun, and was not in itself sufficient to justify military action. The military operations of the Japanese troops during this night, which have been described above cannot be regarded as measures of legitimate self-defence.

—Sara R. Smith, *The Manchurian Crisis, 1931–1932.*

The Japanese seize Manchuria, 1931. The first step on the road to war came in 1931, when the Japanese seized the Chinese territory of Manchuria. Lying at the front door of Japan, this area, rich in minerals and farm land, had long tempted the ambitious Japanese. In September 18, 1931, an explosion occurred on the Japanese-owned South Manchurian Railway near Mukden. The line was slightly damaged, though train service continued on schedule. Japanese leaders blamed the explosion on the Chinese and used it as an excuse for military action. Within a few months Japanese troops had overrun all of Manchuria from the Siberian frontier on the north to the Chinese wall on the south. The invaders renamed the territory Manchukuo and placed it under the puppet rule of Pu-yi, last of the Manchu dynasty.

The League fails to stop Japan. For the first time since World War I a major power had deliberately broken its promises to keep the peace. Japan had violated the League Covenant, the Nine-Power Pact of 1922, and the Pact of Paris of 1928. (See pages 478, 484, 487.) China appealed to the League of Nations. A commission led by the Earl of Lytton investigated the Manchurian affair on the spot and condemned the Japanese military action. The commission recommended that all armed forces be withdrawn and that Manchuria be made a self-governing state under Chinese sovereignty. In February, 1933, the League Assembly adopted the report and the recommendations. The United States announced its agreement with this action. None of the great powers, however, was willing to apply an economic boycott or use force to support the recommendations. Japan felt free to defy the League and to proceed on her path of aggression. In March, 1933, she gave notice that she would drop out of the League.

Meanwhile, China could offer but feeble resistance to the Japanese invaders. China still suffered from the smoldering hatreds of the civil war between the Communists and the

FIGHTING at Mukden, 1931. The Japanese expand into Manchuria.

Nationalist government under Chiang Kai-shek. Long periods of foreign intervention had also contributed to China's weakness and disunity. Moreover, her teeming millions were sadly lacking in modern fighting methods and equipment. The most they could do was to organize a boycott of Japanese goods. At this they were successful for a time; but Japan was not to be stopped in this way.

Japan tries to conquer China. Between 1933 and 1937 Japan moved to get political and economic control of North China. Up to that time Chiang's government had offered little resistance. Early in 1937 Chiang and the Communists patched up their differences so as to present a common front against Japan. In the face of this growing opposition, the Japanese leaders decided that the time had come for the military conquest of China. They soon found an excuse.

Japan overruns the northern provinces. On July 7, 1937, a clash between Chinese and Japanese troops occurred near the Marco Polo bridge outside Peiping. The Japanese armies thereupon began a steady advance southward. They soon overran most of the five northern provinces and captured Shanghai after a three months' siege. The invaders then moved into the Yangtze valley. In December they seized and brutally sacked Nanking, the capital of China. During the fighting around Nanking a Japanese airplane bombed and sank an American gunboat, the *Panay*. Japan apologized and paid damages, but it became increasingly clear that her army would disregard the rights of foreigners in China.

Japan pays a heavy price. By 1939 Japan occupied about one quarter of China, including the principal eastern cities as far south as Canton. But the aggressors had paid a heavy price. As Chiang Kai-shek's armies retreated, they "scorched the earth," leaving nothing of value for the advancing Japanese. Moreover, Chinese guerrillas boldly cut off Japanese supplies and launched attacks inside the enemy lines. Before World War II began in Europe, the war in China had swallowed up a million Japanese lives and ten billion dollars of treasure. Meanwhile, the Chinese had moved their capital far up the Yangtze to Chungking. There they received a thin trickle of munitions overland from Russia, and also from the western powers by means of the Burma Road. England and the United States continued to send Japan such strategic materials as oil and scrap iron. They were not prepared to risk war by denying Japan these vital supplies.

Hitler tears up the treaties. The second country to start on the road to war was Nazi Germany. Hitler's actions grew bolder when he saw that the League was not going to use anything but words against Japanese aggression. In 1933 he withdrew Germany from the Disarmament Conference and gave notice of her withdrawal from the League of Nations. (See page 487.) These steps warned the world that Hitler intended to depart from the policies of Stresemann (strä′zĕ-män), who as foreign minister during the 1920's seemed to accept the Versailles peace terms.

By 1935 Hitler felt strong enough to defy the League openly. In March he announced that Germany had created an air force and had reintroduced compulsory military service. The League Council condemned these outright violations of the disarmament clauses in the Versailles Treaty but took no further action. A year later Hitler dealt a more serious blow to the peace system by marching 35,000 troops into the demilitarized Rhineland zone (March 7, 1936). This move broke not only the Versailles provisions but also the Locarno Pacts (see page 486), which Hitler had repeatedly sworn to respect. In a rousing and boastful speech before the *Reichstag,* Hitler defended his action. He asserted that German troops had entered the Rhineland because Germany was being hemmed in by communism. The French had signed a mutual assistance pact with Soviet Russia in 1935; in doing so, Hitler argued, France had already broken the Locarno Pacts. Now, he said, he

was ready for a "real, honest, and equal European co-operation" except with Russia. "We have no territorial demands to make in Europe."

France favored taking action to compel Hitler to comply with the Versailles Treaty. Britain held back, arguing that Hitler should be given a chance to show that his intentions were peaceful. The League protested but in the end did nothing. Again Hitler had gambled and won.

Mussolini takes Ethiopia. While Hitler was scrapping the Versailles peace settlement, Mussolini, leader of Fascist Italy, started on the path of conquest in Africa. From the beginning of his dictatorship, Mussolini was frankly bent upon expansion and had openly glorified war. (See page 509.) Like Hitler, he harped on the need for living space to accommodate Italy's increasing population. He wanted to get rid of British and French naval control of the Mediterranean and its outlets. He longed to restore the greatness that Italy enjoyed in the days of the Caesars. These ambitions did not spell peace. Moreover, a colonial venture was designed to turn attention from the economic miseries at home.

The first victim of Fascist expansion was Ethiopia. Except for Liberia, that ancient kingdom was the only piece of Africa not yet taken over by a European power. (See map, page 420, Abyssinia.) In December, 1934, Ethiopian and Italian troops clashed at Walwal, on the unmarked borders of Italian Somaliland. This was the "incident" for which Mussolini had been waiting. He made extreme demands on Ethiopia and refused the proposal of Emperor Haile Selassie (hī′lĕ sĕ-lá′sĕ) to arbitrate the dispute. In October, 1935, he ordered his forces to strike. They did — with tanks, planes, and poison gas, against which the barefoot Ethiopians were helpless.

The League fails to stop aggression. The League denounced Italy as an aggressor nation and voted to impose economic sanctions upon her. This meant that League members

SPANISH CIVIL WAR REFUGEES.
This caravan of peasants, led by two soldiers of the Loyalist army, crossed the Catalonian border into France to escape the Nationalists.

were not to send arms or certain raw materials, or to lend money to Italy. It seemed at last that the League had put teeth into a decision. But the sanctions suffered from two fatal weaknesses: (1) Germany and the United States did not participate, and (2) the list of banned goods did not include oil, iron, steel, and coal. The League wished to add these commodities to the list, but Mussolini said this would mean war between Italy and any nation which tried to enforce the sanctions. In December, 1935, another attempt was made to end the conflict. Pierre Laval, the French foreign minister, and Sir Samuel Hoare, British foreign minister, suggested a peace plan by which a large slice of Ethiopia would be given to Italy if Mussolini called off the war. Mussolini rejected the offer. By May, 1936, Ethiopia had been conquered and Emperor Haile Selassie was in exile. Soon after, the League sanctions were lifted. Once again the League had failed to halt aggression.

Rehearsal for conquest in Spain. Emboldened by their successful defiance of the League, Hitler and Mussolini were quick to press their advantage further. The Spanish Civil War gave them an opportunity. (See page 517.) It began in July, 1936, and lasted for three years. Every European power had a stake in its outcome. A victory for Franco would almost surround France with antidemocratic governments and would threaten Britain's hold on Gibraltar. A victory for the Popular Front in Spain would strengthen the French Popular Front government led by a Socialist, Léon Blum. The Blum administration was sympathetic to the Spanish Republicans (Loyalists) and had outlawed several French Fascist groups. Many people both in France and in Great Britain wanted to give aid to the Loyalists.

Claiming that they were saving Spain from communism, Hitler and Mussolini sided with Franco. They poured tanks, planes, guns, and thousands of troops into Spain to fight the Republican armies. Soviet Russia sent help to the Loyalists, but it was only a trifle compared to the aid Franco received. Had France and Britain lined up with Russia, World War II might have begun in the autumn of 1936. British and French leaders hoped to localize the war. They set up a Nonintervention Committee in London in an effort to keep either side in Spain from receiving supplies of men and war materials from the outside. Nonintervention proved a farce from the start. Though they were members of the committee, both Germany and Italy continued to send aid to Franco. France and Britain observed the nonintervention agreement. The United States was bound by its neutrality laws (see page 534) not to export arms to Spain. Thus the Loyalists were unable to get arms and were doomed to defeat.

The Anti-Comintern Pact. Co-operation in Spain drew Hitler and Mussolini into closer partnership. In October, 1936, they joined hands in the Rome-Berlin Axis. They pledged "active and friendly co-operation for European peace and reconstruction." Germany recognized Italy's seizure of Ethiopia, and soon Mussolini indicated that he would no longer stand in the way of *Anschluss*—the annexation of Austria to Germany. A month after the formation of the Rome-Berlin Axis, Germany announced an agreement with Japan to combat the activities of the Communist International, or Comintern. (See page 490.) In 1937 Italy joined Germany and Japan in the Rome-Berlin-Tokyo Anti-Comintern Pact. Three years later they formed a defensive alliance (Tripartite Pact, September, 1940). Outwardly opposed to communism, in fact they were united for aggressive purposes.

Hitler annexes Austria. From the outset Hitler's program had called for the union of all Germans in a Greater Germany. Austria became the first victim of Hitler's drive to enlarge Germany. As we have seen (see page 517), Austrian Nazis had failed in an attempt to seize the government in 1934. Now Hitler was ready to act. Nazi agents filtered into Austria in increasing numbers. In January, 1938, some of their plotting was uncovered by the Austrian government. Hitler was furious. He made demands and threats which finally led the Austrian chancellor (prime minister), Schuschnigg, to resign. When riots broke out, the new chancellor, a Nazi, invited German troops to "restore order." On the night of March 11, 1938, German tanks pounded across the border. Two days later *Anschluss* became a fact. By his "strategy of terror" Hitler had added seven million people to Germany without firing a shot.

The Sudetenland. The next Nazi blow fell upon Czechoslovakia. The German seizure of Austria left the Czech republic dangerously exposed, for the Germans could now strike from the west and the south. About 30 per cent of the population of Czechoslovakia consisted of national minorities, mostly Germans, Hungarians, and Poles. The three million Germans in Czechoslovakia occupied the Sudetenland—the western fringe of the country, which was mountainous and well fortified. Hitler encouraged them to agitate for union with Germany. They organized the Sudeten German party under the leadership of Konrad Henlein, a Nazi sympathizer. Supported by the German press and radio, Henlein proceeded to make trouble for the Czech government. In September, 1938, his men rioted when Hitler demanded self-determination for the Sudeten Germans. The Czech police suppressed the riots. Russia and France indicated that they would help the Czechs against the Nazis, but Britain held back. On September 15 the British prime minister, Chamberlain, flew to Berchtesgaden to see Hitler. He became convinced that the only hope for peace was to let Hitler annex the Sudetenland to Germany. Premier Daladier of France agreed that it would be better to meet Hitler's demand than to go to war.

The Czech government, which was not consulted, could do nothing but accept this decision. But meanwhile Hitler made additional demands. The Sudeten territory must be given up by October 1 without any negotiations, plebiscites, or delays. Areas which had Polish or Hungarian populations must also be surrendered. Hitler stated that the Sudetenland was "the last territorial claim I shall make in Europe." The Czechs prepared to resist the new demands. They mobilized more troops, as did also France and Britain. Feverishly Chamberlain tried to find a way out. At the urging of Mussolini, the Fuehrer agreed to a four-power conference at Munich to settle the details of an orderly surrender of the Sudetenland.

The Munich "peace." The Czechs were not represented at the Munich conference, nor was the Soviet Union. At this historic meeting (September 29–30, 1938), Chamberlain,

Daladier, Hitler, and Mussolini agreed that the Czechs were to leave the Sudetenland by October 10. German occupation was to take place by stages. All areas with a bare majority of Germans were to be ceded. A commission was to settle the final boundaries, which Britain and France offered to guarantee. Feeling humiliated and betrayed by this settlement, the Czech president, Eduard Beneš (bĕ'-nĕsh), resigned and left the country. Chamberlain announced that he had brought back "peace with honor," and added: "I believe it is peace for our time." At home the British and French prime ministers were applauded.

The end of Czechoslovakia. Drunk with success, Hitler soon proceeded to wipe out what was left of Czechoslovakia. After making further demands, he suddenly called the Czech president to Berlin. There, on March 4, 1939, President Hacha was forced to sign a declaration entrusting "the destiny of the Czech people and the Czech country to the hands of the Fuehrer of the German Reich." The provinces of Bohemia, Moravia, and Slovakia promptly became German protectorates. Poland and Hungary had already helped themselves to Czech areas on their borders. When Hitler entered Prague in triumph, he declared: "For a thousand years Bohemian and Moravian lands were part of the *Lebensraum* of the German people." It was now clear that Hitler did not intend to limit himself to territories peopled by Germans.

New Axis aggressions. Within a week after the dismemberment of Czechoslovakia, Hitler struck two more blows. He forced the Lithuanian government to give up Memel, a patch of land on the Baltic where about half the people were of German origin. Next, on March 21, Hitler announced that he expected Poland to permit Germany to reannex the free city of Danzig. He also demanded the right to control a motor road and railway across the Polish Corridor. The Poles felt sure that if they gave in Hitler would soon occupy their entire country. Meanwhile, Mussolini watched with envy the easy victories of his Axis partner. He took advantage of the atmosphere of appeasement by seizing Albania on April 7, 1939. The little kingdom across the Adriatic had been an Italian protectorate. (See page 473.)

GERMAN TROOPS who completed the occupation of Czechoslovakia in March, 1939. At Munich, Hitler had promised to respect the independence of Czechoslovakia if he could have the Sudetenland. He kept his word for six months.

Original German Land

Lands Acquired From 1935 to 1939

GERMAN EXPANSION FROM 1935 TO 1939.
In January, 1935, the people of the Saar voted for reunion with Germany. This was the beginning of the expansion of Hitler's Reich. The map shows the lands brought under German control by the outbreak of World War II.

Appeasement ends. At last Britain and France realized their danger. They saw that Hitler's hunger for territory had no limit, and that his promises were worthless. After the destruction of Czechoslovakia, Chamberlain, the author of the appeasement policy, admitted that his hopes had been shattered. He now made a desperate effort to stop Hitler. On March 31, Britain and France assured the Polish government that they would lend it "all support in their power" if its independence was "clearly threatened." After Mussolini's seizure of Albania in April, Rumania and Greece were given similar guarantees. Shortly thereafter Turkey agreed to co-operate with Britain and France in case of war in the Mediterranean. However, the new "peace front" against the Axis was useless without Russian backing. Britain and France could not send effective help to countries on the other side of Naziland. Only the Soviet Union could block Hitler in the east. In April, Britain and France opened negotiations with Russia for an alliance to protect Poland and Rumania from German attack.

Hitler makes a deal with Stalin. The USSR seemed willing to join the anti-Axis front,

but only on certain conditions. She wanted France and Great Britain to promise to assist her in case of attack by Germany or Japan. Russia also wanted to establish a protectorate over the Baltic states, since in case of a war with Germany the Germans would seek to use these countries as bases from which to attack her. However, these states, like Poland and Rumania, shied away from any alliance which might bring Russian troops on their soil. The western powers, too, could not overcome their old suspicions of Soviet Russia. As a result, the negotiations between Britain, France, and the USSR for an anti-Axis pact ended in failure. Then, without warning, Russia dropped a diplomatic bombshell on the world. On August 23, 1939, the Soviet premier, Molotov, and the German foreign minister, Ribbentrop, signed a ten-year treaty of nonaggression and neutrality. Secret clauses in this treaty provided that (1) Poland was to be divided between Germany and Russia, and (2) Estonia and Latvia were to be in Russia's sphere of influence, while Lithuania was to be in Germany's.

War begins. Hitler's plot against Poland had been taking shape for months. Throughout the spring and summer of 1939 Nazi pressure increased. The Poles were accused of breaking their 1934 nonaggression pact with Germany by accepting British protection. They were charged with mistreating the German minority in Poland. The Nazi press and radio used every device in their bag of propaganda tricks. Poland stubbornly resisted Nazi

WARSAW. The splintered ruins of the main railroad station after the Nazi attack on Poland, September, 1939.

pressure, but her fate was sealed. On August 31 the Nazis published a 16-point proposal to Poland. Before it could be delivered, all wires to Warsaw had been cut. Hitler claimed that his "peace" offer had been turned down. At dawn on September 1, German tanks, siege guns, bombers, and troops poured across the Polish border. On September 3 Britain and France declared war on Germany. The twenty-years' truce was over; World War II had begun.

Axis Aggression Reaches High Tide

German blitzkrieg. How well Hitler had prepared for war was soon clear. His strategy was to attack one nation at a time and strike it down quickly in a *blitzkrieg,* or "lightning war." The German Luftwaffe, or air force, played an important role in the new style of warfare. It bombed and strafed enemy airfields, transportation centers, troop concentrations, factories, and even civilian gatherings. The blitzkrieg was often accompanied by well-organized efforts to sow discord among the enemy and weaken the people's will to resist. Nazi secret agents and sympathizers (known as "fifth columnists") committed acts of sabotage behind enemy lines. The fifth column did still more damage by

spreading false rumors, which caused people to distrust their leaders and one another.

Germany conquers Poland. Blitzkrieg tactics had a telling effect in Poland. The Luftwaffe promptly wiped out the Polish air force. It then bombed cities and communication centers at will. Meanwhile, Nazi ground forces converged on Warsaw, the capital, in a giant pincers movement. Polish troops resisted fiercely but were no match for the Germans in numbers or in equipment. German armies reached the Bug River on September 17. Warsaw held out until September 27, despite a terrific pounding from ground and air.

On September 17, Soviet troops swept across eastern Poland. Shortly after, Germany and Russia divided Poland between them, along a line joining the San, Bug, and Narew rivers. It was the fourth time the nation had been partitioned.

The Russo-Finnish War. Stalin next demanded that Turkey, Finland, and the small Baltic republics join Russia in pacts of mutual assistance. Lithuania, Latvia, and Estonia quickly gave in. They granted Russia the right to establish naval and air bases and to station troops within their borders. (Although Russia had promised to respect their independence, she annexed the Baltic states when France fell in June, 1940.) Turkey refused to meet the Russian terms and Russia did not try to enforce them. The case was different with Finland. When Finnish statesmen turned down the Soviet demand for a naval base at Hanko, for certain islands and part of the Karelian Isthmus, the Russians invaded Finland. The Finns fought heroically with almost no outside help, but by March, 1940, they had lost. Most people in the western nations condemned Russia as an aggressor. In a last gasp, the League of Nations expelled her from membership.

The "phony" war in the west. In the meantime, the western front remained quiet. For about eight months after the war began, the French stayed behind their Maginot Line and the Germans behind their West Wall, or Siegfried Line. This period of inaction was dubbed the "phony" war. However, the term was misleading. Both sides were preparing for large-scale operations. The difference was that Germany was planning an offensive, while Britain and France were strengthening their defenses.

The blitz of Denmark and Norway. The standstill in the fighting came to a sudden end on April 9, 1940, when Hitler launched an attack on Denmark and Norway. He wanted control of these countries to protect Germany's northern flank and to give him naval bases from which to attack British shipping and to run the British blockade. Denmark was defenseless and succumbed within a few hours. The occupation of Norway took longer and was more costly. There the Germans had the help of a Nazi henchman named Quisling, whose name became a byword for traitor. The British fleet tried to prevent the landing of German forces in Norway but failed because it lacked adequate air cover. For a few weeks the British occupied the iron ore port of Narvik in the far north. They abandoned it when disaster faced them in Belgium.

The conquest of the Low Countries. The Nazi offensive now moved into high gear.

On May 10 German panzer (tank) divisions suddenly smashed across the frontiers of Holland and Belgium. Only the day before Hitler had assured these two neutrals that they had nothing to fear. The Luftwaffe swiftly put airports and railways out of action, while parachutists and fifth columnists seized airfields, bridges, and fortresses. Within four days the Germans overran Holland, and the Dutch army had to surrender. The Belgians, supported by large British, Polish, and French forces, put up a stiff fight. They were no match, however, for the mechanized Nazi forces and clouds of enemy bombers. In thirty-six hours the Germans took the great fortress of Eben Emael, pivot of Belgian defense lines. On May 28 King Leopold of Belgium surrendered, as the Allied troops retreated to the French port of Dunkirk. In the face of terrible bombardment the British fleet and a motley host of vessels succeeded in rescuing some 335,000 soldiers. An umbrella of British planes helped to cover the retreat. It was a heroic operation. Still darker days lay ahead.

The fall of France. A huge German force crossed Luxembourg and the Ardennes Forest, flanked the Maginot Line, and raced across northern France to the sea. On June 5 the Germans turned southward from the Somme to strike at the heart of France. The French army, which was supposed to be well trained and equipped, turned out to be ineffective. Its leaders had relied too much on fixed defenses. They were unprepared for the speed and power of tanks and dive bombers. On June 14 Paris fell, and the capital was moved to Bordeaux. While France was reeling from these blows, Mussolini declared war on France and Britain and invaded southern France. A few days later Premier Reynaud (rā'nō') resigned and was succeeded by the aged Marshal Pétain (pā'tăɴ'). Pétain surrendered, declining to continue the war from the colonies. On June 22 French representatives met Hitler in the forest of Compiègne.

The terms were signed in the very railway car in which Foch had delivered the armistice terms to the Germans in 1918. The armistice disbanded the French army and provided for the detention of two million French prisoners in Germany. The French fleet was to be interned. Two thirds of France was to be occupied by German troops and was to pay the costs of occupation. The government of unoccupied France was established at Vichy. The little independence Vichy enjoyed was only on Nazi sufferance. Pétain ruled as a dictator and agreed to collaborate with Hitler. The Third French Republic vanished. Many patriotic Frenchmen refused to accept defeat. Led by General de Gaulle, they organized a resistance movement (later known as the Fighting French). They fought against Germany at home and abroad, armed mainly with American and British weapons.

The Battle of Britain. The fall of France put Britain in a desperate position. Her army had left most of its equipment in France and Belgium. The Royal Air Force (R.A.F.) was vastly outnumbered by the Luftwaffe. Britain was not fortified. Fortunately, she now had a dauntless leader in Prime Minister Winston Churchill. When the outlook seemed hopeless, he inspired his people to make heroic efforts and sacrifices. "We shall defend our island, whatever the cost may be," said Churchill. "We shall fight on the beaches, we shall fight on the landing grounds, we shall fight in the fields and in the streets, we shall fight in the hills; we shall never surrender. . . ."

The Battle of Britain was the first great air contest in history. In an effort to "soften up" Britain for invasion, the Germans rained thousands of bombs on Great Britain. After August 8, 1940, the Luftwaffe filled the English skies with 500 to 1000 planes daily. They not only pounded military targets, but wrecked hundreds of blocks of residential areas. London, Coventry, and Plymouth were particularly hard hit. In less than three

months fourteen thousand civilians lost their lives in London alone. Meanwhile, the weary R.A.F. pilots shot down so many attackers that the Germans shifted from daylight to night bombing. But their worst blows failed to break the British spirit. The survivors courageously dug out of their ruins and continued the fight.

The Battle of the Atlantic. The peril to Britain on the seas soon exceeded her peril from the air. The Germans used planes, terrible new types of mines, and long-range submarines to destroy her shipping and cut off her supplies of food and raw materials. The territory overrun in the spring of 1940 gave the Germans possession of the entire European seacoast from Spain to Norway, including many bases from which to attack enemy ships. By 1941 over 7,000,000 tons of British, Allied, and neutral shipping had been lost.

SCRAMBLE. A line of Spitfires ready for the takeoff during the Battle of Britain.

In the early months of 1941 British losses averaged 500,000 tons a month. The British were already desperately short of ships. The Germans were building submarines at a rapid rate and ship sinkings were increasing. Had the United States government not rushed naval aid, the Battle of the Atlantic would have been won by Germany, and Britain would have been conquered.

The Italians fail in Africa and Greece. While Hitler was trying to finish off Britain, Mussolini was busy in Africa and Greece. Italian troops occupied French and British Somaliland in August, 1940. The following month Marshal Graziani turned eastward from Libya to launch an attack on Egypt. He seized Sidi Barrani, well within the Egyptian border, but there the advance bogged down. Meanwhile, Mussolini demanded bases in Greece. When the Greeks spurned his demand, Italian forces marched into the country from Albania. Instead of gaining an easy victory, they were pushed back into Albania, where for a time the Greeks held the upper hand. The Italians fared no better in Africa. The British under General Wavell drove Graziani's army out of Egypt and destroyed it in a swift pursuit ending at El Agheila. At about the same time, early in 1941, British forces regained Somaliland and captured Eritrea and Ethiopia. Once more Haile Selassie resumed his ancient throne. The Italian

armies had shown a lack of military efficiency and zeal for the war.

Germany seizes the Balkans. By the spring of 1941 Hitler determined to invade the Balkans. He wanted to rescue his faltering Axis partner. Besides, he had already decided to attack Russia and needed to protect his southern flank. Throughout 1940 he had carried on a war of nerves against the Balkan countries. As a result, Rumania, Hungary, and Bulgaria had joined Hitler's "New Order." Only Yugoslavia and Greece remained outside. In April the German war machine rolled through Yugoslavia and into Greece. General Wavell sent 60,000 men from Africa to help the Greeks. The British were poorly equipped and had no air support. When the Germans captured Salonika and Athens, the British hurried to reach evacuation ports. On April 27 the Nazis hoisted the swastika over the Acropolis. A few weeks later they gained command of Crete by dropping thousands of parachute troops on the island. It was the first completely airborne invasion in history.

Hitler turns on Russia. German successes in the Balkans led many people to believe that Hitler would next strike at the Middle East or at Britain. Instead he turned on Russia, with whom he had made a nonaggression treaty less than two years before. The Fuehrer evidently had never given up the dream he had expressed in 1936: "If I had the Ural mountains with their incalculable store of treasures in raw materials, Siberia with its vast forests, and the Ukraine with its tremendous wheat fields, Germany under National Socialist leadership would swim in plenty." Besides, Hitler had always wanted to smash communism. Even more, he wanted to destroy the Russian military machine. Then he could safely launch a drive through the Middle East.

Russia invaded. Undoubtedly Germany wished to strike before Russia grew stronger. Hitler assumed that a war against communism would be popular in Great Britain and the United States.

Excuses for attacking Russia were not hard to find. Hitler said that Stalin had concentrated heavy forces on Russia's western border and had adopted an anti-German foreign policy. On June 22, 1941, without declaring war, Hitler ordered his armies to invade Russia. The Finns, Hungarians, Italians, and Rumanians joined the Germans. Pressing forward steadily along a two-thousand mile front, the Axis forces advanced to an average depth of five hundred miles in five months. They surrounded Leningrad, came within thirty miles of Moscow, and took Rostov, the gateway to the Caucasus. But the Russians were trading territory for time, and "scorched the earth" as they retreated. Hitler's armies, like Napoleon's, found the vast plains of Russia unconquerable. "General Winter" became the ally of the Russians, who were better prepared than the Germans to fight in sub-zero temperatures. Late in 1941 the Russians began a counteroffensive. They recaptured Rostov. By the spring of 1942 they had regained 100,000 square miles of territory, a fifth of that taken by the Nazis. However, the Germans were soon to launch another powerful offensive.

The United States moves toward war. At the outbreak of the war in Europe most Americans sympathized with Great Britain and France. They believed that Germany would be defeated and that the United States

should stay out of the struggle. Isolationist sentiment was still strong. As Hitler won victory after victory, Americans changed their attitude. In November, 1939, Congress amended the Neutrality Act to permit belligerent nations to buy munitions on a cash-and-carry basis. (See page 534.) The change benefited Britain and France, since they needed our munitions. The fall of France made Americans realize the importance of Great Britain to the defense of the Western Hemisphere. Hence the United States decided to give Britain all aid "short of war." In September, 1940, our government transferred fifty over-age destroyers to Great Britain in return for the use of naval and air base sites in Newfoundland, British Guiana, and the West Indies. When England no longer had money to pay for imports, Congress passed the Lend-Lease Act (March, 1941), which provided for "lending" war supplies to Britain and other countries that were fighting the Axis. The American Navy began to convoy British ships part way across the Atlantic. The United States took control of Greenland and Iceland with the approval of the Danish government-in-exile. By early summer, the United States Navy was convoying British merchant ships as far as Iceland. In November, 1941, Congress said that the lend-lease supplies could be delivered in American ships.

Besides acting as the "arsenal of democracy," the United States looked to its own defenses. During 1940 a gigantic program for a two-ocean navy was started. Congress reluctantly passed the Selective Service Act, providing for peacetime conscription. The Office of Production Management for Defense (OPM) was set up to organize the country's industrial resources. The United States and Canada agreed upon a joint board of defense, and the Latin American countries co-operated with the United States in plans for defense of the hemisphere. (See page 537.) Thus the stage was set for active participation in the conflict.

PEARL HARBOR. Japanese planes attacking the American fleet, December 7, 1941.

The Atlantic Charter. In August, 1941, President Roosevelt and Prime Minister Churchill met on shipboard off the coast of Newfoundland and drew up the famous Atlantic Charter. The Charter stated the basic aims of the United States and Great Britain. Later the members of the United Nations declared that they supported the same principles:

First, Their countries seek no aggrandizement, territorial or other;

Second, They desire to see no territorial changes that do not accord with the freely expressed wishes of the peoples concerned;

Third, They respect the right of all peoples to choose the form of government under which they will live; and they wish to see sovereign rights and self-government restored to those who have been forcibly deprived of them;

Fourth, They will endeavor, with due respect to their existing obligations, to further the enjoyment of all states, great or small, victor or vanquished, of access, on equal terms, to the trade and to the raw materials of the world which are needed for their economic prosperity;

Fifth, They desire to bring about the fullest collaboration between all nations in the economic field with the object of securing, for all, improved labor standards, economic adjustment, and social security;

Sixth, After the final destruction of the Nazi tyranny, they hope to see established a peace which will afford to all nations the means of dwelling in safety within their own boundaries, and which will afford assurance that all men in all lands may live out their lives in freedom from fear and want;

Seventh, Such a peace should enable all men to traverse the high seas and oceans without hindrance;

Eighth, They believe that all of the nations of the world, for realistic as well as spiritual reasons, must come to the abandonment of the use of force. . . .

Japan makes ready, 1940–1941. Meanwhile, the Japanese leaders watched hopefully as world events seemed to offer them a golden opportunity. Of the powers which once might have tried to stop Japanese aggression, three soon became helpless to do so: the Dutch and French fell under Nazi domination, and the British needed all their efforts to fight off Nazi bombers. By the summer of 1940 only Russia and the United States remained in a position to oppose Japan's aims in the Pacific. In April, 1941, Japan signed a nonaggression treaty with Russia, and the following June Germany invaded Russia. Thus the United States alone stood between Japan's war lords and their dreams of conquest.

American policy in the Pacific. In the Pacific, as in the Atlantic, the United States used measures short of war to oppose aggression. Lend-lease supplies and loans of money were sent to China, protests were sent to Japan when her troops entered French Indo-China, and much of the American fleet was kept in the Pacific. When Japan moved troops into the southern part of French Indo-China (July, 1941), the United States stopped the sale of oil to Japan and froze Japanese assets in the United States. The Japanese replied by freezing American assets in their country.

Diplomatic fencing. From August to December of 1941 the governments of Japan and the United States exchanged a series of notes in an effort to reach agreement. However, these efforts had no chance of success. The Japanese wanted nothing less than a free hand for conquest in Asia. If the United States had agreed, she would have bought peace for herself at the expense of (1) betraying her long friendship with China, and (2) strengthening Japan. Appeasement had failed against Hitler; the United States refused to try appeasing Japan. Japan prepared for war.

Japanese plans for a "New Order." In spite of American opposition, the Japanese leaders were determined to establish a "New Order" in eastern Asia and the Pacific. By this they meant that Japan would end the influence of the western nations in the Orient and would place herself at the head of the Asiatic nations. A "Co-Prosperity Sphere" was planned, in which Japan would become the manufacturing center of the Far East; the other members of the sphere would supply Japan with labor and raw materials.

If we keep these aims in mind, we can better understand the strategy of the Japanese leaders.

Pearl Harbor. In October, 1941, General Tojo became premier of Japan. Having long advocated direct action to win territory for Japan, he lost no time in starting the action he wanted. Early on the morning of December 7, 1941, more than one hundred Japanese carrier-based planes made a surprise attack on the Pearl Harbor naval base. Several thou-

---

JAPAN MOVES TOWARD WAR

. . . It would seem that from about August 1941, the Army General Staff, even including the highest quarters, began advocating an immediate breaking off of negotiations and opening of American-Japanese hostilities. Seeking in every possible way to contravene these policies, from the latter half of August I repeatedly held consultations with the Army and Navy Ministers and called together countless joint conferences. To a certain degree, the 'National Policy' calling for the breaking off of negotiations and the immediate opening of hostilities against England and America was brought under discussion.

Thus it came about that on September 6th, at a conference held in the Imperial presence, the 'Outline for the Execution of the National Policy of the Imperial Government' was decided upon.

. . . . 1. Determined not to be deterred by the possibility of being involved in a war with America (and England and Holland) in order to secure our national existence, we will proceed with war preparations so that they be completed approximately toward the end of October.

2. At the same time, we will endeavor by every possible diplomatic means to have our demands agreed to by America and England . . .

3. If by the early part of October there is no reasonable hope of having our demands agreed to in the diplomatic negotiations mentioned above, we will immediately make up our minds to get ready for war against America (and England and Holland). . . . Special effort will be made to prevent America and Soviet Russia from forming a united front against Japan.

—Prince Konoye's *Memoirs.*

sand men were killed or wounded, and every one of the eight battleships in the anchorage was sunk or badly damaged. The attack crippled the American Pacific fleet. One of the most tragic aspects of the Pearl Harbor disaster was that it might have been avoided. Several months previously American agents had "broken" the secret Japanese code. From messages which had been intercepted, American officials knew that an attack was coming before long, and had sent warnings to all American commanders in the Pacific. The attack was expected in the Far East rather than in Hawaii, however, and it caught Pearl Harbor unprepared.

Global war. On December 8 the Congress of the United States declared war on Japan, as did Great Britain, the Netherlands government-in-exile, and a number of Latin American republics. Three days later Germany and Italy declared war on the United States, and the United States replied in kind against them. Other countries soon joined the struggle against the Axis. Thus World War II became a truly global conflict, even broader in scope than World War I.

The Japanese Empire at its height. Within six months after Pearl Harbor the Japanese conquered a vast empire in southern Asia and the Pacific. Their specially trained and equipped troops advanced from French Indo-China into Siam (Thailand) and on down the Malay Peninsula. They captured the great British fortress at Singapore in February, 1942. Other troops, moving west from Siam, conquered Burma and cut the Burma Road over which supplies had been moving into China. Meanwhile the Japanese had won a far-flung island empire. Two American outposts in the Pacific, Guam and Wake Island, were taken soon after Pearl Harbor. In the Philippines General Douglas MacArthur conducted a heroic defense against overwhelming odds until he was ordered by President Roosevelt to proceed to Australia. The ill and starving Filipino and American troops fought

on under General Wainwright until the Japanese had taken Bataan and made landings on the last American stronghold, the island of Corregidor. After destroying their remaining ammunition the defenders surrendered in May. By this time the Japanese had overrun most of the Dutch East Indies, had landed on New Guinea in that group, and were pressing into the Solomon Islands northeast of Australia. From their new frontiers they were in an excellent position to attack India and Australia and to finish the war in China.

Japan's early advantage. The astonishing successes of the Japanese may be explained in part by the fact that they held the offensive. They could concentrate upon any point they chose to attack. The Japanese also had the advantage of relatively short supply lines. Distances from Japan to the fighting could be measured in hundreds of miles, whereas the Allied supply lines stretched for thousands of miles. The Allies had to fight for time, using their slender resources to slow the Japanese down wherever possible. Furthermore, in the early months of the war Japan had air and naval supremacy. The new Japanese Empire was safe until the American fleet could be strengthened and until men and supplies could be transported to the fighting fronts.

Coral Sea and Midway. In the spring of 1942 Japan's naval offensive was finally halted in two great naval battles—Coral Sea and Midway. The Japanese had established naval bases in the Solomon Islands, northeast of Australia. From these bases they sent a strong fleet down the east coast of Australia through the Coral Sea. American ships hastened north to meet them and turned them back in a running fight lasting several days (May 4–8). For the time being, at least, the Battle of the Coral Sea had saved Australia and the islands east of it from invasion. The battle opened a new era in naval warfare, for it was the first in which the opposing surface ships did not fire on each other. They struck instead with carrier-based aircraft.

An even greater battle of the same type occurred the following month. A Japanese fleet drove eastward across the Pacific toward Midway Island, an advance outpost guarding Hawaii. The Japanese were ambushed by American vessels which, aided by land-based bombers, inflicted upon them the worst defeat in Japan's naval history up to that time. The Battle of Midway ended the Japanese threat to Hawaii.

The United Nations Drive to Victory

Organizing for victory. Victory over the Axis powers was achieved through a remarkably close co-operation of nations all over the globe. Old grudges were put aside as the menace of Axis aggression forced the nations to unite or lose the war. The foundation for the structure of Allied unity was laid in Washington soon after Pearl Harbor. On January 1, 1942, twenty-six countries signed the Declaration of the United Nations, pledging themselves to fight together to the limit of their resources until they had defeated the Axis. The Allies further pledged themselves to seek a peace based on the Atlantic Charter. Until the end of the war the Allies co-ordinated their efforts through joint planning commissions and meetings of state at which overall strategy was planned.

The Axis forced out of Africa. Nowhere was land warfare more mobile than in North Africa, where the British defended Africa and the Middle East. Six times the tide of battle swept back and forth across the desert sands. After the Italians had been routed in the winter of 1940–1941, the Germans came to their rescue with an army commanded by Marshal Erwin Rommel, a master of desert fighting. His hardened troops drove the British Eighth Army back to Egypt. The British rallied there and then counter-attacked, with Rommel retreating in good order. In May, 1942 (while the Japanese were at the height of their success and German armies were striking deep into Russia), Rommel made his greatest bid for entry into the Middle East. By superb generalship he destroyed most of the British tanks and drove to El Alamein, only sixty miles from Alexandria. New equipment was rushed to the Eighth Army from Britain and the United States, and General Montgomery took command. In October Rommel's lines were broken and the Eighth Army began a pursuit that covered over 1600 miles. While the battle still raged Allied troops commanded by General Eisen-

U. S. NAVY fighter-bomber on a patrol over Mako Island, 1943

hower landed at Oran, Algiers, and Casablanca in northwest Africa. Rommel stood at bay in Tunisia between armies coming in from both east and west. After hard fighting his forces, numbering a third of a million men, surrendered in May, 1943.

The Battle for Italy. Before the African campaign had ended President Roosevelt and Prime Minister Churchill met at Casablanca. Working with their military advisers, they drew up plans for a vigorous prosecution of the war all over the globe until the Axis powers agreed to unconditional surrender. Two months after Tunisia was conquered, the Allied forces invaded Sicily. It was subdued in five weeks. The Allied forces then landed in southern Italy. The Italian government surrendered on September 8, 1943. The Germans, however, rushed troops into southern Italy. Only through bitter fighting were the Allied troops able to inch northward through the mountainous country. They reached Rome in June, 1944. Fighting continued in northern Italy until the collapse of Germany.

The Russians hold at Stalingrad. World War II reached a turning point in 1942. Just as the Japanese were stopped at Coral Sea and Midway and the Germans and Italians at El Alamein, so the Germans in Russia were halted at Stalingrad. In the spring of 1942 Hitler launched a vast offensive aimed at the Caucasus region of southern Russia. Loss of the region might have meant the loss of the war for Russia, for the Caucasus furnished most of her oil and was a vital link in the route of Allied supplies coming up from Iran. Throughout the summer Hitler's armies smashed ahead relentlessly until their goal was almost in sight. The fate of the Caucasus was decided at Stalingrad, a great industrial city on the Volga. Here for three months the Russians threw back massive German attacks, in one of the decisive battles in history. Then the Russians counter-attacked, encircled the German army, and by early 1943 had killed or captured the entire force.

The Russians advance after Stalingrad. Before summer came again the Russians had won back most of what Hitler had taken from them in 1942. They withstood a third German offensive in the summer of 1943, and then began a constant series of hammer blows along the whole German front. Hitler found in the east, not the granary to feed his "thousand-year Reich," but a graveyard for millions of his finest soldiers. Russian losses ran even higher. The Russians developed great striking power through the use of massed artillery, giant tanks, and the Stormovik plane armored for low-level operations; but their chief strength lay in the large number of troops they threw into battle. Women as well as men fought in the ranks and in the guerrilla forces which harried the Germans. For the sake of the war effort Russia's civilians worked long hours for only the barest necessities of life. The goods they produced, plus those sent on lend-lease by their Allies enabled Russia's armies to become far stronger than Hitler had thought possible. By September, 1944, the Russians had swept into Poland as far as Warsaw and had forced Rumania and Bulgaria to surrender.

The air war over Europe. While their armies were meeting defeat in Russia and the Mediterranean basin, the Germans were subjected to increasingly heavy attacks from the air. They fought back with speedy fighter planes and improved ground defenses. Still the bombers came over, British Lancasters by night and American Flying Fortresses by day. In five days of July, 1943, the great city of Hamburg was practically wiped out. Dams, bridges, locomotives, and munitions factories were destroyed throughout German-held Europe. The air war reached a climax in February, 1944, when German fighters made a supreme effort to stop the daylight bombing. For a week the Germans threw into the skies everything that would fly, but the best they could do was not enough. The bombing grew in intensity, hampering German production and transportation and clearing the way for an Allied invasion of the continent.

Opening the second front in Europe. Near the close of 1943 the Big Three—President Roosevelt, Prime Minister Churchill, and Premier Stalin—met at Teheran in Iran. There they agreed to co-ordinate their efforts in a triple thrust aimed at the heart of Germany. Allied forces were to land in southern and western France while the Russians advanced from the east. During the following months an endless stream of men and equipment poured into the British Isles, while Allied leaders planned the details of a cross-Channel invasion. A landing on a hostile coast is the most difficult of all military operations, and this one had to be made in the face of formidable defenses. Command of the invasion fell to General Eisenhower, who skillfully combined diverse Allied forces into an efficient war machine.

D-Day. The Channel crossing began early on June 6, 1944. Under a blanket of planes, the greatest armada ever assembled moved from the English coast and converged on the beaches of Normandy. Shells from warships and bombs from planes struck the coastal defenses while the first troops struggled ashore

through mines and traps and barbed wire. American, British, and Canadian troops took part in several co-ordinated landings. Most soldiers met a hail of bullets from machine guns set up to cover every yard of the beaches. To stop was suicide; to live they had to drive forward. At the end of D-Day the Allies held all four beachheads. During the next few weeks they pressed inland slowly while more men and machines poured ashore behind them. In this critical period Allied airmen bombed the transportation lines of the Germans and kept them from bringing in enough reserves to turn the tide of battle.

Freeing France and Belgium. Seven weeks after D-Day Allied tank forces cut the communications of the German forces on the coast. With strong air support the tanks then turned eastward and raced toward Germany. French and American forces, aided by the men and women of the French underground, liberated Paris with little trouble. Meanwhile, the Allies successfully landed a force on the southern coast of France (August 15) and swept northward through the Rhone valley. Everywhere beaten German armies now streamed across northern France toward the shelter of the Siegfried Line. There they ral-

GENERAL EISENHOWER TALKING WITH PARATROOPERS. The Americans, with faces blackened for battle, were about to enter planes for the invasion of Normandy.

559

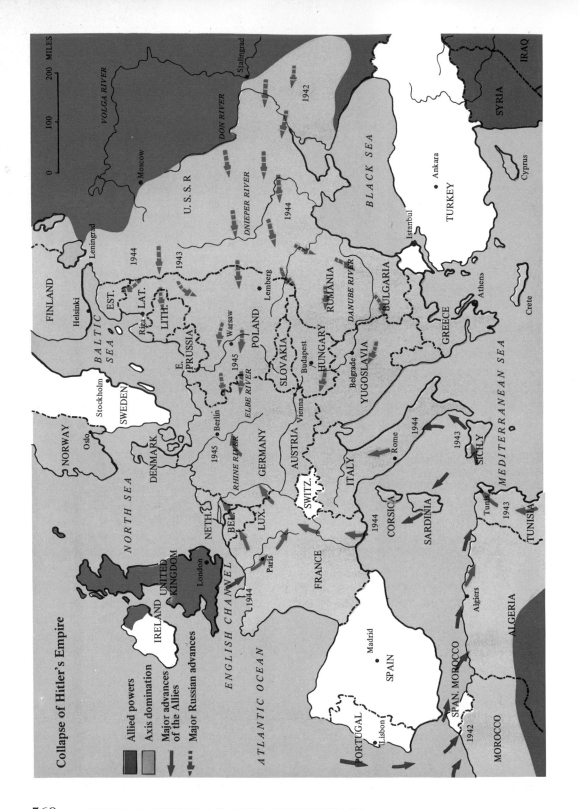

Collapse of Hitler's Empire

Allied powers

Axis domination

Major advances
of the Allies

Major Russian advances

THE LIBERATION OF PARIS. These French students were behind a barricade in the Latin Quarter. The Nazi garrison in Paris surrendered on August 25, 1944.

lied. The Allies had freed most of France and Belgium by early September, but as they crossed the German frontier their pace slowed down. Supplies had to be brought forward and the Rhine had to be reached and crossed before Germany could be beaten.

Germany's secret weapons. Toward the end of the war Hitler told his discouraged people that new and terrible weapons were in preparation which would soon give Germany the advantage. One of these, the flying robot bomb V-1, was used in the summer of 1944, chiefly against England. Another, the high-speed rocket bomb V-2, was used in the fall of 1944 and the winter of 1945. Both caused great destruction of property and heavy loss of life. Had these new weapons been ready early in the war, Germany might have won the Battle of Britain.

The Ardennes counteroffensive. While the Allies prepared for their final assault, Hitler played his last trump. With the utmost secrecy he gathered together all his available reserves and poised them to strike at the thinly held Allied line in the Ardennes Forest area. On December 16, 1944, the blow fell.

Within a few days German tanks drove a wedge sixty-five miles deep into Allied territory, pointed toward Allied supply depots and the Channel ports. The Allies fell back before the furious assault, braced themselves, and then struck hard at the sides of the German wedge. Within a few weeks they won back the lost ground. Hitler's last desperate bid for victory had failed.

Unconditional surrender of Germany. Caught as between the jaws of a vise, Hitler's Reich was crushed by the pressure of armies on both the east and west. In January, 1945, the Russians broke through on the eastern front in Poland and came within sixty miles of Berlin. Shortly afterward the Allies on the western front began an all-out offensive. They reached the Rhine, and on March 7 captured a bridge left standing at Remagen. There and at other points they quickly crossed the river. Their tank columns ranged almost at will behind the German lines. Pounded by constant air attacks, driven into pockets from which there was no escape, the German armies in the west collapsed. Meanwhile the Russians entered Vienna and closed in on

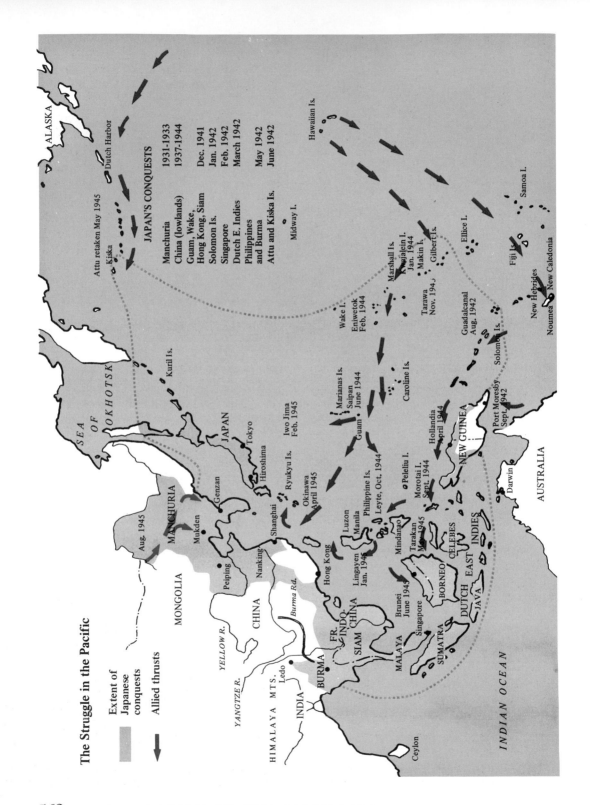

The Struggle in the Pacific

Extent of Japanese conquests

Allied thrusts

JAPAN'S CONQUESTS

Manchuria	1931-1933
China (lowlands)	1937-1944
Guam, Wake,	Dec. 1941
Hong Kong, Siam	Jan. 1942
Solomon Is.	Feb. 1942
Singapore	March 1942
Dutch E. Indies	
Philippines	
and Burma	May 1942
Attu and Kiska Is.	June 1942

ALASKA

Dutch Harbor

Attu retaken May 1945

Kiska

Hawaiian Is.

Midway I.

Marshall Is.

Kwajalein I.
Jan. 1944

Makin I.

Gilbert Is.

Tarawa
Nov. 1943

Ellice I.

Samoa I.

Fiji Is.

New Hebrides

Noumea New Caledonia

Guadalcanal
Aug. 1942

Solomon Is.

Wake I.

Eniwetok
Feb. 1944

Caroline Is.

Aug. 1945

Kuril Is.

SEA OF OKHOTSK

JAPAN

Tokyo

Hiroshima

Ryukyu Is.

Iwo Jima
Feb. 1945

Okinawa
April 1945

Marianas Is.

Saipan
June 1944

Guam

Philippine Is.

Leyte, Oct. 1944

Peleliu I.

Morotai I.
Sept. 1944

Hollandia
April 1944

NEW GUINEA

Port Moresby
Sept. 1942

Darwin

AUSTRALIA

Genzan

Shanghai

MANCHURIA

Mukden

Nanking

Peiping

MONGOLIA

YELLOW R.

CHINA

YANGTZE R.

Burma Rd.

Ledo

HIMALAYA MTS.

INDIA

BURMA

FR. INDO-CHINA

SIAM

MALAYA

Singapore

SUMATRA

Hong Kong

Luzon

Manila

Lingayen
Jan. 1945

Mindanao

Tarakan
May 1945

BORNEO

Brunei
June 1945

CELEBES

DUTCH EAST INDIES

JAVA

INDIAN OCEAN

Ceylon

Berlin. Their advance units made contact with the Americans on April 26. A few days later the German radio announced Hitler's death in the ruins of his capital. By this time northern Italy had been overrun by Allied troops, and German forces everywhere were laying down their arms. Representatives of the German government met the Allied commanders at Reims, France, and agreed to unconditional surrender. V-E Day was proclaimed on May 8, 1945.

Allied strategy against Japan. The Allies defeated Japan by two main lines of attack. In the Pacific they blasted a road to Tokyo through the island empire which Japan controlled. The task of "island hopping" fell mostly to the United States. In their second main line of attack the Allies aimed at the defeat of Japan's armies in China. American, British, and Chinese troops fought to open supply lines into China from India and Burma. In the closing days of the war, with the defeat of Japan assured by atomic bombs, the Russians attacked the Japanese in Asia.

The battle for Guadalcanal. The Allied advance in the Pacific began at Guadalcanal, a tropical island in the southern Solomons. Here in the jungle the Japanese had constructed an airfield as part of their preparations for conquering Australia. In a surprise move the American Navy landed marines on Guadalcanal in August, 1942. For months the battle raged, with both sides sending reinforcements of men and ships to win the strategic island. The fighting at sea reached a climax in November, when Allied ships under Admiral William F. Halsey defeated the Japanese in the greatest naval battle since the Battle of Jutland in World War I. The Japanese were driven out of Guadalcanal early in 1943.

Island hopping toward the Philippines and Japan. Perhaps the best way to understand how we advanced after Guadalcanal is to study the map on the opposite page. Here you will see how the Allied troops under General MacArthur moved into New Guinea, then to Morotai, and finally returned in triumph to the Philippines (Leyte Gulf, October, 1944). Meanwhile, Admiral Chester W. Nimitz directed a similar campaign across the central Pacific. His soldiers and marines stormed ashore and took island after island in the Gilbert, Marshall, Mariana, and Caroline groups. Among their most famous victories, located on the map, were Tarawa, Kwajalein, Eniwetok, Saipan, Guam, Iwo Jima, and Okinawa.

Opening a road into China. While the Allies were advancing toward Japan across the Pacific, they were also moving forward on land in the China-Burma-India theater. Here transportation difficulties and lack of equipment constantly hampered Allied efforts. In 1942 the Japanese invaded Burma and cut the Burma Road (see map, page 562). The Allies were left in a critical situation. They had

THE FLAG is raised on Mount Suribachi, Iwo Jima.

THE JAPANESE SURRENDER. The delegation arrives on the battleship *Missouri* on V–J Day, September 2, 1945, to sign the treaty of surrender presented by the American officers headed by General MacArthur.

to get supplies into China to keep that country in the war and to support American air forces in China. Therefore they sent cargo planes on the costly and hazardous flight from India to China over "the Hump"—the towering Himalayas. The supplies thus carried were not nearly enough; an overland route was needed. General Joseph Stilwell, commander of American forces in China, planned to build a road from India across Burma. To make this possible, American, Chinese, British, and Indian troops began an invasion of northern Burma early in 1944. The Japanese countered by invading India, but were driven back. The Allied soldiers fought their way through northern Burma, with bulldozers and road builders working close behind. Early in 1945 they reached the frontier of China. Fleets of trucks could then carry supplies to China over the new Stilwell Road.

The bombardment of Japan. For Japan, as for Germany, 1945 was a year of appalling reverses. Aided by fresh equipment, China's southern armies took the offensive and inflicted several defeats on the Japanese. Troops

of the British Commonwealth reconquered nearly all of Burma. Meanwhile, American airmen carried on a steady bombardment of Japan. Each advance to a new island base shortened the trips of the bombers and their fighter escorts, and in 1945 American and British aircraft carriers dared to enter the home waters of Japan. The cities and factories of Japan suffered enormous damage under the mounting air offensive.

Atom bombs fall on Japan. In April of 1945, the Russians announced the end of their military pact with Japan; on August 8 they declared war and quickly overran Manchuria. While General MacArthur and Admiral Nimitz prepared for an early invasion of Japan itself, the cities and industries of that unhappy country continued to crumble under the air offensive. Called upon to surrender, the Japanese refused to answer. Their plans for a last-ditch defense of their homeland were changed, however, by the use of the most terrible weapon of war that man had ever devised. On August 6 an American plane dropped an atomic bomb on the city of Hiroshima. Most of the city was destroyed. Three days later a second and more powerful bomb wiped out Nagasaki. Warned of more bombs to follow, Japan asked for peace.

Japan surrenders. In the Potsdam Declaration, issued July 26, 1945, the Allies had stated their terms for the surrender of Japan. Her armed forces were to surrender unconditionally; she was to be disarmed; her war criminals were to be punished; she was to establish a democratic government; her territory was to be limited to the home islands; and she was to submit to Allied occupation. In their request for peace on August 9 the Japanese accepted these terms, asking only that their emperor be allowed to remain on the throne. The Allies replied that if the emperor stayed he would have to take orders from the commander of the occupation forces. The Japanese agreed and ordered all their forces to cease fighting (August 14, 1945). On September 2, on the deck of the battleship *Missouri* in Tokyo Bay, Japanese delegates signed the formal document of surrender. World War II had ended. The victors in the greatest conflict in history now faced the task of bringing order from the chaos of a shattered world.

In Search of Peace

Bringing order out of the chaos of World War II proved as difficult as winning the war itself. As in the past, victory on the battlefield did not really end the battle. Peacemaking was a continuation of the struggle by different means and among different contenders. It was often a frustrating, bitter, and drawn-out process. Yet it offered the only hope that man might in the future save his world from utter destruction.

Laying the foundations of peace. The war had proceeded but a short time when the Allies began to make plans for eventual victory. Even before the United States entered the war, President Roosevelt and Prime Minister Churchill had set forth in the Atlantic Charter some guidelines for a just peace. (See page 554.) These became the basis of the alliance agreed to in the Declaration of the United Nations of January 1, 1942. (See page 557.) A series of wartime conferences followed, all with the purpose of planning for world security after the war.

The United States, Great Britain, and Russia took the first official step toward the creation of a new world security organization. The foreign ministers of the three countries met in Moscow and on November 1, 1943, announced the Moscow Pact. The pact said that the three nations looked forward to the establishment of a general international organization open to all peace-loving nations. The organization was to be designed to keep the peace and promote the political, economic, and social welfare of its members. The next step came in the late summer of 1944, when representatives of the United States, Great Britain, Russia, and China met at Dumbarton Oaks, Washington, D.C. There they drew up specific proposals for a permanent United Nations organization. In February, 1945, Roosevelt, Churchill, and Stalin met at Yalta in the Russian Crimea. They agreed to call a conference of all the United Nations, to be held at San Francisco in April, for the purpose of forming a world peace-keeping organization. (For other agreements at Yalta, see page 570.)

Late in April, 1945, representatives of fifty nations met at San Francisco. The recent death of President Roosevelt on April 12 deprived the conference of a key figure who had shaped both the war and peace plans of the Allies. Nevertheless, President Harry S Truman decided that the conference should not be postponed. During the two months of the sessions that followed, the delegates took up hundreds of suggestions for changing the Dumbarton Oaks proposals. After many of these had been accepted, the delegates unanimously approved the Charter (constitution) of the United Nations. On June 26, 1945, they signed the Charter and then submitted it to their governments to be ratified. The first government to ratify was that of the United States. The vote in the Senate was 89 to 2—a sharp contrast to the refusal of that body to ratify the League of Nations Covenant after World War I. By the end of 1945 fifty-one nations had ratified the Charter. Other countries joined later, bringing the total membership to 126 by 1969.

In 1946 the first session of the United Nations General Assembly met in London. For the important post of Secretary-General it chose Dr. Trygve Lie, then foreign minister of Norway. The General Assembly decided that the headquarters of the U.N. should be in the United States. In 1947 the U.N. accepted a permanent headquarters site in New York City donated by John D. Rockefeller, Jr. The League of Nations turned over its property and assets to the United Nations.

The League buildings at Geneva, Switzerland, have since furnished a convenient site for many international conferences.

The major organs of the United Nations. The organs and agencies of the United Nations were established to carry out its four general purposes. As stated in the Charter, these are (1) to maintain international peace and security, (2) to develop friendly relations among nations, (3) to achieve international co-operation in the solution of economic, social, cultural, and humanitarian problems, and (4) to be a center for harmonizing the actions of nations in the attainment of these common aims.

The Security Council was designed to be the most powerful of the six main organs of the U.N. The Charter says: "In order to insure prompt and efficient action by the United Nations, its members confer on the Security Council primary responsibility for the maintenance of international peace and se-

THE UNITED NATIONS SECURITY COUNCIL

Woodrow Wilson

The Peace Palace at The Hague, Netherlands

World Conflict and Man's Quest for Peace

Periodically the peace of the world has been shattered by wars. Once wars were local affairs with a few nations fighting over a small area of the earth. But in this century our rapidly shrinking world has made it impossible for any nation or people to excape the tragic effects of a modern war.

So terrifying has the prospect of modern war become that nations have increasingly sought to settle their disputes through international cooperation. Even before World War I, keeping the peace became a matter of concern to all nations, not only to those involved in a quarrel. The Hague Peace Palace in the Netherlands stands as a monument to those early efforts.

The spark at Sarajevo, which was to ignite the world into war, fell on a Europe too ready and too willing to be ignited into conflict. Thus, Europe and the world was plunged into a war which was to cost more than 25 million lives and billions of dollars in lost property. The two scenes shown here can only hint at the destruction and cost in human lives which result from modern warfare.

After the horror of World War I nations turned from monuments to the glory of war to institutions for the preservation of peace. Under the leadership of Woodrow Wilson they set up the League of Nations. However, the League was doomed to failure by the bitterness left by the vindictive Treaty of Versailles and by the withholding of support by the United States.

German prisoners and American wounded during the Meuse-Argonne offensive of World War I, October, 1918

"A Coast Defense," by John Lavery. An antiaircraft gun at Tyneside, 1917.

More than one million farmers gathered at Bückeburg, Germany, to listen to the rantings of Hitler in 1938.

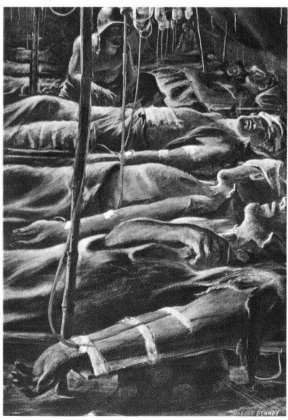

"Shock Tent," by Robert Benney, July, 1944.

566D

The unrest after the war and the effects of the Great Depression aided the rise of dictators who gained power by playing upon the fears and insecurity of their peoples. The stage was set for another conflict, and the League of Nations was powerless to prevent the war.

World War II demonstrated dramatically how an interdependent world becomes involved in a global conflict. Before the war was over almost every nation was involved in some way. It also marked the perfection of old machines of war and the introduction of the most horrifying weapon in the history of warfare, the atom bomb.

Although most realize that only by working together in peace will the world have a good chance to build a truly better world and to avoid the certainty of mass destruction that would result from an atomic conflict, tension in the world continues. All over the globe, one finds the continuing problems of poverty, ignorance, and even conflict much of which seems to result from the "cold war." This ideological split developed soon after World War II between Russia and the western nations.

"The Withdrawal from Dunkirk," by Charles Cundall, June, 1940

The Berlin Wall, a real iron and concrete curtain

Here are two scenes from the period of the "cold war." The first shows a small, lonely boy trudging beside that grim barricade, the Berlin Wall. The wall, erected by the Communists in 1961, divides East and West Berlin. It is a grim reminder that a vast difference still exists between the free world and the world of the Communists.

Below we see the funeral services for John F. Kennedy, 35th President of the United States. Slain by the bullets of a crazed assassin on November 22, 1963, this valiant warrior for peace and world understanding was buried on November 25, 1963. Attending the services were dignitaries from all over the globe, including the late President Eisenhower and DeGaulle of France.

John F. Kennedy, our 35th President, is laid to rest

The United Nations was born in San Francisco after World War II to insure
that the monstrous world conflict from 1939 to 1945 would truly be "a war
to end all wars." In its brief twenty-two years of life, this world organization
has had many successes despite handicaps resulting from its charter. Despite
its problems and handicaps, many still feel that the United Nations is man's
last and best hope for peace. During his brief administration, President Kennedy spoke and acted in support of the United Nations. Situated on the bank
of the East River in New York City, the skyscraper Secretariat building stands
as a monument to man's continuing search for peace.

United Nations Headquarters, New York, N.Y.

curity." Fifteen (eleven until 1965) members hold seats on the Security Council. Permanent seats are held by France, Great Britain, Nationalist China, the Soviet Union, and the United States. The ten remaining members are elected by the General Assembly for a term of two years.

The Security Council may *discuss* a question which any nine of its members have approved. When a dispute seems likely to endanger world peace, the Council may *recommend* arbitration, negotiation, or other means of peaceful settlement. Nine members, including all the permanent members, must vote for such a recommendation before it can become effective. Thus each of the five permanent members has the power to veto any action by the Security Council. This has frequently blocked Security Council decisions. The Soviet Union has used the veto more often than all the other permanent members combined—a total of over a hundred times. The veto has thus shifted the balance of power to the General Assembly.

If a dispute is not settled peaceably, the Council can *take action* to prevent war. It can impose nonmilitary sanctions, that is, cut off trade or communications with one or more of the quarreling nations. When necessary the Council may also use force. The Charter provides that each U.N. member shall furnish military troops for use by the Security Council. Such a standing armed force has never come into being. The major powers could not agree on how it was to be set up and used. To deal with particular emergencies, temporary U.N. forces have been created from time to time.

The General Assembly, sometimes called "a Town Meeting of the World," is the next most important organ of the United Nations. It includes representatives of all member nations and meets at least once a year. Each nation, large or small, may cast only one vote. A two-thirds vote is necessary on matters of special importance, such as a recommenda-tion for using force to maintain peace. Since the General Assembly expresses the conscience of the world, its recommendations carry great weight. The Assembly also controls the budget of the U.N. and elects members of many U.N. agencies. In practice, it has frequently become more important than the Security Council. Although the veto often hampers the latter's work, the Assembly can act whenever a two-thirds majority agrees. It has therefore taken steps toward the solution of a number of thorny problems.

The International Court of Justice, or World Court, gives the nations a convenient means for settling legal disputes. All members of the United Nations may refer cases to the Court; nonmembers may do likewise if the Security Council and General Assembly approve. The Court deals only with disputes between nations, not with questions involving individuals. The cases it considers must be legal rather than political in nature, such as boundary disputes or the interpretation of a treaty. It may also issue "advisory opinions" in reply to legal questions asked by the General Assembly. The Court's fifteen judges are elected by the Security Council and the Assembly for a term of nine years. No two judges may be citizens of the same country. The Court meets in the Peace Palace at The Hague, where the World Court of the League of Nations formerly met.

The Secretariat performs the administrative functions of the United Nations organization. At its head is the Secretary-General, who is elected by the General Assembly for a five-year term. Trygve Lie, the first Secretary, resigned in 1953; he called his office "the most impossible job in the world." His place was taken by a Swede, Dag Hammarskjöld (häm′ar-shüld′), who was killed in 1961 while flying on a U.N. mission in Africa. U Thant of Burma succeeded him and was re-elected in 1966. As chief administrative officer the Secretary prepares an annual report of the U.N.'s activities and supervises

UNITED NATIONS AGENCIES aid many countries with nutrition programs. Here a Guatemalan mother gives her child a glass of *Incaparina*, a high-protein drink.

the work of its various employees, who come from all parts of the world.

Another major organ is the Trusteeship Council, which aims to secure fair treatment for the colonial peoples of the world and help them prepare for self-government. By agreement with certain major powers the Trusteeship Council may supervise the administration of dependent areas which have been assigned to those powers. However, in case the trust territory has military value, it comes under the supervision of the Security Council. Such, for example, are the Pacific islands (Carolines, Marianas, and Marshalls) comprising the United States Trust Territory.

Finally, the Economic and Social Council was set up to create "the conditions of stability and well-being which are necessary for peaceful and friendly relations among nations." The Council studies the social and economic problems of the world, such as food shortages, unemployment, lack of education, and the denial of human rights. For example, it sponsored the drafting of the Universal Declaration of Human Rights, which was adopted by the Assembly in 1948. It urges ratification by member nations of this Declaration, guaranteeing such individual rights as life, liberty, personal security, and freedom from slavery and arbitrary arrest. The Economic and Social Council also ties together the work of a number of commissions and specialized agencies, some of which we shall now examine.

The U.N. specialized agencies. The International Bank for Reconstruction and Development, also known as the World Bank, began operations in 1947. Loans from the Bank at first were used mainly for rebuilding wartorn nations. More recently, its funds have gone into public works and basic industries, especially in underdeveloped countries. Closely related to the World Bank is the International Monetary Fund. It seeks to help all nations maintain a stable currency, so that serious inflation will not hamper world trade.

Another key agency is the United Nations Educational, Scientific, and Cultural Organization (UNESCO). It seeks to promote international understanding through education and the free exchange of ideas and information. Beginning in 1947 UNESCO helped provide school facilities in areas devastated by World War II, and in underdeveloped countries such as Haiti, where most people cannot read or write. Teamed with UNICEF (United Nations Children's Fund), it has helped equip schools and training centers in at least fifty-five countries.

The World Health Organization, set up in 1948, seeks to improve health conditions, particularly among children. Also working closely with UNICEF, it has carried on a program of testing millions of young people for tuberculosis and treating those found to be infected. In addition, WHO has conducted a worldwide campaign against many other communicable diseases, such as diphtheria, scarlet fever, leprosy, yellow fever, cholera, and polio. It has been one of the most effective agencies of the United Nations.

In 1957 the U.N. took an important step by establishing the International Atomic Energy Agency, with headquarters in Vienna. Nearly all U.N. members have approved the "Atoms for Peace" program of the IAEA The program promotes research in the peacetime uses of atomic energy and provides information on new discoveries. IAEA has also set up an international safeguards system and in the future should play an increasingly important part in the inspection of nuclear facilities. In addition, it sponsors annual conferences where scientists may exchange ideas and information.

Plans for setting up U.N agencies originally included an International Trade Organization (ITO). This agency never materialized, but its functions and purposes have been largely fulfilled through the General Agreement on Tariffs and Trade (GATT), begun in 1947. Most of the world's nations have signed this treaty, which provides for the expansion of international trade and the reduction of tariff barriers. Under its sponsorship the "Kennedy round" of negotiations was successfully concluded in 1968.

There are, of course, additional U.N. agencies that deal primarily with the social and economic welfare of the world's peoples, such as the Food and Agricultural Organization (FAO) and the International Labor Organization (ILO). Another group of agencies has as its main purpose the broadening and improving of communication among nations. Among these are the Universal Postal Union (UPU), the International Telecommunication Union (ITU), and the International Civil Aviation Organization (ICAO). Some of these existed before the United Nations began, but all have been made a part of its system in the belief that good communication promotes peace.

The predicament of the U.N. Those who drafted the Charter of the U.N. were faced with an age-old dilemma. It was expressed in the terms of the document itself. One provision declared that members "shall settle their

WORLD BANK aid to farmers. Here a field worker irrigates a cotton field using the siphon pipe method.

international disputes by peaceful means," whereas another emphasized their "sovereign equality." Obviously, a nation that is a law unto itself (sovereign) will not accept the authority of an international body. The framers of the Charter were realistic in recognizing this fact. Hence they left for later decision the setting up of an international police force, which has not materialized. They also provided for a veto by the Big Five in the Security Council, for there was no way of forcing these giants to bow to the will of a majority. Therefore the success of the U.N. has depended on the co-operation among the big powers. The East-West struggle after the cold war began has made such co-operation spasmodic and frequently ineffective. Yet the nations have recognized the need for international order in the risky nuclear age. None has seriously threatened to withdraw from the U.N., and although the world may not be ready for an international government with sovereign authority, the U.N. has at least served as a balance wheel among the superpowers and as a forum for all to air their grievances.

The problem of Germany. While the victorious powers were setting up an international peace organization, they also faced the immediate task of dealing with the defeated nations. Germany, of course, was their foremost concern. At the Yalta Conference (February, 1945) Roosevelt, Churchill, and Stalin outlined a plan for the occupation of Germany after her defeat. The country was to be divided into four zones of control. The Big Four (Great Britain, France, the Soviet Union, and the United States) were each to occupy one zone. Greater Berlin was to be occupied jointly under an inter-Allied authority. At the Potsdam Conference held in the summer of 1945, President Truman, Prime Minister Attlee, and Premier Stalin drew up principles to guide the occupation.

The division of Germany by its conquerors was regarded as temporary. After a period of restoring order, the intention was to reunite the four occupation zones and to make a peace treaty with one Germany. Unfortunately, this was not to be, for the wartime alliance of the Allies was about to fall apart. The ink was scarcely dry on the Potsdam declaration when a series of quarrels began among the Big Four powers. The disagreements found the United States, Great Britain, and France on one side and the U.S.S.R. on the other. Russia was at odds with the other three occupying powers on such basic issues as: (1) Germany's postwar boundaries, (2) the kind and extent of reparations payments, (3) the establishment of a central German government, and (4) the amount of industrial production to be permitted. As a result, the prospects of concluding a peace treaty for Germany were dim.

Meanwhile, in 1946 as part of a "denazification" program, the four Allied powers held a trial of the twenty-two top Nazi leaders at Nuremberg. They were charged with "crimes against humanity," and twelve of the accused were sentenced to be hanged. Many people throughout the world questioned the right of the victorious powers to punish the defeated enemy leaders, especially since Russia, a totalitarian power, was one of the prosecutors. More than twenty years later German courts were still bringing to trial minor war "criminals," mostly in connection with the administration of the dreadful Nazi concentration camps.

Gradually, economic troubles led the western zones of Germany to draw together. On January 1, 1947, Great Britain and the United States merged their zones into a single economic unit. The following year it was agreed that the Germans in the three western zones should set up the West German Federal Republic. Accordingly, an assembly drafted a constitution, which was adopted on May 8, 1949. Bonn, on the lower Rhine River, became the seat of the new government. The Bonn Constitution, as it was called, provided for a

LEAPING THE BARRIER. Looking neither right nor left, this soldier
of the East German Army leaps the barbed-wire barricade
into West Berlin.

system combining the federal features of the
United States government with Great Britain's parliamentary form. Konrad Adenauer
became the federal chancellor, or prime minister. He belonged to the Christian Democratic Union, a middle-of-the-road party. In
May, 1952, Adenauer signed the so-called
"peace contract" with the western powers. It
restored to the West Germans almost complete self-government.

The Russians tried hard to undermine the
West German Republic. Their object was to
prevent West Germany's rearmament and to
prepare the way for communizing a united
Germany. In October, 1949, they set up in
their zones a so-called East German Democratic Republic. It was democratic in name
only. The Russian authorities permitted the
existence of several weak opposition parties,
but at the polls the voters could choose only
from a Communist-approved list of candidates. This puppet state, far weaker economically than West Germany, was declared independent in March, 1954. But Soviet soldiers

remained in the zone and the Communist
party was in full control.

Treaties with the other defeated powers.
Like Germany, Austria was divided into
zones and occupied by the Big Four powers.
At the end of 1945 they set up a constitutional government for the whole country. Six
months later this government was given authority to pass laws on domestic matters. In
May, 1955, Russia reversed her former stand
and agreed with the other three occupying
powers to the terms of the Austrian State
Treaty. The main provisions were: (1) Austrian independence was restored and the occupation troops were to be withdrawn; (2)
Austria was to have her boundaries of 1938
and was not to reunite with Germany; (3)
Austria was to pay for certain industries that
Russia had taken over from the Germans;
and (4) Austria was to be neutral; that is, she
was not to join any defensive alliance. For the
first time in seventeen years, Austria was now
a sovereign nation. Economically, Austria
was in critical condition in the postwar years.

Marshall Plan funds helped to ease the serious lack of food. Relief from hunger was an important buttress, as elsewhere, against Communist influence.

After sixteen months of debate the Big Four finally agreed on a peace settlement for Italy and the wartime satellites of the Axis— Hungary, Rumania, Bulgaria, and Finland. All five lost territory, Italy losing the most. All five were required to pay reparations. The armed forces of all five were sharply limited. In February, 1947, the treaties were signed at Paris. Of the five defeated nations, only Bulgaria was reasonably satisfied with the peace terms. Italy protested that the treaty-makers had not given her sufficient credit for helping the Allies after her unconditional surrender in 1943. Italians were especially bitter over the loss of Venezia Giulia and the city of Trieste. The former was given to Yugoslavia, whereas Trieste and the surrounding countryside were made a Free Territory under the supervision of the United Nations. A revised settlement in October, 1954, gave Zone A on the north, including the city of Trieste, to Italy. The city, however, was to be an international port. Zone B, to the south, plus a small additional strip, went to Yugoslavia. This agreement healed a wound that had threatened to split the western powers, who by now were bound together in the NATO alliance.

Meanwhile, the United States suggested that a peace treaty be negotiated with Japan. As usual, the Soviet Union objected. Therefore the United States drafted a treaty without Russia. On September 8, 1951, the document was submitted for approval to a conference of nations at San Francisco. Forty-eight of Japan's former enemies signed the treaty. India, Burma, and China sent no delegates. Russia and two of her satellites, Czechoslovakia and Poland, refused to sign. (A "peace declaration" with Russia in 1956 officially ended the war with Japan.) The main provisions of the treaty were: (1) Japan was recognized as a sovereign nation; (2) Japan gave up all claim to her former colonies; (3) Japan agreed to abide by the U.N. Charter (in 1956 Japan was admitted to the U.N.); (4) Japan was to furnish labor for war repairs but no cash or goods.

The settlements thus arrived at following World War II were for the most part far from the goals set forth in the Atlantic Charter. Today, thirty years after the end of the conflict, there is still much unfinished peace-making to be done. Why this is so we shall try to make clear in the next three chapters.

REVIEWING THE CHAPTER

TERMS TO UNDERSTAND: *collective security, economic nationalism,* Lebensraum, *appeasement, Anti-Comintern Pact, Munich Conference, blitzkrieg, Luftwaffe, Vichy France, Lend-Lease Act, Atlantic Charter, United Nations, D-Day, V-E Day, Moscow Pact, Yalta Conference, nonmilitary sanctions, veto, trust territory, UNESCO, WHO, GATT, sovereign, Potsdam Conference, denazification, Bonn Constitution, San Francisco Peace Treaty.*

PERSONS TO IDENTIFY: *Haile Selassie, Léon Blum, Chamberlain, Daladier, Beneš, Quisling, Pétain, De Gaulle, Churchill, Graziani, Wavell, Tojo, MacArthur, Rommel, Montgomery, Eisenhower, Halsey, Stilwell, Nimitz, Trygve Lie, Dag Hammarskjold, U Thant, Konrad Adenauer.*

PLACES TO LOCATE: *Sudetenland, Nanking, Burma Road, Chungking, Memel, Danzig, Albania, Luxembourg, Ardennes Forest, Kare-*

lian Isthmus, Dunkirk, Pearl Harbor, Corregidor, Singapore, Coral Sea, Casablanca, El Alamein, Tunisia, Caucasus, Stalingrad, Guadalcanal, New Guinea, Leyte, Saipan, Okinawa, Dumbarton Oaks, Nuremberg, Bonn, Trieste.

QUESTIONS TO ANSWER

1. (a) In what ways were world conditions unfavorable for peace after World War I? (b) Give the main reasons for the failure of the League of Nations to preserve world peace. (c) What did the League do about the Japanese seizure of Manchuria? The Italian attack on Ethiopia? The Russian invasion of Finland?

2. (a) Why did France and Britain not support the Spanish Republic? (b) How did the Non-intervention Committee contribute to Franco's victory?

3. (a) Describe Japan's aggressive actions from 1931 to 1939. (b) Describe Italy's aggressive actions from 1935 to 1939. (c) Describe Hitler's steps toward war between 1933 and March 11, 1938. (d) Outline Hitler's campaign leading to the control of Czechoslovakia. (e) What two countries offered aid to Czechoslovakia in 1938? On what condition? (f) What took place at the Munich Conference? Who was represented there?

4. (a) When and why did Chamberlain abandon the policy of appeasement? (b) What steps did Chamberlain take to stop Hitler in the spring and summer of 1939? (c) What were Russia's terms for joining the anti-Axis front in 1939? (d) What were the principal provisions of the Russian-German treaty of August, 1939?

5. (a) What event was the immediate cause of World War II? What countries promptly declared war? (b) How did Germany and Russia divide the territory lying between them? (c) Trace Hitler's campaigns of conquest in western Europe in 1940. Account for his success.

6. (a) By what two methods did Hitler try to force the British out of the war? (b) What were Hitler's reasons for attacking Russia? When and where did he launch the attack? How far did it penetrate? (c) How did the United States aid Britain, France, and Russia before Pearl Harbor? (d) When, where, and by whom was the Atlantic Charter written? What did it say?

7. (a) What were Japan's aims in the Far East? What was the American attitude toward them? (b) Explain why the Japanese determined to attack the United States. (c) What event brought the United States into the war? When did it occur? (d) Describe the extent of the empire conquered by Japan in 1941 and 1942. (e) Why were the Japanese so successful in the early part of the war?

8. (a) Name the four battles in 1942 which marked the turning point of World War II. (b) Describe the campaigns by which: (1) the Allies won control of North Africa, (2) the Russians cleared their country of Axis forces, (3) the Allies liberated France, (4) Germany was forced to surrender, (5) the "road to Tokyo" was opened, (6) the Stilwell Road was opened, (7) the Japanese were defeated in China.

9. Why did Japan surrender? When was the formal document of surrender signed?

10. (a) Name the main steps which led to the creation of the U.N. (b) What are the four purposes of the U.N.? (c) Name the six major organs of the U.N.

11. (a) Why has the General Assembly been called a "Town Meeting of the World"? (b) What are the two classes of members of the Security Council? (c) Describe the rules which govern voting in the Council. (d) What are the two kinds of decisions issued by the International Court of Justice? (e) What are the duties of the Secretariat? The Trusteeship Council? The Economic and Social Council? UNESCO? World Bank?

12. (a) What plan for the occupation of Germany was outlined at the Yalta Conference and agreed to at the Potsdam Conference? (b) What caused the disputes among the occupying powers in Germany? (c) Trace the steps leading to the setting up of the West German Republic. (d) Why was Italy dissatisfied with her peace treaty? (e) What were the main provisions of the San Francisco Treaty with Japan?

FURTHER ACTIVITIES FOR PART EIGHT

1. Prepare a time line from the armistice of 1918 to 1945. Show the events which have been notable in world history.

2. Debate the question: *Resolved,* that military preparedness leads to war.

3. Imagine that you were a student in Germany in 1936. Write a letter to a friend in the United States, giving the reasons for your enthusiastic support of Hitler. You will find helpful material in Nora Waln's *Reaching for the Stars.*

4. Write a report on the changes made in the Soviet Union by the first and second Five Year Plans. Use references in the library.

5. Prepare a report on international law. Tell how it originated, how it differs from national law, and why it is hard to enforce. Include something about Hugo Grotius and state some of the common rules of international law.

6. Reread the description of the League of Nations and then compare the League and the U.N. in regard to their organization and powers to preserve peace.

7. Report on the trial of war criminals by joint Allied courts in Germany, covering the procedures used, the number of individuals tried, how they were selected for trial, and what the trials accomplished. Consult your librarian for material.

FURTHER READING FOR PART EIGHT

(Stars indicate easier books)

HISTORY

BALDWIN. *Battles Lost and Won: Great Campaigns of World War II.* Harper.

*BARNETT. *The Battle of El Alamein.* Macmillan.

BROME. *The International Brigades: Spain, 1936–1939.* Morrow.

*CAIDIN. *Black Thursday.* Ballantine. (paperback)

———. *The Ragged, Rugged Warriors.* Ballantine. (paperback)

CHRISTENSEN. *The Pictorial History of Western Art.* Mentor. (paperback)

CHURCHILL. *The Second World War.* 6 vols. Bantam. (paperback)

COLLINS and LAPIERRE. *Is Paris Burning?* Simon and Schuster.

*COMAY. *The U.N. in Action.* Macmillan.

*COYLE. *The United Nations and How It Works.* New American Library.

EISENHOWER. *Crusade in Europe.* Doubleday.

*GALT. *How the United Nations Works.* Crowell.

HERSEY. *Hiroshima.* Bantam. (paperback)

HINE and MARSHALL. *D–Day: The Invasion of Europe.* Harper.

HOWARTH. *D–Day, The Sixth of June.* McGraw.

KEITH. *Three Came Home.* Little, Brown.

LAWSON and CONSIDINE. *Thirty Seconds over Tokyo.* Random House.

LORD. *Day of Infamy.* Holt.

———. *Incredible Victory.* Harper.

McNEILL, BUSKE, ROEHM. *The World . . . Its History in Maps.* Denoyer-Geppert.

*NAZAROFF. *Land and People of Russia.* Lippincott.

NEWCOMB. *Iwo Jima.* Holt.

OSADA. *Children of the A-Bomb.* Putnam.

PRATT. *War for the World.* Yale.

PYLE. *Brave Men.* Popular Library. (paperback)

REID. *The Colditz Story.* Lippincott.

REYNOLDS. *The Battle of Britain.* Random House.

*SEARS and PLAYFAIR. *Desert War in North Africa.* Harper.

SHERWOOD. *Roosevelt and Hopkins*. Harper.

*SHIRER. *The Rise and Fall of Adolf Hitler*. Random House. (paperback)

——. *The Rise and Fall of the Third Reich*. Crest. (paperback)

——. *The Sinking of the Bismarck*. Random House.

SIMS. *American Aces*. Ballantine. (paperback)

SNYDER. *The First Book of the Long Armistice, 1919–1939: Europe Between Wars*. Watts.

——. *The Weimar Republic*. Van Nostrand.

TOLAND. *Battle: The Story of the Bulge*. Random House.

TREGASKIS. *Guadalcanal Diary*. Random House.

ULANOFF. *Fighter Pilot*. Doubleday.

*WERSTEIN. *The Battle of Midway*. Crowell.

*——. *Guadalcanal*. Crowell.

*——. *Wake: The Story of a Battle*. Crowell.

WHITE. *They Were Expendable*. Harcourt.

WILLIAMS. *The Wooden Horse*. Abelard-Schuman.

BIOGRAPHY

*ARCHER. *Twentieth Century Caesar: Benito Mussolini*. Messner.

ARMY TIMES (periodical). *Famous American Military Leaders of World War II*. Dodd.

BAKER. *Chaim Weizmann, Builder of a Nation*. Messner.

BLIVEN. *The World Changers*. Day.

BULLOCK. *Hitler: A Study in Tyranny*. Harper.

*CARR. *Men of Power*. Viking.

COOLIDGE. *Makers of the Red Revolution*. Houghton.

EATON. *Gandhi: Fighter Without a Sword*. Morrow.

FERMI. *Mussolini*. Chicago.

FISCHER. *Gandhi*. New American Library. (paperback)

FRANK. *Diary of a Young Girl*. Pocket Books. (paperback)

LOOMIS. *Great American Fighter Pilots of World War II*. Random House.

PAYNE. *The Rise and Fall of Stalin*. Avon Library. (paperback)

SCOTT. *Flying Tiger*. Doubleday.

YOUNG. *Rommel, the Desert Fox*. Harper. (paperback)

FICTION

BEACH. *Run Silent, Run Deep*. Pocket Books. (paperback)

FENNER. *No Time for Glory: Stories of World War II*. Morrow.

FORESTER. *The Good Shepherd*. Little, Brown.

——. *The Last Nine Days of the Bismarck*. Little, Brown.

HERSEY. *A Bell for Adano*. Bantam. (paperback)

——. *The Wall*. Pocket Books. (paperback)

MacLEAN. *Guns of Navarone*. Doubleday. (paperback)

TUNIS. *Silence over Dunkerque*. Morrow.

WOUK. *The Caine Mutiny*. Dell.

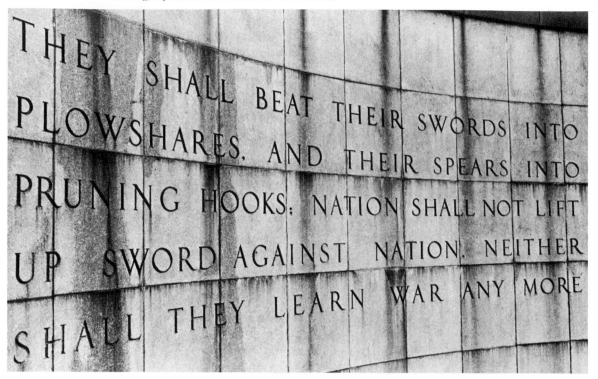

PART NINE

MAN'S SEARCH FOR PEACE AND SECURITY CONTINUES

With the defeat of the Axis powers, new hope for a better world dawned. But the path of peace proved as rocky as before. In Europe both the victorious and the defeated nations struggled to repair and rebuild their shattered cities, their economies, and their morale. With massive United States aid, western Europe recovered rapidly. Meanwhile, the Soviet Union, increasingly distrustful of her wartime allies, expanded her influence by communizing the nations on her western borders. The "cold war" resulted, marked by a series of crises that might have led to World War III. Although a worldwide conflict has been avoided, thanks largely to the "balance of terror" among nuclear powers, limited wars have occurred in Asia, Africa, and the Middle East.

Despite the somewhat gloomy prospects of keeping peace in the world, there have been some hopeful signs that man is concerned about his survival and future happiness. Efforts to achieve at least "peaceful coexistence" have continued. Large-scale foreign aid programs are helping to spread the benefits of advanced technology to the poorer nations of the world.

Meanwhile, man's hopes for the future also rest on his reaching new frontiers of the mind. The knowledge explosion of the twentieth century has emphasized the bewildering speed of change in human culture. In rapid succession the atomic age, the jet age, the computer age, and the space age have seriously affected man's ways of living. His thoughts and his feelings about this new era have been well reflected in his literature, his music, his art, and his educational and religious activities. Man has shown himself remarkably adaptable to the pace of change. Therein lies the hope of a continuing worthwhile existence.

25 The Western World After 1945

DEVASTATED CITY, erected in Rotterdam in 1953, recalls the May of 1940 when Germans bombed the center of the city. The sculpture not only shows the agony of a city destroyed by air raids but also symbolizes how people rebuild their lives and cities.

The defeat of the Axis powers in World War II seemed to mark a decisive triumph for democracy. As after World War I, governments were restored or new ones created along democratic lines. The striking exceptions were, of course, those which had fallen under Soviet control during and immediately following the war. Communist expansion, as we shall see, constituted the major threat to the free nations of Europe. Another challenge they faced was economic—the overwhelming task of rebuilding cities, industries, transportation systems, and farmlands, shattered and disrupted by the devastation of war. The human tragedy was even greater. Nine million homeless, displaced persons had to face the prospect of "starting from scratch" under desolate and discouraging conditions. Even the more fortunate people in war-torn countries had been drained of their ambition and vitality. As Winston Churchill remarked in 1947, "[Europe] is a rubble heap, a charnel house, a breeding place of pestilence and hate." To meet the challenge of recovery and readjustment required heroic effort and leadership as great as that which had been exhibited during the trials of wartime. We shall now examine how the western nations shouldered their burdens and responsibilities in the years after World War II.

Great Britain Faces Economic Crisis

The Labor party comes to power. The leadership which successfully saw Britain through the war was not regarded by the British electors as suitable for the tasks of peace. In July, 1945, Winston Churchill and his Conservative party were voted out of office. The Labor party, with Clement Attlee as prime minister, now came into power for the first time with a clear majority in Parliament. Since the 1920's the Laborites had been gaining strength. Their rise was largely at the expense of the Liberal party, which was less wholeheartedly devoted to the workingman's cause. From 1945 to 1951 the Labor party, committed to democratic socialism, nationalized some major industries and created the broad welfare (social security) system of today.

The early postwar years, however, proved a bitter aftermath to victory. Foreign trade, long the lifeblood of the British economy, had been disrupted. The country had been forced to liquidate (cash in) most of its foreign investments during the war and it lost much of its merchant fleet. Moreover, many industrial areas lay in ruins. Factories that remained had old and outworn equipment and could not produce sufficient goods to pay for the needed imports. Competition with newly industrialized nations, increasing since World War I, was now keener than ever. It took the rigid self-discipline of the British people, plus over four billion dollars in credits and loans from the United States, to stave off economic ruin. Even more disturbing to British composure was the rapid breakup of the Empire. Aside from having certain trade advantages, such as a common currency base in the pound sterling, the Empire served for years as a source of prestige and pride. Now came the time of retreat from colonialism. The last years of empire were 1947–1948, when India, Pakistan, Ceylon, and Burma were granted full freedom. (See pages 619, 623.) Only Burma remained outside the new Commonwealth of Nations, but dissolving ties of allegiance also brought a weakening of economic partnership. Soon a number of other dependent states won the right to self-government. Great Britain became, in fact, what many of its own people referred to as "Little Britain."

The Conservatives return, 1951–1964. The continuation of wartime economic restrictions led in 1951 to the Conservatives' return to power. The party remained in office for nearly thirteen years, under the leadership of its successive prime ministers—Churchill, Eden, Macmillan, and Douglas-Home. The Conservatives gave back the steel and trucking businesses to private owners, but did not disturb the government welfare system. During the 1950's the country's economy recovered and even experienced a boom. Rationing of consumer goods ended in 1954, and general prosperity reached a peak unknown since World War I. Nevertheless, Britain still lagged behind other western European countries in economic growth (the percentage of yearly increase in total output of goods and services). By 1961 an unfavorable balance of trade existed, as production of goods failed to match wage increases. The problem of how to keep its Commonwealth trade and also its markets in western Europe continued to trouble the country. This problem grew as six European nations organized their own trading partnership, the Common Market. (See page 645.) Even though Britain formed a competing free trade group, the European Free Trade Association (EFTA), the desired advantages were not realized. And when her application to join the Common Market was vetoed by President Charles de Gaulle of France, it was a serious blow to British hopes of trade recovery. It also helped bring down the Conservative government in 1964, when labor unrest and unemployment added to the dissatisfaction of the voters.

The Wilson Labor government. The new Labor prime minister, Harold Wilson, and his government faced an economic emergency that had become chronic. He was handicapped by his party's scant majority in the House of Commons, although as time went on the margin increased. To bolster the sagging economy and to overcome the foreign trade deficit, foreign loans had to be made.

Unemployment was down, but wages and prices rose faster than production. Hence more goods were imported than exported. Despite new taxes, an austerity budget, and a freezing of wages and prices, Wilson's government had to devalue its currency in 1967. In United States money the pound fell from $2.79 to $2.40, the first such measure of inflation since 1949. This meant that Britain would have more pounds to spend for its needed imports and for essential government services. Wilson's new bid to enter the Common Market, however, held out little hope of success against De Gaulle's continuing opposition. By 1969 the economic outlook was still bleak. Growing opposition to the Labor government was reflected in the defeat of its candidates in local elections. Yet Wilson managed to keep his government in office and the economy from collapsing.

De Gaulle's France

The unstable Fourth Republic. France emerged from World War II divided and humiliated. General Charles de Gaulle, wartime resistance leader, was head of a provisional government when the war ended. But he would not associate himself with the government set up under the new constitution of the Fourth Republic in 1946. For him it was too weak, and indeed it differed little from that of the Third Republic. With a figurehead president and a premier and cabinet at the mercy of a domineering National Assembly, stability was not assured. One modern feature, however, was the extension of the vote to women. In the first postwar elections the Communist party cast the most votes, but not a majority necessary to form a government. After 1947, shaky coalition cabinets, composed of non-Communist leftists and center parties, struggled to save France from the pitfalls of a rightist dictatorship or of a Communist takeover. The National Assembly, split among six parties of about equal

CHARLES DE GAULLE

strength, forced one cabinet after another to resign. It was the same old headache which had plagued France since 1875. The people became indifferent and even hostile to a government whose factions engaged in what seemed a hopeless tug-of-war. Occasionally, General de Gaulle emerged from retirement to voice his disgust with the unstable political situation. But mostly he bided his time.

Meanwhile, by contrast with the political picture, France's economic recovery was extraordinary. Under the so-called Monnet Plan the government spent nearly forty billion dollars on modernizing the nation's industries. American Marshall Plan aid provided some of the funds. Moreover, France benefited greatly in the 1950's from participation in the European Coal and Steel Community and the Common Market. During the period of the Fourth Republic, France also nationalized some of the major industries and extended social security benefits. These moves, as well as government subsidies to agriculture and to certain industries, put a strain on government income. Furthermore, inflation, tax evasion, and labor strikes tended to cloud the economic sky. Despite these drawbacks, however-

er, the standard of living in France rose to new heights.

The Fifth French Republic. Although the Fourth Republic seemed to weather its political and economic storms, it failed to survive the crisis of empire. It was caught in the worldwide movement for freedom among colonial peoples after the war. In 1954 France suffered defeat at the hands of the nationalists in Indo-China and withdrew. (See page 620.) Two years later it recognized the independence of Tunisia and Morocco. Meanwhile, in 1955 war erupted in Algeria, where Arab nationalists demanded independence and French settlers opposed it. Fearing the French government might abandon them, the settlers and army generals in Algiers seized control and demanded the overthrow of the Paris government. As civil war loomed, French President Coty gave in to popular pressure and appointed General Charles de Gaulle premier. In June, 1958, the National Assembly granted De Gaulle emergency powers for six months.

General de Gaulle proceeded to have a committee draft a new constitution. It increased the powers of the president and premier at the expense of the Assembly, which so frequently in the past had overturned governments. It provided for a new system by which the overseas dependencies received a greater measure of self-government. (See page

---

DE GAULLE'S VIEW OF LEADERSHIP

The Leader must aim high, show that he has vision, act on a grand scale.

—Charles de Gaulle, 1932.

There cannot be a couple at the head of state. Only one man can be in charge. Otherwise the people get the impression that the No. 2 man is doing the steering.

—Charles de Gaulle, 1967.

632.) The French voters overwhemingly approved the constitution of the Fifth French Republic, and in late 1958 elected De Gaulle president. De Gaulle's energetic leadership soon brought order and stability to France. In 1962 he successfully ended the seven-year Algerian War and proclaimed Algeria independent. In the same year De Gaulle scored another triumph by winning a constitutional referendum for the direct election of the French president. And in the following elections for the National Assembly his supporters won a clear majority—a landmark in French history. De Gaulle won a second seven-year term in 1965, although it took a run-off election (for lack of a clear majority) to give him the victory.

Under De Gaulle the French economy continued to flourish for a time. A series of five-year plans boosted production and consumption of goods substantially. But, as in western Europe generally, prosperity tapered off in the late 1960's. It proved more and more difficult to keep wages and rising prices in balance. By 1967, signs of economic trouble appeared. French farmers held "national protest days," blocking railroads and highways into major cities. They said they could not meet the competition of the Common Market countries. Trade unions, too, protested by calling strikes, especially against the government's effort to assume decree power over economic and social matters. Meanwhile, in March, 1967, the Gaullists suffered a setback in the parliamentary elections; their majority in the National Assembly was cut down to a precarious margin. These were signs of dissatisfaction with the De Gaulle regime.

Behind the discontent was also the manner in which De Gaulle operated. His style was that of a benevolent patriarch, making his appeals for support directly to the people. He frequently bypassed the Assembly and the political parties, assigning them a "back seat" in running the government. The bureaucrats (permanent government employees) assumed increasing authority as decision-makers. True, civil liberties were respected, although the government-controlled radio and TV served, for the most part, to back up De Gaulle's policies.

Foreign affairs under De Gaulle. De Gaulle's diplomacy, too, aroused widespread resentment, particularly among France's western allies. Evidently, his primary purpose was to restore France to a position of leadership in Europe and the world, and to have her act as a "third force" between the United States and the Soviet Union. To this end, he kept Britain out of the Common Market, believing that her interests were too closely tied to those of the United States. De Gaulle supported Common Market policies so long as they did not clash with French national interests. For example, he would not agree to reduced Common Market farm prices, since French costs of production were high. Likewise, he vigorously opposed a closer political union of the six nations, for fear that France's (and De Gaulle's) leadership role in Europe might be impaired. He believed Common Market members should stick to economic co-operation. After France joined the atomic power "club" in 1960 by exploding a nuclear bomb in the Sahara, De Gaulle insisted on maintaining his own striking force independent of NATO (the western alliance, see page 643). In the same spirit, France was the only western power to refuse to sign the nuclear test-ban treaty of 1963. De Gaulle further undermined NATO in 1966 by announcing the withdrawal of French forces from NATO's command and by ordering all NATO troops from French soil. "The West is not threatened today as it was when an American protectorate was established in Europe under cover of NATO," he said. Moreover, his Franco-German treaty of reconciliation and co-operation (1963) shocked many Europeans, including some Frenchmen and Germans. On the other hand, he also sought more friendly relations with the Soviet Un-

STUDENTS AND POLICE CLASH IN PARIS. Using clubs and lead-weighted capes, police rush demonstrators. Protesting university regulations, inadequate educational facilities, and alleged police brutality, students hurled cobblestones and chunks of metal.

ion, visiting Moscow in 1966. In Asia, De Gaulle further displeased the free world by extending diplomatic recognition to China (1964). Increasingly, too, he attacked United States policy in Vietnam.

The De Gaulle image fades. De Gaulle's nationalistic show of independence in international affairs and his rather autocratic course at home won him both admirers and enemies. After more than ten years in office his achievements have undoubtedly been impressive. He saved France from possible civil war, stabilized its government, revived its economy, and gave it a new voice in world affairs. But his all-knowing, godlike image was to suffer a reverse.

The greatest challenge to his authority and popularity came in May, 1968, with the outbreak of student riots in Paris. The immediate target of the students' protest was the out-of-date methods and overcrowded conditions in the universities. But there were deeper-seated grievances against the whole "Establishment," the controlling elite in society with its outmoded set of values. (The same rebellious spirit among youth was exhibiting itself throughout the world.) The students were soon joined in their rebellion by strik-

ing workers, whose wages had lagged far behind prices and taxes. As sit-ins were staged in universities and factories, the French economy ground to a virtual halt. The national shutdown lasted for about a month. Rejected by the workers and reviled by the students with such slogans as "To the museum," De Gaulle finally regained his poise. He called for parliamentary elections, emphasizing that the issue was De Gaulle versus the Communists. This was an exaggeration, but it made an effective appeal. Besides, most Frenchmen preferred order to disorder. The election in June gave De Gaulle a new lease on his political life. His supporters won an outright majority in the Assembly while the Communists and other leftist opponents lost more than half of their seats. The General then reshuffled his cabinet, dropping his loyal backer, Premier Georges Pompidou, and replacing him with Couve de Murville. De Gaulle now promised some reforms: for the students, more voice in the administration of the universities; for the workers, the rather vague principle of "participation," which would allow them to share in profits and in decision-making in the factories. But the crisis had been costly and De Gaulle's heroic image had been tarnished. In April, 1969, after losing a referendum on constitutional reforms, the general resigned as president. Evidently the people had rejected the austerity he demanded as the price for French grandeur. France now entered a new era, with Georges Pompidou as president.

Germany: From Ruin to Riches

The "economic miracle." After World War II Germany's future looked very grim. Much of her industrial plant and many of her cities lay in ruins, her territory was zoned off and occupied by the four victorious powers, and millions of Germans lacked the bare necessities of life. Moreover, much of her eastern border region had been lost to Poland and the Soviet Union. From these lost areas, as well as from East Germany (which the Soviets soon turned into a puppet state), thirteen million refugees ultimately fled to the West. For a time, they placed a heavy burden on the limited resources of the Federal Republic.

During the first three years following the war, mere survival was the goal. Then the so-called "economic miracle" began. By 1950 West Germany's industrial production equaled that of 1936 and by 1958 it had more than doubled. Soon West Germany became the foremost industrial country of western Europe. Once again German factory products were finding their way into the far corners of the world and a favorable trade balance resulted. The average citizen now earned higher wages than ever before, and the millions of refugees readily found jobs in the expanding industries.

The nation's rapid recovery can be explained by several favorable conditions. The Germans were always a people of discipline and energy. They had long been noted for their *tüchtigkeit* (thoroughness and efficiency). But they also needed help and inspiration. The former they received from the western allies, once the Soviet Union refused to co-operate in reuniting Germany. American Marshall Plan aid was of crucial importance; ultimately it amounted to more than

GERMANY'S REMARKABLE INDUSTRIAL RECOVERY is well illustrated by this modern industrial section in West Berlin.

3.5 billion dollars. The inspiration came largely from the enlightened leadership of Chancellor Adenauer and his minister of economics, Ludwig Erhard. Unlike the direction taken in Britain and France, Erhard followed the "free enterprise" approach. This evidently gave the Germans the incentive to work harder than before. Their confidence was also restored by the establishment of a sound money system in 1948. West Germany enjoyed other advantages. Many industries had to start from scratch, and therefore were easier to modernize than if the old plants had remained. Furthermore, West Germany did not have to spend money on an expensive armed force, nor on colonies seething with discontent, as did the other great powers. Her unions also co-operated by making only moderate wage demands and by discouraging strikes. Uninterrupted production was the result. Finally, West Germany participated in the European Coal and Steel Community and in the Common Market from their beginning, thus gaining trade advantages over a wide area.

The Adenauer leadership. Much credit for West German recovery must go to Konrad Adenauer, chancellor (premier) from 1949 to 1963. Economic progress would have come much more slowly and painfully without political order at home and harmony in international relations. These were Adenauer's great contributions.

After the establishment of the West German Federal Republic in 1949 (see page 570), Adenauer's CDU (Christian Democratic Union) party had to form a coalition with the conservative Free Democratic party. This was necessary in order to have a working majority in the *Bundestag* (lower house of parliament). The Social Democratic party furnished the chief opposition, but was not effective until 1960, when Willy Brandt became its leader. Meanwhile, the Communist party, never strong, was banned in 1956. Nazi groups occasionally appeared, but at-

KONRAD ADENAUER

tracted relatively few supporters. The Germans seemed committed to parliamentary democracy, and a high percentage of citizens turned out at elections.

In international affairs, Adenauer linked West Germany to the western powers, which had sponsored the founding of the Federal Republic over the objections of Russia. (See page 571.) The Paris treaties of 1954 marked another step in furthering their co-operation. These agreements provided that (1) the western powers would end their ten-year occupation, (2) they could keep troops in West Germany, not as occupiers but as allies, and (3) West Germany would join the defensive alliance, NATO, and rearm itself. At first, the West German parliament resisted these agreements. Many members were against rearmament; they feared it would increase Russia's opposition to German reunification. Moreover, the Bonn constitution had forbidden the draft and a standing army. Then, too, the French, victims of German military might in the past, were reluctant to see Germany rearmed. But as Soviet policy became more aggressive in Europe, opposition to West German participation in NATO declined. In 1955 the Bonn Republic ratified the treaties and thus became fully independent and a member of the western alliance. Adenauer scored a further victory in 1956, when France agreed to return the industrial Saar district to West Germany. Another sign of improving relations with France was the treaty of friendship concluded between De Gaulle and Adenauer in 1963. Meanwhile, as ties between West Germany and the western allies strengthened, hope of reunification of East and West Germany faded. The symbol of disunity since the end of the war was divided Berlin. The building of the Berlin wall in 1961, sealing off the Communist East German sector from the free sector, stood as an unhappy reminder that the goal of reunification was still far off.

Der Alte (old man), as Germans affectionately called Adenauer, served fourteen years as chancellor, retiring in 1963 at age eighty-eight. Under his leadership his people had regained their self-respect and West Germany had become an important bulwark against further Communist expansion.

Since Adenauer. Under Ludwig Erhard, Adenauer's successor, the country's prosperity continued, although by 1965 it had begun to level off. In foreign relations Erhard was less successful than Adenauer. As the United States and France drew apart, German-French relations cooled. The reason was that Erhard backed some United States proposals which De Gaulle opposed, such as the plan for a NATO multilateral (co-operative) nuclear force and British entry into the Common Market. On the other hand, some contacts with East Germany, though unofficial, were maintained. Trade between the two Germanies increased and a limited exchange of visitors on a few holidays was permitted.

Late in 1966 Erhard was forced out of office when the Free Democrats left the coalition government. He was succeeded by Kurt Kiesinger, a former Nazi, whose party, the Christian Democratic Union, now formed a coalition with the Social Democrats. Willy Brandt, leader of the Social Democrats and former mayor of Berlin, became vice-chancellor and later foreign minister. Kiesinger made new proposals to East Germany for lifting travel restrictions and for improving trade and communication. On the whole, the response was negative, for the East German government demanded in return official recognition of its regime—a price West Germany was unwilling to pay. In 1968 Walter Ulbricht, Communist boss of East Germany, imposed new restrictions on passenger and freight traffic between West Berlin and the rest of West Germany. He also banned West German government officials from East Germany. As the parliamentary elections of 1969 approached, Chancellor Kiesinger faced other difficulties. The coalition with the Democratic Socialists proved an uneasy one. Their leader, Foreign Minister Brandt, favored a much more vigorous and independent foreign policy than did the Christian Democrats, particularly toward France and Russia. A new challenge from a rightist party (some called it neo-Nazi), the National Democrats, also arose, as it gained a number of seats in state legislatures. In addition, the economy caused concern; the growth rate declined for the first time in nearly twenty years. Finally, student riots against the established order, as elsewhere, spread across the country in 1968.

Italy's Postwar Road

Economic progress. Like the other European countries, Italy came out of World War II in a state of economic collapse. The road to recovery was a longer and slower one than elsewhere, for Italy's economy before the war had been comparatively backward. Overpopulation and lack of enough good farmland and capital had kept the standard of living low. With the help of Marshall Plan money and supplies, however, Italy's condition soon improved. By the 1960's the country showed the highest economic growth rate in western Europe. Part of the explanation was her membership in the Common Market, which furnished a freer outlet for such Italian exports as automobiles, typewriters, leather goods, and sewing machines. Most of the growing prosperity took place in the industrial north, with Milan as its center. The agricultural south, by contrast, lagged far behind. The government made efforts to balance the regions by passing land reform measures and by encouraging industrialization in the south. Meanwhile, a steady stream of workers moved into the more prosperous industrial north. This helped to reduce Italian regionalism, but it also created problems of housing, education, and overcoming cultural differences. Many Italians, moreover, found jobs in Common Market countries, particularly Germany, where prosperity created labor shortages. But these opportunities declined as the European economic boom tapered off.

The political tug-of-war. After World War II Italy adopted a new constitution which abolished the monarchy and set up a republic. The Communist party, largest outside of Russia and Red China, for a time posed a threat to the new government. But after the cold war began, Communist members were dismissed from the cabinet. The dominant party since 1948 has been the Christian Democrats, who have had to join in coalition governments with other democratic parties. The leader of the Christian Democrats and premier until 1953 was Alcide Gasperi, who did much to stabilize Italian politics in the early postwar period. After his resignation, and under less able leadership, the strength of the leftist parties increased. By 1963 the Christian Democrats had brought into the coalition government the left-wing Socialists, who had previously collaborated with the Communists. The Communists remained a threat, however, as they gained

AUTOMOBILE WORKS in northern Italy exemplifies the economic boom experienced by Italy during the 1960's.

nearly a million votes in the elections of 1963 and again in 1968. The increase was not at the expense of the Christian Democrats but of their Socialist partners. The reasons were that the Socialists had not been able to make good on their promises of social reforms, and prosperity was on the decline. The Communists, on the other hand, ceased to stress the overthrow of capitalism and concentrated on gaining better living conditions for the workers. Furthermore, their supporters increased after Pope John XXIII approved more friendly relations with the Communist world. This made it easier for discontented Italians to express their protest by voting Communist. Under Premier Aldo Moro (1963–1968) and his successor, Mariano Rumor, the government remained shaky. Strikes and student demonstrations reflected the dissatisfied mood of Italians with their government. The survival of any coalition depended on steering a risky course between the Socialist program of extensive reform under government direction and the more moderate program of the non-Communist center and right. To add to the burdens of the government, in 1966 the worst storm in centuries wrecked a third of Italy's economy. Also damaged or ruined were many priceless art and book treasures in Florence, where floodwaters covered most of the city. Funds raised through a worldwide effort helped to restore the objects that could be salvaged.

In foreign affairs, Italy stood firm in its support of the western powers. She was one of the original members of the NATO alliance and the Common Market, and in 1955 was voted into the United Nations. Her relations with Russia, however, took a new turn in 1967 when the two nations signed a pact of friendship. It provided for co-operation in promoting tourism and trade in farm products. Arrangements to construct an Italian automobile factory in Russia had already been made. On the other hand, a thorny dispute continued with Austria over the South Tyrol border region. Terrorists attempted to seize the area for Austria, which had lost it to Italy after World War I. As a result of the trouble, Italy refused in 1967 to approve Austrian membership in the Common Market.

The Soviet Union and Its Empire

The end of the Stalin dictatorship. Stalin's plans for "socialism in one country" (see page 503) had been seriously disrupted by World War II. The staggering loss of life (over six million battle deaths alone) and the massive destruction of homes, factories, and farmlands were greater than those of all of Russia's allies combined. The end of the war brought little relief for the Russian people from the sacrifices of wartime. The fourth Five-Year Plan, begun in 1946, was designed not only to rebuild the nation but also to enable it to catch up with and surpass the capitalist countries, especially the United States. The task required that the workers do without adequate consumer goods, housing, and leisure time. Under the pressure of high production quotas fixed by government planning agencies, the forty-eight-hour week became normal. In industry the results were striking. By 1950 the output of heavy industry—coal, steel, electric power, and oil—surpassed prewar quantities. Agricultural production, on the other hand, lagged behind. Furthermore, Stalin's stepped-up program of organizing large collective farms and mechanizing them still met with resistance from the peasants. Harsh treatment of resisters, as in the 1930's, did not bring the desired results.

In the postwar years the personal dictatorship of Stalin grew even more harsh. In his dual role as premier and first secretary of the Communist party, Stalin made virtually all the important decisions. Those who showed signs of "bourgeois" (capitalistic) influences were forced to confess their "mistakes" and were sent off to slave labor camps. In a new display of nationalism, foreign to Marxist doctrine, the leaders told the people of the glories of Russia's achievements, claiming credit for nearly every important invention ever made. Anti-Semitism, too, in disguised forms, raised its head again. Censorship of news and jamming of foreign broadcasts were designed to keep the people from knowing how the rest of the world lived. True, the government's anti-religious policy had softened during the war, but the reinstated Orthodox Church had to follow the "party line."

In foreign affairs, Stalin now turned to a policy of Communist expansion and infiltration. The confusion and destruction in the aftermath of war aided his efforts. Distrust and obstruction of the western powers characterized Soviet diplomacy more than ever before. As we shall see, this was largely responsible for bringing on the cold war.

Stalin's suspicion and distrust also extended to his own colleagues. He was believed to be making plans for a large-scale purge of his top officials when he died on March 5, 1953. He had been the master of Russia since 1924. Georgi Malenkov succeeded Stalin as pre-

mier, although it was announced that there would be a "collective leadership." Among those who shared authority were Beria, head of the secret police; Molotov, foreign minister; Bulganin, minister of defense; and Khrushchev, Communist party secretary. It soon became clear that a struggle for power was going on among the principal leaders.

The Khrushchev takeover. Malenkov's term was short-lived. In February, 1955, he unexpectedly resigned as premier of the Soviet Union. The reason he gave was the failure of the farm program. But soon it became clear that Nikita Khrushchev, first secretary of the Communist party, had forced Malenkov out. Khrushchev then proceeded to tighten his hold on the reins of power. In June, 1957, he won a close contest within the Presidium (called the Politburo until 1952) against rivals who tried to overthrow him. As a result, three of his enemies were denounced for their "anti-party" views and sent off to minor posts in remote parts of the country. (Under Stalin they would probably have suffered a worse fate.) In March, 1958, Khrushchev made himself premier, still holding on to his position of first secretary of the Communist party. His control of the government now seemed as complete as Stalin's had been.

Meanwhile, Khrushchev had departed from Stalin's policies, though not from Communist goals. At the twentieth congress of the Communist party in February, 1956, he amazed his listeners by denouncing Stalin as a murderer and for establishing the "cult of personality." He also criticized the former leader for turning away from the principles of Marx

and Lenin. This "downgrading" of Stalin, or "de-Stalinization," came as a shock to Communists throughout the world. They had long looked upon him as their idol. It was thought that Khrushchev's startling action was an attempt to make Stalin the scapegoat for the system's failures, particularly in agriculture. Many hard-line Stalinists were soon ousted and trouble brewed among foreign Communist parties.

KHRUSHCHEV DOWNGRADES STALIN

Stalin was a very distrustful man, sickly suspicious; we knew this from our work with him. He could look at a man and say: "Why are your eyes so shifty today?" or "Why are you turning so much today and avoiding to look at me directly in the eyes?" The sickly suspicion created in him a general distrust even toward eminent Party workers whom he had known for years. Everywhere and in everything he saw "enemies, two-facers, and spies. . . ."

—Khrushchev, 1956.

The Soviet new look. The new leadership tried to please the people by producing more consumer goods, reducing workers' hours, ending the tax on private garden plots, and pushing housing construction in the overcrowded cities. Under a new seven-year economic plan, running from 1959 to 1965, a drive was made to pass the United States in butter, milk, and meat production. At the same time Russia made increasing use of technological advances in industry. Although factory output under the plan moved upward, farm production still fell far behind the quotas. So severe did the grain shortage become that from 1963 onward Russia had to import hundreds of thousands of bushels of wheat from the United States, Canada, and Argentina.

Perhaps the most notable departure from the Stalin domestic policies was the greater freedom allowed to Russian citizens. Their privacy now was more respected by the secret police, many slave labor camps were abolished, political prisoners were freed, and regular court trials were substituted for arbitrary police hearings. The authorities also permitted greater freedom to scientists, artists, and writers in pursuing their work. There were limits, of course, and every now and then a "crackdown" served to remind the intellec-tuals of this fact. An example was the case of Boris Pasternak, who was forced to refuse the Nobel literature prize in 1958 because he had criticized Soviet life.

Major changes also came in foreign policy. The most significant development since Stalin was Khrushchev's idea of "peaceful co-existence" with non-Communist nations. He came to realize that nuclear war could destroy the Communist as well as the free world. Hence, war was not inevitable or necessary for the ultimate victory of communism. Maintaining world peace seemed to have become more important than clinging to an ideology drafted in the pre-atomic era. But this revision of Lenin's doctrine did not change the Soviet drive for world domination. Communist victory was now to be achieved by peaceful economic competition and by the support of "just" wars of "national liberation" in developing countries. By 1964, Khrushchev's policy had become the leading cause of a break with Red China.

Meanwhile, Russia's retreat in the Cuban missile crisis (see page 650) and her signing of a limited nuclear test-ban treaty (see page 652) seemed to bear out Khrushchev's desire for "peaceful co-existence." In other ways, too, the trend toward a "thaw" in the cold war was evident. In 1963, Khrushchev sent

RUSSIAN POET
Yevgeny Yevtushenko recites his poems in Tchaikovsky Concert Hall as part of the traditional Day of Poetry in 1963.

condolences to the Vatican on the death of Pope John XXIII; trade treaties were signed with Brazil, France, Italy, and Japan; and direct "hot-line" telephone communication was installed between the Kremlin and the White House for use in case of crisis. It appeared that the Soviet Union had come a long way from the Stalin era.

Although Khrushchev seemed to have a firm hold on the reins of power, all was not harmony within the party Presidium. His tendency to exercise personal rule and the slowing down of economic growth, particularly in agriculture, brought increasing dissatisfaction. In addition, the rift with Red China and the "backdown" in the Cuban affair hurt Russian prestige. In October, 1964, the Presidium abruptly dismissed Khrushchev from his positions of authority. He retired to a quiet life on a *dacha* (country estate) near Moscow. It was a far cry from the treatment accorded fallen leaders by Stalin. Aleksei Kosygin now became premier, and Leonid Brezhnev assumed the key office of party secretary. It looked like a return to "collective leadership."

Since Khrushchev. The new leaders made no basic changes in Soviet policies either at home or abroad. As technicians and economic experts, they showed a primary interest in strengthening Russia's sagging economy. They made a new departure by putting industry under a modified profit system. Supply and demand were now to determine production goals, and factory managers assumed greater control over prices and quality of goods. Some foreign observers viewed this change as "creeping capitalism." The "new economics" included other reforms. Factory workers benefited from the adoption of a five-day work week of forty-one hours. Collective farmers, likewise, were to have improved conditions, with guaranteed monthly incomes. A new Five-Year Plan, ending in 1970, called for reduced goals in both industry and agriculture, but for an increase in output of consumer goods, which were still in short supply.

In foreign affairs the split with Communist China widened as mutual denunciations grew more and more bitter. In 1967 Soviet delegates to China's eighteenth anniversary celebration left the meeting under a barrage of insults. The Chinese also refused to send representatives to the fiftieth anniversary celebration of the Russian Revolution. Soviet-American relations, which had generally improved after the Cuban crisis, were hampered by the escalation of the war in Vietnam and by the outcome of the Arab-Israeli conflict in 1967. (See page 628.) Despite these drawbacks, there were some encouraging gains during 1967–1968. The two nations signed agreements for the permanent disarmament of outer space, for rescuing and returning each other's astronauts, for exchanging consular officers, and for opening direct commercial airline service between New York and Moscow. Still more important were the signing of a nuclear nonproliferation treaty and the proposal to negotiate on the production and use of nuclear missiles. Plans to carry these agreements into effect, however, suffered a setback when Soviet troops invaded Czechoslovakia in August, 1968.

The Soviet empire. In the period immediately after World War II, the Soviet Union turned to a policy of Communist expansion. One major objective was to establish a defensive buffer zone along Russia's western borders. As we have seen, Stalin did not trust his former allies and he also feared a possible resurgence of German aggressiveness. Moreover, both Napoleon I and Hitler had demonstrated that Russia's western frontiers were vulnerable to invasion. Stalin wanted to make sure, therefore, that "friendly governments" were in control of the countries along this boundary. The process of establishing such governments was made easy for several reasons. At war's end, Russian troops actually occupied a large part of the region. The devastation and dislocation created by the conflict had demoralized the Russian people, who already had a long history of national rivalries and bickering. Moreover, the western allies did not fully realize Stalin's purposes, and were under the illusion that wartime co-operation could continue afterward. Hence, by 1947, Poland, Rumania, Bulgaria, and Hungary had fallen under the political and economic domination of Russia. Their governments were run by native Communists, usually trained in Moscow. Yugoslavia had already adopted communism during the war, under the leadership of the freedom fighter Marshal Tito. Tiny Albania soon followed suit. East Germany fell into the Communist camp as a result of the Allied disagreements over the German problem. (See page 571.) To make sure that these satellite countries would pursue uniform policies, a Communist Information Bureau (Cominform) was set up in October, 1947. The Cominform seemed to be a new version of the Communist International (Comintern), which Stalin had dissolved in 1943 as a gesture of goodwill to his allies. The Communists enlarged their front still further in 1948, when infiltrators seized control of the Czechoslovakian government. This *coup d'état* was a shock to the western world because Czechoslovakia had been a stronghold of democracy since World War I. The next month Finland was drawn more closely into the Soviet orbit by signing, at Stalin's request, a mutual aid pact with Russia. Finland, however, was able to retain control over its internal affairs. Thus the Communists had drawn an "iron curtain," as Winston Churchill called it, running from the Baltic Sea to the Adriatic Sea.

The political and economic pattern in the satellites followed closely that of the Soviet Union. The Communist party control became complete in the so-called "people's democracies." Non-Communist leaders were either forced to flee, executed, or otherwise mysteriously made to vanish. The same treatment was in store for any party members who were suspected of "nationalist deviation," that is, of not following the party line as dictated by Moscow. The Communist satellites, imitating Russia, tried to improve their predominantly agricultural economies through rapid industrialization. The emphasis was on heavy industry rather than on consumer goods. Forced collectivization of the farms was also a part of their program. The peasants offered stiff resistance, as in Russia, to collectivization, but in the long run it was generally adopted except in Poland. Despite the pressure and prodding to produce under various five-year plans, the standard of living in the Soviet empire remained low. Moscow saw to it that the puppet states were entirely dependent on the Soviet Union. They were, in effect, merely colonies. The Cominform, the Warsaw Pact alliance, and the Council for Mutual Economic Assistance (Comecon) were designed to keep them in their place.

Cracks in the iron curtain. From the outset, Yugoslavia had been freer from Soviet control than the other satellites. Liberated from Hitler's armies largely through her own efforts, she was in a better position to follow an independent course. Until June, 1948, Marshal Tito, dictator of Yugoslavia, had followed the Communist party line as directed from Moscow. But Russian authorities wanted the country to remain a producer of food and raw materials and urged a speedup in the nationalization of private lands. Tito disagreed. As a result, the Cominform asked Yugoslav Communists to overthrow him. This move failed, and Tito's hold on his nation remained firm. His program was still communistic, but with some modifications. For example, most of the collective farms were broken up and industry returned to a profit basis. The world now witnessed something new—the rise of anti-Russian communism, or Titoism. Economically, for a time

REBELS WAVE THE HUNGARIAN TRICOLOR from a tank captured in the main square in front of the Houses of Parliament in Budapest.

Yugoslavia suffered for her heresy. Cominform countries refused to trade with her. To make up for this loss, the United States, Great Britain, and West Germany extended credits and loans to Yugoslavia. The United States also sent military supplies and received in return strategic raw materials. Instead of joining NATO, Tito signed a twenty-year military pact with two NATO members, Greece and Turkey. After Stalin's death Russia tried to woo Tito back into the Moscow camp. Tito did take some steps toward reconciliation; for example, he exchanged ambassadors and signed a trade agreement with Russia. Nevertheless, his independent communism had become an established fact and an important example.

With Stalin's death, resistance to Moscow's dictation broke out in other iron curtain countries. In 1953 a work speedup in East Germany set off a series of strikes and riots. It required Soviet troops and tanks to put down the disorders. Albania also drifted away from Russia, but for different reasons. She adhered to a strong Stalinist line, as did China, and felt that Russia had betrayed the "true" Marxist-Leninist doctrine. By 1961 the two countries had ended diplomatic relations.

After Khrushchev himself had denounced the Stalin dictatorship in 1956, a new demand for greater freedom arose among the satellites. In June of that year a serious uprising took place in Poznan, Poland. Striking workers demanded higher pay and better living conditions. Exchanges of gunfire between police and strikers left many dead and wounded on both sides. After tanks and troops restored order, the Soviet leaders yielded some ground. They allowed Wladyslaw Gomulka, who had been imprisoned for opposing Moscow controls, to become head of the Polish Communist party. Poland now had somewhat more leeway in managing its own affairs.

The Polish defiance of Russia encouraged the people of Hungary to make a bid for

CZECHS jeer at a Russian tank as troops from the Soviet Union and four other Warsaw Pact nations arrive to put down a short-lived liberal government.

greater freedom from Moscow. Here, however, the outcome was far different. In October, 1956, university students and workers paraded through Budapest streets, demanding release from Soviet control and the return to office of former Premier Imre Nagy. Like Tito and Gomulka, Nagy had supported independent communism. The demonstrations led to riots and bloodshed. The trouble seemed about to end when Nagy returned as premier. Then, in a treacherous move, the Russians brought in reinforcements, shot down thousands of Hungarians, and crushed the revolt. They arrested Nagy, who had been promised safety, and had him executed. A new Soviet dictatorship, under Janos Kadar, was established. As a result, a wave of anti-Russian sentiment spread through the world, even among some of the so-called "neutral nations." The United Nations also condemned the Soviet Union for its brutal military action in Hungary.

The crisis of Soviet communism. Despite its suppression in Hungary, independent communism continued to grow. The new and more liberal course of Stalin's successors in Russia had its influence in the satellite countries. Terrorist methods were abandoned, more emphasis was placed on producing consumer goods, and economic ties with the West were strengthened. Rumania, for example, by 1965 had virtually declared itself free of Soviet economic domination. She refused to comply with Russia's wish to keep the country primarily a producer of raw materials. Rumania's new party leader (1965), Nicolae Ceausescu, went so far as to resist Moscow's pressure to increase the strength of the Warsaw Pact forces. Then, in 1967, Rumania established diplomatic relations with West Germany—a move which caused shivers in Russia and dismay in East Germany. Walter Ulbricht, East German party boss, feared any action that might draw his Communist neighbors closer to his arch enemies in Bonn. Nevertheless, Ceausescu continued to sound a strong nationalistic and independent tone. He differed with Soviet policy concerning the Arab-Israeli War, and in 1969 he further displeased the Russians by warmly welcoming President Nixon to Rumania. For a Communist nation, it was a new departure.

A new crisis in Soviet-satellite relations came in 1968. It developed over Czechoslovakia, more industrialized than the other iron curtain countries and the only one with anything like a democratic tradition. The Czechoslovaks were particularly irritated, therefore, at having to "knuckle under" to the dictates of Moscow. By 1965, as in most satellites, a gradual loosening of the political and economic straitjacket had taken place. The party leader and president, Antonin Novotny, made it clear, however, that Czechoslovakia would continue to follow Soviet wishes.

Signs of trouble appeared in 1967 when the government cracked down on writers and other intellectuals for criticizing the failures of the regime. Some were expelled from the Communist party and others sentenced to prison. The rising unpopularity of Novotny reached a climax in January, 1968, when the party Presidium ousted him. The immediate cause was that the top party leaders lost confidence in his ability to improve economic conditions. Novotny's successor as party secretary was Alexander Dubcêk, the first Slovak to head the Communist party in this country of several minority groups. With unexpected speed Dubcêk put into action a program of liberal reforms that brought a semblance of democracy to Czechoslovakia. Freedom of speech, press, and assembly was restored, political prisoners were released, and special interest groups such as writers, workers, and professional people were permitted to organize and to challenge official party policies. The way now seemed open for non-Communist parties to reappear and compete for political power. Never before had a Communist satellite departed so far from Soviet doctrine. As the clamor for change increased, Moscow and its closest partners (East Germany, Poland, Hungary, Bulgaria) became alarmed. They feared that the democratic contagion would spread to their own countries and even to the Soviet Union. The results not only would be fatal to the Communist system, but would also threaten Russia's defense shield along her western borders. After warnings from the Kremlin and top-level talks between its leaders and Dubcêk, it appeared by July, 1968, that Czechoslova-

kia's democratic revolution might be allowed to succeed. Dubcêk and the new president, Svoboda, had assured Russia and her concerned partners that Czechoslovakia would stay in the Communist camp. But suddenly, on August 20, thousands of Soviet troops, together with Warsaw Pact forces, invaded Czechoslovakia and occupied Prague and other principal cities. The pretext was that they had been invited to come in and quell "counterrevolutionary" groups that were threatening the Communist regime. Despite the courageous show of passive resistance by the Czech people, Russia imposed her will. Summoned to Moscow, Dubcêk and his party colleagues were forced to renounce the program of liberal reforms in return for the promise to remove the occupying forces. The depressed Czechoslovaks again had to accept censorship and all the former restrictions on freedom to assemble and to organize political groups. Moreover, a new seven-year economic agreement bound Czechoslovakia to trade with the Russians. It dashed her hopes of forming more profitable trade ties with the west. Protesting students, workers, and intellectuals continued to resist the takeover. But in the end Dubcêk and his liberal partners had to bend to the Soviet will. In April, 1969, Dubcêk was forced out as party leader. In the words of the Moscow agreement, the situation had been "normalized." Meanwhile, there was no assurance that all Soviet troops would leave the

---

RUSSIA AND THE VIRUS OF REFORM

Seeds sown in Czechoslovakia could in time bear fruit in other areas of the Communist world, perhaps even in the U.S.S.R. itself. Like witch doctors who sought to contain the plague by rushing in to punish an infected tribe, the Soviet leaders may in the long run have done more to spread the virus of reform throughout their empire than to stamp it out.

—James H. Billington, 1968.

1948 YUGOSLAVIA
Tito rejected Moscow's dom-
nation and broke from bloc.

1953 E. GERMANY
Workers rioted in the first
such revolt in a Soviet satellite.

1956 HUNGARY
"Freedom Fighters" fought
Russian tanks but were crushed.

1956 POLAND
Workers staged the "bread"
riots against working conditions.

1961 ALBANIA
Pro-Peking regime broke
from Moscow and the bloc.

1966 RUMANIA
Government moved away
from dependence on Russia.

1968 CZECHOSLOVAKIA
Russian forces invade to
stop liberal reforms.

Communist
countries
Members of
Warsaw Pack

20 SOVIET DIVISIONS

SOVIET UNION

EAST
GERMANY   POLAND

2 SOVIET DIVS.

CZECHOSLOVAKIA

4 SOVIET DIVS.

HUNGARY

RUMANIA

YUGOSLAVIA

BULGARIA

ALBANIA

**THE STORY OF UNREST
IN COMMUNIST EAST EUROPE**

country; some Red Army "defense" units were stationed along the West German border.

The world reaction to Russia's display of naked force was generally one of shock and condemnation. Most significant, perhaps, was the fact that of eighty-eight Communist parties in various countries, only ten approved the Soviet action. There was now a serious question whether Russian leadership of its own Communist camp could last without the use of force.

The Americas after World War II

The United States faces problems of prosperity. The devastation of World War II had not touched the western hemisphere. Recovery, therefore, came more quickly and more easily than in Europe and Asia. This was particularly true in the United States. Here the industrial output, which had doubled during the war, continued to increase, satisfying the huge backlog of demand for consumer goods.

A corresponding rise in national income took place. Though the cost of living also rose, prosperity now reached more people and their standard of living was higher than ever before. Fears that war's end would be followed by a serious depression proved unfounded.

The economic picture was not altogether bright, however. With the removal of wartime price and wage controls in 1946, inflation set in, gnawing away at the purchasing power of the dollar. By 1969 the dollar was worth less than half as much as in 1939. People on fixed incomes suffered the most from the price squeeze. At the same time, taxes remained high. This was necessary mainly to meet the costs of maintaining United States and NATO defenses in the cold war and to carry on the Korean and Vietnam Wars. Well over half the annual budget expenditures went for "major national security," including military defense and foreign aid.

Widespread labor troubles also marked the postwar period in the United States. Fear of unemployment and the rising cost of living brought on a wave of strikes. Labor unions were dissatisfied with the Taft-Hartley Act. It outlawed some union practices and made unions legally liable for violating contracts. Although wages and prices continued to rise, unemployment became serious during the recession of 1957–1958, when seven per cent of the total labor force was out of work. The increasing use of machinery and automation in industry gave little promise of keeping every able-bodied worker employed.

Meanwhile, the farmer was feeling the effects of an old disease—overproduction and declining prices for his products. Scientific and mechanized agriculture made it possible to grow more food than an expanding population required—at least in the United States.

The Eisenhower years. In 1952, after twenty years of Democratic administration, the American people elected Dwight D. Eisenhower as president. The new Republican administration accepted the idea that it was the responsibility of government to promote the welfare of all the people. To that extent, Eisenhower did not abandon the New Deal. But he believed that the states and local communities should assume some of the functions that the federal government had taken over. He also stood for less regulation of business by the federal government.

During his two terms, the Korean War was brought to a conclusion; the Supreme Court issued its historic decision for the integration of Negroes and whites in the nation's schools (1954); and the United States entered the race for space, promoted "atoms for peace," rearmed with nuclear and missile weapons, advocated international control of atomic tests, and met the challenge of the Soviets in the Middle East, East Asia, and Berlin. Moreover, the United States became the fourth largest nation in area, with the admission of Alaska and Hawaii as states. On the other hand, the Eisenhower administration met with less success in dealing with the problems of farm surpluses, lagging employment, an unbalanced budget, and school desegregation in parts of the nation.

The Kennedy administration. In 1960 the Democrats returned to power when Senator John F. Kennedy of Massachusetts defeated Vice-President Richard M. Nixon by a very small margin. In some ways the new administration was pace-setting and precedent-shattering. Kennedy was the second youngest president and the first Catholic to occupy the office. The accent was on youth, both in regard to the men he brought into the service of the government and as to hopes held out to the rising generation by the bold program of the "New Frontier." In less than three years, President Kennedy achieved some substantial successes. The Russians removed their missile bases from Cuba, a limited nuclear test-ban treaty was signed, the Trade Expansion Act was a landmark in reciprocal trade, the Peace Corps marked a new approach to foreign aid, and the first tax cut in years was introduced in Congress (passed under President Johnson). On the other hand, the President's Alliance for Progress proved disappointing; the war in South Vietnam was stalemated; slow economic growth, unemployment, and farm surpluses persisted at home; and the campaign of equal rights for Negroes was marked by bitterness and violence both in the South and in the North.

The Kennedy administration ended in tragedy. While on a speaking tour of the South in November, 1963, the President was struck down by an assassin's bullet in Dallas, Texas.

IN DEFENSE OF LIBERTY

Let every nation know, whether it wishes us well or ill, that we shall pay any price, bear any burden, meet any hardship, support any friend or oppose any foe in order to assure the survival and success of liberty.

—President John F. Kennedy, 1961.

As the nation mourned and began to ask itself *why*, Vice-President Lyndon B. Johnson succeeded to the presidency.

The "Great Society" under Johnson. President Johnson vigorously pursued many of the goals outlined by his predecessor. He overcame congressional opposition with greater success than had President Kennedy and achieved one of the most impressive legislative records of any chief executive. Johnson's first major victory was the passage of the Civil Rights Act of 1964, the most sweeping of its kind in this century. The law banned racial discrimination in employment, schools, voting, and public accommodations. The public accommodations section was the hardest to enforce. While various groups were testing its effectiveness through "sit-ins" and demonstrations, the presidential campaign of 1964 was launched. Senator Barry Goldwater of Arizona, an avowed conservative, was the Republican challenger. After a heated campaign President Johnson won a landslide victory. The voters seemed to approve an active role on the part of the government in trying to improve the social and economic condition of all the people.

Believing that "the Great Society rests on abundance and liberty for all," President Johnson started a "war on poverty" and intensified the drive for racial equality. Under the direction of the Office of Economic Opportunity the federal government poured vast sums of money into antipoverty programs, designed especially to help disadvantaged children and to train unskilled workers. In addition, Congress greatly increased aid to education, particularly in poverty-stricken areas, provided rent subsidies for the poor, and extended hospital and medical care to the elderly under Social Security. As time went on, the war on poverty slowed down because of the cost of the other war, in Vietnam. Charges of inefficiency in running the antipoverty program also caused Congress to cut down its support.

The slow progress in both wars—on poverty at home and in Vietnam abroad—had a direct effect on the so-called civil rights revolution. The 1964 act, already mentioned, was followed by the Voting Rights Act of 1965, providing for registration of qualified voters by federal officials. It gave the Negro greater political power at the polls, especially in the South. In 1968 another landmark was reached in a federal open-housing law, prohibiting racial discrimination in the sale and rental of residential property.

VISTA (Volunteers in Service to America) worker in Alaska teaches adults to read and write.

Despite such legislative victories, the dissatisfaction of the Negro with the pace of improvement increased. Poor housing, inferior schools, and his high unemployment rate were not being remedied fast enough to meet his expectations. Much more needed to be done to make up for the centuries of injustice suffered by the Negro. Frustration and hopelessness led to outbreaks of racial riots in the slum areas of major cities during the years 1965–1968. Dr. Martin Luther King, Jr., clergyman and Nobel peace prize winner, sought to achieve civil rights goals through nonviolent means. But demonstrations, marches, boycotts, and sit-ins did not bring the expected results. The assassination of Dr. King in 1968 set off a new wave of violence in a number of cities, including Washington, D.C. The more militant civil rights leaders now came to the fore, some advocating "black power," that is, greater political and economic control of society by Negroes. The seriousness of the civil rights issue was emphasized by the President's Commission on Civil Disorders. It warned in its report (1968) that "race prejudice has shaped our history decisively; it now threatens to affect our future."

Foreign affairs under Johnson. The Negro protest movement was not the only sign of unrest among the American people. As the cost in lives and money of the Vietnam War mounted, more and more people questioned American policy in pursuing the war. Antiwar groups, especially among college students, became increasingly active, staging demonstrations, marches, and sit-ins. Their opponents generally favored ending the war by escalating the military action. Basically, the question was how far the United States should commit its wealth and armed might in support of freedom throughout the world.

The question was all the more troublesome in view of the widening "dollar gap." This means that the United States was spending more money abroad than it was getting in

MARTIN LUTHER KING, JR.

return. By 1968 a "run" on United States gold reserves had developed. Many foreigners, not trusting the soundness of the American economy, were cashing in their dollars for gold. The government took various steps to remedy the money problem. Cutbacks in loans and investments in foreign countries, restrictions on spending by American tourists, and a tax increase to ease the budget deficit helped to overcome the gold crisis for the time being.

On the other hand, the Johnson administration could claim some solid accomplishments in foreign affairs. Until the invasion of Czechoslovakia by Soviet troops in August, 1968, Russian-American relations showed signs of improving. The treaty to ban nuclear weapons in outer space and military bases on the moon, the treaty to forbid transfer of nuclear weapons to "any recipient whatsoever" (ratified by the United States in 1969), and an agreement to discuss mutual reduction of armaments—all helped to ease tensions between the two superpowers in 1967–1968. Moreover, a meeting of President Johnson and Premier Kosygin at Glassboro, New Jersey, in June, 1967, marked a further step in efforts to maintain friendly contacts with the Soviet Union. The Johnson administration also brought to a successful conclusion the "Kennedy round" of trade negotiations. After four years of talks in Geneva, Switzerland, the member nations of the General Agreement on Tariffs and Trade consented to extensive tariff reductions. Cuts of up to 50 per cent were gradually put into effect beginning in 1968. The benefits for United States and world trade in the years ahead would be substantial.

A hopeful diplomatic move, too, was President Johnson's opening of Vietnam peace negotiations. In April, 1968, North Vietnam leaders agreed to face-to-face talks with American representatives in Paris. By early 1969 no substantial progress had been made, although a breakthrough was expected before long. At first the big stumbling block was the question of unconditional cessation of American bombing of North Vietnam. When, at the end of October, 1968, President Johnson announced a bombing halt over North Vietnam, negotiations still faltered. The South Vietnamese objected to having the National Liberation Front (Viet Cong) admitted to the peace talks on an equal footing with North Vietnam. Although this issue proved an obstacle, South Vietnam, by the end of November, had agreed to send representatives to the Paris peace negotiations. So long as the conference continued, hope for a negotiated settlement did not die.

The election of 1968. The growing dissatisfaction over the war in Vietnam and the civil disturbances in the cities made the election of 1968 a crucial one. Stung by the mounting criticism of his policies, President Johnson surprised the country by announcing in April that he would not seek renomination. This unexpected turn of events intensified the efforts of Democratic contenders for the nomination—Senators Robert Kennedy of New York and Eugene McCarthy of Minnesota, and Vice-President Hubert Humphrey.

The tragic death of Senator Kennedy at the hands of an assassin at Los Angeles in June further complicated the preconvention campaign. It also raised serious doubts about the stability of American society, coming as it did two months after the murder of Dr. Martin Luther King, Jr. In a convention marked by much disagreement, the Democrats nominated Hubert Humphrey. Richard Nixon, the Republican candidate in 1960, was chosen as the standard-bearer of his party. In a vigorous campaign on the issues of law and order at home and the Vietnam War, Nixon won the election by a very narrow margin over Mr. Humphrey, with only 43 per cent of the popular vote. The outcome was affected by the third-party candidacy of George Wallace, former governor of Alabama, who stood for a tough law-and-order policy, states' rights, and an end to forced desegregation. He won the electoral vote in five southern states. Perhaps no President ever faced more challenging problems than Richard Nixon.

Latin America faces hard times. Meanwhile, our neighbors to the south were struggling hard to raise their living standard. World War II had stimulated their industries; but afterward, slumping world prices, declining markets for their goods, the population explosion, and inflation left them in serious economic trouble. They suffered, as the Brazilian president remarked, from the "disease of underdevelopment."

Industrialization seemed the obvious answer to Latin America's problems. This required capital, and the United States had provided no foreign aid program for Latin America as it had for other parts of the world. Private capital proved inadequate to finance the development of the resources of the countries to the south. Trying to help themselves, the Central American republics in 1958 signed a trade treaty which three years later resulted in the establishment of the Central American Common Market (CACM). Another move toward economic co-operation

AGRICULTURAL RESEARCH in Chile. This researcher, supported by funds from the Alliance for Progress, is helping develop a grain that will resist disease, a critical need for Chile which must import nearly twenty percent of its food.

was taken in 1961, when the Latin American Free Trade Association (LAFTA) came into being. Its original members were Argentina, Brazil, Colombia, Ecuador, Mexico, Paraguay, Peru, and Uruguay. They agreed on a twelve-year program of tariff reductions among them as a step toward full economic integration. By 1967 efforts were being made to merge CACM and LAFTA into a hemisphere-wide common market. The prospects were encouraging, but the obstacles that stood in the way of a prosperous Latin America were still overwhelming.

The Latin Americans blamed mostly the United States' trade and loan policies for their economic difficulties. Many also resented the support given by our government to some of the ruling dictators and their wealthy backers. The Communists, although relatively few in number, took full advantage of this resentment to stir up trouble. It took the events in Cuba during 1959 and 1960 (see below), however, to persuade the United States to begin a large-scale economic aid program for Latin America.

The Alliance for Progress. The new program, proposed by President Kennedy, went into effect in 1961. Known as the Alliance for Progress, it set up a ten-year plan for the economic and social development of the Latin American nations. It was viewed as a strong counterweight to Communist subversion. For its purposes, $20,000,000, drawn from private as well as government sources, was to be made available. The United States was to supply over half the amount. All the Latin American nations except Cuba signed the agreement, which pledged them to make reforms in the fields of health, taxation, land, and education. But to the dismay of its promoters, the Alliance for Progress program soon showed signs of stagnation. As with the common market idea, quick solutions to long-standing problems were too often expected. Perhaps the most important stumbling block was the unwillingness of the ruling groups in many of the Latin American countries to make the necessary reforms called for by the agreement. They carefully guarded their positions of privilege. Moreover, periodic revolutions and general political instability handicapped the progress of reform efforts.

Political turmoil continues. In a region long given to unstable politics, it was not surprising that widespread political unrest and violence accompanied economic hard times. Since 1954 the governments in more than half the twenty republics have been toppled at least once. Among the victims were such long-term dictators as Perón in Argentina

(1955), Batista in Cuba (1959), and Trujillo (who was murdered) in the Dominican Republic (1961). Downtrodden people throughout Latin America were in a mood of rising expectations. In the hope of improving their miserable condition, they were willing to listen to radical political leaders. This frequently gave Communists an opportunity to create mischief. The conservatives and military men, on the other hand, in trying to discourage extreme leftist action, sometimes promoted it by opposing needed reforms. In many cases there seemed no middle road between violent revolution and peaceful democratic change. The troublesome problems faced by Latin America can best be illustrated by examining the experiences of several of the countries—Argentina, Brazil, Mexico, and Cuba.

AUTOMOBILE PLANT near São Paulo

Argentina. When Perón was ousted from Argentina in 1955 (see page 537), he left his comparatively rich nation bankrupt. In 1958, after a provisional government had restored order, Arturo Frondizi was elected president. It was the nation's first free election in twelve years. But thereafter the military intervened whenever it felt that its privileged position was threatened. In 1966 the military leaders overthrew the constitutional government of President Illia and installed General Onganía as president. The *coup d'état* came as the result of worsening economic conditions, marked by a staggering inflation and the increased wage demands of the workers. The rising activity of left-wing groups was also the cause of concern. Onganía's government took stern measures to deal with the country's ills. It devalued the peso (the money unit) by about 40 per cent, cracked down on labor unions, dismissed some government employees, and made large loans from the International Monetary Fund and from the United States. For a time conditions improved, as shown by an increasing national product and a favorable trade balance. But by 1969 the economy had again taken a turn for the worse. Unemployment and the cost of living were on the rise, the latter at the rate of 28 per cent a year, and huge government deficits had accumulated. To add to the growing unrest among the people, all political parties were banned, the congress remained dissolved, and universities and students placed under strict control. Furthermore, Onganía removed the more liberal-minded army men from office. The government therefore tended more and more in the direction of one-man rule. The "Argentine revolution" was not fulfilling the people's hopes of economic reform or of a return to democratic politics.

Brazil. Brazil, most populous of the Latin American nations, experienced similar troubles. Under President Vargas' long rule (1930–1945, 1951–1954) the country had begun an ambitious industrialization program.

But the heavy government spending to carry out this program gave rise to a chronic ailment in Brazil's economy—inflation. Vargas' successors faced the same dilemma: how to develop the nation's rich resources without driving the cost of living sky high. President Kubitschek (1956–1961) pushed industrialization still further and spent huge sums of money on roads, dams, hydroelectric projects, and a new capital in the interior, Brasília. Although his efforts raised manufactured goods to a rank second only to that of coffee among the country's exports, the economy suffered. Brazil reached the edge of bankruptcy as the cost of living soared to unprecedented peaks. Corruption in government, tax evasion, and the neglect of education also contributed to a growing popular unrest. Revolution seemed near when in 1964 the army stepped in to place its man in the presidency. The new military regime of General Humberto Castelo Branco took firm action to straighten out the country's economy. Government spending was cut down, taxes increased, tax evaders and corrupt officials punished, and the currency devalued. These stern measures helped to reduce the rate of inflation from 41 per cent in 1966 to 25 per cent in 1967. But at the same time, President Castelo Branco curbed the powers of Brazil's congress, deprived hundreds of citizens of their political rights, and enforced a tight censorship law. The resulting discontent led to riots and demonstrations, especially by students, whose national union was outlawed. Castelo Branco agreed to quit in March, 1967. His army-picked successor, Marshal Arthur Costa e Silva, although promising to take care of the needs of the nation's poor and of its dissatisfied youth, fared little better. Unemployment, low wages, high living costs, illiteracy, and disease continued to plague the country. In 1968 a new wave of student riots broke out in Rio de Janeiro and spread to several other cities. Contrary to tradition, the Catholic clergy lent its support to the anti-govern-

ment protests. In December, 1968, the military government cracked down once more. It suspended Brazil's constitution and the Congress indefinitely.

Mexico. By contrast, Mexico moved far ahead of its Latin American neighbors both in economic progress and in political stability. Ever since the Revolution of 1910 (see page 413), the country has been run by the Institutional Revolutionary Party (P.R.I.). Its long domination may be explained by its support of popular reforms, representing the interests of workers, peasants, and middle-class businessmen. Under the P.R.I.'s special kind of home-grown democracy, the military gradually became a nonpolitical factor in the life of the nation and Mexico enjoyed an unusually long period of domestic peace. This favorable condition enabled the government to carry on an effective program of land reform, industrialization, and expansion of the educational system. Between 1959 and 1964, for example, 38,400,000 acres of land were distributed to landless farmers, as harvests of coffee and wheat climbed to record heights. At the same time, production of petroleum products and steel reached new peaks. In the same period the illiteracy rate was reduced from 53 per cent to 29 per cent. Meanwhile, prices remained steady, so that inflation did not threaten the standard of living. Under President Gustavo Diaz Ordaz, elected in 1964 with 90 per cent of the vote, economic growth continued at a rapid pace. By 1967 the annual rate of increase stood at 7.5 per

---

cent. There were, however, some dark spots in the picture. With one of the fastest rising populations in the world, providing enough jobs for everyone who could work was becoming a serious problem. Moreover, the lot of the rural peasant farmer, who still made up half of the population, was miserable compared to that of the city dweller. In 1968 the government had to put down some minor revolts in rural areas. It also took stern action against the more violent disorders created by protesting students in Mexico City. Their grievances, as elsewhere, stemmed from what they considered an outmoded educational system in which they were not given a sufficient voice. Beyond that, they objected to the ruling party's impatience with dissent and the excessive force used by riot police. The P.R.I.'s long and unchallenged stay in power no longer seemed to satisfy many of the younger generation, who felt left out by the Establishment. By the time the Olympic Games opened in Mexico City in October, 1968, the first to be held in Latin America, student unrest had subsided and order had been restored.

Communist beachhead in Cuba. In Cuba, events after World War II took a different turn. In 1959 the long and cruel dictatorship of General Batista was overthrown. The leader of the revolution was Fidel Castro, who as premier began what seemed to be a sweeping program of democratic reforms. Soon, however, Castro turned on the United States, hurling accusations of "Yankee imperialism" and "economic aggression." He gradually seized almost all United States-owned businesses in Cuba, openly welcomed Communist economic and military aid, and jailed or executed his opponents. In retaliation, the United States virtually cut off Cuban sugar imports, and in October, 1960, placed an embargo on most exports to Cuba. Early in 1961, after Castro admitted he was a Communist, the United States severed diplomatic relations. Eventually, all Latin American nations except Mexico followed suit.

THE OLYMPIC TORCH ARRIVES at ruins in Teotihuacan, an ancient city forty-five miles from Mexico City. Fireworks lit by the torch burst over the Pyramid of the Moon on the eve of the XIX Olympiad.

Thousands of anti-Castro refugees then streamed out of Cuba, mostly to the United States. In April, 1961, some 2000 of them, trained in Central America with the aid of the United States government, attempted to invade Cuba and overthrow Castro. The effort ended in disaster for the invaders at the Bay of Pigs, and the fiasco led to bitter criticism both at home and abroad of the Kennedy administration.

Although his economy approached collapse, Castro sought to export his kind of revolution from Cuba to the other Latin American nations. In the fall of 1963 he supported with arms the Communist guerrillas and terrorists who were trying to prevent election of a democratic government in Venezuela. Cuban-inspired guerrillas also attempted to undermine several other Latin American governments, notably that of Bolivia. There, in 1967, the Bolivian army caught and executed Che Guevara, Castro's revolutionary partner and former war minister. He had carried on an eleven-month guerrilla campaign aimed at setting the torch to Latin American revolution.

The efforts of the OAS. To combat Communist aggression in the western hemisphere, the United States tried repeatedly to get the support of the Organization of American States. (See page 537.) The co-operation of the Latin American nations, however, was often reluctant and halfhearted. The old bugbear of United States intervention seemed to bother them. Nevertheless, the United States in January, 1962, did succeed in getting Cuba expelled from the OAS, but no agreement was reached on imposing collective penalties. During the Cuban missile crisis of 1962 the United States received firmer support when the OAS Council unanimously backed the United States blockade. Two years later an OAS resolution condemned Cuba for its subversive activities in Venezuela and provided for economic and diplomatic sanctions against Castro's government. The OAS also set a

FIDEL CASTRO

precedent by acting as mediator between the United States and Panama in 1964, after a clash of Panamanian demonstrators with American troops in the Canal Zone. The issue was the 1903 agreement which gave the United States permanent rights over the use of the canal. As a result of OAS efforts, discussions were begun which bore fruit in new accords by 1967. Panama was now to have a greater share in the control and financial benefits of the waterway. Finally, after the United States sent troops into the Dominican Republic in 1965 to prevent a Communist take-over, the OAS set up a peace-keeping force there. Only five Latin American nations, however, took part in the action. Later attempts by United States President Johnson to have the OAS establish a permanent military force to prevent similar Communist moves did not succeed. A spirit of close co-operation within the Organization of American States and the Alliance for Progress remained to be achieved.

Trends in Canada. The rapid economic growth of Canada after World War II was in marked contrast to that of Latin America.

Like the United States, which remained her best trading partner, Canada prospered. Her vast deposits of iron, oil, and uranium became of vital importance in an industrial and nuclear age. But her interdependence with the United States brought a business slump during the recession of 1957–1958. Nevertheless, the economic partnership of the two countries received new emphasis in 1959, when through their co-operative efforts the St. Lawrence Seaway and Power Project opened for business. Long in planning and building, the Seaway enabled the passage of all but the largest ships from the Atlantic through the Great Lakes. Thus the "American Mediterranean" was open to four fifths of the world's merchant fleet.

Interdependence and co-operation went beyond economic matters. In 1950 Canada lent its armed support to the United Nations' forces in the Korean War, and as a member of NATO backed the United States in the defense of Europe. Moreover, Canada joined her southern neighbor in building a radar warning system against a polar attack on the continent (the DEW line) and in setting up an air defense command (NORAD).

Although the ties between the United States and Canada have been close, many Canadians for some time have feared that their country might become merely an American dependency. Resentment against United States influence in their affairs was especially strong during the administration of the Progressive Conservative party, from 1957 to 1963. With the return of the Liberal party to power in 1963, continued co-operation with the United States was assured.

A more serious concern of the government was the demand for self-rule by the French Canadians of the Province of Quebec. A renewed mood of unity prevailed, however, as Canada celebrated its one hundredth year as a nation in 1967. The main feature of the celebration was Expo 67, a world's fair held at Montreal. When French President Charles de Gaulle, a visitor at the fair, tried to encourage a "free Quebec," he got a cool reception. The unity of bilingual Canada received additional emphasis when Pierre Elliott Trudeau, a French Canadian, succeeded Lester Pearson as prime minister in 1968. Trudeau opposed Quebec separatism and planned a constitutional reform which would reapportion more fairly the powers of the federal and provincial governments. He expressed the spirit of the new leadership by saying, "Our country deserves more than a blind rush to some imagined utopia, or a blind faith in the prejudices of the past."

MONTREAL. A view of Expo 67 and the St. Lawrence River. Expo 67 celebrated the 100th anniversary of the establishment of Canada and displayed the creative spirit of over a hundred nations.

REVIEWING THE CHAPTER

TERMS TO UNDERSTAND: *EFTA, Monnet Plan, bureaucrats, Establishment, "economic miracle," de-Stalinization, peaceful co-existence, Cominform, iron curtain, Titoism, New Frontier, Great Society, civil rights revolution, black power, dollar gap, CACM, LAFTA, Alliance for Progress.*

PERSONS TO IDENTIFY: *Clement Attlee, Harold Wilson, Charles de Gaulle, Konrad Adenauer, Ludwig Erhard, Willy Brandt, Kurt Kiesinger, Walter Ulbricht, Alcide de Gasperi, Nikita Khrushchev, Aleksei Kosygin, Leonid Brezhnev, Marshal Tito, Wladyslaw Gomulka, Imre Nagy, Alexander Dubček, Dr. Martin Luther King, Jr., John F. Kennedy, Lyndon B. Johnson, Fidel Castro.*

PLACES TO LOCATE: *Algiers, Berlin, Bonn, Milan, Poznan, Brasília, Bay of Pigs, St. Lawrence Seaway.*

QUESTIONS TO ANSWER

1. Summarize the major challenges facing the free nations of Europe after World War II.

2. (a) Name the British prime ministers from July, 1945, to the present and give their political parties. (b) Discuss some of the problems facing Great Britain after World War II.

3. (a) What caused the fall of the Fourth French Republic? (b) What important constitutional changes has De Gaulle brought about in the Fifth French Republic? (c) What were the reasons in the economic, political, and diplomatic fields for resentment against De Gaulle?

4. (a) Discuss some of the problems facing Germany after World War II. (b) Give some of the reasons why the "economic miracle" occurred in Western Germany. (c) Discuss Adenauer's contributions to West Germany.

5. (a) Discuss some of the aspects of Italy's economic recovery and foreign affairs after World War II. (b) Why did the Communist party continue to grow in Italy after World War II?

6. (a) Describe Stalin's rule after World War II in the areas of economics, method of governing, and foreign affairs. (b) Why did Premier Khrushchev "downgrade" Stalin? (c) How, if at all, has Soviet foreign policy changed since 1956? (d) Discuss Communist expansion after World War II. Include its major objective and the ease of obtaining this objective; the European countries which became Communist satellites; the cracks in the iron curtain.

7. (a) What were the main problems accompanying prosperity in the United States after World War II? Draw up a balance sheet of successes and failures in dealing with these problems in each presidential administration from Eisenhower to the present. (b) Discuss the civil rights revolution in the United States, giving its beginnings, its successes, and reasons for continued dissatisfaction. (c) Describe some of the economic and political problems facing the Latin American countries after World War II. How did the Latin American countries and the United States try to solve these problems? (d) Describe Castro's policies in Cuba. (e) Why has Canada prospered while Latin America has not?

26 New Forces and Old Transform the Nonwestern World

INDIA TODAY

In the western world, as we have just seen, the years after World War II brought enormous problems of adjustment to new conditions. In the nonwestern world adjustment was even more difficult. Many parts of Asia, Africa, and the Middle East had been colonies before World War II; after the war they had to learn the skills and disciplines of self-government. In addition, they had to adapt to the economic, cultural, and other changes which were sweeping over the whole world.

As a rule, the new nations sought to keep the best parts of their own cultures and to adopt those new features which met their needs. Often this choice was a difficult one, with opposing groups arguing for conflicting policies. Sometimes the arguments led to violence, with military leaders attempting to take charge, or with Communists seeking to impose their ideology on the nation. Other new countries managed to settle their disputes by democratic means.

Although revolutions and other struggles weakened the new nations, they also enjoyed sources of strength. One such source was economic. Resources such as oil, tin, and uranium were sought by the industrial nations, who gave economic or military aid in return for access to the raw materials. Second, the new nations enjoyed political power, especially through the United Nations. By 1968 they cast over half the votes in the U.N. General Assembly, and thus could influence its actions. Both sides in the cold war wooed the new nations in the hope of gaining their support both in and out of the U.N.

As we shall see, then, the period since World War II has been marked by change in the nonwestern world. Some changes have been peaceful, others violent; some have been constructive, others destructive; some have brought cooperation, and others were divisive. We shall begin with events in East Asia and then move to Southeast Asia, to South Asia, to the Middle East, and lastly to Africa south of the Sahara.

Readjustment in East Asia

Communists seize control of China. Peace in East Asia—and indeed in the whole world —depended increasingly upon conditions in China. With a population totaling more than a quarter of the human race, China's sheer bulk assured her of an important place in world affairs. Furthermore, after World War II China under Communist leadership undertook a vast program of industrialization. As China's industrial power grew, so did her influence.

At the close of World War II China was a great power only in name. Many of her factories and railroads lay in ruins. Manchuria had been industrialized by the Japanese, but when the Russians withdrew they carried away much of Manchuria's heavy equipment. China lost much of its industry. To make things worse, the Chinese people were far from united. Chiang Kai-shek and the Communists had ceased fighting each other in 1937 so that they both could oppose Japan. But in 1945 the truce between the Communist and Chiang's Nationalists ended.

For the United States the situation was difficult. American support had almost alone preserved China's independence at the time of the Open Door Policy, the Boxer Uprising, and Japan's invasion in the 1930's. Now the United States opposed a Communist takeover, but not to the extent of entering a land war in Asia. Instead, it sought by diplomacy

. . . "You are dictatorial." My dear sirs, just as you say. That is just what we are. All the experiences of the Chinese people, accumulated in the course of several decades, tell us to put into effect a people's democratic dictatorship. This means that the reactionaries must be deprived of the right to voice their opinions; only the people have that right.

"Who are the 'people'?" At the present stage in China, they are the working class, the peasantry, and . . . the bourgeoisie. . . .

"Don't you want to abolish state power?" Yes, we do, but not at the present time. We cannot yet afford to. Why not? Because imperialism still exists, and within our country reactionaries and classes still exist.

Our present task is to strengthen the people's state machine—meaning principally the people's army, the people's police, and the people's courts—so that national defense can be made secure and the people's interests protected. . . .

"You are not benevolent." Exactly. We definitely do not adopt a benevolent policy towards reactionaries, or the counterrevolutionary activities of the reactionary classes. Our benevolent policy applies only to the people; it does not apply to such activities or such persons who are outside the ranks of the people.

—Mao Tse-tung, *On the People's Democratic Dictatorship.*

MAO TSE-TUNG

to bring the Chinese factions together. Efforts which had been made before Japan surrendered were followed by sending General George C. Marshall to China in December, 1945. He reported after a year of almost constant conferences that he could find no way to bring the two sides together. In that year fighting between Nationalists and Communists became widespread.

At first Chiang's forces held the advantage. His estimate was that his armies outnumbered the Communists ten to one. His troops were equipped with American arms; all told, the United States provided Chiang with more than two billion dollars' worth of money and supplies after World War II ended.

The Communist armies also had advantages, however. The Russians had allowed them to take over many weapons surrendered by the Japanese in North China and Manchuria. Furthermore, large numbers of the Chinese people seemed to have lost confidence in Chiang and aided the Communists. They were influenced by propaganda which emphasized high taxes and inflation under Chiang, and charged many of his officials with dishonesty. As public support declined, Chiang's armies lost the will to fight. In many cases large groups of soldiers surrendered and turned their weapons over to the Communists. By the end of 1948 the Communists controlled Manchuria. Next they moved against central and southern China, which fell in five more months. In 1949 the Nationalists abandoned the mainland and moved to the island of Formosa, recently retaken from Japan. There were now two Chinas, with the mainland bitterly hostile to the United States.

The thoughts of Mao Tse-tung. Mao Tse-tung ruled as dictator of Communist China. Born in 1893 into the family of a well-to-do farmer, he became a librarian in Peking after attending college. In 1921 he helped to organize China's Communist party. Hard work and persuasiveness made Mao an effective leader. He convinced the party that it should appeal to rural workers rather than to factory workers, as Communists had done elsewhere. His method proved to be successful, for Chiang's government had done little to aid the farmers, and they soon joined with Mao's followers.

When he came to power in 1949, Mao set up a government which he could dominate. The constitution of 1954 gave formal expression to the ideas Mao had put into practice. Chinese government was set up at four levels, with committees called "congresses" at each level sending representatives to serve on congresses at the next highest level. (This plan resembles the system of "soviets" in Russia.) At the highest level was the National People's Congress. At each of the four levels the congress also elected an administrative body called a council. Most powers rested in the councils; at the head of the national council was Mao, who also served as chairman of the Communist party. In theory state and party were separate, but in practice the party directed nearly all activities of the state.

In addition to government and party, many other organizations were formed. Among them were women's leagues and trade unions, student organizations, and the Communist Youth League, with 100,000,000 members. Although Communists held the key offices in these groups, the people were given a feeling that they participated directly in shaping the nation's life. All became familiar with and accepted statements of Mao's philosophy, especially those contained in the booklet entitled "The Thoughts of Chairman Mao." Thus his regime could be described as a dictatorship with a broad base of popular support.

In some respects Mao's policies resembled those of China's emperors. Part of his foreign policy aimed at regaining such lands as Manchuria, Tibet, Mongolia, Indo-China, and others, which China had once claimed. At home he restored the system of examinations (abolished in 1905) by which officials were chosen. The new examinations, of course, tested mastery not of Confucianism but of Communist doctrine, such as that given in the box on page 610.

Domestic policies of Red China. After driving out the Nationalists, Mao and his fellow Communists turned with ruthless brutality to the task of remaking China. Probably 800,000 people accused of opposition met death as "reactionary tools of the imperialists." Many more were punished in other ways. The peasants, on the other hand, were rewarded for having given support to Mao. More than a third of China's farmland was taken from landlords and redistributed. The government took over complete direction of the economy, operating banks, factories, and the transportation system.

Although farm production increased at first, signs of food shortages appeared by 1954. The population was rising at the rate of fifteen million per year—a rate which, if continued, would bring the total to one billion people by 1980. Furthermore, city populations were increasing as industries expanded. Something needed to be done, and Mao chose to apply Communist theory. In 1955, therefore, the government began to organize collective farms. Groups of about two hundred families formed the average number in each collective. Although individual farmers were permitted small plots on which they could raise food for their own use, nearly all the land in the collective was farmed under government direction. This program had only limited success, so in 1958 a far more radical course was adopted. Collective farms were replaced by communes, with about two hundred collective farms to a commune. Private farming was forbidden, and family life was sacrificed for the cause of food production.

Chinese food production declined sharply in 1959, 1960, and 1961. Unfavorable weather conditions were partly to blame, but even the government admitted that the commune sys-

RED CHINA exploded its first hydrogen bomb in 1967. The emergence of China as a nuclear power forced the United States and other nations to re-evaluate their military and political positions.

tem had not worked well. The communes were now reduced in size, to about one hundred families each, and farmers again were allowed small plots of land for their own use. Food production increased, though not to the extent needed, and China was forced to the end of the 1960's to purchase foreign wheat.

Observers generally agreed that China had greater success in a program of industrialization. Between 1952 and 1957 factory output almost doubled. This encouraged the Communists to launch a "Great Leap Forward" in 1958. They intended to use mass labor working at top speed to build new industries. Propaganda spurred the workers to maximum effort in the factory as on the farms. By 1960 the "Great Leap" program, like that of the communes, was in trouble. Crop failures, an end of aid from Russia, and poor planning all helped cause the disaster. The "Great Leap" program was scrapped.

Once the country had caught its breath after the "Great Leap," industrial progress was resumed, though at a slower pace than in the middle 1950's. Under successive five-year plans work went forward on roads and canals and on plants for producing steel, electricity, and other industrial needs. Consumer goods improved in quantity but barely

kept pace with the growth in population, despite a program to encourage birth control. Probably the most important single sign of China's industrial progress from the foreigner's point of view was her entrance into the field of atomic weapons. In 1964 and 1965 China tested atomic bombs, and in 1967 she announced the successful testing of a hydrogen bomb. These developments indicated that major scientific strides had been made.

Other changes involved education. In the past, difficulty of mastering the cumbersome Chinese written characters had limited education to a few. In the 1960's efforts were made to change over to use of the alphabet. Enrollment in schools grew at all levels, and "part-time classes" gave millions of adults the essentials of reading and writing.

To a great extent this educational effort was canceled by the Red Guard. This was an organization of young people who, with Mao's approval, launched a "cultural revolution" in 1966. Apparently Mao felt that communism needed a revival. The Red Guard youths ordered everyone to give up "old ideas, old culture, old customs and old habits." Waving copies of "The Thoughts of Chairman Mao" and shouting Communist slogans, the Red Guard began a reign of terror in

Peking which soon spread to much of China. Buddhist as well as Christian shrines were attacked, as were schools, libraries, art museums, and the persons connected with them. Many schools were closed as the young people left to roam from city to city. By 1968, with the Red Guards fighting pitched battles against more conservative workers and soldiers, Mao called a halt. He gave the army authority to regulate the Red Guard, and ordered the young people to go to work.

Under Mao, China's army expanded until it became one of the largest in the world. Vast reserves of militia made the army capable of great war effort on land. Shortages of ships made seaborne invasions, such as would be needed to capture Formosa, highly unlikely. China also lacked the power to manufacture as much late-model equipment as some industrial nations possessed. In 1966 the loyalty of some of the higher officers came into question. They were removed in a drastic purge and replaced with men known to be ardent Communists. Thus Mao, though aging and rarely seen in public, appeared to have kept his hold on China's millions.

Red China in foreign affairs. The events which shook China also affected every other country in Asia. From the beginning of the Communist movement, Mao's closest ties were with Soviet Russia. For some time Stalin had little expectation that Mao could defeat Chiang Kai-shek. Once it was clear that Mao might win, however, Stalin sent him advisers and military supplies in addition to those taken from Japan in 1945. After 1949 Russian technical assistance increased, and the two countries appeared to be on the best of terms. Mao often spoke of their permanent friendship, and in 1950 the two countries signed a thirty-year treaty of alliance for mutual defense.

To the amazement of many, friendship had turned to open enmity by 1964. Causes of the dispute appeared to be (1) rivalry for leadership of the Communist world, (2) border disputes, and (3) deep disagreement over Communist policy. The Chinese argued for continuing the world revolution by every means, including the use of the atomic bomb. As they expressed it, possibility of nuclear war "does not and cannot alter the law of class struggle, and does not and cannot change the nature of imperialism and reaction." To this the Russians replied that peaceful coexistence was a better policy "because averting nuclear war means saving from death the working class," and because in peace the Communist countries could show their superiority through "magnificent successes in the development of economy, [and] score ever new victories in science and technology."

The split with Russia left China with few friends abroad. As a rule, only little Albania consistently supported Mao's hard-line policies. Although China's name was offered for membership in the U.N. each year, a majority of the members opposed her admission. A major reason for her exclusion to 1970 was that China had fought against U.N. forces in Korea. (See pages 615–616.) Another reason for China's unpopularity was its policy of territorial expansion. Mao made some progress in regaining territories once either ruled or claimed by imperial China. In the north and east, Manchuria, Port Arthur, and other areas which had been held by Japan and Russia were returned to China. (See map, page 614.) To the west, the Communists in 1949 found a number of China's borders to be poorly defined. They settled border questions by peaceful agreements with Burma, Nepal, Mongolia, Pakistan, and Afghanistan. In Tibet, however, they used force.

Tibet for centuries had been a peaceful, semi-independent state ruled by a religious leader called the Dalai Lama. In 1951 the Chinese asserted that they were entitled to govern Tibet; next they installed a communistic government. Tibetans accepted the course of events until 1959, when the Communists attempted to arrest the Dalai Lama.

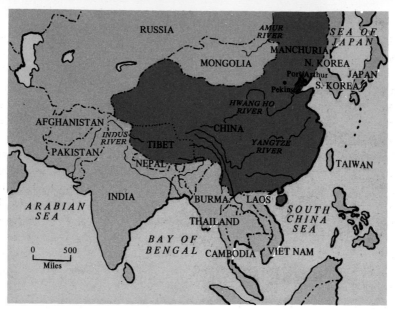

CHINA AFTER 1949

He fled to India with a few followers, while thousands who remained behind were killed.

Perhaps because the Indian people made clear their sympathy with the Tibetans, the Chinese picked a quarrel with India. Their excuse was that the India-Tibetan border had never been agreed upon officially and should be "adjusted." India refused to yield the disputed territory, and in 1962 China attacked high in the Himalayas. Although the fighting ceased early in 1963, Chinese troops continued to occupy most of the territory they had seized.

In the northwest, Outer Mongolia became an object of contention between China and Russia. Outer Mongolia had declared its independence in 1911, at the time of the Chinese Revolution, with Russian support. In 1966, despite Mao's protests, Mongolia signed a mutual defense pact with Russia. Russia also indicated her intention to keep the so-called Maritime Province of Siberia, which once belonged to China.

Korea is freed but divided. Japan's rule over Korea was ended by defeat in World War II. The Koreans had bitterly resented Ja-

pan's policies during forty years of occupation. Japanese had been the official language, Japanese police crushed independence movements, and Japanese "colonists" obtained all the advantages in government, business, and education. Until World War II the Korean economy boomed due to heavy Japanese investment. This economic development was designed to benefit Japan, however, and few of its fruits were passed to the Korean people.

As World War II drew to a close the Koreans hoped for freedom. Some Koreans in the north, led by Communists, set up an underground movement. More conservative Koreans, with Chinese support, met at Shanghai and proclaimed themselves a Korean government in exile. This division of the Koreans into two groups was intensified by arrangements made by the Allies as the war ended. To avoid a chance of conflict between Russian troops coming in from the north and Americans from the south, it was agreed that the Russians would accept the surrender of Japanese north of the 38th parallel in Korea, and the Americans would take over south of that line. Unfortunately, once the Japanese had surrendered, the division of Korea continued. The Russians supported a Communist committee which governed the north, while the American military rule of the south remained in force. Numerous attempts in 1946 and 1947 to unite Korea all failed.

In 1947 the U.N. General Assembly resolved that an election in Korea should choose a government for the whole country. Representatives of the U.N. would supervise, to make sure that the election was fairly held. As election day drew near in 1948, the Russians refused to allow the U.N. commission to enter the north. Voting took place only in South Korea. In August the United States and many other nations recognized the newly chosen government of the Republic of Korea, with Syngman Rhee as president. Rhee had been exiled from Korea in 1897 for leading a demonstration against Japan. In the following years he had worked ceaselessly for Korean independence; now his efforts were bearing fruit.

A month later the Russians announced recognition of the committee which had ruled in the north; it was now known as the Democratic People's Republic, claiming to rule all Korea. Near the close of the year the Russians stated that their troops had been withdrawn. The Americans completed withdrawal from the South in June, 1949. Friends of Korea hoped that the Koreans, left to themselves, would overcome their differences. Communist-controlled North Korea contained much of the industry built by Japan; South Korea had most of the population and raised most of the food. Each section needed the other for economic reasons as well as for the restoration of a unity the Koreans had known for fifteen centuries.

To the North Koreans, unity should come under Communist rule. On June 25, 1950 (June 24, western time) armed forces of North Korea attacked South Korea. The Security Council of the U.N. met in emergency session the following day. With Russia absent in protest because Red China had not been given U.N. membership, the council could act swiftly. It denounced the invasion, ordered North Korea's troops back to the 38th parallel, and asked the U.N. members to help carry out the order. North Korea ignored the U.N. demand. President Truman then directed General MacArthur to use American forces in aiding South Korea. MacArthur was brilliantly successful in defense of South Korea, and in the beginning stages of a move to subdue North Korea. However, as the U.N. forces seemed to be on the eve of complete victory the Korean War entered a new phase. Large numbers of Chinese Communist "volunteers" entered Korea from Manchuria. MacArthur's troops were soon forced southward below the 38th parallel. Here they regrouped and began to move northward again. By the end of January, 1951, the front extended to just north of the 38th parallel and hardly changed for the remainder of the war.

Stalemate in the war led to disagreements over policy. General MacArthur and others believed that the war in Korea could best be ended by striking blows directly at China, now the real opponent in Korea. President Truman and others argued that if the war was extended it might get out of hand and lead to World War III. When General MacArthur's statements were made public, President Truman dismissed him in 1951. Shortly thereafter cease-fire talks with the Communists were initiated. After two years of diplomatic sparring an agreement was reached providing for the exchange of sick and wounded prisoners, and on July 27, 1953, an armistice silenced the guns at last. Terms of the armistice provided that there should be no military buildup by either side and that peace talks would begin.

The peace talks began but soon ended, and rearming in the Communist north led the U.N. command to announce in 1957 that it

THE USS *PUEBLO*, an intelligence ship, was captured by North Korean vessels in 1968. The crew was released eleven months later.

too was modernizing its equipment. Hostile forces continued to face each other while badly needed reconstruction went on in both north and south. A student-led movement in 1960 forced President Rhee from office, and a more democratic government was installed in South Korea. Communist seizure of an American ship off the coast of North Korea in 1968 caused an exchange of threats. Thus until 1970 peace in Korea still had not been restored, and a fair appraisal of the war was difficult.

Opponents of a limited war in Korea charged that nothing had been settled. They felt that greater effort should have been made to bring about a military victory. Defenders of the U.N. policy, on the other hand, asserted that the Korean War made sense. The invaders had not only been repulsed; they had lost a part of their territory and probably more than a million men. More important, the war gave the world its first example of an international organization halting aggression. Which of these two points of view was correct? Only time could tell.

Recovery in Japan. One of the most remarkable events of the postwar world was the revival of Japan. To understand the extent of her revival it is necessary to note conditions at the end of the war. Half of her cities were burned out, three fourths of her

ships had been sunk, and the government was bankrupt. The armistice provided that she should give up Formosa (taken from China in 1895), Korea (given up by China in 1895), the Kurile Islands, Port Arthur, and the southern half of Sakhalin Island (taken from Russia in 1905), the Marshalls, Marianas, and other former German islands given to Japan as mandates after World War I, as well as the territory she had conquered in World War II. Several of these provisions followed terms of the Yalta Agreement shown in the box on page 640, especially those referring to the Kuriles, Sakhalin Island, and Port Arthur.

On the day that Japan surrendered (August 14, 1945) General Douglas MacArthur was appointed Supreme Commander for the Allied Powers. He put into operation the Potsdam Declaration's orders for Japan: that there be established a democratic government with freedom of speech, religion, and thought, which would respect the fundamental rights of humanity. Although the emperor remained on the throne, a new political, social, and economic order in Japan came into existence.

Japan's political changes were summarized in a new constitution which went into effect in May, 1947. It set up a parliamentary government resembling that of Great Britain. A prime minister was chosen by the legislature, and the emperor was forbidden to exercise political powers. Women were given the right to vote, all citizens were guaranteed the right to work and to social equality, and war was renounced forever. Japan thus began a complete turnabout from rule by a few to rule by democracy.

These new policies had the effect of reducing class distinctions. The power of the military leaders—descendants of the *samurai*—and of the business leaders, or *zaibatsu,* was broken. Nearly all titles of nobility were abolished. Landlords had to break up large estates, which were sold to tenant farmers on easy terms. Tenant farming practically disappeared. As a result of these policies, social inequality was reduced in Japan.

Japan's amazing economic recovery grew from a number of causes. Her taxes were reduced, since she no longer had armed forces to support. American investors provided capital for industry, and spending by occupation forces and by the military during the Korean War also brought money to Japan. Government actions also helped, for scarce materials were allocated to firms which were essential to recovery, and businesses were given financial help. Most credit for the recovery, however, belonged to the Japanese people. Their efforts and skills rebuilt Japan. By 1968 Japan had become the world's largest builder of ships, and had surpassed Britain in steel production. Her capital, Tokyo, was the world's most populous city. Trade extending around the globe provided the Japanese people with the highest standard of living of any country in Asia.

Following the war, Japanese leaders tied their foreign policy closely to that of the United States. The two countries signed a mutual assistance treaty in 1951 on the day of the San Francisco treaty, permitting the United States to place "land, air, and sea forces in and about Japan." The United States indicated that it might return to Japan the Ryukyu Islands, including Okinawa. In 1968 the American government promised definitely that Okinawa would be returned to Japanese administration. A possible date was the early 1970's, when the U.S.-Japan Mutual Security Pact was to be reviewed. Nevertheless, some Japanese adopted an anti-American stand. Riots broke out in 1960 when the mutual assistance treaty was renewed, and on a number of later occasions. The Japanese generally supported America in the Korean War but were more divided regarding the fighting in Vietnam (page 621).

Wiping Out Colonialism in Southeast Asia

Postwar events in the Philippines. Dramatic changes also transformed Southeast Asia, as former colonies became free and Communists sought to gain control. First to be freed were the Philippine Islands, as we have seen (page 525). The new government in 1946 resembled that of the United States in form. It faced serious problems: Manila and other cities had been badly damaged by the war, and underground groups plotted a Communist takeover. Both problems were met successfully. Military action against the rebels, plus land reform, brought defeat to the Communists, and American aid helped repair war damages. Assistance took the form of loans, technical aid, and outright grants. Japan also processed some Philippine raw materials free of charge as part of its reparations policy. The Philippine government permitted American armed forces to continue use of bases, under mutual defense treaties.

Although the Filipinos were now politically independent, their economy remained closely tied to that of the United States. About half their foreign trade was carried on with America, and much American capital was invested in Philippine mines and factories. By 1970 in spite of efforts to produce at home the things they needed, the Filipinos still had to import most of their manufactured goods. Some progress had been made, however, in expanding both agriculture and industry. Although a Communist underground movement existed, it seemed to have little chance of success in the face of rising living standards.

Indonesia wins independence. In the Dutch East Indies, just south of the Philippines, native demands for freedom had grown during World War II. After the war the Dutch returned to the East Indies, expecting to govern there much as before. They at once met opposition to their plans, however, and in a short time fighting began. In 1947 the Security Council issued a cease-fire order to both parties and sent a commission to bring them together. This proved to be very difficult. With no settlement in sight, the Dutch in 1948 made the mistake of launching an all-out drive to regain the islands. A wave of world indignation followed, and the Dutch felt compelled to try more peaceful measures. In 1949, at the suggestion of the Security Council, the Dutch transferred sovereignty over all their East Indian islands except New Guinea to the Indonesians. In the following year these islands united under the name "Republic of Indonesia," with a strongly centralized government under President Sukarno. Later he had himself declared president for life. Sukarno showed himself friendly toward the Chinese Communists, and a local Communist movement became very strong. In 1965 Sukarno took Indonesia out of the United Nations. The following year saw a massive Communist attempt to seize Indonesia. A wave of indignation swept over Indonesia. After the army had put down the rebellion, Communists were hunted down and killed—possibly 400,000 in all. Sukarno's powers were stripped from him, and Indonesia rejoined the U.N. Many economic problems remained, however, as a legacy of Sukarno's heavy spending.

General Suharto, sworn in as Indonesia's acting president in 1967, reversed some of Sukarno's basic policies. By 1968 nearly all western-owned industries which Sukarno had seized were back in the hands of their former owners. New investments in Indonesia by Europeans and Americans were growing rapidly, especially those for developing Indonesia's resources of oil, tin, and nickel. The government gave tax holidays and other inducements to foreign investors, hoping that industrial growth would provide jobs and greater prosperity. At the same time, Indonesia ceased to be friendly with Red China and suppressed Indonesian Communists.

The British free Malaysia. Sukarno did his best to weaken British Malaya, on the long peninsula near Indonesia. (See map, page 619.) The British sought to free Malaya on terms agreeable to themselves, the Malays, and the Chinese. (The latter, fewer than the Malays, were concentrated mostly in Singapore.) Many of the Chinese were dissatisfied with an agreement announced in 1947, and began an underground movement. Aided by Sukarno, they attacked plantations, police, and troop patrols. The British might have been driven out had they not made clear that they would give full freedom to Malaya once its citizens agreed among themselves. Support for the rebels dwindled, although fighting lasted for several years. Meanwhile, government in Malaya passed through three stages within a few years: limited freedom in 1948, full self-government in 1957, and membership in the Federation of Malaysia in 1963. The Federation included, besides Malaya, the former British possessions of Singapore, North Borneo (or Sabah), and Sarawak. (Again, see the map on page 619.) Both Indonesia and the Philippines pressed claims to Malaysian territory, and internal disputes also plagued the new republic. After Sukarno's eclipse, Indonesia accepted Malaysia's boundaries. Philippine claims to Sabah were given a "cooling-off period" in 1968, following negotiations with Malaysia. In Singapore events took a different turn.

SOUTHEAST ASIA

Many persons, mostly Chinese, pressed for separation from Malaysia, arguing that they had too little influence with the Malay-dominated government. With British help an agreement was worked out in 1965 by which Singapore became an independent nation—an island republic. She joined with other countries in ASEAN, the Association of Southeast Asian Nations consisting of Indonesia, Malaysia, the Philippines, Thailand, and Singapore. ASEAN, formed in 1967, took on increased importance after the British announced in 1968 that they were removing all their armed forces from areas east of Suez. The independent nations of Southeast Asia would need to co-operate in dealing with mutual concerns, including defense.

Thailand seeks democracy. Thailand (or Siam) alone among the lands of Southeast Asia escaped being "colonized" during the 1800's. This was partly due to the wisdom of her ruler, made famous in the musical "Anna and the King of Siam," who followed a policy of playing the French and British off against each other. A similar policy helped Thailand remain free during World War II. The government co-operated with the Japanese, thus

being spared invasion, but secretly kept in touch with the Allies and thus avoided war with them. After the war the country was plagued by assassinations and revolts. Her problems were not economic, for Thailand prospered from sales of rice, minerals, and forest products. Rather, the difficulties were political: how to achieve democracy at home while avoiding domination by China. A revolution in 1932 had set limits on the king's power, and the constitutional monarchy continued after World War II. Real democracy was not achieved, however, to the dissatisfaction of many. Selection of a foreign policy was also difficult. During the war in Vietnam the Thais permitted American armed forces to build bases in Thailand and to use them for bombing raids on Communist troops in North Vietnam and Laos. Threatened with reprisals by the Communists, Thailand sought security through her membership in ASEAN.

Burma chooses separation from Britain. Burma, Thailand's neighbor to the west, faced strikingly similar problems. Burma chose to separate completely from the British Commonwealth and was permitted to do so

HO CHI MINH

Vietnam, and declared Vietnam a republic. The Allies meanwhile arranged for the surrender of Japanese troops in a manner similar to that followed in Korea: Japanese troops north of the 16th parallel surrendered to the Chinese, and the British took the surrender of troops south of the line.

When French troops arrived they found that nationalist guerrillas held most of the southern countryside. In the north, the Chinese had allowed Ho Chi Minh to keep control of Hanoi. The French agreed to recognize Vietnam as a free state, but soon broke the agreement. After talks with independence leaders broke down in 1946, they bombed Haiphong, a harbor city in North Vietnam, killing many people. Full-scale war broke out in both the north and south, increasing in intensity as other nations became involved. Russia and Red China aided the rebels, particularly after the Korean armistice.

Meanwhile, Laos and Cambodia, the other two states of French Indo-China, were granted greater freedom. Their fate was involved in the Vietnamese war, although they were not fighting. Hostilities ended in 1954, when a French army was completely defeated at Dien Bien Phu. The French met at Geneva with Communist leaders, including the foreign minister of Red China. They agreed to a cease-fire and to practically complete independence for Laos, Cambodia, and Vietnam. The Communists were allowed to keep Vietnam north of the 17th parallel, which Ho Chi Minh thereafter governed separately. He was to take his forces out of the south, and the French were to withdraw from all of Vietnam. Elections were to be held during 1956 in both north and south so as to unite the country, but these did not occur. The leaders of South Vietnam's civilian government apparently believed that the elections, if held, would result in a Communist victory. They argued that they were not bound by the Geneva Agreement because they had not signed it. (The French had signed,

in 1948. Burma's early years of independence proved to be unhappy ones. At one time four separate revolts were under way, and the government held only the capital city. Continued fighting left "the rice bowl of southern Asia" close to bankruptcy. In 1962 a military group seized control and abolished parliamentary government "temporarily"—a condition still in effect in 1970. The military leaders adopted a socialist program, under which the government took over many industries. This program made some appeal to the Communists. However, the government opposed the Chinese Communists in Burma, fearing that they would try to transform Burma into a Chinese satellite. Burma, like Indonesia, tended to move apart from China.

Wars in French Indo-China. The French, like the Dutch, chose to dispute independence movements in Southeast Asia. During World War II the French had of necessity allowed the Japanese to take over French Indo-China. However, an independence league under a Vietnamese Communist named Ho Chi Minh fought the Japanese. With Japan's defeat in 1945 he seized Hanoi, capital city of northern

as had South Vietnam's military leaders, but not the civil officials. The United States also had not signed, having acted only as an observer at Geneva.) Since the parties who had agreed to elections in Vietnam were not in power there, and the men in power had not agreed to the elections, they were never held. Former French Indo-China therefore remained split into the four states of Laos, Cambodia, and North and South Vietnam.

The Geneva Agreement of 1954 failed to satisfy Ho Chi Minh, especially after 1956 passed without elections being held. He seemed to feel that with a little effort he could become master of all Vietnam. For a time, Ho's measures promised victory. His guerrilla forces, the Viet Cong, constantly harassed the south and won the loyalty of many peasants. By 1957 little more than a sixth of South Vietnam was under effective control of the government.

These developments gave increasing concern to the United States. At stake was the freedom of the 240,000,000 people and the rich resources of Southeast Asia. Some Americans thought that Ho might aim at a Vietnam which was communistic but independent of China; others, however, subscribed to the so-called "domino theory." The domino theory got its name from the effect when one sets a row of dominoes on end and then tips the domino at one end of the row—one by one each domino will fall, taking with it the next in line. Believers in the domino theory said that if Vietnam fell to the Communists, other countries in Southeast Asia would likewise fall one by one. As resistance weakened in the south the United States gradually began to aid South Vietnam in checking the Communists.

So it happened that the United States entered the war largely through a series of presidential decisions. President Eisenhower began economic aid to the south in 1954 and in the following year started to train soldiers of South Vietnam. When he left office, American advisers numbered about one thousand. President Kennedy, beginning in 1961, sent combat troops to Vietnam. At the time of his death they numbered nearly fifteen thousand. Aid was increased greatly under President Johnson, especially after two American destroyers were attacked in the Gulf of Tonkin. By the Gulf of Tonkin Resolution in August, 1964, Congress authorized the President to "take all necessary measures to repel any armed attack against the forces of the United States and to prevent further aggression." In

PARIS PEACE TALKS ON VIETNAM, 1969

June, 1965, American commanders were given permission to send their troops into combat, and from that point on the United States was fully at war.

North Vietnam refused to discuss peace arrangements while American troops were present, and continued to send soldiers and arms in increasing amounts to the south. Part of this movement followed the "Ho Chi Minh Trail" through Laos, violating that country's neutrality. The United States played its part in "escalation" of the war by air raids against the north, their intensity at times greater than that of the peak of the air strikes in World War II. Neutral nations as well as Communist ones protested this action. The United States tried bombing halts in an effort to get peace talks started (in 1965, 1966, and 1967), but to no avail.

Unfortunately, the people of South Vietnam were not united. Some of them undoubtedly hoped for a Communist victory. Buddhists, a majority of the population, complained that they were being persecuted, and the Catholic minority feared the Buddhists. During the 1960's several governments came to power in South Vietnam, but none commanded widespread support. High desertion rates among South Vietnamese soldiers suggested that many people were weary after twenty years of war.

War-weariness, in fact, seemed to be general. Americans by 1968 had over 500,000 men in South Vietnam, war costs of about thirty billion dollars a year, a death toll passing that of the Korean War, and no victory in sight. For North Vietnam, also, the war had brought not an easy conquest but ruined cities, a terrible toll of casualties, and the threat of being drawn under tight Chinese control. Under these circumstances, representatives of the United States and of North Vietnam met at Paris in May, 1968, for "talks about talks," that is, for discussions about holding a peace conference.

Little progress was made until November 1 when President Johnson halted American bombardment of targets in North Vietnam. This action helped get the peace talks under way a few weeks later. President Nixon's administration continued to work for a peace based on withdrawal of all foreign troops from South Vietnam so that the South Vietnamese could be free to choose their own form of government. In the fall of 1969, President Nixon began withdrawing U. S. troops as they could be replaced by South Vietnamese.

Facing Independence in South Asia: India, Pakistan, and Ceylon

India freed and partitioned. The people of India long sought freedom from foreign rule. (See pages 523–524.) In 1942, after Japan had overrun Burma and seemed about to invade India, the British promised to give India dominion status after the war was over. For some time the various Indian parties could not agree on any plan for establishing a federal government for India. The chief stumbling block was the Moslem League's insistence on the creation of Pakistan, an independent Moslem state. Finally, in 1947, the Indian constitutional assembly agreed to partition India. As a result, two separate countries emerged—Pakistan (Moslem) and the Republic of India (Hindu). The Republic included most of the princely Indian states. Both Pakistan and India, unlike Burma, chose to remain within the British Commonwealth of Nations, but India inserted the word "Republic" in its official name to show that it did not acknowledge the sovereignty of the British monarch.

Pakistan included two large areas of northern India, one in the Indus valley (West Pakistan) and one on the Ganges (East Pakistan), with a thousand miles between them. There were Hindu minorities in Pakistan and Moslem minorities in what is now the

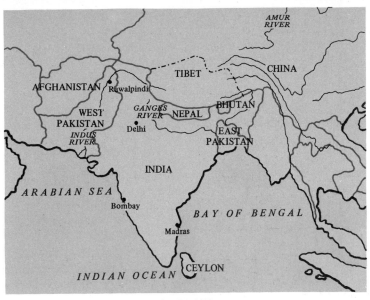

SOUTH ASIA

Republic of India. After the British withdrew (August, 1947), religious riots broke out in both countries and hundreds of thousands of people were killed. Hindus fled from Pakistan and Moslems fled from Hindu territory in this, the greatest migration ever to be held in so short a time. Probably eleven million or more people sought new homes. The inhuman hardships of their journeys and continued mob attacks brought death to many. In an effort to stop the religious strife, Mahatma Gandhi, respected by all parties, went on another fast. He refused food until Moslem and Hindu leaders agreed to make peace. Shortly thereafter, early in 1948, an assassin struck him down.

Friction between Pakistan and the Republic of India has since centered about border disputes. Of these, the most difficult concerns Kashmir, a state in the northwest which is ruled by a Hindu prince, although most of the people are Moslem. Both Indian and Pakistani troops entered Kashmir as the British left, and soon were shooting at each other. In 1949 the U.N. brought an end to the fighting, under an agreement giving India about two thirds of Kashmir, as shown on the map.

Hostilities on a larger scale broke out in Kashmir in 1964–1965. This time an effective cease-fire was negotiated by Prime Minister Kosygin of Russia. Other Indian-Pakistani clashes have occurred along the borders of both East and West Pakistan.

India acted to wipe out remnants of colonial empires once held on her soil by the French and Portuguese. The French peaceably gave up Pondicherry and four other colonies on India's eastern coast. Portugal, on the other hand, refused to accept a World Court ruling in 1960 that she should give up three areas on the west coast south of Bombay. India seized them the following year.

Prime Minister Jawaharlal Nehru took the place of Gandhi as India's spokesman. In economics he steered a middle course. Premier Nehru respected the right to own private property, but he also felt that the government must help raise living standards. In 1950 he launched a series of five-year plans in which the government aided industry, agriculture, and education. Although they were not failures, the five-year plans did not bring the benefits hoped for by Nehru. Part of the difficulty lay with India's population growth, which kept pace with economic growth. In foreign policy, also, Nehru enjoyed but partial success. At first he sought to keep India neutral in the cold war. He advocated the admission of Red China to the U.N., and was therefore suspected by many of being not neutral but pro-Communist. China's attack on India in 1963 only partly dispelled this notion. At his death in 1964 Nehru had achieved limited success.

Nehru's successors continued his policies. His daughter, Mrs. Indira Gandhi, became prime minister in 1966. Her government was plagued by food shortages in 1966 and 1967, caused by droughts and by the steady increase in population. Food shipments from the United States and other countries helped meet the immediate crisis, and the government put increasing emphasis on birth-control programs and food production. New strains of rice and wheat gave promise of much larger yields per acre.

Efforts to modernize Pakistan. Creating a government for Pakistan posed special problems, since the two parts of Pakistan were quite dissimilar. West Pakistan, larger in area, has a dry climate with the result that many areas are desert or semidesert. East Pakistan, with most of Pakistan's people, has extremely heavy rainfall. Although nearly all the people of the two states live by agriculture and are united in the Moslem faith, it has not been easy to forge them into a single country.

A constitution adopted in 1962 gave East and West Pakistan each its own legislature with power to handle local problems. A national legislature was also set up, containing an equal number of delegates from each state. Selection of delegates and of the president was controlled by "electors" from the educated classes who were chosen by the voters. General Mohammed Ayub Khan became president of Pakistan under martial law in 1958 and was later elected to five-year terms in 1960 and 1965. He was supported by the Moslem League, Pakistan's leading political party.

President Ayub made determined efforts to modernize Pakistan. He led moves which ended feudalism and brought a sweeping program of land redistribution. Irrigation projects aided the farmers of West Pakistan, especially after a treaty with India in 1960 provided for sharing water resources of the Indus River. Ayub hoped to build food production to the point where the importing of food would no longer be necessary. His government also encouraged industrial growth, especially the processing of jute, which was East Pakistan's largest export. Although Pakistani living standards in both east and west were low, they were improving steadily.

Despite the gains of his economic program, Ayub's popularity declined. Leftists urged a turn to socialism, and students demanded a more democratic government. Rioting broke out, forcing Ayub to resign early in 1969. Although Ayub had hoped for a new constitution which included election reforms, his successor, General Yahya Kahn, said that democracy could not come soon.

Ceylon and the Colombo Plan. Ceylon, lying eighteen miles off the southern tip of India, chose like India to remain within the British Commonwealth as a republic. Ceylon's position had long made her a natural stopping-place for sailors bound for the Indies. The Arabs, and then the Portuguese, the Dutch, and lastly the English had dominated the island. World War II brought industrial expansion to Ceylon, and the country was prosperous when the British left in 1948. Falling prices on world markets soon hurt Ceylon's economy (based primarily on exports of tea, rubber, and coconuts), although her people still enjoyed a per capita income twice that of India's.

The "Colombo Plan," patterned after the Marshall Plan in Europe and named for Ceylon's capital city, sought to bring prosperity to the nations of southern and southeastern

Asia. The Colombo Plan took effect in 1950, with India, Pakistan, Ceylon, Burma, Malaya, Thailand, and Indonesia as members. They exchanged technicians and information with which they could help each other. "Donor nations"—principally Great Britain—provided money and technical assistance.

During the early 1960's Ceylon's government leaned leftward. It nationalized several industries and also took over some British and American firms. A more conservative party took office in 1965. It agreed to pay for the foreign properties which had been seized, and with western aid launched a program to increase exports.

International co-operation in Asia also took the form of mutual defense agreements. As we have seen, after World War II all of Asia bordering China was in ferment. Korea, Indonesia, Malaysia, Burma, India, and the countries which had once formed French Indo-China all suffered from Communist attacks. North Korea, North Vietnam, and part of northern India fell into Communist hands, and Communist eagerness to seize the rest of Asia was obvious. Hostility between China and Russia could not be counted upon to end the Communist drives. Since most of the new countries in Asia had little military strength, they were vulnerable to Communist pressures. Under these circumstances the United States and other nations of the free world made defense agreements, some with individual nations and others of a regional nature. The most important of these treaties set up the Southeast Asia Treaty Organization (SEATO), which will be discussed in greater detail.

Change Comes to the Middle East

Decolonization in the Middle East. Turning to the Middle East, we find that colonialism also was in full retreat at the time of World War II. Syria and Lebanon, French mandates after World War I, won full independence in 1944. The British gave up their control of Palestine in 1948, and in 1968 gave indepen-

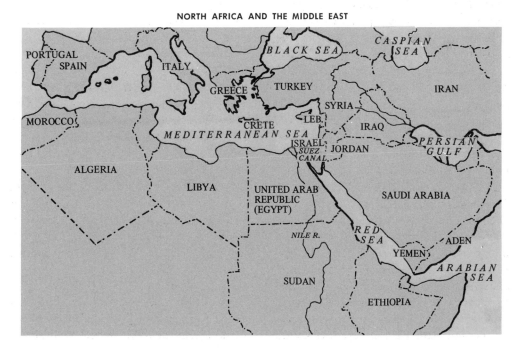

NORTH AFRICA AND THE MIDDLE EAST

dence to Aden and other Arab states which were united in the new country of South Arabia. Aden had been headquarters of British troops in the Arabian peninsula, as Singapore had been their center in Southeast Asia. Withdrawal of British troops meant that the final curtain had fallen on British imperialism in the Middle East. (For the location of Middle Eastern lands today, see the map on page 625.)

Wealth amidst poverty. As in so many parts of the world, the people of the Middle East faced the urgent need to raise their standard of living. But to produce more goods they needed factories and better farming methods; to have factories and modern farms they needed capital and skilled labor; and in most of the Middle East both capital and labor were in short supply. Some countries gave capital and technical assistance individually; other Middle Eastern countries received help from U.N. technical assistance programs. In the long run, however, their chief hope for progress lay in making proper use of wealth

from the sale of oil. Parts of the Middle East seemed to float on a sea of "black gold." In the past, income from oil had tended to remain in the hands of a few while large numbers of people remained ignorant and poor. This pattern began to change in the 1950's and 60's. The Middle East, home of some of man's earliest civilizations, began efforts to catch up with the modern world.

Beginning of changes in Arabia. Saudi Arabia was one of the countries in which oil made the rich richer while the poor stayed poor. King Ibn Saud was said to have an income of a million dollars a day from sale of Arabian oil. He spent most of his income on living expenses for his huge family. In 1964 a "palace revolution" gave the title and power of king to his half brother, Crown Prince Faisal. The new government took a number of forward-looking steps, including much greater emphasis on education, which was made free for everyone. King Faisal inherited an undeclared war in neighboring Yemen. A revolution against Yemen's ruler was backed

DRILLING DERRICK IN SAUDI ARABIA towers over the herd of goats watering at a nearby trough.

by President Nasser of Egypt. To prevent Egyptian domination of Yemen, Saudi Arabia sent aid to the ruler. U.A.R. planes bombed towns in Yemen in 1966, but a truce was reached two years later. During the truce, some Yemen royalists changed sides and joined republican forces.

Iran: world storm center. Oil also flowed plentifully in Iran, once known as Persia. Geography had long made Iran a prize attractive to both Britain and Russia. (See page 428.) During World War II both countries sent forces into Iran to protect the line of Lend-Lease supplies bound for Russia. After the war Russian soldiers stayed on, in spite of Iranian protests. In 1946 Iran appealed to the U.N. Security Council for help in freeing her land from foreign occupation. Debate in the Council followed, focusing world attention on Iran, and Russia withdrew her troops.

Trouble with the British then followed. Iran demanded an increase in payment for oil taken from the ground by a British firm. For a time the company's equipment was seized by the Iranian government. By 1955 the dispute had been settled, and the production of oil was resumed.

However, more than this was needed to improve the lot of Iran's people, who had inherited little more than memories of Persia's glorious past. Demand for a better life for all resulted in the beginning of reform. Land from large estates was distributed to the poor under laws passed in 1949 and 1962, and in 1963 a program of mass education was launched by the government. Taxation of large landholders and other wealthy persons who had not formerly paid taxes was being pushed by 1968.

Israel is reborn. Unrest continued in Palestine after the war. The Arabs sought to retain their dominance in that area; thousands of Jews hoped to find in Palestine a refuge from persecution. In 1947 the British referred the problem of Palestine to the U.N. Assembly, stating their intention to withdraw their troops. The Assembly appointed an investigating committee, which recommended that Palestine be divided into a Jewish and an Arab state.

The plan pleased neither side. In 1948, when the British left, full-scale war broke out in the Holy Land. Dr. Ralph Bunche, an American citizen sent by the United Nations to act as mediator, succeeded in ending the fighting in 1949. The new state of Israel emerged from the war in control of about three fourths of what had been Palestine. The remaining territory, almost entirely Arabic in population, was annexed by the kingdom of Jordan.

Israeli-Arab relations continued to be uneasy. Frequent skirmishes occurred where Israel bordered on Egypt, Syria, and Jordan, as bands of commandos crossed the border to attack the Israelis, who returned the visits with armed raids. In 1956 President Nasser of Egypt seized the Suez Canal and in violation of international agreements barred Israeli shipping from the waterway. Israel invaded Egypt, and Britain and France entered the fighting a few days later. While Egypt's forces were retreating on all fronts, the United States announced disapproval of the invasion. The French and British left, Israel withdrew to her former borders, and a U.N. emergency force kept the peace by occupying disputed territory. Israelis continued to be barred from the Suez Canal.

In 1967 Nasser demanded that the emergency force withdraw. It left in May, and Nasser proceeded to blockade the waters between Israel and the Red Sea. Both sides mobilized troops while the U.N. and individual powers sought to preserve peace. Nasser announced that if war broke out "it will be total and our main objective will be to destroy Israel. . . . At last we feel our might is enough." He appeared to be correct, for Israel was nearly surrounded by enemies and badly outnumbered. The Israelis felt that their best chance for survival lay in striking back. Their forces moved against Egypt, Jordan, and Syria on June 5, following shelling by Jordan and Syria earlier in the day.

The war lasted but six days, and resulted in a spectacular victory for Israel. She seized the Sinai Peninsula, opening the way to the Red Sea for her ships and putting her troops on the eastern edge of the Suez Canal. Territory held by Jordan west of the Jordan River, including part of Jerusalem, fell into Israeli hands. The "Six-Day War" ended with a cease-fire arranged by the U.N. However, the Arabs refused to discuss peace terms directly with Israel. Troops exchanged occasional bursts of fire across the Suez Canal, and terrorist raids continued in the desert. Russia hurriedly replaced the many planes and tanks lost by the Arabs, and peace in the Holy Land seemed far from secure.

In spite of handicaps, Israel achieved remarkable economic growth in the 1950's and 1960's. Land area under cultivation increased more than two and one-half times between 1955 and 1970, port cities were built, mines and wells were opened, and forests were planted. Industry also expanded and provided goods for export. Caring for many immigrants placed a burden on the Israeli economy, but aid also came from abroad through foreign grants and reparation payments by Germany.

Egypt becomes leader of the Arab world. Misrule for centuries retarded progress and kept Egypt's middle class from growing. As a result the people were mostly very rich or very poor and unskilled. Population pressure made conditions worse, for the high birth rate contributed to a low standard of living. The suffering of the people, coupled with reports of extravagance and corruption in the government (contributing to defeat by Israel in 1948–1949), finally brought revolution in 1952. King Farouk fled into exile, and military leaders took over. Colonel Gamal Nasser emerged as the "strong man."

In 1953 Egypt began a series of five-year plans for economic development. Some progress resulted, especially in increased industrialization. Nearly all of Egypt's industries were nationalized in 1961. Nasser hoped for gains in both agriculture and industry from the Aswan High Dam on the Nile, begun in 1960. The dam was designed to produce great quantities of electricity for the cities and to irrigate two million acres of new farmland. American aid for the project was shelved in 1956 because it was felt that Nasser had become too friendly with the Soviet Communists. The Russians then stepped in with financial and technical aid, amid much publicity. In 1964 the first stage of the dam was opened, with completion likely about 1970.

MIDDLE EAST TROUBLE SPOTS as photographed 175 miles above the earth during the flight of *Gemini XI*.

THE GREAT TEMPLE OF ABU SIMBEL was dismantled and moved when waters behind the Aswan Dam began to rise.

As waters rose behind the dam, an international effort succeeded in raising ancient Egyptian monuments to safety.

Egypt pursued an ambitious foreign policy under Nasser. His first project was one of his most successful—that of forming the Arab League. Egypt's capital city, Cairo, was the scene of a meeting in 1945 at which the states of Egypt, Syria, Saudi Arabia, Yemen, Iraq, Jordan, and Lebanon agreed to form a loose association. Later Tunisia, Libya, Morocco, and Sudan also joined. League members usually voted as a bloc in the U.N. General Assembly, and thus exerted considerable influence there. They also stood together on most other international matters, including hostility toward Israel.

To increase his popularity, Nasser needed international triumphs. He scored a success over the British by gaining control of the Suez Canal. In 1956 the British left the canal zone, at Nasser's insistence. Three months later he seized the canal, although by treaty the canal was not to become Egypt's until 1968. Britain and France protested vigorously at this unlawful act and joined with Israel when she invaded Egypt, as we have seen.

After the British, French, and Israelis withdrew, the fact of Nasser's control of the canal was accepted.

Nasser now sought to unite other countries with Egypt in a federal union. In 1958 Egypt merged with Syria to form the United Arab Republic. Egyptians dominated the new government, so the Syrians withdrew after three years. (Egypt continued to call itself the U.A.R., however.) Advantages of closer cooperation continued to attract some Arabs. In 1963 new plans for a merger of Egypt, Syria, Iraq, and Yemen were agreed upon briefly and then dropped because of fear of Egyptian dominance.

Nasser's diplomatic box score shows several failures. Syria backed out of the U.A.R., and attempts to control Yemen by force were blocked by Saudi Arabia. In 1956 the region south of Egypt known as the Anglo-Egyptian Sudan became independent, and continued its connection with Egypt only through the Arab League. The disastrous "Six-Day War" with Israel also hurt Nasser's prestige badly, and he moved toward closer relations with Russia to gain military, economic, and diplomatic aid.

Libya, Tunisia, and Morocco gain independence. Libya, just west of Egypt, was ruled by Italy before World War II. Italy's defeat led the United Nations to acknowledge Libya's independence, effective in 1952. Four years later Libya's neighbor, Tunisia, succeeded in ending a French protectorate. The Tunisians afterward deposed their king, and set up a republican government.

Morocco, opposite Gibraltar, had been a protectorate of France and Spain ever since the Moroccan crises of 1905 and 1911. Arab pressure forced an end to the protectorate in 1956; a united kingdom of Morocco resulted.

The problem of Algeria. By 1960 a line of independent Arab nations stretched along the entire Mediterranean coast—a line unbroken except for Algeria. Algeria presented a problem bristling with difficulties. After France seized Algeria in 1830, many Frenchmen moved there and built Algeria into a productive land of farms and cities. Arab immigration more than kept pace with that of the French, so that the Arabs continued to be in the majority.

Political control remained, however, in French hands. To tie Algeria more closely to France, the French proclaimed it an official part of their mother country. Algerians elected delegates to the French parliament, just as was done in other parts of France. However, carefully restricted balloting left the Arabs with little influence in the government.

Most Arabs in Algeria resented this political arrangement. Some took up arms and attacked the French, either openly or as guerrilla warriors. The demand for a free Arab Algeria met stone-wall opposition from the French colonists. They argued that their labor and investment had brought prosperity to Algeria. A promising beginning of oil production in southern Algeria made the French even more anxious to protect their interests.

In 1958, when General de Gaulle took power in France (see page 581), he faced the Algerian question with boldness. Risking the displeasure of many Frenchmen, he permitted Algerians to vote on the question of separation from France. More than seventy per cent of the voters chose independence in 1962.

Within a few years after 1962 all but about ten per cent of the Europeans emigrated, leaving the governing of Algeria to the Arabs. In the first three years of independence, Algerians followed leftist policies. The government took over many factories and farms and aligned itself with Russia in foreign relations.

Some Algerians became alarmed at the direction which the government was following. In 1965 the army rebelled and placed one of its leaders, Colonel Boumedienne, at the head of the country. He continued to govern with the aid of a 26-man Revolutionary Council; no opposition party was permitted.

Unlike Indonesia, which returned seized properties to their former owners, Algeria under Boumedienne kept them. The state appointed a director over each business or farm, with committees of workers aiding in management. Most of Algeria's foreign trade continued to be carried on with France, and the Algerians and French co-operated in developing oil and other mineral resources in the Sahara Desert.

Arabian nightmares. At the beginning of 1970, no clear solution appeared to a series of dilemmas facing the Arabs. A proud and sensitive people, they had no wish to be dominated by the Russians—yet Russia offered them arms and economic aid. They fervently wished to destroy Israel—yet Israel could not be conquered. They could best reach their goals by uniting under a strong leader—yet Nasser, the logical leader, had not been successful. They might have negotiated a settlement with Israel—yet they could not negotiate, since they refused to recognize Israel's existence. Everyone suffered from these Middle East dilemmas, but the most unfortunate victims were the Arab refugees who had been made homeless in the wars with Israel. Thou-

PALESTINEAN REFUGEE CAMP IN JORDAN. The refugees live in tents, with no electricity or hot water.

sands of them continued to live in "temporary" camps, fed year after year by U.N. grants of a few cents per day for each person. For them and for millions of others, peace in the Middle East would permit a return to productive lives. However, rearmament by both sides and continued border clashes in much of 1969 made war seem more likely than permanent peace.

A New Africa South of the Sahara

New African states are formed. As we have just seen, several new states appeared along the Mediterranean coast of Africa. Many more were formed south of the Sahara after World War II. More than any other part of the earth, Africa was transformed by decolonization. In 1914 only two independent states (Ethiopia and Liberia) existed in the entire continent. By 1969 this number had grown to 37.

British withdrawal. In general, Britain's policy in Africa was that used in Asia: giving freedom to states which were ready for self-government. Three different situations illustrate British actions. Nigeria, in west central Africa—an area occupied by African empires during Europe's Middle Ages—had been prepared by the British for independence. Native Nigerians had been trained for work in public administration, and had been given increasing responsibility. For years they had owned and managed most of the farms and businesses. In 1960, therefore, when Nigeria became free, the move was an orderly one. The Nigerians chose not to break completely with Britain, and took a place beside the other dominions in the British Commonwealth of Nations.

In Kenya, across the continent in East Africa, conditions were quite different. Beginning in 1952 a society known as the Mau Mau attacked the government and landowners, nearly all of whom were white. The British in Kenya, while using force to suppress the Mau Maus, admitted the justice of some Mau Mau complaints. They therefore provided better homes for city workers, more land for farming tribes, and greater voice in the government for all. After peace had been restored, Kenya became independent (1963), but remained in the British Commonwealth of Nations.

Kenya's first prime minister was Jomo Kenyatta, who had led the Mau Maus. Kenyatta purchased farms from Europeans who left Kenya, and divided the land among Africans. He was especially interested in promoting education, and joined with Uganda and Tanzania in developing the University of East Africa at Nairobi.

A third example of British policy in action may be seen in Rhodesia, a landlocked country in southern Africa. Rhodesia had been a member of the Federation of Rhodesia and Nyasaland. Much dissatisfaction on all sides led to separation in 1963, with the Federation being split into three states: Zambia, Nyasaland, and Rhodesia. The first two became independent countries, with governments controlled by their black citizens.

In Rhodesia the whites (225,000 out of a population of about 4,000,000) sought to keep control. They had written a constitution in 1962 which would guarantee them a majority vote in Rhodesia's legislature. This arrangement the British refused to accept; they delayed granting independence until a fairer arrangement could be worked out. The white Rhodesians then defied the British. In 1965 they declared their independence, as the United States had done in 1776. A United Nations order called on U.N. members not to trade with Rhodesia, and many members complied. However, white-dominated governments of countries bordering on Rhodesia continued to keep vital supplies flowing into the country. Premier Ian Smith, leader of white Rhodesia, seemed to have been little hurt by the U.N. sanctions. His regime was threatened also by guerrillas from countries with black governments, but this danger subsided after several public executions. In June, 1969, Rhodesia felt strong enough to adopt a new constitution, naming her an independent republic under white rule.

Closing down the French colonies. The British had followed a quite consistent policy of giving independence to people who were ready for it. The French, on the other hand, changed policies rather abruptly. The French had opposed independence movements in Africa until De Gaulle became president, as we noted in the story of Algeria (page 582). Late in 1958 De Gaulle, convinced that the past policy was a failure, ordered elections to be held in all French Africa. Each territory, except Algeria, could vote for either (1) complete independence, (2) membership in the French Overseas Community, or (3) continuing as a French colony. Only French Guinea chose independence; only French Somaliland chose to remain a colony—a vote reaffirmed in 1967. The remaining twelve French colonies made individual agreements which spelled out their relationship with France. Most of them received practically complete independence in a situation similar to that of the British dominions. By 1970 France continued to hold only a few small islands in addition to Somaliland, now renamed the French Territory of the Afars and the Issas. Most of the members of the Overseas Community had dropped out.

Belgium gives up the Congo reluctantly. Belgium's government held the Congo after World War II with no indication of plans to free the colony. However, riots in 1958 convinced the Belgians that they must make concessions. In June, 1960, they turned the government over to the Congolese without having prepared them for self-government. Unrest now turned to violence. Most Belgian civilians fled in panic, and Belgium flew troops to the Congo.

The Congo became a battleground of the cold war when Russia rushed technicians there and threatened to send troops. The United States promised to do "whatever is necessary" to keep Russian soldiers out. At this point the United Nations hurried a force of 18,000 soldiers to the Congo. They restored a measure of order but could not solve the central problem: the unreadiness of the Congolese to govern themselves. Dag Ham-

UNITED NATIONS troops were sent to the Congo to maintain public order and prevent civil war.

marskjöld, Secretary-General of the U.N., tried without success to settle disputes between rival native leaders.

Congo affairs became further complicated when Katanga, the richest province (state), seceded from the Congo. Without revenues from Katanga's mines and industries, the central Congolese government could not hope to be self-supporting. U.N. forces finally secured the surrender of Katanga in 1963, amid much criticism. Some people charged that the U.N. had exceeded its authority by interfering in the Congo's domestic affairs.

After the U.N. troops departed, a new revolt broke out and was suppressed by the army of the central government. The head of the army deposed the president and prime minister, appointed himself president, and took over the powers of the legislature so that he could rule by decree. The Congo had exchanged colonial status for dictatorship, an action copied in several other African states within the next few years.

Italy loses her colonies. Defeat in World War II cost Italy all her overseas possessions. Libya, in North Africa, became independent in 1952 under U.N. sponsorship. Libya permitted Britain and the United States to main-

tain air bases on her soil with the understanding that they would be closed down in 1969 or soon afterward.

In East Africa, Italian officials had been driven out of Ethiopia by British and Ethiopian troops during World War II. Emperor Haile Selassie returned to Addis Ababa in triumph and resumed the leadership of Ethiopia. The U.N. later voted to cede to Ethiopia the former Italian colony of Eritrea, and the colony known as Italian Somalia was merged with British Somaliland to form the new country, the Somali Republic. Italy and other countries later gave economic aid to the Somali Republic.

Spain and Portugal oppose independence movements. Both Spain and Portugal took neutral positions in World War II and thus avoided the punishment given to Italy. Independence movements therefore came from the colonies rather than from the U.N. Spain and France by joint action gave up their claim over Morocco, long an international trouble spot; it became an independent state in 1938. In 1968 Spain also freed her possessions near the equator.

Portugal, on the other hand, controlled two large and important possessions, Angola and

Mozambique, and governed all as if they were part of the mother country. In practice, this meant that government was almost exclusively in the hands of the whites. Their policies included limiting the voting and citizenship rights of Negroes, and the use of forced-labor contracts which virtually made slaves of the laborers. African protests changed to violence in 1960, when armed uprisings caused much loss of life in Angola.

In 1961 the U.N. Assembly voted overwhelmingly to call on Portugal to halt "the repressive measures against the people of Angola." Portugal paid no heed to the request, and by stern measures put down the rebels. Some escaped to neighboring states with black governments. By 1969 there were "governments in exile" claiming to represent the people of both Angola and Mozambique, and carrying on border raids against the whites in both colonies. This aid of blacks by blacks was countered by the white government of Mozambique, which sent help across the border to the white government of neighboring Rhodesia.

Racial tension in South Africa. Rhodesia's needs for oil and other products were also

ALBERT LUTHULI

met by the Republic of South Africa. After World War II, elections in South Africa gave control to the Nationalist party. Its members were largely of Dutch descent, and its policies were far less liberal than those of previous administrations. The Nationalists followed a policy called *apartheid,* meaning complete separation of the races. Whites made up about one fourth of the population in this country of South Africa. Racial problems were most serious in the cities, where many natives had come to work. Their demands for better housing, schools, and the right to vote led to a tightening of white control and the forcible resettlement of nonwhites.

Criticism from the outside world merely led South Africa's segregationists to withdraw into themselves. They left the British Commonwealth in 1961, taking the new name Republic of South Africa. Similarly, South Africa ceased all but token connection with the United Nations.

The government in power after 1961 ruled that black citizens could not own land, sit in Parliament, or travel without permission. The two million persons of Asian or mixed descent had representatives in Parliament, but they were required to be white. A complicated law effective in 1963 gave blacks in rural areas representative assemblies of their own, but with little power. Stern laws against black meetings and protests were strengthened further in the late 1960's. Albert Luthuli, a black nationalist and leader in passive resistance, the winner of a Nobel prize in 1960, was kept under "house arrest" until his death in 1966. Others who spoke up for freedom often received harsher treatment from the government.

South Africa and the U.N. came into opposition over the question of governing South West Africa, which had been taken from Germany after World War I and given to South Africa as a mandate. South Africa's repressive racial policy was also practiced in South West Africa. Ethiopia and Liberia therefore sued in the World Court to have South West Africa freed. In 1966 the court dismissed the suit, saying that Ethiopia and Liberia had no direct concern with conditions in South West Africa. A storm of protest followed. The U.N. General Assembly voted to end the mandate and bring South West Africa under direct U.N. administration. South Africa, like Portugal, ignored the U.N. and continued to govern as before.

South Africa's racist policies did not prevent her from seeking to have good relations with her black neighbors. Trade agreements were made with several countries, and independence was given to two black nations within what had been South Africa (Lesotho in 1966, and Swaziland in 1968).

Meanwhile, South Africa enjoyed an economic boom. She profited from a worldwide gold shortage, and opened new mines in the 1960's. Other mines also brought wealth, as did the increase in factories which made South Africa "the industrial giant of the continent." Geographic position and economic strength made her the mainstay of the white colonies and countries of southern Africa.

Facing Africa's Problems

Establishing the O.A.U. As one who first begins to walk must expect to stumble, so the new black governments in Africa sometimes made errors. They faced enormous problems and sought to deal with them better through united action. Organization began in 1963 when the heads of thirty African states met in the capital of Ethiopia. There they signed the Addis Ababa Charter of the Organization of African Unity. Some of the signers had hoped to set up an African federation; others wished for a confederation such as that of the American states in the 1780's. (See page 267.) Instead, the Addis Ababa Conference organized an association similar to that of the United Nations. The African organization aimed at freedom, equality, and solidarity of all Af-

rica, and provided for action through an Assembly of Heads of State which would meet annually. A Secretariat to handle day-to-day affairs of the Association was located at Addis Ababa, as was a commission charged with settling disputes between African states. Partly through O.A.U. support the African Development Bank was established in 1965 with the goal of aiding economic growth.

Africa's economic needs. Like the Arab states of North Africa, the new nations south of the Sahara could be classed as "underdeveloped." All Africans, white and black, in 1967 had an average income of only thirty cents per day. Economic difficulties stemmed from a host of causes. European rule had drained rather than built up the colonies; falling prices of raw materials exported by Africa cut into African incomes after World War II; shortages of capital, skilled laborers, and managers hindered industrial and agricultural development; and revolutions often interrupted economic life.

Russia, the United States, and other countries, as well as the U.N., gave money and skilled help to the new nations, but much remained to be done. For instance, health conditions had to be improved, and educational needs were particularly pressing. Yet governments could not afford schools or hospitals when their people needed all their energies just to stay alive.

Africa's political needs. Many of the colonial powers, as we have seen, gave little attention to training black Africans for self-government. Consequently, the new governments often suffered from mismanagement. Tribal divisions served to sharpen African political troubles. African society had centered about the tribe, which gave the individual a feeling of "belonging." Africans often had no real understanding of national needs, and gave their loyalties to the tribe rather than to the nation. The situation can best be understood by examining events in Nigeria, where tribalism had tragic consequences.

... Tribal lines, not national boundaries, make up the true map of Black Africa. The Congo's latent disorder stems more than anything else from its stubborn attempt to throw a skein of nationhood over no fewer than 200 tribes. Even tiny Dahomey numbers more than a dozen tribes within its borders. Worse for national unity, tribalism is growing almost everywhere as a cushion against the shocks of transition into the 20th century. In Africa's multiplying ghettos, tribal "unions" or associations flourish as a kind of foreign embassy in the city for dazed tribesmen from the country. When things go wrong, the tribe itself remains, as Robert Frost said about home, the one place where, "when you have to go there, they have to take you in."

Says Ivory Coast President Felix Houphouet-Boigny: "Tribalism is the scourge of Africa." Unless tribalism goes, adds Kenya's Minister of Economic Planning Tom Mboya, "much of what we have achieved could be lost overnight." Yet no African leader would stamp out tribalism overnight, even if he could. For safety's sake, the leaders themselves pack their governments with fellow tribesmen. . . . So it goes: the central fact of Africa is that no leader can ignore the tribal grouping of peoples linked by common ancestors, speech and customs. . . .

—*Time*, August 23, 1968.

As we noted on page 631, the British made a genuine effort to prepare the Nigerians for independence, and observers expected that Nigeria would become a successful nation. One tribe, that of the Ibo people, had responded brilliantly to British training. The Ibos welcomed a chance at education, and their young people quickly mastered studies in government and business administration. Ibo villages spent about 40 per cent of their tax money on education. After Nigeria became independent in 1960, the Ibos took over much of the nation's business and government. Other Nigerians became jealous of the Ibos' success. When in 1966 a group of army officers from the Ibo tribe killed several non-Ibo leaders, including the prime minister, others reacted fiercely. Ibo soldiers and civilians were murdered by the thousands. Surviving Ibos retreated to their homeland in southeastern Nigeria, a region known as Biafra. In 1967 they proclaimed Biafra a republic, separate from Nigeria.

The federal government, with the backing of the O.A.U. and several western countries, acted to suppress the rebellion. The government blockaded the Biafran coast and sent troops toward the main Biafran cities. Atrocities against civilians were many as the troops advanced, but worse still was the effect of cutting off shipments of food. Since Biafrans could not raise enough food for their needs, they had depended upon air and sea deliveries. When these were stopped, the Biafran people began to starve. Deaths mounted, especially among children. Although the world's conscience was touched, little could be done in relief work until after hostilities ceased.

Other countries faced the tribal problem in a different way. They set up one-party rule, usually with a military man at the head of the state, and thus achieved unity at the expense of democracy.

Summarizing the chapter. Africa, like Asia and the Middle East, included millions of people to whom life offered little except poverty, hunger, disease, and endless toil. Before World War II great numbers of them lived under the rule of foreigners. After 1945 nearly all of them achieved political independence. Many problems remained, however: the fighting off of attacks, either open or underground, by Communists; the building of democratic governments and prosperous economies; and the establishing of peaceful relations with their neighbors. Many of the new nations formed regional organizations so that they could work together in meeting common problems. To a great extent, world peace depended upon how well they succeeded.

REVIEWING THE CHAPTER

TERMS TO UNDERSTAND: *Great Leap Forward, commune, Red Guard, ASEAN, domino theory, Colombo Plan, Six-Day War, Arab League, Mau Mau,* apartheid, *OAU.*

PERSONS TO IDENTIFY: *Chiang Kai-shek, Mao Tse-tung, Dalai Lama, Syngman Rhee, Douglas MacArthur, Sukarno, Suharto, Ho Chi-Minh, Jawaharlal Nehru, Mrs. Indira Gandhi, Mohammed Ayub Khan, Gamal Nasser, Ralph Bunche; Jomo Kenyatta, Ian Smith, Dag Hammarskjold, Arthur Luthuli.*

PLACES TO LOCATE: *Red China, Nationalist China, Tibet, Outer Mongolia, North and South Korea, Indonesia, Sabah, Singapore, Vietnam, Laos, Cambodia, Dien Bien Phu, Republic of India, Pakistan, Kashmir, Israel, Yemen, U.A.R., Aswan Dam, Nigeria, Biafra, Kenya, Congo, Rhodesia, Republic of South Africa.*

QUESTIONS TO ANSWER

1. (a) Trace the struggle for power in China after World War II. How did the United States try to halt the Communist advance? (b) What have been the policies of Communists in dealing with China's internal affairs? In foreign affairs? (c) What have been some of the causes of the dispute between Red China and the Soviet Union? (d) How was Korea governed immediately following World War II? (e) Summarize the events of the Korean War. What are the two opposing points of view on the results of the war?

2. (a) Summarize the postwar changes in Japan in the fields of government, social classes, and economic reconstruction. (b) What were the provisions of the San Francisco Treaty?

3. (a) To what extent have postwar events in the Philippines, Indonesia, Malaysia, Singapore, Thailand, and Burma been influenced by the spread of communism? By the retreat of colonialism? By political instability? (b) How did Laos, Cambodia, and Vietnam get their independence from France? Why did the United States get involved in the war in Vietnam?

4. (a) Since 1945, what changes have taken place in India politically? Economically? In relations with Pakistan? (b) Give some examples of international co-operation in Asia.

5. (a) How has the economy of the Middle East been complicated by each of the following: the retreat of colonialism; the presence of natural resources; Israeli-Arab nationalism? (b) Explain the causes and results of four of the postwar crises in the Middle East. (c) Give examples of international co-operation in the Middle East. (d) Summarize the series of dilemmas facing the Arabs at the beginning of 1969.

6. (a) Discuss Britain's policy toward her colonies after World War II and show how her policy worked out in three African countries. (b) Summarize the political events which have occurred in the following parts of Africa since World War II: in French possessions; in the Belgian Congo; in the Italian possessions; in the Spanish and Portuguese possessions; in the Republic of South Africa. (c) Give examples of international co-operation or regional organizations in Africa. (d) Summarize Africa's economic and political needs.

7. What are some of the many problems facing African and Asian nations today?

27 Conflict and Co-operation in the Space Age

EARTH, 1969

After World War II the so-called cold war developed between Russia and her satellites on one side and the western nations on the other. It was primarily a power contest between the two remaining superpowers, the United States and the Soviet Union. In Europe it was fought mostly with economic and political weapons, taking on the characteristics of an international chess game, with check and checkmate, challenge and response. In Asia it turned into two serious shooting wars. Furthermore, it influenced the international relations of nations in almost every other part of the globe. The United States and its supporters charged Russia with trying to communize the world by methods of infiltration and the threat of force. Russia and its satellites accused the United States of imperialism and warmongering. No other big power rivalry in history has had such far-reaching effects.

In the last two chapters we have repeatedly referred to the cold war as it related primarily to the domestic affairs of the world's nations. It remains now to show how the cold war began and how it led to a series of international clashes and crises, with intermittent attempts at co-operation and peaceful coexistence. Finally, we shall have a brief look at what man has accomplished in science and the arts in recent times, despite the tensions of the cold war.

The sources of conflict. The wartime alliance of the western powers and Russia had been an unnatural and uneasy one. Ever since the Bolshevik Revolution of 1917, a strong fear prevailed among the nations of the West that communism might undermine their way of life. A feeling of mutual distrust had marked their relations with the Soviet Union for nearly a quarter of a century. The alliance, therefore, had been one of convenience, held together only by the threat of defeat at the hands of a common enemy. Winston Churchill justified it when he remarked, "I would ally myself with the Devil himself if it would help me defeat the Nazis." Moreover, until military victory was achieved, all major decisions about postwar adjustments had been postponed. This gave the Soviet Union an advantage, since at the end of the war it was able to back its demands with increased armed strength and its military occupation of much of eastern Europe.

Basically, the peace aims of the world's two superpowers were entirely different. The United States, with its closest ally, Great Britain, held to the principles of the Atlantic Charter as the guideline for a just peace. (See page 554.) The Charter, later accepted by all the countries in the United Nations alliance, pledged that the rights of self-government and self-determination of nations would be respected. In terms of the western democratic tradition, these were idealistic and worthy goals. But to Stalin these noble principles were unimportant compared with the need for Russian security.

The Yalta concessions. Since the era of Peter the Great, a major concern of the Russians had been the danger of invasion across their western borders. Three times in the twentieth century alone enemies had surged into Russia through Poland. Before the end of World War II, Stalin made it clear that he would insist on having governments in eastern Europe "friendly" to the Soviet Union, especially in Poland. When the Red Army "liberated" Poland, the Soviet-sponsored Lublin Committee was set up as the provisional government. Britain and France, on the other hand, recognized the Polish government-in-exile in London. At the Yalta Conference in 1945 (see pages 565 and 570)

Stalin had his way when the western powers agreed to a new government based on an enlarged Lublin Committee. President Roosevelt and Prime Minister Churchill did get from the Russians a promise that the new Polish government would hold "free and unfettered elections." The same pledge was made with regard to the other occupied countries of eastern Europe. As we have already seen, these promises were not kept. Where Soviet forces were in control at the end of the war (in Poland, Czechoslovakia, Rumania, Bulgaria, and Hungary), inevitably governments friendly to Russia were set up, that is, governments run by Communists. In addition, at Yalta Roosevelt and Churchill yielded to Stalin much of eastern Poland, in return for which Poland received a large slice of Germany east of the Oder-Neisse line. This concession further assured the Soviets of a strong defense buffer against future invasions from the West.

At Yalta, Russia likewise secured its Far Eastern frontiers. Stalin agreed to enter the war against Japan "two or three months" after Germany's surrender in return for the territories and rights lost in the Russo-Japanese War of 1904–1905. (See pages 404 and 433.) Stalin's price was a heavy one, and the charge has been made that Roosevelt yielded too much to Russia unnecessarily. But at the time, the United States did not yet have the atomic bomb, and the President's military advisers persuaded him that Russia's help was needed to defeat Japan. Roosevelt also seemed to believe that he could keep the Anglo-Soviet-American wartime friendship alive. The fact was that the Soviet Union held the trump cards. With its newly won military strength, it was determined to satisfy age-old territorial ambitions as well as to spread the doctrines of the Communist revolution. Short of another war, there was no way to stop Soviet expansion. As James F. Byrnes, one of America's delegates at Yalta, said, "It was not a question of what we would let the Russians do, but what we could get the Russians to do."

1947—year of decision. Russia's aim to achieve national security in the postwar world did not stop with domination of eastern Europe and the strengthening of her position in Asia. Her major concern was the possibility of a revived and powerful Germany which again might threaten her safety. The chief goal of the Soviet Union, therefore, was to set up a friendly government, meaning Communist, in Germany as well. It was disagreement over the German problem that set the stage for a widening conflict between Russia and the western powers.

As we have already noted, the Potsdam Conference in July, 1945, led to a series of quarrels over the future of Germany. (See page 570.) A major dispute developed when the Soviet Union insisted on stripping Germany of her industrial equipment and refused to regard the defeated nation as an economic unit. As a result, the British and Americans merged their zones of Germany for economic purposes. This was the beginning of a divided Germany and virtually put an end to four-power co-operation in controlling the country. The final effort to settle differences over Germany came at the Moscow Conference in March, 1947. After a few weeks of angry argument the meeting ended in failure.

Meanwhile, the Soviets were consolidating the occupied nations of eastern and southeastern Europe into a solid Communist bloc. Winston Churchill, now out of office, had warned against this rising Communist tide in his "Iron Curtain" speech of March, 1946, at Fulton, Missouri. Winston Churchill's plea for stronger western defense measures went largely unheeded until a new Communist threat developed in southeastern Europe. Throughout 1946, Communist-led guerrillas had been challenging the authority of the Greek government. They received supplies from the neighboring Soviet satellites

THE YALTA CONFERENCE

of Albania, Yugoslavia, and Bulgaria. At the same time, the Soviet Union had been carrying on a propaganda campaign against Turkey, seeking to gain control of part of the Caucasus borderlands and the straits leading from the Black Sea into the Mediterranean. The British, long the opponents of Russian expansion in this area, had been sending help to the Greek government and giving moral support to the Turks. But early in 1947, plagued by economic troubles at home, the British government announced it would have to end its support to Greece. At that time the United States made its first open move in the cold war. President Truman, who the year before had said, "I'm tired of babying the Soviets," told Congress in March, 1947, that "it must be the policy of the United States to support free peoples who are resisting attempted subjugation by armed minorities or by outside pressures." This became the Truman Doctrine, or policy of "containment," that is, the policy of preventing further Communist expansion. To put it immediately into effect, Congress voted 400 million dollars for military and economic aid to Greece and Turkey. With American equipment and funds, by October, 1949, the guerrilla bands in Greece had been defeated and scattered. In the case of Turkey, the United States sought to bolster that country's strength against any attempt by Russia to secure control of the strategic Dardanelles or to take any other Turkish territory.

The new "get tough" policy of the Truman Doctrine aimed to prevent Communist victories in countries under immediate threat and pressure. But a more positive long-term approach was needed to bolster Europe's economic defenses against communism. As American Secretary of State General Marshall saw it, without ". . . the return of normal economic health in the world, . . . there can be no political stability and no assured peace." When the wartime agency, the United Nations Relief and Rehabilitation Administration (UNRRA), ended its activities in 1947, Europe was still far from recovery. Further stopgap help by the United States government was not enough. Early in June, 1947, Secretary Marshall suggested a fresh approach to the problem of European reconstruction. He proposed that the European nations hold a meeting (1) to list their economic resources and needs, (2) to work out a blueprint for aiding one another, and (3) to decide how the United States might best help them to help themselves. In response to Secretary Marshall's suggestion, the delegates of sixteen nations met at Paris in July, 1947. The nations of eastern Europe were not excluded, but Russia and her satellites, as well as Spain, refused to participate. The conference drew up a plan to make the participating countries self-supporting in four years. The United States Congress voted to provide sixteen billion of the twenty billion dollars needed to finance the program. It was called the European Recovery Program (ERP), or, more commonly, the Marshall Plan.

By the end of 1951 the Plan had largely achieved its main purpose—the economic recovery of postwar Europe. Industrial and farm production had exceeded prewar levels, and the standard of living had greatly improved in all Marshall Plan countries. From their point of view the program was an act of generosity and far-sighted statesmanship. In Russia's eyes it was part of an imperialist conspiracy. The Soviet Union responded with two countermeasures. In September, 1947, the Communist parties of eastern Europe, as well as those of France and Italy, established the Communist Information Bureau, or Cominform. (See page 592.) And in January, 1949, the Molotov Plan, or Council for Mutual Economic Assistance (COMECON) was

FARM MACHINERY provided by the Marshall Plan helped Turkish farmers recover quickly from the war.

launched as a Communist bloc counterpart of the Marshall Plan.

Strengthening Europe's Military and Economic Defenses

The anti-Communist alliance system. A series of events in 1948 further widened and deepened the East-West conflict. The Communist seizure of Czechoslovakia in February was a serious blow to free government. It reminded the West that ten years earlier the fall of Czechoslovakia to Hitler had been the signal for a new wave of aggression. In June, 1948, followed the first Berlin blockade and the massive American airlift in reply.

Meanwhile, Mao Tse-tung's Communist forces were in the final stages of defeating the Nationalists in China, while the British in Malaya were being plagued by Red terrorists. It seemed that no part of the world was to escape the inroads of communism.

The response of the western powers to the danger of Communist expansion now took a more forceful turn. They gradually built a military security system that reached around the world. It consisted of a series of mutual defense treaties and a large-scale rearmament program.

The pattern for mutual defense pacts against Communist aggression had already been established by the American republics in 1947. The Rio Treaty of that year pledged its signers to take common action against aggressors from without or from within. In 1948 its principles were reaffirmed and strengthened in the Charter of the Organization of American States (OAS), drawn up at Bogotá, Colombia. The OAS is a regional organization under the United Nations and the successor to the Pan American Union.

Meanwhile, a similar collective defense organization was taking shape in western Europe. In March, 1948, Great Britain, France, Belgium, the Netherlands, and Lux-embourg signed a fifty-year mutual defense alliance at Brussels. The Brussels Pact set up what became known as the Western European Union. It could not become effective, however, without the means to rearm. The United States promised assistance, and out of the diplomatic talks that followed emerged the North Atlantic Treaty (ratified in July, 1949). The original signers of the alliance were the United States, Canada, Great Britain, France, Belgium, the Netherlands, Luxembourg, Norway, Denmark, Iceland, Italy, and Portugal. Later Greece and Turkey became members of the treaty organization, commonly called NATO. The parties agreed to "promote the stability and well-being in the North Atlantic area" by collective efforts for defense. Article 5 of the treaty stated that "an armed attack against one or more of them . . . shall be considered an attack against them all," and that "each of them . . . will assist the party or parties so attacked." Russia condemned the pact and advised the Scandinavians not to join. Of these, only Sweden stayed outside. The first Supreme Commander of the NATO armed forces was General Dwight Eisenhower, whose great prestige helped to inspire confidence and co-operation.

NATO's changing role. The Paris Agreements (1955) provided for the admission of a rearmed West Germany into NATO and the Western European Union (WEU). The original five-member WEU group (see page 585) was increased to seven, to include not only West Germany but also Italy. Originally, WEU was aimed at German aggression; now it was directed against Communist attack. Under the new agreement West Germany was allowed to contribute a 500,000-man army to NATO forces.

By 1958, however, the NATO defense army was disappointingly small. The Algerian war took away some French troops, while Britain cut down its German force because of financial difficulties. West Germany, too, had not filled its quota. To make up for lack of ground troops, it was agreed that the United States could build missile bases in NATO countries. In fact, the development of nuclear and rocket weapons caused NATO leaders to revise their entire defense plan. They now emphasized smaller, specially trained ground forces, equipped with atomic weapons. They also counted heavily on a ring of air and missile bases surrounding the Soviet Union. But France strongly opposed a United States suggestion for a NATO multilateral striking force with unified personnel and using nuclear weapons. As we have seen, De Gaulle wished to maintain an independent French nuclear power and in 1967 withdrew France's forces from the NATO organization.

By early 1968, rifts within the Communist bloc of nations tended to cast doubt on the necessity for a strong anti-Communist alliance system. The Soviet invasion of Czechoslovakia in August, 1968, however, suddenly changed this feeling. When the NATO foreign ministers met in Brussels in November, they warned that "any Soviet intervention directly or indirectly affecting the situation in Europe and the Mediterranean would create an international crisis with grave consequences." They also pledged renewed support of NATO alliance forces. The changed mood was reflected by France's co-operation in air and naval patrols of the Mediterranean, where the Soviet navy had sharply built up its squadron of ships. To all intents, NATO had gotten a new lease on life.

Other defense pacts. Areas outside Europe were not overlooked in building a barrier against further Communist expansion. In 1951, three mutual defense pacts were signed. These were between the United States and the Philippine Republic, between the United States, Australia, and New Zealand (ANZUS), and between the United States and Japan. Of greater scope and importance was the Southeast Asia Collective Defense Treaty (SEATO). Eight countries signed this

agreement in September, 1954. They were the United States, Great Britain, France, Australia, New Zealand, the Philippines, Pakistan, and Thailand. Unlike NATO, SEATO does not require its members to use armed force, nor does it have a standing army or a supreme commander. Its members also promised to promote self-government and higher living standards in Southeast Asia.

Finally, as a barrier against Soviet extension southward, Turkey, Iran, Iraq, Pakistan, and Great Britain signed the Baghdad Pact in November, 1955. When Iran dropped out in 1958, it became the Central Treaty Organization (CENTO). The United States became a member the following year.

To counteract the anti-Communist pacts, in May, 1955, Russia and her seven satellites formed an alliance called the Warsaw Pact. It permitted Russia to station troops in the Soviet bloc nations and to assume command of united alliance forces. It was under Warsaw Pact sponsorship that Czechoslovakia was invaded in 1968.

The arms race continues. Rearmament on all sides accompanied the postwar alliances. The United States, the chief source for NATO armaments, retained the military draft after the war and stockpiled quantities of new atomic and missile weapons. These included the fearsome H-bomb, or hydrogen bomb, first successfully tested in November, 1952. The Russians were not long in competing for arms supremacy. They exploded their first atomic bomb in 1949 and had mastered the secret of the H-bomb by 1953. Others, too, joined in the nuclear weapons race—Great Britain, France, and Red China. Meanwhile, disarmament efforts were persistent but achieved only limited success. A quarter of a century after World War II the world still faced the grim prospect that if another war came, no place on earth would be safe.

Western Europe moves toward economic unity. A more constructive safeguard against

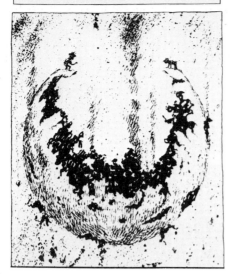

THIS PULITZER PRIZE-WINNING CARTOON (1963) illustrates the possible outcome of international tensions.

Communist expansion was building economic defenses. The success of the Marshall Plan had shown the promise of this approach. Now the countries of western Europe moved toward closer economic co-operation of their own accord. The first step in this direction was the adoption of the Schuman Plan. Brain child of the French economist Jean Monnet, it was negotiated by the French foreign minister, Robert Schuman, and went into effect in 1951. It provided for a European Coal and Steel Community composed of France, West Germany, Italy, and the three Benelux countries. They were to pool their coal and steel resources and give to all consumers in the participating countries equal access to coal and steel at uniform prices. The Schuman Plan Treaty was to last for fifty years. By the spring of 1953 the European Coal and Steel Community (ECSC) was in full operation.

The next step toward European economic unity came in 1957, when the same six nations signed the Rome treaties, setting up the European Economic Community (EEC), or Common Market. Its plan was to form a free-trade area in which people, goods, and money could move across national boundaries without hindrance. A beginning was made in 1959 by mutual tariff reductions of 10 per cent and the free exchange (convertibility) of national currencies. A landmark was reached on July 1, 1968, when the Common Market countries removed the last of the tariff barriers among them and adopted a common external tariff. With a combined population of more than 185 million, the EEC has been one of the fastest growing economic areas in the world. In the first ten years of its existence the six countries' gross national product increased at a higher rate than that of the United States. The governing authority of the Community is the Common Market Commission, which is responsible to a Council of Ministers and the same European Parliament which serves the Coal and Steel Community and Euratom. A supreme court of seven judges also acts for the three European communities.

In 1957 the six Common Market nations formed a third co-operative organization, the European Atomic Energy Community, or Euratom. Its purpose was to pool the atomic knowledge and resources of the member countries in order to provide atomic power especially for civilian use. In 1958 the United States signed an agreement with Euratom to lend money for nuclear reactors and to supply uranium for twenty years. It was predicted that by 1980, twenty to twenty-five per cent of the electricity within the Community would be produced by nuclear power.

European Community politics. Almost from its beginning, the British urged that the Common Market be expanded into a seventeen-nation free trade area. France objected because she feared that her high-priced goods would suffer from the competition. Thereupon, in 1959, Britain led in forming another free-trade group, the European Free Trade Association (EFTA), or the "Outer Seven." Its members included Great Britain,

Norway, Sweden, Denmark, Switzerland, Austria, and Portugal. Like the Common Market countries, their plans called for the gradual elimination of trade barriers. But unlike the Common Market, the Outer Seven would retain control of their own tariff regulations on the goods of nonmembers, and they had no overall governing body. Nevertheless, substantial tariff reductions were achieved among EFTA members.

Fear of a trade war between the two economic blocs led to plans for a merger. As a beginning, Great Britain took an historic step in 1961 by applying for EEC membership. As we have seen, however, France in 1963 and again in 1968 blocked the British application. President de Gaulle, determined to establish French leadership of western Europe, said that Britain was not "ready" to fit its economy into the Common Market. De Gaulle's generally unpopular action was a blow to European unity, but hope of progress toward this goal was revived as an economic crisis hit France in 1968. (See page 583.) Some authorities felt that to save the franc from devaluation, France would need to depend more and more on the co-operative efforts of a united Europe.

Meanwhile, the idea of a political union for western Europe, growing out of economic co-operation, was constantly in the minds of some of the Common Market leaders. Jean Monnet, father of the European Community plan, and his Action Committee for the United States of Europe, promoted the goal of a western Europe without national boundaries. Jean Rey, President of the Common Market Commission, in 1968 called on the six member countries to take action toward political union by strengthening Community agencies, especially the European Parliament. Plans for the direct election of members to the Parliament by universal suffrage had been drawn up in 1960, but no action was taken on the proposal. National differences and deep-seated traditional rivalries have stood in the way of realizing the dream of political union for western Europe. In the foreseeable future, these barriers would probably remain.

Conflicts and Crises of the Cold War

Goals and aspects of the cold war. The cold war passed through a number of crises and calms, of freeze-ups and thaws. The events can become confusing unless we remember the basic aims of the opposing sides. For the Russians and their allies, these were a desire to expand, to break out of their territorial limits, and to bring the whole world into the Communist system. For the United States and the free world, the goal was one of *containment*—of halting Communist expansion.

We should also remember that the war took many forms. In part it was a propaganda war, designed to win the hearts and minds of neutral or uncommitted peoples. In part it was an arms race, with each side seeking military superiority or, at a minimum, equality in a "balance of terror." Both major powers spent hundreds of billions of dollars on elaborate systems of attack and defense. At all times the cold war was a contest to see who could produce the highest standard of living and the most advanced technology. Thus even the factories and the laboratories were cold war battlefields. Although the cold war was fought without a declaration of hostilities and without the leading powers shooting at each other, it was a contest as deadly as any war in the past. Upon its outcome depended the future of mankind.

Crises over Berlin. The city of West Berlin was an island of democracy in a Communist sea. Its high standard of living attracted thousands of East Germans who hoped for a better life. Many of them were skilled workers or professional people who were badly needed by the Communists. They fled to the West by way of Berlin—a flight the Communists wished to halt.

When Hitler was defeated and Germany was divided into occupation zones, the western authorities failed to provide for guarantees of travel rights to and from Berlin. In 1948 the Russians took advantage of this lapse by announcing a blockade. They sealed off all land and water routes by which food and raw materials came from the West to Berlin, hoping to starve West Berlin into submission. Taking over West Berlin would have been a major propaganda stroke. Recognizing this, the United States turned to the one remaining avenue to Berlin—the air. A tremendous airlift brought supplies of food, coal, and other necessities; in one period of twenty-four hours, British and American planes landed 1,398 cargoes. Without the atomic bomb the Russians dared not risk war over Berlin, and within a year lifted the Berlin blockade. However, by 1961 the increasing flow of refugees led the East German government to take further measures. They proceeded to build a massive wall of concrete, topped by barbed wire, along the boundary line dividing the city. Heavily guarded at all times, the wall was very effective in virtually stopping the flow of East German refugees to the West. By its very existence, however, the wall became a symbol of the continued tension between East and West.

Conflict over Korea. The scene of conflict now moved from western Europe to East Asia. Here the balance of power had shifted radically when China fell to the Communists in 1949. Both China and Russia hoped to see all Korea made Communist. The Russians assisted North Korea to prepare and launch an invasion of the South in June, 1950. They expected a quick victory, partly because American officials had indicated an unwillingness to defend Korea. However, the Korean invasion failed as a result of United Nations action on South Korea's behalf.

Tension continues over the arms race. If the 1949–1953 period brought stalemate in Berlin and Korea, it also brought the two sides in the cold war near equality in military strength. After the defection of Yugoslavia the Russians realized that they must not rely too heavily on the satellite countries for defense forces. The Russians therefore tripled their army and nearly tripled their naval and air strength. In the fall of 1949 they reached a long-awaited goal by exploding their first atomic bomb. The United States at this time also decided to work at building a hydrogen

THE BERLIN AIRLIFT. Berliners watch from a rubble pile as an airplane flies in vital supplies to the sealed-off city.

bomb. The first H-bomb test occurred in November, 1952, and blew away an entire Pacific island. Russia exploded its first hydrogen bomb in 1953. During these years the United States and Britain stayed supreme on the sea and in the air; the Russians with their massive army had superiority on land. In addition, the Russians possessed a powerful fleet of submarines.

A new phase begins. When General Eisenhower became President in January, 1953, he brought to the office great prestige as leader in World War II and in NATO, together with a genuine desire for peace. He sought ways of reducing the heavy expenditures of arms, and within a few months arranged for an armistice in Korea. The United States now cut spending on conventional weapons, relying instead on the "deterrent power" of nuclear bombs. By coincidence, Joseph Stalin died at about the time of Eisenhower's inauguration. His successors, with Nikita Khrushchev clearly the leader by 1957, sought a thaw in the cold war. In Europe they withdrew Russian forces from East Austria (occupied since 1945) and made peace with Tito in Yugoslavia. In the following year Russia dissolved the Cominform and signed a peace settlement with Japan.

In mid-1955 a "summit meeting" of the American, Russian, British, and French leaders was held at Geneva. Although it accomplished very little, the meeting was a polite one and indicated a thawing of the cold war.

This period of relative calm ended suddenly on October 4, 1957, when the Russians launched *Sputnik I*, a man-made satellite circling the earth. In November they launched *Sputnik II*, six times larger than the first and carrying a live dog. The implications of the satellites were of the greatest importance. In the propaganda field, they demonstrated that Russia had built a highly advanced scientific and industrial system. This fact impressed many people who had thought of Russia as being technologically backward. In military matters the *Sputniks* posed a chilling threat. They showed how, with a few refinements, atomic weapons could be put into orbit and held there, awaiting only the push of a button before plunging down to destroy any target on earth.

The Americans' reaction to the *Sputniks* was one of alarm. Just as the Russians had exerted themselves to catch up in the atomic weapons field, so now the Americans sought to make up for lost time in the "space race." In the nation's schools, study of mathematics and science was encouraged by federal grants of money. Work on rockets went ahead at a forced pace. Thus the arms race entered a new phase, involving the scientists and production systems of the two sides in work on rocketry.

Weakening alliances. One factor working against a world war in the late 1950's was the weakening of alliances on both sides. Disputes in the Middle East helped to separate Britain and France from America. When Britain, France, and Israel invaded Egypt in 1956, the United States showed strong disapproval. Calling back their troops weakened the prestige of France and Britain, especially the latter, where the crisis led to Prime Minister Anthony Eden's being forced from office. In effect the Atlantic Alliance, as it was called, now began to break up. The Russians were happy to hasten the process. In 1957, five days after *Sputnik* went up, they warned Britain of the danger of being caught in the middle and destroyed if she stayed allied to the United States. Similar warnings were sent to France. Officially the warnings brought no result, but they did make many people question the wisdom of being allied with America.

The Russians, however, had similar problems. In trying to end Stalin's reign of terror they relaxed controls, which encouraged young people in the satellite countries to hope for freedom. Uprisings occurred in East Germany and in Czechoslovakia in 1953, and in Poland and Hungary in 1956. They were crushed, especially in Hungary, with a brutality that shocked the world. In the East the Russians faced even greater difficulties, as Red China became less and less willing to follow Russia's lead. As we have seen (page 590), the break between the two countries was complete by 1959. China's hostility undoubtedly kept Russia from being more aggressive in Europe.

Toward the end of President Eisenhower's administration, he and Khrushchev made efforts to improve relations. The two men agreed to a "summit conference" in Paris which met on May 16, 1960. As the meeting was about to begin, however, newspapers carried stories of a startling event; the shooting down of a U-2 plane. The world now learned that the American Central Intelligence Agency (CIA) had developed an airplane capable of flying at extremely high altitudes while photographing ground activities. The U-2 planes had been flying over Russia since the summer of 1956, taking amazingly detailed pictures which showed Russian activities in the atomic and missile fields. The Russians had been unable to hit the planes until a missile succeeded on the eve of the Paris conference. Khrushchev, although he had known of the U-2 flights for years, pretended shock and anger in Paris and broke up the meeting before it began. Thus at the end of the Eisenhower years the cold war was as cold as ever.

Crises over Cuba. Within little more than a year of taking office (1961), President Kennedy had to deal with the gravest crisis of the cold war. The trouble grew out of events in Cuba, just off America's Florida coast. Here the long and brutal dictatorship of General Batista had been overthrown in 1959. Leader of the rebels was Fidel Castro, who began what at first seemed to be democratic reforms in Cuba. Soon, however, Castro turned against the United States. He gradually seized almost all United States-owned businesses in Cuba, openly welcomed Russian military and economic aid, and jailed or executed his opponents. Early in 1961, after Castro admitted he was a Marxist, the United States cut off diplomatic relations.

Thousands of anti-Castro refugees then streamed out of Cuba, mostly to the United States. In April, 1961, some two thousand of them, trained in Central America with the aid of the CIA, attempted to invade Cuba at the Bay of Pigs and overthrow Castro. The effort ended in disaster for the invaders, and the Kennedy administration received biting criticism both at home and abroad.

CUBAN MISSILE CRISIS. This display of Russian missile bases in Cuba, arranged by U.N. American Ambassador Adlai Stevenson, increased world tension as the U.S. and the Soviet Union faced major policy decisions in October 1962.

Meanwhile Cuba's economy came near to collapse and was increasingly dependent upon Russian aid. Khrushchev seized the opportunity to make Cuba a base for offensive and defensive missiles aimed at the United States.

Russian advisers had been coming to Cuba at a rapid rate, sometimes as many as a thousand a month. The United States had been sending U-2 flights over Cuba to check on developments there. Pictures taken in August, 1962, disclosed that some missiles were in place and that arrangements were being made for others. President Kennedy warned the American people of the grave situation facing them, and announced that the American Navy would stop on the high seas Russian ships carrying missiles and nuclear weapons to Cuba. Kennedy demanded that the missile bases be dismantled, while Khrushchev threatened war. For a few days, the world watched with fear and alarm while the United States and the Soviet Union stood "eyeball to eyeball."

A solution to the Cuban crisis was possible because, as Robert Kennedy later said, "The missiles in Cuba, we felt, vitally concerned our national security, but not that of the Soviet Union." In other words, the administration felt that American firmness plus patience would make the Russians see that their course would cause a war they did not want. The policy succeeded, for Russian missile-carrying ships turned back from Cuba. Russia agreed to dismantle and remove the rockets already in Cuba in return for an American pledge not to invade that island. Having saved face, each country stepped back from the brink of war.

East-West tensions continue. Once the Cuban crisis passed, relations between the United States and Russia improved. In 1963 both sides agreed to halt atmospheric tests of atomic weapons. Five years later they agreed that atomic weapons would not be given to countries which did not already have them.

These agreements did not mean that the arms race had ended. By 1969 the United States was experimenting with missiles which carried multiple warheads of atomic bombs, as well as with nerve gases. The race to the moon also carried military implications, and both the Americans and Russians were building expensive defenses against nuclear attack. The arms race also led to increased naval activity, with the United States pressing ahead on construction of nuclear-powered submarines. The Russians also built both nuclear and non-nuclear submarines supplementing their surface fleet. By 1969 they had a number of warships in the Mediterranean Sea, partly in order to annoy the American naval vessels there and partly to increase their influence in the Middle East.

During the 1960's Russia was generally blocked in efforts to communize Latin America, Africa, and South Asia. Her attempts at expansion aimed next at the Arab world. By subsidizing the Aswan High Dam and other projects and by arming the Arabs, she hoped to win their gratitude and with it a dominant position in the Middle East. These hopes suffered a setback in 1967, when in the Six-Day War Israel destroyed or captured most of the Arab weapons. Russia, however, quickly supplied new ones. She appeared quite willing to aid the Arabs against Israel, but not herself to enter a war in the Middle East. In fact by 1969, she was making some efforts toward arranging a peace settlement for that explosive area with the United States, Britain, and France.

In late 1968 there were signs of a revival of cold war tensions with the invasion of Czechoslovakia by Russia and the other Warsaw Pact countries. However, in the early months of 1969 both American and Russian leaders continued to indicate a willingness to place limits on the arms race, giving hope for keeping the cold war under some control. Tensions were also eased by progress in the talks at Paris over peace in Vietnam.

International Co-operation in the Space Age

If the years after 1945 brought crises and conflicts between nations, they also witnessed examples of international co-operation. Encouraging progress was made in meeting human needs through the United Nations and other agencies, and through the actions of individual countries. In this section we shall look at some examples of progress, beginning with the work of the United Nations.

Weighing the record of the United Nations. In the postwar world the United Nations stood at the center of efforts to advance international co-operation. In 1970 the U.N. record had finally reached the quarter-century mark, and it became possible to make some estimate of the organization's work. How had it actually performed as a peace-keeper and as a leader in solving problems of hunger, ignorance, and disease?

The U.N. as a peace-keeper. Supporters of the U.N. could argue that its record included solid achievements in the cause of peace. Perhaps the most notable single action was the use of force to halt aggression in Korea in 1950–1953. Here for the first time the world saw an army fighting under the flag of an international organization in an effort to uphold international law.

Other peace-keeping activities occurred in many parts of the world. As we have seen, they included helping to pacify the Congo after the Belgians withdrew (1960–1964) and the work of policing or securing "cease-fire" agreements during disputes in Iran, Indonesia, Yemen, Greece, Israel, and other countries. A typical example of U.N. action occurred in Cyprus. The British ended their rule over Cyprus in 1960, giving the island its independence. Although Cyprus lay near Turkey, only about one-fifth of its inhabitants were of Turkish descent. The great majority of the inhabitants were Greek.

In 1963 the two groups began fighting, and soon the Greek and Turkish governments became involved. Turkish Cypriots charged that the Greeks planned to change the constitution of Cyprus so as to reduce the rights of the Turks and that the Greeks had massacred some Turks. Planes from Turkey bombed Greek positions in Cyprus, and war seemed near. U.N. troops landed in Cyprus in the spring of 1964 to restore order and helped bring about a cease-fire later in the year. Their presence through 1969 in all probability prevented a war between Greece and Turkey. It should be noted that in actions such as these the U.N. soldiers and officials usually came from small nations, and did not represent any interest other than that of peace.

Besides sending troops for peace-keeping or for actual fighting, the U.N. acted to limit armaments, especially those of nuclear weapons. People had shuddered at the horrors

THE UNITED NATIONS PEACE-KEEPING FORCE in Cyprus, where they helped maintain order and prevent a recurrence in fighting.

caused by the use of atomic weapons against Japan in 1945. Yet within a few years, far more destructive weapons appeared. Russia, the United States, and other nations raced to increase their weapons stockpiles and to build airplanes and rockets which would deliver "payloads" anywhere on earth. Perfect defense systems were not found, and it was obvious that an all-out nuclear war would cause the destruction of millions of human lives.

To counter this danger the U.N. had no power other than the force of world opinion, and no field of action other than U.N. meeting rooms. Yet these were enough to start bringing nuclear weapons under control. It seems fair to say that the U.N. was at least partly responsible for the following actions:

(1) *Calling for "denuclearization."* In 1965 the General Assembly asked that all countries refrain from "testing, manufacturing, using or deploying nuclear weapons on the continent of Africa." (This action was aimed at France, which had held nuclear tests in the Sahara. France shifted her tests to the Pacific.) The U.N. also considered proposals for the denuclearization of Latin America. Although full agreement could not be reached in the U.N., largely because of Castro's Cuba, efforts bore fruit in 1968 with the signing of a treaty by fourteen Latin-American nations banning nuclear weapons from their soil. In this way *area* limits were put on atomic bombs.

(2) *Calling for limitation of the number of weapons.* Although the U.N. Disarmament Commission was concerned mainly with the control of atomic weapons, it was also interested in control of what were called "conventional" or customary weapons. This concern grew out of awareness, not only of the damage weapons can cause, but also of their cost. By 1969 the world's annual expenditures for weapons amounted to nearly the total annual incomes of all the under-developed countries. If the arms race could be halted, the money saved could be used to improve greatly the living standards of the poorer nations.

Under Security Council supervision, the Eighteen Nation Disarmament Commission held talks for years. Results finally appeared in the field of atomic weapon testing. In 1958 the United States announced a halt in its tests. The Russians then followed suit until 1961, when a renewal of their testing led the United States to do the same. Worldwide complaint about the poison in the atmosphere, which could cause genetic damage to future generations, helped bring a test-ban treaty two years later. Under the treaty the United States, Great Britain, and Russia agreed not to conduct tests in the atmosphere.

In 1968 the Disarmament Commission announced agreement on a vastly more important matter. This was a treaty banning for twenty-five years the giving of nuclear weapons to nations which did not already have them. This Non-Proliferation Treaty was endorsed by the Security Council and the General Assembly, and was presented for ratification to the world's governments. It was hoped that the treaty would take effect in 1969.

U.N. peace-keeping—the debit side. For an accurate appraisal of the U.N. we must list not only its achievements; we must also consider the other side of the ledger. Here we find that, far from guaranteeing world peace, the U.N. at best has limited war. In every year since 1945 at least one war has been waged. U.N. action has been most effective when the United States and Russia remained aloof, as in Cyprus, or have agreed (as they did in opposing the British-French-Israeli invasion of Egypt in 1956, which ended with a U.N. cease-fire). In cases concerning one of the great powers directly (Russian entrance into Czechoslovakia in 1968, the United States and the Cuban missile crisis of 1962, and China's invasion of Tibet in 1959), the

U.N. has been ineffective. As for control of nuclear weapons, the U.N. has failed to touch the most important point—that of beginning nuclear disarmament. Bacteriological and other new weapons has also remained uncontrolled.

Several reasons help account for U.N. ineffectiveness against the great powers. One was lack of funds. Each member nation contributed voluntarily to the U.N. treasury; if an action was disliked by one nation, that nation might withhold its contribution. For example, the Russians objected to U.N. actions in the Congo, where they had hoped to gain a foothold. The Russians claimed the U.N. action was illegal and refused to pay for special Congo forces. As a result, money shortages severely hampered U.N. peacekeeping efforts in the Congo and elsewhere.

A second reason may be found in use of the veto in the Security Council. Russia by 1969 had cast more than a hundred vetoes. Resulting loss of Council effectiveness was somewhat balanced by giving more power to the General Assembly, but the over-all effect was a hampering of the U.N.

Third, even when the U.N. operated to the peak of its effectiveness, it had only limited authority. It could not pass laws binding on its members, it could not bring treaty-breakers to justice before the World Court, and it could not tax. The U.N., in short, was not a world government. Rather, it depended on persuasion, on appeals to the good intentions of national governments. Governments, unfortunately, do not always base their actions on good intentions.

Perhaps the U.N. record could be summarized by saying that it contained some successes and some failures. If it had not prevented wars, at least it had helped to prevent World War III. By giving most of the nations a chance to band together at times, by bringing opponents to the conference table, by helping to work out agreements on the use of atomic weapons, by sending troops into troubled areas, it had reduced international tensions and increased international understanding.

Other activities of the U.N. If there was disagreement about the U.N.'s success in keeping peace, there was little question of its effectiveness in other fields. In its first quarter-century the U.N. scored important gains on man's age-old enemies of ignorance, hunger, and disease, and by 1969 was spending 80 per cent of its budget on programs to combat them.

Approximately two-fifths of the world's adults were unable to read or write in the 1960's, and in some countries the figure ran much higher. This rate of illiteracy condemned many persons and nations to poverty. Recognizing that success and progress could come only to the educated, the U.N. set about raising educational standards through training of teachers, improvement of educational materials, and building of schools. The fight against illiteracy was directed by UNESCO (see page 569). Three large-scale regional programs were set up— for Africa, for Asia, and for Latin America. Although UNESCO's educational budget was limited, many countries were helped to improve their schools. A world congress on illiteracy, held at Teheran in 1965, served to focus world attention on educational needs.

Even more numerous than those who cannot read and write are those who are poorly fed. The results of malnutrition may be listlessness, an inability to learn, and lack of resistance to disease. In order to increase world food production, the U.N. in 1945 set up the Food and Agriculture Organization. The FAO attacked the problem of hunger in a variety of ways. Food production was increased by distributing improved seeds, as in new types of rice and wheat. Animal diseases were studied and controlled, fisheries were developed, and aid was given to countries for use in school lunch programs and for nutrition education.

In 1960 the FAO began a Freedom from Hunger campaign to heighten world awareness of nutrition needs. As a result, private individuals contributed millions of dollars to aid the FAO. The additional money enabled the Freedom from Hunger campaign to expand its work in land clearing, irrigation, agricultural education and research, and home economics programs. Although studies showed that "impressive gains" were made in the total amount of food produced, the gains were nearly wiped out by population increases.

The U.N. had greater success in fighting disease. Through the World Health Organization (WHO) an effort was made to raise health standards and combat disease. It helped wipe out malaria, for example, in Burma and other countries where the disease had been a major problem. WHO has con-

ducted a world-wide campaign against diphtheria, tuberculosis, scarlet fever, yellow fever, leprosy, polio, and cholera.

Health work has also been carried forward by UNICEF, originally a Children's Emergency Fund set up at the end of World War II. When the emergency in Europe was over, the Fund continued on a permanent basis. It fights malnutrition, sets up health centers, and supports schools. UNICEF is supported entirely by voluntary contributions, such as "trick or treat" collections on Halloween, and by projects such as the sale of UNICEF Christmas cards.

The United Nations Development Program. In 1965 the United Nations decided to merge many of its agencies into a single organization known as the Development Program. Combining all the activities into one agency eliminated overlapping and made for more efficient use of funds. The Development Program included WHO, the International Bank for Reconstruction and Development, the Universal Postal Union, and the International Atomic Energy Agency, to name a few. The organization trained persons for work in technical fields, such as operating electric generating plants, and helped private investors build factories in poorer nations. By 1969, projects were carried out in more than 150 countries and territories.

Individual countries give aid. The United States and other countries also acted independently to improve living conditions in underdeveloped countries. Immediately after World War II President Truman announced the "Point Four" program. It consisted

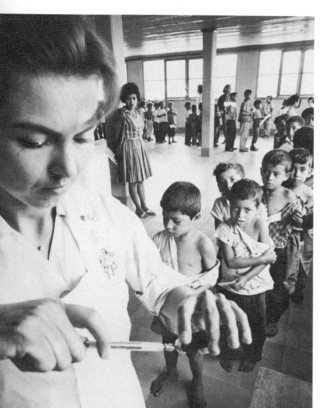

THE WORLD HEALTH ORGANIZATION provides BCG vaccinations in Honduras. In order to aid countries in drawing up their tuberculosis programs, the United Nations provides medical staff, laboratory and X-ray technicians.

mainly of furnishing technical experts who showed people how to help themselves, and was notably successful. Under later administrations foreign aid was carried on under the International Co-operation Administration. It provided loans, grants of money or food, and military and technical aid.

Skilled help to underdeveloped nations was also given through the Peace Corps. The Corps began in 1962 under the Kennedy administration. The President called for volunteers "who will live at the same level as the citizens of the country to which they are sent, eating the same food, speaking the same language. We are going to put particular emphasis on those men and women who have skills in teaching, agriculture, and in health." Within a short time Americans were at work in many parts of the world. They served so well as good-will ambassadors that the Peace Corps was made a permanent agency.

Although weary United States taxpayers sometimes complained of the cost of foreign aid, America's opponents recognized its effectiveness and attempted to copy the programs. Both Red China and Russia, for example, gave aid to Castro in Cuba, and Russia financed construction of Egypt's High Dam at Aswan. Although the amount of aid given by the Communist countries was not known, it appeared to be high in relation to their resources.

Other co-operative efforts. Scientific and financial problems also helped bring nations together. In the field of science, the International Geophysical Year was a joint effort to better understand man's home, the earth. Co-operation was especially high in Antarctica, where an American stayed at the main Russian base and a Soviet scientist stayed at Little America. In the late 1960's, as exploration of outer space advanced, it appeared that some co-operation might take place as a means of keeping costs down for each country.

Problems with national currencies also led countries to work together. In 1947 an International Monetary Fund was set up to provide a means of keeping currencies stable. Since trade is carried on in terms of money, unstable currencies can upset international trade. Members of the Fund made deposits of gold and currency, with the right to make withdrawals to meet emergencies. Crises occurred in 1968 and 1969, when the British pound and the French franc came under attack. Speculators weakened the pound and franc by demanding gold for their paper money. The Monetary Fund helped prevent drastic declines in the values of the two currencies.

Science and the Arts in Today's World

Continuing forces in today's society. The rapid changes which distinguish today's society are the result of the continuing impact of the Scientific and Industrial revolutions. They affect the way contemporary man thinks, feels, and acts. These changes have created an environment that at the same time offers great hope of human betterment and great risk of human destruction.

Today's urbanized and technological civilization developed first in the western world, but it has spread in some degree to all parts of the earth. The extension of western culture has posed new problems not only for nonwestern peoples but also for western man. Let us examine some of the milestones in the shaping of that culture in modern times.

The atomic revolution. Man speculated about the atomic theory of matter over a period of more than two thousand years (see page 341). Not until the twentieth century was the theory transformed into technology, that is, adapted to practical use. The atomic age came into being when scientists found out how to split atoms by artificial means. They learned that they could do this by bombarding the atom nucleus with particles of other atoms. For this purpose, in 1932 an American, Ernest O. Lawrence, built an

SCIENTISTS study the effects of rain on a model of the San Fernando Valley.

atom-smashing machine, calling it the "cyclotron." Soon scientists in a number of countries were making headway in the fission, or splitting, of the atom. By 1939 German scientists had learned that the nucleus of the uranium atom, when split, released enormous energy. The problem was to create a "chain reaction," or a continuous explosion of uranium atoms. On December 2, 1942, this was accomplished at the University of Chicago. There a team of scientists, led by Enrico Fermi, produced the first sustained chain reaction in an atomic reactor, or oven. This accomplishment soon resulted in the invention of a terrible weapon of war—the atomic bomb. Ten years later, research in nuclear power created a still more destructive weapon, the hydrogen bomb. It is based on the *fusion,* or uniting, of hydrogen atoms instead of *fission,* or splitting, of uranium atoms.

Creative uses of atomic energy. Fortunately, the peaceful uses of atomic energy hold great promise of serving mankind. Already scientists have used the atom to generate electric power, propel ships, create rare metals and earths, and produce radioactive isotopes for medical and other research. Knowledge gained from the study of fission has also led to methods for determining the age of objects from the remote past. Radioactive dating systems have made us revise our estimates of the age of ancient rocks, pieces of wood and bone, mummies, and other relics.

Some of the greatest benefits to mankind have come from the production of radioactive isotopes. A number of these are new elements, unknown before the development of atomic fission. Thus the alchemist's dream of changing one element into another has been realized. But most of the radioactive isotopes are elements long known, which have been made radioactive by exposing them to the radiations of an atomic pile. The radiations of a radioactive isotope may be detected by an instrument called a "counter." Hence these isotopes may now be used by doctors and biologists as "tracers." For example, researchers "tag," or label, living bacteria with radioactive phosphorus in an effort to find how the germs inflict damage in the human body. Likewise, if a scientist wishes to see what happens to a new drug when it is injected into the body, he can tag the drug with a radioactive tracer. No matter where the drug lodges, it reveals its presence by its radioactivity. Through the use of radioactive isotopes, medical men have made encouraging progress in their attack upon cancer. Scientists have also been able to "map" oil pools in the earth, study the action of fertilizers on plants, preserve food by irradiation, and determine what happens to metals when subjected to friction and wear.

More recently, atomic power plants have become an important source of electricity. In 1956 Great Britain opened the world's first atomic power station at Calder Hall. In the following year the United States put into operation at Shippingport, Pennsylvania, its first commercial atomic power plant. Thereafter the building of such plants to produce electricity spread rapidly throughout the world. It has been estimated that by 1980 about a third of all electricity used in the United States and in Sweden will be produced by nuclear fission.

The first steps in developing hydrogen energy for peacetime uses have also been taken. When once a power plant based on fusion of heavy hydrogen atoms becomes a reality, man will have an endless source of power from sea water. Certainly man has entered a wonderful, but dangerous, era. If he misuses nature's energy, he might well destroy himself.

Dawn of the space age. The rapid development of the rocket engine during World War II foreshadowed a new age in man's conquest of the skies. Near the end of the war, rocket research in Germany produced the deadly V-2 missile. (See page 561.) The Germans had learned much from the pioneer work of an American physics professor, Dr. Robert H. Goddard, who had launched a rocket as early as 1926. Following World War II, several countries successfully tested long-range rockets and ballistic missiles for military purposes. Some reached far beyond the earth's atmosphere. Then, in 1957, came a remarkable new achievement for the rocket. It was used to fire a man-made satellite into an orbit around the earth. The Russians launched the first ones, called *Sputnik I* and *II*, in October and November. This news excited the world, for few people had suspected that Russian technology was so far advanced. Soon after, the first successful United States satellite, *Explorer I*, was shot into space on January 31, 1958, from Cape Canaveral, Florida (now Cape Kennedy). These satellite launchings were a part of the activities of the International Geophysical Year (IGY). During this period (July 1, 1957–December 31, 1958), scientists of sixty-four nations joined in an attempt to solve some of the mysteries of the universe. Radio signals from the artificial satellites sent back valuable information on atmospheric density, cosmic rays, temperature, radiation bands, and meteorites. Man had entered the space age.

The space race. The race into space moved ahead rapidly, with the United States and Soviet Russia engaged in a zig-zag contest. Both nations now stepped up their programs of earth satellite launchings and space probes. In 1959 each fired rockets into orbit around the sun, and the Russian *Lunik II* hit the moon. The number of satellites shot into orbit nearly doubled in 1961, with the United States leading the Soviet Union by more than three to one. The latter's booster rockets, however, admittedly had greater thrust.

1961 also became the year of *manned* space flights. On April 12, Russian Major Yuri Gagarin successfully returned from a one-orbit circuit of the earth in a bullet-shaped capsule, *Vostok I*. He was the first human being to leave the earth's atmosphere. Within the following two months the United States fired two manned space vehicles into suborbital flights. Then, in August, Russia sent her second man into orbit, circling the earth seventeen times.

The United States soon closed the space gap with Russia. In 1962, pioneered by the three-orbit flight of John Glenn, the United States launched three manned satellites. Its Project Mercury series ended in May, 1963, with the twenty-two-orbit flight of Leroy Cooper, Jr.

By 1965 both the United States and the Soviet Union were preparing to send manned spacecraft to the moon. In preparation for the manned landings, they made a number of exploratory flights. During one, in 1965, Soviet cosmonaut Alexei Leonov performed the first "space walk" outside his capsule. Soon after, American astronaut Edward White accomplished the same feat. During 1966 and 1967 a series of Russian and American unmanned spacecraft orbited the moon and made soft landings on its surface. They sent back to earth thousands of photographs via television. They also made the first chemical analysis of lunar soil. Such probes were to help in selecting suitable landing sites.

New breakthroughs in space exploration soon followed. In December, 1968, the United States spacecraft *Apollo 8,* containing three astronauts led by Colonel Frank Borman, made the first manned flight around the moon. Telecasts and photos from *Apollo 8* revealed what man had never viewed before. Soon after, in January, 1969, the Russians achieved the world's first crew exchange in earth orbit by docking two manned spacecraft, the *Soyuz 4* and *Soyuz 5.* But these space feats were merely the prelude to the most spectacular feat of them all. On July 20, 1969, the American spacecraft *Apollo 11,* landed the first men on the moon, completing what was described as "the most momentous journey in man's history." As Astronaut Neil Armstrong first set foot on the lunar surface, he uttered the memorable words, "That's one small step for man, one giant leap for mankind." The peoples of the world seemed to

THE BREATHTAKING FEAT of landing men on the moon will impress itself slowly on our minds for as long as we live. The tangible results, in communications, and the use of the moon as a research station, may quickly be taken for granted.

agree. Four days later the three *Apollo 11* astronauts successfully returned to earth, bringing back samples of lunar rock for scientists to study. NASA (National Aeronautical and Space Administration) immediately made plans for further lunar landings.

Of more immediate benefit to earth dwellers were the communications and weather satellites. In 1962 the *Telstar* relay satellite first made telecasts possible between continents. In 1965 much more effective transmission of live television came with relays from the *Early Bird* satellite, stationed 22,300 miles above the Atlantic Ocean. In the following year a similar relay satellite was positioned over the Pacific. These two transmission systems were part of the program of an international organization of fifty-seven nations (Intelsat) to set up a global satellite communications system. The year 1966 also marked the launching by the United States of the *Essa II* weather satellite. It orbits the earth, sending back photographs of cloud formations to more than 150 ground stations in forty-five countries.

Meanwhile, man's curiosity led him to probe ever deeper into space. In 1962 the United States sent *Mariner II* thirty-six million miles to gather data about Venus. In 1965 and 1969 other *Mariner* spacecraft passed close to Mars, beaming back pictures more than 60 million miles to earth. Some scientists hinted that life might exist there. Venus was reached by United States and Soviet unmanned spacecraft in 1967. These were the first landings on a planet outside the earth's orbit.

However, the same rocket missiles that probed outer space could serve as deadly instruments of war. Here, too, the United States and Russia are in competition. Both have developed intercontinental ballistic missiles with atomic warheads and have fired them with remarkable accuracy. Whether these are to become the "ultimate weapons" remains to be seen.

The wonders of electronics. Radio, television, and radar are products of electronics— the science which deals with the activity and control of electrons. After the invention of the wireless, or radiotelegraphy, it was a short step further to radiotelephony. In 1906 R. A. Fessenden and in 1908 Dr. Lee De Forest succeeded in sending the human voice "over the air." Regularly scheduled commercial broadcasting did not come until 1920, when Station KDKA opened in Pittsburgh. Radio rapidly became a big business. Meanwhile, the radiotelephone has proved of great value in communicating across oceans, between ships and from ship to shore, and in directing the flight of aircraft. Photographs are also transmitted by radio and by telegraph to newspapers.

When radio waves were also made to carry moving images, television resulted. Developed chiefly by Zworykin and Farnsworth in the 1930's, it was not used commercially until 1941. Since then, color television has been added (1951) and the satellite relays have made international telecasts possible.

Radar (an abbreviation for "radio detection and ranging") is a device for the detection of distant objects. It also measures the distance or range of the objects. For example, an aviator flying over a heavy layer of clouds may receive accurate information about the ground below by looking at a radarscope, or screen, in the cabin of his plane. Rivers, land, buildings, and mountains appear as patterns or lines on the screen. In World War II this instrument enabled airplanes to bomb targets through overcast skies and find their way home again, permitted antiaircraft guns to find their targets and fire automatically, and helped surface vessels to locate submarines. In peacetime it increases safety in air and sea navigation.

The peaceful uses of electronics have multiplied rapidly. One is *automation* in industry, a system by which electronic signals regulate machines and make them automatic.

THE STRUCTURE OF A DNA MOLECULE. The first synthetic DNA molecule was produced in 1967.

Electronic computers, or "mechanical brains," are the center of automation systems. By means of their "memory units," which store all sorts of information, they can make the calculations to carry out a great variety of tasks. Among these are keeping records, translating languages, landing airplanes, detecting crime and apprehending criminals, and controlling re-entry of spacecraft.

Automation has also come to the farm. It is now possible, for example, to feed livestock and poultry by means of push-button devices. One man, making use of such equipment, can do in ten minutes what it used to take five men a half day to accomplish.

The computer can save much human labor and speed up production. On the other hand, it can also reduce the number of jobs available, creating technological unemployment. Some people also predict that in time man's leisure may be almost entirely "automated."

An even more significant development of electronics is the laser beam. It resulted from the experiments with high-frequency light waves by an American, Charles H. Townes, in the 1950's. The secret of the laser lies in the amplification of light waves, so that the power of a single beam is enormously concentrated and thereby increased. By 1962 the laser had come into commercial use. Its possibilities are staggering. Because of the number of "frequency bands" available in lasers, a single beam could accommodate numerous television channels and thousands of telephone circuits. Relayed through satellites like *Early Bird*, lasers could interconnect the world instantaneously with countless lines of television and telephone communication. A laser range finder and obstacle detector, much more accurate than radar, could track satellites and spaceships and improve automatic guidance systems. With a concentration of light hundreds of millions of times as bright as the sun, the laser beam can drill microscopic holes through any known substance in a fraction of a second. In medicine the use of the laser "knife" for bloodless surgery and the application of the beam in the treatment of cancer have already been demonstrated. Unfortunately, as with the splitting of the atom, the laser could be used for man's destruction. As a "death ray," it could penetrate the heaviest armor, seek out and explode nuclear missiles, spacecraft, aircraft, and any object of military or human value.

The march of medicine. The 1960's saw important new breakthroughs in medical science. One was a remarkable series of discoveries about the structure and functions of a nucleic acid molecule called DNA. This is the basic chemical in every living cell that controls growth and heredity. It manufactures the proteins which give all living things their specific traits, such as sex, hair and skin color, blood type, etc. Late in 1967 a team of American biochemists at Stanford University produced a synthetic (artificial) DNA molecule. In doing so, they "unlocked a fundamental secret of life." The possibility that man might create life and artificially control heredity poses some awesome problems for human society. At this stage, the consequences can only be guessed at.

Another medical breakthrough came with the transplantation of human organs. In what was described as "the most dramatic feat of modern surgery," the first successful human heart transplant was performed in December, 1967, at Capetown, South Africa. There Dr. Christian Barnard and a team of surgeons removed the heart of an auto crash victim and placed it in the body of a man who was dying of heart disease. The patient soon died of other complications, but the surgical technique had proved successful. During the following year, surgeons in a number of countries performed heart transplant operations. The survival rate is still low, but progress is being made in using drugs to combat the body's natural tendency to reject foreign tissue.

The operation that made medical history also raised a basic ethical question. Since there are comparatively few donors, how is the recipient of a transplant to be selected? The responsibility for making that decision is a grave one. Some men of medicine think that a better solution to the problem would be found in using the artificial heart. Such a device proved temporarily successful in 1966. Meanwhile, transplantation of other human organs—kidney, lung, liver—has also achieved limited success.

Progress on other medical fronts has also been noteworthy. Cancer research occupies the efforts of many scientists. No real breakthrough is in sight, but treatment with drugs, radiation, and surgery has made significant advances. Immunization against additional contagious diseases, such as mumps in 1967, has become common. Computerized machines to perform various chemical tests of body elements have quickened the pace and reduced the work in laboratories. Medically related problems, such as air and water pollution, still defy man's will but not his knowledge.

The population crisis. Another problem related to the health of the world's peoples is the population explosion. Until recently, Malthus' pessimistic prediction that population growth would outrun food supply was taken seriously by few people. (See page 332.) Advanced technology has, for the most part, taken care of increased food needs. But the remarkable progress of medical science has brought a sharp drop in the death rate. Industrial nations now have death rates of about ten per thousand and birth rates of fifteen to twenty. By contrast, the poverty-stricken areas of Asia, Africa, and Latin America have death rates of fifteen to twenty but birth rates of forty to forty-five. It is not surprising, therefore, that population experts predict that the present world's population of about 3.7 billion will more than double by the end of this century. Moreover, the food surpluses in such great agricultural countries as the United States, Canada, Australia, and Argentina have been exhausted. Two thirds of the world's peoples have no food reserves, and their chances of importing sufficient grains have been growing slimmer. Man is now beginning to realize that Malthus was not so wrong after all.

The solution, according to most experts, lies in controlling population growth, especially in the underdeveloped countries, where 85 per cent of the births take place. Governments and private organizations have begun large-scale voluntary family planning programs. The big stumbling blocks are religious, cultural, and political traditions. Whether the multiplication of human beings will bring man to the brink of ruin remains to be seen.

Major trends in contemporary literature. The discontent and protest which marked early twentieth-century literature and the arts have continued beyond mid-century. In literature there are two principal styles— realism and formalism—with many variations, and each is linked closely to the preceding period. The realists still emphasize content, relating it at every point to the life of the times. The target of much realistic fiction is the middle class, now frequently referred to as the Establishment. For example, the Italian novelist Alberto Moravia has continued to criticize the emptiness of bourgeois society. Likewise, the German Günter Grass and the Englishman Joyce Cary have exposed the ridiculous in current life by the use of pointed satire. Grass' *Dog Years,* for instance, portrays the madness of the Hitler era. Some realists, like the Irishman Samuel Beckett, have followed the existential pattern made famous by the French writers Albert Camus and Jean-Paul Sartre. That is to say, they see no particular purpose in the universe and stress the importance of personal decision and individual attitudes in making sense out of life. Their characters behave in very unpredictable ways. Still other realists, like the Frenchman Alain Robbe-Grillet, have rejected the storytelling

VOTE VICTIM by Calvin Burnett

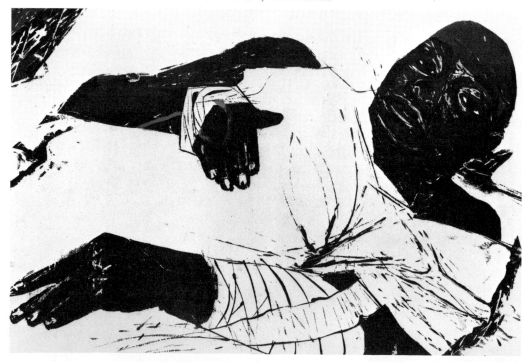

People in Today's World

Today, through the marvels of modern transportation and communications, people around the world know more about one another than ever before. To understand other people, their hopes, their fears, their way of life is the only certain way to build understanding and co-operation among nations.

Around the world people express their gaiety and enthusiasm in different ways. They make their livings by many methods. They express themselves artistically in countless styles. They adhere to hundreds of different faiths and claim loyalty to governments diverse as they are numerous. Traditions and environment are as varied as the peoples of the world.

But in the midst of these differences people around the world have similar hopes and fears and goals. From Quebec to Kuwait, from India to the arctic, people are found working hard, enjoying themselves together, and struggling to make their lives better.

Americans parading on Fifth Avenue in New York

662A

Seal hunting in the bleak winterland of the arctic

Indian women in colorful saris coming out of a mosque

May Day in Red Square, Moscow

662D

However, there are still significant differences in the way people live in the world. Some of these differences tend to divide people into hostile camps. Others show the glory in being a person who lives in time-honored ways, satisfied with being himself.

The picture in 662D shows a holiday in the Soviet Union, May Day. This day is chosen to honor the "saints" of the Communist movement. Notice the banner which highlights Karl Marx and Lenin, both of whom are honored in the Soviet Union, as in much of the Communist world, as great heroes.

Below shows a family in Eastern Europe harvesting grain by hand, using time-honored methods. This family still must rely on methods used a hundred years ago to make a living from the soil.

Harvesting wheat in Central Europe

Nevertheless, change in some form is sweeping across every corner of the globe. Few places are isolated and only a few places have not heard or seen at least something that seems to promise revolutionary change. Now that so many have seen or heard what things one can have and what things one should have in order to lead a better life, the world is experiencing what has been called "A Rising Tide of Expectations."

In Kuwait, for example, women herding sheep in ancient ways now must dodge traffic which streams over superhighways. The automobile which was developed less than a century ago, is quickly becoming a universal sight throughout our world. While in Italy, where automobiles and television sets are commonplace, modern apartments are now available for industrial workers, once crowded in ancient slums.

Yesterday meets today in Kuwait on the Persian Gulf.

662F

The Olivetti Company's employee housing project.

Africa, once called the Dark Continent, is also feeling the "winds of change." With almost thirty new nations since World War II, this continent has seen more change in the last decade than it saw for three centuries of European domination. Africa is no longer exclusively the place of isolated native villages. Modern cities and new factories dot Africa's landscape.

However, one can still see in the outskirts of many African cities, villages which seem to reflect little of the modern world. In the Republic of South Africa, the split between the world of the white European and that of the black African is especially exaggerated by the unjust governmental policy of apartheid.

Native village near Pretoria, Africa

NIGHT, a ceramic tile mural by Miró, decorates one of two walls outside the UNESCO headquarters in Paris. The dominating image is a blue crescent, reinforced by hollowed out passages and checkered compositions and figures.

pattern and described small pieces of human experience. They, among others, have used what some call antiplots, regarding life as not having much order or sequence in it. The socialist realists, mostly in Communist countries, see life as predetermined by historical conditions like the class struggle. The "good guys" always follow the party line. It must be said, however, that some socialist writers have begun to break out of this straitjacket, even in the Soviet Union. Since the death of Stalin (see page 588), some criticism of government policy has been permitted. Writers like Boris Pasternak (author of *Doctor Zhivago*), however, have gone too far in the eyes of official censors and have been forbidden to publish their works in their own country. Russian authors have increasingly spoken out for the right to publish freely what they regard as having literary value.

In the United States the civil rights movement brought forth in the 1960's another kind of realistic writing. For example, the "sociological" novels of James Baldwin have made an eloquent case in angry terms for equality of the Negro.

The writers who have followed the mood of formalism have separated themselves from history, nature, and their immediate surroundings. For them the outer world of re-

ality only serves to give their imaginations some raw material. The times do not create the art, but art creates the times, they believe. The old idea of "art for art's sake" has become their guide. The emphasis, therefore, is on style rather than content. *Giles Goat-Boy,* by the American John Barth, is an example. Barth claims, "Language is the matter of books." Or, in the case of poetry, as Archibald MacLeish expresses it, "A poem should not mean but be." As an offshoot of romanticism and symbolism, formalism owes much to these two movements. Essentially escapists, the formalists frequently distort the events and characters drawn from the current scene. Regardless of their attitudes, however, they cannot escape the fact that art is inseparable from life and also represents a view of life.

The visual arts. In painting and sculpture, experimentation was still apparent in the 1950's and 1960's. Rebellion, and even anarchy, might describe the mood of many of the artists. Of the older abstract painters and sculptors, Picasso (see page 360) and his countryman Joan Miró (1893–) still flourished. Miró was probably the chief inspirer of the so-called postcubists. His diverse genius has produced a wide variety of subjects and styles, from the primitive folk-art of "The Farm," the social realism of "Still Life with Old Shoe," to the ultraminimal "Paint-

ing," which consists simply of three blobs of
color. The latter has opened up a new field
for many painters and sculptors of today,
namely, minimal art. It makes use of a very
small (minimal) number of lines, objects,
and colors. These artists have also been influenced by the computer era, emphasizing
mathematical shapes and forms. The work
of a Dutch painter, Pieter Mondriaan, is a
good example of how geometrical arrangements of line, shape, and color can excite and
also baffle the imagination of the viewer. The
"Mondriaan look" was adopted even by
some dress designers. This style has lent itself particularly to sculpture, in which cubes,
rectangles, spheres, and numerical propor-

tions seem to have become the fashion. Recently, sculpture has also become constructivist; that is, it creates things of new industrial materials (iron, stucco, glass, tin, zinc,
cables, etc.), reflecting the machine age. The
father of this style was probably the Russian
Vladimir Tatlin (1885–1956), whose monument to the Third International looks "like
a cross between the Eiffel Tower and the
Leaning Tower of Pisa." Meanwhile, poster
art attracted the attention of serious painters,
giving new quality to an old form of advertising.

Avant-garde art, however, does not mo-
nopolize the stage. The popular American
painter Andrew Wyeth, for example, has
won acclaim for his realistic lonely landscape
scenes and his portrayal of simple people.

Architecture has continued its "form follows function" techniques. And "functional"
no longer has to mean box-shaped, or built
merely of steel and glass. A new departure
in skyscrapers, for example, is the one-hun-
dred-story John Hancock building in Chicago, with its giant cross girders to protect
against wind stress and its tapered lines.
The number of new buildings of this kind
and the growing interest of architects in
urban planning indicate that cities are not
dying, as some critics have charged. Other
purposes and other settings call for vastly

BOSTON CITY HALL. By combining stark geometric forms with fundamental hues and textures, the
architects have created a structure which harmonizes with the Early American atmosphere of its
surroundings.

different styles. The Trans World Airlines Terminal in New York, by Eero Saarinen, has soft, wavy lines; and the General Time Corporation headquarters in Stamford, Connecticut, assumes the shape of a flying saucer, but is surrounded by a romantic throwback—a moat. In designing their ingenious structures, architects have used a whole battery of technological aids: precast concrete beams, cable-hung roofs, mass-production methods, and a host of new materials, such as spun plastic, rust-sealing steel, aluminum, and glare-proof glass. Concrete as a finished building material has also proved versatile and popular. United States architects have often been the leaders of innovation, and the most important of these is probably the German-born Ludwig Mies van der Rohe.

Musical moods continue to change. In music, as in art and architecture, older styles have been modified and some new ones have emerged. The twelve-tone technique and atonal system made famous by Schönberg and Stravinsky (see page 365) are here to stay. But this kind of music has become more melodic, lyrical, and restrained in the works of younger composers, such as the Frenchman Pierre Boulez (1925–   ) and the German Karlheinz Stockhausen (1928–   ). These two also pioneered in experimenting with electronic music, which has become a striking characteristic of current "pop" (popular) music. Consisting of tape-recorded sounds, usually selected to accompany vocal performances, electronic music reflects the influence of a technological age.

POP MUSIC

What I like of the new pop music is maybe 5 per cent of the whole output . . . it's mostly trash. But that 5 per cent is so exciting, and . . . so significant, that it claims the attention of every thinking person.

—Leonard Bernstein, 1967.

Pop music represents by far the most inventive form of the listening art in recent times. Based originally on the jazz of the 1920's (see page 365), it has gone through various phases and styles—rhythm and blues, rock 'n' roll, and folk-rock. It is music of and for the young, expressing their disillusionment and anger with what they consider the shortcomings of the adult world. The chief performers and composers have been members of small vocal groups with unconventional names, and the favorite accompanying instrument has been the guitar (electronic, of course). The sometimes deafening noise—produced by percussion, amplified guitars, and shrieking voices of singers dressed in "far-out" clothes—gives evidence that, in the words of Bob Dylan's song, "The Times They Are A-Changin'." This is not to say that pop music has no enduring qualities. Some of the voices of protest against the Establishment convey their messages in subtle and delicate poetry. Many represent an honest effort to search for their identity in a world of scrambled values. Moreover, Negro groups have made an important contribution to the pop scene by reflecting the temper of the times in "soul music." It is based on the older jazz and blues patterns and expresses the way of life of those who have had to suffer and endure.

Perhaps the pop revolution has been best exemplified in the works of the Beatles, an English singing and instrumental quartet that burst upon the music world in 1963–1964. They (and their numerous imitators) have made rock music an international language. Their range of topics has been wide, from a romantic ballad like "Michelle" to the more serious presentation of the generation gap in "Sergeant Pepper." Meanwhile, that gap is being bridged to some extent in the still-popular Broadway-show theme songs, patterned after the older and more sedate styles of George Gershwin, Irving Berlin, and Cole Porter.

AUDIO DNA, a Peter Max poster inspired by psychedelia, pays tribute to the generative forces of modern rock and roll.

Education adapts to the times. In this age of advanced technology, education the world over has taken on new meaning and importance. The reasons are fairly clear. As pointed out before (see page 337), the machine age has created a need for additional knowledge and new skills. Machines and automation have eliminated to a large extent much of the backbreaking labor of past generations. Unskilled jobs have been disappearing. Moreover, as the percentage of workers producing goods has declined, the number producing services has sharply increased. Those who repair and maintain products, who sell and transport them, who work in banks, insurance companies, schools, etc., now outnumber those who work in factories. All these people require special training in some degree. Technology has also created entirely new industries and fields of work—space,

computer, and microelectronic, to name only several of a large and growing list. With the so-called knowledge explosion has come the population explosion (see page 332), requiring that increasing numbers of people be given "marketable skills." Mass education, therefore, seems to hold the answer. For the person with little or no education, job opportunities are scarce. In the United States it is estimated that, by 1975, youths who do not finish elementary school will have an unemployment rate seven times higher than that of college graduates. In practical terms this means that education pays. The job outlook for the school dropout is bleak in all industrialized nations, as well as in those on the way to becoming industrialized.

Faced with skyrocketing enrollments and the need to adapt their curricula to the demands of the machine age, schools have slowly broken with tradition. Some common trends are evident throughout the western world, although in general the United States has led the way in experimenting with new methods and courses. After World War II an increasing emphasis was placed on education in science and mathematics. Nuclear fission, the space race, and the cold war stimulated this emphasis. Nations regarded it as a matter of national security to strengthen their military technology, based on scientific research. Another pressure came from the fact that science and mathematics have played key roles in producing the wonders of the machine age, promoting prosperity in most industrialized nations. The effort to recruit better-trained teachers of science and mathematics and to build well-equipped laboratories has been the result. It requires that more and more money be spent on education at every level. Governments now set aside higher percentages of their budgets for educational purposes. Private foundations, too, spend larger and larger amounts in promoting experimentation in the schools.

It has also come to be realized throughout the world that if education is to be an important national resource, it must provide equality of opportunity. Whether they are gifted or slow learners, from urban slums, wealthy suburbs, or rural areas, each individual should have the opportunity to develop his ability to the limit. The comprehensive high school, long established in the United States, Japan, and Sweden, tends to serve this end. It is spreading slowly to other western countries, where education has been largely for the elite. In this kind of school, regardless of ability, all have a better chance to know how to live and work together.

Learning devices and procedures in the schools have also been undergoing marked changes. Increasing emphasis has been placed on the use of educational "hardware," such as closed-circuit television, tape recorders, teaching machines, electronic information storage systems, and a battery of audio-visual aids. The object has been to improve the efficiency of learning and to free teachers from mere drill chores. More recently, educators have renewed an interest in the humanities, recognizing that narrow training in vocational skills and technical knowledge overlooked the development of the total person. A broader liberal arts schooling, it was held, would make individuals more adaptable to the pace of change in modern society. To that end, also, independent study projects and "discovery learning" techniques have become more and more common. These seem to give new life to the educational theories of Pestalozzi and Dewey.

One aspect of the contemporary educational scene is especially noteworthy—an international exchange program. In 1946 the United States Congress passed the Fulbright Act, which proved a milestone in international relations. It provided for the financing of an exchange of students, teachers, and professors between the United States and forty-nine foreign countries. After the first twenty years of its operation the program had enabled more than eighty thousand persons to study and teach in countries other than their own. The purpose has been to promote mutual understanding among the peoples of the world. Although the results cannot be

---

TOWARD A FEELING OF COMMON
HUMANITY

I do not think educational exchange is certain to produce affection between peoples, nor indeed is that one of its essential purposes; it is quite enough if it contributes to the feeling of a common humanity, to an emotional awareness that other countries are populated not by doctrines that we fear but by individual people—people with the same capacity for pleasure and pain, for cruelty and kindness, as the people we were brought up with in our own countries.

—Senator J. W. Fulbright

---

measured in exact terms, learning how different peoples think, feel, and act is bound to furnish a sound basis for the preservation of peace.

Toward religious unity. In the twentieth century the materialistic values created by an industrialized society have continued to lessen the influence of organized religion. Although church membership has kept pace with population increases, active church participation of Christians and Jews has declined. The distractions of mass culture (the automobile, movies, television, recreational facilities, etc.) have served to compete with religious activities. Furthermore, from the beginning of the Industrial Revolution churches have been slow to take an active interest in solving urgent social problems (slums, bad working conditions, race relations). On these questions they generally supported the views of their most influential members. World Wars I and II further disillusioned the common man as to the ability of organized religion to contribute to world peace.

Nevertheless, to counteract these forces and to revive interest in religion, several important steps have been taken. All of them point toward a larger measure of co-operation among the various religious sects and groups. In 1908 United States Protestants put their efforts together in founding the Federal Council of Churches of Christ in America. This organization was the basis for the World Council of Churches, founded in 1948. Interreligious co-operation had already been extended in 1928 with the establishment of the National Conference of Christians and Jews. Its programs to combat intolerance and promote human brotherhood have had a widespread influence.

The most significant religious event of recent times, however, was the calling of Vatican Council II by Pope John XXIII. (Vatican Council I met in 1870.) Beginning in 1962, its sessions continued during the following four years, coming to an end under the papacy of Pope Paul VI. One of its chief concerns was Christian unity. This ecumenical spirit, as it is called, was shown by the presence of observers from major Protestant groups, who took part in discussions and in public events and services. The most important decision of the Council was the decree supporting religious freedom. It represented a sharp break with previous official policy, opening the way for increased interreligious co-operation. It also foreshadowed further changes in the relations between church and state. A decree condemning anti-Semitism likewise improved Jewish-Christian relations. The Council also departed from the past in authorizing the use of modern languages instead of Latin in church services. The spirit of brotherhood (ecumenism) stimulated by the Council sessions has spread in many directions, from setting up common theological studies and Biblical research to holding interfaith services and meetings of the clergy. Pope Paul himself visited the Greek Orthodox Patriarch in Istanbul, Turkey, the first such contact with Eastern Christendom in nearly a thousand years. He also made trips to the Holy Land, India, and the U.N., and received the Anglican Archbishop of Canterbury in a "new spirit of Christian fellowship." In 1968, however, unity within the Catholic Church itself received a setback when Pope Paul issued his encyclical (decree) "On Human Life." It reasserted the traditional opposition of the Church to artificial limitation of human births. Many clergymen and laymen protested that this position was unrealistic in the face of the critical population explosion.

In the meantime, the nonwestern world has failed to show the same tendency toward ecumenism. The Arab-Israeli War of 1967 (see page 628), the clash of the older religious values with the Maoist Cultural Revolution in China, and the continuing bitterness between Hindus and Moslems in India and Pakistan have made the goal of human brotherhood seem more distant than ever.

REVIEWING THE CHAPTER

TERMS TO UNDERSTAND: *cold war, Lublin Committee, Truman Doctrine, containment, ERP, COMECON, OAS, NATO, SEATO, CENTO, Warsaw Pact, Schuman Plan, EEC, Euratom, Berlin airlift,* Sputnik, *U–2, Non-Proliferation Treaty, Point Four, Peace Corps, cyclotron, chain reaction, fusion, fission, Calder Hall, satellite, IGY, Intelsat, KDKA, radar, automation, laser, DNA, formalism, minimal art, constructivist, Vatican Council II, ecumenism.*

PERSONS TO IDENTIFY: *George Marshall, Dwight Eisenhower, Robert Schuman, Ernest Lawrence, Enrico Fermi, Robert Goddard, Yuri Gagarin, John Glenn, Lee De Forest, Charles Townes, Christian Barnard, Gunter Grass, Boris Pasternak, James Baldwin, John Barth, Joan Miró, Pieter Mondriaan, Andrew Wyeth, Ludwig Mies van der Rohe, Ray Charles, the Beatles, Pope John XXIII, Pope Paul VI.*

PLACES TO LOCATE: *Oder-Neisse line, Cyprus, Shippingport, Cape Kennedy.*

QUESTIONS TO ANSWER

1. (a) Briefly describe what the cold war is. (b) Account for its beginning. (c) What concessions were made to the Soviet Union at Yalta and why were these concessions made? (d) Show how 1947 was a year of decision in the cold war. (e) Give evidence to show that the Marshall Plan was successful. What were Russian countermeasures to the Marshall Plan?

2. (a) Why did the non-Communist nations adopt collective defense measures? (b) Give a brief account of the development of NATO. (c) What other defensive pacts have been signed by the non-Communist nations? (d) How effective have these defense pacts been in "containing" communism? (e) How did Russia react to these anti-Communist pacts?

3. (a) What steps have been taken to promote economic unity in western Europe? (b) What progress has been made toward political union in western Europe? What obstacles have stood in the way?

4. (a) What were the basic aims of the opposing sides in the cold war? (b) Explain the major events in the cold war from 1949 to 1960. (c) Explain the "Berlin question" as part of the cold war conflict. (a) What were some of the implications of the *Sputniks*? (e) Did the cold war change in nature or intensity in the 1960's? Include the Cuban crises and the arms race in your explanation.

5. (a) Summarize some of the successes and failures of the United Nations as a peace-keeper, including the limiting of armaments. (b) Why has the United Nations been ineffective against the great powers? (c) Explain how and with what agencies the United Nations has worked against ignorance, hunger and disease. (d) In what ways has the United States helped to improve living conditions in underdeveloped countries?

6. (a) What is atomic fission? Fusion? (b) What are some peacetime uses of atomic energy? (c) Explain key developments in each of the following fields: space, electronics, medicine. (d) Why does the twentieth-century face a population crisis?

7. (a) Distinguish between realism and formalism in twentieth-century literature. Name authors of each style. (b) Briefly describe the contribution of four artists mentioned in Chapter 27. (c) What are some of the recent trends in architecture and music? Give specific examples.

8. (a) Why has education taken on new meaning and importance in the twentieth century? Give some recent trends in education. (b) What forces have tended to lessen the influence of organized religion in the twentieth century? Explain some of the steps which have attempted to revive interest in religion.

9. Explain in your own words what you think is the real challenge of the future.

FURTHER ACTIVITIES FOR PART NINE

1. Draw a time line from 1945 to the present. Indicate on the line the events which have been notable in world history.
2. Prepare (by yourself or with three classmates) a series of four maps showing Europe in 1914, in 1919, in 1939, and today.
3. Debate: *Resolved,* that the United Nations has been a failure.
4. Prepare a map of Africa and a map of Asia, indicating the political boundary changes which have occurred between 1914 and the present.
5. Prepare a report on the most recent inter-American conference. Consult periodicals listed in the *Readers' Guide.*
6. Consult the current magazines in the library to obtain information on problems up for consideration by the United Nations. Report orally to the class on your findings, using a map to show where the problems exist.
7. Prepare a debate on the question: *Resolved, that the world would have been happier without nuclear fission and fusion.*
8. Make a chart of the various international organizations (defensive or economic) mentioned in Part Nine. Name the organization, its date of founding, its members, and its purpose.
9. On a map of the world name and show by shading the various areas taken over by the Communists since 1945.
10. Prepare a written or oral report on one of the people mentioned in Part Nine. Consult the biographies listed below.

FURTHER READING FOR PART NINE

(Stars indicate easier books)

HISTORY

BARACH. *1975: and the Changes to Come.* Harper.

BOWLES. *At Home in India.* Harcourt.

BROGAN. *France.* Time-Life.

BRONOWSKI, ed. *The Doubleday Pictorial Library of Technology.* Doubleday.

*BROWN. *India.* Time-Life.

CHRISTENSEN. *The Pictorial History of Western Art.* Mentor. (paperback)

CLARK. *The Coming Explosion in Latin America.* McKay.

——. *Impatient Giant: Red China Today.* McKay.

CLENDENIN. *Music History and Theory.* Doubleday. (paperback)

*COUGHLIN. *Tropical Africa.* Time-Life.

CROW. *Mexico Today.* Harper.

DEAN. *New Patterns of Democracy in India.* Harvard.

DILL. *Germany: A Modern History.* University of Michigan.

DMYTRYSHYN. *USSR: A Concise History.* Scribner.

ELLIS. *The Arabs.* World.

FALL. *The Two Viet-Nams.* Praeger.

——. *Viet-Nam Witness, 1953–1966.* Praeger.

FESSLER. *China.* Time-Life.

FISCHER. *The Story of Indonesia.* Harper.

*FORMAN. *The Land and People of Nigeria.* Lippincott.

FOSTER. *Africa South of the Sahara.* Macmillan.

GALANTE and MILLER. *The Berlin Wall.* Doubleday.

GATTI and ATTILIO. *The New Africa.* Scribner.

GUNTHER. *Inside Africa.* Harper.

——. *Inside Europe Today.* Harper.

——. *Inside Russia Today.* Harper.

HEAPS. *The Wall of Shame.* Duell.

HISCOCKS. *The Adenauer Era.* Lippincott.

HUGHES. *The First Book of Africa.* Watts.

ISENBERG, ed. *Ferment in Eastern Europe.* Wilson.

JOY. *Young People of South America.* Duell.

*KARNOW. *Southeast Asia.* Time-Life.

KING. *Why We Can't Wait.* Signet. (paperback)

KITTLER. *Equatorial Africa.* Nelson.

KUH. *Break-Up: The Core of Modern Art.* New York Graphic Society.

*LARRALDE. *Land and People of Mexico.* Lippincott.

LAVINE. *Central America.* Time-Life.

LAWSON. *The United States in the Korean War.* Abelard-Schuman.

McKINNEY. *Music in History, the Evolution of an Art.* American Book.

McNEILL, BUSKE, ROEHM. *The World . . . Its History in Maps.* Denoyer-Geppert.

MARSHALL. *The Military History of the Korean War.* Watts.

*MATTHEW. *Land and People of Thailand.* Lippincott.

MATTHEWS. *Cuba.* Macmillan.

MICHENER. *Bridge at Andau.* Random House.

*MYRDAL and KESSLE. *Chinese Journey.* Beacon. (paperback)

NIELSEN. *Africa.* Atheneum.

*PATON. *The Land and People of South Africa.* Lippincott.

*ROSS. *Land and People of Canada.* Lippincott.

SALISBURY. *Russia.* Atheneum.

SAVAGE. *The Story of Africa South of the Sahara.* Walck.

*STEWART. *The Arab World.* Time-Life.

STILLMAN. *The Balkans.* Time-Life.

THOMAS. *Men of Space.* Chilton.

TREGASKIS. *Vietnam Diary.* Holt.

WADSWORTH. *The Glass House: The U.N. in Action.* Praeger.

WARD. *The Rich Nations and the Poor Nations.* Norton. (paperback)

WESTON. *Afghanistan.* Scribner.

WESTWOOD. *Russia, 1917–1964.* Harper.

BIOGRAPHY

ABRAHAMS. *Tell Freedom: Memories of Africa.* Knopf.

ALEXANDER. *Prophets of the Revolution: Profiles of Latin American Leaders.* Macmillan.

BINGHAM. *U Thant.* Knopf.

CLARK. *The Man Who Is France: The Story of General Charles de Gaulle.* Apollo.

DALAI LAMA. *My Land and My People.* McGraw.

DEAN. *Builders of Emerging Nations.* Holt.

DOOLEY. *The Night They Burned the Mountain.* Farrar, Straus.

EDWARDES. *Nehru, a Pictorial Biography.* Viking.

GOLLOMB. *Albert Schweitzer: Genius of the Jungle.* Vanguard.

KAYIRA. *I Will Try.* Doubleday.

LAMB. *The Nehrus of India.* Macmillan.

LEVINE. *Champion of World Peace: Dag Hammarskjold.* Messner.

LUTHULI. *Let My People Go.* McGraw.

MAURIAC. *DeGaulle.* French and European Publications.

MOSLEY. *Hirohito, Emperor of Japan.* Prentice-Hall.

NKRUMAH. *Ghana: The Autobiography of Kwame Nkrumah.* Nelson.

RAMA RAU. *Gifts of Passage.* Harper.

SANSAN. *Eighth Moon.* Harper.

FICTION

*BENARY–ISEBERT. *Rowan Farm.* Harcourt.

*BLATTER. *Cap and Candle.* Westminster.

BOJER. *The Last of the Vikings.* New American Library.

BURDICK and WHEELER. *Fail-Safe.* McGraw.

CHAMBERLAIN. *More Combat Stories of World War II and Korea.* Day.

DEIGHTON. *Funeral in Berlin.* Dell. (paperback)

HERSEY. *A Single Pebble.* Knopf.

HUXLEY. *Brave New World.* Bantam. (paperback)

LE CARRÉ. *Spy Who Came in from the Cold.* Coward-McCann.

LESSING. *African Stories.* Ballantine. (paperback)

MICHENER. *The Bridges at Toko-ri.* Random House.

NARAYAN. *The Bachelor of Arts.* University of Michigan.

SINGH. *Train to Pakistan.* Grove. (paperback)

VAN DER POST. *Flamingo Feather.* McGraw.

Reference Section

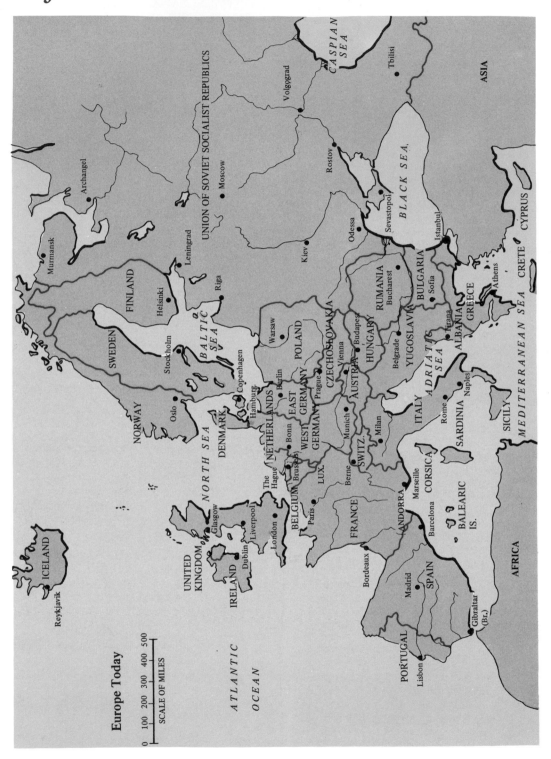

Europe Today

SCALE OF MILES

0   100   200   300   400   500

ICELAND

Reykjavik

ATLANTIC

OCEAN

UNITED KINGDOM

IRELAND

Dublin

Glasgow

Liverpool

London

NORTH SEA

NORWAY

Oslo

SWEDEN

Stockholm

Murmansk

Archangel

FINLAND

Helsinki

BALTIC SEA

Leningrad

Riga

UNION OF SOVIET SOCIALIST REPUBLICS

Moscow

Volgograd

Tbilisi

CASPIAN SEA

ASIA

Rostov

Kiev

Odessa

Sevastopol

BLACK SEA

Istanbul

DENMARK

Copenhagen

Hamburg

NETHERLANDS

The Hague

BELGIUM

Brussels

LUX.

Paris

FRANCE

Bordeaux

ANDORRA

SPAIN

Madrid

Barcelona

BALEARIC IS.

Marseille

CORSICA

SARDINIA

Berlin

EAST GERMANY

WEST GERMANY

Bonn

Munich

SWITZ.

Berne

POLAND

Warsaw

CZECHOSLOVAKIA

Prague

AUSTRIA

Vienna

HUNGARY

Budapest

Milan

ITALY

Rome

Naples

SICILY

MEDITERRANEAN SEA

YUGOSLAVIA

Belgrade

ADRIATIC SEA

ALBANIA

Tirana

GREECE

Athens

CRETE

CYPRUS

RUMANIA

Bucharest

BULGARIA

Sofia

AFRICA

PORTUGAL

Lisbon

Gibraltar (Br.)

672

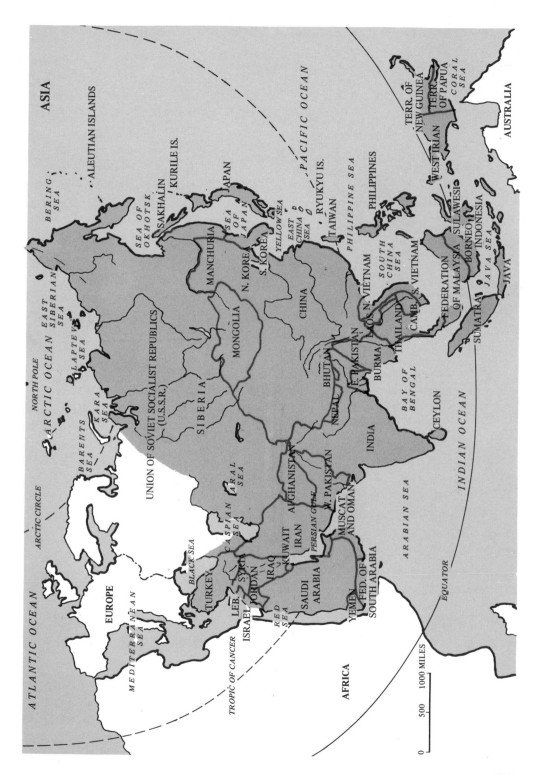

673

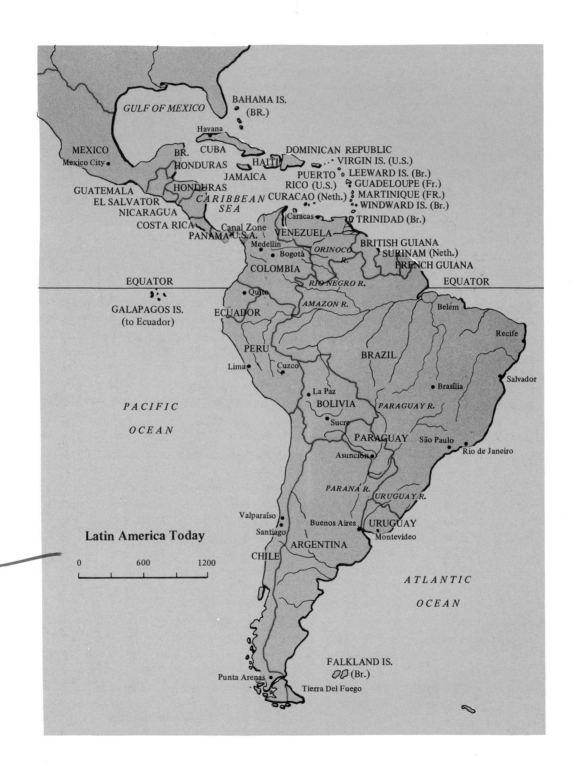

Latin America Today

0   600   1200

674

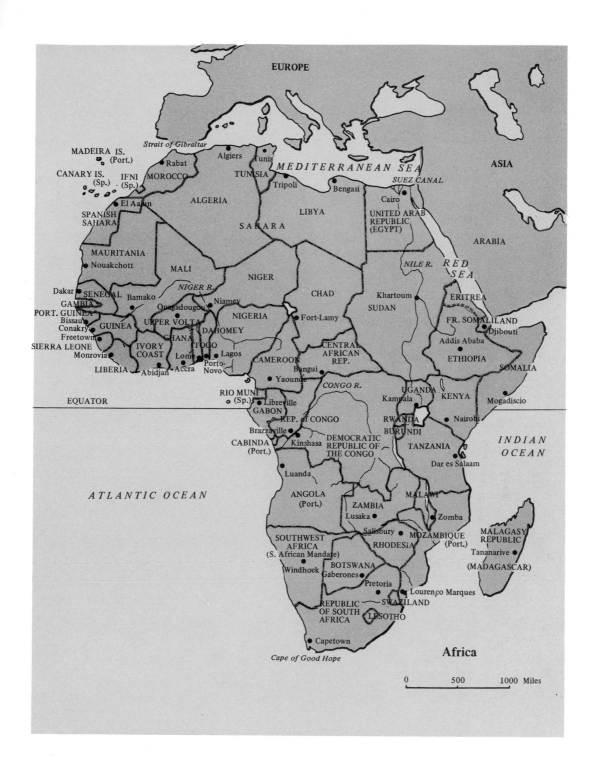

Africa

| 0 | 500 | 1000 Miles |

675

SIGNIFICANT DATES IN WORLD HISTORY

Political and Military	*Industrial, Agricultural, Commercial*	*Intellectual, Religious, Humanitarian, Scientific*
B.C.	**B.C.**	**B.C.**
	c.**3000** A high civilization existed in Mesopotamia, Turkestan, Egypt, and India. Copper used	*c*.**3000** Egyptians had alphabet of 24 letters. Written records kept by Egyptians. Soon after by Sumerians
c.**2850** Menes became king over Upper and Lower Egypt	*c*.**2800**–*c*.**2100** Pyramids built in Egypt	
c.**2000** Indo-Europeans settled in Greece	*c*.**2000** Egyptians dug canal connecting the Nile and the Red Sea. Also built large irrigation basins	*c*.**2000** Egyptians had considerable knowledge of medical science, algebra, plane geometry, and solid geometry
c.**1750** Code of Hammurabi at Babylon	*c*.**1600**–*c*.**1100** Aegean civilization at peak. Commerce and art highly developed	
1580–1150 Empire Age in Egypt		
c.**1500** Aryans entered India	*c*.**1500** Iron used in Western Asia and in Egypt	*c*.**1500** Written records kept by the Chinese
c.**1025** Hebrew tribes united under Saul		
	c.**1000** Mayas began to develop first great civilization in America	*c*.**1000** Phoenician alphabet reached the Greeks
c.**973**–*c*.**933** Reign of Solomon in Palestine	*c*.**1000**–*c*.**700** Phoenicians had commercial supremacy in Mediterranean. Planted numerous colonies on its shores	
		c.**850** Homer composed *Iliad*, the world's greatest epic
753(?) Rome founded		**776** First recorded celebration of Olympian (Olympic) games. Authentic Greek history begun
	c.**750** Greek city-states began to plant colonies along shores of Mediterranean and Black seas	
		c.**600** Mayas had remarkably accurate calendar
612 Destruction of Nineveh. End of Assyrian Empire		*c*.**563** Birth of Buddha
		c.**551** Birth of Confucius
	c.**530**–*c*.**330** Persian Empire at its height. Persians built widespread system of roads and carried on far-flung commerce	
509(?) Roman Republic established		
	c.**500** Darius I restored canal linking the Nile and Red Sea	*c*.**500** Darius I created a great medical school in Egypt
490 Marathon, **480** Salamis **479** Plataea, and Mycale		*c*.**484** Birth of Herodotus, "father of history"
479–405 Period of Athenian Empire		*c*.**469** Birth of Socrates, martyr to freedom of thought
	461–429 Athens a center of manufacturing and trade	**461–429** Age of Pericles in Athens. Athens regarded as "the school of Hellas"
		460 Birth of Hippocrates, "father of medicine"

Political and Military	Industrial, Agricultural, Commercial	Intellectual, Religious, Humanitarian, Scientific
B.C. **459–404** Peloponnesian Wars. Downfall of Athens **451–449** Laws of the Twelve Tables in Rome	**B.C.**	**B.C.**
390 Gauls sacked Rome		**427**(?) Birth of Plato, author of *The Republic*
338 Macedonia conquered Greek city-states **333** Battle of Issus, **331** Battle of Arbela. Macedonians overthrew Persian Empire **323** Death of Alexander	**332** Alexander founded city of Alexandria, Egypt, soon a center of commerce and learning **312** Appian Way begun. First important link in a great system of Roman roads	**384** Birth of Aristotle, foremost scholar of ancient world *c.***360** Praxiteles, greatest Greek sculptor
264 Rome supreme over the Italian peninsula. Began to fight Carthage for control of Sicily		*c.***300** Euclid wrote *Elements of Geometry*
246 Shih Huang-ti began reign in China **206** Han dynasty began rule in China **202** Battle of Zama. Ended Second Punic War. Rome triumphant over Carthage **146** Rome destroyed Carthage and Corinth and became mistress of the Mediterranean	**214** Great Wall of China begun **206**–A.D. **220** Ancient Chinese civilization at its peak	**160**(?) Birth of Hipparchus, greatest of Greek astronomers
	*c.***120** Romans began to use concrete	**133** Tiberius Gracchus tried to reform the landholding system of Rome
44 Death of Julius Caesar **31** Battle of Actium. Octavian defeated Antony **27** Octavian became Emperor Augustus. Established Roman Empire **27**–A.D. **180** Pax Romana (Roman Peace)	**31**–A.D.**180** Mediterranean world enjoyed flourishing commerce	**46** Caesar reformed the calendar used by the Romans **4**(?) Birth of Christ

Political and Military	Industrial, Agricultural, Commercial	Intellectual, Religious, Humanitarian, Scientific

A.D.

A.D.

A.D.
29(?) Crucifixion of Christ

98–117 Reign of Trajan. Roman Empire reached greatest extent
117–138 Reign of Hadrian. Noted for systematic organization of Roman government

122–127 Hadrian's Wall built in England

130 Birth of Galen, author of medical encyclopedia

284 Diocletian assumed absolute rule in Roman Empire. Revived emperor worship

313 Edict of Milan. Constantine made Christianity a legal religion in Roman Empire
325 Council of Nicaea. Framed creed of Christian beliefs

330 Constantinople made the capital of Roman Empire
378 Battle of Adrianople. Visigoths defeated Romans and began to overrun Roman Empire
395 Final division of Roman Empire into Eastern and Western Empires

392 Christianity became state religion in Roman Empire

*c.*400–*c.*1100 Constantinople was the greatest city of Europe and a center of world trade

451 Battle of Châlons. Romans defeated Huns under Attila
476 Romulus Augustulas deposed by the Germans. Ended line of Roman emperors in the West
529–534 Code of Justinian

476 Beginning of so-called Dark Age in western Europe

618–907 China under the T'ang dynasty was the most civilized state on earth
*c.*700–*c.*1100 The Arabs developed an imposing civilization

622 Hegira (flight) of Mohammed from Mecca to Medina

711 Moslems entered Spain from Africa
732 Battle of Tours. Franks under Charles Martel stopped advance of Moslems in western Europe
800 Charlemagne crowned emperor of the Romans. An attempt to revive Roman Empire in the West
843 Treaty of Verdun. Charlemagne's empire divided into three parts

678

Political and Military	Industrial, Agricultural, Commercial	Intellectual, Religious, Humanitarian, Scientific
A.D.	**A.D.**	**A.D.**
962 Otto I, the Great, crowned Roman emperor. Holy Roman Empire founded	**1000** Leif Ericsson, a Viking, touched North America	*c.*1000 The epic *Beowulf* was written in Old English
1066 Battle of Hastings. Norman conquest of England		**1054** Final separation of Greek and Roman churches **1096** First crusade begun **1122** Concordat of Worms *c.*1198 University of Paris founded
*c.*1200 Mayas conquered by Toltecs. Aztecs began conquest of central Mexico **1206** Genghis Khan established Mongolian Empire **1215** Magna Carta, first great charter of English liberties	*c.*1200 In Europe towns were growing larger. Workshop industries were increasing in variety and importance. Craft guilds were being organized. Annual fairs had become common	*c.*1214 Birth of Roger Bacon. Suggested use of observation and experiment as guides to truth *c.*1225 Birth of Thomas Aquinas
1280 Kublai Khan made himself emperor of all China	**1271–1295** Travels of Marco Polo in Far East	
1337–1453 Hundred Years' War. English expelled from France	**1348** Black Death appeared in Europe. Hastened decline of serfdom	*c.*1307 Dante began the *Divine Comedy* **1309–1377** "Babylonian Captivity" of the popes. Removal to Avignon, France **1378–1417** The Great Schism. Weakened authority of popes over western Christendom *c.*1387 Chaucer began *Canterbury Tales*
1453 Ottoman Turks captured Constantinople. End of Byzantine Empire **1455–1485** Wars of the Roses. As a result, Henry VII started Tudor line in England **1492** Conquest of Granada. Moors driven out of Spain	**1486** Diaz rounded Cape of Good Hope **1492** Columbus discovered America. Beginning of Atlantic period of European history **1497** John Cabot reached mainland of North America. Established English claim **1498** Da Gama reached India around Africa. Portuguese opened all-water route to Far East	**1454(?)** Gutenberg printed Latin Bible. First large book printed with movable type

Political and Military	Industrial, Agricultural, Commercial	Intellectual, Religious, Humanitarian, Scientific
A.D.	A.D. **1513** Balboa discovered Pacific Ocean	A.D. **1513** Machiavelli wrote *The Prince*, an outstanding work on politics **1517** Luther's *Ninety-five Theses* posted. Beginning of Reformation in Germany
1519–1521 Cortés conquered Mexico for Spain. End of Aztec Empire **1531–1533** Pizarro conquered Peru for Spain. End of Inca Empire	**1519–1522** Magellan sailed around world	
		1543 Copernicus published theory of sun-centered universe **1545–1563** Council of Trent. Beginning of Catholic Counter Reformation **1555** Peace of Augsburg
1558–1603 Reign of Elizabeth in England **1588** Defeat of Spanish Armada. Gave England control of seas	**1577–1580** Drake became first Englishman to sail around the world	**1561** Birth of Francis Bacon, advocate of the scientific method **1591–1613** Shakespeare wrote thirty-six plays **1598** Edict of Nantes
	1607 Settlement of Jamestown. First permanent English colony in America **1608** Settlement of Quebec. First permanent French colony in America	
1613 Romanov family came to power in Russia **1618–1648** Thirty Years' War. Religious and political **1619** First representative assembly in America established at Jamestown	**1620** Settlement of Plymouth by Pilgrims	**1625** Grotius published *On the Law of War and Peace*. Founded international law **1628** Harvey published work on blood circulation
1635 Japan closed doors to Europeans	**1634** Lord Baltimore established Maryland as home of religious freedom	**1636** Harvard College established **1637** Descartes published his *Discourse on Method*
1642–1649 Puritan Revolution. Dealt blow to absolutism in England **1643–1715** Reign of Louis XIV in France		

Political and Military	Industrial, Agricultural, Commercial	Intellectual, Religious, Humanitarian, Scientific
A.D. **1644** Manchu dynasty began rule in China	**A.D.**	**A.D.**
	1681 William Penn founded Pennsylvania	**1685** Birth of Bach. Edict of Nantes revoked **1687** Newton published theory of universal gravitation
1688–1689 Glorious Revolution **1689** Bill of Rights. Made Parliament supreme in English government and protected civil rights of people **1689–1725** Reign of Peter the Great in Russia. Europeanization of Russia begun		**1689** English Act of Toleration **1690** Locke published *Two Treatises of Civil Government.* Advocated government by consent of the people
1713 Peace of Utrecht. Ended War of Spanish Succession. A Bourbon placed on throne of Spain. England won Gibraltar	**1701** Jethro Tull invented seed drill	
1740–1786 Reign of Frederick the Great. Prussia became a leading power **1756–1763** Seven Years' War	**1733** Kay invented flying shuttle. First of the inventions which brought about Industrial Revolution **1740** Enclosure of English farmlands hastened by act of parliament	**1752** Diderot's *Encyclopedia* appeared in France **1762** Rousseau published *Social Contract* **1764** Publication of Beccaria's *On Crimes and Punishment*
	1764 Hargreaves invented spinning jenny **1769** Watt's improved steam engine was patented. Arkwright patented "water frame" for spinning	**1774** Priestley discovered oxygen **1776** Adam Smith published *Wealth of Nations,* attacking mercantilism and advocating laissez-faire
1776 Declaration of Independence by the United States		
1783 Peace of Paris and Versailles. Ended War of American Revolution	**1779** Crompton invented spinning "mule" **1785** Cartwright invented power loom	
1787 Constitution of United States framed **1788** George Washington elected first U.S. President **1789** Estates-General summoned in France. Beginning of French Revolution		

Political and Military	Industrial, Agricultural, Commercial	Intellectual, Religious, Humanitarian, Scientific
A.D. **1791** French Declaration of the Rights of Man	A.D. **1793** Eli Whitney invented cotton gin **1797** Newbold invented cast-iron plow **1800** Volta invented electric cell	A.D. **1796** Jenner used vaccination for smallpox
1803 Louisiana purchased by United States from Napoleon **1804** Code Napoléon. The most enduring work of Napoleon **1810–1825** Latin American revolutions for independence	**1807** Fulton's steamboat, the *Clermont,* launched on Hudson River	
1814–1815 Congress of Vienna. Remade map of Europe after Napoleonic era	**1814** Stephenson built successful locomotive First steam printing press installed Jethro Wood built iron plow of replaceable parts **1816** Davy invented miner's safety lamp	**1813** Birth of Richard Wagner, originator of the music drama
1815 Battle of Waterloo. Final defeat of Napoleon I	**1819** Steamship *Savannah* crossed Atlantic	**1818** Mary Shelley published *Frankenstein*, a warning that man would be overpowered by his machines **1821** First public high school in the United States opened at Boston **1824** British repealed laws against combinations of wage earners
1823 Monroe Doctrine announced, warning Europe to keep "hands off" the Americas		
1830–31 Uprisings in various parts of Europe. Overthrew Bourbons in France and made Belgium independent **1832** First Reform Act in Great Britain. Gave vote to middle class	**1831** Faraday produced an electric current	**1830–1833** Lyell's *Principles of Geology* published
	1833 McCormick patented the reaper	**1833** Britain abolished slavery in empire. Third English Factory Act limited child labor **1836** America's first women's colleges founded **1838–1839** Cell theory by Schleiden and Schwann **1840** Liebig published first of his great works on soil chemistry
1839 Lord Durham's Report	**1839** Goodyear invented vulcanization of rubber **1844** Morse's telegraph successfully operated **1846** Repeal of British corn laws. Beginning of free trade policy	**1844** YMCA founded in England **1846** Long and Morton used ether for anesthesia

Political and Military	Industrial, Agricultural, Commercial	Intellectual, Religious, Humanitarian, Scientific
A.D. **1848–1849** Revolutions swept Europe. Second Republic set up in France. Uprisings failed in Italy, Germany, and Austrian Empire **1852** Louis Napoleon set up Second Empire in France **1853–1856** Crimean War. Russia defeated in effort to weaken Turkey **1854** Commodore Perry opened up Japan	A.D. **1851** Livingstone discovered Zambezi River in Africa **1856** Bessemer process **1858** Aniline dyes produced from coal tar **1859** First oil well sunk (in Pennsylvania)	A.D. **1855 and later.** Pasteur proved that certain diseases are caused by microbes **1858–1861** Alexander II abolished serfdom in Russia **1859** Darwin published *Origin of Species*, setting forth theory of evolution
1860 Abraham Lincoln elected U.S. President **1861–1865** Civil War in the United States	**1862** Nobel invented dynamite **1866** Atlantic cable laid **1869** Completion of first transcontinental railroad in the United States Suez Canal opened Invention of first plastic (celluloid)	**1863** Lincoln's Emancipation Proclamation **1865** Lister began practice of antiseptic surgery Publication of Mendel's work in heredity **1867** Publication of first volume of Marx's *Das Kapital* **1869** Mendeléef worked out Periodic Table of elements
1870 Rome occupied by Italian troops. Unification of Italy completed **1871** German Empire proclaimed at Versailles	**1874** Universal Postal Union established **1876** Bell's telephone **1877** Stanley traced course of Congo River **1879** Edison invented incandescent electric lamp	**1870** Great Britain established national system of education
1878 Treaty of Berlin		**1879** Ibsen's play *A Doll's House* gave impetus to the feminist movement **1880** William Booth founded Salvation Army in England **1881–1886** Free public education established in France **1883–1889** Germany adopted system of social insurance
1882 Triple Alliance		

Political and Military	Industrial, Agricultural, Commercial	Intellectual, Religious, Humanitarian, Scientific
A.D.	**A.D.** **1884** Invention of artificial silk, or rayon *c.***1885** Combination harvester and thresher invented **1887** Daimler patented successful gasoline engine	**A.D.**
1890 Pan American Union **1894–1895** Chinese-Japanese War. Japan won Formosa		**1895** Freud published first book dealing with psychoanalysis
	1896 Marconi obtained first patent for wireless telegraphy **1897** Diesel engine invented	**1897** Discovery of electrons **1898** The Curies discovered radium William James formulated pragmatism
1899 Meeting of First International Peace Conference **1899–1902** Boer War. British extended control over South Africa	**1900** Trans-Siberian Railroad completed **1903** Wright brothers made first successful flight in heavier-than-air machine	**1901** Planck originated quantum theory
1904–1905 Russo-Japanese War. Japan established herself as major power		**1905** Einstein published formula for conversion of mass into energy ($E = mc^2$)
1907 Triple Entente completed	**1906** De Forest invented the audion, or vacuum rectifier Human voice first sent "over the air" **1909** North Pole reached by Peary **1911** South Pole reached by Amundsen	**1906** Finland became first nation to grant suffrage to women **1908** Boy Scout movement begun
1911–1912 China declared a republic **1912–1913** Balkan Wars		**1913** Rockefeller Foundation established **1916** Einstein published general theory of relativity
1914–1918 World War I	**1914** Panama Canal opened	
1917 Russian Revolution. Communist regime begun	**1918** Air mail service established between New York and Washington	
1919 Third International founded by Communists Peace Conference met at Versailles **1920** First meeting of League of Nations		**1919** Women in the U.S. given right to vote International Labor Organization established
1921–1922 Washington Arms Conference	**1920** Regularly scheduled broadcasting begun	
1922 World Court organized. Mussolini controls Italy		

Political and Military	Industrial, Agricultural, Commercial	Intellectual, Religious, Humanitarian, Scientific

A.D.
1925 Locarno Conference

1928 Pact of Paris. Outlawed war as an instrument of national policy

1931 Japan invaded Manchuria

1933 Hitler came to power in Germany. End of German Republic
Roosevelt announced Good Neighbor policy
1935–1936 Italy seized Ethiopia. Mussolini defied League of Nations
1936 Formation of Rome-Berlin Axis
1936–1939 Civil war in Spain. Franco became dictator
1937 Japan moved into northern China

Germany annexed Austria

Munich Pact. Britain and France agreed to Hitler's seizure of Czech Sudetenland
1939 Italy annexed Albania
Russo-German nonaggression pact
World War II began
Russo-Finnish War began
1940 Blitzkrieg in the West. Fall of Denmark, Norway, Holland, Belgium, and France

Air war over Britain
Japan joined the Axis
1941 Germany overran Balkans and invaded Russia

Roosevelt and Churchill drew up Atlantic Charter

Japan attacked Pearl Harbor

United States joins Allies

A.D.

1926 First successful projector for sound movies
1927 Lindbergh made solo flight across Atlantic
1928 First Five Year Plan begun in Russia
1929 Stock market crash in United States. Beginning of world-wide depression
1930 Nylon plastic invented. Synthetic rubber invented
1932 E. O. Lawrence invented cyclotron, or atom-smasher
Great Britain abandoned its historic policy of free trade

A.D.

1929 Discovery of penicillin

1934 United States joined the International Labor Organization
1935 Social Security Act in the United States
1936 Sulfa drugs used in medicine

1938 Hahn and Strassman split uranium atom

1941 The war years brought remarkable advances in medicine, surgery, and psychiatry. Rapid advance continued after the war

685

Political and Military	Industrial, Agricultural, Commercial	Intellectual, Religious, Humanitarian, Scientific
A.D.	**A.D.**	**A.D.**
1942 Japan conquered Philippines, East Indies, and Burma		**1942** First sustained atomic chain reaction produced at University of Chicago. Led to invention of atom bomb
Russians stopped Germans at Stalingrad		
Germans and Italians halted in North Africa		Nationwide program for collecting donations of blood begun by American Red Cross
Allied forces landed in northwest Africa		
1943 Russian counteroffensive against Germans begun		**1943** United Nations Relief and Rehabilitation Administration established
Allies drove Germans from North Africa and invaded Sicily and Italy		
Italy surrendered		
Air attack on Germany		
Allies began island hopping toward Japan		
Teheran Conference. First meeting of Roosevelt and Churchill with Stalin		
1944 Second front opened in France		**1944** Streptomycin used in medicine
Germans driven out of Russia		
MacArthur's forces landed in the Philippines		
1945 Yalta Conference. Big Three decided on disarmament of Germany	**1945** United Nations Food and Agriculture Organization established	
Franklin D. Roosevelt died		
Unconditional surrender of Germany		
United Nations Charter drafted at San Francisco		
Atom bombs destroyed Hiroshima and Nagasaki		
Unconditional surrender of Japan		
1946 First meeting of United Nations in London	**1946** International Bank for Reconstruction and Development came into operation	**1946** Synthetic penicillin produced
United Nations Atomic Energy Commission established	**1946–1947** Byrd expedition to Antarctica. Mapped over half the continent	Radioactive isotopes used in medicine and in other fields
Civil war renewed in China		United Nations Educational, Scientific and Cultural Organization established
Italy set up republic		
Philippines became independent		
France established Fourth Republic		
1947 Peace treaties signed with Italy, Hungary, Rumania, Bulgaria, and Finland	**1947** British Labor government nationalized all coal mines	**1947** 200-inch telescope put into operation at Mt. Palomar, California
Truman Doctrine	International Trade Organization established	Chloromycetin used in medicine
Britain freed India		

686

Political and Military	Industrial, Agricultural, Commercial	Intellectual, Religious, Humanitarian, Scientific
A.D.	**A.D.**	**A.D.**
1948 Marshall Plan adopted	**1948** New synthetic fiber, orlon, developed	**1948** Comprehensive health insurance program went into effect in Great Britain
Ninth Inter-American Conference at Bogotá, Colombia		World Health Organization established
Berlin blockade broken by airlift		First international congress on poliomyelitis
Yugoslavia expelled from Cominform		International Refugee Organization established
British withdrew from Palestine. War between Jews and Arabs followed		U.N. Assembly adopted Declaration on Human Rights
1949 Council of Europe organized		**1949** Cortisone and ACTH reported effective against arthritis
West German Republic established		
North Atlantic Treaty signed		
1950 India became a republic within British Commonwealth	**1950** First turbojet transport plane flown in U.S.	**1950** Two new chemical elements, 97 and 98, created artificially
Korean War began		Largest U.S. atomic furnace for research went into operation at Brookhaven National Laboratory
Chinese Communists entered Korean War		
1951 Schuman Plan adopted	**1951** British iron and steel industry nationalized	
Japanese Peace Treaty signed	First commercial color television broadcast took place	
Egypt denounced Suez Canal Treaty with Britain		
1952 Bonn Agreement with West Germany signed	**1952** First commercial jet flight in history, from London to Johannesburg	**1952** U.N. headquarters buildings completed in New York
EDC Treaty signed	Liner *United States* set new world record for trans-Atlantic crossing	Gamma globulin used for prevention of polio
General Naguib forced King Farouk of Egypt to abdicate		Archeologists found more Sumerian tablets
General Eisenhower elected U.S. President		
U.S. conducted hydrogen bomb experiments in Pacific		
1953 Premier Stalin died	**1953** U.S. rocket plane set altitude record of sixteen miles	**1953** British expedition climbed Mt. Everest
Coronation of Queen Elizabeth II of England		
Korean War ended		
Russia announced she had H-bomb		
1954 Indo-China truce signed at Geneva. Cambodia, Laos, and Vietnam became independent	**1954** First atomic-powered submarine launched by U.S. Canada and U.S. joined in St. Lawrence seaway project	**1954** Funeral boat of Cheops discovered near Great Pyramid
SEATO treaty signed		
Paris Agreements signed, giving West Germany membership in NATO and WEU		

Political and Military	Industrial, Agricultural, Commercial	Intellectual, Religious, Humanitarian, Scientific
A.D. **1955** Afro-Asian Conference held at Bandung Austrian treaty signed Big Four "summit" conference held at Geneva Perón ousted in Argentina West Germany became a sovereign state, joined NATO Warsaw and Baghdad pacts signed **1956** Khrushchev "downgraded" Stalin Suez Crisis resulted in first use of international police force (UNEF) Hungarian revolt brutally crushed by Russia **1957** Eisenhower Doctrine for Middle East announced First U.S. ICBM successfully fired	**A.D.** **1955** First international conference on peaceful uses of atomic energy held at Geneva Nuclear-produced electricity used in U.S. Solar battery used to send telephone messages **1956** First large-scale atomic power plant opened in England **1957** Common Market and Euratom pacts signed First nonstop round-the-world jet plane flight made by six U.S. fliers First U.S. large-scale nuclear power plant opened	**A.D.** **1955** Molds for Phidias' statue of Zeus found in Greece Salk polio vaccine proved effective Dr. Albert Einstein died at 76 **1957** International Geophysical Year began Russians launched first Sputnik International Atomic Energy Agency established
1958 Khrushchev assumed premiership in Russia U.S. and British troops entered Lebanon and Jordan France established Fifth Republic New Berlin crisis arose **1959** Fidel Castro led successful revolution in Cuba Big Four Foreign ministers meeting on Berlin crisis ended without agreement Tibetan revolt put down by Chinese Communists Premier Khrushchev visited the U.S. **1960** Khrushchev killed Paris summit conference U.N. intervened in Congo crisis John F. Kennedy elected U.S. President Seventeen newly independent African countries joined U.N. **1961** U.S. ended diplomatic relations with Cuba Cuban invasion by exiles failed Berlin Wall crisis begun Soviets resumed nuclear tests	**1958** "Commune" system spread through Red China Transatlantic commercial jet plane service begun by British and Americans **1959** Central American common market agreement ratified St. Lawrence Seaway opened **1960** European Free Trade Association established **1961** Alliance for Progress went into effect	**1958** First U.S. earth satellite launched First U.S.-Soviet cultural exchange agreement signed First land crossing of Antarctica completed Pope John XXIII is elected **1959** First known radar contact with Venus made by U.S. scientists Two monkeys returned alive after flight to outer space in U.S. rocket Russian satellite photographed the "other" side of the moon **1960** France tested its first atomic bomb First Polaris missile fired from submerged submarine **1961** U.S. Peace Corps created Russia's Gagarin became first space man Russia exploded 50-megaton hydrogen bomb

688

Political and Military	Industrial, Agricultural, Commercial	Intellectual, Religious, Humanitarian, Scientific
A.D. **1961** U.N. Secretary Hammarskjold killed in plane crash **1962** Algerian independence achieved after 7-year war Russia agreed to remove missile bases from Cuba Communist China opened attack on India along Himalayan border	**A.D.** **1962** U.S. Trade Expansion Act passed Boring of Mont Blanc Tunnel between France and Italy completed	**A.D.** **1962** U.S. orbited its first astronaut, Col. John H. Glenn First international satellite fired into orbit by U.S. and Britain Telstar communications satellite launched by U.S. 21st Ecumenical Council opened by Pope John XXIII in Vatican
1963 France rejected NATO nuclear force France and West Germany signed Treaty of Reconciliation Katanga secession from Congo ended with aid of U.N. forces Organization for African Unity formed at Addis Ababa conference East-West Nuclear Test Ban Treaty signed by U.S., Britain, and Russia U.S.-Soviet "hot line" connected President Kennedy assassinated	**1963** France vetoed Britain's entry into European Common Market U.S. and Canada agreed to sell wheat to Russia	**1963** U.S. Syncom satellite launched Pope John issued encyclical *Pacem in Terris* Pope John XXIII died. Succeeded by Pope Paul VI Civil Rightists marched on Washington
1964 Greek-Turkish conflict on Cypress Sino-Soviet rift widened Prime minister Nehru of India died Gulf of Tonkin incident led to full-scale American entry into Vietnam War Khrushchev overthrown	**1964** First stage of Egyptian Aswan Dam opened U.S.-Soviet treaty for exchange of consuls signed	**1964** U.S. Ranger VII rocket took pictures of moon's surface **1964** Russia orbited space vehicle carrying three men China conducted first atomic bomb test End of third session of Ecumenical Council U.S. and Russia launched space probes toward Mars
1965 3,500 U.S. Marines landed in Vietnam (first U.S. combat troops) U.S. Marines landed in Dominican Republic Indonesia seized all foreign firms	**1965** Early Bird satellite television relay set up over Atlantic	**1965** Ranger 8 sent back 7,000 pictures of the moon before crashing on lunar surface Russian cosmonaut became first man to step from spacecraft into space Russia detonated underground nuclear blast

Political and Military	Industrial, Agricultural, Commercial	Intellectual, Religious, Humanitarian, Scientific
A.D.	A.D.	A.D.
American troops directed to fight in Vietnam U.S. urged suspension of atomic tests Six days of rioting in Watts, California **1966** Sukarno removed from power in Indonesia French withdrew all forces from NATO U.N. General Assembly revoked South Africa's mandate over Southwest Africa U.N. General Assembly called for ban on nuclear tests **1967** 62 nations signed treaty limiting use of outer space for military purposes Biafra seceded from Nigeria Israeli-Arab Six-Day War	**1966** Executive bodies of European Common Market, European Atomic Energy Community, and European Coal and Steel Community were merged **1967** 53 nations agreed to drastic tariff cuts as result of "Kennedy Round" of tariff talks	Death of Albert Schweitzer Ecumenical Council closes **1966** Russia's Luna 9 made first "soft" landing on the moon First weather satellite launched by U.S. U.S. Medicare program begun U.S. Gemini 10 performed first docking maneuver in space **1967** Synthetic DNA Molecule produced at Stanford University China exploded first H-bomb Russian spacecraft parachuted instrument package to Venus surface Dr. Christian Barnard performed first human heart transplant
1968 Student and worker riots in Paris Nuclear non-proliferation (A-ban) treaty signed Assassination of Senator Robert F. Kennedy Russia crushed liberalization program in Czechoslovakia Richard Nixon elected **1969** DeGaulle resigned as President of France and George Pompidou elected	**1968** Tariff cuts resulting from "Kennedy Round" negotiations begun "Miracle" wheat and rice produced record crops where used in Asia	**1968** Assassination of Dr. Martin Luther King, Jr. U.S. Apollo 8 orbited first man around moon **1969** U.S. landed first men on the moon Mariner VI and VII relayed readings and pictures of Mars back to earth Ho Chih Minh, president of North Vietnam, died

ACKNOWLEDGMENTS

Permission to use illustrative material in *The Record of Mankind*, Fourth Edition, has been courteously granted by the following sources:

BLACK AND WHITE PHOTOGRAPHS

PAGE

2 Department of Antiquities, Ashmolean Museum, England
4 Odyssey Studio (top); Bettmann Archive (bottom)
8 J. Allan Cash (top); Johnny Hart and Field Enterprises, Inc. (bottom)
18 The Mansell Collection
20 British Museum
24 Radio Times Hulton Picture Library
25 Bettmann Archive
26 Trans World Airlines
27 Louvre
28 Acme Newspictures, Inc.
29 McLaughlin Air Service
32 New York Public Library
35 Radio Times Hulton Picture Library
36 Gettysburg College Oriental Art Museum, Pennsylvania
39 Department of Tourism, Government of Pakistan
41 Archaeological Survey of India
45 Museum of Fine Arts, Boston, Ross Collection
46 Peabody Museum, Salem, Mass. (top); Museum of Fine Arts, Boston (bottom)
47 Peabody Museum, Salem, Mass.
48 Bettmann Archive
52 D. A. Harissiadis
54 Biblioteca Ambrosiana, Milan, Italy
56, 57 Metropolitan Museum of Art
58 Three Lions
60 Metropolitan Museum of Art
62 D. A. Harissiadis
65 Harold M. Lambert (bottom)
68 Radio Times Hulton Picture Library
70 Monkmeyer
72 Alinari
74 British Museum
75 Museum of Fine Arts, Boston
79, 81 Alinari
83 D. A. Harissiadis
84 Bettmann Archive
85 Museum of Fine Arts, Boston
86 Lateran Museum
88, 102, 104 Alinari
107 Boston Public Library
108 Alinari
112 Ewing Galloway
113 Museum of Fine Arts, Boston
116 Three Lions
122 Victoria and Albert Museum, London, Crown Copyright
124 Museum of Fine Arts, Boston
128 John Carter Brown Library
131 Martin Hurlimann
132 Radio Times Hulton Picture Library
136 LIFE, Eric Schaal, © Time, Inc.
138 Bettmann Archive (left); Museum of Fine Arts, Boston (right)
141 New York Public Library
142 ENIT
143 ENIT
145, 147 Metropolitan Museum of Art
148 Bettmann Archive
149 Bodleian Library, Oxford, England
150 From *Grand Banquier de France*, by Bertrand-François Barrême, 1685
152 The Mansell Collection
155 Bettmann Archive
157 New York Public Library
158 LIFE, Hans Wild, © Time, Inc.
162 New York Public Library
165 Harvard University Library (left); Alinari (right)
167 Bettmann Archive
169 University of Paris
170 Bibliothèque Nationale, Paris
171 Courtesy of Livermore and Knight Company
173 Giraudon
178 Cabinet des Estampes, Antwerp
180 Bulloz
183 Painting by Vasari
188 Radio Times Hulton Picture Library
190 Brown Brothers
191 Black Star (left); Monkmeyer (right)
194 The Mansell Collection
198 Pierpont Morgan Library
200 New York Public Library
203 Brooklyn Museum
204 "La Rochester," Mexico City
205 Pan American Airways
209 Black Star
210 National Maritime Museum
211, 215, 216 Bettmann Archive
218 Museum of Fine Arts, Boston, Fenollosa-Weld Collection
221 Saudi Arabian Public Relations Bureau
224 Department of Tourism, Government of India
228 Victoria and Albert Museum, London (left); Metropolitan Museum of Art, Kennedy Fund, 1926 (right)
229 Museum of Fine Arts, Boston (top); Mario Andi (bottom)
230 Japanese National Tourist Organization
233 Immedia
236 Alan Band Associates
242 Metropolitan Museum of Art
244 Bulloz
249 The Mansell Collection
258 Culver Pictures, Inc. (top left); Giraudon (bottom)
261 Brown Brothers
262 Three Lions
265 Yale University Press
268 Cliché des Musées Nationaux
273 New York Public Library
274 Brown Brothers
277 Musée Carnavalet
279 Bettmann Archive
281 Paul Rodier: *The Romance of Weaving*
282 Bettmann Archive
293 Historical Picture Service, Chicago
294 Pan American Union
297 Culver Pictures, Inc.
298 L. C. Handy Studios
302 Smithsonian Institution
304 Brown Brothers
306 Bettmann Archive
308 Benjamin Butterworth: *Growth of Industrial Art*
310, 311 Three Lions
312, 314 Brown Brothers
318 George Eastman House
321 Northern Natural Gas Company Collections, Joslyn Art Museum, Omaha, Nebraska
322 Bettmann Archive
324 Ford Archives, Henry Ford Museum, Dearborn, Michigan (top left); National Archives (top right); Ford Motor Company (bottom left); David W. Corson from A. Devaney, N. Y. through E. P. Jones (bottom right)
327 Monsanto Public Relations Department, St. Louis, Missouri
329 Ford Motor Company
330 Courtesy of the U.S. Naval Institute
332 *Harper's Monthly*, 1870
334 Radio Times Hulton Picture Library

337 Wide World Photos
341, 344 Radio Times Hulton Picture Library
347 Wide World Photos
350 Collection of the Whitney Museum of American Art, New York
354, 357 Bulloz
358 Victoria and Albert Museum, London
359 Staatliche Museum, Berlin
361 A. Renger-Patzsch Wamel-dorf Uber Svest, West Germany, courtesy of TAC
363 The Mansell Collection
369 Photo Researchers, Inc.
374, 376 Radio Times Hulton Picture Library
379 The British Museum
383 Bettmann Archive
385 Radio Times Hulton Picture Library
393 Brown Brothers
399 Painting by Camphausen
400 Bettmann Archive
404 Soviet Life from SOVFOTO
405 Radio Times Hulton Picture Library
411 Canadian Government Travel Bureau
416, 421 Radio Times Hulton Picture Library
422 Bettmann Archive
425 Culver Pictures, Inc.
426 Radio Times Hulton Picture Library
429 Wide World Photos
430 United Press International
431 From Admiral Matthew Perry's *Report*, 1856
433 J. Allan Cash
435, 437 Brown Brothers
438 Wide World Photos
440 Radio Times Hulton Picture Library (top); Brown Brothers (bottom)
443, 445 Bettmann Archive
446, 450 Brown Brothers
456 *The New York Times*
458 Wide World Photos
460 International News Photo
462 Western Newspaper Union Photo Service
466 National Portrait Gallery, Smithsonian Institution, Washington, D.C.
468 U.S. Signal Corps
470 Keystone View Co.
471 Radio Times Hulton Picture Library
475 Acme Photo
477 Radio Times Hulton Picture Library
480 Black Star
483 Wide World Photos
485 From *Since 1900* by Macmillan Co., by Harding in *The Brooklyn Eagle*
492 *Guernica* (mural), 1937. On extended loan to The Museum of Modern Art, New York, from the artist.
494 Acme Photo (top)
498 Press Association, Inc. (left); Wide World Photos (right)
502, 504 SOVFOTO
509 Black Star
512 Wide World Photos
517 Black Star
519 Monkmeyer
520 Black Star
522, 527 Radio Times Hulton Picture Library
532 © Hammond Incorporated

535 San Francisco Gallery of Art, Gift of Dr. Grace L. McCann Morley
536 CIAA
538 United Nations
540 U.S. Army Photo
543 Historical Picture Service, Chicago
545 Wide World Photos
547 Brown Brothers
549 Wide World Photos
552 The Mansell Collection
554, 557 U.S. Navy Photo
559 International News Photo
561 Rapho Guillumette
563 Defense Department Photo
564 U.S. Army Photo
566, 568, 569 United Nations
571 Wide World Photos
576 Anna Kaufman
578 Netherlands Information Service
581 Wide World Photos
583 Georges Bendrihem, *Christian Science Monitor*
584 German Information Center
585 United Press International Photo
587 Fiat
589 United Press International Photo
590 Tass from SOVFOTO
592 Wide World Photos
593 United Press International Photo
598 OEO Photo by Joan Larson
599, 601 United Press International Photo
602, 604 *Christian Science Monitor*
605 Wide World Photos
606 Jack Manning
608 Werner Bischof of Magnum, from *The Concerned Photographer*
610 Culver Pictures, Inc.
612, 616, 620 Wide World Photos
621 *Christian Science Monitor*
626 Arabian American Oil Company
628 *Christian Science Monitor*
629 United Nations
631 *Christian Science Monitor*
633 United Nations
634 Alan Band Associates
638 NASA
641 Culver Pictures, Inc.
642 United Press International Photo
645 Frank Miller cartoon, *Des Moines Register*, from Wide World Photos
647 Wide World Photos
649, 651, 654 United Nations
656 Ralph Crane, LIFE Magazine © Time, Inc.
658 NASA
660 Museum of Science, Boston
662 Boston Public Library Print Collection
663 UNESCO from MASS
664 Owen Franken
665 Peter Max Poster Corporation, New York

COLOR PHOTOGRAPHS

PAGE
22-A LIFE © 1959 Time, Inc.
22-B Henry C. Heniman
22-C Saul S. Weinberg
22-F J. Barnell from Shostal
22-G J. Barnell from Shostal
22-H Metropolitan Museum of Art
118-A Freda Closs from Shostal
118-B Edwards from FPG
118-C Edwards from FPG
118-D Henry C. Heniman
118-E Edwards from FPG
118-F and G Elliot Erwitt from Magnum
118-H Allan R. Sloan from Shostal
182-A Bradley from Shostal
182-B British Museum and Three Lions
182-C Morgan Library
182-D Three Lions
182-E Alinari
182-F Iris Verlag
182-G Shostal
182-H Louvre and Giraudon (top); National Gallery of Art, Washington, D.C. (bottom)
214-A Staatliche Landesbildstelle, Hamburg
214-B Shostal
214-C Three Lions
214-D and E Rijksmuseum, Amsterdam
214-F Huntington Library
214-G Lowry Aerial Photo Service
214-H Grace Lines
278-A Courtesy of the Duke of Bedford
278-B National Cash Register Company
278-C Barnell from Shostal
278-D Camera Clix
278-E Jerry Cooke from Photo Researchers
278-F European Art Color Slides, Inc.
278-G Burstein
278-H Fritz Henle from Photo Researchers
342-A Monkmeyer (top); New England Telephone and Telegraph Company (bottom)
342-B U.S. Air Force Photo
342-C LIFE, by Yale Joel
342-D FPG
342-E SOVFOTO (left); House of Photography (right)
342-F LIFE, by Kessel
342-G Thomas S. Cash from Shostal
342-H LIFE, by Kessel and Grehan
566-A Library of Congress (left); McDermott from Black Star (right)
566-B Smithsonian Institution and *American Heritage*
566-C Imperial War Museum, London
566-D Hugo Jaeger (top); Abbott Laboratories Collection (bottom)
566-E Imperial War Museum, London
566-F Pix
566-G Fred Ward from Black Star
566-H Lowry Aerial Photo Service
622-A FPG
662-B Ward W. Wells from Shostal
662-C Photo Researchers
662-D FPG
662-E Round the World Photos by Bernardine Bailey
662-F LIFE, by Joseph McKeown
662-G Olivetti Corporation of America
662-H Lowry Aerial Photo Service

INDEX

Bolívar, Simon, 294, 439
Bolivia, 204, 414
Bombay, 213
Bonapartists (France), 290
Book of the Dead, 25
Boris III (King: Bulgaria), 520
Borman, Frank, 658
Borough system, England, 381
Bosnia, Austria seizes, 408; Austria-Hungary annexes, 444; revolution in, 407; WW1, 441
Bosporus, 406
Boston Tea Party, 265
Botany, 82
Botany Bay, 425
Boulez, Pierre, 665
Boulton, Matthew, 308
Bourbon family, 246
Bourgeoisie, 296, 271, 290, 322
Boxer Uprising, 430, 436, 609
Bracque, Georges, 360
Brahms, Johannes, 363
Branco, Humberto Castelo, 603
Brandenburg; & Austria, 254; Russians occupy, 255
Brandenburg-Prussia, 254
Brandt, Willy, 585, 586
Brasília, 603
Brazil, dictatorship in, 537, 602; formation of, 413; government of, 143; independence of, 297; rubber industry, 328, 413; silver in, 215; slavery abolished, 413–414; social insurance, 338; trade with, 202
Brest-Litovsk, treaty of, 498
Brezhnev, Leonid, 498
Briand, Aristide, 487
Britain, Caesar conquers, 97; China trade, 227. *See also* England, Great Britain, United Kingdom.
Britain, battle of, 551
British Columbia, 411
British Commonwealth of Nations, 386, 441
British East India Company, 212, 213, 424
British Empire, 210–214, 527, 528
British Guiana, 530
Bronze age, 16, 236
Brook Farm, Mass., 320
Brown, A. W., 330
Browning, Robert, 355
Brunswick Manifesto, 276
Brussels Pact, 643
Bryan, William Jennings, 477
Bubonic plague, 153–154
Budapest, 400
Buddha, Gautama, 41–43, 49, 223, 228
Buddhism, 41–43; in China, 228; decline of, 223; in India, 224; in Japan, 231; Southeast Asia, 232, 233
Buenos Aires Conference (1936), 535
Buffon, Count Georges de, 344

Bunsen, Robert, 340
Bulganin, Nikolai, 407, 589
Bulgaria, 408, 448, 519–520, 552, 562, 592, 640
Bulge, battle of, 561
Bülow, Count Bernhard von, 443
Bunche, Ralph, 627
Bundesrat, 399
Bundestag, 585
Burke, Edmund, 265
Burma, 232, 426; Chinese expansion, 230, 429; Colombo Plan, 625; communism in, 620; independence, 579, 619–620; Red China border, 613
Burma Road, 544, 556, 563
Bushmen, 235, 236
Byrnes, James F., 640
Byron, Lord George, 353, 354, 364
Byzantine Empire, 125–126, 129
Byzantium, 61, 101, 125

Cairo, 129
Calais, 160, 162
Calcutta, 213
Calendar, errors in, 114; Julian/Roman, 252; Moslem, 127; Romans improve, 97
California, annexation of, 410
Calvin, John, 189–190, 195
Camacho, Manuel Ávila, 538
Cambodia, 232, 426, 620
Cameroons, 419
Campo Formio, treaty of, 280
Camus, Albert, 662
Canada, American boundary dispute, 484; & British Commonwealth, 386; dominion status, 411; emigration to, 410; ceded to England, 212; family allowance system, 338; France acquires, 248; French rule in, 210; government of, 411; independence of, 410–411; law in, 411; Loyalists &, 266; Quebec separatism, 606; self-government, 411; unification of, 410, 411; U.S. relations, 410, 606; WW2, 605
Cannae, battle of, 94
Canning, George, 289, 298
Canon law, 113
Canova, Antonio, 358
Canterbury, Archbishop of, 144
Cantigny, battle of, 460
Canton, 227, 428, 543
Cape Colony, 421, 287
Cape of Good Hope, 199, 208
Cape Kennedy, 657
Cape Town, 208
Capet, Hugh, 161
Capital, 336; labor and, 317
Capital punishment, 253, 366
Capitalism, 315–317
Caporetto, battle of, 454
Caracas, 294
Cárdenas, Raul de, 437–438

Carmona, Antonio, 517
Carnegie, Andrew, 476
Carol II (King: Rumania), 520
Carpeaux, Jean, 358
Carthage, 32, 93–94
Cartier, Jacques de, 209
Cartwright, Edmund, 307, 308, 315
Carver, George Washington, 328
Cary, Joyce, 662
Casablanca, 558
Caspian Sea, 37, 249
Caste system, 39, 40–41
Castro, Fidel, 604, 649
Catherine of Aragon, 191
Catherine the Great (Empress: Russia), 220, 253, 256, 257
Catholic Church, 119; split in, 142. *See also* Greek Orthodox Church, Roman Catholic Church.
Catholic Reformation, 185
Cavendish, Henry, 341
Cavour, Count Camillo, 392, 393
Ceausescu, Nicolae, 595
Cell theory, 342, 344
Censorship, 312
Central America, 199, 202, 296–298, 412
Central Intelligence Agency, 649
Central Powers, 444, 451
Central Treaty Organization, 644
Ceres, 92
Cervantes, Miguel de, 184
Ceylon, 37, 197; Colombo Plan, 624; Congress of Vienna, 287; independence of, 579; trade, 200
Cézanne, Paul, 359, 360
Chaeronea, battle of, 67, 69
Chagall, Marc, 360
Chaldeans, 32, 34
Chamberlain, Neville, 494, 536, 548
Charlemagne, 129, 130, 132–133, 380
Charles I (Emperor: Austria-Hungary), 400
Charles I (King: England), 260, 261
Charles I (King: Spain), 200
Charles II (King: England), 261, 262
Charles V (Holy Roman Emperor), 189, 191
Charles V (King: Spain), 245–246
Charles X (King: France), 289, 290, 389
Charles Albert (King: Sardinia), 292
Château-Thierry, battle of, 459
Chaucer, Geoffrey, 165
Cheka, 499
Chemistry, atom and, 344; in India, 223–224; modern, 326, 328, 340

Crécy, battle of, 162
Crete, 23, 55, 56, 408, 552
Crimean War, 388, 407
Cro-Magnon man, 12
Crompton, Samuel, 306, 315
Cromwell, Oliver, 260–261
Crucé, Eméric, 478
Crusades, 148–151, 219, 476
Cuba, Bay of Pigs, 605, 649; communism in, 604–605; missile crisis, 590, 597, 605, 649, 650; OAS &, 605; revolution (1895), 436; U.S. protectorate, 535; U.S. troops in, 438
Cubism, 360
Cuneiform writing, 20, 28
Curie, Marie, 342
Curie, Pierre, 342
Cyprus; 23, 408, 651, 652
Cyrus the Great, 34, 62
Cuzco, city of, 204
Czechoslovakia, 471; emergence of, 495; French treaty, 532; Germany absorbs, 546; republic of, 496; revolt in, 291; Soviets invade, 590, 592, 594 595, 613, 644, 650; & Sudetenland, 547; uprisings in, 648; Yalta Conference, 640

Da Gama, Vasco, 199, 200, 216
Daladier, Édouard, 546, 547
Da Vinci, Leonardo, 182, 330
D-Day (June 6, 1944), 559
Daimio, 231
Daimler, Gottlieb, 329
Dali, Salvador, 360
Dalton, John, 342
Daniel (prophet), 34
Dante, Alighieri, 166
Danton, Georges Jacques, 276 277, 278
Danzig, 471, 547
Dardanelles, 62, 67, 406, 454, 642
Darius I (Emperor: Persia), 20, 32, 39, 62, 68
Darius III (Emperor: Persia), 68
Darwin, Charles, 344, 352
Das Kapital (Marx), 321
Daumier, Honoré, 358
Davy, Sir Humphry, 308
Dawes, Charles G., 474, 513
Déak, Ferencz, 400
Debussy, Claude, 366
Declaration of Independence (U.S.), 263, 266, 275
Declaration of the Rights of Man (France), 263, 275, 371
De Forest, Lee, 659
De Gaulle, Charles, 551, 572, 580–582, 606, 630, 632, 644, 646
Delacroix, Eugène, 358
Delian League, 63
Demeter, 78
Democracy, 375, 377–378, 383; in Athens, 64; dictatorship replaces, 496; direct/representa-

tive, 377; gains in, 292; in Great Britain, 385; Greek, 59, 64; growth of, 376–415; modern, 377–378; in North America, 410–414; political, 380–385; post WW1 gains, 495; in Rome, 92–93; U.S., 410
Democritus, 82, 341
Demosthenes, 67, 111
Demography, 332
Denmark, 283, 365, 377, 397, 550
Depression, 317, 337, 474, 526, 533, 541
Descartes, René, 351
De Soto, Hernando, 202
Despotism, 56, 257, 282, 288, 388, 394, 408
Dewey, Admiral George, 436
Dewey, John, 352, 369, 667
Díaz, Bartholomew, 198–199
Díaz, Porfirio, 412
Dickens, Charles, 355
Dictatorship, Argentina, 537, 602; in Balkans, 519; Brazil, 537, 602; Communist, 504; defined, 496; replaces democracy, 496; Estonia, 519; in Germany, 514; in Hungary, 518; Italian, 508; Latin America, 411, 601; Latvia, 519; Lithuania, 519; Poland, 519; Portugal, 517; Spain, 516; spread of, 516; Stalinism, 588; & WW2, 541
Diderot, Denis, 270, 340
Dien Bien Phu, 620
Diocletian, 101, 116
Dionysius, 78
Directory, 278, 280
Disarmament, conference on (1898), 446; Geneva conference (1932), 487; Germany, 468; League and, 483; naval, 486. See also Arms limitation.
Disraeli, Benjamin, 383–384, 408, 423
Divine right of kings, 259, 267, 286, 288, 377, 399
Dix, Dorothea, 367
DNA molecule, 660
Dollfuss, Engelbert, 518
Dom Pedro I (Emperor: Brazil), 297
Dom Pedro II (Emperor: Brazil), 413
Dominican Republic, 437, 605
Dostoevski, Fedor, 356
Douglas-Home, Sir Alec, 580
Draco, 60
Drake, Sir Francis, 211
Drama, 85, 86, 107, 229
Dreyfus, Alfred, 391
Drug traffic, 428, 480
Dubcêk, Alexander, 595
Dubois, Dr. M. Eugene, 12
Duma, 404, 497
Dumbarton Oaks Conference, 565

Dunant, Henri, 368
Dunkirk, evacuation of, 550
Dupleix, Joseph, 209–210, 213
Dürer, Albrecht, 193
Durham, Lord, 410
Dylan, Bob, 665

Earth, 184, 343
East Indies, 197, 198, 200, 230, 233, 267, 413, 525, 556
Ebert, Friedrich, 461, 511
Economic activities & feudalism, 137
Economic reform, 226, 249
Ecuador, 204, 414, 294
Eden, Sir Anthony, 580, 648
Edict of Milan, 116, 117
Edict of Nantes, 370
Edison, Thomas Alva, 325, 331
Education, Arabic, 120; Babylonian, 30; Byzantine, 125; Charlemagne &, 132; Chinese, 226; Church &, 144; & colleges, 370; contemporary, 368–370, 666–667; Egyptian, 26; in Great Britain, 369; Greek, 59, 75–77; Japanese, 231; post WW1, 495; Prussian, 254, 256; Red China, 612; Roman, 99, 110; Russia, 251; Saudi Arabia, 626; Soviet, 505; universities &, 370
Edward III (King: England), 162
Edward VII (King: England), 442
Egypt, agriculture, 24; Anglo-French invasion (1956), 648; & Arab League, 629; leads Arab world, 628; architecture, 25; British in, 442; class system, 23; & Cleopatra, 99; culture, 23; economic development, 628; economic life, 24; education, 26; engineering, 25; foreign policy, 619; gods, ancient, 23; government, 23; history, 21–23; houses of, 25; independence, 423, 530; irrigation, 22; law, 23; literature, 25; monotheism, 23; mummies, 24, Napoleon in, 280; Nile river, 21; & Ottoman empire, 220; religion, 23; schools, 26; science, 26; society of, 27; & Suez Canal, 423, 627, 629; trade, 25; & Yemen, 626–627. See also Nasser, United Arab Republic.
Einstein, Albert, 341, 343
Eisenhower, Dwight David, 557–559, 621, 648–649
El Agheila, battle of, 552
El Alamein, battle of, 557
Elba, 285
Electricity, 342
Electron, 342
Electron microscope, 346
Electronics, 659

697

Laos, 232, 426, 620
Latin America, communism in, 643, 650; democracy in, 537; denuclearization of, 652; dictatorship, 411, 601; education in, 370; French influence, 293; independence of, 292–298; industrial progress, 537, 600; social reforms, 537; supports U.S., 537; U.S. commercial relations with, 535; & WW1, 411, 533; revolutions, 279, 411; unstable, 298; woman suffrage, 368; WW2, 600
Latvia, 470, 495, 519, 548
Lausanne, Treaty of (1923), 521
Laval, Pierre, 545
Lavoisier, Antoine, 341
Law, Anglo-Saxon, 134; in Athens, 64; Babylon, 28; Canada, 411; common law, 160; ecclesiastical law, 144; England, 160, 261; France, 247, 280; Germany, 387; Greece, 60; India, 223; international, 195; Italy, 391; Japan, 231; legal system (England), 160; Prussia, 256; reform in, 257; Roman, 93, 113, 159; Russian, 252, 401; Solon, 60
Lawrence, Ernest O., 655
Lawrence, Colonel T. E., 455
League of Nations, 478; aggression, failure to stop, 544; Article Ten, 469, 481; Assembly of, 479; Council, 479; drug traffic, 480; economic activities, 480; failures of, 482; forerunners of, 477; "Fourteen Points," 461, 467–468; & Germany, 513, 544; & Japan, 542; Manchuria, 542; mandates, 469, 479; membership in, 478; & minorities, 479, 480; organization of, 479; Peace of Paris &, 468; peace structure, 483; political disputes, 482; purposes & duties, 479; & Russia, 483; Secretariat, 479; slave traffic, 480; social activities, 480; & Soviet, 506, 550; successes of, 482; & U.S. Senate, 469; weaknesses of, 541; withdrawals from, 482
Leakey, Louis S. B., 235
Lebanon, 625, 629
Le Corbusier, 361
Leeuwenhoek, Anton van, 345
Lend-Lease, 536, 553, 555
Lenin, Nicolai, 497, 498, 500, 505
Leningrad, 252, 500
Leo I (Pope), 142
Leonidas, 63
Leonov, Alexei, 658
Leopold I (King: Belgium), 290
Leopold II (King: Belgium), 419, 550

Lesseps, Ferdinand de, 422–423, 436
Lexington, battle of, 266
Leyte, battle of, 563
Libby, Willard F., 11
Liberia, 419, 423
Libya, 220, 522, 630, 633
Licinius, 116
Lie, Trygve, 566, 567
Liebig, Justus von, 314
Lincoln, Abraham, 410
Lindbergh, Charles A., 330
Linnaeus, Carolus, 344
Lister, Joseph, 347
Liszt, Franz, 364
Literature, Babylonia, 30; Chinese, 47, 229; contemporary, 662; discontent in, 355, 356; Egyptian, 25; French, 247; Greek, 85; Indian, 222, 223; Islamic, 221; in machine age, 350–373; protest, 355, 356; Reformation &, 181; Renaissance, 183; Roman, 110; romanticism in, 352
Livy, 111
Luthuania, 401, 470, 495, 519, 548
Litvinov, Maxim, 506
Livingstone, David A., 418–419
Lloyd George, David, 384, 459, 478
Locarno Pact, 486, 513, 544
Locke, John, 263, 266, 269, 270
Lollards, 187, 190, 476
Lombard, Peter, 144
Lombards, 142
Lombardy, 393
London (city), 157
London Company, 211
London, Peace of (Balkan wars: 1913), 408
London Economic Conference (1933), 534
London Naval Conference (1930), 534
Long, Crawford, 347
Lorraine, 248, 447, 469. See also Alsace.
Loubet, Émile, 442
Louis XIV (King: France), 243, 247, 248, 249, 271, 370
Louis XV (King: France), 271, 272
Louis XVI (King: France), 271, 273–277
Louis XVII (King: France), 287
Louis XVIII (King: France), 288, 289, 386
Louis Napoleon, 291, 387; & French Republic, 386. See also Napoleon III.
Louis Philippe, 289, 290, 291
Louisiana, 210, 248, 297, 410
L'Ouverture, Toussaint, 297
Loyola, Ignatius, 192
Ludendorff, Erich, 459
Lumière Brothers, 331
Lunar probe, 657

Lusitania, 456, 457
Luther, Martin, 187–189, 195
Luthuli, Arthur, 634
Luxembourg, 388, 455, 550
Lydians, 31
Lyell, Sir Charles, 323

McAdam, John, 309
Macadamized process, 310
Macao, 227
MacArthur, Douglas, 556, 563, 564, 615, 616
McCarthy, Eugene, 600
McCormick, Cyrus, 313
Macedonia, 67, 95, 407–408
Machiavelli, Niccolò, 183
Machine Age, 324–349; arts in, 350–373; literature in, 353–373
MacLeish, Archibald, 663
MacMahon, Marshall, 389
Macmillan, Harold, 580
Madagascar, 232, 234, 235, 421
Madero, Francisco, 413
Madison, James, 267
Madras, 213
Magellan, Ferdinand, 200
Maginot Line, 532, 550
Magna Carta, 160–161, 260, 262, 263, 378, 385
Magyars, 135, 291, 401
Mahmud II, 406
Maine, sinking of, 436
Malagasy Republic, 235
Malay Peninsula, 37
Malaya, 7, 232, 235
Malaysia, federation of, 615, 618, 643
Malenkov, Georgi, 588
Mali, 237
Malta, 282, 287
Malthus, Thomas, 332
Man, adaptability of, 7; environment, prehistoric, 13; migration by, 7; prehistoric, 10–17; search for, 11; primitive, 11–12; unity of, 9
Manchu dynasty, 44, 227, 230, 525
Manchuria, 44, 227, 426, 429, 434, 482, 487, 525, 542, 610
Manet, Édouard, 359
Mann, Horace, 369
Mantinea, battle of, 67
Mao Tse-tung, 610–611, 613, 643
Marat, Jean Paul, 276
Marathon, 62
Marcus Aurelius, 116
Mardonius, 63
Marco Polo, 197, 226, 233
Marconi, Guglielmo, 331
Marengo, battle of, 281
Maria Theresa (Queen: Austria), 254, 255, 256, 257, 271
Marie Antoinette (Queen: France), 271, 274, 275, 276, 278
Mark Antony, 99

704

Portugal, 246, 285–288, 366, 370, 418, 517, 623, 633
Poseidon, 57
Post impressionism, 359
Potsdam Conference, 565, 570, 616, 641
Poznan, 593
Pragmatism, 352
Prague, post WW1, 471
Praxiteles, 85
Predestination, 190
Prehistoric man, 10–17
Priestley, Joseph, 341
Priests, medieval, 144
Primitive man, 11–12
Printing, 183, 225, 226, 229
Prison reform, 366, 367
Prohibition, 367
Proletariat, 322
Protestant Reformation, 179, 187–192
Protestantism, 185; attacks on, 210; Calvinism, 190; divisions within, 194; extent of, 193–194; free thinkers among, 370; Inquisition &, 193; Lutheranism, 189; & warfare, 476
Protons, 342
Proust, Marcel, 356
Prussia, 253–257, 277, 286–288, 388, 395
Psychiatry, 347
Psychology, 337, 348
Ptolemic system, 185
Ptolemy, 82, 84, 199
Public schools, 369
Pueblo incident (1968), 616
Puerto Rico, 436
Pullman cars, 311
Punic Wars, 93–94
Puritan Revolution, 260, 261–262, 278
Puritanism, 216, 260
Pushkin, Alexander, 354
Pygmies, 236
Pyrrhus, 91, 93

Quadruple Alliance, 288, 289; Monroe Doctrine &, 298
Quakers, 216, 365, 476
Quebec, 209, 212; nationalism in, 606
Queen Anne's War, 214
Quisling, Vidkun, 550

Racial equality, 598
Racial groups, 235
Racial tension, South Africa, 634
Radar, 659–660
Radio telescope, 340
Radioactive isotopes, 436, 656
Radioisotopes, 346, 656
Radium, discovery of, 342
Rama, 223
Rapallo, Treaty of, 486
Raphael, 182
Rasputin, 404
Rastadt, treaty of, 214
Ravel, Maurice, 364

Reactionary, 286
Realism, 354–355, 356, 358
Reaper, invention of, 313
Reason, 351
Reciprocal tariff, 334, 335
Reciprocal Tariff Act, 335
Reciprocal Trade Agreements Act (1934), 335, 484, 486, 534
Red China, 609–614, 620, 624, 649
Red Cross, 368
Red Guard, 612
Red Shirts (Italy), 394
Reform Acts (GB), first (1832), 381; second (1867), 384; third (1884), 384
Reformation, 180–195; Crusades &, 150; education following, 368; in England, 210; freedom of thought, 195; Germany, 245; Lutheranism &, 189; New World, 185; Protestant, 187–192; results of, 194–195. *See also* Catholic Counter Reformation; Protestant Reformation.
Reichstag, 399, 511; fire in, 514
Reign of Terror (France), 278, 352
Relativity, theory of, 343
Religion, Arabic, 127; African, 237, 238; Aztec, 204; Babylon, 29–30; basis of, 32; China, 48–49, 227, 228; colonization &, 205; conversion, 204; effect of discoveries on, 216; Egypt, 23; England, 262; fascist Italy, 510; freedom to worship, 370; Greek, 57; Hindu, 40; India, 34, 39, 41–43, 222, 223, 224, 242, 622, 623; Japan, 231, 432; modern, 368, 370–371; Moguls, 222; Mohammedism, 127–129; monotheism, 23, 127; Moslem, 128, 129; nationalism &, 379; Philippines, 233; pre-destination, 190; Prussia, 256; Red China, 613; reform in, 257; in Rome, 91–92; Russia, 250, 253, 402, 406; salvation &, 188, 231; Southeast Asia, 232, 233; in Soviet, 505; wars over, 194
Religious art, 223
Religious freedom, 211, 216, 247, 495
Religious music, 362
Religious toleration, 189, 253, 270, 370–371
Reparations, WW1, 468, 473–475; WW2, 541, 572
Renaissance, 179, 180–195; Crusades &, 150; Italy, 391; Petrarch &, 181
Renoir, Pierre Auguste, 359
Restoration (England), 261, 262
Revolution, defined, 243
Revolution of 1905 (Russia), 404
Revolutionary War, 214

Rey, Jean, 646
Reynaud, Paul, 550
Rhee, Syngman, 615–616
Rhenish Palatinate, 388
Rhineland, 248, 516, 544
Rhode Island, 371
Rhodes, Cecil, 421
Rhodesia, 632
Ribbentrop, Joachim von, 548
Richard the Lion-Hearted, 149
Richelieu, Cardinal, 247
Richthofen, Manfred von, 460
Rickenbacker, Eddie, 460
Rio Conference (1932), 536
Risorgimento, 392
Rivera, Primo de, 516
Riza Khan, 523
Robbe-Grillet, Alain, 662
Robespierre, Maximilien, 276, 277, 278
Rockefeller, John D., 566
Rodin, Auguste, 359
Roland, Jeanne Manon, 278
Romagna, 393
Roman Catholic Church, 186; Babylonian Captivity, 186; Bismarck &, 398–399; conflict within, 186; Counter Reformation, 192–193; deprived of land & property, 412, 413; despotism, 394; disunity in, 186, 187; in England, 259, 263; equality for, 256; excommunication, 187; feudalism &, 145; in France, 275, 276, 281; in Germany, 398–399; Great Schism, 186; Henry VIII &, 259; indulgences, sale of, 187, 188; & Italian unification, 384; in Maryland, 216; not tolerated, 370; organization, 148; privileged, 210; Reformation, 179, 185, 192–193; rise of, 142–148; sacraments, 144; state religion, 371; simony, 187; Vulgate Bible, 193; & warfare, 144
Roman empire, 94–97; cities of, 108–109; commerce, 109; conquests, 95; decline of, 96–97, 102–103; in the east, 94–95, 101; industry, 109; landholding, 109–110; law, 113; politics, 109; road building, 110; taxation in, 109; violence in, 101; in the west, 95, 101. *See also* Julius Caesar.
Romanov family, 251, 290, 401–405, 496
Romantic music, 362
Romanticism, 352
Rome, agriculture in, 91, 95; Allies capture, 558; amusements, 107–108; architecture, 111, 182; art, 111, 112; building in, 106, 112; citizenship, 93; civilization, 181; clothing, 105; democracy in, 92–93,

377; divination, 92; eating habits, 106–107; economic conditions, 91; education, 99, 110; engineering, 111; fall of, 96–97, 102–103; family in, 91; fascist march on, 508; founding of, 70, 90; French in, 292; houses, 105, 106, 112; gods, 92; government of, 91–92; Greek influence, 89, 95; law, 93; Italian unification &, 394; life in, 91; looting of, 91; luxury of, 95; mob control, 96; Napoleon annexation, 283; North African domination, 235; paintings, 106, 112; population, 108; rise of, 90–91; sculpture, 112; seaport, 109; Senate, 92, 96; slavery, 91, 95, 105; social classes, 105; standard of living, 106–108; state religion, 92; statues, 106; university at, 110; & women, 91, 105

Rommel, Erwin, 557–558
Romulus, 90
Romulus Augustulus, 102, 132
Roosevelt, Franklin D., 534, 554, 565, 640
Roosevelt, Theodore, 433, 434, 437, 443
Rosas, Juan Manuel de, 413
Rosetta Stone, 20, 38, 203, 280
Rossini, Gioacchino, 363
Roundhead, 260, 261
Rousseau, Jean-Jacques, 257, 270, 275, 279, 293, 352, 356, 478; French Revolution, 270
Rubáiyát of Omar Khayyám, 221
Rubber, 413; synthetic, 328; vulcanization, 309
Rubens, Peter Paul, 358
Rubicon, Caesar crosses, 97
Ruhr, 474, 512
Rumania, 101, 401, 405, 407, 408, 444, 472, 486, 518, 552, 572, 582, 640
Runnymede, 160
Rush-Bagot agreement, 484
Russia, agriculture, 249; Alaskan claim, 251; Allied invasion (WW1), 499; anti-French coalition, 388; autocracy in, 401, 402; Bolshevik turnover, 498; capital punishment, 253; & Catherine the Great, 253; & Central Asia, 428; China defeats, 251; China trade, 227; civil war in, 499; Congress of Vienna, 286–288; corrupt government, 404; Crimean War, 407; culture, 252; dictatorship, 338; & Duma, 404; education, 251; emergence of, 401–405; emigration from, 250; Europeanization of, 251–252, 253; foreign policy, 252; France, war with, 283, 285;

geography of, 249; German challenge, 375; government of, 253; impressionism in, 364; independence of states in, 250; industrialism, 404; Japan, war with, 433, 434; manufacturing, 252; March revolution, 498; Mongol rule, 226, 250–251; nationalities comprising, 401; natural resources, 249; 19th century, 401; novelists in, 355–356; November Revolution, 498; October Revolution, 498; & Ottoman Empire, 406; Peter the Great, 251; Poland, partition of, 253; political terrorism, 403; provisional government, 497; Quadruple Alliance, 288; radicalism in, 405; Red terror, 499; reform in, 253; religion, 250, 253, 402, 406; revisionism in, 322; romanticism, 354; seaport, need for, 252; serfs in, 253; Seven Years' War, 255; & Siberia, 251; Slavs in, 250; socialism in, 322; strike epidemic (1905), 404; Swedish conquest, 135, 252; Swedish influence, 250; trade, 250; trade unionism, 404; Turkey, war with, 253; unification of, 249–253; WW1, 449–465. *See also* Soviet Union
Russian Revolution, 251, 404, 453, 495, 639
Russo-Finnish war, 549
Russo-Japanese war, 404, 433, 434
Russo-Turkish war, 407
Ryswick, treaty of, 214

Saar, 469–470, 586
Saarinen, Eero, 665
Sadowa, battle of, 397
Sahara Desert, 234, 235, 421, 635
Saint Augustine, 191
Saint Benedict, 147
Saint Dominic, 147
Saint Francis of Assisi, 147
Saint Francis Xavier, 231
Saint-Gaudens, Augustus, 360
Saint Germain, treaty of, 468
Saint Helena, 285
Saint Lawrence River, 209
Saint Lawrence Seaway, 606
Saint Lawrence Valley, 265
Saint Peter's Church, 132, 182, 188
Saint Petersburg, 252, 402
Saint-Simon, Claude Henri, 320
Saint Sophia, Cathedral of, 126
Saipan, 563
Sakhalin Island, 428, 434
Saladin, 149
Salamis, 63
Salazar, Antonio de, 517
Salonika, 552

Samnites, 91
Samoa, 435
Samurai class, 231, 432, 617
San Martin, José de, 194–195
San Salvador, 199
San Stefano, Treaty of, 407
Sanskrit, 39, 223
Santa Anna, Antonio, 412
Santiago (Cuba), battle of, 324
Sappho, 85
Saratoga, battle of, 267
Sarawak, 617
Sardinia, 280, 289, 392, 394, 407
Sarajevo, 448
Sarmiento, Domingo Faustino, 413
Sartre, Jean-Paul, 662
Saskatchewan, 411
Saudi Arabia, 522, 626, 629
Saul, 32
Saul of Tarsus, 114
Savery, Thomas, 307
Savoy, 388, 392
Saxons, subdued, 132
Saxony, 255, 396
Sazonov, Sergei, 449
Schiller, Friedrich von, 353, 363, 367
Schleiden, Matthias, 344
Schleswig, 470
Schleswig-Holstein, 397
Schliemann, Heinrich, 55, 56
Schubert, Franz, 363
Schuman Plan, 645
Schumann, Robert, 363
Schurz, Carl, 292
Schussnigg, Kurt von, 518, 546
Schwann, Theodor, 344
Science, Aztec, 203; Babylon, 30; Egypt, 26; India, 223; & industry, 325; in Machine Age, 324–349; modern, 339; Renaissance &, 183, 184; Roman, 111; & warfare, 445
Scientific method, 339–340
Scientific Revolution, 351
Scipio, 94
Scotland, 160, 161, 190, 380, 385
Scott, Sir Walter, 354
Sculpture, African, 238; American Indian, 203; Buddhist influence, 229; experimental, 359; Greek, 85; India, 222; Renaissance, 182; Roman, 112; romanticism in, 358
Second Balkan War, 408
Second Empire (France), 389
Second French Republic, 387
Second Hundred Years' War, 212
Second International, 323
Second Punic War, 93–94
Security Council (UN), 570
Sedan, battle of, 389
Selassie, Haile, 544, 545, 552, 633
Selim III (Sultan: Ottoman Empire), 606
Seljuk Turks, 130, 219